# JERUSALEM: THE TOPOGRAPHY
# ECONOMICS AND HISTORY

# THE LIBRARY
# OF
# BIBLICAL STUDIES

Edited by

Harry M. Orlinsky

TWO VOLUMES IN ONE

# JERUSALEM

THE TOPOGRAPHY, ECONOMICS AND HISTORY
FROM THE EARLIEST TIMES TO A.D. 70

BY

## GEORGE ADAM SMITH

D.D., LL.D.

PROFESSOR OF OLD TESTAMENT LANGUAGE, LITERATURE
AND THEOLOGY, UNITED FREE CHURCH COLLEGE, GLASGOW

Prolegomenon by
SAMUEL YEIVIN

*IN TWO VOLUMES*

*VOL. I.*

WITH MAPS AND ILLUSTRATIONS

KTAV PUBLISHING HOUSE, INC.
1972

*First Published 1877*

NEW MATTER

COPYRIGHT © 1972

SBN 87068-105-2

LIBRARY OF CONGRESS CATALOG CARD NUMBER: 68-19734
MANUFACTURED IN THE UNITED STATES OF AMERICA

# CONTENTS OF VOLUME I.

# BOOK II

## THE ECONOMICS AND POLITICS

# Contents

# LIST OF MAPS AND PLANS IN VOLUME I.

# LIST OF PLATES IN VOLUME I.

# TABLE OF CONTENTS
# FOR PROLEGOMENON

# 1

## INTRODUCTORY

Before embarking on an introduction to a reprinted work of any kind, it is not enough to ask oneself what sort of a book it is that is being reprinted, and what are its merits, that demand and justify its recirculation among new generations of readers. One must also find out as much as possible about the personality of the author of the reprinted *opus,* so as to try and understand his appeal to the reading public, and what makes his book interesting or valuable, or both.

The author of this prolegomenon was rather surprised to find that the only biography of George Adam Smith had been written, shortly after his death, by his widow, Lady Lilian Adam Smith, née Buchanan.[1] As Lady Lilian puts it very aptly in her introduction to the small biographical volume (p. 5): "A wife is not the right person to assess her husband's work, and I have not tried to do this; but I have tried to give a living picture of him in the doing of it." And in that little book she very honorably acquitted herself of this task. As one reads the biographical sketch with its numerous quotations from George Adam Smith's

---

1. Lilian Adam Smith, *George Adam Smith, A Personal Memoir and Family Chronicle* (London, 1943); for details, see pp. 28 ff. Hereafter, all page references otherwise unindicated derive from this biography.

personal diaries and several humorous "asides" put in by its
author, there emerges, and materializes before the reader's eyes,
the life-like image of the subject of this biography, a warm personality with its merits and defects, the active social worker, the
passionate preacher, the serious scholar, the devoted family man—
all of it seen through the loving eyes of an admiring and revering
wife, but not distorted at all by any unbalanced bits of uncritical
marital adoration.

As will be seen in the following pages, the present writer has
drawn fully from this source on the life of the author of *Jerusalem,*
in order to present a true image of the man and his work, each
explaining and helping to understand the other. He has tried to
make the image as true as an outsider can grasp it on the basis
of contemporary auxiliary material.

A short time before the publication of Lady Smith's volume,
Professor Stanley A. Cook eulogized G. A. Smith at a session
of the British Academy, of which both were Fellows.[2] Besides
very short notes on biographical facts, this speech contains some
acute observations on Smith the scholar, and various testimonials
to his powerful gifts as a speaker. It was Cook who first introduced (p. 1) the notion "of the great Scottish trio, who . . . enabled
their country, and not their country alone, to bridge the gulf
separating the Biblical studies, inaugurated by the Renascence and
Reformation, and their present situation. Andrew Bruce Davidson
(1831-1902), William Robertson Smith (1846-1894), and G. A.
Smith were the three outstanding figures in the days when the
Bible lost much of its inherent value . . . G. A. S[mith], the Doyen of
Old Testament scholars, notable as preacher and teacher . . . has
left his mark as an outstanding personality by his exposition of
the prophets, his knowledge of the geography, topography, history
and economic condition of Palestine, and his understanding of
the Oriental mind."

---

2. S. A. Cook, "George Adam Smith, 1856–1942" (24 pp.); reprinted from *The Proceedings of the British Academy,* vol. XXVIII.

# PART I:

# THE AUTHOR: GEORGE ADAM SMITH

*Parents and Birth, Early Childhood*

George Adam Smith was born in Calcutta, India, on the 19th of October, 1856. He was the oldest of the ten children, five brothers and five sisters, of Dr. George Smith (1833-1919) and his wife Janet, née Adams (died 1888). The family came from Restalrig, near Leith, in Scotland. George Smith, the father, with very liberal leanings, had been at the time principal of the Doveton College for Eurasian boys in Calcutta, which he later left to become editor of *The Calcutta Review,* and then of *The Friend of India,* and Indian correspondent of *The Times.* Only in 1875 did Dr. George Smith and his wife return home to settle in Edinburgh, where Dr. Smith became editor of *The Edinburgh Daily Review.*[1]

When he was two years old, George Adam Smith was brought to Scotland by his mother, and left at Leigh, together with his next brother, in the care of his paternal aunts Mary and Hannah Smith. Gradually other brothers and sisters came to join him there.

It seems that the two aunts exercised great influence on Smith during his formative years. Hanna, more practical and with a keen and caustic wit, took care of the physical needs of the young

---

1. *Biog.,* p. 14.

children, while Mary, the older of the two, looked after their
spiritual needs. She helped the children "with their homework,
and she went so far as to study Latin herself in order to assist
them properly. When lessons were done, she would tell them
stories of their own folk . . . and . . . would read Shakespeare's
plays to them, giving them parts to act or to recite; and on one
occasion she took them to hear Dickens giving a reading from
some of his own tales.

"On Sundays the children were allowed to read a Bible story
and then to act it as a play. These stories were chiefly from the
Old Testament, and Aunt Mary would give graphic descriptions
of places and people" (pp. 12-13).

In later years, Smith acknowledged his debt to his aunt by
dedicating to her these two volumes on *Jerusalem*.[2] Moreover,
there is little doubt that it was this early interest in the Bible,
and the vivid actualization of its stories due to Aunt Mary Smith,
that made George Adam decide quite early in his school days
to choose the ministry as his career, when he would grow up.

## Further Education; Faith and Criticism

George Adam attended in due course the Royal High School
in Edinburgh, "walking three miles there and three miles back
every day" (p. 12). He then went to Edinburgh University, where
he took a course in Arts, including Greek, Latin, English Literature, and Philosophy. Already then he showed his independent
turn of mind and his great interest in actual social questions, by
adding to these a totally unrequired subject, namely, lectures
on Political Economy, given at the time by Professor Hodgson.

---

2. The printed fly-leaf has actually a very short dedication "To the
Memory of M. S."; Lady Lilian Smith, in her biography (p. 13), gives
a much more elaborate version, adding: "the dear kinswoman, my first
teacher, to whose guidance I owe my introduction to the history of
Jerusalem and my earliest interest in it." A slightly different and shorter
version of this addition is incorporated in Smith's preface to his book
(p. xv). Of course, the discrepancy may be due to Lady Lilian's writing
from memory.

Having graduated in Arts at the age of eighteen, Smith proceeded to realize his boyhood ambition to enter the ministry. He went to New College, the Divinity Hall of the Free Church, where he immediately came under the influence of Professor A. R. Davidson, "whose keen mind and wide outlook made the study of Hebrew and the Old Testament one of special fascination" (p. 16). During the summer holidays he traveled about in Germany in the company of some of his University mates, attending summer courses on theology at Leipzig and Tuebingen under Delitzsch and Harnack. This was the period when Protestant German scholarship was developing its school of Higher Criticism with great enthusiasm. Though this school was quite firm in its fundamental religious convictions, it was taking great liberties with the Massoretic Text of the Hebrew Bible. Helped frequently by an imperfect realization of what is possible and what is impossible in Biblical Hebrew idiom, and its almost total ignorance of Post-Biblical Hebrew (with very few exceptions)—as well as by its frequently quite conscious, and sometimes possibly unconscious but inborn, Judeophobia—this school developed some most unlikely theories concerning the origins and composition of the Books of the Old Testament, some of the scholars going to fantastic extremes in the "pulverization" of Scriptural verses in multiplicity of so-called primary sources.[3]

Discoveries in the new fields of archaeology and Near Eastern philology, as well as progress in the study of the then newly deciphered languages and the unfolding of their literatures, helped to stimulate a critical approach to the text of the Bible. As usual, the conservative attitude of the Established Churches helped to push the pendulum of critical research to greater and greater extremes.[4]

---

3. Cf. now C. H. Gordon, in *A Christianity Today Reader* (New York, 1966), pp. 67 ff.

4. It is only within the last forty years that the pendulum of research began to swing back toward more conservative attitudes in the Higher Criticism of the Bible; but the period under discussion here aims at the latter part of the nineteenth century.

Small wonder, therefore, that young Smith and his companions succumbed to the general trend. He became, and all his life remained, an ardent follower of the German school of Higher Criticism. And yet his Scottish upbringing in the path of unwavering faith, and his belief in the Divine nature of biblical inspiration and revelation, stayed with him. This, to many of us somewhat strange symbiosis of faith and criticism frequently found rather naïve expression in his writings. Thus, in discussing the inaugural prayer of King Solomon, as preserved in the Hebrew text, he noted some of its apparently late features, but at the same time added: "... *we cannot believe* [emphasis added] that the consciousness of either [*viz.*, the historical and ethical elements] was absent from the men who built the Temple or that it failed to find some expression on so great a festival as that of the Dedication."[5] Or, again, in analysing seemingly contradictory attitudes to the erection of the first Temple, he noted: "But in the second [*viz.*, tradition] the description of so sudden a change in the *Divine purpose* [emphasis added] can hardly be a pure invention."[6] Quite obviously, neither of the two is pure invention, but both are reflections of the attitude of court circles on the one hand, and the stand of the majority of the common people on the other, both ascribed by biblical tradition, as usual, to Divine intervention.[7]

Incidentally, his summer vacation in Germany brought Smith into his first contact with writing: "... in Germany ... he was unexpectedly called upon to fill the role of journalist and foreign correspondent. The Berlin Congress met that year (1878), and his father's friend, Henry Lucy, then editor of *Mayfair,* commissioned him to report on it. The young divinity student made the most of his opportunities, and was able to send to the paper some interesting and entertaining accounts of the various personalities and proceedings."[8]

---

5. G. A. Smith, *Jerusalem,* II (1907), p. 77.

6. Idem, pp. 78-79.

7. For a more detailed exposition of the subject see S. Yeivin, *apud* B. Z. Lurie, ed., *Studies in the Books of Samuel* (Hebrew; to appear shortly).

8. *Biog.,* p. 17.

## *Extra-Curricular Activities*

Smith was not by nature merely a research scholar, a theoretician, content with the attitude of those whom our forebears so graphically described as: *ḥovshe safsal* "bench-'huggers.' " [9] His energetic character demanded action. And for that pressing need he found two outlets: personal and public. Thus, "While pursuing his theological studies he was an ardent member of the Queen's Edinburgh Rifle Volunteers, and at their Camp Sports he won" several prizes; this aspect of his endeavors was merely a continuation of his enthusiastic activity in sports during his school and university days (*Biog.*, pp. 12-16).

As far as public activities were concerned, we learn that "During his days at the New College, George had been active in home mission work," in the course of which he met, on his own testimony, "some of the poorest but the bravest people I have known, and learned more from them than they could have learned from me." [10] This last statement is very characteristic, revealing the man George Adam Smith was: essentially modest, well intentioned, and always ready—for the love of his neighbor—to extend a helping hand, be it to a friend or a student, or any human being in need of succor.

## *First Steps; First Visit to The Holy Land*

When Smith completed his course at New College, he was invited by Dr. Lansing, a missionary of the United Presbyterian Church of America, to come to Cairo to assist in missionary work, different in nature from what he had been doing in his Mission at Edinburgh. [11] This phase of his work gave him the opportunity to realize one of his early dreams, to pay a visit to the Holy Land.

---

9. See, e.g., A. Even-Shoshan, *Ha-Milon He-Ḥadash* (*The New Dictionary;* Jerusalem, 1969), s.v. חובש ספסל, according to whom it is a modern phrase coined on the pattern of חובש בית־המדרש (as in Ḥagiga 14a).

10. *Biog.*, p. 17 (quotation of Smith's oral communication).

11. *Biog.*, pp. 17-18; Cook, *PBA*, XXVIII, p. 5.

Like two of his famous predecessors, Rabbi Estori Ha-Pirḥi in the fourteenth century, the unwitting and unacknowledged father of modern Israelology, and Edward Robinson in the early nineteenth century, Smith "tramped the country on foot . . . going from place to place as the spirit moved him . . . And so the land unfolded itself to him in all its many aspects. His eyes were opened to see the reasons and the meanings of words and events which, until then, he had only partly understood, and there is no doubt that the idea of writing a book upon the country was born in his mind from that first solitary journey." [12] For Smith lived to impart knowledge, and to share with others his views on the Bible and its background, meaning, and message.

Back in Scotland he became assistant for a short time to a minister at Brechin, but soon thereafter was appointed to the Free Church College in Aberdeen to teach Hebrew and the Old Testament. This appointment was made to replace Professor Robertson-Smith, who had been asked to resign his chair because his views on the subject of religion were considered too "heretical" for a Free Church college.

Smith's sense of fairness, and his desire to be on good terms with people whose scientific achievements he held in appreciation and reverence, made him visit the older scholar, whom he was called to succeed, in order "to seek his advice as to the conduct of the classes." Robertson Smith "seemed not too well pleased to see him, which was scarcely surprising. 'What would you do,' he demanded fiercely, 'if I should refuse to obtemper . . . and insist on taking the class myself?' 'Then,' said George, 'I would be proud to go and sit among your students'" (*Biog.*, p. 19). Thereafter, the two became good friends.

But Smith's yearning to disseminate his knowledge and understanding of the Bible, as the basis of a sincere religious conviction, among the largest possible circles could not find satisfaction in a mere teaching position. So that immediately after being ordained by the Presbytery of Aberdeen, on April 20, 1882, he accepted

12. *Biog.*, p. 18. This visit dates to the spring of 1880; see G. A. Smith, *Historical Geography of the Holy Land,* 25th ed. (London, 1931).

the invitation of the congregation of the then newly built Queen's Cross Church, at the west end of Aberdeen, to become their minister. The next Sunday evening, April 23, he preached his first sermon there. "That was the beginning of a ten years' ministry that is spoken of with admiration and gratitude even to this day" (*Biog.*, pp. 19-20).

### Academics and Ministry; Marriage

This position offered Smith for the first time opportunity and scope for his undoubted gifts as a speaker and preacher. He possessed what is vulgarly known as the "gift of gab" to the highest degree. His sermons and general lectures were models not only in content, vocabulary, and form but also as regards voice, tone, articulation of speech, and accompanying gests. Numerous testimonies of friends, pupils, even strangers in random audiences bear witness to the magic of his influence. One of his students in later years wrote: "His eloquence, his religious passion, the vivacity and infectious enthusiasm of his manner, his unflinching application of great ethical principles, his searching appeal to the conscience made him a great force in the pulpit." [13] But probably the most eloquent testimony was from an anonymous member of "a working-class congregation who were looking for a minister ... 'Gin we could hae yon man wha preached last Sabbath, there wadna be a dissentient voice amang us'" (p. 23).

He also became Secretary of the Scottish Geographical Society, of which his father had been one of the founders, thus adding another field of activity to his diversified interests. One of the early fruits of this interest was a very detailed review of Doughty's *Arabia Petrea* published in *The Spectator* (1888).

His early work at Aberdeen brought Smith into contact with Scottish churches abroad, especially in Switzerland; and there he had become involved in a new form of sport, namely, mountaineering, ever since his first visit to that country in 1883. In 1886 he was admitted to membership of the Alpine Club, where he had already several friends. Characteristically he found in that sport not only a physical relaxation, but also a spiritual re-

---

13. Prof. William Manson, as quoted in *Biog.*, p. 21.

juvenation, as he noted in his diary: "... To myself it is a great deliverance. All the year round I am in a groove, pretty much mentally and more so physically ... in such conditions you feel your manhood oozing gradually out of your fingers ... Then you go to Switzerland ... and you are a boy once more! That is only the prospect of the hills, but when you are on them, what a health, and what a glory it is! A gymnastic for every muscle in your body, and for anything that corresponds to muscle in your mind, and imperial vision for the eyes at every step" (p. 26).

Through his interest in Alpine mountaineering, Smith was destined to meet the young lady who became his wife and life-companion, Miss Lilian Buchanan, daughter of Dr. George Adam Buchanan and his second wife Alice Mary Asmar (née Seaton). They soon became engaged, and in December 1889 were married at the Parish Church of St. Marylebone, London (pp. 30-36). They had seven children, three sons—two of whom fell in battle in World War I—and four daughters.

The years that Smith served as a minister of Queen's Cross Church were a period of tense and multisided activity. One of his assistants during that time, John Kelman, who became a life-long friend, wrote some years later of that period: " 'The memory of a Queen's Cross winter gives one the feel of a snow-plough driving on through everything, with its constant spindrift of things done flying to right and left . . .' Sunday services, Bible classes, young men's and young women's classes, four Sunday schools, lectures on an astonishing variety of subjects, visiting and social work in the congregation, besides all kinds of work outside—everything . . . accomplished with a thoroughness and individual care ..." (p. 38). This was a true pen-sketch of the first foretaste of Smith, that remained true throughout his active life.

### Second Visit to The Holy Land; Literary Activity

In the latter part of his term of service at the Queen's Cross Church, Smith received many calls from other, larger congregations in different parts of the United Kingdom, including London and Edinburgh. He refused them all, and his grateful congregation offered him a six months' leave of absence in the spring of 1891 to enable him to pay a second visit to Palestine.

Smith and his small party, including his young bride, traveled by way of Cairo, where they stayed but a few days, then took ship from Alexandria to Jaffa, and proceeded on horseback inland, visiting Masada and Engedi, and ending up at Jerusalem. Their stay there was comparatively long, exploring both the old and the new parts of the city, drinking in the peculiar atmosphere of the holy town. The traveling party then went on to Samaria, Galilee, the Buqa'a, Damascus, Transjordan, and back to Jerusalem. Then they continued to Jaffa, Haifa, and Beyrouth, whence they sailed to Cyprus. Throughout the voyage Smith made copious notes and took numerous measurements concerning climatic conditions, geographic features, ethnic context, and archaeological sites of the Holy Land, all of which stood him in good stead later when he finally settled down to write his *magnum opus, The Historical Geography of The Holy Land* (*Biog.,* 46 ff.).

But before turning to a discussion of that volume, one should note a prior result of Smith's years of ministry at Aberdeen: "One of the chief features of his ministry," wrote Cook, "was the Sunday evening after-service symposium with the young men of the congregation, when discussion ranged the whole field of knowledge, and by his criticism and exposition he made their reading a lasting pleasure. Among his sermons those on the Book of Isaiah and the personality of the prophet who has given his name to it, deeply impressed his hearers. They led to the two volumes of the *Expositor's Bible* (1888 and 1890), which went through many editions."[14] That was to mark the beginning of Smith's career as interpreter and expositor of Holy Writ. Later he produced also volumes on Jeremiah (1923),[15] the Twelve Minor Prophets,[16] and Deuteronomy.[17]

---

14. Cook, *op cit.,* p. 6.

15. *Biog.,* p. 205.

16. *The Expositor's Bible,* ed. W. Robertson-Nicoll, 2 vols. (London, 1896 and 1898); later reprinted in G. A. Smith's *On the Prophets,* 5 volumes (1927-1929).

17. *The Book of Deuteronomy* (Cambridge, 1918), in the series *The Cambridge Bible for Schools and Colleges,* ed. A. F. Kirkpatrick.

On these and similar works, Cook (*op. cit.*, p. 24) pronounced a very penetrating verdict: "G. A. S[mith] . . . was never a prodigy of learning; he had not the profound erudition and dialectical incisiveness of W[illiam] R[obertson] S[mith], and his scholarship, which came to the fore in his more technical writings, underlies his work as an expositor, though the scholarship is not always of the last decade or so . . . On the other hand, the synthesis which he [W.R.S.] had hoped to complete, G.A.S. himself accomplished with the first of his expository writings." For this was the gist of Smith's endeavors in the field of biblical research, namely, to reconcile the outlook of an advanced scientific scholar with the spirit of devout reverence. He did it by never renouncing his sincere belief in the Divine inspiration of the Book, which remained to him topical for all ages.[18] Quite unwittingly, he was following in the footsteps of the early medieval Hebrew *Darshanim*, who used scriptural quotations to inculcate into their listeners ethical principles of behavior, and to expound on the events of the present by enlarging on the quite dissimilar past.

To return now to the *Historical Geography of the Holy Land*. The book was the product of pioneering endeavor, a successful effort to find a new approach to biblical studies. Numerous scholars and exegetes of the Bible had tried to describe the geography of the Holy Land and to identify on the ground the various settlements and geographical features mentioned in the Bible, beginning with scattered references in Post-Biblical Hebrew literature and the first systematic attempt to summarize such information made by Eusebius in the fourth century. But Smith was the first to combine all the various aspects of geographical research connected with the Bible into one so-to-speak multicolored spectrum, thereby giving rise to a new field of research. Here, for the first time, geographical data were discussed and related one to another, whether in their permanent or changing aspects. Here, for the first time, too, was an attempt to understand the vicissitudes of the *history* of the land *sub specie geographica*, and to draw possible conclusions concerning the environmental conditioning of national culture and development.

18. Cf. above; and see also Cook, *op. cit.*, pp. 19-20; *Biog.*, pp. 20 ff.

Smith himself expressed quite clearly what he aimed at in composing his volume. In the Preface to the first edition (p. 9) he wrote: ". . . What is needed by the reader or teacher of the Bible is some idea of the outlines of Palestine—its shape and disposition; . . . its rains, winds and temperatures; *its colours, lights and shades* [emphasis added]. Students of the Bible desire to see a background and to feel an atmosphere; to discover from the 'lie of the land' why the history took certain lines . . . *above all* [emphasis added] to discern between what physical nature contributed to the religious development of Israel, and what was the product of moral and spiritual forces . . ." It is interesting to find here special emphasis not only on the actual physical milieu but especially on the religious aspect of the problem, which is the central concern of all that Smith wrote as scholar and active worker in other fields.

This work became at once one of the indispensable tools for anyone who aspired to study and understand his Bible. Within less than forty years (1894-1931) it was printed in twenty-five editions, many of them revised and brought up to date. In spite of the fact that the last edition (1931) is antiquated and newer works on the same subject have since appeared,[19] it still retains its value and freshness of approach, and deserves serious reading by anyone studying the subject.

### *At Glasgow; Third and Fourth Visits to The Holy Land; Voyage to India*

In the spring of 1892 Smith was appointed Professor of Hebrew and Old Testament at his alma mater, New Church College, in Glasgow, where he remained for twelve years. But as he pointed out in his inaugural address, ". . . If my call to this Chair were a call away from practical work, I would not be here. I have not left a pulpit which I loved and found freedom in, for any other ultimate purpose than the one for which the Church sent me to it, or with any other confidence than that the free and full study

---

19. Suffice it to name two: F. M. Abel, *La géographie de la Palestine,* 2 vols. (Paris, 1933 and 1938); Y. Aharoni, *The Land of the Bible,* 2nd ed. (Philadelphia, 1967).

of the Old Testament by teachers and scholars together has for its inevitable result the preaching of God's simple Word to the people . . ." [20] The appointment to a professorial Chair did not mean abandonment of his activity as preacher, expositor, and social worker. However, his new post left Smith more time for the literary part of his scholarly work, and his written output grew apace in Glasgow.

In addition to the *Historical Geography*, which appeared when he was already in Glasgow, Smith's twelve years' stay produced also the *Book of the Twelve Prophets* (2 vols., 1896-1898), the *Life of Henry Drummond*, his late teacher and friend (1899), *Modern Criticism and the Preaching of the Old Testament* (1901), and many sundry articles. He continued his call as a preacher, toiled arduously as a social worker (championing the cause of ill-paid women workers),[21] joined the work of the Toynbee House Settlement to "encourage the atmosphere of understanding and friendliness between the West and East of the great city," and did much to further the ends of the Boy's Brigade, etc. (*Biog.*, pp. 68 ff.); in addition, he went on lecture tours, three times to the United States (1896, 1899, 1903).

During this period he was honored by the University of Aberdeen, which conferred on him in 1895 the Honorary Degree of LL.D. His path, however, was not always smooth, for after the publication of his book on *Modern Criticism and the Preaching of the Old Testament*, he was accused by some circles in the United Church of Scotland of "undermining the teaching of the Bible and of denying its divine inspiration." The accusation was brought before the General Assembly, which met at Glasgow in 1902. Smith was given the opportunity to explain his views, and "he told the eager audience how his own faith had been strengthened by critical, intelligent study of the Bible, and how he believed with all his heart and mind that the Bible was one of the most potent forces of God's revelation of Himself to man" (pp. 82 ff.).

---

20. *The Preaching of the Old Testament to the Age;* quoted from *Biog.*, p. 64.
21. *Biog.*, p. 68.

After this the Assembly rejected (by 534 to 263 votes) [22] any notion to institute proceedings against him, or to forbid him freedom of criticism. Though the storm had been weathered, and even evoked positive comment in Church circles, "it left its mark upon him, for he found it hard to understand how the Church, which he had served so faithfully, and to which he had dedicated his great gifts of heart and mind, should have so misunderstood him" (*Biog.*, p. 84).

In 1901 Smith visited Palestine for the third time. On this occasion, on his way to Nablus, he chanced to meet Dr. F. J. Bliss of the Palestine Exploration Fund, who greeted him by saying: "I came here seeking for jar-handles, and I have found George Adam Smith!" (*Biog.*, p. 81).

Already then Smith was struck by the rapid destruction and disappearance of ancient remains, which were still to be seen on his previous visits, and he noted that "if the ancient sites of Palestine are to be explored and the civilisations they contained brought to light, this must be done as soon as possible." How much truer this is today, when a good deal of what Smith had seen has since been irretrievably lost. This visit to the Holy Land is also memorable for another reason, for it was on this occasion that he and his companions discovered in the mud wall of the village of Tell-ish-Shehab in the Hauran the slab of black basalt which proved to be part of Seti I's now famous stele (pp. 81 ff.).

A serious bout of illness during his third lecture tour in the United States gave Smith the opportunity to go on a short voyage of recuperation to India, the land of his birth, which he left at the age of two. Perhaps the most illuminating statement of this voyage comes from some disconnected notes he made in his diary following a conversation he had with the then Viceroy, Lord Curzon: "Psychologists discovering phenomena in all religions which resemble each other; the mistake made by many of our fellow-countrymen who had been brought up to believe that all religions except their own were wrong; their surprise at finding these faiths governing the lives of millions. Practical matters— the great responsibility of our country towards the native races;

---

22. Cook, *op. cit.,* p. 11.

British government, while preserving liberty in religion, had not been afraid to put down the greater forms of immorality and cruelty; work of the missionaries, meeting on great human levels, ethical and spiritual; the fine and saintly characters in other faiths than our own, and generous minds . . ." [23] It is somewhat surprising to find that even a personality like Smith, who was broad-minded enough to see common ethical principles of widely differing religious beliefs, could not rid himself of the idea of the so-called "white man's burden," closely coupled with the partly paternalistic, partly condescending, and fully snobbish attitudes of the Colonial Service. Or is one to view his approach as deriving from the same fundamental, irradicable doctrines subconsciously imbued as a traditional spiritual heritage, like his unshakable faith in the biblical truth and its Divine inspiration?

On the return voyage from India Smith visited the Holy Land for the fourth time, devoting most of his stay to traveling in Moab, but spending also many days in Jerusalem, where he was observing, discussing, and making notes on detailed material for a special study concerning Jerusalem, planned as a culminating supplement of his *Historical Geography*.

With the years, the fame of New Church College spread, and large numbers of students were attracted to it. Numerous testimonies of old students bear witness to Smith's activity and inspiration as a teacher. One South African student wrote: "He had genius which was inspiration and imagination. Many a time in the Hebrew class, perhaps reading Jeremiah, did he inspire me. Almost carelessly he would scatter his jewels. He would open a text just as a skillful fisherman in my old Highland home would 'shell' a mussel, and then he would say, 'Gentlemen, I make a present of it to you' . . .". Another student, an Irishman, said in his letter: "I was a member of his Hebrew class, he was to me most kind. He was the first professor who ever took me by the arm—he did this the first day I arrived . . . with another Irish student. We knew no one there and were introduced to him by the Janitor . . . He made us sit on either side of him that day as he presided at the College dinner, and he had us often up at his

---

23. *Biog.*, pp. 85 ff.

house. Forgive this letter, I could not refrain from this expression of my feelings for a revered teacher to whom I owe so much." [24]

## The End of Smith's Term at Glasgow

To the latter part of Smith's professorship at Glasgow belongs the final draft and printing of his second great historico-geographical work: *Jerusalem* (in two volumes). He considered this work as a supplement, nay culmination, of his *Historical Geography*. He began his preface to Volume I by saying: "In the *Historical Geography of the Holy Land* it was not possible, for reasons of space, to include a topography of Jerusalem, an appreciation of her material resources, or a full study of the historical significance of her site and surroundings. The present volumes are an attempt to deal with these subjects, and to give in addition a history of the City's politics, literature and religion."

As Lady Smith so aptly put it (*Biog.,* p. 106): ". . . *Jerusalem* was in circulation . . . It did not have the wide and speedy recognition that had greeted the *Historical Geography;* much of it was too detailed and too technical for general reading, but it was welcomed by students and scholars, and took its own place in the literature of Jerusalem. To my mind the second volume is one of the best pieces of work George ever did. The comment has often been made that it is more the history of the people than an account of the city; but the city was so essential a background to their history that it seems impossible to dissociate them."

A similar evaluation is given by Cook (*op. cit.,* p. 12): "Hitherto there had been no specific study of Jerusalem . . . The whole was the first great work of its kind, and, as ever, G. A. S[mith] had in view preacher, teacher, and student, and his book leaves a powerful impression as one reads his chapters on the Jerusalem of Isaiah, Ezra, and Nehemiah, the Greek period, and ultimately of Jesus and the Apostles . . ." The religiously colored bias creeps in here, too, for Cook ends this paragraph with the following words: "One reaches the last tragedy of the people, zealous and gifted, but fanatical, ignorant, and blind; and the curtain is rung down when

---

24. *Biog.,* p. 92.

Zion was 'a sunset to herself, but the dawn of a new day to the world beyond.' " The fact that this was not the last tragedy, but was followed by countless other tragedies, some of them wrought by Cook's own forebears and contemporaries, in the life of a people that survived for nearly 2,000 years, to return and start to rebuild its ancient glories, does not bother Cook at all.

In 1909 Smith was offered, and he accepted, the Principalship of the University of Aberdeen. One of the reasons for accepting the offer was economic, for the family had been growing in number and Smith was a devoted family man who strove to give the family the best he possibly could. He very plainly pressed this point in answering his wife's remonstrations about his over-working himself: "We need every penny I can make, and thou knowest how I rejoice to work for thee and the bairns" (pp. 108 ff.). Characteristically, he did not abandon his old college at Glasgow on short notice; during the first year he commuted weekly between Aberdeen and Glasgow till the end of the academic session, so as to give New College the respite necessary to find a suitable replacement.

## Return to Aberdeen

On Nov. 8, 1909, Smith was nominated and appointed Principal and Vice-Chancellor of the University of Aberdeen, and held this post for the rest of his active career. In spite of the fact that the new post put a heavier burden on his shoulders, his fields of activity remained as numerous and varied in Aberdeen as previously at Glasgow.

His literary output included the manuscript of his Schweich Lectures delivered in 1910, which was published in 1912 under the title, *The Early Poetry of Israel in its Physical and Social Origins,* a commentary on *Deuteronomy* (published in 1918), and a commentary on *Jeremiah the Book, the Man, and the Prophet* (1923).

Smith's early years at Aberdeen were marred by World War I. He served part of it as a chaplain to the troops, and his two oldest sons fell in battle. Smith spoke frequently of the war which was "to lead to the victory of right over wrong," and finally went on an official mission in that connection to the United States (early in 1918), where he emphasized that "to put peace before justice, before honour, before rescue of the oppressed, before the security of women and children, is to turn Christianity upside down" (*Biog.,* pp. 169 ff.). How true, even today, and not only of Christianity.

There were also compensations. In 1916-17 he was appointed Moderator of the General Assembly of the United Free Church, an appointment entailing a heavy burden of duty, for that year. In 1916 he was elected a Fellow of the British Academy, and a member of the Athenaeum. In the same year he was also Knighted (pp. 159-165).

After a long service of strenuous work at the University, both as teacher and administrator, and additional endeavors on various public committees, institutions, and causes dear to his heart, Smith finally retired from public life in 1935.

He continued his literary and Church work. But his health was failing. On Dec. 18, 1939, Lady Lilian and Sir George celebrated their Golden Wedding. The World War II was already in progress, and probably events left their mark on the ailing scholar. On March 3, 1942, in his 86th year, Sir George Adam Smith quietly passed away (*Biog.,* pp. 258 ff.).

Thus came to an end the most fruitful and busy career of a fervent exponent and enthusiastic interpreter of the Old Testament.

# PART II:

## THE SUBJECT: JERUSALEM

### Chapter 1: *Jerusalem, the Book*

Volume I of *Jerusalem* describes the geographical features of the site of the city and its immediate surroundings, discusses its economic possibilities and their changing conditions throughout the ages, and deals finally with what Smith designates as politics, namely, the organized administration of the city and kingdom in its historical development. Of course, in the purely geographical part much space is devoted to discussing the plausible identification of various topographical details on the ground. In agreement with several predecessors, Smith opted for identifying the "citadel of Sion" (*Meṣúdát Ṣiyyón*) with the "city of David" (*'ir Dávíd*), and placed them on the southeastern hill; he also agreed with those scholars, who identified the two with the Ophel (*Jerusalem, I,* 34 ff.). The present writer ventures to mention that his own suggested interpretation of the term *Siyyon* as "Water Town"[1] clinches the argument for the identification of both on the southeastern hill.[2] One should also consider the possibility that all three terms —*Ophel, Meṣudat Ṣiyyon,* and *'ir David*—really apply to the royal citadel of the Jebusite city, and so are to be looked for inside the

---

1. Cf. II Sam. 12:27 (the "Water Town" of Rabbath-ammon).

2. S. Yeivin, *Yerushalayim,* I (1948; Hebrew), p. 15, n. 103; *JNES,* VII (1948), p. 41, n. 102.

central eastern part of the Summit inside the fortified perimeter of Jebus/Jerusalem, immediately overlooking the spring of Gihon, rather than to the city as a whole.

Book I of Volume I (chaps. IV-V, pp. 71-133) includes an excellent description and discussion of the water resources of the city of Jerusalem. In this connection it is surprising to find Smith, while correctly surmising that *'Eyn ha-tannin* (the Dragon's Spring) should be connected with an earthquake, and probably the one associated with King Uzziah, nevertheless denied its identification (on the ground) with *Bir 'Ayyub* (p. 74). It remained for a much later investigation, carried out on the spot by Dr. M. Hecker, the city engineer of Jerusalem in the second quarter of the current century, to prove the identity of *'Eyn Rogel, 'Eyn Ha-tannin,* and *Bir 'Ayyub,* and by pointing out the existence of a spring at the bottom of this well ( = *bir*) to connect it definitely with the earthquake in the days of King Uzziah.[3]

There are also excellent chapters on Commerce and Imports (I, 310 ff.), royal revenues (337 ff.) and administration (377 ff.). It is not strange at all that Smith, with his proper sense of realities, should have perceived at once that Jerusalem, as well as the whole state of Judea, could not possibly eke out even the most meager of subsistence living from its natural resources, mainly agriculture, and must have had recourse to commerce and industry, the latter in a very much restricted sense. But it is rather surprising to find him emphasizing the role played by the transit-trade in the economy of the country (335 f.), the royal trade monopolies (p. 340), and other features of the economic circumstances in the country (352 f.).

These chapters contain also some very suggestive philological remarks. Thus, in discussing various metals, in connection with the problem of imports, he makes the following remark on gold (p. 328, n. 2): *"zahav sagur,* closed, that is probably *stanch* or *sterling* gold, but compare the Assyrian expression as to silver, *Kanku,* 'sealed', or enclosed in sealed packs . . ." He not only anticipated Eisler in connecting this gold with the stamped nuggets from

---

3. M. Hecker, *Bulletin of the Jewish Palestine Exploration Society* ( = *BJPES*), IV (1936-1937; Hebrew), pp. 95 ff.

Phoenician mines, but probably felt (rather than logically decided) the connection of *sagur* with *sealing, stamping,* rather than with traditional *closing.*[4]

Smith made quite frequent use of the Hebrew postbiblical literature, quoting freely from the Mishna, Tosephta, the Talmud, and even Midrashim; but it is obvious that he uses only second-hand information (quotations in translations, or from articles in European languages).[5]

The most valuable and interesting part of *Jerusalem* is, however, Volume II (Book III), which unveils before the reader the whole canvas of the vicissitudes of the city from its beginning until the destruction of the Second Temple (70 C.E.).

The beginnings, for Smith (Vol. II, pp. 3 ff.), meant the rule of Arad-Khib/pa (Abd-Khiba as Smith spells it) of Tell el-Amarna correspondence fame. Parker's ill-fated dig, that revealed something of the prehistory of the town, was still to come at the beginning of the second decade of the twentieth century, as was also the first season of Weill's excavations (see-below), while the discovery and publication of the Egyptian Execration Texts, which make mention of Jerusalem and its kings in the nineteenth (and possibly early twentieth) century B.C.E., did not occur till the late twenties and early forties of this century.[6]

Fresh approaches to numerous historically very interesting problems abound in this volume. There are numerous stimulating remarks, and a sincere striving to uncover the roots of various phenomena, and examine their whys and wherefores. Thus, we find that Smith, dealing with the problem of the Jebusites, remarks (II, p. 28): "... This compact little tribe is of interest, not only because of the stand which it made for centuries against the Israelite invaders, but because, upon David's capture of their

---

4. This problem is discussed in greater detail in the present author's forthcoming book on *The Temple.*

5. *Jerusalem,* I, p. 114, n. 6; p. 407, n. 3.

6. K. H. Sethe, *Abhandlungen der Preussischen Akademie der Wissenschaften, Phil.-Hist. Klasse,* Berlin 1927; G. Posener, *Princes et pays d'Asie.et de Nubie* (Bruxèlles, 1942).

stronghold, it became a constituent of that strange medley, the
Jewish people, and doubtless carried into their life the tough
fibre of its tribal [*sic!*] character and some of the temper of its
immemorial religion [*sic!*]" Surprisingly, Smith asserts, "There
is small doubt that the tribe was Semitic"—an assertion that
strikes the present writer as being very doubtful. There seems to be
more and more evidence that the Hurrian element was current
among them.[7] But, alas, over sixty years after the publication of
*Jerusalem*, we are no nearer the solution of that enigma.[8]

As usual, Smith's ear is attuned to the economic problems; and
he considers King David as the father of the commercial activity
in ancient Israel (II, p. 37). But such a conception of David's
activity is hardly reconcilable with the detailed list of David's
fiscal officials, which contains only officers connected with agriculture,[9] and one official appointed over the treasury of the king.[10]

One can agree or disagree with many of the conclusions drawn
by Smith from the very acute and penetrating analyses of all data
having any relevance for the history of Jerusalem. But one cannot
fail to notice his deeply emotional approach to the main figures
that appear in that history. In summing up, in a very warm
paragraph, David's role in the making of Jerusalem, he concludes
(II, p. 47): "The drama of Jerusalem is never more vivid than
while David is its head." And again, in the evaluation of Solomon's activity in the city, Smith writes (p. 51): "He (*viz.*, Solomon) found her (*viz.*, Jerusalem) little but a fortress, and he left
her a city."

---

7. Cf., e.g., the present writer's discussion of ארונה in *Encyc.
Biblica* (Hebrew), I, 552 f., and his forthcoming article in *Tarbiz*.

8. *Pace* A. Reubeni's attempts, *The Peoples of the Ancient Near
East* (Jerusalem-Tel-Aviv, 1969; Hebrew), pp. 140 ff., who connects
this name (Jebus) with the *wšš* of the Sea Peoples mentioned by Ramses
III—a rather unlikely surmise.

9. In its wider meaning, embracing also agricultural industry (such
as the manufacture of oil and wine) and cattle husbandry.

10. Involving mainly war spoils and tribute; for the whole list see
I Chron. 27:25-31, and cf. S. Yeivin, in *The Kingdoms of Irael and
Judah,* ed. A. Malamat (Jerusalem, 1961), pp. 59-60.

Some chapters of this volume rise to a very exalted prose. Such are, e.g., chaps. V ("Isaiah's Jerusalem"), IX ("Jeremiah's Jerusalem"), and XI ("The Ideal City and the Real"). But there is always a very strong and deep religious feeling that underlies the whole structure of the book, and this leads Smith to accept all scriptural statements (including variant readings of the Septuagint) as equally inspired; and where they don't agree with each other, he takes refuge in statements which, from his point of view, undoubtedly reflect sincere convictions, but which, to some readers at least, would appear somewhat equivocal, and in certain cases contradictory. Thus, e.g., in discussing various statements concerning Solomon's building activity, Smith says (II, pp. 70 f.): ". . . These fragments, so variously placed and rendered in the Hebrew and the Greek texts,[11] apparently belong to one original statement from an ancient source, probably the annals of Solomon's reign; there is no reason to doubt it." And yet in another case, the assassination of King Joash, he finds that: ". . . The Hebrew text of Kings [at II Ki. 12:21] . . . as it stands . . . gives little sense, and the versions testify to so early a corruption . . . that it is perhaps vain to attempt to restore it" (p. 112). However, the corruption, if it is one, concerns only the last word of the verse in question, and was incomprehensible already to the early translators.[12] But the text makes very good sense (with the exception of the attempt to identify the exact spot where the murder had been perpetrated), and hardly justifies the very strong expression of Smith's disapproval of it.

This urge to "improve" texts by emendations, clear influence of the practice so largely made use of by the German schools of Higher Criticism, very frequently led Smith astray, so that emendations are accepted, or suggested, where there is not the slightest reason for introducing them. One typical example will suffice. II Kings states (at 15:5; cf. also II Chron. 26:21): "The Lord smote the king (*viz.,* Azariah) and he became a leper till the

---

11. Note the implicit placing of the Massoretic Text and the Septuagint variants on an equal footing.

12. The word in question, מִלֹּא , may perhaps indicate some topographical feature of Jerusalem, otherwise unknown to us.

day of his death, and dwelt in *beth ha-ḥophshith,* while Jotham the king's son was over the house, governing[13] the people of the land." Clearly the term *beth ha-ḥophshith,* literally "the house of the freed one" (f.; in a neuter or abstract sense), is a euphemistic appellation for some sort of a detention compound (probably outside the confines of the city) for the permanently stricken people, who could not be allowed regular contact with the healthy, not only because of their illness but also on account of their permanent religiously unclean state. The actual purpose of the compound was the absolute antithesis of the literal meaning of the name. There exist innumerable examples of such euphemistic expressions. Klostermann's emendation, *be-betho ḥophshith,* i.e. (he lived) in his own house relieved (of the duties, etc.), and adopted by Smith (II, 117. f.), is not only redundant and without any justification, but actually defeats its own purpose; for *ḥophshith* (as an adv.) does not mean "relieved" but "freed," and that is exactly what the king was *not.*

In this historical part of his *Jerusalem,* Smith displays quite frequently a very pronounced intuition in connection with historical situations, e.g., when he assesses Jehoshaphat's relations with his contemporaries in Israel: "The terms in which he (*viz.,* King Jehoshaphat) did so [i.e., agreed to the suggestions of the kings of the Northern Kingdom], are, however, no stronger than the forms of Oriental politeness demand from an ally" (II, p. 97).

Smith's religious inclinations and his determination to view every phase from this point of view, sometimes led him into bizarre statements in spite of his historical insight. These frequently make strange reading (II, p. 112): "We see then that the Deuteronomic exaltation of Jerusalem was no sudden or artificial achievement . . ."; but the name Jerusalem does not occur in the book of Deuteronomy at all! All that the book speaks of is the cen-

---

13. Literally "judging." Though the figurative use of this verb, as translated here, is quite plausible (cf. S. Yeivin, *Lesonenu,* XXXIII (1968/9 Hebrew), pp. 3 ff.), it may be that allusion is made to the judiciary powers of the regent, replacing the king, as separate and final judicial authority.

tralization of worship at a single place, without attaching any name to it.

This same approach, characteristically Christian, culminates in the closing sentence of *Jerusalem* (II, p. 579): "... the awful siege and destruction which He (*viz.*, Christ) foresaw; while all her spiritual promises, thronging from centuries of hope and prophecy, ran out from her shining into the next: a sunset to herself, but the dawn of a new day to the world beyond." To such a statement no historian can subscribe. The destruction was to come in the year 70 C.E., followed by another in 135 C.E.— but followed also by the return of the exiles and the rebirth of the city, to become a new Metropolis of the State of Israel on the threshold of the second half of the twentieth century C.E.

## Chapter 2: *Jerusalem the City, Then and Now*

### A. Area and Population

The world has changed since 1907, and Jerusalem with it. In 1907 Jerusalem was a small provincial town in the hinterland of a derelict Turkish empire—the "sick man of Europe"—riddled with corruption and inefficiency, overburdened by an enormous external debt to which its income had been mortgaged, and tottering under a regime of indecision that stultified any attempt at reform and regeneration. By 1970 Jerusalem has become the reunified capital of a small but dynamic independent republic, a modern metropolis pulsing with economic and cultural vigor, and looking forward to still greater achievements.

Quantitatively, in 1907 the population of the town was estimated at some 61,000 inhabitants: 40,450 Jews, 10,000 Moslems, and about 10,500 Christians. In September 1967 Jerusalem counted 269,000 inhabitants: 198,000 Jews, 57,500 Moslems, 12,000 Christians, and the remaining 1,500 of unknown or other religions.[1]

---

1. A. M. Lunz, *Luaḥ 'Eres Yisra'el* (Hebrew), vol. XIII. The author owes these references to the kindness of Dr. U. Schmeltz, of the Central Bureau of Statistics in the Prime Minister's Office, to whom he wishes to express his gratitude for the assistance so willingly offered.

In area, too, the city grew immensely. In 1902[2] the municipal area covered 12,720 dunams, i.e., 12.72 sq. km.[3] The Mandatory Government amended the Town Planning Projects several times.[4] After the armistice of 1948 Jerusalem was temporarily divided between the State of Israel and the Kingdom of Jordan, with two strips placed under direct control of the U.N. (a total area of 1.33 sq. km.). The area of Jerusalem under the control of the State of Israel had been fixed then at 25.76 sq. km., while that occupied by Jordan had been 2.6 sq. kms.[5] Since 1967, after reunification, the municipal area of Jerusalem is about 110 sq. km.[6]

## B. *Domestic Architecture and Street Planning*

Much more important were the changes that may perhaps be termed "qualitative," both on the material as well as the spiritual plane. At the beginning of the century the prevalent type of domestic architecture in the Jewish quarter outside the "Old City" was still the so-called *"khotzer"* (*ḥaṣer*, "courtyard"), wherein a large inner court formed a common unroofed square into which opened numerous small appartments, the surrounding structure being sometimes two or even three stories high, approached by open staircases (inaccessible from outside the courtyard); these common courtyards communicated with the narrow lanes, on which they were built, through a gate, that could be closed at will. This type of building was evolved for security reasons, but really

---

2. Only five years before the publication of Smith's book, near enough to be taken as the figure for that time.

3. See the comprehensive article by M. Hecker, in *Sefer Yerushalayim* (Hebrew), I, ed. M. Avi-Yonah (Jerusalem, 1956), pp. 5-7. The late M. Hecker served for many years as the Municipal Engineer of Jerusalem. On the book see below.

4. For details see Henry Kendall, *Jerusalem, the City-Plan* (London, 1948).

5. Hecker, *op. cit.*, pp. 5 ff.

6. The author wishes to thank Mr. Th. Kollek, Mayor of Jerusalem, for kindly passing on his enquiries to the office of the municipal engineer.

represented a new adaptation of the current oriental type of house, the inner courtyard house, closed to the outside.

In the second decade of this century individual buildings appeared, sometimes, again, two or three stories high (and containing each several more spacious apartments), each standing in its own grounds, with porches opening either onto front gardens, or directly onto wider streets. During the Mandatory period (1920-1948) modern apartment houses were introduced, and wider tree-lined streets in new quarters; widening of streets and hard surfacing were attempted also in older quarters. The exclusive use of Jerusalem stone as building material, at least for surfacing the exterior walls, was enforced by a by-law.[7] However, this later restriction had to be abandoned, in spite of its beautifying aspect, when the State of Israel came into being, since it became imperative to speed up building activity as a result of intensified and immediate growth of population.

## C. *Communications*

In 1907 Jerusalem was connected with the open roadstead of Jaffa by a narrow-gauge railway, on which a "toy" train, drawn by a tiny steam engine, took four hours to puff its way into the outskirts of the city, over a winding track of 80 km. Two so-called highways passed through the town: one came up from the maritime plain (Jaffa—64 km. away) through the "Gateway of the Vale" (*Sha'ar Ha-gay; Bab'l-Wad*), and continued eastward to Jericho and the Jordan River; the other ascended from the Negev, the then recently refounded Beersheba, through Hebron, along the

7. Shortly after the conquest of Jerusalem by the British Army in December 1917, the then Military Governor, Col. (later Sir) Ronald Storrs, was instrumental in founding the *"Pro-Jerusalem Society"* (1918-1922). Its records were published by C. R. Ashbee, its civil adviser and Secretary: *Jerusalem* I, *1918-1920;* London, 1921; II, 1920-1922 (mostly a collection of essays by members of the Society), London, 1924. These contain much information on the actual and proposed changes. Mr. Ashbee was succeeded in 1922 by Mr. A. C. Holliday.

The Society ceased functioning in the late twenties since it failed to rouse local interest in its work, owing to a variety of political and ethnical tensions.

watershed of the mountainous backbone of the country, and continued northward to Shechem (*Nablus*) and Beth Ha-gan (*Jenin*). Both were rickety tracks of badly laid paving stones, the maintenance of which left much to be desired, in spite of the toll levied on the so-called "Highway" outside Jaffa. Heavy goods could not be moved over either railway or highroad; they were hauled by camel caravans, but accordingly restricted.

Nowadays a large-gauge railroad, laid by the Mandatory Government, connects Jerusalem not only with the roadsteads of Tel-Aviv and Jaffa, but also with the two ports of Haifa and Ashdod, permitting the movement of heavy goods in trains drawn by diesel engines introduced by the Israel Railways.

Road communications have also immensely improved, partly during the Mandatory period. Jerusalem is now connected by a six-lane highway (being gradually completed) with Tel-Aviv-Jaffa. A second metalled road leads first northward to Ramallah, then westward over the two Beth-Horons to join the main highway to Tel-Aviv-Jaffa at Latrun. A third metalled road runs southwest over Ein-Kerem to Beth-Guvrin to join there the highway from Hebron to Ascalon. Another metalled road branches off at the Gate of the Vale, leading southward to Beth-Shemesh and finally to Beth-Guvrin, while some 6 km. south of the "Gate of the Vale" another branch of the same highway turns west to Ramle, there joining the main Jerusalem-Tel-Aviv-Jaffa road. To the east a new metalled road from el-Bireh leads through Bethel into the Jordan Valley north of Jericho.

## D. *Economic*

The fact that Jerusalem became the capital of the territory (after 1918) led to a great change in the occupations of its population already under the Mandatory Government. Not only was there a large influx of civil servants, but there was a marked rise in commercial activity. This resulted in comparatively large numbers of members of the free professions settling in the city, medical practitioners, dentists, lawyers, engineers, and the like.

Lately, attempts to introduce light industrial plants into the city, to bolster its economic viability, have been crowned with some success.

XXLPROLEGOMENON

## E. *Cultural*

Jerusalem soon became also the center of cultural and academic activity. In 1925 the Hebrew University was formally inaugurated on Mount Scopus. A few years later it opened its doors to students in the Faculties of Humanities and Science, incorporating a number of specialized institutes. With the establishment of the State of Israel, the University, now cut off from its original campus on Mount Scopus, managed not only to continue its activity in a number of hired buildings in the city but to erect a new and vast campus at *Giv'at Ram,* to incorporate the Mandatory School of Law on a vastly improved academic level as a Faculty of Law, and to build up an efficient Faculty of Medicine, mainly with the help of, and based on, the Hadassah Hospital, which soon moved to a new location above *'Ein Kerem.* More faculties were added in the course of time.

The Art School of Bezalel, founded in 1906 by the late Professor Boris Schatz, continued to grow. Following his death, the Museum of Jewish Art which Schatz had established at his School was maintained by the Jewish Agency, and in 1963 merged with the Israel Museum. The Rubin Musical Academy was opened in 1947. The Schocken Institute was established in 1929, and in 1969 it became affiliated with the Jewish Theological Seminary of New York; it houses a large library of some 90,000 volumes. In 1951 the Hebrew Language Academy was created by law, succeeding the voluntary Committee of Hebrew Language, which had been functioning since 1889. In 1959 another governmental law established the National Academy of Sciences.

Only two foreign archaeological institutions were located in Jerusalem in 1907, namely, the École biblique et archeologique française de St. Étienne, of the Dominican Order (founded 1892), and the American Schools of Oriental Research (founded 1900). Since then several other archaeological institutions have been established in the city, foremost among them the British School of Archaeology in Jerusalem (founded 1919), the Biblical Pontifical Institute (*Institutum Pontificum Biblicum;* founded 1927), and the latest newcomer—the Biblical and Archaeological School of the Hebrew Union College-Jewish Institute of Religion.

## Chapter 3: Archaeological Activity in Jerusalem

## A. 1907-1920

One thing that did not change was Jerusalem's significance as the fountainhead of Judaism and monotheism in general, and the deep attachment of world Jewry to it, both as the seat of their independence in the past, and the beacon-light of their revival as a rejuvenated nation in the present and for the future.

The religious significance of the city always attracted international archaeological bodies. And indeed, archaeological investigation and excavation continued there almost uninterruptedly.

The summer of 1909 saw the arrival of the adventurous Montague Parker expedition, that continued its investigations until the summer of 1911. Its motive and ultimate aim remain obscure; fortunately, however, the Rev. Father L. H. Vincent of the École biblique was able to follow the course of its work almost from the beginning, and his publication is the only record of the achievements of that investigation involving the source of Gihon (the Virgin's Spring) and the Siloam Tunnel.[8] They discovered in the tunnels, running from the spring in various directions, remains attesting the presence of a population from the fourth millennium B.C.E. onwards.

It seems that in 1911, not satisfied with the course of his work till then, Parker attempted to bribe his way into excavating by night within the area of the Temple Mount. This incensed the local populace to such a degree that the members of the expedition had to flee for dear life to Jaffa, board their yacht, and leave the country for good.[9]

---

8. Leon-Hugues Vincent, *Jérusalem sous terre* (London, 1911); available also in English translation: *Underground Jerusalem* (London, 1911).

9. B. Maisler (Mazar), *Toledoth Ha-meḥqar Ha-' arkhe'ologi Be-'eres Yisra'el* (The History of Archaeological Exploration in Palestine; Hebrew) (Jerusalem, 1936), pp. 80 ff., who also evaluates there Parker's contribution to the exploration of Jerusalem.

The ill-fated end of Parker's expedition was followed by the beginning of an exploration marking the first Jewish participation in archaeological work in Jerusalem. The "Father of the Yishuv," Baron Edmond de Rothschild of Paris, equipped an archaeological expedition under the French-Jewish scholar Raymond Weill, which was to excavate in the SE hill outside the "Old City." The expedition was active for two seasons (1913-1914) before the First World War, and resumed its work a decade later with the same backing, for one more season (1923-1924). Weill's work was executed in strip investigations in the southern part of the SE hill of Jerusalem, outside (and south of) the south-eastern part of the Suleimanian wall of the so-called "Old City."[10] His main discovery during the earlier seasons was a monumental series of ruck-cut tombs, which he took to be the burial place of the Davidic line.[11] However, most scholars rejected this identification.[12] The present author would suggest that these tombs represent the burial places of the pre-Israelite kings of Jerusalem.[13]

Another important discovery during the early seasons of excavation was an almost complete Greek inscription on a marble slab (broken into two halves), unfortunately not found *in situ*.[14] It commemorates a certain Theodotos, Priest and Archisynagogos, who "built the synagogue for the reading of the Law and for the teaching of the Commandments".[15] Its importance lay in the fact that it proved the existence of synagogues as congregational meeting places before the destruction of the Second Temple. Much more questionable, important as it is, is Weill's interpretation, dating, and reconstruction of the various fortification remains uncovered by him.[16]

---

10. R. Weill, *La Cité de David,* I (Paris, 1920); II (Paris, 1947), with a valuable bibliography on pp. 2-6.

11. *Op. cit.,* I, pp. 157 ff.

12. See, e.g., L. H. Vincent, *RB,* XXX (1921), pp. 412 ff.

13. For a discussion of the problem, see S. Yeivin, *JNES,* VII (1948), pp. 30 ff.

14. Now on exhibition at the Museum of the Dept. of Antiquities and Museums (the so-called "Rockefeller" Museum).

15. Weill, I, pp. 186 ff.; pl XXV, A. For the early literature discussing this inscription and its significance, see vol. II, p. 2.

16. Vol. II, pp. 27 ff.

## B. *1920-1948*

It was the idea of the late Professor John Garstang, the founder and first director of the Dept. of Antiquities of the Civil Mandatory Administration, to prepare a blueprint for international cooperation in the exploration of the site of ancient Jerusalem (the SE hill, south of the so-called "Old City"). Thus it happened that Baron de Rothschild's renewed expedition, led by Weill, was assigned the area of its former investigation in the southern sector of the SE hill, while a permit for the exploration of the northern sector was issued about the same time to the Palestine Exploration Fund. The latter put the veteran excavator, Prof. R. A. S. Macalister in charge of the expedition, which was financed largely by a contribution of the *Daily Telegraph* of London, and later supplemented by contributions from Sir Charles Marston and the British Academy. Macalister was assisted by the Rev. John Garrow Duncan, who later took over the directorship of this undertaking.

This expedition investigated two fields (nos. 5 and 7) on the eastern edge of the SE hill, some 140-280 m. due south of the SE angle of the Suleimanian wall of the "Old City." Macalister found the limits of the Jebusite town on the north, protected by an artificial moat cut across the ridge from east to west. But his investigations of the fortification works on the eastern edge of the excavated area were less successful. He failed to examine the remains underlying both the "sloping rampart" and the square tower abutting on it on the south, and was led to date the former to the Jebusite (pre-Davidic) period, and the latter to Solomon's days. His account of the associated pottery is confused, and in no way indicates the correctness of his chronological conclusions.[17] His published assumptions confused the issues on Jerusalem's history for over forty years, until Prof. Kathleen M. Kenyon's recent excavations put the facts into their proper perspective (see below).

---

17. R. A. S. Macalister and J. Garrow Duncan, *Excavations on the hill of Ophel, Jerusalem, 1923-1925* (London, 1926; = *Annual of the Palestine Exploration Fund* [*APEF*], IV), pp. 65; 73-74.

The work of the Palestine Exploration Fund ( = PEF) on the SE hill, this time in conjunction with the then newly established British School of Archaeology in Jerusalem, was renewed in 1927. It was then conducted on the western edge of the hill and down its western slope (field No. 10), under the direction of J. W. Crowfoot, the Director of the British School of Archaeology, ably assisted by G. W. Fitzgerald, and again largely financed by a contribution from Sir Charles Marston. Though the remains of a massive wall and western gate flanked by two towers, which Crowfoot uncovered along the lower western slope of the SE hill, on which Macalister investigated its eastern edge (see above), obviously dated to the Hasmonean period, it seems that the western limit of the Jebusite and Israelite towns apparently ran on the same line, as Crowfoot endeavoured to prove.[18] However, Miss Kenyon does not agree with his view, suggesting instead that the Jebusite-Davidic limit of the city, and by inference also the earlier occupations, ran farther up the slope (to the east).[19]

In the early twenties a new group entered the field of archaeological exploration of Jerusalem, the Jewish Palestine Exploration Society (now: Israel Exploration Society). Founded in 1913 by local Jewish scholars, it perforce suspended its activity during the years of the First World War. It started its field work with excavations at Hammath (south of Tiberias) under the direction of Prof. Nahum Slousch in 1920-1921.[20] In 1924 the Society began its work in Jerusalem, uncovering, cleaning, and exploring the funeral monument popularly known as *Yad Avshalom* ( = The Memorial of Absalom). This enterprise definitely established the connection of the freestanding monument with the burial-cave in the NE corner of the leveled rock-platform on which the mono-

---

18. J. W. Crowfoot and G. M. Fitzgerald, *APEF*, V (1927), pp. 15 ff.

19. Kathleen M. Kenyon, *Jerusalem, Excavating 3000 Years of History* (London,.1967), pp. 25 ff.

20. N. Slousch, *Journal of the Jewish Palestine Exploration Society* ( = *JPES;* Hebrew), I/1 (1921), pp. 5 ff.; I/2 (1922-24), pp. 49 ff.

lithic monument stands. The cave was explored and a complete plan of it published for the first time.[21]

In 1925 the widening of the Richard Coeur-de-Lion Rd. revealed, at the corner where it enters Nablus Rd., opposite the building which then housed the Mandatory Department of Antiquities, a large drafted ashlar stone typical of the so-called Herodian masonry, which seemed to be *in situ* as part of a monumental wall. When trenching started on an adjacent plot preparatory to building activities, more antique remains were uncovered, and the Department of Antiquities stopped further work on the site. The Jewish Palestine Exploration Society then commissioned two of its members, Professors L. A. Mayer and E. L. Sukenik, to investigate these with a view to determining their nature. In three seasons (1925-1927) they revealed several sections of a large fortification wall, of an average thickness of 4.00-4.50 m., running in a general direction southwest to northeast. At irregular intervals there were square towers jutting out of the wall, one of them 7.50 m.; their length varied from 12 to 16 m. A gateway in this wall (opposite the American School of Archaeology) was flanked by two towers. The excavators rightly identified these with the "third wall" of Jerusalem, and the gateway as that near the "towers of the women" mentioned by Josephus.[22] Later, additional fragments of the same wall were uncovered, both east and west of those investigated by Mayer and Sukenik; and long-known foundations of what seems to have been the northwestern corner tower of this wall east of the so-called "Russian Compound", in the

---

21. N. Slousch, *The Excavations round the Memorial of Absalom*, *Journal of the JPES*, I/2 (1922-24), pp. 5-48, and plan—fig. 5 (on p. 26). Cf. also the latest discussion in N. Avigad, *Ancient Monuments in the Kidron Valley* (Jerusalem, 1954; Hebrew), pp. 97 ff., especially pp. 120 ff.

22. L. A. Mayer-E. L. Sukenik, *Excavations of the Third Wall* (Hebrew), (Jerusalem, 1931).

vicinity of Prophets' Street, were coordinated with the newly uncovered remains.[23]

The publication of Mayer and Sukenik's results immediately
brought on a very spirited controversy. First and foremost among
the antagonists of the proposed identification of these remains
was one of the greatest authorities on ancient Jerusalem, the
Rev. Father L. H. Vincent.[24] Although his criticism seems to be
based on archaeological objections, one cannot somehow escape
the impression that it stems first and foremost from the fact that
this discovery was likely to shake the authenticity of the Christian
tradition concerning the Holy Sepulcher. The articles are un-
necessarily emotional, sometimes rising to vehement crescendo,
making free with sarcastic personal remarks about the excavators.
Vincent's suggestion that the wall discovered represents remains of
hasty fortifications carried out at the time of Bar-Kokhba's war
against the Romans[25] cannot be considered seriously, for the
simple reason that at that period Jerusalem had been desolate
for over 60 years, and admitting a small settlement of onhangers
on the Legionary camp, and scanty Jewish squatters among the
ruins, there was no justification whatsoever to enlarge the fortified
area to such an extent. (See further below.)

It may have been with a view to shedding more light on the
problem of Jerusalem's ancient fortifications in Herodian times—
though he himself gives a different reason—that R. W. Hamilton
undertook, in 1937, some soundings along the present north
wall of the "Old City," in the vicinity of the "Shechem (Damascus) Gate" (*Bab$^i$ l-'Ammud*) and "Herod's Gate," or "The Flower
Gate" (*Bab$^i$ z-Zahra*). He reports that these soundings "were
outside the North Wall of Jerusalem." But his results are very

----

23. C. S. Fisher, *BASOR,* No. 83 (Oct. 1941), pp. 4 ff.; E. L.
Sukenik, *PEQ,* 1944, pp. 145 ff.; L. A. Mayer and E. L. Sukenik,
*Qedem,* I (1942; Hebrew), pp. 24 ff.; R. B. Scott, *BASOR,* No. 169
(Feb. 1963), pp. 61-62.

24. *RB,* XXXIV (1925), pp. 588 ff.; XXXVI (1927), pp. 576 ff.;
XXXVII (1928), pp. 80 ff.; 321 ff. For further literature on this controversy, see M. Avi-Yonah, *IEJ,* 18 (1969), pp. 98 ff.

25. Vincent, *RB,* XXXVII (1928), pp. 334 ff.

significant for the problem on hand, for according to him, "there is no evidence of a wall that could have belonged to any city earlier than Aelia Capitolina."[26] It seemed then that the present-day north wall of the "Old City" could not be taken into consideration in discussing Josephus' description of the three walls of Jerusalem at the time of the Roman siege in 69-70 C.E. (See further below.)

With the appointment of E. T. Richmond as the Director of the Mandatory Dept. of Antiquities in 1927, a new policy of excavations was instituted.

It had become obvious by then that foreign expeditions were interested mainly in the exploration of prehistoric or biblical sites.[27] So the Dept. of Antiquities decided to concentrate its efforts on the exploration of post-biblical sites. Following an extensive spell of work at the Pilgrim's Castle (Crusaders' Period), northwest of 'Athlith, and its immediate surroundings, Mr. C. N. Johns, of the Dept. of Antiquities, transferred his attention to the Citadel in the "Old City" of Jerusalem. Excavations here continued intermittently from 1934 to 1948.[28] The results of these investigations proved that the area of the Citadel covered the remains of the three large towers erected by Herod, namely, those of Phasael, Hippicos, and Mariamne (west to east); and that these were built into an earlier fortification wall of the late Hellenistic and Hasmonean periods, probably going back to the early second century B.C.E.[29] The Herodian fortifications were much built-over in Roman times, beginning with the camp of the Xth Legion and ending with Byzantine reconstructions. The Citadel was in con-

---

26. R. W. Hamilton, "Excavations against the North Wall of Jerusalem 1937-8," *Quarterly of the Department of Antiquities, Palestine* (= *QDAP*), X (1944), pp. 1-53, and pls. I-XI.

27. Only one Crusader site had been investigated by foreign excavators till then, namely Montfort (near *Mi'iliye*); this was an expedition sponsored by the Metropolitan Museum of Art, New York, and directed by B. Dean, in 1926.

28. C. N. Johns, "The Citadel, Jerusalem," *QDAP*, XIV (1948), pp. 121 ff.

29. *Idem.*, p. 131.

tinuous use during the Early Arab period, while under the Crusaders it served both as Citadel and Royal Residence.[30]

However, perhaps the most significant result of this exploration was the discovery (in the lowest reaches of trial pits) of late Middle Israelite pottery (of the 7th-6th centuries B.C.E.). These, however, were found in the fill and could not be connected with any building remains dating to the same age.[31]

Apart from the problems of fortifications, and consequent upon them the extent of the walled city at various periods of its existence, two more fields of exploration were pursued in the years following World War I, namely, (a) various restricted excavations at different spots in the "Old City" and its surroundings, mainly within the precincts of various churches; (b) uncovering and cleaning numerous tombs belonging to many periods all round the "Old City," as well as in and around its newer quarters and suburbs.

The former group includes the uncovering and investigation of the Eleone Church on the western slope of the Mount of Olives. This was carried out by the *Pères Blancs* in 1910 and again in 1918. Only foundations, or foundation-cuttings in the rock, of this building remained, revealing a plan that includes a largish courtyard surrounded by porticoes, and a basilica of 72 x 12 m. ending in an "inner" apse before which there was a crypt. The erection of this church is attributed to Constantine (4th century C.E.).[32]

Another church of the same period, restored and built over by the Crusaders, was investigated during the years 1909-1920 by Father Orfali and the architect Barluzzi, on behalf of the Franciscan Order, at Gethsemane, at the western foot of the Mount of Olives. The Byzantine church, here too, is a basilica, 22.5 x 16 m.,

---

30. *Idem.*, p. 163.
31. *Idem.*, p. 130, and fig. 6 (on p. 129). However, see further below.
32. Fathers L. Hugues Vincent and F.-M. Abel, *Jérusalem nouvelle,* I (Paris, 1914), pp. 339 ff. For the investigation in the adjacent Russian Compound, see Elisabeth Loukianoff, *Mémoires presentés à l'institute d'Egypte* (= *MIE*), XLII (1932).

with a large protruding apse in the center, flanked by two "inner" apsides.[33]

West of the YMCA building on King David St. were found in 1932 remains of a Georgian monastary and nearby a cemetery of the 5th-7th centuries C.E., investigated at the time by Dr. Baramki of the Mandatory Dept. of Antiquities.[34] Additional architectural fragments of the same monastary came to light in the early fifties.[35]

Up to 1912 the Assumptionist Fathers continued the exploration of the remains in their plot at the eastern slopes of the Western Hill south of the Suleimanian wall of the "Old City"; investigations actually had begun as far back as 1889. The remains represent a large house, 31 x 21 m., of the type of an inner courtyard, with an underground cistern in the center, surrounded by halls. Here and there in the halls were uncovered remains of mosaic floors. The façade on the north had a portico supported on pillars, and a large *kantharos* in the center. Though Father Germer-Durand, who discussed these remains,[36] dates the house to the late years of the Second Temple, Avi-Yonah is of the opinion that comparative material rather justifies its attribution to Aelia Capitolina.[37]

In 1937 D. C. Baramki investigated a small chapel (6.10 x 3 m.) of the Byzantine period near the "Third Wall" of Jerusalem.[38]

Of the large number of tombs excavated between the two World Wars[39] only a few call for especial mention. In 1929

---

33. P. Gaudence Orfalli, O.F.M., *Gethsémani* (Paris, 1914); Vincent-Abel, *op. cit.,* pp. 328 ff.

34. See *apud* M. Avi-Yonah, in *Encyclopaedia of Archaeological Excavations in the Holy Land* (= *EAE*), vol. I (Jerusalem, 1971; Hebrew), p. 230.

35. In the files of the Israel Dept. of Antiquities.

36. *RB,* XI (1914), p. 223.

37. See p. 224 of article cited in n. 34 above.

38. D. C. Baramki, *QDAP,* VI (1938), pp. 56 ff.

39. For a general survey of Jerusalem tombs, by no means complete, see N. Avigad's article in *EAE,* I, pp. 232-241.

Prof. E. L. Sukenik investigated a small rock-cut tomb near Giv'at Ram (*Sheikh Badr*), on the northwestern approaches to Jerusalem, dated to the second century C.E. In a small compartment of this one room, one *kokh* (niche) tomb was found together with a stone ossuary, a terracotta ossuary, and iron nails attesting the original presence of a wooden one as well.[40]

Another accidental discovery of a tomb in 1934 was also investigated by E. L. Sukenik. There, one of the *kokhs* was still stopped up by a stone closure plastered over, while above it an Aramaic inscription warned: "This niche had been made for the bones of our progenitors, its length (being) two ells (*'ammin*), and it should not be opened on them (*viz.*, the bones)." Here was an opportunity to determine the length of the contemporary ell;[41] however, the resultant size (78 cm.) seems too large, and the question of the exact size of the ell at that period is still unanswered.[42]

In 1945 a one-room tomb with five *kokhim* was accidentally discovered near Talpioth on the southern outskirts of the town. Again investigated by Sukenik, it caused a short-lived flutter in the foreign press. The finds, pointing to the first century C.E., included 11 ossuaries; the outside of one bore large crosses, marked in coal, on another were written the words $I\eta\sigma\upsilon\varsigma\ \iota\upsilon$, and on a third the words $I\eta\sigma\upsilon\varsigma\ \alpha\lambda\omega\theta$. The explorer saw in these symbols and inscriptions an expression of grief on the death of Jesus,[43] but many scholars disagreed with him.[44]

## C. *1948-1967*

Following the Israeli War of Independence (1947-1949) Je-

---

40. E. L. Sukenik, *Tarbiz*, I (1930; Hebrew), pp. 122 ff.

41. Idem, *Tarbiz*, VI (1935; Hebrew), pp. 190 ff.

42. This author would suggest that the given length possibly does not refer to the *kokh* itself, but to its opening, in which case its length (across) being about 66 cm. (measured on the plan, fig. 1 in Sukenik's article cited in n. 41 preceding) will yield an ell of 33 cm., which is the standard Ptolemaic cubit.

43. Sukenik, *AJA*, 51 (1947), pp. 5 ff.

44. N. Avigad, in *EAE*, I, p. 240, § 11.

rusalem was temporarily divided. The eastern part of the city, including the whole of the "Old City," was held by Jordan, while the new city on the northwest and the southwest remained in Israel. The building which housed the Palestine Archaeological (Rockefeller) Museum and the Mandatory Dept. of Antiquities remained in the territory held by Jordan. Officially, in preparation for the division suggested by the UN Commission, the then High Commissioner of Palestine issued in 1948 an order-in-council, by which the Museum was placed in the hands of an international body of twelve commissioners representing archaeological bodies, various Arab Governments, and the residents of Palestine, including a Jewish representative of the Hebrew University.[45] Actually, this body acquiesced in the Jordanian refusal to allow the Jewish representative to take part in its deliberations. Though it made several attempts to persuade the present author, who was appointed in 1948 to head the Israel Dept. of Antiquities, to return to them a few files and a museum card-index, which accidentally remained in the hands of former Jewish employees of the Mandatory Dept., because they were working on these at home under the specific instructions of R. W. Hamilton, the Mandatory Director of Antiquities at the time, this body never even acknowledged the proposals made by this author for the exchange of these materials against material belonging to Jewish owners that remained in the Palestine Archaeological Museum, and for arrangements enabling the Jewish representative to participate in the meetings.

Thus, twice repeated offers of Israeli cooperation with this body came to naught. In 1966 the Government of Jordan nationalized the Palestine Archaeological Museum, and dissolved the international board of commissioners without the latter voicing the slightest protest or objection, as far as publicly known.

Following this temporary division of the city in 1949, archaeological activity continued on both sides. In the eastern part, occupied by the Jordanian authorities, many tombs, mainly east of the city, were investigated, and the results published in various

45. *The Palestine Gazette,* No. 1666, April 22, 1948.

scientific periodicals.[46] Only some explorations inside and in the vicinity of the "Old City" of Jerusalem need especial mention here. During the years 1949-1958 Father Sylvester J. Sallers, of the Franciscans, excavated on the property of the Custody of the Holy Land at Bethany, on the eastern slopes of the Mount of Olives, where he uncovered tombs and cisterns dating from the Late Israelite ( = Persian) Period onwards. He also cleared some features in and around the ancient church and monastary of St. Lazarus.[47]

In 1955 the site of Dominus Flevit, on the western slope of the Mount of Olives, was investigated by Father B. Bagatti. A small chapel (14 x 7 m.) was uncovered with a mosaic pavement of geometric patterns in which was incorporated a Greek inscription mentioning a priest in the church of St. Anastasis. There were foundations of one apsis, and an altar with a chancelscreen in front of it. According to Father T. J. Milik, this chapel was erected in the seventies of the 7th century C.E.[48] In addition, a cemetery of the Middle and Late Canaanite and the Roman Periods on the property was investigated in the course of the same operation.[49]

In the years 1956 and 1962 the White Fathers resumed the investigation of the remains in their grounds near the Church of St. Anne, begun a long time before that. An underground passage between the two large cisterns, uncovered previously, was decorated with painted scenes. These paintings, together with inscribed dedication objects, suggest the existence of a shrine of one of the oriental divinities, the cult of which had been so common in the Roman period.[50]

---

46. See Avigad's article cited in n. 39 above.

47. Fr. Sylvester J. Saller, O.F.M., *Liber Annuus,* II (1951/2), pp. 119 ff.

48. Father B. Bagatti, *Liber Annuus,* VI (1955/6), pp. 240 ff.; his measurements are smaller, since he gives the inner size.

49. For the Late Canaanite tomb, see C. Lemaire, *Liber Annus,* V (1954/5), pp. 261 ff. For the Middle and Late Canaanite Periods, see F. J. Sallers, *The Excavations of Dominus Flevit,* Vol. II (Jerusalem 1964); for the Roman age, see B. Bagatti and J. T. Milik, vol. I (Jerusalem 1958).

50. See in Avi-Yonah's article, *EAE,* I, p. 226.

In 1960 Father Corbo of the Franciscan Order explored the remains of the Church of Ascension on the summit of the Mount of Olives. His excavations proved that the original church was of the *rotunda* type (about 25 m. in diameter). Inside the building there was an inner circle of columns that supported the domed roof. The church had been destroyed by the Sassanians after their conquest of the city (614 C.E.), but reconstructed according to its original plan by Bishop Modestus after the Byzantine reconquest of the land. A dedicatory inscription mentioning his name was found in the corner of these excavations.[51]

In 1962 reconstruction work was carried out under the auspices of the Greek Government in the Church of the Holy Sepulchre. In the course of this work, several points concerning the plan of the earlier basilical church, erected on this spot by Constantine in the early fourth century C.E., were revealed.[52] Recently, reports in the local press announced the uncovering of part of the original apse of the Constantinian basilica.[53]

As far as Jewish remains are concerned, the Jordanians not only destroyed the Jewish quarter in the "Old City," ruining and desecrating its numerous synagogues, but carried this desecration to the large Jewish Cemetery on the western slope of the Mount of Olives, which goes back to the early days of the Kingdom of Israel. Part of the cemetery was built over by contractors of the modern Intercontinental Hotel; and tombstones from all over the cemetery were torn up and reused by the Jordanian army for various purposes in the neighborhood. While all this was going on, quite openly, the various pious international bodies, who were quick to raise an outcry against alleged and imaginary misdeeds of the Government of Israel, maintained absolute silence about this desecration.

In 1961, Professor Kathleen M. Kenyon started, on behalf of an enterprise jointly sponsored by the British School of Archaeology in Jerusalem, the Palestine Exploration Fund, the British Academy, and the École biblique, and with Perè Roland de Vaux as codirector, a new rëexamination of the ancient fortifications

---

51. P. V. Corbo, *Liber Annuus,* X (1959/60), pp. 205 ff.
52. See *apud* Avi-Yonah, in *EAE,* vol. I, p. 227.
53. *Jerusalem Post,* March 3, 1971,.p. 8.

of Jerusalem. Prof. Kenyon's point of departure were certain topographic considerations that did not quite square with Macalister's conclusions.[54] To check her doubts she cut a broad trial trench down the eastern slope of David's city, starting on the eastern edge of Macalister's field no. 5 of investigations on top of the slope, and going down to the vicinity of the Gihon Spring (the Virgin's Fountain). The trial trench was 11 m. wide and 48 m. long. She also sunk several trial pits along the northern and southwestern edges of the southeastern hill of ancient Jerusalem.[55]

Miss Kenyon soon realized that the fortifications attributed by Macalister to the Jebusites, David, and Solomon, were in fact Hasmonean, and that their foundations rested on tumbled down stones, below which came to light remains of "very massive stone buildings . . . with associated pottery of the seventh century BC."[56] At the bottom of the trench she found remains of a heavy wall "built of rough *wadi* boulders of great size . . . It was built slightly in advance of a scarp in the natural rock, and between the rock face and the wall was a filling containing only Middle Bronze Age pottery, about 1800 BC."[57] This proved to be the Jebusite wall, and it continued in use till the seventh century B.C.E., when it was superseded by another wall, remains of which were found crossing the early wall at a higher level in the excavations.[58]

---

54. Mainly, the question of water supply from the Gihon Spring whenever trouble started, which did not square with Macalister's results (see above); for a detailed discussion, see her volume on *Jerusalem, 3000 Years of History* (London, 1957), pp. 19 ff.

55. *Idem*, fig. 5 (on p. 29).

56. *Iden*, p. 24. About Macalister's Jebusite ramp, see there pp. 115-116.

57. *Idem*, p. 24.

58. This reconstruction, coupled probably with the top layer of houses, may possibly be attributed to the time of King Manasseh (cf. II Chron. 33:14), though this is nowhere stated by Prof. Kenyon. She seems inclined (pp. 68 ff.) to ascribe this phase to King Hezekiah; but since her chronology—720-685 B.C.E.—is impossible, and should be emended to 727-698 B.C.E. (S. Yeivin, *Chronological Tables* [Hebrew], Tel-Aviv University, 1962, pp. 10-11), her suggestion seems hardly possible.

Though the above-mentioned Jebusite-Israelite wall was still a good deal west of (and higher up than) the spring, a tunnel and a shaft, already discovered by the Parker expedition, would have provided a protected access to the water even under siege conditions.[59] The built-up area between the Jebusite-Israelite wall down the slope and the top of the southeastern hill rose in tiered terraces protected by retaining walls and connected by flights of stairs.[60] Prof. Kenyon describes also some of the private buildings, which conform to the very common pattern of the "four-spaced" (or the so-called ח) house, in which she considers the middle space roofed,[61] though evidence from other sites definitely points to its being a small inner courtyard open to the sky.[62] The excavator's identification of supposed cultic places seems also rather questionable.[63] Of course, it is a well-known and persistent tendency among archaeologists (not only those dealing with Israelite archaeology) to see in every upright stone a *maṣṣebah,* in every flat stone an altar, and in every slightly unusual pottery vessel or even sherd a relic of cultic significance; but these should usually be taken *magno cum grano salis.*[64] This is true also of the cultic interpretations of the very numerous fragments of figurines. Though the excavator seems ready to admit "that an animal figurine has no greater significance than that of a toy," the lady persists in ascribing the female figurines to the "elemental mother-goddess type"[65] for which there is not the slightest evidence.[66]

---

59. Kenyon, *op. cit.,* p. 25 and figs. 3-4.

60. It should be mentioned that such a suggestion about Jerusalem in the days of the Second Temple was made by the architect M. Kon in a private conversation with the author.

61. *Op. cit.,* pp. 82-83.

62. M. Avi-Yonah and S. Yeivin, *The Antiquities of Israel* (Tel-Aviv, 1955. Hebrew), pp. 90 ff., and figs. 17-20d. Cf. now also Y. Shiloh, *IEJ,* 20 (1970), pp. 180 ff.

63. Kenyon, *op. cit.,* pp. 65-66.

64. Discussed in some detail in the author's forthcoming article in *EI,* XI (Dunayevsky Memorial Volume).

65. Kenyon, *op. cit.,* p. 101.

66. The author has dealt in detail with this question in *Proceedings of the American Academy for Jewish Research* [*PAAJS*], XXXIV (1966), pp. 148 ff.

Much happier and extremely interesting are the excavator's surmises concerning the probability that the Pool of Siloam was originally a covered (cave) cistern,[67] though not for the reasons propounded by Prof. Kenyon. (See further below.)

This problem focuses the reader's attention on the limits of the Davidic city on the north and west. On the north Prof. Kenyon's delineation agrees more or less with that suggested by Macalister; but her delimitation of the western edge of the Jebusite and Davidic city—resting as it does mostly on negative evidence[68]—seems, at least to this author, rather doubtful; in his opinion Crowfoot's suggestion about this limit (see above) still stands.

A second undertaking by the same expedition in the years 1964-1966 was intended to clarify the problem of the "Third Wall." It was helped by the investigation instituted by the Jordanian Dept. of Antiquities and entrusted to one of Prof. Kenyon's assistants, Dr. J. B. Hennessy.[69]

Hennessy, who dug at the Shechem (Damascus) Gate, exposed the foundations of the present gate, and just east of it, "below a totally unexpected gate of the Crusader period on a different plan and preceding Byzantine levels, was found an accumulation of the time of Aelia Capitolina.[70] Below that came the original surface and then the foundation trench of the original wall . . . The lower part of the eastern tower proved to be preserved to a considerable height . . . It has not been possible to uncover the central arch of the gateway, corresponding to the present gate, but to the north of it the side arch for foot-passengers, flanked by engaged columns, survives to half its height in the original masonry."[71]

This, of course, flatly contradicts Hamilton's statements; but it

67. Kenyon, *op. cit.*, pp. 71-72.

68. Kenyon, *op. cit.*, pp. 25-28 and fig. 5.

69. Kenyon, *op. cit.*, p. 162; J. B. Hennessy, *Levant*, II (1970), pp. 22 ff.

70. This was the top of the arched gateway to which Hamilton had referred in his investigations; see above.

71. Kenyon, *op. cit.*, p. 163, and pl. 76. See also *RB*, LXXV (1968), pp. 250-251.

still does not prove Hennessy's contention that the lower part of
the gateway (its upper part was reconstructed in Hadrian's time
by the builders of Aelia Capitolina) had been erected by Herod
Agrippa I, and consequently represents the Third Wall.[72] It could,
and most probably does, represent the Second Wall of Jerusalem,
for Hennessy's arguments against such an earlier date are archaeologically rather weak.

Prof. Kenyon's conclusion—based as it was on Hennessy's arguments—that the wall uncovered by Meyer and Sukenik represents the remains of the Roman circumvallation has been definitely
refuted by Prof. M. Avi-Yonah in his summarizing article on the
problem.[73] Apart from cogent topographic reasons, the remains,
if they represent the circumvallation, flatly contradict Josephus'
statement that the whole circumvallation was erected and finished
in three days. This assumption can also be hardly squared with
some of the findings of a second assistant of Prof. Kenyon, E. W.
Hamrick, who reports on his re-examination of a section of the
wall already dug by Mayer and Sukenik: "The problem of identifying the wall is complicated by the fact that one cannot determine
conclusively the direction in which the wall faces. Miss Kenyon
has taken the position that the wall faces south, but the present
writer is unconvinced"; and further on: "The towers ... suggest,
moreover, that the wall faces north." [74] A further stretch of the
wall accidentally discovered during building operations in 1966
confirmed Hamrick in his abovementioned doubts, though he
still insists that the wall postdates the period of Agrippa I.[75]

Summarizing, one might agree with Prof. Avi-Yonah's conclusions that the remains uncovered by Prof. Mayer and Sukenik
seem to be those of the Third Wall, while the exact line of the

---

72. Hennessy, *Levant,* II (1970), p. 24.

73. M. Avi-Yonah, *IEJ,* 18 (1968), pp. 98 ff., pp. 111 ff.

74. E. W. Hamrick, "New Excavations at Sukenik's 'Third Wall,' "
*BASOR,* No. 183 (Oct. 1966), pp. 25-26.

75. Hamrick, "Further Notes on the 'Third Wall,' " *BASOR,* No.
192 (Dec. 1968), pp. 21 ff.

Second Wall is still unclear, though it did pass under the present-day gateway of the Shechem Gate.[76]

Prof. Kenyon's investigations included some trial pits along the eastern slopes of the Western Hill (so-called "Mount Zion"), but she could not shed new light on the southern limits of the city in the days of the Second Temple.[77]  Prof. Kenyon also dug some trial pits in the garden of the Armenian Patriarchate, where her investigation produced "A considerable amount of Iron Age II [= Middle Israelite Period] pottery . . . but on rock there was only evidence of extensive quarrying," which she ascribes for what seem cogent reasons to the Maccabean period.[78]  However, her negative conclusion about the inclusion of the Western Hill in pre-exilic Jerusalem proved at elast partly wrong in light of later excavations.  (See further below.)

The manifold building activities that took place in the Israeli part of the city necessitated a constant vigil on the part of the newly created Dept. of Antiquities; for though many public bodies and private citizens were very archaeologically minded and reported immediately any accidental discoveries made in the course of such work, thus enabling the Dept. to step in and investigate, others, less publicly minded and fearing complications and delays, involving possible financial losses, concealed such information, sometimes without being discovered until too late.

On the other hand, there were institutions that even initiated and financed investigation of sites which they intended to include in their building projects. Thus the Jewish Agency, before starting on its construction of *Binyene Ha'umma,* at the northwestern approaches to the city, financed a Dept. of Antiquities expedition, which was assisted by the Israel Exploration Society, to investigate *Giv'at Ram (Sheikh Bader).* A small force, working under Drs. M. Avi-Yonah and P. P. Kahane successively, uncovered scanty remains of a large mosaic-paved Byzantine church of St. George

---

76. Avi-Yonah, *loc. cit.* (above, n. 73), pp. 120-125; see also below.

77. Kenyon, *op cit.,* p. 144 and figs. 5 and 14.

78. Kathleen M. Kenyon, in *Near Eastern Archaeology in the Twentieth Century,* ed. James A. Sanders (New-York, 1970), p. 246; cf. also above, n. 54; and see further below.

and the adjacent monastary, a tenth legion workshop for producing tiles (?), and some additional buildings.[79]

Another exploration initiated by the Dept. of Antiquities, with the assistance of the Israel Exploration Society, in the near vicinity of the city, in an area "threatened with development," was the continuation of a half-hearted exploration started some thirty years before, on behalf of the American Schools of Oriental Research, in one of the large heaped-up stone "cairns."[80] Mrs. Ruth Amiran intended to start on the large tumulus, across the top of which Albright had dug a shallow trench; but technical reasons persuaded her to abandon her original intention, and to excavate instead a similar large "cairn" in the vicinity (no. 5), in the spring of 1953. She removed the whole mass of heaped-up rubble, which was surprisingly clean of earth, sand, or any other materials, and entirely devoid of potsherds in the major part of its height. Only toward the lowest layers of the heaped-up stone rubble were there some sherds of the late-seventh cent. B.C.E. (late Middle Israel III). Below the heaped-up stone "cairn" was uncovered a polygonal (17-sided) stone structure, consisting of dry rubble masonry, its wall standing in part to a maximum height of 1.45 m., while its thickness was 1.00 m. Its inner face was unfinished. It enclosed an area of uneven surface, in the middle of which was an irregular hexagonal cavity lined with stones, some 90 cm deep, and in the middle of the eastern part of which were remains of a filled-up, flagstone-paved platform. The cavity had been filled with red earth mixed with ashes and charcoal bits. On the lower rock surface to the east there were again traces of burning, fragments of charcoal and quantities of ashes mixed with sherds of the above-mentioned period. Two entrances led into this walled-in. enclosure. One, on the east, opened on to five stone steps built over a fill, rising to the level of the flagstone-paved platform exactly opposite the lined hexagonal cavity; the other, on the northwest, was preceded by two shallow steps over the thickness of the wall of the enclosure.

79. A. Avi-Yonah, *Bulletin of the Israel Exploration Society* (= *BIES*), XV, (1950. Hebrew), pp. 19 ff.

80. W. F. Albright, *BASOR,* No. 10 (Apr. 1923), pp. 1-3.

Another "cairn" (no. 6), of somewhat different construction, some 150 m. northwest of the former, was investigated in the autumn of the same year. A trial trench was also run toward a third "cairn" (no. 4), some 500 m. east of the former. That revealed a polygonal enclosure wall similar to that of no. 5.[81]

There can be little doubt that we have here a series of "desecrated" high-places; and the meager quantity of pottery discovered in connection with these places makes it likely that they were desecrated and abandoned under King Josiah (640-609 B.C.E.). Hence the present writer has suggested that this series of high places is the one to which the biblical narrative refers (II Ki. 23:13): "Moreover the high places that overlook [so for the phrase *'asher 'al-p^e-ne,* and not traditional "before," and certainly not "east of" as in the American, Chicago Translation] Jerusalem, to the south of the hill of the destroyer [not traditional "destruction"[82]] which Solomon built for Ashtoreth the abomination of the Sidonians, and for Chemosh the abomination of Moab, and for Milkom the abomination of the Ammonites, the king defiled." This mountain might have been dedicated in Jebusite days to the cult of some warrior deity (e.g., Resheph, Haddad, Moth) associated with death and destruction; or "the destroyer" might have been merely a pejorative term for a pagan deity (cf., e.g., *bosheth,* "shame" for Baal); or the site might have been associated in popular legend with the spot over which David saw

---

81. Ruth Amiran, *BIES,* XVIII (1954. Hebrew), pp. 45 ff.

82. The "Mount of the Destroyer" should probably be identified with Mount Ora (848 m.), which was popularly known in Jerusalem as *Miss Carry,* after its owner, who erected there a building dedicated to all monotheistic religions. From this peak one could overlook the immediate heights surrounding the old city of Jerusalem, before lately erected high buildings obstructed the unimpeded view and concealed most of the panorama on the east. The current identification of the Mount of the Destroyer (*Har Ha-mashḥit*) with Mount Olives (*Har Ha-mishḥah*), while based on early Post-Biblical tradition (cf., e.g., Mishna, *Rosh Hashanah* 2:4; *Encyclopaedia Biblica,* V [1968; Hebrew], *s.v.* [*Har Ha-*]*Mashḥit,* col. 506), seems to be based on a doubtful popular philological analogy.

the destroyer-angel in his vision at the threshing floor of Araunah the Jebusite.[83]

Investigations necessitated by construction projects uncovered remains of nymphaeia at *Giv'at Ram* and on the slope west of the "Valley of the Cross" (the "Masleva")[84]; remains of an agricultural farm (in the northeast corner of the complex of the new Ezrath-Nashim Hospital for the Mentally Ill) of the first-second cent. C.E.;[85] and a building of uncertain use, which included a ritual bath, a room the southern and eastern walls of which were covered with "columbarium" niches, and a burial (?) cave underneath, within the precincts of the *Giv'at Sha'ul* cemetery (*Khirbet Ras'l-'Alawy*), the remains perhaps dating to the third-fourth cent. C.E.[86]

Another large-scale undertaking by the Israel Dept. of Antiquities in association with the Israel Exploration Society was the investigation of Tel Ramat Rahel (*Khirbet Saleh*) at the entrance to the communal settlement of the same name, on the southern border of the Municipal Area of Jerusalem. Dr. Y. Aharoni was in charge of the excavations, begun in the autumn of 1954.[87] Later, the enterprise was continued with the participation of the Hebrew University and the University of Rome during five more seasons, 1959-1962 under the direction of the same scholar.[88] The site revealed five main strata of occupation: Middle Israelite II-III

---

83. For the details of that episode see S. Yeivin, in *Studies in the Book of Samuel* (to appear shortly), ed. B. Z. Lourie. In this connection it should be noted that the proposed peak of "The Mount of the Destroyer," almost in view of the Temple Mount, is just about where the glow of the sunset would be seen by a man standing on the "threshing floor of Araunah."

84. S. Yeivin, *A Decade of Archaeology in Israel, 1948-1958* (Leiden, 1950), p. 39.

85. J. Leibowitch, *Bulletin of the Department of Antiquities of the State of Israel (BDASI)*, V-VI (Sept. 1951; Hebrew), pp. 24-25.

86. Ruth Amiran, *BDASI,* III (June 1951; Hebrew), pp. 43-44, and pl. V, b-c.

87. Y. Aharoni, *BIES*, XIX (1955), pp. 147 ff.; *IEJ*, 6 (1956), pp. 102 ff.

88. *Idem, Excavations at Ramat Rahel,* I (Roma, 1962); II (1964).

(layer V; VIIIth-VIIth centuries B.C.E.); Post-Exilic (layer IV; Late Israelite-Early Roman; Vth century B.C.E.-70 C.E.); Late Roman-First Byzantine phase (layer III; IInd-IVth centuries C.E.); Second Byzantine phase (layer II; Vth-VIth centuries C.E.); Third Byzantine phase (of layer II; VIth-VII centuries C.E.); Early Arab (layer I; VIIth-VIIIth centuries C.E.).[89]

The latest phase of occupation seems to have been sparse and of a temporary nature.[90] Those of the two preceding layers have revealed the remains of a large basilical church, rightly associated with the Kathisma church (mentioned in written sources) and two phases of the adjacent monastary.[91] The most interesting find here was a large cruciform slab of stone, identified by Father B. Bagatti as the church altar.[92] In the third layer was unearthed a large Roman bath-house.[93] The most interesting feature of layer IV was undoubtedly the impressions of seals of the Late Israelite (Persian) period found there. Among them were numerous impressions of a previously unknown class, with the names of Jewish governors of the sub-province (*medinah*) *Yehud*. These produced material evidence for the title *peḥwa'* (a hitherto unattested Aramaic title) for the governor of a sub-province, and names

---

89. This author does accept the archaeological chronology propounded by Aharoni (*op. cit.*, I, p. 2, n. 2; cf. also *op. cit.* II, p. 38, n. 2). In this author's opinion, the Israelite period is to be divided into three main phases: Early (*ca.* 1200-970 B.C.E.), Middle (*ca.* 970-586 B.C.E.), and Late (mainly Persian, 586-332 B.C.E.), with the Middle phase further subdivided into three: Middle Israelite I (roughly 970-840 B.C.E.), MI II (roughly 840-720 B.C.E.), and MI III (roughly 720-586 B.C.E.). On the possible subdivisions of Late Israelite, see now S. Weinberg, *Proceedings of the Israel Academy of Sciences and Humanities,* IV (1969), pp. 78 ff.

90. Y. Aharoni, *Excavations at Ramat Raḥel,* I, p. 2. This represents some modifications and refinements of the stratification proposed in the earlier report (*IEJ,* 6 (1956), p. 105). For a still more refined table of layers, see *idem, Excavations,* II, p. 38.

91. P. Testini, *apud* Y. Aharoni, *Excavations,* I, pp. 73 ff.

92. Father B. Bagatti, *Liber Annuus,* VII (1957), pp. 71-73.

93. Aharoni, *Excavations,* I, pp. 24 ff.; and esp. A. Ciasca, *apud* Y. Aharoni, *op. cit.,* pp. 69 ff.

of at least two unknown Jewish governors: Yehoazar (or Ye-hoezer?) and Aḥio.[94]

But the most interesting and spectacular finds came to light in the lowest layer (V; Middle Israelite II-III). Here were uncovered remains of two phases of a royal palace within a large enclosure. The latest plan, published by the excavator, shows a rather irregular enclosure constructed so as cleverly to utilize the topographic features of the ground. This was protected by a solid stone wall, mostly 2 m. thick. Inside this, and mostly adjacent to the eastern part of the outer northern wall, where it forms a re-entrant angle, was an inner enclosure surrounded by a casemated wall, some 6 m. thick on the north and south, nearly 14 m. thick (with a double row of casemates) on the west, and about 8 m. thick on the east; here it was pierced by two gateways: one (about the middle of the wall) paved, a little more than 3 m. wide, and flanked by two projecting wide buttresses on the outside; this gateway had apparently been intended for the passage of chariots; and, south of it, a narrower side-gate, about 1.20 m. wide, intended for pedestrians. The northern part of the central area, the "inner courtyard" of the citadel, paved with a layer of chalk, was occupied by a large rectangular building, some 25 x 15 m., the palace, constructed on a plan of a central courtyard surrounded by rooms on all four sides. In its northwestern part a large corridor led to a low postern, semi-subterranean, giving exit to the exterior of the citadel. The postern survived almost intact, and presents an interesting example of roofing in stone slabs; but it is not at all clear why the excavator considers this building as "reminiscent of the Assyrian-type edifices," [95] and not the ordinary central-court house, quite common on several Middle Israelite sites.[96]

---

94. *Idem,* I, pp. 7 ff.; 32 ff.; II, pp. 21 ff.; 44-45; cf. also *Encyc. Biblica,* VI, *s.v.* פקידות (Hebrew; to appear shortly). [See now, cols. 561–2.]

95. Aharoni, *op. cit.,* I, pp. 35 ff.; II pp. 27-28.

96. See, e.g., M. Avi-Yonah and S. Yeivin, *The Antiquities of Israel* (Tel-Aviv, 1955; Hebrew), pp. 90, 95 ff. Note also in this connection levels IX-VIII at Tel 'Erany, which date to the IXth—very early VIIIth cent. B.C.E., at the latest (from the author's excavations; material as yet unpublished).

The western part of the inner courtyard was occupied in the Middle Israelite period by a large edifice; but being on the highest ground and much built over in later times (Roman and Bryzantine), it was so ruined that apart from its outlines (36 x 18 m.) nothing else could be determined, except the probable existence of ornamental windows in its façade.[97]

The most interesting objects found in the Middle Israelite layers were undoubtedly the little stone colonettes (23.5 cm. high), which formed part of a small balustrade skutting off the lower parts of recessed window frames in upper stories; such windows are illustrated by ivory insets of furniture from Samaria and elsewhere in Hither Asia.[98] A large rectangular stone slab, decorated on both sides with balustrades of rows of similar colonettes in relief, found on the surface of the *tell* in 1929, must have served a similar purpose.[99] This latter piece must have come from the earlier palace (layer V a).[100] Other interesting finds include a complete proto-Aeolian stone capital and fragments of several others; fragments of crenellation stones from the outer wall of the inner citadel[101]; many impressions of seals including the *"lamelekh"* ones, and one of the well known "steward of King Jehoiakin" type ["(belonging) to Elyaqim / (the) steward (= *na'ar*) (of) Yokan"][102]; and a painted sherd portraying a seated man,[103] which indicates the high standard achieved by Judaean artists at the end of the eighth century B.C.E.

97. Aharoni, *op. cit.,* II, p. 49.

98. *Ibid.,* pp. 56 ff.

99. B. Maisler (Mazar) and M. Stekelis, *Qobes, (Journal of the Jewish Palestine Exploration Society;* Hebrew), III (Mazie Memorial Volume, ed. N. Slousch); Jerusalem, 1934-1935), pp. 14, 27-29, and pl. 3. For the whole problem of such windows and balustrades, see S. Yeivin, Lesonenu, XVI (1948/1949; Hebrew), pp. 128 ff.

100. About this earlier phase, see Aharoni, *op. cit.,* II, pp. 58 ff., 119.

101. *Op. cit.,* pp. 54 ff.

102. *Op. cit.,* I, pp. 15 ff.; 43 ff.; II, pp. 32 ff.; 60 ff.

103. *Op. cit.,* I, pp 42-43.

The excavator has suggested the identification of this site with
biblical Beth-(hac)cherem (Jer. 6:1; and other references); but
his evidence seems insufficient. Two other propositions put forward
by Prof. Aharoni seem to be much more plausible and reasonable,
namely: (a) that the second phase of the citadel (layer V A) was
reconstructed by King Jehoiakim (608-597 B.C.E.) and was in
use until the final Babylonian conquest (586 B.C.E.), and this
building activity may have been the cause of Jeremiah's diatribe
against that king (Jer. 22:13 ff.);[104] (b) that the first phase
(layer V B) is to be ascribed to King Uzziah ( = Azariah) and
identified with *beth-ha-ḥophshith* ((lit. the house of liberation),
in which the king spent his life in seclusion after having been
stricken with leprosy.[105] The Hebrew term, however, is not a
derogatory appellation,[106] but a euphemistic term.[107]

Apart from those explorations, field-work in Israeli Jerusalem
during the years 1948-1967 was concerned with the clearance and
exploration of numerous tombs uncovered in the course of building operations, and the restoration and further exploration of such
as were known before.[108] Some of these undertakings deserve
special mention.

While excavating foundations for a building on an empty plot
(12 Alfasi St.), the contractor unwittingly broke the roof of a
burial cave. Neighbors interested in archaeology reported this
to the Dept. of Antiquities. Work was stopped; and the excavations
that were conducted on behalf of the Dept. by Dr. M. Dothan
and Mr. L. Y. Rahmani revealed an extremely interesting tomb

---

104. *Op. cit.*, II, pp. 122 ff.

105. *Op. cit.*, I, pp. 50-51, in spite of the postscript on pp. 59-60.
The window balustrades of the two types (see above) definitely point
to the existence of two phases of a palace, an earlier and a later one.

106. *Op. cit.*, I, p. 59.

107. For the whole question of King Uzziah's seclusion, see this
author's chapter on the history of the Divided Kingdoms, in vol. III,
ed. A. Malamat, of *The World History of the Jewish People* (to appear
shortly).

108. A summary of such work is given in S. Yeivin, *A Decade of
Archaeology in Israel, 1948-1958* (Leiden, 1960), pp. 5; 12-13; 38-39;
45-46.

of the Late Hasmonean period. It belonged to one Jason, who seems to have been a naval officer under the Hasmoneans, and his family.

The plot was expropriated after the end of the excavation, and the whole monument restored by the Conservator of the Department, architect A. Hiram. It shows an entrance *prodromos* running south to north, through which one approaches an inner courtyard leading to an unusual façade with only one column between two antae opening into an entrance vestibule; in the back wall of this, a small square doorway gives access into a large and high square burial chamber. On the west wall of the vestibule there is a charcoal sketch showing two battleships that guard (?) a captured (?) merchantman, all with full flying sails, but at least two of them with anchors weighed down. On the back wall (north) of the vestibule there were several Aramaic and Greek dipinti (giving the name of the erstwhile owner of the tomb). It seems that the tomb continued in use till the second century C.E., when a second burial chamber with several loculi was carved out of the rock in the west wall. Above the vestibule and the original burial chamber there rose once a pyramid, which was fully restored according to indications of several architectural fragments found in the debris that filled the inner court.[109]

Large-scale exploration, cleaning, and partial restoration were undertaken, with some assistance from the Ministry of Religions, in connection with the group of Herodian tombs on the northern outskirts of the city, known popularly as the Sanhedriah group, for legend had it that the most decorative of these rock-cut tombs, containing numerous "loculi," was the burial place of the members of the Sanhedrin, the High Court during the days of the Second Temple. The municipality of Jerusalem participated in the landscaping, and turned the whole area into one of the most pleasant municipal gardens of the city.[110]

The long-known rock-cut tomb near the King David Hotel, property of the Greek Patriarchate and used by the Mandatory

---

109. L. Y. Rahmani *et alii, Atiqot,* IV (Jerusalem, 1964; Hebrew).
110. Cf. S. Yeivin, *Short Guide to the Rock-Cut Tombs of San-hedriyya* (Jerusalem, 1956).

Government in 1948 for some special purpose, was taken in hand. The exploration of the area immediately in front of its entrance revealed the rock-cut base of a very large pyramid built up to an unknown height in courses of local ashlar (very little of which survived). An additional area has been landscaped as a small garden and an entrance to it built, the tomb itself was protected by a gate, and the site opened to visitors; then he area was handed back to its previous owners upon their request.[111]

Another accidental discovery in the autumn of 1952 should be mentioned. While excavating a sewage drain in the area of *Beit Safafa*, on the outskirts of the city, the workmen revealed remains of a mosaic floor and bases of columns. J. Landau, of the Israel Dept. of Antiquities, excavated the site, and found a burial under-structure divided into seven (possibly eight?) loculi paved with small white mosaic tesserae and covered with flat stone slabs. Four of the loculi contained each a lead sarcophagus; one contained two small lead sarcophagi (a medical examination revealed that one of them contained the remains of an infant several months old); the two other loculi were empty. All the sarcophagi were ornamented—in relief—with rope patterns, small wreaths, and crosses. North of the underground burial structure were remains of a mortuary chapel (?) some 7 x 8 m., paved in larger stone tessarae. The mid-part of the floor mosaic had at its western end a tabula-ansata inlaid in mosaics with a Greek inscription in four lines naming the owner of the tomb "Samuel and members his family" and giving the date as June of the XIVth indiction of the year 206; this era is uncertain. The interesting feature of this inscription is that its lines run backwards, i.e., its lowest line is line 1, and its uppermost is line 4. The finds date this structure to the end of the fifth century C.E. at the earliest, so that the date of the start of this era should be looked for at the end of the third or beginning of the fourth century C.E.[112]

---

111. *Bulletin of the Dept. of Antiquities, Israel,* III (June 1951), pp. 15-16.

112. J. Landau, *Bulletin* (see preceding note), V-VI (Sept. 1957), pp. 40-42. It would make for too long and too tedious a catalogue to enumerate here all the other investigations of tombs in and around Jerusalem; for a summary, see above, n. 100.

Finally, in repairing and restoring war damage around the so-called "Tomb of David" on Mount Zion, an investigation inside the so-called "Tomb" was undertaken by architect J. Pinkerfeld, the then Conservator of Monuments in the Dept. of Antiquities, on behalf of the Dept. and the Dept. of Moslem and Druze Affairs in the Ministry of Religions. Repairing of the floor of the "Tomb" chamber (in 1951) revealed that the original floor of the structure lay 70 cm. below the present-day floor. To that original building belonged the whole eastern wall of the present tomb chamber, and the eastern ends of the northern wall, with its niche, 1.22 m. above the present-day floor (1.92 m. above the original floor), and the southern wall of the adjacent chamber on the south. The high niche is oriented to the north with slight deviation (of a few degrees) to the east, i.e., to the Temple Mount. Below the present plaster covering the niche was revealed monumental ashlar masonry of the late Roman age. The original hall, the eastern part of which still stands, is 10.50 m. long (s.-n.). Its width could not be ascertained, since the original western wall had disappeared, the present western wall having been erected in late Arab times, while the southern partition wall, dividing the present "Tomb" chamber from the room south of it, had been built in the late Turkish age. No signs of a burial were found outside the extant sarcophagus on a lower level; this must, therefore, be considered a cenotaph, probably placed there by the Crusaders. The orientation of the building points to its having originally been a synagogue.[113] This was first turned by the Arab conquerors into a mosque, as witness the added *miḥrab* ( = niche) on the floor level in the room south of the present "Tomb" chamber. The Crusaders, apparently basing themselves on a medieval Jewish tradition, erected there, in front of the niche, the present cenotaph, and built on top of this building the present-day church, oriented east.[114]

---

113. Epiphanius, in his book *On Weights and Measures,* reports seven synagogues on Mount Zion; cf. S. Yeivin, *The War of Bar Kokhba,* 3rd ed. (Jerusalem, 1957; Hebrew), p. 186.

114. Cf. J. Pinkerfeld, *In the Paths of Jewish Art* (Tel-Aviv, 1958 [?]; Hebrew), pp. 128-130. "A Table of the Major Excavations in Jerusalem" (up to 1968) was worked up by Y. Shiloh, in *Qadmonioth,* I, 1-2 (1968; Hebrew), 71-78.

## D. *1967-1971*

The reunification of Jerusalem, after the Six Days War in June 1967, brought a new impetus to archaeological work in the city. In the autumn of 1967 Professor Kenyon returned to complete her investigation in the large trench down the eastern slope of the southwestern hill.[115] But all such work was dwarfed by the large-scale excavations undertaken by the Israel Exploration Society—in cooperation with the Dept. of Antiquities and the Archaeological Institute of the Hebrew University—and directed by Professor B. Mazar, in the area lying south of the temenos wall of the Temple Area and on both sides of the southeastern part of Sultan Suleiman's fortification of the "Old City" on the one hand, and along the southernmost part of the Western Wall westwards, an area almost completely "out of bounds" to archaeological excavation until then.[116] The excavations began on Feb. 28, 1968, and have been continuing without interruption ever since, all year round—except, of course, on holy days, very rainy days in the winter, and the like.[117]

The first season revealed the fact that the area had been derelict ever since the Mameluke period (twelfth century C.E.). Below this topmost thin accumulation of debris the excavators have uncovered to date four main periods of occupation: Arab [= A, subdivided into eight layers, A I—A VIII (the topmost)];

---

115. See above; and Kathleen M. Kenyon, *Hadashoth Archeologioth* (Archaeological News), XXV (Jan. 1968), pp. 16–18.

116. With the exception of Warren's deep pits and Professor Kenyon's two trial pits: the former on behalf of the Jordan Dept. of Antiquities, about 60 m. southeast of the temenos wall of the Temple Area, and the latter in collaboration with the late Rev. Father R. de Vaux, near the southeastern angle of the Suleimanian wall; see Kenyon, *Jerusalem* (see n. 54 above), p. 192.

117. For a first preliminary report, see B. Mazar, *Eretz-Israel* (Annual of the Israel Exploration Society; the Albright Volume), IX (1969), pp. 168 ff. (Hebrew; published as a separate pamphlet in English [Jerusalem, 1969], 24 pp., xv pl.); information culled also from press releases. The author is indebted to Prof. Mazar, who kindly consented to read this condensed report of the discoveries in this area, and agreed to its publication.

Byzantine ( = B, subdivided into four layers, B I—B IV); Roman ( = R, subdivided into two layers, R I—R II); and Herodian = H, lasting until Titus' conquest of Jerusalem and the destruction of the Second Temple, 70 C.E.).[118]

The uppermost Arab layer (VIII), which can be dated to the Crusader and Mameluke periods, shows only remains of an installation of sorts, the nature of which is not obvious; these confirm the fact that from that period onwards the area had lain derelict. The layer below it (A VII) could be dated to the Fatimid period (tenth-eleventh centuries C.E.). Here again the only remains were a storage pit for gravel and a slaked-lime pit, which were probably used for building activity in the Temple Area, whereas the large plot south of the temenos wall had not been in use. In layers AI—A VI there was a lane running along the southern temenos wall and gradually rising eastward, between it and a large building to the south. That building had been first erected in the Ummayad period, was apparently destroyed in the earthquake of 748 C.E., rebuilt in the Abbasid period (the second half of the eighth century C.E., layer A II), and partly continued in use through the following layers A III—A IV. Prof. Mazar very wisely refuses to define the nature of this impressive building as long as it has not been fully uncovered, nor as long as the adjacent remains to the northwest have not been fully investigated, though various suggestions have been made by his assistants and consultants.[119]

The underlying four Byzantine layers did not reveal remains of buildings, but numerous coins, sherds, and other finds help to date these levels: B-4 (the topmost) to the days of Justinian I (527-566 C.E.) and until the Persian conquest of Jerusalem (614 C.E.); B-3 to the period between Empress Eudokia's activities until the days of Justinian; B-2 to the period between Theodosius I (379-395 C.E.) and Theodosius II (408-450 C.E.); and B-1 to the days of Constantine I and his successors. An interesting find in this layer, a terra cotta lamp adorned with Jewish symbols (menorah, shofar, and calix [?]), facing the temenos wall and resting against it, may represent a Jewish pilgrim's visit to the

---

118. Mazar, *loc. cit.,* pp. 163 ff.
119. *Ibid.,* pp. 171 ff.

site (perhaps under Emperor Julian?). The two Roman layers testify to occupation from the founding of Aelia Capitolina under Hadrian (R I overlies immediately the ruined remains of Titus' sack of the place) until the reign of Diocletian, when the Legio X Fretensis left Jerusalem. No finds were uncovered that could be definitely dated to the period between the destruction of the Second Temple (70 C.E.) and the war of Bar-Kokhba (132-135 C.E.).[120]

But undoubtedly the most interesting and spectacular finds were made in the lowest layer uncovered to date, the Herodian. Apart from dramatic single finds, like the stone beaker marked *qorban* (sacrifice),[121] or discoveries like the Hebrew grafitti, the excavations have revealed a large area of the flagged Herodian piazza south of the Temple, its northern wall limiting (to the south) the paved and partly stepped street, running south of the temenos wall of the Temple Area eastward toward the Hulda Gates. Along the southern part of the Western Wall was uncovered another street running along it, and continuing southward, while on the opposite side of that street were unearthed, opposite the spring of Robinson's Arch in the wall, the foundations of a large pier. Subsequent investigations showed that this pier supported a two-flight (at right angle) staircase, that led from this street to a gate in the southern part of the western temenos wall, giving access to the Temple Area proper, above the "Robinson Arch" (in the Western Wall). The full width of this arch, that served together with the above-mentioned pier to support those stairs, has been exposed by the excavators.

On the pavements of the southern and western streets were found numerous stones and architectural fragments that were thrown there when the Temple had been destroyed; and these help in gaining some idea of the upper finishing of the temenos wall. At one spot below the above-mentioned paved Herodian piazza, to the south of the Temple Area, came to light remains of the late days of the Period of the Kings, judging by the ceramic remains revealed there in a trial pit.[122]

---

120. *Ibid.*, p. 165 (col. II).
121. *Ibid.*, pp. 168-170, pl. 45, 5.
122. *Ibid.*, pp. 168 (col. I)–170. Similar finds are reported by Professor Kenyon in a small trial pit excavated by her, together with the late R. de Vaux, in 1963-4; see Kenyon, *Jerusalem*, fig. 6 (on p. 57).

In July 1971 the area east of the Suleimanian wall of the "Old City," in the re-entrant southeast corner of those fortifications, has been uncovered, revealing a large monumental staircase ascending from the ancient "Lower City" to the eastern Hulda Gate. A covered passage near it served the priests, who could go, after cleansing immersion, straight into the Sacred Area without coming in contact with potential defiling factors.[123]

The excavation also revealed the fact that the bottom of the original valley, which bounded the Temple Mount on the west in the Period of the Kings, runs east of the Western Wall, proving that the Herodian reconstruction of the Temple Area extended it a good deal westward.

On the opposite (western) slope of that limiting valley, which ran through ancient Jerusalem (Josephus calls it the Tyropoion, the Valley of the Cheese Makers), were uncovered some rock-cut tombs, which by their type and the scanty sherds found in them, could be definitely dated to eighth century B.C.E., thus proving that at least until the second half of that century the area was outside the perimeter of the city (See also below.)

The reconstruction of the largely ruined Jewish quarter within the "Old City" gave rise to the archaeological investigation of several areas (A-E) within this quarter, carried out by Professor N. Avigad on behalf of the Institute of Archaeology of the Hebrew University, the Dept. of Antiquities and Museums, and the Israel Exploration Society. Area A (excavated in September-December 1969), some 250 m. west of the Temple Compound (northwest of the ruined *Tif'ereth Yisra'el* Synagogue) revealed "nine stages of building operations apparently belonging to six periods."[124] The foundations of the uppermost large building of the Crusader or Mameluke periods penetrated to the virgin rock, destroying much that lay beneath it. Since the site was levelled by a bulldozer, prior to the beginning of the excavations, it is no longer possible to say what Byzantine and later remains were present here (except for the deep foundations mentioned above). Only few remains of the Roman period survived, mainly a large number of terra cotta

123. Recent press releases; and see above, n. 117.
124. N. Avigad, "Excavations of the Jewish Quarter . . . 1969/70 (Preliminary Report)," *IEJ*, 20 (1970), p. 3.

tiles, stamped with the "Legio X Fretensis" mark. Below that there were two "well-preserved floor levels of beaten *hawwar*". In the debris between the two floors were uncovered numerous fragments of painted plaster, showing decorative imitations of marble paneling, of architectural designs in three-dimensionally graded shadings, and rich patterns of foliage and clusters of pomegranates and apples.[125] Here, too, were found two fragments of unpainted plaster, incised with a reproduction of a seven-branched candelabrum (of which the three on the left are missing). This portrayal may possibly be closer to the true form of the temple candelabrum, but it definitely does not agree with the representation of the *menorah* on the Arch of Titus in Rome. On the upper of the two floors was found a decorated stone slab, picturing two crossed cornucopia with a pomegranate branch and fruit in between, which must have been part of a decorative frieze, that ornamented possibly a movable object, according to Avigad. In the opinion of the present author it may have run along a wall of an important building (public? or large private residence?) on this spot. Below these two floors, were remains of a Hasmonean level (late second or early first century B.C.E.). No Early Hellenistic and Persian remains were found, but on the virgin rock were remains of walls and floors of the Late Middle Israelite period (seventh century B.C.E.), with a massive substructure of large stone blocks in the western part of this Area.

Excavations resumed here in April-November 1970, with a view to further defining the wall of the Israelite period, revealed "a massive city wall 6.40-7.20 m. thick situated about 275 m. west of the Temple enclosure, opposite its southern end." A continuous stretch of 35 m. of this wall was exposed, revealing a maximum height of about 3.30 m. It runs in a general line north-east-southwest, with the southern end of the exposed section

---

125. Such decorations have already been uncovered elsewhere. For the first mentioned kind (at Masada) see Y. Yadin, *IEJ*, 15 (1965), pp. 11-12; and an even earlier discovery by Bar-Adon in a Hellenistic building at Beth Yeraḥ (uncovered in the early fifties; unpublished). For the latter kind, see S. Yeivin *apud* L. Waterman, *Preliminary Report of the University of Michigan Excavations at Sepphoris, Palestine, 1931* (Ann Arbor, 1937), p. 28.

showing a distinct bend westward. It can be dated to the end of
the eighth-seventh centuries B.C.E.[126] Later investigations (August
1971) of another area lying to the southeast of Area A revealed
remains of well-built Israelite houses on stepped terraces of the
virgin rock on the eastern slope of the western hill, which could
definitely be dated to the reign of Hezekiah. Consequently
one may assume that the defensive city wall of Area A was built
by this king. Avigad has thus proved that at least the eastern
half of the Western Hill had already been included in built-up
Jerusalem toward the end of the eighth century B.C.E.[127]

No less noteworthy were the remains uncovered in Area B
(excavated in January-February 1970), some 170 m. from the
Temple Compound, opposite Robinson's Arch. Here, too, a bulldozer removed the late debris before the excavators were called
in, but "No Byzantine sherds or building remains could be traced
in the sections."[128] The earliest uncovered remains date to the
early Roman period. The main structure was a house of the first
century C.E., sacked and burned during the Roman conquest of
the city in 70 C.E.; it has been dubbed "The Burnt House." Since
the ruin had not been disturbed by later building activity, a large
number of finds was made there. Of special interest are two
rectangular stone tables, one complete with decorated borders,
and one of a number of stone weights, on which was incised an
Aramaic inscription giving the name of its owner:  דבר / קתרס
(= that of Bar Kathros). This priestly family is mentioned in
post-biblical sources, where they are blamed because of "their
(reed-)pen"; as Rashi explains it: "since they were writing letters
for evil."[129] It seems that the excavators stumbled on their home.
West of this house were uncovered remains of a Middle Israelite
foundation built on the bedrock; it still stands 2-3 m. high, is
1-1.20 m. thick, and was revealed along a length of 11 m. termi-

126. N. Avigad, "Excavations in the Jewish Quarter . . . 1970 (Preliminary Report)," *IEJ*, 20 (1970), pp. 129 ff.
127. The author wishes to thank Professor Avigad for this communication, for his consent to read and check the summary of his work
presented here, and for agreeing to have it published.
128. Avigad, *op. cit.* (n. 124 above), p. 6.
129. At Bab. Talmud, Tractate Pesaḥim, 57 a.

nating on the south in a tower-like projection. The ceramic remains in its earth abutment, above it, and between its stones,
"point to the seventh and perhaps also the eighth centuries
B.C." [130]

Site D, in the courtyard of "Batei Maḥse", revealed the presence
of a large Byzantine church which is probably to be identified
with the "Nea" church (New Church of the Theotokos), built
by Justinian in 543 C.E., and destroyed by an earthquake in the
late eighth century.[131]

A third enterprise of the same three archaeological bodies, with
the assistance of the Municipality of Jerusalem, was centered
on the courtyard of the Citadel. The work was directed by Mrs.
Ruth Amiran and A. Eitan. They continued the exploration
started by C. N. Johns (see above) against the inner face of his
"first wall" of the city.[132] The present excavation revealed eight
layers (including the one uncovered and removed by Johns, apparently late Byzantine.[133] The second (II) dates to the foundation
of Aelia Capitolina under Hadrian (after 135 C.E.). The third
seems to belong to the living quarters of the Tenth Legion established in this corner of the city after its conquest and sack by
Titus (70 C.E.). The fourth (III B) is marked by fragmentary
floors covering the ruins of Herodian buildings. The fifth (IV)
revealed a short stretch of a street running southeast-northwest
at an angle to the strengthened city wall, with houses on both
sides, the western one abutting on the city wall. In this structure
of the Herodian period (first century B.C.E.-first century C.E.)

---

130. Avigad, *op. cit.,* p. 8.

131. Avigad, *op. cit.,* pp. 137-138.

132. Ruth Amiran and A. Eitan, "Excavations in the Courtyard of
the Citadel . . . ," *IEJ,* 20 (1970), pp. 9 ff.

133. The above report seems slightly confusing on this point; on
p. 9 it is stated: "In the present excavation eight strata have been uncovered," but the enumeration (on the same page) marks the lowest
layer as *"Stratum VII."* This is probably due to the fact that in count-
ing the strata the authors considered phases IIIb-IIIa as two separate
strata, while in the description on p. 15 they marked them as two
phases of the same layer, since both date to the end of the first century C.E.

there is a complete change of plan and orientation of buildings, built on massive foundations containing in between a deep fill, in which were found large quantities of sherds ranging from the seventh century B.C.E. to the Herodian period, as well as a carnelian seal of the seventh century B.C.E. that belonged to one "Mattanyahu (the son of) Azaryahu." In the houses themselves the floors were partly paved with flagstones, and "fragments of painted plaster . . . indicated that the walls had been decorated with stripes and panels in red, yellow, black, and green." [134] The latest coins found date "to before A.D. 70." In the fill there were remains of a floor, possibly used during the construction of the foundations and fill, which has been counted as the sixth stratum (V). Below this a differently constructed wall and several rooms abutting on it represented the seventh stratum (VI). This was dated to the Hasmonean period, "but accurate dates for its beginning and end are as yet difficult to propose." [135] However, the most interesting discovery of this exploration was the presence of the eighth stratum (VII). It lies on the bedrock, some 9 m. below the present surface; and therefore it "could be excavated only in a very limited area." Here an accumulation of 1.50 m. revealed five superimposed floors, the lowest of which, "of white lime, lay directly upon the rock; the other floors" above it "were of beaten earth, the top one containing an ash-filled pit 0.50 m. deep. Preliminary examination of the pottery . . . would ascribe it to the 7th century B.C." [136]

Now, this discovery is extremely important for the delimitation of Jerusalem in the last decades of the Kingdom of Judah. Both C. N. Johns and Kathleen M. Kenyon reported finding potsherds of the seventh century B.C.E. on this western hill (see above), but these could not be associated with any structural remains, and might have indicated merely refuse heaps. The investigation by Amiran and Eitan of the stratified floors, if indeed they prove to be such (as they undoubtedly seem at present), provides certain

---

134. Amiran and Eitan, p. 13. And see above for similar decorations in private houses of the period uncovered under the "Jewish Quarter."

135. Amiran and Eitan, p. 11.

136. *Idem,* p. 10.

evidence of living quarters, testifying to the expansion of a suburb of Jerusalem as far west as this, already under the last kings of Judah.

A new investigation by Mr. Dan Bahat, continued by Mr. Magen Broshi, on behalf of the Dept. of Antiquities, was started in the summer of 1971 in the garden of the Armenian Patriarchate, prior to the construction of an Armenian Theological Seminary there. They have found, so far, the same deep foundations of a large Herodian building (palace) that Amiran and Eitan uncovered in their fifth stratum (IV), with the same sort of fill in between them.[137]

In the autumn of 1967 Professor Kenyon put some finishing touches to her protracted exploration of the eastern slope of the southeastern hill of ancient Jerusalem, revealing possible Solomonic remains, an artificially cut cave east of the earliest eastern town wall which the excavator took to be connected with a repository for rejected ritual vessels. At a third spot on the slope on the western hill was uncovered a long stretch of Byzantine wall underlying the Suleimanian wall of the "Old City" at its southwest corner.[138]

Some additional trial pits were sunk by Y. Margovsky, on behalf of the Dept. of Antiquities with the assistance of the Municipality of Jerusalem, south of Burj el-Kibrit, in the southern wall of the "Old City," between the Zion and the Dung Gates. Underlying the present Burj, there is a Medieval tower (Mameluke or Crusder), while below its floor there were Byzantine remains overlying a Herodian building, with fragments of frescoes painted in black and red on plaster. Adjacent pits showed the same stratification of Byzantine over Herodian remains.[139]

Many tombs have been investigated since June, 1967 in various parts of the city. Only one is of especial interest as far as its

---

137. *Ḥadashoth Archeologioth* (Archaeological News), 37 (Jan. 1971), p. 20.

138. *Ḥad. Archeo.,* 25 (Jan. 1968), pp. 16 ff.

139. *Ḥad Archeo.,* 36 (Oct. 1970), p. 14; 37 (Jan. 1971), pp. 19-20.

contents are concerned. It was uncovered in connection with building activities on Giv'at Ha-mivtar (*Ras'l-Maṣaref*) in northeast Jerusalem. Of the four tombs excavated there by V. Tzaferis, on behalf of the Dept. of Antiquities in June 1968,[140] one (No. 1) contained several limestone ossuaries. On ossuary No. 1 were two graffiti designating the remains as those of "Simon the mason of the Temple." Another ossuary bore a very rough graffito in two lines; the first of these raises no problems: "the ossuary of Salom(e) the daughter of Saul." The second line is read by Naveh די שברת שלום ברתה and translated (on rather tenuous speculations) as "who failed to give birth (i.e. died in childbirth). Salome his (Saul's) daughter. (Or: Salome the daughter. Or: Peace, Daughter!)"[141] The present author would suggest a different division of letters: ש ברת שלום ברתה (looks much more probable) ו(more probable ר, =) ד i.e., "Dush (or Rush, admittedly a rather problematical n. per. f.[142]) the daughter of Salom(e) his (viz. Saul's daughter," meaning that the bones of both mother and daughter were placed in the same ossuary.

Ossuary No. 4, from the same tomb marked with the name Yehoḥanan,[143] contained the remains of a crucified adult male, some 24-28 years old: "The shins were found intentionally broken" and "Both the heel bones were found transfixed by a large iron nail."[144]

---

140. V. Tzaferis, "Jewish Tombs . . . ," *IEJ*, 20 (1970), pp. 18 ff.

141. J. Naveh, "The Ossuary Inscriptions . . . ," *IEJ*, pp. 33-34.

142. ("Simon, builder of the Sanctuary") and pp. 36-37. Another explanation is possible, if it is assumed that the woman Shalom (Salome) died in childbirth. The word רוש may be a "simplified" spelling of ראש, or else read ריש, the Aramaic for "head;" if the infant child died as well, the bones would hardly survive the decay of the flesh, so that only the skull remained and had been placed in the ossuary, and hence the graffito: "head (of the) daughter (of) Shalom(e) his (viz., Saul's) daughter."

143. Naveh, *op. cit.,* p. 35.

144. Dr. N. Haas, "Anthropological Observations on the Skeletal Remains . . . ," *IEJ*, 20 (1970), pp. 38 ff., devotes a detailed study to this "case of crucifixion" (pp. 49-59); the quotations are from p. 42.

Excavations in Jerusalem are continuing, both large-scale undertakings such as at the "Western Wall" and in the Jewish Quarter of the "Old City," and more modest activities and investigations in connection with accidental discoveries.

What would one wish to achieve by such future work? In the first place, one would like to see in Professor Mazar's future excavation the uncovering of as large an area of the Israelite layers of the ancient city as possible. Such investigations will probably provide the scholarly world with data on the actual plan of the Royal Citadel of Solomon and his descendants in regard to the palace, storage facilities (the House of the Forest of Lebanon or/and its successors), and other buildings within its perimeter (cf. I Ki. 7:1-12).

In the second place, seeing that the northern and eastern limits of the city at most periods of its existance have already been traced in most stretches—though new excavations tend to raise new problems—it would be desirable to continue spot investigations along its southeastern, southern, and southwestern edges, as well as along the outer sides of the present western Suleimanian wall, with the view to defining its limits on the south and west at various periods. The extension of Professor Avigad's work along the wall, which he tentatively dated to Hezekiah's reign (see above), would contribute to such delimitation at least during the seventh-sixth centuries B.C.E.

Spot investigations by various Christian and Moslem public bodies within and between existing buildings in the Christian and Moslem Quarters of the "Old City" could help to improve our knowledge of the alignment of the first and second walls of Hasmonean and Herodian periods, described by Josephus.

One must hope that all those will be forthcoming in due time.

## PART III:

## BOOKS ON JERUSALEM

Qoheleth noted long ago (12:12) that "there is no end to making many books." There is hardly a subject under the sun to which this maxim could apply more aptly than "Jerusalem." A multitude of all sorts of books has appeared on the subject since 1907, dealing with numerous aspects: fiction, utopia, history, archaeology, guides, etc., etc. Four works are singled out here for especial mention.

In 1909 Condor published a compact volume on Jerusalem Throughout the Ages: "to present in a convenient form the results of research and exploration concerning the history and building of the city of Jerusalem . . . The story of forty centuries is carried down to the present year, and reliance is chiefly placed on monumental history."[1] But in doing this Condor seems to have lost sight of the fact that he was dealing with a living and developing body, and not a mausoleum of embalmed history. This grudge against the living begins in his Introductory Chapter (p. 1): "The view [in 1872—S.Y.] . . . was not then obstructed by the row of Jewish cottages since built. The population was only about a third of what it now [1909—S.Y.] is. The railway station was not thought of, and only a few villas outside the gate existed, while the suburbs to the north and south had not grown up, and

---

1. C. R. Conder, *The City of Jerusalem* (London 1909), Preface.

Olivet was not covered with modern buildings." He even introduces a prophetic note at the end of his volume (p. 326): "We have thus traversed the long ages during which Jerusalem has been, for four thousand years, a holy city. It can never be anything else." Yet even so, he sensed its future fate, for he concludes (*ibid.*): "But the Holy City may still be described in the words of the Psalmist: 'Jerusalem is builded as a city of gathering together to itself; for thither the tribes go up' (*Psalms* CXXII, 3)."

It is interesting to note that in his discussion of the fortifications of Jerusalem at the time of Agrippa I, Condor thinks of the third wall as being where Mayer and Sukenik later uncovered it: ". . . large stones, with well-dressed faces and drafts after the Herodian style, have been found in several places towards the north-west outside Jerusalem [Condor means the "Old City"], and these may have belonged to Agrippa's wall . . ." [2] The book, in spite of its shortcomings, is still the only one that tells the *story* of the city till the beginning of this century.

In 1952 Father J. Simons published his monumental volume on *Jerusalem in the Old Testament.*[3] Specifically confined to Old Testament times, the book is a mine of information, presenting all the historical and archaeological data available at the time. On only one point does this volume exceed the time limit that its author imposed on himself, namely, in discussing: "The 'Second Wall' and the Problem of the Holy Sepulchre" (ch. V), and "the 'Third Wall' or the Wall of Herod Agrippa" (ch. VIII). The volume is a very useful and comprehensive compendium, up to the time of its publication, though the theories advanced there do not always seem plausible, e.g., those propounded in discussing the burial place of the members of the Davidic Dynasty,[4] or in discussing the "Second Wall" (though he more or less anticipated the discovery of Hezekiah's wall; see above).[5]

---

2. Conder, p. 166; and see his very balanced discussion, pp. 162-167.

3. Dr. J. Simons, S.J., *Jerusalem in the Old Testament, Researches and Theories* (Leiden, 1952).

4. *Op. cit.,* pp. 198 ff.

5. *Op. cit.,* pp. 282 ff.

In 1945 the now defunct Jewish Jerusalem Society planned the issue of a comprehensive study on Jerusalem, from its beginnings until the present day. Professor M. Avi-Yonah was appointed editor. Unforseen circumstances delayed the publication; however, the first volume appeared in 1956, entitled *The Book of Jerusalem*.[6] It includes articles dealing with the physical and ecological aspects of the city and its immediate surroundings, as well as its history and archaeology until Titus' conquest and destruction of the city and Temple in 70 C.E. In the extent of time with which this volume is concerned, and the wide scope of aspects it embraces, this publication probably comes nearest of all to Smith's *Jerusalem*, though it is somewhat differently arranged and is not the work of a single author, being a compendium of 24 articles written by 20 scholars.

In 1967 Professor Kenyon published her *Jerusalem: Excavating 3000 Years of History*, which—as the subtitle indicates—is a record of archaeological work in the city during the century 1867-1967; and "It is on the results of these excavations," she asserts (p. 11), "based over the years on such wide-scale support, and carried out by the energy and enthusiasm of such a large staff, that the history of Jerusalem is re-written in this book."[7] It is the

---

6. *Sepher Yerushalayim (The Book of Jerusalem)*, edited by Michael Avi-Yonah; editorial Board: L. A. Mayer, the late I. Press, S. Yeiven; Volume One: *The Natural Conditions and the History of the City from its Origins to the Destruction of the Second Temple* (Jerusalem and Tel-Aviv, 1956).

7. Jerusalem, to Prof. Kenyon, consists of an "Old City and two new cities. The Old City is the lineal descendant of the medieval city . . . still enclosed by the majestic circuit of walls built by Suleiman the Magnificent in 1535. The two new cities have been divided by the De-militarized Zone . . . the *Israel-occupied part* [emphasis mine—S.Y.] . . . lapping the walls of the Old City on the west, the *Arab city* [as above] extending north . . ." (p. 12). Apparently the writer's anti-Israeli bias does not extend to Biblical Israel, of whose career there is a very detailed and, on the whole, correct account.

latest epitome of archaeological work in the city, and attempt to draw historical conclusions from such work. It is written by an acknowledged master of archaeological technique and expertise; and though some of her conclusions have been questioned above and elsewhere, and while others need correction in the light of the results obtained by later excavations, it is the best and most authoritative summing up of the problems involved, up to 1967.

Withal, none of the books discussed above matches the literary style of Smith, which frequently rises to almost poetic lyricism, and yet never falls into bombastic bathos. As a work of sound scholarship and masterly expression, Smith's *Jerusalem* remains an outstanding book, always worth serious perusal.

Samuel Yeivin
Jerusalem

Aug. 15, 1971.

# PREFACE

IN the *Historical Geography of the Holy Land* it was not possible, for reasons of space, to include a topography of Jerusalem, an appreciation of her material resources, or a full study of the historical significance of her site and surroundings. The present volumes are an attempt to deal with these subjects, and to give in addition a history of the City's politics, literature and religion.

In order to prepare the reader for the long and often intricate discussions of so vast a subject, extending over more than fourteen centuries, I have thought it well to present first of all a picture of the essential Jerusalem. This will be found in the Introduction.

Book I. comprises the Topography of the City and the various questions, which this raises, of position and nomenclature, along with some account of the Climate, a chapter on the Geology and another on Earthquakes. For the earthquakes which we know to have visited Jerusalem not only may have affected that exact distribution of the waters on which so many topographical questions depend, but have certainly by their *débris* masked other features of the site, while the

folklore connected with them has possibly influenced
some of the names. There were unfortunately no
previous studies of which I could avail myself in dealing
with these matters. I have come to no definite conclusions—which, indeed, from the nature of the subject are impossible—but have been content to make a
few suggestions and to enforce the need of caution in
topographical argument, in face of the disturbance
which the earthquakes of Jerusalem have undoubtedly
introduced into the tradition of her topography. I have
besides quoted the criticisms which the late Sir Charles
Wilson kindly sent to me when my views on the subject
were first published, so that the reader may judge for
himself whether I have gone too far in estimating the
influence of the earthquakes. As to the topography
itself, one cannot give an adequate idea of it without
the details of the controversies—topical, textual and
historical—which have been more numerous and more
keenly debated in the case of Jerusalem than in that
of any other site in the whole world. Recently, however, the main issues have been cleared of much irrelevant
reasoning, and there is a remarkable tendency towards
agreement upon many of the conclusions.

The following pages, with their innumerable references,
will exhibit the greatness of my debt to all who have
worked on the site and, in only a less degree than this,
to many who have argued about it. I most heartily
express my gratitude to the Palestine Exploration Fund
and their pioneers in the survey and excavation of the
site—especially Sir Charles Wilson, Sir Charles Warren,

Colonel Conder, M. Clermont-Ganneau (whose other works are equally valuable), and Dr. F. J. Bliss. For the last thirty years all work on the topography of Jerusalem, whether in English or other languages, has been based on the Fund's Ordnance Survey, its Maps, Plans and Memoirs. These can never cease to be indispensable to the student. In addition, I thank the Executive Committee of the Fund for their generous permission to me to base the large plan of the City which will be found in the pocket of Volume I. upon their Plan of Jerusalem reduced from the Ordnance Plan made by Sir Charles Wilson. I would also record my indebtedness, like that of every other worker on the subject, to the publications of what is now the 'Deutscher Verein zur Erforschung Palästinas.' In particular, the chapter on the Geology and the geological map, by which Mr. Bartholomew has illustrated it, could not have been prepared without the materials supplied in Dr. Blanckenhorn's treatise on the Geology of Jerusalem which appeared in their *Zeitschrift*; and every student of the subject knows the value of Dr. Guthe's excavations on Ophel carried out under their auspices. I also owe much to the *Revue Biblique* and the work of the Dominican Fathers and their colleagues in Jerusalem ; and among other individuals especially to Dr. Merrill, who has generously laid his stores of knowledge at the disposal of inquirers, and whose book we eagerly await ; to the late Herr Baurath Schick, whose labours on the topography and architecture were so long and constant ; to the Rev. J. E. Hanauer, Dr. Masterman, and other residents in Jerusalem; to Mr. R. A. S. Macalister; and to various Directors of the American Archæological School.

In the following treatment of the topography the reader will not find any novel theories of the cardinal questions. Brought up in the traditional views of the position of Ṣion on the South-west Hill, I have been constrained by the Biblical evidence to conclude with the majority of modern scholars that the original Ṣion lay on the East Hill somewhere above the Virgin's Spring; and also to agree with those who find the rock of the Altar of Burnt-Offering in the present eṣ-Ṣakhra, and consequently place the Temple to the west of this. Nor have I many fresh suggestions upon the details of the topography. I found, however, that the Biblical evidence as to the name Ṣion had not received the exhaustive treatment which I have attempted to give it; and the reader will be interested in at least one of the results of this examination, viz. that the name Ṣion for the East Hill appears to be avoided by a school of Old Testament writers, and that *the 'Ophel* seems to have been once a synonym for it. As to the Walls of the City, all I have attempted is an elucidation of the results of the excavations and an exegesis of the relevant passages in the Old Testament and Josephus. I think I have given all the evidence that is extant, except in the case of certain alternative theories of the course of the Second Wall, because in my judgment we do not yet possess sufficient material for deciding among them. The question of the Second Wall involves that of the site of Calvary

and the Sepulchre of our Lord.   It may disappoint some
readers that I offer no conclusion as to this.   But after
twenty-seven years' study of the evidence I am unable to
feel that a conclusion one way or other is yet possible, or
perhaps ever will be possible.   In this negative result
I am confirmed by the opinion of an authority of much
greater experience, the late Sir Charles Wilson, whose
posthumous work, *Golgotha and the Holy Sepulchre*, edited
by Sir Charles Watson, and published last year by the
Committee of the Palestine Exploration Fund, is a
lucid and exhaustive treatment of this difficult subject.   After this, to attempt even to restate the evidence
would be superfluous and wearisome.   Sir Charles
Wilson's volume is invaluable to the student and to
the visitor to Jerusalem, not only upon this question
but on many others in the topography of the City.
Nor have I been able, in the present state of our information, to treat many of the details of the structure
and arrangement of Herod's Temple; though I am
clear that its actual site, size and appearance were as
I have described them.   But upon these and all other
questions of the topography, I must here remind the
reader, as I have done several times in the following
pages, that the excavation of Jerusalem, though it has
been profuse and thorough so far as it has gone, is
nevertheless still incomplete, and that much of the
ancient site remains unexplored.   Whether surprises are
in store for us, who can say?

   To the topography proper I have added two chapters
on the history of the name Jerusalem and on other names

for the City. The former is founded on a study of the name which appeared in the *Encyclopædia Biblica*, article 'Jerusalem,' § 1, and which has received the approval of so great an authority in philology as Dr. Eberhard Nestle.

Book II. The Economics and Politics.—As I put the chapters on the topography into shape, I found that my first design of adding to them one on the material resources of Jerusalem, her agriculture, industries and commerce, would not be sufficient for its subject. The very difficult problems of the City's economy are immediately suggested by the topography; they run through every phase of her ethics and politics; the character and organisation of her religion are deeply involved in them; and their materials survive even in the most spiritual forms of its symbolism—which are in use at the present day. How was so large a community, especially with the enormous additions made to it on the occasions of the great festivals, able to subsist on such a site in such surroundings? What lands had the City, and what did she grow on them? Devoid as her territory is of many of the necessaries of life, and beset by obstacles to trade, how did she secure the former and overcome the latter? After supplying their own needs, what surplus of natural products did the citizens possess with which to purchase the commodities denied to them by their own soil? What other revenues came to them? There has been no full answer to these problems in the histories of Jerusalem; some of them have hardly been raised by any historian. Yet they are radical to the life of the City, relevant (as I have said) to every phase of her history, and greatly intensified by the growth of her peculiar religious institutions. Each of them requires a chapter to itself; and as among them they start the whole subject of the City's administration, I have added two other chapters upon the constitutional history of Israel from the earliest times to the Roman dominion. For these last there are, of course, many precedents; but as in the economic portions of this work I was without guides, I can hardly have done more than suggest to others fuller and more accurate ways in which to treat the subject.

Book III. The History.—Part of my original design was a sketch of the general history of Jerusalem, without which neither the significance of the site nor the details of the topography, differing as they did from age to age, could be made clear. But I found that this would not be sufficient to accomplish such aims, involving as these do the determination of so many points of historical and literary criticism. And if such a sketch were inadequate to declare the things in Jerusalem that may be seen, handled and physically measured, in so far as they affected the character of her people and the course of her history, still less could it do justice to the things that are unseen, the ethical and religious elements of that history; which, while sometimes determined by the material conditions, often wonderfully transcend both the aids and the obstacles that the latter contribute to them. It became necessary, therefore, to provide what is virtually a political and religious history of Israel from the time when with David the City was first identified with the fortunes of the People, to that of Titus when such an identification came to an end. This I have done in Book III.

It was impossible to prevent some overlapping among these three divisions of the work. The reader will find not a few anticipations of the general history of Book III. in the chapters of the first two Books. The history of the City under the Romans is treated with great brevity in Book III. because so much of it is already given in Book II. under 'The Government and Police' and 'The Multitude.'

The most of chapters vi., vii., ix. and x. in Book I., of chapter ix. in Book II., and of chapters ii. and iv.-xiii. in Book III., and of Appendices I. and II., along with portions of the Introduction, of chapters iv. and v. in Book I., and of chapters ii. and iii. in Book III., have appeared in the *Expositor* for 1903, 1905, 1906. Chapter x. Book II. was delivered as the Inaugural Lecture for Session 1907-8 of the Board of Theological Studies in the University of Liverpool. All the rest of the work is now published for the first time.

The thirteen Maps and Plans for the volumes have been prepared, like those of the *Historical Geography of the Holy Land*, by the eminent Scottish cartographer, Mr. John George Bartholomew, and warm thanks are due to him for all the trouble he has taken in their preparation, as well as for the clearness and impressiveness with which they have been achieved. Of the fifteen Plates, thirteen are from photographs by myself. The two others are of coins (except in two cases) from my own collection. To Mr. George Macdonald, LL.D., Honorary Curator of the Hunterian Coin Cabinet in the University of Glasgow, I owe the reproductions of the two coins from that collection, as well as assistance in determining other coins. My thanks are also due to Messrs. T. and R. Annan and Sons, Glasgow, for their beautiful reproduction of the photographs in collotype.

Two other debts I desire to acknowledge as the greatest of all. As my introduction to the history of Jerusalem, and my earliest interest in it, were due to the guidance of the dear kinswoman, my first teacher, to whose memory I have dedicated this work; so the work would never have been completed but for the constant assistance and counsel of my wife, who, besides reading all the proofs, has prepared the General and Special Indices to both volumes.

I have sought to make the work as useful as I could by giving the greater number of the dimensions and distances stated in the topography in metres as well as in feet, and by multiplying the references to the relevant literature. I have tested all these twice or thrice, but I cannot have escaped falling sometimes into error, and I will be grateful for corrections.

I have appended to this a table of the transliteration of Oriental names.

GEORGE ADAM SMITH.

GLASGOW,
*19th October* 1907.

# TRANSLITERATION OF SEMITIC NAMES

IN volume I. a number of the familiar historical names have been left in the usual English spelling. The following table explains such of the spelling adopted as may be unusual to the English reader.

| HEBREW | ARABIC | ENGLISH TRANSLITERATION |
|--------|--------|-------------------------|
| Aleph | Elif | When initial not expressed, when medial ' |
| Gimel | | g |
| | Gim | j |
| He | Hā | h |
| Wāw | Wāw | w (in a few cases v) |
| Ḥeth | Ḥā | ḥ |
| | Ḥā | kh (in a few cases ḫ) |
| Ṭeth | Ṭā | ṭ |
| | Zāy | z |
| Yodh | Yā | usually i or y (but in the Divine and other proper names j) |
| Kaph | Kāf | k (but in familiar proper names ch) |
| 'Ayin | 'Ain | ' |
| | Ghain | usually gh |
| Ṣadhe | Ṣād | ṣ |
| Qoph | Ḳāf | ḳ |

Final *he* (silent) is generally expressed, but not always; *e.g.* in titles of the tractates of the Mishna and Talmud. Some of these titles, too, have been given in the notes in the conventional spelling; the accurate transliteration will be found in Special Index III. In the text the Arabic definite article *el* (*en*, *esh*, etc.) is so spelt—with an *e*. But in a number of names on the large Plan of Jerusalem it appears with an *a*—*al* (*an*, *ash*, etc.).

# ADDITIONS AND CORRECTIONS TO VOLUME I.

INTRODUCTION

*THE ESSENTIAL CITY*

# THE ESSENTIAL CITY

HIGH up on the back of a long mountain range, between its eastern flank which is the last bulwark against the Arabian desert, and its western which is the side of the vaster basin of the Mediterranean, lies Jerusalem, facing the desert and the sirocco, yet so close to the edge of the basin as to feel the full sweep of its rains and humid winds. The sea is some thirty-four miles away, washing a bleak coast without harbours. On the other side, the range is separated from the Arabian plateau by the profound trench of the Jordan and Dead Sea; but the desert has crossed the trench, and climbs to within a few miles of the City-gates. The site is a couple of rocky spurs, lower than the surrounding summits of the range, but entrenched from them on three sides by abrupt ravines, in one of which lies the only certain spring of the district. There is no river nor perennial stream, and no pass nor natural high-road across the mountain. The back of the range offers a rough pasture, which in the rainy season spreads out upon the desert, but is suitable only to the smaller kinds of cattle. The limestone terraces and slopes are among the best in all the world for the olive and the vine, but there are comparatively few fields for grain. The broad plains of Palestine are far off, and more open to other countries than commanded by her own hills. Even further away are the nearest metals and salts.

Geographically considered the City is the product of two opposite systems of climate and culture.  She hangs on the watershed between East and West, between the Desert and the Sea : central but aloof, defensible but not commanding, with some natural resources but bare of many of the necessaries of life.  Left alone by the main currents of the world's history, Jerusalem had been but a small highland township, her character compounded of the rock, the olive and the desert : conscious, by right of such a position, of her distinctness and jealous of her freedom ; drawing, from her cultivation of that slow but generous tree, the love of peace, habits of industry and the civic instinct ; but touched besides by the more austere and passionate influences of the desert.  Sion, 'the Rock-fort,' Olivet and Gethsemane, 'The Oilpress,' the Tower of the Flock, and the Wilderness of the Shepherds, would still have been names typical of her life, and the things they illustrate have remained the material substance of her history to the present day.

But she became the bride of Kings and the mother of Prophets.  The Prophets, sons only of that national and civic life of which the Kings had made her the centre, repaid her long travail and training of their genius by the supreme gift of an answer to the enigmas of her life : blew by their breath into imperishable flame the meaning of her tardy and ambiguous history.  She knew herself chosen of God, a singular city in the world, with a mission to mankind.  And though her children became divided between a stupid pride in her privilege and a frequent apostasy to other faiths, for she had heathen blood in her from the beginning, God never left Himself without witnesses in her midst, nor ceased to strive with her.  She felt

His Presence, she was adjured of His love, and, as never another city on earth has been, of His travail for her worthiness of the destiny to which He had called her.

Few cities have been so often or so cruelly besieged, so torn by faction, so sapped by treachery, so inflammable to riot, so drenched with blood. The forces of her progress and her re-actions have been equally intolerant, and almost equally savage in their treatment of each other.

Yet it has not been in this ceaseless human strife that the real tragedy of Jerusalem has consisted—except in so far as both sides were together but one side of the more awful contest through the ages between the Spirit of God and the spirit of man. Nowhere else has this universal struggle been waged so consciously, so articulately as in Jerusalem. Nowhere else have its human responsibilities and its Divine opportunities been so tragically developed. The expostulations of souls like Jeremiah's and Habakkuk's with the decrees of Providence and the burdens of Its will have been answered from their own hearts, and those of other prophets, in the assurance of an infinitely more anxious travail and agony waged by God Himself with reluctant man for the understanding of His will, the persuasion of His mercy, and the acceptance of His discipline towards higher stages of character and vision. It is to-day the subject of half the world's worship and of the wonder of the rest, that both these elements in the long religious history of Jerusalem culminated and were combined in the experience of Jesus Christ within and around her walls: on the one hand, in His passionate appeals to the City to turn to Him, as though all the sovereign love and fatherly yearning of God were with Him; and on the other, in His Temptation, His agony of submission to the Divine will, and His Crucifixion. So that Sion and Olivet, the Wilderness and Gethsemane, their earthly meanings almost forgotten, have become the names of eternal facts in the history of the relations of God and man.

From another point of view, and with more detail, we may present this essential history of the City as follows.

The life of even the meanest of towns cannot be written apart from the general history of the times through which it has flourished. While still but a hill-fort, with centuries of obscurity before her, Jerusalem held a garrison for the Pharaoh of the day, and corresponded with him in the characters of the Babylonian civilisation.

When such a town, suddenly, without omen, augury or promise of national renown, becomes, as Jerusalem did under David, the capital of a kingdom, her historian is drawn to explore, it may be at a distance from herself, the currents of national life which have surprised her, and the motives of their convergence upon so unexpected a centre. His horizon is the further widened, if the capital which she has become be that of a restless nation upon the path of great empires : tremulous to all their rumour, and provoking, as Jerusalem did from the days of Sennacherib to those of Hadrian, the interference of their arms.

Yet this range of political interest opened to our City only as the reflection of that more sacred fame which dawned upon her when, with Isaiah, the one monotheism of the ancient world was identified with the inviolableness of her walls ; when with Deuteronomy and Josiah the ritual of that religion was concentrated upon her shrine, and the One Temple came to be regarded as equally essential to religion with faith in the One God. Not only did the Country, already much diminished, shrink in consequence to be the mere fringe of the City, within whose narrow walls a whole nation, conscious of a service to humanity, henceforth experienced the most powerful crises of their career; not only did her sons learn to add to the pride of such a citizenship the idealism and passionate longing which only exile breeds ; but among alien and far away races the sparks were kindled of a love and an eagerness for the City almost as jealous as those of her own children.

So lofty an influence was exercised by Jerusalem some centuries before the appearance of Jesus Christ; yet it was only prophetic of the worship she drew from the whole world as the scene of His Passion, His Cross and His Grave.   Though other great cities of Christendom, Antioch, Alexandria, Carthage and Rome, were by far her superiors in philosophy and spiritual empire, Jerusalem remained the religious centre of the earth—whose frame was even conceived as poised upon her rocks—the home of the Faith, the goal of most distant pilgrimages, and the original of the heavenly City, which would one day descend from God among men.   By all which memories and beliefs the passions of mankind were let loose upon her. She became as Armageddon.   Two world-wide religions made her their battle-ground, hurling their farthest kings against her walls and shedding upon her dust the tears and the blood of millions of their people.   East and West hotly contended for her, no longer because she was alive, but in devotion to the mere shell of the life that had gone from her.   Then, though still a focus in the diplomacy of empires and the shrine of several forms of faith, her politics were reduced to intrigue and her religion overlaid with super-

stition, for generations hardly touched by any visible
heroism or even romance.

In all it has been thirty-three centuries of history,
climbing slowly to the Central Fact of all time, and then
toppling down upon itself in a ruin that has almost
obliterated the scenes and monuments of the life which set
her Alone among the cities of the world.

The bare catalogue of the disasters which have overtaken
Jerusalem is enough to paralyse her topographer. Besides
the earthquakes which have periodically rocked her
foundations,[1] the City has endured nearly twenty sieges
and assaults of the utmost severity, some involving a considerable, others a total, destruction of her walls and buildings ;[2] almost twenty more blockades or military occupations, with the wreck or dilapidation of prominent edifices ;
the frequent alteration of levels by the razing of rocky
knolls and the filling of valleys ; about eighteen reconstructions, embellishments, and large extensions, including
the imposition of novel systems of architecture, streets,
drains and aqueducts, athwart the lines of the old ; the
addition of suburbs and the abandonment of parts of the
inhabited area ; while over all there gathered the dust and
the waste of ordinary manufacture and commerce. Even
such changes might not have been fatal to the restoration
of the ancient topography, had the traditions which they
interrupted been immediately resumed. But there also
have happened two intervals of silence, after Nebuchadrezzar and after Hadrian, during which the City lay
almost if not altogether desolate, and her natives were
banished from her ; five abrupt passages from one religion
to another, which even more disastrously severed the con-

---

[1] Below, Bk. i. ch. iv.     [2] For these and following statistics, see App. I.

tinuity of her story ; more than one outbreak of fanatic superstition creating new and baseless tradition; as well as the long, careless chatter about the holy sites which has still further confused or obliterated the genuine memories of the past.

Before we put our hands to this *débris*, and stir its dust with the breath of a hundred controversies, it is necessary to fill in that general view of the position of the City which we have just taken with some detail of her surroundings and atmosphere ; and of the common life which, under every change of empire and of religion, has throbbed through her streets to the present day.

Jerusalem lies upon the mountain-range of Judæa, about 2400 feet above the sea, and some thirty-four miles from the coast of the Mediterranean. From the latter she is separated by a plain, which during the greater part of her history was in the hands of an alien and generally hostile race ; by low foot-hills ; and by the flank and watershed of the range itself. From the west, therefore, except for its rains and its winds, we must realise that Jerusalem stood almost completely aloof. The most considerable valley in the mountains on this side of her, after starting from the watershed a little to the north of her walls, drives its deep trench southward, as if to cut her off more rigorously from the maritime plain and the sea. Travellers by the modern road from Jaffa will remember how after this has seemed, by a painful ascent from Bab-el-Wâd, to attain the level of the City, it has to wind down the steep sides of the Wady Bêt-Ḥanînâ or Ḳuloniyeh, and then wind up again to the watershed. The only pass from the west that can be said to debouch upon Jerusalem is a narrow and easily defended gorge, up which the present railway has been forced, but which can never have been used as a road of approach either by armies or by commercial caravans. Hence nearly all the great advances on Jerusalem have been made, even by Western Powers in command of the plain, either from further north, by the Beth-horon road, or from further south—by the passes upon Hebron and Bethlehem ; and then, in either case, along the backbone of the range, by the one main route near which the City stands.

Nor is Jerusalem perched upon the watershed itself, but lies upon the first narrow plateau to the east of this. As you stand at the Jaffa gate and look west, the watershed is the top of the first slope in front of you, and it shuts out all prospect of the west even from the towers and house-tops. The view to the north is almost as short—hardly farther than to where the head of the hidden Wâdy Bêt-Ḥanîna—the precise water-parting—comes over into the faint beginnings of the valley of the Ḳidron, draining south-east to the Dead Sea. Above the course of this valley and between it and the watershed the ground slopes obliquely from the north-west. Just before the city-walls are reached, it divides into two spurs or promontories running south between the Ḳidron and the Wâdy er-Rabâbi and separated from each other by the now shallow glen, El-Wâd, once known as the Tyropœon. These spurs form the site of the city. Without going into the details of their configuration, we find enough for our present purpose in observing that the western is the higher of the two, and that running as they do southwards, the dip of them[1] and therefore the whole exposure of the city is to the east.

[1] According to Conder the dip of the strata is about 10° E.S.E.

JERUSALEM: LOOKING S.E. BETWEEN OLI

JERUSALEM: LOOKING E. ACROS
Taken from

*Plate I.*

IR ABU ṬOR TO THE MOABITE PLATEAU.

*Plate II.*

SHERÎF TO THE Mt. OF OLIVES.
n Synagogue.

Jerusalem faces the sunrise, which strikes across the Mount of Olives and over the Ḳidron.

Yet this downward tilt towards Olivet does not exhaust the eastern bent and disposition of the City. We have seen that the west and north are entirely shut off. The blockade is carried round the north-east and east by Scopus and Olivet: the south is equally excluded by the ridge between the city and Bethlehem. In fact there is but one gap in the low and gentle horizon of hill tops, and this is to the south-east: giving view across the desert of Judæa and the hollow of the Dead Sea to the high range of Moab, cut only by the trench of the Arnon and battlemented towards its far southern end by the hill of Kerak. In certain states of the atmosphere, and especially when the evening sun shortens the perspective by intensifying the colour and size of the Moab mountains, the latter appear to heave up towards the city and to present to her the threshold of the Arabian desert immediately above the hills of her own wilderness. Thus, what Josephus says of the tower Psephinus is true of most of the housetops of Jerusalem. Their one 'full prospect is towards Arabia.'[1] The significance of which is obvious. It is as if Providence had bound over the city to eastern interests and eastern sympathies. Hidden from the west and the north, Jerusalem, through all her centuries, has sat facing the austere scenery of the Orient and the horizon of those vast deserts, out of which her people came to her. If the spell of this strikes even the western traveller as he passes a few evenings on her house-tops, he can the better understand why the

---

[1] *Vide* v. *B.J.* iv. 3: ἐπὶ γὰρ ἑβδομήκοντα πήχεις ὑψηλὸς ὢν Ἀραβίαν τε ἀνίσχοντος ἡλίου παρεῖχεν ἀφορᾶν καὶ μέχρι θαλάττης τὰ τῆς Ἑβραίων κληρουχίας ἔσχατα. For the outlook to Moab, see Plate I.

Greeks were not at home in Jerusalem, and why Hellenism, though not forty miles from the Levant, never made her its own ; why even Christianity failed to hold her; and why the ˙Mohammedan, as he looks down her one long vista towards Mecca, feels himself securely planted on her site.

The desert creeps close to the city gates. The blistered rocks and the wild ravines of the Wady of Fire[1] are within a short walk of the gardens of Siloam. From the walls the wilderness of Judæa can be traversed in a day, and be-beyond are the barren coast and bitter waters of the Dead Sea. The sirocco sweeps up unhindered ; *a dry wind of the high places of the desert towards the daughter of my people, neither to fan nor to cleanse* ;[2] gusty, parching, inflammatory and laden with sand when it comes from the south-east, but clear, cold and benumbing when in winter it blows off the eastern or north-eastern desert plateaus. It is difficult to estimate what effect this austere influence

---

[1] Wâdy-en-Nâr, the continuation to the Dead Sea of the Ḳidron valley.

[2] Jer. iv. 11. 'It is when the wind blows from the south-east that it acquires the peculiarities which Europeans usually signify by the term *sirocco*. The more the wind tends to the south the more dull and overcast is the sky, and the more disagreeable to the feelings the state of the atmosphere. The worst kind dries the mucous membrane of the air passages, producing a kind of inflammation resulting in catarrh and sore throat ; it induces great lassitude, accelerated pulse, thirst, and sometimes actual fever. It dries and cracks furniture, and parches vegetation, sometimes withering whole fields of young corn. Its force is not usually great, but sometimes severe storms of wind and fine dust are experienced, the hot air burning like a blast from an oven, and the sand cutting the face of the traveller. This kind of air has a peculiar smell, not unlike that of the neighbourhood of a burning brick-kiln. Sometimes the most remarkable whirlwinds are produced. Clouds of sand fly about in all directions, and the gusts of wind are so violent as to blow weak persons from their horses and to overturn baggage animals.'—Abridged from Dr. Chaplin's account in *P.E.F.Q.*, 1883, p. 16. Sometimes towards harvest a day of this wind will prematurely ripen the grain. But the effect is precarious, and may readily pass into the result of blasting it.—*Diary*, 6th May 1904.

has exercised on the temperament of the City. A more
calculable result in her history was produced by the convenience of the desert as a refuge when the native garrisons
of Jerusalem could no longer hold out against their besiegers. Not only was the east the most natural direction
of flight for David before Absalom, and for Zedekiah[1]
when he broke with a few soldiers through the blockade
of the Babylonian army; but the desert sheltered both the
troops of Judas Maccabæus when Jerusalem was taken by
the Seleucids, and those bands of zealots who escaped
when Titus stormed the citadel and the sanctuary.

Conversely the life of the desert easily wanders into
Jerusalem. There are always some Arabs in her streets.
You will see one or two of the few Christians of that race
worshipping—like Amos at Bethel—on some high festival
about the Holy Sepulchre; and through the environs you
will meet a caravan, with salt, skins, wool or dates from
the Dead Sea or Ma'an, or even from Sinai. Except
Damascus or Gaza no Syrian town gathers to itself more
of the rumour of Peræa, or of Arabia, from the borders of
Hauran to Mecca.[2] In was in or somewhere near Jerusalem that an observer wrote the lines:

*I saw the tents of Kushán in affliction:*
*The curtains of Midian's land were trembling,*[3]

—one of the finest expressions in any literature of the
electric passage of tidings through the tremulous East.

---

[1] David and Zedekiah the first and last kings: 2 Sam. xv. ff., 2 Kings
xxv. 4 f. See further Bk. ii. ch. x.

[2] Cf. Robinson, *B.R.* i. 366. In 1896, when the Turks were at war with
the Druzes of Hauran and the Government had stopped the telegraphs, news
of the conflicts reached the Jerusalem bazaars within a few days.

[3] Habakkuk iii. 7.

And so, too, it is Jerusalem, fully hidden from nearly every point of view in Western Palestine, which, of all sites on the latter, except Bethlehem, remains in most frequent evidence to the traveller on the east of the Jordan. From Machaerus I have seen her buildings with the morning sun upon them round the end of Olivet, and I believe that on a clear day they are also visible from Kerak. From Mount Nebo, from the hills above 'Arâḳ-el-'Emîr or Rabbath-Ammon, and I think, too, from the Jebel 'Ôsha' above es-Salṭ, the Russian tower on the Mount of Olives is always prominent.

The single trunk route which Jerusalem commands runs along the backbone of the western range, from Hebron to the north. It is one of the least important in Palestine. No passage by the city connects the east and west. The nearest—from the maritime plain by the Beth-horons and past Michmash to Jericho—is almost twelve miles away. Jerusalem, therefore, cannot be regarded as a natural centre of commerce. When she commanded the transit trade of Western Asia, and was in Ezekiel's words *the gate of the peoples* ;[1] or when, in the days of her weakness, she excited the jealousy of her enemies lest she should again become strong enough to exact tribute and toll from them,[2] such an influence must have been due, not to the virtues of her site, but to her political rank as the capital of a strong and compact people entrenched upon the paths between Phœnicia and Edom. Nor was Jerusalem ever, so much as Damascus, Hebron or Gaza, a desert port or market for the nomads, from which they bought their cloth, pottery and weapons ; nor, like Antioch or Mecca, had she (except for a very short period) a harbour of her

[1] Ezekiel xxvi. 2 ; LXX.    [2] Ezra iv. 20 f.

own upon the sea. Even when she swayed the commerce of Palestine and Arabia, her influence was political and financial rather than commercial;[1] the only trade that came to her was due to her comparatively large population, or to her Temple and the multitude of its annual pilgrims. Her industries were also local—potteries, weaving, fulling and dyeing and, later, soap-making. Beyond oil she exported nothing of her own except to the neighbouring villages.

Another feature of life, conspicuous by its meagreness in the district in which Jerusalem stands, is the water supply. The upper strata of the neighbourhood are of that porous limestone, through which, as in the greater part of Western Palestine, the rain sinks to a considerable depth and living springs are far between. The only point in the environs of the City where the lower, harder rocks now throw up water to the surface is in the Ḳidron Valley immediately under the wall of Ophel; and this supply, secured for the City even in times of siege by a tunnel through the rock, was supplemented by the reservoirs, for which Jerusalem has always been famous, and which were fed from the rain caught upon the multitude of her roofs. These gave the city, when blockaded, an advantage over most of her besiegers, who found no springs in her immediate neighbourhood, and in several cases were ignorant of any even at a distance.[2] To which facts we may attribute the brevity and failure of several blockades,[3] as well as the unwillingness of every great

---

[1] This is especially obvious in Josephus.

[2] Such as the copious well at 'Ain Kârim, from which the upper classes in Jerusalem still carry water because of its purity.

[3] Such as those of the Nabateans in 63 B.C., and of Cestius Gallus in 66 A.D.

invader to come near to Jerusalem till he had made very sure of his base of supplies in the lower country round about.[1] The City's strength, then, was this: that, while tolerably well watered herself, she lay where her besiegers could find not much food and scarcely any water. Strabo describes her thus: 'The site is rocky, and surrounded by a strong *enceinte*; within well provided with water, but without absolutely arid.'[2]

The immediate surroundings of Jerusalem are bare and rocky; with some exceptions they can hardly ever have been otherwise. The grey argillaceous soil is shallow, stony, and constantly interrupted by scalps, ledges and knolls of naked limestone. In the sides and bottoms of the wadies green patches are visible; but the only natural gardens are those fed from the overflow of the one spring in the valley of the Ḳidron. On the north-west of the City, the winter rains render the ground swampy: for example, in the Khallet el-Kasabe 'the little valley of the reeds,' where reeds still grow, and in the Khallet eṭ-Ṭarḥa. Here and there the environs show fields of grain or vegetables; and one of the northern gates was called Genath, 'the garden.'[3] The foliage to-day is nearly altogether that of the olive-trees, scattered at intervals in the stony orchards on the hill-sides, or down the Ḳidron and the Wâdy er-Rabâbi. The vineyards are few. Within the walls

---

[1] Cf. *H.G.H.L.* 298 ff. for Vespasian, Titus and Saladin. Thus also may be partly explained the long delay of Richard I. in the Shephelah, and his ultimate abandonment of the advance on Jerusalem.

[2] *Geog.* xvi. 40. Dion Cassius (lxvi. 4) puts the same fact more vividly in his account of the siege by Titus: τὸ δὲ δὴ πλεῖστον οἱ Ῥωμαῖοι τῇ ἀνυδρίᾳ ἐκακοπάθουν, καὶ φαῦλον, καὶ πόρρωθεν ὕδωρ ἐπαγόμενοι· οἱ δὲ Ἰουδαῖοι διὰ τῶν ὑπονόμων ἴσχυον. Similar evidence from the Crusades, Will. of Tyre *Hist.* viii. 4, 7, 24. The water-supply of Jerusalem forms the subject of ch. v. of Bk. i. of this volume. [3] Jos. v. *B.J.* iv. 2. See below, p. 243.

there are less than half a dozen palms, exotic at this altitude, and some other trees in the garden of the Armenian monastery. The sycomore, the chief source of timber in Judæa, does not grow at so high a level. Whether in ancient times the groves of olive were more numerous, or whether trees of other species ever clothed the surrounding hills, are questions difficult to answer. Olivet has almost lost its title to the name, by the Jewish graveyards and Christian buildings which have recently multiplied on the face opposite the City, and is now excelled in greenery by the western slope towards the watershed. But in ancient times the Mount of Olives would hardly have been called so, had it not stood out in conspicuous contrast to the other hills. One can well believe that its north-western flank, the high basins between it and Scopus, and its eastern folds towards Bethany were once covered with trees. They are still fertile and support a number of orchards.[1] The Jews who returned to Jerusalem after the Exile were bidden *to go up into the mountain and bring wood*[2] for building, but this may not have been in the immediate neighbourhood. Josephus mentions a timber-market;[3] but probably it was for imported beams, and even most of the fuel may have come from a distance. Where the royal park lay from which Nehemiah was empowered to obtain timber,[4] we do not know. It is striking how seldom any tree appears in the present place-names of the immediate environs.[5] One has to walk several miles before encountering the

---

[1] Jerome, on Jerem. vii. 30, mentions groves in Hinnom where olives still flourish. See Plate III.
[2] Haggai i. 8.    [3] ii. *B.J.* xix. 4.
[4] Neh. ii. 8, cf. 1 Chron. xxvii. 28.    [5] See below, Bk. ii. ch. iv.

name of the oak, the plane-tree, the tamarisk or the thorn, and the nearest wood is three miles down the railway.[1] The latter instances prove that such trees could grow around Jerusalem, and the bareness of her suburbs during the Arab period may be due to the number of her sieges. We know that Pompey cleared away the trees, and one hundred and thirty-three years later Titus is said to have done so for a distance of ninety stadia from the walls, and, in particular, to have cut down all the groves and orchards to the north on the line of the main assault.[2] There may, therefore, have been periods in which the hills engirdling the City were much more green than they are to-day ; but if this was the case, it has left no reflection in literature. We do not read of woods about Jerusalem. It is *mountains* which stand round her ;[3] and except for Olivet, and perhaps Bezetha and Bethphage, there is in the neighbouring place-names of the Bible no trace of trees.[4]

The climate of Jerusalem is easily described, especially since the details have been reduced to statistics by the scientific observations of the last forty years.[5] As through-

---

[1] *P.E.F. Large Map,* Sheet xvii., and Schick's *Karte der Weiteren Umgebung von Jerusalem, Z.D.P.V.* xix., with the list and explanation of names accompanying.

[2] Josephus vi. *B.J.* i. 1, viii. 1 ; v. *B.J.* iii. 2.          [3] Ps. cxxxv. 2.

[4] Bezetha may equal Beth-zaith, *house of olives* : Bethphage may be *h. of the green fig.* In 680 A.D. Arculf found few trees on Olivet except vines and olives. In Crusading times woods of any importance were found near Jerusalem only on the west of its territory, Belle-fontaine, St. Jean des Bois, Emmaus, and also north of Hebron.—Rey, *Colonies Franques, etc.,* 239.

[5] The observer to whom we owe most of these is the late Dr. Chaplin, whose vivid paper, ' Observations on the Climate of Jerusalem,' *P.E.F.Q.,* 1883, pp. 8 ff., accompanied by numerous tables giving the result of observations between 1860-1 and 1881-2, ought to be studied by all who wish to understand the climate, not of Jerusalem only, but of all Palestine (cp. O. Kersten, *Z.D.P.V.* xiv. 93 ff.). See also the works quoted below, p. 77 f., on the ' Rainfall.'

out Syria, the year is divided into two seasons, a rainy
winter and a dry summer, but at so high an elevation the
extremes are greater and the changes more capricious
than in the rest of Palestine. With an annual rainfall
about that of London,[1] the city receives this within
seven months of the year—a quarter of it in January
alone [2]—and through the other five, May to October, is
without more than a few showers. July is absolutely
rainless; June, August and September practically so.
The drought is softened by heavy dews and by dense
mists, which trail away swiftly in face of the sunrise.
The temperature, with a mean of 62°,[3] has also its extremes. Not only is winter colder than on the plains,
but the summer heat mounts higher and is more trying.
In fifteen years there was an average of thirty-eight days
on which the thermometer was above 90°—on twenty-
eight occasions from 100° to 108°; and an average of
fifty-five nights on which it fell under 40°, with 107
descents to or below freezing-point.[4] Ice is therefore
formed but does not last through the day. Snow has
fallen in fourteen seasons out of thirty-two; for the most
part in small quantity, and soon melted; but sometimes

[1] 25·23 inches on an average of thirty-two years, 1861-1892; Glaisher,
*P.E.F.Q.*, 1894, p. 41. Hilderscheid (p. 34) calculates the average of thirty-
nine years at Dr. Chaplin's station within the walls as 26·05 (661·8 mm.).

[2] December, February and March are the next most rainy months in that
order. The rains begin to fall either in October or November, the latter
rains in the end of March, but lessening through April.

[3] Fahrenheit; 1882-1896, *P.E.F.Q.*, 1898, 202 f.

[4] Glaisher, *P.E.F.Q.*, 1898, pp. 183 ff. In Sarona, near Jaffa, the number of
days in which the mercury rose above 90° in ten years varied annually from
8 to 39 (average 23·6); the nights in which it fell below 40° varied from 2 to
15 (average 6·5), *P.E.F.Q.*, 1891, pp. 165, 170. Chaplin (*P.E.F.Q.*, 1898,
p. 184) reports for Jerusalem once 112° and (*id.* 1883, Tab. xiv.) once 25·0°
(in January).

there are heavy snowstorms, and the drifts lie in the
hollows of the hills for two or three weeks.¹ After both
snow and rain the clayey soil will be muddy for days, but
the porous limestone prevents the formation of swamps;²
and although the air may continue damp, it is not in
itself unhealthy. The present malariousness of the City
at certain seasons arises from the masses of *débris*. Rain
and snow have been known to last for thirteen or fourteen
days in succession, but usually the winter rains fall for
one or two days at a time, and these are followed by one
or more of fine weather, 'some of the most enjoyable that
the climate of Palestine affords.'³

One rainy day I vividly remember; it was typical of
many. Clouds coming up from the sea on a westerly
wind, their skirts were caught upon the watershed, while
the rest hurried raining over the City. Blue sky broke
between; the wet house-tops and the green and grey of
the surrounding hills glistened with a brief reflection. Then
the gap closed, and beneath the compact pall all became
dark, the olive-groves turning to black and the limestone
ridges by contrast to a white as of long-bleached bones.
The wind was chill and mournful, and brought up to one
the keynote of the ancient dirge—

> '*When the Lord beclouds with his wrath*
> *The daughter of Sion.*'⁴

When the winter east wind comes, it is clear and dry,
but sometimes benumbing. The sirocco, or south-east

---

¹ Chaplin, p. 11. In December 1879 the fall of snow was 17 inches. On
March 14, 1880, it was 5 inches; and I remember the consequent mud and
cold when I reached Jerusalem in the end of the month.

² With the transient exceptions mentioned above, p. 16.

³ Chaplin, *op. cit.* p. 9.                    ⁴ Lam. ii. 1.

wind, with its distressing heat and dull atmosphere of sand,[1] blows at frequent intervals in April, May and October. The daily breeze from the sea during summer[2] does not always reach Jerusalem, and when it does, has often been robbed of its refreshing qualities:[3] the reason of the excess of the summer heats over those of the coast. The summer dusts are thick: at that height easily stirred and irritating. The long drought, exhausting many of the reservoirs, and the sultry nights, robbed of moisture by the failure of the west wind, are more dangerous to health than the rainy season. From May till October 'the climatic diseases of the country, such as ophthalmia, fevers and dysentery, are most prevalent.'[4]

On the whole, then, the climate of Jerusalem is temperate and healthy; but with rigours both of cold and heat. Except during the sirocco and some dusty summer days, the atmosphere is clear and stimulating. There is no mirage in the air, nor any glamour, save when, sometimes at evening, the glowing Moab hills loom upon

[1] See above, p. 12.  [2] *H.G.H.L.* p. 520.

[3] Chaplin, p. 15. The west wind has been observed 55 times in a year. The prevailing wind at Jerusalem is the north-west, blowing from 100 to 150 days in the year. Dr. Masterman kindly writes me, 'Your note implies that the west wind is rare; this is of course quite a mistake, as it is almost a constant feature from midday onwards. Now in June, for example, we have quite a stiff breeze almost daily from noon till the small hours of the next morning. Many days, and still more nights, it amounts to quite a gale. Dr. Chaplin's figures only refer to the direction of the wind at nine in the morning. As the observations are made in my own house for the Fund, I know this well.'

[4] Chaplin, p. 20. Dr. Masterman writes:—'I suppose any medical man now would be apt to cavil at the idea of any "air" [see previous page] being malarious, but that Jerusalem is an extremely malarious place, especially, of course, in the summer months, my daily work shows. I could fill our hospital here several times over with malaria cases only. There is no season free from this scourge, and travellers in the spring, not at all infrequently, are affected.'

the City, or when the orange moon rises from behind
them, and by her beams you feel, but cannot fathom, the
awful hollow of the Dead Sea.  But these touches of
natural magic are evanescent, and the prevailing impression is of a bare landscape beneath a plain atmosphere, in
which there is no temptation to illusion nor any suggestion of mystery.  This is no doubt part of the reason why
the visitor is so often disappointed by an atmosphere
which he expected to fascinate him.  Let him reflect that
this very plainness is significant.  He must bring the
spell with him out of the history ; and his appreciation of
it will only be enhanced by the discovery that Nature has
lent almost nothing to its original creation.

In such surroundings and such an atmosphere, Jerusalem
sits upon her two promontories in the attitude already
described : facing the Mount of Olives and looking
obliquely through the one gap of her encircling hills
towards the desert and the long high edge of Moab.  The
ravines which encompass the promontories—the valley of
the Ḳidron and the Wâdy er-Rabâbi—determine the extreme limits of the town on the east, the south and the
west.  They enclose a space, roughly speaking, of about
half a mile square.  It will be our duty to inquire how
much of this was occupied by houses or girdled by walls
at successive stages of the history : questions which are
the subject of much dispute.  But for our present purpose
—which is to recall some image of the Essential City,
the same which through so many centuries has grown
and adorned herself, and been trampled and suffered ruin
—it is sufficient to take as much as we can of the present
town and its most prominent features.  Virtually upon
her ancient seat Jerusalem still sits and at much the same

slope; rising, that is, from the edge of the Ḳidron valley
up the same easy ascent to the constant line of her
western wall. Only her skirts do not extend, as they did
in ancient times, over the southern ends and declivities of
the two promontories; but these lie bare and open, even
the ruins of their walls being buried out of sight. As we
shall see, the present shape of the City is no natural
growth, but the stamp which her Roman conquerors impressed upon her. Along with the mouth of the Tyropœon, that opens between them, the inferior parts of those
southern declivities formed the lowest portion of the
ancient city, from which stairs and steep lanes led to the
Temple terrace over the Ḳidron. This terrace is now the
lowest stretch of the city; it remains what it always was,
a large court with a sanctuary, and at its north-west corner
there are barracks and a tower on the site of what was
once a citadel.[1] To the north the ground, after a depression representing an ancient fosse is passed, rises somewhat
quickly and is covered with houses: once a suburb, but
now within the walls. To the west of the sanctuary-plat-
form the houses, also thickly clustering, dip for a little—
above the once deeper depression of the Tyropœon, the
line of which is still visible across the city from north to
south—and then the roofs slowly but steadily rise till they
culminate in the tower of Herod and the present citadel
by the Jaffa gate.

Looking down upon this sloping city, either from one
of its own towers or from the Mount of Olives, we are
struck by the crowding of its houses. Except round the
sanctuary, and for almost imperceptible intervals at the
gates and a few other sites, there are no open spaces or

[1] Antonia of the Roman period.

even open lines; for there are no streets or squares, but only close and sombre lanes, climbing steeply from the Temple Court to the west, or, at right angles to these, dipping more gently from north to south.[1]  And so it must nearly[2] always have been.  *Jerusalem is builded as a city that is compact together.*[3]  The locusts, besiegers and death are pictured by the Prophets as entering the windows and houses directly from the walls.[4]  Throughout the Old Testament we read of *streets* very seldom, and then probably not in the proper sense of the name, which is *broad places*, but under a poetic licence.[5]  Even in Isaiah's time it is only on the housetops,[6] or on the walls,[7] that we see the whole population gathered for a purpose which is not religious.  Josephus frequently mentions the ' narrow streets,' and the fighting from the housetops.[8]  Through these lanes, ever close, steep and sombre as they are to-day, there beats the daily stir of the City's common life : the passage of her buzzing crowds, rumour and the exchange of news, the carriage of goods, trading and the smaller industries, the search for slaves and criminals, the bridal processions, the funerals, the tide of worshippers to the Temple, and occasionally the march of armed men.  And through them also raged, as Josephus describes, the fighting, the sacking, the slaughter : all the fine-drawn pangs and anguish of the days of the City's overthrow.

Above these narrow arteries, through which her hot

[1] Cf. Lam. iv. 1 ; *the top of every street.*
[2] The early Christian Jerusalem showed a line of columned street, from the present Damascus gate southwards.
[3] Ps. cxxii. 3.      [4] Joel ii. 9 ; Jer. ix. 21 [20].
[5] Lam. ii. 11, 12 ; iv. 18 ; Jer. ix. 21 [20] : ' rĕhōbŏth.'
[6] xxii. 1. : *What ailest thou that thou art wholly gone up to the housetops!*
[7] xxxvi. 11.
[8] *B.J.*, e.g. I. xviii. 2 ; II. xv. 5 ; V. viii. 1 (*bis*) ; VI. viii. 5 : οἱ στενωποί.

blood raced, Jerusalem, to the outside world, showed clean and fair: a high-walled white city; steep and compact, but with one level space, where since the time of Solomon her Temple rose, and since the Exile there were no secular buildings.

This is as much of the ancient City as by light of day we dare reconstruct from her present condition. For the strong eastern sun aggravates the nakedness of those slopes to the south which were once covered with houses and girt by walls; emphasises the modern buildings and the fashions of western life that everywhere obtrude; and flattens still further the shallow ravines, which, before they were choked with the *débris* of so many sieges, lifted the city high and gallant above their precipitous sides. He who would raise again the Essential City must wait for night, when Jerusalem hides her decay, throws off every modern intrusion, feels her valleys deepen about her, and rising to her proper outline, resumes something of her ancient spell. At night, too, or in the early morning, the humblest and most permanent habits of her life may be observed, unconfused by the western energies which are so quickly transforming and disguising her.

It was a night in June, when from a housetop I saw her thus. There was a black sky with extremely brilliant stars; the city, not yet fallen asleep, sparkled with tiny lights. I could scarcely discern the surrounding hills. Moab was invisible. After an hour a paleness drew up in the south-east, the sky gradually lightened to a deep blue, the stars shone silver, and a blood-red gibbous moon crept suddenly above the edge of Moab, and looked over into the Dead Sea. The sleeping city was now dark, lying in huddled folds of black, save where, through a wider gap, one palm and the dome of the Ashkenazim synagogue stood out against the pearly mist of the Moab hills. But as the moon fully struck her, Jerusalem seemed to turn in her sleep, and in something of her ancient outline, lifted herself, grey and ghostly, to the light. I descended, and issuing by the Jaffa gate, saw her in another aspect: the western wall alive, erect and grim against the sky, while its shadow deepened the valley below. The wall is Turkish, and only a few centuries old, but even so must the ramparts and the towers of Herod have looked to the night-guards in the Roman trenches. A caravan of camels came up from the Hebron road; the riders in white abbas swaying over the necks of their beasts, that with long strides paced noiselessly upon the thick dust. They stopped outside the gate, the camels were made to kneel, the bales were loosened from their backs, and stacked upon the ground; the men lay down beside them, and in a few minutes were asleep. No wind stirred, and except for spasms of barking from the street dogs, answered now and then from a far-away village, scarcely a sound broke the silence. The moonshine at last turned the wall and touched the muddy water at the lower end of the great reservoir beyond. A pair of jackals stole down to drink, but fled before the yelp of the dogs. For the next two hours nothing stirred but the wash of breeze through the olives on Nikophorieh; till the cocks crew, and two horsemen came through the gate, the first apparently for the long ride to Jaffa, the second by the Birket Mamilla for the Gaza road down the Wâdy el-Werd. Looking up to the edge of the citadel, one could see how Herod had built his tower there to command these approaches, as well as that from Hebron and the south.

I returned to the housetop. The sky had grown blue in the lower east, and above that from purple to pink. Swifts began to fly past the houses : thronging at last till the air was thick with them. A bugle rang out from the citadel, and was answered up the town from Antonia ; challenge and answer were several times repeated. In the hollow between Scopus and the Mount of Olives the sky grew red. Two camels entered the Jaffa gate laden with lemons, and knelt groaning upon the pavement; the netting burst and the lemons spilt into the shadow. A fruit-seller set out his wares on a basket. A black woman, some porters, and a few sleepy soldiers, crossed the open space inside the gate. In the eastern sky the crimson had spread to pink, which was followed by a deep yellow, and the first beams of the sun broke across Olivet. The Latin clock struck five. A detachment of soldiers were threading their way up from Antonia, invisible, but bugling loudly. They broke on the street near the castle, and, forming fours, passed over to the drawbridge. The lower city, the sanctuary and its court, caught the sunshine, and life grew busy. Lines of camels laden with charcoal stalked through the gate ; followed by donkeys with wood for fuel. A man swept the street, and a boy put the refuse in a bag on a donkey's back. The barber and the knife-grinder took up their posts on the pavement. A small flock of sheep, peasants with eggs and cucumbers, and (since it was a summer of more than usual drought) a line of water-carriers from 'Ain Kârim, entered together in a small crowd. There was a shuffling of many feet on the pavements, and in the bazaars the merchants were opening their booths.

So Jerusalem must have looked by night to Herod when

his dreams drove him to the housetop.   So Solomon's
caravans may have come up in the moonlight from Elath
and from Jaffa.   So the sick king must have heard the
swifts screaming past his window.   So, in the Roman
occupation, the bugles rang out from the tower, and were
answered from Antonia.   And, so through all the centuries,
the dawn has broken upon Jerusalem, and the hewers of
wood and drawers of water, the peasants with their
vegetables, the sheep for the temple sacrifices, and all the
common currents of the City's life, have passed with the
sunrise through the gates, and stirred the gloom of the
narrow lanes with the business of another day.

# BOOK I
## *THE TOPOGRAPHY*
### SITES AND NAMES

# CHAPTER I

## THE SITE OF THE CITY

JERUSALEM lies (as we have seen) immediately to the east of, and slightly below, the main ridge or water-parting of the Judæan range. That ridge running southwards at an average height of The Hills over 2600 feet trends a little to the west, just round about. south of the village Sha'fât about a mile and a half from the north wall of the City, and then runs south again at 2685 (818·58 m.), 2669 (813·71 m.), and slightly lower elevations past the City till it falls to about 2450 feet (746·95 m.), on the plain el-Buḳei'a, commonly held to be the ancient Rephaim. The main ridge thus forms the western side of a rough triangle, of which the eastern is a spur of its own that leaves it where it trends west, and running south-east and south at about 2680 feet (c. 817 m.), culminates in the summit of the Mount of Olives, 2693 (c. 821 m.) ;[1] while the southern side is formed to the east of el-Buḳei'a by a hill running eastward, the Jebel Deir Abu Ṭôr, traditionally known as the Hill of Evil Counsel, 2550 feet high (777·43 m.). These are the mountains that are round about Jerusalem.

[1] This appears to be the figure on the Large P.E.F. map at the village et-Ṭor. The Memoirs, iii. p. 2, give the highest elevation as 2680 (817 *m.*), Baedeker's and Schick's maps of the nearer environs of Jerusalem, have 812 m., 2664 at the Russian Tower, but further n. at Karm eṣ-ṣaiyad 818 m., 2684 ft. (*Z.D.P.V.* xviii. 157); Wilson (Smith's *B.D.* 1587) gives 2641 feet at Ch. of Ascension.

The space they enclose is about $2\frac{1}{2}$ miles, north and south, by $1\frac{1}{2}$ at its greatest breadth. It may be roughly described as a triangular basin declining from its north-western

The Basin within them. side, that is nearly on the level of the main ridge or about 2550 feet (777 m.), to its south-eastern angle, where its only outlet runs by the W. en-Nâr, between the Mount of Olives and the Jebel Deir Abu Ṭôr at a level of about 1980 feet (603.6 m.). At first a high plateau, it hollows eastward with the beginnings of the W. Sitti Mariam, here known as the W. ej-Jôz, and recovering for a little, just outside of the present north wall of the city breaks up into three distinct valleys or gorges with two promontories between them, all in the main running south. The eastmost valley is the W. Sitti Mariam, along the base of the Mount of Olives. The middle one is el-Wâd, which separates the two promontories. The western one is the W. er-Rabâbi, which first runs south under the main ridge and then turns sharply eastwards under the Jebel Deir Abu Ṭôr, to join the other two at the outlet from the basin.

The two rocky promontories running south from the plateau, with the valley el-Wâd between them, form the site of the City proper. On the north they merge across

The City's Site Proper. its head in the plateau. But the Wâdies Sitti Mariam and er-Rabâbi deeply entrench them on the east, south and west; by their steep sides providing almost impregnable bulwarks against siege, as well as impassable limits to the City's building. The north, therefore, is the only direction from which a foe can attack Jerusalem or towards which the City may extend herself. Of the two promontories, that between the Wâdies Sitti Mariam and el-Wâd is known, in the topography of Jerusalem, as

THE VALLEY OF

V. of Hinnom.                    S.W. Hill.

Mouth

THE HILLS AND VALL

The site of the Pool of Siloam is in

E. Hill.                    S.E. Corner of Temple Area.          *Plate IV.*

Valley of Kidron.

FROM THE SOUTH-EAST.
aret in the mouth of the Tyropoeon.

the East Hill; that between el-Wâd and er-Rabâbi as the West Hill. The West Hill is the higher and more extended of the two, overlooking, and on the south overreaching, the end of the other. The two may be roughly likened to a thumb and forefinger pointing south, the latter somewhat curved. The hand in which they merge to the north is the plateau.

The East Hill, or promontory, really starts from the plateau north of the present city-wall near the Church of St. Stephen, and runs between the W. Sitti Mariam and el-Wâd southward to its lowest point at Siloam: approximately 1968 yards (1800 m.) long, or nearly a mile and an eighth; narrow and falling steeply on either side into the Wâdy Sitti Mariam and el-Wâd, which are now choked with *débris*, but were once 20 to 40 feet deeper. The East Hill has now four summits; but anciently had perhaps five. The northmost is outside the present City: the knoll el-Edhemîyeh 2549 feet (about 777 m.) above the sea. The long trench between it and the city-wall is artificial, some think on the line of an ancient, natural gully running east into the W. Sitti Mariam. The second summit of the East Hill is within the north-east angle of the present City, the Mohammedan quarter, anciently Bezetha: on which some of the levels, above the entrance to the Royal Quarries, are 2524 feet (769·5 m.)[1] East of this summit the East Hill was cleft from north to south in ancient times by a ravine which begins to sink from the plateau outside the north wall, north-east of el-Edhemîyeh, and may be traced under that

The East Hill.

[1] According to the Ordnance Survey; see *P.E.F. Mem.*, 'Jerus.' 279, No. 90. Kuemmel (*Materialien zur Topogr. des Alten Jerus.* p. 21) quotes from Karl Zimmermann a slightly higher level here: 771 m.

wall, past the Church of St. Anne (where it is 2411 feet or 735 m.) into the present Birket Israil (2344 or 714·3 m.), from which it bends eastward a little, and beneath the north-east corner of the Ḥaram area issues on the W. Sitti Mariam, just north of the Golden Gate, at a level of about 2230 feet or 680 m.[1]  On the west of this gully the East Hill runs south by a narrow saddle to the prominent rock (2462 feet, 750·3 m.)[2] on which the castle Antonia was built, the site of the present Turkish barracks.  From this point the original gradients of the East Hill are masked by the artificial platform of the Ḥaram esh-Sherîf, the ancient Temple area, the general level of which is about 2420 feet (*circa* 737 m.).[3]  The next original summit, however, the fourth, may be taken to be the Rock eṣ-Ṣakhra, beneath the great Dome, 2440 feet or nearly 744 metres.  From this the natural hill declines rapidly southwards beneath the present mosque el-Akṣà and (I reserve in the meantime the question whether it originally rose once more into a hump or knoll south of the Ḥaram) more gradually falls to about 2100 feet (640 m.) at Siloam.  On this last slope, a triangle between the W. Sitti Mariam and el-Wâd, which join at its lowest point, stood the ancient Ophel, south of the Temple area.

The West Hill really starts from the watershed itself and declines south-east along the Jaffa road to the north-
The West Hill.west angle of the present walls.  From this to its southern limit in the W. er-Rabâbi, just below the eastward curve of the latter, it measures some

---

[1] Sir Charles Wilson has given the name 'St. Anne's' to this ravine: *Golgotha and the Holy Sepulchre*, 25 f. and Plan.  Some take it to be the Chaphenatha of 1 Macc. xii. 37.

[2] *P.E.F. Mem.*, 'Jerus.' 16.

[3] But the central platform averages 2434 to 2435 feet, 742 m.

1,300 yards (about 1189 m.) but diagonally to its furthest point below Siloam at the junction of the three valleys 1614 yards (*c.* 1476 m.), while of course if we take it from the watershed it is much longer still. The West Hill was like the East, divided by a ravine, in this case a second head of the valley el-Wâd, which, descending from a saddle by the site of the present Jaffa Gate, followed the line of the present David Street. The hill to the north of this ravine, known as the North-west Hill, on the slope of which the Church of the Sepulchre lies, rises in the north-west corner of the City as high as 2581 feet (or 786·5 m.). The hill to the south of the ravine, known as the South-west Hill, the traditional Sion, is disposed in three terraces running north and south. The western and highest, on which the Citadel, the Armenian gardens and the Cœnaculum now stand, is from 2550 to 2520 feet (777 to 768 m.); the second, to the south of the street leading north from Sion Gate, varies from 2500 to 2430 (762 to 740·5 m.); there is then a sudden drop over a long scarp to the third, 2400 to 2360 feet (731·5 to 719·5 m.), which is nearly on the present level of the valley el-Wâd, where this passes the south-west corner of the Ḥaram. But further south the South-west Hill descends from the Cœnaculum, 2519 (768 m.), even more rapidly and deeply to the level of Siloam, about 2080 (634 m.).

We take now the central valley, el-Wâd, between the the East and West Hills. Of all the natural features of the site, this—one of the most important The Central historically, for there can be no doubt that it Valley: el-Wâd. is the Tyropœon of Josephus—has suffered most from the manifold wrecking and waste of the City. Choked with the *débris*, that has rolled into it from the ruined slopes on either side, its original bed lies from 20 to 90 feet below the present surface; while the houses which fill its northern part enhance the first casual impression that the West Hill sweeps over to the Temple Area on the East Hill without a break.  Yet from any of the towers or housetops on the former, which command a view of all Jerusalem, the line of the central valley is still visible down the whole of its course from just outside the Damascus Gate, where it first sinks in the plateau, to its fall into the W. en-Nâr below Siloam; in all about 1640 yards (*c.* 1500 m.)[1]  This faintly perceptible line of valley is one of the first features of the City which the visitor on his arrival should master; and he must then deepen his impression of it by a study of the following figures, which show the differences between the levels of the present surface and those at which the officers of the English survey found the rock below, on approximately the original bed of the valley.[2]  Just outside the Damascus Gate, or Gate of Columns, the ground is 2474, and just inside 2462 feet (754 and 750'6 m.).  Down the long 'Street of the Gate of Columns,' it sinks gradually till past the barracks—the ancient Antonia.  Opposite the north-west angle of the Temple area it is 2413 (735'5 m.), but the rock is here only 2369 (722 m.).  Opposite the summit of the East Hill, eṣ-Ṣakhra, 2440 feet (744 m.), the present level of the valley is about 2400 feet (731'5 m.),

---

[1] That is, measuring from about 66 yards to the north of the Damascus Gate, but perhaps the measure should start from even a little further north.

[2] The contours of the rock are taken from the 'Rock Contours of Jerusalem,' by Lieut.-Col. [now Major-Gen. Sir] C. Warren, R.E., 'from the records of the Excavations, from the Ordnance Survey, and from levels supplied by Herr C. Schick and others,' Plates II. and III. in the *P.E.F.* portfolio of *Excavations at Jerusalem.*  The surface levels are, as before, from the *P.E.F. Plan of Jerusalem*, by Sir Charles Wilson.

but the rock is found below the 2349 contour (716 m.):
more than 50 feet of difference. Below the south-west angle
of the Temple area (under which the bed of the valley
passes) the ground is about 2382 (726 m.), the rock is
just on the 2289 contour (697·8 m.), and from this the
descent is rapid to the Lower Pool of Siloam: ground
about 2100 (640 m.), rock 2049 (624·6 m.).[1] These figures
prove that in the earliest times the central valley, el-Wâd,
must have run from 20 to 90 feet deeper than it does
to-day between the East and the West Hills.

Taking together all these details of the three principal
constituents of the Site of Jerusalem, the East Hill, the
West Hill, and the Valley between them, we *Results of the*
are able to form a general view of the City, and *foregoing.*
to grasp the dominant features of her site. *First*, then, we
notice that the extreme slope or fall of the site is from the
north-west angle of the present City (which is the summit,[2]
within the walls, of the North-west Hill) 2581 feet (786·5 m.),
diagonally to the south-east angle at the mouth of el-Wâd
between the ends of the two hills, just under 2100 feet
(640 m.): a difference of 480 feet (*c.* 146 m.). *1. Main Dip*
The whole exposure and prospect of the Site *of the Site—*
is thus to the south-east, and towards what we *S.E.*
have seen to be the only break in the ring of higher hills
which encircle it. *Second*, we notice that the crowning elevation of the North-west Hill is—after the *2. Dominance*
narrow ravine is passed which descends from *of the West*
the Jaffa Gate to the middle valley—fairly sus- *Hill.*
tained along the whole of the long top of the South-west

---

[1] Here of course there was probably always more soil than in the upper
stretches of the valley.

[2] Ḳala'at or Ḳaṣr Jâlûd, 'Goliath's Castle.'

Hill, 2550[1] to 2520 feet (777 to 768 m.); or from 200 to
260 feet (61 to 79 m.) above the levels of the middle valley
below the Temple area, and even 110 feet (33·5 m.) above
the summit of the East Hill, eṣ-Ṣakhrah.  *Third*, though
this is so, and the West Hill is altogether more massive and
commanding than the East, yet the original depth of the
valley between them must, in the conditions of ancient war,
have rendered the East Hill completely free of the West,

3. Indepen-
dence of the
East Hill.

and capable of independent occupation and defence; and in connection with this we must not
fail to note, that while the whole of the West Hill
is without natural water supply, the one good spring of the
district lies immediately at the base of the East Hill in the
Wâdy Sitti Mariam.  But, *fourth*, while the East Hill is thus
independent of the West Hill, the mouth of the valley between them is not.  The South-west Hill absolutely commands it.  These are facts which we shall find critical when

4. But not of
the Pool of
Siloam.

we come to determine the size of the City at
various periods.  In the ancient conditions of
war the East Hill might be held by itself independently of the West; but so soon as its inhabitants brought
the waters of their only spring by the well known rock tunnel
under the East Hill to the Pool of Siloam, they must for the
security of the latter have held the South-west Hill as well.

We proceed now to the two great valleys which surround
the site of Jerusalem upon three sides and meet at its south-

The Encom-
passing
Valleys.

east angle: the W. Sitti Mariam or Valley of
the Ḳidron, and the W. er-Rabâbi, which is
most generally identified with the valley of the
Son of Hinnom.

[1] This is the present surface.  Warren's highest *rock* level on the S.-W.
Hill is 2532.

The Valley of the Ḳidron starts (as we have seen) well
to the north of the present City, on the plateau, and not far
from the main watershed itself. The Nablus  Wâdy Sitti
road, slightly rising from the Damascus Gate  Mariam.
(2474 feet, 754 m.), begins to fall again between the
Dominican Church of St. Stephen and the Anglican
Bishop's residence (highest point 2533 feet, 772 m.), into
a shallow basin just north-west of the Tombs of the Kings.
This basin on the west of the road is known as W. ej-Jôz
and has a level of about 2490 feet (759 m.).[1]   Descending
eastward under the name W. 'Akabet es-Sāwān, it has fallen
at the 'Anâta road (600 yds. north of the north-east angle of
the City) to about 2350 (716·3 m.).   Here it turns sharply
south, running between the East Hill of the City and the
Mount of Olives: about a mile and a half from the turn to
the Bîr Eiyûb.   While under the East Hill, it is known as
the W. Sitti Mariam, or Valley of our Lady Mary.   The
name W. en-Nâr, which is sometimes applied to the whole
of it, properly begins after its junction with the W. er-
Rabâbi.   As, owing to the accumulations of rubbish in it,
the present surface is always from 10 to 50 feet above the
ancient bed, it will be necessary to give the rock levels
throughout this part of its course, as well as the rock levels
under the line of ancient wall along the edge of the East
Hill, in order to form an idea of the depth to which the
Valley entrenched the Hill.

[1] Schick's Map of the near environs gives 749 m.

COMPARATIVE TABLE OF ROCK AND SURFACE LEVELS ON THE
EAST HILL AND KIDRON VALLEY.

\*\*\* The Metres are approximate within ·4.

| | Rock Levels under East City Wall. | | Rock Levels in the Bed of the Kidron. | Levels of present Surface of the Bed of the Kidron. |
|---|---|---|---|---|
| 1. At N.-E. Angle of City, . . . | Feet, Metres, | 2,457 749 | 2,289 698 | 2,300 (?) 701 (?) |
| 2. At Fragment of Ancient Wall before 'the Golden Gate,'. | Feet, Metres, | 2,339 713 | 2,229 679·5 | 2,279 695 |
| 3. Opposite the 'Tomb of Absalom,' . . | Feet, Metres, | 2,329 710 | 2,189 667 | 2,229 679·5 |
| 4. At S.-E. Angle of Ḥaram Area, . . | Feet, Metres, | 2,279 695 | 2,169 661 | 2,193 668·5 |
| 5. At Well of our Lady Mary, . . . | Feet, Metres, | 2,229 679·5 | 2,079 634 | 2,111 (?) 643·5 |
| 6. At Mouth of El-Wâd under old Wall, . | Feet, Metres, | 2,039 621·5 | 1,979 603 | 2,033 (?) ·619·5 |
| 7. At Bîr Eiyûb, . . | Feet, Metres, | | Below 1,929 588 | 1,979 603 |

We thus see that the rock bottom of the Ḳidron Valley,
which is approximately at the same level as the original
bed of the valley, lies from 10 to 50 feet[1] below the present
surface and, at various points, 110, 140, 150 and 168 feet,[2]
below the base of the ancient East Wall of the City. Moreover, the eastern bank or wall of the Wâdy was very much
steeper than it is to-day. In some parts naturally precipitous or nearly so, in others it was scarped by the early

[1] From 3 to 15 metres.
[2] Or about 33·5, 42, 46 and 51 metres.

defenders of the City, so as to make the whole of it practically impregnable.

The W. er-Rabâbi, the western and southern trench of the City's site, begins like the W. Sitti Mariam The Wady very close to the watershed itself, but much er-Rabâbi. further south, viz. about 660 yards west-north-west of the

COMPARATIVE TABLE OF ROCK AND SURFACE LEVELS ON THE SOUTH WEST HILL AND ON THE W. ER-RABABI.

|  | Rock Levels under Wall on South West Hill. | Rock Levels in the Bed of W.er-Rababi. | Levels of present Surface of W. er-Rabâbi. |
|---|---|---|---|
| 1. At the Jaffa Gate, . | Feet, 2,528<br>Metres, 770·5 | 2,469<br>752·5 | Above 2,470<br>753 |
| 2. S.-W. Angle of Citadel, | Feet, 2,479<br>Metres, 755·8 | 2,449<br>746·5 | Above 2,450<br>747 |
| 3. S.-W. Angle of present City Wall, . | Feet, 2,499<br>Metres, 761·9 | 2,379<br>725 | About 2,382<br>726 |
| 4. S.-W. Curve of S. W. Hill (north end of ancient scarp), . . | Feet, 2,480<br>Metres, 756 | 2,339<br>713 | About 2,349<br>716 |
| 5. Fragment of ancient Wall, 200 yards S.-E. of Cœnaculum, . | Feet, 2,409<br>Metres, 734 | 2,199<br>670 | 2,202<br>671 |
| 6. Fragment of ancient Wall at east end of Jewish Cemetery, . | Feet, 2,279<br>Metres, 694·8 | 2,129<br>649 | *‚* |
| 7. Gate at S.-E. angle of ancient Walls, . . | Feet, 2,080<br>Metres, 634 | 2,039<br>621·6 | *‚* |

*‚* I have left the last two spaces in the third column vacant, because I have been unable to determine accurately the figures. But Dr. Bliss measured 55 feet of *débris* just south of the south-east angle of the ancient walls above the scarp and baths which he excavated.[1]

---

[1] *Excav. at Jerus.*, 1894-97, 225-230, with Plate xxi. : Section 'A.B. Kuemmel's figure of 7·6 metres for the *débris* 'at the end' of the W. er-Rabâbi (*Materialien zur Topogr. des Alt. Jerus.* 44) must refer to a little further west up the W. er-Rabâbi.

Jaffa Gate, under the name of the W. el-Mes (Nettle-tree)
at a height of about 2520 feet (768 m). Curving south as
it approaches this Gate, opposite which its bed is 2470 feet
high, it runs between the watershed and the South-west
Hill for almost half a mile (805 m.), sinking rapidly. Then
sharply running east, it continues for another half mile
between the South-west Hill and the Jebel Deir Abu Ṭôr
to its junction with the Ḳidron Valley at about 2050 feet:
a fall of 420 feet (128 m.) in the mile.

In one important respect this table shows a remarkable
difference from the corresponding table on the Ḳidron
Valley. While in the Ḳidron the differences between the
present surface of the valley and its ancient bed below
were as much as from 10 to 50 feet, the analogous differences
in the W. er-Rabâbi amount for the most part
to only 2 or 3 feet, at one part reach 10 feet,
and we do not come to a great accumulation
of *débris* till we are out of the W. er-Rabâbi
into the Ḳidron Valley again, opposite the
south-east angle of the walls, where we find 55 feet.
Whether this last is due to gradual artificial causes or to an
earthquake it is impossible to say; Dr. Bliss points out
that the accumulation must be later than the Roman baths
he found beneath it. But in the W. er-Rabâbi itself it is
clear that far less *débris* has been shot than into the
Ḳidron Valley. This goes to confirm what we shall
find indicated by the history of the City, that the City on
the East Hill and the walls there were older and more
frequently overthrown than those on the South-west Hill.
As to the difference in height between the bottom of this
great western and southern trench of the City and the base
of the walls on the South-west Hill immediately above it,

*Different depths of débris in Ḳidron Valley and W. er-Rabâbi.*

MAP 3

# COMPARATIVE PROFILES OF THE EAST AND WEST HILLS

## Mainly from the Rock Levels

## WITH THE ROCK-BED OF THE ḴIDRON

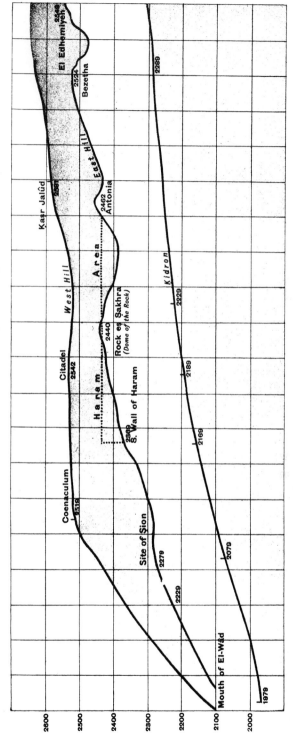

Vertical Scale 100 feet to the Square

Horizontal Scale 100 yards to the Square

The Top Line is the West Hill
The Middle Line is the East Hill
The Lowest is the line of the Ḵidron

London: Hodder and Stoughton.

the table shows that at the three points selected on the western side it was respectively 59, 50 and 120 feet (about 18, 15'18 and 36'6 metres); and at the four points selected on the southern side, 210, 140, 150 and 41 feet (64, 42'7 and 12'5 metres). This last, the smallest of the differences, is at the south-east angle of the City walls, where the South-west Hill sinks to its lowest point.

These are all the most important features of the Site of the City. In the next chapter we shall see which among them can be certainly identified with the data of the ancient topography, and what are the questions that remain over for discussion.

# CHAPTER II

## FACTS AND QUESTIONS IN THE
## ANCIENT TOPOGRAPHY

H AVING surveyed the natural features of the Site, it will be convenient for us at this stage to separate the certain from the uncertain elements in the ancient topography: to define what points in this are practically beyond doubt, and to make a preliminary statement of questions which still form the subject of controversy, and which we shall try to answer in the following chapters.

Certain and Uncertain points in the Topography.

There is no doubt that Jerusalem always occupied in whole or in part the Site whose natural features and limits we have been tracing: the so-called East and West Hills, separated by the valley el-Wâd, and bounded on the east, west, and south by the Wâdies Sitti Mariam and er-Rabâbi. There are other towns in Palestine which in the course of their history have wholly changed their sites. This Jerusalem never has done. No one now wants to discuss whether the City ever lay outside the two encircling Wâdies. These forbid, as we have seen, all expansion east, south or west. We have not to inquire, therefore, whether Jerusalem ever lay on any of the encircling hills, the main watershed, Jebel Abu Deir Ṭor or the Mount of Olives; though it will

1. General Permanence of the Site.

44

always be a question whether, at the foot of the latter, 'Ain Silwân and its ancient caves may not represent a settlement as primitive as any within the site of the City proper. On the north of the City the questions are more open. This is the only direction in which the expansion of the City is possible. Expansion is taking place there now; cisterns, alleged remains of walls, and the foundations of ancient churches have been found outside the present north wall in some quantity. It is, therefore, a question whether the suburb enclosed by Agrippa within the so-called Third Wall may have lain out there.[1]

Again, there is no doubt that the boundary valley on the East, the W. Sitti Mariam, is the Ķidron Valley of the Old and New Testaments and of Josephus.[2] The caves at 'Ain Silwân on its East bank may 2. Wâdy Sitti (as said above) represent a primitive settle- Mariam = Ķidron ment; but from an early point in the history Valley. of the City the bed of the Ķidron formed her eastern limit,[3] and down till the end there is no word of anything beyond it except a small village, and scattered houses and tombs. In the Ķidron Valley lies the one certain spring of the district, the 'Ain Sitti Mariam, under the base of the East Hill of the City. We shall have to inquire to which of the wells named in the Old Testament it corresponds.[4] Its importance as a landmark of the Topography is second to almost none other.

Nor is there any doubt that the East Hill was the Temple

---

[1] See further on this below, p. 48.
[2] Though some distinguish between the Valley of the Kidron, and 'the ravine of the Kidron,' *i.e.* Wilson's 'St. Anne's Ravine.' Sandie, *Horeb and Jerus.* ch. x. See Plate IV.
[3] See below, under David, Bk. iii.
[4] See below, on ' The Waters of Jerusalem,' Bk. i. ch. v.

Hill.   It is agreed that the threshing floor of Araunah, on which Solomon built the Temple, and on which the
3. East Hill =<br>Temple Hill<br>and Ophel<br>with Siloam<br>at S. end. Second Temple and Herod's rose, lay somewhere about the summit of the East Hill, the rock eṣ-Ṣakhra, and that the present Ḥaram esh-Sherîf represents more or less the successive Temple areas.   The following points on the East Hill are also clear.   The present barracks at the north-west angle of the Ḥaram are on the site of the castle Antonia, of Roman or Herodian times.   The 'Ophel was part of the slope south of the Temple.   And Siloaḥ or Siloam lay at its foot, at the issue of the tunnel which carries the waters of the 'Ain Sitti Mariam beneath Ophel to the mouth of el-Wâd.   Moreover, the line of the ancient wall, which ran along the East Hill above the Ḳidron Valley as far as Siloam, has been for parts exactly and for parts approximately ascertained.

The Middle Valley, el-Wâd, between the East and West
4. El-Wâd =<br>the Tyropœon. Hills, is certainly the Tyropœon of the Roman or Herodian period.   Whether it is mentioned in the Old Testament, and if so under what name or names, is a question we shall have to discuss.[1]   As will be easily understood, a good deal of the topography of the ancient City turns upon it.   Some hold that the lower part of it, at least, lay outside the Old Testament City, and that it was the Hollow of the Son of Hinnom, or, The Hollow, Hag-Gai. Others think that at the very earliest period it was outside the City, which was then confined to the East Hill, but that it was brought within the walls built by the early Kings of Judah, others that it was within walls even before David.

But this raises the whole of the questions regarding the

---

[1] Below, Bk. i. ch. vii.   See Plate IV.

South-west Hill, among the most vexed in the topography of Jerusalem. It is agreed that this Hill was all enclosed within the City Walls in the Roman or Herodian period, and that the present citadel by the Jaffa Gate contains one of Herod's towers; 

5. South West Hill, the 'Traditional Sion.'

that from this a wall upon the edge of the W. er-Rabâbi ran round the South-west Hill on the line ascertained by Mr. Maudslay and Dr. Bliss till it met the wall down the East Hill at the south-east angle, and enclosed the mouth of the Tyropœon ; and that another wall bounded the South-west Hill along its northern edge above the ravine which sinks from the Jaffa Gate into the Tyropœon. This is the so-called First Wall. But when it was built, or rather, when the South-west Hill became an integral part of the City, is one of the serious questions in the topography of Jerusalem, subsidiary only to that which is one of the two most important, viz :— whether Sion, the Jebusite stronghold captured by David and called after him the 'City of David,' lay on the South-west Hill on the site of the present citadel, or must be placed on the East Hill and on the part called Ophel immediately above the Virgin's Spring. The former view is the traditional one, Christians having called the South-west Hill ' Mount Sion' since the fourth century, and Josephus having placed the 'City of David' on the site of the present citadel. The latter is the view of modern scholars arguing from the Biblical evidence. The question is so fundamental that we shall discuss it in a separate chapter.[1]

As to the North-west Hill, there is also difference of opinion about its inclusion in the city. It is agreed that at some period subsequent to the erection of the First Wall on

[1] Below, Bk. i. ch. vi.   See Plates III. and IV.

the north of the South-west Hill, and before our Lord's time, a Second Wall (as it is called) was run across the North-west Hill from near the Jaffa Gate to the castle at the north-west angle of the Ḥaram area. But both the date and the course of this Second Wall are questions under keen debate, and, since they partly involve the question of the site of Golgotha and the Holy Sepulchre, of equal importance with the questions raised by the South-west Hill. Some authorities trace the Second Wall by ancient remains on a zig-zag line to the south and east of the Church of the Sepulchre. Others, also following ancient remains, trace it to the west and the north of the Church on a line from David's tower to the Ḳala'at Jâlûd (Goliath's Castle), thence on the line of the present north wall to near the Damascus Gate, and thence south-east to the corner of the Ḥaram area. Here again I only state the question : its discussion will come later.[1]

*6. North-west Hill; the questions of its enclosure. The Second Wall.*

The North, where the East and West Hills merge on the plateau, we have seen to be the only direction possible for the expansion of the City. The City is rapidly extending there now. Old cisterns, the foundations of churches, and the mosaic floors of sumptuous dwellings found in considerable quantity to the north of the present wall, prove that, at least in the Roman and Christian periods, Jerusalem spread over part of the northern plateau. Where then did the Third Wall run, built by Agrippa to protect a suburb beyond the Second? Some hold that it was nearly coincident with the present north wall, others that its course lay some 530 yards to the north, where a line of wall is said to have been found.

*7. The Plateau to the N. The Third Wall.*

[1] Below, Bk. i. ch. viii. pp. 247 ff.

This is a minor question in the topography of Jerusalem, though not without its bearings on the others; we shall reserve it to the Chapter on the Walls of the City.[1]

Finally, there is the western and southern boundary of the Site of the City: the W. er-Rabâbi. The common opinion is that this is Hag-Gaî, the Hollow, or Hollow of the Son of Hinnom, at least on its lowest and eastward stretch. But some, as we have seen, hold that Hag-Gaî was el-Wâd. This question, involved in that of the date of the inclusion of the South-west Hill in the City, will be treated partly under the latter, and partly in a separate chapter on the Hollow of the Son of Hinnom.[2]

8. W. er-Rabâbi and the Valley of Hinnom.

---

[1] Below, Bk. i. ch. viii.     [2] Below, Bk. i. chs. vi. and vii.   See Plate III.

# CHAPTER III

## THE GEOLOGY

'Ανάγκη δ' ἐπὶ τῶν ἐνδόξων τόπων ὑπομένειν τὸ περισκελὲς τῆς τοιαύτης γεωγραφίας.—Strabo XIV. i. 9.

TO understand the Geology of the site of Jerusalem, and of the basin in which it lies, is necessary to the student of her history for more than one important

Geology in-
dispensable to
the Historian.

reason. The character and disposition of the strata determine the surface and subterranean directions of the water which has fallen on the basin, with the positions of pools, streams and springs; and on these in turn depend some of the cardinal questions of the topography. Again, the character of the water-supply, and the resources of clay, stone and metal, together with the nature of the soil, govern the economy and the industries of the City. And finally, the quality of the rock, besides influencing the architecture and ornament of the buildings, will determine, as every epigraphist who has worked in Palestine is aware, the number of surviving inscriptions, or account for their absence. In all departments of his work, therefore, the historian is dependent on the geologist.

Edward Robinson, who was a pioneer in this as in

50

everything else connected with the historical geography of Palestine, had at his disposal the scattered observations by himself and other travellers: The Authorities. Seetzen, Russegger, Anderson, von Schubert, and John Wilson. His description of the geology of the land, though characteristically faithful, is necessarily far from complete;[1] and he died before he was able to add, to his outlines of the general formations and his section on earth-quakes, the remarks which he intended on caverns, minerals and soils. To Jerusalem he devotes only a few sentences. Karl Ritter had the same materials before him as Robinson; his arrangement and review[2] of them possesses the value which distinguishes all the work of this famous geographer. The outlines which these two writers traced by 1860 have since then been corrected and largely filled in by a number of expert geologists and engineers. Dr. Oscar Fraas[3] not only published geological descriptions of Egypt, Sinai and Syria, but gave details, with sections, of the strata about Jerusalem. M. Louis Lortet added an immense amount of valuable material to the general geology.[4] Sir Charles Wilson, who had an opportunity of examining the structure of the basin of Jerusalem with Dr. Fraas, and who was down every cistern in the Ḥaram, and many others inside and outside the City, including the Ḥammâm esh-Shefâ and the Bîr Eiyûb, has published summaries of the geology of Jerusalem,[5] and has kindly supplied me with

[1] *Physical Geography*, 284-299.
[2] Eng. Transl.: *The Comparative Geogr. of Palestine*, iii. 12 f., 196, iv. 183.
[3] *Aus dem Orient*, Stuttgart, 1867 : on Jerusalem, 50-59.
[4] *Essai sur la géologie de la Palestine*, Paris, 1869, 1873 ; *Exploration géologique de la Mer Morte, de la Palestine et de l'Idumée*, Paris, 1877 ; and other works. Lortet's *Essay on the Formation of the Bed of the Dead Sea*, etc., is translated by Grove in vol. iii. of Ritter's *Comp. Geog. of Pal.*, 351 ff.
[5] Especially that in his article ' Jerusalem,' Smith's *D.B.* (²) i. 1588.

some valuable manuscript notes.  Similarly Colonel Conder, whose examination of the site and environs has been no less thorough, has published several descriptions.[1]  In 1888 the Palestine Exploration Fund issued their *Memoir on the Physical Geology and Geography of Arabia Petræa, Palestine, and Adjoining Districts*, by Professor Hull; and Sir J. William Dawson included in his *Modern Science and Bible Lands*[2] an appendix on the Geology of Palestine. In 1905, the German geologist, Dr. Max Blanckenhorn, published the most detailed and illustrated study of what immediately concerns us, 'The Geology of the Nearer Environs of Jerusalem.'[3]  From all these and my own observations during five visits to Jerusalem, I have compiled the following description.[4]  Dr. Blanckenhorn has not carried his detailed study into the region where, for our topographical purposes, it would be of most use to us —the effect of the character and disposition of the strata on the distribution of the water.

In Jerusalem and its surroundings the strata belong to well-defined limits of the geological scale.
The Strata of Jerusalem exclusively limestone and chalk. There are no rocks of primary or palæozoic age ; no granite, porphyry, gneiss, nor schist; and no volcanic rocks, lava, nor the like.  The 'Nubian' sandstone, on which the limestone ranges of

---

[1] *e.g. Enc. Bibl.* 'Jerus.' § 5 ; and article 'Jerus.' in Hastings' *Dict. of the Bible*, ii. 584.        [2] London, Hodder and Stoughton, 587 ff.

[3] *Z.D.P.V.*, 1905, 75-120, with a coloured geological map and four profiles of the strata, cf. R. Sachsse *Z.D.P.V.* 1897, 1 ff.

[4] For other studies and observations before 1883 see the summary in *P.E.F.Q.* for that year of Professor Huddleston's address to the Geologists' Association, vol. viii. No. 1, on 'The Geology of Palestine.'  I have consulted also other geological notes in the *P.E.F.Q.* (especially 1887, p. 80, by Schick) and in the *Z.D.P.V.*  I regret not to have seen any of the works of Paul Lortet, given on p. 587 of Röhricht's *Bibliotheca Geogr. Palæstinæ*.

# GEOLOGICAL MAP OF JERUSALEM
### *after Dr Blanckenhorn*

MAP 4

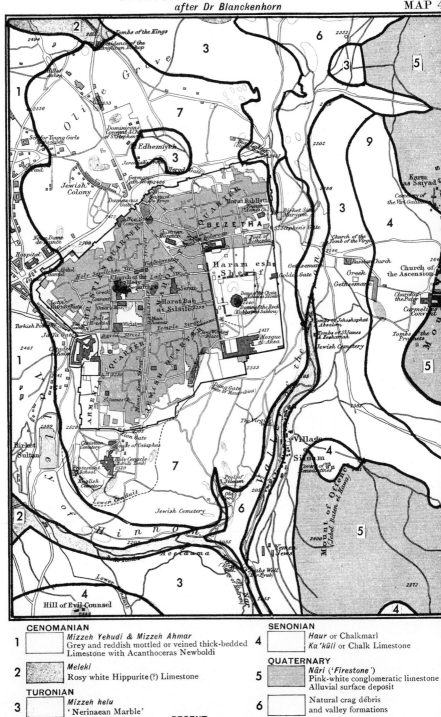

**CENOMANIAN**

1    *Mizzeh Yehudi & Mizzeh Ahmar*
Grey and reddish mottled or veined thick-bedded
Limestone with Acanthoceras Newboldi

2    *Meleki*
Rosy white Hippurite(?) Limestone

**TURONIAN**

3    *Mizzeh helu*
'Nerinaean Marble'

**RECENT**

7    Building débris and
ash-heaps of Jerusalem

**SENONIAN**

4    *Haur* or Chalkmarl
*Ka'kûli* or Chalk Limestone

**QUATERNARY**

5    *Nâri* ('Firestone')
Pink-white conglomeratic limestone
Alluvial surface deposit

6    Natural crag débris
and valley formations

Numbers have been added alongside each of the different
shades and inserted also in the map itself.

Syria rest, passes, it is calculated, from 1500 to 2000 feet below the City, not to appear till the further coast of the Dead Sea, where you can see it from Jerusalem refulgent in the evening sun. Everything above this in the Judæan range is limestone and chalk of the secondary and tertiary systems, with a crust from the post-tertiary or quaternary. Dr Blanckenhorn has defined six or seven different formations or stages ranging from the Cenomanian of Continental geologists, the Lower Chalk of the English,[1] up through the Turonian and Senonian (corresponding to the Middle and Upper White Chalks of Great Britain) to the crust of calcareous breccia, which is not found in position in Britain, but still covers the summits of southern lands untouched by glacial action. The stone-masons of Jerusalem have long distinguished these varieties of rock, with the marls, bituminous limestones, and harder constituents which are found among them, and have given them the following names: *Mizzeh Yehudi* and *Mizzeh 'Aḥmar*, *Meleki*, *Mizzeh Helu*, *Ka'kûli*, and *Nâri;* with *Haur* for the marls, *Nebi Mûsa* for the bituminous limestones, and *Mizzeh 'Akhdar* or *'Akhdar-'Aḥmar* for some marble-like varieties in the upper chalks. Employing these harmonious data of the scientific geologists and of the practical stone-workers, we may, most conveniently for our present purpose, arrange the series under four divisions and start from the highest downwards.

On the summits of Olivet and of the Hills of Offence and Evil Counsel there is a thin stratum of conglomeratic limestone of the post-tertiary period, pinkish-white in colour, soft and friable, but fireproof, known locally as *Nâri*, or 'Firestone.' 'All

1. Upper Chalks—Nâri and Ka'kûli.

---

[1] James Geikie, *Outlines of Geology*, 327.

others crack when heated or become lime; not so this one,
so all fire-places are made with it when bricks cannot be
had.'[1]  As the stones from it are specially light, they
are used for the inner arching of vaults.  With the *Nâri*
many take the *Ka'kûli,* as only an alternate name for it,
but Schick distinguishes the two, and Blanckenhorn defines the latter as a separate Senonian stratum in two
layers: an upper of soft cretaceous limestone with deposits
of *Haur* or marl, which is used in mortar, and a lower more
tenacious but still soft stone, used for Jewish and Mohammedan gravestones, and also in the building of houses.  It
is in a number of layers of these upper chalks that are
found the deposits of bituminous limestone, the beautiful
marble-like stone known as green or blue-green Mizzeh, as
well as the numerous flints which were used by the primitive
inhabitants of Jerusalem as weapons.[2]  None of these
various strata are found within the City.

Below these there is a Hippurite limestone, nongranu-
lous, with bands of flint, hard, reddish-grey, and
capable of a good polish, a 'Nerinæan marble'
known locally as *Mizzi*[3] (or *Mizzeh*) *helu*, 'the
sweet Mizzeh.'  This is found within the City

2. Turonian, Hippurite Limestone— Mizzi helu.

on the rock eṣ-Ṣakhrah, and under other parts of the
Ḥaram, under the barracks, in Bezetha, in the knoll el
Edhemîyeh (known as 'Jeremiah's Grotto'), and according
to Conder in the 'cliff of the traditional Calvary.'[4]  Outside
the City it may be seen at the railway station, in the W.
er-Rabâbi, and in the lower strata of Olivet along the

---

[1] Schick, *P.E.F.Q.*, 1887, 50; cf. Fraas, 57.
[2] Germer-Durand, *L'Age de Pierre en Palestine.—Rev. Bib.* 1897, 439.
[3] I cannot get the meaning of this term: Can it be from mazz, to suck, with the signification porous? Fraas, 53, takes it from mazz, to excel.
[4] Hastings' *Dict. of the Bible*, ii. 584.

Ḳidron. It has been measured in depths from 72 to 82 feet (22 to 25 m.). The colossal stones of the Ḥaram wall, and the stones of some of the churches, are of this rock. It is quarried at the present day from the Frank Mountain, principally for the larger stones round the windows and doors of houses.

Below this Upper Mizzeh lies a stratum of granulous limestone or ' marble,' also called Hippurite[1] by some : a white chalk with a rosy complexion, so soft underground that it can be cut with a knife, but 3. Cenomanian, granulous hardening upon exposure and therefore valuable Limestone—Meleki. for building ; locally known as *Meleki*, ' Royal.' Its breadth averages 328 yards (300 m.), its depth about 35 feet, and it forms the basis of the whole City. The great quarries under Bezetha ('The Cotton-Grotto'), the deeper cisterns beneath the Temple area, and other cisterns of the City have been excavated within it, being reached from the surface by narrower shafts through the harder Upper Mizzeh.[2] According to Blanckenhorn it forms the rock under the Church of the Holy Sepulchre. Some of the scarps under the Wall above the W. er-Rabâbi, the Pool of Siloam, the caves under the village of Silwân, the base of the so-called Tomb of Absalom, the pyramid of Zechariah, and other monuments in the Ḳidron valley, are of this rock. It is also found on the surface of the Buḳei'a and on the Bethlehem road by the English eye-hospital, from which it extends into the W. er-Rabâbi.

Below the Meleki lies a harder Cenomanian limestone, partly dolomitic, known like the rock above the Meleki by

---

[1] 'Genuine Hippurites,' says Blanckenhorn, 'I have not recognised in Meleki.' He calls it a 'Rudistenmarmor.' On the contrary Fraas, 52.

[2] Schick, *Z.D.P.V.* i. 140.

the name of *Mizzi* or *Mizzeh*, but distinguished locally
as *Mizzeh Yehudi* or ' Jewish Mizzeh ' ; *Mizzeh*
*'Aḥmar* or ' red Mizzeh,' and *Dēr Yâsîni*, from
a village where there are quarries of it.   These

*4. Cenomanian Limestone— Lower Mizzeh.*

names represent three distinct divisions of it. *Mizzeh Yehudi*
is dark grey, sometimes of a yellowish, sometimes of a reddish complexion, with veins of calcareous spar and occasionally 'instead of pure limestone, dolomitic limestone, and
genuine finely crystallised dolomite.'   At the present day
it is the ' stone most used for building,' [1] yet ' the hardest
stone in Palestine, a cold compact limestone, most difficult
to work, chisels of finest tempered steel breaking on it like
glass.' [2]   It lies directly under the Meleki.   Of the *Mizzeh*
*'Aḥmar* there are two varieties, a limestone irregularly red,
found on the watershed, where it may be traced in the
graves of the Nikophorieh, in Hinnom and the Birket es
Sulṭan and elsewhere, much used in building and to be
seen in the columns of the Bethlehem Basilica ; and ' a
crystalline limestone or real marble with glistening grains
of a quite regular red,' [3] not found in Jerusalem.   The *Dēr*
*Yâsîni* is a laminated limestone (Plattenkalk), grey or
reddish, used for lintels and the outer stones of arches.
All these divisions of the Lower Mizzeh, when they appear
on the surface, resist atmospheric influences and are hardy
rocks ; they form the foundation of many of the cultivated
terraces.   The inference is that underground they (or some
of them) resist or divert the waters which penetrate
to them through the Meleki.   Yet they are divided and
streaked with layers of soft limestone marls, useful, when
they break to the surface, in forming soil, and below

[1] Blanckenhorn.
[2] Clermont-Ganneau, *Archæol. Researches*, ii. 225 f.   Schick, *loc. cit.*, also
calls it ' the hardest.'                                    [3] Blanckenhorn.

easily permeable by water. As the strata appear (on Dr Blanckenhorn's coloured map) in the Ḳidron Valley a little to the north of the Virgin's Spring, they probably extend thither from the Hinnom valley right under the City. But how much of the marl they contain, or whether they are at all fissured and broken, as they are sometimes in their outcrops, we do not know. We shall have to take this into consideration when we inquire into the character of that fountain and the reason of its position.

All these strata are disposed with tolerable regularity. Dr. Blanckenhorn says: 'The disposition of all the strata which here make their appearance remains on the S. of Jerusalem, within the town itself, and on the N. in general the same.' But while (as Regular Disposition of these Strata. we have seen) the watershed in passing the basin of Jerusalem forms a curve or bow with its opening eastward, the groups of strata which compose the ground of the basin are so extended as to form a curve in the opposite direction, with its opening westward (as Dr. Blanckenhorn's coloured map clearly shows). There are no noteworthy distortions, nor any 'faults,' and no intrusive dykes. It is worth noticing, again, with regard to the bearing of the geology on the water-distribution, that according to Dr. Blanckenhorn's observations, the soft Meleki limestone appears to reach its lower limit exactly at the Bîr Eiyûb in the Ḳidron Valley. Finally, with a few minor interruptions, the strata all dip regularly eastward or south-eastward, at a general angle of 10°, Their Dip, E.S.E. thus forming what we have seen to be the eastward decline and exposure of the city's site, as well as giving both the surface and underground waters of the basin their main bent in that direction.

Before we get entangled among the topographical questions which are connected with the waters, it will be well to discuss these in their purely geological relations, particularly with regard to the possibility of natural springs or fountains.

Very little of the water which falls on the earth's surface finds its way immediately to surface beds of rock or clay impervious enough to hold it up in the form of lakes or streams ; the most is absorbed in the first instance in the ground. Where the upper strata, as in the basin of Jerusalem, are all of porous chalk, capable of retaining water to a third of their own bulk and passing the remainder downwards, there is no opportunity for the formation of tarns or rivulets except for a short period after a heavy downpour. As we shall see, the historical evidence reveals no lake or stream at Jerusalem, with the exception of the *naḥal,* or *fiumara,* or winter-brook of the Ḳidron, the lowest or most easterly of the valleys of the basin, where (as we have seen) the lower, impervious limestone appears in the bed of the wâdy.

Sometimes the porous rocks, such as those of which at least the upper strata of our basin are composed, when they have absorbed water beyond their power to retain it, will 'weep' or 'sweat' it forth again above the surface where they crop out from this, or where the hollowing of a valley lays them bare, or underground where a natural fissure or artificial receptacle has been formed. There are many instances of this percolation upon, under, and around the site of Jerusalem. Some at least of the water which gathers in the bed of el-Wâd, in the Ḥammam esh-Shefâ and in the Bîr Eiyûb, are demonstrably due to this surface percolation. But we may easily mistake its effects in a gathering of water for those of a real spring or fountain, particularly if it takes place, as now in el-Wâd, beneath a mass of rubbish.

Springs or fountains proper, which originally are due, of course, to the percolation of water through porous strata, happen only when the watery content of these is refused further passage underground by impermeable underlying rocks and somehow or other is forced up to the surface. But springs may vary from something very little different from percolation to forms quite distinct and separate. For instance, water absorbed by one of the softer superficial strata, and finding no passage downward because the underlying stratum is impermeable, may with the softer stratum itself, and without ever having left it, emerge on the side of a valley, where the softer stratum is exposed and truncated. Except by their waters being concentrated in a single outlet, such openings do not differ from the percolation sketched above. Others spring from greater depths, where a water-laden stratum has encountered an uprise of impervious rock, along whose ascent its contents make way by their own pressure to the surface. Others, found mainly in regions of massive rocks like granite, are formed of water which has found its way downward by long cracks and fissures, often to great depths ; whence, encountering other fissures of easier gradient or lower issue than those by which it has descended, it also reaches the surface by its own pressure.

Now in and around Jerusalem, with its exclusively limestone geology, there is no possibility of this last, and generally deepest, kind of spring. Our consideration is limited to the other two. And the sole question which arises geologically, is

*[margin note: Springs or Fountains proper.]*

*[margin note: Are there any in Jerusalem?]*

whether either of these forms of spring proper is present, or whether any underground gathering of water or its issue to the surface may more scientifically be described as due to percolation only.   It is on the latter ground that some authorities on the topography have doubted the existence in or about Jerusalem of any spring properly so-called,[1] and that others refuse the name to the Virgin's Fountain.[2] The question is one of difficulty, both because of the nearness of all the possible springs to the surface of the strata from which they spring, and because (as I have shown) the shallowest form of spring proper is not easily distinguishable from the results of mere percolation.   But it will turn upon the question of the presence among the limestone strata of one more or less impermeable by water, below the porous others.   Now the lowest of the strata, the Cenomanian, *Mizzeh Yehudi* and *'Aḥmar*, is (as we have seen) at least in part a hard stone, insensible to rain or other atmospheric influences when lying on the surface, and therefore presumably able underground to withstand and divert the passage of water from the softer strata above it.   But this harder limestone underlies the City, and forms in part at least the bed of the Ḳidron valley, in which precisely the disputable springs of Jerusalem are found.

We have up to this been considering the constant factors in the geology of Jerusalem, but before we can complete

Earthquakes.    our subject we must discuss a possible fac- tor of disturbance introduced among them by Earthquakes.   This leads to so many questions both of topography and mythology, that we devote to it a separate chapter.

---

[1] Sir Charles Wilson in an MS. communication to the author.
[2] See below, p. 87 ff.

# CHAPTER IV

## EARTHQUAKES, SPRINGS AND DRAGONS

Καὶ ἰδοὺ φωναὶ καὶ θόρυβος, βρονταὶ καὶ σεισμός, τάραχος ἐπὶ τῆς γῆς, καὶ ἰδοὺ
δύο δράκοντες μέγαλοι ἕτοιμοι προῆλθον ἀμφότεροι παλαίειν. [Apocryphal]
Esther xi. 4 f.

*And, behold, noises and tumult, thunderings and earthquake, uproar upon
the earth ; and, behold, two great dragons came forth, both of them ready to
fight.*

I T is necessary to explore, so far as materials exist for
the purpose, the subject of earthquakes in Jerusalem,
not only because of the certain influence of Extent of the
these upon the fortunes of the City and her Subject.
buildings, but because of their possible effects upon the
geology we have been studying, and especially upon the
water-springs, on the positions of which so much of the
topography turns.   And as in the name of one of the
springs there is a remnant of the ancient mythology about
earthquakes, we must learn what we can of this latter
subject.

Here again Edward Robinson led the way in an instructive section on earthquakes in his *Physical Geography.*
Admiral Smyth, in his valuable memoir *The* The Materials
*Mediterranean,*[1] has a number of observations and
on earthquakes experienced by himself and Authorities.
others within the great basin of which Syria is the eastern

[1] London, 1854.

slope. In Diener's monograph on the physical geography
of Central Syria, entitled *Libanon*, there is a list of earthquakes in that region.[1] But with the view of checking and
increasing their data, I have looked through, besides the
Bible and Apocryphal and Apocalyptic works, — the
latter of which are especially instructive on the mythology
of earthquakes, a subject practically untouched by modern
scholars—Pliny and Strabo, Appian, Polybius and Dion
Cassius, Jerome's works, the early histories of the Church,
the French collection of Historians of the Crusades, Röhricht's *History of the Kingdom of Jerusalem*, a number of
recent Travels through Syria, and Dr Chaplin's meteorological records ; besides Von Hoff's *Chronik der Erdbeben*
and Perrey's Memoir.[2] On the general subject of earthquakes, I have consulted Prof. James Geikie's *Outlines of
Geology*, and I have communications from Sir Archibald
Geikie and Sir Charles Wilson as to the effects on water
supplies. Beyond some hints in that extremely useful work
by Stark on Gaza and the Philistine Coast,[3] I found nothing
in modern writers on the religion and mythology of the
Semites as to the influence of earthquakes, although these
have been so frequent in the natural history of Syria,
and so impressive upon the religious feelings of her inhabitants.

Through those periods of the history of Syria of which
we have records, we find earthquakes frequent and destructive. Northern Syria and its cities,
especially Urfa (Edessa), Aleppo, Antioch
and Hamath, the skirts of the Lebanons and

Lines of
earthquake,
Syria.

[1] *Libanon, Grundlinien der phys. Geogr. u. Geol. von Mittelsyrien.* Wien,
1886 ; 258 ff.     [2] *Mémoires, publ. par l'Acadèm. de Belg.* xxii.
[3] *Gaza u. die philistäische Küste,* Jena, 1852.

the Jordan valley, the coast of Palestine and its cities from Beirût to Ascalon and Gaza, have been especially scourged by them.[1] But just as, in South America, the Chilian coast of the Pacific is devastated by earthquakes, while the Andes to the east altogether escape or are little shocked, so while the maritime plain of Palestine and the volcanic districts in the Jordan valley have suffered ruinously from the disturbances, the Judæan range between them has been far less visited.[2] 'It is singular,' says Robinson, 'how amid all the terrific earthquakes with which Syria has been afflicted for so many centuries, the City of Jerusalem has been comparatively spared, in consequence perhaps of its position and distance from the volcanic regions.' That the Greek and Latin historians do not include Jerusalem among the many Asiatic cities which they record as ruined by earthquakes in the centuries immediately before or after the birth of Christ, may be due to the fact that they were comparatively so ignorant of her affairs. But when we take the period of the Crusades, to the historians of which Jerusalem was the central point of interest, we find that of all the convulsions recorded on the coast or in North Syria, only two are definitely said to have affected Jerusalem.[3]

Still the immunity of Jerusalem was only comparative. Besides being visited at irregular intervals by fits and starts of earthquake, the City has suffered several convulsions of disastrous magnitude. Of one of these which happened in Uzziah's reign, the tremors and the ruins it left are visible through the

*Earthquakes in Judæa.*

---

[1] Diener, *op. cit.* 260.

[2] Unfortunately for our present quest Diener's statistics are confined to Middle and North Syria, and do not extend to Judæa.

[3] Röhricht, *Geschichte des Königreichs Jerusalem*, 59, 100, 114, 118, 218, 290, 348, 681, 695, 993.

prophetic writings of the eighth century,[1] while the memory of it lasted into the Christian era. The description by Josephus, whether really of this earthquake or not, is at least evidence of the havoc which some shaking of the earth had caused before his day to the site of Jerusalem.[2] 'Before,' that is, on the east of, 'the City, at what is called Eroge,'[3] that is Enrogel, 'half of the mountain broke off from the remainder on the west, and rolling four furlongs came to a stand at the eastern mountain, till the roads as well as the King's Gardens were blocked.' This means at least that at some time before the other great earthquake, of which Josephus knew, the East Hill and the Kidron valley had suffered from geological disturbances of considerable severity. The other earthquake he describes, took place in Judæa, 'in the seventh year of the reign of Herod,' 31 B.C., and brought a great destruction on the cattle in that country: about ten thousand men also perished by the fall of houses.[4] The account in Matthew's Gospel of what happened at the Crucifixion at least implies the liability of Jerusalem to severe shocks during the first century of our era.[5] We know nothing of the effect on Judæa of the great earthquakes which devastated Asiatic cities in B.C. 62, A.D. 17, 115[6] (which destroyed Antioch), 320, 419.[7] But Socrates and Sozomen describe an earthquake in 362 A.D., which 'tore up the stones of the old foundations of the Temple' of Jerusalem, and 'threw

---

[1] Amos iv. 11, viii. 8; Isaiah ix. 9, xxix. 6. Cf. Zech. xiv. 4 f.

[2] ix. *Ant.* x. 4.    [3] Πρὸς τῇ καλουμένῃ Ἐρωγῇ (Ἐῤῥωγῇ).    [4] xv. *Ant.* v. 2.

[5] Matt. xxvii. 51, 52. Cf. Jerome epist. 150 *ad Hedibiam* and the story of the fissure created in Calvary by the earthquake, with all that was afterwards told of this, in Quaresmius, *Elucidatio Terræ Sanctæ*, lib. v. cap. xli.

[6] Strabo, xii. 8, 18; Pliny. *Hist. Nat.* ii. 86 (84); Tacitus, *Ann.* ii. 47; Dion Cassius, lvii. 17; lxviii. 24.

[7] Marcellinus, *Chron.* p. 38, quoted by Von Hoff.

down the houses and public porticos' near its site.[1]  The
Christians interpreted this by the anger of God at the
Emperor Julian's attempt to rebuild the Temple.  In the
infancy of Jerome, there were heavy shocks in Moab,
destroying the walls of Areopolis,[2] but neither of them,
nor of the great earthquakes in Justinian's time, 526 and
551 A.D.,[3] the first of which destroyed Antioch, the second
Beirût and other Syrian towns, do we hear that they affected
Jerusalem.  In the early Moslem centuries there were at
least eight great earthquakes in Syria, 631, 658, 713, 718,
746,[4] 856, 1016, and 1034.[5]  The two last must have worked
great havoc in Jerusalem ; for the colonnade of Ibn Tahîr,
described by Muḳaddasi in 985, on the north of the 'Aḳṣa
mosque, is not mentioned by Nasir-i-Khusrau in 1047, and
while the former counts 15 gates along the north side, and
11 on the east, the latter gives only 7 and 10 respectively.[6]
By earthquakes in 1105 and 1113,[7] but apparently not by
those of 1115, 1138, 1157, 1170, 1182, Jerusalem was dam-
aged.  I find no mention of damage by earthquakes of the
sixteenth and two following centuries.[8]  In 1834 a spasm
'shook Jerusalem, and injured the Chapel of the Nativity
at Bethlehem '; while the great earthquake of 1837, which
overthrew Safed, and shattered the walls of Tiberias, 'was
felt as far as Bethlehem and Hebron.'[9]  Between 1860
and 1882 Dr. Chaplin observed in the City twelve shocks,
apparently not serious.

[1] Soc. iii. 20 ; Soz. v. 22 ; cf. Gibbon, ch. xxiii.
[2] Jerome on Is. xv. ; cf. Perrey, p. 5.
[3] Theophanes, p. 192 ; Cedrenus, p. 376, quoted by Von Hoff.
[4] Theophanes, 258, 320, 331, 354, quoted by Von Hoff.
[5] Cedrenus, 737 (Jer. shaken 40 days ; many churches fell).
[6] Guy le Strange, *Pal. under the Moslems*, 102 f.        [7] Perrey, p. 16.
[8] Jer. escaped the shocks of 1759, Perrey, 30, 70.
[9] Robinson, *Phys. Geog.* 298 ; Ritter, *Comp. Geog.* ii. 248.

The influence of earthquakes upon the history of springs is natural, and has been well attested. The difficulty begins

Effects of Earthquakes on Springs. where, as in the case of the Jerusalem springs, the records are defective. There is no doubt that by causing landslips, or creating fissures in the ground, earthquakes have the power to 'interrupt or revolutionise the drainage system of a country.'[1]

We have innumerable observations of their interference with warm springs in volcanic regions. Demetrius

On Hot Springs. of Callatis reports that the hot springs of Ædepsus in Eubœa, and of Thermopylæ, were suppressed for three days, and when they began to run again those of Ædepsus gushed from new fountains.[2] Many other instances from the ancient geographers might be given. Two modern ones may be cited. About 1710 the hot springs by Tiberias are said to have remained dry, in consequence of an earthquake, for nearly three years ;[3] and the converse result happened after the convulsions of 1837, for the volume of water was temporarily increased.[4]

But the effect of earthquakes on the much shallower cold springs is less frequent and more uncertain. The

And on Cold Springs. Semites, who (as we shall see presently) identified the untameable power of the sea with that which periodically shook their lands, and who, unlike the Greeks, imagined the sea as flowing beneath the whole foundations of the earth, and feeding the fountains of the latter, could not have failed, therefore, to think of a connection between earthquakes and springs. They do not, however, always notice it. Some passages of the Old and

[1] J. Geikie, *Outlines of Geol.*, 167, R. Mallet, Herschel's *Manual of Scient. Enquiry*, 354, Perrey, 59.

[2] Quoted by Strabo, I. iii. 20 ; cf. *Frag. Histor. Græc.*, Müller, iii. 380.

[3] Ritter (quoting Reland), *Comp. Geog.* ii. 249.     [4] *Ibid.* ; Perrey, 47, 57.

New Testament, which detail the ruin wrought by earthquakes, do not speak of the wells as affected.[1]  It is uncertain whether this is intended in such sentences as: *Tremble, thou earth, at the presence of the Lord, which turneth the rock into a pool of water, the flint into a fountain. We fear not though the earth bubble and mountains shake in the heart of the sea.*[2]  But in other passages the Divine power in shaking the earth is associated with the appearance of springs where before there were none.[3]  The Book of Enoch, too, appears to connect *a great convulsion*, not only with a *swelling of the waters*, which in this case are sulphurous springs, but with *a change of temperature in the water springs*;[4] and the author of II. Esdras says, *earthquakes make the deeps to tremble*—the deeps which, according to the cosmogony described above, are the reservoirs of the fountains.[5]  In most of the accounts of earthquakes by Greek and Latin geographers or historians, with which I am acquainted, no mention is made of the ordinary fountains of cities as affected,[6] even where the statement of eyewitnesses is given; but both Strabo and Pliny assert the general effect of earthquakes in disturbing underground water-passages and changing the course of rivers,[7] and they cite some instances in which these particulars have happened.[8]  Athenæus quotes from the *Histories* of Nicolas

[1] Ezek. xxxviii. 19 ff.; Rev. vi. 12, viii. 5, xi. 13, 19, xvi. 18.

[2] Ps. cxiv. 8, xlvi. 2 [Eng.], the latter after Wellhausen's and Furness' translation, Polychrome Bible.

[3] Is. xli. 18; Ps. cvii. 33 ff., lxxiv. 15.

[4] Bk. of Enoch, lxvii. 5-11.

[5] II. Esdr. iii. 19.

[6] In none of the following by Strabo, V. iv. 9; VI. i. 6; VIII. vii. 2; XII. viii. 16-19; XIII. iv. 8; XVI. ii. 26, etc.

[7] Strabo, IX. ii. 16, XV. i. 19; Pliny, II. 82 (80).

[8] Strabo, I. iii. 16, Arethusa by Chalcis in Eubœa, obstructed and reopened through other vents; XVI. ii. 7, a new spring for the Orontes.

of Damascus, that : 'About Apameia in Phrygia, at the
time of the Mithridatic wars, earthquakes having happened, lakes appeared where none were formerly, and
rivers and other fountains were opened by the motion, but
many also vanished.'[1]   Dion Cassius, describing the great
earthquake at Antioch in 115, when Trajan was present,[2]
says : 'Other mountains collapsed, and much water, not
there before, burst up, and much that had been flowing
ceased.'   In the accounts of earthquakes which I have
read in the early church histories, some of whose writers—
like Evagrius on his marriage day at Antioch[3]—were eyewitnesses of the convulsions produced, I have not noticed
any mention of the disappearance of old springs or the
emergence of new ones.   Yet, although these writers are
often more concerned with the effect of the earthquakes
in postponing Church Councils, or with their religious
significance, they communicate besides a considerable
amount of physical detail.   There are instances, too, of the
agelong persistence of fountains in spite of frequent earthquakes.   One of these Sir Archibald Geikie has quoted to
me, with some observations on the general question :—
'The question you ask me is one to which no confident
reply either way can be given.   On the one hand it is well
known that springs are sometimes seriously affected by
earthquakes, being closed up or opening out from new
vents in the rocks underneath.   On the other hand it is
equally certain that even after violent earthquakes old

---

[1] Athenæus, viii. ; see *Fragmenta Histor. Græc.*, Müller, iii. 416.

[2] Dion Cassius, lxviii. 24, 25, the quotation is at the end of the latter
section : ὄρη τε ἄλλα ὑφίζησε καὶ ὕδωρ πολὺ οὐκ ὃν μὲν πρότερον ἀνεφάνη, πολὺ
δὲ καὶ ῥέον ἐξέλιπε.

[3] *Eccl. Hist.*, vi. 8.   The earthquake was that of 389 A.D., and Evagrius
describes its effects very fully.   It is not mentioned in Perrey.

springs may continue to maintain their old exits. Of this persistence we have a good example in the Roman Forum. The Fons Juturnæ, at which Castor and Pollux watered their horses when they came to announce the victory of Lake Regillus, is still flowing, and has recently been laid open once more to light by the removal of the church, etc., built over it. Yet during the last 2000 years Rome has been visited by many earthquakes, some of them severe enough to shake down buildings and do much damage.' One other bit of evidence may be added. At Gezer Mr. Macalister reports the disappearance of one well and the comparatively late appearance of another, and suggests that this was due to the disturbance of the strata by an earthquake.[1]

The bearing of these data on the question of the springs, real or reputed, at Jerusalem is somewhat delicate and difficult to compute with certainty. On the one hand, Jerusalem does not lie in a volcanic district, such as those in which many of the above instances of the change of fountains occurred; on the other hand, the effects of at least several earthquakes in Jerusalem were otherwise the same as I have quoted. Sir Archibald Geikie continues (it is in answer to a question I had addressed to him, more particularly with regard to the Virgin's Fountain): 'I do not think much stress can be laid on the position of the Jerusalem spring. It *may* have maintained its position in spite of all the earthquakes, but on the other hand it *may* have had its passage opened for it within historic time, and other springs may have existed which have had their passages closed up. Of course a close study of the ground might

*Possibility of conclusion from these data as to Jerusalem.*

[1] *P.E.F.Q.*, 1903, 216 ff.

enable a geological expert to express an opinion a little more definitely in one direction or the other, but I hardly think he would feel himself justified in expressing any confidence either way.' After reading a paper I published upon ' The Waters of Jerusalem,'[1] Sir Charles Wilson sent me the following criticism :—' I think you have given too much weight to the effect of earthquakes on the springs. There is no trace of any important geological disturbance visible, and though a violent earthquake might have a slight temporary effect on the flow of the Siloam Spring, it could not from the conditions under which the spring is supplied have a permanent one. In the case of deep-seated hot springs such as are found in and near the Ghôr, the case is different.' I confess that after this double witness to the impossibility of any certain conclusion, I would have abandoned my attempt to reach one, but for an additional piece of historical evidence, the value of which I have appreciated only since the paper alluded to was published. The possibility of a disturbance by earthquakes of the natural water-supply of Jerusalem is not, and cannot be denied ; on the other hand, it is clear that such a disturbance would reasonably explain some of the existing uncertainty as to the positions and characters of the historical springs or wells. But so much being granted, I think we can now argue in addition, from the name of one of these springs or wells, that one such disturbance did take place in the early history of the City. To explain this name, and the evidence I find in it, it is necessary to consider the effect of earthquakes on ancient mythology.

So frequent and serious a phenomenon in Syria must have left its stamp on the popular religion. The mono-

[1] *Expositor*, March 1903.

theism of the prophets and psalmists includes the earthquake among the signs of the Almighty's
power and the instruments of His wrath upon
the wicked children of men ; it is even possible
that this violence was the origin of the divine name El
Shaddai.[1]   In any case the God worshipped by Israel
holds in His hand the power that quakes the earth,
and the prophetic scenes of the Divine judgment
shake with its tremors and convulsions.   It would be
singular if the popular religions of Syria, clinging closer to
the earth, and even more in awe of the violences of Nature,
had not also found a place for the earthquake in their
mythologies, and after their manner assigned it to some
special being or beings.   For proofs of this we need not
go beyond the Old Testament, and the later works of
Judaism ; though they have been somewhat overlooked.
In the materials for their imagery which prophets or
psalmists have not refused to draw from the folk-lore of
their times, there figures frequently a Dragon—*Tannin*,
as he is called in Hebrew.   He is properly a
sea-monster, born of the element which seemed
to the Semites to perpetuate the turbulence and arrogance
of primeval chaos.   He personifies the sea : *Art thou*

*Earthquakes and myth-ology.*

*The Dragon.*

---

[1] Robertson Smith, *O. T. in the Jewish Church* (1st ed. 424), after pointing
out how the vocalisation of the name may be due to a later mistaken etymology
of it, suggests that it is an intensive form from שׁדד to *pour out*, and in that
case the derivation assumed in Is. xiii. 6, Jer. i. 15, from שׁד would be
wrong.   But the many passages in the O. T. (outside P., in which the name
stands for the name by which God revealed Himself to the Patriarchs before
His new name to Moses, Ex. vi. 3, and passages in which it is used con-
ventionally as by Job's friends or in mere parallel to *God*) in which the
name is used along with the divine affliction, or violent possession, of a man
(Num. xxiv. 4, 16, Ruth i. 20, 21, Ps. lxviii. 15, Ez. i. 24, x. 5 ; cf. Gen. xlix.
25, where it is associated with the *blessings of the deep*), support the derivation
from שׁד, and this word, meaning violence that leads to *havoc* and *ruin*, is often
used in connection with earthquakes or in the imagery derived from them.

*not it that ... pierced the Dragon, that dried up the sea? Am I the sea or the Dragon, that thou settest a watch over me?* [1] And the name in the plural is given to the great sea-monsters, whales and sharks.[2]    But we must keep in mind that the sea was supposed by the Semites to roll under the whole earth, and wash with ceaseless tides the roots of the mountains.    We must remember that to the Greeks Poseidon was not only god of the sea, but the great earth-shaker as well, and worshipped as such in cities far inland;[3] and that the mythical sea-serpent Typhon 'filled the earth *as well as* the sea with evils,'[4] 'deeply furrowed the earth, and formed the bed of the Orontes,' and as he 'lay beneath the island of Prochyta and turned himself, caused flames and water to rush forth, and sometimes even small islands to rise.'[5]    And we must understand that all this attribution to the same being of the powers of the sea-storm or the earthquake is due to the frequent experience of the inhabitants of the Mediterranean basin, where in the great convulsions sea and earth rise together, and enormous 'tidal waves' accompany the earthquakes.[6]    After this, we shall not be surprised to find in the Old Testament, too, that the Dragon is also the earth-shaker. *He swallows*

[1] Isa. li. 9; Job vii. 12.   The definite article after the poetic fashion is omitted in the original.

[2] Gen. i. 21, and perhaps elsewhere.

[3] As Strabo points out in the case of the earthquake-riddled Apameia in Phrygia (XII. viii. 18.): whence no doubt Poseidonius of Apameia got his name, the geographer upon whom Strabo draws so much, and who, conformably to his name, was of all Greek philosophers the one that, next to Aristotle, contributed most to the subject of earthquakes.   See Tozer, *Hist. of Ancient Geogr.*, 199.      [4] Plutarch, *De Is.* 27, quoted by Stark, *Gaza*, 276.

[5] Strabo, XVI. ii. 7. (cf. Robertson Smith, *Rel. of the Semites*, 161, in which however nothing is said of earthquakes), V. iv. 9.

[6] Strabo, I. iii. 17. f.; V. iv. 9.; VIII. vii. 2.; XVI. xi. 26, etc.   Pliny II. 82 (80)—88 (86); II. Esdras xvi. 12; Smyth, *The Mediterranean*, 107, 108, 179, 498.

*and casts out,*[1] he is introduced among or near other symptoms of earthquake:[2] and Psalm cxlviii. calls out definitely: *Praise the Lord from the earth* (not the sea), *ye Dragons and ye Deeps.* This association is even plainer in the Apocryphal writings : *Thou didst shake the earth and madest the Deeps to tremble.*[3] *Behold noises and tumult, thunderings and earthquake, uproar upon the earth ; and behold two great Dragons came forth, both of them ready to fight, and their cry was great.*[4]

Moreover it was to these Dragons, as the authors of earthquake, that both Semitic and Greek folklore attributed the appearance of springs and rivers. Dragons and Psalm cxlviii. implies this when it links the Springs. Dragons and Deeps, for it was from the *Deep that coucheth beneath*[5] that the fountains of the land were fed.[6] The Apocryphal Book of Esther associates dragons and springs in the use it makes of both in its imagery.[7] We have seen that the springs and bed of the Orontes, the Nahr el-'Aṣi or 'River of the Rebel,' were supposed to be the work of a Dragon, and to Typhon the Greek myths attribute the issue of many springs.[8] Other springs in Syria are called by the name of Serpent,[9] and a Moslem legend has it that the rebel angels Hārūt and Mārūt are entombed under a well at Babylon.[10] It is strange that

---

[1] Jer. li. 34. Here the myth has passed into political history, and the Dragon is Nebuchadrezzar.   [2] Ezek. xxxii. ; Isai. xxvii. 1.
[3] II. Esdr. iii. 18.   [4] (Apocryphal) Esther xi. 5 f.
[5] Deut. xxxiii. 13.   [6] Amos vii. 4.
[7] (Apocr.) Esther x. 6 ; cf. xi. 5 f. with 10.
[8] Strabo and Pliny in the passages cited above on Typhon.
[9] *e.g.,* near Ruâd ; Maundrell's *Journey,* 1697, under March 7.
[10] Cited by Robertson Smith, *Rel. of the Semites,* 161, from Cazwīnī, i. 197. Compare the curious Moslem story of the origin of the flood at Gezer : Cl.-Ganneau, *Arch. Res.* ii. 237 ff.; R. A. S. Macalister, *P.E.F.Q.,* 1903, 217 f.

these instances—and they could be multiplied—along with the prevalence of earthquakes in Syria, should not have suggested to modern writers on Semitic mythology this fruitful side of the subject of springs and religion.[1]

But now we come to the point of our argument. In Jerusalem also there was, in Nehemiah's day, a Dragon's

*The Dragon-Spring at Jerusalem.*

Fountain, somewhere (as we shall see) between the Valley Gate and the Dung Gate, in the Valley of the Son of Hinnom. It has been identified with the modern Bír Eiyûb, which is therefore also sometimes called Nehemiah's Well. But this does not suit the data which Nehemiah gives for its position. All the analogies of the name suggest a spring caused by an earthquake,[2] and this conclusion is supported by the fact that neither the name nor a well in that position occurs either before or after the time of Nehemiah.

One, therefore, inclines to the probability that we have here, at Jerusalem, a case of a spring opened by earthquake

*Earthquakes may have changed the Jerusalem Springs.*

—Uzziah's or another—and afterwards disappearing, as so many wells thus caused have done. But this gives further ground to believe that earthquakes *may* have affected the other springs of Jerusalem ; which result of our examination of the subject of earthquakes and springs we carry over into our next chapter on the Waters of Jerusalem.

---

[1] On 'voices,' 'bellowings,' 'groans,'etc., in earthquakes see a number of citations from Greek and Latin writers in Bochart's *Phaleg*, bk. i. ch. 8, pp. 408 ff.

[2] Cheyne, *Enc. Bibl.* coll. 1132, 1133, seeks to show that since there are two classes of serpent-myths, one which takes the reptile as hostile, the other as friendly, to man, and serpents are often associated with wells, Nehemiah's Dragon Spring must belong to the latter. But this is a case, not of a serpent, but of the Dragon, a monster, who is never friendly to man.

# CHAPTER V

## THE WATERS OF JERUSALEM

I N the introduction to this volume some account has been
given of the water-supply of Jerusalem. But a more
detailed examination of the hydrography is Topographical
needed to prepare us for the discussion of the and Economic
Importance of
topographical problems. Nowhere so much as the Subject.
in the East do such problems depend on the position and
possible alteration of the water sources ; but in the case of
Jerusalem, the meagreness of these enhances their topographical importance to a degree unusual, even in the
Orient. In fact we cannot describe them without at once
starting some of the most radical questions concerning the
place-names of the City and her environs. The study will
also furnish us with material for our subsequent discussion
of the economy of Jerusalem : the endowment of the site
in the necessaries of human life.

The authorities on the subject are almost too numerous
to mention. I confine myself to the principal. Robinson,
as elsewhere, ought to be carefully studied ;[1] The
although his treatment of the subject is warped Authorities.
by his erroneous location of Gihon on the west of the city,
and although like Tobler[2] he worked before the days of

---

[1] *Biblical Researches*, i. ii. ; *Later Bibl. Res.* 196 ff. 243 ff.
[2] *Topogr. von Jerusalem*, ii. 84 ff.

excavation. Sir Charles Wilson, Sir Charles Warren, Colonel Conder, and M. Clermont-Ganneau afford the first results of the latter in the volume of the Survey Memoir on Jerusalem,[1] in many papers in the Quarterly Statement, and in other works.[2] Some materials are supplied by Pierotti, an Italian architect employed by the local authorities.[3] Then come the results of a life-long inspection and study of the springs, pools and aqueducts by Dr. Schick, the practical architect and high authority on the topography of Jerusalem;[4] the results of Dr. Guthe's excavations on Ophel,[5] Dr Bliss's excavations on the South-west Hill and at Siloam;[6] a paper by Dr. Masterman, a resident for some years in the City;[7] Dr. Guthe's article in Hauck's *Realencyclopädie*;[8] and a summary of results in Kuemmel's Materials for the Topography of ancient Jerusalem.[9] Except for certain stretches of the two long-distance aqueducts, the centre of the Siloam Tunnel, Warren's Shaft, the Ḥammam esh-Shefâ and the bottom of the Bîr Eiyûb, which I have not examined, the following study is based on my own observations made during my five visits to the city. For the measurements where they are not taken from the Fund Memoir, references are given below.

[1] *P.E.F. Mem.*, ' Jerus.'

[2] Especially *The Recovery of Jerusalem* (1871) 233 ff., and Wilson, *The Water Supply of Jerusalem*, an address to the Victoria Institute, 26th May 1902; Clermont-Ganneau, *Archæological Researches in Palestine*, vol. i.; Conder's and Warren's Articles in Hastings' *Dictionary of the Bible*, Wilson's in the 2nd ed. of Smith's *Dictionary of the Bible*; and that by Robertson Smith, Conder, and the present writer in the *Enc. Bibl.*

[3] *Jerusalem Explored;* to be used with discrimination.

[4] *Z.D.P.V.* i. (1878) 132 ff. : ' Die Wasserversorgung der Stadt Jerusalem,' with a Map and Plans.     [5] *Id.* vol. v. with plans.

[6] *Excavations at Jerusalem*, 1894-1897, especially 24, 53, chs. ii.-v. and ix.

[7] *Biblical World*, 1902.     [8] Vol. viii. 1900.

[9] Published by ' Der Deutsche Verein zur Erforschung Palästinas,' 1906.

## 1. THE RAINFALL AND OTHER NATURAL CONDITIONS.

The natural causes which affect the water-supply of Jerusalem are four; three of which may be regarded as practically constant: the Rainfall, the Height and Shape of the Basin in which the City stands, and its Geological Formation; and one which, as we have seen, introduces some uncertainty into the subject, the Earthquakes that have periodically rocked the foundations of the City.

*Natural Conditions of the Water-Supply.*

We have seen that the average rainfall upon Jerusalem is rather over 25 inches (practically 635 millimetres), or about as much as that of London; but that it falls in winter only, and leaves a long summer drought. One calculation of thirty-two years' observations at a station within the walls gives 25·23 inches (640·8 mm.), another on thirty-nine years gives 26·05 (661·8 mm.).[1]

*1. The Rainfall.*

[1] Besides Chaplin's article quoted above, p. 18 *n.* 5, see Glaisher 'On the Fall of Rain at Jerus., 1861-1892,' *P.E.F.Q.*, 1894, 39 ff.; in subsequent volumes Glaisher's collections of observations since 1892; H. Hilderscheid, 'Die Niederschlagsverhältnisse Palästinas in alter u. neuer Zeit,' *Z.D.P.V.* xxv. (1902), 1 ff.; also Benzinger *M.u.N.D.P.V.*, 1904, 78 ff. and other papers. Both Chaplin and Hilderscheid present the Biblical data, the latter more fully along with those from the Mishna. The longest series of observations, those of Dr. Chaplin, continued by Mr. J. Gamel, were taken 'in a garden within the City, about 2500 feet above the sea.' Glaisher reckons from them the average of 25·23 inches. They differ curiously from others taken for a period of three years at a lower station in the German Colony on the Buḳeiʻa to the S.-W. of the City; and from a third series, taken on a higher point, the Syrian orphanage to the N.-W. of the City. Hilderscheid (p. 34) calculates the average of thirty-nine years, as taken at the first of these stations, at 661·8 mm. (26·05 ins.), and those at the two others reduced to the same rate as respectively 547·2 mm. (21·54 ins.) and 579·4 mm. (22·41 ins.). The difference may be due to the different instruments; but Hilderscheid adds the report of a resident, that it 'frequently rains within the City when only a few drops fall at the German colony; also the reverse case was already observed.'

Did the rainfall in ancient times differ from this? The
Old Testament data are, of course, not specific, but at least
sufficient to justify a negative answer. Some authorities
on the climate and fertility of Palestine have, indeed,
argued that, as in the Mediterranean basin as a whole, so
throughout Palestine in particular, the climate has suffered
a change for the worse through the diminution of the
rainfall.[1] One of the reasons given for this conclusion is
the alleged decrease of the woodlands of the country. I
have elsewhere shown that in all probability these were
never much greater on Western Palestine than they are
to-day.[2] The other natural features by which the rainfall
is influenced—the position of the City relatively to the sea,
and the prevalent winds—have remained the same; while
the references to climate and weather in the Bible and the
Mishna are fully consistent with the present conditions.
We may conclude, therefore, that the rainfall upon Jerusalem in ancient times must have been very nearly the same
as it has been observed to be during the last forty-six
years.[3] Even if it was a little greater, the difference cannot
have been of much practical moment.

[1] So Hull, *Memoir on Phys. Geology and Geogr. of Arabia Petræa, Palestine,*
*etc.* (in the *P.E.F. Memoirs*), pt. v. ch. ii. ; Th. Fischer, *Studien über das*
*Klima der Mittelmeerländer* in Petermann's *Mittheilungen, ergänz. heft* 58,
p. 41 ; and Zumoffen, *La Météorologie de la Palestine, etc.*, in the *Bulletin de*
*la Société de Géogr.* 1899, 467. Cf. Blanckenhorn, *Z.D.P.V.* xv. 8, 40, and
Buhl, *G.A.P.* 54 f. See also O. Fraas, *Aus dem Orient*, i. 196.

[2] *H.G.H.L.* 80 ff.

[3] Among those who agree that the climate has not much changed, or is
virtually the same as in ancient times, are Robinson, who does not argue the
question, but generally assumes this answer, or illustrates it (*e.g.*, *B.R.* ii. 97,
*Phys. Geog.* 263, 267, 279 f.); similarly Thomson (*L. and B.* 90 f. 395, etc.),
and Chaplin, who notes at least the harmony between Scripture references and
present conditions, *op. cit.*; Lortet in the Duc de Luynes's *Voyage d'Explora-*
*tion à la Mer Morte, etc.*, iii. 212 ; Conder, *P.E.F.Q.*, 1876, 131 ff. ; Ankel,
*Grundzüge der Landesnatur des Westjordanlandes*, iv. Das Klima ; Rindfleisch,

This rainfall of about 25 inches annually happens upon a large basin, from brink to brink some 2½ to 3 miles by 1 to 1½, which lies on the summit of a mountain range. The highest levels of the basin are from 2600 to 2700 feet, the lowest under 2000 feet, above the sea. The fall is therefore for the most part very rapid. 2. Height and Size of the Basin of Jerusalem. The principal hollows by which the basin is drained, begin above the City (as we have seen), deepen round or through its site, and join below its south-east angle upon the one outlet towards the Dead Sea. The City, therefore, is placed where any water that falls in the basin, and runs on or near its surface, must gather before leaving it. Here, then, is one of the reasons why Jerusalem stands exactly where she does. A large town is less possible anywhere else on this part of the range. But while enough water falls within the basin to sustain, if not her full population, yet a considerable one, the limits of the basin, the nearness of the watershed and the rapid slope forbid the formation of any stream or lake.

A more efficient cause for their absence, however, we have already seen in our examination of the geology of the district.[1] In the upper strata of this formation no hard impervious rocks are found, but the soft porous limestone greedily absorbs the rain, and that is the full reason why neither lake nor steady stream has ever blessed the neighbourhood of Jerusalem. Pools formed by the winter rains soon 3. The Geology.

*Z.D.P.V.* xxi. 46 (very sensible remarks on the subject) ; with great force of detailed argument, Hilderscheid, *Id.* xxv. 99 ff. ; and Guthe ('Palästina' in Hauck's *Realencycl. für prot. Theol. u. Kirche,* xiv. 590 ff.), who admits, however, a decrease in the woodland, and in consequence a possible diminution in rainfall.　　　　　　　　　　[1] Chapter iii.

disappear[1] and there are but one or two quickly-drying swamps.[2]  Except for a brief interval after heavy down-bursts of rain, water does not run above ground outside the Ḳidron Valley.  It is in the latter therefore that we must seek for the only stream of the district of which we read in the Bible—not of course on the present bed of the valley, which is of shot rubbish, but some 30 feet below,

The Brook Ḳidron.  and 240 to the west.  Here the rock—porous as it still is, but with impervious strata immediately below, which tend to turn the waters back—has been found to be moist and in parts covered with mud,[3] while wherever it is exposed it bears marks of having been swept by occasional torrents.[4]  Opposite the City these are quickly absorbed by the *débris*; but lower down, beyond the Bîr Eiyûb, they will flow on the surface for several days at a time after the heavy rains of spring.[5]  This is the only approach to a stream which is now found in the environs of the City; that it was not otherwise in ancient times is proved by the literature. We have seen Strabo's emphasis on the aridness of the surroundings, and that Dion Cassius gives a still more vivid account of the stagnancy of the water on which Titus had to draw in the neighbourhood.[6]  In none of the other classical authorities is there any reference to a perennial stream.  Josephus, who several times mentions the Ḳidron,

[1] Schick mentions one which gathers every winter for a few weeks near the Nâblus road, north of the City, *P.E.F.Q.*, 1892, 9; but this is due to the remains of an artificial pool: see below, p. 119.

[2] See above, p. 16.

[3] *Recovery of Jerusalem*, 135.

[4] Cf. Robinson, *B.R.* i. 402.

[5] Thomson, *L. and B.*, 659; 'gushing out like a millstream'; *P.E.F. Mem.*, 'Jerusalem,' 371; Masterman, *Bibl. World*, 1902, 89 f.

[6] Above, p. 16.

THE LOWER KIDRON VALLEY: LOOKING SOUTH.

On the left the Village of Silwân: on the right near the Valley-bed the position of the Virgin's Spring: beyond, the Jebel Deir Abu Tôr.
Taken from the *débris* near the S.E. Corner of the Temple Area.

*Plate V.*

describes it generally as a valley or gorge, and once by the Greek word for 'winter' or 'storm torrent,'[1] by which it is also called in the New Testament.[2]   It is in this sense that we must take the Hebrew term *naḥal* as applied to the Ḳidron in the Old Testament.[3]   Translated *brook* in our versions, *naḥal* means no more than a valley down which a transitory stream may flow after heavy rain ; and in fact the Ḳidron is only referred to in the Old Testament as something to be crossed or passed up, or as a place for casting out rubbish : except in one verse which, if the text be sound, speaks *of the Naḥal which rushes* or *gushes in the midst of the land*.[4]   But this description is very suitable to the present outbursts after the winter rains below the Bîr Eiyûb.  That before the bed of the Wâdy was choked with *débris* these began further up, opposite the City, is very probable.  In ancient times when the water of the present Virgin's Spring ran into the Wâdy, there must have been a fitful rill even in the dry season. In the light of this it becomes significant that the Chronicler should include the *naḥal which gusheth* or *overfloweth through the midst of the land* with *the fountains outside the City* that Hezekiah sealed up ; for, as we shall see, it was in all probability this king who diverted the water of the Virgin's Spring by a tunnel to a pool within the City.  It is true that water has sometimes been found by excavators running down the

---

[1] Κεδρών or ὁ κεδρών simply v. *B.J.* vi. 1, vii. 3, xii. 2 ; φάραγξ ix. *Ant.* vii. 3, v. *B.J.* ii. 3, iv. 2, vi. 1, vi. *B.J.* iii. 2 ; Χειμάρροος or—άρρος viii. *Ant.* i. 5.
[2] John xviii. 1, Κεδρών.
[3] נַחַל קִדְרוֹן : 2 Sam. xv. 23, 1 Ki. xv. 13, 2 Ki. xxiii. 6, 12, Jer. xxxi. 40, 2 Chr. xv. 16, xxix. 16, xxx. 14.  Or הנחל alone, *the* Wâdy *par excellence,* 2 Chr. xxxiii. 14, Neh. ii. 15.
[4] 2 Chron. xxxii. 4.

rock-bed of the Tyropœon.[1]   But the fact that the
Ḳidron is called in two passages *the* Naḥal, and that no
other Jerusalem Valley gets the name, implies that neither
in the Tyropœon nor elsewhere about the City was
there a flow of water worthy of even the name *storm* or
*winter-brook*.[2]

The last paragraph has already brought us to the subject
of the Springs of Jerusalem.   Before beginning this we
must recall the great uncertainty introduced
into it through the possible disturbance of the
subterranean drainage by earthquakes.   From
our investigation of these,[3] the conclusion was reached

4. Earth-
quakes and
Springs.

---

[1] *Recovery of Jerus.*, 77 ; Warren here sums up his experiences as follows :
'It would appear then that there is still a stream of water, whether from rainfall or from springs, percolating through the Tyropœon Valley.'   Warren was
working after heavy rain ; but we must keep in mind also the leakage and
overflow from Hezekiah's Pool and other reservoirs in the north-west of the
City.

[2] The passage to which 2 Chron. xxxii. 4 belongs is a difficult one, and
objections have been taken to it.   But that it represents a sound tradition is
probable from what has been said above.   The LXX. read the description of
the stream differently : τὸν ποταμὸν τὸν διορίζοντα διὰ τῆς πόλεως.   If on any
grounds this could be argued to be the original meaning, it might refer to a
stream flowing down the Tyropœon, which Mommert, for instance, has
taken to be *the brook flowing through the midst of the land*.   But the Chronicler
would hardly have spoken of *a brook flowing through the midst of the land*,
along with the fountains outside of the City, had the brook been in the
Tyropœon, nor would there have been any use in Hezekiah's sealing such a
brook.   We may therefore take the Hebrew text to be the original, and the
Greek as an emendation made when the fact of a stream, which once flowed
from the Virgin's Fountain into the Ḳidron, but was diverted by Hezekiah,
had been forgotten ; and since it seemed absurd to speak of a stream through
the midst of the land, the reading of the Greek was altered to suit the stream
Hezekiah made through the tunnel, which in a sense *makes a division through
the City*.   Sir Charles Wilson would refer the Hebrew phrase to the conduit (see
below), which, before the tunnel was constructed, carried the water of the
Virgin's Fountain round the base of Ophel to Siloam (*Water Supply of Jerus.*,
page 6), and this view is apparently shared by Benzinger on 2 Chron. xxxii.
3.   It is not likely, however, that the Chronicler would have described a
conduit as a naḥal.                              [3] See above, ch. iv.

that the earthquakes with which Jerusalem was visited
were associated with the name of one spring—the Dragon's
Fountain, and that, in all probability, they have affected
others; while the *débris* they have caused may mask some
ancient vents of water, and cause their overflow to appear
to-day as mere surface percolations.

## 2. THE SPRINGS—REAL AND REPUTED.

In the topography of Jerusalem, few points have raised
so much controversy as her various real and reputed
springs. In such a basin it is evident that Reputed
springs are not probable, except where the Springs about
hard *Lower Mizzeh* comes near the surface. Jerusalem.
The most natural place to look for them is this same
Ḳidron valley; also possibly in the natural grooves which
in ancient times descended into it from the East Hill; and
in the mouth of the Tyropœon. Everywhere else the
porous strata prevail for a great depth below the surface,
and we must be on our guard against mistaking their
filtrations of water for a real spring.[1] It is true that in
recent times, as well as in ancient, rumours have arisen of
the existence of fountains about Jerusalem, elsewhere than
in the Ḳidron valley; but these have been due either to
the exigencies of topographical theories, or to forgetful-
ness of the distinction just noted, or to a misinterpretation
of Biblical texts. Robinson and others have placed the
Biblical Giḥon on the west of the City, by the head of the
Wâdy er-Rabâbi;[2] and this used to be the common
opinion. Others have sought for Giḥon on the north, and

---

[1] See above, p. 59, on this distinction.
[2] Robinson, *B.R.* i. 323-329, *L.B.R.* 247 ff.; Schultz, 79; Thomson, *L. and B.*, 655, etc.; Pierotti, *Jerusalem Explored*, 241; and many others.

have taken the aqueduct which runs from the Damascus
Gate towards the Temple Area as a channel for its waters.[1]
And Pierotti calls the Ḥammam esh-Shefâ, the water-pit
in the Tyropœon to the west of the Temple, a spring.[2]
But, as Robinson remarks, 'the nature of the ground on
the north of the Damascus Gate, shows that no sources of
living water ever existed there:'[3] the same objection holds
good against his own location of Giḥon on the west, and,
as we shall see, Giḥon is to be found, without doubt, in the
Ḳidron valley.   Careful examination of the Ḥammam esh-
Shefâ proves it to be a mere reservoir for the surface
waters and percolations immediately under the surface,
and no true spring.[4]   Other reports of real springs within
the City hardly need refutation.   The statements by Timochares (2nd cent. B.C.), and Xenophon the topographer,
both quoted in the fragments of Alexander Polyhistor
(1st cent. B.C.),[5] that the whole town abounds in running
water, and that there is 'a spring within the place which
throws up water in abundance,' probably refer, the former
to the existence of the aqueducts, the latter to the pool of

[1] Williams, *Holy City*, ii. 474.   In connection with this may be mentioned
the theory of the Rev. George Sandie (*Horeb and Jerus*. Edin. 1864, 275),
who locates the City of David on the East Hill, that Giḥon was in the
Central Valley, el-Wâd.

[2] *Jerus. Expl.*, 15, 257.

[3] *L.B.R.*, 244; cf. 245, where he shows that the name Mount Giḥon, as
applied to a ridge of land on the N.W. of the City, does not appear to go
farther back than Brocardus, 1283 A.D.; *B.R.* i. 39.

[4] So several writers who have examined the cistern.   *E.g.*, Chaplin,
*P.E.F. Mem.* 'Jerus.,' 262 ff.; Sir C. Wilson (see below, p. 120); Masterman
(*Bibl. World*, 1905, 95 f.).   'An underground tank . . . it contains only
dirty water, greatly impregnated with sewage . . . it has no true spring.'
K. Furrer's identification of it with the Pool of Bethesda (*Zeitschrift f. N.T.
Wissenschaft*, 1902, 260), is based on the assumptions, 1, of a Temple-Spring,
2, of its being intermittent, and 3, of a real spring in the Ḥammam.

[5] Müller, *Fragm. Histor. Graec.* iii. 228 f.

Siloam, still regarded as an 'Ain by the Arabs, because of the issue from the tunnel which fills it.

The question of a real spring within the Temple Area rises from data of somewhat different value. The 'Pseudo-Aristeas' states that the Temple had an in-exhaustible supply of water, not only in its wonderful cisterns, but from a copious natural spring within itself.[1] Tacitus speaks of a 'fons perennis aquæ,'[2] apparently also within the Temple. Both these statements may be mere inversions of the prophecy that a fountain of living water would issue from the Sanctuary. At the same time a very deep well beneath the Temple Area, descending far enough to tap some gathering of living water upon the Lower Mizzeh, is perfectly possible. 'It has often occurred to me,' writes Sir Charles Wilson, 'that the Bir el-Arwa, under the Ṣakhra, may be a deep well going down below the floors of the adjacent valleys, and so having an almost constant supply. Such wells are not uncommon in northern Syria, and there is a good example at Shobek in Edom.'[3] Against this hypothesis, so reasonable in itself, there stand the following facts. First, the great complex of cisterns under the Temple Area, in which, so far as they have been explored, no trace of such a well has been found, and second, the aqueduct or aqueducts by which water was brought to the Temple from distant sources.[4] That all these were necessary seems to prove that there never was any considerable spring of water discovered by boring beneath the Temple

*The question of a Temple Spring.*

[1] Thackeray's ed. in Swete's *Introd. to the O.T. in Gr.*, 535. Eng. Trans., 21.

[2] *Hist.* v. 12.

[3] From a private letter to the author, 1903.

[4] See below, p. 120, and p. 124 f.

Area itself; unless such a spring existing in the earlier
times disappeared through the influence of the earthquakes,
and substitutes for it had to be provided.   A more
formidable reason against the hypothesis would be the
existence of the Water Gate, if it could be proved that
this was a Temple Gate, for, if such a spring existed, there
would be no need to descend for water into the Ḳidron
valley.   But a comparison of the passages in which the
Water Gate is mentioned convinces me that those are
right who take it to have been a City Gate on the eastern
wall, even although Nehemiah does not mention it in his
account of the rebuilding of that wall.[1]   The Water Gate
cannot therefore be used in the present argument.  Yet the
two other facts, or rather our *present* evidence for them,
are sufficient to make very doubtful the existence of a
fountain within the Temple *enceinte.*   The rumours of it
are to be explained as above.

We turn now to the Springs, real or reputed, in the
Ḳidron valley.   Both the Chronicler and Josephus report
springs (in the plural) of Jerusalem : the Chronicler when
he describes how Hezekiah *took counsel to stop the waters
of the fountains which were without the City . . . and they
stopped all the fountains and the naḥal which overflowed
through the midst of the land* ;[2] and Josephus, who reports
that when exhorting the Jews to surrender to Titus, he
said, 'You know that Siloam as well as the other springs
without the City had (before the siege) so failed that water
was sold by the jar, whereas they now produce in such
abundance for your enemies, that they suffice not only

[1] This opinion is contrary to that which I previously expressed in *Enc.
Bibl.*, 'Jerusalem,' § 24, *fin.* col. 2,425.

[2] 2 Chron. xxxii. 3, 4, הַמַּעְיָנוֹת הָעֵינוֹת

for these and their cattle but for their gardens as well.'[1] Both writers have been charged in this with exaggeration, and we are not concerned to defend the accuracy of Josephus, especially on such an occasion; it would certainly be hard to reconcile his statement with those quoted above from Strabo and Dion Cassius, and with the difficulties in finding water to which all other besiegers of the City are known to have been subject. Probably Josephus is referring to the water which Titus brought in sufficiency from distant sources; the aqueducts from the south were then in operation. With regard to the Chronicler's report of *fountains*, the alternatives are either that he uses the plural of *'ain*, the Hebrew word for a real spring, with the same looseness with which it is used in modern Arabic; or that there were, in Hezekiah's time and his own, several springs in the Ḳidron valley which have disappeared as a result of earthquakes; or that he speaks of other wells further off from the City.[2] To-day there are only two wells in the Ḳidron valley which have been claimed to be real springs: the Virgin's Fountain and the Well of Job. These we will now examine.

The 'Ain Sitti Mariam, or Fountain of our Lady Mary, lies in a cave in the west wall of the valley in the rock of the East Hill, some 353 yards south of the south-east angle of the Temple Area. It is also The 'Ain Sitti Mariam.

---

[1] Jos. v. *B.J.* ix. 4 (409, 410) πηγαί.

[2] Dr. Masterman suggests (in a letter to the author) that the curious rock-tunnels connected with so many springs in the neighbourhood, *e.g.* 'Ain Kawrar, 'Ain el Khanduk [*P.E.F.Q.* 1902, 245, descriptions and plan by Macalister], 'Ain Ḳaryet es-Sa'ideh, may have been made at least partially to hide these springs on the approach of a hostile force. A similar kind of tunnel has just been found at 'Ain Ḥôḍ, 'The Apostles' Fountain.' Compare what is said below on the 'Ain el-Lôzeh.

known as the 'Ain Umm ed-Deraj, or Fountain of Steps,[1]
which lead down to it from the present surface of the valley.
The steps are in two flights.  The upper flight of sixteen
ends upon a level landing beneath a vault.  The lower of
fourteen ends under the roof of the cave, and projects seven
feet over a rocky basin thirty feet long by eight broad,[2]
which fills with water from a hole near its centre.  In 1901,
in consequence of a diminution of the water, the municipality of Jerusalem had the basin cleared of a large accumulation of rubbish.  At the invitation of the late Yusuf Pasha
I had the opportunity of accompanying him and Dr. Schick
upon an inspection of the well, the results of which have
been described by Dr. Schick.[3]  Almost six feet west of
the lowest step is the opening of the source, a hole in the
rock apparently natural and about a foot wide.  The cliff
above projects eastward over the lower flight of stairs about
seventeen feet from the source.  The basin, thus situated in
a cave on the eastern wall of Ophel, appears to be the
original pool of the spring, and is like that of many other
springs in Western Palestine.

As is well known, the flow of water in the 'Ain Sitti
Mariam is intermittent: the water breaks from the hole in
Its Character; the basin three to five times a day during the
a real Spring. rainy season, but during summer twice a day,
and after any failure of the spring rains (as in 1901, as well
as in other years) less than once.  Even when the spring

---

[1] The legend that Mary washed here the swaddling clothes of her infant is first
met with in the fourteenth century.  But as far back as the sixth (Antoninus
Plac. 590) the house and grave of Mary were pointed out a little higher up
the Ḳidron Valley; and no doubt this earlier legend gave rise to the later (cf.
Guthe, Hauck's *Realenc.* 'Jerus.' viii. 670).  I do not know how far back
the earlier name goes.

[2] Baedeker, 5th ed. 1898, gives the dimensions as 3·5 metres by 1·6 or about
11½ feet by 5.          [3] *P.E.F.Q.*, 1902, 29.

rains do not fail, the flow in autumn frequently falls to this minimum. The volume of the water therefore depends immediately on the rain - fall and the ultimate source cannot be deep-seated. But it is useless to deny to the issue the name of Spring, as some have done.[1] The cause cannot be the mere overflow of some of the many cisterns beneath the Temple Area ; we shall find evidence that the issue existed at an earlier date than that at which these can have been constructed. Nor does the water gather by mere percolation. It breaks, as we have seen, through what is no artificial conduit, but, to all appearance, the mouth of a natural fissure in the rock. At the other end of this fissure we must assume that there is a cavity in which the volume of water sent forth at each out-burst of the spring has room to gather ; a cavity which receives water from the porous strata above, but being itself in the harder rock prevents the further passage of the water downwards, and sends it along the fissure to the hole in the cave ; the hole, we must remember, occurs on a level not far beneath which the impervious Lower Mizzeh is lying.[2] To water issuing under such conditions we can as little refuse the name of Spring as to scores of other water-sources in Western Palestine ; and indeed nearly all modern observers are agreed upon the fact.[3] The inter-

[1] *e.g.* Mommert, *Topographie des alten Jerusalem* erster Theil, 13. His hypothesis, that the Bir Eiyûb or 'En Rogel was the original spring in the Ḳid-ron valley, and that the 'Ain Sitti Mariam was opened in later times as a vent for the subterranean waters of the Ḳidron valley, close to the City, has no evidence to support it. On the contrary, we shall find proof of the very early existence of the 'Ain Sitti Mariam under the name of Giḥon.

[2] See above, p. 56 f.

[3] *e.g.* Wilson, *Recov. of Jerusalem*, 19 ; Warren, Hastings' *D.B.* ii. 387 ; Conder, *Enc. Bibl.* § 11 ; Socin and Benzinger in *Baedeker*, 5th ed. 98 ; Buhl, *G.A.P.* 93, etc. ; Lagrange, *Revue Biblique*, 1892, 17-38 ; Masterman, *Bibl. World*, 1905, 91 f. ; Guthe, Hauck's *Realenc.* viii. 670. f. ; etc. etc.

mittent flow is generally explained as due to the cavity and fissure forming between them a natural syphon. When the water has risen in the former high enough to cover the mouth of the outflow fissure, the whole drains off rapidly till the mouth of the inflow fissure is exposed; and the flow then ceases till water sufficient to repeat the process has again gathered.[1] Colonel Conder thus describes the outburst of the Spring itself: 'When we first entered there was not more than a foot depth of water in the pool, but the rush of water was now very rapid, and the depth increased just after we had reached the foot of the steps to four feet seven inches.'[2] From what we have seen of the connection in folk-lore between dragons and springs, it will not surprise us that the common people explain the intermittent flow of the Virgin's Spring by the story of a Dragon, in the interior of the rock, who swallows the water, but when he sleeps it rushes past him to the issue. Finally the water is clear, but to the taste brackish, as if tainted with the sewage of the City above.

At present the water is prevented from flowing out of the cave into the valley of the Ḳidron by the vast accumulation of rubbish, upon which the steps descend to the spring. But before this rubbish was gathered, the water must have flowed out of the cave on the natural surface eastward or south-eastward into the bed of the *naḥal* Ḳidron, thus forming the rill mentioned above.[3] Dr. Schick has reasonably supposed

Original direction of the outflow.

---

[1] Guthe (*op. cit.* 671) assumes a double source in the interior of the rock, an irregular as described above, and a regular.

[2] *P.E.F. Mem.*, 'Jerus.' 357. Masterman (*op. cit.*) describes the intermittent spring el-Fûwarah 'The Bubbler' in the Wâdy Kilt, where 'the water rises three or four times an hour in a group of natural stony basins.'

[3] P. 61. The bottom of the basin in the cave is, I believe, at least 12 or

that at one time it was intercepted by an artificial pool, somewhere to the south of the present mosque. Sir Charles Wilson has objected[1] that there is no trace or tradition of such a pool, but, as Dr. Masterman points out,[2] there is abundance of room for it in this situation, and the whole ground has yet to be excavated. When we come to discuss the position of the Pool of Bethesda, this possibility must be kept in mind.

Shut off, however, by the accumulation of rubbish from this its natural direction into the *naḥal* Ḳidron, the water of the Virgin's Spring flows at present, and for ages has flowed, through the celebrated rock-tunnel under Ophel to the Pool of Siloam in the mouth of the Tyropœon. A shaft, communicating between the surface of Ophel and this tunnel, a short distance from the Spring, suggests that this part alone was first made, and that the rest of the tunnel was completed later. And, recently, traces of another artificial conduit have been discovered running outside, down the edge of the valley, southwards. We shall now examine in turn these three, beginning with the last named.

*Conduits from the Virgin's Spring.*

Some years ago, Dr. Schick discovered the lower end of an aqueduct issuing near the Lower Pool of Siloam, and followed it up towards the Virgin's Spring. The upper end of it, he believed, might be found to start from the landing between the

*1. Surface Conduit in the Valley.*

15 feet below the natural rock in the valley outside. Therefore, either the water gathered to a great depth in the cave, or escaped into the valley by a rift in the rock. The former alternative is supported by the fact that the mouth of the ancient conduit, described below, is at the top of the lower flight of steps, to which, or above which, the water in the basin must have originally risen.

[1] Art. 'Bethesda' in Smith's *D.B.*
[2] *Bibl. World*, 1905, 101.

flights of steps.[1]  Here, accordingly, in 1901, a shaft was sunk and the entrance opened to a conduit running south on the edge of the valley towards the Lower Pool of Siloam. This was traced by Messrs. Hornstein and Masterman for a distance of 176 feet, and found to be partly excavated in the rock and partly built with rough stones.[2]  Whether it is actually the upper end of Dr. Schick's aqueduct is not yet certain; but, in any case, Dr. Hornstein and Dr. Masterman have proved the existence of a conduit from the Spring along the edge of the valley, southwards, at or near the natural surface.  Colonel Conder regards the portion discovered by Dr. Schick as modern ; but it would be difficult to discover a reason for the construction of the other portion, which lay exposed outside the ancient wall of Ophel, if the tunnel was already in existence which carries the water under Ophel to Siloam.  We may therefore take Hornstein and Masterman's conduit to be the older of the two, and perhaps the first artificial channel carrying the water of the Spring southward.

In the famous Tunnel under Ophel which carries the water of the Virgin's Spring south-west to the Pool of

2. Warren's Shaft and connected Tunnel.

Siloam, there are possibly two different stages from different epochs.  First, there is that part of the Tunnel immediately contiguous to the Spring which runs in a main direction of a little north of east for 50 feet as far as a great shaft discovered by Sir Charles Warren in 1867, and named after him.  This shaft runs straight up through the rock for 44 feet, to a horizontal passage, from the end of which a flight of steps or very steeply sloping passage leads to the surface of

[1] *P.E.F.Q.*, 1891, 13 ff.; cf. 1886, 197 ff.
[2] *P.E.F.Q.*, 1902, January.

Ophel just where, we shall see, the original fortress of Ṣion must have been situated. The purpose of the shaft is clear: it was to enable the garrison to draw upon the Spring from within their wall, which ran upon Ophel above the cave of the Spring. Sir Charles Warren's opinion, that the shaft and the portion of the Tunnel between it and the Spring is of earlier date than the rest of the Tunnel to Siloam, has been generally accepted.[1]

From the Virgin's Spring to its mouth in the Upper Pool of Siloam, the length of the Tunnel has been measured several times by competent hands, with results varying from 1700 to over 1750 feet (about 518 to 535 metres).[2] 3. Tunnel to Siloam. The direct distance between the two points is only some 1090 feet, or little over 332 m.[3] The Tunnel, therefore, winds considerably, in part probably by the intention of its makers, but also in part from their inability to preserve a straight direction. They began the work from both ends. From the Spring the mine was run almost due east for over 250 feet (this may have been an earlier bit of work), and was then turned to the south. From the Pool, after a few feet north-north-east, the tunnel was driven south-east till the miners reached the line on which their fellows were working southwards, and turned sharply north to meet them at a point discovered by Colonel Conder approximately half-way between the points where each had curved.[4] The

---

[1] *Recovery of Jerus.*, 238. *P.E.F. Mem.*, 'Jerus.' 353 ff.

[2] Warren, *Recov. of Jerus.* 212, 1708 feet, 520·58 m.; Conder, *Enc. Bibl.* § 11, 1708 feet ; Robinson, *B.R.* i. 503, 1750 feet, 533·5 m., cf. Baedeker, 5th ed. 99; Conder, *P.E.F.Q.*, 1882, 122 ff., 1757 ft. 4 in., 535·6 m. ; the difference seems due to the exclusion from the smaller estimate of 50 ft. at the N. end.

[3] As in Sir Charles Wilson's *Plan of Jerus.*, red. from the Ordnance Survey.

[4] But about 945 feet from the Pool and 813 from the Spring, according to his measurement (*i.e.* 287·7 and 247·9 metres respectively).

great curve on the south M. Clermont-Ganneau and Dr.
Bliss supposed to have been due to the wish of the miners
to avoid the Tombs of the Kings of Judah.[1]  Whether this
was the exact cause remains uncertain ; but the intentional
character of the curve seems clear from the fact that the
two parties afterwards worked on the same line north and
south.   Indeed, from the point at which they met, it appears as if the northern party started on their southward
turn to meet the southern party only when these had
turned their curve.   But the winding of their courses as
they approached each other, with the fact that more than
once they deserted directions in which they were travelling,
proves that they were not always sure of their way.
Nevertheless, allowing, as we cannot help doing, that the
great curve was intentional, and considering that the
miners had to work without a compass, we cannot but
wonder at their skill as well as their enterprise and industry.   The present height of the tunnel varies from over
11 feet at the south end, and over 6 at the north, to
under 2 at various other points, and at one place to as
low as 16 inches (about 410 mm.).   But as in these last
cases the bottom is hard chalky mud, and the rock has not
been reached, the original height of the channel must have
been greater.   The fall of the bed has been reckoned by
Colonel Conder as under a foot, or about 300 mm.

In the year 1880 an inscription, now in the Imperial
Museum at Constantinople, was discovered on
a prepared surface on the right wall of the
Tunnel, some 19 feet from the Siloam outlet.   It

The Inscrip-
tion of the
Tunnel.

---

[1] Clermont-Ganneau, *Rev. Critique*, 1887, *Athenæum*, Sept. 11, 1897,
361, and *Les Tombeaux de David et des Rois de Juda et le tunnel-aqueduct
de Siloé* (Extrait des Comptes Rendus de l'Acad. des Inscript. et Belles
Lettres), 1897.   See F. J. Bliss, *Excav. in Jerus.*, 1894-1897, 230 f.

consists of six lines of Hebrew prose, of pure classical style, in the ancient script used by Israel up to the time of the Exile, and recounts the completion of the Tunnel. There is no doubt that it is from the makers themselves, but it contains, remarkably, no royal or official name. The few lacunae can be easily supplied, and among the many epigraphists who have studied the inscription there remains no doubt as to the meaning, except of a word or two. There have been several reproductions of the inscription, and numerous translations, descriptions and treatises on the subject.[1] The following is the text with a translation. The *lacunæ*, which can be supplied with some certainty, are given in brackets; the others are represented by dots. Dots also separate the words.

1. ‧‧‧ ‧ הנקבה ‧ וזה ‧ היה ‧ דבר ‧ הנקבה ‧ בעוד ‧ [מניפם ‧ החצבם ‧ את]
2. הגרזן ‧ אש ‧ אל ‧ רעו ‧ ובעוד ‧ שלש ‧ אמת ‧ להנקֶ[ב ‧ נשמ]ע ‧ קל ‧ אש ‧ ק
3. רא ‧ אל ‧ רעו ‧ כי ‧ הית ‧ זדה ‧ בצר ‧ מימן ‧ ו ‧‧‧ ‧ אל ‧ ובים ‧ ה
4. נקבה ‧ הכו ‧ החצבם ‧ אש ‧ לקרת ‧ רעו ‧ גרזן ‧ על ‧ גרזן ‧ וילכו
5. המים ‧ מן ‧ המוצא ‧ אל ‧ הברכה ‧ במאתים ‧ ואלף ‧ אמה ‧ ומ ‧ [א]
6. ת ‧ אמה ‧ היה ‧ גבה ‧ הצר ‧ על ‧ ראש ‧ החצב[ם]

## TRANSLATION.

1. . . . the boring. And this was the matter of the boring: when yet [the hewers were lifting]

[1] First reports of the discovery in *P.E.F.Q.*, 1881, 141 ff., and *Z.D.P.V.*, 1880, 3, 54 f.: see further *P.E.F.Q.*, 1882, 122 ff. (Conder), 1890, 208 ff., 1897, 204 ff.; and *Z.D.P.V.*, 1881, 102 ff., 250 ff., 260 ff., 1882, 205 ff. Full accounts with facsimiles and translations, Guthe, *Z.D.M.G.*, 1882, 725 ff. Clermont-Ganneau, *Recueil d'Archéologie Orientale*, i., Pl. xvi.; Euting in Gesenius-Kautzsch, *Hebr. Grammar;* Driver, *Notes on the Text of the Bks. of Samuel*, xv.; Stade, *Gesch. des Volkes Israel*, i. 594 (1897); Lidzbarski, *Handbuch der nord-semitischen Epigraphik*, 1898; Socin, *Z.D.P.V.*, 1899, 61, and (separate ed.) *Die Siloahinschrift z. Gebrauch bei akad. Vorlesungen*, 1899; G. A. Cooke, *Text book of North Semitic Inscriptions* (without facsimile, but with alphabet), 1903. Cf. D. M. Ross, *The Cradle of Christianity*, 1893.

2. the pick, each towards his fellow, and when yet there were three cubits to be bored, [hear]d was the voice of each

3. calling to his fellow; for there was a fissure (?) from south even [to nor]th.[1]   And on the day of the

4. boring, the hewers struck, each to meet his fellow, pick against pick ; then went

5. the waters from the issue to the pool for two hundred and a thousand cubits, and a

6. hundred cubits was the height of the rock above the head of the hewer[s].

The word translated ' fissure (?) ' is of uncertain meaning ; but the meaning given is a possible one,[2] and suits the preceding phrase to which it is the explanation, ' the voice of the one party was heard calling to the other.' The point at which they met was, as we have seen, about half way up the north and south stretch of the tunnel. If just before meeting, and while still three cubits, or about four and a half feet, distant from each other, they broke into a north and south fissure, this, and only this, would enable them to speak to each other. They might hear the picks through four and a half feet of solid rock : hardly the human voice. The figures in the last two lines are evidently round numbers.[3]   On ' the hundred cubits of rock above the head of the hewers,' Col. Conder remarks : ' towards the north, the rock surface is 170 feet above the roof of the tunnel.'[4]

---

[1] Literally : ' from the right hand even [to the le]ft.

[2] זִדָּה has been suggested by Blake, *Journ.* of Amer. Orient. Soc. xxii. 1. (1901), 52 f., as if from זָנַד with the radical meaning 'narrow.'   G. A. Cooke translates ' split.'   Socin leaves the word untranslated.

[3] G. A. Cooke, p. 17.

[4] *P.E.F.Q.*, 1882, 127.

The water, then, of the Virgin's Spring was brought by this Tunnel to a Pool (Hebrew *bĕrekah*) represented to-day by the Birket Silwan, usually called the Upper Pool of Siloam. As it issues into this, spasmodically because still under the influence of the intermittent flow described above, the people give it the name of Spring; it is in Arabic the 'Ain Silwân. The Pool, according to Dr. Bliss, who was the first fully to excavate it, was originally about fifty feet square; and he assigns its construction to the Herodian period. Subsequently it was so built upon, that the present pool is an oblong of some fifty by fifteen feet. What the size was of the pool which preceded it in the days when the tunnel was constructed, we are unable to say.[1] Dr. Guthe had previously, in 1882,[2] reported the discovery of a pool to the north-east of the present Birket Silwân, with an inlet in its west wall; but this does not appear in Messrs. Bliss and Dickie's plans. Either it is only the north-east corner and part of the eastern wall of their Herodian pool, or else the remains, as Dr. Guthe himself takes it, of the pool which preceded the Herodian.[3] Against the latter alternative is the fact that the Tunnel does not run into it. An outlet from the Birket Silwân on the south—as well as one on the south wall of Guthe's pool[4]—admits the water

*(marginal note: 'Ain and Birket Silwan.)*

---

[1] *Excavations at Jerus.*, 1894-97, chs. iv. v. and p. 330. The Pool, as excavated by Dr. Bliss, was surrounded by an arcade (cf. the evidence of the Bordeaux Pilgrim). The western and the northern sides were in large parts hewn out of the solid rock, and Dr. Bliss thinks that the rudely hewn scarps indicate the sides of the pool, before it was built up in Roman times (p. 157).

[2] *Z.D.P.V.* v. 59 ff., 355 ff. with Tafel ii. Hauck's *Realencycl.* viii. 681, lines 55 ff., and 686, lines 45 ff. See also Kuemmel, *Materialien z. Topogr. des alt. Jerus.* 149.

[3] Hauck's *Realencycl.* viii. 681, lines 55 ff., and 686, lines 45 ff.; cf. Kuemmel, *Materialien z. Topogr. des alten Jerus.* 149, and Plan.

[4] *Z.D.P.V.* v. 131, with Tafel ii. and Kuemmel's Plan.

to a conduit which carries it, not into the Lower Pool of Siloam, but past this into the Ḳidron valley.

The so-called Lower Pool of Siloam, the Birket el-Ḥamrâ, lies to the south-east of the Birket Silwân, in the very mouth of the Tyropœon valley; about 150 feet by 110. This has never been thoroughly excavated; but occupies, in all probability, the site of an ancient reservoir, in which the surface waters of the Tyropœon, as well as those brought from the Virgin's Spring by the Ḳidron valley aqueduct, were stored for the irrigation of the gardens below. At present it is an open cesspool, receiving that part of the City's sewage which succeeds in reaching it down the Tyropœon. But in ancient times, as Dr. Bliss has shown, the great drain of this valley passed it on the west.

Birket el Ḥamrâ.

Down the Ḳidron valley, nearly 1000 feet from the Birket el-Ḥamrâ, lies the Bîr Eiyûb, or Well of Job (sometimes also called Nehemiah's Well, from an erroneous location of his Dragon Spring). This is a great well, 125 feet deep or 38·1 metres, the water in which has seldom been known to fail, and can be drawn upon all the year round.[1] From an overflow near this well,[2] the stream spoken of above breaks down the valley for a few days after the Latter Rains, and its appearance is taken as the token of a fruitful year. Whether we have

Bir Eiyûb.

[1] 'In the height of a particularly dry summer I have known of a hundred and twenty animals—donkeys, mules, and horses—being employed night and day carrying goatskins of water (two or three to each animal) up to Jerusalem. On an average every animal made four or five journeys within the twenty-four hours. In addition great quantities of water were taken locally—for Silwān and for the vegetable gardens near the well.'—Masterman, *Bibl. World*, 1902, 89.

[2] *P.E.F. Mem.*, 'Jerus.' 371.

in the Well only the gathering of the surface water or a true spring, and whether a spring existed here in ancient times, are questions which have been much discussed. Some take the Bîr Eiyûb not only to have been a real spring, but in early times at least the only one about Jerusalem.[1] It is true that the quality of the water is distinctly better than that of the Virgin's Spring, but this may be due to the further filtration of such supplies as reach it from the latter, and to additional percolations from the surface of the valleys, which meet above it. Is there besides a deep natural spring still undiscovered? Sir Charles Wilson, who descended and carefully examined the Well, answers in the negative. 'There can be no doubt,' he says, 'as to its not being a true spring. The bottom of the well is cemented so as to form a collecting basin, and it is quite apparent that the well has been deepened at least once, and possibly oftener, to obtain infiltration. When I went down there was hardly any water in the basin, and I could see water "weeping" into the shaft between the strata. The upper part of the well, in the rubbish, has been lined with masonry.'[2] Nevertheless we cannot altogether dismiss the possibility of a real spring in former times in this the lowest level of the district round Jerusalem, and a spot too where, as we have seen, the soft *meleki* strata suddenly come to an end.[3] The sites of such large wells are not chosen without there being some special attraction in them to the seekers for water. This attraction may have been the annual outburst of the stream in the immediate neighbourhood ; or it may have been a small more constant spring,

---

[1] Mommert, *Topogr. des alten Jerus.* i. 13 f.
[2] From a letter to the author.
[3] Above, p. 57.

which has now disappeared through the influence of the earthquakes, or whose presence has been masked by the building of the Well. The question is certainly not closed.[1] The underground conduits leading down the valley near the Well which were discovered by Sir Charles Warren are, as Sir Charles Wilson has written, 'almost certainly the drainage system of the ancient City,' with 'a series of tanks for the deposit of the solid matter, and steps by which they could be cleaned.'[2]

Some 585 yards (about 535 metres) south of the Bîr Eiyûb, by the junction of the Wady Yasûl with the W. en

'Ain el-Lôzeh.

Nâr, is the 'Ain el-Lôzeh, or Almond-tree spring. I have myself never seen it flow; and I believe that it does so only after heavy rain. Near is an ancient shaft, blocked with earth which is said to lead to a long subterranean channel hewn in the rock.[3]

Returning now to the Wâdy er-Rabâbi and its southern

Possibilities of Water in the W. er-Rabâbi.

portion, immediately about its junction with the Kidron valley, we find that there is here neither a spring, nor the name nor trace of a spring. But some 460 yards up from the mouth of the Wâdy we come, in the bed of it, upon the remains of an ancient rock-cut conduit, about 126 yards in length: whether to carry off the surface water, or water from a now vanished spring, it is impossible to say. Nor must we omit to notice the great accumulation of *débris* at the issue of the W. er-

---

[1] I had formerly suggested (*Expositor*, March 1903, 218) that we might expect a spring to issue on the east edge of the Kidron valley, for the Mount of Olives above this must receive an immense amount of water. But Sir Charles Wilson has rightly pointed out to me that the dip of the strata eastward contradicts this suggestion.

[2] From a letter to the author.

[3] *P.E.F. Mem.* iii. 372 f. ; Schick and Benzinger, *Z.D.P.V.* xviii. 150, with Schick's Map of the nearer surroundings of Jerusalem.

Rabâbi into the Ḳidron valley.[1] Relevant to our present subject of the hydrography are the questions whether this unusually large heap of rubbish may not be due to an earthquake, and whether it may not mask, on what is not an unlikely place for a spring to issue, some ancient spring now forgotten.

### 3. THE IDENTIFICATION OF THE SPRINGS.

Such are the essential details of the waters, and of the system of water supply, which are discoverable in the valley of the Ḳidron, and the mouths of Identification the Tyropœon and Hinnom. Our next duty of foregoing with Bible is to inquire whether any of them are identical names. with the Biblical sources, channels, or pools of water about Jerusalem, and in particular with the names Shiloaḥ, Giḥon, 'En-rogel, and the Dragon's Spring. In undertaking this inquiry we have, as before, to keep in mind the uncertainty introduced into the question by the earthquakes, one of the worst of which, as described by Josephus, affected especially this part of the environs of the City. We have seen that earthquakes may have seriously altered the subterranean drainage of this region as a whole; while it is still more possible that the deep *débris* cast here, a large part of which has not yet been excavated, may have choked or masked vents of the underground waters, which in ancient times were known and named.

Some facts, however, are clear, and we shall start with the most undoubted. The surface aqueduct, the short tunnel and shaft, and the long tunnel, all lead- Date of the ing from the Virgin's Spring, prove that when Tunnel. they were executed the Spring was already a considerable

[1] See above, p. 41 f.

source of living water. The characters of the inscription, describing the excavation of the Tunnel, are archaic, and the writing may be of any date before the Exile. There is a general agreement among scholars to assign it to the eighth century B.C., a period when great public works were executed by at least three kings, Uzziah, Jotham and Hezekiah. The Biblical evidence that Hezekiah was the author appears to me as conclusive as could be expected for so remote a date. According to the annalists of Judah, Hezekiah *made the pool and the conduit, and brought water into the City.*[1] In the time of the Chronicler, whatever be the date of his sources, the tradition was that this conduit and pool were the Tunnel and a Pool on the site of, or near to, the present Birket Silwân. No other conclusion seems possible from the Chronicler's words: *And he sealed the issue of the waters of Giḥon the upper, and directed them down westwards to the City of David;*[2] *he built an outer wall to the City of David, west of Giḥon, in the Naḥal, even up to the entry of the Fish Gate, and he surrounded the 'Ophel and made it,* the wall, *very high.*[3] Another passage, which we have already quoted, explains his purpose: *they sealed all the springs, and the Naḥal flowing through the midst of the land, saying, Why should the Kings of Assyria come and find much water?*[4] We have seen that in the Old Testament the *Naḥal* is always the Ḳidron valley, with its winter or storm brook. Ophel is universally identified with the ridge of the East Hill, at the eastern foot of which the Virgin's Spring issues. The 'City of David,' we shall see in the next chapter, stood upon Ophel. *An outer wall to the City of David, west of*

[1] I Ki. xx. 20.  [2] 2 Chron. xxxii. 30.
[3] 2 Chron. xxxiii. 14.  [4] 2 Chron. xxxii. 4.

*Giḥon*, would run along just the natural line for such a wall, to the west of and above the Virgin's Spring. The Spring lay, therefore, outside this wall, and Hezekiah's purpose to prevent besiegers from using it could be achieved only by the stoppage of its natural or artificial issue into the Ḳidron valley, and the conveyance of its waters to the pool in the Tyropœon by the Tunnel, the course of which is more or less exactly described by the words, *he directed the waters of Giḥon the upper, down westwards to the City of David.* The Tunnel, therefore, was made by Hezekiah, and at his date, the eighth century B.C., the present Virgin's Spring was in existence.[1]

But if the Tunnel was made by Hezekiah, and is so obviously intended to supersede both the surface aqueduct in the valley, traced by Messrs. Schick, Horn- The Shiloah stein and Masterman, and the shaft discovered —Siloam. by Sir Charles Warren, these must date from still earlier periods. The surface aqueduct ran to the mouth of the Tyropœon, either into a pool on the site of the Birket el Ḥamrà, or in order to feed, along with the surface waters of the Tyropœon itself, a number of channels for the irrigation of the gardens in the valley of the Ḳidron. Now we have contemporary evidence that in the reign of Ahaz, the immediate predecessor of Hezekiah, there was here a conduit, or system of conduits. In an oracle of that reign Isaiah says:[2] *forasmuch as this people despises*

---

[1] This opinion is now generally accepted. I need only quote the names of some of its supporters: Warren (*Recov. of Jerus.*, 238; cf. *P.E.F. Mem.*, 'Jerus.' 6, 94, by Warren and Conder), Robertson Smith (*Enc. Brit.*, 9th ed.), Sir Charles Wilson (*Water Supply of Jerus.*, 7, 'probably'), Socin. and Benzinger (*Baedeker*, 5th ed., 98, 'höchst wahrscheinlich'); Buhl (*G.A.P.* 138 ff.), Guthe (Hauck's *Realencycl.* viii. 681 f., where the identification is taken as 'a fixed point'). From the epigraphic side of the question, G. A. Cooke (*N. Sem. Inscr.* 16) and others.          [2] Isaiah viii. 6.

*the waters of the Shiloah, which flow gently and . . .*[1]
*therefore, lo, the Lord will bring up against them the waters
of the River*, the Euphrates. *The Shiloah*, or (according
to another ancient spelling) *Shilloah*,[2] is a passive form,
and means the *sent* or *conducted*.[3] No one doubts that
it applies to the water-system in or about the mouth of
the Tyropœon, where the name has always been at home.
In Josephus *Siloa* or *Siloam*, when used with the feminine
article,[4] is a copious spring of sweet water, obviously the
issue of water from the Tunnel into the Birket Silwân,
which in Arabic is still called 'Ain Silwân. But Josephus
also uses Siloa with the masculine article,[5] which has been
held to mean 'the district of Siloa';[6] and this wide sense
is that in which Dr. Guthe interprets Isaiah's *Shiloah*.
*The waters of the Shiloah which go softly* would accordingly mean, all the water artificially controlled and led
about the mouth of the Tyropœon, in order to irrigate the
gardens in the Ḳidron valley.[7] But whether we put this

[1] This clause is uncertain: see Cheyne in *S.B.O.T.* and Marti's commentary.

[2] So the *Cod. Babyl.*, the *Complutensian Bible*, and other early eds. This
reading is accepted by Baer, but not in Kittel's edition.

[3] In later Hebrew שֶׁלַח means *outpouring irrigation*, בֵּית הַשִּׁלָחִין *an
irrigated field*.

[4] ἡ Σιλωά so in Niese's text (the oblique cases), but some MSS. have
Σιλωάμ; v. *B.J.* iv. 2. Cf. vi. 1, ix. 4; vi. *B.J.* viii. 5. And ἡ Σιλωάμ v. *B.J.*
xii. 2.

[5] Μέχρι τοῦ Σιλωά (Niese: some MSS. have Σιλωάμ), ii. *B.J.* xvi. 2; vi.
*B.J.* vii. 2.

[6] Sc. χῶρος: cf. Guthe, *Z.D.P.V.* v. 359 ff. The masculine article is also
used in the N.T. with the form Σιλωάμ, Luke xiii. 4, John ix. 7. The form
Σειλωάμ or Σιλωάμ is that used in the LXX. of Isai. viii. 3, though some codd.
read Σιλωά.

[7] But of course, at the time Isaiah used it, the name would not cover the
Tunnel, which was made after this by Hezekiah. Buhl is therefore right
in taking the name as older than the Tunnel (*G.A.P.* 139, 139).

or a more particular meaning upon the name, the *Shiloah* implies the existence in the reign of Ahaz of a conduit, or conduits, inclusive of the surface-conduit from the Virgin's Spring to the mouth of the Tyropœon. This latter also suits *the conduit of the upper pool towards the highway of the fuller's field*,[1] mentioned in another passage of the same date; in that case *the upper pool* would be the basin of the Virgin's Fountain, to which, as we have seen, the Chronicler applies the epithet *upper*.[2] Yet this conduit of the upper pool on the highway of the fuller's field is described later on as the place where the envoy of Sennacherib met the representatives of Hezekiah; and on the ground that 'no general commanding an army would go down to the mouth of the Tyropœon valley, but would speak to them from some point on the plateau to the north,' Sir Charles Wilson holds that this conduit must be placed on the north of the City.[3] I appreciate the military reason, but it is not conclusive. The parley was possible in the valley beside what was still the principal part of the City; and it is hard to think of the *fuller's field* as anywhere but on this lowest level of the environs, where alone water abounded.[4] A gloss to one of the later oracles of Isaiah[5] records *a lower pool*, and *a reservoir*

[1] Isai. vii. 3.

[2] Stade, Marti, etc., identify *the upper pool* with the pool which Guthe (*Z.D.P.V.* v. 355 ff.) claims to have discovered a few feet to the N.E. of the Birket Silwân; but, as we have seen (above, p. 97), this may be only part of the wider ancient pool which extended on both sides of the present Birket Silwân, and was excavated by Bliss.

[3] In a letter to the author. Cf. Guthe in Hauck's *R.-E.* viii. 681.

[4] Note the cavern south of the Triple Gate described by Warren (*Rec. of Jerus.*, 306 ff.). He suggests it may have been a fuller's shop, and cites the tradition that St. James was thrown over the outer wall of the Temple enclosure, and that a fuller took the club with which he pressed the clothes and beat out the head of the Just One.    [5] xxii. 9b-11a.

*between the two walls for the waters of the old pool.* But
as these references are of uncertain date, and an intrusion
into their context, it is impossible to define their data.
Nehemiah mentions as immediately north of the Fountain
Gate (which lay immediately south of the mouth of the
Tyropœon, at the extreme south-east angle of the City),
*the pool of the Shelaḥ,*[1] that is, *aqueduct* or *irrigation.*
This must have been one of the two in the mouth of the
Tyropœon, probably the pool into which Hezekiah's
conduit led ; and the other *the king's pool,*[2] which he also
mentions there. He also gives *the made,* or *artificial, pool*[3]
to the north of *the pool of the Shelaḥ,* that is, nearer to the
Virgin's Spring.

Except that, as we have seen, it must be earlier than
Hezekiah's tunnel, the date of Warren's shaft, with the
portion of the tunnel leading from it to the
Virgin's Spring, is quite uncertain. Its purpose
was to enable the water to be drawn by buckets
to the summit of the rock above, at a position which was
probably that of the fortress Ṣion.[4] It has consequently
been assigned by some to David's or Solomon's time, by
others to that of the Jebusites, and in the latter case has
been taken to be the very *ṣinnôr* (E. V. *gutter* and *watercourse*), by which David urged his men to take the fortress.[5]
The text of this passage, and the meaning of *ṣinnôr* are,
however, too uncertain to confirm the latter suggestion ;
and the other more general date remains only a probable
conjecture.[6]

*Date of
Warren's
Shaft.*

---

[1] iii. 15 : but see Guthe, *Z.D.P.V.* v. 371 f.     [2] ii. 14.

[3] iii. 16.     [4] See below, ch. vi.

[5] 2 Sam. v. 8. צִנּוֹר used in Ps. xlii. 8, as a torrent or cataract, but in
N. Heb. as a watercourse or conduit.

[6] On the identification of Warren's shaft with the *ṣinnôr,* see Birch,

We have seen that in the Chronicler's time, about 300 B.C., the Virgin's Spring was known as *Gihôn the upper.* The name Gihon, derived from a verb meaning to *burst* or *bubble forth,* exactly suits the intermittent violent action of the Virgin's Spring, and may be compared with the Arabic El-Fûwarah, 'The Bubbler,' applied to the intermittent spring in the Wâdy Kelt.[1] That it is called *Gihon the upper* is, of course, due to the fact that, in the Chronicler's day, the water issuing from the other end of the tunnel would be known as *the lower Gihon.* And in fact the connection of Gihon with the Shiloah is from this time onwards a close one. The Targum gives *Shilloah* or *Shillôhā* as an equivalent for *Gihôn,*[2] and both D. Kimchi and Rashi take them as identical. It is difficult to understand how, even under the strong influence of tradition, earlier explorers were led to place Gihon in the west or north of the City,[3] when the Biblical evidence we have quoted, supported by later Jewish opinion, so definitely marks the Spring as on the east and in the Kidron valley; where now nearly all the leading authorities are agreed as to its identification with the Virgin's Spring.[4]

*(margin note: Gihon the Virgin's Spring.)*

---

P.E.F.Q., 1891, 80, and previous papers. Guthe has recently adhered to the view of a date in David's or the Jebusite period (Hauck's *Real-Enc.* viii. 682, line 11).

[1] גִּחוֹן from גִּיחַ *gîḥ*;—ôn being a common termination in place-names. The derivation by Chaplin (*P.E.F.Q.* 1890, 124) from גחן, *to creep,* is not probable etymologically, and the meaning, ' place one needs to creep through,' as due to the tunnel, is open to the objection, stated by Birch (*ibid.* 200) that the name, as we shall see, is older than the Tunnel.

[2] 1 Ki. i. 33, 38; Reland and De Vogüé adhered to the identification.

[3] See above, p. 83 f.

[4] Furrer in Schenkel's *B.L.* ii. 463 ; Conder, *P.E.F. Mem.,* 'Jerus.' 366 ; Chaplin, *P.E.F.Q.,* 1890, 124; Birch, *P.E.F.Q.,* 1889, 208; Robertson Smith,

There is, however, still earlier Biblical evidence for
Gihon. King David sent Solomon *down* to be crowned

Early
evidence for
Gihôn.

at Gihon, and after the ceremony was over the
company *came up* from Gihon to David.[1]  As
the king was in the ' City of David ' on Ophel,[2]
this is further proof, if it were needed, that Gihon lay in
the valley of the Kidron.  By David's time Gihon must
have been a sacred and therefore an ancient well.  We
have thus every reason to believe that it was the original
well of the City, whose position underneath the ridge of
Ophel determined the choice of this ridge as the site of
the earliest fortress.  Upon the heaped rubbish at the foot
of the now naked hill, and amid the squalid bustle which
prevails there to-day, one forgets that this was the scene
of Solomon's coronation.  But in that day the precipitous
rock with the fortress above it, the open cave with the
mysterious intermittent fountain, apparently directed by
an immediate supernatural agency, must have formed a
fitting theatre for the first coronation of an Israelite King
in Jerusalem.

We now turn to the other name for a spring in the
neighbourhood : 'En-rogel.  This is usually rendered *Ful-*

'En-rogel.

*ler's Spring* ; but *rogel* is not the Hebrew for
*fuller*, and a more probable meaning is offered

---

*Enc. Brit.* 9th ed. ; Stade, *Gesch.* i. 294 ; Socin and Benzinger in *Baedeker*,
5th ed. 98 ; Buhl, *G.A.P.* 93, etc. ; Guthe, Hauck's *R.-E.* viii. (1900) 670 ;
Wilson, *Water Supply, etc.*, 1902, 7 ; the author's paper, *Expositor*, March
1903, 224 ; Masterman, *Bibl. World*, 1905, 99.  Of course both Wilson
and Guthe reached this conclusion much earlier than the date of their statements referred to above.

[1] See below, p. 110.

[2] 1 Ki. i. 33, 38, 45; בְּגִחוֹן.  The Heb. preposition means *in*, but that,
with the name of a well, it may be used for *beside* is seen from 1 Sam. xxix. 1:
the Israelites pitched בָּעַיִן, *beside the fountain.*

by the Syriac, *rogâlo*, 'current' or 'stream.'[1] 'En-rogel was either the Virgin's Spring or the Bîr Eiyûb, or some other spring in the Ḳidron valley now lost. The Biblical data are these. When David fled before Absalom, Jonathan and Ahimaaz stayed in 'En-rogel, out of sight of the City, to obtain news of the progress of the revolt.[2] When Adonijah set himself up as David's successor, on the same day as Solomon was crowned, *he sacrificed sheep, oxen, and fatlings by the stone of the Zoheleth, which is beside 'En-rogel*.[3] And the Priestly Code mentions 'En-rogel as the southmost point of the border between Judah and Benjamin, which thence turned north up *the valley of Hinnom to the shoulder of the Jebusite*.[4] On these data some have identified 'En-rogel with Gihon and the Virgin's Spring, because the latter is the only known spring now in the valley, or because the name Zoheleth is 'still attached to the rocky ascent to the village of Silwân,'[5] opposite the spring; or because the Spring cannot be seen from the City, where Absalom was in power.[6] But the identification of the Virgin's Spring, which we have seen to be Gihon, is excluded by the narrative of Solomon's coronation there, from which the simultaneous feast of Adonijah at the stone Zoheleth was at such a distance that Adonijah's company could not see Solo-

---

[1] Levy, *Chald. Wörterbuch*, ii. 406. We need not ask, therefore, whether 'En-rogel had any thing to do with the *field of the fuller* (כֹּבֵס) which must have lain outside the mouth of the Tyropœon. See above, p. 105.

[2] 2 Sam. xvii. 17.     [3] 1 Ki. i. 9.

[4] Josh. xv. 7, cf. xviii. 16. The issues of the border were at 'En-rogel, that is to say, its furthest point in the southerly direction.

[5] In the form Zeḥweileh ; Cl.-Ganneau in *P.E.F. Mem.*, 'Jerus.' 293.

[6] Supporters of the identification of the Virgin's Spring with 'En-rogel are Cl.-Ganneau, as above, Wilson ('possibly'), *Water-Supply, etc.*, 6 and elsewhere ; Warren in Hastings' *D.B.* art. 'Hinnom.'

mon's, but only heard the noise of their jubilant return to the City; nor did they learn what had taken place at Gihon till messengers came and told them.[1]　Besides, the position assigned by the Priestly Code to 'En-rogel must either be at the mouth of the valley of Hinnom or to the south of that; and with this agrees the statement of Josephus, that the spring near which Adonijah feasted lay in the king's paradise or garden.[2]　The Zoheleth, too, was *a stone*, that is, probably, a separate rock or boulder, not such a rocky incline as stands opposite the Virgin's Spring on the ascent to Silwan; and if the name Zehweileh is to be brought into the argument, Dr. Masterman informs me that, though always pointed out by the villagers of Silwân as one definite smooth surface of rock, just below their houses, it appears to cover the 'long ridge running all the way on a definite line of strata, even as far as the Bîr Eiyûb.'[3]　Besides, if the name is the same, it has drifted up the valley.　On all these grounds, then, we are justified in concluding that 'En-rogel was not the Virgin's Spring, but lay some way off down the valley, and is either represented by the Bîr Eiyûb, which, as we have seen, may represent an ancient spring,[4] or was a fountain now lost. It is possible to account for the disappearance of 'En-rogel, *the spring of the current* or *stream*, and the presence in its place of the deep well Bîr Eiyûb, by such an earthquake and displacement of the hill-side, as Josephus describes having taken place at 'En-rogel.　But if 'En-rogel was elsewhere in the neighbourhood, the same causes may now mask its true position; and send its waters trickling

[1] 1 Ki. i. 41-46.

[2] vii. *Ant.* xiv. 4.　On the other hand, in ix. *Ant.* x. 4, Josephus seems to place Eroge or 'En-rogel to the east, not the south, of the City: this, however, is not certain.　　　　[3] From a letter.　　　　[4] See above, p. 100.

through the *débris* to feed the Bîr Eiyûb and the stream which in spring breaks out close by.[1] The 'Ain el-Lôzeh seems rather far off to be identified with 'En-rogel.

It is possible that 'En-rogel is not always used in the Old Testament as the name of a spring. While waiting for information from the City to carry to David, Jonathan and Ahimaaz, anxious as they were to escape the notice of the people of Jerusalem, 'En-rogel possibly also a village. would hardly choose so public a place as a frequented Spring.[2] A suburban village would better suit their purpose, and the 'En-rogel of their story may well be such a village standing on the eastern bank of the Ḳidron valley, either on the site of the present Silwân or further to the south. It may also be a village which is intended by 'En-rogel in the delimitation of the frontier between Judah and Benjamin.[3]

The question of Nehemiah's Spring of the Dragon we have already sufficiently discussed.[4] Nehemiah went towards it after coming out of the *Gate of the* The Dragon *Gai* or *Hollow,* that is the Gai ben Hinnom, the Spring. present Wâdy er-Rabàbi;[5] and before he reached the Dung Gate towards the end of the Ravine. The spring

---

[1] Among those who, on the Biblical data, place 'En-rogel at or near the Bir Eiyûb, are Robinson, Tobler, Thomson, Mommert, Socin and Benzinger ('probably'). Buhl, p. 94, agrees that the Bîr Eiyûb suits the Biblical evidence for 'En-rogel, and Guthe (671) says the latter was evidently near the conjunction of the Ḳidron and Hinnom valleys. The author feels that the additional arguments given above remove the objections candidly felt by some of the above writers to this the only location for 'En-rogel which suits the Biblical data.  [2] 2. Sam. xvii. 17.

[3] Josh. xv. 7, xviii. 16.

[4] See above, p. 74. The Spring of the Dragon עֵין הַתַּנִּין. The LXX. has Well of the Figs, תְּאֵנִים, but the Hebrew text is confirmed by Lucian: τοῦ δράκοντος.  [5] See below, p. 175 f.

was, therefore, in the Ravine, either some way up it, and if so, perhaps connected with the detached length of watercourse we have seen there, or more probably near the mouth, where the considerable *débris* may now easily mask it.[1]

### 4. THE RESERVOIRS AND AQUEDUCTS.

I turn now from the real and reputed Springs of Jerusalem to the extraordinary artificial provision which The artificial the City shows for collecting the rain and surwater-supplies. face water, and for bringing in supplies from a distance. Nothing of the ancient building has been so well preserved as the reservoirs, cisterns and conduits; among all the remains none are so impressive as these vast and intricate monuments from every stage of the history. They prove how insufficient for the needs of the population the few springs were found to be; and they, and not the springs, even when these waters were brought by conduits within the City, explain what several ancient writers have reported, that Jerusalem was a well-watered fortress within surroundings arid and waterless.

The first of these monuments which strike the eye of the visitor are the great tanks round and within the City. The Great For number and size the like of them, all either Surface now or once above ground, are to be seen in Tanks. no other city of Palestine. 'It must be remembered,' writes Sir Charles Wilson,[2] 'that in time of war the water in all the collecting pools outside could be

---

[1] See above, p. 100 f. Guthe (Hauck's *R.-E.* viii. 672) says: 'Either it is now sealed up, or is to be identified with Giḥon or 'En-rogel.' The latter alternative is impossible on Nehemiah's data.

[2] In a letter to the author.

run into reservoirs within the walls: save that in the Birket es-Sultân, which could be run to waste down the valley.' The difficulty about them is that we are so little able to fix the dates of their construction.

We may begin with the Birket es-Sultân in the Wâdy er-Rabâbi, beneath the western city-wall and the road to Bethlehem, which crosses the Wady by the dam on the south of the Pool. This 'Pool of the Sultân' is 555 feet N. to S. by 220 E. to W. (just over 169 metres by 67). The northern wall is ruined. Here the depth was some 36 feet (nearly 11 m.), but the bed declines, partly with the natural slope of the valley and partly by an excavation in the rock at the southern end, to a depth of over 42·5 feet (13 m.). The pool is named either from the fact that it is the 'great' or 'grand pool,'[1] or from its reconstruction by the Sultân Sŭleiman ibn Selim, in the middle of the 16th century. By the Crusaders it was called Germanus, after the Frank Knight who recovered the Bîr Eiyûb and is said to have built the Pool in 1176 A.D.[2] A Pool, however, may have existed here from an early Jewish period. Sir Charles Wilson writes: 'I think it is ancient, or that there was a pool in the same position to receive surplus water from the Low Level Aqueduct, which seems to be the oldest conduit bringing water from a distance.'[3]

*1. The Sultân's Pool.*

To the north-west of this, in the Wâdy el-Mês, the head of the W. er-Rabâbi, is the Birket Mâmilla. Lying from east to west, it is 292 feet (89 m.) long by 193 (almost 59 m.) broad, and 19·5 (6) m. deep.

*2. The Pool Mamilla.*

---

[1] Masterman.

[2] Röhricht, *Gesch. d. Königr. Jerus.* 415; *Regesta Regni Hieros.* 133, 143, 147.

[3] In a letter to the author. Cf. Benzinger, in *Baedeker*, 5th ed. 25, 103.

Its age and origin are unknown.  It has been identified with *the upper pool* of the Book of Isaiah,[1] but for this it seems too far from the city walls ; and in all probability *the fuller's field* mentioned in connection with *the upper pool* lay in the Kidron valley.[2]  Equally uncertain is the identification of the Mamilla Pool with the Serpent's Pool of Josephus.[3]  Sir Charles Wilson, who judges this Pool to be also old,[4] supports the identification.[5]  Others have suggested the Beth Memel of the Talmud.[6]

In the east wall of the Mamilla Pool is an outlet from which a conduit leads south-eastward by the Jaffa Gate[7] to a great Pool lying in the cross valley, between the West and South-west Hills, and known to-day as the Birket Ḥammâm el-Baṭ-

*3. Pool of the Patriarch's Bath.*

rak, or Pool of the Patriarch's Bath.  It is about 240 feet long from north to south, 144 broad, and from 19 to 24 feet deep (73 by 44 by 6 to 7½ metres).  The porous rock of the bed has been levelled and covered with a cement of small stones and lime.  The eastern wall, against which, as the lower side of the pool, the chief weight of the water rests, has been proved by Dr. Schick's observations to be especially massive.[8]  There are some indications that the Pool may have formerly extended further to the north.  Some 60 feet in this direction of it, a cement was

---

[1] vii. 3 ; xxxvi. 2 (2 Ki. xviii. 17).

[2] See above, p. 105.

[3] v. *B.J.* iii. 2 : Titus levelled 'all the place from Scopus to Herod's monuments which adjoin the Pool called that of the Serpents,' τῇ τῶν ὄφεων ἐπικαλουμένῃ κολυμβήθρᾳ.

[4] In a letter to the author. [5] *Water Supply*, etc., 9.

[6] 'Erūbīn,' 51 b, 'Sanhedrin' 24 a ; cf. 'Bereshith Rabba,' li. : cited by Kuemmel, *Materialien z. Topogr. des alt. Jerus.* 152.

[7] Warren, *Recovery of Jerus.* 237.

[8] *Z.D.P.V.*, 1885, 270 ; 1891, 49 ; *P.E.F.Q.*, 1891, 276 f. with plan ; 1897, 107.

uncovered of the same character as that on the bottom of
the Pool, and beyond it a massive wall, nearly 11 feet
thick, in which the squared stones resemble some of apparently the most ancient in the Ḥaram wall.  For these
reasons a high antiquity has been ascribed to the Pool.  It
is tolerably certain that it is identical with the Amygdalon
Pool or Pool of the Towers, mentioned by Josephus[1] as
the scene of the labours of the Tenth Legion under
Titus.  As their occupation took place after Titus had
captured the Second Wall, the latter apparently ran outside
the Pool; but to this we shall return.  By calling the pool
Hezekiah's Pool, recent explorers have assigned it to his
reign: *he made the pool and the conduit, and brought water
within the City.*[2]  They have even identified with it the *lower
pool* of the Book of Isaiah in distinction from the *upper pool,*
the Pool Mamilla.[3]  But we have seen reason to place
Hezekiah's Pool and Conduit in the Ḳidron Valley; and
there is no evidence to carry back the Pool of the Patriarch's Bath to so remote a period.

In this north-western part of the City, outside the course
of the First Wall, other tanks have been discovered by
excavation, or are recorded in documents.  To 4, 5, 6. Three
the east of the Pool of the Patriarch's Bath, or other Tanks
lower down the same branch valley south of in Upper
the Muristan, lies an old tank about 130 feet from east to
west, and 50 north and south (about 40 by 15 metres).
To the north-east of it lies another, which is, at least, 130
feet north and south, by 15 east and west.  In the twelfth
century there appears to have been a large pool near the

[1] v. *B.J.* xi. 4: κολυμβήθραν Ἀμύγδαλον, that is ברכת המגדלין.  See
*P.E.F. Mem.,* 'Jerus.' 8.
[2] 2 Ki. xx. 20.     [3] Isai. vii. 3, xxxvi. 2, xxii. 9.

head of the Tyropœon valley. A charter of 1177 names it the Lacus Legerii;[1] and in ancient Arab title-deeds, the vicinity is called Ḥaret el-Birkeh, the 'Quarter of the Pool.'[2] No trace of it has been discovered. Sir Charles Wilson suggests that it fed the rock-hewn conduit on the East Hill, which 'may have been *the conduit of the upper pool.*'

North of the Temple Area, on the line of the subsidiary valley that in this quarter ran down to the Ḳidron, are other reservoirs. The so-called Twin-Pools, closely adjoining the north-west corner of Antonia, lie side by side. The longer, to the west, is 165 feet by 20 (just over 50 metres by 6), the shorter is 127 feet by 20 (nearly 39 metres by 6). They are fed by the conduit from the north, which has been traced to beyond the present wall, just opposite the west end of the knoll Ed-hemiye. They are covered by arches of unknown date, but M. Clermont-Ganneau identifies them with the Pool Strouthion, over against the middle of which Josephus says that the fifth legion, under Titus, raised a ramp against Antonia,[3] and thinks that they were roofed over during the period of Aelia Capitolina. Some have taken them to be the Twin Pools, which Eusebius, Jerome, and the Bordeaux Pilgrim identified with Bethesda.[4] Dr. Masterman thinks it probable that they did not exist until after the destruction of the City by Titus, 'for they are made inside the great moat of the fortress Antonia.'[5]

*7. The Twin-Pools.*

---

[1] Röhricht, *Reg. Regni Hieros.* No. 543 p. 144. But see *Z.D.P.V.* i. 96.
[2] Cl.-Ganneau (who was the first to point out the reference); Wilson, *Water Supply*, 8, 11.
[3] v. *B.J.* xi. 4: τῆς Στρουθίου καλουμένης κολυμβήθρας.
[4] *P.E.F. Mem.*, 'Jerus.' 209 ff., 263 f. with plan.
[5] *Bibl. World*, 1905, 96.

East from these, and against the eastern wall of the City and the north side of the Ḥaram, lies the Birket Isra'il or Isra'in, the Pool of Israel: a large open reservoir, 360 feet from east to west, by 126 from north to south (about 110 metres by 38). It has long been dry and has filled up with rubbish, the present level of which is about 69 feet (21 metres) below that of the Ḥaram area. As in the case of the Pool of the Patriarch's Bath, the eastern wall, the lower courses of which form the continuation of the Ḥaram wall, is a massive dam some 46 feet (14 metres) in thickness. Two outlets gave passage to the waters into the Ḳidron valley. Sir Charles Warren, who explored the walls, describes the arrangements for the regulation of the outflow and the alterations upon the original structure.[1] The Pool has a double bottom, the lower of small stones in mortar, the upper of a hard cement. The masonry of the thick dam, like that adjoining in the north-east corner of the Ḥaram, appears to be from the Roman period, to which also Antonia belongs. Josephus does not seem even to allude to such a Pool, which would be strange if this existed at the time of the siege of Titus; and yet it is impossible to assign to it an origin subsequent to this, before the alterations on the original structure which Sir Charles Warren reports as Byzantine. Messrs. Socin and Benzinger do not hesitate to carry it back to the pre-exilic Jewish period.[2] It was identified by pilgrims with the Sheep-pool of John's Gospel,[3] and from the twelfth century

8. Pool of Israel.

---

[1] *Recovery of Jerus.* 163 ff.; *P.E.F. Mem.*, 'Jerus.' 122 ff.; Masterman, *Bibl. World*, 1905, 94; Kuemmel, *Materialien z. alt. Topogr. Jerus.* 114 ff., 150 f.

[2] *Baedeker*, 5th ed., 25; also Kuemmel, *Materialien*, etc., 151.

[3] John v. 2, if indeed Sheep-pool be meant here.

with Bethesda, but, as Dr. Masterman observes, there is no evidence of arcades around it.

North of this, and on the west side of the Church of St. Anne, beneath vaults on which rest the remains of 9. Twin Pools probably two Churches, is a pool cut out of at St. Anne's. the rock on at least two sides, 55 feet long and 12½ broad (almost 17 metres by 3.8), with another beside it.[1] No trace of a spring has been found or an aqueduct: the water, which gathers sometimes to the depth of 20 feet, is immediately drawn from the surface. There can be no doubt that we have here the twin pools which, from the time of Eusebius[2] at least till the end of the sixth century, were identified with the Pool of Bethesda; but from that to the pool actually intended by S. John is, as we shall find, a far cry indeed.[3]

A little to the east of this, but outside the City wall, is the Birket Ḥammam Sitti Maryam, the Pool of the Bath 10. Pool of of our Lady Mary; 93 feet by 75, and 13 the Virgin. deep (28.3, 23, and 4 metres). It is 'quite modern, and made in the rubbish':[4] yet old enough to have attracted to itself, besides its usual name, several others of equal value: Pool of the Tribes, Dragon-well, and Hezekiah's Cistern: a remarkable proof of how quickly absolutely false traditions spring up from this teeming soil.

In his excavations upon Ophel, Dr. Guthe discovered on the back of the ridge two small tanks, one 11, 12. Two south-west of the Virgin's Spring, measuring Tanks on Ophel. about 66 feet by 10 (20 by 3 metres), and the other, lower down near Siloam, 50 feet by 16 (about

---

[1] *P.E.F.Q.*, 1888, 117 ff. ; *Z.D.P.V.* xi. 178 ff.   [2] *Onom. Sacr.* βηθεσδα.
[3] See below, chapter on the Gospels.   [4] Sir Charles Wilson in a letter.

15 by 4.9 metres).[1]  It is natural that in this older and narrower part of the City, the tanks should be smaller than the others we have surveyed, which had larger areas to draw from, and probably belonged to a later age.

Of the real and reputed pools in the mouth of the Tyropœon valley and in the Ḳidron valley, I have written sufficiently above.[2]  The Upper and Lower Pools of Siloam, the Birket Silwan and the Birket el-Ḥamrā, are the only two in existence on the surface to-day, and no doubt represent pools in the same position in the time of Hezekiah and earlier.  But there were other pools in connection with the same water system or Shiloah : and probably, as we have seen, one near the Virgin's Spring itself.  But the whole valley region here, on which rubbish has so deeply gathered, requires further excavation. 13, 14. Upper and Lower Pools of Siloam.

Besides all these open, or once open, reservoirs within or immediately round the City, two others have been discovered at some distance from the northern wall.  One is in the Wâdy ej-Jôz, near the Nablus road,[3] where a pool still forms in winter.  This 'is part of an old pool once connected with the water supply of the City.'[4]  The other one lies in the neighbourhood, and is hewn entirely in the rock.[5] 15, 16. Two Pools to the North of the City.

Next to the open tanks of Jerusalem must be mentioned the equally remarkable series of reservoirs under the Temple Area.  Of these some thirty-six or thirty-seven are known, and have been surveyed.  Full lists and descriptions of them will be found The Temple Cisterns.

[1] *Z.D.P.V.* v. 334 f. ; see Tafel viii.
[2] Pages 97, 98, 105, 106.
[3] *P.E.F.Q.*, 1892, 9 ff.
[4] Sir Charles Wilson in a letter to the author.
[5] *P.E.F.Q.*, 1892, 289.

in the under-mentioned works.[1]   Here we may confine
ourselves to their general characteristics and outstanding
features.   They may be distinguished into the smaller
surface pits arched over, and probably not all originally
cisterns; and the great deep basins hollowed out of the
lower-lying *meleki* rock,[2] 30, 40, 50, and 60 feet deep (one
of them, 'the Great Sea,' with a capacity of two million
gallons) carefully cemented; their roofs of the harder
upper *mizzeh* rock, occasionally supported by heavy piers
of masonry; with channels of communication, passages
for inspection, and conduits for draining the water at
different levels.[3]   Sir Charles Wilson has noted that none
of these larger basins are found north of the Dome of the
Rock.[4]   Their enormous capacity was fed by the great
aqueduct from Bethlehem.   When they were full, one can
understand how even a very large garrison could face a
siege without fear of a famine of water, while their besiegers suffered in the waterless environs.

Beneath the rest of the City there are some public
reservoirs, one of which, the Ḥammâm esh-Shefā, was
The Ḥammâm once perhaps a surface basin, whose walls, as
esh-Shefā.   the rubbish rose through various generations,
were heightened yard by yard, and finally roofed over.
'There is no trace,' writes Sir Charles Wilson, 'of a pool
or cistern in the Ḥammâm esh-Shefā shaft and gallery.
There is only a small cemented basin in which the water
collects.   Most of the water is certainly derived from
surface drainage, that is, water percolating through the

---

[1] *Recovery of Jerus.* 204 ff.; *P.E.F. Mem.*, 'Jerus.' 217 ff., with plan,
(Conder); *P.E.F.Q.*, 1880, with plans; Schick, *Stiftshütte u. Tempel*, 292
ff. (not seen); and a clear and detailed catalogue founded on the foregoing in
Kuemmel's *Materialien*, etc., 153 ff.
[2] See above, p. 55.   [3] *P.E.F. Mem.* 162, 165.   [4] *Recovery of Jerus.* 17.

rubbish, but some may possibly be derived from a small spring in the valley.'[1]   Other larger cisterns exist in Antonia, and to the east of the Church of the Sepulchre; and two were examined by Dr. Schick outside the Damascus Gate.[2]

Even more characteristic of Jerusalem than all these more or less public works, are the innumerable domestic cisterns.  The modern excavator may be said to come upon them everywhere in the living rock, or in the rubbish of all possible ages.  Upon Ophel, the site of the primitive City, Dr. Guthe uncovered a great number.[3]  To the north of the City the Survey Plan is dotted with the name.[4]  To-day virtually all the houses have cisterns, fed from the rain which falls on the vaulted roofs or trickles through their surroundings.[5]  In the new town, to the north and north-west, no house of any size is built without one or more.  A hotel-keeper in that quarter told me during the drought of 1901, that he had water stored sufficient for all his purposes for three years!  The cisterns of Jerusalem are of various kinds. Four of these have been distinguished by Sir Charles Wilson and Sir Charles Warren: the flagon or bottle-like cisterns, with a wide body in the soft *meleki* rock, but with narrow necks in the harder upper *mizzeh*; cavities hewn

*Domestic Cisterns.*

[1] In a letter to the author.  But see above, p. 84.
[2] *P.E.F.Q.*, 1890, 11 f., with plan.
[3] *Z.D.P.V.* v. 336, with Tafel viii.
[4] Cf. Schick's plan *P.E.F.Q.*, 1890, opposite p. 9, and Schick's Map of the nearer environs of the City, *Z.D.P.V.*  See below, Bk. ii. ch. iii., on the City Lands.  For cisterns on S.W. Hill see Schick, *Z.D.P.V.* viii. 42 ff.
[5] That in earlier times the roofs were not all, at least, of stone, is proved by the discovery during an excavation in the Tyropœon of one of the stone rollers commonly used in Palestine for keeping hard and close the clay-covered timber roofs.  *P.E.F. Mem.* 182 f.

in the rock, of irregular form, with natural roofs and man-
holes through them ; shallower basins in the rock covered
by vaulted masonry ; and pits built in the rubbish.[1]

Dating as they do from all periods of the history—repeated, altered, and replacing each other on different
levels of the gradually rising surface of the
city—these innumerable cisterns, public and
private, prove very distinctly that the people
of Jerusalem have always depended for their water, *in the
main*, upon the collection and storage of the rains and
the surface percolations.   Their springs, as we have seen,
were and could only be few, hardly more than two or
three in number.   These sprang besides on the lowest step
of the city's rapidly descending site, and were liable to
be tainted, as the Virgin's Spring is to-day, with sewage
from the town above them.   Hence the dependence of the
inhabitants upon the rain itself, and the carefulness with
which they gathered its direct supplies.

*Significance of the Cisterns.*

But even these, in addition to the springs, proved insufficient as the population increased, and water had to
be introduced into the city from other sources.
If we take a circle with a radius of ten miles
(about sixteen kilometres) from Jerusalem as
a centre, we find, besides many weak or inconstant
springs, several that are both copious and steady.   We
may pass over such as the 'Ain el-Muhandis and the
'Ain el-Ḥôḍ on the east of, the 'Ain el-Mudawara and
'Ain es-Ṣûwân on the north of, the Mount of Olives, the
'Ain er-Rawâs due west of the city, the springs about
Welej, the 'Ain Yalô and the 'Ain el-Ḥaniyeh by the
railway in the Wâdy of the latter name—for these are

*Water Supplies at a Distance.*

---

[1] *Recovery of Jerus.* 23.

all unsuitable either from their size or the level at which they stand. And in this western direction, there is no use crossing the Wâdy Ḳuloniyeh to the springs on its other side. The water of the springs at Liftâ, 'Ain Kârim and Bittîr is often carried into Jerusalem in skins on the backs of donkeys; but the springs themselves lie too low to be tapped by aqueducts to the City. Perhaps the most remarkable fountain in the neighbourhood of Jerusalem is the 'Ain Fârah in the Wâdy of that name, about five and a half miles (nine kilometres) to the north-east of the City. Here a considerable stream of pure water bursts from the rocks; but the source is several hundred feet below the level of the City.[1] At ej-Jib, the Biblical Gibeon, there are eight springs, some of them large, and a great ancient reservoir. The place is only five and a half miles (or nine kilometres) from Jerusalem, but the difference of level—the village itself stands 2533 feet (772 metres) above the sea—does not seem to have been great enough, or the intervening difficulties were too great, for the construction of an aqueduct.

On this side of the City there remains the good spring at el-Bîreh, the ancient Be'eroth, eight and a half miles (nearly fourteen kilometres) north of the City, and 2820 feet (about 860 metres) above the sea. It has been supposed that an aqueduct once led from this into the north of Jerusalem. There are cuttings in the rock here and there along the ancient road between them; there is the old reservoir in the Wâdy ej-Jôz, and aqueducts have been traced upwards out of the City beyond the north wall. All this

*Possible Aqueduct from the North.*

[1] One is sorry to hear of buildings recently erected at this beautiful spring in the desert of Benjamin.

makes plausible the hypothesis of an aqueduct from el-Bîreh, or possibly, if the levels suit (but of this I am ignorant), one from ej-Jîb. Yet, as Sir Charles Wilson has pointed out to me,[1] 'some traces of a work of such magnitude would surely have been noticed before; one finds many cuttings like aqueducts'; and the reservoir in W. ej-Jôz and the underground aqueducts coming up under the north wall may have been only for the gathering and direction of the surface waters.

From this uncertainty on the north of the City we turn to the two very certain and considerable aqueducts which

Springs in the Wâdies 'Artâs, Bîâr, and 'Arrûb. reach it from the south; and first we consider the groups of springs which feed them. About six and a half miles (nearly eleven kilometres) south-west of Jerusalem, and nearly two miles from Bethlehem, lies the small Wâdy 'Artâs, distinguished by the three great reservoirs known as Solomon's Pools, 2616 feet (797 metres) above the sea. About these there spring five good sources of water: furthest west and close to the present Hebron road, the 'Ain Ṣaleḥ, known for the last three centuries as *the Sealed Fountain*,[2] near it an unnamed spring, in the lowest reservoir the 'Ain Farûjeh,[3] on the slope to the south-west the 'Ain 'Aṭân, and further east the 'Ain 'Artâs, by the village of the same name. A mile and a half south of the Pools, in the Wâdy el-Bîâr on the *old* Hebron road, is the 'Ain el-Maghârah, to the south-east of it high up the 'Ain Faghûr,[4] and a mile and a half further south, but in the same Wâdy, the 'Ain ed-Derej. Two miles further south or nearly twelve from Jerusalem, in the Wâdy 'Arrûb, there is another remarkable group of

---

[1] In a letter, 1903.  [2] Song of Sol. iv. 12.
[3] So Baedeker, 129.  [4] The Phagir of the Greek version of Josh. xv. 29.

springs, the Ras el-'Ain or Fountainhead, the 'Ain el 'Arrûb and others ; with a reservoir, the Birket el-'Arrûb : all about 2740 feet (835 metres) above the sea. All of these clear, and most of them copious, springs, were in ancient times built in and connected by conduits with the two great aqueducts which we have now to consider, and which are known respectively as the Low and the High Level Aqueducts.

The Low Level Aqueduct has been wholly preserved, and after several alterations, ancient and recent, still carries water from Solomon's Pools to the Temple Area. But before we follow this aqueduct, it is necessary to speak of a later one which was formed from the springs in the Wâdy 'Arrûb in order to increase the supply for Solomon's Pools. Leaving the reservoir in the Wâdy 'Arrûb, this aqueduct runs southeast, and then east on the left bank of the Wâdy, turning at last north up the Wâdy Menje, and so across the Biḳ-'at Teḳua', and round the various hills and Wâdy banks to the north on countless curves, till at last it issues into the middle pool of the three called Solomon's.[1] This extraordinary channel covers the direct distance of a little over five miles (8.3 kilom.) in a winding course of something over twenty-five miles (over 40 kilom.). The fall is approximately from 2740 feet in the W. 'Arrûb to 2600 feet at the middle Solomon's Pool ; 140 feet or nearly forty-three metres. Starting from the lowest Pool, the Low Level Aqueduct receives almost immediately, by a conduit, the water of the 'Ain 'Aṭàn, and

*The Low Level Aqueduct.*

---

[1] This may be easily followed on the *large P.E.F. Map*, Sh. xxi., or on Schick and Benzinger's Map of the ' Weitere Umgebung von Jerusalem,' *Z.D.P.V.* xix. 1896.

proceeds down the bed of the Wâdy till it has passed 'Artâs. Then it bends northwards, and piercing the hill of Bethlehem by a tunnel encompasses in many a curve the hill on which Ṣûr Bâhir lies. Then passing through a second tunnel[1] on the west of Râs el Maḳâbir, it winds round the Jebul Deir Abû Ṭôr, and so along the right bank of the Wâdy er-Rabâbi to above the Sultan's Pool, where on arches[2] it crosses the Wâdy about the 2409 contour.[3] From this it bends south and runs round the South-west Hill for the most part in a rock-cut channel. The course is outside the ancient City wall till it has passed the south-west angle of this. At 147 feet east of the angle, 26 feet east of his Tower II., Dr. Bliss found that the smooth-faced masonry of the wall had been broken to effect the entrance of the aqueduct, and then repaired.[4] But before the conduit enters the ancient City, he discovered, running above and more or less parallel to it, an older aqueduct hewn wholly in the rock, which sharply bends into the ancient City immediately under Tower II.,[5] and continues north-east on a line previously unearthed by Sir Charles Warren,[6] to a great tower round which it curiously twists to avoid either the tower itself or the rock chambers over which this is built. Further on Sir Charles Warren 'found it to be crossed and used by the later Lower Level Aqueduct; the two follow parallel courses for a long distance.'[7] Dr. Bliss has lucidly stated

---

[1] Recently turned into a tank in connection with the new water-works.— Wilson, *Water Supply*, etc., 3, 9.

[2] *Recovery of Jerusalem*, 23.

[3] On the Ordnance Survey Map; between the 732 and 735 metre contours on Kuemmel's Map.

[4] *Excav. at Jerus.* 24.    [5] *Id.* 54.    [6] *Ibid.* and *Recov. of Jerus.* 233.

[7] *Excav. at Jerus.* 56.

the different dates, from Solomon to Pontius Pilate, which the curious relations of this aqueduct to the tower and rock chambers suggest,[1] but no certain conclusion is possible on the data. The anterior puzzle remains, why the aqueduct was driven so far north as to encounter the Great Tower and the chambers. It touches the 2,429 contour line at Tower II., and returns to that after its excursion to, and singular embrace of, the Great Tower. Only this seems clear, that the aqueduct in question is an older line of the Low Level Aqueduct than that now in use. The Low Level Aqueduct, after bending round the Burj el-Kibrit about the 2,419 contour line,[2] passes north on the great scarp above the Tyropœon valley,[3] and finally crosses this by Wilson's Arch to the Temple enclosure, where it fed the great cisterns south of the Ṣakhra rock.

The High Level Aqueduct started from a reservoir at the 'Ain ed-Derej in the Wâdy el-Biâr. By a long tunnel reached from the surface by many shafts, and by con-
duits from the other springs in the Wâdy, it reached the Wâdy in which the Pools lie on a level about 150 feet above that of the Low Level Aqueduct. The High Level Aqueduct. Here it could receive the water of the 'Ain Ṣaleḥ. Running down the 'Arṭâs Wâdy to opposite 'Arṭâs, it turned north, passing Bethlehem about three-eighths of a mile to the west, to the Tomb of Rachel. Here it had to descend into and climb out of the valley. The passage of the water was effected in ' an inverted syphon of perforated limestone blocks, forming a stone tube fifteen inches in diameter.'[4]

---

[1] *Id.* 332.

[2] Between the 726 and 729 metre contours on Kuemmel's Map.

[3] See above, p. 35.

[4] Wilson, *Water Supply*, etc. : about 381 mm.

Over the hill Ṭanṭûr it proceeded to cross the plain Buḵeiʿa, where, however, its course is not certain.[1] How it entered the city we cannot tell. Possibly its water flowed into the Pool Mamilla (or round this) and by the conduit which enters the City north of the citadel and feeds the Pool of the Patriarch's Bath. Or its course may have been an ancient conduit discovered through the Russian property on the north-west of the City and entering the latter at Goliath's Castle. In either case it arrived upon a level from which it was possible for the water to reach both the North-west Hill and the gardens of Herod's Palace on the South-West Hill. Here were deep conduits bronze-fitted, and large enough to serve as refuges.[2]

The dates of these two Aqueducts from Solomon's Pools to Jerusalem, and of the two conduits which fed them from the Wâdy el ʿArrûb and the W. el Biâr respectively, have formed the subject of much discussion. It is doubtful if even approximate results can be reached. A few years ago Père Germer Durand discovered on one of the perforated blocks of the syphon in the High Level Aqueduct the letters ʿcos I. Clement,' which is the name of Tineius Clemens, consul in 195 A.D. under the Emperor Severus ;[3] and on other stones the names of several centurions have been carved. The aqueduct was accordingly assigned to the reign of Severus with ʿconsiderable certainty.'[4] But these inscriptions may

*Dates of the Two Aqueducts.*

---

[1] The *large P.E.F. Map*, Sh. xxi., traces it parallel to the highroad on the west.

[2] Josephus, v. *B.J.* iv. 4, ii. *B.J.* xvii. 9.

[3] *Revue Bibl.*, 1903, 106 ff. ; Cl.-Ganneau, *Rec. d' archéologie Orientale*, iv. 206 ff.   For other inscriptions recently found see *P.E.F.Q.*, 1905, 75 ff.

[4] Schürer, *Gesch.* (3) 490 *n.* 146 : further on in the same note the possibility that the names attest only the repair of the Aqueduct is admitted.

record not the construction but only the repair of the Aqueduct; a hypothesis which is rendered certain by the need of assuming the existence of the Aqueduct in Herod's time in order to feed the conduits in the gardens of his palace on the South-west Hill.[1]   Roman engineers, it seems certain, used the inverted syphon, as well as the aqueduct raised on arches to bring water across valleys. But there is also evidence that the syphon was possible in Palestine at an earlier date, either under Herod or even before him.[2]   Herod's reign may therefore be taken as the lower limit for the date of the construction of the High Level Aqueduct.   As to the date of the Low Level Aqueduct, running into the Temple area, the lowest limit is the Procuratorship of Pontius Pilate.   According to Josephus Pilate brought water to Jerusalem.   By which aqueduct and to what exact destination is not noted ; but, as he used the sacred money for the purpose (and even he would hardly have dared to do this for an aqueduct that did not directly supply the Temple) we may take it as probable that the Low Level Aqueduct is the one intended.   The distance of 200 stadia (fifteen miles) which Josephus gives to it in one passage[3] is fairly suitable to the length of the Low Level Aqueduct, including its windings, from the Pools to the Temple, but rather much for the direct distance from its furthest supplies in the W. el 'Arrûb to Jerusalem. In another passage, if the reading be correct, he says it was 400 stadia.[4]   But if Pilate's work relates to the Low Level Aqueduct between the Pools and the Temple, it can only have been a work of restoration ; for there is evidence

---

[1] Jos. v. *B.J.* iv. 4, ii. *B.J.* xvii. 9.
[2] Wilson, *Water Supply*, 10 f.   *P.E.F.Q.*, 1905, 77.
[3] Jos. xviii. *Ant.* iii. 2.
Jos. ii. *B.J.* ix. 4 : the Lat. and Euseb. *Prep. Evang.* viii. 2, 122 read 300.

that the Aqueduct was the construction of Herod. Josephus says that Herod brought water at great expense to his fortress of Herodeion,[1] Jebel el-Fureidîs, south-west of Bethlehem, and this is apparently the Aqueduct traced by the Ordnance Survey from the Pools to the site in question.[2]   But Dr. Schick states that the structure of this Herodian aqueduct is the same as that of the Low Level Aqueduct.[3]   If this be correct Herod was the author of the latter,[4] and in that case probably of the older branch of it, uncovered by Dr. Bliss on the South-west Hill,[5] while the other and later one at that place may have been the work of Pilate.[6]   The Talmud states that water was brought to the Temple from 'En Ethâm,[7] in which we may recognise the 'Ain 'Atan, whose waters, we have seen, feed the Low Level Aqueduct a little below the Pools.[8]   The Low Level Aqueduct thus being in all probability the work of Herod (along with the two lower Pools, as we may presume), we may take the High Level Aqueduct, extant in his day, to be the work of an older generation : for it is very unlikely that Herod should have constructed both. Dr. Schick is of opinion that the structure of the High Level Aqueduct is the older.[9]   Yet we are quite without evidence as to what earlier age than Herod's to attribute it. The remarkable fact is, that no record should have survived

---

[1] Jos. xv. *Ant.* ix. 4, 1 *B.J.* xxi. 10.

[2] *Large P.E.F. Map*, Sheets xvii. xxi.        [3] *Z.D.P.V.* i. 132 ff.

[4] So too Guthe, Hauck's *R.-E.* 686.        [5] See above, p. 126.

[6] But there have been at least three other restorations of the viaduct, by Mahmud ibn Kilawûn about 1300, by Süleiman the Magnificent about 1542, and in 1865.

[7] *Talm. Jer.* 'Yoma,' 31*a* ; cf. 'Zebáhîm' 54*b*, and 'Pesâhîm' 109*b*.

[8] See above, p. 125.

[9] Compare also the very definite opinion of Socin and Benzinger in *Baedeker*, 5th ed. 129.

of the construction of so considerable a public work. The syphon upon it tempts one to put it in the Greek Period, and here the long reign of Hyrcanus I. (135-125), who had stores of money, enlarged his territory by conquests in all directions, and achieved some considerable water-works,[1] provides us with the possibility. Yet had Hyrcanus been the author, Josephus would surely have said so. The high priesthood of Simon, the son of Onias, with its great public works [2] is also tempting, but had the High Level Aqueduct been made by him or one of his predecessors we should surely have heard of its existence during the Maccabean campaigns in that quarter, or the siege of Jerusalem by Antiochus VII. (135-4 B.C.). Of this only can we be sure, that there is no evidence in the Bible of either aqueduct as the work, or as extant in the days, of the pre-exilic Kings of Judah. Dr. Bliss's suggestion that the older branch of the Low Level Aqueduct on the South-west Hill may be perhaps the work of Solomon,[3] rests on conditions which we do not yet understand. The name ' Solomon's Pools,' of course, proves nothing ; and even if the Mamilla Pool and its conduit into the City were extant in the days of Hezekiah,[4] they would not involve the existence of the High Level Aqueduct. Neither this nor the Low Level Aqueduct can be traced in time behind the reign of Herod the Great. It is very probable that the latter is his work : and the most likely date for the former is the previous century, when Timochares tells us that the whole town abounded in running water.[5]

---

[1] Jos. xiii. *Ant*. x.
[2] Ecclesiasticus l. 1 ff.
[3] *Excav. at Jerus.* 332.
[4] See above, p. 114 f.
[5] See above, p. 84.

The long study we have pursued is full of dark details, and we leave it baffled by many of the answers of which Moral Results we have been in search. Yet it has its own of this study. prizes, and they are more precious than those of topographical certainty. We cannot have worked through this series of water-systems without a vivid imagination of the secular, ceaseless labours which produced them, or devoid of a profound sympathy with the hopes which their meagre results excited in the hearts of their authors.

In casting our imagination along the history of Jerusalem, we are apt to be content with recalling her walls, temples, The ceaseless palaces and markets, and with the endeavour struggle for to reconstruct from these alone the full picture water. of her interests and activities. But preliminary to war, worship, trade and every kind of art, woven through them all and—on those high and thirsty rocks—more constant than any, was the struggle for water. Nature lent but a grudging assistance. Nor if we go behind Herod and the construction, at his comparatively late date, of the great Aqueducts which we have just been following, are there any arches or other imperishable structures to bear witness that genius for architecture, imperial wealth, or the power which could command hordes of slaves ever atoned, as in other waterless cities, for the absence of physical resources. The work, outside the great aqueducts, was all done by the citizens under pressure of their daily needs, by petty kings hurriedly providing against sieges, by statesmen with limited revenues in a nation of small capacity for building. What thrift and storage of scanty supplies! The dykes of Holland, piled to keep the water out, tell no more eloquent tale of the labour of centuries, the piety and resolution of many generations, than does this story of what Jerusalem has done to keep the waters in—the rock cisterns of her early days; the desperate care to bring the springs within the walls out of reach of besiegers; the execution of tunnels and pools by men hardly apprenticed to the art of engineering; the struggle to keep pace with the rise of the City's levels above the sunken sources of the past; and finally, the long aqueducts and deep reservoirs of more numerous and civilised generations.

When all these labours, before the last, resulted in such moderate achievements, when the reservoirs and springs were liable to be exhausted by the failure of Effect on the the rains, and the parched gardens scarcely hope of the relieved the barrenness of the landscape, do we people. wonder, that as the mirage of the desert appears to the parched traveller like pools and lakes, so the hopes of this thirsty people assumed the form of streams and rivers about their Holy City? It is only such a study as we have come through that can furnish us with full sympathy for these words of Psalmist and Prophet:

*There is a River which gladdens the City of our God.*[1]
*And he brought me back to the door of the House; and lo, waters issued from under the threshold of the House eastward . . . and it was a river I could not pass through, for the waters were risen, waters to swim in, a river that could not be forded.*[2]

*But there the LORD will be with us in majesty, a place of broad rivers and streams; wherein shall go no galley with oars, neither shall gallant ship pass thereby. For the LORD is our Judge, the LORD is our lawgiver, the LORD is our King: He will save us.*[3]

[1] Ps. xlvi. 4.　　[2] Ezek. xlvii. 1, 5.　　[3] Is. xxxiii. 21 ff.

# CHAPTER VI

## ṢION, OPHEL AND 'THE CITY OF DAVID'

ONE of the two cardinal questions of the topography of Jerusalem stated in Chapter II. is that of the

Rival Sites— position of Ṣion, the Jebusite fortress which
South-west David captured, and which was called there-
and East
Hills. after *The City of David*, or (more properly translated) *David's-Burgh*. To this question there are two possible answers. *First*, till a few years ago it was the general opinion, received by tradition from the time of Josephus, that the South-west Hill, the most massive and dominant of the heights of Jerusalem, was not only an integral part of the City from before the days of David, but contained also the citadel he captured from the Jebusites and remained the centre of political and military power under the kings of Judah. This traditional view is expressed in the present nomenclature of the South-west Hill. The Tomb of David is believed to lie there, and there is placed the site of the Palace of Solomon, from which a bridge or raised causeway across the central valley is supposed to have served for the passage of the king when he *went up* to the Temple. The southern gate of the present City opening on the Hill is called Bab en-Neby Daûd, 'Gate of the Prophet David,' or Bab Ṣahyun, 'Ṣion-Gate.' The Citadel-tower is known as 'David's Tower,'

134

and the Hill, as a whole, is called by Christians 'Mount Sion.' *Second*, the opposite view is that Sion, and by consequence the 'City of David,' lay on the East Hill on the part called Ophel, just above the Virgin's Spring; that Mount Sion came to be the equivalent in the Old Testament of the Temple Mount; that the location of the 'City of David' by the present Jaffa gate was due to an error by Josephus, and that there is no trace of the name Sion being applied to the South-west Hill till we come some way down the line of Christian tradition. The supporters of this second view are divided as to when the South-west Hill was brought within the City; some think in Jebusite times, some by David, some by Solomon, some by the eighth-century kings, and some not till the Greek or Maccabean period. These subsidiary questions may be postponed till we reach their periods in the history. But the other, whether the South-west or the East Hill was the site of Sion and the 'City of David,' is so fundamental as to require a separate and preliminary treatment.

There is more than one way of conducting this important debate. We might follow the interesting course which it has taken in modern times from the date of The Course Robinson, when the South-west Hill was of the following generally accepted as Mount Sion, to the argument. present day, when the most of the authorities, some of whom had previously taken the other view, place the original Sion upon Ophel. Or we might start, as so many of the controversialists on both sides do, with the description of Josephus, who was the first definitely to place the 'City of David' on the South-west Hill, and work back through the Maccabean and the Biblical data to the earliest times. It seems to me that the more lucid and convincing method is to leave at first the evidence of Josephus alone, for, valuable as this is for his own day, he was not a trustworthy guide among the ancient conditions; and to start with the topographical and military arguments for the two sites, then to follow the Biblical evidence and that from the Books of the Maccabees, and by these earlier witnesses to test the statements of Josephus and the claims of ecclesiastical tradition.

### I. THE ARGUMENTS FROM TOPOGRAPHY AND ARCHÆOLOGY.

We can have little doubt about two things: *first*, that the earliest settlers in this district would select the sides of the only valleys in which water was present in any quantity; **that is,** as we have seen, the Kidron, and, more **doubtfully,** the sheltered mouth of the valley running into it, the Tyropœon; and, *second*, that when it became necessary to fortify themselves, they would do so on one or other of the two promontories, which, except at their north ends, sink steeply, if not precipitously, into the gorges below them. Our choice clearly lies between the South-west and the East Hills. Although from a very early time dwellings may have been excavated on the eastern bank of the Kidron valley, the site of the present village of Silwân, where there are still cave-dwellings, the place is not suitable for fortification, and the dip of the strata makes it improbable that springs ever broke in the valley immediately below.[1]

*Earliest Settlement on either the E. or the S.W. Hill.*

[1] It is to be wished that excavations were made along this bank of the Kidron valley. Cf. Cl.-Ganneau, *Arch. Res.* i. 305.

Those who support the claims of the South-west Hill as the site of Ṣion, placing this either on the northern edge of the Hill where the present citadel stands, or on the southern end,[1] rest their case, apart from tradition, on these grounds: the *The Claims of the South-west Hill.* height of the hill above its flanking valleys, W. er-Rabâbi and el-Wâd, and the steepness of the slopes by which it rises from the latter; its dominance of the other hills of Jerusalem, and its fitness for fortification. But it is doubtful whether so broad and long a hill, without any outstanding eminence, would have been suitable for such a citadel as that of the Jebusites.[2] Sir Charles Wilson says: 'The western spur is broad-backed, and so far as the original form is known, there is no broken ground or conspicuous feature upon it that would be naturally selected as the site of a castle such as those usually erected for the protection of an ancient hill-town.'[3] Again, the South-west Hill is waterless and lies aloof from the ancient source or sources of water in the Ḳidron valley. Unless the earthquakes have closed or masked some former vent, there was no spring in el-Wâd or the Wâdy er-Rabâbi; and indeed the geology, as we have seen, renders very improbable the existence there, at any time, of a fountain. It is true that some towns in Palestine are planted at as great a distance from their springs as the South-west Hill is from the Ḳidron valley; but in no instance (I think) does this happen where a more, or equally, suitable site for the town lies nearer the spring, as is the case in Jerusalem. The tradition that Ṣion lay

---

[1] So Georg Gatt and Karl Mommert : for their works see below, p. 165.

[2] מְצֻדַת צִיּוֹן, *meṣudath Ṣion, stronghold* or *hill-fort of Sion.*

[3] Art. 'Zion' in Hastings' *D.B.* iv. 983.

on the site of the present citadel is associated with, and
dependent on, the other, that the spring Gihon lay in the
head of the Wâdy er-Rabâbi; but we have seen that
Gihon is undoubtedly the same as the Virgin's Spring in
the Ḳidron valley.  Finally, no remains have been discovered on the South-west Hill which can be assigned
with certainty to the pre-Israelite period.  The rock
cisterns are few compared with those in other parts of
Jerusalem ; the walls and aqueducts that have been traced
may be referred to a later age ; and this is also true of the
rock cutting known as Maudslay's Ṣcarp, above the western
slope.  It is true that the Hill has not yet been thoroughly
excavated; and the Great Tower with the rock-chambers
beneath it, discovered by Dr. Bliss, forms a perplexing
problem.[1]  But so far as the archæological evidence at
present goes it supports the other view.  Consistent with
this is the comparative absence of *débris* in the W. er-
Rabâbi which we noted before, and which seems to
indicate that the South-west Hill had not so remote a
history as the East Hill.[2]  Summing up, we may say that
while there is no positive evidence for an early settlement
on the South-west Hill, it is also improbable that the
Jebusite citadel was built there.

The East Hill is not so high as the South-west, which
dominates it.  But, as we have seen,[3] it is high and aloof
enough to have been, in the conditions of
Argument
for the East  ancient warfare, quite independent of the latter,
Hill.  and capable of being held by itself.  That the
position immediately above Gihon is suitable for a fort has

[1] See above, p. 126.
[2] See above, p. 42.  Of course there remains the possibility that the
greater *débris* in the Ḳidron and Tyropœon was partly due to earthquakes.
[3] See above, p. 37 f.

been affirmed by several eminent military engineers.[1]  But even the eyes of those who are not soldiers nor engineers may perceive the possibility of the Canaanite fort on that position.  Down either side the ground falls abruptly to the Tyropœon and the Ḳidron.  The position is nearly 200 feet above the bed of the Ḳidron, and the descent very steep, about 30°;[2] while it is 100 feet above the bed of el-Wâd.  Southwards there is a steep slope to the point between the junction of the two valleys.  The sole difficulty is to the north.  Immediately above the Virgin's Spring (2087 feet, or 636 m. above sea level), there is a contour line on the Survey Map of Ophel of 2279 (695 m.), from which the rock gradually ascends to 2299 (701 m.), 2312 (704'5), and finally, at the foot of the Ḥaram Wall 2370 (722).  Such an ascent is certainly not very suitable for carrying the northern wall of the fort.  Dr. Guthe indeed claims to have discovered a trench or gully running across the hill immediately north of the Virgin's Spring.[3] But his data were drawn from only two shafts, and others familiar with the ground deny that any such trench exists.[4] Yet even with the surface as it stands at present Sir Charles Wilson, Sir Charles Warren and other authorities in engin-

---

[1] Including Generals Sir Charles Wilson and Sir Charles Warren.

[2] Warren, *P.E.F. Mem.*, 'Jerus.' 368 : and the natural surface of the rock, it must be remembered, is covered with *débris* from 10 to 50 feet in depth.

[3] *Z.D.P.V.* v. 166, 316. Hauck's *R.-E.* viii. 668 f. : ' By two shafts it was then [1881] clearly determined that the original rock-bottom immediately north of the Virgin's Spring, opposite the upper part of the village Siloah, lies from 12 to 13 metres deeper than the adjoining height on the south, and 25 to 30 m. deeper than the neighbouring height on the north' ; cf. *Id.* 675 lines 45 ff.

[4] *E.g.* Wilson and Warren.  Kuemmel also has recently (*Materialien z. Topogr. des alt. Jerus.*, 1906, 82) expressed doubts of the existence of this gully.

eering, or the topography of the hill-forts of Palestine,
believe that the Jebusite stronghold stood above Gihon.
In Gihon, too, we have the only certain spring of the
district.   It is true that if their fort was built on the East
Hill, the Jebusites could not include the Spring within its
walls, nor be able to prevent its use by an enemy besieging them.   Gihon lies at the foot of a steep rock on which
a wall could not run, except high above the Spring.   But
at least, even with primitive means of warfare, the besieged
could seriously harass an enemy in his use of Gihon ; and
we have the evidence of Warren's shaft to prove that, at
a date certainly earlier than the construction of the Tunnel
by Hezekiah, the garrison of the town on Ophel above
the Spring made a passage to the latter through the rock,
such as would secure to themselves the use of its waters
during a time of siege.   Moreover, the needs of times of
peace must be taken into consideration.   It is most
probable that the earliest settlement was as near to the
Ḳidron Spring or Springs as possible, that is upon Ophel ;
and that therefore, when a fort became necessary, it was
built on the same hill, somewhere above Gihon, rather than
on a hill farther away.

We have now to ask whether any of the ancient remains,
discovered on the ridge of Ophel, indicate the Jebusite
period.   Both the English surveyors and Dr.
Guthe discovered lines of wall in various forms
of masonry, rock-dwellings, cisterns, reservoirs,
steps and scarped rocks.   Of the seven kinds of masonry
which Dr. Guthe distinguishes on the encompassing
walls, he is inclined to ascribe the second class of ' ashlar
with regular margins and bosses' to a period when the
Israelites worked under Phœnician example, that is

*Archæo-
logical
Evidence.*

from Solomon's time onward;[1] but his first class of
' regular blocks, but rough-hewn and without mortar,' which
is met with everywhere on the east coasts of the Mediterranean, he assigns to an earlier period.[2] We have seen
that Warren's shaft must be earlier than the eighth century,
and that there is no objection to ascribing it to the Jebusites. Near this, just above Giḥon, Dr. Guthe unearthed
what is apparently the oldest relic, a bit of wall or tower
with a thick layer of black cement, seemingly ancient,
but whether Jebusite or not he wisely abstains from
affirming.[3] Round cisterns he found only among those
hewn in the rock:[4] such a shape of cistern is assigned
by some to the Canaanites, but this also is uncertain. Of
more significance are 'rock chambers, with doors and
openings for light,' and the dwellings half cut in the rock
and half built against it. Some of these, Dr. Guthe
thinks,[5] go back to the earliest period. There can have
been little building in stone before Solomon's time, or he
would not have had to bring masons from Phœnicia, and
no traces have been found of building in timber.[6] But
even from the rock-dwellings it is precarious to infer a
very early date; for the habit of living in houses half
hewn in the rock and half built against it, continued in
Greek times, as is proved from the mosaic under some
of these hybrid constructions, and persists still in the
village of Silwân. On the whole, then, while nothing
has been found on Ophel which is indubitably Jebusite, many of the remains are possibly so, and certainly
earlier than the eighth century; and there is not a little

---

[1] *Z.D.P.V.* v. 284, 287-289.  [2] *Ib.* 286 f.
[3] See point E on Tafel viii. *Z.D.P.V.* v.; cf. 319 f.
[4] *Id.* 336.  [5] *Id.* 341.  [6] *Id.* 344 f.

which suggests the primitive practice of dwelling in caves.

The probability of the position of the original fortress of Jerusalem, on the East Hill, having been shown from the topographical and archæological evidence, there remains, before we leave this department of our argument, the subsidiary question whether Ophel presents a large enough surface for the Jebusite town. It is a frequent contention on the part of those who support the claims of the South-west Hill that the ridge of Ophel is too small to have held the ancient City, that the size of the South-west Hill is more suitable for this, and that accordingly we ought to seek for the Jebusite stronghold on its more dominant height.[1] The force of this contention depends on what one conceives the size of Jerusalem under the Jebusites to have been. If one has large views of this, the contention will prevail. But the probability is that before David's time Jerusalem was but an ordinary hill-town. Now we happen, just recently, to have been furnished with some data as to the size of another important Canaanite city which, like Jerusalem, defied the attempts of Israel to take it before the period of the monarchy. In his report, in January 1905,[2] on his excavations at Gezer, Mr. R. A. S. Macalister gives some estimates of the length and date of the outmost of the city walls which he has laid bare: 'I estimate its total length,' he says, 'at about 4,500 feet, which is rather more than one-third of the length of the modern wall of Jerusalem.' 'After a careful study of the masonry of all the exposed parts' of the walls, and

*Ophel sufficient for Jebusite town.*

[1] So Colonel Conder, art. 'Jerus.,' Hastings' *D.B.* ii. 591.
[2] *P.E.F.Q.* of that date.

of ' the associated antiquities,' he assigns the houses built
over the ruined *inner* wall to the middle of the second
millennium, ' every dateable object being contemporary
with Amenhotep III.' But ' as it is inconceivable that a
city of the importance of Gezer should have existed at
any period without a wall, the ruin of the inner wall must
have been synchronous with the erection of the outer wall,
which superseded it.' Though repaired from time to time,
this outer wall is ' fundamentally of the respectable antiquity of the Tell-el-Amarna correspondence,'[1] ' and lasted
from about 1500 to 100 B.C.' If, then, Mr. Macalister's
observations and reasoning be correct, we know the size
of a royal Canaanite city, contemporary with the Jebusite
Jerusalem, and, like the latter, holding itself from the
Israelites till about 1000 B.C. Its walls measured approximately 4500 feet round (about 1372 metres). Now if we
take Dr. Guthe's or Dr. Bliss's plans of Ophel, and
measure from the scarp, at the lowest point of the East
Hill, northwards along the line of discovered and inferred
wall on the eastern edge of the ridge, to the 2329 feet
contour (710 metres), where the level rises rapidly towards
the Ḥaram wall, and thence 520 feet (about 159 metres)
to the same level on the Tyropœon side of the ridge, and
thence southward along the line of ascertained rocks and
scarps, on the west of Ophel, to our starting-point, we
get a circumference of approximately 4250 feet (about
1295 metres). This means a space for the Jebusite town,
if it was confined to Ophel, not much less than the
Canaanite Gezer, which, so far as we can discern from
the Tell-el-Amarna correspondence, was at the time at
least of equal political importance with Jerusalem, and

[1] *Circa* 1400 B.C.

from its more favourable position, both for agriculture and for trade and other communications with Egypt and Phœnicia, may well have held a larger and wealthier community.

## 2. The Biblical Evidence as to Ṣion.

To the topographical and archæological evidence stated above we may now add that of the Biblical history from the time of David onwards. It starts from the verse which records his capture of the Jebusite stronghold, and runs along the history of the two names which the verse assigns to the stronghold: *David took the stronghold of Ṣion* or *Ṣîyôn, the same is the City of David* or *David's-Burgh*;[1] and it includes the use of the name *The 'Ophel* as practically a doublet for Ṣiôn.

In the verse quoted the name is given (as throughout the Old Testament) without the definite article ; that is,
as already a proper name. This has not
prevented the attempt to derive it from a
Semitic root expressive of the character of the site to which it was originally attached. In early Christian literature it has been variously translated ' watch-tower,' ' peak,' ' dry place,' ' impassable,' and ' fixed ' or ' ordained.'[2]   The meaning ' dry ' has been revived by Gesenius and Lagarde ;[3] and that of ' ordained ' or ' set

*Meaning of the name Ṣion.*

---

[1] 2 Sam. v. 7.

[2] So Jerome (*Liber Interpr. Hebr. Nom.*, see Lagarde *Onom. Sacr.* pp. 70-73, etc.) : ' Sion, specula vel speculator sive scopulus,' ' vel mandatum vel inuium.'   *Onomastica Vaticana*, see Lagarde, *id.* p. 204: Σιων σκοπευτήριον ; p. 211 : Σ. διψῶσα; p. 222 : ἡ ἐντολὴ σκοπιᾶς.

[3] Ges. *Thes.* 1164; Lag. *Bildung Hebr. Nomin.* 84, as if צִיּוֹן were a contraction of צָהְיוֹן from צהה; cf. Graetz's emendation of צִיּוֹן in Jer. xxx. 17 to צִיּוֹן.

up' by Delitzsch.[1] Another derivation is from the root which appears in the Arabic Ṣan, 'to guard';[2] another compares the Mishnic Hebrew Ṣiyyûn, 'the act of making anything conspicuous by marking it.'[3] I think that a much more probable derivation may be reached through the Arabic equivalent for Ṣiōn : Ṣahyun or Ṣihyun.[4] In Boha-ed-Din's *Life of Saladin*[5] a castle near Laodicea in northern Syria is described, under the name Ṣehyun, as 'well-fortified on the edge of a hill.' Now the Arabic Lexicons give Ṣahweh as the 'highest part' or 'ridge of a mountain or hump or shoulder,' or even as 'a citadel or bastion.' That there was a second castle of the same name, also on a narrow ridge,[6] encourages the belief that in this Arabic form we may find the correct etymology of Ṣion or Siyōn ; the termination -ōn being that which occurs in so many place-names. Ṣion would then mean 'protuberance,' or 'summit of a ridge,' and so 'fort' or 'citadel.' In itself such a meaning is most probable.

When Israel, in possession of the Jebusite citadel,

---

[1] *Psalmen*, 3rd ed. 170, as if from צָוָה.

[2] Wetzstein, see Delitzsch, *Genesis*, 4th ed. p. 578.

[3] From this no doubt came the meaning 'tomb' (cf. Cruden's *Concordance*), for tombs were marked white.

[4] The present name for the Mount Sion of Christian tradition, the S.W. hill. Bab Ṣihyûn is, in Muḳaddasi, the present Bab en-Nabi Dāūd, and Kenisah Ṣihyun the name in Mas'ûdi for the Christian Church on the traditional Mount Ṣion ; see Le Strange, *Palestine under the Moslems*, 203, 212-217. In the *P.E.F.Q.*, 1877, p. 21, Col. Conder points out that the name still exists in the neighbourhood of Jerusalem, Wady Ṣahyun, about 1¾ miles S.W. from the Jaffa Gate, and quotes Isaac Chelo as describing Ṣion not *at* but *near* Jerusalem.

[5] Ch. 43, opening sentence, ed. Schultens, p. 82.

[6] Yaḳut, *Geogr. Lex.*, tells us that the Syrian castle was sometimes confused with the Jerusalem Ṣion.

changed its ancient name to that of their own king, its
History of the conqueror, they may have expected that the
Name.           former, a foreign and obscure designation,
would disappear behind a title so illustrious and, as
it proved, so enduring as 'the City of David.'   Instead
of this, the name Ṣion, as if emancipated from the rock
to which it had been confined, began to extend to the
neighbourhood, and, advancing with the growth of
Jerusalem, became more identified with her final extent
and fame than that of David himself.   The name of
David appears to have remained on the limited area on
which his people had placed it: Ṣion not only spread
over the Temple Mount, the whole city and her population, but even followed the latter during their exile to
Babylon.   It is a remarkable story which we are now to
trace.   An epithet, originally so limited in application and
apparently so concrete in meaning, gradually becomes
synonymous with Jerusalem as a whole, is adopted as one
of Israel's fondest names for the shrine of their religion,
and is finally idealised as an expression of the most
sacred aspects of their character as the people of God.
Yet even across so wide a career there lie scattered proofs
that the spot from which the name started was a narrow
summit of the East Hill above Giḥon.

In the history of Solomon's reign Ṣion, still equivalent
to the 'City of David,' is described as distinct from the
Under        site of the Temple and as lying below it.
Solomon.     According to 1 Kings viii. 1 ff. Solomon
gathered the heads of the people to *bring up the Ark out
of the City of David which is Ṣion* to the Temple.   The
other verb used in verse 6 of the conveyance of the Ark,
after it had reached the Temple level, to the Holy Place,

viz., *brought in,* proves that the verb *brought up* in verses
1 and 4 is to be taken in its obvious sense and not (as
some argue, who place the original Ṣion on the South-
western Hill)[1] as if it merely meant *started out with* or
*brought on its way.* To the writer of this passage Ṣion
evidently lay *below* Solomon's Temple : that is, on the
site on which topographical reasons have led us to place
it, on the eastern ridge above Gihon.[2]

 The next appearances of the name are in the writings
of the Eighth-Century Prophets, some two hundred and
fifty years after David. Amos says : *Yahweh
roars from Ṣion and utters his voice from* In the 8th-
*Jerusalem,* and speaks of *those who are at ease* Century Prophets.
*in Ṣion and secure in the mount of Samaria.*[3] The former
passage certainly includes in Ṣion the Temple as the
residence and oracle of the God of Israel. Isaiah records
a word of Yahweh : *I lay in Ṣion a foundation stone ;* that
is, the intimate spiritual relation between Himself and His
people, on which He calls their faith to rest.[4] Micah
mentions Ṣion as equivalent to the whole town of
Jerusalem, and adds, as if it were distinct from this, *the
Mount of the House* or Temple.[5] Both Micah and
(probably) Isaiah speak of the City and her population as

---

[1] For example, Rückert, *Die Lage des Berges Sion,* p. 32.

[2] To the above passages may be added 2 Sam. xxiv. 18 ff., 1 Chron. xxi.
18 ff. ; according to which David *went up* from his residence in the city of
David to the threshing-floor of Araunah, subsequently the site of the
Temple.

[3] Amos i. 2, vi. 1. The genuineness of both passages has been contested,
but on insufficient grounds.

[4] Isaiah xxviii. 16 : accepted as genuine by all critics. Other oracles
mentioning Ṣion might be added to this one, for there is not much reason to
doubt that they are Isaiah's own. But as they are not accepted as such by
all critics, I refrain from using them here.   [5] Micah iii. 10, 12.

the *Daughter of Sion.*[1]   Another form, *Mount Sion*, occurs
in a number of oracles attributed to Isaiah, but assigned
by many scholars to exilic or post-exilic times.   I do not
feel, however, that the reasons which the latter give
against the authenticity of some of these passages are
conclusive.   Ch. viii. 18 appears to be genuine, in spite of
Volz's and Cheyne's arguments to the contrary, and if so,
affords evidence that the Temple Hill was called Mount
Sion in Isaiah's time.[2]

How the
name spread.
   Thus it appears that the name Sion, which till
Solomon's time at least had been confined to the
Jebusite fort, had spread during the next
two hundred and fifty years across the whole
of Jerusalem.   The reasons for this extension are
obvious, even if we cannot define the successive stages
of the process.   Either the name followed the expansion
of the population, and (as Micah iii. 12 seems to show)
only subsequently to this included the site of the Temple ;
or more probably it first accompanied the Ark to the
latter (as we might infer from Amos i. 2) and thence
spread over the rest of the City.   But we must not forget
the possibility of a third alternative : that the name
Sion had covered the whole of the East Hill from the
earliest times.   In any case it would be more natural for
it to spread first across this, and only then over the rest
of Jerusalem.

   In the Seventh Century Jeremiah uses *Sion* as

---

[1] Micah i. 13 ; Isaiah i. 8.   See below, p. 269.

[2] In Isaiah xxix. 8 and xxxi. 4, which are also probably genuine, *Mount Sion* may be even interpreted as covering the whole of the City.   Other occurrences of the name in prophecies which till quite recently were generally regarded as Isaiah's own, are iv. 5, x. 12, xviii. 7.   In x. 32 and xvi. 1 is found *Mount of the Daughter of Sion.*

equivalent to Jerusalem, City and Temple;[1] and the
*Daughter of Ṣion* as the personified City and
her population.[2]   He does not give the name
*Mount Ṣion.*   Coming to writers of the Exile,

we find that Ezekiel nowhere mentions Jerusalem or the
Temple Mount by the name of Ṣion ; a remarkable
omission, as if this rigid theologian had purposely excluded from the holy precincts a title of Gentile origin.
But in Lamentations, on the contrary, *Ṣion* and *the
Daughter of Ṣion* are frequent designations not only of
the City, ruined and desolate, and, as personified, *spreading forth her hands,*[3] but also of the community carried
away captive.[4]   Once there is mention of *Mount Ṣion,*
the deserted site trodden by foxes.[5]   As in Jeremiah so in
the great prophet of the Exile, Isaiah xl.-lv., *Mount Ṣion*
does not appear : but *Ṣion* is used both of the City,[6] as
parallel to Jerusalem,[7] and of her exiled people,[8] who are
also addressed as *the daughter of Ṣion.*[9]

All these instances of the name in its various forms
increase throughout the later literature (except in certain
books presently to be noted).   *Ṣion* is become
the full equivalent of Jerusalem,[10] and the

name is as closely attached to the Lord as to His people.
Ṣion is Ṣion of the Holy One of Israel,[11] His Holy Mount,[12]
and dwelling place ;[13] the mother of the nation,[14] the nation
herself ;[15] the pure and holy nucleus of the nation.[16]   To

---

[1] Jer. iv. 6, viii. 19, xiv. 19, xxvi. 18 ; and probably also xxxi. 6.
[2] iv. 31, vi. 2, 23.    [3] Lam. i. 4, 17, ii. 1, 6, v. 11., etc.    [4] iv. 22.
[5] v. 18.    [6] *e.g.* li. 11., lii. 7 f.    [7] xl. 9, xli. 27, lii. 1.
[8] li. 16 ; cf. Zech. ii. 7.    [9] lii. 2.
[10] Zech. i. 14, 17, viii. 3. Zephaniah iii. 16 (a late passage).
[11] Isa. lx. 14.    [12] Joel ii. 1, cf. 15.    [13] Joel iii. 17.
[14] Isa. lxvi. 8 ; Joel ii. 23.    [15] Zeph. iii. 14, daughter of Ṣion = Israel.
[16] Isa. lix. 20.

Ṣion the Gentiles look, and from her goes forth the true religion.[1] The fuller name *Mount Ṣion* is sometimes employed as covering all Jerusalem;[2] and sometimes apparently in the narrower sense of the Temple Mount where Yahweh reigns.[3] Instances of such applications of the name in the Psalms are too numerous for citation. We meet them also in the Apocrypha, in which Mount Ṣion is the Temple Hill, but Ṣion the holy community, in contrast to Babylon.[4]

To this frequent reference to Ṣion in post-exilic literature, there is one remarkable line of exceptions. Just as *Writers who refrain from the use of the name.* Ezekiel does not use the name, so it is absent from Chronicles, Ezra and Nehemiah. Except as the Jebusite designation of the citadel[5] which David took, the Chronicler does not mention Ṣion. To him the mountain of the Temple is Mount Moriah.[6] Even in passages describing the gathering of the people to sacrifice or to the cleansing or repair of the Temple, in which we might have expected the use of the name Mount Ṣion,[7] it is constantly avoided; and the worshippers are described as *coming to Jerusalem* or *going up to the house of the* LORD.[8] In Ezra the formula frequently used is *the house of God* or *of Yahweh which is in Jerusalem*;[9] and Nehemiah speaks of *Jerusalem* and the *courts of God's house.*[10] That the Chronicler, who knew of Ṣion as the name of the Jebusite fort, and who introduces the 'City of

---

[1] Isa. ii. 3 (if indeed this be a post-exilic oracle, and not one, as is probable, from an earlier date), Micah iv. 2.

[2] 2 Kings xix. 31 ; Obad. 17, 21 ; Joel ii. 32(?).

[3] Isa. xxiv. 23 ; cf. xxvii. 13, the holy mount ; Micah iv. 7.

[4] *e.g.* 2 Esdras ii. 40, 42 (Mt. Sion), iii. 2, 31, x. 20, 23, 39, 44, xiii. 35 (Mt. Sion), 36.      [5] 1 Chr. xi. 5; 2 Chr. v. 2.

[6] 2 Chr. iii. 1.      [7] *e.g.* 2 Chr. xx., xxiii. f., xxxiv.

[8] *e.g.* xxix. 20.      [9] i. 3, 5, iv. 24, etc.      [10] xiii. 7.

David,' 'Ophel and Moriah ; that Ezra and Nehemiah, who
also give so many of the topographical names of Jerusalem,
neglected by accident to call the Temple Mount Ṣion,
appears incredible. Doubtless, like Ezekiel, they had some
religious reason for refusing the name to so holy a place.
Were it not for the frequent use of Ṣion in the Psalms, we
would be tempted to say that Ṣion was exclusively a prophetic designation; which the priestly school of writers
avoided.

One other witness to the use of the name in the Old
Testament period, is the author of First Maccabees (about
100 B.C.). In this Book Mount Ṣion is always Maccabean
the Temple Mount[1] distinct both from the Period.
City of David and from the rest of Jerusalem. So in
other parts of the Apocrypha.[2]

Neither in the Old Testament nor in the Apocrypha is
there any passage which can be interpreted as applying the
name Ṣion specially to the South-west Hill. 'Ṣion' never
The attempt to do so has indeed been made. applied to
the S.W.
Verses of the Psalms, which, according to the Hill.
parallelism of Hebrew poetry, place within the same
couplet *Ṣion* and *Yahweh's Holy Hill*, have been interpreted as if they thereby designated *two different localities*;
viz., the South-west Hill and the Temple Hill. But this
would imply that within ancient Jerusalem there were
actually two sites of equal sacredness, an impossible
conclusion. The only natural inference from the parallelism just quoted is that Ṣion and the Temple Hill were
identical.

---

[1] iv. 37, 60, v. 54, vi. 48, 62, vii. 33, x. 11, xiv. 27.
[2] 1 Esdras viii. 81 ; Ecclesiasticus xxiv. 10 (Sion=holy tabernacle) and
(apparently) Judith, ix. 13.

### 3. HISTORY OF THE NAME THE 'OPHEL.

The Biblical history of the name The 'Ophel so curiously supplements that of Ṣion, for which, indeed, it appears in certain writers to be the equivalent, that we must take it next, and before we deal with the name *City of David*. The meaning of the word is well-known. It signifies *lump* or *swelling*, and was applied in Hebrew to a mound, knoll or hill, in one case with a wall round it.[1] It is, therefore, exactly synonymous with Ṣion or Ṣahyûn, but unlike the latter, which is always used without the article as a proper name, the Old Testament writers always (except in two passages) talk of *The 'Ophel*. And everybody agrees that this was the name of part at least of the East Hill, south of the Temple, where, as we have seen, Ṣion stood.

*The 'Ophel* does not certainly occur in pre-exilic writings,[2] though there is no other reason against its early origin, save that after the Exile, when it comes into use, it has still the definite article: that is, it is still an epithet and not a proper name. The Book of Nehemiah — probably not that part which is Nehemiah's own memoirs, but the work of the Chronicler[3] —gives the name as already familiar, and places it south of the Temple. The only other occurrences of the name

The 'Ophel synonymous with Ṣion;

and a later substitute for it.

[1] 2 Ki. v. 24: *the 'Ophel* on which Elisha lived; Moabite stone, line 22, *the wall of the 'Ophel* in Daibon or Kirḥah(?).

[2] Of its two occurrences in prophecy, Isai. xxxii. 14, and Micah iv. 8, the former is not found in the LXX., and is probably a later insertion in the text, while the latter cannot be confidently assigned to Micah. In addition, it is to be noted that these are the only two passages in the O.T. in which the name is used in connection with Jerusalem, in the generic sense.

[3] Neh. iii. 26 f., xi. 21: see below, Bk. iii., the chapter on Ezra and Nehemiah.

in the Old Testament are in Chronicles,[1] where we are told that King Jotham *built much on the wall of the 'Ophel,* and that King Manasseh *compassed about the 'Ophel.* But we have seen that these are the very books whose author, or authors, avoid the name Sion except in the two cases in which it is used of the old Jebusite citadel. It cannot be by accident that it is in these books that The 'Ophel appears. The two names apply practically to the same site, and are almost exactly synonymous. Naturally, therefore, the following questions arise. Were *Sion* and *The 'Ophel* contemporary and alternative names for the part of the East Hill below the Temple? Or when the name Sion was removed from this locality and applied to the Temple Mount as a whole, did the name The 'Ophel succeed it in its narrower designation? If the former question be answered affirmatively, then we have an explanation of the appearance of The 'Ophel only in writings which avoid the use of Sion; if the latter, then we understand the confinement of the name The 'Ophel to the post-exilic literature. I am inclined to prefer the latter alternative.

The name reappears in Josephus as Ophlas, and The Ophlas, to the south of and adjoining the Temple. He seems indeed in one passage to limit it to the Ophlas in northern part of the ridge running down from Josephus. the Temple to Siloam.[2] But his accounts of the Ophlas,

---

[1] 2 Chron. xxvii. 3, xxxiii. 14.

[2] Jos. v. *B.J.* iv. 2 describes the city wall which runs north from Siloam as bending east at ' Solomon's Pool,' the site of which is unknown (see above, p. 119), running on μέχρι χώρου τινὸς ὃν καλοῦσιν 'Οφλας, and joining the east colonnade of the Temple. Cf. Schlatter, *Zur Topogr. u. Gesch. Paläst.* 211. The other passages in Josephus are v. *B.J.* vi. 1: John held the Temple and the parts adjoining for not a little way, τόν τε

and the whole south end of the East Hill are too general for a definite inference to be drawn from them. The name does not occur in the Apocrypha or the New Testament.

Both the names Ṣion and ʿOphel mean ʿ protuberance,' ʿswelling,' ʿmound,' or ʿknoll,' and apply either to the whole of the East Hill south of the Temple, or to some part of it. In the latter case we must assume that anciently that ridge did not slope down from its summit on the Rock eṣ-Ṣakhra to Siloam so regularly as it does now, but bore upon it, between these limits, a considerable outcrop of the rock, like that on which Antonia stood to the north of eṣ-Ṣakhra. Such a ʿswelling' on the ridge would give originally a fifth summit to the East Hill,[1] and provide us with a sufficient site for the Jebusite fort of Ṣion, without any need of what we have seen to be the very doubtful trench across the East Hill to the north of the Virgin's Spring.[2] And for the disappearance of such a ʿswelling,' the original Ṣion or ʿOphel, we shall see that we can account by the measures which the Hasmoneans are said to have taken for the removal of the rock on which the Syrian citadel stood that had threatened the Temple.

*Sion or The ʿOphel originally a Knoll on E. Hill above Gihon.*

### 4. HISTORY OF THE NAME DAVID'S-BURGH OR ʿCITY OF DAVID.'

While the ancient Canaanite name *Ṣion* left the citadel

Ὀφλᾶν καὶ τὴν Κεδρῶνα καλουμένην φάραγγα; and vi. *B.J.* vi. 3: the Romans set fire to the ἀρχεῖον, καὶ τὴν ἄκραν καὶ τὸ βουλευτήριον καὶ τὸν Ὀφλᾶν καλουμένον.

[1] See above, p. 33 f.          [2] See above, p. 139.

on the knoll above Giḥon and spread first across the
Temple Mount and then over Jerusalem as a Corrobora-
whole, the Israelite title of *David's-Burgh* or tion of
preceding
*City of David* appears to have remained, con- evidence.
fined to that fort, its complex of buildings, and probably
the town which clustered about it.   We are, therefore,
able to discover, in the use of this title in Old Testament
times, corroboration of the preceding evidence that the
citadel lay south of the Temple on the East Hill.

David brought the Ark into the *City of David* and was
buried there.[1]   Solomon lodged there the daughter of
Pharaoh, till he should have built *his palace* The City of
*and temple and the wall of Jerusalem round* David in
O.T.
*about.*[2]   When the Temple was finished he Writings.
*brought up* to it (as we have seen) the Ark from the City
of David,[3] and was buried in the City of David,[4] as were
also in the next centuries many of the kings of Judah.[5]
Except in an oracle of Isaiah [6] (which, however, does not
define its position, save in holding it distinct from Jerusalem as a whole),[7] the City of David is not mentioned in
the prophets of the eighth century.   We find it, however,
in the Chronicler's account of that period, as distinct from
the City at large,[8] but also as lying upon the East Hill
above Giḥon.   For he tells us, as we have seen, that

---

[1] 2 Sam. vi. 12; 1 Kings ii. 10.
[2] 1 Kings iii. 1; xi. 27 also implies that David's-Burgh was a particular
part of Jerusalem.
[3] 1 Kings viii. 1.                                          [4] xi. 43.
[5] 1 Kings xiv. 31, etc.   Thenius (*Bücher der Könige*, ed. 2, p. 15) quotes
Theodoret (4th cent.) as placing these graves near Siloam.
[6] xxii. 9.                                                  [7] v. 10.
[8] 2 Chron. xxviii. 27, which states that Ahaz was buried in Jerusalem,
but not in the sepulchres of the kings, which, we have just seen, lay in the
City of David.

Hezekiah, in stopping the fountains outside the City so as to deprive the besiegers of water,[1] closed *the vent* or *issue* of the waters of the upper Giḥon, and *brought them straight down* or *underneath, to the west of the City of David.*[2]  This can refer only to the tunnel hewn under the East Hill from Giḥon to the Pool of Siloam, and it places the City of David above the tunnel and between its two ends.  The Chronicler adds that Manasseh built a wall on the west side of Giḥon in the valley of the Ķidron ; that is, on the most natural site for such a wall, immediately above the fountain, and *compassed about the 'Ophel.*[3]  After the Exile Nehemiah also places the City of David here, for he mentions the *stairs which go down from it* in close connection with Siloam,[4] and describes a procession as entering by the gate at Siloam, the Fountain Gate, and thence ascending these stairs towards the Temple.[5]  Sir Charles Wilson does not write too strongly when he says :[6] 'The statements of Nehemiah, which place the stairs of the City of David, the palace of David and his tomb between the Pool of Shelaḥ (Siloam) and the Temple, absolutely exclude the western spur as a possible site for the City of David.'

In the First Book of Maccabees David's-Burgh or ' the

---

[1] 2 Chron. xxxii. 3; cf. 2 Kings xx. 20; Ecclus. xlviii. 17.

[2] 2 Chron. xxxii. 30 : or *westwards, to the City of David*, the English versions do not give the exact meaning.  In the *P.E.F. Quart. Statement* for 1877, 178 f., Colonel Conder admits that according to this verse the City of David was on Ophel : but he regards the name as transferable.

[3] *Id.* xxxiii. 14.

[4] Neh. iii. 15, 16.  The latter verse adds the datum, *and unto the house of the Gibborim ;* but these were David's mercenaries, and their quarters were either in the David's-Burgh or close to it.

[5] xii. 37.

[6] Article 'Zion' in Hastings' *Bible Dictionary.*

City of David'[1] still stands distinct from the Temple
Mount, and both of them from the rest of ₍In First
Jerusalem. In 168 B.C. the forces of Antiochus Maccabees.
Epiphanes, after sacking and burning Jerusalem, *fortified
the City of David with a great and strong wall, with strong
towers, and it became unto them an Akra or citadel.*[2] A
Syrian garrison was put into it, who, *storing arms and
victuals, and gathering the spoils of Jerusalem, laid them up
there. And it became a great trap, an ambush against the
Sanctuary, and throughout an evil adversary to Israel.*[3] In
165, when Judas Maccabeus and his men went up to
Mount Ṣion, they saw the Sanctuary lying desolate, and
while they cleansed it they had to tell off certain of their
number *to fight against those in the Akra.*[4] Again, in 164,
as *those out of the Akra were confining Israel to the holy
places,*[5] Judas laid siege to the Akra, making mounds to
shoot from and engines of war.[6] About 161 Bacchides
strengthened and re-victualled the Akra, and imprisoned
in it certain Jewish hostages,[7] who were restored out of
the Akra to Jonathan in 153, when he took up his residence in Jerusalem and re-fortified the Sanctuary.[8] About
146 Jonathan besieged the Akra,[9] but could not take it,
and besought King Demetrius to withdraw the garrison,
for they were fighting against Israel.[10] Demetrius promised

---

[1] ῾Η πόλις Δαυείδ.   [2] Εἰς ἄκραν.

[3] 1 Macc. i. 33-36 ; cf. ii. 31, where either the word Ιερουσαλήμ is a gloss,
or the words πόλει Δαυείδ have been added as a more exact description of the
position of the garrison.

[4] *Id.* iv. 37-41.

[5] Οἱ ἐκ τῆς ἄκρας ἦσαν συγκλείοντες (for the Heb. סגר) τὸν Ισραὴλ κύκλῳ
τῶν ἀγίων.

[6] *Id.* vi. 18 ff.; cf. 26 : τὴν ἄκραν ἐν Ιερουσαλήμ.

[7] *Id.* ix. 52 f.   [8] *Id.* x. 7-11.

[9] *Id.* xi. 20-23.   [10] *Id.* xi. 41-53.

but broke his word.   Jonathan tried to starve out the
garrison by raising *a great mound between the Akra and
the City so as to separate it from the City, that it might be
by itself, alone, and men could neither buy nor sell.*[1]   Some
time after, the garrison, in want of victuals, sent an embassy
to Tryphon to relieve them by way of the wilderness, but
a snowstorm prevented him.[2]   Continuing to starve, a
number of them perished, and at last they surrendered to
Simon[3] in 142 B.C.   Simon occupied *the Temple-Hill that
was by the citadel,*[4] and made it stronger than before.
Although none of these passages define the exact site of
the Akra, the most of them imply that it was a particular
quarter of Jerusalem, distinct from both the Temple-Mount
and the rest of the City, and that it lay close beside the
former, a rival and a threatening fortress.   But the first of
the passages makes the Syrian Akra identical with the
*City of David,* which, as we have seen, was still recognised
in Nehemiah's time as lying immediately to the south of
the Temple.   The supposition is natural that in the
time of the Maccabees the name remained where it lay
from David's day to Nehemiah's.   It is true that more
than two and a half centuries separate Nehemiah from
the year 168 B.C., and that the possibility must not be
overlooked of the shifting of the name *City of David* from
its Biblical position to some other spot, say, on the north
of the Temple.   But, with this possible reservation, we
must hold that the Akra of the Maccabean period lay on
the same spot as Nehemiah's City of David, that is, on the
East Hill to the south of the separate Temple-Mount, or
just above Gihon.

[1] *Id.* xii. 36.          [2] *Id.* xiii. 21 f.          [3] *Id.* 49-51.
[4] *Id.* 52 : τὸ ὄρος τοῦ ἱεροῦ τὸ παρὰ τὴν ἄκραν.

We are, then, confronted with the problem of its disappearance, for no eminence rises there now which could
be separately fortified as a citadel, and menace
the Temple. But a statement of Josephus,
which supplements and concludes the history

The Syrian
Akra in
Josephus.

of the Akra under the Maccabees, comes to our assistance.
He has thrice stated that the Jews after taking the Akra,
and in order to avoid any further danger from it to the
Temple, reduced, or even abolished, the mound on which
it stood.  In one passage of the *Wars* he says : ' Simon
digged down' or 'rased the Akra';[1] but in another, that
the ' Hasmoneans . . . having worked down the height of
the Akra, made it lower than it was before, so that the
Temple should dominate even it.'[2]  In the *Antiquities* he
goes into more detail; he says that Simon, anxious 'that
the Akra should no more be a base from which the foe
might storm or harass Jerusalem, thought it the best way
to cut down also the hill on which the Akra stood, so
that the Temple should be the higher.  Having called
the people to an assembly, he persuaded them to set
themselves to the work, which cost them three whole
years, night and day, before they reduced the hill to
its base and made it a perfect level.  Thereafter the
Temple overtopped everything, both the Akra and
the hill on which it stood being demolished.'[3]  In these
passages Josephus writes of what had disappeared two

---

[1] Jos. I, *B.J.* ii. 2: κατέσκαψε τὴν ἄκραν.

[2] Jos. v. *B.J.* iv. 1: οἱ ᾿Ασαμωναῖοι . . . τῆς ἄκρας κατεργασάμενοι τὸ ὕψος
ἐποίησαν χθαμαλώτερον, ὡς ὑπερφαίνοιτο καὶ ταύτῃ τὸ ἱερόν.

[3] Abridged from xiii. *Ant.* vi. 7: the words, 'thereafter the Temple overtopped all the' other buildings or places are consistent only with the view
that the City was then confined to the East Hill.

centuries before his own day. He implies that the
Akra had dominated the Temple; but this it cannot
have done if, as First Maccabees states, it was on
the site of the City of David.[1] Also, his ascription
of its demolition to Simon is not compatible with the
statement of First Maccabees, that Simon garrisoned
and fortified the Akra.[2] In his second passage he
attributes the demolition to the Hasmoneans; and the
suggestion has been made that the work, whatever its
extent may have been, was due to Hyrcanus I., who built
another castle, the Baris at the north-west corner of the
sanctuary.[3] The erection of the Baris led to the demolition of the Syrian Akra. In any case, this disappeared,
and the thrice-repeated statement of Josephus that part,
at least, of the rock on which it stood was also removed,
cannot be a pure invention. His closing remark, that the
reduction of the Akra to a level left the Temple higher
than everything, is hardly consistent with his other
descriptions of the City.

We find, then, that the Biblical data and the testimony
of the Apocrypha agree with the conclusions at which we
arrived from the topographical and archæological evidence. The Jebusite stronghold of
Sion, afterwards called David's-Burgh, lay on
the East Hill above Gihon, the present Virgin's Spring;

Conclusions from foregoing.

---

[1] On the Akra in Pseudo-Aristeas see below, Bk. iii. Sir Charles
Watson (*P.E.F.Q.*, 1906, 50 ff.) places the Akra=Sion within the Haram
area, above 'the Great Sea,' partly because he thinks it lay N. of 'the City
of David'; but as we have seen above, Sion='City of David.'
[2] 1 Macc. xiv. 37.
[3] Wellhausen, *Israelit. u. Jüd. Gesch.* 227; Guthe, Hauck's *R.-E.* viii.
684; cf. Schürer, *Gesch.* 247 *n.* 14.

and probably on a more or less isolated rock, a ' swelling ' or mound into which the ridge originally rose, but which was removed under the Hasmoneans.   There is no trace in the Old Testament, let me repeat, of the application of the name Şion to the South-west Hill in distinction from the rest of Jerusalem, any more than there is a trace of the name Ophel ever having been attached to that Hill.   Nor is there any evidence of the South-west Hill ever having been regarded in Old Testament times as sacred.[1]   We have also, by the way, found that there is no compulsion to seek a larger area for the primitive Jerusalem than the East Hill offers south of the Temple. But this subsidiary question will have to be re-opened when we come to the relevant point in the history.

5. THE TRADITION, FROM JOSEPHUS ONWARDS, THAT THE 'CITY OF DAVID' LAY ON THE SOUTH-WEST HILL.

With Josephus, however, there started another tradition, which placed the ' City of David ' on the South-west Hill. Adopted by the Christian Church, which, from the fourth century, called this Hill Mount Şion, the tradition was, till a few years ago, *Josephus and the ' City of David.'* universally accepted, and is still held by some experts in the topography of Jerusalem.   Like some of the Old Testament writers, Josephus nowhere uses the name Şion,

---

[1] It is not necessary to use Baron von Alten's argument (*Z.D.P.V.* ii. 29) in support of this.   He quotes Ezekiel's description of the removal of the offended God of Israel from the Temple Hill to the Mount of Olives (xl. 23, xliii. 1 ff.), as if that proves that the South-west Hill had no special sacredness before Ezekiel's time ; for he thinks that if it had been sacred Ezekiel would have named it, instead of the Mount of Olives, as the Deity's resting-place.

either for a part of Jerusalem or in its wider Biblical
meaning, but he places David's-Burgh on the South-west
Hill. 'The City,' he says,[1] 'was built over two hills
divided by a middle valley. Of the hills, that which held
the Upper City was much the higher, and in length the
more straight.[2] On account, therefore, of its strength it
was called by King David the Fort,[3] but by us the Upper
Agora.' This is also his view of the topography in his
account of the capture of the City by David ;[4] for he says,
that after David 'took the lower City,' in his view the
East Hill, 'the citadel held out still,' that is on the South-
west Hill, till Joab took it. He adds that 'when David
had cast the Jebusites out of the citadel, he also re-built
Jerusalem and named it the City of David.' The contra-
dictions of this with the Biblical account are obvious.
In the latter there is no mention of an upper and a lower
City; nor did David call the whole of Jerusalem, but only
the Jebusite stronghold, the 'City of David.' It is evident
that Josephus has read into those ancient times the conditions of his own, when there were a lower and an upper
City on the two hills, and when the citadel built by Herod
so completely dominated Jerusalem from the latter, that
it was natural to suppose that the ancient stronghold had
occupied the same site.[5] The Biblical tradition had lasted
till the time of First Maccabees, 100 B.C. But between
that date and the time of Josephus, over 150 years, there
had happened the siege and capture of the City by Pompey,

[1] Jos. v. *B.J.* iv. 1. He adds the epithet ἀντιπρόσωπος. See above, p. 32 ff.

[2] Or 'level' (?) ; he means by this both the N.W. and S.W. Hills together.

[3] Φρούριον. It is significant that he does not call it Akra, conscious as he was of a citadel elsewhere.          [4] Jos. vii. *Ant.* iii. 1 f.

[5] *Enc. Bibl.* col. 2420, § by the present writer. Cf. von Alten, *Z.D.P.V.* ii. 20 f.

the siege, capture and great devastation by Sosius, and the very extensive rebuilding by Herod, which included the erection of Antonia, of the Temple, and of the great towers and fort on the west of the City. And before all these there had been the extensive building by Hyrcanus I. We have, therefore, more than sufficient to account for this transference by Josephus of the centre of power in Jerusalem from the East to the West Hill.

But if there was excuse for Josephus' contradiction of the Biblical statements about ' David's-Burgh,' there was even more for the Christians, who followed The Growth him in his error, and heaping change on of the change, as has been too often the case with tradition. geographical tradition in Palestine, removed the name Mount Sion from the Temple-Mount to the South-west Hill. Titus destroyed at least half the city.[1] According to Josephus, the whole was ruined except Herod's three towers and part of the west wall;[2] and other writers testify to a thorough devastation.[3] For sixty years the Temple area, Ophel, and other parts lay under *débris*, while the Tenth Legion held part of the Upper City as a fortified camp. Then came Hadrian's suppression of the revolt of 132. He destroyed most of what Titus had left, reducing Jerusalem to a waste,[4] forbidding it to its Jewish inhabitants, and colonising it with a different race.[5] The Temple-Mount was desecrated by the erection of a fane to Jupiter Capitolinus. The Legionary Camp remained to emphasise the supremacy of the South-

---

[1] Eusebius, *Demonstr. Evang.* vi. 18.
[2] Jos. vi. *B.J.* ix, 1, 4; vii. *B.J.* i. 1.
[3] Appian, *Syr.* 50.                    [4] Just. Mart., *Apol.* 47.
[5] Eus., *Eccl. Hist.* iv. 6; *Theophania*, iv. 20; *Chron.* (in Migne, *Patrol. Gr.* xix. 557 f.).

west Hill, and on the same hill the Church cherished the site of the institution of the Lord's Supper and the descent of the Spirit at Pentecost.[1] In a land in which names have continually drifted from their original sites, all these events, aided by the example of Josephus, render explicable the transference of the name Mount Sion to the South-west Hill. The transference did not happen immediately. Origen takes the Temple Hill and Sion as identical,[2] and so, apparently, even Jerome in one passage.[3] But the Bordeaux Pilgrim (333 A.D.) and, in the *Onomasticon*, both Eusebius (c. 350) and Jerome (c. 400) place Sion on the Western Hill; and from them onwards this became the accepted opinion among Christians. As Sir Charles Wilson has pointed out,[4] its acceptance was probably facilitated by the building of the Church of the Resurrection on the West Hill. But the statements of Josephus, the lapse of time, the destructions and changed conditions, the ignorance of pilgrims new to the city, careless talk and fallacious reasoning, all contributed. Such a tradition slowly accumulates and is fed from a hundred trickling sources. We need not impute deliberate fraud. 'There was no falsification of tradition, but an adaptation of an ancient term to a new situation.'[5]

For Christians, and afterwards for Mohammedans, the South-west Hill continued to be Mount Sion, and the citadel on it David's Tower down to the middle of the nineteenth century. These identifications were accepted by the first scientific geographers: Robinson, Ritter, Tobler, De Vogüé, and

Modern supporters of the tradition.

[1] Cf. Wilson, *Golgotha*, etc., 146 ff.      [2] Ad Joannem, iv. 19 f.
[3] *Ad Esai.* xxii. 1 f.
[4] Smith's *D.B.* 2, 'Jerusalem,' 1651.
[5] Lagrange, *Rev. Bibl.*, 1892, 17-38, 'Topogr. de Jérus.,' near the end.

others. They were also at first taken for granted by the excavators of the Palestine Exploration Fund, and by the late Dr. Schick. With various modifications, they are still defended by Colonel Conder,[1] Consul Merrill, Dr. Archibald Henderson, Dr. Stewart ; and, more recently, with fresh argument against the defenders of the East Hill theory, by Herr Georg Gatt, Dr. Rückert,[2] and in greatest detail by Dr. Carl Mommert.[3]

### 6. THE RETURN TO THE EAST HILL.

In 1856, Robinson, after his second journey to Palestine, and a fresh study of the topography of Jerusalem, wrote that 'amid the many diversities of opinion which have of late been advanced, it is gratifying to find a few points yet unassailed, and which in general are still admitted by most writers.' *Earliest assailants of the S.W. Hill Tradition.* The first of these, he says, is, 'that Sion was the south-western hill of the city.'[4] But the previous year there had appeared a volume by the Rev. J. F. Thrupp,[5] in which the author questioned Robinson's topography, and maintained that the earlier or true Ṣion, equivalent to the 'City of David,' was the Temple Hill, that the old Jebusite fortress stood on the northern part of the Hill, and the Temple in the south part of the Ḥaram area. In

[1] Hastings' *D.B.*, 'Jerusalem.'
[2] Gatt, *Die Hügel von Jerusalem*, Freiburg i. B., 1897, 1 ff; *Sion in Jerusalem*, 1900, 34, 38 ff; *Z.D.P.V.* xxv.; Rückert, *Die Lage des Berges Sion*, Freiburg i. B., 1898.
[3] *Topographie des alten Jerusalems, Erster Theil ; Sion u. Akra die Hügel der Altstadt*, n.d. (pref. dated Dec. 1900), with plan ; *Z.D.P.V.* xxiv. 183 ff.
[4] *L.B.R.*, 1856, 206.
[5] *Antient Jerusalem*, by J. F. Thrupp, M.A., vicar of Barrington (late Fellow of Trin. Coll., Camb.). Cambridge, Macmillan, 1855. Cf. Röhricht, *Bibl. Geog. Pal.*, 447.

1861 Mr. Thomas Lewin published his *Jerusalem*, in
which the claims of the East Hill were also advocated ;
and in 1864, the Rev. George Sandie,[1] after an independent examination of the sites and with fresh argument, showed that Ṣion was a separate part of the City,
and lay on the East Hill, emphasised the presence of
a ravine across the Hill to the north of the Temple
area, and assigned the castle Ṣion or 'the City of
David' to the site of Antonia. The same year Dr.
Ch. Ed. Caspari identified Ṣion with Moriah, and placed
the Syrian Akra on the Temple Hill ;[2] and in 1871,
Dr. Furrer presented a summary of the argument for
the East Hill.[3]

The earliest assailants of the traditional theory had
to support their argument for the East Hill without the
aid of the recent excavations, which have
supplied so many new data in support of
their main contention, and in correction of
some of their subsidiary views. The most of them had
placed Ṣion to the north of the Temple Area, but after
the discoveries on Ophel by the English engineers and
Dr. Guthe, and after a more thorough examination of
the Biblical evidence, the case we have presented for

*Trend of
recent
opinion.*

---

[1] *Horeb and Jerusalem*, by the Rev. George Sandie. Edinburgh, Edmon-
ston and Douglas, 1864. This little-known volume is well written, and is still
interesting and instructive, anticipating many points that have been elaborated
in the subsequent discussion, venturing also on conclusions that have received
little or no support, such as that Giḥon lay in the central valley el-Wâd, and
that the site of the Crucifixion was the north-west corner of the Temple Hill.
He follows Fergusson as to the site of our Lord's grave. Fergusson's first
work, *Essay on the Anc. Topogr. of Jer.*, appeared in 1847.

[2] *Theol. Stud. u. Krit.*, 1864, 309-328 : 'Zion u. die Akra der Syrer :' cf.
*Chronolog. Geogr. Einleitung in das Leben Jesu Christi*, 1869.

[3] Schenkel ; *Bibel-lexikon*, 1871 : art. 'Jerus.' ; cf. *Theol. Liter. Zeitung*,
1907, 258.

the position of Sion to the south of the Temple has
become increasingly strong.    Credit must first be given
for the use of the new materials to the Rev. W. F. Birch,
who in 1878 began a numerous series of articles,[1] in which
he argued independently on the Biblical and archæological
data for the location of 'the City of David' on Ophel;
to Baron von Alten, who in 1879[2] gave at length reasons,
good or less good, for identifying Sion with the East Hill;
and to Dr. Klaiber's two lucid articles in 1880-81.[3]    They
were followed in 1881 by Professors Stade and Robertson
Smith,[4] and in 1883 by Professor Sayce.[5]    Since then the
opinion has come to prevail with the great majority
both of the excavators of Jerusalem and of Old and New
Testament scholars.    It has been adopted by Sir Charles
Wilson and Sir Charles Warren,[6] who had previously
taken the other view, although the latter from the first felt
its incompatibility with the data of Nehemiah.[7]    Professor
Guthe adhered to it as early as 1882,[8] maintaining, as
we have seen, the existence of a gully between the site
of the fortress Sion and the Temple area, which, however,
is not certain, and requires further investigation.    In
addition may be mentioned the names of the following
authorities on the Old Testament or the topography of
the City:  Socin, Benzinger, Ryle, Driver, Buhl, Ryssel,
Bliss, H. G. Mitchell, and practically also A. B. Davidson.[9]

[1] In the Pal. Expl. Fund Quarterly Statement.        [2] *Z.D.P.V.* ii. 18 ff.
[3] *Id.* iii. 189 ff., iv. 18 ff.
[4] *Gesch. des Volkes Israel,* i. 267 f. ;  *Encycl. Brit.*[9] xiii. : art. 'Jerusalem.'
[5] *P.E.F.Q.*
[6] Wilson in *City and Land,* 1892, 19 f., and other works;  Warren in
Hastings' *D.B.* ii. 386 f.                        [7] *Recovery of Jerus.* 289.
[8] *Z.D.P.V.* v. 7-204, 271-378: cf. *Ausgrabungen bei Jerusalem,* Leipzig,
1883.
[9] Socin and Benzinger in Baedeker's *Palästina,* the latter also in *Hebr.
Archäol.,* 1894; Ryle on Neh. iii. 15, in *Camb. Bible for Schools,* 1893;

The most notable of recent adherents to the support of the East Hill is the Dominican scholar, Père Joseph Lagrange, in an able and lucid article, of date 1892.[1] Till the appearance of this, Roman Catholic opinion had almost unanimously[2] adhered to the ecclesiastical tradition in favour of the South-west Hill. There is no one more familiar with the site of Jerusalem than Père Lagrange; his estimate of the Biblical evidence and that of Josephus is temperate and judicious; and his explanation of the transference of the name a natural one. That such a scholar should have been compelled, by a careful review of the evidence, to abandon the church tradition is as significant as that explorers like Sir Charles Warren, who also for so long accepted it, have made the same change.

In forming a judgment on the question at issue, the reader will keep in mind that excavations have before now
Final Conclusions. overturned conclusions as widely accepted as is to-day the position of the original Ṣion upon Ophel; and that a great deal of excavation still remains to be done in Jerusalem. Till then we must be content with holding many of the topographical questions in suspense. But for those now before us, both the Biblical and the topographical data are too strong for doubtful answers. The Biblical evidence indubitably identifies Mount Ṣion with the Temple-Mount, which, there

Ryssel in his ed. of Bertheau's Commentary on Nehemiah; Buhl, *Geogr. des Alt. Paläst.*, 1896, 132; Driver, Hastings' *D.B.* ii. 554; Bliss, *Excav. at Jerus.*, 1894-97, 287 ff.; H. G. Mitchell, *Journ. of Bibl. Liter.*, xxii., 1903, 101; A. B. Davidson, *The Exile and Restoration*, in T. and T. Clark's *Bible-Class Primers*. The list could easily be multiplied.

[1] *Revue Biblique*, i. 17-38: 'Topographie de Jérus.'

[2] Another Rom. Catholic, Riess, *Bibl. Geog.*, had adopted the E. Hill theory, but this has been abandoned in a new ed. of his *Atlas Scripturæ Sacræ*, 1906, by Rückert.

has never been any doubt, was on the East Hill; and almost as clearly places the ' City of David ' below it. The topographical evidence from the present surface, and still more from excavations, tends wholly to the conclusion that this lower position lay to the south of the Temple upon Ophel, and with this the Biblical accounts agree. The position on the north, which the earlier advocates of the East Hill selected [1] does not suit the Biblical data ; Antonia is not below but above the Temple level. It is true that further excavations in the choked valley bed beyond it might unmask an ancient spring, which could have served as the centre of the earliest settlement and the Jebusite town. But against this there is the fact that the Virgin's Fountain was already in David's time a sacred and therefore an ancient spring; and had then or shortly after a tunnel and shaft communicating with the surface of Ophel above it. Thus everything at present points to the Jebusite Ṣion, the Israelite David's-Burgh, having been situated there; while, as we have seen, its disappearance can be accounted for.[2] The data, whether Biblical or topographical, appear to me too clear for indecision on the main points. Subsidiary is the question whether Jerusalem in the Jebusite period was confined to the East Hill. We have seen that this confinement was possible ;[3] whether it was actual either then or under the Kings are questions that will best be treated at the relevant points in the history.

[1] So even v. Alten, *Z.D.P.V.* i. 60 ff.　　　[3] Above, p. 142 ff.
[2] Above, p. 159 ff.

# CHAPTER VII

## THE VALLEY OF HINNOM

I N Chapter I., on the Site of the City, a detailed account has been given of the two encompassing valleys, the Topographical Wâdy Sitti Mariam and the W. er-Rabâbi, importance and of the dividing or central valley, el-Wâd. of the Valley. In Chapter II., on Facts and Questions in the Topography, it was pointed out, that no one doubts that the W. Sitti Mariam, the valley which runs down the east of the City, and separates it from the Mount of Olives, is the Ḳidron of Scripture and Josephus, or that el-Wâd is the Tyropœon of Josephus ; but that while the majority of experts in the topography of Jerusalem identify the lower part of the W. er-Rabâbi with the Biblical Valley of Hinnom or Gehenna, there are some who place the latter in the W. Sitti Mariam, and others in el-Wâd. It is to the discussion of this question, the location of the Valley of Hinnom, that we are to address ourselves in the present chapter. Interesting in itself because of the superstitious practices which, under Ahaz and Manasseh, found their scene in Hinnom, and because of the eschatology which later Judaism associated with the name Gehenna, the question of the position is also of very great importance in the topography of Jerusalem. On our

170

answer, and especially on whether we place the Valley in el-Wâd or the W. er-Rabâbi, will depend our views as to the size of the City under the later kings of Judah ; as to the line of her western and southern walls, and as to the position of such important points as the Valley-Gate, the Dung-Gate and the Dragon's Spring. If el-Wâd be the Valley of Hinnom, Jerusalem was confined, down to the Exile and for long after the Return, to the East Hill, and the western wall with the Valley-Gate and Dung-Gate upon it ran up the western slope of Ophel. But if the Wâdy er-Rabâbi be Hinnom, the South-west Hill was an integral part of Jerusalem under the kings, the western and southern walls ran round the edge of the Wâdy, and the two gates named must be sought for on the latter, above the lower stretch of the valley.

The name of this sinister valley has also been the subject of discussion. It is never described in the Old Testament as a *naḥal*, a valley with a winter-brook, but always as a *gai"*, a valley without such a brook, for which we have no equivalent in English, but which, because as a rule it is smaller than the other, we may translate *hollow*,[1] *glen* or *ravine*. Of the name, there are various forms : Gê-ben-Hinnom,[2] *Hollow* or *Ravine of the Son of Hinnon ;* Gê-bnê-Hinnom,[3] *Hollow of the Sons of Hinnom ;* Gê-Hinnom ;[4] and Hag-Gai

*The Name Gê-ben-Hinnom.*

---

[1] This indeed may be the radical meaning of gai' גַּיְא from גָוָה *to be hollow:* cf. Aram. גַּוָּא, *the inside.*

[2] Heb. text of Josh. xv. 8, xviii. 16; 2 Chron. xxviii. 3, xxxiii. 6; Jer. xix. 2; and the Heb. and Gk. of Jer. vii. 31, 32, xix. 6, xxxii. 35.

[3] Kethibh of 2 Ki. xxiii. 10 (but the Keri and Gk. have *son*), and the Gk. (Cod. B) of 2 Chron. xxxiii. 6, and Jer. xix. 2.

[4] Josh. xv. 8, xviii. 16 (once each in Heb., twice in Gk.), and Neh. xi. 30 (omitted in Gk. Cod. B).

or *The Hollow*.[1]   The last two of these occur only in late
passages and are doubtless abbreviations of the first, which
from its frequency is to be preferred to the second.[2]
Whether Ben-Hinnom was the name of a man or of a
deity it is impossible to say.   The reading is too often
confirmed in both the Hebrew and the Greek of the Old
Testament[3] to leave room for emendation (Canon Cheyne
has on religious grounds proposed Na'aman),[4] and the
attempts to translate it as *wailing*,[5] in reference to the
cries of the sacrificed children, are fanciful and have
received little support.   It must be admitted that no
name corresponding to Hinnom, either human or divine,
has been found in Hebrew or any other Semitic language;[6]
and it is not impossible, therefore, that the term was originally geographical or botanical.   It occurs only from the
time of Ahaz (? or Manasseh[7]) to that of the Chronicler.
In the Targums it appears not in a geographical but in
a theological sense;[8] and in the same sense the gorge
is described without being named in the Apocalyptic
literature.[9]   The Books of Maccabees and Josephus do
not give the name, nor is it employed geographically in

[1] 2 Chron. xxvi. 9 ; Neh. ii. 13, 15, iii. 13; perhaps also Jer. ii. 23.

[2] The plural Bnê may have risen from assonance with the preceding Gê.

[3] Heb. always הִנֹּם ; Gk. Ελνομ (most frequently), Ουνομ, Ονομ, and in
Josh, xviii. 16, Γαιεννα (B) and Γαι Ουνομ (A).

[4] *Encyc. Bibl.*, art. ' Hinnom, Valley of.'

[5] הִנֹּם, as if connected with Arab. *hanna* ' to sigh ' or ' whimper ' : cf.
Graf on Jer. vii. 31.

[6] Unless the Babylonian Ennam, cited by Hommel (*Altisrael. Überlieferung*,
142, referred to by Guthe, Hauck's *R.-E.* viii. 669), is the same.

[7] See below.   It has been proposed as an emendation to the *Valley of
Vision* in Isa. xxii. 1, 5.

[8] On Psalm cxl. 11: גֵּיהִנָּם.

[9] R. H. Charles, Hastings' *Bible Dictionary*, art. ' Gehenna.'

the Talmud, except perhaps to designate a valley of hot springs east of Jordan.[1]  Apparently it had ceased to be used of the gorge at Jerusalem after 300 B.C.

The Hollow of Hinnom has been placed by different authorities in each of the three valleys of Jerusalem : the eastern Ḳidron or Wâdy Sitti Mariam, the central Tyropœon, el-Wâd, and the southern (and western) Wâdy er-Rabâbi; while some have sought to unite these views, so far as Topheth is concerned, by placing the latter on the open junction of the three valleys below Siloam.

I. In the *Onomasticon* Eusebius and Jerome place Γαιεννουμ or Gehennom under the eastern wall of Jerusalem ; the Moslem geographers Muḳad- dasi and Nâsir-i-Khusrau call the Ḳidron- valley Wâdy Jahannum ; the Jewish com- mentator, Kimchi,[2] identifies the valleys of Jehoshaphat and Hinnom ; and on Fuller's Map in his *Pisgah Sight of Palestine* the ' Vallis Ben-Hinnom ' runs between the City and the Mount of Olives.  Dean Stanley and Sir Charles Warren have revived this identification.[3]  But their argument for it is defective in all the premises.  The identification does not ' follow from Jeremiah xix. 11.'  The gate Ḥarsith, which opened on Hinnom, does not mean Eastgate.  The identity of 'En-rogel with the Virgin's Fountain, on which Sir Charles Warren depends, is contradicted by the narrative of Solomon's coronation.[4]  And the Mohammedan tradition, which he quotes, is not only balanced by another, for Idrisi places Jahannum in the W. er-

1. Location in Ḳidron inadmissible,

---

[1] Neubauer, *Geog. du Talmud*, 36 f.

[2] On Isa. lxvi. 24.

[3] Stanley, *Recovery of Jerusalem*, xiv. ; Warren on ' Hinnom ' in Hastings' *Dict. of the Bible*.

[4] See above, p. 109.

Rabâbi;[1] but the origin of it, as well as of the statement in Eusebius, may be easily accounted for—and in this way. When the Gê-ben-Hinnom, as a place-name, had disappeared from the surroundings of Jerusalem, the theological Gehinnom as a state of torment for apostate Jews could not remain in the air, but demanded a local habitation; and this was found for it, if one may judge

and due to the from Isaiah lxvi. 24, somewhere near the
theological Temple, and in all probability in the valley
Gehenna
being placed of the Ḳidron.[2] As we see from the story of
there. Josiah's reforms, the bed of the Ḳidron was
already a place for refuse and regarded as unclean. The offal of the Temple, according to the Old Testament and the Talmud,[3] was cast into it, and probably in part consumed by fire. In any case, we may see how the theological Gehinnom came to be located here; the more so, that according to the belief about it, the sufferings of its victims were to take place in sight of the righteous, of whose eternal habitations the Temple-courts were the natural symbol. But this location of the theological Gehinnom in the Ḳidron Valley (from which probably arose the modern name, Wâdy en-Nâr[4]), is no argument for placing there the actual Gê-ben-Hinnom. On the contrary, such a geographical identification is excluded by these two data of the Old

---

[1] Robinson, *Bibl. Res.* i. 403; *Z.D.P.V.* viii. 127.

[2] So Kimchi on this passage: cf. the late identification of Ḳidron with the valley of Jehoshaphat, Joel iii. 12; note also Zech. xiv. 3 ff.

[3] Jer. xxxi. 40: *Jerus.* 'Nazir,' 57, 4; *Babyl.* 'Yoma,' 58, 2. Buhl's identification (p. 94) of the *'emek* of Jer. xxxi. 40 with the Gorge of the Son of Hinnom is on the ground of the name impossible. The *'emek* is the more open space of the Ḳidron-valley.

[4] In April 1904 I was informed that the Bedouin about Mar Saba sometimes carry the name Wâdy en-Nâr up the W. er-Rabâbi to the Jaffa-gate. Robinson was told the same, but I cannot find his reference to this.

Testament: that the Ḳidron is never called Gai but Naḥal, and that the gate which Nehemiah calls the Gate of the Gai lay not on the east of the City over Ḳidron, but on the west over either the Tyropœon or the W. er-Rabâbi.

2. The Gê-ben-Hinnom has been identified by the Rev. W. F. Birch,[1] Professors Robertson Smith[2] and Sayce,[3] and Dr. Schwartz[4] with the Tyropœon. This 2. Not in the is not unsuitable to the place assigned to the Tyropœon. Gai in the record of the boundary between Benjamin and Judah,[5] nor to the data provided by Nehemiah.[6] But it is only possible if the Tyropœon lay outside the City at the time of Manasseh, for human sacrifices never took place within the walls of a town. But, as we have seen, Siloam in the lower Tyropœon was within the City by the time of Hezekiah ; and its reservoir, to which that monarch brought the waters of Giḥon by a conduit beneath Ophel, could have been of no use to the citizens in time of siege unless they also held the Western Hill.[7] Under Manasseh, therefore, the Tyropœon was well within the City and could not have been the scene of the sacrifice of children.

3. There remains the third of the valleys, the Wâdy er-Rabâbi. This suits the direction assigned to the Gê-ben-Hinnom on the border between Benjamin 3. But in the and Judah ; and under the later monarchy, as W. er-at all other times, it lay outside the City walls. Rabâbi. By far the greatest number of modern authorities accept

[1] *P.E.F.Q.*, 1882, 53 ff; 1889, 38 ; 1893, 330 ; 1898, 168, etc.
[2] *Enc. Brit.* (⁹) xiii. 'Jerusalem' ; *Enc. Bibl.* 'Jerusalem,' § 24.
[3] *P.E.F.Q.* 1883, 213.
[4] *Das Heilige Land*, cited by Warren, Hastings' *D.B.* ii. 387.
[5] Josh. xv. 8, xviii. 16.
[6] Which Robertson Smith, indeed, thinks a proof of the identification.
[7] See above, p. 38.

it as the Gai.[1]  Sir Charles Wilson has suggested that the name Hinnom may have extended to the flat ground where all three valleys meet.[2]  Here, in fact, it was placed by Jerome in his Commentary on Jeremiah:[3] among the gardens watered from Siloam, a place 'amoenus atque nemorosus, hodieque hortorum delicias praebet.'  And mediæval writers argued that Topheth and Hinnom both meant pleasure, and supported the argument by an alleged antithesis between these names and the *Valley of Slaughter* in Jeremiah vii 32.[4]  Hence Milton's 'pleasant valley of Hinnom.'  But the junction of the three valleys is practically part of the Naḥal Ḳidron and too open to be designated a Gai.  The designation fully suits the W. er-Rabâbi a little way up from its mouth, where the rocks are high and the passage narrow.  Certainly the scenery is there more consonant to the gloomy superstition and its savage rites than are the gardens and groves watered from Siloam.  On the ridge to the south lies the traditional Aceldama, the Field of Blood, and the rock around is honeycombed with graves.  Melander argues that the traditional Aceldama was the site of Topheth.[5]

Professor Robertson Smith argued for the identification of the Tyropœon with the Hollow of Hinnom on this 'The Gate of the Gai.' ground, among others, that Nehemiah describes the Gate of the Gai or *Valley-Gate* to have been 1000 cubits from the Dung-Gate, which he implies lay close to the Fountain-Gate at the south-east angle of the City.[6]  Now the Gate of the Gai used to be

[1] Quaresmius, Barclay, Robinson, Wilson, Socin, Buhl, Benzinger, etc.
[2] Smith's *Dict. of the Bible* (2nd ed.), 1373.
[3] On vii. 31 f.
[4] Quaresmius, lib. iv. cap. xviii.
[5] *Z.D.P.V.* xvii. 25 ff.     [6] Neh. ii. 13, iii. 14 f.

placed by those who supported the identification of the Gai with the W. er-Rabâbi[1] high up the latter at or near the present Jaffa Gate, an impossible distance from the Dung and Fountain gates, according to Nehemiah's data. It was reasonable therefore for Professor Robertson Smith to suppose that the Gate of the Gai lay up the Tyropœon, and that the latter was the Gai itself. But his hypothesis becomes unnecessary if we can prove, or indeed may only reasonably suppose, the existence of an ancient city-gate above some lower stretch of the Valley of Hinnom. In itself such a position for a gate is more than probable. On the theory (for which the evidence is irresistible) that Jerusalem of the Kings covered the South-west Hill, the western and southern city wall cannot possibly have run the whole way round from the present Jaffa Gate to Siloam without another gate some-where between these points. The most natural position for such a gate is about the south-west corner. Near this, in 1894, Dr. Bliss began his celebrated excavations, which revealed a line of wall running south-east from the end of the Protestant Cemetery, and then, still on the edge of the Hill, eastward to the south-east corner of the ancient City. In this wall, just before it turns east, that is practically at the south-west corner, he laid bare an ancient gateway,[2] with four sills, one above the other, representing four different periods: and from these he traced north-east into the ancient City a line of street.[3] On the first reports of this Gate, Professor Guthe in 1895 identified it with the Gate of the Gai.[4] In the spring of 1901, with Dr.

---

[1] *E.g.* Robinson, *B.R.* i. 423; Schick, *Z.D.P.V.* viii. 272.
[2] The first to suggest a gate here was, I believe, Professor Stade, in 1888 : *Gesch.* ii. 167.
[3] *Excav. at Jerus. 1894-97*, 16 ff.     [4] *M.u.N.D.P.V.*, 1895.

Bliss's book before me, I twice carefully examined the
course of the excavations, once under the guidance of Dr.
Bliss himself, and, ignorant of Dr. Guthe's identification,
came to the same conclusion.   In 1901-2, Professor
Mitchell of Boston, then in residence as head of the
American Archæological School, also independently
reached this identification.[1]  These separate arrivals at the
same point illustrate how probable a position this is for
the Gate of the Gai.   But the four sills of the gateway
seem all to belong to the Christian era;[2] if Nehemiah's
Gate of the Gai stood exactly here, none of its masonry
has survived.   Moreover, the distance to the south-east
angle of the City, near which Nehemiah's Dung Gate
opened, is still rather great for Nehemiah's datum of 1000
cubits between the gates.   Dr Bliss's work has disclosed
certain alternatives round the south-east corner nearer
the Siloam end of the wall, and more in harmony with
Nehemiah's statement of its distance from the latter.
One of these is between his Towers III. and IV., but
here he marks no sign of a gateway in either his higher
or lower line of wall.    Another alternative is between
his Towers IV. and V., the proximity of which, as he
says, favours the idea 'that they once flanked a gate
midway between them, at a point where a drain coming
from the north butts against the rubble foundation,' and
where there are other signs of a gate.[3]   No gate was here
found by him, and he says the presence of a gate between
the corners remains uncertain.   Yet it is to be noted
that to the north, on the eastern slope of the South-west
Hill, he laid bare a line of paved street running north and

[1] *Journal of Bibl. Liter.*, 1903, 108 ff., with plan.
[2] See below, pp. 215 ff.                    [3] *Excav. at Jerus.* 27.

south.[1] From its crossing certain terrace pavements, he gathers it was late, and he did not follow the line of it south to his walls ; but we must remember the tendency of successive streets in Jerusalem to follow the same ancient lines, 'and a slight diversion of this street to the west would bring it to a point midway between Towers IV. and V.'[2] This point is distant from the gate opened by Dr. Bliss not far from the south-east corner, which may be Nehemiah's 'Dung Gate,' about 1280 feet, while the distance of the Gate at the South-west corner is nearly 1900 feet. Neither figure is near to the 1000 cubits, about 1600 feet, which Nehemiah gives presumably (but not necessarily) as the distance from the Gate of the Gai to the Dung Gate.[3] But in any case, it is clear that the Gate of the Gai must have opened over the Gai-ben-Hinnom somewhere near the south-west corner of the South-west Hill, where what has always been a main line of street through the City from north to south terminated ; and where a pathway used by men and laden animals still passes down the brow of the hill, not far from the Gate unearthed by Dr. Bliss, into the W. er-Rabâbi, the bed of which is from 130 to 170 feet below the sills of the Gate. In the bed it meets a path up and down the valley, and another which climbs southwards the opposite hill. With such an approximate position for the Gate of the Gai, there is removed the last objection to identifying the Gai with the Wâdy er-Rabâbi.

We have now made it clear that, although Șion, or David's-Burgh, and the earliest city lay upon the East

---

[1] *Excav. at Jerus.* 78 : part of this was previously uncovered by the Augustinians : cf *P.E.F.Q.*, 1894, 18.

[2] *Id.* 80.  [3] Neh. iii. 13.

Hill, Jerusalem extended under the Kings of Judah
over the South-west Hill also; and found her

Conclusions as
to the extent   limits, as we have assumed in previous chapters,
of the City.
on the edges of the two Hills of her site
above the W. Sitti Mariam and the W. er-Rabâbi
respectively.    We are now therefore ready for the
fourth of the great topographical questions we have to
consider before we attack the details of the history; the
exact course of the City Walls.

# CHAPTER VIII

## THE WALLS OF JERUSALEM

HAVING now before us the extent of ancient Jerusalem within at least her eastern, southern, and western boundaries, we are able to state—even if we find it impossible wholly to answer—the The Facts questions connected with the City walls. and Questions. While the Jebusite fortress of Sion, afterwards called David's-Burgh, lay upon Ophel, and this part of the East Hill may also have held the rest of Jebusite Jerusalem;[1] the City of the Jewish Kings covered both the East and West Hills along with the Central Valley: or all between the Ķidron on the east and the Valley of Hinnom on the west and south.[2] Above these 'impassable ravines,' Josephus tells us that a single line of wall sufficed for the defence of the City;[3] while from Nehemiah we learn many of the details of its course along the edge of them.[4] The natural direction for this single wall to take is so obvious that there has been virtual agreement as to its general course, especially since the excavations of Sir Charles Warren and Professor Guthe on the East Hill and of Mr. Maudslay and Dr. Bliss on the South-west Hill. In this quarter of the City

---

[1] See above, Chapter vi.　　　　　　[2] Chapter vii.

[3] Τρισὶ δ' ὠχυρωμένη τείχεσιν ἡ πόλις καθ' ἣν μὴ ταῖς ἀβάτοις φάραγξι κεκύκλωτο, ταύτῃ γὰρ εἰς ἣν περίβολος: v. B. J., iv. 1.

[4] See below, pp. 195 ff.

the only uncertainties are : at what times the line of wall included, and at what times it excluded, the Pools of Siloam in the mouth of the Tyropœon valley; and whether a line of wall also ran up the western edge of Ophel. Much more difficult to determine is the course of the north wall or walls. On the north, as we have seen, the natural features are not so positive as are the ravines on the east, south and west of the City; both within and since our period, building, destruction and rebuilding have been much more frequent here than on the south; and it is not possible to conduct, as there, long continuous lines of excavation. Nehemiah indicates along the northern face of the City only a single line of wall, but we are told by the Chronicler of a *second wall* in preexilic times (built by Hezekiah),[1] which is now generally understood as a north wall enclosing a suburb of the earlier City in the only direction in which (as we have seen) the City, after it had occupied the South-west Hill, could expand into suburbs. But Josephus reports for his time no fewer than three northern walls. Of these the First Wall[2] was the inmost and most southerly, the earliest northern rampart of the City; before Hezekiah built out in front of it his second wall. Modern opinion is generally agreed as to the course of this First Wall: the natural line for it was the north edge of the Southwest Hill above the ravine which runs from the present Jaffa Gate eastward into the Central Valley. The Second Wall of Josephus would then be Hezekiah's *second wall*, and if this be correct, it is the single northern

---

[1] 2 Chron. xxxii. 5.

[2] It must be kept in mind by the student that when describing the advance of Titus into the City, Josephus reverses the above order of the three walls, and that his Third, or Agrippa's wall, is then called by him the First.

line of wall described by Nehemiah. The course it
followed is still one of the least understood and most
hotly debated questions of the topography. Nehemiah's
description implies that it ran from the north-east corner
of the City, that is from the north of the Temple enclosure
of his time (or somewhere to the south of the ravine that
falls into the Kidron Valley, under the present Ḥaram
area, north of the Golden Gate)[1] across the East Hill and
the Central Valley to some uncertain point above Hinnom
on the South-west Hill. Josephus describes it as starting
from Antonia, on the north-west of the Temple enclosure,
and following a curved line to the Gate Genath on the
First Wall, somewhere near the north-western corner of
the latter. The beginning and end are therefore more
or less fixed points; but, for the reasons given above, the
intervening course is, and at present cannot but be, much
disputed. Though probable on one or other of two widely
differing lines—one of which excludes the Church of the
Holy Sepulchre, but the other, partly following the present
north wall of the City, includes it—the course of the
Second Wall is still unknown to us. The Third Wall of
Josephus was built by Agrippa north of the Second,
in order to cover a new suburb: all we certainly know of
it is that it included Bezetha: the rest of its course
is largely a matter of inference.

These are the main certainties and uncertainties of the
subject before us. Minor questions must be separately
discussed in the historical part of this volume,
at the dates at which they arise. But it will be Course of the
following in-
convenient to give in the present chapter a quiry.
general statement of the data, topographic, archæological,

---

[1] See above, pp. 33 f.

and literary, and the more certain conclusions which may be drawn from them. I propose to start from the present walls, define the kind of evidence on which we seek to identify the ancient walls, and summarise first the literary and then the archæological evidence.

## 1. THE PRESENT CITY WALLS.

It will be most convenient to start with the present City walls and their predecessors back to the time of Titus, because it is the present City walls, complete and dominant as they are, which tend to govern the mind of the student, but which, nevertheless, except in so far as they follow the natural boundaries of the site, he must ignore in his quest of the ancient lines of fortification. The walls of Jerusalem, with their towers and gates, owe their present form (*circa* 1540) to the Sultân Suleiman[1] the Magnificent, the successor of Selim I. who, in 1517, brought Syria under the dominion of the Turks. The variety of their construction is no less apparent than that of the character of their course. On the east, and partly on the west, this follows the natural line of fortification above the encompassing valleys, and the mixed, and largely modern, masonry rests in many parts upon courses of an ancient date. The north wall also contains some lower courses of an ancient character still *in situ ;* and with some exceptions, to be afterwards noted, coincides with an old line of wall within a great rock-hewn ditch, which entrenched it against the plateau to the north. But the present south wall follows no natural or intelligible

*The Present Walls and their Predecessors back to Titus.*

[1] An inscription on the Damascus Gate ascribes its rebuilding to Suleiman in the year 1537.

line of fortification. Leaving the edge of the W. er-Rabâbi just above the Pool of the Sulṭân, it strikes east across the middle of the back of the South-west Hill on an average rock-level of just over 2500 feet (762 m.) for 275 yards (251 m.). Descending a little to the Burj el-Kibrît, 2388 feet (728 m.), the wall turns thence north and north-east, on pretty much the same level, to a point from which it strikes nearly due east across the Tyropœon valley (traversing the rock-bed of this at about 2250 feet, 686 m.) to a point on Ophel 2326 feet (709 m.). Here it turns at a right angle north to the southern wall of the Ḥaram. There had never been a satisfactory explanation of the curious course of this south wall till Sir Charles Wilson, from a reasonable argument as to the position and size of the Legionary Camp on the South-west Hill (A.D. 70-132), suggested that the Wall follows the southern limit of that camp, and then crosses the Tyropœon on the line of Hadrian's city of Aelia.[1] This was also the southern line of the Crusaders' Jerusalem. But it excludes from the City the half of the South-west Hill, all Ophel and the lower Tyropœon, which were enclosed, as we have seen, by the First Wall of Josephus : the wall which Titus left ruined, and which was doubtless further destroyed by the commanders of the Legionary Camp and by Hadrian. Between Hadrian and the Crusaders the following changes took place in the south wall of the City. In the fourth century it still ran upon the south line of the Camp and Hadrian's City across the back of the South-west Hill.[2] But by the fifth century all the South-west Hill, now

[1] *Golgotha*, etc., 143 ff. These arguments as to the Camp and Hadrian's City, and their conclusions, should be studied by all who seek a clear view of the later topography.

[2] So the Bordeaux Pilgrim, 333 A.D.

called Mount Sion,[1] was again included within a wall,
which, however, left Siloam outside as it crossed to
Ophel;[2] and the Empress Eudocia, consort of Theodosius
II., who resided in Jerusalem about 450 A.D., is said to
have added walls which brought Siloam within the City.[3]
These, which must have run down the edge of the South-
west Hill to the mouth of the Tyropœon, across this and
up the eastern edge of Ophel, remained probably till the
capture of the City by the Persians under Chosroes II.
514 A.D., who effected much ruin of the public buildings,
and doubtless of the walls as well. After this the south
City-wall was again drawn upon the line of Hadrian's,
along which it has remained to the present day.[4] It is
interesting that the City thus owes its present southern
shape, not to its ancient and native growth, but to the
stamp of its Roman conquerors.

The City walls just described all rose outside of our
period, or subsequent to the destruction by Titus. Their

Their
character-
istics.
dates within the Christian era are marked by
several signs: Byzantine, Crusading or Saracenic architecture and ornament, either on
themselves, or on other buildings which their position may
prove to be earlier than themselves; or the insertion
in them of Roman inscriptions, evidently out of place;[5]

---

[1] See above, pp. 161 ff.

[2] The Epitome ascribed to Eucherius, Bishop of Lyons, 430-450: *P.P.T.*
vol. ii. p. 10: on the preferred reading, Siloam is said to be 'infra muros';
another reading, 'intra muros,' may be a later emendation to suit the change
brought about by the Empress Eudocia's wall: cf. Bliss, *Excav. at Jerus.*
307, 318; Wilson, *Golgotha*, 147.

[3] Antoninus Martyr (560-570 A.D.), xxv.; cf. Theodosius (c. 530), xlvii.:
*P.P.T.* vol. ii.

[4] Cf. Guthe, Hauck's *R.-E.* viii. 690, lines 15-22.

[5] As, for example, the presence of an inscription of Hadrian upside down

or their position above rubbish containing remains of the Christian era, or other similarly obvious proofs. All such walls must be put aside from our inquiry into the walls before and up to Titus, except (as I have said) in so far as they follow lines of fortification older than themselves, and contain the material of the latter still *in situ.*

## 2. Proofs of the Ancient Walls up to Titus, and their Limits.

But where we find remains of walls on the natural lines of fortification or (which is much the same) on lines indicated by Josephus, and without any sign of The Marks the Christian era in or below them, we may of earlier examine these in the expectation of detecting Walls. in their structure or surroundings some further evidence that they belong to our period. We know the natural lines of fortification, and Josephus has traced along them, at least on the east, south and west of the City, the course of the walls which were standing in his day.[1] He also describes their structure. They rose from precipitous rocks. At intervals there were towers, with solid bases, built of huge blocks so carefully joined to each other as to appear one mass of stone.[2] We know also that it was the custom at the time to protect these bases by revetments (as engineers call them) of masonry, 'built at the angle of slope best calculated to resist the ram and projectiles, and to render escalade difficult,' and that opposite gates and the more assailable parts of the line, ditches, counterscarps and other outworks were cut in the rock.[3]

in the south wall of the Haram, *P.E.F. Mem.*, 'Jerus.' 9; Schick, *Die Stiftshütte u. der Tempel z. Jerus.* 340 f.

[1] v. *B.J.* v. 1.       [2] *Ibid.* 2-4.

[3] Wilson's summary of Philo of Byzantium (*circa* B.C. 150) in *Golgotha*, 122.

Tacitus, too, describes the walls of Jerusalem as carried round the two hills and ingeniously drawn with curves and re-entrant angles. They rose, he adds, on scarps which added greatly both to their height and that of the towers,[1] besides lifting the masonry beyond reach of rams and miners. He refers, of course, to the rocky slopes above the valleys where scarps were possible. On level ground the wall was built much broader, and was entrenched by a rock-cut ditch. Now where such features of fortification—thus reported either of Jerusalem herself in the Roman period or as usual at the time—are discovered to-day along any of the natural lines of wall described by Josephus, without recognisable remains of the Christian era about them, we may safely identify the remains as earlier than the siege by Titus. Position on one of the known ancient lines of wall, foundation upon the rock itself beneath the virgin soil, with scarps below where scarps were possible, and, where they were not, with extremely thick and solid masonry; the stones large, finely drafted and fitting exactly to each other, and with no appearance of being anything else than *in situ*—these are the marks which experienced excavators consider to be justifications for assigning a wall to the period before Titus.[2] Sometimes, indeed, there may be additional

---

[1] 'Sed urbem, arduam situ, opera molesque firmaverant, quis vel plana satis munirentur. Nam duos colles in immensum editos claudebant muri per artem obliqui aut introrsus sinuati, ut latera oppugnantium ad ictus patescerent. Extrema rupis abrupta, et turres ubi mons juvisset, in sexagenos pedes; inter devexa in centenos vicenosque attollebantur, mira specie, ac procul intuentibus pares.'—Tacitus, *Hist.* v. 11.

[2] Dr. Guthe (*Z.D.P.V.*, 1882, 273 ff.) suggests another sign for determining the ancient lines of wall. Quoting Strabo's report (see above, p. 16), that while the City had abundant supplies of water within its walls, the environs were waterless, he argues that the course of the ancient walls cannot have run far outside the region of frequent cisterns. But Strabo's words are rather

evidence in the presence of a layer of *débris* above these remains of wall and below the foundation of another and later wall; for, as Dr. Bliss has reasonably argued in the case of such a superimposed wall round the South-west Hill, the *débris* may represent the ruin and waste in this quarter during the long period between Titus and the fifth century, and in this case the lower wall is that which Titus overthrew. But we must remember that while the data we have quoted may suffice to prove an origin within our period for the remains of walls on the southern end of the City's site, where we know the ancient and natural lines, and where our knowledge of subsequent building is comparatively good, the same data are not so conclusive upon the North-west Hill, on which, along now unknown lines, a good deal of building and rebuilding was effected in the early Christian centuries, upon, it may have been, the same principles which characterise the ancient architecture. And this is part of the reason of the difficulty of identifying any remains of walls found on the North-west Hill with the Second Wall of Josephus.

As yet we have only discovered evidence sufficient to prove ancient remains as portions of the walls extant in the time of Josephus. The further attempt to assign their construction to some definite period or periods before his date is a much more difficult and, in great part, an impossible task. Mr. Dickie, an expert architect and the colleague

*Difficulty of assigning them to definite Periods.*

to be understood of the distribution of springs (compare passage of Dion Cassius quoted above on the same page); and, in fact, the large P.E.F. map, as well as Schick's and Benzinger's, show the remains of many ancient cisterns outside the City, especially on the northern plateau. The evidence from cisterns is therefore limited by Dr. Guthe himself to the steep southern flank of the City; yet, even here, it is in some cases uncertain owing to our defective knowledge of the rock surface, and in others superfluous.

of Dr. Bliss in the excavations on the South-west Hill
and Ophel, has recently warned us against the use of a
standard on which much reliance was once placed:[1] the
style of the masonry and stone-dressing. His conclusions
are, that whatever light may have been thrown on the
subject by his investigations, 'it does not help us to define
the date of a building by its dressing. On the contrary,
it tends to encourage scepticism as to the possibility of
fixing periods by any hard and fast rules of masonry
alone. Each succeeding style has mingled with its predecessor from the time of its introduction. Boss and
margin work may have been used in early Jewish times,
but was undoubtedly used in later Jewish, Roman times,
and afterwards. Comb-pick margin with pick-centred
dressing was certainly used contemporarily with the boss
and margin, and may have been used before. Quarry-
pick dressing is universal. The delicate pick-centre and
comb-picked margined dressing of the Haram area is
certainly characteristic of one great building period, such
as that of Herod might signify.'[2] And Sir Charles Wilson
has pointed out how boss and margin work—the bosses
left to weaken the force of the ram, the margins made to
assist the exact fitting of the stones—prevails from the
very earliest times down to the castles of the Crusades.[3]
Thus stone-dressing and masonry become minor means of
proof as to the dates of the walls, and can be used only

[1] *P.E.F.Q.*, 1897, 61 : 'Stone-Dressing in Jerusalem, Past and Present';
republished in Bliss and Dickie's *Excav. at Jerusalem*, 1894-97, 273 ff.

[2] Mr. Dickie adds that 'the plain-faced styles with comb-pick and chisel-
pick dressings may have been introduced into Jerusalem in Roman times, and
have been used since. The furrowed Crusading dressing seems alone to
definitely date its origin, and its after-use is beyond doubt.'

[3] *Golgotha*, 124.

along with other lines of evidence; such as inscriptions Greek, Hebrew, or Phœnician; pottery; styles of architecture analogous to those of buildings in other parts of the country known to be archaic ; and the literary or historical evidence that at certain periods certain lines of wall were built. But, unfortunately, no inscriptions have been found connected with any masonry in Jerusalem earlier than the Greek notice which stood on a fence in Herod's Temple to warn Gentiles from entering further ;[1] the argument to dates from analogies of style is precarious; and we are left with the Phœnician marks on the lower courses of the east wall of the Haram ;[2] with the pottery; and with the historical evidence that at certain dates the walls of Jerusalem ran on certain lines, were breached, ruined or restored, and that the reigns of certain kings were periods of fine and extensive building.

## 3. The Historical Evidence.

The first of these periods which we come to behind the time of Josephus is the Herodian ; and upon the historical evidence, it is possible to identify as Herod's not a little masonry still extant in Jerusalem. The Herodian Period.
The solid basis of the so-called 'David's Tower' in the present citadel is certainly the platform from which Herod's Tower of Phasael arose.[3] The dimensions approximate to the round numbers which Josephus gives.[4] The stones

---

[1] See below, Bk. ii. ch. ix.

[2] *Recov. of Jerus.* 139, 142 ff.; *P.E.F. Mem.*, 'Jerus.' 150 ff.

[3] Schick, *Z.D.P.V.* i. 226 ff., xi. 49; *P.E.F. Mem.* 8, 267 ff. ; Socin and Benzinger in *Baedeker*, 81 f. ; Wilson, *Golgotha*, 127 (and earlier works); Guthe, Hauck's *R.-E.* viii. 685, line 59. See Plate VI.

[4] Jos. v. *B.J.* iv. 3 : he makes the Tower base a cube of 40 cubits (approximately 60 feet). The actual dimensions are 65·6 feet (20 m.) high ;

with bosses and margins are cubes of just over four feet
(1·25 m.), and are closely set to each other without mortar.
The Greek influence which we should expect under Herod
is 'very apparent . . . the beautifully-dressed and jointed
stones of the sloping revetment are essentially Greek
in character.'[1]    But Herod's greatest work was the rebuilding of the Temple and its courts.    Josephus says that
he made the sacred area twice as large as before.[2]    As the
rock sloped downwards from all sides of the old Temple
courts, this extension can only have been effected by the
inclusion of the slopes within retaining walls, and the
covering of them with rubbish or great substructures.    It
is generally agreed that the result was the present Ḥaram
area, as far north as 'Solomon's Throne,' and parts of its
surrounding walls.    The south-west corner of the area lies
over the bed of the Tyropœon valley, and Sir Charles
Warren found that the portion of the wall which encloses
it, or all between the Bâb el-Mughârib on the west wall and
the Double Gate on the south, was not only of different
construction from the walls on either side of it, but must
have been built after the valley had been filled with
rubbish to the height of 23 feet (7 m.) from the rock; for
up to this level (which is that of the pavement under
Robinson's arch and the foot of the pier of that arch) the
wall is built with rough-faced stones not intended to be
seen, and only the portion above has been made to
resemble the other parts of the wall.[3]    This masonry,

---

55·78 (17 m.) broad and 70·21 (21·40 m.) long.   These numbers are taken
from *Baedeker*.                          [1] Wilson, *Golgotha*, 123.

[2] Jos. i. *B.J.* xxi. 1.    He gives details of the building in xv. *Ant.* xi.

[3] *Recov. of Jerus.* 119 f., and especially 122 f.; cf. 325; *P.E.F. Mem.*
175; cf. Jos. v. *B.J.* v. 1, on the filling of the valleys; that of the Tyropœon he ascribes to the Hasmonæans, *id.* iv. 1.

*Plate VI.*

THE NORTH-EAST TOWER OF THE CITADEL.
Called 'David's Tower' but really Herod's Tower, Phasael.

along with Robinson's Arch and the pavement below it, Sir Charles Warren ascribes to the Herodian age, and the ascription has been generally accepted. It is probable that the northern wall of the Ḥaram is not of the same period. There is no report of any work by Herod upon the City walls, but from his building of the great towers, we may infer that he not only repaired but in parts wholly rebuilt them ; and that the strength of the fortifications which Titus found so formidable was largely due to him. Herod was an experienced builder of fortresses, and one cannot become familiar with the walls of those which he raised in other parts of the country, without feeling assured that no yard of the fortifications of Jerusalem was overlooked by his vigilance or neglected by his engineers.

From Herod back to Nehemiah, we meet with a series of reports of destructions both of the City and the Temple walls, and of their restorations, which, if we took them literally, might well fill us with despair of finding extant any considerable portion of the pre-Herodian or Biblical walls. *Frequent destruction and rebuilding in the centuries behind Herod.* These reports speak not only of breachings but of repeated 'overturnings,' 'pullings down,' and 'razings' of the walls 'round about'; and not merely of Jewish 'repairs' and 'heightenings,' but of complete 'rebuilding' or 'fortifying round about,' till behind these restorations, after such apparently thorough demolitions, the Jews were able to resist new sieges by large forces. But even if we give only a little credence to these strong statements, they are so frequent, that the walls which Nehemiah restored can have reached the days of Herod only in patchwork and after many partial divergences from their original lines. Here again, however, we must make a distinction between the wall on the South - west Hill and the walls on the north and the east of the City. Round the South-west Hill, as we have seen, far less rubbish has been shot than on those other lines; the assaults from the north were much more frequent, and there, therefore, the destruction of the walls must have been much more thorough. Probably the wall on the South-west Hill was often spared when the northern and eastern walls were ruined or even razed to the ground.

Behind Herod's time the first destruction we reach is that of 64 B.C. Though admitted to the City and The List of obliged to take only the Temple Mount by these back to storm, Pompey is said to have overturned the Nehemiah. walls of the City, and Hyrcanus II. or Antipater got leave from Caesar to restore them.[1] Behind this there is the breaking down of the fortifications, that encompassed the City, by Antiochus VII. (Sidetes) after his siege in 134, and the rebuilding of the walls by John Hyrcanus.[2] Behind this are the destructions and rebuildings of the Maccabean period; the pulling down of the walls by Antiochus Epiphanes in 168;[3] the 'fortification' of the Temple Mount 'round about with high walls and strong towers' by Judas Maccabeus in 165,[4] so that he was able to withstand a siege by Antiochus VI. till the latter promised him favourable terms, but broke his word and 'pulled down the wall' of the sanctuary 'round about.'[5] In 153 Jonathan 'rebuilt the walls and Mount Sion round about';[6] and some seven years later heightened

---

[1] Jos. xiv. *Ant.* iv. 4, viii. 5; 1 *B.J.* vii. 1 ff., x. 3, τὰ τείχη . . . ἀνα-κτίσαι κατεστραμμένα.      [2] Jos. xiii. *Ant.* viii. 3; 1 Macc. xvi. 23.
[3] 1 Macc. i. 31; καθεῖλεν τὰ τείχη.      [4] *Id.* iv. 60; cf. vi. 26.
[5] *Id.* vi. 51-62      [6] *Id.* x. 10 f.

the walls and raised a great mound between the Akra and the City. When there fell down part of the 'wall of the winter-brook,' that is of the east wall above Kidron, he repaired that which is called Chaphenatha.'[1] Simon also heightened the walls of the City.[2] Behind the Maccabean period lie two more or less severe injuries to Jerusalem : by Artaxerxes Ochus about 350, when the City is said to have been sacked and the Temple burnt,[3] and by Ptolemy I. (Lagi) who is reported to have torn down or destroyed the City ;[4] and there was at least one period of reconstruction under the high priest Simon, the son of Onias (*c.* 250), who by repairing and fortifying the Temple, making a reservoir and building a wall, *took thought for his people against the spoiler, and strengthened his City against siege.*[5]

These are all the destructions and rebuildings of the walls reported during the four centuries back from Herod to Nehemiah, with whom we again secure Nehemiah's detailed data of the lines of the walls and their construction. These data are valid, not only Walls. for Nehemiah's time, but for the pre-exilic period, as will appear from the following reasons. What Nehemiah describes is not the building of new walls, but as his explicit statements declare, the restoration of the old walls, whose ruin had so stirred his pious heart. That with some few exceptions he carefully followed the old

Nehemiah's Restoration of the Pre-exilic Walls.

---

[1] I Macc. xii. 35-37. There seems to have been some manipulation of the text here. One would expect after the clause, ' part of the winter-brook wall fell down,' the simple statement that 'he repaired it' ; but a later hand seems clumsily to have added 'that which is called Chaphenatha.' See above, pp. 33 f.

[2] *Id.* xiv. 37.

[3] Syncellus, ed. Dindorf, 1486 ; but see below, Bk. iii., under the Persians.

[4] Appian, *Syr.* 50.      [5] Ecclesiasticus l. 1-4 (Hebrew text).

lines, is further proved by his finding that the enclosed space was too large for the meagre population who had returned to the City from exile, as well as by the fact that so many of his landmarks can be identified as already extant in pre-exilic times. His discriminating diction reveals that while his restoration may here and there have been from the rock upwards, in large part it was but a *strengthening* or fortifying, a *healing* or a stopping, of the breaches in the old wall.[1] There are three passages in the Book of Nehemiah in which the course of the wall is defined or indicated, all of them, except for certain interpolations and corruptions of the text, from Nehemiah himself: ii. 13-15, Nehemiah's inspection of the walls; iii. 1-32, the account of the rebuilding; xii. 31-41, the account of the two processions at the Dedication.[2] From these passages we learn that the wall of Jerusalem, which Nebuchadrezzar destroyed and Nehemiah restored, followed on the west, south, and east the natural boundaries of the site above the Gê-ben-Hinnom and the Naḥal Ḳidron; and enclosed the north of the City on a line not so determinable across the two Hills and the Central Valley.

We may start our tour of this wall from the point at

---

[1] See below, Bk. iii., under Nehemiah.

[2] See for the text and criticism of these the Commentaries (Ryssel's edition of Bertheau, Ryle, and Bertholet), and also the valuable study by H. G. Mitchell, 'The Wall of Jerusalem according to the Book of Nehemiah' in the *Journal of Biblical Literature*, xxii. 1903, pp. 85-163, with plan and numerous photographs. Dr. Mitchell offers reasons (88 ff.) for believing that the account of the rebuilding, iii. 1-32, did not form a part of Nehemiah's own story, and Dr. Torrey (see below, Bk. iii.) had previously argued on the same lines. But their reasons do not appear to me to be conclusive. The passage is accepted as substantially authentic by the commentators and analysts of the Book. Dr. Mitchell allows that it contains valuable material.

which Nehemiah began his inspection: the Gate of the
Gaî or Gê-ben-Hinnom, the Valley Gate of our   The South
English versions.[1] We have seen that this   Wall.
gate opened in the City wall either at the south-west
corner where Dr. Bliss discovered an ancient gateway, or
somewhat further to the east.[2] From here the wall ran
east on the southern edge of the South-west Hill, 1000
cubits, or about 1800 feet, to the Dung Gate.[3] Here, near
the south-east corner, where he could see both their
southern and eastern lines, Nehemiah *viewed the walls of
Jerusalem*, and from this view-point he *crossed* or *went on
to the Fountain Gate and the King's Pool.*[4] His language
does not enable us to decide whether the Fountain Gate
lay at the end of the South-west Hill, the south-east
corner, that is south of the mouth of the Tyropœon
Valley; or whether by *crossing* he means he crossed the
latter and came to the Fountain Gate on its north side.[5]
My own judgment is that his *crossing* or *passing on* has
nothing to do with the mouth of the Tyropœon, on the north
of which no gate has yet been verified, but refers to his
passage from the point from which he took his view of the
walls back to their south-east corner, at which Dr. Bliss
unearthed an ancient gate, and that then, as he says,

---

[1] Neh. ii. 13.      [2] See above, pp. 177 ff.

[3] שַׁעַר הָאַשְׁפֹּת (Neh. ii. 13, iii. 14, xii. 31) Gate of the Ashheaps; acc.
to Robertson Smith (*Rel. of Sem.*, 357 n.; 377 n.) originally 'hearth,' from
שפת : in which case it was possibly named after the neighbouring Topheth.
In Neh. iii. 13 it is שַׁעַר הָשְׁפֹת, from which some have thought the name
Tyropœon = 'cheesemaking,' is derived: as if שְׁפוֹת = 'curds' or 'cheese'
had been substituted for אַשְׁפֹת. It may originally have been 'Gate of the
Topheth.'          [4] ii. 14.

[5] So Guthe, Hauck's *R.-E.* vii. 679, lines 24 f., Mitchell (*op. cit.* 116).

he came to the King's Pool, one or other of the two Pools of Siloam, intending to proceed inside the City walls; but finding the road there so blocked with ruin that *the beast under him had no place to pass*, he came out of the wall again and *went up by the Naḥal* or Ḳidron valley.[1]

In any case the wall turned north across the mouth of the Tyropœon below the two pools to the east edge of Ophel, up which it ran *past the sepulchres of David and the made Pool*[2] to the *House of The Gibbōrim*, the barrack of David's guards, in or close to David's-Burgh, which, as we have seen, lay above Giḥon, the Virgin's Spring. The next point mentioned on the wall is an *angle* or *turning*, after the wall had passed the *ascent of the arms* or *armoury*.[3] The configuration of the hill requires an angle in the wall above Giḥon, and here Dr. Guthe discovered ancient remains which indicate one.[4] Passing there the house of the High Priest, and those of other priests—an indication that it was

The East Wall.

---

[1] ii. 15. The King's Pool may be the same as the Pool of the Shelaḥ or that at the mouth of the tunnel. Guthe (*Z.D.P.V.* v. 357) takes it as the older pool, of which he thinks he discovered remains here, but as we have seen (above, p. 97), this is uncertain. Or it may have been the Birket el Ḥamrâ (above, p. 98); or if the Fountain Gate was on the north side of the Tyropœon valley, the Virgin's Spring as Robinson (*B. R.* i. 474) supposes, or more correctly the pool which, as we found, possibly existed once near that Spring. The existence of this pool would remove 'the serious objection' which Mitchell (p. 120) takes to Robinson's view.

[2] iii. 16. Positions quite uncertain. The tombs of David, as we have seen above, p. 94, are still to be found. There is probability in Clermont-Ganneau's suggestion that the great curve on the tunnel was made in order to avoid them. Guthe holds that the Made Pool was one of the reservoirs he found on Ophel (*Z.D.P.V.* v. 334 f.), but as Mitchell remarks, these appear too small. Schick (*id.* xiv. 54) places this pool on the east of the ridge above the tombs; see Plan.

[3] iii. 19: text uncertain; Mitchell (155) emends to *past the chamber of arms to the angle*.

[4] *Z.D.P.V.* v. 298.

approaching the Temple Mount [1]—the wall reached another angle [2] equally required by the configuration of the hill just south of the end of the remains discovered by Sir Charles Warren. Here three, if not four, prominent features are named: the *Water-Gate, Wall of the 'Ophel,* and one *tower that standeth out,* if not two.[3] The Water-Gate must have been so called because it opened on the path descending from the City to Gihon, and it probably stood not far from where the path by which water is still carried from the Virgin's Spring into Jerusalem approaches the top of Ophel. Close by, Sir Charles Warren found the remains of a great tower, which he identifies with *the tower that standeth out.*[4] Thrice is this phrase used in these verses, and it is doubtful whether the same tower is always meant by it, or whether two different projecting towers are intended. *The Wall of the 'Ophel* was probably the ancient wall which ran across the north end of the ridge and enclosed the earliest site of the City.[5] From here the East wall continued north *above the Horse-Gate,* which was connected with the palace,[6] and therefore stood near the south-east corner of the present Ḥaram area. From the Horse-Gate the wall ran past priests' houses in the more sacred precincts just opposite the Temple, and then past the houses of Temple servants and mer-

---

[1] iii. 20-23.  [2] iii. 24.  [3] iii. 25-27 ; xii. 37.
[4] *Recov. of Jerus.* 295.  [5] See above, p. 143.  Cf. Mitchell, 159 f.
[6] שַׁעַר הַסּוּסִים, iii. 28, cf. 2 Ki. xi. 16, 2 Chron. xxiii. 15, Jer. xxxi. 40.

The discriminating preposition *above* or *over* may mean either that the Horse-Gate was an entry in the lower courses of the wall leading to some sub-structions of the palace, or lay below the line of wall repaired by Nehemiah on an outer and older line. It can hardly imply *both* of these, as Mitchell suggests. But perhaps to make either of these inferences is to force the preposition, which may only imply that the Horse Gateway itself needed no repair, but only the wall which ran over it.

chants in the less sacred precincts to the north, and *over against the Gate of the Muster*,[1] to the *high chamber* or *turret of the corner*, apparently the north-east angle, and *the Sheep Gate*, also placed by Nehemiah on the north.[2] Now at this time the Temple area did not extend so far north as does the Ḥaram area, whose north-east corner lies over the ancient ravine tributary to the Ḳidron. The Temple precincts must have come to an end on the south of this ravine. We shall not be far wrong, therefore, if we place the north-east angle of Nehemiah's wall very little north of the present Golden Gate.

From the Sheep Gate, close to the north-east corner of the City, the first twelve verses of Chapter iii., and (in the reverse direction) the route of the Second Procession, Chapter xii. 38 f. give us the course of the wall round the north and west of the City to our starting-point at the Gate of the Gaî. On the northern stretch of this route we find ourselves among the uncertainties spoken of in the beginning of the chapter, for we no longer follow the margin of the encompassing valleys, but strike across the East Hill, the Central Valley and the West Hill, where there are no such natural features to determine the line. If the north-east corner and the Sheep Gate lay, as we have seen probable, on the

*Nehemiah's North and West Wall.*

---

[1] שַׁעַר הַמִּפְקָד, iii. 31 : cf. Ezek. xliii. 21, where Hammiphkadh seems to be a place just outside the Temple.

[2] שַׁעַר הַצֹּאן, Neh. iii. 1, 32, xii. 39. These are conclusive for its position on the north. K. Furrer in *Z.N.T.W.*, 1902, 260, sets the Sheep Gate on the west wall of the Sanctuary as a gate that led from the industrial quarter of the City, once a suburb, into the Temple area, near the present Bab el Kattânîn, but this is irreconcilable with Nehemiah's data, and the only reason for it appears to be the author's location of Bethesda in the Hammâm esh Shefâ, for which we have already seen there is no evidence.

northern slope of the Temple summit above the ravine
into the Ḳidron, the most natural line for the wall to take
westwards from them would either be over the *col* between
the Temple summit and Antonia, or else round the rock
on which the latter stands, and across the other *col* to the
north.[1]  The statement of Josephus that the Second Wall
started from Antonia favours the second alternative.  In
that case the two *Towers, Hammeah* and *Ḥananeʾ-el,* the
next features on Nehemiah's wall after the Sheep Gate,
would stand on the rock on which Antonia stood, north-
west from the Sheep Gate.  This relative position suits
the other Biblical references to them.  In Zechariah xiv.
10, the north and south extent of the City is given from
the *tower of Ḥananeʾ-el unto the king's wine-presses*
(probably at Siloam); while the east and west extension
is given as *from the gate of Benjamin,* probably identical
with the Sheep Gate, *to the place of the First Gate,* near the
north-west corner of the City; similarly in Jeremiah xxxi.
38, as *from the tower of Ḥananeʾ-el* to the *Gate of the
Corner,* another name for the First Gate.  From Ḥananeʾ-
el the wall would dip and cross the Tyropœon, on the
road down the bed of which we most naturally seek for
the site of its next feature, *the Fish Gate.*[2]  The references
given below explain this name as due to the Tyrians, who
sold dried fish, and found their nearest market or entrance
to the City on the north;[3] and associate it with the *Mishneh*
or *Second City,* most intelligible as the name of the northern
suburb, and with the *Maktesh,* or *Mortar,* a term which

[1] See above, p. 34.
[2] שַׁעַר הַדָּגִים: Neh. iii. 3, xii. 39, Zeph. i. 10, 2 Chron. xxxiii. 14; cf.
for the name, Nehemiah xiii. 16.
[3] See below, Bk. ii. ch. v., on Imports.

suggests the shape of the northern Tyropœon. The Fish
Gate thus corresponded to the modern Damascus Gate,
opening on the same natural line of road down the
Tyropœon, but further south : it is impossible to fix the
exact position. The next gate westward is stated on
Nehemiah's line, only after a considerable interval. This
is unfortunate, for the stretch between these gates is precisely that portion of the wall, upon the exact line of
which the most serious topographical questions depend.
The Gate is called (as the text stands) by the puzzling
name of *Gate of the Yeshanah*,[1] that is (if the latter word
be really what it seems, a feminine adjective meaning *old*),
*the Gate of the Old* . . . (?) It is usually translated *The Old
Gate*, but the genitive construction forbids this. Various
proposals to supply a noun have been made :[2] *the Old City*
or *Wall* or *Pool;* and in supporting this last, Dr. Mitchell
argues for its identification with the Pool of Hezekiah or
the Patriarch's Bath.[3] One is tempted, by change of a
single consonant to emend *Yeshanah* to *Mishneh*, and to
read *Gate of the Second City*, the earliest northern suburb.
This Gate has been identified with the Corner Gate and
the First Gate.[4] If so, it stood near the north-west corner
of the City, and we now turn down the western stretch of
the wall. The next landmark mentioned in the course
of the procession (but not in that of the rebuilding of

---

[1] שַׁעַר הַיְשָׁנָה, Neh. iii. 6, xii. 39.

[2] Schultz ; Cheyne, *Enc. Bibl.* 1972, suggests this as the original of
Hassenaah, הַפְּנָאָה.

[3] *Op. cit.* 134. On the Pool, see above, p. 114. As we have seen, the
Old Pool was more probably the Lower Pool of Siloam.

[4] שַׁעַר הַפִּנָּה, 2 Ki. xiv. 13, שַׁעַר הָרִאשׁוֹן, Zech. xiv. 10. W. R. Smith,
*Enc. Bibl.* col. 2424 ; W. F. Birch, *P.E.F.Q.*, 1879, 177.

the walls) is the well-known *Gate of Ephraim,* which was 400 cubits, about 600 feet (or 183 m.) from the Corner Gate. That this Gate is not given in the line of the rebuilt wall, and that a slightly different preposition is used for its relation to the passage of the procession from that used of the gates common to the procession and the rebuilding, induces one to suppose that the gate was not on the line of Nehemiah's wall, but below this on an inner and lower wall. And, in fact, a Gate of Ephraim was in existence on the first north wall before Hezekiah's time,[1] to whom, as we have seen, the second of the north walls is attributed. The Gate of Ephraim is usually placed a little to the south-east of the present Jaffa Gate ; but one expects a gate with such a name to have stood further east, on the line of street running east of the Muristan to the Damascus Gate, or on the other line of street thither up the Tyropœon, in either case corresponding to the present Ephraim Gate of the City, and in the latter case representing on the First or inmost wall the Fish Gate of the Second Wall. The former alternative is the more probable. In the account of the rebuilding the next point after the Corner Gate is *the Broad Wall,* about which many conjectures have been made. A most natural one is that its unusual thickness was due to the outward ascent of the ground at the north-east corner.[2] But another cause may have been the overlapping of the First and Second Walls for some distance, and the subsequent filling up with masonry of the space between them. It is also possible that the name is a corruption of the *Wall of the Broad Place,* such as lay by the Gate

[1] 2 Kings xiv. 13 ; 2 Chron. xxv. 23.      [2] Stade, *Gesch.* ii. 167.

of Ephraim.[1] The last landmark on the west stretch of wall, before the Gate of the Gaî is reached, is the *Tower of the Furnaces* or *Ovens*,[2] so called, perhaps, because the Bazaar of the Bakers, mentioned by Jeremiah, was situated there.[3]

Thus we return to our starting-point at the Gate of the Gaî, having completed our circuit of the pre-exilic wall which Nehemiah restored. Except for the manner in which the Gate of Ephraim is introduced, we have found no recognition of anything but a single wall. But the course which his accounts indicate for the northern stretch of the wall appears to have followed the line, not of the First Wall of Josephus on the northern slope of the South-west Hill, the earliest rampart of Jerusalem to the north, but rather the line of the Second Wall of Josephus, which curved from Antonia to the Gate Genath, somewhere near the present Jaffa Gate.

*The North Wall of Nehemiah = the Second Wall of Josephus.*

Such, then, is the course of the Pre-Exilic Wall which Nehemiah restored. It would be vain to attempt to determine exactly the various modifications of line and structure which it had received under the kings of Judah from Solomon to the Exile, partly because we may be sure that we have the reports of only some of these, and partly because what is reported is either vague or has come down to us in dilapidated texts. Still, for the sake of completing this history of the ancient walls of Jerusalem, we may

*The Walls from Solomon to Manasseh.*

---

[1] So the Vulgate of Neh. iii. 8.  Cf. Neh. viii. 16.  St. Clair, *P.E.F.Q.*, 1889, 99.  Broad wall = הָרְחָבָה הַחוֹמָה

[2] מִגְדַּל הַתַּנּוּרִים :  iii. 11.

[3] Jer. xxxvii. 21.  See below, Bk. iii., on Jeremiah.  On the custom of sending the domestic dough to be fired at the bakers' ovens, see below, Bk. ii. ch. viii.

here give a list of the buildings, destructions and rebuildings of the City walls between Solomon and the
Exile. Solomon himself is said to have built *the wall of
Jerusalem round about*.[1] On the ground that *Jerusalem* is
distinct from David's-Burgh, and that the latter lay on
the East Hill, Dr. Guthe holds that no other position is
left for *Jerusalem* except the South-west Hill, and that
it must have been this which Solomon in whole or in
part enclosed, as Josephus asserts.[2] But while David's-
Burgh was indeed an entity distinct from Jerusalem, it
was a citadel and not a town,[3] and, as we have seen,
there was room on the East Hill for the town to lie below
and round it. There is no evidence that the name Jerusalem was confined to the South-west Hill, either in
Solomon's or any other period; and the statement of
Josephus, that David and Solomon surrounded the whole
of the South-west Hill, cannot be taken as conclusive. At
the same time, as we shall see when we come to deal
with Solomon's reign, it is probable that the great increase
of the population which his policy effected involved an
extension of Jerusalem from the East to the South-west
Hill ; and it is also possible that Solomon's wall enclosed
this extension. But how great the extension was, or
what line the wall took, round or across the Hill, are
questions we have no means of answering ; and it may
be doubted whether Josephus was any better informed.
In that state of uncertainty, we must leave the question of

---

[1] I Kings iii. 1 ; cf. ix. 15.
[2] Hauck's *R.-E.* viii. 678, lines 40 ff. ; Jos. v. *B.J.* iv. 2. This view has,
of course, been frequently and, in fact, generally taken. Cf. Wilson in
Smith's *D.B.*
[3] Above, p. 155. Also 2 Chron. xxxiii. 14 distinguishes it from the rest
of Ophel.

Solomon's wall round Jerusalem.[1]  The next great building period in the pre-exilic history of the City was the
eighth century; during which the commerce and wealth
of Judea rapidly increased, the literature abounds in
reports of architectural enterprise, and metaphors drawn
from building became frequent in the prophets.  Moreover
Israel's widened horizon then included a knowledge of the
military architecture of the Phœnicians and Assyrians;[2]
and we have in the Siloam tunnel an example of the
engineering ambitions and resources of the Judean kings.[3]
About 790, Joash of Israel, attacking Jerusalem from the
north, broke down *four hundred cubits of the wall from the
Gate of Ephraim to the Gate of the Corner.*[4]  This was, of
course, upon the earliest and most southerly of the three
northern walls of Josephus.  On this face of the City, then,
a wall was already standing, probably since Solomon's
time.  Of the next King, Uzziah (*circa* 780-740 B.C.) the
Chronicler[5] reports that *he built towers in Jerusalem, over
the Gate of the Corner and over the Gate of the Gai, and
over the angle* or *turning* of the wall *and fortified them.*
As explained below,[6] this notice is credible both from
the great increase in building which distinguished Uzziah's
reign, and from the development which military architecture had achieved by this period throughout western
Asia.  The Palestine fortresses, attacked by the Assyrians
in the eighth and ninth centuries, are represented as polygonal, sometimes with double or even treble walls, but
their main feature is the tower projecting from the wall
We cannot think that the Jerusalem of Uzziah was any

[1] The question of what and where the Millo was, we must reserve for the
History.          [2] See below, Bk. iii., under Uzziah.
[3] See above, p. 93.          [4] 2 Ki. xiv. 8-14, from an Israelite document.
[5] 2 Chron. xxvi. 9.          [6] See below, Bk. iii., under Uzziah.

less strongly or finely fortified than, for example, Lachish, of whose walls we have an Assyrian picture in the eighth century. The Chronicler tells us that the next king, Jotham, *built much on the wall of the 'Ophel.*[1] Ahaz also attended to the defences of the City ;[2] and we have seen already what Hezekiah did for these, including (the Chronicler states) the building of an outer wall—*he built all the wall which had been breached and raised upon it towers, and to the outside another wall*[3]—which is generally, but perhaps too easily, assumed to be the Second Wall of Josephus round the first northerly extension of the City; the northern stretch of Nehemiah's wall. As the walls of Jerusalem under Ahaz resisted the attempt of the Arameans, so, after their strengthening by Hezekiah, they resisted, alone among all the cities of Judah and the coast, the blockade of the Assyrians. Even more important for our present purpose is the proof which Hezekiah's tunnel and pool afford, that by his time the wall encompassed the whole of the South-west Hill. It would have been vain for him to bring the water of Giḥon beneath Ophel to a pool in the mouth of the Tyropœon, in order to secure it for the use of the City in times of siege, if the South-west Hill had been wholly or partially open to the besiegers; for, under the conditions of ancient warfare, that hill commands the pool at the mouth of the Tunnel. By the eighth century then the South-west Hill and the mouth of the Tyropœon was all enclosed within a wall ; and it is just possible that this is the *other outside wall* which the Chronicler's tradition assigns to Hezekiah himself. We must keep in view such an alternative to the

[1] 2 Chron. xxvii. 3.　　　　[2] Isaiah vii. 2 ff., xxii. 8-11.
[3] 2 Chron. xxxii. 5.

theory which identifies it with the Second Wall of Josephus. Finally, in the seventh century, Manasseh (*circa* 685-640), according to the Chronicler, *built an outer wall to the David's-Burgh, on the west of Gihon in the Nahal, even on to the entry of the Fish-Gate, and he compassed the 'Ophel, and made it very high.*[1] This can only mean that outside the existing rampart of the Citadel, on the ridge above the present Virgin's Spring, Manasseh constructed another line of fortification which he carried northwards past the Temple Mount, and round its northern slope to the Sheep Gate.[2] These are all the reports, sometimes vague sometimes definite, that we have of those walls of Jerusalem; which were gradually developed from David to Manasseh; which Nebuchadrezzar destroyed, and which Nehemiah rebuilt.

Such is the literary evidence for the walls of Jerusalem between the time of David and that of Herod and of the reports of Josephus. Some definite conclusions Conclusions from the Literary or Historical Evidence. may be drawn from it: that before the eighth century, nothing beyond Ophel is certain as to the course of the walls; that by the eighth century the whole of the South-west Hill and the mouth of the Tyropœon were enclosed; that by the Exile the wall, with perhaps an outer and inner line, ran up the edge of Kidron past the Temple Mount, and turned east up the tributary ravine to the north of the latter; that probably two walls protected the north face of the City, one the earliest, which there is no reason for denying to Solomon, from the western Temple wall up the north slope of the South-west Hill; and the other further north, probably from the rock on which Antonia afterwards stood, to join

[1] 2 Chron. xxxiii. 14.          [2] See above, p. 200.

the inner wall somewhere east of the present Jaffa Gate : the course which Nehemiah followed in his rebuilding of a *single* line of wall round the city. Besides this, *the Ophel, the swelling* on which Ṣion or David's-Burgh stood, had been encompassed with a wall of its own from the earliest times, the north stretch of which, across the ridge between David's-Burgh and the Temple Mount, was probably *the wall of the 'Ophel* mentioned by Nehemiah ; while Manasseh built an outer wall to *the 'Ophel* and continued it to the Fish-Gate. But besides affording these more or less definite data, the literary evidence reminds us no less by the length of time over which it stretches than by the large number of thorough or partial destructions of the City walls which it records, that their repair and reconstruction were very frequent if not almost constant, and that the masonry of earlier generations must have been employed by their successors, till in parts an inextricable mixture of styles of stone-dressing and building must have resulted. The rapidity with which Nehemiah accomplished his reconstruction is evidence that he used the squared stones of the older walls. Dr. Schick thinks it improbable that he used mortar ;[1] yet some of his technical expressions seem to point to this.[2]

## 4. THE EVIDENCE OF THE EXCAVATIONS.

With all this literary evidence before us, and these conclusions from it, we pass to an examination of the archæological evidence uncovered so profusely and yet so partially by recent excavation : keeping especially

[1] *Z.D.P.V.* xvii. 78.      [2] See below, Bk. III., under Nehemiah.

in mind the last warning that, after so long and troubled
a history as the walls have passed through, it will be

Their bearing on the archæological evidence. extremely difficult, to say the least, to determine the different styles in their remains, and
to assign them to different sections of our
period. Sir Charles Warren, the first of the excavators,
writes: ' The stones in the south wall are probably not
*in situ*, nor, I think, are those of the Ophel wall : that is
to say, they appear to be stones used in the building of
a previous wall.'[1] And the same authority warns us of
another difficulty in reaching the archæological facts :

Another necessary warning. ' As the earth about here [Ophel] only covers
the rock to a depth of from twelve to fifteen
feet, it is possible that the wanting portion of the wall
may have been taken up and sold for building stone by
the fellahin who at the present day frequently go down
to that depth in search of cut stone. Cut stone in
Jerusalem is much in demand, and in the grounds of the
fellahin all traces of wall at or near the surface are fast
disappearing. The rock-cut steps and caves which
existed along the slopes of Ophel are also fast becoming
obliterated ; the farmers find that these are the places
where they have least trouble in blasting and quarrying
the rock, and within the last few years many old features
on the southern side of the old city have vanished ; thus
year by year the old Jerusalem will become more difficult
to be understood.'[2] But these processes of change and
obliteration have been at work for nearly three thousand
years since Solomon *built the wall of Jerusalem round about.*

---

[1] *Recovery of Jerusalem*, 300. Dr. Bliss, too, gives several instances of
the same.

[2] *Recovery of Jerusalem*, 298. Cf. Bliss, *Excavations at Jerusalem*, 22,
118, 120, 186.

The archæological evidence as to the walls has been provided by the excavators of the last forty years. Though not a few valuable observations had been made above-ground by earlier scholars and engineers,[1] the necessary basis of the work was first accurately laid down by Captain, afterwards Lieutenant-General Sir, Charles Wilson of the Royal Engineers, in his ordnance survey of the City's site, buildings, and surroundings.[2] The area of this survey was 'surveyed and drawn on the same scale and with the same accuracy as the cadastral or parish plans of

*List of excavations and discoveries.*

---

[1] As the result of a visit to Jerusalem and careful examination in 1833, Catherwood made a plan of the Ḥaram area, which, except for an error at the north-west angle made in joining his detached sketches, is, according to Wilson (*Recovery of Jerusalem*, 30), 'minutely accurate.' Among several others, a list of which is given in *Recovery of Jerusalem*, 30, we may mention here Robinson's and Barclay's, both of 1856, and Van de Velde's, of 1858, with memoir by Tobler. Robinson on his first visit discovered the ancient arch, since known by his name, and the remains of apparently a wall to the north of the present city. Barclay discovered an ancient gate, since known by his name, north of Robinson's arch. Signor Erm. Pierotti, employed by the native authorities as architect and engineer, was able between the years 1854 and 1862 to make a number of investigations into the remains of the ancient city, the results of which are given in two volumes, one of text and one of plates, entitled *Jerusalem Explored*, translated by T. G. Bonney, London, 1864. This work contains valuable observations and suggestions, but its data require to be used with great discrimination (cf. *Recovery of Jerusalem*, 30 f., Wilson's criticisms ; 204 f., Warren's—both severe).

[2] *Recovery of Jerusalem*, 1871, 3-32 ; *P.E.F. Memoir, Jerusalem*, by Warren and Conder, 1884; with portfolio of *Plans, Elevations, Sections, etc., of Excavations at Jerusalem*, 1867-70, by Warren. The original plans were :— *Plan of Jerusalem, etc.*, $\frac{1}{10000}$, or 6·33 inches to the mile ; *Plan of Jerusalem, with Streets, Buildings, and Contours*, $\frac{1}{2500}$, or 25·34 inches to a mile ; *Plans of Haram esh Sherif, with Cisterns, Vaults, and Contours*, $\frac{1}{500}$, or 10·56 feet to a mile ; *Plans of the Church of the Holy Sepulchre and Dome of the Rock*, $\frac{1}{200}$ ; *Plans of the Citadel, etc.*, $\frac{1}{500}$. In 1900 there was also published by the Palestine Exploration Fund *Plan of Jerusalem, reduced by permission from the Ordnance Plan*, $\frac{1}{2500}$ scale, *made by Major-General Sir Charles Wilson, K.C.B., etc., to illustrate recent discoveries*, from which the plan in this volume, by kind permission of the Committee of the Fund, has been prepared.

England.' Captain Wilson also began excavations, and by the Bab es-Silsile discovered the arch which now bears his name. From 1867 to 1870 the first prolonged excavations were made by Captain, now Lieutenant-General Sir, Charles Warren, R.E., chiefly round the walls of the Ḥaram and on Ophel, partly also on the South-west Hill and at numerous points in and around the City, with a view of determining the rock-contours.[1] From 1872 to 1875 Lieutenant, now Lieutenant-Colonel, Conder, R.E., conducted further explorations in and around the City.[2] In 1875 Mr. Henry Maudslay, an English engineer, discovered and examined the Great Scarp, since known by his name, and other scarps and rock-cuttings on the edge of the Wâdy er-Rabâbi, west of the Cœnaculum.[3] In 1881 Dr., now Professor, Hermann Guthe conducted excavations of considerable extent upon Ophel.[4] From 1894 to 1897 Dr. F. J. Bliss, along with the architect, Mr. A. C. Dickie, excavated from Maudslay's Scarp round the edge of the South-west Hill, and in various lines across the Hill, also across the mouth of the Tyropœon round Siloam, on the southern end of Ophel, and for some distance up the Tyropœon.[5] To all these it is necessary to add the many observations and measurements made during the last thirty or forty years by various residents

[1] *Recovery of Jerusalem*, 35-329; *P.E.F. Memoir, Jerusalem*; *with Plans*, etc., in the *P.E.F.* portfolio. Cf. *Underground Jerusalem.*

[2] *P.E.F. Memoir, Jerusalem*; *Tent-Work in Palestine*; art. 'Jerusalem' in Hastings' *Dict. of the Bible*, and other works.

[3] For accounts of this see Conder's article 'The Rock Scarp of Zion,' *P.E.F.Q.*, 1875, 81 ff. ; and Bliss, *Excavations at Jerusalem*, 1 ff.

[4] *Z.D.P.V.*, v. 1882, 7-204, 271-378, republished under the title of *Ausgrabungen bei Jerusalem*, 1883.

[5] *Excavations at Jerusalem 1894-1897*, by Bliss and Dickie, 1898. For the quarterly reports on which this volume is founded see *P.E.F.Q.*, 1894-1898.

in Jerusalem, and among them to mention especially the work of the late Baurath Schick, and that of Consul Merrill, both of which have been extremely valuable with respect in particular to the course of the north walls.[1] M. Clermont-Ganneau's *Archæological Researches*[2] must also be consulted. Finally, the ancient remains discovered are marked on the plan reduced by the Palestine Exploration Fund from Sir Charles Wilson's ordnance survey;[3] and on Herr A. Kuemmel's map to his *Materials for the Topography of Ancient Jerusalem*, in the text of which detailed accounts are given.[4]

Upon our survey of the remains of walls or scarps discovered in the course of all these systematic operations and scattered observations, it will be most convenient to start where we started for our circuit of Nehemiah's wall, about the south-west angle of the city, yet so as to include in our beginning Maudslay's Scarp, a little to the north of Nehemiah's Gate of the Gai. From a point[5] 100 feet (30·5 m.) north of Bishop Gobat's School this great scarp was traced south, with one small projection, to the school, which is built over a second

*Maudslay's Scarp.*

---

[1] For Schick's long and patient work, valuable as that of a trained architect familiar with the literature, and resident for a long time in the city, see numerous papers in the *P.E.F.Q.* and *Z.D.P.V.*, particularly in the latter, viii. 245 ff. : 'Die Zweite Mauer Jerusalems,' etc. (by Schick and Guthe), xiv. 41 ff. : 'Nehemiah's Mauerbau,' and xvi.-xviii. : 'Die Baugeschichte der Stadt Jerusalem.' Consul Merrill's valuable experience and observations of many years, so generously communicated to visitors to the city, will also be found in numerous contributions to the *P.E.F.Q.* as well as the *Biblical World*, and are eagerly expected in fuller form in his forthcoming work on Jerusalem.

[2] London, *P.E.F.*, 1899, vol. i.

[3] See above, p. 211 *n.* 2.

[4] *Materialien zur Topgr. des alten Jerusalem*, by August Kuemmel ; Halle, 1906. The map is on the scale of $\frac{1}{500}$.

[5] The scarp probably continues farther north than this point.

and larger projection of the scarp, 45 feet square and 20 feet high. Thence it runs south-east, with one projection, above the school garden and cemetery to the end of the latter, where, with outside steps leading up to it, another great rock-projection occurs, the face of which is some 43 feet long. 'For at least a third of its length, and presumably throughout its whole extent, the great scarp is a parapet of rock, in places 40 feet high on the outside and at least 14 feet within.'[1] No masonry appears to have been found *in situ* along the top of the scarp ; but if, as is probable, a wall once ran along the latter, the result, as Colonel Conder justly says, 'must have been a splendid and impregnable fortification which might well defy any attempt to take Jerusalem from the south.' Parts of an outer scarp on a line running parallel to Maudslay's were uncovered by Dr. Bliss. Dr. Bliss began his excavations on the projection of Maudslay's Scarp at the south end of the cemetery. He found this to be the rock-base of a great tower, several courses of whose masonry are *in situ*. The stones, varying in length from 2 feet 10 inches ('86 m.) to 4 feet 8 inches (1'42 m.), and from 27 to 28 inches high ('68 to '71 m.), have great bosses and long deep-set margins or drafts with the 'pock-mark dressing,' a style which (as we have seen) prevails from the earliest to a late age in Jerusalem. Outside were found fallen stones of the same style, but also others with 'the diagonal fine comb-pick dressing of crusading work.' On the rock-base of the tower the pottery 'points to early times.' Now, instead of finding the scarp to continue south-east from the tower on the edge of the Hill, as from its previous line Dr. Bliss naturally expected it to do, he discovered a

---

[1] *P.E.F.Q.*, 1875, 84.

COURSES OF ANCIENT CITY WALL ON THE SOUTH-WEST HILL (Near the Protestant Cemetery).
Discovered by Dr. Bliss.

Plate VII.

deep rock-cut fosse on the south-west of the tower turning round its south-east face and crossing the back of the Hill in a north-easterly direction. On the north side of this fosse a scarp runs on from the tower, on its south side a lower counter-scarp. It has been suggested that this fosse was originally a rock-hewn road, with a gate, therefore, at the tower. But, however this may have been, it is clear that at some period the strong line of defence marked by Maudslay's Scarp turned at the tower northeast across the back of the Hill.[1]

Having sufficiently ascertained that direction of the fosse, Dr. Bliss started upon those excavations round the edge of the Hill which resulted in his great discovery of two lines of wall. From the fosse, one of those lines, 9 feet thick of fine masonry on a rubble base, runs south-east 105 feet (32 m.) to the Gate described above.[2] The fine masonry is of stones from one foot to three in size, well set in lime, 'smooth-faced, without margins and dressed with the comb-pick.' The Gate has four superimposed sills of four different periods, of which the highest is 8 feet wide (2·44 m.) and the three lower 8 feet 10 inches (2·89 m.) : 'the smooth-faced masonry described above was characteristic of the wall during the four gate periods'; below the pavement leading to the highest sill was a pilaster with a Roman *graffito*. From the Gate a drain and street ran into the City north-eastwards. From the Gate the wall continues for 31 feet (9·45 m.), in two styles of smooth-faced masonry resting on rough-dressed work, to a tower, which shows these to belong to two periods. From this tower, its

The south-west Wall.

---

[1] For above details see *Excavations at Jerusalem*, 4-14.
[2] P. 177.

extreme south-west angle, the line of wall sets in the direction of Siloam, its extreme south-east angle, down to which it was traced by Dr. Bliss, except where it passes under the Jewish cemetery. Like the tower above mentioned, the wall consists of two distinct and separate constructions, one above the other, and often with a thick layer of *débris* between them. The upper wall, sometimes resting on this *débris*, sometimes on the lower wall, and of smooth-faced masonry, belongs to the gate of the four sills, representing four different periods. It was, therefore, a wall of long standing ; the upper sill, from the remains below it, is clearly post-Roman ; and it may be inferred from the sameness of the masonry in the gateway and upper wall throughout that the whole of both belong to the Christian era. Dr. Bliss reasonably, therefore, takes them to be the remains of the wall of the Empress Eudocia.[1] Unfortunately, the remains cease some 300 feet (about 91 m.) west of the Jewish cemetery. The thick *débris* below them is the record of a time when no city wall existed here, which condition suits the age between the destruction by Titus and the wall of Eudocia.[2] In the lower wall, always resting on the rock and running the whole way to the south-east corner of the City, Dr. Bliss detected three systems of construction. The earliest is of stones with broad margins, carefully comb-picked, while the centres are pick-dressed, without mortar, but with jointing ' so close that a pin-point can hardly be inserted.' Bonded into this is the masonry of a later period of lower courses, rough and with different kinds of dressed stones, some of which have evidently been borrowed from the earlier system. And there is a

[1] See above, p. 186.    [2] Above, pp. 185 f.

third period in which (if I understand Dr. Bliss aright) occur the fragments which he found, 'of Græco-Jewish mouldings, like those in the Hasmonean monuments in the Ķidron valley.'[1]

This lower line Dr. Bliss takes to be the wall which Titus destroyed, and the patch-work in which the Græco-Jewish mouldings occur, to represent some of the latest repairs on that wall during the Hasmonean and Herodian or Roman periods.[2] No one familiar with the literature of ex-cavation can fail to feel that Dr. Bliss's methods of work on this line of wall were as thorough, or that his reason-ing so far on the question of dates is as convincing, as any in the whole range of the literature; especially if one has had the good fortune to examine any of the dis-coveries for himself. But to go behind this general conclusion and to seek to determine the dates of the earlier systems of construction which the wall contains is precarious. To which of the many repairs of the wall between Nehemiah and the Hasmoneans,[3] that we have found reported, are we to assign the lower courses of rough masonry containing older stones of several styles : Dr. Bliss's second system? It is impossible to answer. It ought to be less difficult to ascertain the date of the 'exquisitely dressed and jointed masonry' of his first system. This must belong to one of the few epochs of original and massive building in Jerusalem. The Herodian is excluded. There remain those of Solomon's reign and the Eighth Century B.C.[4] Dr. Bliss discusses the following alternatives for the earliest of the three

Date of the lower south-west Wall and Maudslay's Scarp.

---

[1] For all these details, see *Excavations at Jerusalem*, 14-47, and 314.
[2] *Ibid.* 319.
[3] See above, pp. 194 ff.      [4] See above, pp. 204 ff.

systems in the wall, along with the question of Maudslay's Scarp, and its turn at the great tower to the north-
east across the Hill.   If the lower wall be the later, then
the rock-base of the tower, he thinks, will represent the
south-west angle of the City in Solomon's time, in which
case this king's wall did not enclose the whole of the
South-west Hill.   If the lower wall be contemporaneous
with the Scarp, the latter represents a citadel on the line
of the City wall with a fosse partly within and partly without the City.   The want of connection between the wall
and the Scarp would probably be due to the builders of
the thirteenth Christian century, who ran a wall across the
Hill north of the Cœnaculum, to which wall the stones
with the Crusading dressing found on the fosse would
belong.   That Maudslay's Scarp is later than the lower
wall, Dr. Bliss thinks impossible, because Hadrian's wall
was farther to the north, and there is no other period to
which so magnificent a fortification as the Scarp could
be assigned after the date of Titus.   To Dr. Bliss's
argument I have only this to add—that, as we have seen
that the South-west Hill and Siloam[1] must have been
enclosed within the City wall by the eighth century, the
oldest masonry in Dr. Bliss's lower wall is probably at
the latest of that date.   Whether we can carry it or
Maudslay's Scarp back to Solomon,[2] it is impossible in
my judgment to say.   A line of wall which Dr. Bliss
discovered on the South-west Hill east of the Cœnaculum
he assigns, because of its Byzantine moulding and its
agreement with the line of the south wall of the City
upon Marino Sanuto's map (1321 A.D.), to the thirteenth
Christian century.

[1] See above, p. 207.                    [2] So Dr. Bliss, p. 334.

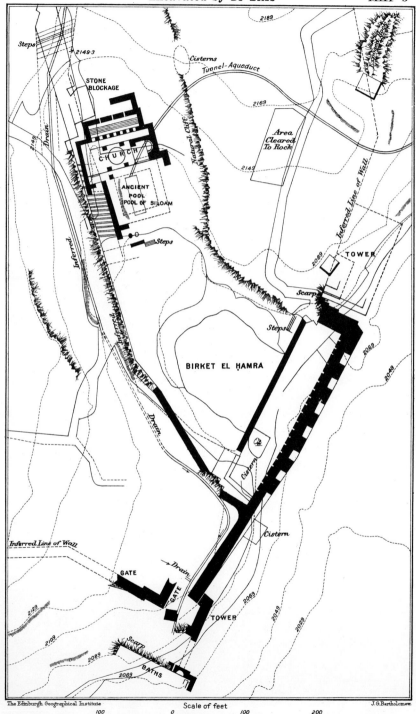

We turn now to the difficult complex of walls discovered round the south-east angle of the ancient City,
and across and in the mouth of the Tyropœon.
We have seen that Dr. Bliss traced the lower  South-east<br>Angle of the<br>Ancient Wall.
and more ancient south wall along the edge
of Hinnom all the way (except under the Jewish cemetery) to the south-east angle of the ancient City. About
150 feet (46 m.) before this angle is reached by the wall,
there opens in the latter a little gate which it would be
tempting to identify with Nehemiah's Dung-Gate, but
that Dr. Bliss considers it too small to have been 'an
exterior gate of the city.'[1] Close to the south-east
angle (due south from the Pool of Siloam), Dr. Bliss
uncovered a more massive gateway, which, both from its
position and construction, must have been for long one
of the great gates of Jerusalem. It lies at the end of a
branch of the main street up and down the Tyropœon,
and beneath it the great Tyropœon drain leaves the
City. The construction, with three different sills, represents three periods. The earliest Dr. Bliss takes to be
that of the Jewish kings, and the Gate itself to be
Nehemiah's *Gate of the Fountain* or *Spring*.[2] The second
period he judges was that of Eudocia's wall, whose
builders, since their characteristic masonry[3] is lacking
in the gateway, must have used here the masonry of the
ancient Jewish wall.[4] The third period, according to him,
is also of the Eudocian wall, which, he infers from Bede,
lasted till the eighth Christian century.[5] Dr. Mitchell

---

[1] *Excavations at Jerusalem*, 87 f. This small gate is omitted both by
Mitchell, *op. cit.*, and on Kuemmel's map.
[2] 'Perhaps.' Kuemmel, *Materialien*, etc., 72.      [3] See above, p. 216.
[4] Alternatively their masonry here has been wholly destroyed.
[5] *Excavations at Jerusalem*, 327 f.

identifies the Gate as Nehemiah's Dung‑Gate, on the grounds that it lies at the mouth of the Tyropœon, further up which the present Dung-Gate opens, and that the ancient drain runs beneath it.[1]  To protect the Gate, a tower was added in both of the last two periods, and formed the precise south-east angle of the wall.

From this tower Dr. Bliss followed the wall north-east across the mouth of the Tyropœon to the toe of the East

*Ancient Walls across the mouth of the Tyropœon.* Hill.[2]  It runs nearly parallel to the line of the present dam of the Birket el-Ḥamrâ, but some 50 feet (over 15 m.) to the east, and at its north end, turns round a tower or corner buttress north-west to the line of the dam.  Originally this wall was 8 or 9 feet (2·44 to 2·74 m.) thick, but besides the corner buttress it had six others which added to its thickness 11 feet (3·35 m.).  After being ruined it was rebuilt flush with the face of the buttresses, and later still a rough supporting wall was constructed against the front of it. The many buttresses, unnecessary for military purposes ; the subsequent filling of the spaces between them ; and the supporting wall, prove that this stretch of wall across the mouth of the Tyropœon served also as a dam to the Pool.  Indeed, Dr. Bliss found not only that the original wall had burst or bulged from internal pressure, but that there are signs of the action of the water even on the outside supports.[3]  The Pool, therefore, extended at

---

[1] *Op. cit.* 114.  Guthe, Hauck's *R.-E.*, viii. 679, lines 14 f., contents himself with stating that the Dung-Gate was in this region, and that here Dr. Bliss uncovered a gate.

[2] *Excavations at Jerusalem*, 96-115.

[3] *Ibid.* 101, 105 f. along with Plate xii., shaft K2 (signs of bulging and wrenching) ; 106 f., 115 (signs of action of water on exterior wall).

one time 50 feet (15 m.) east of the present dam.  But
Dr. Bliss also discovered what some previous excavations
by Dr. Guthe had rendered probable, that at another time
the wall had crossed the valley on the line of the present
dam, and that after it had reached the toe of the East
Hill a tower (of two periods) had projected from it over
the Ḳidron valley.  The result is to prove that at many
different periods—Dr. Bliss thinks five—the main city
wall crossed the mouth of the Tyropœon *below* both the
Pools of the Siloam.  That it was a city wall and not
merely a dam is proved by the convergence of all its lines
upon the scarp at the toe of the East Hill, from which it
continued up the edge of the latter.  In none of these
lines was any indication of a gate discovered.  No gate
was possible, of course, opposite the Pool.  South of this
Dr. Bliss found the wall continuous, though after a study
of his and Dr. Guthe's excavations at this point of the
South-west Hill I am not prepared to say a gate never
existed here.  On the north of the Tyropœon, where the
presence of the tower (of the two periods) might lead us
to suppose a gate, and where Dr. Mitchell would place
the Fountain-Gate,[1] nothing of a gateway was seen.  It
is true that the remains here are much ruined and mixed,
but the high, stepped scarp, which exists on the toe of the
East Hill, just where Dr. Mitchell would place the
Fountain-Gate, seems, with Dr. Bliss's description, to
preclude all possibility of a gate.[2]

These massive city walls of various periods across the
mouth of the Tyropœon were, however, not the only
ancient walls in this region.  Just where the outer line

[1] *Op. cit.* 116, and plan on p. 162.
[2] *Excavations at Jerusalem*, 108 ff. with Plan xiii.

leaves the South-west Hill, about 130 feet (over 39 m.) from the tower at the south-east angle, Dr. Bliss found

Ancient Wall up the West of the Tyropœon.

another wall[1] at right angles to the outer one, and traced it, wall and scarp, north-west up the edge of the South-west Hill above the Tyropœon, and therefore on the west of the two pools of Siloam, to a point above the upper Pool. From here it remains undecided whether the wall continued in the same direction, and was therefore part of a wall encompassing the South-west Hill, or whether (as Dr. Bliss thinks) it struck east above the Upper Pool to Ophel. If this was ever an exterior city wall, it left the two Pools outside. In parts it is 10 feet thick, but Dr. Bliss says it may have been only an interior wall. Unfortunately the remains have been recently much removed by the fellahin, and except for the stepped scarps the line of it may soon vanish.

The attempt to identify all these remains of walls in and about the mouth of the Tyropœon is not one which

Attempts to identify all these Walls.

we can hope to make successful. All we can say with certainty is that the City wall after turning its south-east angle, where there was always an important gate, crossed at many periods, if not all, of its history the mouth of the Tyropœon so as to include the two pools, and then ran (as we shall see) right up the east edge of Ophel above the Ḳidron. And it is at least reasonable to hold that the original wall with six buttresses across the Tyropœon existed in Hezekiah's day, because unless the mouth of the Tyropœon was then enclosed there would have been no object in

---

[1] *Excavations at Jerusalem*, 116-126. Dr. Bliss was here following previous excavations by Dr. Guthe and Herr Schick.

bringing the waters of Gihon under Ophel to a pool in
the mouth of the Tyropœon in order to secure them from
besiegers. In this case it is natural to take the gate of
the south-east angle as the Fountain-Gate, a position
which does not disagree with Nehemiah's data,[1] and
to suppose that the Dung-Gate opened upon Hinnom
further up the south wall, where the line of this was not
excavated by Dr. Bliss. I admit, however, that the position of the Fountain-Gate is not certain. Yet we seem
shut up to its identification with the gate at the angle by
the absence of any trace of a gateway on the wall across
the Tyropœon, unless one opened on the south of the
latter.[2] There remains the question of the wall up the
Tyropœon and its relation to the wall across. Was that
wall up the Tyropœon ever an exterior City wall built
when the wall across was in ruin, so as to leave outside
the two Pools which the latter had included? Dr. Bliss
thinks it was, and takes it as the line of the City wall in
the times of Herod and Josephus.[3] In the latter's description of that line, on which Dr. Bliss founds his argument,[4] the data are not quite clear, and in fact except for
one proposition, ' *above* the fountain Siloa,' on which it
would be unwise to build a great argument, they suit
both a line which includes and a line which excludes
Siloam. But putting that passage aside, I do not
think that another passage—in the exhortation which
Josephus claims to have made to the Jews to surrender
to Titus—can be interpreted except as meaning that
the spring of Siloam (as the issue of the waters from

[1] Above, p. 197.     [2] Above, p. 221.
[3] *Excavations at Jerusalem*, 326, 335 ; Plate xxix. No. 3.
[4] Jos. v. *B.J.* iv. 2.

the tunnel into the pool is still called by the Arabs) lay
outside the walls. He says: 'For Titus those springs
run more plentifully, which before were for you dried up ;
you know that Siloa failed and all the springs outside the
city, so that water was sold by the jar, but now they so
abound for your enemies that they are sufficient not only
for themselves and their cattle but for their gardens.'[1]
Assuming that this sentence means that Siloam, as well
as 'all the springs outside the city,' was available for the
Romans, and therefore like them *extra muros*, we have to
ask, is it correct?   In reply we have already seen that it
is contradicted by the testimony of Strabo, Dion Cassius,
and others ;[2] and I may now add that Josephus himself
elsewhere implies that Siloam lay within the walls under
command of the besieged, for he says that Simon, one
of their leaders, held, along with other parts of Jerusalem, 'as much of the old wall as bent from Siloam to
the east[3] . . . and he also held the fountain.'[4]   According
to this, then, Siloam was within the wall at the time of
the siege.[5]   There is further the following consideration.
As it would have been unnatural in the time of Hezekiah
to leave the one running water of the district outside the
wall, so also in the days of Herod and Josephus, especially
when it was so much easier to carry the wall across the
mouth of the Tyropœon on the old foundations than to
carry it up the Tyropœon, round the spring and down
again to the toe of the East Hill.   On these grounds, then,
we may, in opposition·to Dr. Bliss, assume that the wall

---

[1] Jos. v. *B.J.* ix. 4 (409 f.).
[2] See above, pp. 16, 80, 87.                    [3] Or 'north-east.'
[4] Jos. v. *B.J.* vi. 1.
[5] Since writing the above I see that Kuemmel (*Materialien*, etc., 71)
comes to the same conclusion.

followed at the time of Titus's siege the same line as it
did in Hezekiah's day: that is, across the mouth of the
Tyropœon so as to include the two Pools. What, then,
are we to make of Dr. Bliss's line of wall up the Tyropœon? It seems to me there are three alternatives
possible. Either (1) it was originally laid down before
the ancient wall across the mouth of the Tyropœon and
the tunnel and the upper pool were constructed, in
which case we should have to think of it as built to
encompass the South-west Hill, and as rendering that Hill
a separately fortified town, with the valley open between it
and the equally fortified East Hill; or (2) it was built by
the Maccabees round Jerusalem when the Syrians held the
Akra on the East Hill,[1] and the wall across the Tyropœon
had been destroyed by Antiochus Epiphanes; or (3) it is
some later wall built in the Christian era after Titus had
again destroyed the wall across the mouth of the Tyropœon. The last alternative is attractive, but for the
first there is this evidence in the Old Testament that
under the Jewish kings *two walls* existed in this region,
one of whose pools was called *a reservoir between the two
walls* made *for the water of the old pool* after the people
had *held back the water of the lower pool.*[2] This seems a
suitable description of Hezekiah's diversion of the water
of Gihon (which had flowed by Schick and Masterman's
conduit into the Birket el-Ḥamrâ,[3] or lower pool) by the
tunnel to the new upper pool. But if so, the *two walls*
existed from Hezekiah's time onwards. Either they were
the one up the Tyropœon and the one across the mouth
of it,[4] or else the former and the wall on the west of

---

[1] See above, pp. 194 f.    [2] Isaiah xxii. 9, 11.    [3] See above, p. 9. f., 98.
[2] So Bliss (apparently : pp. 326 f.) and Benzinger.

Ophel.[1]  In either of these cases it would be difficult to place *the gate between the two walls* by which Zedekiah and his soldiers, upon their escape from the City, emerged upon the King's Gardens.[2]  Another alternative for the two walls, however, presents itself in connection with their use as the name for this exterior Gate. They might be the south wall above Hinnom and the east wall across the Tyropœon, which meet at the south-east angle, and *the gate between the two walls* would be an appropriate name for the great gate Dr. Bliss discovered at the angle. Among these uncertain alternatives we must leave the subject.  Unfortunately, the nature of the little masonry left on the wall up the Tyropœon has not been sufficiently ascertained; nor did the remains at the point where the wall across, and the wall up, the Tyropœon diverge allow Dr. Bliss to determine anything decisive as to their relation.[3]

We pass now to the ancient lines of wall which excavators have traced upon the ridge of the East Hill south of the Ḥaram area.  At the toe of the East Hill, upon a scarp, we saw that all the lines of ancient wall crossing the mouth of the Tyropœon valley northward converged, and that Dr. Bliss found here the remains of a tower

The East City Wall. Guthe's Excavations on Ophel.

---

[1] So Duhm, Marti (one alternative), Guthe (Hauck's *R.-E.* viii. 679), and Paton.  [2] 2 Kings xxv. 2-5 = Jer. lii. 5-8 ; Jer. xxxix. 2-5.

[3] As this sheet goes to press there has appeared, in the *Journ. for Bibl. Liter.*, xxv. 1906, 1-13, an interesting paper on the 'Meaning of the Expression "between the Two Walls,"' by Prof. Lewis B. Paton.  He takes the 'Gate between the Two Walls' (equivalent to the Fountain Gate) as having stood above the Upper Pool in the wall round Ophel, the Fountain of Siloam being outside it.  But as (for the reasons given above) we must think of the exterior wall of the City as having crossed the mouth of the Tyropœon from Hezekiah's time onwards, and as the 'Gate between the two walls' was an exterior city gate through which Zedekiah and his men emerged on the King's Gardens, I am unable to agree with Prof. Paton's identification.

projecting from the wall over Ḳidron. From this point
the east wall of the City must have run northwards on
the edge of the Hill above Ḳidron. On this line Dr.
Guthe conducted a number of excavations in 1881.[1]
About 90 feet (over 27 m.) from the scarp he came
upon a fragment of wall, finely and very firmly constructed, the original breadth of which must have been
about 13 feet (4 m.). Unfortunately this fragment, undoubtedly part of the City wall, was only about 10 feet
6 inches long (3·2 m.).[2] The next discoveries were much
further north, still on the edge of the Hill, from a point
immediately above the Virgin's Spring for about 370
feet (113 m.) southwards.[3] They consisted of many
fragments of wall and signs of scarped and levelled rock.
For the most part the fragments of wall rested upon
rock, but some of them upon concrete.[4] Their various
directions show that the wall, or walls, here must have
been built with various angles and perhaps projecting
towers, just as one might have expected. Dr. Guthe
distinguishes seven kinds of masonry, which he assigns
to all ages from the most remote antiquity to the
Byzantine period.[5] The general result may be accepted,
that all these periods are represented on this most
ancient portion of the City's site. For here the Jebusite
citadel stood, afterwards David's-Burgh and the Syrian
Akra; walls encompassing *the 'Ophel* are attributed to at
least one Jewish king; Nehemiah rebuilt the wall here,
and here it stood, being destroyed at intervals, till
the time of the siege by Titus; and here it was after-

---

[1] *Z.D.P.V.*, 1882, 7-204, 271-378.
[2] *Ibid.* 42 f., 279, Tafel viii. K.　　[3] *Ibid.* 145 f., 150-166.
[4] *Ibid.* 161 f., 286.　　[5] *Ibid.* 284 ff.

wards rebuilt by Eudocia. But these very facts, to
whose multitude the huge masses of *débris* shot into
the Ķidron valley below bear impressive witness, prove
how impossible it is to distinguish exactly among the
different dates. A fuller excavation than Dr. Guthe
accomplished would hardly lead to success, for the
remains here have always been within reach of the
quarrying fellahin, and even since Dr. Guthe worked
heaps of old stones have been dug out, and portions
of the rock itself have been blasted away.[1] But we
may accept his identifications of the very ancient un-
mortared masonry as primitive, and the next most
ancient as that of the masonry of the Jewish kings
working under Phœnician influence; as also his recognition of Byzantine work in the smooth-faced stones
without bosses or margins which he uncovered;[2] for this
is the same as we have seen in the wall on the South-
west Hill, which Dr. Bliss has reasonably assigned to the
Empress Eudocia. But Dr. Guthe's other distinctions,
into work respectively of Solomon, Hezekiah, Nehemiah
and the Maccabees, are much more precarious. One
suggestion I feel to be untenable: that of a certain
double layer of squared stones to Jonathan,[3] for as long
as the Akra stood in the possession of the Syrians, it is
very improbable that any of the Maccabees built walls so
near to it.

From the north end of Dr. Guthe's discoveries, the
line of the east wall can only be inferred for some 295
feet (90 m.) northwards past a rocky knoll near which
' some massive walls have been uncovered,'[4] till we

[1] *Excavations at Jerusalem*, 127.    [2] *Z.D.P.V.*, 1882, 310 f.
[3] *Ibid.* 147.    [4] *Recovery of Jerusalem*, 298.

reach, upon the same edge of Ophel, the south end of
the wall discovered by Captain Warren [1] in 1867.  Com-
mencing at the south-east angle of the Ḥaram,
he traced it in prolongation of the east
wall southwards for 76 feet (23·18 m.) to a
small tower, at which it turns with the
The East<br>City Wall.<br>Warren's Ex-<br>cavations on<br>Ophel.
ridge south-west for 700 feet, and then stops abruptly.
At the base 14 feet 6 inches thick (4·42 m.), it rises from
the clay, on which it rests, 50 feet, or 74 above the rock.
The lower 20 feet (6·09 m.) are of rubble masonry, with
a plinth course of a 6-inch (15 cm.) projection above
it, and then smooth-faced masonry without margins or
bosses.  Whatever may have been the origin of the
lower rubble—whether an older wall or a foundation
for the upper masonry—this latter, as Dr. Bliss points
out,[2] resembles the masonry of his upper line of wall on
the South-west Hill: the proportions of the stones and
the spaces between the towers on the two walls are also
much the same.[3]  But further, this Ophel wall rests like
the south-west wall on the line of an older construction: besides its own small towers, Sir Charles Warren
found the remains of two towers with large boss-and-
margin stones corresponding to the masonry of the
lower wall on the South-west Hill.  One of these towers,
projecting 41½ feet (12·65 m.) from the rubble line to
a face of 80 feet (24·39 m.), Sir Charles Warren has
suggested, may be *the tower which lieth out.*[4]

[1] *Recovery of Jerusalem,* 294 ff. ; *P.E.F. Memoirs,* ' Jerusalem,' 226 ff.,
with plates v. and xi.        [2] *Excavations at Jerusalem,* 129.
[3] All this would indicate that from the plinth upwards at least, Warren's
wall is that built by the Empress Eudocia.  Kuemmel (p. 89) thinks it must
go back at least to the time of Herod.
[4] See above, p. 199.

Of other lines of wall on Ophel, of which we read at
least once that it was encompassed,[1] few traces remain.
Other Walls    Sir Charles Warren found a wall running west
on Ophel.    from the east wall, 15 feet (4·57 m.) south of
the Ḥaram wall.  It is but 4 feet (1·21 m.) thick.  No
traces of a wall with masonry *in situ* have been found along
the west edge of Ophel above the Tyropœon or round the
south end ; but scarps stand here and there upon this
line, and the disappearance of the masonry is well
accounted for by the fact that in later ages the wall was
not required for the defence of the city, and must have
been destroyed without being rebuilt.

We have now, with Warren's wall, reached the south-
east angle of the Ḥaram area.  Here we strike what in
The Ḥaram    one shape or another was always a separate
Area and the    part of Jerusalem, enclosed, as to-day, within
Temple
Walls.    its own walls, and forming a distinct keep or
citadel within and partly upon the walls of the City.  If
I abstain from giving a detailed description of this
Temple area, its buildings, substructions, and surrounding wall, that is not only because such a description
would require almost a volume to itself, but because with
the data at present before us I am unable to come to
conclusions upon many of the details.  For our present
task, the survey of the City walls, only a general outline
is necessary of what the excavations have shown to be
probable concerning the area and its boundaries.  It is
universally agreed that the threshing-floor of Araunah
upon which Solomon built the First Temple and its
courts lay somewhere within the present Ḥaram area.
The Biblical descriptions, as well as the tenacity with

[1] See above, p. 208.

which sanctuaries in the East hold through all changes of religion to the same sites, form sufficient premises for this conclusion. Further, the investigation of the contours of the original hill under the Ḥaram area has shown that the site of the First Temple and its courts must have been upon the highest portion of the hill, round the Rock eṣ-Ṣakhra, where indeed Josephus places it.[1] On this site also lay the Second Temple, and by consequence, the Temple of Herod. But Herod practically doubled the sacred precincts.[2] According to Josephus, the perimeter of the area under Solomon had been four stadia,[3] but after Herod's reconstruction was six, including Antonia.[4] Thus, while Solomon's Temple area had been a square, one stadium in each direction,[5] Herod's became an oblong, probably by extension north and south. The dimensions which Josephus gives are not trustworthy, nor reconcilable with those of the Ḥaram area. Some think that in *extent* the present Ḥaram area is the same as Herod's Temple area; but, for reasons given below, the latter probably did not extend much further north than the present 'Golden Gate,' thus excluding the space east of Antonia. The Ḥaram area forms not a quite perfect rectangle; only the south-west and north-east angles are right angles.[6] Exact measurements have been attempted several times, but their results differ. Approximately the south side is 920 feet, the east 1540, the north 1035, and

---

[1] v. *B.J.* v. 1. A study of the contours shows the improbability of the theory of Fergusson, Thrupp, Lewin, and others, advocated by W. R. Smith, art. 'Temple,' *Enc. Brit.*, that Solomon's Temple, and, according to the last-named, Herod's also, lay in the south-west angle of the Ḥaram area, which projects on substructions over the Tyropœon.

[2] Jos. i. *B.J.* xxi. 1; cf. xv. *Ant.* xi. 3.

[3] xv. *Ant.* xi. 3 (near the end).  [4] v. *B.J.* v. 2 (§ 192).

[5] xv. *Ant.* xi. 3.  [6] *P.E.F. Mem.* 119.

the west 1605 (about 280, 470, 315, 490 m.), which do not
agree with the round figures of Herod's area given by
Josephus, nor are the proportions of length to breadth
nearly the same. Herod surrounded his area by a great
wall with battlements,[1] round all the inside of which ran
colonnades or porticoes,[2] destroyed by Titus, and never
rebuilt. It is not impossible that, in constructing this wall,
Herod had made use of at least the foundations of the old
Temple area wall on the west and east. But, to obtain the
extension of the area, especially on the south, he must
have had to form great substructions, and surround these
parts with a wall new from the bottom. So far as they
go, the excavations confirm, and nowhere contradict, this
assumption. They have revealed the present walls
round the area to be of very composite structure, indicative of building and rebuilding at many different periods.
Sir Charles Warren's researches have determined forty-
one courses of stone,[3] of which from six to twenty are at
various points still above-ground, the rest being covered
by masses of shot *débris*, or lying deeper still in the
original soil above the rock on which the foundation
courses rest. Of the courses above-ground, from three
to twelve are of comparatively modern masonry, either
Turkish, with stones of irregular form and many kinds of
dressing, some of which have evidently been borrowed
from older structures; or else uniformly Byzantine,
smooth-faced, without margins or bosses. But other
courses are as evidently older; large stones with margins
and very fine joints. These can be seen to-day in the

---

[1] iv. *B.J.* ix. 12.                    [2] xv. *Ant.* xi. 5; v. *B.J.*, v. 2.
[3] See the interesting table, Appendix iii. of the *Recovery of Jerusalem*,
332 f.

lowest course above-ground in the south wall west of
the Single Gate, or better still, from this eastward to
the south-east angle, where the present surface falling
rapidly away leaves several courses of them visible.
Below-ground, according to Sir Charles Warren's reports,
the courses everywhere exhibit an ancient character.
All these older pre-Byzantine courses are as ancient *at
least* as the Herodian age, in which the Temple area was
so greatly extended, chiefly (as we have seen) by substructions and walls new from the foundation on the
south and south-west, so as to cover the bed of the
Tyropœon valley above which the present south-west
angle of the area lies. The masonry resembles that of the
extant base of Herod's Tower, Phasael, and of other
remains of buildings constructed under the Greek influences which prevailed during this period. Whether any
part of the surrounding walls goes behind the Herodian
age, or any is Maccabean, or even Solomonic, cannot be
declared with certainty. Sir Charles Warren has shown
how different the masonry round the south-west angle
from the Bab-el-Mughârib to the Double Gate is from
that to the north of it, on the west wall; and we have
seen that, on other grounds, this angle of the area was
Herod's work. But probably the whole south wall was
his. The north wall has not been sufficiently examined,
but is later than even Agrippa. Some think that the
portions of the west and east walls, which are opposite the
site of Solomon's Temple, are Solomon's original Temple
walls. In their lower courses there is nothing to conflict
with the theory of his date, but the archaic letters found
on them cannot be used in evidence of this; these may
be as late as Agrippa. Solomon's Temple-court had its

southern limit some 300 feet north of the south wall of
the Ḥaram.　As his Palace was to the south of and below
his Temple,[1] it must, as Sir Charles Warren long ago
pointed out, have lain within the south Ḥaram wall—he
thinks at the south-east angle, but probably further north,
immediately adjoining the Temple.

　　From these observations of the Temple walls we return
to the east City wall, one line of which, we saw, ran up the
east margin of Ophel to their south-east angle.
This east City wall is independent of the east
Temple wall, though built in a line with it.
It is of very different construction, rising
perpendicularly, while the Temple wall has a
batter ; and it is founded on the clay above the rock,
while the Temple wall is founded on the rock itself.
These facts point to the Ophel wall as the later of the
two; and indeed we found that it resembled, and was
probably the continuation of, the wall of Eudocia, uncovered by Dr. Bliss on the South-west Hill.　In the fifth
century, then, as to-day, the east City wall, after coming
up Ophel, was continued by the east Ḥaram wall in line
with it.　But it is extremely probable that this was also
the case in the Herodian age, and at the siege by Titus.
The fact that the south-east angle of the Herodian wall
is not a right angle, like that at the south-west, can be
explained by the east wall of Herod's Temple area having
been built in line with the City wall up Ophel, which
Herod found, and the line of which Eudocia followed.
And indeed Josephus expressly says that the City wall
coming up Ophel 'joined on to the east cloister of the
Temple.'[2]　Nor does he contradict this datum by any-

*Side note:* East City Wall coincident with East Wall of Temple area in the Herodian period.

[1] See below, Bk. III. ch. iii.　　　　[2] Jos. v. *B.J.* iv. 2.

thing else he says in his description of the Temple and account of the siege, but, on the contrary, rather confirms it; for he nowhere mentions an east City wall outside of the east wall of the Temple area, but describes how one looked down from the top of the latter, a giddy height, into the valley below.[1] Nor do I think all this is contradicted by his statement that Agrippa's wall, coming round the north of the City, 'joined to the old wall and came to an end in the ravine called Kedron,'[2] because *the old wall* is too vague a phrase from which to infer a separate City wall east of and below the east Haram wall, and (as just said) Josephus nowhere describes a course for the City wall independently of the latter, but, on the contrary, leaves a gap just where the east Haram wall comes in. On these grounds we may assume that in the Herodian age, and at the siege, the east wall of the Temple area had no City wall to the east of it, but lay above Kidron, the only rampart of Jerusalem upon that quarter.[3] And this view is further confirmed by the fact that Sir Charles Warren found the east Haram wall running on continuous to the north after the north-east angle of the Haram area was passed,[4] that is, into the line of Agrippa's wall.

But probably it was different in Old Testament times,

[1] xv. *Ant.* xi. 5. His remark that one could not see the bottom of the valley from the top of the Temple walls does not mean, of course, that a city wall came in to break the view, but that the height was so great as to strain the spectator's eyes in reaching to the bottom—a characteristic hyperbole.

[2] v. *B.J.* iv. 2. Does ' ravine called of the Kedron ' mean here, as Sandie (263 f.) holds, 'the tributary ravine'?

[3] Kuemmel takes a contrary view, on the ground of the phrase, *the old wall* (*Materialien*, etc., 89).

[4] *Recovery of Jerusalem*, 162: 'There can be no doubt that the ancient wall below the surface runs several feet to the north of the north-east angle without break of any kind.'

and that then a separate City wall did run above Ḳidron
below the east wall of the Temple area.   Some 46 feet

East City Wall
in O.T. times
ran below East
Wall of
Temple.

(14 m.) to the east of the Golden Gate of the
Haram wall (which is comparatively modern,
but rests on an ancient Temple gateway) Sir
Charles Warren came upon 'a massive masonry
wall' running from south to north, but with a bend westwards; on the line, that is, of the contours round the
Temple Mount up the gully which here comes into the
Ḳidron : the line round which we have seen the pre-exilic
wall of the City to have bent.[1]   Sir Charles tried to break
through this wall of massive masonry, but had to desist
after penetrating for 5 feet 6 inches (1·67 m.).   The stones
are so far similar to the lower course seen in the Ḥaram
wall near the Golden Gate, that their roughly dressed
faces project about 6 inches (152·39 mm.) beyond the
marginal draft, and that they are over 5 feet (1·52 m.)
long and 2 feet 6 inches (·76 m.) high.   The joints are
about 12 inches (·30 m.) apart, and filled with stones
packed in a curious cement of lime, oil and the virgin
red clay of the site, still used in dressing cisterns.   It is
possible that this wall continues up to the surface, as
immediately above it, upon the road, Sir Charles Warren
found 'some large roughly bevelled stones lying on the
same line.'[2]   Taking all these facts into consideration,
that the masonry is ancient, that it is worthy to have
been part of a City wall, and that it follows the natural
direction for the pre-exilic City wall, as this turned from
the Ḳidron valley round the north of the Temple Mount,

[1] See above, pp. 200, 208.
[2] Abridged (except so far as the indication of its following the contour is
concerned) from the *Recovery of Jerusalem*, 156-169.

we may assume, fragmentary as it is, that it represents
the approach to the north-east angle of the City wall laid
down above Kidron, but below the east Temple wall, by
the Kings of Judah, and repaired by Nehemiah. We
may almost dare to identify it with the wall which the
Chronicler says Manasseh carried north from Ophel as
far as the Fish-Gate.[1] Where on the south it left the
Ophel wall (which was afterwards carried higher on the
slope to join the eastern Temple wall) we cannot tell:
most probably about the first ancient tower which Sir
Charles Warren found south of the Ḥaram area. The
theory that on the north this wall turned up out of the
Kidron westward on the north slope of the Temple Mount
and to the south of the tributary gully (crossing, as I
think, the line of the present Ḥaram wall a little south
of the tower called Solomon's Throne, and curving
thence to the rock Antonia[2]), was first suggested to me
by Mr. Sandie's volume.[3] Dr. Schick follows the same
line on his Plan of 1891-2.[4] This is the natural line, and
it suits the data of Pompey's assault on the Temple from
the north. The only fact which leads to hesitation about
it is that Sir Charles Warren concluded that the wall at
the north-east angle of the Ḥaram area, that is on the
north of the tributary gully, is the work of the Kings of
Judah,[5] and that therefore their east wall did not turn
away from Kidron till north of that: Sir Charles thinks
it turned in near St. Stephen's Gate.[6] But this view is
opposed by the almost certain fact that if not Herod
then Agrippa made a northern extension of the Temple

---

[1] See above, p. 208.  
[2] See above, p. 200 f.  
[3] See above, p. 166.  
[4] *Z.D.P.V.* xvii. ; Plan opposite p. 1.  
[5] *Recovery of Jerusalem*, 324.  
[6] *Ibid.* 170 f.

area, and that (this is quite certain) the Birket Israel,
which now lies on the tributary gully, was not there in
Pompey's time.   Sir Charles Warren has himself proved
that the east wall of the Ḥaram does not stop at the
north-east angle, but continues several feet (at least) to
the north 'without break of any kind.'[1]   It seems to me
that all the work here is of the Roman age, and that
Colonel Conder and Dr. Schick are right in bringing[2] the
wall of Agrippa round Bezetha south across the mouth
of the tributary gully.[3]

We have seen, then, that the ancient east wall of the
City turned round to the north wall south of the tributary
gully which enters the Ḳidron valley under
the north-east angle of the Ḥaram, and that
Agrippa's wall crossed the mouth of this gully
to meet it just as Josephus describes.[4]   Following the
line of this northward from the Ḥaram, the line of
the present City wall, we reach St. Stephen's Gate
(*Bab Sitti Mariam*), and here meet with unmistakable
proof that we have left the more ancient and frequently
destroyed walls of Jerusalem behind us, and are pursuing
a line of wall comparatively modern and very seldom
destroyed.   For while from this gate southwards to the
south-east angle 'the *débris* varies in depth from 50 to

*East City Wall North of the Ḥaram.*

---

[1] *Recovery of Jerusalem*, 162 ; apparently 26 feet (7·92 m.).

[2] *P.E.F. Mem.*, 'Jerus.' 245 ; *Z.D.P.V.* xvii., plan opposite p. 1.

[3] Warren found Phœnician letters in red paint (like those found near the
other end of the east Ḥaram wall) on a stone below the original surface of
the tributary gully some 72 feet (22 m.) south of the Tower (*P.E.F. Mem.*,
129, 141).   But it is precarious to draw any inference of date from these.
The old Phœnician script was in use in Israel, on coins, down to 130 A.D.,
and may easily have persisted also as a tradition among masons.   Note the
tesseræ 'similar to those supposed to be Roman,' which Warren found below
a drain running along the Ḥaram wall on top of course Z (*Recovery of Jerusalem*, 186).                          [4] Josephus, v. *B.J.* iv. 2.

Part of Olivet.                                    Bezetha.

Entrance to Royal (
THE PRESE

Kasr Jalûd.                                          *Plate VIII.*

Damascus Gate.
JERUSALEM.

over 100 feet' (15 to 30 m.), north of the gate 'there are only a few feet of *débris* and often none at all; this rather implies that to the north of this gate there has been very little destruction of old walls.'[1] At St. Stephen's Gate the present wall does not rest upon rock, but only goes for 10 feet (3·04 m.) below the surface, and then rests upon 10 feet of concrete above the rock.[2] He thinks, therefore, that St. Stephen's Gate 'may not stand upon the site of the old wall.' But the construction he has noted may be due to the haste with which Agrippa's wall was completed by the Jews after he had left it unfinished. From St. Stephen's Gate the wall runs by the east of Bezetha northwards to the Burj Laḳlaḳ, its north-east angle, with a rock-cut ditch on the outside. The ditch never went further north than this, but turns almost at right angles to the west and the wall with it.

The latter, now the north wall of the present City, runs west on a high scarp to the so-called Herod's Gate (or *Bab es-Sâhire*), west of which it recedes for a space, but its original line, to judge from ancient remains,[3] ran straight to a point above the *The Present North City Wall.* entrance to the Royal or Cotton Grottoes (*Maghâret el Kettân*), where its foot is some 65 feet (19·8 m.) above the level of the ditch below. Between this and the Damascus Gate or Gate of the Pillars (*Bab el-'Amûd*) several courses of the ancient masonry are still *in situ*.[4] The gate is Turkish work, and bears an inscription of Suleiman the Magnificent.[5] With a mainly west-south-west direction, the wall and ditch run from the Damascus Gate up to the

---

[1] *Recovery of Jerusalem*, 170 and 160.   [2] *Ibid.* 161, 170.
[3] *P.E.F.Q.*, 1889, 38.
[4] Baedeker says that the Turks have modernised their appearance (104).
[5] See above, p. 184.

extreme north-west angle of the present City, and then turn sharply south-east upon Goliath's Castle (the *Kasr* or *Kala 'at Jalûd*). For the greater part of this stretch the present wall runs inside the line of the old wall, but follows largely the same angles as the latter.[1]  Goliath's Castle is a complex of remains of a powerful fort from

Goliath's Castle.

several periods. The rock base and part of the masonry probably represent Herod's Tower, *Psephinus*. Herr Schick would carry back part of it to at least Maccabean times,[2] but according to Sir Charles Wilson and others this part is of Crusading origin[3]—an illustration of the extreme diversity of views which it is possible for authorities to reach on the archæological and literary evidence. To the north-west of the Kasr Jalûd a line of ancient wall has been discovered coming south on the present north wall at an obtuse angle. There must have been a gate about here.[4]

From this point the west wall of the City, with a stretch of old wall parallel to it on the outside (which Dr. Schick

The present West City Wall.

attributes to Hadrian) runs south-east to the Jaffa Gate (*Bab el-Khalîl*), a Turkish structure, and south of this, till the recent gap was made in it, joined on to the present citadel of which the north-west tower was probably Herod's *Hippicus*, and the north-east certainly Herod's *Phasael*. The great outside ditch, of which there has been no trace for some time, reappears again outside the Citadel.[5]  From the Citadel the wall

---

[1] Schick, *Z.D.P.V.*, 1878, 16 ff. ; Merrill, *P.E.F.Q.*, 1903, 155 ff.  For discovery of part of a crypt or ancient monastery outside the wall near the Damascus Gate, see Barton, *Jour. of Bibl. Lit.*, xxii. 176 ff.

[2] *Z.D.P.V.*, 1878, 21.

[3] *Ordnance Survey of Jerusalem, Notes*, 1865, 73 ff. ; cf. *P.E.F. Mem.* ' Jerus.' 266.           [4] Schick, *Z.D.P.V.*, 1878, 22.

[5] For a curious theory of Uzziah's constructions on this part of the city's perimeter, see Schick, *Z. D.P. V.* xvii. **17** ; cf. Plan.

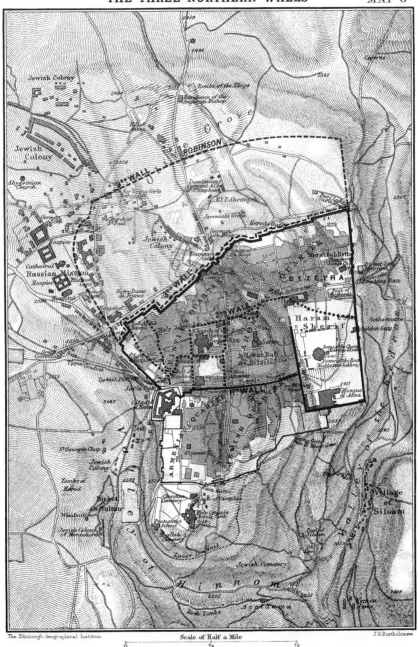

The Edinburgh Geographical Institute

Scale of Half a Mile

0      ⅓      ½

J.G.Bartholomew.

1st WALL ———     2nd WALL········     3rd WALL – – – –

(Alternative Lines)

London; Hodder and Stoughton.

runs on a scarp above Hinnom, till it suddenly turns from this eastwards across the South-west Hill, probably upon the direction of Hadrian's south wall. The stretch between the north-west corner of the Citadel and this point is the most ancient and constant stretch in the whole *peribolos* of the City, representing the west wall of Jerusalem perhaps as early as Solomon's time, and certainly as early as Hezekiah's, the west Hasmonean wall, the west wall of Herod's citadel and fortified palace, the west wall of the Legionary Camp and of Hadrian's Aelia, and the west wall of the city ever since through the Byzantine, Moslem and Crusading periods. From the present south-west angle the natural and more ancient line continues above Hinnom south to Maudslay's Scarp. And so we arrive again at our starting-point upon this long archæological survey of the City walls.

## 5. THE THREE NORTH WALLS.

We have now to examine only the remains of ancient walls within the northern section of the City, and to inquire how far they and the ancient remains we have just noted on the present encircling wall help us to determine the courses of the three north walls described by Josephus.[1] These (as has been already said) he calls the First, Second and Third, numbering them from the inmost and most southerly, the earliest continuation across the north face of the City of the wall which encircled the South-west Hill and Ophel. The Second or middle Wall started from the Gate Genath on the First, and curved to Antonia. The Third or most northerly was that begun

The Three North Walls of Josephus.

[1] v. *B.J.* iv. 1, 2.

by Agrippa, and finished by the Jews before the siege of Titus; it ran round Bezetha. But when Josephus is recording the advance of Titus into the City from the north, he reverses these numbers: the Third Wall he calls the First, and the First he calls the Third.[1]

Of the course of the First or most southerly of these we can have little doubt. Josephus says that it began

The First Wall of Josephus.

at the tower called Hippicus,[2] probably in the north-west corner of the present Citadel, by the Jaffa Gate, and ran east, by Phasael, the present 'David's Tower,' and by the Tower Mariamne,[3] the site of which is unknown, towards the Xystos which lay in the Tyropœon, and then, joining the Boulē or Council-House, finished upon the west colonnade of the Temple. That is to say, if we add to these data those of the natural features between the present Citadel and the west Ḥaram wall (so far as they have been ascertained), the First Wall ran along the north edge of the South-west Hill above the cross-valley which declines from the Jaffa Gate into the Tyropœon,[4] and then traversed the latter to the Temple Mount and the west Temple wall. On this line several ancient remains have been found. To begin with, there is the base of Herod's Phasael, already described.[5] Some 440 feet (134 m.) farther east, on the continuation of a line drawn from Hippicus to Phasael, under the Ḥaret eḍ-Ḍawâyeh and on its north side, there is a stretch of ancient wall about 160 feet (49 m.) with two towers projecting northwards 8 feet 7 inches (2·61 m.), and having faces of 9 feet 10 inches (3 m.).[6]

---

[1] v. *B. J.* vi. ff.  [2] *Id.* iv. 2.  [3] *Id.* 3, 4.
[4] See above, p. 35.  [5] See above, p. 191.
[6] *P.E.F. Mem.* 271 ; cf. De Vogüé, *Le Temple de Jérusalem,* 112 ff.

At the east end of the same street some ancient remains (often called the Gate Genath) have been proved by Sir Charles Warren to be Roman or Byzantine.[1] No further remains have been uncovered, but probably the wall crossed the Tyropœon somewhat on the line of the street Bab es-Silsile to Wilson's Arch and the other ancient remains about this.

In this First Wall there opened, according to Josephus, the Gate Genath.[2] If we knew the exact position of this Gate, many of the most difficult and unsettled points in the topography would become fixed and clear. But we do not know ; and even if excavation ever becomes possible in so crowded a part of the City, it will be a piece of rare fortune to discover this Gate after the thorough destruction of the wall by Titus. Josephus mentions the Gate Genath only once as the starting-point of the Second Wall. The name, if it means Garden Gate, would be suitable for a gateway opening upon the North-west Hill outside of the Second Wall, for the ground there was unoccupied by houses. The Gate Genath has been placed by some between the towers Hippicus and Phasael, that is close to the Jaffa Gate,[3] and by others at the latter tower.[4] But Sir Charles Wilson argues that the interval between Hippicus and it must have been considerable.[5] Present theories about the position of the Gate depend entirely upon

The Gate Genath.

[1] *Recovery of Jerusalem*, 10, 274-6, with Plan ; *P.E.F. Mem.* 234 f.
[2] v. *B.J.* iv. 2. Γενάθ, as though it were the Aram. Ganatha (Heb. and Talm. Heb. Gannah or Ginnah)=Garden. But the root-meaning of the word is *protection*, and this is not lightly to be excluded where the name of a gate is concerned.
[3] The earlier view and Robinson's, *B.R.* i. 461 f.; *L.B.R.* 212 ff.
[4] *Eg.* Schick, *Z.D.P.V.* xvii. 19 ; cf. Guthe, Hauck's *R.E.* viii. 679, line 58.
[5] *Golgotha*, etc., 128. At Hippicus there was a 'secret gate,' v. *B.J.* vi. 5.

what their authors think the course of the Second
Wall to have been.

Before discussing this, the most difficult and contested
line in all the topography of the City, it will be best to
try to determine the line of the Third or outmost wall of Josephus.  The 'beginning of it
was the tower Hippicus, whence extending
northwards to the tower Psephinus, it then marched
down right opposite the monuments of Helena,[1] . . . and,
prolonged through the Royal Caverns, bent at the corner
tower beside the monument called the Fuller's, and joining
the ancient *peribolos* came to an end at the ravine called
Kedron.  This Agrippa laid round the increase of the
City, which was all unprotected ; for [the City] overflow-
ing in population, had gradually crept beyond its *periboloi.*
Especially the parts to the north of the Temple towards
the hill, becoming one with the City, advanced not a little
till the fourth hill was surrounded with houses.  This
hill, which is called Bezetha, lies opposite the Antonia,
but is divided from it by a deep fosse, dug on purpose to
prevent the foundations of the Antonia adjacent to the
hill from being easily approached from and dominated
by the latter.'[2]

In his account of the attack of Cestius on the City,
Josephus calls the quarter thus enclosed by Agrippa's
wall Betheza (or Bezetha), or New-City, and implies that

*The Third Wall of Josephus.*

[1] 'The same was queen of Adiabene, daughter of King Izates.'
[2] v. *B.J.* iv. 2.  I have omitted the strange meaning which Josephus
gives to the name Bezetha: 'This recently built quarter is called in the
vernacular Bezetha, which, if interpreted in the Greek tongue, would be called
New-City.'  More correctly, in ii. *B.J.* xix. 4, Josephus says that Bezetha
(here in Niese's text spelt Betheza) was *also* called New-City.  Bezetha
cannot mean New-City: probably it stands for Beth-zaith, 'house' or 'district
of olives.'

it contained the Timber-Market,[1] and in his account of
the capture of it by Titus he calls it 'the northern parts '
of the City. Titus, he adds, now 'camped within [the
City] at the so-called "Camp of the Assyrians," having
seized all the intervening parts as far as the Kedron.'[2]
Also he tells us that opposite the monuments of Queen
Helena there was a gate in the Third Wall beside the
towers, called 'The Women's Towers.'[3] The course
which Josephus describes for Agrippa's wall shows more
than one remarkable correspondence to that of the
present City wall round 'the north parts of the City';
and though this wall is mostly of Saracenic construction,
we will keep in mind that we have seen ancient remains
sometimes in its own lower courses and sometimes
following a line parallel to it, a few feet to the outside.[4]
Agrippa's wall ran north from Hippicus (probably the
north-west tower of the modern Citadel), just as the
present wall does, to Psephinus, from which it ' descended '
as the present wall does from Ḳaṣr Jalûd, and was prolonged like the present wall past the Royal or Cotton
Caverns to a corner tower where it turned, and arrived,
just as the present wall arrives, at the ancient *peribolos*
above Ḳidron, most probably on the south of the tributary gully.[5] It thus enclosed Bezetha just as the present
wall does. Like other defences of the period, it had a
ditch on its outer side,[6] like the present wall. There are
besides the following considerations. It is unlikely that
even the Herodian Jerusalem was so large as to extend
beyond the present north wall of the City ; as it was, there

[1] ii. *B.J.* xix. 4.   [2] v. *B.J.* vii. 2, 3 (§§ 302, 303).
[3] v. *B.J.* ii. 2.   [4] Above, p. 239 f.
[5] See above, p. 237 f.   [6] Wilson, *Golgotha*, etc., 140.

was still a great deal of vacant ground within Agrippa's
wall.  Moreover, it does not appear that the plateau north
of the present wall was ever built upon sufficiently to
justify our assuming that it formed part of the City.
Compared with the soil inside the present wall, there is
very little *débris*, except at isolated points, mixed with or
lying over the reddish earth of the original surface of the
district.[1]  The many cisterns which dot the plateau on
the ordnance map are not nearly so frequent as those
within the City, and are to be accounted for by the custom
of having cisterns in suburban gardens, or as belonging
to the villas which, from Josephus's description, probably
stood among the gardens to the north of Agrippa's wall.[2]
Dr. Robinson, indeed, traced the course of the Third Wall
from 900 to 1800 feet (274 to 548 m.) north of the present wall,[3] so as to coincide with some ancient remains
which appear to have been much more numerous in
Robinson's day than they are now.   In 1864-5 these were
investigated by the Ordnance Survey officers, with the
result that in their opinion they 'could not have formed
part of a wall of defence.'[4]   The theory is besides
opposed by the fact that the Third Wall ran 'through

[1] Cf. Kuemmel, *Materialien*, etc., 53 f.

[2] v. *B.J.* ii. 2 (gardens and hedges); iii. 2 (hedges and walls); vi. 2
(trees and suburbs); cf. vi. *B.J.* i. 1.

[3] *B.R.* i. 464 ff. ; *L.B.R.* 179 f., 188, 193, and Map of Jerusalem.
Robinson (*B.R.* i. 458) places Psephinus not at 'Goliath's Castle,' but from
700 to 1350 feet further north, near the east end of the present Russian
cathedral.  A similar extended line has been advocated by Schultz, Fergusson,
Thrupp, Tobler, and recently with still more forcible arguments by Merrill.
Conder, agreeing with Robinson as to the position of Psephinus, traces the
Third Wall east from this, and so as to join the present City wall at the
Royal Caverns. *Handbook to the Bible*, 352 ; *P.E.F.Q.*, 1883, 77 ; but
cf. Hastings, *Dict. of Bible*, ii. 595.  Wilson, *Golgotha*, etc., 204, states
strong, and, as it appears to me, final, answers to this theory.

[4] Wilson, *Golgotha*, etc., 204. Kuemmel, *Materialien*, etc., 54, says

the Royal Caverns.' As already said, it implies an extension of the City, improbable even in the Herodian age, and for which no evidence has been found in the soil outside the present wall. On the whole, then, it appears to me that the Third Wall most probably followed the line of the present City wall.[1]

Those who support Robinson's theory of the Third Wall as having embraced a vast portion of the northern plateau outside the present wall, suppose that the line of the Second Wall coincided, or nearly coincided, with the latter on the stretch *The Second or Middle Wall of Josephus.* west of the Damascus Gate, from which it ran to Antonia, either direct or over the highest point of Bezetha (as Robinson thinks).[2] As Sir Charles Wilson points out, this course is not compatible with Josephus's statement that the wall 'went up' to Antonia;[3] and, besides showing no ancient remains between the Damascus Gate and Antonia, is just there of doubtful military value. But if, as we have seen, it is probable that the Third Wall of Josephus followed the line of the present City wall, we must seek for the course of the Second Wall somewhere to the south between it and the course of the First Wall,

that it is supposed that the wall, of which there are remains, was erected by the Crusaders, and refers to *Recovery of Jerusalem*, 278 ; but on this page Sir Charles Warren is writing not of the remains in question, but of others at the Damascus Gate.

[1] This view is very fully argued by Sir Charles Wilson, *Golgotha*, etc., 137 ff. It is also that of Schick, *Z.D.P.V.* xvii. 87 (see Plan opposite p. 1) ; of Guthe, Hauck's *R.-E.* viii. 686, lines 58 f. ; Kuemmel, *Materialien*, etc., 53, etc. ; and, on the whole, Robertson Smith, *Enc. Bibl.* col. 2430. Of course, as remarked above, the original line of the wall was sometimes coincident with the present line, and sometimes lay outside, but exactly parallel to it, as proved by the ancient remains. Between Hippicus and Psephinus it may have lain inside the present wall on the line traced by Schick on his map.

[2] *L.B.R.* 217-220.          [3] *Golgotha*, etc., 128.

which we have traced from the Citadel along the north slope of the South-west Hill, and across the Tyropœon to the Ḥaram area. Josephus says, 'it took its beginning from the gate which they called Genath, on the First Wall, and encircling the northern quarter [of the City] alone it went up as far as the Antonia.'[1] That is, it must have reached the Antonia from the hollow of the Tyropœon on the west. This is all we certainly know about it; for, as we have seen, its starting-point at the Gate Genath is uncertain. Various courses have been laid out for it, of which a detailed description has lately been given by Sir Charles Wilson.[2] They depend upon their supporters' opinions of the character of lines and clumps of ancient masonry, worthy to be parts of a city wall, discovered at various points between the line of the First Wall and the latitude of Antonia. As we have seen that the character of a bit of masonry can be by itself no clue to its date; as Titus himself is said to have 'thrown down the whole northern stretch' of the wall;[3] and as this is the part of the City where there has been the most frequent destruction and rebuilding of walls both exterior and interior, and where prolonged and thorough excavation has been least possible, the most sound position to take up is that of scepticism with regard to all these remains. It would have been generally agreed that we can know but little of the course of the Second Wall after it crossed the Tyropœon from the Antonia, had not the question of the genuineness of the Holy Sepulchre depended on how the wall passed from the Tyropœon to the First Wall, and where it struck the latter. More or less probable assumptions as to the line of this passage

---

[1] v. *B.J.* iv. 2.    [2] *Golgotha*, etc., 127 ff.    [3] v. *B.J.* viii. 2.

can be made from the natural lie of the rock on the North-west Hill (whose present contours, however, may not have been exactly those which shaped it in ancient times), and from the account by Josephus of the Roman assault under Titus upon the Second Wall. But on our present data it is hopeless to attempt to decide between the rival and contradictory arguments; and my own conclusion after a study of the remains, so far as they are still visible, and of the literature on the subject, is that we do not know how the Second Wall ran from the First to the Tyropœon; we do not know whether it ran inside or outside the site of the Church of the Holy Sepulchre.

# CHAPTER IX

## THE NAME JERUSALEM AND ITS HISTORY

THE English spelling of the name Jerusalem—
which is common to many modern languages
—was derived by the Authorised Version of 1611 A.D.,
Various forms through the Vulgate, from the Greek Ierou-
of the Name. salem, and approximates to what was in all
probability the earlier pronunciation in Hebrew, Yĕru-
shālēm. The Old Testament form, however, vocalises
the last syllable differently: Yerushālaim. Other
Semitic dialects give the type Urusalem with several
modifications. And even in Greek and Latin, besides
Ierousalem, there are Hierousalem, Hierusalem, Hierosolyma, and Solyma, most of which reappear in one or
other of the modern European languages. The history of
all these forms, along with a discussion of the questions,
which is the original or nearest the original and what the
derivation of the latter may be, forms the subject of the
present chapter.[1]

---

[1] Of recent literature the following may be cited :—by J. Grill, *Z.A.T.W.*,
1884, 134 ff. : 'Ueber Entstehung u. Bedeutung des Namens Jerusalem'
(written before the discovery of the name in the Tell el-Amarna letters, which
contradicts much of the argument); by Haupt, *Götting. Gelehrt. Nachrichten*, 1883, 108, and *Isaiah, S.B.O.T.* (Hebrew), Excursus on אריאל,
xxix. 1; by Marquart, *Z.A.T.W.*, 1888, 152; by myself, *Enc. Bibl.*, 'Jerusalem,' § 1, and *Expositor* for February 1903, 'The Name Jerusalem and
other Names'; by F. Prätorius, *Z.D.M.G.* lvii. 782; and by Nestle,
*Z.D.P.V.* xxvii. (1904) 153 ff. ; 'Zum Namen Jerusalem.' Other relevant

In the consonantal text of the Old Testament, the Hebrew letters for the name are ירושלם Y-R-U-S[1]-L-M. The Massoretes have vocalised them as יְרוּשָׁלַ͏ם,

The Hebrew Yerushalaim a late form.

Yĕrûshāláim, which takes the fuller form ירוּשָׁלַיִם, Yerushāláyim in three late passages.[2] This (without vowels) appears on coins which belong either to the reign of Simon, 142-135 B.C., or to the Jewish revolt against Rome, 66-70 A.D.;[3] and also sometimes in the Talmudic literature.[4] The termination -aim or -ayim used to be taken as the ordinary termination of the dual of nouns, and was explained as signifying the upper and lower cities, of which Jerusalem was composed at least in the later periods of her history.[5] But either it is a mere local ending, for it appears in other place-names, in which it is not natural to conjecture a dual,[6] or a purely artificial form confined to the reading of the Scriptures and other solemn occasions. In any case Yerushalaim is a late Hebrew form, and appears in no other dialect.

literature will be cited in the course of this chapter, which is based on the *Expositor* article mentioned above. The forms of the name in various dialects are spelt as in my article in the *Enc. Bibl.*, of which Nestle says that, of the modern Encyclopædias, it 'geht am genauesten auf die Schreibung des Namens ein.' *Cf.* also Guthe in Hauck's *R.-E.*, viii. 673 f.

[1] Or SH.

[2] According to Baer: Jer. xxvi. 18; Esther ii. 6; 2 Chron. xxxii. 9. Other recensions of the text add two more: 1 Chron. iii. 5; 2 Chron. xxv. 1—in both of which Baer reads לֵם-. The Babylonian vocalisation gives the ל with a *Pathah* (short *a*); in Codex B it has a *Seghol*, 2 Kings iv. 7. (*Cf.* Bleek, *Einl.*, 6th ed. 588; Nestle, *op. cit.* 154.)

[3] On these coins and the question of their date, see Bk. II. ch. ix.

[4] E.g. *Tosephta* 'Kethuboth,' 4. Usually the form is ירושלם, *Mishna* 'Zebahim,' xiv. 8; 'Menahoth,' x. 2, 5; 'Arakîn,' ix. 6, etc. etc.

[5] Gesenius, *Thesaurus s.v.*; though another explanation might be found in the legendary explanation of the name given below.

[6] Barth, *Die Nominalbildung der Semitischen Sprachen*, § 194 c. note 1.

The evidence is conclusive for an earlier and more common pronunciation, Yĕrûshâlém.[1]   This suits the

Yĕrûshālém<br>the original<br>Hebrew form. Hebrew consonants; it is confirmed by the Septuagint and New Testament translitera-tion, Ierousalēm, and by the earliest appear-ance of the name in classic Greek;[2] it appears in the Biblical Aramaic, Yerûshlem,[3] and in the Hebrew con-traction, Shālēm.[4]   It must, in fact, have been the pro-nunciation in ordinary use; and if we could only abolish our senseless abuse of the letter *j* as a soft *g*, we might congratulate ourselves on possessing, as the French and Germans do, a close approximation to the musical Hebrew form used by prophets and psalmists.

But there was another ancient form of the name, which has also had its tradition, lasting till the present

The Baby-<br>lonian Form<br>—Urusalim. day.   In the Tell el-Amarna letters, written about B.C. 1400, in the Babylonian script and language, the spelling is U-ru (or Uru)-sa-lim.[5]   On the Assyrian monuments of the eighth century, the transliteration is Ur-sa-li-immu.[6]   This has descended through the Aramaic 'Urishlem,[7] occur-ring in a Nabatæan inscription discovered by Mr. Doughty not far from Hejra, in Arabia, the Mandaic

---

[1] יְרוּשָׁלֵם.

[2] Ιερουσαλημη.  See below, p. 260.

[3] יְרוּשְׁלֵם, Ezra iv. 20, 24, v. 1; לֵם-, Ezra v. 14, vi. 9; Baer, םִ- throughout.

[4] Psalm lxxvi. 3; LXX. ἐν εἰρήνη; cf. Genesis xiv. 18.

[5] Berlin collection, Nos. 103, 106, 109; Winckler, *Thontafeln von Tell-el-Amarna*, 306, 312, 314; Sayce, *Records of the Past*, second series, v. 60 ff., 72 f.

[6] Delitzsch, *Par.* 288; Schrader, *C.O.T.*, ii. 214.

[7] אורשלם; *Corpus Inscriptionum Semiticarum*, ii. 1, 294.  The exact spot is El-Mezham.  The inscription is of one נתנוי=נתניה, Nethaniah, apparently a Jewish name.

Urashelam (?), the Syriac Urishlem,[1] and the Arabic Aurishalamu.[2]

There are thus in the main two lines of tradition as to the original form of the name. Since the *s* of the Babylonian is to be taken as the equivalent of the Hebrew *sh*, the difference between them is confined to the first part of the word. *[Whether the Babylonian or the Hebrew is the original?]* The question to which we have to address ourselves is: Which of the two was original? Though the distinction turns on a letter or two, it involves a matter of no little historical importance. For it opens up the larger question: Was the name of the City a native, that is a Canaanite, name, or given by the Babylonians during a period when, as we know, the Babylonian culture pervaded Palestine?

Assyriologists take the first part of Uru-salim as meaning 'city.'[3] Sayce interprets the second part as the name of a god, and translates 'City of Salim.'[4] But the determinative for deity is wanting, and the introduction of a divine name is *[Meaning of Urusalim.]*

---

[1] Mandaic, אוראשלאם; Syriac, ܐܘܪܫܠܡ.

[2] اورسلمو : this is an old Arabic form quoted by Yāḳūt (*Muʿǧam-el-Buldan*, ed. Wüstenfeld, 317) from a pre-Islamic poet. It occurs also in Idrisi: Robinson, *B.R.* i. 380. Robinson spells it Aurûshlim.

[3] 'Vielleicht': Delitzsch, *Wo lag das Paradies?* 226 f. Others without any qualification: Sayce, *Records of the Past*, second series, v. 61; *Academy*, 7th February 1891; Haupt as below. Nestle, *Z.D.P.V.* xxvii. 155, gives some other references.

[4] See references in last note and compare *Early History of the Hebrews*, 28: 'The figure and name of the god Salimmu, written in cuneiform characters, are on a gem now in the Hermitage at St. Petersburg. The same god, under the name Shalman, is mentioned on a stela discovered at Sidon and under that of Selamanês in the inscriptions of Shêkh Barakât, north-west of Aleppo (Cl.-Ganneau, *Études d'Archéologie Orientale*, in the *Bibliothèque de l'École des Hautes Études*, cxiii. vol. ii. 36, 48; Sayce, *P.S.B.A.* xix. 2, 74).'

opposed by Dr. Zimmern,[1] who, however, elsewhere admits the possibility of it.[2] Dr. Haupt translates the name in analogy to the Arabic Dâr es Salam and Medinet es Salâm as 'Place of Safety,' 'præsidium salutis.' He recalls the term *stronghold*[3] as applied to the town in Hebrew, and compares the name of 'the southernmost Babylonian port, Bâb Salimêti, "safe entrance."' 'Urusalim is thus a compound of the Sumerian word for "fortified place," "city," and the Semitic *Shalim*, "safety." The *u* after the *r* is the Sumerian vowel of prolongation; the *i* in Urishalim (Syriac Urishlem, Arabic Aurishalamu) substitutes the *i* of the genitive as termination of the construct state, and is therefore more correct from a Semitic point of view.'[4]

This Babylonian form Urusalim or Urisalim Dr. Haupt takes to be the original name of the City, and the Hebrew

The theory that Jerusalem is derived from it.

Yerushalem or Irûshalim to have been derived from it either by dissimilation, that is avoidance of the repetition of the same vowel, or as a dialectic modification; *eri*, a dialectic form of *uru*, passing

---

[1] *Zeitschrift für Assyriologie*, 1891, p. 263. Sayce's argument that Salim is a divine name is based upon his reading *Issuppu* in l. 12 of Letter 102 (of the Berlin collection), which he renders 'prophecy' (of the mighty king); and on his rendering *Zuruh*, in ll. 14, 34 of 104, 'oracle' (of the mighty king); and on his rendering of l. 16, Letter 106, 'the temple of the god Uras (whose) name (there is) 'Salim.' But Winckler, *Die Thontafeln von Tell-el-Amarna*, reads in l. 12 of 102 (Wi. 179), Zu-ru-ukh, which both there and in ll. 14 and 34 (Wi. l. 33) of 104 (Wi. 181) Zimmern and he render 'arm': taking 'the mighty King' not as a deity, but as Pharaoh. Winckler reads, Letter 106 l. 16 (numbered by him 15) differently from Sayce: (alu) Bit-Ninib.

[2] *K.A.T.*, 3rd ed., 475.    [3] מְצוּדָה.

[4] 'From the Assyrian point of view Urusalim is less correct than Urisalem.'—Haupt; and he compares Penuel and Peniel. So also יְרוּאֵל, 2 Chron. xx. 16; יְרִיאֵל, 1 Chron. vii. 2; יְחוּאֵל, Kt. and יְחִיאֵל, Kr., 2 Chron. xxix. 14; יְעוּאֵל, 1 Chron. ix. 6; and יְעִיאֵל, 1 Chron. xv. 18.

into Hebrew as *'îr* (עיר). Similarly Dr. Nestle says: 'Since from the genealogies of Genesis I learned to equate Yaradh (ירד) with 'Iradh (עירד), I have felt disappear every objection to see in Yerushalem (ירושלם) an older Irushalem (עירושלם). If the letter 'Ayin (ע) can vanish in the middle of a word, why not also at the beginning of a name, which often enough will be spoken together with a preposition?' If these arguments be sound, the name Jerusalem was not a native or Canaanite name, but given by the Babylonians during one of the early periods of the supremacy of their arms or of their culture in Palestine. And we should have to seek for the native name of the town among such as the Stronghold, Sion, the 'Ophel, or Jebus.

In itself such a conclusion is by no means impossible. There is à little evidence of the impress of Babylonian names upon Palestine: for example, Nebo, Beth 'Anâth, 'Anathoth, and (according to some), even Bethlehem.[1] But this is both meagre and ambiguous, and affords no support to Dr. Haupt's theory. Indeed, if the *Bit Ninib* mentioned in the Tell el-Amarna letters as in the territory of Jerusalem (No. 183) be Jerusalem herself,[2] then that was the Babylonian name of the town, and Jerusalem was the native name. Nor does Dr. Haupt's theory derive support from

*Supported by no external evidence and purely linguistic.*

---

[1] Even Nebo, the most likely, is not certain, and for Bethlehem, in which one or two scholars trace the name of the god Lahmu, there is, to say the least, an equally probable etymology, *house* or *domain of bread*. It has, indeed, been argued that in a place-name compounded with Beth- and another word the latter is either a divine name or had a divine name attached to it in a fuller form of the word (G. B. Gray, *Hebrew Proper Names*, 127, 324). But for reasons against this argument see *The Critical Review*, 1898, 20.

[2] As Haupt himself supposes, *Joshua, S.B.O.T.* (Engl.) 54; though Zimmern thinks this improbable, *K.A.T.*, 3rd ed. 411 *n.* 4.

the fact of the survival of the form *Uri* in Aramean and Arabic; for such a survival only proves the derivation of these forms from the Babylonian (a derivation historically probable, as the Arameans were in close intercourse with Babylonia and carried their language far into Arabia), and does not furnish independent evidence for the originality of the Babylonian form. There is, therefore, no external or independent evidence for Dr. Haupt's conclusion, which is entirely drawn from the Babylonian language.

Coming then to the linguistic evidence, we have to observe first that if the form Irushalem had been derived *Linguistic* from Urusalim, and the equivalent in Hebrew *objection to it.* of the Babylonian Uru be 'Ir (עיר), with an initial 'ayin, we might have expected in the Hebrew name an initial 'ayin, or at least, as in the Syriac and Arabic derivations from the Babylonian, an initial 'aleph. The absence of this seems to prove that in Irushalem or Yerushalem we have a form on another line of tradition altogether than that which the Babylonian started.

But more important still, Dr. Haupt's hypothesis is confronted with an alternative, for which there is some evidence in other Palestine place-names. He *Possible* *alternative—* says that the Hebrew Yerushalem (Irushalem) *Urusalim a* *corruption of* was produced from Urusalim either by dis- *Jerushalem.* similation or, more probably, as a dialectic variety. But not only is it equally possible on phonetic grounds that Urusalim is a corruption, by assimilation of the vowels, from Yerushalem; there are, besides, actual instances of such a change in the Assyrian transliteration of the native names of other places in Palestine. For while it is true that the long, or otherwise well-marked, vowels in such native names are correctly reproduced in the cuneiform transliterations, as in the cases of Lākhîsh, Ashdôd, Yāphô (Joppa) and Sîdôn, which in Assyrian appear as Lā-kî-s-u, As-du-du, Ya-ap-pu-[u], and Si-du-n[u], it is also very significant that when in a native name a weak vowel precedes a strong one, as in the first part of Yĕrûshālēm, it is very often in the Assyrian transliteration assimilated to the sound of the latter. Thus 'Edom (אֱדוֹם) becomes U-du-um[u],[1] Pĕkôd (פְּקוֹד) Pu-kû-d[u];[2] Bĕnê-Bĕrak (בְּנֵי־בְּרַק) Ba-na-a-a-bar-ak; and 'Elul (אֱלוּל the name of the month) U-lu-l[u]. Even a long vowel is sometimes assimilated to another long one as in Môāb, which in one Assyrian form is Ma-'-aba; Ammôn (עַמּוֹן) which becomes Am-ma-n[u];[3] and the Talmudic 'Ushā (אוּשָׁא),[4] which becomes U-s-u-[u]. An instance of assimilation is also found in the Assyrian Ma-ga-du-[u] (but elsewhere Ma-gi-du-[u]) for Megiddo, and perhaps in mi-ṣir and mu-ṣur for the name of Egypt, which the Hebrew gives as Maṣôr. The last instance reminds us that in several cases the Assyrian shows a fondness for the vowel *u*, where there does not appear to have been any trace of this in the original: as in Al-ta-ku-[u],[5] from 'Eltĕkēh (אֶלְתְּקֵה), and Gu-ubli,[6] from Gĕbal (גְּבָל). In face of all these—really a large proportion of the few place-names of Palestine of which we possess Assyrian forms—it is clear that Urusalim may possibly have been produced by assimilation from Yĕrû- or Iru-shalem. And this alternative to Dr. Haupt's derivation

---

[1] Delitzsch, *Par.* 295.
[2] The name of a tribe (Jer. l. 21 ; Ezek. xxiii. 23).
[3] Though in this case the native pronunciation may have been 'Ammân.
[4] Sukka, f. 20a.     [5] Del. *Par.* 288.     [6] *Ibid.* 283.

has a further superiority over the latter in that it implies
for Yerushalem what we find for all but a very few and
doubtful place-names in Palestine, a native origin.

What the etymology of Yerushalem may be it is almost
impossible to descry.　Various derivations have been
suggested, some ludicrous, none satisfactory.
Suggested
Derivations for The latter half of the word is usually taken
Yerushalem—
ancient and　as meaning *peace* or *security*; but while the
modern.
early rabbis and earliest Christian writers
interpreted the first part as *vision* or *fear*,[1] modern ety-
mologists have been divided between *the possession* and
*the foundation—of peace* or *security*.[2]　The resemblance of
the first part of the name, *Yĕru*, to the imperfect of the
verb, and the composition of instances of the latter with
a divine title in so many of the Palestinian place-names,
suggests a similar derivation for Yĕrûshālem : as if it were
from the verb Yarah, and should mean Shalem or Shalman, *founds* ; or rather, since this meaning for *yarah* is
not certainly possible, *Shalem casts the lot*.　On the whole
however, *shalem* is more probably a noun *peace* or an adjective *perfect* or *secure*.　*Yeru* might be either a verb, *he*
(the god) *casts a perfect* or *peaceful* (*lot*), or a noun, as if
*secure lot*.　There are, however, other alternatives.　The

---

[1] There is one curious Rabbinic explanation in the *Midrash Bereshith
Rabba*, ch. 89.　Abraham called the place יִרְאֶה (Gen. xxii. 14), but Shem
(*i.e.* Melchisedec) had called it שָׁלֵם (Gen. xiv.).　The Almighty, unwilling to
disappoint either Patriarch, gave it both names, Yireah-Shalem = Yerushalem.
The numerical value of יראה and ירו is the same.　In the Greek and Latin
*Onomastica* (see Lagarde, *Onom. Sacra*, and Nestle, *op. cit.* 154), Jerusalem is
usually explained as ὅρασις εἰρήνης, *visio pacis*.

[2] ירוש שלם, *possession of peace*, Reland and others ; ירו שלם (from ירה,
*to throw down*) *the foundation of peace*, Gesenius *Thes.*, Gesenius-Buhl.,
*Lexicon*, 12th ed. (cf. Grill, *Z. A. T. W.* iv. 134 ff.); or *the foundation of security*,
Merrill, *Bibl. World*, 1899, 270.

Arabic 'Arya means *abiding, continuous* ; *'iryu*, a *stable* or *stall*. And there is the common Semitic root *'ûr* or *'îr*, *to lighten*, from which we have the Hebrew *'ûr* (אוּר), *fire* or *hearth*, and the Arabic *'Irat, focus* or *hearth*, and *'awwar*, *to kindle*. The probability of this latter derivation is increased if we read (with Canon Cheyne and others) Isaiah's name for Jerusalem, 'Ariel,[1] *God's Lion*, as 'Uriel, *God's Hearth*, and suppose that the prophet formed it in analogy to the name of the City. Yerushalem would then signify *hearth of peace* or *inviolate hearth*. But all these are suppositions, none of which we have any means of proving. It is interesting that Saadya sometimes renders the name by Dār es-Salām, and sometimes by Medīnat es-Salām : the House or City of Peace.[2] Worth noticing also is the suggestion that Yerushalem was originally a personal name ; as is well known, it is used as such in the present day.[3]

We have now to pursue the history of the name through Greek and Latin to the languages of modern Europe.

The Hebrew Yĕrûshālēm appears in the Alexandrian translation as Ιερουσαλημ (Ierousalēm): the constant form in all those books of the Greek canon which have been translated from the Hebrew. As in the case of so many other proper names in the Septuagint, it is an exact transliteration of the original, made before the vowel-points were inserted in the Hebrew text, and reflecting (as we have seen) the early

*[side note:]* Ierousalēm in the Septuagint and Clearchus.

---

[1] xxviii. 2 ; אֲרִיאֵל.

[2] Nestle, *op. cit.* 154 ; cf. Medinat es-Salām, the Khalif Mansur's official name for Baghdad (Nöldeke, *Sketches from Eastern History*, 129).

[3] Franz Prätorius, *Z.D.M.G.* lvii. 782, quoted by Nestle, p. 153.

and common pronunciation of the name. The earliest appearance of this form in other Greek, which I have been able to discover, is that in a passage of Clearchus of Soli,[1] a pupil of Aristotle, which is quoted by Josephus.[2] He gives it accurately, but with a Greek termination: Ierousalēm-ē. Since he says that it is ' altogether awkward ' to pronounce—which he would hardly have asserted of the Hellenised form Hierosolyma—and since Josephus everywhere else uses Hierosolyma, we may be sure that in ' Ierousalēm-ē ' we have the original spelling of Clearchus himself.[3]  And if this be so, it is another proof of the original pronunciation of the name.[4]

In the Septuagint and the citation by Josephus from Clearchus the light breathing should probably be prefixed to Ierousalem ;[5] but in any case the rough breathing came early into use : Hierousalem. This may have been originally due to an effort to express the consonantal force of the first letter ;[6] but more probably arose from—and was at least confirmed by— the fashion prevalent in Western Asia from the third and second centuries B.C., of Hellenising proper names.

*Hierousalem.*

---

[1] End of the fourth and beginning of the third century B.C.

[2] *C. Apion*, i. 22 : Τὸ δὲ τῆς πόλεως αὐτῶν (*i.e.* οἱ Ἰουδαῖοι) ὄνομα πάνυ σκολιόν ἐστιν· Ἱερουσαλήμην γὰρ αὐτὴν καλοῦσιν.  In the meantime the initial breathing is purposely omitted from Ιερουσαλημη.

[3] Therefore Niese's note—' suspectum '—to the reading Ιερουσαλημη (see Index to Niese's ed. of Jos. *s.v.*) is unnecessary.

[4] See above, p. 252.

[5] The edd. of the LXX. (except Swete's), and Niese's ed. of Jos., prefix the *spiritus asper*.  But in his ed. of the LXX. and *Introd. to the O.T. in Greek* Swete gives the light breathing, pp. 305, 313 : and so Reinach in the excerpt from Clearchus (*Textes d'Auteurs Grecs et Romains relatifs au Judaïsme*, p. 11), but Müller (*Frag. Hist. Gr.* ii. 323) the rough.

[6] Yet initial *yod* is usually transliterated with the light breathing (*e.g.* Ἰορδάνης, Ἰησοῦς, etc.) except in such Hellenised forms as Ἱεροβοάμ, Ἱερεμιάς.

To the same source we may trace the further modification of the name into the plural noun Ἱεροσόλυμα (with or without the article), Hierosolyma. When this first appeared it is impossible to discover.

Hierosolyma.

The earliest, directly recorded, instances of it, so far as I can trace, belong to the first century B.C. In Maccabees ii.-iv., in which the Septuagint spelling of proper names is so often followed,[1] we find not ᾽Ierousalem but ᾽Ierosolyma; and so in the ‘Letter of Aristeas’[2] (date doubtful) and in Strabo, quoting probably from an author who wrote soon after the Syrian campaign of Pompey in 63 B.C.[3] In Latin Cicero has it,[4] and subsequent writers, for example Pliny, Tacitus and Suetonius:[5] still in a plural form Hierosolyma. It was therefore in common use from the first century B.C. onwards. But it appears so uniformly in quotations from earlier Greek writers,[6] that

[1] Swete, *Introd.* 313.

[2] Both with and without the article. See Thackeray's ed. in Swete's *Introd.* pp. 525 f. In this edition of Aristeas the rough breathing is prefixed; and it is a question whether the rough breathing should not also be prefixed in Maccabees ii.-iv., as in Tischendorf's ed. Swete gives the light breathing.

[3] See Reinach, *op. cit.* p. 97. It occurs, too, in Philo (*Legat. ad Cajum,* § 23), Plutarch, and so through Appian (*Syr.* 50), Dion Cassius, *Hist. Rom.* (xxxvii. 15 f., etc.), and subsequent writers: always as a plural and generally with the article. The edd. give the rough breathing.

[4] *Pro Flacco,* c. 28 §§ 68 f.

[5] Pliny, *H.N.* v. 14 f.; Tac. *Hi.* ii. 4, v. 1; Suet. *Tit.* 5. We find it also on an inscription in the time of Claudius: [Hi]erosolymitana (*Corp. Inscr. Lat.* x. No. 1971).

[6] From Hecataeus of Abdera (*c.* 300 B.C.), in a fragment of Diodorus Sic. preserved by Photius; from Manetho (third cent. B.C.) in Jos. *C. Ap.* i. 14 f.; Berosus (under Antiochus Soter, 280-261 B.C.) in Jos. *C. Ap.* i. 19; from Menander of Ephesus (probably early in second century B.C.), and Dios (?) in Jos. viii. *Ant.* v. 3, cf. *C. Ap.* i. 17; from Agatharchides of Cnidus (under Ptolemy VI., 181-146 B.C.) in Jos. *C. Ap.* i. 22; from Polybius (*c.* 210-128 B.C.) in Jos. xvi. *Ant.* iii. 3; from Timochares (probably second century B.C.); Xenophon the topographer (? before the first century B.C.), and Philo ‘the Elder,’ a poet—all three in Eusebius, *Praep. Evang.* ix. 35,

we are justified in tracing its origin to some distance
behind the first century; and all the more so that the
materials for its formation were present in Greek literature
and were quoted in connection with the Jews as early as
the fifth century B.C.　Josephus, who in his Hellenic
fashion constantly employs the form Hierosolyma[1]—
though he must have known better—derives it more than
once[2] from Solyma, that is the Salem of Melchisedec.[3]
He spells it Solyma because Greek writers had already
used this shorter form and found for it an etymology of
their own.　He quotes[4] the Greek poet Choerilos, who, he
thinks, in the fifth century B.C. had spoken of the Judæan
range as the ' Solyman mountains ';[5] and Manetho,[6] who
speaks of the Hebrews, leaving Egypt, as the Solymites.[7]
It was natural for classic writers to identify this name
with that of the Lycian Solymi mentioned by Homer.[8]
This appears to have been the origin of the form Hierosolyma, though we cannot help wondering if its resemblance to the name of Solomon had anything to do with

36, 37, cf. 20, 24; from Posidonius of Apamea (*c.* 135-51 B.C.), in Diod.
Sic. xxxiv. (preserved by Photius).　The historical Greek writers quoted
here are all given in Müller, *Fragmenta Historicorum Graecorum*.　But the
student will find more convenient the collection of these extracts, and of.
those of pagan Latin writers given above and below, which has been drawn up
by Théod. Reinach in his useful *Textes d'Auteurs Grecs et Romains relatifs
au Judaïsme*, Paris, 1895.

[1] Both with and without the article: e.g. *Ant.* V. ii. 2; VII. ii. 2, iii. 2;
VIII. x. 2, 4; X. vii. 1; XI. i. 1, 3, iii. 1, 10, iv. 2, v. 6, 8.

[2] I. *Ant.* x. 2: ὁ τῆς Σολυμᾶ βασιλεύς: τὴν μέντοι Σολυμᾶ ὕστερον ἐκάλεσεν
Ἱεροσόλυμα.　vi. *B.J.* x. 1.　　　[3] Gen. xiv.

[4] *C. Apion,* i. 22.　　　[5] Ἐν Σολύμοις ὄρεσιν.

[6] *C. Apion,* i. 26.　　　[7] Οἱ Σολυμῖται.

[8] Cf. Tacitus, *Hist.* v. 2.　Jos. VII. *Ant.* iii. 2: ἐπὶ γὰρ Ἀβράμου . . .
Σόλυμα ἐκαλεῖτο, μετὰ ταῦτα δὲ αὐτὴν φασί τινες, ὅτι καὶ Ὅμηρος ταῦτ' ὠνόμασεν
Ἱεροσόλυμα· τὸ γὰρ ἱερὸν κατὰ τὴν Ἑβραίων γλῶτταν ὠνόμασε τὰ Σόλυμα, ὅ
ἐστιν ἀσφάλεια.

its rapid acceptance.[1] The form Solyma, which Josephus [2] also uses as a feminine singular (indeclinable), appears as a plural neuter in Martial,[3] and as an adjective, Solymus, in Valerius Flaccus, Statius, and Juvenal [4]—all at a time when the siege by Titus had made the name of the city very familiar throughout the Roman world. In Greek, Pausanias, in 175 A.D., also gives the form Solyma.[5]

So much, then, for the history of a false form. It is curious to observe that the one pagan writing in which the correct spelling, Ἱερουσαλήμ, is found (except the extract from Clearchus), is that ascribed, rightly or wrongly, to the pedantic Emperor Julian.[6]

The New Testament employs both forms, Ιερουσαλήμ and Ιεροσόλυμα. The former (indeclinable) is used mostly in the writings of Luke (about twenty-seven times in the Gospel and forty in Acts, as against the use of Ιεροσόλυμα four times in the Gospel and over twenty in Acts [7]) and Paul; also in the Apocalypse and Hebrews. Grimm [8] has suggested that it has been selected where a certain sacred significance is intended,[9] or in solemn appeals.[10] It has the article only when accompanied by an adjective.[11] The form Ιεροσόλυμα appears as a singular feminine only once.[12] Elsewhere it is a neuter plural, as in Josephus

*Ιερουσαλημ and Ιεροσολυμα in the New Testament.*

---

[1] Compare Menander of Ephesus: Σολόμων ὁ Ἱεροσολύμων βασιλεύς; and Dios: τυραννῶν Ἰ. Σολόμων; both quoted in Jos. VIII. *Ant.* v. 3, and *C. Ap.* i. 17 f.

[2] Above, p. 262 *n*. 2.     [3] *Epigram.* xi. 94 (written in 96 A.D.).

[4] Val. Flaccus (fl. 70-90 A.D.), *Argonautica*, i. 13; Statius, v. 2, 138; Juvenal, *Sat.* vi. 544.     [5] *Perieg.* viii. 16, 4.

[6] *Epist.* 25.     [7] Knowling on Acts i. 4.     [8] *Lex.* s.v.

[9] Gal. iv. 25.     [10] Matt. xxiii. 37 ; Luke xiii. 34.   Add Luke xxiii. 28.

[11] Winer, *Gram.*, E.T., 125 ; yet see Acts v. 28.

[12] Matt. ii. 3.   Here, as in Matt. iii. 5, it stands for the inhabitants of the city.

and Greek writers; so in all the Gospels,[1] and Acts and Galatians. It occurs only in John with the article in the oblique cases.[2] It is doubtful whether either of the two forms should have the aspirate. Blass gives it to the Greek alone; Westcott and Hort deny it to both.

Following the Greek Testament the Vulgate has both the Hebrew and Greek forms, in some codices with the aspirate, in some without : Hierusalem and Hierosolyma, Ierusalem and Ierosolyma (fem. and neut.); these continue through the Christian centuries. The Pilgrim of Bordeaux[3] and Eucherius[4] write Hierusalem ; Eusebius, Ἱερουσαλημ ; Jerome, Ierusalem, Iero- and Hiero-solyma (fem. and neut.: Lag. *Onom. Sacr.*) ; Antoninus[5] and Arculf,[6] Hierosolima; Willibald, Bernard and Theodoric,[7] Ierusalem ; Chroniclers of the Crusades, Hierosolyma and Hierusalem and Ierusalem ;[8] documents of the Crusades, Hierosolyma.[9] The earliest French writings have Iherusalem,[10] Jerusalem, Jerusalen, and Jerusalam.[11] Barbour's *Brus*[12] has Ierusalem, and Spenser's *Faërie Queene*,[13] Hierusalem. The English Authorised Version of 1611 has Ierusalem

*Forms of the name in Christian literature.*

[1] *eg.* Matt. xx. 17 ; xxi. 1. (?) ; Mark iii. 8 ; Luke xxiii. 7 ; John ii. 23, v. 2. Ιεροσολυμα always in Mk. and John.

[2] John v. 2, x. 22, xi. 18. So Winer, *op. cit.* p. 125. John v. 1 the acc. is without the article. On the whole N.T. use see Zahn, *Einl. i. d. N.T.* ii. 311.

[3] 333 A.D.   [4] *c.* 427-440.   [5] *c.* 570.   [6] 680.

[7] Wil., *c.* 722 ; Bern., 867 ; Theod., *c.* 1172.

[8] Bongars, *Gesta Dei per Francos.*

[9] Röhricht, *Regesta Regni Hieros.*

[10] In the *Cité de Ih.*, 1187.

[11] *L'Estoire de la Guerre Sainte,* from the end of the twelfth century; but in a revised form of somewhat later date (edited by Gaston Paris, 1897).

[12] iv. 29.   [13] Bk. 1. canto x. 57.

in the Old Testament and Apocrypha, but Hierusalem
in the New Testament.[1]

Thus Jerusalem (with some variants) comes to be the
form in the languages of Europe. Hierosolyma, and the
shortened Solyma, treated now as feminine, appear occasionally in poetry and romance.

We have seen that an early Arabic form of the name
was 'Aurishalamu, of which also there were abbreviations Shalamu and Shallamu.[2] The Arabs, The Arabic
however (as we shall see in next chapter), forms.
commonly designate the City by epithets expressive of
its sanctity, el Mukaddas, el Ḳuds, and the like. But
modern Jews, Levantines, and native Christians throughout Palestine frequently use Yerusalem.[3]

---

[1] On the use of the name in the Latin Version of the N. T., see Wordsworth
and White, *Nouum Test. . . . Latine sec. ed. S. Hieronymi*, notes to Marc.
iii. 8, Luc. ii. 22, Ioh. i. 19, and Index.

[2] Le Strange, *Palestine under the Moslems*, 83.

[3] *Z.D.P.V.* xvii. 257.

# CHAPTER X

## OTHER NAMES FOR THE CITY

FROM first to last a number of other names and epithets have been given to Jerusalem, either derived, like Jebus, from her lords previous to Israel ; or like Ṣion, extended from some point within her site ; or expressive of her sanctity, like the series founded on the root K-D-SH ; or imposed by her conquerors, like Aelia Capitolina and its derivatives. Of one of these, Ṣion, we have already traced the progress from its original use for the citadel on the East Hill to its extension over the whole City and the sacred community.[1] The others will be described in this chapter.

*Other names for the City, of various origins.*

Of the first of them little requires to be said. We will discuss elsewhere the name of the Jebusite predecessors of Israel.[2] In Judges xix. 10 f., and in 1 Chronicles xi. 4 f., the name Jebus[3] is applied to the City : *the same is Jerusalem.* There is, however, no other instance of it in the Old Testament, and its appearance in these two passages has been suspected. The second is certainly late, the work of the Chronicler about 300 B.C., and there is cause to doubt the integrity of the text of the first. The town, we know, had long before the time of the Judges been called Jerusalem ; and

*Jebus.*

---

[1] See above, ch. vi.       [2] See below, Bk. III. ch. i.

[3] יְבוּס, LXX. Ιεβους.

when a second name appears only in what are probably
late texts, the inference is reasonable that it has been
suggested by the name of the tribe which Israel found in
possession of the site. At the same time, there can
be no doubt about the Jebusites themselves—they are
accredited by every line of the Hebrew tradition—nor
that they held a certain amount of territory round their
fortress. To this territory the name Jebus may easily
have been given in the common speech both of the
Canaanites and the Hebrews; and it would be rash to
assert that it was never used of the town, and is only
a late and artificial suggestion. In such uncertainty we
must leave the question.[1]

Another possibly mistaken application of an ancient
name to Jerusalem may be mentioned here. The chronicler calls the Temple Hill, *Mount of the Moriah,*
*where a vision was made unto David*[2] (?).
Josephus identifies it with the place in *the land of the
Moriah,*[3] where Abraham prepared to sacrifice Isaac,[4] and
this was also a Rabbinic tradition.[5] Accordingly Mount
Moriah has become a usual name among both Jews and
Christians for at least the East Hill of Jerusalem. But,
in the first place, Abraham's *land of the Moriah* (if that
be the proper reading, which is doubtful)[6] is unknown,
the identification of it with the Temple Mount is very

Mount
Moriah.

---

[1] See G. F. Moore, *Judges* (*International Critical Commentary*), 1895;
K. Budde, *Das Buch der Richter* (*Kurzer Hand-Commentar*), 1897;
S. R. Driver, 'Jebus,' in Hastings's *D.B.*; G. A. Smith, *Enc. Bibl.* col. 2416;
H. Guthe, Hauck's *R.-E.* viii. 638.

[2] 2 Chron. iii. 1 : ‏הַר הַמּוֹרִיָּה אֲשֶׁר נִרְאָה לְדָוִיד‎.

[3] Gen. xxii. 2.

[4] Josephus, i. *Ant.* xiii. 1, 2 : τὸ Μώριον ὄρος.

[5] Levy, *Neuhebr. u. Chald. Wörterbuch*, iii. 58 ; *Bereshith Rabbath*.

[6] See Driver's *Genesis*.

late, being ignored even by the Chronicler ; and the Chronicler's own use of the name, to which he gives another origin, is also late and unsupported by any earlier passage in the Old Testament. Whatever place it belongs to, the name probably has nothing to do with vision.

Next in order we may conveniently refer to two foreign designations, both by conquerors of Judah. At the head of the list which Shishak[1] gives of the cities he took in Judah, stands the name *Rabbat,* with which some have suitably identified Jerusalem ;[2] for the word means 'chief town' or 'capital.' And by the time that the Israelite territory had so shrunk as to become the mere suburbs of Jerusalem, Asarhaddon called Manasseh king not of the land, but of *the City, of Judah.*[3]

Rabbat (?)<br>and the City<br>of Judah.

A number of names and epithets given by the Prophets and Psalmists may now be mentioned. Isaiah addresses Jerusalem as *'Ariel,*[4] which as it stands may mean *The Lion of God,* and is often so translated. But as in Ezekiel the same word is used for *the altar-hearth,*[5] and as Isaiah himself speaks elsewhere of God having *a fire in Ṣion* and *a furnace in Jerusalem,*[6] and in his inaugural vision beheld the Divine Presence above the burning altar of the Temple, it is more probable

O.T. Epithets:<br>Ariel.

---

[1] See below, Bk. III. ch. IV.

[2] Sayce, *Academy,* 1891, Feb. 4 and 28.

[3] *Records of the Past,* cf. 2 Chron. xxv. 28 ; the parallel passage, 2 Kings xiv. 28, has *city of David.*

[4] xxix. i. : אֲרִיאֵל, 'Αριήλ.

[5] Ezek. xliii. 15 f. (Kethibh) ; cf. אראל on the Moabite stone, lines 12, 17. Cf. above on the Arabic 'Irat or 'Iryat = 'hearth,' p. 259.

[6] xxxi. 9, unless, as some think, this is a later addition.

that the name means *the hearth of God.* The Hebrew *Bath* or *Daughter* is often applied to the popu- Daughter of Ṣion, etc. lation of a town or country, and in this sense we are to take as names of Jerusalem the following: *Daughter of Ṣion,*[1] *Daughter of Jerusalem,*[2] *Daughter of my people,*[3] *Virgin daughter of Ṣion.*[4] Also it is called *The City of Righteousness* by Isaiah,[5] City of Right- eousness and of God. and by the Psalms *The City of God,* or *of our God,* or *of Jahweh of Hosts,* or *of the Great King.*[6]

By the time of the Exile Jerusalem had come to be known among her people as *The City,* in distinction from *The Land*;[7] and this is usual also in the Mishna. It is significant of the growth of The City. her importance both material and spiritual, and of the absence of other cities in the rest of the now much diminished territory. Townships there were, and not a few fenced ones; but Jerusalem stood supreme and alone as The City.

In Deuteronomy Jerusalem is not named, but frequently implied as *the place where Jahweh will cause His Name to dwell.*[8] This concentration of the national worship upon her Temple, preceded The Holy City 'Ir haḳ- Ḳodesh. as it had been by Isaiah's visions of the divine presence, and his declaration of God's purposes for His

---

[1] Lam. ii. 1 ; iv. 22 ; Isa. lii. 2, etc.   On this name see above, pp. 148 ff.

[2] Isa. xxxvii. 22 ; Lam. ii. 13, 15, etc.     [3] Lam. iv. 6.

[4] Isa. xxxvii. 22 ; Lam. ii. 13.       [5] i. 26.

[6] Psa. xlvi. 4 ; xlviii. 1, 2, 8 (the references are to the English Bible); cf. Isa. lx. 14.

[7] Ezek. vii. 23 ; Jer. xxxii. 24 f. ; Ps. lxxii. 16 (*they of the City*)—הָעִיר; Isa. lxvi. 6 (עִיר).

[8] Cf. Ps. lxxiv. 7 : *dwelling-place of Thy Name.*

inviolable shrine, led to the name *The Holy City*, *'Ir hak-
Ḳōdesh*[1] (compare *My Holy Mount*[2]); and from this has
started the long series of names meaning the same in
many languages, which has continued to the present day.
On the coins which are variously assigned to Simon
Maccabaeus and to the First Jewish Revolt (66-70 A.D.),
the legend is *Yerushalaim Ḳĕdoshah*, or *Haḳ-Ḳedoshah*,
Jerusalem the Holy.   Matthew twice calls it Ἡ Ἁγία
Πόλις[3]—so still in the Mosaic Map of Medeba (sixth
Christian century).   Philo has Ἱερόπολις,[4] a form which
suggests the origin of the form Ἱεροσόλυμα (with the
rough breathing).[5]   So in Arabic the commonest designation is derived from the same Semitic root for *holy*,
Ḳ-D-S.   It appears in various forms *Bêt el-Maḳdis*,
el-Muḳaddas   'domain or place of the Sanctuary'; *el Muḳad-*
el-Ḳuds.        *das* or *el Muḳaddis*, 'the Holy';[6] or (in the
modern vernacular) *el-Ḳuds esh-Sherîf*, or more briefly
*El-Ḳuds*, 'The Sanctuary.'   In the East this is by far the
commonest name to-day.[7]   The suggestion made by M.
Clermont-Ganneau[8] that el-Muḳaddas or el-Ḳuds betrays
a reminiscence of a dedication of the sanctuary at Jerusalem to a Canaanite deity Ḳadish is interesting, but
there is no evidence for it.   And the derivation of the
name from the immemorial sanctity of the City is
sufficient.

To complete this list of names we may add, though it
really lies beyond our period, the name imposed on

---

[1] Isa. xlviii. 2; lii. 1; Neh. xi. 1; cf. Dan. ix. 24.
[2] Joel ii. 1.                        [3] Matt. iv. 5; xxvii. 53.
[4] *In Flaccum*, § 7.                 [5] See above, pp. 261 ff.
[6] Yaḳut, iv. 590; Taj el 'Arus, iv. 214.
[7] Cf. the Syriac *Ḳudsch*, *Ḳúdusch*, or *Ḳudúsch*.
[8] *Archæo. Researches in Palestine*, i. 186.

Jerusalem by her Roman conquerors. When the Emperor Hadrian destroyed so much of the City and gave her another shape than that of her native growth, he strove also to destroy the native name by substituting *Aelia Capitolina*.[1] Till the time of Constantine, and for at least two centuries later, *Aelia* remained the official name[2] and usual geographical designation;[3] was still longer continued in Christian writings;[4] and even passed over into Arabic as *'Iliya*.[5] From the other part of Hadrian's name came Ptolemy's Καπιτολίας.

Aelia Capitolina, Kapitolias, 'Iliya.

[1] Dion Cassius, lxix. 12. On the coins of Hadrian (and his successors down to Valerian) bearing the legend Col[onia] Ael[ia] Kapit[olina] and the like, see Madden, *Coins of the Jews*, ed. 1903, ch. xi. Aelia was from Hadrian's own family name, Capitolina from Jupiter Capitolinus, to whom he erected a temple on the site of the Jewish Temple.

[2] *e.g.* in Canons of the Council of Nice, A.D. 325, vii. ; and in Acts of Synod held in Jerusalem, A.D. 536 (cited by Robinson, *B.R.* ii. 9).

[3] *Onomasticon* ; Eusebius, Αἰλία ; Jerome, Aelia.

[4] *E.g.* Adamnanus, *De Locis Sanctis*, i. 21.

[5] Yaḳut, iv. 592.

BOOK II

*THE ECONOMICS*

*AND POLITICS*

# CHAPTER I

## A GENERAL STATEMENT OF THE ECONOMIC PROBLEMS

AMONG the countless questions raised by the history of Jerusalem—the appearance and persistence of such a city on exactly such a site—none are more radical or pertinent to all the rest than those of her material resources and economy, the area of her supplies and the methods of her finance. How was the City fed? What were the extent and character of her own fields, woods, quarries and supplies of clay? Where were her markets, what her exports and imports? What purchasing-power had her government and her citizens respectively? What taxes did the former draw? On what industries did the latter depend?

*The usual economic problems of a city.*

The importance of such questions, obvious as it is in the history of every city, is intensified in the case of Jerusalem by the peculiarities of her political and religious development. At first merely one of several highland towns, with her own chief, and possessed of a limited area of the surrounding country, in these conditions her economy is easy to understand. The primitive Jerusalem fed herself from her own fields, and by the petty trade which she

*Peculiarly intensified by the religious history of Jerusalem.*

conducted with her neighbours and with the great centres of civilisation, whose caravans passed to and fro upon the plains about a day's journey from her gates. When she became the capital of a considerable kingdom, with a court and standing army, she commanded at the same time a wider area of resources from which these might be easily sustained. But when in the course of time, from being but one of several shrines of her people, Jerusalem was elevated to the rank of the only altar at which their sacrifices were lawful and the nation periodically assembled for worship, then the problems of her economy were aggravated to an intensity experienced by hardly any other city in the ancient world. For, situated as she was in a district comparatively poor and with a limited water supply, Jerusalem had not only to provide for a large permanent priesthood and their servants, but thrice a year also entertained great crowds of pilgrims. In these circumstances, how were her finances regulated, and whence did she draw provision both for so numerous a non-productive population and for the temporary but immense additions to it caused by the Temple festivals? Altogether the economic questions are among the most important in the history of Jerusalem. They not only form the standing physical problem of that history—the survival of so large a city upon a site economically so unfavourable—but they penetrate everywhere the subject of her religion. They form the texts of the most ethical discourses of the prophets. They are closely entangled with the organisation of the priesthood and with the whole system of the national worship.

For answers to these questions the Bible contains no little amount of material. Some of this, relevant to the

support of the monarchy and of the priesthood, is carefully stated in the legal codes of the Old Testament.
The rest, referring to the more fundamental
matters of the natural resources of the
City, the people's foods, trades, industries

and finance, is given incidentally in the historical and
prophetic literature. To the former the Talmud contributes much elucidation of detail; upon the latter the
information of Josephus is a little more generous than
that of the Bible, and there is something to be gleaned
from the Greek and Latin geographers and the accounts of the imperial administration. But, because
till a few years ago the economy of the City had very
little changed, we may illustrate and supplement the
information from all these sources by data derived from
the works of the Arab geographers; from the charters
and laws of the Latin kingdom of Jerusalem; from the
reports of modern pilgrims and travellers; and from the
present systems of land-tenure, cultivation and taxes.
Through all the ages to which these sources of information belong, the political and religious ideals of Jerusalem
have profoundly altered; but the physical conditions
of her life, very much of the economy of her citizens, and
in consequence the fiscal measures of her governments,
have remained substantially the same as in Biblical
times. It is remarkable, for instance, how much of the
system of land-tenure which prevails under the Turkish
government resembles, and may be used to illustrate, the
fragmentary notices of the disposition and inheritance of
the soil which we find in the Old Testament.

Before we start upon the details of our inquiry, it may
be well to add to our statement of the economic questions

particular to Jerusalem a general description of the main stages of economic development through which the

The general economic development of Israel.

people of Israel as a whole passed, during those periods of their capital's history with which we have to deal. Like all the Semites who preceded and followed them, Israel entered their Promised Land as a pastoral or nomad people, with the family or the tribe as the social unit.[1] Gradually they exchanged their pastoral and nomadic habits for those of agriculture. They settled in villages and townships to the cultivation of definite areas of soil, surrounded by almost equally definite areas of uncultivated land on which they pastured their flocks. We must keep in mind, however, that the agriculture on which Israel entered was not that of a virgin soil. They found the country already richly cultivated, and succeeded not only to the inheritance of *goodly towns which they did not build, full of all good things which they filled not, of cisterns which they did not hew, of vineyards and olive trees which they did not plant,*[2] but to all the habits and tempers of this long-established civilisation. More or less gradually they became absorbed in a life mainly agricultural indeed, but already permeated by the influences of commerce and partly moulded by the forces of an ancient and pervasive system of culture, the Babylonian, which had long ago passed the merely agricultural stage and was imposing upon the peoples of Syria the tempers, if not

---

[1] It must be kept in mind that the tribe was seldom a *pure* one, *i.e.* consisting only of individuals and families all descended from a common ancestor. There were numerous amalgamations of families descended from different stocks; and grafts, more or less artificial, of individuals or families upon tribes to which by blood they did not belong.

[2] Deut. vi. 10 f.

also some of the institutions, of its civic and imperial economy. Under all these influences, the ancient Hebrew constitution slowly altered. The tribe was replaced by the village or township; the social principle of kinship was crossed and broken by that of neighbourhood. In the sparseness of the information which the Old Testament affords, and the difficulty of dating much of it, a complete understanding of the system of land-tenure in Israel is impossible to us; but some light is reflected from the methods prevalent to-day. On the one hand we have clear testimony to the existence of private or family property in land (or at least in the fruits of definite areas of the soil), and to the tenacity with which the piety of the individual, the urgency of the prophets, and the skill of the great law-codes sought to preserve to each family its ancestral estates.[1] On the other hand, there is evidence of the existence of communal or village property in land, the rights to the tillage of which were disposed among individuals or families by lot; but it is not clear whether this evidence is proof of the continuance of the custom throughout the later ages of Israel's history, or is only the memory that such had been the form of land-tenure

---

[1] 1 Kings xxi. 3; Ruth iv.; Jeremiah xxxii. 6 ff.; 1 Kings iv. 25 and Micah iv. 4; Isaiah v. 8 ff.; Micah ii. 1 ff. The earliest code, the Book of the Covenant, Exodus xxi. ff., which plainly reflects the agricultural state of life, does not make it clear whether private property, which it implies in the rights of pasture and tillage and in the fruits of the land, extends to the soil itself. Deut. xix. 14 (cf. xxvii. 17) forbids the removal of landmarks *which they of old have set*: a remark which implies that at least the rights to cultivate certain fields descended from generation to generation in the same family. In the Priestly Code the preservation of landed estates in the same family is provided for by the rule that even daughters may succeed to it (Numb. xxvii. 1-11); and the inalienableness of land is further emphasised in Lev. xxv. 23 f. : *the land shall not be sold in perpetuity, for the land is mine.*

in the earliest times.[1]  To-day both systems prevail.
Lands, which are not devoted to the purposes of religion,
are of two classes.  First, they may be *mulk*, 'governed'
or 'owned,' that is 'real or freehold property, . . . lands
generally in close proximity to, if they do not immediately surround, a village or town, and almost invariably used as gardens and orchards.'  Or, second,
they are *amîriyeh*, 'Amîr's' or 'government land,' belonging to the Imperial State, but held in common by all the
members of the village or community, and called *Arâdi
Mashâ'a* or 'undivided lands,' the tillage rights of which
are annually apportioned by lot among the village
families : 'these lands are invariably arable.'  It may be
that the double evidence of the Old Testament, which
we have quoted above, is to be explained by some similar
arrangement.[2]  Besides these two kinds of land there are
to-day the *Wâḳuf* or *Waḳf*, 'stopped' or 'inalienable,'
lands devoted by gift or will to the maintenance of a
mosque or religious institution ; the like of which existed,
as we shall see, in Old Testament times, and had an
important influence on the economy of the capital and
its Temple.  To return to the other two kinds in Israel—
the tenacity of the system under which lands were family
property, either through freehold possession and right of

[1] Micah ii. 5 ; Jer. xxxvii. 12 ; Ps. xvi. 5-6 ; Josh. xv.-xix., xxi. ; Ps.
cxxv. 3 ; 1 Chron. vi. 55, etc.  All of these passages imply the division of
land by lot, but whether as a custom in the writer's own time, or as metaphor
reminiscent of an ancient custom, is uncertain.

[2] The whole subject lies outside the scope of our present task, and therefore I give only the outlines.  For the details see two papers on the Turkish
system by Bergheim in the *P.E.F.Q.*, 1894, 191 ff. (from which come the
extracts in the text above), and by Graf Mülinen in *Z.D.P.V.* xxiii. 159 ff. ;
Fenton, *Early Hebr. Life*, §§ 17-20 ; Buhl, *Die Soc. Verhältn. der Israeliten*,
55 ff. ; *Z.D.P.V.* xxx. 152, 207, describes the sale of village lands to individuals and corporations.

inheritance or by lot as part of the communal or village property, gradually yielded to or was ruptured by the passage of Israel from a purely agricultural economy to one that was increasingly commercial. The prophets of the eighth century complain of the loss of their estates by the old yeoman families of the country to rich men, who were no doubt produced by the growth of trade, the increase of taxation, and the consequent necessity of mortgaging land : *ye who range homestead on homestead and lay field to field, till no place is left,* that is for the independent yeomen, *and ye be the sole householders in the midst of the land.*[1] We shall see how the capital, which was Jerusalem, thus grew at the expense of the provinces, in spite of the laws specially framed by the latest code to counteract the tendency ;[2] and how the agricultural conditions of the people became subordinated, for good and evil, to a centralising policy and a civic economy. The rural militia upon which the national defence had rested in earlier days were reinforced under the monarchy by a standing army of mercenaries, always in Eastern states the result of a growth of commerce;[3] and the king, imitating in this and other ways foreign examples, grievously increased the people's taxes. Finally, there fell upon Israel the dominion of the great empires, which imposed their own fiscal measures, and in some cases their own system of conveying and registering landed estates.[4] The Imperial authorities frequently farmed out

---

[1] Isa. v. 8 (the verse is elliptic, but the above appears to be the proper meaning of it) : cf. Micah ii. 1 ff.   For modern instances, *Z.D.P.V.* xxx. 152, 207.

[2] See above, p. 279 *n.* 1.

[3] See the author's article, 'Trade and Commerce,' in the *Enc. Bibl.* §§ 11, 48, 63 *n.* 1, 66, 75 *n.* 2, for instances of this.

[4] See below in Bk. iii., the chapter on Manasseh's reign.

the taxes to native Israelites, and thus in the latest periods we meet with a class of *publicans*, whose existence had, as we shall see, serious economic and political effects upon the character of the capital and the life of the country as a whole.

Having thus made clear the general lines of Israel's economic development, in addition to the particular problems of the economic history of Jerusalem, we may now pass to a detailed account of the latter from the earliest times up to the end of the Biblical period, illustrating it as far as is possible from the later sources of information indicated above.

# CHAPTER II

# THE ETHNIC AND ECONOMIC ORIGINS
# OF JERUSALEM

SEVERAL years ago, in caves of the Lebanon, there were discovered some remains of primæval men using stone implements and hunting a fauna which has long disappeared from Palestine.[1] More recently Mr. R. A. Stewart Macalister has unearthed at Gezer the remains of another and much later race (for the only animal fragments found among them are those of animals of the present epoch), but also cave-dwellers, without metals and using only stone implements. The men were remarkably smaller than their Semitic successors. Mr. Macalister assigns them to a date 'not much later than 3000 B.C.,' and suggests a possible identification of them with the Horim, usually translated *Cave-men*, whom Hebrew traditions place in Eastern Palestine and Edom prior to the immigration of the Semites.[2] 'For perhaps five hundred years this primitive race occupied the hill'; then came the great Semitic invasion of Syria and Babylonia, to which archæologists give the name of Amorite or Canaanite. With this we

*(margin note: The Stone Age in Palestine.)*

[1] Dawson, *Modern Science in Bible Lands*, ch. iii., 1888.
[2] *P.E.F.Q.*, 1902, 347 ff. ; 1903, 13, 20 ff. ; 1904, 107 ff.  *Bible Side-Lights from the Mound of Gezer* (Hodder and Stoughton, 1906), 25 f. and ch. iii.

find, though stone implements continue to be used, the first introduction of metals. We may, therefore, provisionally conclude that before the Semitic immigrations Palestine had, as a part at least of its population, some of the races known as Palæolithic and Neolithic: the latter short of stature, living in caves, and using the surface rocks and caves (as Mr. Macalister has shown) as their sanctuaries; cremating their dead; unused to metals, and employing only stone implements.[1] Whether they were the same as the Biblical Horim seems to me doubtful.

Remains of these races have been found at Jerusalem. A great many cave-dwellings have been uncovered both on the East and West Hills of the City's site, and under the village of Silwân.[2] But the use of caves for dwellings lasted to a late period in the history of Jerusalem, and nothing (so far as I know) has yet been discovered in the layers of their floors which gives proof of their use in the Stone-age. Round the City, however, large numbers of flints have been picked up, rudely shaped as weapons.[3] From these and other specimens Father Germer-Durand has formed and classified a collection of over five thousand pieces in the museum of Notre-Dame de France, which represents virtually every distinguishable phase of the Stone-age. Among them are the 'chipped flints,' or flints shaped entirely by

*Probable Stone-age Remains at Jerusalem.*

---

[1] On the subject of the Semitic migrations see Winckler, *Die Völker Vorderasiens* (in *Der Alte Orient*, vol. i. Heft 1); Paton, *The Early History of Syria and Palestine*, ch. i.

[2] See Dr. Guthe on his excavations on Ophel, *Z. D. P. V.* v. ; Cl.-Ganneau on ancient caves on the South-west Hill, *Arch. Res.* i. 291 ff.

[3] Germer-Durand, 'L'Age de Pierre en Palestine' in the *Rev. Bib.* 1897, 439 ff. ; cf. *Actes du II<sup>e</sup> Congrés Intern. des Orientalistes*, 'Ethnogr. de l'Orient,' 276 ff. For other sites see Bliss and Macalister, *Excav. in Pal.* 26, 142 ff., pl. 71 ; cf. Blanckenhorn, *Z. f. Ethn.* 1905, 447 (not seen); Vincent, *Canaan d'après l'exploration récente* (1907), ch. vi.

chipping, which, in distinction to 'flaked flints,' archæologists recognise as dating from a more remote antiquity. On the back of the Olivet range, about two hundred metres east of Râs el-Meshâref, M. Clermont-Ganneau reports 'a prodigious quantity of flint chips,' evidently broken from a reef a few steps off. He found among them no perfect specimen of chipped flint, but numbers 'which seemed to have been roughed out and prepared ; others again seemed to have been begun and then thrown away' ; and he thinks 'there must have been a workshop for chipped flints in this place.'[1] In all probability, therefore, the first settlements at Jerusalem were of Stone-age men, inhabiting caves, somewhere on the banks of the Ḳidron valley as the position nearest to the natural water-supply.

This race was succeeded in Palestine, as we have seen, somewhere about 2500 B.C., by Semites,[2] men of a higher economy, at first inhabiting tents and occupied   The Semitic with the rearing of sheep and cattle, but after   Settlements. they swarmed from Arabia into Palestine, settling down to agriculture and building. Whether in the east or the west, the earliest towns—as the Biblical story of Cain reminds us—were the foundation not of shepherds, nomads content with easily shifted camps, but of husbandmen who had settled to the cultivation of a definite area of soil. These, after a period of alternating between summer tents and winter caves or huts, built themselves (often with the help of the caves) permanent dwellings of stone or clay, and fortified their settlement first with a tower and then with a rampart. In describing this

---

[1] *Arch. Res.* i. 273 ff: 'Rujûm el B'hîmeh.'

[2] We need not here discuss the question whether there was an earlier Semitic invasion of Palestine, corresponding to that of Babylonia in the fourth mill. B.C.

process we are not left to imagination. Through all but its latest stage of wall it is pursued at the present day upon Moab and other frontiers of the desert by the same race to which the earliest historical inhabitants of Jerusalem belonged. Thus at 'Araḳ el-Emîr, in April 1904, I found the son of a pure Bedawee tent-dweller, who told me that his family had begun to cultivate the soil three generations before. His father left off tent-dwelling in winter, and before he died had charged the son to build from the ancient ruins of the place a permanent house of stone, which the latter was now doing. Other instances of the kind I found the same year in Moab, as I had found them in 1891 in Southern Judæa and in Ḥauran.[1]

The first fortification which the converted nomad builds for his new settlement, often before he has abandoned his tents, is a tower: there is no better or more universal refuge in Western Asia against the sudden desert razzias.[2] There are towers in Northern Moab built to protect their grain by the 'Adwân, who are otherwise content with 'their houses of hair.' When Uzziah sought the protection of his shepherds as well as his trade roads to Elath, he built towers in the southern desert.[3] We may,

---

[1] For another instance of the transition see Libbey and Hoskins, *The Jordan Valley and Petra*, ii. 19: 'The inhabitants [of Tafileh] are nearly all in the middle stage between dwellers in tents and dwellers in cities.' Cf. *H.G.H.L.* p. 10; and see also for Ḥauran, *Z.D.P.V.* xx. 96 f., and *M.u.N.D.P.V.*, 1900, 69; Burckhardt, *Travels in Syria, etc.*, on Kerak, 387, for the Jôf in Arabia, App. iv. p. 663; for Carmel see *Z.D.P.V.* xxx. 151.

[2] Cf. 2 Chron. xx. 24, and Doughty, *Arabia Deserta*, i. 13: 'The tower was always the hope of this insecure Semitic world'; 285: 'Every well-faring person, when he had fortified his palms with a high claybrick wall, built his tower upon it. . . . In the Gospel parables, when one had planted a vineyard, he built a tower therein to keep it. The watch-tower in the orchard is yet seen upon all desert borders.'

[3] See below, Bk. III., under Uzziah.

therefore, conclude that the earliest strong building erected by the Semites who first settled in Jerusalem was a tower. Of this we find a symbol, if not the actual echo, in the name by which a prophet calls the city long after, *Migdal 'Eder, the Tower of the Flock*.[1] But in time the tower would have a wall attached to it running round the rough dwellings of the community, and the primitive village would become a town. This would stand upon some small ridge or knoll within easy reach of the water sources in the valley of the Ḳidron and elsewhere. I have given reasons for supposing that the ridge or knoll must have been Ophel, above the present Virgin's Spring.[2] Indeed the prophet we have quoted identifies *the Tower of the Flock* with *the 'Ophel of the daughter of Sion*.

---

[1] Micah iv. 8 ; cf. Gen. xxxv. 21.          [2] See above, pp. 138 ff.

# CHAPTER III

## THE CITY LANDS

THE village or town, whose economic development we have sought to sketch in the preceding chapter, had a territory, which its inhabitants cultivated and upon which they pastured their cattle. The size of this
The Territory of the City. territory varied, of course, with the political influence of the town, and with the different economic processes which developed among the inhabitants. At first the territory of Jerusalem would be small, not more than four or five square miles, if we may reckon by the neighbouring villages, which we have no reason to presume were less ancient than what afterwards became their metropolis. But when the site was fortified, being much stronger and almost as well watered as any other within a radius of six or eight miles, the area possessed or controlled by Jerusalem would substantially increase, the villages upon it becoming in the Biblical phrase *her daughters*,[1] and contributing to her supplies. The Tell el-Amarna letters of 1400 B.C. state that the chief of Jerusalem had lands and a territory, but unfortunately they do not provide data from which we might reckon even the approximate extent of his domains.[2] That chief acknowledges that he held his lands on no hereditary right, but by direct gift of the King of Egypt, to whom he paid

[1] Num. xxi. 25, 32; xxxii. 42; Josh. xvii. 11; 2 Sam. xx. 19, etc.
[2] See below, Bk. III. ch. i.

288

tribute. It is of interest that the only form of tribute
which he mentions is slaves: nothing is said as to
the fruits of the soil. How the chief allotted the rights
of tillage among his people, or whether the fruit-trees
were private property, we do not know. The pasture-
grounds were probably common; but the construction of
cisterns by individuals or families would naturally lead to
an exclusive use of certain stretches of pasture. In
the East, property in water is of far more importance,
and probably of earlier origin, than property in land.[1]
In the environs of Jerusalem there are numerous
cisterns where nothing but pasture could ever have been
possible.

It is most convenient to give here the Old Testament
data relevant to the territory or 'liberties' of a town. The
references chiefly belong to the latest post-
exilic writings and to ideal arrangements for
the land, which were perhaps never actually
carried out. We must, therefore, beware of transferring
their definiteness to the much earlier period of which we
are now treating, or indeed to any actual stage of the
economic life of Palestine.[2] Still they reflect certain
principles which had probably always prevailed, and the
terminology of the subject which they include is un-

O.T. data as
to suburban
territories.

---

[1] As Robertson Smith has pointed out, *Religion of the Semites*, 2nd ed.
104 f.

[2] Cl.-Ganneau, *Arch. Res.* ii. 270, points out the remarkable similarity
between the dimensions of the *migrash* or *suburbs* of the Levitical towns,
with rights of refuge, and the figure formed by the four boundary stones
discovered by him round Gezer. But, in the first place, it is doubtful
whether the interpretation that he gives of Num. xxxv. 2-5 in which the
*migrash* is defined is correct; and *secondly*, the Gezer instance of boundary
stones is the only one yet discovered, and is not earlier than the Hasmonean
kingdom.

doubtedly more ancient than the documents themselves. The Old Testament, then, implies that every
town had its surrounding territory, its liberties—*suburbs*,
as our version calls them—and we may assume that
they consisted of two classes: arable fields or gardens,
and pasture-lands. For these the Old Testament has, in
addition to several general terms, two more or less definite
names, *migrash* and *sadeh*, or *sadai*, both of them used also
in the plural, *migrashîm* and *sadôth*.

The most obvious derivation of *migrash* or *migrashîm*, rendered 'suburbs' by the English version, is
from *garash*, 'to drive forth.'[1]  In that case
the term would mean originally *pasture-land*;
and indeed it is expressly said that the *migrashîm* of
certain cities are to be assigned to the Levites *for their
cattle and their substance and all their beasts*.[2]  But
the *migrash* also included cultivable fields.[3]  By Ezekiel
the name is applied to that part of the land common to
the city, which he distinguishes from the *môshab* or
*inhabited* part,[4] but also to the open space round the
Temple.[5]  From the law that the *migrashîm* assigned
to the Levites were not to be sold,[6] we may infer that (at

1. The Mig-
rash.

---

[1] מִגְרָשׁ from גָּרַשׁ, just like מִדְבָּר from דָּבַר, also to *drive* or *lead forth*,
with which is usually compared the German *Trift*, as if from *treiben*. The
Arabic term corresponding to *garash* appears to be *gashar*, 'to send out
the cattle to pasture so that they shall not return at evening,' and in another
form 'to lead cattle to pasture'; *gishshâr* is 'the overseer of a meadow in
which horses feed,' etc. (Freytag): cf. Barth, *Etym. Stud.* 47.  For another
derivation see Cheyne, *Jew. Quart. Rev.*, July 1898, 566.

[2] Num. xxxv. 3; cf. 1 Chron. v. 16.

[3] 2 Chron. xxxi. 19, שְׂדֵי מִגְרָשׁ עָרֵיהֶם, where the plural שְׂדֵי cannot have
any meaning but *fields* for cultivation: see next page.

[4] Ezek. xlviii. 15.          [5] Ezek. xlv. 2.

[6] Lev. xxv. 34.  The same law holds good of the modern *Wâkuf*, or lands
held for religious purposes.  See above, p. 280.

least in later times) the *migrash* of ordinary towns was
alienable, and therefore private property. In the earlier
period, as already remarked, such private property in the
pastoral portion of the *migrash* would arise only through
the construction or possession of cisterns.

The second word used in the Old Testament for this
territory is *sadeh*, in the plural *sadôth*, of the *fields* of
a town.[1] But in reaching this meaning the 2. Sādeh or
word had an interesting career. To judge Sadôth.
from the Hebrew and kindred languages, the original
signification was perhaps *mountain*, but at least *wild-land*
—whence the phrases *flowers of the field* and *beasts of the
field*—as contrasted with cultivated soil, and *open-land*
as contrasted with cities.[2] Then it was applied in a
political sense to the lands or territory of a people,[3] or
estate of a family.[4] But as land in possession of a tribe
implies cultivation, that which had originally meant uncultivated land passed into the very opposite signification,
and is used from at least the time of the Book of the
Covenant onwards as *arable field* (along with vineyards),
ploughed, sown and yielding harvest.[5] In this sense we
must take it when it is connected with towns. The *sadôth*
of a town were its arable fields and gardens. The *migrash*, as we have seen, included them and the common
pasture-land besides.

It has been necessary to give these definitions in

---

[1] שָׂדֶה or שְׂדֵי, Neh. xi. 30; xii. 29, 44 (of cultivated fields); 2 Chron.
xxxi. 19. In the singular, field of Zoan, Ps. lxxviii. 12.

[2] Micah iv. 10, *out of the city into the field*; cf. Gen. xxv. 29.

[3] Judges v. 4; Hosea xii. 13, etc. etc.

[4] 2 Sam. ix. 7; xix. 30: the domains of Saul's house.

[5] Exod. xxii. 4; xxiii. 16; Num. xx. 17; Is. v. 8; Micah iii. 12;
Joel i. 11.

detail, because several writers have assumed the opposite :
that *migrash* means arable and *sadeh* pasture.[1]

Several other terms are used in the Old Testament for
the district or environs of a city, but they are of less

3. Other terms for the suburban territory.

definite signification. Nehemiah seven times
uses the word *pelek* (the root meaning of which
is probably *circle*) for a district of a city, but
whether within or without the walls is not quite clear ;
the Assyrian analogy supports the latter.[2] Nehemiah also
speaks of the *kikkar* or *circuit of Jerusalem*,[3] in what seems
to be not a geographical but a political sense. The Book
of Jeremiah distinguishes from other districts of Judah
the *sĕbîbîm* or *sĕbîbôth*, the *surroundings* of Jerusalem.[4]
On the other hand, the term *gĕlîlah*, also meaning *circuit*, appears to have been used only of districts wider
than urban ones.

That the boundaries of these urban territories were
from very early times definitely known, there is sufficient

Definite Civic bounds.

evidence. In all probability they were as
distinctly marked as we know the boundaries
of private fields to have been.[5] The early story of the
return of the Ark from Philistia speaks of its arrival at
the *gĕbûl*, or *border*, *of Beth-Shemesh*, where it was first
noticed by the men of Beth-Shemesh, who were reaping
their harvest within the border.[6] And in the late portions

---

[1] So Fenton, *Early Hebrew Life*, § 20, and others following him.

[2] פֶּלֶךְ, Neh. iii. 9, 12, 14-18, of Jerusalem and other towns. The
Assyrian *pulug[g]u* and *pilku* both seem to mean districts outside cities. See
Delitzsch, *Assyr. Wörterbuch*, sub vv.

[3] כִּכָּר, Neh. xii. 28.

[4] סְבִיבִים and סְבִיבוֹת, Jer. xvii. 26 ; xxxiii. 13.

[5] Deut. xix. 14 ; xxvii. 17 ; Prov. xxii. 28 ; xxiii. 10.

[6] גְּבוּל or גְּבֻל, 1 Sam. vi. 12.

of the Books of Numbers and Joshua we read of the
definite borders of many other cities,[1] and once generally
of the *gĕbulôth*, or *borders, of the cities of the land*.[2] The
Targums translate *gĕbûl*, which is not found in post-
biblical Hebrew or Aramaic, by the word *tĕḥûmâ*, which,
with another form *tĕḥûm*, is a common word in the
Talmud for boundary ; *tĕḥum Shabbath* is the limit of the
legal Sabbath-day's journey, 2000 cubits (1000 yards).[3]
The word occurs in all the North Semitic languages and
in Arabic for the boundary of a village, town, or province.[4]
It is the term used in the boundary inscriptions of Gezer
discovered by M. Clermont-Ganneau, and dated by him
' at or near the first century' before Christ.   M. Clermont-
Ganneau reckons one of these inscriptions as 3000 cubits
from the foot of the Tell of Gezer, which is the same as
his calculation of the *migrash* assigned to the Levitical
cities.[5]   However this may be, we cannot, of course,
suppose that the boundaries round different cities
or villages were either uniform with each other or
constant.

   In the New Testament the Greek words by which the
Septuagint renders *migrash*[6] do not occur, and, except
in one doubtful case, *Perichōros* is always used of larger

---

[1] Num. xxxv. 26 (a city of refuge) ; Josh. xiii. 3 (Ekron) ; 26 (Lidebir) ;
xvi. 3 (Beth-horon, the nether) ; xix. 12 (Chisloth-Tabor).

[2] גְּבֻלֹה, Num. xxxii. 33.

[3] תְּחוּמָא, for the Targ. cf. Deut. iii. 16, etc.   תחום שבת, 'the Sabbath
limit,' *Erub.* 51 *b* : cf. Acts i. 12.

[4] Assyr. taḫumu (Delitzsch) ; Syriac tḫûmâ (Maclean, *Dict. of Vernac.
Syr.*).   Palmyrene תחומא (Cooke, *N. Sem. Inscr.*, a Tariff inscription
from Palmyra, ii. *a* 3 ; ii. *b* 14, 31 : pp. 322, 326).   Arabic taḫm and
tuḫm (Freytag).

[5] *Arch. Res.* ii. 26 ff., 270 ff.

[6] Προάστειον, περισπόριον, περιπόλιον.

regions than suburban territories.[1]  But the *fields*, the
*sadôth*, are frequently mentioned in connection with

Suburban
territories in
the N.T.

*towns and villages*, or in contrast to the town.[2]
Also, not only is *chorai* used for the open country in opposition to the city,[3] but there is
mention of the *chora* of a city in which lay its tombs and
pasture-ground running down to the Lake of Galilee.[4]  If
we take this particular city, according to one reading, to
have been Gadara, we know that it bore a trireme on
some of its coins, which implies rights on the coast and
the lake.[5]  The Synoptics also call the territory of a city
the *patris* or *fatherland* of its citizens.  Thus when Jesus
returned to Nazareth, it is said that *He came into His patris
and taught in their synagogue.*[6]  The last clause proves
that *His patris* cannot refer to any of the larger divisions
of Galilee, in each of which there were several cities and
synagogues, but must be the definite territory belonging
to Nazareth.  Luke describes Jesus as coming to the
*city called Bethsaida* ; yet what follows there happens in
a desert place, and there are villages and fields round
about.[7]

The suburban lands, however, were not the only possible

Extra-sub-
urban terri-
tory of a
town.

property of a village or town.  In the course
of their history many a community came into
possession of and cultivated fields at a distance
from themselves.  This was due to one or other of

---

[1] Περίχωρος.  The doubtful case is Luke viii. 37.

[2] Mark vi. 56, *villages, cities, fields* ; Mark v. 14 ; Luke viii. 34, πόλις and
ἀγροί, besides pasture.  Cf. τὰ σπόριμα, Matt. xii. 1, etc.

[3] Luke xxi. 21, χώραι contrasted with Jerusalem, verse 20.

[4] Matt. viii. 28 ff. ; Mark v. 1 ff. ; Luke viii. 26 ff.

[5] *H.G.H.L.* 601 ; also my article on 'Decapolis,' *Enc. Bib.*

[6] Matt. xiii. 54, 57 ; Mark vi. 1, 4 ; Luke iv. 23 f.

[7] Luke ix. 10 ff.

several interesting causes. A village might become de-
populated in the course of a war or by the banishment
of its inhabitants, and in that case its fields fell to its
neighbours. As I learned in 1901 when visiting Tell el-
Ash'ari in Hauran, the fertile land round this ruined and
abandoned site is cultivated by the inhabitants of Taffas,
five or six miles away; and M. Clermont-Ganneau has
shown from two inscriptions which I discovered, one at
Taffas and the other at Tell el-Ash'ari, that a similar
condition of affairs existed there in 69 A.D.[1] Or the
sovereign authority of the land might make a grant, to
some local chieftain, of villages or towns and their fields
at a distance from his own domains: this was frequently
done by the Romans to Herod and others. Or such
grants might be made from religious motives. Jerusalem
especially profited by these, as we shall see in the case
of the Church of the Holy Sepulchre and the Mosque of
Omar; we may presume that this happened also in favour
of the Jewish Temple. Or, finally, a town growing rich,
but finding the produce of its suburban territory too
meagre for its growing population, might purchase the
lands and villages of other towns ; or this purchase might
be effected by wealthy individuals. Very recently, on
the Plain of Esdraelon, the rights of the tillage of the
lands of several villages were sold to a firm of Greek
bankers, who now employ the villagers as their tenants
and farm servants.[2] These last processes were of course
natural in the case of such a capital as Jerusalem, and it

---

[1] See *P.E.F.Q.*, 1902, 21 f. Of course it is possible, as M. Cl.-Ganneau
points out, that both inscriptions, which are by the same man, originally were
raised at the same spot.

[2] For the same on Carmel, see *Z.D.P.V.* xxx. 152.

was in fact the purchase of the yeomen's estates by rich men, many of whom must have been resident in the capital, which led to the economic problems and the agricultural distress deplored by the prophets of the eighth century.

We have now sufficiently traced the fundamental lines on which a community in Palestine like that of early Jerusalem was formed and held its lands, and may proceed to a consideration of the natural resources of the territory of the City.

# CHAPTER IV

## THE NATURAL RESOURCES OF JERUSALEM

IT is curious what opposite appreciations have been given of the neighbourhood of Jerusalem. The City has been described as lying 'upon barren mountains,' as 'the centre of a stony waste,' as 'having a few fertile spots within sight,' but the rest 'dry and arid,' 'a great plain, part

Opposite appreciations of the country round Jerusalem.

stony, part of good soil'; as 'the most fertile portion of Filastin,' 'a country where on the hills are trees, and in the plains fields, which need neither irrigation nor the watering of rivers, . . . "a land flowing with milk and honey."' Such differences of opinion are explicable partly from the difference of the seasons and partly from the different economic conditions during which the writers quoted have visited the City; but principally from the fact that the favourable opinions are those of Mohammedans accustomed to the more desert regions of their world, while the unfavourable are by travellers, ancient Greeks or mediæval pilgrims, fresh from the greater fertility of Europe. The truth is to be ascertained only by an examination of the various products, which agriculture when diligent and unharassed has been able to raise among these high summits of the Judæan range.

Grain may be grown, and is grown, on every plain, such as those to the south-west and north, and in the wider valley bottoms. But withal the space for cereal crops is comparatively limited.[1] Wheat can be raised and raised well, but the conditions are so much less favourable to its growth than they are in other parts of Palestine within easy reach of Jerusalem—for example, Philistia and Esdraelon with their offshoots among the hills like Ajalon and Sorek; the Plains of Jordan, where these are irrigated; and the Plain of Mukhneh to the east of Shechem—that wheat can never have abounded in the immediate neighbourhood of the City. Among all the place-names within a radius of ten or twelve miles from Jerusalem I have found only one which is a monument to the presence of wheat: the Joret el-Ḳamḥ, in the Wâdy south of 'Anathoth,[2] and this is the more significant that all the other products of the district are so frequently found among its place-names. To-day the bent of the higher towns and villages of Western Palestine towards the wheatfields or harvests of the lowlands is everywhere visible,[3] and it proves how largely dependent for wheat ancient Jerusalem must have been upon the neighbouring valleys and plains. The most accurate summary of the facts I have seen is that given by Martin Kabátník, the Bohemian pilgrim of 1492 A.D.:[4] 'Round Jerusalem there is little level

*Cereal Crops: 1. Wheat.*

---

[1] Thomson (*L. and B.* 667) says: 'These rides about Jerusalem reveal the ruggedness of this territory. It could never have been a corn-growing region, but is admirably adapted to the olive, the fig, the vine, the pomegranate, and other fruit-trees.' See below.

[2] Joreh = a valley-bottom where water is found during the rains. Ḳamḥ = wheat, Heb. חִטִּים, חִטָּה.

[3] *e.g.* Carmel, *Z.D.P.V.* xxi. 152.

[4] German translation by Prášek in *Z.D.P.V.* xxi. 56.

land, mostly great mountains and valleys; good grain, however, flourishes here; only one can cultivate little of it, wherefore the bread is very dear.'

The common grain of the highlanders was barley, regarded as characteristic of Israel when Israel was confined to the hills,[1] and besides barley there were millet and vetches, with beans, onions, cucumbers and other vegetables. But against barley, millet, vetches and beans the same comparative want of space would tell as against wheat.

*2. Barley, Millet, etc.*

Far more than any grain the staple products of the Judæan range have been its fruit-trees, and especially the great triad of the Olive, the Vine and the Fig. These are the three which in the ancient parable the trees desire in turn to make their king.[2] They are celebrated throughout the poetry of the Old Testament, and in proverbs which speak of the comfort of the home and the prosperity of the land. They form the full, bright vestures of all but the desert landscapes of Judæa. And from first to last it is they alone which have not only sustained her inhabitants, but by their surplus supplied these with the means of exchange for goods in which their own land was lacking. None of the three grows either in Babylonia[3] or Arabia.

*Fruit-trees the staple.*

The chief place among them belongs to the Olive,[4] which upon the fatter plains below is much less fertile

---

[1] Judges vii. 13, barley-fields at Jerusalem 2 Sam. xiv. 30; barley= שְׂעֹרִים, שְׂעֹרָה    [2] Judges ix. 8 ff.

[3] So Hommel (*Geogr. Vorderasiens*, p. 12), who derives all three from Eastern Asia Minor. Other authorities trace the fig from the southern coasts of the Mediterranean.

[4] Hebrew זַיִת, *zaith*, or עֵץ הַזַּיִת: oil זֵית יִצְהָר, שֶׁמֶן, *zaith, yiṣhar*, and *shemen*; wild olive עֵץ שֶׁמֶן.

in oil than when it grows upon high rocky slopes or terraces, in a wash of wind and sunshine. The most favourable conditions for its culture are a warm, porous, limestone soil, where the winter frosts are moderate or

1. The Olive.

transitory, and where the summers, when the berries ripen, have either little or no rainfall. The tree flourishes on stony declivities that will produce no other fruit, and is also at home on marly soil and among the shot *débris* of hills and even of ruined towns.[1] Round Jerusalem these conditions are all present, and the Palestine olive reaches its best.[2] A large number of place-names, ancient and modern, attest its prevalence,[3] along with the numerous olive-groves of the present day and the frequent traces of ancient oilpresses.[4] To *the labour of the olive*, then, we may believe that the earlier like the later inhabitants of Jerusalem

[1] I take these, and a few of the other particulars I have given, from the monograph by Prof. Theob. Fischer, *Der Ölbaum, seine geogr. Verbreitung, seine wirthschaftliche u. kulturhistorische Bedeutung.* Gotha : Justus Perthes, 1904, in *Petermanns Mitteilungen*, Ergänzungsheft Nr. 147.

[2] So I have been told by fellahin. Cf. Ritter, *Compar. Geogr. of Palestine*, iv. 184. ' The olive tree seems to have its natural home here ; for seldom are very old olives met which yield so good an oil as those of this district. When the Koran swears by the fig and the olive, it is as if it swore by Damascus and Jerusalem.'

[3] Besides Mount of Olives (which, though now called Jebel eṭ-Ṭur, was still called Jebel ez-Zaitun in the earlier Moslem period), Gethsemane (and perhaps Bethzetha), the following are given in Schick and Benzinger's map : *Weitere Umgebung von Jerusalem* (founded on the large P.E.F. map), *Z.D.P.V.* xix. 145 ff. : Sheikh Abu Zaitûn (Kh. el Meiṭā) N.E. of, and W. ez-Zait W. of, Bethhoron the Upper ; Bir ez-Zaitunât on the road from Jerusalem to Anathoth ; W. ez-Zaitûn, running S.E. from under Bethany ; Beit Zaitâ, a ruin on Hebron road almost due west from Teḳoaʻ ; and Ḳaʾat ez-Zitûneh west of the Hebron road.

[4] Probably the finest work of its kind in the neighbourhood of the City is a large rock-cut press with several vats for the extraction of wine or olive oil in the garden known as ' Abraham's Vineyard,' on the N.W. side of Jerusalem. It is fully described by Mr. Macalister in *P.E.F.Q.*, 1902, 248 and 398-403, with plan and photograph.

mainly applied themselves, and reaped not only the
wealth which the tree ultimately yields to its possessor,
but those moral endowments which observers, ancient
and modern, have justly attributed to the discipline of
its slow and skilful cultivation.   The berries yield their
farmer food and light,[1] ointment for cleansing, healing and festival ; the timber provides his furniture and
fuel.   But if his farm be a highland one, the olive, besides
thus fulfilling so many domestic uses, is practically the
only one of his crops which yields a surplus over his
yearly wants, and is therefore ready for export or
exchange.   The Pseudo-Aristeas, writing about 200 B.C.,
places the olive at the head of the products of Judæa,
which he says 'is thickly wooded with masses of olives.'[2]
Nâsir-i-Khusrau reports in the eleventh century 'that
many of the chief men harvest as much as 50,000 Manns
weight of olive oil,' about 16,800 gallons.   'This is kept
in tanks and cisterns and they export thereof to other
countries.'[3]   The harvest of the olive, however, comes
only to a long patience.   The young plant is carefully
cultivated for seven or eight years, before engrafting, and
even then for three years more before it bears fruit, but
it is only after fifteen to twenty years that it reaches its
full value.   Watering is necessary in the earlier stages,
and frequent digging, as much as three and five times a
year.[4]   After this the tree may endure for centuries,
for 'it possesses with its very slow growth, so enormous a

---

[1] The oil is little used for this since the introduction of petroleum.

[2] ἐλαικοῖς πλήθεσι σύνδενδρος, Thackeray's ed. in Swete's *Intro. to the
O. T. in Greek*, 539.   Corn, pulse, vines, and honey are the other crops
he mentions, with numberless fruit-trees and palms and rich pasture.

[3] Le Strange, *Pal. under the Moslems*, 88; for to-day cf. *P.E.F.Q.*, 1903, 338.

[4] Fischer, 30 f.   Manure is also frequently applied.

vitality, that we may call it imperishable.'[1]   How all this
makes for the increase of caution and foresight in a community, for habits of industry and love of peace, may be
easily realised.  'The olive-tree is one of the educators
of mankind towards a higher civilisation.'[2]   It was not
arbitrarily that the ancient Mediterranean peoples selected
the olive as the symbol of peace and the civic virtues ;
or that the poets of the Old Testament took it as a figure
of the health both of the nation and of the individual
Israelite.[3]   Its appearance in so many place-names about
Jerusalem, and some of these among the most historic, is
a proper token not only of the City's means of subsistence,
but of the elements of her people's character.  The divine
source of these was symbolised by its oil in the anointing
of kings and priests, expressive as this was of the conveyance of the grace and authority of God.  When
Zechariah illustrated the fulness of Revelation through
Israel, he did so by the seven-branched lamp of the
sanctuary, fed (as he saw it) from two olive-trees, the
anointed prince and priest of the people, *the two sons of oil
which stand before the Lord of all the earth.*[4]  The olive
does not appear in the Parables of our Lord, nor its oil
in the Sacraments He instituted.  But it is enshrined in
His Name, *The Christ* ; and it is the symbol of the consecration and endowment of His Church by His Spirit.[5]
Nor can the Christian heart forget that it was beneath
olive-trees and hard by an olive press that the Divine
Passion was accomplished, and the Saviour bowed Himself to His sacrifice for the life of men.

---

[1] Fischer, 31.                           [2] Fischer, 32.
[3] Hos. xiv. 6 ; Jer. xi. 16 ; Ps. lii. 10 [Eng. 8].
[4] Zech. iv. 14.                          [5] 2 Cor. i. 21 ; 1 John ii. 20, 27.

With the olive we must emphasise the Vine,[1] and all
the more that, under the ban which Islam has put upon
wine, vineyards are less prevalent in Judah
than undoubtedly they were in ancient times.    2. The Vine.
In the Old Testament Judah is *par excellence* the province
of the grape;[2] vines and vineyards appear frequently
in its parables and poetry, as well as in the Judæan
parables of our Lord.    The language has blossomed
into an unusual, almost an Arabic, luxuriance, upon the
parts of the vine and the various forms of its products.
Not only for wine was the plant cultivated.    Raisins
have always been a common article of food; and the
*d'bash* of the phrase translated *flowing with milk and
honey* is very probably the same as the Arabic *dibs*: a
thick syrup of grapes.[3]    The place-names round Jerusalem which record the vine are numerous, but even less
so than the diminished vineyards of the present day,
and these still less than the remains of ancient vine-
terraces.    The largest plantations seem to have been
on the north-west of the City, and at the south-western
end of the Buḳeiʻa, the ancient plain of Rephaim, where
about Bittir and Weljeh they are numerous even to-day;
but place-names with *grape* or *vine* in them come close

---

[1] Hebrew: vine, גֶּפֶן *gephen*; cluster of grapes, אֶשְׁכֹּל *'eshkōl*; grapes,
עֲנָבִים *'anabîm*; vineyard, כֶּרֶם *kerem*; wine-press, גַּת *gath*; wine, יַיִן
*yayin*, חֶמֶר *ḥemer*, תִּירֹשׁ *tîrōsh*, etc.    There are other words for vine-
shoots, vine-rows, etc.    Raisins, צִמּוּקָה *ṣimmûḳah*.

[2] Gen. xlix. 11 f.; Isaiah vii. 20 ff.; Micah iv. 4; 1 Kings iv. 25; Hab.
iii. 17; Isaiah lxi. 5, lxv. 21; also in Malachi, Joel, etc.    For details see
*H.G.H.L.* 308 ff.

[3] The question is not yet settled.    See *H.G.H.L.* 673, additional note to
p. 83; and the discussion by Nestle, Dalman, and others in the *M.u.N.D.P.V.*
for 1902 and 1905.

to the City walls, as no doubt the vineyards always did : there are plantations down the Wâdy en-Nâr, and the name of a vineyard still survives on the top of Olivet.[1] The grapes of Jerusalem were large and fine ; to this we have a singularly constant testimony especially from the Moslem geographers and mediæval travellers ; the latter of whom also certify to the good quality of the wine. Martin Kabátník, already quoted, says that 'at Jerusalem they have enough of good and cheap wine. In the Jerusalem vineyards I have seen extraordinary vine-branches.' He came from a wine-growing country and gives some interesting particulars as to its cultivation compared with that of the Jerusalem vineyards.

The third of the great triad of the fruit-trees of Palestine is the Fig.[2] No homestead was complete without it ;[3] and the subtleties of its fertilisation appear to have been known from the earliest times.[4] Like the olive and the vine, it afforded the Judæan peasant a possible article of exchange. Round Jerusalem the place-names carrying *fig* are not so numerous as those with *vine* or *olive*.[5]

Other fruits in Judæa were the sycomore figs, food

---

[1] Near the city are the following place-names : Karm (vineyard) Aḥmed, N.W. not far from the Jaffa road ; Karm esh-Sheikh, just N. of N.E. corner of the walls ; Ḳaṣr el Karm and W. Umm el 'Anab, N. on the Nebi-Samwil road ; Magharet el 'Anab, N. and W. of the Nablus road ; Karm es-Seiyâd (V. of the hunter), on the north summit of Olivet ; further away Kuryet el 'Anab, etc. The plantations down the W. en-Nâr are found at Kh. Deir es-Senne. It is, of course, impossible to give a full list of the extant or ruined vineyards round Jerusalem.

[2] Hebrew : תְּאֵנָה *tĕʾēnah* ; early fig, בִּכּוּרָה *bikkûrah*, פַּגָּה *paggah*.

[3] 2 Kings iv. 25 ; Micah iv. 4.

[4] See the instructive article in the *Enc. Bibl.*

[5] Bethphage ; 'Ain et-Tine, far S.W. of Bethlehem on the Hebron road ; W. et-Tin, S. of Bethlehem.

only for the poor, the pods of the locust or carob-tree, nuts and almonds, pomegranates, apples, apricots, mulberries.[1] In a burst of exaggeration pardonable to a native of the city, Mukaddasi, the Arab geographer (*c.* 985 A.D.), exclaims: 'As for the Holy City being the most productive of all places in good things, why, Allah—may He be exalted!—has gathered together here all the fruits of the lowlands and of the plains and of the hill country, even all those of most opposite kinds: such as the orange and the almond, the date and the nut, the fig and the banana, besides milk in plenty, and honey and sugar.'[2] It will be noticed that nothing is said of wheat or other grain.

Other fruits.

Of the more difficult question of the prevalence of trees for timber about the City, the data have been already given in the general description of Jerusalem.[3] The environs have been so often stripped by besiegers that a definite answer to the question is now impossible. On the one hand, there never can have been much large timber; the Old Testament reflects but little—in fact nothing beyond Isaiah's allusions to oaks and terebinths—and speaks of wood for building as brought from a distance. On the other hand, the present place-names testify to the growth of the oak,[4] the walnut, the plane, the tamarisk, the nettle-tree,[5] and the willow. The sycomore,[6] so much used in Old Testament times

Trees for timber.

---

[1] On sycomore figs see Amos vii. 14; 1 Chron. xxvii. 28. The upper part of the Ķidron valley is called W. ej-Jôz or 'Nut-Vale.' There is an 'Ain el-Lōzeh or almond-tree well, and Khurbet el-Lôz. The pomegranate scarcely occurs in the place-names. The Carob or Khârrub tree is frequent. W. el Khokh is 'Peach-Vale.' Burj et-Tut=mulberry tower. There is a Ķaṣr Umm Leimun at Teķoʻa and a Kh. Leimun N.W. of Jerusalem.

[2] *Palestine under the Moslems*, p. 85.   [3] Above, pp. 16 ff.
[4] *Quercus ilex.*      [5] *Celtis.*      [6] *Ficus Sycomorus.*

U

for building, had to be brought from a distance. It does not grow above one thousand feet above the sea.[1]

In the immediate territory of Jerusalem there are no deposits of salt : the word does not occur in any place-name nearer than the Wâdy el-Malḥa, south-

Salt.

east of Herodium, where there may be a few precarious 'salt-licks.' But as the damp sides of caves often yield a slight saline crust, mixed with soil, the primitive inhabitants of Jerusalem, as well as some of her poorer citizens up to the end of the history, may have scraped off the meagre and dirty stuff for their own use in cooking : the like is still done in other parts of Syria.[2] The great deposits on the Dead Sea, however, were not far away, and have been constantly imported to the City during historical times. But this belongs properly to our next chapter, on the commerce of Jerusalem.

In Syria 'the best honey,' says Muḳaddasi, 'is that from Jerusalem, where the bees suck the thyme.' One

Honey.

of the Tell el-Amarna letters includes honey in a list of ordinary foods.[3] The honey of the Old Testament is that of wild bees, *honey from the rock*.[4] By New Testament times the cultivation of honey is implied in the use of the phrase *wild honey*, the food of John the Baptist in the desert;[5] and from other sources we know that by that time apiculture

---

[1] Cf. Diener, *Libanon*, 173 f., where the limit is given as 300 m.

[2] Libbey and Hoskins, *The Jordan Valley and Petra*, ii. 110.

[3] Winckler's edition, No. 138, l. 12, *dishb*. Of course it is possible that this is grape-syrup. See above, p. 303.

[4] Deut. xxxii. 13 ; Ps. lxxxi. 16 ; cf. Judges xiv. 8 ff. ; 1 Sam. xiv. 25 ff. Cf. Thomson, *L. and B.*, 566.

[5] Matt. iii. 4 ; Mark i. 6 ; cf. Nestle on Luke xxiv. 42, *Z.D.P.V.* xxx. 208 f.

was practised.[1] The art is so ancient that it may have been known to the Canaanites and early Israel, but the Old Testament references, as given above, point the other way. In any case, honey was a common product of the district round Jerusalem.

In the land of Judæa the shepherd was a prominent figure, who frequently came to the very front of her religious and political life, and whom her Cattle-breeding. literature takes as the type of the highest qualities of the ruler of men, whether human or divine.[2] The cause of his capacity and the reason of the honour paid him is largely due, however, to the difficulty of his field. The waters of Judæa are few and far between ; the pasture is sparse and uncertain. Sheep and goats thrive upon it, but except in the district to the west of Hebron such large flocks are not met with as in other parts of Palestine. The oxen and the cows are small and sometimes even stunted-looking.[3] For the larger and finer cattle the country is quite unsuitable. They have to be imported. Of fowls for food pigeons abound, and in some parts partridges are fairly numerous. The domestic fowl was not introduced till the Persian period.

As everywhere in the early East so at Jerusalem the Ass was the common animal for riding and loading. Josephus, in reply to Apion's absurd charge that the Jews worshipped the head of an ass, The Ass. says : ' Asses are the same with us as they are with other

---

[1] See the evidence from Philo and the Mishna, given by A. R. S. Kennedy, art. 'Honey,' *Enc. Bibl.* For modern apiculture, *Z.D.P.V.* xxx. 162, 166.

[2] *H.G.H.L.* 310 ff.

[3] Every traveller will observe this. Ritter says : ' the bullock is small and ugly-looking ; veal and beef are seldom eaten.'

wise men, creatures which bear the burdens we lay upon
them; but if they come to our threshing-floors and eat
our corn, or do not perform what we lay upon them, we
beat them with a great many stripes; for it is their
business to serve us in our husbandry.'[1]   The ass in
several varieties forms as frequent a figure in the streets
and landscapes of Jerusalem to-day, as he does in the
stories of the City from the time of the Judges to those
of the Gospels.[2]   The poorest peasant owned his ass;
troops were included in the property of the rich.  Besides
their employment in agriculture, they were used in the
caravans of commerce and sent from Jerusalem even
upon the longest expeditions through the desert.  As
contrasted with the horse the ass was the symbol of
humility and of peace : *Rejoice greatly, O daughter of Sion,
shout aloud, O daughter of Jerusalem, for thy King cometh
unto thee vindicated and victorious, meek and riding on an
ass and a colt the foal of an ass.*

Horses and mules were not introduced to Jerusalem
till a comparatively late period.  And the same is probably true of camels.  It is to be remarked that asses alone
are mentioned as used in ordinary agriculture even in so
late a passage as I Sam. viii.[3]   All the others, therefore,
fall to be considered in our next chapter under the
imports of the City.

[1] *C. Apion*, ii. 7.

[2] *e.g.* Gen. xlix. 12 ; Ju. xix. 3, 10; I Sam. ix. ; 2 Sam. xvi. i. ; Is. xxx.
6 ff. (in caravans sent from Jerusalem through the desert) ; Zech. ix. 9 ; Matt.
xxi. 2 ff. ; Mark xi. 2 ff. ; Luke xix. 29 ff.  The Hebrew terms are חֲמוֹר
*hămôr*, אָתוֹן *'āthôn, she-ass,* עַיִר *'aîr*=πῶλος, *young ass* (also of the grown
animal, Ju. x. 4, etc.).  In Judges v. 10, אֲתֹנוֹת צְחֹרוֹת, *red-white asses* of
a better kind, for riding.  Wild-ass is פֶּרֶא or עָרוֹד.

[3] Verse 16.

Of good workable stone, as we have seen in the chapter on the geology, the inhabitants of Jerusalem had an unlimited quantity under the city itself, though Stone, Clay, in these latter days they prefer to draw their and Metals. supplies from quarries further off.[1]  The *meleki* stone, so much used under the monarchy, is no longer drawn upon. Of the flints we have spoken.  There is neither basalt nor granite.  The clay of the surroundings is of poor quality.  The Nâri, or upper chalk, is strong, to withstand heat, and therefore to this day fire-places and ovens are made of it, but so friable that its clay is bad for water-jars and other vessels of the potter.[2]  There are no metals in the rocks, neither gold nor silver, neither copper nor iron ; they will therefore be considered under the imports.[3]

Such are the natural resources of the territory of Jerusalem.  While some of them yield a considerable surplus over the domestic needs of the inhabi- Summary: tants, others barely fulfil the latter ; and the the need and absence from the list of a number of the the means of necessaries of life implies the existence in the city, from the earliest times, of a certain amount of commerce with other districts, which, as the population, and especially its unproductive elements, increased, must have grown to a great volume.  The commerce of Jerusalem will therefore form the subject of the next chapter.

[1] Baldensperger, *P.E.F.Q.*, 1904, 133.       [2] See above, pp. 53 f.
[3] There is an interesting paper on the mineral and chemical resources of the Dead Sea coasts and Wilderness of Judæa (petroleum, asphalt, sulphur, phosphates, etc.) by Blanckenhorn in the *M.u.N.D.P.V.*, 1902, 65 ff.

# CHAPTER V

## COMMERCE AND IMPORTS

I N the primitive community of Jerusalem every family would roast and rub or grind their own grain,[1] bake their own bread, make their own curds and cheese, and weave their own clothing. Each house-father slaughtered the beasts needed for the family or guests. Wine and oil presses they may have held in common, or separately. The men roughly cured the hides of their beasts, as the Arabs do to-day, and stitched them into water-vessels; these skins preceding jars of pottery, as we see from the leather shapes and seams which are still imitated on the latter. They also fashioned their own flints and clubs, and carved other implements out of bone.

*How far early Jerusalem depended on her own resources.*

So far the primitive Jerusalem lived upon herself. Yet even from the beginning and for some of the necessaries of life a modest amount of trade was inevitable: trade with the farmers of the plains, with the desert nomads, and with the nearest centres of civilisation. The first of these, as we have seen, must have furnished some wheat, and as Jerusalem grew the imports of this constantly increased.

*Trade inevitable from the first.*

---

[1] For a specimen of the primitive corn-rubbers which preceded the hand-mill, see photographs in Bliss and Macalister, *Excav. in Pal.*, 143; *M.u.N.D.P.V.*, 1905, 24; also Cl.-Ganneau, *Arch. Res.* i. 292; and Mac-alister, *Bible Side-Lights*, etc., p. 98, fig. 28.

The clay of the neighbourhood, being poor, can hardly have initiated among the inhabitants the art of pottery apart from the imitation of imported jars, which, perhaps along with the raw clay, came also from the lowland villages. The desert nomads would bring salt from the coasts of the Dead Sea, along with cattle, butter, cheese, alum, alkali and medicinal herbs, and receive in exchange oil and various fruits. But Jerusalem never was such a market for the Bedouin as either Hebron or Gaza. The wandering workers in metals, who have always ranged the less civilised regions of the Semitic world, would furnish vessels for cooking and ploughshares ; while the travelling weapon-smiths of Egypt, also visible in that earliest history,[1] and probably too those of Phœnicia, would supply lances and swords. In the second millennium before Christ there was a busy trade across Palestine, and the products of Syria found a ready market in Egypt. The caravans between the Nile and the Euphrates had to be fed on their way through Canaan, and in exchange would drop upon it a certain proportion of their goods. They passed to and fro less than thirty miles from Jerusalem, and it is more than probable that many of the simpler comforts and embellishments of life, with a certain store of the precious metals, would drift into the possession of her inhabitants even when she was little more than a village and a hill-fort. Neither the Egyptian records nor the Hebrew accounts of Palestine at the time of Israel's arrival warrant us in minimising the local or foreign trade of the land, or the wealth which the petty clans were able to draw from it. To such travelling forms of

---

[1] Cf. the story of Seny-hit, and see *Enc. Bibl.* article 'Trade and Commerce' by the present writer, for this and further details of trade.

commerce each township would add in time the booths of some settled dealers, blacksmiths and potters,[1] and thus a little *sûk* or bazaar would be formed. In the earliest cases these would probably be foreigners familiar with other markets. Whether images and amulets were the work of priests or other specialists, because of a required conformity to orthodox patterns, or whether each family fashioned its own household gods, we cannot tell. At the best the amount of trade cannot have been capable of sustaining the community when the not infrequent droughts or famines visited their fields. One town had then to buy water from another, but as the crops of the whole country usually, though not always,[2] suffered equally from such a plague, grain had to be sought in far lands like Egypt, which were under different meteorological influences. What had the peasants of Palestine, then, wherewith to purchase food and seed, but the hoarded ornaments of their women or their spare homespuns, or, when these were exhausted, their children? Syrian slaves were highly prized in Egypt.[3]

All this is clear enough while Jerusalem is but one of the many mountain townships of Western Palestine; and these remain the essential factors of her economy to the very end. But difficulties arise as we begin to inquire how far these factors

Increasing need of trade.

[1] To-day in Palestine the earliest shops to be opened in a growing village are that of the grocer, *sammān*, or dealer in butter, salt, spices, dried fruits, and small wares, and that of the smith. So Van Lennep, *Bible Lands and Customs*, p. 775, and Baldensperger in *P.E.F.Q.*, 1903, 68, etc. Burckhardt found in Kerak that the 'only artisans who keep shops are a blacksmith, a shoemaker, and a silversmith,' p. 388.

[2] The Sirocco will sometimes blight the crops of one district in Judæa and leave those of another untouched, or at most only prematurely ripe.

[3] W. Max Müller, *Asien u. Europa*, 37 f., 150, 352.

developed, and how much they had to be supplemented when Jerusalem became a capital, political and religious, with large non-producing elements among her population—courtiers, priesthood and a mercenary garrison—always, be it remembered, in a territory less fruitful of some of the necessaries of life than the surrounding regions, with no opportunity for large industries, and aloof from the great trade routes of the country.

That serious economic problems arose in Jerusalem from the very beginning of her history as a capital, and persisted, because of the conditions just mentioned, down to the very end of our period, is seen from David's immediate organisation of the trade of his kingdom and his conquests of the rich corn-lands east of Jordan; from Solomon's cultivation of foreign trade, and his arrangements for feeding the non-producing classes in his capital; from the successive attempts of later Jewish monarchs to re-open Solomon's lines of traffic; from the criticisms by the prophets upon the cruelties which commerce, and especially corn-dealing, inflicted upon the poor; from the witness of Ezekiel to the commercial influence of Jerusalem in the seventh century and the traditions of the same preserved in the Book of Ezra; from the economic difficulties of the returned exiles as recorded by Haggai and Zechariah; from the grants of food and materials for building made by the Persian monarchs; from the fiscal and customs arrangements of the Seleucids, with the attention given by the Maccabees in their campaigns to the lines of trade; from the financial relations of the Hasmonean kings and Herod with the Nabateans; and from the large importations

Evidences of commercial expansion.

of corn which Josephus records from Egypt and from
Cyprus during the Roman period.  With the details of
these we shall have to deal at the proper points of the
history.  Here it is needful to give a general account of
how the growing population of Jerusalem, much of it
non-producing, supplemented the inadequate supplies
of her immediate neighbourhood, and even of Judah as
a whole.  We keep in mind the fact, which in the course
of this study we shall be able frequently to illustrate,
that the population of royal and post-exilic Jerusalem
could not possibly be sustained by the produce of their
own lands—the *sadeh* or *migrash*[1] of the City—nor
even by what they drew in tribute or by purchase from
the rest of the territory of Judah.  Imports from other

Imports necessary. states were necessary even in the best of
times ; during drought or after war had
devastated the fields they must have been enormous.
We shall, in this chapter, inquire what were these
imports into Jerusalem, and whence they came ; and in
others, what industrial products and collections of
money the city had wherewith to pay for them.

Although the territory of Jerusalem may have grown,
and the land of Judah did grow, some wheat, the soil (as

Import of wheat. we have seen[2]) was not so favourable to cereals
as was that of neighbouring states, and
throughout its history the City must have imported wheat
from abroad, as it does at the present day.  To-day
wheat comes into Jerusalem from Nablus, the produce
of the fertile Mukhneh to the east of that town, from
Hebron,[3] and from the east of Jordan, particularly Moab.
In Moab, as I learned from personal observation, corn-

---

[1] See above, pp. 290 f.     [2] P. 298.     [3] Robinson, *B.R.* ii. 95.

dealers from Jerusalem buy up the harvests before they
are reaped. At the bridge over Jordan, near Jericho
you will meet with caravans of from thirty to fifty asses,
or of mules with the peculiar yoke of Kerak—where, as
Doughty says, 'corn is as the sand of the sea'—all laden
with the grain and bound for the Jerusalem market.
Herod sent for corn to the people about Samaria.[1] In
Moslem times it was regularly imported from 'Ammân.[2]
For the pre-Christian era we have even wider evidence.
Eupolemus, a Jew, who flourished between 140 and
100 B.C., reflects, in a supposed letter from Solomon to
the King of Tyre concerning food supplies for the
workmen sent by the latter to Jerusalem, what must have
been the condition in his own time and for many centuries
before: 'I have written also to Galilee, Samaria and the
country of Moab and of Ammon and to Gilead, that there
should be supplied to them what they require, month by
month ten thousand *kors* of wheat. Oil and other
things shall be furnished them from Judæa, but cattle
to be slaughtered for food from Arabia.'[3] So probably
it was also in more ancient times. For this conclusion
we must not depend, as some continue to do, on the story
of the assassins of Ish-bosheth in Mahanaim, who, according to the English version, got into the house of their
victim under pretence of *fetching wheat*; for the Hebrew
text thus conjecturally translated is corrupt, and the

---

[1] Jos. i. *B. J.* xv. 6.     [2] *Pal. under the Moslems*, 18, 391-393.
[3] Quoted by Alexander Polyhistor, Müller, *Fragmenta Historicorum
Graecorum*, iii. 226. The passage is so important for the illustration of the
economics of Jerusalem at all times that I give the original: Γέγραφα δὲ καὶ
εἰς τὴν Γαλιλαίαν καὶ Σαμαρεῖτιν καὶ Μωαβῖτιν καὶ 'Αμμανῖτιν καὶ Γαλαδῖτιν
χωρηγεῖσθαι αὐτοῖς τὰ δέοντα ἐκ τῆς χώρας κατὰ μῆνα κόρους σίτου μυρίους . . .
Τὸ δὲ ἔλαιον καὶ τὰ ἄλλα χορηγηθήσεται αὐτοῖς ἐκ τῆς 'Ιουδαίας, ἱερεῖα δὲ εἰς κρεο-
φαγίαν ἐκ τῆς 'Αραβίας.

Greek version gives a better and a wholly different account.[1]   But the Chronicler mentions tribute of wheat and barley.   Ezekiel, in recounting the exports of Judah to Tyre, mentions wheat, not her own,[2] but from Minnith on the east of Jordan.[3]   So that pre-exilic Jerusalem imported wheat not only for her own use—it is clear from many passages of the Old Testament that the people, and especially the landless poor, had to purchase wheat,[4]—but in order to sell it again to the Phœnicians; the proof that in those days she was a centre of exchange, *the gate of the peoples*, as Ezekiel himself calls her.[5]   The business gave rise to speculation.   *He that withholds corn*, says one of the Proverbs, *the people curse him, but blessing is on the head of him that selleth it.*[6]   Prices, as often in the East, rapidly fluctuated, and the farmer or dealer held his stores against a rise.   The same is done to-day, as I learned, among the farmers of Sharon.[7] Ordinary fellahin will store great quantities of corn in ancient cisterns or cemented pits.   One fellah, I was told, kept his wheat for ten years; another sold at one time ' 100,000 bushels, or two shiploads.'   But there are risks, for the grain is liable to spontaneous combustion; if this has just begun, the fellahin say that even the chickens refuse it.[8]   In times of general drought these stores and these imports from other parts of Palestine

---

[1] 2 Sam. iv. 6.   Read with Wellh. and Driver after the LXX. : *and lo ! the portress of the house was cleaning wheat, and she slumbered and slept and Rechab and Ba'anah slipt past.*

[2] The wheat which Solomon exported to Tyre (1 Kings v. 11) would come not from Judah but from other parts of the then extended kingdom of Israel.

[3] Ezek. xxvii. 17.              [4] *e.g.* Amos viii. 5 ; Prov. xi. 26.

[5] Ezek. xxvi. 2 ; LXX.         [6] Prov. xi. 26.

[7] Cf. Robinson, *Phys. Geog.* 252, with further references.

[8] This last from a communication by Mr. R. A. Macalister at Gezer.

failed. Herod the Great brought corn from Egypt not only for bread 'for the cities of Jerusalem,' but for seed; and Queen Helena of Adiabene, to meet a similar necessity, had it imported from Egypt and Cyprus.[1] In Moslem times, as we have seen, grain was imported from 'Ammân. Whence the kings of Judah obtained their means of purchase we shall inquire later.

An important article of diet in Jerusalem was Fish. The evidence for the post-exilic period is found in Nehemiah xiii. 16, where it is said that a colony of Tyrians *brought in* the fish and sold Fish. it both to the citizens and the country folk. From their market the Fish Gate on the northern wall, the natural entrance for Phœnicians to the City, took its name. But this name is also pre-exilic,[2] and the Deuteronomic code had already directed what kinds of fish might be eaten.[3] The sources of supply, the Jordan, the Lake of Galilee, the Mediterranean coast and the Delta, are too distant for the fish to be brought to the city either alive [4] or fresh. The arts of drying and salting fish were practised in Egypt and along the Syrian coast from a high antiquity. In Egypt 'dried fish were a great feature of housekeeping. They were the cheapest food of the land, much cheaper than corn, of which the country was also very productive. The heartfelt wish of the poorer folk was that the price of corn might be as

---

[1] Jos. xv. *Ant.* ix. 2 ; xx. *Ant.* ii. 5.

[2] Neh. iii. 3 ff.

[3] Deut. xiv. 9. Cf. in the J. document of the Pentateuch, Num. xi. 5, the people's desire in the wilderness for the fish of Egypt.

[4] Fishponds were unknown among the Jews till Roman times ; *teste*, the Talmudic name for them, ביבר, *i.e.* βιβάριον, *vivarium* ; A. R. S. Kennedy, *Enc. Bib.* 1529. There were, of course, fishponds much earlier in the sanctuary at Ashkelon and elsewhere.

low as that of fish.'[1]    There were also saltpans and
villages of fishermen upon the lagoons of the desert coast
between Egypt and Palestine,[2] and further north the
Phœnicians preserved part of the harvest of their fisheries.
The Phœnician fish seem not to have been so good[3] as
those of Egypt, which had a great reputation in Israel,[4]
and in later times were largely imported to Jerusalem.[5]
From all these sources the Tyrian dealers brought to
the City's markets what must have been one of her
cheapest and most abundant supplies of food.    Dried fish
formed a convenient ration for journeys and pilgrimages.
They were a staple nourishment of the hosts which visited
the City for the great festivals.    The enormous rise in the
demand for food upon these periodic occasions was most
suitably met by supplies which came so abundantly from
so many sources and were capable of being stored.    After
the Greeks introduced the art of curing fish to the Lake
of Galilee,[6] a large proportion of the supplies would come
from its prolific waters.    The rights of fishing on these
were granted during the Latin Kingdom of Jerusalem to
the Canons of the Holy Sepulchre before Easter.[7]    In
Mohammedan times a favourite pickle was made at
Jericho from the fish of Jordan.

Another constant article of import into Jerusalem was
Salt.    The nearest sources—except for a few precarious

---

[1] Erman, *Life in Ancient Egypt*, E.T., 239, with references to
Wilkinson and others.

[2] *H.G.H.L.* 157.

[3] Rawlinson, *Hist. of Phœnicia*, 45.                    [4] Num. xi. 5.

[5] *Mishna*, 'Makshîrîn,' vi. 3, quoted by Kennedy *ut supra*, speaks of
Egyptian fish that come in baskets (barrels ?).

[6] Cf. the Greek name ταριχεῖαι, which in Pliny's time gave the lake its
name ; *H.G.H.L.* 450-455.

[7] Röhricht, *Regesta Regni Hieros.* 36, No. 142, A.D. 1132.

'salt-licks' east of Bethlehem[1] — were, of course, on the Dead Sea coasts: Jebel Usdum, the mountain of rock-salt,[2] the deposit at Birket el-Khalîl, south of 'Ain Jidy,[3] the pools and deposits round the northern end of the sea,[4] and on the south-eastern coast.[5]  So long as the Kings of Judah held sway on the western shores, their own caravans would bring up the salt to Jerusalem.  It may have been a royal monopoly, as it was in the times of the Seleucids and during the Latin Kingdom, when King Fulke gave liberty to the peasants of Teḳoa' to gather bitumen and salt from the Dead Sea.[6]  But when the influence of the City was limited to her immediate neighbourhood, the salt supplies would be furnished precariously by the citizens themselves bringing it up on their asses,[7] or by the Arabs of the Judæan wilderness, or later by the Nabatean traders. But the Dead Sea salt is much mixed with earth, and it is probable that, as at the present day, purer qualities were imported to Jerusalem from more distant sources. When in Moab, I found that the salt used by the villagers was not all brought from the Dead Sea coasts, near as they lie, but mainly from the salt-pans of the Wâdy Sirhân in Arabia, which Mr. Forder describes in the account of his journey to Ej-Jôf.[8]  With the salt came nitre,[9] alum,[10] and asphalt.

Salt.

---

[1] Cf. the W. el Mālḥa, S.E. of Herodium.

[2] Robinson, *Bib. Res.* ii. 481-485.

[3] *Ibid.* 226 ; *Phys. Geog.* 199.  [4] Ezek. xlvii. 11.

[5] Irby and Mangles, *Travels*, ch. viii. p. 139. Cf. p. 107.

[6] Röhricht, *Regesta Regni Hierosolymitani*, No. 174, A.D. 1138.

[7] Robinson, *Phys. Geog.* 199, mentions that he saw it brought up on asses by the inhabitants of villages near Jerusalem.

[8] *With Arabs in Tent and Town*, chaps. v.-viii.  Cf. Burckhardt, p. 662.

[9] Irby and Mangles, *Travels*, ch. viii. p. 139.

[10] στυπτηρίας μέταλλα, Jos. vii. *B.J.* vi. 3.

The manufacture of Soap, now so great an industry in Palestine, and once practised at Jerusalem, as the large

Alkali. heaps to the north of the City certify, was introduced to the country only after the beginning of the Christian era. Previous to that people used oil and lime, fuller's earth, and the mineral and vegetable alkalis.[1] The vegetable alkali has always been an important article of Bedouin trade in the towns of Palestine. Hasselquist[2] reports 'a kind of the Arabian *kali*' on the northern shores of the Dead Sea. In a Bedouin camp in the south of Edom, Burckhardt was astonished 'to see nobody but women in the tents, but was told the greater part of the men had gone to Gaza to sell the soap-ashes which these Arabs collect in the mountains of Shera.'[3] Seetzen reports that the inhabitants of the land between Anti-Lebanon and Palmyra conduct a considerable trade in the potash products of the *kali*,[4] and Diener that the plant, called by the Arabs *abû sabûn*, 'father of soap,' is collected in great masses, especially in the neighbourhood of Jêrûd.[5] One of the principal sources of the alkali used to-day in the soap-manufactures of Western Palestine is the steppes south of Ḥauran, where, as I learned when travelling there, it is obtained from the ashes of the *kilu* and other plants and carried to Nablus by the Arabs. Ancient Jerusalem, then, would receive alkali from the Ishmaelites or Midianites, and use it for tanning skins, or, when mixed with oil, for washing.

[1] It is these last two which are usually understood by the names נֶתֶר and בֹּרִית, *nether* and *bōrîth*, in Jer. ii. 22.

[2] *Voyages and Travels in the Levant*, 131.
[3] *Travels in Syria*, etc., 411.
[4] *Reisen*, i. 279.
[5] *Libanon*, 369.

We have seen that, while Judæa affords fair pasture for sheep and goats, her native breed of cattle is of a small and meagre kind, and that the finer species had to be imported.  As the popula- Import of animals for food. tion of the City grew, the native supplies even of sheep became insufficient, and consequently all kinds of animals for food and sacrifice were introduced from abroad in increasing numbers.  The chief pasture-lands were those of Bashan, celebrated for its breeds both of rams and bulls;[1] of Moab, whose king, like the chiefs of to-day, was a great sheep-master;[2] and of Mount Gilead, reputed for its goats.[3]  'More famous than the tilth of Eastern Palestine is her pasture.  We passed through at the height of the shepherd's year.  From the Arabian deserts the Bedouin were swarming to the fresh summer herbage of these uplands. . . . The herds of the settled inhabitants were still more numerous.  In Moab the dust of the roads bears almost no marks but those of the feet of sheep.  The scenes which throng most our memory of Eastern Palestine are (besides the threshing-floors of Ḥauran) the streams of Gilead in the heat of the day with the cattle standing in them, or the evenings when we sat at the door of our tent near the village well, and would hear the shepherd's pipe far away, and the sheep and goats and cows with the heavy bells would break over the edge of the hill and come down the slope to wait their turn at the troughs. Over Jordan we were never long out of the sound of the

[1] Deut. xxxii. 14; Ezek. xxxix. 18; Micah vii. 14; Jer. l. 19; Ps. xxii. 13 [Eng. 12].

[2] 2 Kings iii. 4; compare the passages on Reuben and Gad, Judges v. 16; Num. xxxii. 1 ff., etc.

[3] Cant. iv. 1; vi. 5.

lowing of cattle or of the shepherd's pipe.'[1]  Consequently the import of sheep and other cattle from
Eastern Palestine and Arabia to Jerusalem has been
constant through the centuries.  The greater amount of
the spoil taken by kings of Judah from Arab tribes was
in sheep.[2]  A prophet of the period immediately after
the Exile looks to Arabia for the City's supplies of sheep
in the days of her coming glory : *all the flocks of Kedar
shall be gathered unto thee, the rams of Nebaioth shall
minister to thee: they shall come up with acceptance on mine
altar.*[3]  In the extract we have already quoted from
Eupolemos, a Jew of the second century,[4] we are told
that while the wheat was brought from Samaria, Galilee,
and Eastern Palestine, and there was sufficient oil in
Judæa herself, 'cattle to be slaughtered for food shall
be supplied from Arabia.'  Similarly in Mohammedan
times Jerusalem imported lambs from 'Ammân.[5]  And
during the Latin kingdom of Jerusalem raids were made
by the Crusaders upon the Arab and Turkoman shepherds of the pastures to the north-west of the Lake of
Galilee for the purpose of carrying off their flocks.[6]

As for riding and draught animals, we have seen that
the only one in use in Jerusalem from the first was the
ass.  The horse, the mule and even the camel were not
introduced to the Judæan hills or Jerusalem till a period

---

[1] *H.G.H.L.* 523 f.

[2] 1 Chron. v. 21 (the tribe Reuben from the Hagrites, but it illustrates
the experience of the later monarchy) ; 1 Sam. xxvii. 9 (David from the
Amalekites, etc.) ; 2 Kings iii. 4 (Mesha's tribute to Israel) ; 2 Chron. xiv. 15
(Asa's spoil from the Kushite Arabs, not *Ethiopians* as in E.V.) ; xvii. 11
(Jehoshaphat's tribute from the Arabians), etc.

[3] Isa. lx. 7.          [4] Above, p. 315.          [5] Above, p. 315 *n.* 2.

[6] *e.g.* the treacherous attack during a time of peace in 1157, Röhricht,
*Gesch. des Königreichs Jerusalem*, 287.

which, in each case, it is possible to define with tolerable certainty. This was not because the region is very unsuitable to any of them. They abound there to-day, and are usefully employed for all sorts of traffic and agriculture. But none of them is indigenous to Syria, and the directions of their appearances in Western Asia may be clearly traced.

Import of riding and draught animals.

Not indigenous to Syria, the Camel must have been familiar to her inhabitants from a very early period through the desert traders with whom her primitive commerce was chiefly conducted.

1. The Camel.

So great an authority as W. Max Müller says that 'the assertion that the ancient Egyptians knew the camel is unfounded.'[1] Nor, curiously enough, is there any mention of the beast in the Tell el-Amarna letters, even when these speak of the caravans that pass through Syria. In the Old Testament, camels are first assigned to the Ishmaelites, and included among the property of the Patriarchs. But there is no mention of them in connection with Israel either throughout the wanderings in the wilderness or on the entry into Canaan. The first of the settled Israelites to whom they are attributed is David, and it is significant that the keeper of his camels was an Ishmaelite. They became common in the later history, for caravans if not for agriculture, till they were almost as familiar as the ass. Numbers were in the spoil Sennacherib took from Hezekiah. The camel was, of course, the one-humped variety.[2]

[1] *Enc. Bibl.*, 'Camel,' § 3.

[2] Hebrew גָּמָל *gāmāl*; as the property of the Patriarchs, Gen. xii. 16; xxiv. 19, etc.; xxx. 43; of the Arabs, xxxvii. 25; cf. Judges vi. 5; vii. 12; viii. 21; 1 Sam. xv. 3; 1 Ki. x. 2, etc.; David's camels, 1 Sam. xxvii. 9; 1 Chron. xxvii. 30; not used in agriculture, Deut. xxii. 10; forbidden as

The Horse was probably not used in early Jerusalem. Introduced into Egypt by the Hyksos after 1800 B.C.,

2. The Horse. horses were never very common there.[1] By 1600 B.C. they were used in war, with chariots, in Palestine;[2] and in the Tell el-Amarna letters they are mentioned as imported to Egypt from Mesopotamia and Cyprus, and as used in Syria for journeys.[3] None of these notices, however, refers to Jerusalem. King Solomon appears to have been the first to introduce them there, or at least into his kingdom, for the neighbourhood of Jerusalem is unfitted for chariots, and the depôts of the royal chariots were, as we shall see, in other cities. The true reading of the passage relative to their introduction is as follows: *the export of horses for Solomon was out of Muṣri and Ḳuë; the dealers of the king brought them out of Ḳuë for a price.*[4] Muṣri here is not Egypt, but the north-Syrian state of that name: Ḳuë is Cilicia. Horses came from north to south in Western Asia, probably first from Asia Minor, and at the hands of the Hittites. The Phrygians are called by Homer 'they of the fleet steeds.' According to Ezekiel, the Phœnicians traded in them with the people of Togarmah, perhaps part of Armenia. It is probable, however, that some were brought into Israel from Egypt, where the breed was good.[5] By the ninth century the

food, xiv. 7; Lev. xi. 4; in caravans, Isa. xxx. 6; lx. 6; Ezra ii. 67; Neh. vii. 69; 1 Chr. xii. 40; Zech. xiv. 15; Sennacherib's Inscr., *Taylor Cylinder*, iii. 18.

[1] W. Max Müller, *Enc. Bibl.*, 'Egypt,' § 9.

[2] Annals of Thothmes III.; cf. Judges v. 22.

[3] *e.g.* Nos. 16, 26, 27, 51. Cf. the phrase *thy groom*, 224-227, 235, etc.

[4] 1 Kings x. 28 f., according to the Greek; cf. Winckler, *A. T. Untersuch.* 108 ff.

[5] *Iliad*, iii. 185; Ezek. xxvii. 14; Deut. xvii. 16, where Miṣraim is evidently Egypt; cf. W. Max Müller, *Enc. Bibl.*, 'Egypt,' § 38.

horse and the chariot were sufficiently identified with
the armaments of Northern Israel to form a figure
for the two prophets who had so materially contributed
to the national defence : *my father, my father, the chariot
of Israel and the horsemen thereof.*[1]  By the eighth century, horses and chariots had become very numerous
in both kingdoms.  They are nearly always mentioned
by the prophets in connection with war or foreign sub-
sidies for war.[2]  An ancient proverb speaks of the horse
as *prepared against the day of battle* :—

> ' *As oft as the trumpet soundeth he neigheth,*
> *And smelleth the battle afar off,*
> *The thunder of the captains and the shouting.*' [3]

The prophets always include the cavalry as a formidable
element in the hosts of the northern invaders of Palestine.[4]  Naturally the Israelites used horses less in the
highlands of Judah than in other parts of the country :
the instances of horses or chariots at Jerusalem are
extremely few compared with those given for the broad
avenues of Northern Israel.[5]  Still, as early as Athaliah's
time there was *a horse entry* to the palace in Jerusalem,
and a Horse-gate on the Wall.[6]  Under Manasseh we
shall see the introduction of the worship of the horses
of the Sun.[7]

---

[1] 2 Kings ii. 12 ; xiii. 14 ; cf. 1 Kings xviii. 5, 44 ; xxii. 34 ff. ; 2 Kings
ix. 16 ff.    [2] Amos iv. 10 ; Hosea i. 7 ; xiv. 3 ; Isa. ii. 7 ; xxxi. 1, 3.

[3] Prov. xxi. 31 ; Job xxxix. 25 ; cf. Jer. viii. 6 ; Nah. iii. 2.

[4] Especially Jeremiah.

[5] Cf. *H.G.H.L.* 330 ; and add 2 Sam. xv. 1, Absalom's *one* chariot.

[6] 2 Kings xi. 16 ; 2 Chron. xxiii. 15 : the reading, however, in both cases
is not quite certain.

[7] Hebrew names for the horse are (1) סוּם *sûs* ; (2) פָּרָשׁ *pārāsh* ; (3)
רֶכֶשׁ *rekesh* (uncertain) ; (4) perhaps also בְּנֵי הָרַמָּכִים, Esth. viii. 10.
For other possible names see *Enc. Bibl.* col. 2114.  Poetically the horse
was called אַבִּיר *'abbîr*, mighty.

Before Solomon's time Jerusalem had become ac-
quainted with the Mule.	When mules were introduced

3. The Mule.

to Syria and Egypt from Asia Minor we do
not know.	There is a possible, but ambiguous,
piece of evidence for their appearance in Egypt as early as
the reign of Thothmes III.[1]	In Jerusalem they first ap-
peared in the time of David, ridden by the King and the
King's sons;[2] only later did they become baggage animals,[3]
as they are chiefly to-day in Syria, though sometimes, as
in David's time, used for riding by officials.	Sennacherib
carried away many from Judah, and in the post-exilic
period their use seems to have been very frequent
in spite of the law against breeding them.[4]	The one
Hebrew name does not distinguish between the mule, the
offspring of the he-ass and mare, German *Maulthier*, and
the hinny or burdown, child of the stallion and she-ass,
German *Maulesel*.[5]	The most able and interesting of
all the animals of the East, the mule is almost as closely
associated with the landscapes round Jerusalem as the ass,
and it is interesting to find it there in the history as

---

[1] W. Max Müller, *Neue Darstellungen mykenischer Gesandter, etc.*, *in
altägypt. Wandgemälden* (*Mitteil. der vorderasiat. Gesellschaft*, 1904, 2),
p. 33 *n.* 1.	This, along with *Beiträge z. Assyr.* iv. 542, and Anderlind's
paper on the Mule in *M.u.N.D.P.V.*, should be consulted in addition to the
articles ' Mule' in the *Enc. Bibl.* and in Hastings' *D.B.*

[2] 2 Sam. xiii. 29; xviii. 9; 1 Kings i. 33, 38, 44.

[3] 2 Kings v. 17; Isa. lxvi. 20; 1 Chron. xii. 40; Judith xv. 11.

[4] Sennacherib, *Prism Inscription*, iii. 18 ff.	Post-exilic references, Ezra
ii. 66; Neh. vii. 68; Ps. xxxii. 9 (compare the modern Arabic proverb,
'keep away from both ends of a mule'), etc.	Ezek. xxvii. 14 says they
were imported by Phœnicians from Togarmah.	Law against breeding them,
Lev. xix. 19.

[5] Heb. פֶּרֶד *pered* (fem. *pirdah*), from which comes the mediæval Latin
*burdo*, Old Eng. *burdown*.	On the proper use of the German terms, often
confused, see Anderlind as above.

early as David. But neither horses nor mules were much used as pack-animals in Palestine in ancient times. In the days of Josephus, camels and asses were still the common beasts of lading. Mules, however, are also mentioned by him.[1]

As we have seen, there are no minerals in the rocks of the surroundings of Jerusalem; whatever metal was used by the inhabitants had to be imported. For early Babylonia and Egypt the sources of gold—besides the mines of Egypt and Nubia —were mainly in Arabia;[2] in harmony with which one of the earliest Old Testament records of gold, after the settlement of Israel, is that of the earrings and other ornaments which Gideon took from the Ishmaelites.[3] In the spoil which Achan stole was a *tongue of gold of fifty shekels' weight.* Professor Cheyne's ingenious emendation of the word for tongue[4] is unnecessary, since Mr. R. A. S. Macalister's discovery at Gezer of a bar of gold whose weight, 860 *grammes,* is 'not far from fifty shekels . . . its shape was long, narrow, and slightly curved; it might well be described as a *tongue.*'[5] We may conclude from these two instances that the shape was a usual one. David brought gold to Jerusalem among the spoils which he took in war;[6] and no doubt the tradition is sound which implies a great increase of this precious metal

*Imported Metals: 1. Gold.*

[1] *Life,* 24, 26.
[2] See § 7 of the author's article on ' Trade and Commerce ' in *Enc. Bibl.,* with the references given there. The following may be added : Ezek. xxvii. 22 ; Pseudo-Aristeas, Thackeray's ed. in Swete's *Introd. to O. T. in Greek,* 539.
[3] Judges viii. 24 ff.
[4] *Enc. Bibl.* col. 1751 ; Josh. vii. 21.
[5] *Bible Side-lights from the Mound at Gezer,* 122.
[6] 2 Sam. viii. 7, 11 ; 1 Kings vii. 51.

through the policy and the trade of Solomon.[1]  In these, other monarchs imitated him.  The hunger for gold was no doubt the motive of the many attempts to re-open his commerce with the Red Sea and Arabia.  Other sources were spoil of war, tribute, and tolls upon the caravans which passed through Israel between Arabia and Phœnicia.  The gold of Arabia must have been in large part the secret of the wealth of the Nabateans, who in the first century before Christ financed Antipater and Herod. The metal was hoarded either in *tongues* or men's and women's ornaments, or, chiefly, in the ornament and furniture of the Temple.  But, as we shall see, these stores of it were periodically depleted for payment to the conquerors and liege-lords of Israel.  The number of terms for gold in Hebrew prove at once the number of sources from which the metal came and the people's familiarity with the working of it.[2]  Of the caravans which now enter the Holy City, the most interesting and picturesque are those which come up from Arabia; but the costliness of many of their burdens in ancient times adds to

---

[1] I Kings vi. ff.

[2] The oldest terms seem to be (1) חָרוּץ *ḥârûṣ*, archaic and poetical in Hebrew, usual in Phœn. and Ass., cf. χρυσός, and (2) כֶּתֶם *kethem*, poetical in Hebrew, also found in Egyptian and Sabæan, and probably from the name of a land: *e.g.* 'the good gold of Katm' (Erman, *Life in Ancient Egypt*, 464; cf. W. Max Müller, *As. u. Eur.* 76 *n.* 1).  The commonest term is (3) זָהָב *zāhāb* (also in Aram. and Arab.), both alone and with a number of epithets, thus: זָהָב מוּפָז, *refined gold*, of which פַּז *paz* may be an abbreviated form; זָהָב טָהוֹר, *clean gold*, a synonym for the preceding; זָהָב שָׁחוּט, *beaten gold*; זָהָב סָגוּר, *closed*, that is probably *stanch* or *sterling gold*, but compare the Assyrian expression as to silver, *kanku*, 'sealed,' or 'enclosed in sealed sacks' (Joh   *Bab. and Ass. Laws*, etc., p. 253); and זָהָב אוֹפִיר, *gold of Ophir*.

their vividness, and in that remote haze picks them out in gold to our eyes.

In contrast with its many words for gold the Hebrew language has but one for Silver, *keseph,* usually understood to mean the pale metal in distinction from its ruddy fellow. This is plausible, for ² Silver. in post-Biblical Hebrew the word has the signification of whiteness, but not at all certain. The primary meaning may be, as in Arabic, 'to cut off,' and the name have been given to the metal because it was the first to be cut off into definite *pieces*: the name of several coins.[1] Silver was rare in Egypt before 1600 B.C., and had a higher value than gold: its sources were Asiatic.[2] But soon thereafter the supplies must have enormously increased, for by 1400, according to the Tell el-Amarna letters, the metal was in pieces used for payments.[3] In the time of the Judges it was common enough in Israel to be employed in the definite form of *shekels* or *weights.*[4] David stamped shekels, presumably of silver.[5] According to the tradition, silver was even more plentiful than gold in Jerusalem under Solomon: the quantity of its import would prevent that enhancement of its value which otherwise must have followed from the great increase of gold under the king: for *silver was nothing*

---

[1] כֶּסֶף; on the root as meaning 'pale' see Robertson Smith, *Journ. of Philol.* xiv. 125, but in the *Book of the Twelve Prophets,* ii. 39 *n.* 5, it is shown how even the meaning of נכסף, *ashamed* or *baffled,* is more easily derivable from the root sense of *kasaph,* 'to cut off,' than from 'paleness.' Barth (*Etym. Studies,* 61) derives נכסף from the same root *kasaph,* but in the sense of 'to be deprived.' The chief support of the derivation from *paleness* lies, of course, in the undoubted use of *kasaph* in post-Biblical Hebrew for *whiteness.* In support of the other derivation is the O.T. use of כֶּסֶף in the plural as meaning *pieces* of silver.

[2] *Enc. Bibl.,* 'Egypt,' § 38.      [3] No. 280, 8; cf. 11, 21.
[4] Judges xvii. 2, etc. ; 1 Sam. ix. 8.      [5] 2 Sam. xiv. 26.

*accounted of in the days of Solomon ; he made silver to be
in Jerusalem as stones.*[1]  Certainly after this it continues
to rank as the second of the precious metals, and virtually
to mean money.   According to Ezekiel and the Book of
Jeremiah, Tyre imported silver from Tarshish.[2]

On the relative values of gold and silver, and on the
various weights made from these metals and in current
use, a full account has been given by Professor A. R. S.
Kennedy in his article on 'Money' in Dr. Hastings's
*Dictionary of the Bible.*

Besides gold and silver the Jews, at least in Babylonia,
appear to have known that mixture of the two metals

3. Electrum.
Precious
Stones.
which was called by the Greeks Elektron.[3]
How many of what we count the precious
stones were known or used by the Jews is
uncertain : the reader must be referred to the Bible dictionaries and encyclopædias.[4]

Of what we call the useful metals, Copper was used
universally in Canaan at the time of Israel's arrival, nearly

4. Copper
and Bronze.
pure and with alloy of tin as bronze.[5]   It is
the latter which is meant by the Old English
term *brass* used in our versions : 'in the Old Testament
this never refers to the alloy of zinc to which the term is
now confined.'[6]   The sources of copper for Palestine and

---

[1] 1 Kings x. 21, 27.          [2] Ezek. xxvii. 12 ; Jer. x. 9.

[3] חַשְׁמַל, Ezek. i. 4, 27 ; viii. 2.

[4] *Enc. Bibl.*, 'Stones (Precious),' J. L. Myres ; Hastings' *D.B.*, Flinders
Petrie.          [5] Bliss, *A Mound of Many Cities*, 39, 60, 67, 80, 188 f.

[6] J. H. Gladstone, *P.E.F.Q.*, 1898, 253 *n.* 1, in a paper on the metals
of antiquity, reprinted from *Nature.*   See also *Athenæum*, Feb. 3, 1906,
4084, for report of a paper on 'Copper and its Alloys in Antiquity,' by the
President of the Anthropological Institute.   In his opinion, bronze was made
directly from a copper ore containing tin long before the two metals were
artificially mixed.   There are other interesting details.

Egypt were Cyprus, the Lebanons, where was the land of Nuhashshi or bronze, and also Edom and North Arabia.[1] From the country of Zobah, at the foot of Hermon, identified with 'the land of Nuhashshi,' David brought away much bronze,[2] but there seems to have been no Israelite worker in the metal, for Solomon had to import Huram-abi from Tyre.[3] From that time onwards bronze was too prevalent in Jerusalem for all manner of purposes to require detailed notice.[4] In Egypt, as in parts of Africa to-day, copper wire was used as a standard of exchange.[5] But we have no record of a similar use in Syria. In the Tell el-Amarna letters and the Old Testament the shekels seem to be invariably of silver or gold.

The Bronze age in Palestine appears to have lasted at least till about the date of the arrival of Israel in the land; then, or perhaps later, Iron was introduced. Like copper, iron also came out of the North,[6] 5. Iron. where in Lebanon there were mines of it worked by the Phœnicians.[7] But it was probably imported to Babylonia as early as 2500 B.C. from Arabia.[8] There were other sources nearer to Judah. Some have denied that the promise to Israel of finding iron in the rocks of their

---

[1] For Cyprus (Alasia) see Tell el-Amarna letters, Nos. 25, 27, 31 ff. For other references see the author's article 'Trade,' etc., in *Enc. Bibl.*, § 7.

[2] 2 Sam. viii. 8.

[3] 1 Kings vii. 13 ff. ; 2 Chron. ii. 12.

[4] The Hebrews had but the one word נְחֹשֶׁת, *nĕhosheth* (with the adjective נָחוּשׁ), for both copper and bronze.

[5] Erman, *Life in Ancient Egypt*, 494 ff.

Jer. xv. 12.

[7] One is mentioned above Beyrut by Idrisi, *Z.D.P.V.* viii. 134. Ramman-Nirari III., King of Assyria, mentions iron as well as copper among the tribute he received from Aram-Damascus.

[8] Hommel, *Geogr. u. Gesch. des Alten Orients*, 13.

land is justified by the geological facts.[1]  But ancient sources of the ore have been discovered at Ikzim on Mount Carmel and near Burme, north of the Jabbok; and Josephus mentions in the Eastern Range a mountain 'called the Iron Mountain, which runs in length as far as Moab.'[2]  The Pseudo-Aristeas says that both iron and copper used to be brought before the Persian period 'from the neighbouring mountains of Arabia.'[3] The Hebrew name for it (*barzel*) is not native,[4] and in estimating the number of passages in which it occurs in the Old Testament we must keep in mind that the same name was applied to basalt, as it is to-day by the Arabs east of Jordan.[5]  David is said to have had iron in abundance, but in any case, by the ninth and eighth centuries the metal was known, and by the seventh was common in Israel, and smelting-furnaces were used.[6]  The excess of the number of references in Jeremiah and Deuteronomy over those in previous writers may point to a great increase of the metal in Israel at some date shortly before 650 B.C.

Lead appears to have been used in Israel partly for the mason's plummet, as wire, for purifying silver, and as writing-tablets.[7]  It was probably not always distin-

[1] Deut. viii. 9.          [2] *Z.D.P.V.* xxx. 129; iv. *B.J.* viii. 2.

[3] Thackeray's ed. in Swete's *Introd. to O.T. in Greek*, 540.

[4] Heb. בַּרְזֶל.

[5] *E.g.* Og's bedstead, *i.e.* sarcophagus (cf. 2 Chron. xvi. 14), was of basalt, not iron, Deut. iii. 11; and the threshing sledges of barzel were no doubt the same as the sledges of the present day, toothed with sharp fragments of basalt, Amos i. 3.  Similarly perhaps Jer. i. 18, Ezek. iv. 3.

[6] 1 Kings xxii. 11; Isa. x. 34; Micah iv. 13; Jer. i. 18; xv. 12; xvii. 1; xxviii. 13; Deut. viii. 9, etc.; Ezek. iv. 3; xxvii. 12; smelting furnaces, Jer. xi. 4; Deut. iv. 20; Ezek. xxii. 17 ff.; but cf. 1 Kings viii. 51 (Dt.).

[7] Ex. xv. 10; Amos vii. 7 f.; Jer. vi. 29; Ezek. xxii. 18 ff.; Job xix. 23 f.  Heb. עֹפֶרֶת, *'ophereth.*  Lead-wire, Bliss, *A Mound, etc.*, 189.

guished from Tin, known from early times as an alloy
of copper to make bronze.[1]   Antimony was probably
very rare, and it may not have been this but    6. Lead, Tin,
some oxide of lead or sulphide of copper which    etc.
was used in the eye-paints employed by Hebrew women.[2]

As necessary to the domestic uses of the citizens were
the harder forms of stone for their corn-rubbers and hand-
mills.   Basalt and the firmer sandstone are,
as we have seen, not found in Judah.   They    Basalt.
must have been imported.[3]   But it is very singular that
in the remains of a town where 'the dull rumour of the
running millstone' was constantly heard, almost no old
rubbers or querns should yet have been recovered, and
so few other pieces of ancient basalt.[4]

Incense, perfumes, spices and drugs were imported
from Arabia ;[5] but, as we shall see, it is doubtful whether
incense was used in Israel till the seventh    Incense,
century B.C., or adopted in the regular worship    spices, etc.
of the Temple till after the return from Babylon.   The
rest were imported into Israel from the earliest times.

Other possible imports for common use were Wool and
Flax.   On these as articles of trade, the Biblical data are
meagre and difficult.   On the one hand, Amos
of Ṭeḳoaʿ seems to have carried the fleeces of    Wool.
his sheep to markets beyond Judah ;[6] but on the other,

---

[1] Tin is בְּדִיל, *bĕdhîl*, the separated metal ; Ezek. xxii. 18, 20 ; xxvii.
12 ; Zech. iv. 10 (as a plummet) ; Num. xxxi. 22.

[2] For this the Hebrew was פּוּךְ, *pûkh*, the N. Heb. כָּחוֹל *kāhol* (cf. Jer. iv.
30 ; Ezek. xxiii. 40).          [3] See above on Iron.

[4] Clermont-Ganneau, *Arch. Res.* i. 292, a piece of a laver or sarcophagus
of basalt ; cf. 137.   Ossuaries found are always of limestone, 134.

[5] Incense, לְבֹנָה, Gr. λιβανωτός, Jer. vi. 20 ; Isa. lx. 6 ; cf. Pseudo-Aristeas,
Thackeray's ed. as above, 539 ; Pliny, *H.N.* xii. 30.   Spices, etc., Gen.
xxxvii. 25 ; Ezek. xxvii. 22.          [6] *Book of the Twelve* (*Exp. Bible*), vol. i.

wool is not mentioned by Ezekiel in his list of Judæan exports to Tyre, and we may therefore conclude that just before the Exile the population used all that their own flocks produced, as well as the fleeces of the numerous animals imported from abroad.[1] Probably the whole of the surplus stock was turned into home-spun, which we know was sold to Phœnician pedlars for export.[2] The woollen garments of Syria were prized in Egypt.

In Judah proper Flax cannot have been cultivated. The Jordan valley is favourable to its growth, and we find *Flax.* it there both in the earliest times and in the latest.[3] It was probably thence that it came into Judah, where it was spun for their own use and for sale by the women of the families.[4] But flax was also largely and finely cultivated in Egypt.[5] It is interesting that out of the half-dozen references to it in the Old Testament two should occur in Isaiah xl.-lv., which was written in Babylonia.[6]

These, then, are the certain and probable imports of Jerusalem during the period when she was a political and religious capital. The next stage of our inquiry is that concerning the sources from which the City derived her

[1] Wool, צֶמֶר *ṣemer*, Hos. ii. 7, 11; Prov. xxxi. 13; Ezek. xxxiv. 3; 2 Ki. iii. 4 (tribute). The shorn fleece, גֵּז גִּזָּה, Deut. xviii. 4; Judg. vi. 37 ff. Sheep-shearing, 2 Sam. xiii. 23 ff.

[2] Prov. xxxi. 24.

[3] Josh. ii. 6; Hos. ii. 7, 11 (in N. Israel); Deut. xxii. 11; Prov. xxxi. 13; פֵּשֶׁת *pēsheth. Totius Orbis Descriptio* (anonymous work of fourth Christian century, which places it about Bethshan).

[4] Prov. xxxi. 24.      [5] Ex. ix. 31; Isa. xix. 9.

[6] Isa. xlii. 3; xliii. 17.

purchasing-powers: the means of paying for these imports, necessary and nearly necessary to her life. Such means were various. *First* came her agriculture, in The Power which, as we have seen, her fruit-trees, and wherewith to Purchase especially her olives, furnished her with a these Imports. surplus for exchange. We need not believe all that we are told by Jewish and Mohammedan writers as to the productiveness of Jerusalem's territory in oil 1. The Sur- and wine ; but at least the City's output of oil plus of Oil. must have been very great in all but the most disastrous periods of her industry. There is evidence enough that in their oil alone the inhabitants enjoyed a rich means for the purchase of foreign products, and that their surplus stores were at least sufficient to pay for the wheat and the salt which they required to import. *Secondly*, there were the crafts and industries of the City which, as we shall see, very much increased 2. Crafts and from the eighth century onwards ; and which, Industries. while productive of very few articles desired by foreign lands or cities, at least manufactured those that were necessary to the life of the surrounding villages, and could be exchanged for country produce. *Thirdly*, there was the commerce, for which Jerusalem, by her elevated position and aloof from the great trunk roads, 3. Commer- was peculiarly unfitted, but which political cial Profits. and fiscal interests attracted to her as the capital of a kingdom or a province. Besides that portion of her trade which had to do with the needs of her own citizens, there was, as we shall see, at certain periods, no inconsiderable amount of through traffic and exchange between the merchants of the Mediterranean coast and those of Arabia. The commissions upon all this, and the price of handling, storing and passing it on, must have added in some degree to the purchasing-power of the community. But, above all, we must remember how much of the imported produce, by which the life of the City was sustained, came to her in the long periods of her prosperity without money and without price. So we must 4. The Royal have regard, *fourthly*, to the revenues which Revenues. her kings and governors derived either in kind or 'money' from their domains, or by tribute or taxation or customs; and *fifthly*, to the revenues of her Temple 5. The Temple and Priesthood, who also had their domains Revenues. beyond the City territory, and who enjoyed almost as many kinds of tribute and offering as the Crown itself.

Because in early times the king was himself the chief trader, and indeed to the end of our period continued Order of to conduct commerce on his own behalf; and following because the receipts from taxes and tribute inquiry into these. were always one of the chief sources of his capital's income, it will be most convenient to consider the royal revenues first, then those of the Temple, then the riches of traders and other wealthy citizens, and then the common industries and crafts for which the City was never famous. As for the local agriculture, which lay behind all these and supplied the City's one natural surplus of oil, we have already sufficiently studied that in the chapter on her natural resources.

# CHAPTER VI

## THE ROYAL REVENUES:
## ESTATES, TRIBUTE, TITHES, TAXATION

IN pursuance of the plan laid down in the end of the preceding chapter, we begin our inquiry into the sources
of the City's powers of purchase with an ap- The Fluctua-
preciation of the royal revenues, the bulk of tions of these.
which flowed into Jerusalem as the capital of the kingdom.
In the course of the varying fortunes of the people—their
independence and prosperity at some periods, the subjection of their kings as vassals of the great empires at
others, at another the position of the City as a poor,
hunger-bitten colony, and then, somewhat improved, as a
small province with a foreign governor, and again as the
seat of an independent kingdom—we can understand how
the character and degree of her political revenues varied
fundamentally from time to time. Here we give only
a general view, reserving the details of the different
periods for the subsequent chapters on the history.

From the first the kings of Israel and Judah had their
own domains partly within the territory of the City, but
mostly beyond it. These domains consisted The Royal
partly of the ancestral estates of the royal Domains.
family—thus David appears to have given land to
Chimham the son of Barzillai, in the neighbourhood of
Bethlehem[1]—partly of lands taken by force or fraud
from the people,[2] and partly of lands legally assigned to

---

[1] 2 Sam. xix. 31-39, compared with Jer. xli. 17.
[2] 1 Sam. viii. 14 ; 1 Kings xxi. 16 ; also Nehemiah v.

the Crown. On this last Ezekiel, in his picture of the ideal state, lays emphasis as a means of preventing the temptation of the prince to oppress the people.[1] These estates varied in size, but under powerful monarchs were extensive. An apparently trustworthy tradition, preserved by the Chronicler, gives a list of officials under David who had the oversight of the king's tillage, of his vineyards, olives and sycomores, of his herds in Sharon and the valleys, of his flocks, camels and asses, of his olives in the fields, cities, villages and forts, and of his cellars of wine and oil.[2] It is a very considerable inventory of royal property, which must have increased under Solomon, and can never have been wholly lost by even the most unfortunate of their successors. The king, as we have seen, had his own officials for these estates, but it was also his custom to enlist for their cultivation the servants and the animals of the people.[3]

Besides this private property in lands and cattle, the king is said to have received the tithes of the fields, vineyards, olive-yards and flocks of his people.[4]

*Tithes on Agricultural Produce.* The fact is disputed,[5] but appears to be certain at least for the later kingdom. The proportion is a small one in light of the one-third delivered as rent to the Crown by the holders of *amîriyeh* land under the present system of land-tenure; but the probability is that there was a land-tax in addition (see below), and that in any case unscrupulous officials found means of seriously increasing the amount. Under the

---

[1] Ezek. xlv. 7 f.; xlvi. 18.

[2] I Chron. xxvii. 25-31 ; see Benzinger *in loco.* The King's son Absalom had fields near Jerusalem, 2 Sam. xiv. 30, and sheep-shearers at Baal-hazor, xiii. 23.          [3] I Sam. viii. 16 ; cf. I Macc. x. 31 ; xi. 35.

[4] I Sam. viii. 15, 17.          [5] Wellh., *Isr. u. Jüd. Gesch.* 63.

Persian governors of Judah this was actually the case, to such an extent that the people had to borrow money to pay the king's tribute, and so their lands became mortgaged.[1] The king, too, had his mowings off the spring herbage:[2] probably the same duty which the Roman governors of Syria annually imposed in the month Nisan.[3] Solomon (as we shall see) divided his kingdom into twelve provinces, each of which was bound to supply a month's victuals to his household;[4] and in the Persian period Nehemiah speaks of the *governor's bread* as *a bondage heavy upon the people*, which he himself demanded not of them.[5]

Another, though more irregular, source of the royal revenues was the tribute of vassal chiefs, paid both in cattle or wool, and in metals;[6] and whatever of this came to Judah in the days of the kingdom Tribute must have mostly found its way to Jerusalem. When Judah was a province of the Persian or of the Seleucid Empire, grants of material or of money were made by the sovereign lord for the repair of the city or other purposes.[7] Another source was spoil of war. As was the case in the Latin kingdom of Jerusalem, part of the booty taken in successful campaigns fell to the king,[8] and it is probable that, like David, the king would always, when and Spoil of possible, select his portion from the precious War. metals. From these two sources alone David and Solomon must have accumulated considerable treasure. Although many of the later kings were not so fortunate,

---

[1] Neh. v. 4.      [2] Amos vii. 1 f.
[3] Robertson Smith, *Religion of the Semites*, 228.
[4] 1 Kings iv. 7 ff.      [5] Neh. v. 14, 18.
[6] 2 Kings iii. 4; 1 Kings x. 10, 25.      [7] Neh. ii. 8; 1 Macc.
[8] 2 Sam. viii. 10 f. ; xii. 30.

and the palace treasuries were frequently depleted to
pay the indemnity of war or tribute, they also must have
found means for replenishing these, because, as we shall
see, there was nearly always a store of the metals either
at the Palace or at the Temple, to which the kings
invariably devoted some of their wealth.

In ancient times, as in Europe to a late date and still
in some Eastern states, the king kept at least the foreign
trade in his own hands.[1]  David's regulation
Royal Trade.
of trade is proved by his stamping of shekels
used as weights.[2]  More explicit are the statements about
Solomon.  It was Solomon's own agents who managed
the importation of horses from Cilicia and the Syrian
Muṣri, and who undertook the voyage down the Red
Sea.[3]  The annals of other kings of Judah record the
royal initiative in the same direction.  Imports resulting
from such enterprises would naturally be paid in olive
oil,[4] but part of the payment may have been in gold or
silver ; and in one case we are told that land was ceded
in exchange.[5]  Conversely, some of the imports were
themselves in gold and silver.  We are safe in assuming
at certain periods a considerable accession to the royal
revenues from the direct trading of the kings.  As in later
times, salt also may have been a royal monopoly.

Again, a considerable part of the royal revenues which
flowed into Jerusalem was derived from taxation, in
addition to the king's tithes.  The data sup-
Taxation.
plied by the Old Testament are so defective
that it is best before considering them to review the fuller

---

[1] See the author's article, 'Trade and Commerce,' *Enc. Bibl.*, §§ 11, etc.
[2] 2 Sam. xiv. 26.　　　　　　　　[3] See above, p. 324.
[4] 1 Kings v. 11.　　　　　　　　[5] 1 Kings ix. 11.

information which is at our disposal from the later periods of the City's history. We may begin with the indirect taxation, and take first of all the duties levied on the transit trade of the country.

The position of Palestine, between Arabia with its stores of incense, salt, balsam and some of the precious metals, and the Phœnician cities on the Levant, Customs and and between Egypt and Damascus, with the Tolls further trade to the Euphrates, has conferred upon the masters of the land constant opportunities for levying dues on the transit trade. Of these the Seleucids, the Maccabees, the Herods, the Romans and the Crusaders took full advantage. We have seen that the Maccabees in their campaigns paid attention not only to in later ages the military opportunities of the soil, but to in Palestine; the lines of traffic across it. Two of the passes through the Judæan and the Samarian hills were strongly fortified by Herod the Great, who also held the tolls at Gaza for Arabia by Petra and for Egypt.[1] Later Strabo describes how the Phylarchs on the Syrian border of the empire exacted heavier customs than did the independent chiefs of the nomads from the caravans passing from Babylonia,[2] and Pliny mentions the imperial customs at Gaza for the through trade in incense between Petra and Europe.[3] To use Pliny's phrase, it was the 'imperii nostri publicani' who lifted these dues for the imperial treasury at the borders of those provinces that were directly governed by Rome, such as Judæa in our Lord's time. Therefore Zacchæus of Jericho, an *architelones*, or *chief publican*, in that border town of Judæa, was a 'publicanus

---

[1] *Enc. Bibl.*, 'Trade and Commerce,' 5189.
[2] *Geogr.* xvi. 1, 27.　　　　[3] *Hist. Nat.* xii. 32.

imperii.'[1]　　But, with the restriction that Roman citizens should be free, the empire granted the customs of in N.T. Times; cities and kingdoms confederate with Rome to their own governments.　And therefore Matthew at Capernaum[2] was an official or lessee of the customs of Herod the Tetrarch.[3]　There is, indeed, still extant the list of the duties levied on goods entering one of these semi-independent states : the very full and exact Tariff of Palmyra, of the year 137 A.D., in Greek and Palmyrene Aramaic.[4]　The Christian kingdom of Jerusalem, lying as it did between Egypt and Damascus, both of which were Mohammedan, furnishes instances more exactly illustrative of the Old Testament conditions. From the year 1116 at least[5] Moslem caravans traversed the Christian territories.　As William of Tyre under the Latin King- dom; informs us, the crusading fortress of Darum was erected not only for the defence of the villages in its neighbourhood, but in order to exact a toll from traders who passed it.[6]　In the north, Toron and other castles served the same purpose,[7] and eastwards, Montroyal on the road from Egypt to Damascus.[8]　In assigning the latter to one of the nobles, Baldwin III.

---

[1] Luke xix. 1, 2.　　　　　　　　　　[2] Matt. ix. 9, etc.

[3] So Schürer, *Hist.*, div. i. vol. ii. 67 f.

[4] The full text, with translation and notes, in G. A. Cooke's *North Semitic Inscriptions*, 313-340.

[5] *Historiens Orientaux des Croisades* (in the *Recueil des Hist. des Croisades*), iii. 498 : extract from Nojûm ez-Zahîreh.

[6] *Hist.* xx. 20 : 'ut . . . de transeuntibus statutas consuetudines plenius et facilius sibi posset habere.'

[7] Ibn Jobair, *Hist. Orientaux des Croisades*, iii. 447 ; Rey, *Colonies Franques*, 260.

[8] Charter of Baldwin III. in Röhricht's *Regesta Regni Hieros.*, No. 366: 'salvis regis caravanis quaecunque de partibus Alexandriae et totius Aegypti in urbem Baldach et e converso transeunt.'

distinctly reserves for himself the tolls upon caravans passing from Egypt to Damascus or *vice-versâ*.

All these instances reflect upon certain passages of the Old Testament.   Under their light we cannot doubt that Solomon fortified Hazor, Megiddo, Gezer, Beth-horon the nether, Baalath, and Tamar— and in the Old Testament. cities commanding important lines of traffic[1] —not so much for the defence of his kingdom as to secure the payment of customs by merchants bringing in goods to his country and of tolls by those who would pass through it.[2]   The Judæan narrative of Jacob and his sons (as early at least as the eighth century) implies that traders to a foreign land took with them a *gift* or *tribute* to the king.[3]   Among the duties which the Book of Ezra declares to have been levied by the pre-exilic kings of Judah, one, *hălāk*, is evidently *way-money* or *toll*; the other two, *middah* and *bělō*, may be different forms of customs, though as the three seem to cover all the royal taxes, it is probable that one of them is the name of a direct tax, and *bělō* is explained by some as a poll-tax.[4]

Whether in addition to these customs and tolls levied at some guard-house near the frontier of the country duties were also paid as the goods passed through the gates of the capital and other *Octroi* Duties. towns, the Old Testament does not say, unless either the *middah* or the *bělō* was *octroi*.   But Antiochus the Great

---

[1] See below, Bk. III. ch. iii.   Baalath is the only one whose position is unknown.

[2] Such duties appear to be mentioned in 1 Kings x. 15, but the list is too corrupt to permit us to be certain.

[3] Gen. xliii. 11, מִנְחָה *minḥah*, at first only *a present*, came to mean a statutory tribute.

[4] Ezra iv. 13, 20; vii. 24.   See the vocabulary to ‘Trade and Commerce,’ *Enc. Bibl.* col. 5198, הֲלָךְ, בְּלוֹ מִדָּה.

decreed that the materials for repairing the Temple should be admitted duty free, as well those that come *out of Judah* as those from elsewhere;[1] which proves that under the Seleucids at least gate-moneys or *octrois* were levied at Jerusalem. Whether Matthew the publican who *sat at receipt of custom* in Capernaum lifted *octroi* duties, or tolls from caravans traversing the Via Maris from Damascus, or customs on goods entering Galilee from the territory of Philip, is uncertain ; and the tax imposed by Herod and removed by Vitellius seems to have been one levied on sales in the market.[2] But under the Latin kings dues were levied at the gates of Jerusalem and other towns in their realm. These are mentioned in a number of charters. Baldwin II., upon the Patriarch's representation that the customs hitherto exacted ' in the gate from those who brought in wheat, barley and vegetables,' are very hard upon the pilgrims, remits the same, and 'absolves from all exactions any who wish to bring in through the gates of Jerusalem wheat, barley, beans, lentils and peas.'[3] Amalrich I. grants to the house of St. Lazarus seventy-two besants ' to be annually received from the gate of David.'[4] The *Assises de Jérusalem* contains a list of articles on which duty was payable, whether they were brought by land or sea, into Acre;[5] and of the Acre *douane* we have an interesting description from the Arab, Ibn Jobair.[6] These illustrations from Crusading times are useful not

[1] Jos. xii. *Ant.* iii. 3.

[2] Jos. xvii. *Ant.* viii. 4; xviii. *Ant.* iv. 3.

[3] This document is given in *Assises de Jérusalem*, Tome II. (in the *Rec. des Hist. des Croisades*), on pp. 485 f. ; cf. Röhricht's *Regesta*, etc., No. 91, and Cartulaire du Saint-Sépulcre, No. 45.

[4] Röhricht, No. 487.

[5] Tome II., chapter ccxlii. : of the *Assises de la Cour des Bourgeois*, cf. 485 *n.a.*      [6] *Hist. Orient. des Crois.*, iii. 449.

only in showing how *octrois* were levied in the towns of Palestine, but in illustrating how they might be remitted in favour of pilgrims, and even assigned in part to religious institutions, of which Jerusalem was the home from the time of Solomon onwards.

We have evidence that certain Babylonian dues called *miksu* were *octroi* duties, for they were levied at the quays and ferries.[1]

Besides these forms of indirect taxation of the people, it would appear that the monarchs of Judah raised other taxes directly from families, individuals, and upon property.

*Family, Poll, and Property Taxes.*

That a family tax existed from an early period of the monarchy may be argued from the promise that any successful champion of Israel against the Philistine grant shall have his *father's house* made *free in Israel.*[2] This, however, may mean only that the fruits of his field were to be free from the king's tithe. Wellhausen thinks that 'the land-tax was unknown in Palestine,'[3] and in this opinion is supported by Benzinger.[4] The reason given, the account of Joseph's introduction of it into Egypt, appears insufficient. It is also a fair inference from David's numbering of the people that he had a poll-tax in view; and in a great emergency a property-tax was exacted by the King.[5] Under the Persians an assessment was made for the governor;[6] and besides land-taxes (1 Macc. x. 30) the Seleucids imposed a poll-tax,[7] which, however, in part, was really a trade tax.[8] The Romans levied both a

---

[1] Johns, *Babyl. and Assyr. Laws,* etc., 206.
[2] 1 Sam. xvii. 25.
[3] *Israel. u. Jüd. Gesch.* 63.
[4] *Enc. Bibl.* col. 1908.
[5] 2 Kings xxiii. 35.
[6] Neh. v. 14.
[7] Jos. xii. *Ant.* iii. 3, iv. 1.
[8] See Schürer, *Gesch.*, § 6 *n.* 14.

property and various poll-taxes.[1]   But to the direct
taxation of the kings of Judah a nearer analogy than all
these is found in the fiscal measures of the Latin kings,
both because the methods were similar and the results
immediately affected Jerusalem, in both cases the seat of
the royal treasury.   Just as Jehoiakim raised a direct tax
to meet an extraordinary emergency, so Baldwin IV. in
1177 decreed a levy to rebuild the walls of Jerusalem,[2] and
in 1182 to replenish the exhausted treasury a graduated
tax was imposed of 2 per cent. on incomes from rents, 1 per
cent. on wages and all properties above 100 besants, less on
those below, with 1 besant for each hearth in a *casale*.[3]

By all such fiscal institutions the kings of Israel fed
the treasury, and laid up from time to time stores of the
precious metals. *I gathered me*, says Ecclesiastes, *silver
and gold, and the private property of kings and of the
provinces*.[4]  But as we shall see in the course of the
history, the military misfortunes of Judah, as well as her
prolonged subjections to the Assyrian empire, drained the
palace treasury.  To meet these emergencies the monarchs
had recourse to the stores of precious metals accumulated
in the Temple partly by their own gifts and partly from
other sources.  To the Temple treasures we shall turn
in the next chapter.

But before we do so, we must look at one department
of the royal administration for which many of its taxes
were exacted from the people, and upon which
both these and the royal profits from trade
were bestowed, with a proportionate effect
upon the spending-powers of the City.  The department

Mercenary
Garrisons in
Jerusalem.

---

[1] Schürer, *Gesch.*[3], § 17, excursus 1, pp. 511 ff.

[2] William of Tyre, *Hist.* xxi. 25 ; cf. Gaston Dodu, *Histoire des Institutions monarchiques dans le Royaume Latin de Jérusalem*, 256.

[3] William of Tyre, *Hist.* xxii. 23 ; cf. Dodu as above.        [4] Eccles. ii. 8.

I mean is a military one: the mercenary garrison which, from David onwards, the most, if not all, of the kings of Judah sustained in Jerusalem. In the history of Western Asia this is a phenomenon which regularly appears in every state upon any considerable increase of its commerce.[1] The native militia, proper to agricultural conditions of life, is supplemented or even replaced by a mercenary army, often largely composed of foreigners. The history of Jerusalem, as the capital of Israel, began with such a garrison.[2] David, whose earlier political fortunes had required him to raise a troop of freebooters,[3] gathered from the detached and discontented among his countrymen, had no sooner established his kingdom than he enlisted a force of guards, partly, no doubt, from among the tried comrades of the days of his wanderings, who were sons of Judah, and partly from foreigners.[4] Under his successors these guards are found on duty round the person of the king, in the Palace and in the Temple.[5] Isaiah

[1] See the author's 'Trade and Commerce' in *Enc. Bibl.*, §§ 11, 48, 55 *n.* 1 (a reference to Nebuchadrezzar's mercenaries should have been added to 56), 63, etc. (both footnotes), 66 ; cf. W. H. Bennett's 'Army,' § 7, and G. F. Moore's 'Cherethites' in the same encyclopædia.

[2] There is one earlier instance in the history of Israel, that of Abimelech, Judges ix. 4.

[3] 'Perkin was not followed by any English of name, his forces consisted mostly of base people and *freebooters*, fitter to spoil a coast than recover a kingdom.'—Bacon.

[4] 1 Sam. xxii. 1 f. ; 2 Sam. viii. 18 ; xv. 18 ; xx. 7, 23 ; 1 Kings i. 38, 44 ; and see G. F. Moore as above ; also the many foreign names among David's servants (they cannot all have been traders), and especially Uriah the Hittite and Ittai the Gittite.

[5] 1 Kings xiv. 27 f. ; 2 Kings xi. 4-19. The Hebrew term was רָצִים *rāṣîm*, runners ; on כָּרִי *kārî*, see below in the history under Joash. 2 Chron. xxv. 6 says that Amaziah of Judah hired out of N. Israel for 100 talents of silver, 100,000 *gibbôr ḥātl*, E.V. *mighty men of valour* ; but the use of *gibbôr* here confirms its technical meaning of hired soldier. The term, however, is used in a wider sense in 2 Chron. xiii. 3.

counts the *gibbôr* or mercenary soldier along with the *man of war* as one of the standing elements of the population.[1] In addition, Hezekiah hired a number of Arab mercenaries for the defence of the City against Sennacherib,[2] a measure which was probably adopted at other crises of her history. We have no data on the subject from the period when the High Priests bare rule in Jerusalem, but besides their unpaid levies the Maccabees employed mercenaries native and not foreign;[3] and the Hasmonean kings, especially Hyrcanus I. and Alexander Jannaeus, hired large numbers of foreign soldiers.[4] Herod's forces were recruited from many nations, among them even Thracians, Germans and Gauls, and he paid them liberally; not otherwise could he have carried out his many enterprises, garrisoned his fortresses, or kept himself secure when in Jerusalem.[5] Of all such enlistments a number, of course, had little to do with the City economically, yet the native rulers would always have a garrison there, and when in residence their own guards. These mercenaries were paid partly in rations, partly by distribution of the booty, and partly in money.[6] Till the entry of Vespasian's great army the Romans employed only auxiliary troops in Judæa; the garrison at Jerusalem in Paul's time consisted of one cohort of infantry, from 500 to 1000 men, with sometimes at least a similar detachment of cavalry, largely recruited from the region

---

[1] Isa. iii. 3 f.

[2] Sennacherib's Inscription on the *Taylor Cylinder*, col. iii. lines 31-33, or Schrader, *C.O.T.*, i. 286.

[3] 1 Macc. xiv. 32.

[4] Josephus, i. *B.J.* ii. 5; iv. 3, 5; v. 4.

[5] *Ibid.* xv. 6; xvi. 3; xviii. 3; xxxiii. 9.

[6] See especially i. *B.J.* xv. 6; xviii. 3.

of Sebaste or Samaria. Many of them had been taken over by the Romans from the forces of Herod and Archelaus.[1] It was doubtless to such soldiers that John the Baptist addressed the exhortation to be content with their rations.[2]

In all the periods we have surveyed, the Jerusalem garrison, paid no doubt mainly in rations, but also, as we have seen, by money, and by a share in the booty of victorious campaigns, must have added not inconsiderably to the spending and purchasing powers of the City.

Similarly in Jerusalem there was round the Kings of Judah, as round the later foreign governors, a large number of civil officials and servants, the description of which would carry us beyond our present task. To give an idea of their number it is enough to mention the high officials named in the ancient Court of Judah, *The Servant of the King*,[3] the *Scribe* or *Secretary*, the *Recorder* or *Remembrancer*, the *Chief of the Palace* or *Steward*,[4] all of them with their households resident in Jerusalem. To these must be added the other *sarîm* or *nobles*[5] who attended the court; several of lesser rank, the *mashḳeh* or *cupbearer*, the

The Court and Civil Officials.

---

[1] On the Roman garrisons of Judæa see Schürer in *Z.f.w. Th.* xviii. 413-425, and *Hist.*, div. i. vol. ii. 49-57.

[2] Luke iii. 14 : ὀψώνια.

[3] 2 Kings xxii. 12 ; cf. 2 Sam. xv. 34. This separate and perhaps highest office is confirmed by the discovery of several seals belonging to different holders of it in Judah and N. Israel ; for an exhaustive study of these by Kautzsch, see *M.u.N.D.P.V.*, 1904, 1-14, 81-83. It is possible that the *'ebhed ha-melekh* was only the chief eunuch, or that the title was applied to more than one office under the king.

[4] 2 Kings xviii. 18, 37 (=Isaiah xxxvi. 3, 22) ; Isaiah xxii. 15 ; 2 Kings xxii. 12.

[5] Jer. xxvi. 10 ; xxxvi. 12, 14.

keepers of the treasures and of the robes;[1] the *sérisîm*, probably, but not certainly, eunuchs; and a crowd of minor officials, *soṭerîm* and *sopherîm*, *clerks* and *secretaries*, and so forth. Other names meet us under the Persian and Greek governments. The City, too, as Nehemiah tells us, had its own officials. Like the ancient kings, the Hasmonean kings and Herod must have had their servants in residence. The seat of the Roman procurator was in Cæsarea, but he came with his officials periodically to Jerusalem. Many of the *nobles* had their own country estates, the income of which they would draw to the capital. But below them were those large numbers of officials who, as much as the mercenary soldiers, had to be sustained by the state.

---

[1] 1 Kings x. 5 ; 2 Kings x. 22 ; 1 Chron. xxvii. 25 ff.

# CHAPTER VII

## THE TEMPLE REVENUES, PROPERTIES
## AND FINANCE

IN stating the general economic problems which arise in the course of the history of Jerusalem, we included that of the sustenance of the priesthood, their families and their servants, whether personal or attached to the service of the Temple. From the earliest times to the latest, careful provision, both in kind and in money, was made for all these classes. That very class which, after the national worship had been centralised by Deuteronomy, became the most numerous of the non-producing classes of the population of the City, was supported by the system which created it. The same laws which developed a large priesthood and host of followers provided that they should be fed by the tribute of the whole nation ; and the more they increased in number, the more did the law enhance and secure their incomes. We may divide our consideration of the subject into the periods before the Exile, immediately after the Return, and during the last stages of the Temple history.

That during the period of the First Temple the king had the supreme direction of its arrangements and finance, and provided for its upkeep and embellishment, whether

The Support of the Priesthood.

351

from his own private resources or the people's tribute, is proved by many passages in the history. It was
**1. Pre-exilic Period—The Crown and the Temple Finances.** Solomon who built the Temple, just as actually as he built the Palace and other royal buildings. He gave the furniture, vessels and ornaments, many of which were of gold, and brought into the sacred treasuries the silver, the gold, and the vessels which David, his father, had dedicated.[1]

Partly depleted by the exactions of Shishak, King of Egypt, the Temple treasuries were refilled by Asa, and emptied again by the same king for tribute to the King of Aram:[2] fluctuations which, as we shall see, happened frequently in the course of the history. The king had as ready a command over the treasuries of the Temple as he had over those of the Palace, but when he drew upon them to meet emergencies, he seems as soon as possible to have filled them once more. At least there was always treasure in the Temple to meet fresh emergencies. In the reign of Joash we learn that the people paid moneys directly to the priests, consisting of an assessment on individuals, voluntary gifts, and quit-moneys.[3] Joash ordered that the first two of these classes of revenues should be devoted to the repairs, and directed the priests to see to this individually—each from his own *transactions*, or *takings*, or *possessions* (the meaning of the term is uncertain). Such a direction implies at least the beginnings of those individual and hereditary rights in the Temple revenues which we know to have existed in other sanctuaries of the time.[4]

[1] 1 Kings vi.-ix.    [2] 1 Kings xv. 15-18.
[3] 2 Kings xii. 4 ff. ; for details see below in the history, chapter on Joash.
[4] For Babylonia compare Johns, *Bab. and Assyr. Laws*, etc., 215.

But the story also illustrates the king's jurisdiction over the Temple finance, for with the consent of the priests Joash afterwards arranged that they should resign their interests in the two sources of income above mentioned, and these were administered by the king's secretary for the repair of the House of the Lord. Uzziah and Ahaz both asserted the royal supremacy over the service of the Temple; Joash and Ahaz the right of the king to draw, in emergency, on the Temple treasures.

At this time there is no notice of Temple estates. But we shall probably be right in assuming that the kings, who made grants of lands to individuals, did so in the case of the Temple as well, especially in payment or pledge for the sacred treasures which they appropriated to meet military or political emergencies. We know that in Babylonia from the earliest times, and in Assyria at dates contemporary with those of the kings of Judah, the Temples owned lands which they could cultivate or let, but not alienate.[1] There are examples of the same in the cases of other Semitic sanctuaries.[2] The Priestly Code speaks (as we shall see) of the consecration of houses and lands to the Lord, and this may well be held as implying the existence of the practice in times earlier than the date of that code. In the Latin kingdom of Jerusalem a number of *casales*, or villages with their lands, were assigned by the Crown, and gifted or bequeathed by individuals to the Church of the Holy Sepulchre and other religious corporations in Jerusalem;[3]

*Temple Lands.*

---

[1] Johns, *Bab. and Assyr. Laws*, etc., 209. For Egypt, cf. Gen. xlvii. 22.

[2] Cooke, *North Semitic Inscriptions*, Têma, 196, 198; cf. 40, 48, 241.

[3] Of these there are many instances in the collection of charters published by Röhricht, *Regesta Regni Hierosolymitani* (1893), with *Additamentum* (1904), *e.g.* Nos. 43, 52, 57, 58, etc. etc.

and under Mohammedan law, as we have seen, certain villages are *wakf*, to the Mosque of Omar; and *wakf* land, like the landed property of the ancient Babylonian Temples, is inalienable.[1]

In ancient times temples were used as places for the deposit of money, not only by kings but by private individuals as well. In Babylonia 'the temples did a certain amount of banking business,' and lent money on interest. They also advanced all kinds of raw material, derived from their tribute and rents, and did a considerable amount of trade.[2] And the like, as we shall see, was true of the Temple at Jerusalem in its later history. There is no evidence of the pre-exilic Temple having served as a bank for private depositors, unless we so interpret the fact that garments were left in pledge by the altar.[3] Even if we assume the practice as likely, we cannot prove that the priesthood derived revenues from such a source. But we can be sure that about the Temple, as about every other sanctuary of that early period, a considerable commerce tended to gather, of the profits of which the priesthood would have their share.[4]

*The Temple as a Bank and Trade Centre.*

It was universally recognised in antiquity that they who wait upon the altar shall have their portion with the altar. The daily food of the priests and their families was found in a share of the sacrifices made at their sanctuaries. In the earliest times the process of delivering these shares was rude and unsatisfactory. When an offerer had set apart the fatty portions of his animal for consumption on the altar,

*The Priests' Portions in Kind.*

---

[1] Above, p. 280.   [2] Johns, *op. cit.* 211.   [3] Amos ii. 8.
[4] See 'Trade and Commerce,' *Enc. Bibl.*, § 24.

and had put the rest to boil, that he and his friends
might eat before their God, the priest's servant came
with a flesh-hook of three teeth and stuck it into the
caldron, taking for his master all that the hook brought
up ; and in Shiloh the sons of Eli were blamed because
they sought to select their portion more definitely from
the raw meat.[1] Yet this innovation, regarded then as
sin, came to be the established law. No provision for
priests is specified in the earliest laws ;[2] but in the
Deuteronomic Code the priest's portion, whether of
sacrificed ox or sheep, is defined as *the shoulder, the two
cheeks, and the maw.* In addition, the people are to give
the priesthood the *rēshîth,* the *first* or *best,* usually translated *first-fruits,* of their corn, wine, oil, and fleece.[3]
Deuteronomy separately provides for the According to
*maʿăsēr* or tithe of corn, wine, and oil. Two Deuteronomy.
years out of three this is to be brought to the Temple
along with the firstlings of the herd and flock, and eaten
by the worshippers themselves before the Lord, the priest
getting his portion of the animals as above. Or if the
Israelite lives at a distance from Jerusalem he is to turn
the tithes and the firstlings into money, carry this to
the sanctuary, and buy for consumption by himself, his
household, and domestic Levite whatsoever he pleases.
The third year the tithe is to be stored within his own
doors for the poor and the Levites.[4] The offerings named
in Deuteronomy are the *zebah,* the common name for any
slaughtered and dedicated animal ; the *ʿolah,* or *offering on*

---

[1] I Sam. ii. 12-17.    [2] Exod. xxi. ff.

[3] Deut. xviii. 1-8, *rēshîth,* רֵשִׁית or רֵאשִׁית.

[4] Deut. xiv. 22-29 ; xii. 6 ; xxvi. 1-15 ; *tithe,* מַעֲשֵׂר ; *firstling,* בְּכֹר. The
exact relation of *tithe* and *rēshîth* is obscure.

*the altar of the whole victim*; the *terûmah of the hand*, or *contribution*; the *neder* or *vowed thing*; the *nĕdebah* or *free-will offering*; and the *shelem* (uncertain), all of which, except the *'olah*, were consumed by the offerers, less the portions laid on the altar and given to the priests.[1]

In Deuteronomy no mention is made of money offerings to the priests—they may, however, be included

Priests' Receipts in Money.

under the voluntary contributions—nor of money dues either given in payment for the *torôth*, the priestly decisions, or for the Temple upkeep. We have seen, however, from the story of the king's administration of the finance, that the priests individually made moneys from the people's offerings and that their interest in one class of these, the quit-moneys, was recognised and continued to them. It is this method of personal income which the prophets of the eighth century declare to be full of abuses. Hosea says the priests *fed on the sin of the people*.[2] Micah blames them for teaching for hire;[3] and Jeremiah charges them with covetousness and fraud, calling the Temple, even after the Deuteronomic reforms, *a den of robbers*, the market of an unholy trade, from which doubtless the priests were the principal beneficiaries.[4]

From the earliest times the priests of Jerusalem had their family estates, and it was the priest Jeremiah's

Estates in Land.

anxiety, even when he was in prison and though the country was derelict to the enemy, to exercise his right of pre-emption to his ancestral fields.[5]

---

[1] Deut. xii. 6, זֶבַח, עֹלָה, תְּרוּמָה, נֶדֶר, נְדָבָה; Deut. xxvii. 7, שֶׁלֶם.

[2] Hosea iv. 8; cf. the assignment of the *guilt* and *trespass* offerings (in kind) to the priests by the later law. Cf. Amos ii. 8; Isa. xxviii. 7; 1 Sam. ii. 27-36.    [3] Mic. iii. 11.    [4] Jer. vi. 13; xxiii. 11; vii. 11.

[5] 1 Kings ii. 26; Jer. xxxii. Cf. Amaziah, priest at Bethel, Amos vii. 17.

The pecuniary incomes, just described, must have enabled some priests to add to such estates. Probably no class in the community were more able to take advantage of the frequent mortgage of the peasants' lands.

The foreign rulers of Judah after the Exile made grants of material and money for the building, and occasionally for the furnishing, of the Temple. Under Nehemiah the Jews imposed upon themselves the third part of a shekel yearly for the service of the House,—the furnishing of the shewbread, the continual offerings, the periodic feasts, the holy things, the sin-offerings—and for all the business of the House, and they agreed to supply by turns wood for the fires. To the priests they assigned annually *the first-fruits of our ground and all manner of trees*, the *first* or *best of our meal* or *dough, the firstlings of our herds and of our flocks, with the first-born of our sons*, redeemable, of course, by money. But to the Levites, now distinct from the priests, as they are not in Deuteronomy, fell the tithes of the ground, and a tithe of these tithes the Levites handed over to the priests. The contributions of corn, wine and oil were stored in the *lĕshakôth* or Temple-chambers. Officials were appointed to superintend the storage and distribution, and with Nehemiah's thoughtfulness for the poor, the singers and doorkeepers received their daily portion. Indeed, by order of the king himself, a *settled provision* was made for the singers.[1]

> 2. Post-exilic, under Nehemiah.

---

[1] Neh. x. 32-39 (*first fruits*, בִּכּוּרִים); settled provision for singers, xi. 23 ; portions for them and doorkeepers, xii. 47 ; officials over the chambers, xii. 44. For earlier royal gifts, cf. Ezra vi. 8-10.

In the Priestly Code we find the arrangements for the
provision of the Temple and Priesthood, which were

Immense
Extension by
the Priestly
Code.
accepted under Nehemiah, codified along with
many additions and modifications all tending
to the further endowment of the priesthood,
on a scale far beyond that fixed by Deuteronomy. To
begin with, instead of the portions of the ordinary sacrifice assigned by the latter to the priests, these were to get
the better *breast and right shoulder*,[1] and in addition the
whole of some new offerings unknown to Deuteronomy,
*the sin and trespass offerings*, with besides the *meal
offering*.[2] But the law continues, still addressing the
priest: *and this is thine, the contribution or oblation of
their giving with all the wave-offerings of the children of
Israel*, the *tĕnûphôth* or breasts of the beasts which were
waved before the altar:[3] further, the *fat* or *best* of the oil,
vintage and corn, the *first-ripe fruits* of all that was in
the land;[4] further, anything that was *ḥerem* or *devoted* to
the Deity: all the first-born of men and animals.[5] As
with Nehemiah, the tithe belongs to the Levites, who
again give a tithe of it to the priests;[6] and, according
to another and later section of the law, this tithe shall not
be only of the ground as under Deuteronomy and in
Nehemiah's time, but shall include the tithe of cattle.[7]
The people also brought to the sanctuary a *contribution*
from their *meal* or *dough* and their *threshing*-floor;[8] and

[1] Lev. vii. 30-34.

[2] Num. xviii. 9, 10; sin o. חַטָּאָה; trespass o. אָשָׁם; meal o. מִנְחָה.

[3] Num. xviii. 11: תְּנוּפוֹת must be limited here to the breasts of the
beasts. See G. B. Gray *in loco*.

[4] Verses 12, 13. It is possible that the one is distinct from the other.

[5] Verses 14-20.   [6] Verses 21-32.

[7] Lev. xxvii. 30-33; cf. 2 Chron. xxxi. 6.   [8] Num. xv. 20.

to the priest fell the *skins* or *fleeces* of the animals sacrificed.[1]

All this represents an increase in the dues to the priests to an amount which Professor Wellhausen is right in calling 'enormous. What originally were alternatives are thrown together ; what originally was left free and undetermined becomes precisely measured and prescribed.'[2] Nor did it all come in kind. The Priestly Code arranges for the redemption of the first-born of men at five shekels a head, and of unclean beasts at the value of each *plus* one-fifth :[3] similarly the tithe might be redeemed for a fifth over its value.[4] Moreover, in the skins or fleeces of the sacrificed beasts the priests had a negotiable asset that, especially upon the great festivals, must have risen to a huge amount. They would dispose of those, after satisfying their own domestic wants, to the tanners and weavers of the town, probably for money. The Priestly Code fixes the Temple tax for each Israelite, which we saw under Nehemiah to be a third of a shekel, at half a shekel.[5] Thus, after meeting the necessary repairs to the Temple fabric, and their own personal expenses, there must have been in possession of the priesthood under the Second Temple a considerable store of money and other negotiable metal both as common Temple property and in possession of individual priests. If even Jeremiah could buy land, as we have seen, one may assume that those in closer connection with the Temple than he was had their private fortunes, some modest, some, in the case of the principal

*Revenues in money of the Temple and Priesthood.*

---

[1] Lev. vii. 8.          [2] *Proleg. to the Hist. of Israel* (E.T.), 158.
[3] Num. xviii. 15, 16 ; Lev. xxvii. 27.        [4] Lev. xxvii. 31.
[5] Ex. xxx. 13-16 : a shekel = 2s. 9d. (nearly).

priests after the Return, very considerable. Eliashib's
dealings with Tobiah [1] were no doubt profitable to him,
and later high-priests, by themselves or members of their
families, mingled largely in the trade and finance both of
the Temple and of the country as a whole. What opportunity they had may be realised from the particulars
given above.[2] On the subject of the revenues from the
Levitical cities, nothing can be said, as we do not know
whether the system was ever put into practice. But it
presupposes the possibility of the holding of estates in
land by the priestly class, and justifies us still further in

Temple
Estates.
assuming that besides their family estates,
the priesthood of the Second Temple held
domains, like the priests of other ancient sanctuaries, for
behoof of the general interests of the Temple. For this,
indeed, there is distinct proof in the law which provides
for the redemption of houses and lands consecrated by
individuals to the Lord.[3]

The embodiment of all these codes and separate laws,
dating from different stages of the development of the

[1] Neh. xiii. 4 ff.

[2] The above account is based on the generally accepted scheme of the date
of the Deuteronomic Code as (in the main) complete in the seventh century
before the Exile, and of the date of the Priestly Code in the Exile or after the
Return. Nehemiah's data thus occupy an intermediate position. So do
those of Ezekiel, which I have not included. The best authorities on the
subject will be found by the English reader in Wellhausen's *Prolegomena to
the Hist. of Israel* (trans. by Black and Menzies), ch. v.; in Robertson
Smith's *O.T. in the Jewish Church* (2nd edit.), Lectures xi.-xiii., with
App. F, and *Relig. of the Semites*, esp. Lectures vi., vii., xi. ; in W. R.
Harper's *The Priestly Element in the Old Testament*; in Driver's *Com-
mentary on Deuteronomy* (esp. on chs. xii., xiv., and xviii.), and G. B.
Gray's on *Numbers* (esp. on ch. xviii.), both in the *International Critical
Commentary*; and in Ryle's *Ezra and Nehemiah* in the *Camb. Bible for
Schools*. A useful summary will also be found in Schürer's *Hist, of the Jewish
People*, div. ii. vol. i. 230-234 (trans. by Taylor and Christie).

[3] Lev. xxvii. 14 ff. In verse 28 lands are *ḥerem* ; cf. *C.I.S.* ii. 199, etc.

Israelite ritual, in one law-book, all parts of which were
equally binding on the Jewish community from the fifth
or fourth century onward, gave opportunity <sub>3. Provision</sub>
to the authorities of later Judaism, destitute <sup>for Temple</sup> <sub>and Priests</sub>
as they were of the sense of historical <sup>in New</sup> <sub>Testament</sub>
discrimination, to augment and exaggerate <sup>Times.</sup>
the dues to Priesthood and Temple to an extraordinary pitch. The result, aggravated by the additions
which successive interpretations of the law effected, was
no small part of those burdens upon the national life in
New Testament times, of which we hear complaints
through the Gospels. Professor Schürer, in his *History of
the Jewish People in the Time of Jesus Christ*, has given
so admirable a summary of the Temple and priestly
imposts of the period, with full reference to the authorities,[1] that it is not necessary to do more here than
provide a general sketch of the various resources of the
Priesthood and Temple, in so far as these supported the
largest non-producing class of the population of Jerusalem,
and added to the City's purchasing-power. It is well to
note that for the Greek period we have two
estimates of the number of the priesthood. <sup>Number of</sup> <sub>Priests in the</sub>
Writing in this period, the author of the <sup>Greek Period.</sup>
Pseudo-Aristeas describes seven hundred ministrants as
at one service, besides a multitude of those who brought
forward the victims.[2] The author of the work on the
Jews, wrongly ascribed to Hecatæus of Abdera, but probably earlier than 200 B.C., for it is quoted by the Pseudo-

---

[1] Eng. transl., div. ii. vol. i. 234-254. The chief authorities on the subject
are Josephus, iii. *Ant.* ix. 1-4 ; iv. *Ant.* iv. 4 ; viii. 22 ; Philo, *De Praemiis
Sacerdotum et Honoribus*, and several treatises in Talmud and Mishna.
The latter I have consulted in the ed. of Surenhusius, 1703.

[2] Edition by Thackeray in Swete's *Introd. to the O.T. in Greek*, 536.

Aristeas, says, ' All the Jewish priests who are in receipt
of the tithe of the produce [of the soil] and administer
the public moneys [or affairs] are at the most fifteen
hundred.' [1] This does not seem to include the Temple
servants. Philo does not venture on numbers, but enables
us to infer how large they must have been from his
emphasis upon the innumerable multitude of sacrifices,
private and public, which were offered both every day,
and especially at the national assemblies and feasts. [2]
Josephus states that there were four tribes of priests,
each more than five thousand in number, but he may
mean to include the Levites and servants. [3] So numerous
were the priesthood, that they were divided throughout
this period into twenty-four courses. [4] These data do not
assist us to a definite idea of the number. The most
probable figure appears to be the fifteen hundred of the
Pseudo-Hecatæus, but if correct for the third century
before Christ, we should need to increase it considerably for
the Herodian period ; and if we add the Levites, singers,
gatekeepers and servants, we must estimate the non-producing classes attached to the Temple at many thousands.

As to the nourishment of these—the priests alone could
eat the flesh of the sin and guilt offerings, the meal-
offerings and the supplies of the shewbread,
but they could share with their families and
servants the breasts and right shoulders of the
thank-offerings, the flesh of the male firstlings of the cattle,

*The Priests' Receipts in kind.*

[1] Quoted from ' Hecatæus ' by Josephus, *C. Apion.* i. 22 ; cf. Reinach,
*Textes d'auteurs Grecs et Rom. relatifs au Judaïsme,* 229.

[2] Philo, *Vita Mosis,* iii. 19.

[3] *C. Apion.* ii. 8 ; Schürer (219 f.) suggests this is a corruption of the usual
*twenty-four,* but Josephus with all his love for great numbers would hardly
have ventured on twenty-four times 5000. Ezra ii. 36 ff. gives 4289.

[4] 1 Chron. xxiv. 7-18 ; *Talm. Jerus.,* ' Ta'anith,' iv.68.

and of every beast slaughtered extra-officially the maw, two cheeks and shoulder (for to this class of butcher-meat tradition transferred the Deuteronomic directions as to sacrificial victims), all cattle specially devoted as *ḥerem* to the sanctuary, and perhaps the tithe of the increase of cattle as well.[1] Of the produce of the soil they had besides the shewbread and their portion of the meal-offerings, the first-fruits of 'the seven kinds,'—these are wheat, barley, olives, vines, figs, pomegranates and honey;[2] the *terûmah* or *contribution* of these and other fruits from one-fortieth to one-sixtieth of the whole crop;[3] and, when these had been deducted, the tithe of the rest of the crop for the Levites, who (as above) had to hand on a tithe of what they received to the priest;[4] and a portion of the dough, one twenty-fourth from private individuals and half as much from public bakers.[5] Besides these supplies in food, the priests received the skins of the *ʿolah* and other victims,[6] and a proportion of the produce of the annual sheep-shearing. Josephus says that some priests, contemporaries of his, had 'gotten great riches from these tithes, which were their dues.'[7]

In money the priests enjoyed revenues from the payments already described under the law for the redemption of the male firstlings of man, and the animals which could not be eaten—ass, horse, and camel; and, according to Josephus, the quit-money

*Receipts in money.*

---

[1] *Mishna,* 'Zebaḥim,' v. 7 f.; 'Ḥullin,' x. 1; 'Ḥalla,' iv. 9.

[2] 'Bikkurim,' i. 3; Deut. viii. 8.     [3] 'Terumoth,' iv. 3.

[4] 'Maʿaseroth'; the *second tithe* was then taken off the crops on the basis of Deut. xiv. 22-26, but that, in accordance with this passage, was consumed by the worshippers 'Maʿaser sheni.

[5] 'Ḥalla,' ii. 7; *Tosephta,* 'Ḥalla,' i.

[6] Jos. iii. *Ant.* ix. 1; 'Ḥullin,' xi. 1 f.; 'Zebaḥim,' iv. 41, xii. 3; 'Sheḳalim,' vi. 6.     [7] *Life,* 12.

as well of persons who had been vowed to the sanctuary,[1] fifty shekels for a man and thirty for a woman; with various indemnities and fines. When the loyal Jew, who was anxious to fulfil all his debts to the sanctuary, lived at a distance from Jerusalem, he either paid them in kind to a resident priest, or, doubtless following the precedent set in Deuteronomy, sent their equivalent in money to the Holy City.

The mainstay of the support of the Temple service continued to be the tax of half a shekel imposed on every male adult by the Priestly Code.[2] This General Temple Revenues. was not only paid by the resident Jews in Palestine, but regularly gathered from those of the most distant Diaspora, and forwarded as convenient to Jerusalem.[3] Profits on things vowed went to the Temple treasury.[4] Voluntary gifts of money were also deposited in boxes in the Temple courts,[5] or sent from abroad; and there were frequent donations, by Gentiles as well as Jews, of gold, silver and other precious materials,[6] which were devoted to the embellishment of the holy fabric as well as to the support of the ritual. As in Nehemiah's time, the wood for the altar was furnished by certain families in rotation.[7]

According to the Mishna, when any one consecrated his properties to religion, after the portion fit for sacrifice

---

[1] iv. *Ant.* iv. 4.

[2] Matt. xvii. 24. In the Greek it is called τὸ δίδραχμον, or double drachma, of the coinage valid in Syria under the Romans. The half-shekel was almost equivalent to this. See above, p. 359 *n.* 5.

[3] On Babylonia, Josephus xviii. *Ant.* ix. 1; on Egypt, Philo, *De Monarch.* ii. 3; cf. *Mishna*, 'Shekalim,' ii.

[4] *Ibid.* iv. 6-8.　　　　　[5] Mark xii. 41 ff.; Luke xxi. 1 ff.

[6] Jos. xiii. *Ant.* iii. 4; v. *B.J.* v. 3; xiii. 6; 'Middoth,' iii. 8; 'Yoma,' iii. 10.　　　　　[7] *Mishna*, 'Ta'anith,' iv. 5.

was sold to worshippers and the money put into the treasury, the rest was to go to the treasury, also for the support of the Temple.[1] The language is vague, but 'the rest' may be held to include those Temple Lands. lands and houses which, as we have seen, it had been the custom from early times to devote to the Lord.[2] In all probability these gifts of land increased greatly during the last periods of the Temple's history. When Hecatæus of Abdera, in the beginning of the third century, says[3] it was forbidden to the Jewish priests to sell their lots of land, he probably refers to the Temple estates.

Finally, from this latest period we have ample evidence of the Temple as a place of safe deposit for money, not only by the rulers of the people but by private individuals. Josephus says that on the de- The Temple as Bank. struction of the City by Titus there was in the Temple treasuries 'an immense quantity of money, garments, and other precious goods there deposited ; . . . there it was that the entire riches of the Jews were accumulated, while the wealthy had there built chambers for themselves.'[4] A much earlier writer records a report that in the Greek period 'the treasury in Jerusalem was full of untold sums of money, so that the multitude of the funds was innumerable, and that they did not pertain to the account of the sacrifices' ; which report the high priest qualified by explaining 'that there were deposits of widows and orphans, and moreover something belonging to Hyrcanus, son of Tobias . . . and that, in all, there

---

[1] 'Shekalim,' iv. 7 f.

[2] Above, p. 360 ; see also 'Arakin,' viii. 1, 4, and other passages of the *Mishna.*

[3] Quoted by Diod. Siculus ; Müller, *Fragmenta Histor. Graec.* ii. 391.

[4] vi. *B.J.* v. 2 ; cf. i. *B.J.* xiii. 9.

were four hundred talents of silver and two hundred of gold.'[1] As we have seen, the Babylonian Temples lent money, grain and other goods. Burckhardt says that loans are sometimes required of the convents in Kesrouan, but these are regularly reimbursed in the time of the next harvest.[2]

From all this we see not only how large in these later times the revenues of the priesthood and Temple had become, but what a busy centre the latter was both of trade and finance. Among the chief priests there were many with large fortunes. The High Priest and his counsellors were trustees and accountants on a large scale—the more so that there was, except for a part of the period, no separate civil authority. But they were also great traders. To assist them in the reception, investment and distribution of the funds, they had a great staff of officials, duly organised and entitled.[3] But indeed in those days nearly every priest must have been a trader.

*Greatness of the Temple Finance and Trade.*

[1] 2 Maccab. iii. 6, 10 f.

[2] *Travels in Syria*, etc., 188.

[3] The best account of these in the Roman period is by Schürer (Eng. trans.), div. ii. vol. i. 260 ff.

# CHAPTER VIII

## TRADES, CRAFTS AND INDUSTRIES

OUTSIDE the royal and priestly classes, with their hosts of dependants, whose purchasing-power we have appreciated in the preceding chapters, lay the bulk of the citizens. The residence in Jerusalem of numbers of the landed *sarim* or nobles has already been noted. The attraction of the wealthier landowners to the court and capital began from the earliest days of the kingdom,[1] and was not always resisted as Barzillai and that lady of Shunem, who preferred to dwell among her own people, resisted it. As the old tribal system gave way, and still more when the great changes in the rural economy took place in the eighth century, and foreign invasions swept the country, the capital drew to herself more and more of the energy, the talent and the wealth of the nation.[2] The land even passed out of the hands of the older families into those of merchants, usurers and rulers, whose official position gave them opportunities to acquire estates mortgaged by their owners to pay the heavy taxes,[3] and the natural centre of all those classes was the capital. Such economic pro-

*Concentration of the national wealth and energy.*

---

[1] Mephibosheth and David, 2 Sam. ix. ; Barzillai, Chimham, and David, 2 Sam. xix. 31-39 ; *I dwell among mine own people,* 2 Kings iv. 13.

[2] See above, p. 281, and below, Bk. III. ch. ii.

[3] Neh. v.

cesses must have repeated themselves at different periods of prosperity and adversity after the Return from Exile. Others with the same results sprang from the opportunities of finance offered to the Jews under the fiscal administration of their foreign rulers. The story of how Joseph of Jerusalem amassed riches by farming the taxes of Ptolemy IV. or V.[1] (between 221 and 184 B.C.), affords the first instance of what afterwards became so notorious a profession in the nation, gaining for individual Jews at once a large fortune and the deep hatred of their fellows.[2] Though these farmers of the customs resided during office on the borders of the province of Judæa, like Zacchæus at Jericho,[3] they would naturally gravitate with their gains to the capital. Thus there was at all times in Jerusalem a class of well-to-do and even wealthy persons drawing much money towards the City.

*Financiers and Publicans.*

We turn now to the commercial and industrial classes of the population.

We have already seen what was the probable formation of the earliest *Sûk* or bazaar in the primitive Jerusalem: the settlement of a smith, a butter and salt dealer, a potter, all of them foreigners and confined to the supply of what the townsmen could not produce by their domestic industries.[4] Jerusalem lies aloof from the great trade-routes of the land, and whatever further commercial activity she

*The Beginnings of the Bazaar.*

---

[1] Jos. xii. *Ant.* iv. ; cf. Büchler, *Die Tobiaden*, etc., 43 ff., 91 ff.

[2] As in the Gospels, so in the *Talmud* and *Mishna*, e.g. 'B. Kama,' 94*a* : 'tax-gathers whose repentance is difficult.' 'Demai' 23*a*, 'an associate' (of the company of scholars or scribes) 'who becomes a tax-gatherer, shall be expelled.' Cf. *Mishna*, 'Baba Kama,' x. 2 ; 'Nedarim,' iii. 4.

[3] See above, p. 341       [4] See above, p. 312.

developed must have arisen in spite of the natural disadvantages of her site, and in consequence of her political rank and the mercantile and financial measures of her kings. A new capital is no sooner formed in an Oriental state than its lord invites or compels a number of foreign traders to settle about him. If his people be still mainly agricultural and unversed in the crafts, it is, as we shall see, builders and archi- Royal Patron-tects, dealers in gold ornaments and the like, age of Trade. whom he will chiefly select; as also traders in those foods and animals which his people do not produce, but which they have come to require, owing to their growing numbers and increased military ambition.[1] There can be no doubt that David adopted this policy, that Solomon extended it—witness his dealings with horse-traders—and that they were imitated by their successors in Judah. That these traders were chiefly Phœnician is both probable in itself, and confirmed by the fact that the earlier Hebrew for *dealer* is *Canaanite*. But the Hebrews soon learned their busi- Foreign and ness and rivalled their ability. Amos— Native perhaps himself a wool-seller, as well as a Traders. shepherd[2]—appears to describe the chief merchandise of his own countrymen as wheat;[3] but Hosea calls Northern Israel a very *Canaan*, as if expert in every form of trade.[4] The merchants of the City mentioned by Zephaniah[5] may be either Phœnician or Jewish; but her bazaars, through which Jeremiah seeks in vain for

---

[1] In illustration, take the case of Hayil in Arabia, cited below.
[2] *Book of the Twelve Prophets*, i. 79.
[3] Amos viii. 5 f.     [4] Hosea xii. 7.
[5] Zephaniah i. 11: *people of Canaan*, he calls them, but the name may have here its professional and not its ethnic meaning.

an honest man, are certainly those of Jewish traders, who falsely guarantee their goods with the oath, *As Jahweh liveth.*[1] The business in which all those engaged comprised both commodities consumed by the citizens themselves, and that transference of wheat and other goods to the Phœnicians which is mentioned by Ezekiel.[2] After the institution of the Deuteronomic festivals, the trade of Jerusalem was three times a year enormously enhanced. For Deuteronomy provides that pilgrims from a distance shall not bring their own stock with them, but turning it into money shall take this to Jerusalem and purchase there the material of the required sacrifices.[3] As we have seen, this material was largely sold to the pilgrims by the priests themselves, but there must have been many other traders, especially in salt, incense and such goods as the priests could not provide. On their return from exile the Jews could not at once have resumed their commerce, and the transit trade had altogether ceased. Nehemiah describes Tyrians as settled in the City and selling not only fish, but all manner of wares. Joel describes Jerusalem as a thoroughfare of strangers, and a still later prophet, writing in the beginning of the Greek period, implies that even the sanctuary contains them.[4] With the right of citizenship granted in Antioch and Alexandria to the Jews, very many of whom were traders, and with the growth of the crowds of pilgrims from the Greek world to Jerusalem, the number of Jewish traders having agents and correspondents of their own faith abroad must have increased through

---

[1] Jeremiah v. 1 ff.    [2] xxvii. 17. See above, p. 316.
[3] Deuteronomy, xiv. 24 ff. ; cf. above, p. 354 f.
[4] Nehemiah xiii. 16; Joel iii. 17 [Eng.]  'Zech.' xiv. 21.

the Greek period. Jesus ben-Sira finds it necessary to make many warnings against covetousness and fraud in trade.[1] By the Christian era the prevalence in Hebrew of Greek, and to a less extent of Latin, names for the objects and means of trade is very striking.[2] But it would be a mistake to conclude from this that all the trade with which the Jews had to do was in the hands of Greeks or Hellenised Syrians. Even in the Greek period the Jews had risen to great influence in Antioch, Alexandria and Cyrene;[3] while those of Asia Minor deposited in Cos 800 talents, or about £192,000.[4] Herod drew largely on the resources of his fellow-believers of the Diaspora, and Josephus gives an interesting account of the trade, finance and wealth of the Babylonian Jews.[5] All these results can hardly have been achieved without a considerable participation by the people in the trade of the time. Perhaps our Lord had this in view when He spoke of the Galilee of His time as a place in which a man could gain the whole world but lose his own soul. Still there were many obstacles against trade becoming characteristic of the Jewish people as a whole: as the strictures of the law, and especially the precepts relating to the Sabbath and things clean and unclean. Those against writing and carrying and putting a value on anything on the Sabbath must have made trade on that day impossible except

---

[1] Ecclesiasticus xxvi. 29 ff.; xxxvii. 11; viii. 13; xxix. 4 ff.; xli. 18; xlii. 3 f.; cf. Wisdom xv. 12.

[2] *Enc. Bibl.*, 'Trade and Commerce,' § 77. The fullest list of Greek terms will be found in Schürer, div. ii. vol. i. 33 f., 36 ff.

[3] Strabo, quoted by Jos. xiv. *Ant.* vii. 2.

[4] See Reinach, note 2, p. 91 of *Textes d'Auteurs Grecs et Romains relatifs au Judaïsme.*

[5] xviii. *Ant.* ix.; xx. *Ant.* ii. 3.

by desperate subterfuges, while the laws against unclean things operated still more widely. Moreover, the bulk of the brains of the nation were absorbed in other directions. To Greek observers of the time, the Jews are a nation given to sacred things and the service of their Deity; and Strabo, when recording the different peoples of Syria and their characteristics, speaks only of the Phœnicians as merchants.[1]

Parallel with the development of trade at Jerusalem was that in industrial and manufacturing pursuits.

Natural Unfitness of Jerusalem for Industries.

There never was a city which by its position was more unfitted than Jerusalem was to be the home of industries. About her lie none of the materials of manufacture nor any of the aids to it. Stone, hides and wool abound, but neither metals, clay, pigments, nor, in any quantity, timber. Nor are the roads suitable for wheeled vehicles. Here again the acute observer whom we have already quoted may be taken as summarising what must impress every intelligent visitor. Martin Kabátnik, writing in 1491-92, says: 'Jews and Christians have a poor subsistence, for there are few artisans at Jerusalem, and that because it does not lie on the high-road. For this reason industrial enterprise is hard for the people.'[2] Throughout her long and varied history, the name of Jerusalem has never been linked with any product of man's hands or original invention. When the Greeks first met with the Jews, this want of mechanic and artistic ability struck them in a nation from that ingenious East out of which they had derived so many arts and inventions. Apollonius of Rhodes, a teacher of Cicero,

[1] *Geogr.* xvi. 2.       [2] *Z.D.P.V.* xxi. 58.

declared 'that the Jews are the most inept of the Barbarians, and the only ones who have not contributed any invention useful to life.'[1] The apparent testimony to the contrary by the Pseudo-Aristeas that Jerusalem was a 'city of many crafts,'[2] does not refer to the technical originality of the citizens; and the writer, who is an obvious Jew, would in any case naturally exaggerate the abilities of his city.

David and Solomon, like other Oriental masters of new kingdoms, brought to their capital various skilful artisans from abroad : stone, wood and metal workers, weavers and dyers.[3] Some of these would settle permanently in the City and bequeath to their children the practice of their crafts. Native families of artisans on the same lines would spring up: masons, carpenters, blacksmiths and coppersmiths, all of whom with ruder capacities had been there from the first; potters, though one theory of the stamps upon old jar-handles implies that the best potteries were elsewhere ;[4] goldsmiths and silversmiths. Gradually, too, the various industries which in an agricultural society had been discharged within each household would severally become the business of specialists —such as weaving, tanning, fulling, and even baking.

*Crafts actually mentioned.*

---

[1] Quoted by Josephus, *Contr. Apion.* ii. 15 ; cf. Celsus in *Origen. Contr. Cels.* iv. 31.

[2] Πολύτεχνος. Thackeray's edition in Swete's *Introduction to Old Testament in Greek,* 539.

[3] According to 2 Chron. ii. 14, Huram-abi was skilful to work *in purple, in blue, in fine linen, and in crimson,* as well as in stone, wood and metals ; cf. iv. 16.

[4] Bliss and Macalister, *Excavat. in Palestine,* 1898-1900, 108 ff. But Macalister (*P.E.F.Q.,* 1905, 243 f. ; 328 ff. 'The Craftsmen's Guild of the Tribe of Judah' ; cf. *Bible Side-Lights from the Mound of Gezer*) takes the names as those of the potters, not of places.

Spinning was still done on the domestic distaff, but from an early time the phrase the *weaver's shuttle* seems to indicate the special workman. In Jeremiah's day there was a *Bakers' street,* to the ovens of which, as in New Testament times and to-day,[1] the women would send the dough kneaded in the household, and the *House of the Potter.*[2] Doubtless the gold- and silver-smiths, who were also image-makers, the weavers, dyers, all of whom Jeremiah mentions,[3] and the workers in stone, wood and metal, whom Nebuchadrezzar carried away, had each their own bazaar in the City. Harness and trappings were largely imported from Arabia,[4] where in El Jôf they are still a staple manufacture; but there must have been harness-makers, as there were shoemakers, in Israel.[5] The lowest of all classes, as is well known, were *the hewers of wood and drawers of water*: both of them very necessary elements in the life of Jerusalem. But the good artificer is not despised in the Old Testament: on the contrary, his gifts are regarded equally with those of the husbandman as from God.

In the Greek period the industries of Jerusalem continued to be similar to those given above. The smith, the potter, the moulder of copper, the gold- and the silver-smith, and the engraver, are all mentioned.[6]

The Crafts in the Greek Period.

> 'Without these shall not a city be inhabited,
> And men shall not sojourn nor walk up and down;
> They will maintain the fabric of the world,
> And in the handiwork of their craft is their prayer.'[7]

---

[1] *Mishna*, 'Ḥallah,' i. 7; Baldensperger, *P.E.F.Q.*, 1903, 75.
[2] Jeremiah xviii. 2.  [3] vi. 29; x. 9, 14; xxiv. 1.  [4] Ezek. xxvii. 20.
[5] Amos ii. 6.  [6] Wisdom xv. 7, 9; Ecclesiasticus xxxviii. 27-30.
[7] Ecclesiasticus xxxviii. 32, 34.

But the son of Sira, who speaks thus, adds that the craftsmen 'put their trust in their hands, and each becometh wise [only] in his own work; they shall not be sought for in the council of the people, and in the assembly they shall not rise on high.' They are far beneath the Scribe, whose 'wisdom cometh by opportunity of leisure.' Only 'he that hath little business shall become wise.'[1] A different spirit was manifested by later Rabbis. Rabban Gamaliel III. urged on the scribes engagement in some business besides the study of the Law, 'for exertion in both keeps from sin.'[2] Paul sustained himself by tent-weaving. The industries of Jerusalem must have remained during the Roman period the same as formerly. They were still incorporated in guilds, of whom the weavers and wool-workers had a 'bad reputation.'[3] Yet the chief industry of Judæa was the manufacture of woollen goods, while that of Galilee was of linen.[4] It is singular that in all the parables of our Lord, which contain many references to trading, there is none to a handicraft, though He was Himself the *son of a carpenter*.

The Western eye will be struck by the absence from this list of traders and craftsmen of the Miller, who in the history of Europe is one of the earliest specialists in industry. Nor is there any name for him in Biblical Hebrew, which yields us only *mill-maids*.[5] The work was done in each home by the women. *The sound of the millstones*—the peaceful

No Miller.

---

[1] Ecclesiasticus xxxviii. verses 31, 33, 24.    [2] 'Aboth,' ii. 2.

[3] See Delitzsch, *Jüdisches Handwerkerleben*.

[4] *Mishna*, 'Baba Kamma,' x. 9.

[5] The feminine participle טֹחֲנוֹת, Eccl. xii. 3; cf. Isaiah xlvii. 2; Exodus xi. 5, and (perhaps) Job xxxi. 10; cf. Matthew xxiv. 41.

drone and humming which still reaches the traveller's ears out of the doorways of the people—was as much domestic music in the days of Jeremiah as *the voice of the bridegroom, the voice of the bride, and the light of the candle.*[1] It is uncertain when the Miller first appeared in Palestine: that is when running water or a horse or ass was first used to turn the stones, and it became possible to employ very large ones. This was certainly before the Christian era, for the name miller appears in post-biblical Hebrew, and the Gospels use the phrase *ass-millstone.*[2] To-day water-mills are found only on the streams of the maritime plain, of Esdraelon and of Eastern Palestine. At the great waterfall of Tell-esh-Shihâb there are enough for the whole Ḥauran, and there I found a miller at the head of the community.[3] But in Jerusalem there is no running water, and in the place-names of the neighbourhood no memory of mills till you come to the Wâdy of Mills below Artas, along which ancient aqueducts run from the Pools of Solomon.[4] There are now in Jerusalem some ass- and horse-mills;[5] but down to the recent introduction of steam, the drone of the domestic quern continued to be almost as characteristic of the City's life as it was in the days of Jeremiah.

[1] Jeremiah xxv. 10.

[2] Miller in N.H., טַחֲנָא, *ṭaḥônā.* Ass-Millstone, μύλος ὀνικός, Matthew xviii. 6 ; Mark ix. 42.

[3] In Moab, on the Wâdy Waleh and elsewhere, I learned that the miller receives one-twelfth of the grain he grinds.

[4] W. eṭ Ṭawâḥîn. The only other name of the kind I ever heard about Jerusalem is the Ras eṭ-Ṭāḥûne, a hill covered with olives north-west from el-Bireh, which appears to owe its name rather to some rocky formation.

[5] Baldensperger, *P.E.F.Q.*, 1903, 76.

# CHAPTER IX

## GOVERNMENT AND POLICE

### I. BEFORE THE EXILE

JERUSALEM was the creation of a king, and kings of his dynasty *reigned in Jerusalem*—the formal phrase of their annalists—for over four hundred years. They built her walls and towers, her Temple and other public buildings; her conduits and reservoirs. They brought to her traders and artisans; they directed her imports and endowed her with treasures. Therefore it is not surprising that till the time of the Exile we hear of no civic assembly or constitution in Jerusalem, nor of any government of the town except by the monarch's own, and generally direct, administration. In the City's history there was no room for that gradual transition from the tribal to the royal authority, which took place in other towns of Israel. For Jerusalem had not been occupied by an Israelite tribe before David took her by force of arms, and gave her citadel his own name. While the elders of other cities or of the nation or of the land as a whole are frequently mentioned,[1] pre-exilic documents speak of *Elders* in Jerusalem only four or five times, and then but once are

*Pre-exilic Jerusalem: a Royal Administration.*

---

[1] *e.g.* Judges viii. 14; I Sam. xxx. 26; 2 Sam. xvii. 4; xix. 11; I Kings xx. 8; xxi. 8; 2 Kings vi. 32; Deut. xix. 12; xxi. 2 ff. etc. etc.

they called by the name of the City.[1]  No doubt there
were elders of the capital as of other towns, with their
functions among the minor matters of justice, but their
influence was overborne by the presence of the Crown
and Court.   In lists of authorities in which we should
expect them to appear, they are not present.   Even the
Chronicler, who imputes so many of the institutions of
his time to the pre-exilic period, speaks not of Elders
of Jerusalem under the monarchy, but always of those of
*Israel, Judah* or *the land*.   In arraigning the wickedness
of the City, Isaiah singles out her *rulers, princes, judges*
and *counsellors* ;[2] and the authorities in Jeremiah's time
were the *princes of Judah*,[3] or rather the *officers*, for,
though they may have included the king's sons, Jeremiah
identifies them with the high state officials.   Of notable
families, these held their posts from the king, were part
of his court, *his servants*,[4] and gave decisions in cases of
law—for instance, in the case in which Jeremiah was
defendant and the priests and prophets prosecutors.
Isaiah's *rulers, judges* and *counsellors* were doubtless of
the same class.   It is singular that among them pre-
exilic documents never mention a governor of the City—
not even in lists of high officials and on occasions on which
we might expect to find such an officer had he existed.[5]

[1] Isa. iii. 2, *elder* as a constituent of the strength of the state ; 14, *elders of
his people* ; Jer. xix. 1, *of the people* ; xxvi. 17, *of the land* (but here only as
witnesses) ; 2 Kings xxiii. 1, *elders of Judah and Jerusalem* (but the date of
this verse is uncertain : it is not clear that it belongs to the annals of Judah).
Neither in 2 Sam. xii. 17, *elders of his household, i.e.* David's, nor in 1 Kings
xii. 6, the elders *which had stood before Solomon*, are the elders of the City
meant.         [2] קְצִינִים, שָׂרִים, שֹׁפְטִים, יֹעֲצִים, Isa. i. 10, 23, 26 ; xxii. 3.

[3] Jer. xxvi. 10 ff., 16 ; xxxvi. 12, 14, 19.                [4] Jer. xxxvi. 24.

[5] 2 Sam. xxiii. 8 ff.; 2 Kings xi.; xviii. 18 ff.; xxiii. 1 f.; xxiv. 14 ff.; xxv. 18,
19 ; nor in 1 Chron. xviii. 14 ff. (David's officers) ; 2 Chron. viii. 9 (Solomon's
officers) ; 2 Chron. xix. 8 ff. (under Jehoshaphat).

Once, however, the Chronicler gives the title *Sār ha‘Ir*, *Prince*, or *Officer*, *of the City*, to Maaseiah under Josiah,[1] in a passage which we shall find reasons for considering reliable. But if the title be not an anachronism, the office was held like those of the other *Sārîm* from the king, just as was the case in the other Israelite capital of Samaria.[2] Yet it is strange that we do not find any holder of it upon one or other of the lists or occasions already referred to. Thus the government of the City under the monarchy was royal, and for the most part directly so. The fact is confirmed by the absence of all mention of watchmen other than the one in the king's house;[3] or of police, or executioners, other than the royal guard, the mercenaries of the palace.[4] As we see from the story of Jeremiah, the prisons were within the courts of the palace,[5] though the priests also had penal powers. Between the royal administration, then, and those whom the documents of the time call the *men*, or *inhabitants of Jerusalem*, there was no other governing body. When opposition to a reigning monarch arose, it was either from his own *servants* or courtiers, or from the priests with the garrison on their side, or from the whole body of the people. Unlike other towns, whose *elders* enjoyed a certain independence of the Crown, pre-exilic Jerusalem had no constituted authority from among her own citizens.[6]

---

[1] 2 Chron. xxxiv. 8.        [2] 1 Kings xxii. 26.

[3] 2 Sam. xiii. 34; cf. xviii. 24; 2 Kings ix. 17.

[4] 2 Kings xi. Similarly in N. Israel, x. 25.

[5] Palace: Jer. xxxii. 2; xxxvii. 15, 21; xxxviii. 6, 13; Temple: xx. 1 ff.; xxix. 26.

[6] This opinion would have to be modified if it could be proved that the Chronicler in 2 Chron. xix. 8-11 were drawing his details from a genuine pre-exilic source. That, however, is doubtful. Of the supreme court which Jehoshaphat is here said to have set up in Jerusalem, consisting of Levites,

## 2. AFTER THE RETURN, 536-444 B.C.

A very different state of affairs meets us in Jerusalem after the Exile.  In the first place, those who returned from
Very different Constitution after the Exile. Babylonia—the *Gôlah* or *Bnê ha-Golah*, as they called themselves, *The Captivity* or *Sons of the Captivity*—came back not to a kingdom but to a *mĕdînah* or *district* (and city) of the Persian Empire : to what so far as they themselves were concerned was but a colony (though on their fathers' lands) of the Jewish nation, the material bulk of which, as well as its spiritual authority, still resided in Babylonia.   The hopes which prophecy revived among them[1] of a crowned head for themselves, a prince of the house of David, were dissipated by the death or fall of Zerubbabel, and the Persian kings gave them no more governors from their own royal house.  Secondly, the returned Exiles were organised by their families.   That is to say, the old tribal organisation of the people, modified by the principle of locality or neighbourhood, was anew defined ;[2] and elders and heads of households, who had been the only instruments possible for the administration of the Law in Exile,[3] returned to Palestine invested with habits of authority which had already been restored to them for two generations.   But, thirdly, if the Jews who settled in Jerusalem and her

priests and heads of houses, there is no word in the Book of Kings ; and the whole language is the Chronicler's own (Wellh., *Hist.*, E.T. 191).   Even the name Zebadiah, given to the prince of the house of Judah who presided over this court on its civil side, is one which occurs only in Chronicles and other post-exilic writings.  See further, below, pp. 387 f.

[1] See below under Zechariah, p. 381.        [2] Neh. vii. 6 f. = Ezr. ii. 1 f.

[3] Ezekiel viii. 1 ; xiv. 1 ; xx. 1.   Elsewhere it is *the house of Israel* that he addresses, iii. 1, etc. ; iv. 3 ; xvii. 1 ; xx. 27 ; xxxvi. 17 ; or *the children of thy people*, xxxiii. 1.

neighbourhood after the Exile were thus a democratic colony—democratic, that is, in a patriarchal sense— they were governed, as the people had not been governed even under the Deuteronomic régime, by their religious authorities.[1] Their hopes of a king were shattered, but their priesthood remained; and to the High Priest they transferred at a very early date the crown which the prophet Zechariah had at first designed for the monarch. They built a Temple in Jerusalem, but no palace; and the Temple had its courts fortified upon the most defensible hill in Jerusalem long before the City walls were rebuilt. At first the High Priest may have exerted little authority. But the law which the people accepted under Ezra and Nehemiah gave him the highest rank in the community; and in the absence of a prince of the people, the subsequent holders of the office, aided by the large priesthood under them, soon realised their legal rights. In the Greek period the High Priest was the civil as well as the religious governor of Jerusalem. The following are the details of the process.

The forces to which Haggai appeals are Zerubbabel the prince, Jehoshua' the priest, and the *rest of the people*.[2] To Zechariah God and the City are the two units of religion (520-518 B.C.).[3] Virtue, symbolised by the chief product of the district, flows from Him to her through *two olive branches, two sons of oil*, the prince and the priest. The prince has the precedence and the crown. The priest is at his right hand: if he is worthy he shall judge God's house and keep His

Haggai, Zechariah, and 'Malachi.'

---

[1] Ezekiel xliv. 23 f. had already directed that the priests should judge, not only in ceremonial, but in civil cases.    [2] Hag. i. 12, 14; ii. 2.

[3] Zech. i. 16 f. (*I am returned to Jerusalem*); ii. 1-13; iii. 2; viii. 2 (*I am jealous for Sion*), 3 f.

Courts.[1] When Zerubbabel failed, Zechariah himself, or
a later hand, changed this, and gave the priest the crown.
Even before this the priest had a number of colleagues,
*men of omen*, who *sit before him*.[2] But according to
'Malachi' some sixty years later, the priests are unworthy; the discipline of the sacrifices and the Temple
is decayed. 'Malachi' complains of priests and worshippers, but of no rulers or judges.[3]

### 3. UNDER NEHEMIAH, 444-432 B.C.

When Nehemiah came to Jerusalem he found the same
unworthiness among the priests, and even in the High
Priest, who seems to have had no good influence on the government of the City.[4] Nehemiah himself was invested with the powers of
*Peḥah* or governor of the *Mĕdînah*, under the Satrap of
the trans-Euphrates Province of the Empire. The local
authorities in Jerusalem he calls *Sĕgānim*: *rulers, magistrates* or *deputies*.[5] These are clearly Jews, for they are
reckoned in the genealogies of Israel, and charged with
trespass in marrying foreign wives.[6] With them were
associated—or perhaps the terms were convertible—what

*Civil Administration under Nehemiah.*

[1] Precedence of the prince, iv. 6 ff.; vi. 9-15 (the original text of which
assigns the crown to Zerubbabel). The office of the priest, iii. 1-7 (not
attained without controversy); vi. 13 (LXX., at right hand of prince). See
*Book of the Twelve*, ii. 309. [2] Zech. iii. 8.
[3] 'Mal.' i. 6; ii. 1-9; iii. 3 (priests); i. 13 f.; iii. 5-11 (worshippers).
[4] Neh. xiii. 4 ff., 10 ff., 28 ff. Cf. Ezra ix. 1, x. 18.
[5] Neh. ii. 16: סְגָנִים; an Assyrian or Babylonian term, *Shaknu*, one
appointed or instituted to an office (Del. *Assyr. Handwörterbuch*). On the
cuneiform inscriptions and in Jer. li. and Ezek. xxiii. applied to generals and
governors of provinces. The Greek form was ζωγάνης.
[6] Neh. vii. 5, Ezra ix. 2. Neh. v. 17 must therefore be read so as to make
*Jews* and *rulers* synonymous; *besides those which came from the heathen about
us.* So the Vulgate.

Ezra calls the *Sārîm, officers* or *princes*, but Nehemiah the *Sārîm* and *Horîm, nobles* or free-born Jews, so that the whole congregation as registered and taking upon themselves the law are said to consist of *Horim, Sĕganim, and the People.*[1]  Elsewhere the popular assembly, which gathers to discuss reforms and to ratify the law it is to live under, is described as *all the men of Judah and Benjamin; the Sarim of the whole Congregation* or *Kahal; the people gathered as one man; the children of Israel assembled; all who have separated themselves from the peoples of the land unto the Law of God, their wives, sons and daughters, every one having knowledge and understanding, who cleave to their brethren the Horim and enter into ban and oath to walk in God's Law.*[2]  *Elders* are named as such only under Darius I., and by Ezra on his arrival.[3]  Thus we may conceive of the authority in all religious and local affairs as emanating from the whole adult population, who covenanted with their God to live by the Law; while from the *elders* of the *noble* or *free-born* families would be selected the *Sarim,* whom we may define as *persons in office,* or *Sĕganim, deputies* (that is of the Persian authority). To these would be committed the local administration of justice and other affairs in Jerusalem and the townships of the country.  But all were under the power and subject to the direct interference of the *Peḥah,* or Persian governor.  When he had set up the walls and the gates, Nehemiah gave his brother Ḥanani and Ḥananiah, *the Sar,*

---

[1] Neh. vii. 5.  The other references are Ezra ix. 2; Neh. ii. 16; iv. 8 [14 Eng.], 13 [19 Eng.]; v. 7, 17; vi. 17; vii. 5; ix. 38; xi. 1; xii. 40; xiii. 11, 17.  *Heads of families,* Ezra i. 5; ii. 68; Neh. vii. 70.  *Rulers,* a moneyed class, v. 7.

[2] Ezra x. 1, 9, 14; Neh. viii. 1; ix. 1; x. 28.

[3] Ezra v. 9 (Aramaic Document); x. 8; cf. 14, *elders and judges of every city.*

or *Officer, of the Castle, charge over Jerusalem,* with the particular duties of seeing to the shutting and opening of the gates and of appointing *Mishmĕrôth* or *watches* from among the inhabitants, *every one in his own watch, and every one over against his own house.* He also instituted a special police from among the only classes whom, as we shall see, he could thoroughly trust: the *Levites, singers and gatekeepers* of the Temple.[1] Further, he gave direct orders for the shutting of the gates upon the Sabbath to the exclusion of foreign traders; and in his great energy he did not hesitate to take into his own hands the enforcement of other laws.[2]

It is well to remind ourselves here of how a town was watched in those early days. The people selected *a man*
The City Watchman. *from among themselves, and set him for their watchman;* and he warned the people of the approach of danger by blowing a horn.[3] During the rebuilding of the walls *he that blew on the horn* stood by Nehemiah.[4]

### 4. FROM NEHEMIAH TO THE MACCABEES, 431-168 B.C.

I have called the government in Nehemiah's days a 'system,' and it proceeded under the sanction of an accepted law, written and detailed. But
Factions in the Community. some of the last details I have quoted, and indeed all the records, make it clear that for the time the 'system' was held together and enforced largely by the energy of Nehemiah himself, who had no successor; and that within the covenanting community there were

---

[1] Neh. vii. 1-3.                    [2] xiii. 15-31.
[3] Ezek. xxxiii. 2 ff.; cf. Amos iii. 6.        [4] Neh. iv. 18 [Hebr. iv. 12].

classes or factions which were certain to break loose when Nehemiah was no longer present. On the one hand were the chief priestly families and some of the lay nobles, even among those lately returned from Babylonia, who were far from loyal to Nehemiah's purposes, and related themselves in marriage, or conducted correspondence, with the hostile forces outside the community.[1] Nor were these lay and priestly factions, though thus bound by a common temptation, wholly at one among themselves; their particular interests must have frequently diverged. But over against the ambition and licence of both lay the stricter party, devoted to the law, either professionally because they were its scribes and doctors, or with that real conscience for its authority which never died out of the mass of the Jewish population. These we may consider as the more democratic party. Finally, the law itself was not yet complete; there is evidence that it received additions after Nehemiah's time. Here, therefore, was not only room for such a development of the constitution as we shall find taking place up to the time of the Maccabees, but all the materials for that controversy and struggle between factions, through which we may be equally sure the development proceeded.

Though the priests set their seals to the law along with the rest of the Jews, Nehemiah assigned to them no posts among the executive officers of Jerusalem ; and indeed while the High Priest himself was traitorous to the measures of the reforming governor, there is evidence that the latter could almost as little rely on the general body of the priest-

The Constitution in the Priestly Law.

---

[1] See below, Bk. III., chapter on Nehemiah.

2 B

hood.[1]  But the Law, which Ezra and he had induced the
people to accept, gave to the priesthood, and in particular
to the High Priest, with that branch of the tribe of Levi
to which he belonged—for the office was now hereditary—
a supremacy not only over the Temple and its ritual, but
over the nation as a whole.   The priestly legislation,
which was the new element introduced into the Law by
Ezra, knows no king.   The High Priest (to whom the
earlier ' Law of Holiness ' ascribes a peculiar sanctity, but
whom it still regards as one among his *brethren*[2]) is, in
the body of the Priestly Code and in its later additions,
*the Anointed*,[3] and is invested with, besides the oil, the
turban and the diadem.[4]   He stands before God an
equivalent unit with the nation : *thyself and the people* ;[5]
his offering for pardon is equal to theirs ;[6] and the
term of a high priest's life determines the period during
which a homicide must dwell in a city of refuge.[7]   On the
other hand, the Priestly Code hardly mentions the elders
by that name.[8]   The High Priest is to surround himself with the *princes of Israel* or *of the congregation, heads
of families*, elsewhere numbered as twelve, to represent the
different tribes.[9]   They are described as the *chiefs of the*

---

[1] See below, under Nehemiah, Bk. III.

[2] Lev. xxi. 10-15 ; cf. xxi. 1-9.

[3] הַמָּשִׁיחַ, Lev. iv. 3 ; viii. 12 ; cf. Exod. xxix. 7 ; Num. xxxv. 25.

[4] Ex. xxix. 6.    [5] Lev. ix. 7, etc.

[6] Lev. iv. 3 f., 13 ff.    [7] Num. xxxv. 25.

[8] Lev. iv. 15 is really the only passage (*elders of the congregation*, עדה), for
in Lev. ix. 1 the phrase is probably a later insertion.

[9] Num. vii. 2 ; cf. i. 4-15.   The term *princes of Israel*, נְשִׂיאֵי יִשְׂרָאֵל,
seems to belong to the supplementary parts of P.   The body of the document
calls them *p. of the congregation*, נ" הָעֵדָה, Ex. xvi. 22 ; Num. iv. 34 ; xvi. 2
(250 of them) ; xxxi. 13 ; xxxii. 2 ; Jos. ix. 15, 18 ; xxii. 30.   See Driver,
*Introd.* 132 f., and G. B. Gray on Num. vii. 2.

*thousands*, or *clans of Israel*, and as *those who are called to the Diet* or *Assembly* ; they attend the national leader and hear petitions with him from the tribes ; they represent the nation in engagements with other peoples.[1]  In other words, they are the same as the *elders* or *Sarim* of Ezra, Nehemiah, and the earlier Old Testament writings.  But we must not fail to notice the higher dignity of the name given to them by the Priestly Code; this has hitherto been reserved for the royal head of the nation.[2]  The change appears to represent a step in the political evolution which we are following ; the selection, perhaps, when a civil governor ceased at Jerusalem, of the most notable chiefs of families to assist the High Priest in the govern-. ment.  But just as in the data supplied by Nehemiah there is no evidence of the incorporation of the *Sarim* in a definite court or college, so with the *Nĕsî'îm* of the Priestly Code, although it numbers those who are to stand round Moses as twelve.  The Elohist states a number destined to prevail in the later history, *seventy elders* whom Moses was bidden to take with him to the mountain, and again to the door of the Tabernacle, where the spirit of prophecy descended upon them.[3]

The Chronicler (*circa* 300) attributes to King Jehoshaphat (873-849) the institution of a definite court with a double jurisdiction, secular and sacred :[4]  *In Jerusalem did he set up of the Levites and the priests, and of the heads of the families of Israel for the mishpat, or cultus, of Jahweh, and for judging the*

The High Court of the Chronicler.

---

[1] For these references see in previous note the passages on *the princes of the congregation*, and note 2 on p. 390.

[2] The King, 1 Kings xi. 34 ; Sheshbazzar, Ezra i. 8 ; and especially by Ezekiel vii. 27 ; xii. 10 ; xlv. 7 ff., etc.

[3] Ex. xxiv. 9 ; Num. xi. 16, 24 : with Moses, 71, *Mishna*, ' Sanh.' i. 6.

[4] 2 Chron. xix. 8-11.

*inhabitants of Jerusalem* [1] *. . . Whensoever any controversy
shall come to you from your brethren, that dwell in their
cities, between blood and blood, between law and commandment, statutes and judgments, ye shall advise them. . . .
Amariah the chief priest is over you in all the matters of
Jahweh, and Zebadiah, the son of Ishmael, the ruler of the
house of Judah, in all the King's matters, and the Levites shall
be scribes,* or *officers, before you.* There is no doubt that the
Chronicler sometimes employs ancient and reliable sources
of information, not drawn upon by the editors of the
Book of Kings. Is this one of them? The definiteness
of the information, and the division of the presidency
between the secular and sacred heads of the community
(which did not exist in the Chronicler's own day), pre-
dispose us in favour of the passage. But on the other
hand, the diction is the Chronicler's own; and we may
feel sure that if an institution so basal and definite had
existed before the Exile, the Books of Kings would not
have failed to notice it,[2] and some remnant of such a
court would have survived in the days of Nehemiah.
The division between secular and sacred seems to exclude the theory that the passage is a mere reflection
of the conditions in the Chronicler's own day; for then,
as we shall see, the High Priest presided over both
Temple and Nation; but the passage may be the
Chronicler's protest against this monopoly. Otherwise
it is the recollection of something that really prevailed
after the Exile, and before the High Priests had absorbed
the civil supremacy. Levites and priests have a place in
this Court not given them by the Priestly Code.

[1] With LXX. read יֹשְׁבֵי ירוּשָׁלַם for "י וַיֵּשְׁבוּ.
[2] Cf. Wellhausen, *Prol.* (E.T.) 191.

No further light is thrown upon the subject by any other Old Testament writer. Joel, about 400 B.C., and the author of ' Zechariah ' ix.-xiv., some eighty years later, are too engrossed with disasters to the land, physical and political, and too hurried into Apocalypse, to give thought to the institutions of their City. The *assembly of the congregation* which Joel summons is for worship. In the Book of Proverbs none but kings and princes,[1] a *Sar*, a judge, and a ruler are mentioned. Bribery and false witness are condemned ; going to law is deprecated ; but there is a singular absence from these popular sayings of the names of the national institutions.

Consequently our next witness is a Greek, the first of Greeks to have any real information about Jerusalem. Hecatæus of Abdera, *circa* 300 B.C.,[2] reports that 'the Jews have never had a king, but committed the presidency of the people throughout to that one of the priests who was reputed to excel in wisdom and virtue ; him they call Chief Priest, and consider to be the messenger to them of the commands of God. It is he who in the *ecclesiae*, and other synods, transmits the precepts' or orders.[3] The Jews prostrate themselves before this ' interpreting Chief Priest.' Moses ' chose the most genial and able men to preside over the nation, and instituted them as priests' for the service of the Temple, but also as 'judges in the most serious cases, and entrusted them with the care of the laws and morals.'

---

[1] נדיב and נגיד.

[2] Quoted in a fragment of Diod. Siculus, Müller, *Fragm. Histor. Graecorum*, ii. 391 f. ; cf. Reinach, *Textes . . . Relatifs au Judaïsme*, 14 ff.

[3] Τὰ παραγγελλόμενα.

Hecatæus adds, that while all the citizens had the national territory distributed among them by lot, 'the lots of the priests were the greater that they might enjoy the more considerable revenues, and so give themselves without distraction to the worship of the Deity.' Here, just as with the Chronicler, is a regular court of priests. Not only is it presided over by the High Priest, but is subject to his absolute powers as mediator and interpreter of the Divine will. Like other Greek writers on the Jews, Hecatæus was blinded to the share of the laity in the conduct of affairs, probably by the brilliance of the national worship and the priesthood. Yet that share, as we have seen, was a considerable one, and it was secured to the laity by the Law.

The next evidence may be taken from the Greek translation of the Law, which was made in the third Greek Version of the Law. century. Sometimes this version renders the Hebrew words for *elders* and *princes* by their Greek equivalents, *presbuteroi* and *archontes*, or *archēgoi*, but sometimes also by the collective term *Gerousia* or *Senate*;[1] and translates the description of them as *summoned to the Diet* by the phrase *called together to the Boulē* or *Council*.[2]

In the 'Letter of Aristeas to Philokrates' we have not, as it pretends, the testimony of a Greek ambassador from The Pseudo-Aristeas. Ptolemy Philadelphus, 286-247, to the High Priest Eleazar; but the work, perhaps about 200, of a Jewish writer, well acquainted with the City and

---

[1] Γερουσία, Ex. xxiv. 9 (cf. 1); Lev. ix. 1, of the elders of the nation, and always, save once in Deuteronomy: xix. 12; xxi. 2-4, 6, 19; xxii. 15-18; xxv. 7-9, the Γερουσία τῆς πόλεως. In xxi. 20, for *elders* the LXX. reads *men*.
[2] קְרִיאֵי מוֹעֵד (or קְרוּאֵי), σύγκλητοι βουλῆς, Num. i. 16; xvi. 2; xxvi. 9.

the land.[1]  He represents Ptolemy as treating with
Eleazar alone, and describes the power and splendour of
the latter, ' the ruling chief priest,' in terms which recall
those of Hecatæus.  The High Priest consults with an
assembly ' of the whole nation.'  The constituents of the
nation are the host of priests ; the Temple servants ; the
carefully selected garrison of the Akra, which, 'standing
on a very lofty spot with many towers, dominated the
localities about the Temple'; and the citizens.[2]

Ecclesiasticus, or the Wisdom of the Son of Sira, about
180 B.C., sheds little light on the exact forms of government in Jerusalem ; the spirit of the author is Jesus ben
more concerned with their moral influence. Sira.
It was *Simon the son of Joḥanan, the priest, great one of
his brethren and the glory of his people,* who by repairing
and fortifying the Temple, making a reservoir and building the wall, *took thought for his people against the spoiler,
and strengthened his City against siege.*[3]  His glory in his
robes at the altar, surrounded by the sons of Aaron in
their glory, the choir and all the people of the land, who
bowed down before him as he blessed them, is vividly
described.[4]  The *congregation* or *assembly* is mentioned
under both of its Hebrew names, and in one case called
*the congregation of God's gates* (?) ;[5] associated both by

[1] Swete, *Introd. to the O. T. in Greek*, 10-16.  The text of the letter edited
with introd. by H. St. J. Thackeray will be found in the Appendix, 499-574.
[2] The High Priest, 519, 521, 525-527, 533-536 ; the citizens, 519, 527; the
other priests and Temple servants, 534-536 ; the Akra and garrison, 537, of
the above edition.  The presiding chief priest (τοῦ προστατοῦντος ἀρχιερέως,
533) convenes the whole people (συναγαγόντες τὸ πᾶν πλῆθος, 527).
[3] L. 1-4.  I have followed the Hebrew text from the edition in *The
Wisdom of Ben Sira*, by Schechter and Taylor (Camb., 1899, p. 19).
[4] L. 5 ff.
[5] Both עדה, συναγωγή, and קהלה, ἐκκλησία, iv. 7, vii. 7.  עדת שערי אל.

this name and otherwise with judicial processes.[1] The *congregation* is also equivalent to *the people*.[2] There are *elders*,[3] *great men of the people*, and *leaders of the City* or *of the Ecclesia*;[4] *dynasts* or *men in power*,[5] whom the Hebrew calls *rulers* and *judges*.[6] It is evident from more than one passage that the common man most in the way of promotion to these dignities is *the scribe*.[7] Among the worst evils to be feared in Jerusalem are the *slander of the town, mob law, and false accusation*.[8] On the whole, the Son of Sira may be said to write from a democratic point of view, and in a popular temper, but with special emphasis on his own profession, the scribes.

Such is the literary evidence as to the government of the City and Nation, which dates from within the period itself. I turn now to the later histories. It

Josephus, 1st and 2nd Maccabees.

is in this very period, and towards the end of the third century B.C., that Jewish historians begin to speak of a *Gerousia* or *Senate* beside the High Priest. Josephus quotes a letter of Antiochus the Great, 233-187, in which the king reports that upon his approach to Jerusalem the Jews came out to meet him with their *Gerousia*, and that he has discharged *the Gerousia*, the priests, the Temple scribes, and the sacred singers, from all taxes.[9] The Second Book of Maccabees states that the *Gerousia* sent three men to Antiochus Epiphanes in

---

[1] xxiii. 24, and especially xxxviii. 33. The adulterer, too, is punished in the broad places of the City, xxiii. 21 ; the adulteress brought *out* to the congregation, 24.

[2] xxxiii. 18 [19] ; xliv. 15 ; l. 20.    [3] vi. 34 not in the Hebrew.

[4] Μεγιστᾶνες (also found in the LXX.), Heb. שָׁלְטוֹן, iv. 7 ; xxxiii. 18 [19], and ἡγούμενοι, x. 2 ; xxxiii. 18 [19].    [5] iv. 27 ; x. 3, δυναστῶν, מוֹשְׁלִים.

[6] x. 2, κριτής.    [7] x. 5 ; xxxviii. 24-xxxix. 11.

[8] Διαβολὴν πόλεως καὶ ἐκκλησίαν ὄχλου καὶ καταψευσμόν, xxvi. 5, not in Hebrew.    [9] Jos. xii. *Ant.* iii. 3.

170, and quotes a letter from Antiochus, of date 164, addressed to the *Gerousia of the Jews and the other Jews.*[1] The First Book of Maccabees speaks, to begin with, only of *rulers and elders*[2] in Israel; but of the letter, which it quotes as sent to the Spartans about 144, the superscription runs: *Jonathan the High Priest and the Gerousia of the nation, and the priests and the rest of the people of the Jews.*[3] The formal inscription of the national gratitude to Simon is dated as follows: *In the third year,* 139 B.C., *of Simon the High Priest and Prince of the People of God* (?), *in a great Congregation of Priests and People, Rulers of the Nation and Elders of the Land.*[4]

From all this evidence we may reasonably infer that the formation of a definite Synod or Senate at Jerusalem came about in the following manner. First, the High Priest, whose rank was hereditary, extended his civil power: partly no doubt through the absence of a Persian governor of Jerusalem, partly by the great ability of some holders of the office, but chiefly by the support of the large priesthood and the possession of a fortified temple; under the sanction of the Law accepted by the people from Nehemiah, and with those opportunities of adding to it, which were taken advantage of in the generations subsequent to Nehemiah. Such a president of the nation and interpreter of the Law would seek to fortify his growing office by a council not merely of his own profession and family, but of the leaders of the foremost lay families, the *elders of Israel*, or at least of those of

*Conclusions from the foregoing evidence,*

*as to the growth of the Senate:*
*1. Under the Persians.*

---

[1] 2 Macc. iv. 44; xi. 27.   [2] 1 Macc. i. 26; the date referred to is 168 B.C.
[3] xii. 6 (cf. the equivalent, *elders of the people*, 35; *elders and nation of the Jews*, xiii. 36; *high priest, elders, priests, and residue of the people*, xiv. 20.
[4] xiv. 27 ff.; for εν Σαραμελ read perhaps ישר עם אל.

them who, as *Sarim* and *Seganim*, had vested rights to
official positions, and were recognised by the law as
*Něsî'îm* or *Princes*.  And it would be in his interest, as
well as conformable to the tendency of the Law, to have
their eligibility, their number and their functions more or
less clearly defined.  As for their number, the Law gave
precedents : *the seventy elders* and the *twelve princes*.  No
doubt there were many controversies over the matter
between the priests on the one side and the laity on the
other.  But the High Priest had the advantage.  He was
*The Anointed*; and among a people so absorbed in
worship, whose only legal temple was a citadel within
their capital, the impression of his sacred rank and of his
splendour as he performed the rites, as well as of his
material power, must have been, as several of our witnesses
both Greek and Jew testify, not less than overpowering.
On the other hand, there were the long-established rights
of the heads of the principal lay families to a voice in
public affairs ; and behind all was the splendid consciousness which, as we shall see, Israel never lost, that the
ultimate source of authority was the people itself, the
whole congregation and assembly of the faithful.  How
far the balance of power and interest among these forces
was crossed or disturbed by political crises, such as the
disasters to the City, we have no means of knowing ;
but it is extremely probable that such crises would give
now one faction and now another the advantage.  On the
whole, as we see from nearly all our witnesses, the
High Priest prevailed and strengthened his supremacy.
Probably, as in the Greek period, he was responsible to
Persia for the taxes of his people.  Whether in the
records of the period itself or in the histories of Josephus,

he stands wonderfully on high.   Yet we must remember that the lay leaders passed into the period with ancient and well-confirmed habits of governing ; that the Law had partly organised them ; that both it commands, and some of our witnesses testify to, their presence round the High Priest on many national occasions; and that others associate with them the priests.   Josephus cannot be wrong when, with all the precedence he gives the High Priest, he describes the general result as ' a form of government that was an aristocracy, but mixed with oligarchy, for the chief priests were at the head of affairs.' [1]

But, secondly, there arose in Palestine, from the invasion of Alexander the Great onwards, an increasing number of Greek cities, each with its democratic council ;   2. Under the and the example of these, perhaps along with   Ptolemies. the advice or pressure of the Greek sovereigns of Judæa, cannot but have told on the institutions of the Jews, who, whether willing or unwilling, became more and more subject to Hellenic influence.[2]   Kuenen gives a somewhat different explanation : in the goodwill towards Jews of the Ptolemies, their masters during the third century, as contrasted with the smaller amount of independence vouchsafed them by the Persians.   The contrast is by no means so certain as he assumes.   In Nehemiah's time, at least, the Jews had favour shown them by the Persian king, sufficient to have permitted the formation of an organised senate had other influences been existent to lead to the creation of this.   The interested kindness of the Ptolemies may have provided the opportunity, but it is more probable that the stimulus itself came from the example of the Greek or Hellenised towns in Palestine.

[1] xi. *Ant.* iv. 8.          [2] Hecatæus (§ 9) admits this.

The names which are given to the new institution are Greek, *Gerousia* and *Boulē* : no insignificant evidence as to the influences which had assisted to mould it.

In any case, by the end of the period we have surveyed, there was associated with the High Priest in the govern-

A definite Senate in existence by the beginning of the 2nd century.

ment of the nation a definite senate composed of priests, scribes and the heads of families, which in the name of Israel conducted nego- tiations with other states. That they are regarded by the First Book of Maccabees as equivalent to the *elders and rulers of the people*, there can be no doubt.[1] Therefore we may add to the Senate's adminis- trative functions the supreme judicial power : this is supported by the Septuagint's use of the term *Gerousia*.

From the facts that some of our witnesses do not use the term *Gerousia*, and that those who do nowhere record

Possible objections and alterna- tives.

the creation of a senate, nor offer a definition or statistics of it, the argument might reason- ably be urged, that the writers who speak of a *Gerousia* of the Jews are only following a fashion to which Jews were prone, of giving Greek names, often far from appropriate, to their own institutions. This is possible, but I do not feel that it is certain. The Jewish constitution, it is true, was not Hellenised to the same extent as those of the surrounding Semitic states.[2] The City never received, like the others, a Greek name ; she

---

[1] See above, p. 393 note 3.

[2] Gustav Hölscher, *Palästina in der persischen u. hellenist. Zeit*, 68, has, in my opinion, gone too far when he concludes that 'Jerusalem was also ranged in the Hellenistic organisation of the land, and with its territory may have been called νομός.' He founds this, p. 74, on the supposition that of the four *nomoi* mentioned in 1 Macc. xi. 57, Judæa is the fourth. Much more probably this is *Ekron* ; cf. x. 89.

kept her own religion, and was governed by her own High
Priest. But with this seclusion the formation of a senate
in imitation of Greek models was compatible, and I feel
that on the whole the evidence is in favour of the fact
that such a senate was formed in Jerusalem before 200 B.C.
The alternative is that it first appeared on the organisation of Jerusalem as a Greek town by Antiochus in 168.

There were, of course, local courts as well. The elders
of each township continued to sit in its gates as of old
and as sanctioned by the law. It is perhaps No evidence
to such a burgh-court in Jerusalem that the of another
Supreme
Son of Sira alludes as *the congregation of* Court.
*the gates,*[1] *the leaders of the City.*[2] In that case the
supreme court may also have been the town's court.
Unfortunately, the data of the Son of Sira are ambiguous. The only other gathering for judgment which he
mentions is one of the whole people, who are also mentioned as a whole in the list of national authorities in the
Books of Maccabees. There is no trace of a select body
of leaders distinct from the *Gerousia,* and possessing
only spiritual or religious authority.[3] Such a division of
jurisdiction would have been contrary to the principle
which runs through the Jewish law, of the identity of the
secular and sacred. That the *Gerousia* divided itself, as
the Chronicler asserts of Jehoshaphat's supreme court,
into—not two courts—but two different kinds of sessions,
one to deal with religious matters and one to deal with
civil, is of course possible. But upon the evidence it is
as impossible to separate (as he does) the High Priest's
supremacy from the secular as from the sacred cases.

---

[1] vii. 7 (Heb.). See above, p. 391.     [2] x. 2.
[3] As suggested in the *Jewish Encycl.,* art. 'Sanhedrin.'

The fiscal administration of Judah was in his charge.[1] We must also note that in religious matters, not priests only but scribes had already a great and a growing influence.

## 5. The Reconstitution of Israel, 168-142 B.C.

We have seen that out of the priesthood and those elders of Israel whom the Priestly Law appointed as councillors of the High Priest and his colleagues in dealing with other states, and whom it dignified with the name of *Nesî'îm* or *Princes*, there was probably developed by the close of the third century B.C., under the influence of Greek models, a definite *Gerousia, Boulē,* or Senate, which was associated with the High Priest in his government of the nation. In the words of Josephus already quoted, the Jewish government was 'an aristocracy with an oligarchy.' In the period of the constitutional history of Israel which we are to traverse in this section, the first facts to be appreciated are that whatever institutions the Jews hitherto had were broken up by the persecutions of Antiochus Epiphanes (175-164) and subsequent events; and that a fresh system of national authority, following of course the old lines, had to be organised from the foundation by Judas Maccabeus and his brothers. These are facts not sufficiently emphasised by the historians, many of whom too readily assume the continuity of the Jewish constitution from the age of Nehemiah to that of Christ.

Under the Ptolemies the High-priesthood had been

*Destruction and Restoration of the Jewish Institutions.*

---

[1] Jos. xii. *Ant.* iv. 1.

hereditary in the Aaronite family of the Oniadæ, and so
continued under the reign of the Syrian Their destruc-
Seleucus IV. (187-175), the High Priest being tion by Anti-ochus IV. in
still Onias, son of that Simon who is probably 168 B.C.
praised by Ben Sira.   Even when Antiochus IV., soon
after his accession in 175, deposed the virtuous Onias, it
was a brother of the latter, Jeshua (Jesus) or Jason, who
succeeded.   But the means which he employed to oust
his brother, outbidding him in the amount of tribute he
promised, and undertaking to introduce Greek fashions
among his people, prepared the way for his own downfall,
and was the beginning of all the national troubles.
Another family, the Tobiadæ, had in the meantime, by
the management of the royal taxes, risen to great influence
in Jerusalem.   An adherent of theirs, Menelaus, was sent
by Jason with the annual tribute to Antiochus, and
Menelaus, who according to one account (but this seems
incredible) was not even a member of the priestly tribe,
seized the opportunity to get the High-priesthood for
himself, outbidding Jason by 300 talents of silver.[1]   The
struggles between Jason and Menelaus—each of whom
had his own faction in Jerusalem, while both disgusted
the pious Jews by their Hellenising, and the body of the
people by their tyranny—led to the interference of Antiochus, who shattered the whole system, of which, by these
irreligious and illegitimate means, they sought the presi-

---

[1] There are two divergent accounts : 2 Macc. iii., iv., according to which
Menelaus was the brother of Simon a Benjamite (iii. 4 ; iv. 23), and Josephus,
xii. *Ant.* v. 1, according to which he was a younger brother of Jason.   But
Josephus allows that the support of the Tobiadæ was given to Menelaus.
Many take him, therefore, to have been a Tobiad, but this is nowhere stated,
and the opposite is a natural inference from the words of Josephus ; cf.
Schürer, *Gesch.* [3] i. 195 *n.* 28.

dency. It is well to note that till this catastrophe, the *Gerousia* or Senate continued to exist, and they protested against the conduct of Menelaus.[1] But in 168 the Temple was desecrated, Jerusalem organised as a Greek town, and the worship of Hellenic deities enforced throughout Judæa. Numbers of Jews had already volunteered apostasy,[2] others now succumbed to the persecution.

Those who remained faithful to the Law, and *pursued righteousness and judgment*,[3] fled to the mountains and the desert. In the wilderness the constitution of Israel, without City, Temple or High Priest, formed itself anew from those primal elements, the consciences of a people faithful to their God, from which it had been originally created. The description of the process carries us back not only to the time of Nehemiah and Ezra, for they had a City, a Temple and a High Priest, but rather to that of Gideon and Deborah, with this difference, however, that there was now a written and a fixed Law. The remnant which went down into the wilderness were a number of the ordinary families of Israel : men, *their sons, wives, and cattle* ;[4] those who fled to the mountains were doubtless of the same class. At first their zeal for the Law would not allow them to fight on the Sabbath, and on that day a large number were slain unresisting. But a family of priests, of the order of Jehoiarib—Mattathias and his five sons, John, Simon, Judas, Eleazar and Jonathan—had signalised themselves by starting at their own village of

*New Birth of the Congregation.*

---

[1] 2 Macc. iv. 44.  [2] *Id.* 10, 13 ff.

[3] 1 Macc. ii. 29, δικαιοσύνην καὶ κρίμα, evidently for the Hebrew צדק ומשפט, though the latter is usually in the inverse order. *Judgment* covers the religious and ceremonial law as well as justice.

[4] 1 Macc. ii. 30.

Modein, in the Shephelah, an active revolt against the officers of Antiochus, and by advocating armed resistance even though it should involve disregard of the Sabbath. Mattathias was accepted as leader of the fugitives, and mustered an army. He was joined by a more or less organised group of men of position in Israel, zealots for the Law, calling themselves *Hasîdîm*, that is *Pious* or *Devout*.[1] All this happened in 167.[2] In the following year Mattathias died, exhorting his followers to faithfulness to the Law, even unto death, and advising them to take Simon for their counsellor and Judas for their captain.[3] The simple words of the historian emphasise how Israel was resolved into its elements. The *people and their sanctuary were in ruin*; but *the congregation was gathered for battle and for prayer*.[4]

They had, too, the Law, with its prescribed institutions and its examples and precedents from the heroic age of the national history. At Mizpeh, *a place of prayer aforetime for Israel*, Judas arranged a Reorganisation by Judas. pathetic ghost of the legal service of the Temple, and effected a closer organisation of his forces also with scrupulous respect to the directions of the Torah.[5] After a solemn fast and reading of the Book of the Law they gathered, as if in sacramental remembrance of their immediate duty, the ineffectual remnants of the Temple ritual: priests' robes, first-fruits, tithes, and such Nazarites

---

[1] The term is difficult to translate by one English word, as the noun from which it comes signifies not only *love* (in this case towards God), but fidelity also to their covenant with Him.

[2] ii. 1-30.      [3] ii. 49-70.

[4] ' Άναστήσωμεν τὴν καθαίρεσιν τοῦ λαοῦ ἡμῶν καὶ τῶν ἀγίων.' Καὶ ἠθροίσθησαν ἡ συναγωγὴ τοῦ εἶναι ἑτοίμους εἰς πόλεμον καὶ τοῦ προσεύξασθαι, κ.τ.λ., 1 Macc. iii. 43 f.

[5] iii. 46-56.

as had accomplished their days.[1]   After this Judas
appointed *leaders of the people,* later on called *scribes of the
people,*[2] which is but the Greek translation of the ancient
*shôṭĕre ha'am*—the captains or tribunes of the nation
when it was mobilised for war—*officers of thousands,
hundreds, fifties and tens.*   By 165 B.C. the army amounted,
we are told, to 10,000 men.[3]   In the restoration of the
Temple and the renewal of the services that same year
nothing is said of the rank of the priests employed, only
that they were selected as *being blameless and well-
wishers to the Law.*[4]   The legislative power is described
as *Judas, his brethren and the whole Ecclesia of Israel* ;[5]
and again it is said that *a great Ecclesia was assembled* to
consult as to what should be done for the Jews in Gilead
and Galilee.[6]

We need not linger over the appearance in 161 of the
High Priest Alcimos or Eliakim, a man of the seed of
Aaron but not of the family of Onias; nor
upon his leadership of the Hellenising faction,
his institution to the office by Demetrius, his
acceptance by the Hasîdîm, or the struggles between
him and Judas, who rightly never trusted him.[7]   They

The High
Priest
Alkimos.

---

[1] Verse 49 reads ἤγειραν, which modern versions render by the senseless
*stirred up,* as if from ἐγείρω.   Wellhausen ingeniously suggests the emendation ἔκειραν, *shaved,* but with a very necessary query after it in view of verse
50, which goes on to say that the people then asked God with despair what
they should do with the Nazarites.   The proper reading, of course, is ἤγειραν,
the aor. of ἀγείρω, frequent in Greek for the mustering of men.

[2] v. 42, γραμματεῖς τοῦ λαοῦ=שׁוֹטְרֵי הָעָם.

[3] iv. 29.                                          [4] iv. 42.

[5] iv. 59.                                          [6] v. 16.

[7] 1 Macc. vii. 5 ff. ; Jos. xx. *Ant.* x. 3 ; cf. xii. *Ant.* ix. 7, from which
and from 2 Macc. xiv. 3 we learn that Alcimos, or Jacimus, had already acted
as High Priest.

passed away within a short time of each other—
159 B.C.

Two points, however, require emphasis. The High-
priesthood was now vacant, and for seven years remained
so.[1] Moreover, the Seleucids now saw that it was impossible to extirpate the Jewish religion, and gave the
Jews formal permission to practise it in the Temple and
elsewhere, upon which the Hasîdîm withdrew from the
active revolt. Henceforth this was carried on as a political
movement, hardly, as Wellhausen judges, for the mere
sovereignty of the Maccabean house, but rather for the
independence of the Jewish nation.

Jonathan took the leadership in place of his brother,
and, after several campaigns, ruled Israel in peace from
Michmash for three or four years (156-152).[2] Jonathan,
In 153 King Alexander Balas, outbidding his High Priest
and Gover-
rival Demetrius for the support of Jonathan, nor.
appointed the latter High Priest, with a purple robe and
crown of gold; and at the Feast of Tabernacles in that
year Jonathan put on the holy garments.[3] In 150 he was
further empowered to act as *military and civil governor of
the province* of Judæa.[4] Thus the High-priesthood, which
had already passed from the house of Onias, fell to a
family of priests, whose representatives by their religious
energy and valour had won an indubitable right to it, and
who secured in addition civil and military titles not

---

[1] The death of Alcimos was after that of Judas, according to 1 Macc. ix.
54, but before that of Judas, according to Josephus, who adds that Judas was
made by the people High Priest in his stead, but afterwards contradicts this
by affirming that after Alcimos the office was vacant seven years and then
filled by Jonathan (xii. *Ant.* ix. 7 ; xx. *Ant.* x.).

[2] 1 Macc. ix. 23-73 ; Jos. xiii. *Ant.* i.        [3] 1 Macc. x. 18 ff.

[4] Καὶ ἔθετο αὐτὸν στρατηγὸν καὶ μεριδάρχην, 65.

before granted to any High Priest by any sovereign of
Israel. In 146-145 the Jewish territory was enlarged,
and for the payment of three hundred talents was relieved
of the king's tithes, tolls and other taxes.[1] Jonathan
removed his residence to Jerusalem, and in counsel with
the elders of the people strengthened the walls.[2] We
may be sure also that he did for the Holy City what we
are told that Simon did for Gezer : *cleansed the houses
where idols were, put all uncleanness away, and placed in
it such men as would keep the Law.*[3] Like Nehemiah, he
would enlist a special police.

On his succession to Jonathan in 143-2 Simon was
confirmed in the High-priesthood and freedom from taxes
by Demetrius II., and the Jews began to write
on their contracts and other documents, *In the
first year of Simon the great High Priest,
Captain and Governor of the Jews.*[4] For the last of these
titles the more definite *Ethnarch* is also given,[5] while the
formal proclamation of his people's gratitude invests
Simon with (so far as they are concerned) absolute power
and dignity.[6] In all but name he was King of the Jews.
But the authority which under God conferred his power is
called *a great convocation of priests and people and of
rulers of the nation and elders of the country.*[7] If the
definite *Gerousia* or Senate had been reconstituted, the
name was probably purposely avoided, and the more
ancient designations substituted. A difficulty remains

*Simon, High Priest and Ethnarch.*

---

[1] xi. 28-37.   [2] x. 10, xii. 36 ; 'approved by τὸ πλῆθος,' xiii. *Ant.* v. 11.
[3] xiii. 47 f.
[4] xiii. 42 ; cf. xiv. 28 (on which see above), 47.
[5] xiv. 47 ; xv. 2.    [6] xiv. 27-47.
[7] Ἐπὶ συναγωγῆς μεγάλης τῶν ἱερέων καὶ λαοῦ καὶ ἀρχόντων ἔθνους καὶ τῶν
πρεσβυτέρων τῆς χώρας, xiv. 28.

# DESCRIPTION OF COINS ON PLATE IX.

1. Silver Siglos or Daric, of a Phœnician town (?) under the Persians, probably between 424 and 338 B.C. Archer kneeling and stretching bow; galley on waves. A. R. S. Kennedy, in Hastings' *D. B.* iii. 421 f.

2. Silver Octadrachm (=Double Shekel) of Ṣidon under Persia (probably of the reign of Artaxerxes Ochus, 359-338 B.C.); galley on waves; the King in a chariot with an Asiatic behind him. See Head, *Historia Numorum*, 672, and for other types Macdonald, *Catalogue of Greek Coins in the Hunterian Collection, University of Glasgow*, iii. 249, Nos. 3. 4.

3. Silver Drachm (=Quarter Shekel) either of Alexander the Great's time or later by some Syrian city. Head of Alexander; Zeus throned and holding eagle right and sceptre left; ΑΛΕΞΑΝΔΡΟΥ. See Eckhel, *Doctrina Veterum Numorum*, ii. 98 ff.; Head, 199.

4. Silver Tetradrachm (=Shekel) of Tyre under Antiochus VII. (Sidetes), 138-129 B.C. Bust of Antiochus; ΑΝΤΙΟΧΟΥ ΒΑΣΙΛΕΩΣ; eagle standing on beak of galley with wings closed, over right wing a palm, in field left IE above a club, in field right ΑΨ, IOP (=135 B.C.). See Macdonald, iii. 84, Nos. 59-60.

5. Silver Tetradrachm (=Shekel) of Tyre. Laurelled head of Herakles Melkart (see 2 Macc. iv. 19); ΤΥΡΟΥ ΙΕΡΑΣ ΚΑΙ ΑΣΥΛΟΥ; eagle standing on rudder with closed wings, above the right a palm branch, in front club downwards, in field left, date BI (=114 B.C.), right M. See Head, 675 f.; Macdonald, iii. 263, Nos. 2 and 3.

6. Silver Didrachm (=Half-Shekel) of Tyre. Similar to the preceding. Date seems to read LK.

7. Bronze Coin of Tyre. Head of Herakles(?); galley with what seems to be ΙΕΡΑΣ ΜΗΤΡΟΠΟΛΕΩΣ above and ΤΥΡΙΩΝ below. Cf. Macdonald, iii. 267, No. 35.

8. Silver Shekel of Simon Maccabæus (but see pp. 405 f.). Chalice with broad rim, above it the date ב [נת]שׁ 'year 2'=137 B.C., round the edge שקל ישראל, 'shekel of Israel'; lily (?) with three blooms, round the edge ירושלים הקדושה, 'Jerusalem the Holy' (see pp. 251, 270). From the Hunterian Collection, University of Glasgow, Macdonald, iii. 285, No. 1. Cf. Madden (ed. 1903), 68; Kennedy, 424 f.

9. Bronze Coin of John Hyrcanus (135-106 B.C.). Two cornua-copiae with a poppy-head between; for the Hebrew legend on the other side see p. 408. Madden (ed. 1903), 76 ff.; Kennedy, 425.

10. Bronze Coin of Alexander Jannaeus (103-78 B.C.) An anchor with two bars; on other side eight spokes of a wheel (not the sun's rays, as usually interpreted). For the Greek and Hebrew legends see p. 409. Madden, 90; Macdonald, iii. 287.

*Plate IX.*

SPECIMENS OF THE EARLIEST COINS CIRCULATING IN SYRIA AND JUDAEA.

Nos. 1—7, 9, 10 from the Author's Collection.
No. 8 from the Hunterian Collection, University of Glasgow.

with regard to the mention of a *Gerousia* of the nation in the superscription of the letter to the Spartans, under Jonathan, about 144 B.C.[1] This is the only use of the title in First Maccabees, and may be due to the fact that the letter, if genuine, was addressed to foreigners and Greeks. In the same chapter the same body is called *the elders of the people*,[2] and elsewhere *the elders and nation of the Jews*,[3] and *the high priest, priests and people, rulers and elders*.[4] These terms are in harmony with the Maccabean spirit, democratic and tenacious of ancient forms.

In 138 B.C. Antiochus VII., Sidetes, granted to Simon the right *to coin money for his country with his own dies*,[5] and this is the first coinage of their own the Jews ever had; having used before the Exile stamped The Right of Coinage. weights of metal, and since the Return first the gold darics and silver shekels of the Persian kings, or the coins which these allowed Phœnician cities to strike, and then the gold staters, silver tetradrachms and drachms of Alexander, the Ptolemies and the Seleucids.[6] Whether certain silver shekels and half-shekels, with the legends 'Shekel of Israel' and 'Jerusalem the Holy' upon them,[7] discovered at Jerusalem, Jericho and elsewhere, are Simon's or not, is a question which still divides numismatists. Those who maintain the negative emphasise these facts : that the Seleucid sovereigns reserved the coinage of silver, their standard, to themselves, permitting to some privileged cities the right only of coinage in bronze ; that no successor of Simon coined in silver ; that the shekels, which are numbered in years from 1 to 5, cannot be fitted

---

[1] xii. 6.    [2] xii. 35.    [3] xiii. 36.    [4] **xiv. 27 f.**
[5] Καὶ ἐπέτρεψά σοι ποιῆσαι κόμμα ἴδιον νόμισμα τῇ χώρᾳ σου, xv. 6; Codd. ℵ V.
[6] For specimens of some of these see Plate ix. 1-7.    [7] Plate ix. 8.

into the chronology of Simon's reign, because the right
of coinage was granted to him only four years before his
death; but if we suppose that he anticipated it and coined
money from the first year of his reign onwards, coins of the
sixth and seventh years are wanting; and that the shekels
are not so like Seleucid coins of the period as they
are to the imperial moneys of the first century B.C., to
which, accordingly, they must be relegated as belonging
to the first revolt against Rome, 66-70 A.D.  Those of the
opposite opinion appeal to the archaic aspect of the
shekels, the fact that not a single specimen occurs restruck
on a Roman coin, and the impossibility of extending the
first revolt against Rome beyond four years, September
66 to September 70.  The only other period possible for
them is the reign of Simon; a royal licence to coin mere
bronze money would not have been recorded; the difference between the fabric of the shekels and that of contemporary Seleucid coins is explicable by the newness
of the Jewish mint; the coins of the first four years
belong to Simon, and those of the fifth to John Hyrcanus;
then they cease, which implies the surrender of Jerusalem
in that year.[1]  The question is still open, and perhaps

---

[1] The question, on which I hesitate to give an opinion, has been discussed
both by Hebrew scholars and numismatists.  Of the former, Ewald, Schürer
(who gives a thorough résumé of the discussion and list of the literature,
*Gesch.*, 3rd ed. i. 243 ff. App. iv.) and A. R. S. Kennedy (who in the best
treatise in English on the money of the Bible (in Hastings' Bible Dictionary)
works upon great numismatic knowledge as well) all decide against Simon's
reign.  So do a minority of numismatic authorities, Théod. Reinach (at first),
Imhoof-Blumer, and Babelon.  Nearly all the rest, from Eckhel onwards
by De Saulcy (*Num. de la Terre Sainte*), Merzbacher (quoted by Madden and
Schürer), Madden (*Coins of the Jews*, 2nd ed. 1881, 3rd ed. 1903, 65 ff.), and
Head (*Historia Numorum*, 681), decide for Simon's reign; and recently
Reinach, *Jewish Coins* (Eng. Trans. by Mary Hill, with App. by G. F. Hill,
on forged shekels 12 ff.), who has changed from his previous position, and
whose fresh reasons for Simon's reign are among those given above; George

will always be so; but if I may venture an opinion on the opposing arguments, the balance is in favour of Simon's reign. It will be noticed that these coins bear no ruler's head or name, but only that of the nation and of the City. There are also bronze coins which some attribute to Simon, in his fourth year. They bear on the reverse the legend : For the Redemption of Sion.[1]

From those popular and religious elements, then, and by those successive stages, so largely the efforts of the individual Maccabees, was the constitution of Israel re-created. Simon's rank was by popular acclaim fixed *for ever, until there should arise a faithful prophet*:[2] that is till the voice of God Himself, whose hand had been so manifest in the advancement of this family, should take away the kingdom from them and give it to another.

## 6. THE HASMONEAN DYNASTY, 142-63 B.C.

Simon's dynasty received the name not of Maccabean, which was rather reserved for Judas (and his brothers), but of Hasmonean, derived from Hashmon, the great-grandfather or grandfather of Mattathias.[3] On our present task they need not detain us long. Their coins will be

---

Macdonald (*Catalogue of Greek Coins in the Hunterian Collection, Univ. of Glasgow*, iii. 285) and Von Sallet, who says (as quoted by Schürer) that because of the antique character of the coins and of the script of their legends they 'must fall in the time of the Maccabees.' From the later coins of the Jewish revolt they are 'completely different.'

[1] Madden, 71 ; Head, 682.                [2] 1 Macc. xiv. 41.

[3] Wellhausen, *Pharisäer u. Sadd.* 84 reads בֶּן חַשְׁמוֹן as the Hebrew original of τοῦ Συμεών in 1 Macc. ii. 1. Jos. xii. *Ant.* vi. 1 says that Mattathia's great-grandfather was Asamonaios, and in xv. *Ant.* xi. 4 he calls the family (to which he says he himself belonged, *Life*, i.) Asamonaioi. In the *Mishna* בְּנֵי חשמונאי or בֵּית, 'Middoth,' i. 6, cf. *Talmud* 'Sabb.' 21*b*. Cf. Targ. of Jonathan to 1 Sam. ii. 4.

found in the works already cited.[1]   The Hasmonean
kings kept their hold over the City and her factions from
the castle on the north of the Temple, and by means of
their mercenary guards.   In his account of their campaigns and enterprises Josephus hardly mentions ‘the
leading men’ or ‘elders’ of Jerusalem.[2]   There is no
mention of the *Gerousia* by that name.   The active forces
under the prince are the nation, the nobles, and the now
definite parties of the Pharisees and Sadducees.

The reign of John Hyrcanus (135-104) began with
a siege of Jerusalem, and her surrender to Antiochus

John
Hyrcanus.
Sidetes.   But as the Syrian power decreased
and became divided, and still more as Rome
was appealed to by the Jews for protection, but was not
yet able to interfere with their actions, Hyrcanus made
the large additions to the Jewish territory and people
which distinguish his reign, till his power came to resemble that of an independent king rather than of an
ethnarch.   Though he did not take the title, the presence
of his own name upon his coins marks the nearest possible
approach to its assumption.   The legend of the earlier
issues runs ‘ Jehoḥanan the High Priest and the Ḥeber (or
Association) of the Jews ’; that of the later, ‘ Jehoḥanan
the High Priest, Head of the Ḥeber of the Jews.’   The
change may mark an actual growth of power.   ‘ Ḥeber ’
has been taken to denote the *Gerousia*,[3] whose history
we have followed above, and by others the whole People
or the Ecclesia of Israel.[4]   But recently Dr. A. R. S.

---

[1] Two specimens are given on Plate ix. Nos. 9 and 10.

[2] xiii. *Ant.* xvi. 5.

[3] *E.g.* Madden and Wellh., *Gesch.* 236 ( =the Synedrion of Antioch or
Alexandria).

[4] Nestle (*Z.A.T.W.*, 1895, 288 ff.; חבר $=\xi\theta\nu\sigma s$, ראש חבר $=\xi\theta\nu\dot{\alpha}\rho\chi\eta s$).
Schürer (269 f.) emphasises the analogy of ‘ the congregation of the Jews.’

Kennedy has suggested that it is the equivalent of the Greek τὸ κοινόν, in one of its meanings, as either the state as a whole, or its executive authorities, or a confederation.[1] As Schürer has pointed out, the increase of the prince's political interests and powers illustrates the gradual passage of his favour from the Pharisees, 'the party of the multitude,' to the Sadducean or aristocratic party.

Engaged as we are with the history of the constitution, it is interesting to note that while Hyrcanus in his will nominated his eldest son, Judas Aristobulus, as High Priest, he left the whole of the government to his wife.[2] This novel experiment was not yet to be realised. Aristobulus starved his mother and became prince himself (104-103). He was the first of his dynasty to take the title of king, but not upon his coins, on which he is styled like his father High Priest, and associated with the ' Ḥeber.' The devices are a double cornucopia, poppy-head and wreath of laurel. As his father enforced the Law upon the Idumæans to the south, so he began to do with Galilee.[3]

*Judas Aristobulus.*

Alexander Jannæus (103-76 B.C.), besides issuing coins with a legend similar to those of his two predecessors, struck others, with the royal title[4] his grandfather had never used, and his father though using had not ventured to put on coins. The legend runs in Hebrew 'Jonathan the King,' in Greek 'Of King Alexander.' It was a natural gradation, especially in the growing weakness of the Seleucids. The incongruity lies rather in the other and more sacred title. There never

*Alexander Jannæus.*

---

[1] Hastings' *D.B.* iii. 425.    [2] Jos. xiii. *Ant.* xi. 1.    [3] *H.G.H.L.* 414.

[4] יהונתן המלך, ΒΑΣΙΛΕΩΣ ΑΛΕΞΑΝΔΡΟΥ: anchor and flower and wheel: for coins of John and Jonathan, Pl. ix. 9, 10; of Judas, Madden, 82.

was a greater monstrosity among all the rulers of Israel than this brilliant drunkard, who at the same time was High Priest in Jerusalem. No wonder the people pelted him with citrons when he stood beside the altar on the Feast of Tabernacles.[1] He was constantly in controversy with the Pharisees, who at last kindled a rebellion against him; but in spite of their rapidly growing influence, he quelled it.

The experiment which the dead hand of Hyrcanus had failed to start was also bequeathed by Jannæus to his people, and this time it was carried out.[2] His widow, Alexandra, became Queen, his son Hyrcanus II., High Priest. They submitted themselves to the Pharisees, and under such influence the queen's reign (76-67) was prosperous and popular ; but a certain balance of power between the factions was sustained by the adhesion of her second son, Aristobulus, to the Sadducees. She stamped at least small bronze coins with an anchor and the legend in Greek,[3] 'Queen Alexandra,' on the reverse a star or eight spokes of a wheel [4] with some Hebrew.

*Queen Alexandra.*

The history of the reign of Aristobulus II. (67-63), to whom his brother at first yielded both the dignities, is full of constitutional interest : the conflict between the two princes ; the adoption of the cause of the weaker brother, the more pliable instrument, by the ambitious governor of Idumæa, the Idumæan Antipater, aided by many of the nobles ; and when Pompey

*Hyrcanus II. Aristobulus II.*

---

[1] Jos. xiii. *Ant*. xiii. 5 ; 1 *B.J.* iv. 3.

[2] xiii. *Ant*. xvi. 1 ff. ; i. *B.J.* v.

[3] Madden, 91 f., with specimen ; Head, 682.

[4] So Macdonald, iii. 287, on a coin of Alex. Jannæus, on which there is the same device ; pointing out that 'surely the heavenly bodies came under the ban of the Second Commandment, the influence of which is obvious in all early Jewish coins.' But see the stars on coins given by Madden, 96 f.

entered as judge into the quarrel, the appearance before
him not only of the two claimants to the throne, but of
‘ the nation against them both ; which did not desire to be
ruled by kings, for what was handed down to them from
their fathers was that they should obey the priests of the
God they worshipped ; but these two, though the descendants of priests, sought to transfer the nation to another
form of government, that it might be enslaved.’ [1]

## 7. UNDER THE ROMANS : B.C. 63 ONWARDS

After Pompey took the City (63 B.C.), the Romans, who
in other towns dealt with the magistrates, senate and
people,[2] delivered, along with authority to rule   Pompey's
the Jewish people in their own affairs, all powers   rearrangement. The
in Jerusalem itself to the High Priest Hyr-   Synedrion.
canus II. (63-40), who was later styled Ethnarch.[3] But they
continued, or possibly reconstituted, a Senate or Council,
with powers of life and death. That now after Pompey's
and Cæsar's rearrangement of affairs we meet for the
first time with the word *Synedrion* or *Sanhedrin*, as the
name for the supreme Jewish court, is very significant.
Josephus so styles the court in his account of the young
Herod's narrow escape from its sentence of death in 47
or 46.[4] The name Synedria, as well as Synodoi, had
already been given to the five districts, fiscal or judicial,
into which Gabinius had divided the Jewish territory.[5]
With all Palestine Judæa was placed under the Governor
of the province of Syria, and obliged to pay tribute.[6]

---

[1] xiv. *Ant.* iii. 2.          [2] *e.g.* Sidon xiv., *Ant.* x. 2.
[3] xiv. *Ant.* iv. 4, 5, viii. 3, 5, ix. 2, x. 2-7, xii. 3 f. These powers were conferred by Pompey in 64, withdrawn by Gabinius, and restored by Cæsar in 47.
[4] *Ibid.* ix. 3-5.          [5] *Ibid.* v. 4 ; 1 *B.J.* viii. 5.
[6] xiv. *Ant.* iv. 4, 5 ; 1 *B.J.* vii. 7. See Schürer, *Gesch.* i. 338 ff.

In 40 the Parthians having taken Jerusalem, deposed Hyrcanus, and appointed as King the son of Aristobulus II., Mattathiah or Antigonus, who styled himself on his coins High Priest and King (40-37).[1]   Herod, who had been appointed Tetrarch by Mark Antony,[2] and (in 40) King by the Roman Senate,[3] took Jerusalem in 37 from Antigonus, who was executed.[4]   From Herod's accession to power up to his death it ceases to be possible to talk of constitutional government in Jerusalem.  He ruled by force, tempered by arbitrary pretences of justice,[5] by cajoling the mob,[6] by gifts of corn, of a theatre, a circus and a new Temple,[7] and by a general, though inconstant, respect to the prejudice of the citizens against statues.[8]   His new towers and his palace dominated the City from its highest quarter ;[9] his soldiers in the castle commanded the courts and colonnades of the Temple.[10]   He forbade public meetings, spread abroad his spies, skulked himself in disguise among the people,[11] and used his guards to torture and execute suspects in sight of their fellow-citizens.[12]   The High Priests were his puppets, and he had begun his government by slaying most of the Sanhedrin.[13]   He also enforced a severer law against housebreakers![14]   His coins —only bronze, since he was the vassal of Rome—bear the

*(margin note: Herod's Arbitrary Government.)*

---

[1] The coins, of bronze, bear the earliest representation of the seven-branched candlestick, with a bare base, while that on the arch of Titus has griffins figured on it : Madden, 102 f.  Cf. vii. *B.J.* v. 5.

[2] xiv. *Ant.* xiii. 1 ; 1 *B.J.* xii. 5.

[3] xiv. *Ant.* xiv. 4 f; 1 *B.J.* xiv. 4.

[4] xiv. *Ant.* xvi. 1 ff. ; 1 *B.J.* xvii. 9 ; xviii. 1 ff.

[5] xv. *Ant.* vi. 2; vii. 4; xvii. *Ant.* v.   [6] xv. *Ant.* viii. 2 f., xi. 1; xvi. ii. 4, etc.

[7] *Ibid.* viii. 1, ix. 2, xi.   [8] *Ibid.* viii. 2, ix. 5, xvii. *Ant.* vi. 2.

[9] v. *B.J.* iv. 3.   [10] xv. *Ant.* xi. 4.

[11] *Ibid.* viii. 4, x. 4.   [12] viii. 4 ; xvi. *Ant.* x. 5.

[13] xiv. *Ant.* ix. 4, xv. *Ant.* i. 2 ff., iii. 1, ix. 3.   [14] xvi. *Ant.* i. 1.

# DESCRIPTION OF COINS ON PLATE X.

1. Bronze Coin of Herod Archelaus, B.C. 4—A.D. 6 (rather than of Herod the Great). Bunch of grapes with legend HPΩΔOY; helmet with plumes and cheek-pieces. On other specimens of this type EΘNAPXOY is legible below the helmet, and the bunch of grapes does not occur on any known specimen of a coin of Herod the Great. See Madden (ed. 1903), 117, No. 8; Macdonald, iii. 288, No. 2.

2. Bronze Coin (Quadrans?) of a Roman Procurator under Augustus. An ear of wheat with legend KAICAPOC; a palm-tree with two bunches of dates; the date, stamped on the field on either side of the stem of the palm, is illegible, but the wheat ear is the same as that on coins of the Procurator Coponius, dated 8 A.D. Macdonald, iii. 292, No. 1; cf. Madden (ed. 1903), 174.

3. Bronze Coin (Quadrans?) of the Procurator Felix under Nero. Within a wreath of laurel NEPΩNOC; a palm-branch, and on either side LΣ KAI-CAPOC; date year 5=58-59 A.D. See Madden, 185; Macdonald, iii. 293.

4. Bronze Coin of Agrippa I. (41-44 A.D.). An umbrella with deep fringe with the legend from right down BACIΛEΩC AΓPIΠA (only the first letters are legible); three ears of wheat, with date illegible.

5. Small Bronze Coin, uncertain; possibly a specimen of the λεπτόν or 'mite,' but more probably a coin of one of the towns of Palestine outside Judæa.

6, 7, 8. Three specimens of bronze coins struck in second year of the Jewish Revolt against Rome, 67-68 A.D. Vase with two handles and cover, legend from left down and then up right. שנת שתים=year 2 (on 6 the last letter *mim* is legible above the vase, and the first *shin*; on 7 the *shin* of שתים; and on 7 ים of שתים); vine-twig and leaf hanging down, legend from left down and up right חרות־ציין=freedom of Ṣion (on 6 only the *nun* is legible, on 7 and 8 חרות, and also on 8 צי־. See Madden (ed. 1903), 206; Macdonald, iii. 293 f., Nos. 2 to 10.

9. Silver Shekel (Tetradrachm) of the Second Jewish Revolt against Rome (132-135 A.D.). Representation of the Temple, legend from right up ירושלם =Jerusalem; a *lulab* with *ethrog* or citron-branch to left, legend from right up ישראל [ות] לחר לשב=ʻYear 2 of the Freedom of Israel.' From the Hunterian Collection, University of Glasgow, Macdonald, iii. 295. Second Revolt, No. 1.—This coin bears no marks of being re-struck, as was all the silver coinage of the Second Revolt, but for a specimen of a quarter-shekel or drachm, on which traces of the original type are obvious, see Macdonald, iii. 296, No. 4, Pl. lxxviii. 16; and for a tetradrachm of Antioch, Kennedy, Pl. 20.

10. Bronze Coin of Second Revolt. Vine-leaf inverted, with legend from right up לחרות ישראל (only the יי־רא־ of ישראל are legible on the left); palm-tree with bunches of dates; of the legend שמעון=Simon [Bar-Cochba] only the ש to right of the tree-stem and מ to the left are legible. See Madden (ed. 1903), 204, and Macdonald, iii. 296, for similar types.

*Plate X.*

SPECIMENS OF COINS USED BY THE JEWS FROM HEROD ARCHELAUS
TO THE SECOND REVOLT B.C 4—A.D. 135.

Nos. 1—8 and 10 from the Author's Collection.

No. 9 from the Hunterian Collection, University of Glasgow.

legend 'King Herod,' or simply 'King.' They bear only
a Greek legend, like those of his successors.[1]

All this, sufficiently monstrous in itself, shows even
more flagrant when contrasted with the state of affairs
which followed, on the assumption of Judæa
as a Roman province. The nightmare of
Herod's tyranny falls upon the earliest chapters
of our Lord's life; it is the authority of the Romans, with
their respect for the native laws of their foreign subjects,
which we feel through the rest of the New Testament.
The few references of Josephus to the Sanhedrin under
Herod expand to many in the Gospels and the Acts.
Throughout these it is the chief Jewish court, their relation
to the Roman Governor, their procedure, and the gradation
of the inferior tribunals, which are in evidence. We have
passed from the passions and caprices of a tyrant to the
influence of settled institutions. If justice is still abused, the
forms, at least, of the law are observed or taken for granted.

*The difference in the New Testament.*

In 6 A.D., when our Lord was a boy, and just before
His visit with His parents to Jerusalem, Judæa was taken
from Archelaus, the son of Herod, and constituted a Roman province with a governor
of its own, of equestrian rank, called Procurator, but in the New Testament Governor, and subject, in cases of emergency, to the Legate of the Province
of Syria.[2] The capital of the Province and usual residence
of the governor was Cæsarea,[3] but for the great Jewish
feasts he came up to Jerusalem. He was in command of

*The Roman Province of Judæa.*

---

[1] Madden, 105 ff. ; for coin of Herod Archelaus see Pl. x. 1.

[2] See the full exposition by Schürer, *Hist.* (Eng. Transl.), div. i. vol. ii.
44 ff., 3rd Germ. ed. 454 ff. The Greek for Procurator is ἐπίτροπος, literally
'curator' or 'steward'; Governor, ἡγεμών, Lat. *praeses.* Josephus besides
using these calls the governor ἔπαρχος, Praefectus.   [3] See *H.G.H.L.* 141.

all the soldiers in the province, in charge of all the finance, and, while the lesser law was usually left to the native courts, he or his representative could interfere at any point of their procedure,[1] and he alone could render valid their sentences of death.[2] The coinage of the province was kept, of course, by the Romans in their own hands. We have coins of the Procurators from 6 to 41 A.D., when the province was given to Agrippa, and again from 44 to 66 A.D., the date of the beginning of the First Jewish revolt. They are all bronze with palms, palm-branches, ears of corn and laurel wreaths upon them, but no heads, out of respect to the Jewish feeling against images. The legends are in Greek ; either the simple καισαρος under Augustus, or the name of the reigning Emperor, and once that of Julia Agrippina. Those struck by Augustus are dated in the years 33, 35, 36, 39, 40 and 41 of the Augustan era, which began 27 B.C., those by Tiberius bear dates from 1 to 18, that is from 14-15 A.D. to 31-32.[3]

Under such imperial authority the High Priest and Sanhedrin resumed that actual government of Jeru-

High Priest and San-hedrin.

salem and the Jewish people, of which during Herod's reign they had enjoyed only the appearance. From 6 A.D. the Jewish 'Politeia' (says Josephus in his review of the history of the High-priesthood) 'became an Aristokrateia, and the High Priests were entrusted with the "Prostasia" or Presidency of the Nation,'[4] now a very limited distinction.

---

[1] See below, p. 420.

[2] An exception to this we shall see below, p. 424.

[3] De Saulcy, *Numism. de la Terre Sainte*, 69 ff., Plates iii. f. ; Madden, *Coins of the Jews*, ch. vii. ; Head, *Hist. Num.* 684 ; Macdonald, *Catalogue, etc.*, iii. 292. See Pl. x. 2, 3.

[4] xx. *Ant.* x. (§ 251). In iv. *Ant.* viii. 17, Josephus makes Moses say :— Ἀριστοκρατία μὲν οὖν κράτιστον, καὶ ὁ κατ' αὐτὴν βίος.

The powers and procedure of the Sanhedrin[1] during this period of their guarantee by Rome are fully illustrated in the New Testament, Josephus, and several tractates of the *Mishna*. That the powers included authority over the local Synedria or Sanhedrins,[2] not only of Judæa, but of Galilee, Peræa, and even of Jewish settlements beyond is indisputable so far as the interpretation of the Law and similar abstract questions are concerned, and is extremely probable in regard to other judicial cases. Professor Schürer states that 'since the death of Herod the Great at least, the civil jurisdiction of the Sanhedrin of Jerusalem was confined to Judæa proper,' Galilee and Peræa forming since that time independent spheres of administration.[3]   But Galilee and Peræa continued to be under a Jewish tetrarch, who was on good terms with the native authorities of Jerusalem, and would be ready to carry out their wishes. It is significant that addressing Galileans our Lord made use of a metaphor which implied the subjection of their local courts to the Council or Synedrion;[4] and Luke tells us that Saul the Pharisee *asked of the High Priest letters to Damascus unto the synagogues, that if he found any that were of the Way, he might bring them bound to Jerusalem.*[5]  This was not a civil case, but it involved civil penalties, and illustrates how difficult it is to draw the distinction which Dr. Schürer suggests.  It is true that John's Gospel de-

*The Area of their Jurisdiction.*

[1] סַנְהֶדְרִין =συνέδριον, so often in N.T., also πρεσβυτέριον, Luke xxii. 66, Acts xxii. 5, γερουσία (v. 21); cf. βουλή, Jos. ii. *B.J.* xv. 6, βουλευτής, Mark xv. 43; *Mishna,* סנהדרין גדולה or בית דין הגדול.
[2] *Mishna,* 'Sanhedrin,' i. 5, x. 2, 4.: סנהדריות לשבטים. In iv.*Ant.* viii. 16, the local authorities of a city =αἱ ἀρχαὶ καὶ ἡ γερουσία; cf. *ibid.* 14, where the supreme court is curiously described as ὁ ἀρχιερεὺς καὶ ὁ προφήτης καὶ ἡ γερουσία.
[3] Div. ii. vol. i. 162; cf. 185.     [4] Matt. v. 21 ff.     [5] Acts ix. 2.

scribes our Lord as withdrawing from Judæa to Galilee in
order to avoid the designs of the Pharisees,[1] who by
this time had great influence in the Sanhedrin. But
this does not mean that the Sanhedrin 'had no judicial
authority over Him so long as He remained in Galilee.'[2]
For, according to Matthew, when *the Pharisees and scribes
came from Jerusalem* to Him, and *were offended* at
His answers, He *went out thence and withdrew into the
parts of Tyre and Sidon*.[3] In Galilee the arm of the
Sanhedrin might take longer to act than in Jerusalem
—just as it might take longer to act in the remote
Judæan village of *Ephraim, near the wilderness*, to which
for the same reason, according to John, our Lord also
once withdrew,[4]—but ultimately it could reach Galilee
equally with the furthest borders of Judæa.

The influence of the Sanhedrin everywhere haunted
our Lord and His little band of disciples. Just as Herod

How the San-
hedrin
haunted our
Lord.

had spread abroad his spies and himself played
the eavesdropper among the people, so they
with this new prophet. A definite gradation
is observable in their measures.[5] At first, according to all
the Gospels, it was the popular and pervasive Pharisees
who were startled by His influence, began to dog and
question Him, and take counsel how they might destroy
Him.[6] Then deputations of scribes, or of scribes and

---

[1] John iv. 1 ff. ; vii. 1 ; cf. 45.　　[2] Schürer as above, 185.
[3] Matt. xv. 1, 12, 21.　　　　　　　[4] John xi. 53 f.
[5] This in answer to Keim, *Jesus of Nazara*, who in direct contradiction of
the facts says, that 'the Gospels are fond of bringing on the stage from the
very beginning the whole Sanhedrin' (*Eng. Tr.* v. 132).
[6] Matt. xii. 2, 14, 24 (*Pharisees*); 38 (*scribes and Phar.*); Mark ii. 24
(*Phar.*); 16 (*scr. and Phar.*); iii. 6 (*Phar. and Herodians*); Luke v. 17
(*Phar. and doctors of the Law*); 21, 30; vi. 7, 11 (*scr. and Phar.*); John ii.
18 (*the Jews*); iv. 1 (*Phar.*); vi. 41 ff. (*Jews*); vii. 32 (*Phar.*).

Pharisees, came down from Jerusalem with questions,[1] upon which, as fearing the power of the Sanhedrin even in Galilee, He withdrew to the Gentile territory of Tyre and Sidon.[2]  From this point Matthew uses a more formal term for the questioning of the Pharisees: they *tried* or *tested* our Lord.[3]  How aware He was of all the steps they would take in their graded procedure appears from His many allusions to them: first the hatred of one's own family; then the stirring up of the local courts, *when they persecute you in this city, flee ye into the next*;[4] the delivery to the provincial synedria with their prisons and tortures, and to the synagogues with their scourgings;[5] and in the ultimate background *governors and kings* with their powers of life and death.[6]  That capital sentence lowered from the beginning: *be not afraid of them which kill the body.*[7]  Nor was the great intermediate court out of sight.  When at last our Lord felt the net about Him, and said to His disciples that He must go up to Jerusalem, the seat of the Sanhedrin, He described it by the names of its oldest and most executive members, *elders, chief priests and scribes,*[8] who *shall condemn Him to death and shall deliver Him unto the Gentiles* — an exact reflection of their regular procedure.  *It cannot be that a prophet perish out of Jerusalem.*[9]

[1] Matt. xv. 1 ; Mark iii. 22 ; vii. 1.

[2] Matt. xv. 21.  See previous paragraph.

[3] πειράζω.  Matt. xvi. 1 ; xix. 3 ; xxii. 18 ; Mark as early as viii. 11 ; Luke xi. 16 ; cf. John viii. 6.

[4] Matt. x. 21, 23 ; cf. xxiii. 34.

[5] x. 17 : *torturers* (βασανισταί), even in the case of debt ; xviii. 25, 34.

[6] x. 18.

[7] x. 28.

[8] xvi. 21 ; xix. 18 ; Mark x. 33.

[9] Luke xiii. 33.

But our immediate task is to learn the powers and procedure of the Sanhedrin within the City herself.

Here there were really three forces for keeping order and dispensing justice: the supreme Sanhedrin, and the local courts under it ;[1] the Priesthood charged with the watching and discipline of the Temple, but subject of course to the Sanhedrin's interpretation of the law relating to them ; and when he was present, the Procurator, or in his absence the Chiliarch commanding the garrison, with five hundred to a thousand infantry and a cohort of cavalry.

The scholarship of our time has been sharply divided over the question of the character and organisation of the Great Sanhedrin of Jerusalem. Our information on the subject is derived, as has been said, from three sources: the Gospels, Josephus, and the Talmudic literature. The evidence of the last differs in many respects from that of the two former: the question is, which of them are we to trust ? To cite only recent disputants, Jewish scholars like Zunz and Grätz accept the tradition of the Talmud that the Sanhedrin was presided over not by the High Priest, but by successive 'Pairs' of leaders, whose names it gives ; and with them some Christian scholars like De Wette are in agreement. On the other side, Winer, Keil and Geiger have, in contradiction to the Talmud, asserted either the constant, or the usual, presidency of the High Priest; while Jost has defended an intermediate view that the Sanhedrin enjoyed its political rights only in theory, but was prevented from putting them into practice through the usurpation of

---

[1] For a tradition of these, see *Mishna*, ' Sanh.' x. 2.

them by the High Priests and others. Another question
is, when was the Sanhedrin definitely constituted? But
after our survey of the historical evidence we need not
go into this. The whole subject has been admirably expounded and discussed by Kuenen in his essay on 'The
Composition of the Sanhedrin.'[1] His results are hostile
to the Talmudic account of the Sanhedrin, for he
believes he has proved that a Sanhedrin of the type
described or implied in the New Testament and Josephus,
not only coincides with the Jewish form of government
since Alexander the Great, but actually existed since
the third century B.C., and that the modifications which
it underwent before its collapse in 70 A.D. may be stated,
if not with certainty, at least with great probability.
Kuenen's conclusions were generally accepted till recently
Dr. Adolf Büchler, in *The Synedrion in Jerusalem*, etc.,[2]
offered an argument for the existence of two great
tribunals in the Holy City, with separate authorities,
religious and civil; and this view has been adopted by the
*Jewish Encyclopædia* in its article 'Sanhedrin.'

The view, of which Kuenen was the chief exponent
and which has been generally accepted, is that the Great
Sanhedrin in Jerusalem was a single court, the supreme
tribunal of the Jewish nation, which met usually in a
hall in the southern part of the Temple enclosure known

---

[1] See Budde's German edition of Kuenen's *Gesammelte Abhandlungen*,
49-81 : 'Über die Zusammensetzung des Sanhedrin.' The previous
literature I have referred to will all be found there with much more
cited. Useful summaries on the same lines are given by Schürer (*Gesch.
des Jüd. Volkes*, etc.,[3] § 23 (*Eng. Trans.*, div. ii. vol. i. 163-195), with
additional evidence ; and in Robertson Smith's article 'Synedrion' in the
*Ency. Brit.*[9]

[2] *Das Synedrion in Jerusalem und das Grosse Beth-Din in der Quader-
kammer des Jerusalemischen Tempels.* Wien, 1902.

as the *Lishkath hag-Gāzîth* or Chamber of Hewn-
Stone,[1] but which under stress of circumstances might
also meet elsewhere.[2]   There they interpreted
the Law, and in criminal cases gave sentence.
Their power over Jews was, subject to the Procurator's approval of their sentences of death,
unlimited; and in certain cases they did not
wait for references from the lower courts, but acted
directly.   According to the *Mishna* they alone could try
a false prophet or an accused High Priest, or decide
whether the king might make an offensive war; and
Josephus adds that the king was to do nothing without
the High Priest and the opinion of the Senators, and if
he affected too much luxury, was to be restrained.[3]   Also,
they judged directly accused priests and other persons.[4]
The *Mishna* adds that Jerusalem or the Temple Courts
could not be extended without the consent of the Sanhedrin.[5]   The number of the latter was seventy-one.[6]

This view of the Sanhedrin rests upon the evidence of
the New Testament and Josephus, with illustrations from

*(margin note)* Prevalent Conception of the San-hedrin—a single supreme court.

---

[1] *Mishna*, 'Sanh.' x. 2; 'Middôth,' v. 3; the βουλή of Jos. v. *B.J.* iv. 2.
On the origin of the name and on the position of the place, see Schürer,
Eng. Tr., div. ii. vol. i. 191.

[2] Whether the migration related in the *Talmud*, 'Shabbath,' 15a and elsewhere, that forty years before the destruction of the Temple the Sanhedrin
sat in the bazaars, *ḥanuyôth*, be historical or not, it implies that the Sanhedrin
could meet elsewhere than in the Temple Courts, unless by the *ḥanuyôth* we are
to understand the merchants' booths in the outer court : see Schürer, p. 192.

[3] 'Sanhedrin,' i. 5; ii. 2, 4; Jos. iv. *Ant.* viii. 17.   The directions of
the *Mishna* may be partly, but cannot be 'purely theoretical' (so Schürer),
as the witness of Josephus proves.   Yet we learn that Agrippa removed and
set up high priests (as Herod had done), Jos. xix. *Ant.* vi. 2, 4—whether
after consulting the Sanhedrin is not stated.

[4] Besides 'Sanhedrin' as above, see 'Middôth,' v. 3.

[5] 'Sanhedrin,' i. 5; 'Shebuoth,' ii. 2; cf. Maimonides, *Beth hab-Bechereh*,
vi. 10 f.                              [6] 'Sanh.' i. 5 f. : above, p. 387 *n.* 3.

Talmudic literature, when this agrees with it; and with
the rejection of the rest of the Talmudic evidence as
late and unhistorical. Dr. Büchler, however,
has made a fresh examination of the Tal- Büchler's View of two Sanhedrins.
mudic evidence, and has come to the conclusion
that there were two great Jewish tribunals at Jerusalem,
possessing different powers: one with civil authority, the
Sanhedrin of Josephus and the Gospels, one a Sanhedrin
with purely religious functions.[1] The former, he thinks
Josephus indicates, sat in the town, or on the west
edge of the Temple mount.[2] The latter was entitled
'the great Beth-Din, which is in the Lishkath hag-
Gāzîth,' or 'the great Sanhedrin, which sits in the
Lishkath hag-Gazîth.'[3] This second tribunal had to
decide on the purity of priests and other exclusively
religious matters.[4] Neither Josephus nor the Gospels
report of their Sanhedrin that it judged cases concerning
priests, the temple-service, or any religious questions, but
ascribe to it exclusively judicial processes, penal sentences,
and perhaps cases of a political nature. With these the
Talmud does not associate the 'Great Beth-Din in the
*Lishkath hag-Gāzîth.'*[5] Dr. Büchler bases his theory on
no meagre foundation of evidence; his argument is generally reasonable, and his conclusion that there were two
supreme courts meets some difficulties, which are not
removed by the view that there was only one. Still, the
following considerations appear to me to be hostile to it.
Neither in the Gospels nor in Josephus is there any proof
of this duality in the supreme national authority. Had it

[1] Büchler, 4.  [2] *Ibid.* 33.
[3] *Mishna*, 'Sanhedrin,' x. 2; *Sifra*, 19a; Büchler, 34.
[4] Büchler, 33 ff.  [5] *Ibid.* 36.

existed, the descriptions of the Jewish constitution by
Josephus would certainly have contained some explicit
notice of it; nor do the citations by Dr. Büchler from
Josephus necessarily imply it.[1] Nor have we found any
evidence of a second supreme court in our survey of the
constitutional history previous to New Testament times.
Nor does the Talmud itself afford an unambiguous statement that there were two courts—a curious phenomenon,
which would certainly have articulated itself somewhere
in that vast literature as it would in Josephus, had it
actually existed. There is, too, the fundamental idea of
the Jewish system that the civil and religious sides of life
were not separate but everywhere interpenetrating, if not
identical; and the impossibility, as we have seen, of
deciding what matters were religious and what not. To
these considerations may be added the fact, as Dr. Büchler
admits, that the *Lishkath hag-Gāzîth* was so situated, on
the southern edge of the inner court of the Temple but
with a door into the outer court, that a body, partly consisting of laymen, might have gathered in it.[2] The
solution of the problem may be in some such arrangement as we found[3] the Chronicler to record or suggest,
whereby cases purely of the ceremonial law were decided
by the priestly members of the Sanhedrin only. But in
that case the High Priest would surely have presided;
while in the Beth-Din, which Dr. Büchler takes as the
supreme religious court, the Talmud says he did not
preside!

The Sanhedrin and other courts had a certain number
of officers to make arrests and execute their decrees—

[1] ii. *B.J.* xvii. 2-4; xx. *Ant.* ix. 6: Büchler, 36 f.
[2] Büchler, 19; cf. Maim., *Beth hab-Bechereh*, v. 17.  [3] Above, p. 387 f.

'hyperetai,' as the Gospels call them, *constables* or *bailiffs*,[1] and *servants of the High Priest*,[2] whom Josephus describes as enlisted 'from the rudest and most restless characters' both by the High Priests for the collection of tithes, and by the leaders of factions, 'the principal men of the multitude of Jerusalem.'[3] There were in every town town-officers; *watchmen, head of the watch*, and *bailiff*;[4] those of Jerusalem may be included under the general expression Hyperetai. Josephus speaks of the 'public whip,' probably in charge of a special officer.[5] Matthew even mentions *torturers*.[6] *Suborned spies* are spoken of by Luke, one of the several features which he alone introduces to the Gospel narrative.[7] That the *public ward* or *prison* at the disposal of the Sanhedrin[8] was in the town and not in the Temple is implied both by the adjective and by the other details of the story. But besides all these, their own agents and resources, the Sanhedrin could enlist those of the Temple as well.

> The Servants and Instruments of the Sanhedrin.

The Temple discipline is fully set forth in the *Mishna*. Here we are concerned only with that part of it which may be called the Police, and had to do with the watching of the Courts and the control of the crowds who filled them. Josephus and the Book of

> The Temple Guards.

---

[1] Matt. v. 25. In Luke xii. 58 called πράκτωρ, *exactor*, collector of debts, and probably also of tithes.

[2] Matt. xxvi. 51; Mark xiv. 47; John xviii. 10.

[3] Jos. xx. *Ant.* viii. 8, ix. 2.

[4] רִישׁ מְטַרְתָּא, נְטוֹרָא, and סַנְטְרָא (prob. σημαντήρ). See Levy, *Neuheb. u. Chal. Wörterbuch*, under מְטַרָא.

[5] τῷ δημοσίῳ σκύτει, iv. *Ant.* viii. 21.

[6] Matt. xviii. 34.   [7] Luke xx. 20; cf. Jos. xv. *Ant.* viii. 4.

[8] Acts iv. 3; v. 18 ff. It is the hyperetai of the Sanhedrin who go to the prison for the apostles: the captain of the Temple acts only later.

Acts mention a Stratēgos, or Captain of the Temple,[1]
who appears to have belonged to one of the chief priestly
families, and has been reasonably identified with the
*Sĕgān,* who in rank was next to the High Priest himself.[2]
With him were other *Segānîm* or *Stratēgoi.*[3]  The *Mishna*
mentions two officials: the 'Man of the Mountain of the
House,' and the 'Man of the Bîrah' or Temple proper.[4]  It
was the duty of the former to go round the night guards
and watches, and see that none was asleep.   Priests kept
watch at the inner posts, in three 'houses' or rooms (in
one of which, 'the house Moked,' slept the keepers of
the keys of the court); and Levites at twenty-one posts:
ten gates, eight corners, the chambers of the offerings and
the veil, and behind the house of atonement.[5]   Thus by
night the Temple was entirely closed and carefully
watched.   By day a still greater number of guards were
on duty to watch the gates and keep order in the courts.[6]
They had to see that no foreigner passed the fence
which divided the inner court from that of the Gentiles;
they could immediately put to death even Roman citizens
who transgressed this rule, plainly inscribed on the fence
in Greek and Latin.[7]   One of the several copies of this

---

[1] στρατηγὸς τοῦ ἱεροῦ, Jos. vi. *B.J.* v. 3 (294); Acts iv. 1, v. 26; but
στρατηγῶν, xx. *Ant.* ix. 3; ii. *B.J.* xvii. 2; cf. 2 Macc. iii. 4, προστάτης τοῦ
ἱεροῦ καθεσταμένος; 1 Chron. ix. 11; 2 Chron. xxxi. 13, נגיד בית האלהים;
LXX. ὁ ἡγούμενος οἴκου θεοῦ.   In Jer. xx. 1, Pashhur is described as פקיד נגיד
בבית יהוה, and as a priest.

[2] Schürer, ii. i. 257 f.           [3] 'Bikkurim,' iii. 3; Luke xxii. 4, 52.

[4] איש הר הבית, 'Middoth,' i. 2, etc.   איש הבירה, 'Orla,' ii. 12.
Schürer, p. 267, argues that the latter was the Stratēgos of the Temple, the
former a captain who had charge of the outer court; but in *Jer. Talm.* 'Pes.'
vii. 38*a*, כל הר הבית=בירה.

[5] *Mishna,* 'Middoth,' i. 1-9; 'Tamid,' i. 1; cf. Jos. iv. *B.J.* iv. 6; vi.
*B.J.* v. 3, etc. : οἱ τοῦ ἱεροῦ φύλακες.

[6] Philo, *De Praemiis Sacerdotum,* vi.

[7] Acts xxi. 28; Jos. xv. *Ant.* xi. 5; v. *B.J.* v. 2; vi. *B.J.* ii. 4; *Con.
Apion.* ii. 8 f. ; *Mishna,* 'Middoth,' ii. 3.

inscription, in monumental characters, has been discovered :—[1]

ΜΗΘΕΝΑ ΑΛΛΟΓΕΝΗ ΕΙΣΠΟ

ΡΕΥΕΣΘΑΙ ΕΝΤΟΣ ΤΟΥ ΠΕ

ΡΙ ΤΟ ΙΕΡΟΝ ΤΡΥΦΑΚΤΟΥ ΚΑΙ

ΠΕΡΙΒΟΛΟΥ ΟΣΔ' ΑΝ ΛΗ

ΦΘΗ ΕΑΥΤΩΙ ΑΙΤΙΟΣ ΕΣ

ΤΑΙ ΔΙΑ ΤΟ ΕΞΑΚΟΛΟΥ

ΘΕΙΝ ΘΑΝΑΤΟΝ.

'No foreigner is to enter within the railing and
enclosure round the Temple. Whoever is caught will be
responsible to himself for his death which will ensue.'

We have seen that, under the Strategoi of the Temple,
it was the Priests and Levites who attended to the duties
of the watch. Josephus says it required twenty men to
shut the 'eastern gate of the inner shrine (?), which was
of brass,'[2] and two hundred to close 'the doors of the
shrine, which were all overlaid with gold, and almost
entirely of beaten gold';[3] but his words are large, and it
is difficult to see how so many as two hundred men could
be effectively employed upon twenty cubits, the breadth
he gives to the doors. There were besides many lay
servants for the outer gates and courts, and for service
abroad.[4]

---

[1] By M. Clermont-Ganneau in 1871, *P.E.F.Q.*, 1871, 132. *P.E.F. Mem.*,
'Jerusalem,' 423 f.
[2] vi. *B.J.* v. 3.
[3] *C. Apion.* ii. 10. Hudson reads *twenty* for *two hundred*.
[4] Acts v. 26 : ὁ στρατηγὸς σὺν τοῖς ὑπηρέταις.

But as the Temple was 'a Keep overhanging the City, so was Antonia to the Temple.'[1]  This fortress stood on a rock some seventy-five feet high at the north-west corner of the Temple enclosure, to the cloisters of which its garrison descended by two gangways or flights of stairs, and 'taking up position in open order round the colonnades, they kept guard over the people at the Feasts, so that no revolt might take place.'[2]  Luke calls the commander of these troops by his regimental rank Chiliarch, but Josephus, Phrouriarch or commander of the garrison.[3]  That they garrisoned other towers in Jerusalem and so acted as the City police, is both likely in itself and affirmed by Josephus,[4] and that some of them assisted in the arrest of our Lord on Olivet would not be surprising.  But John's Gospel says that Judas received the *Speira* as well as the officers of the chief priests[5]—*Speira* being in the Book of Acts[6] the whole cohort, but in Polybius a *manipulus* or two centuries—and adds that the *Chiliarch* himself was present. No other Gospel includes Roman soldiers among the band which arrested Jesus.

*Antonia and the Roman Garrison.*

[1] Jos. v. *B.J.* v. 8; cf. xv. *Ant.* xi. 4, where he calls it an ἀκρόπολις, but says that the Kings of the Hasmonean family and the High Priests, who had built it before Herod, called it Baris, *i.e.* בִּירָה, *Castle.*  In xviii. *Ant.* iv. 3 he attributes it to Hyrcanus.  In the Book of Acts (*e.g.* xxi. 34, 37) it is called παρεμβολή, which Polybius uses both of an army drawn up for battle, and of a camp, like στρατόπεδον.  Cf. xv. *Ant.* vii. 8: fortified places were two, one to the City itself, the other to the Temple.

[2] Jos. v. *B.J.* v. 8: the whole chapter is on the Antonia.  Josephus calls the gangways or stairs καταβάσεις.  In Acts xxi. 40 they are called ἀναβαθμοί.

[3] Acts xxi., etc. ; xv. *Ant.* xi. 4 ; xviii. *Ant.* iv. 3.

[4] That only part of the Jerusalem garrison was usually in Antonia is expressly stated by Josephus, xx. *Ant.* v. 3.  Some, no doubt, were in Herod's palace and towers, and the cavalry cohort may have had their barracks outside the walls. 　　　　　[5] John xviii. 3. 　　　　　[6] x. I.

The administration of Judæa by Procurators was interrupted in 41 A.D., when Herod Agrippa I., who had already received from Caligula, in 37 and 40, Herod the tetrarchies of Philip, Lysanias and Herod Agrippa I. Antipas, with the title of King, was further endowed by Claudius with Judæa and Samaria; and thus entered upon the full domains of his grandfather, Herod the Great.[1] A repaired profligate, Agrippa reigned three years: benevolent and magnanimous, loyal, in act at least, to Rome, favourable to the Pharisees, sedulous in worship, and enjoying an almost unmixed popularity. His coins are of two kinds. On some, for use in Jerusalem, there is the plain title 'King Agrippa,' with an umbrella and three wheat ears.[2] Others, for circulation in the maritime cities and elsewhere, bear his own image or that of Claudius, with the title 'Great King,' and with epithets expressive of his devotion to Rome.[3] Josephus estimates his annual revenues at twelve millions of drachmæ, about £475,000, but adds that he was often compelled to borrow; his expenses were enormous. He had his own military force, commanded by Silas, the companion of his earlier misfortunes and extravagance. Other events of constitutional interest were his appointment of High Priests; his persecution of the Christians;

---

[1] Agrippa (so on his coins and in Josephus) is called Herod in Acts xii. He was the son of Aristobulus, son of Herod the Great.

[2] See Plate X. No. 4: the legend ΒΑΣΙΛΕΩΣ ΑΓΡΙΠΑ runs from right of the umbrella downwards; such are mostly of the year 6, reckoning from 37 A.D. On the coins of Agrippa see Madden (ed. 1903) 129 ff.; Reinach, *Jewish Coins* (E.T.), 34 ff.; and compare Schürer's note, § 18 *n*. 41.

[3] Βασιλεὺς μέγας 'Αγρίπας φιλόκαισαρ, to which certain inscriptions add εὐσεβὴς καὶ φιλορώμαιος. Another type of coin (or perhaps medal) has on one side 'King Agrippa, friend of Cæsar,' on the other 'Friendship and alliance of King Agrippa with the Senate and the People of Rome.'

his policy against certain citizens of Doris who brought a statue of Cæsar into a Jewish synagogue, and the consequent decree for their punishment by Petronius the Legate of Syria;[1] his building of the Third Wall of Jerusalem,[2] stopped by Claudius on the report of Marsus the successor of Petronius; and his attempt to hold at Tiberias a conference of the Asiatic vassals of Rome, which was suspected and frustrated by the same Marsus. The accounts of Agrippa's sudden death, given by Luke and Josephus, agree in their essential features. It happened at Cæsarea, where he appeared before a great multitude in a splendid robe, and was acclaimed as divine. Josephus adds certain details calculated to win our admiration for the stoicism of the smitten monarch.[3]

When the news reached Rome, Claudius was inclined to bestow the kingdom on Agrippa's son of the same name, but was dissuaded by his counsellors on account of the latter's youth; and Palestine was resumed into the direct administration of the Emperor, with a Procurator over it, as Judæa and Samaria had been governed from B.C. 6 to 41. According to Josephus, the first two of the new series of Procurators, Cuspius Fadus and Tiberius Alexander (44-48), by a scrupulous respect for the Jewish laws, kept the nation tranquil. There followed the unfortunate and blundering govern-

Return of the Procurators.

---

[1] This contains, as reported by Josephus, these phrases: ' It is but a part of natural justice that all should have authority over the places belonging to themselves; both I and King Agrippa, whom I hold in the highest honour, have nothing more in our care than that the Jewish nation may have no occasion for getting together . . . and becoming tumultuous.'

[2] See above, p. 244.

[3] Acts xii.; Jos. xix. *Ant.* iv.-viii.; ii. *B.J.* xi.

ment of Cumanus (48-52); the tyranny of Felix (52-60);
the brief improvements of Festus, terminated by his
death in 62; the venal and hypocritical administration
of Albinus (62-64); and the exasperating cruelties of
Gessius Florus (64-66), which, executed in open and
unashamed alliance with the most turbulent of 'the
Robbers,' estranged from Rome many of the hitherto
patient Jews and provoked the War of Independence
(66-70).[1]

We have seen that the Procurators from 6 to 41 A.D.
issued bronze coins.[2]  This was also done by those
from 44 to 66, who likewise avoided types  <small>Procuratorial</small>
offensive to the Jewish conscience.[3]  These  <small>and other coinage in</small>
Procuratorial bronzes are 'apparently all of  <small>N.T. times.</small>
one denomination, the quadrans (?),'[4] the kodrantēs of the
Gospels.  The *quadrans* was the fourth part of the *as* or
*assarion*;[5] or about five-eighths of a farthing of our money,
and was double the *lepton* or *mite* of the Gospels.[6]  Silver
coins in circulation under the Procurators and mentioned
in the Gospels were: the Tyrian *staters* or *tetradrachms*,
the usual tender in payment of the Temple-tax, of which
one being equal to a shekel paid the tax for two persons,

[1] Jos. xx. *Ant.* i.-ix., xi. ; ii. *B.J.* xi.-xvii.

[2] Above, p. 414.

[3] See Plate x. No. 3 for a coin of Felix with Nero's name on one side and
on the other LE KAICAPOC and a palm-branch.   Year 5 = 59 A.D.

[4] Kennedy, 'Money,' Hastings' *D.B.* iii. 428; 'they may be termed
*quadrantes*': Reinach, *Jew. Coins*, 41 *n.* i.  Κοδράντης, Matt. v. 26; Mk.
xii. 42.  E.V. *farthing*: known popularly by the name of its tariff equivalent,
Chalkos, *copper*.

[5] ἀσσάριον, E.V. *farthing*, Amer. Rev. more properly *penny*; Matt. x. 29;
Luke xii. 6.   Kennedy argues that there were two values of the *assarion*,
'the tariff' as above—the אִיסָר אִיטַלְקִי of the *Mishna*—and the 'current' of

half that amount.   He spells it אִסָּר, iṣṣar.

[6] λεπτόν, Luke xii. 59, xxi. 2; Mk. xii. 42.

as, for example, our Lord and Peter;[1] the Græco-Roman
*tetradrachms* of Antioch; some, but comparatively few,
*didrachms*;[2] *drachms*, which were very numerous, and their
Roman equivalents the *denarii.* It was a *denarius* with *the
image and superscription of Cæsar*, which the Pharisees and
Herodians, the parties respectively of the theocracy and
the Idumean dynasty, brought to our Lord when they
asked Him *if it were lawful to pay tribute to Cæsar*, and
He replied *show Me the tribute money.*[3] The value of the
*denarius* in our money was 9½d. : a fair day's wage for a
labourer.[4] For commercial purposes the *drachm*[5] bore
the same value, but for tariff purposes was fixed at three-
fourths of the *denarius.*[6] In the New Testament silver is
money *par excellence*; it is significant that gold coins are
hardly mentioned.[7] The weight of the Roman *aureus*
varied from 19s. 6d. under Augustus to 18s. 8d. of our
money under Nero. It is the gold dinar of the Talmud,
the 'gold-piece' of Josephus.[8]

　　In A.D. 44, on the death of Agrippa I., his brother Herod
Herod of　　of Chalcis obtained from Claudius authority
Chalcis.　　over the Temple, the sacred treasure and
the appointment of the High Priests.[9] He died in 48,

----

[1] στάτηρ, Matt. xvii. 27; Rev. Vers. shekel. See above, p. 405, Pl. ix.

[2] τὰ δίδραχμα, Matt. xvii. 24, *tribute-money, i.e.* Temple-tax=half shekel :
so rightly in the Rev. Ver. See above, p. 359 *n.* 5.

[3] Ἐπιδείξατέ μοι τὸ νόμισμα τοῦ κήνσου. Οἱ δὲ προσήνεγκαν αὐτῷ δηνάριον.
Matt. xxii. 15 ff. The *Penny* of E.V. is of course inadequate. The
American revisers more happily suggest *shilling.* The *denarius* is in Greek
δηνάριον, in the *Mishna* דִּינָר

[4] Matt. xx. 2 ff. ; Kennedy, pp. 427 f. 432.

[5] Luke xv. 8, *piece of silver*; also probably in Acts xix. 19.

[6] Kennedy, 428; Reinach (39) says 'the d. had been made equivalent to
the Attic drachm.'　　　　　　　　　　　　　　　[7] Matt. x. 9.

[8] *Talm. Jer.*, 'Kidd.' I. 58^d ob. ; v. *B.J.* xiii. 4. For the whole of the
above paragraph I have consulted Madden, Reinach, Kennedy and
Macdonald.　　　　　　　　　　　　　[9] Jos. xx. *Ant.* i. 3.

and was succeeded in all these powers by his nephew
Agrippa II. Resigning Chalcis in 53, this great-grandson
of Herod the Great received what had been
the tetrarchies of Philip and Lysanias, and
Agrippa II.
later from Nero part of Galilee, including Tiberias and
Taricheae.[1] The difference of five years between his
accession to his first and that to his second and greater
dignity may be the explanation of a double date upon
an inscription at eṣ-Ṣanamein in Ḥauran: 'in the 37th
which was also the 32nd year of King Agrippa'; but some
are inclined to read this rather of two other eras beginning
in 56 and 61 respectively.[2] More Roman than any of his
predecessors, Agrippa II. issued coins which do not conform to the Jewish law against images. They display his
own head or that of one of the Emperors on whom this
last of the Herodian dynasty, with all the astuteness but
none of the strength of his fathers, fawned up to his death
about 95.[3] Even before he became King he exerted his
influence at Rome on behalf of his countrymen, by
securing to them the guardianship of the sacred vestments and by persuading Claudius to punish Cumanus.
Down to 66 A.D. Agrippa II. continued to depose and
appoint the High Priests.[4]

The Revolt of the Jews against Rome was undoubtedly

---

[1] Josh. xx. *Ant.* vii. f.

[2] Copied by me in 1901 and described (with a different explanation of the
two eras, as if from 44 and 48 or 49) in the *Critical Review*, ii. 56 (previously
recorded in *Z.D.P.V.* vii. (1884), 121 f. ; cf. *P.E.F.Q.*, 1895, 58). For the
other explanation see Schürer, *Gesch.*, 3rd ed., § 19, Anhang, *n.* 7 ; Macdonald,
*Catalogue of Gr. Coins in the Hunterian Collection*, iii. 290 ; Reinach, *Jewish
Coins*, 37 *n.* 2.

[3] That is the last year found on any of the coins, the year 35, if we take
61 as the era (see above, *n.* 2). Photius says he lived to 100 A.D.

[4] Jos. xx. *Ant.* i. viii. ff.

a revolt of the People, stirred indeed by individuals of the ruling class, but yet in opposition to the main influences of the latter, which were often but vainly exercised in the interests of peace.

When Florus withdrew from Jerusalem, he left the City in charge of the chief priests and Sanhedrin with a cohort to support them.[1] 'The multitude' professed allegiance to Rome in one Assembly called by Neopolitanus, an emissary from the Legate Cestius, and in another under Agrippa;[2] but they refused to obey Florus, and on the incitement of Eleazar, the Temple-Strategos and son to the High Priest, they discontinued the daily sacrifice for the Emperor.[3] 'Influential persons'[4] in conference with chief-priests and notable Pharisees tried to dissuade them, tried then to hold against them the Upper City ; but, reinforced by Sicarii, 'the seditious' overpowered the whole of Jerusalem. A few months later, in the flush of their victory over Cestius, they organised a government. A number of 'the most eminent men' had already deserted the City, but it was from those who remained that a popular assembly elected two governors for Jerusalem, as well as generals for the provinces. Josephus,[5] who was appointed to Galilee, declared that he took his authority from 'the commonwealth of the people of Jerusalem' and from the Sanhedrin ;[6] and it was the High Priest, acting, however, under compulsion from the zealots, and as many of the influential men as were not of the Roman party, who organised the defence of the City.[7] After the Romans

[1] Jos. ii. *B.J.* xv. 6.
[2] *Ibid.* xvi.
[3] *Ibid.* xvii. 2.
[4] Οἱ δυνατοί ; ii. *B.J.* xvii. 3-6.
[5] *Ibid.* xx. 3, 4.
[6] *Vita*, 12, 13.
[7] ii. *B.J.* xxii. 1.

had subdued Galilee in 67, the defeated patriots who escaped him thronged to Jerusalem, to inflame her zeal but to dissipate her strength by the factions which they formed.[1] Their seizure and abuse of the Sanctuary, their outrageous appointments to the High-Priesthood, roused 'the People,' 'the Multitude,' against them, and, with the help of these, two chief priests, Ananias and Jeshua, seemed likely to gain the mastery. They were defeated by the treachery of John and the introduction of the Idumeans.[2] With some brief pretence of the forms of justice, assemblies and other courts, the Zealots started a reign of terror, destroying many of the chief men and other citizens. Then 'John began to tyrannise,'[3] and prevailed in the City till the return in April 69 of Simon Bar-Giora from those raids which Vespasian's delay permitted him to make through the south of Judah.[4] Finally, Jerusalem was divided into three hostile camps, or rather fortresses, of which Simon held the Upper City and a great part of the Lower, John the Temple Mount, and Eleazar, whose party had separated from John, the Inner Court of the Temple. So violently at last did the constitution of Jerusalem break up, at the very hour at which Titus with his legions appeared before the walls, April 70.

In addition to the precious metals stored in the Temple, a great amount of treasure fell to the Jews on their defeat of Cestius in 66, and their authorities coined money down to the end. Some of their bronze coins, uniform in weight and type, are still extant, dated from the second and third

*Coins of the First Revolt, B.C. 66-70 ;*

---

[1] iv. *B.J.* iii.  [2] *Ibid.* iv. f.
[3] *Ibid.* vii. 1.  [4] *Ibid.* ix.

years of the Revolt, with the legend 'Freedom of Sion.'[1] Even in the fourth year, and after the siege had commenced, they continued to issue money. But their silver and copper, if not their gold, had run low, and the coins of this issue in bronze had merely nominal values attached to them—'in fact the equivalent of modern paper money offered by bankrupt states.'[2] They bore a legend rather more intense than that of the earlier years: 'For the Redemption of Sion, year 4.' A number of other coins which used to be attributed to this Revolt[3] are now generally ascribed to the Second Revolt, 132-135 A.D. During this the Jews, possessing little or no treasure, used the silver denarii and Imperial tetradrachms, re-striking them with orthodox Jewish types : vases, palm-branches, citrons, bunches of grapes and trumpets. Bar-cochba's denarii have the legend 'Simon, year 2 of the Freedom of Israel,' his shekels[4] the same (sometimes with 'Jerusalem' substituted for Simon), and 'Year 1 of the Redemption of Israel' with a representation of the Temple and often above it a star in allusion to his name.' One denarius carries on one side a vase and palm, on the other a bunch of grapes with the legends 'Eleazar the Priest' and 'Year 1 of the Redemption of Israel.' Others have on one side Eleazar's, on the other Simon's die. From this Revolt there are also bronze coins, which exhibit similar types and legends.[5]

*and of the Second, A.D. 132-135.*

---

[1] See Pl. x., Nos. 6, 7 and 8, for coins of the second and third year.
[2] Reinach.          [3] See Madden, 198 ff.
[4] See Plate x. No. 9.          [5] See Plate x. No. 10.

# CHAPTER X

## 'THE MULTITUDE'

THROUGHOUT the political history, which we have followed in the previous chapter, we have observed the constant, often the dominant, influence <sub>Meaning of</sub> exercised by the common people; either <sub>the term.</sub> through an assembly of their representatives or by a revolt in mass. Our English version of the Gospels and the Acts designates them as *the multitude*, thus translating two Greek terms: ὁ ὄχλος, *the crowd* or *mob*, and τὸ πλῆθος, *the masses, the body and bulk of the nation.* To realise the political atmosphere of Jerusalem it is not enough to be aware of this restless, ominous background to her great personalities and parties. We must attempt a distinct appreciation of the power of the people, from which every form of the constitution originally derived its authority; to which prophets and tyrants alike appealed; and the influence and methods of which were especially significant in the times of Herod, of our Lord, and of the revolt against Rome.

Although during this last period the constitution of Israel betrays the influence of those Greek and Græcised communities of which Palestine had long been full,[1] it

---

[1] See above, pp. 395 f.

would be a grave error to ascribe to Hellenism any large degree of the Jewish consciousness of the rights and powers of the people. In fact, the Greeks ruled Asia as much by conquest as by culture; and it was not in imitation of their civic institutions, but against the forms of despotism which they developed, that Israel under the Maccabees evinced to the world the vigour and the conscience of her democracy. Of these the Semitic ancestry and the religion of the nation were the original and the most copious sources.

*Sources of democracy in Israel.*

The primitive Semitic tribe was as democratic a society as existed in the ancient world. A blood-brotherhood with an economy mainly communal; its chief but a *primus inter pares*, dependent on the counsel and goodwill of his fellow-tribesmen—under such conditions a tyranny is hardly conceivable. In the camps of the nomads there are neither police, guards, nor a citadel. Behind the sheikh's authority there is nothing but the force of public opinion; to influence the individual nothing but 'shame,' as one has expressed it, 'before the face of his kin.'[1] The effects of so free a discipline, operative perhaps for millennia, before the ancestors of Israel appear in history, were bound to endure in the national temper, and in fact are precipitated in many of the written laws. Even in the rude days of the Judges there was a public conscience among the tribes, and outrages were stamped as *wantonness* or *folly in Israel.*[2] The local courts and national assemblies sanctioned by the

*(1) Racial;*

---

[1] Cf. Wellhausen, *Reste des arab. Heidentums*; Robertson Smith, *Religion of the Semites*, 60, etc.; G. A. Barton, *A Sketch of Semitic Origins*, ch. ii.

[2] Ju. xx. 6, 10, etc.

Law are probably among its most primitive institutions, the equivalents among a people settled to agriculture of the daily conferences of nomads before the tent of their sheikh. When a monarchy was established in Israel it was in answer to the desire of the people. The crown was offered to David through their representatives ; and the movement which constituted the ten tribes into a separate kingdom was a popular revolt. The government of Jerusalem herself was directly royal, but for that (as we have seen [1]) there were reasons ; and even so it was the people of Jerusalem who more than once determined the succession to the throne of Judah.

In the same direction, if with a different character, conspired the influences of religion. The prophets of the ninth and eighth centuries, inconceivable except in a large and free public life, at once (2) Religious. rose from and appealed to the people. It is true that while some of the merely professional members of this class were the servile flatterers of the court, others, almost as basely, were demagogues with no higher ideals than those of a vulgar and unethical patriotism. But the true prophets, who spoke in the name of a God exalted in righteousness, equally aimed at the people ; and in their indictments of unjust rulers and the vices of the crowd, relied upon the existence of a public conscience. They rewakened the people's memory of their divinely guided history, the people's instincts of justice and of duty ; addressing them in the mass and setting before them the ideal of a nation wholly devoted to righteousness. While he insisted upon the need of just and strong princes,

[1] Above, pp. 377 ff.

Isaiah equally emphasised the necessity among ordinary citizens of character and the power to discriminate character. The prophets had no programme of political rights. But in their protests against the policy or the character of the rulers and in the confidence with which they appealed to their fellow-citizens upon the righteousness of their message, they illustrated at once the duty of the individual conscience to assert itself, and the example of reliance upon the soundness of popular opinion when the leaders of the nation have gone astray. Nor could the prophets enforce as they did the legal and economic rights of the poor, without exciting in the latter some sense of their political power as well. In one direction their energy operated powerfully towards democracy, and may be illustrated by a similar movement in Western society. M. Fustel de Coulanges[1] has remarked that with the rise of the *plebs* to power in Greece and in Rome a new dogma appeared in politics. Loyalty to the national ritual, and to tradition in general, was replaced by 'the public interest,' from which there followed, of course, the necessity of popular discussion and national suffrage. The Hebrew prophets were also hostile to ritual, and equally they gave to Israel in its place a dogma of 'the public interest': ethical service, the discharge of justice and the ministry of the poor. These, instead of sacrifices and rites, they proclaimed as the demands of God upon His people. In the following century the provisions of Deuteronomy for the expression of public opinion, with its emphasis upon domestic religion and education, and above all, the individualism which Jeremiah and Ezekiel developed in the national religion, were strong factors in

---

[1] *La Cité Antique*, 19th ed., 376 f.

the same direction. Throughout the course of history nothing has contributed more powerfully to the political enfranchisement of the masses than such conviction as the prophets express of the common man's immediate relation to God : *they shall teach no more every man his neighbour, and every man his brother, saying Know the Lord, for they shall all know me, from the least of them to the greatest of them, saith the Lord.*

It was with reason, therefore, that the pioneers of democracy in Europe appealed for their principles and sought their precedents rather in the Old Testament than in the New (which does not concern itself with the liberties of a nation), and chiefly in the history of Israel under the Kings.[1] The pilgrim to Jerusalem from the free communities of the West, as he contemplates the few remains of her ancient walls or treads the great platform on which in face of their Temple her people once gathered to listen to their prophets, and make covenant with their God, cannot but be stirred by emotions even deeper and more grateful than those aroused upon the Areopagus or among the ruins of the Forum. The student of the prophets, as he realises their equal insistence upon the Word of God, upon the need of strong and just rulers, upon the religious and economic rights of every common citizen, and upon the substitution for confidence in ritual of the ethical service of men, must recognise principles, of which all social philosophies and systems since constructed present only the fragments and details.

The Debt of the Peoples to Jerusalem.

[1] Cf. the author's *Modern Criticism and the Preaching of the Old Testament,* 260 ff.

*For that the leaders took the lead in Israel,*
*For that the people offered themselves willingly,*
*Praise ye the Lord.*

In the reconstitution of Israel after the Exile we trace the working of these same forces : the influence of the Divine Word, the justice and energy of heroic personalities, the consent and participation, not of the heads of families alone, but of every adult in the community : *all the men of Judah and Benjamin, the children of Israel assembled, all who had separated themselves from the peoples of the land unto the Law of God, their wives, sons and daughters, every one having knowledge and understanding.*[1] This covenant of the whole people, upon which Israel was freshly built, was never forgotten ; the *Assembly* or *Congregation*[2] remained a Jewish institution to the end. For the period from Nehemiah to the Maccabees we have little evidence, but such as exists shows us *the multitude* in *assembly*; sometimes in consultation with the High Priest and his immediate council,[3] sometimes, when he abused his civil power, assuming this to themselves. The Pseudo-Aristeas makes the High Priest write to Ptolemy that he had convened 'the whole body of the people'[4] to hear the request for scribes learned in the law and to select such as should be sent. And Josephus narrates that when the High Priest Onias endangered the commonwealth by withholding the national tribute to Ptolemy Euergetes, B.C. 246-221, Joseph

The Power of the People under Nehemiah

and under the High Priests.

---

[1] See above, p. 383 : on the popular power a few years before this under Haggai and Zechariah, p. 381.

[2] הָקָהָל, ἐκκλησία or συναγωγή.　　[3] See above, pp. 383, 386, 397, 401.

[4] τὸ πᾶν πλῆθος : see above, pp. 390 f.

son of Tobias went into the Temple and 'called together the multitude to an Assembly,'[1] who took the financial responsibilities of their ruler upon themselves and sent ambassadors of their own to their Greek suzerain. And this reminds us that while the High Priests and the ruling families farmed the taxes of the nation and used other opportunities of finance to their own profit and power, there were in these last the occasions also of the common citizen, and the origins of fortunes outside the oligarchy.[2] The increase of commerce, consequent on the wide Diaspora of the Jews, did not fail to work to the same result. For further evidence of the popular power in the Greek period, and especially in the growing influence of the scribes, see what has been said above on the political temper and atmosphere of Ecclesiasticus.[3]

We have seen how, when the Nation was ruined by Antiochus Epiphanes and the Sanctuary desecrated, *the Congregation gathered for battle and for prayer*; and how the Maccabees reconstituted Israel <sub>Under the Maccabees</sub> from the conscience and energy of the common people.[4] It was these who gave the High-Priesthood to Jonathan,[5] it was *the multitude* who approved of his proposals to re-build the wall and appointed Simon his successor,[6] and it was a convocation of priests, people, rulers and elders who invested Simon with absolute power.[7]

Under the Hasmonean kings the Pharisees were the party trusted by 'the multitude';[8] the nation rose against

---

[1] Jos. xii. *Ant.* iv. 2 : συγκαλέσας τὸ πλῆθος εἰς ἐκκλησίαν.
[2] See above, pp. 368, 399.      [3] Above, pp. 391 f.
[4] See above, pp. 400 f.      [5] Jos. xii. *Ant.* x. 6.
[6] *Ibid.* xiii. v. 11, vi. 3 : τὸ πλῆθος.      [7] See above, p. 404.
[8] xiv. *Ant.* xv. 5 : cf. xiii. *Ant.* xi. 6 ; xiii. *Ant.* xiii. 5, τὸ ἔθνος.

Alexander Jannæus; and appeared through ambassadors before Pompey to oppose both Hyrcanus and Aristo-

and Has-monean kings. bulus, rivals for the throne.[1] Aristobulus muti-lated Hyrcanus, from fear that 'the multi-tude might make him king.'[2]

But the instances which most distinctly illustrate the meaning of the New Testament *multitude* are those

The Multi-tude under Herod. described by Josephus in his histories of Herod the Great and of Archelaus. Josephus ap-plies the words ὄχλος and ὄχλοι, *crowd* and *crowds*, to any throng of the people at the religious feasts, games or spectacles;[3] but also to their gatherings for armed revolt,[4] to the mass of an army,[5] and even to the populace as a whole.[6] In the same general meanings he sometimes employs τὸ πλῆθος,[7] but at others uses this term in a more formal sense—the people organised for petition, or for consultation with the king, or for the trial of accused persons. On such occasions the details of the popular procedure are of the greatest interest.

Herod's troubles with 'the multitude' began on his embellishment of Jerusalem in honour of Augustus, about

The People's feeling against Images. B.C. 25. When the people cried out against what they supposed to be images among the trophies he set up, he summoned 'their most eminent men,' and showed that the trophies stripped of

---

[1] xiv. *Ant.* iii. 2.    [2] *Ibid.* xiii. 10.

[3] xvi. *Ant.* i. 2, v. 1; xvii. *Ant.* viii. 4 (where ὁμίλος is also used : cf. Rev. xviii. 17).

[4] xvii. *Ant.* v. 5; cf. under the Romans xx. *Ant.* vi. 2.

[5] xv. *Ant.* v. 2, 3.

[6] *Ibid.* vii. 7 (a pestilence carried off 'the greater part τῶν ὄχλων,' of the masses): cf. xx. *Ant.* viii. 5; *Vita* 31.

[7] xv. *Ant.* vii. 10; xvii. *Ant.* vi. 3 (almost synonymous with ὄχλος), ix. 2, x. 5, 10; xviii. *Ant.* i. 4, etc.

their ornament were but pieces of wood—a happy jest
to the majority, who were disposed by it to change their
feelings towards him.   But ten of the citizens were not
thus propitiated, and formed a conspiracy to slay the
king, which he discovered by his spies, and put the conspirators to the sword.   They died undauntedly protest-
ing their piety in seeking the death of so great an enemy
to the nation and corrupter of its customs.[1]

When 'the multitude' were unwilling to assist him in
building the Temple, Herod won them over to his vast
designs, not without difficulty, by 'calling
them together' and explaining his motives
and the methods he proposed to meet their
objections.[2]   Again, in B.C. 14, when he returned to
Jerusalem from his visit to Marcus Agrippa, the Emperor's
son-in-law, 'he brought together an Assembly of the
whole people, the crowd from the country was also great';
made what Josephus calls 'an apologia of his whole
journey,' dwelling on his assistance to the Jews of Asia
Minor and all his good fortune; and remitted to the
people one-fourth of their taxes—'so they went their
ways with the greatest gladness.'[3]   In B.C. 12 he made
another 'apologia' to an Assembly on the favourable
results of his visit to Augustus, and explained his dis-
positions with regard to his sons; but while the greater
part of his audience accepted these, the rivalry of the
young princes excited among the rest revolutionary
ambitions.[4]

About B.C. 8 Herod appealed to the people in another
form.   Two of his guards having under torture charged

Herod's
Apologias to
the People.

---

[1] xv. *Ant.* viii. 1-4.
[2] *Ibid.* xi. 1, 2.
[3] xvi. *Ant.* ii. 5 (§§ 62-65).
[4] *Ibid.* iv. 6.

his sons, Alexander and Aristobulus, with designs on his life, Herod, apparently with respect to the Law which

'The Multitude' as Judges.

directed the parents of a rebellious son to bring him before the elders of their township to be stoned by all the men,[1] produced the tortured witnesses to declare their accusations before 'the multitude in Jericho,' and the latter stoned them. They would also have stoned the two princes had not Herod, through his friends, 'restrained the multitude,' and put his sons into prison to await the orders of the Emperor.[2] Augustus directed him to call a special court, which met at Beyrout. Of the 150 members, Roman officials and Herod's own friends, the majority voted for death, but Saturninus the president and his three sons for imprisonment. While Herod hesitated to inflict the capital

The case of Tero.

sentence, an old soldier of his, Tero by name, spoke openly what many others thought, 'crying out among the multitudes that truth was perished and justice abolished from among men, while lies and malice so prevailed and brought such a fog upon affairs that the guilty became blind to the very greatest mischiefs men can suffer.' Tero even faced the king himself, reproaching his methods of government, and daring him to slay the princes. 'Dost thou not notice that the silence of the crowds at once sees the sin and abhors the passion, that the whole army and its officers commiserate the unfortunates and detest the men who have brought about these things?' Tero, after being tortured with his son and the king's barber, who had volunteered an accusation, was with 300 officers brought before an Assembly, and by the fickle multitude stoned to death. The conspiracy

[1] Deut. xxi. 18 ff.       [2] xvi. *Ant.* x. 5.

alarmed Herod, and he had Alexander and Aristobulus immediately strangled.[1]

Again in 4 B.C. two teachers of the Law, Judas and Matthias, celebrated for their eloquence and beloved by the people, incited their disciples to destroy the works which Herod had erected contrary to the Law. When the Temple courts were thronged with people they cut down the golden eagle; but forty were arrested by the king's soldiers and apparently brought before an Assembly at Jericho. On their asserting their readiness to die for the Law they had vindicated, Herod declared to 'the principal men among the Jews' that the accused had at once affronted himself and done sacrilege against God, whereupon 'the people,' in fear of the dying lion, disowned the deed and approved the punishment of its authors.[2] But the fate of their beloved teachers rankled in the minds of 'the seditious'; and these, after vainly appealing to Archelaus on his accession, took action at the next Passover when 'an innumerable throng had come up out of the country.' Archelaus sent a regiment, but the multitude stoned them off, and went on with the sacrifices 'which were already in their hands.' The whole army was ordered out, and the revolt quelled with the slaughter of 3000 people: the rest fled to their homes or to the mountains.[3]

The People's Devotion to the Law.

These instances prove how even the most unscrupulous tyrant of the Jews found it necessary to conciliate the people, and expedient to employ the consultative and judicial courts through which their ancient constitution allowed them to express their

Summary under Herod.

[1] xvi. *Ant.* xi. 4.     [2] xvii. *Ant.* vi. 1-4.
[3] *Ibid.* ix. 1-3.

will. We also see that while it was possible for Herod to influence their prominent representatives, less by his casuistry than by the power of death he held over them, and while a large proportion of the masses were easily flattered, there was always a remnant incorruptible in their devotion to the Law. Among these were private individuals of great piety, lofty eloquence and a supreme contempt of death.

It was the body of the Jewish people who besought the Romans to take the government of Judæa into their own hands. After the massacre at the Pass-over of 3 B.C., ambassadors were sent 'by authority of the nation' to Augustus. 'The head and front of their demand was this: to be delivered from the kingly and similar forms of government; that being annexed to the Province of Syria they might be subject to the Governors sent thither; for thus it would become manifest whether they were really seditious and given to revolt or not, when they had moderate men set over them.' Their plea was met by Nicolaus, the royal advocate, with charges of incurable seditiousness; and, as is well known, Augustus compromised the matter by taking the crown from Archelaus, but appointing him ethnarch of half his father's domains. In 6 A.D., on a second accusation both 'by his kinsmen and the principal men of Judæa and Samaria,' Archelaus was banished and Judæa became a Roman province.[1] The mass of the people were induced by the High Priest Joazar to accept the fiscal measures of the first Procurator, Cyrenius; but Judas of Gamala and a Pharisee named Saddok persuaded many

*The People's Hope in Rome and their first Seditions.*

[1] xvii. *Ant.* xi. 1-4, xiii.; see above, pp. 413 f.

that obedience was no better than slavery, and effected a wide sedition. In these men Josephus marks the rise of a fourth sect among the Jews. After explaining the piety and popular religious doctrines of the Pharisees and their influence with the multitude, the consequent obligation of the Sadducees, when in power, to conform to the Pharisaic doctrines, and the separate communion of the Essenes; he describes the party of Judas as in general agreement with the Pharisees, but 'with an invincible love of liberty, maintaining that God is their only Governor and Lord, despising every form of death, nor allowing the fear of it to make them call any man lord.'[1]

There can be no doubt that Josephus is right in discriminating here a new departure in the politics of the people. This started indeed with the religious character which had always dis-tinguished popular movements in Israel, but was gradually warped, by the new shapes of foreign despotism with which it contended, into the attitude and temper of a mainly political revolution. There is ample evidence that the mass of the people were content to live quietly under the Roman rule, so long as this was exercised with due respect to the religious forms of the nation and their own courts of law, and without oppression of their poverty. But any phase of despotism, however mild, was intolerable to the new party, who more or less consciously substituted a political for a religious ideal; and then, partly by the perversion of their contempt for their own death into a disregard of human life in general, partly by association with all the reckless spirits of the time, and partly because embittered

The New Departure in Popular Politics.

---

[1] xviii. *Ant.* i.

by the cruelties of some of the governors, degenerated into groups of desperadoes at war with society and often with each other. Although the body of the people and their wiser leaders showed wonderful patience under the religious or fiscal oppressions inflicted by certain of the governors, and even preferred a passive death to revolt, every abuse of power by the Romans drove more of them over to the parties of violent measures, till, as Josephus says, under the exactions of Gessius Florus the whole nation 'began to grow mad with this distemper,' and rose in that revolt, from the factious zeal of which, no less than by the success of Titus in breaking it, Jerusalem perished.

Some illustrations may be given of this development of sixty years from 6 to 66 A.D., and first of its nobler Illustrative factors. In the Procuratorship of Pilate Instances. multitudes of Jews came to Cæsarea to beg him to remove the 'images of Cæsar' from Jerusalem. He surrounded them with soldiers, but they bared their throats, willing to die rather than have their laws broken.[1] When Vitellius would have marched his army through Judæa, 'the principal men' met and dissuaded him because of the images the soldiers would carry.[2] When Caligula ordered that his statue should be erected in Jerusalem, and Petronius the Legate of Syria was on his way to fulfil the command, 'many ten thousands of Jews' met him at Ptolemais, and besought that he would not force them to transgress the laws of their fathers. When they followed him to Tiberias and he asked if they meant war, they said No, but we rather die than break our laws, and threw themselves on their faces ready to be

---

[1] xviii. *Ant.* iii. 1.                    [2] *Ibid.* iv. 3.

slain.  This they did for forty days, neglecting the tillage
of their lands although it was seed-time.[1]  When some of
their leaders impressed upon Petronius the resoluteness of
'the multitude,' he promised to write to Caligula and risk
the attraction of the Imperial anger upon himself, if they
would but go back to their fields.  The result was that
Caligula withdrew the order, and Petronius escaped the
consequences of his intrepidity only through the Emperor's
death.[2]  The letter of Claudius concerning the sacred
vestments is addressed 'to the rulers, senate, people of
Jerusalem, the whole nation of the Jews.'[3]  Under
Cuspius Fadus, about 45 A.D., Theudas, who gave himself
out as a prophet, persuaded a great part of the people to
follow him to the Jordan and see him divide the river,
but Fadus, suspecting a political movement, sent cavalry
in pursuit, and Theudas with many of the people was
slain.[4]  The Procurator Cumanus (A.D. 48-52) had several
conflicts with the multitude.  Anticipating sedition at a
Passover, he drew up a regiment in the Temple cloisters,
and on one of the soldiers using an indecent gesture
to the crowds of worshippers, a tumult ensued in which
many were crushed to death.  On their flight from the
City, some of the rioters robbed an imperial servant.
Upon the principle of communal responsibility, still
enforced in the East, Cumanus sent soldiers to punish
the nearest villages and arrest their chiefs.  In these
proceedings a copy of the Law was torn to pieces by

---

[1] Philo, *Legat. ad Caium*, says it was near harvest.
[2] xviii. *Ant.* viii. 2-8.  There is also an interesting instance of the gathering of the multitude to an Assembly by one Simon ($\pi\lambda\hat{\eta}\theta$os εἰς ἐκκλησίαν
ἁλίσας), learned in the Law, to accuse King Agrippa of not living holily, but
Agrippa conciliated the man, xix. *Ant.* vii. 4.
[3] xx. *Ant.* i. 2.                                    [4] *Ibid.* v. 1.

a soldier with insulting language.  A large popular
gathering marched on Cæsarea, asking Cumanus for
vengeance, not for themselves but for God whose laws
had been affronted, and the Procurator appeased them
by ordering the soldier to be executed.[1]  On another
occasion, when he refused satisfaction to the Galilean
pilgrims to Jerusalem for the slaughter of some of their
number by the Samaritans, they persuaded the Jewish
commonalty[2] to take arms and regain their liberty, for
'in itself slavery was a bitter thing, but when joined with
wanton violence it was altogether unbearable.'  They
would not listen to some principal men, who tried to
pacify them, but sought the assistance of Eleazar, a
bandit, and plundered many Samaritan villages.  Cumanus
attacked them with four infantry regiments and many
were slain.  After this sharp lesson they yielded to the
expostulations of 'the most eminent men of Jerusalem,'
that by such conduct they would utterly subvert their
country, and returned to their homes, while the bandits
withdrew to their mountain fastnesses.  But, adds
Josephus, after this time all Judæa was filled with
robberies.[3]  Again, one Doctus induced a crowd to revolt
from Rome, and for a time Cumanus feared the whole
commonalty of Jerusalem would join them.[4]  Affairs grew
worse, as they could not but do, under Felix, A.D. 52-60,
'who with every cruelty and lust exercised the power of
a king in the temper of a slave.'[5]  'The Robbers' mixed
with the crowds at the Temple festivals, and proved how
inadequate is the name that Josephus gives them by

[1] xx. *Ant.* v. 2-4.          [2] τὸ πλῆθος τῶν ᾽Ιουδαίων.
[3] xx. *Ant.* vi. 1.          [4] *Ibid.* vi. 2.
[5] Tacitus, *Hist.* v. 9.

'persuading many to follow them into the wilderness' to
a political revolt.  For the moment Felix broke their
power by wholesale crucifixion and imprisonment.  But
they were succeeded by 'the Sicarii,' secret assassins, who
rendered life in Jerusalem absolutely insecure ; while
'prophets' continued to appear, 'prevailed with the
multitude to act like madmen, and went before them into
the wilderness promising that God would show there
the signals of liberty.'  We shall never understand the
history of the City without appreciating this conspiracy
between its people and the free, wild desert at their gates.
An Egyptian 'prophet' led up thousands[1] from the
desert to the Mount of Olives to show them how at his
command the walls of the City would fall, with the destruction, of course, of the Roman power.  But Felix dispersed them.  There arose, too, a conflict between 'the
principal men of the multitude and the chief priests.'[2]
Under Festus the Sicarii grew more bold, and captured
some officers of the Temple as hostages against those of
their own number who had been arrested.[3]  Quarrels
about the high-priesthood and the oppression of the
people by members of the royal family increased the
disorder.  To propitiate the multitude Albinus, the next
Procurator, A.D. 62-64, emptied the prisons but thereby
filled the country with violence.  The completion of the
works on the Temple let loose a large number of men
without employment—Josephus says 18,000.  Then came
the last and the worst of the Procurators, Gessius Florus,

---

[1] Acts xxi. 38 says 4000 ; Josephus, ii. *B.J.* xiii. 5, 30,000 ; and in xx.
*Ant.* viii. 6 he says this man persuaded $\tau\hat{\varphi}$ $\delta\eta\mu\sigma\tau\iota\kappa\hat{\varphi}$ $\pi\lambda\hat{\eta}\theta\epsilon\iota$, the masses of
Jerusalem, to go with him.

[2] xx. *Ant.* viii. 5-8 ; ii. *B.J.* xiii. 2-5.

[3] xx. *Ant.* viii. 10, ix. 3.

A.D. 64-66, ' who compelled us,' says Josephus, ' to take up arms against Rome.' The reason is obvious. Florus disgusted the respectable members of the populace by conniving at ' the Robbers' ' operations for a share of their spoil, and thus drove some of the best friends of Rome among the Jews over to the more active and fanatic groups.[1] We have seen from Josephus how he was appointed to the command of affairs in Galilee by an Assembly in Jerusalem; and how he invoked for his measures the authority sometimes of the Sanhedrin, sometimes of ' the commonwealth of the people of Jerusalem.' But he was compelled also to pay blackmail to ' the Robbers.' That he represents his rivals as exciting the populace to revolt, and himself as, at first at least, exercising restraint, may be due to his wish, when he wrote his life, of standing well with his Roman patrons. Yet when this is allowed for, there remains sufficient evidence that the nation, exasperated by the atrocities of Florus and inflamed by its fanatic and reckless members, whether in the name of religion or of liberty, forced the more staid of its leaders, and even the most astute and influential among these, into open war against Rome.[2]

Such, then, were the political conditions among which the Gospels describe our Lord as entering on His These Political ministry. Below, there teemed a restless and Conditions obvious in the an ambitious people—in part, at least, educated Gospels. by the Pharisees, and in part blindly following this sect which had risen from among themselves. Accustomed to discussion and the expression of their own will through local courts and national assemblies; sensi-

[1] xx. *Ant.* xi. I ; ii. *B.J.* xiv. f.          [2] See above, pp. 432 ff.

tive to eloquence and beneath its spell aware of their sheer
weight and movement; straining, beyond all hold of their
teachers, for the appearance of prophets, and (1) The Jewish
throbbing to the promises of a great leader People.
with which their sacred books abounded; they felt the
brute blood and strength in them as the omen of that
divine suddenness with which the Apocalypses, so
popular at the time, declared that the Kingdom of
Heaven, the redemption of Sion, should arrive. Among
them were many of a devout temper whose ideals were
spiritual, and who were content, as were others not so
spiritual, with their foreign yoke, so long as it was
moderately exercised. All were jealous for the Law
and the purity of the national worship; but the mass
were possessed in addition with a passion for political
freedom that sometimes intensified and sometimes overwhelmed the other elements of their faith. Fickle,
therefore, and beyond most 'multitudes' frankly fickle,
they swung now to the spiritual and now to the material
goals of their hope; ready to acclaim any prophet
who promised deliverance, but as ready to turn on
him if they found that his purpose did not include their
political enfranchisement. Above, hung the Roman
power, armed, vigilant, menacing; anxious at heart to
understand the people and to conserve their (2) The Roman
laws and customs; but blundering by accident, Power.
or through the insolence and greed of its agents, into cruel
insults and oppressions; always provocative to the pride
and defiling to the conscience of the nation; the embodiment of every worldly force that had ever crushed their
liberties or polluted their religious life. Around, lay in
the first place those Greek communities, which must have

infected the Jewish townships of Galilee and Jerusalem herself with their particular restlessness and love of change—
(3) The Greek that *neoterismos* which Josephus feels increas-
Communities. ing among his countrymen through all this
period ;[1] and in the second place those great deserts,
(4) The Deserts. their spaces so near and so free for large
popular rallies, their scenery so native to
fanaticism, their air so redolent of the origins and most
heroic recoveries of Israel.

We see it all in the Gospels.   In Galilee *the multitude*
is always ready to gather; always about Jesus.   Weaned
Jesus and the from their homes, their tillage, their fishing,
Multitude. careless even of their food, they follow Him
into desert places.   The most sane among them want to
know when the Kingdom shall be given to Israel; the most
mad call the spirits that possess them by the name of the
nation's incubus, the Legion.   The people desire to make
Him king, by the same force with which their fathers had
deposed and appointed monarchs for untold ages.   And
they had a conscience among them—a rough moral
instinct which Herod Antipas feared when he did wrong,
and to which Jesus confidently appealed from the religious
authorities.   But till He came they had no true leader,
and He had compassion on them as sheep without a
shepherd.   When He went up to Jerusalem it was still
with the crowds, 'the innumerable throng from the
country,' who would keep festival, and it was not a city

---

[1] It is very doubtful how much Greek example influenced the Jews.   Their
frequent cry for liberty, when it sounds alone, sounds more essentially
human than particularly Greek, and is generally accompanied by a religious
pretext.   The leaders, whether 'prophets' or 'robbers,' have practically all
Hebrew names, and the trend of the movements they start is not towards the
(Greek) city, but towards the (Semitic) desert.

which He addressed there, but a nation concentrated like a city beneath one man's influence. The mountains were around, the deserts lay near. Had He ordered them to the wilderness they would have followed Him as they followed the Egyptian and Theudas. Had He promised that the walls of Jerusalem would fall before Him and the Roman garrison be swept to the sea, they would have died for Him by their thousands as they died for others. But He never spoke against Rome. He recognised their duty to Cæsar. He said that His kingdom was not of this world, and that only the truth could make them free. Therefore they turned against Him, and within a week of welcoming Him as king to the City—though Judas and the priests still feared their uncertain temper[1]—they haled Him, a criminal, before the Roman governor, and with Rome they shared the guilt of His death.

In the Book of Acts the same mobility and power of the 'multitude' of Jerusalem are several times visible, and we are reminded in addition by the danger of Paul, when he introduced (as was supposed) Greeks to the Temple, of the one occasion on which the multitude had summary powers of death with which even Rome hesitated to interfere.[2] Stephen's murder, on the other hand, was not within the powers permitted to the Jews by Rome. It is also of interest that in the Book of Acts the Christian Church works officially upon the democratic precedents set her throughout the law and history of the Old Covenant. The hundred and twenty gathered to elect an apostle in place of Judas are called *a crowd*; the πλῆθος of them that believed were of one heart and one soul ;[3] when there

*'The Multitude' in Acts.*

---

[1] Luke xxii. 6.     [2] Acts xxi.: above, pp. 414, 424 f.     [3] Acts ii. 15; iv. 32.

arose a murmuring of the Hellenists against the Hebrews, the twelve called *the multitude together*, and when they had made their proposals, *the saying pleased the whole multitude*, and they chose the seven deacons.[1]  *The Multitude* is the name for the Christian community at Antioch.[2]  The same Greek term which Luke uses for the populace of Greek cities[3] and for the men of Israel,[4] he applies to the body of the faithful in Christ Jesus.

[1] Acts vi. 1-5 : τὸ πλῆθος.

[2] xv. 30 ; cf. verse xii.

[3] xiv. 4 ; xix. 9, etc.

[4] xxi.

# GENERAL INDEX TO VOLUME I.

civil power, 381 *f.*, 386, 393 *f.*,
404 *f.*, 414 *f.*, 423 ; responsible for
the taxes, 394, 399, 440 *f.*
High Level Aqueduct, 127, 128,
130.
Hilderscheid, on the rainfall at Jerus.,
19 *n.*, 77 *n.* ; on the climate, 79 *n.*
Hill, G. F., and Mary Hill, Eng.
trans. of *Jewish Coins*, 406 *n.*
Hill of Evil Counsel, 31, 53.
—— of Offence, 53.
Hinnom, Valley of, 38, 46, 49, 56,
241, Book I. chap. vii. *See also*
Gai.
Hippicus, the tower, 240, 242, 243,
243 *n.*, 244 *f.*
Hittites and horses, 324.
Hölscher, *Palästina in der pers. u.
hellenist. Zeit*, 396 *n.*
Holy City (the name), 269.
—— Sepulchre, 48, 248, 249.
Homer, on the Solymi, 262 ; on the
Phrygians, 324.
Hommel, *Alt-Isr. Ueberlieferung*,
172 *n.* ; *Geog. u. Gesch. des Alt.
Orients*, 331 *n.* ; *Geog. Vorder-
asiens*, 299 *n.*
Honey, 306.
Horim, the cave-men, 283.
—— the free-born Jews, 383.
Hornstein, Dr., 92, 103.
Horses, import of, 308, 322, 324 *f.*,
340.
Horse-Gate. *See* Gates of City.
Hort, 264.
Hosea, 356, 369.
Hoskins, 286 *n.* *See* Libbey.
Huddleston, Professor, 52 *n.*
Hudson on Josephus, 425 *n.*
Hull, Professor, *P.E.F. Memoir on
Geology*, etc., 52, 78 *n.*
Huram-abi, 331.
Hyksos, the, 324.
Hyperetai, 423.
Hyrcanus I., or John Hyrcanus, 131,
160, 163, 194, 348, 408 *f.*, 410.
—— II., 194, 410 *f.*, 442.
—— son of Tobias, 365.

Ibn Jobair, 344.
—— Tahîr, 65.
Idrisi, 173, 331 *n.*
Idumeans, subdued by Hyrcanus I.,
409 ; Idumean force in Jerus., 433.

Imhoof-Blumer, on Jewish coins,
406 *n.*
Imports of Jerusalem, 314, Book II.
chap. v.
Incense, 333.
Industries of Jerusalem, 335, 372 *f.*,
Book II. chap. viii.
Inscription from Herod's Temple,
425.
—— in Siloam Tunnel, 94.
Irby and Mangles, *Travels*, 319 *n.*
Iron in Lebanon, Palestine and
Arabia, 331 *f.*
Isaac Chelo, 145 *n.*
Isaiah, 104 *n.*, 147, 347, 378.
Ish-bosheth, 315.
Ishmaelites, 320, 323, 327.

Jabbok, remains of iron mines, 332.
Jacob, 343.
Jaffa Gate. *See* Gates of City.
Jason, or Jeshua, High Priest (175
B.C.), 399.
Jebel Deir Abû Tor, 31, 32, 42, 44,
126.
Jebel el-Fureidis, 130.
Jebel 'Osha, 14.
Jebel Usdum, 319.
Jebus, 266.
Jebusites, 135, 137 *f.*, 140, 227, 266.
Jehoiakim, 346.
Jehoshaphat, 387.
Jehoshua, the Priest, 381.
Jeremiah, 148 *f.*, 330, 332, 356, 369,
378 *f.*, 438.
Jeremiah's Grotto, 54.
Jericho, trade and trade routes, 14,
315, 318, 341, 368 ; assembly at, 444.
Jerome, 17 *n.*, 62, 64 *n.*, 65 *n.*, 116,
144 *n.*, 163, 173, 176, 264, 271 *n.*
Jêrûd and the Kali plant, 320.
Jeshua, chief priest in 68 A.D., 433.
Jesus ben-Sira, 371, 375, 391, 397.
Jesus Christ, God and Man, 5 *f.* ;
and Jerusalem, 7 ; Nazareth His
*Patris*, 294 ; the olive and olive
trees, 302 ; vines and vineyards,
303 ; on Galilee, 371 ; does not
refer to any handicraft, 375 ; His
birth under Herod, 413 ; boyhood
and ministry under Rome, 413 *ff.* ;
on the Council, 415 ; haunted by
the Sanhedrin, 416 *f.* ; His arrest
on Olivet, 426 ; on the Temple-

# SPECIAL INDEX I.

## PASSAGES OF THE BIBLE AND THE APOCRYPHA

# SPECIAL INDEX II.

## JOSEPHUS

### I. THE ANTIQUITIES OF THE JEWS

(Cited as *Ant.*)

490

## II. THE JEWISH WARS

(Cited as *B.J.*)

## III. AGAINST APION

(Cited as *C. Ap.* or *C. Apion.*)

## IV. LIFE OF JOSEPHUS

(Cited as *Vita*)

# SPECIAL INDEX III.

## TALMUDIC LITERATURE

### I. THE MISHNA (ed. Surenhusius)

✱✱✱ The Tractates are given below in the order in which they
are arranged in the Mishna.

## III. THE TALMUD

## IV. THE MIDRASHIM

# LIST OF ABBREVIATIONS USED
# IN THE NOTES

*Ant.* . . . . . *Antiquitatum Judaicarum Libri xx.*, by Josephus. Vols. i.-iv. of his works in Niese's edition. Berlin, 1887-90.

*Arch. Res.* . . . *Archæological Researches in Palestine*, 1873-74, by C. Clermont-Ganneau, LL.D. London : Pal. Expl. Fund, vol. i., 1899 ; vol. ii., 1896.

*Assyr. Wört.* . *Assyrisches Handwörterbuch*, by Friedrich Delitzsch. Leipzig, 1896.

*Baedeker*[5] . . Fifth edition of *Pälastina und Syrien, Handbuch für Reisende*, by I. Benzinger (1st and 2nd edd. by Socin). Leipzig : Baedeker, 1900.

*Bib. Geogr. Pal.* *Bibliotheca Geographica Palæstinæ*, by R. Röhricht. Berlin, 1890.

*B.J.* . . . . . *De Bello Judaico Libri vii.*, by Josephus, vol. vi. of Niese's ed. Berlin, 1894.

*B.L.* . . . . . *Bibel-Lexikon.*

*B.R.* . . . . . *Biblical Researches*, by Edward Robinson. London, 1841.

*C.* . . . . . . *Circa.*

*C. Apion.* . . *De Judæorum Vetustate sive Contra Apionem Libri ii.*, by Josephus. Vol. v. of Niese's ed. Berlin, 1889.

*Chald. Wörter-* ⎱ *Chaldäisches Wörterbuch*, by J. Levy, 3rd ed. Leipzig,
*buch* . . . ⎰ 1866.

*Comp. Geog. of* ⎱ *The Comparative Geography of Palestine*, by Carl Ritter.
*Pal.* . . . ⎰ Edinburgh (T. and T. Clark), 1866.

D. . . . . . Various Deuteronomic Portions of the Old Testament.

*D.B.* . . . . *Dictionary of the Bible.* Hastings' *D.B.*, Edinburgh (T. and T. Clark), 1898-1904 ; Smith's *D.B.*[2] (sometimes *B.D.*), 2nd ed. London (Murray), 1893.

E. . . . . The Elohist Document of the Hexateuch.

*Enc. Bibl.* . . *Encyclopædia Biblica*, edited by T. K. Cheyne and J. S. Black. London (A. and C. Black), 1899-1903.

*Etym. Stud.* . *Etymologische Studien zum Semitischen . . . Lexicon*, by J. Barth. Leipzig, 1893.

*Excav. at Jerus.*    *Excavations at Jerusalem 1894-1897,* by F. J. Bliss and A. C. Dickie. Publ. by Committee of the Pal. Explor. Fund. London, 1898.

*Frag. Hist.* ⎫ *Fragmenta Historicorum Græcorum,* by C. and T. Müller. 
*Græc.* . . . ⎭ Paris (Didot), 1841-51.

*G.A.P.* . . . Geographie des Alten Palästina, by F. Buhl. Leipzig, 1896.

*Geog.* . . . . Geographica, by Strabo : ed. by G. Kramer, Berlin, 1852 ; another ed. by A. Koraē, Paris, 1815, etc.

*Geog. Lex.* . . . Geographisches Lexikon (Mu'jam el-Buldân), by Yakût, ed. Wüstenfeld. Leipzig, 1866.

*Gesch.* . . . Geschichte (Schürer's, Guthe's, Stade's, and Wellhausen's).

*Gesch.*[(3)] . . . Third edition of Geschichte des Jüdischen Volkes im Zeitalter Jesu Christi, by E. Schürer. Leipzig, 1901. See also *Hist.*

*Gesch. d.* ⎫ Geschichte des Königreichs Jerusalem (1100-1291 A.D.), 
*Königr. Jerus.* ⎭ by R. Röhricht. Innsbruck, 1898.

*Golgotha.* . . . Golgotha and the Holy Sepulchre, by (the late) Major-General Sir Charles W. Wilson, K.C.B., etc. ; ed. by Colonel Sir C. M. Watson. London (Pal. Expl. Fund), 1906.

*Gram.* . . . A Grammar of the New Testament Diction, by G. B. Winer, trans. by E. Masson. Edinburgh (T. and T. Clark), 1859.

*Hebr. Arch.* . Hebräische Archäologie, by I. Benzinger. Freiburg-i.-B. 1894 ; 2nd ed. 1907.

*H.G.H.L.* . . The Historical Geography of the Holy Land, by the present writer. London (Hodder and Stoughton), 1894 ; 13th ed., 1906.

*Hist.* . . . . Wellhausen's. See *Prol.*

*Hist.* . . . . Schürer's. A History of the Jewish People in the Time of Jesus Christ. Edinburgh (T. and T. Clark), 1890, being the Eng. transl. of the 2nd ed. of the work given above against *Gesch.*[(3)].

*Hist.* . . . . William of Tyre's Historia Rerum in partibus transmarinis gestarum a tempore successorum Mahumeth usque ad A.D. mclxxxiv., edita a venerabili Willermo Tyrensi archiepiscopo ; in the Recueil des Historiens des Croisades : Historiens Occidentaux. Tome Ier. Paris, 1844.

*H.N.* . . . . Caii Plinii Secundi Naturalis Historiae Libri xxxvii. Paris, 1685.

*Isr. u.*   *Jüd.* ⎫ Israelitische und Jüdische Geschichte, by J. Wellhausen. 
*Gesch.* ⎭ Berlin, 1894. See also *Gesch.*

*J.* . . . . . . The Jahwist Document of the Hexateuch.

*K.A.T.*[(3)] . . *Die Keilinschriften und das Alte Testament*, by E. Schrader; 3rd ed. by H. Zimmern and H. Winckler. Berlin, 1903.

'Kidd.' . . . Ḳiddushîn, tractate of the Mishna and Talmud.

*L. and B.* . . *The Land and the Book*, by W. M. Thomson. London (Nelson and Sons), 1877.

*L.B.R.* . . . *Later Biblical Researches*, by Edward Robinson. London (Murray), 1856.

*Luc.* . . . . Lucian's Greek version of the Hebrew Scriptures.

LXX. . . . The Greek or Septuagint Version of the Hebrew Scriptures, ed. by H. B. Swete: *The O.T. in Greek according to the Septuagint.* Cambridge, 1887-94.

LXXA. . . . Codex Alexandrinus of the same.

LXXB. . . . Codex Vaticanus of the same.

LXXℵ . . . Codex Sinaiticus of the same.

*Mater. zur To-* ⎫ and similar abbreviations, *Materialien zur Topographie des*
*pogr. des Alt.* ⎬ *Alten Jerusalem*, by A Kuemmel, Halle (Deutscher
*Jerus.* . . . ⎭ Verein zur Erforschung Palästinas). 1906.

*M.u.N.D.P.V.* *Mittheilungen und Nachrichten des Deutschen Palästina Vereins.* Leipzig (Baedeker).

*Neuhebr. Wör-* ⎫ *Neuhebräisches u. Chald. Wörterbuch*, by J. Levy.
*terbuch* . . ⎭ Leipzig, 1876.

*N. Sem. Inscr.* *A Textbook of North-Semitic Inscriptions*, by G. A. Cooke. Oxford (Clarendon Press), 1903.

*Onom. Sacr.* . *Eusebii Pamphili . . . Onomasticon . . . Graece cum Latina Hieronymi interpretatione*, edition of Larsow and Parthey: Berlin, 1862; also in *Onomastica Sacra* by P. de Lagarde, 2nd ed., Göttingen, 1887.

*O.T.J.C.* . . *The Old Testament in the Jewish Church*, by W. Robertson Smith. 2nd ed. London (A. and C. Black), 1892.

P. . . . . The Priestly Document of the Hexateuch.

*Pal. under the* ⎫ *Palestine under the Moslems*, by Guy le Strange. London
*Moslems* . . ⎭ (for the Pal. Expl. Fund), 1890.

*P.E.F. Large* ⎫ *Map of Western Palestine in 26 sheets*, by C. R. Conder
*Map* . . ⎬ and H. Kitchener, 1872-77. Scale, one inch to the
. . ⎭ mile. London, Pal. Explor. Fund, 1880.

*P.E.F. Mem.* ⎫ *The Survey of Western Palestine* (Memoirs of the Palestine
'Jerus.' . . ⎬ Exploration Fund), the Jerusalem volume by Warren
. ⎭ and Conder. London, 1884.

*P.E.F.Q.* . . *Palestine Exploration Fund Quarterly Statement*, published at the office of the Fund, 38 Conduit Street, London, W.

*Phys. Geog.* . *Physical Geography of the Holy Land*, by Edward Robinson. London (Murray), 1865.

Plans of Jeru- ⎫
salem . . . ⎭ For these, see vol. i. p. 211.

2 I

| | |
|---|---|
| *Præp. Evang.* | *Præparatio Evangelica* of Eusebius, ed. Gaisford. Oxford, 1843. |
| *Prol.* (also sometimes *Hist.*) | *Prolegomena to the History of Israel* by J. Wellhausen, translated by J. S. Black and A. Menzies. Edinburgh (A. and C. Black), 1885. |
| *R.E.* *Real. Enc.* . . | *Realencyclopädie für Protestantische Theologie und Kirche*, edited by A. Hauck. Vol. viii. Leipzig, 1900. |
| *Recov. of Jerus.* | *Recovery of Jerusalem*, by C. W. Wilson, C. Warren, and others. London, 1871. |
| *Rec. d'Arch. Orient.* . . | *Recueil d'Archéologie Orientale.* C. Clermont-Ganneau. Paris, 1888 (not seen). |
| *Reg. Regn. Hieros.* and *Regesta* . . | *Regesta Regni Hierosolymitani* (*MXCVII.-MCCXCI.*), ed. R. Röhricht. Innsbruck, 1893. *Additamentum*, 1904. |
| *Rel. of the Sem.* | *Lectures on the Religion of the Semites*, by W. Robertson Smith. Edinburgh (A. and C. Black), 1889 |
| *Rev. Bib.* . . | *Revue Biblique.* |
| ' Sanh.' . . . | Sanhedrin, tractate of the Mishna and Talmud. |
| *S.B.O.T.* . . | *The Sacred Books of the Old Testament*, ed. with the assistance of Horace Howard Furness, by Paul Haupt. London (J. Clarke and Co.). |
| ' Shabb.' . . | Shabbath, tractate of the Mishna and Talmud. |
| *Talm. Bab.* . . | The Babylonian Talmud. |
| *Talm. Jerus.* . | The Jerusalem or Palestinian Talmud. |
| *Theol. Stud. u. Krit.* . . . | *Theologische Studien und Kritiken.* Gotha. |
| *Thes.* . . . . | *Thesaurus . . . Linguae Hebraeae et Chaldaeae Vet. Test.*, by Gesenius. Leipzig, 1835. |
| *Vit.* . . . . | *Flavii Josephi Vita*, Niese's ed., vol. iv. Berlin, 1890. |
| *Z.A.T.W.* . . | *Zeitschrift für die alt-testamentliche Wissenschaft.* Giessen. |
| *Z.D.M.G.* . . | *Zeitschrift der Deutschen Morgenländischen Gesellschaft.* |
| *Z.D.P.V.* . . | *Zeitschrift des Deutschen Palästina Vereins.* Leipzig (Baedeker). |
| *Z.N.T.W.* . . | *Zeitschrift für die neu-testamentliche Wissenschaft.* Giessen. |
| *Zur. Topogr. u. Gesch. Pal.* . | *Zur Topographie und Geschichte Palästinas*, by A. Schlatter. Stuttgart, 1893. |

Other works referred to in the text or notes are cited by their unabbreviated titles.

# JERUSALEM: THE TOPOGRAPHY
## ECONOMICS AND HISTORY

# JERUSALEM

THE TOPOGRAPHY, ECONOMICS AND HISTORY
FROM THE EARLIEST TIMES TO A.D. 70

BY

## GEORGE ADAM SMITH

D.D., LL.D.

PROFESSOR OF OLD TESTAMENT LANGUAGE, LITERATURE
AND THEOLOGY, UNITED FREE CHURCH COLLEGE, GLASGOW

*IN TWO VOLUMES*

*VOL. II.*

WITH MAPS AND ILLUSTRATIONS

KTAV PUBLISHING HOUSE, INC.
1972

# PREFATORY NOTE TO VOLUME II.

THIS volume contains Book III. of the present work—
the History of Jerusalem, with such portions of the
topography as are proper to particular periods. The
size to which the volume has grown has rendered
necessary the omission of a detailed history of the City
through the Roman period and of a separate chapter on
the siege by Titus. But in the last two chapters of
Book II. a summary has already been given of the
principal political events under the Romans and during
the War of Independence, thus bringing the history
down to 70 A.D.

I regret that the first proof of Chapter xiv. on the
Rest of the Persian Period was corrected before
Dr. Sachau's publication of the three papyri from
Elephantine, and that in consequence I was unable to
make any but the briefest allusion to these very important documents. They confirm the chronology
adopted in Chapter xiii., that Nehemiah lived under the
first Artaxerxes. But it has been impossible to discuss their bearing on the critical questions of the age of
the Pentateuch. With regard to these I need state only
one remarkable result of the discovery of the papyri. It
has convinced Professor Nöldeke, who has so long resisted
the Graf-Wellhausen hypothesis, of the impossibility of

assigning the close of the Pentateuch to an earlier date than that of Ezra (*Zeitschrift für Assyriologie*, January 1908). Professor Nöldeke does not discuss how far the papyri affect the question of the date of Deuteronomy, a question which I hope to have other opportunities of discussing. I also regret that Professor Kittel's *Studien zur Hebräischen Archäologie und Religionsgeschichte*, containing treatises on the Rock eṣ-Ṣakhra, the Serpent-stone in the Ḳidron Valley and the movable lavers in Solomon's Temple (Leipzig, 1908), did not come into my hands till after this volume was passed for press.

In the History I have thought right to give a more exact transliteration of the Hebrew proper names than the conventional English spelling adopted in Volume I. ; but some of the more important names, such as Solomon, Isaiah, and Jeremiah, I have left in their familiar forms. I have also altered one or two forms of reference to ancient works : for instance, the document cited in Volume I. as the Pseudo-Aristeas appears in this volume as the Letter of Aristeas.

To the list given in the Preface of those to whom I have been indebted for assistance in the preparation of this work, I wish to add the names of my colleague Professor Denney, whose suggestions on the New Testament period have been very helpful; Dr. D. M. Ross of Glasgow, Professor C. A. Scott of Cambridge, Dr. John Kelman of Edinburgh, and Mr. W. Menzies of Glasgow. I also thank, for the care and ability with which they have treated the somewhat intricate materials, the compositors and proof-readers of Messrs. T. and A. Constable, the printers of these volumes; and I owe a very special debt of gratitude to Messrs. Hodder and Stoughton and to Mr. J. Sinclair Armstrong of New York for their great patience with the many delays in the completion of the work, as well as for their generosity in the matter of its illustrations.

I call the attention of the reader to the list of Additions and Corrections to Vol. I. inserted in that volume ; and to the list of those to Vol. II. on page xiv. I regret that the Appendix referred to on pages 327, 331, 333, and 334 has been crowded out.

GEORGE ADAM SMITH.

GLASGOW,
*7th April* 1908.

# CONTENTS OF VOLUME II.

## BOOK III

### THE HISTORY

# LIST OF MAPS AND PLANS IN VOLUME II.

---

# LIST OF PLATES IN VOLUME II.

## ADDITIONS AND CORRECTIONS TO VOLUME II.

PAGE

68, footnote 2 : xi. *read* xli.

97, line 18 : *delete* second.

175, footnote 1 : 1 Kings *read* 2 Kings.

253, line 21 : *read* 'Ebed-Melek.

253, footnote 2 : *read* xxxviii. 13.

278, footnote 3 : the last sentence belongs to the next footnote.

281, verse 11 : for *It* read It.

309, footnote 6 : see, however, 2 Chron. iv. 9.

327, lines 16 ff.⎫ The Appendix referred to in these passages has been
331, footnote 1. ⎬ crowded out. Instead of it I beg to refer the reader to
333, footnote 1. ⎭ my article on the subject, *Expositor*, July 1906.
334, line 9.

# TABLE OF THE PRINCIPAL STAGES IN THE HISTORY OF JERUSALEM

| | B.C. |
|---|---|
| Settlements of the Stone Age . . . | *c.* 3000 |
| Settlement of a Semitic Tribe . . . | *after* 2500 |
| (With mixture of other elements, *e.g.* Hittite, according to some authorities.) | |
| Chief Town of a small principality, under 'Abd Khiba, a vassal of Egypt . . . | *c.* 1400 |
| The Capital of All-Israel, under David . . | *c.* 1000 |
| The Building of the Temple under Solomon . | *c.* 970 |
| The Struggling Capital of Judah from Rehoboam to Uzziah . . . . . | *c.* 930-720 |
| Isaiah interprets the History of the City and vindicates her sacredness . . . . | *c.* 740-685 (?) |
| The National Worship concentrated in the Temple: Deuteronomy and Josiah . . | 621 |
| The Destruction of the City and Temple by Nebuchadrezzar . . . . | 587-586 |
| Idealisation of the City during the Exile of her Inhabitants . . . . . | 586-538 |
| First Return of the Exiles . . . | 538 |
| Rebuilding of the Temple . . . | 520-516 |
| Reconstitution of the Community and Rebuilding of the Walls . . . . . | 444-431 |

# BOOK III

## *THE HISTORY*

# CHAPTER I

## THE PRELUDE—ABD-KHIBA

### *c.* 1400 B.C.

THE histories of most famous cities melt back, through the pride of their peoples or the hatred of their foes, into legendary tales of their origins, which find their exact moulds sometimes in the memory of an actual fact, sometimes in a religious symbol, but often in more or less fantastic etymologies of the city's name. Of such legends Jerusalem has her share. We have seen the rabbinic fable associating her name with two of the early Patriarchs.[1] Josephus, followed by many Jews and Christians, identified the Temple Mount with a 'Mount Moriah,' which he took to be the scene of Abraham's sacrifice of Isaac; but the Biblical story of the latter knows no 'mount' so called.[2] The accounts of Jerusalem's origin, which are due to the fancy, not untouched by malice, of Egyptians or Greeks, either connect the late form Hierosolyma with the Solymi of Homer, or ascribe the formation of the City to a band of refugees from Egypt, some say in the leadership of Moses.[3] We now know that

*Legends of the City's Origins.*

---

[1] Vol. i. 258 *n.* 1.          [2] Vol. i. 267.

[3] For Manetho's story, see Jos. *C. Apion.* i. 14 f., 26 f. (Müller, *Frag. Hist. Gr.* ii. 511 ff.). Of Greek accounts these are samples: Hecatæus of Abdera (Müller, *Frag. Hist. Gr.* ii. 391); Posidonius of Apamæa (*Id.* 256); Lysimachus of Alexandria (Jos. *C. Ap.* i. 34; Müller, iii. 334 f.); cf. Tacitus, *Hist.* v. 2. Plutarch (*De Iside et Osiride,* 31) dismisses a curious legend as a confusion of Egyptian and Jewish reports. On the Solymi see vol. i. 262.

Jerusalem, under that name, existed before the arrival of Israel in the land; and the sole fact of importance which these legends reflect—the most wandering fancy could not have missed it — is her debatable position between Egypt and Babylonia. For the compound name Jerusalem various etymologies are possible. But there is no doubt of its Semitic origin; and, as we have seen, it was bestowed more probably by Canaanite settlers than by Babylonian conquerors of Palestine.[1]

We have also seen that these Semitic settlers from Arabia had, about 2500 B.C., succeeded men of another race belonging to the Stone-Age. The presence of this race in Palestine is beyond doubt. Something of their personal appearance and manner of life has been illustrated by discoveries on other parts of the land; while their occupation of the site or neighbourhood of Jerusalem is proved by the great numbers of flint weapons and tools which have been picked up within her surroundings.[2] But the Stone-Men lie beyond the limits of history proper.

*The Stone-Age.*

If we leave aside the ambiguous narrative in Genesis xiv., the earliest written records of Jerusalem present her as entering history with a plain and sober air, singularly in keeping with that absence of glamour which we have noted in her clear atmosphere and grey surroundings.[3] Among the archives of the Egyptian court, about B.C. 1400, there have been discovered a small number of clay tablets, seven or eight in all: letters from Jerusalem which describe her condition in plaintive detail and with no

*Sober Entrance of Jerusalem into History, c. 1400 B.C.*

[1] Vol. i. 253-58.   [2] Vol. i. 283-88.   [3] Vol. i. 22.

touch of the ideal. They invoke no deity, they assert
no confidence, material or spiritual. They speak only
of the City's loneliness, her disappointment in her pro-
tectors, her abandonment to an approaching foe. Yet
even so, these tablets are more symbolic of the history
of Jerusalem than any legend or prophecy could have
been. Their tone is in unison with the dominant notes
of the long tragedy to which they form the prelude.
They express that sense of betrayal and of vanishing
hope in the powers of this world which haunts Jerusalem
to the very end.

Nor is it less typical of the course of her history that
the tablets reveal Jerusalem as already under the influence of the two great civilisations, which, Already in
between them, shaped the fortunes and touch with Babylon and
coloured the character of her people. The Egypt.
tablets are written in the cuneiform script, and in the
language, of Babylonia: a proof that the influences of
this most ancient seat of human culture already ran
strong across Western Asia. The politics, which the
tablets reveal, have their centre at the other side of
the world, with Babylonia's age-long rival. Jerusalem
is a tributary and outpost of Egypt; and Egypt is
detected in that same attitude of helplessness towards
her Asian vassals which is characteristic of her throughout history. As in the days of Isaiah, she is *Rahab that
sitteth still*; promising much, but when the crisis arrives,
inactive and unwilling to fulfil her pledges.[1] As in the
days of Jeremiah, the expected *King of Egypt cometh
not any more out of his land*,[2] and Jerusalem is left alone
to face a foe from the north. Other instances may be

---

[1] Isaiah xxx. 7.      [2] 2 Kings xxv. 7.

cited. When Antiochus Epiphanes took Jerusalem in 168 B.C., and desecrated the Temple, Judæa was still claimed by the Ptolemy of the time, but he did not stir to her help. Down to the retreat of Ibrahim Pasha in 1841, Egypt, whether because of the intervening desert or the fitful prowess of her people, has been unable, for any long period, to detach Palestine from Asia and bind it to the southern continent.

Soon after 1600 B.C. Egypt, under the Eighteenth Dynasty, began a series of campaigns in Syria, which
Egyptian<br>Dominion in<br>Palestine,<br>1600-1200 B.C. carried her arms (on one occasion at least) to the Euphrates, and reduced the states of Palestine for four centuries to more or less regular dependence upon her. No fewer than fourteen of these campaigns were undertaken by Thutmosis III. about 1500 B.C. He defeated, at Megiddo, a powerful Canaanite confederacy, but left to his successors, Amenhotep II. and Thutmosis IV., the reduction of some separate tribes. So far as we know, the next Pharaoh, Amenhotep (Amenophis) III., enjoyed without interruption the obedience of his Asian vassals. By his only possible rivals, the kings of Mesopotamia and Babylonia, he was recognised as sovereign of Syria, and his influence extended northwards to Armenia. His vast empire, his lavish building throughout Egypt and Nubia, his magnificent temples at Thebes, his mines and organisation of trade, his wealth, along with the art and luxury which prevailed under all the monarchs of his dynasty, and their influence on the Greek world—represent the zenith of Egyptian civilisation. Whether, in his security and under the zeal with which he gave himself to the improvement of his own land, Amenhotep III. neglected

the Asian provinces of his empire, is uncertain.  In any
case he was succeeded by a son whose interests in
Egypt were still more engrossing, and who for this or
other reasons was unable to preserve the conquests of
his predecessors.  Amenhotep IV. was that Amenhotep
singular monarch who effected a temporary IV., *c.* 1400 B.C.
revolution in the religion and art of Egypt.  Turning his
back upon Amōn and the other ancient gods, he spent his
reign in the establishment of the exclusive worship of
Aten, the Sun's Disk, and in the construction of a centre
for this and a capital for himself.  He introduced styles of
art as novel as his religious opinions ; free and natural,
but without other proofs of ability.  Absorbed in these
pursuits, Amenhotep IV. was the last kind of ruler to
meet, or even to heed, the new movements in Asia which
threatened his empire.  Across the Euphrates lay three
considerable kingdoms : Babylonia, then under a Kassite
dynasty ; Assyria, her young vassal, but already strong
enough to strike for independence ; and Mitanni, a state
of Hittite origin in Northern Mesopotamia.  It was not,
however, from these, divided and jealous of each other,
that danger had to be feared by Egypt.  From Asia
Minor, the main branch of the Hittite race, the Kheta
or Khatti were pushing south-east, alike upon their
kinsfolk of Mitanni, and upon the Egyptian tributaries
in Northern Syria.

It is beneath this noontide, and approaching eclipse,
of Egypt's glory that Jerusalem emerges into history.
The correspondence, of which her eight clay
tablets form a small portion, was discovered The Tell el-
Amarna
at Tell el-'Amarna, in Middle Egypt, the site Letters.
of the capital of Amenhotep IV.  It was conducted

between his father and himself on the one side, and the Trans-Euphrates kingdoms and the Syrian feudatories of Egypt on the other.[1] Through it we see, passing over Palestine, a close and frequent communication between the Nile and the Euphrates.

The human interest of these Letters is intense: kings at peace, but in jealous watch of each other, their real *Their human* tempers glowing through a surface of hypo- *interest.* crisy. They marry and give in marriage; they complain that they cannot get evidence whether their daughters or sisters sent abroad for this purpose are alive or well treated; they appeal to the women of the courts which they seek to influence. Above all they are greedy of gold, of which Egypt is the source; one alleges that a present of gold-ore, when it arrives, yields less than the promised value, another that wooden images have been sent instead of golden. One even grumbles that his royal brother has not inquired for him when he was ill.[2] There is some humour, much cunning, and once (if the interpretation be correct) a

---

[1] The tablets of Tell el-Amarna are now in Berlin and London. The following facts, recorded in them, are taken from H. Winckler's transliteration and translation in *Die Thontafeln von Tell-el-Amarna*: Berlin, 1896. In the following references B., followed by a figure, signifies the Berlin collection; L. the London collection; and W. Winckler's rearrangement and numbering of the letters. Knudtzon, in the *Beiträge zur Assyriologie*, iv. pp. 101 ff., 279 ff., gives some revision of the tablets, with corrections of earlier readings and translations. An account of the substance of the tablets is given by C. Niebuhr in *Die Amarna-Zeit*, the second Heft of vol. i. of *Der Alte Orient*, and by Wallis Budge in the last chapter of vol. iv. of his *History of Egypt*. See also Winckler, pp. 192-203 of the third edition of Schrader's *Die Keilinschriften und das Alte Testament*, and Sayce on 'Canaan in the Century before the Exodus,' *Contemporary Review*, lxxxviii. (1905) 264-277.

[2] B. 7: W. 10.

frank proposal of villainy.[1] Between these very human courts and their countries there moves a constant commerce: 'Write me what thou desirest from my land, they will bring it thee, and what I desire from thy land, I will write thee, that they may bring it.'[2] For the Egyptian gold and oil, the states of the Euphrates send manufactured gold, precious stones, enamel, chariots, horses, and slaves. These are not all royal presents. A Mesopotamian king complains that his merchants have been robbed in Canaan, Pharaoh's territory. Caravans cross Palestine or pass from it into Egypt. Phœnician ships, not without danger from Lycian corsairs, bring to Egypt copper, bronze, ivory, ships' furniture, and horses from Alashia, either Cyprus or Northern Syria. They take back silver, oil and oxen.[3] One letter begs the king of Egypt not to allow the writer's merchants to be wronged by his tax-gatherers (?).[4] Such are a few of the many details: so many, and so intimate, that it may be truly said, before the Roman Empire there is no period for which we have records more replete with the details of social intercourse or with revelations of personal character and policy. All is vivid, passionate, frank. Of this busy, human life, thirty-three centuries ago, Jerusalem was a part, lying not far from one of its main arteries.

[1] B. 9: W. 15: 'Why should the ambassadors not remain on the journey, so that they die in foreign parts? If they remain in foreign parts, the estate belongs to the king. Therefore when he (thy present ambassador) remains on his journey and dies, then will the estate belong to the king. There is therefore no [reason why we should fear] that the ambassadors die in foreign parts, whom we send . . . the ambassadors . . . and . . . and die in foreign parts.'
[2] B. 1: W. 6.
[3] L. 5-7 and B. 11-15: W. 25-33.    [4] B. 12: W. 29.

The letters from the chiefs of Palestine, among whom
the ruler of Jerusalem was one, reveal the duties that

The Letters
from
Palestine.

Egypt required of her feudatories, the awe
in which they held her power, the dangers
which threatened them through her inaction,
and all the intrigue and duplicity arising from so ambiguous a situation.  Some of the writers have Semitic
names; that is, they are native Canaanites or Amorites.
Others have non-Semitic names: interpreted by some
scholars as Hittite or Mitannian.[1]  They profess themselves
slaves of Egypt, and address the Pharaoh with fulsome
flattery.  They prostrate themselves before him—'seven
and seven times.'  He is their lord, their king, their gods
and their sun.[2]  They are his slaves, and the grooms of
his horse.[3]  They hold their hereditary domains by his
gift.[4]  They send tribute,[5] and are obliged to certain
services, such as provisioning the royal troops who march
through the land,[6] and maintaining royal garrisons.[7]
They guard the posts entrusted to them by the king,
and the king's chariots; but also the gods of the king.[8]
In return they expect to be protected by Egypt, and to
receive supplies.[9]  One of the chiefs, Iabitiri of Gaza,
says that in his youth he was taken to Egypt.[10]  In
short, the position of these feudatories of Pharaoh is
analogous to that now occupied by the semi-independent rajahs of India under the British Government.  And
just as the latter places, at the courts of the rajahs,
political agents with great powers, so Egypt had at that

---

[1] Sayce, *Contemporary Review*, lxxxviii. 267, 269 ff.
[2] A frequent formula.     [3] B. 118-22: W. 210-13.     [4] Frequent.
[5] *e.g.* L. 67 : W. 198.     [6] L. 52, 54: W. 207, 209 ; B. 114: W. 194.
[7] B. 113, 121 : W. 193, 212: L. 52, 53: W. 207, 208.
[8] B. 122 : W. 213.          [9] Frequent.     [10] L. 57 : W. 214.

date in Palestine her own officials, who went from place to place as advisers and superintendents of the feudatories.[1]

Dushratta, king of Mitanni, had written to Amenhotep III. (Nimmuria) of the pressure of the Hittites on his kingdom.[2] Correspondents of the Egyptian court in Northern Syria give warnings The Khabiri. of the same danger. But these and the chiefs in Palestine intimate other foes. 'The power of the Khabiri[3] is great in the land,' advancing from the north; and with the Khabiri are sometimes named the Suti.[4] These enemies are not without allies among the Canaanite chiefs. A certain Lapaya of Megiddo and his sons are chiefly accused by such Egyptian vassals as remain or pretend to remain loyal.[5] Biridiya of Makida writes that since the royal troops were withdrawn the sons of Lapaya have so closely watched his town, that his people cannot get vegetables or go outside the gates.[6] But indeed no man is sure of his neighbour. The letters of the vassals are full of accusations of each other, and

---

[1] Pakhamnata, Shûta, Pakhura and Iankhamu are named. A title for these officials is *rabiṣ*.     [2] L. 9 : W. 16.

[3] B. 68 : W. 113 ; L. 49 : W. 204, etc. etc. An unknown people, identified by some (as is well known) with the Hebrews; cf. Niebuhr, *Die Amarna-Zeit*, 23 f. They were Semitic immigrants into the land, and belonged to the same movement as, or more probably to an earlier movement than, that which brought Israel there: 'Tribes,' says Winckler (*Keilinschr. u. das A. T.*[(3)] 198), 'represented as in the process of immigration and invasion of civilised territory, the same *rôle* taken up later by the Israelites.' Sayce takes them to have been marauding Hittite bands, whose name, phonetically but not historically identifiable with that of the Hebrews, is found elsewhere in Assyrian texts in the sense of 'confederates.' *Contemporary Review*, lxxxviii. 272.

[4] L. 51, 74 : W. 206, 216.

[5] B. 111, 115 : W. 192, 195 ; L. 72 : W. 196, etc. Sayce reads the name Lapaya as Labbawa.     [6] B. 115 : W. 195.

of excuses for the writers.  Iapahi of Gezer says that his younger brother has revolted from him to the Khabiri,[1] and Tagi writes that he would have sent his brother to the king, but he is full of wounds.[2]  Some, perhaps all, must be telling lies.

Among the chiefs of Southern Palestine who thus accuse each other is Abd-Khiba, the writer of the seven or eight Jerusalem letters.  In Letter I.[3] he defends himself against some one who has been accusing him as a rebel (lines 5-8).[4]  Yet it was neither his father nor mother who set him in this place, but the strong arm of the king[5] which introduced him to the territory of his father [bît (amilu) abi-ia] (9-13).  Why then should he rebel against the king? (14 f.)  By the life of the king he is slandered; because he had said to the king's official [rabiṣ sharri], 'Why do you favour the Khabiri and injure the tributary princes [khazianutu]?'[6] and 'The king's territory is being ruined' (16-24).  The king knows that he had placed a garrison[7] in Jerusalem, but Iankhamu (the king's deputy or general) has removed it (25-33).  Let the king take thought and trouble for his land, else his whole territory will disappear, the king's towns under Ili-milku having already revolted (34-38). Abd-Khiba would come to court, but he dare not unless the king send a garrison (39-47).  He will continue his warnings, for without royal troops the king's territories will be wasted by the Khabiri (48-60).  The letter con-

*(margin note: Abd-Khiba of Jerusalem— Letter I.)*

---

[1] L. 50: W. 205.
[2] L. 70: W. 189.       [3] B. 102: W. 179.
[4] The accuser appears to have been a neighbouring chief Shuwardata.
[5] See below, p. 22 *n.* 5.
[6] Lehnsfürsten: Winckler; heads of the tribes of the country: Budge.
[7] Besatzung: Winckler; outpost: Budge.

cludes with a message to the king's secretary to impress the contents on him.

Letter II.[1] describes the dangers to the king's territories as increased—all the states have conspired against Abd-Khiba; Gezer, Ashḳelon and Lakish have given the enemy provisions (4-24)—and repeats the assurance that Abd-Khiba holds Jerusalem solely by the king's gift (25-28). Melk-ili and others have yielded his land to the Khabiri (29-31). Abd-Khiba is innocent in the affair of the Kashi, who are themselves to blame by their violence (32-44). They appear to have been the Egyptian garrison in Jerusalem, and were perhaps Kushites or Ethiopians.[2] Paura the Egyptian official came to Jerusalem when Adaya, along with the garrison, revolted, and said to Abd-Khiba, 'Adaya has revolted: hold the town.' So the king must send a garrison (45-53). The king's caravan has been robbed in the territory[3] of Ayyalôn. Abd-Khiba could not send the king's caravans on to the king (54-59). The king has set his name on Jerusalem for ever, he cannot surrender its territory (60-63). The postscript to the secretary of the king says that the Kashi remain in Abd-Khiba's territory.

In Letter III.[4] Abd-Khiba, after again repudiating the slander against him (7-8), describes himself as no prince [*khazianu*] but an *u-i-u*[5] of the king, and an officer who brings tribute, holding his territory not from father or mother, but by the king's gift

*Letter II.*

*Letter III.*

---

[1] B. 103 : W. 180.
[2] Winckler, *Thontafeln*, etc., p. xxx. *n.* 1.   Sayce takes them as Kasians from the Hittite Kas in Asia Minor (*Contemporary Review*, lxxxviii. 269).
[3] Shati-i ; W. compares Heb. שׁדֵּרָה.
[4] B. 104 : W. 181.       [5] Niebuhr, 'stabsofficier'; cf. *As. u. Eur.* 276.

(9-15).   He has sent the king slaves, male and female
(16-22).   Let the king care for his land, it is all hostile
as far as Ginti-Karmil (23-39).   Some chiefs, presumably
loyal, have been slain (40-45).   If the king cannot send
troops, let him fetch away Abd-Khiba and his clansmen
that they may die before the king (47-60).

Letter IV.[1] is broken: its fragments report chiefs as
fallen away from the king, and beg for troops.   Letter V.[2]

Letters<br>IV.-VIII.  repeats the loss of the king's land to the
Khabiri, with (among other places) Bit-Ninib,
in the territory of Jerusalem (5-17), and asks for troops
(18-28).   Letter VI.[3] repeats the assurances of Abd-Khiba's
submission, and complains that the king has not sent to
him.   Letter VII.,[4] two-thirds of which are wanting, after
telling the same tale of disasters to the Egyptian power,
and the wish of Abd-Khiba to repair them (1-16), adds
that the garrison which the king sent by Khaya has been
taken by Adda Mikhir into his territory of Gaza.   Letter
VIII.,[5] which, like Letter VII., does not in its present state
yield the name of the writer, and by many is not attributed to Abd-Khiba, deals with the two rebels already
mentioned in Letter VII., Melk-ili and his father-in-law
Tagi.[6]   All of these tablets have more or less of the usual
introduction, in which the writer does homage to the
king.

The composition of the name Abd- or Ebed- Khiba [7] is

[1] B. 105: W. 182.            [2] B. 106: W. 183.
[3] B. 174: W. 184.
[4] B. 199: W. 185; Sayce, *Contemporary Review*, lxxxviii. 272 f.
[5] B. 149: W. 186.
[6] The territories of these chiefs seem to have lain on what was afterwards
Southern Judah or on the Philistine Plain near Gath.
[7] Hommel (*Grundriss der Geogr. u. Gesch. des Alten Orients*, 55) reads
Arad-Chiba.

Semitic: *slave* or *worshipper of Khiba.* The same forma-
tion with the names of many deities is, it need   The Name
hardly be stated, common in Phœnician and   Abd-Khiba.
Arabic as well as Hebrew. In the Old Testament we have
'Obed-Edom, 'Obadiyah, 'Abdeēl, 'Ebed-Melek, and others.
But if Khiba be a divine name, is it Semitic or otherwise?
Professor Sayce says that it is that of a Mitannian (or
Hittite) deity.[1] The Tell el-Amarna letters give the
names compounded with *khipa* of two Mitannian prin-
cesses.[2] We know so little of the Mitannians and Hittites
that no certain inference can be drawn from these data,
and there is the possible alternative of a Semitic origin
for the name Khiba. The suggestion that it disguises an
original Iahu, a form of Iahweh, which would make
Abd-Khiba equivalent to Obadiyah is purely imagina-
tive.[3] But the Semitic root *habah* (Hebrew) or *khabah*
(Assyrian[4] and Arabic), *to hide* or *hide oneself*, is not unsuitable for a divine title, and it is possible to see this root
in the name El-Iaḥba, one of David's heroes, from the
Canaanite town of Sha'albim.[5]

These alternative derivations for the name Abd-Khiba

---

[1] *Contemporary Review*, lxxxviii. 269.

[2] Gilukhipa, wife of Amenḥotep III.; L. 9: W. 16, lines 5 and 41; cf.
W. M. Müller, *As. u. Eur.* 286, 288. Tâtum or Tadu-khipa, apparently
wife both of Amenḥotep III. (L. 10: W. 20) and A. IV. (B. 24: W. 21).
W. M. Müller adds Pu-u-khipa from Bouriant's copy of the Hittite-Egyptian
treaty, and Khipa from an amulet (K. 3787) in the British Museum.

[3] The radical *h* is not the same in the two cases, and although suggested it
has not been proved that a possible link between the two forms, Iba, which
appears in certain compound names, is a corruption of Iahu. See Johns
(after Jensen), *Assyr. Deeds and Documents*, iii. p. xvi., and Zimmern,
*K.A.T.*[(3)] 467.

[4] Delitzsch, *Assyr. Handwörterbuch*, 265 f.

[5] 2 Sam. xxiii. 32; Josh. xix. 42; Judg. i. 35. The proper name Khabi also
occurs in the Tell el-Amarna letters, L. 28: W. 150, line 37; and Winckler
gives a place-name I-khibi from a letter (B. 27) not reproduced by him.

open up the question of the racial character of the early
Were these early Masters of Jerusalem Hittite? masters of Jerusalem.   Were they Semitic
or Hittite?   And if the latter, were they a
Hittite aristocracy ruling a Semitic population,
or did they and their subjects together form part of a
Hittite migration which had settled in several centres in
Southern Palestine?   The existence of a Hittite state or
states in Northern Syria, and as far south as the Lebanon,
is indubitable between 1500 and 700 B.C.; it is recorded
by Egyptian and Assyrian inscriptions,[1] and by the earlier
historical books of the Old Testament.[2]   But the Priestly
Document also describes a people of the same or a similar
name as living in Southern Palestine along with the
Jebusite and Amorite, and possessing land about Hebron,
for which Abraham treated with them;[3] two Hittites are
mentioned among David's warriors,[4] and Ezekiel emphasises the congenital wickedness of Jerusalem by the
words *thy father was an Amorite, thy mother a Hittite.*[5]
We have seen that Abd-Khiba's name is asserted to contain that of a Mitannian deity; and that both the Kasian
troops of which he speaks and the Khabiri are held by
some to be Hittite.[6]   And finally, it has been pointed out
that several of the prisoners taken by Rameses II. (1275-

---

[1] The earliest notice is Egyptian, under Thutmosis III., *c.* 1500, and the
Kheta or Kh'ta, as the Egyptians call them, reappear under Sethos I.,
Rameses II., and Rameses III. (*c.* 1200).   On Assyrian inscriptions they
appear as the Khatti from 1100 to 700.

[2] Judg. i. 26; 2 Sam. xxiv. 26 (read with Lucian קדשה החתים ארץ אל),
and even 1 Kings x. 28 f. (see vol. i. 324); cf. Josh. xi. 3, Judg. iii. 3, in
both of which read Hittite for Hivite.

[3] חת בני or חתי, Gen. xxiii. 3-10; cf. xxv. 10, xlix. 29, l. 13, xxvi. 34
(Esau takes wives of the H.), xxvii. 46 (daughters of H.); cf. xxxvi. 2.

[4] 1 Sam. xxvi. 6; 2 Sam. xi. 3.

[5] Ezek. xvi. 3 (LXX.).          [6] Above, pp. 13, 15.

1208 B.C.) from Ashḳelon, and represented on a bas-relief at Karnak, have the features which Egyptian artists consistently give to the Hittites. On all these grounds the theory of early Hittite conquests in Southern Palestine has been maintained by several scholars,[1] and in particular Professor Sayce has inferred that the Jebusites, whom Israel found in possession of Jerusalem, were 'descendants of the Hittite Arzawaya.'[2] If this be proved, we have to read Ezekiel's statement that the mother of Jerusalem was Hittite as exactly historical, and to illustrate it by the observations of Dr. von Luschan that the features of modern Jews and Syrians indicate an ancient mixture of their Semitic blood with that of the primitive Hittite inhabitants of Asia Minor.

There is, however, much to be said on the other side. Ezekiel's statement and the application of the term Heth or Hittite to tribes in Southern Palestine by the Priestly Writer were made at a time when Or Semitic? the names Amorite, Canaanite and Hittite appear to have been employed in Hebrew not for particular peoples, but each of them as a general designation for all the tribes whom Israel found in the land; and it is probable besides that Ezekiel meant by the use of two of them merely to emphasise the incurable heathenishness of the people of Jerusalem. Moreover, the *Hittites* of Hebron and David's two Hittite warriors have Semitic names; the Deuteronomic phrase, *all the land of the Hittites*,[3] means simply the whole of Syria, which the Assyrians also meant by 'the land of the Khatti'; the Hebronites, whom

[1] See especially Hommel, *Grundriss der Geogr. u. Gesch. des Alten Orients*, 55.

[2] *Contemporary Review*, lxxxviii. 274.   [3] Josh. i. 4.

the Priestly Writer calls *Hittite*, are called *Amorites* by the Elohist,[1] and Esau's *Hittite* wives are in another Priestly passage called *daughters of Canaan*.[2]

As for the Jebusites, everything we know about them, except, perhaps, the name 'Araunah, points to their Semitic

The Jebusites. character. By the Jahwist and Elohist writers who lived when Jebusites were still found in Jerusalem,[3] they are associated with other Semitic tribes.[4] Their chief Adoni-ṣedek [5] and their citadel Ṣion [6] have also Semitic names, and at least the formation of the name Abd-Khiba is Semitic. Adoni-ṣedek, too, is called by the Elohist a *king of the Amorites*.[7]

We may, therefore, come to the following conclusion. While it is possible that in the second millennium before

More probably Semitic. Christ there were Hittite conquests and settlements in Southern Palestine, and that in Jerusalem and elsewhere a Hittite aristocracy dominated the Semitic population;[8] yet, since we know so little about the Hittites, and since the earlier Hebrew documents give so many indications that the Jebusites were Semitic, while only the later Hebrew documents speak of Ḥeth or Hittite in Southern Palestine (and do so at a time when

---

[1] Josh. x. 5.      [2] Gen. xxxvi. 2.      [3] Josh. xv. 63 (J).

[4] JE: Gen. x. 16 (J, perhaps an addition); Num. xiii. 29 (E); Josh. x. 5 (E); xv. 63 (J); Judg. i. 21; xix. 11 (J). Ex. iii. 8, 17; xxiii. 23; xxxiii. 2; xxxiv. 11 are generally assigned to JE, but may be from the Deuteronomist. To the latter belong Ex. xiii. 5; Deut. vii. 1; xx. 17; Josh. iii. 10; ix. 1; xi. 3; xii. 8; xxiv. 11 *b*; Judg. iii. 5 (?); 1 Kings ix. 20 (=2 Chron. viii. 7); and to the Priestly Writer Josh. xv. 8; xviii. 16, 28. In 2 Sam. see v. 6; xxiv. 16, 18; and compare Zech. ix. 7. The notices in Chronicles, Ezra, and Neh. are taken from the earlier documents.

[5] Josh. x. 1 (E). See below, p. 25.

[6] See vol. i. 144 ff.      [7] Josh. x. 5.

[8] 'This is the utmost concession to be made to modern theories,' Robertson Smith, *Religion of the Semites*, 11 f.

*Plate XI.*

STELE OF SETY I OF EGYPT.

Discovered by the Author at Tell esh-Shihâb, May, 1901.

it is probable that *Hittite* in Hebrew had no particular ethnical meaning), it is more reasonable to believe that the pre-Israelite masters of Jerusalem were, like Israel themselves, Semitic.[1]

Before describing the political position of Abd-Khiba, we may pursue the religious question started by his name. That the states of Palestine at this time had native deities is a fact certain in itself, and confirmed by the theophorous names which several of the princes bear.  Their silence about these gods is explained by the fact that the king, to whom their letters are addressed, not only belonged to a different race, but conceived himself to be an incarnation of the deity. Hence the fulsomeness of the terms in which they write to him : 'their sun, their gods.'  The only gods whom the Syrian chiefs mention are the gods of Egypt.  One chief calls himself the guardian of these gods.[2]  This phrase is explained by a stele of Sety I. (about 1350 B.C.), which I discovered at Tell esh-Shihâb, in Hauran, in 1901, and which is here reproduced.[3]  Of this Professor W. Max Müller writes that 'it has no *graffito* character, but is a carefully and expensively executed monument . . . of the purest Egyptian workmanship, and not an imitation by an Asiatic sculptor.'  On the right the king is offering

*Religious Questions.*

---

[1] The reader may be further referred to Driver's art. 'Jebus' in Hastings' *D.B.*, and *Genesis*, 228 ff. ; G. B. Gray, *Numbers*, 147 ff. ; *Expositor*, May 1898, 340 ff. ; *Enc. Bibl.*, 'Jerusalem,' § 13, by the present writer; and Hittites by M. Jastrow, junior, who thinks that P.'s Hethites or Hittites of Hebron had beyond the name nothing in common with the Hittites of Northern Syria and Asia Minor.          [2] B. 122: W. 213.

[3] See Plate XI.  *P.E.F.Q.*, 1901, 344 ff: 'Tell esh-Shihab, and the discovery of a Second Egyptian Monument in Hauran,' by G. A. Smith, with a reading of the monument by Mr. (now Sir) Herbert Thompson ; 1904, 78 ff: 'The Egyptian Monument of Tell esh-Shihab,' by W. Max Müller, Philadelphia.

two libation vessels. In the rectangle above his hands
are the two royal cartouches with his names Ra-men-maat,
'Son of the Sun,' and Ptaḥ-meri-en-Sety, 'Sety beloved of
Ptah.' Above the names are the titles 'Lord of the two
lands' and 'Lord of Glories'(?); below are the words
'Giving life like Ra.' On the left the god, to whom the
libations are offered, is Amōn, whose name with some
titles is inscribed before him. Behind stands the goddess
Mut with her name. Similar representations of their
gods were doubtless set up by Egyptian conquerors in
other towns of Palestine. As Sety's stele is of basalt,
the rock of the district in which it was erected, those in
Southern Palestine may have been in limestone—the
reason of our failure to discover any of them. Abd-
Khiba founds one of his appeals to Amenḥotep IV. not to
desert Jerusalem on the fact that 'the king has set his
Name on Jerusalem for ever.'[1] With some probability
Dr. Winckler argues that he means that Amenḥotep IV.
had instituted in the City the worship of Aten, of whom
he conceived himself to be the incarnation.[2] If this be
correct, a monument was erected in Jerusalem analogous
to that of Sety I. at Tell esh-Shihâb. It is worth a passing
notice that the form of Egyptian religion, which most
nearly approached Monotheism,[3] should have been imposed, for however brief a period, upon Jerusalem. How
was the worship performed? Were its high hymns[4]
chanted by the Egyptian officials and soldiery? Its
Asiatic origin,[5] we are tempted to infer, may have helped

---

[1] B. 103 : W. 180, line 60 f.   [2] *K.A. T.*(3) 194 f.
[3] Sayce, *The Religions of Ancient Egypt and Babylonia*, 92 ff.
[4] See Budge, *History of Egypt*, iv. 125; Sayce, *op. cit.* 95 f. ; W. M.
Müller, *Enc. Bibl.* 'Egypt,' § 56: 'The hymns now composed in praise
of the Sun-god are the best productions of Egyptian religious literature.'
[5] Sayce, *op. cit.* 92.

its acceptance by the Canaanites. Yet how were they to understand its language? Would they comprehend more than what their letters express—that it was the adoration of the Egyptian monarch himself? We can hardly think so ; but, however this may have been, no trace of the worship of Aten survived. Overthrown in Egypt, it cannot have persisted in Syria. Amōn and Mut were the gods whom, half a century afterwards, Sety I. set up at Tell esh-Shihâb.

There are traces of the worship of another foreign deity at Jerusalem at this time. Either in the town or its territory stood Bit-Ninib, Bit-Ninib. that is the sanctuary of the Babylonian deity Ninib. So much for the religion.

Abd-Khiba held Jerusalem by appointment of the King of Egypt. Dr. Winckler says that the tablets distinguish between *Amelu*, princes ruling Abd-Khiba's in their own right, and *Khazianûti*, not the old Powers. hereditary princes, but others selected for the headship by Pharaoh out of the princes or families of the towns or tribes ;[1] and that Abd-Khiba was such a *Khazianu*. Yet the latter describes his lands, although he had not received them from father or mother, but from Pharaoh, as his ancestral domains. The phrase expressing this is so often repeated that it seems to have been a formula of submission. To Jerusalem there was attached a certain ' territory.' The town itself appears to have been fortified. At least it contained an Egyptian garrison, and even without that it might hold out against the king's enemies.[2] Taking this bit of evidence along with others, viz. that Abd-Khiba appears to have been held responsible for the

[1] *K.A.T.*(3) 193 f.  [2] Letter II. 45-53.

disaster to a caravan in Ayyalôn,[1] and that he maintained
his post against a universal hostility, we may infer that
Jerusalem was already a place of considerable strength.
Its chief could send caravans of his own to Egypt ; but it
is to be noted that no products of the soil are described
among his tribute, only a number of slaves, perhaps
captives of war.   Definite data are wanting as to the size
of Abd-Khiba's territory and the number of the troops
needed to defend it.[2]   Neither Abd-Khiba's anxiety for
the whole territories of the king,[3] nor the opposition to
him of all the other chiefs,[4] can be taken as evidence that
his responsibility to the king was greater than theirs ;
and there is nothing else în his letters to prove that
' Jerusalem was already the dominant state of Southern
Palestine.'[5]

The question of the site of the primitive Jerusalem
has already been sufficiently discussed.   We have seen

The Site of
Abd-Khiba's
Town.

that the citadel most probably lay on the
East Hill, above the one certain spring of
the district, the Old Testament Giḥon, the
modern 'Ain Sitti Mariam, and that this part of the
East Hill, between the southern limit of the Ḥaram
area and Siloam, was a sufficient site for the City down
to the time of David.   The area is nearly as large as

---

[1] Letter II. 54-59 ; above, p. 13.

[2] Winckler's translation of B. 103 and 105 does not support W. M. Müller's
(*As. u. Eur.* 276) inference that only a very small garrison was required to
defend the territory of Jerusalem.

[3] W. 179, 180.                    [4] W. 180, line 12.

[5] Sayce, *Early History of the Hebrews*, 28 f.   This hypothesis was combined with the other that Abd-Khiba was not under Egyptian rule, but was
the friend of the Pharaoh and derived his power from the god directly—
Professor Sayce taking the phrase ' mighty king ' to mean the god.   But this
is denied by other Assyriologists.   Certainly the terms in which Abd-Khiba
submits to the latter are as humble as those of any other chief.

that of the ancient Gezer, with which, as Gezer also
continued to remain a Canaanite *enclave* in Israelite territory, we may most suitably compare Jerusalem.[1] Among
the ancient remains discovered on the area some may
be, none indubitably are, pre-Israelite.[2] No cuneiform
tablets similar to those sent by Abd-Khiba to Egypt
or those found in Lakish or Taanach have come to
light in Jerusalem. It is possible that more extended
excavations may unearth them; but the chance of this
will be felt to be slender when we remember how often
the East Hill has been besieged and its buildings
destroyed, and how constant have been the rebuilding
and the quarrying upon it.[3]

[1] See vol. i. 142 ff.  [2] See vol. i. 140 f.
[3] See vol. i. 210, 227 f.

# CHAPTER II

## THE CONQUEST BY DAVID

### *c.* 1000 B.C.

W E have seen that about 1400 B.C. Jerusalem under
that name was a fortress and town with an
uncertain extent of territory. The inhabitants
Summary
of previous    were Semitic, under a hereditary chief Abd-
Chapter.
Khiba, who, however, ascribed his position
neither to his fathers nor his people but to the lord-
paramount of the land, the King of Egypt. The fortress
was sometimes occupied by an Egyptian garrison; and
the Pharaoh, Amenhotep IV., had placed his name'
upon it. That is, he had imposed on Jerusalem the
worship of himself as the incarnation of Aten, the Sun's
Disk, in favour of whom he had sought to disestablish
the other gods of Egypt. There must have been a
local deity of Jerusalem, but Abd-Khiba prudently re-
frains from alluding to this in letters addressed to a
sovereign who entitled himself Khu-en-Aten, 'Glory of
Aten,' and who regarded Aten as the sole god. The
worship of the local deity, however, can hardly have
been interrupted by that of the Pharaoh, and probably
continued at least till David brought to the town the
Ark of Jahweh.

Who was this predecessor of the God of Israel on the high place of Jerusalem ? We are left to conjectures from the theophorous names of her chiefs and perhaps of herself. Besides Abd-Khiba,[1] one other chief bore such a name, Adoni-Sedek, who was reigning when Israel entered the land.[2] Sedek was a deity of the Western Semites,[3] and appears in several men's names both Aramean and Phœnician.[4] It is worthy of notice that a priest of Jerusalem in David's time was called Sadok, and natural also to compare Melki-Sedek, king of Salem, in the story of Abraham.[5] Again, if the latter part of the name Jerusalem be that of Shalem or Shulman, another deity of the Western Semites,[6] this may have been the local god

The earlier gods of Jerusalem.

---

[1] See above, p. 15.

[2] Joshua x. 1 ff. This passage is from J E, and substantially from E. The parallel in Judges i., from J, names the king Adoni-Bezek, and the LXX. have this form in both passages. On which ground some prefer the reading Adoni Bezek. This is, however, improbable, since in personal names Adon is always compounded with the name of a deity, and no deity Bezek is known, while Sedek occurs several times as the name of a Western Semitic god. Besides, the reading Bezek may easily have arisen in Jud. i. 5, through confusion with the name of the place where Israel encountered the king. Moore, Bennett and Nowack read Adoni-Sedek. Budde, who previously preferred Adoni-Bezek, leaves the question open in his recent commentary on Judges.

[3] See Zimmern, *K.A.T.*[3] 473 f.

[4] Kemosh-Sedek, Sedek-Rimmon, Sedek-Melek. Also as a Canaanite name in the Tell el-Amarna letters, No. 125 (W.), line 37 : Ben Sidki (spelt by the Canaanite scribe Zidki), for which Knudtzon (*Beitr. z. Assyr.* iv. 114) reads Rab-Sidki.

[5] Gen. xiv. 18. Winckler, *K.A.T.*[3] p. 224, takes Salem in this passage, not as an abbreviation for Jerusalem, but as a form of the divine name Shalem, and Melek-Salem as only another form of Melki-Sedek, whom he assigns to the city of Hazazon Tamar=Banias (*Gesch. Isr.* ii. p. 37). All this is very precarious : yet Winckler founds upon it the identity of the god Sedek with the god Sulman or Shalem.

[6] Zimmern, *K.A.T.*[3] 474 f., where the Assyrian Shulman is regarded as probably a title of the god Ninib, of whom, as we have seen, a sanctuary

of whom we are in search.　Other less probable names
have been proposed.[1]　But whoever he was, it is remarkable that no direct mention of the Amorite god of
Jerusalem has survived, although his worshippers were
spared when Israel took the City and continued to live
there.　Either the later scribes took care to eliminate
from the Hebrew records every trace of this predecessor
of Jahweh; or his influence was so restricted and unimportant that his name and his memory disappeared
of themselves.　It is significant that except for the
ambiguous reference to Shalem in Genesis xiv., early
Jerusalem is not regarded in the Old Testament as
having been a famous shrine, such as Beersheba', the
various Gilgals, Gibeon and Bethel continued to be
down to the eighth century.　On a site so crowded and
so disturbed during all the following centuries it is
hopeless to search for remains of the Amorite sanctuary
in Jerusalem.　It may have been about Gihon, for this
spring, as we have seen,[2] was regarded as sacred; or
it may have stood in the valley of Hinnom, where the
sacrifices of children, a feature of Canaanite worship,
afterwards broke out among the Israelites.[3]

　　But if unimportant religiously—at least as compared

The Jebusite with Bethel, the Gilgals and Beersheba'—Jeru-
Jerusalem. salem must have been in those early days a
fortress of no ordinary strength.　We have seen[4] that

existed at or near Jerusalem.　Winckler, *id.* p. 224, sees in Shelomoh, the
Hebrew for Solomon, a form derived from the divine name Shalem.

　[1] Winckler, *K.A.T.*[(3)] 225, 230, supposes that in the names of *David* and
the *City of David* there lurks a *Dōd*, either a divine name or an appellation
for the *genius loci*.　But this would imply that David received his name only
after the capture of Jerusalem, or else that there was a remarkable coincidence
between his name and that of the city he took.　　　[2] Vol. i. 108.

　[3] See below, p. 40, on Millo.　　　　　[4] Vol. i. Bk. i. ch. vi.

her citadel lay upon the East Hill, just above Giḥon, where on all sides save one the ground falls from the ridge to a considerable depth. Apart from what may be an editorial gloss, the Old Testament traditions are unanimous that before David the Israelites failed to capture the citadel;[1] the garrison felt themselves so secure that they laughed at the challenge of David.[2] In fact, through the earliest centuries of Israel's history Jerusalem was the most easterly of a line of positions—Gezer, Beth-Shemesh, Sha'albim, Ayyalôn, Ḳiriath-ye'arim (Kephira, Gibe'on, Be'erōth), Jerusalem—from which Israel did not succeed in ousting their occupants, but which, during the period of the Judges, formed a barrier between the children of Judah to the south, and the rest of Israel.[3] The Elohist document calls those tribes who thus maintained their position against Israel *Amorites*; the Jahwist document, *Canaanites*: both of them general terms for the Semitic populations which preceded Israel in Palestine. More

---

[1] The gloss above mentioned is Judges i. 8: *and the men of Judah fought against Jerusalem and took it, and smote it at the edge of the sword and set fire to it.* But this seems contradicted by Jud. i. 21: *and the Jebusites who dwelt in Jerusalem the children of Benjamin did not drive out, but the Jebusites have dwelt with the children of Benjamin in Jerusalem to this day*; and by Josh. xv. 63: *and the Jebusites, the inhabitants of Jerusalem, the children of Judah did not drive them out, but the Jebusites have dwelt (with the children of Judah*: omit LXX.) *in Jerusalem till this day.* The substitution in Jud. i. 21 of *Benjamin* for *Judah* of Josh. xv. 63 is usually supposed to be due to an editor who thereby strove to remove the contradiction with Jud. i. 8. It is possible to effect a technical conciliation between Jud. i. 8 on the one hand and Jud. i. 21 and Josh. xv. 63 on the other (cf. *e.g.* Sayce, *Early Hist. of the Hebrews*, p. 246 f.; Ottley, *Hist. of the Heb.* 87 f.). But even those who propose this either interpret Jud. i. 8 only of the town, and agree that the Hebrew invaders did not capture the citadel of Jerusalem; or suppose that the Hebrew occupation was only temporary.

[2] 2 Sam. v. 6. See below, pp. 31 f.

[3] In the Song of Deborah Judah is not mentioned.

particularly the Jahwistic document defines the inhabitants of Jerusalem and some neighbouring states as Jebusites, a name not found outside the Old Testament, but sufficiently accredited within that.[1]   This compact little tribe is of interest, not only because of the stand which it made for centuries against the Israelite invaders, but because, upon David's capture of its stronghold, it became a constituent of that strange medley, the Jewish people, and doubtless carried into their life the tough fibre of its tribal character and some of the temper of its immemorial religion.   There is small doubt that the tribe was Semitic, and that it subsisted by agriculture —the Jebusite is called *the inhabitant of the land*[2]—and by the simpler industries of the long-settled Canaanite civilisation.   Beyond these indications there is little to enable us to define the relation of the Israelites to the Canaanite *enclaves* which endured for centuries in their midst.   In the story of Judges xix. the Levite refuses, though night is near, *to turn aside into this city of the Jebusites and lodge in it*, for it is *the city of a stranger, where are none of the children of Israel.*[3]   Israelite and Jebusite, therefore, kept apart, but they talked what was practically the same dialect ; there must have been traffic between them, the less settled Israelites purchasing the necessities and some of the embellishments of life from the townsfolk, as the Bedouin do at the present day ; and, in addition, there may have been occasional intermarriage.   So affairs lasted till the time of David.

[1] The name Jebusite has been handed down all along the main lines of the tradition.   See above, p. 18 *n.* 4.   On Jebus, see vol. i. 266 f.

[2] 2 Sam. v. 6.   Therefore, as formerly under Abd-Khiba, so now Jerusalem must have commanded some extent of the surrounding territory.

[3] Verses 11 and 12.

The story of David's capture of Jerusalem, about 1000 B.C., raises a number of chronological and other questions which lie outside our present aims. Capture by These are rather to discover David's reasons David. for the choice of Jerusalem as his capital, and the effect of this choice on the subsequent history of Israel. We may, however, give a brief statement of the former.

The account of the capture comes to us as part of the Second Book of Samuel, chapters v.-viii., which present a summary of David's reign written from a The Order religious point of view.[1] The order, in which of Events. the events now of interest to us are arranged, is as follows. After Ishba'al's death Northern Israel submits itself to David, who is king in Hebron. He then takes Jerusalem, and has to sustain a double attack of the Philistines, whom he defeats. He brings the ark to Şion, and proceeds with the rebuilding of the city. If this is meant by the editor to be the chronological order, it implies that the Philistines were moved to attack their former vassal by the extension of his power over the northern tribes, which also had been subject to them,[2] and by his capture of a fortress, which must have threatened Israel from the rear in all their previous campaigns against Philistia. But this order seems contradicted by the details from which the summary account has been composed. One of these, v. 17, states that the Philistine attack upon David followed the submission to him of Northern Israel, and that when he heard that the Philistines were advancing he *went down to the hold.* But

---

[1] See the Commentaries, especially Driver's *Notes to the Books of Samuel,* H. P. Smith in the *International Critical Commentary,* and Budde in the *Kurzer Hand-Commentar.*

[2] As Kamphausen was the first to point out.

a hold to which he had to *go down* cannot have been
Jerusalem,[1] but was some fortress at the foot of the hill-
country, perhaps 'Adullam.   If he was already in possession of Jerusalem, such a procedure is hardly intelligible.
We may infer therefore that David's capture of Jerusalem
was subsequent to his defeat of the Philistines.   Again,
this victory (according to v. 17) followed the anointing of
David as king of all Israel.   And yet the phrase in
verse 6, *the king and his men went to Jerusalem against
the Jebusites*, seems to imply that David attacked that
fortress before he had all Israel behind him, and when he
was only a southern chief with a band of followers.[2]
Accordingly other arrangements of the chronological
order than that followed by the editor of chapters v.-viii.
have been offered by modern scholars.   Professors Kittel
and Budde suppose that when David became king of all
Israel the Philistines opened war upon him, and that only
after defeating them he took Jerusalem and brought in
the ark.[3]   Others[4] place the capture of the city first, and
find in it the provocation of the Philistines to attack
David, who defeats them, and is only then joined by
Northern Israel.   Whichever of these arrangements be
the right order of the events—and perhaps it is now
impossible to determine this—the capture of Jerusalem
is closely connected, either as preparation or as conse-

[1] As Ottley and others maintain.

[2] For this phrase the Chronicler (1 Chron. xi. 4) has substituted *David and
all Israel went to Jerusalem*, which seems to be an effort to reconcile the
above difficulties.

[3] Cf. G. W. Wade, *O. T. Hist.* 246 ; W. F. Burnside, *O. T. Hist.* 182.

[4] R. L. Ottley, *Hist. of the Hebrews*, 138.   Winckler dates the capture of
Jerusalem before a forcible conquest of Benjamin, which he imputes to
David, and the effects of which he traces in the subsequent life of the king
(*K.A.T.*[3] 230).

quence, with the renewed hostility of the Philistines and David's assumption of the kingship of all Israel.

The narrative of the actual capture of the stronghold also raises questions. The text is uncertain, and, as it stands, hardly intelligible. It reports that Narrative of the Capture. when David and his men went up against the Jebusites these taunted him. By a slight change in one of the verbs their taunt most naturally runs thus: *Thou shalt not come in hither: but the blind and the lame will drive thee off:*[1] *meaning David cannot come in hither.* *Nevertheless David took the stronghold of Ṣion*—the first appearance of this name in the history. The next verse (8) is both uncertain in its text and impossible to construe as it stands. Our English translation, even in the Revised Version—' And David said on that day, Whosoever smiteth the Jebusites, let him get up to the watercourse and *smite* the lame and the blind, that are hated of David's soul '—is conjectural, as may be seen from the word introduced in italics and from the marginal alternative. Besides, we should not expect directions to take the *hold*, after the statement of its capture in verse 7. The original has *a Jebusite*, and the word translated *watercourse* means rather *waterfall*,[2] of which there was none in Jerusalem; while the consonants of the text read the active form of the verb: *they hated.* The first clause can only be rendered *Whosoever smiteth a Jebusite*, and the rest, as Dr. Budde and others have inferred, ought to be emended so as to express some threat against the slaughter of a Jebusite, in conformity with the testimony that David spared the defenders of the

---

[1] 2 Sam. v. 6, reading with Wellhausen יְסִירְךָ for הֱסִירְךָ.

[2] So Ps. xlii. 8. But in Mishnic Hebrew the word does mean ' conduit.'

City when he took it.[1]  Dr. Budde's own emendation, though not quite satisfactory, for it introduces a negative, may stand in default of a better.  By omitting one letter and changing the vowel points,[2] he gets rid of the difficult *waterfall* (which, besides, is not what the Greek translators read) and substitutes *his neck*, rendering the whole thus : *Whoso slayeth a Jebusite, shall bring his neck into danger, the halt and the blind David's soul doth not hate.*[3]  We thus lose a picturesque yet difficult account of how the citadel was taken, with all occasion for the topographical conjectures that have sprung from it ; but we gain a sensible statement following naturally on the preceding verse and in harmony with other facts.  The concluding clause of verse 8 : *wherefore they say a blind man or a halt may not enter the House*, is obviously an insertion which attempts to account for the later Levitical exclusion of blemished persons from the Temple.[4]  *And David dwelt in the stronghold and called it David's-Burgh.*

From these details we turn to the larger questions of David's policy in regard to Jerusalem.  For clearness' sake we may distinguish between his capture of the City and his choice of it as his capital.

The capture of Jerusalem—whatever he might afterwards make of the City—was necessary for David in

The Military Value of Jerusalem to David.

respect equally of his dominion over Northern Israel, and of his relations to the Philistines.  The last of the alien *enclaves* on the hill-country of the Hebrews, the Jebusite fortress, stood

---

[1] 2 Sam. xxiv. 16.

[2] Instead of וְאֶת- בְּצִנּוֹר, he reads בְּצַוָּרוֹ אֶת-.  The Greek version has 'with a dagger.'          [3] לֹא שָׂאנה.          [4] Lev. xxi. 18.

between the two portions of David's kingdom, and hard
by the trunk-road which ran through them. If, as is
likely,[1] the capture happened before David's accession to
the united sovereignty, it is proof of his political foresight and of the fact that he already cherished the
ambition of being ruler of all Israel; while its achievement may have helped the attraction of the northern
tribes to his crown. Most probably the capture did not
happen before his campaign or campaigns with the Philistines,[2] his experience in which must have shown him
the inexpediency of leaving an alien stronghold on his
rear so often as he should have to descend to meet the
Philistines on the border of the Shephelah. Besides,
Jerusalem lies near the head of one of the passes leading up from the Philistine territory. David had himself
encountered the Philistines on the plain of Rephaim near
the Jebusite fortress, and by that alone must have felt
the indispensableness of the latter. Plainly, therefore,
the capture of Jerusalem was as necessary to Israel's
independence of Philistia as it was to their unification.

The same motives must have worked towards the
selection of the captured City for his capital—but along
with others. As king of all Israel David His Choice
could not remain in Hebron. This town lay of it as his
too far south and its site possesses little Capital.
strength. On the other hand, to have chosen one of
the fortresses of Ephraim, or even to have settled in
Shechem, the natural centre of the country, would have
roused the jealousy of his own southern clans. His
capital had to lie between the two: most fitly between
Bethlehem and Bethel. But upon this stretch of country

---

[1] From 2 Sam. v. 6, see p. 30.      [2] See above, pp. 29 ff.

there was no position to compare for strength with Jerusalem. Bethel, indeed, was better situated for the command of roads and the trade on them, but the site has little military value. Bethlehem, again, might have made a better fortress than Bethel, and lay in a district of greater fertility than Jerusalem. But it had not even the one spring which Jerusalem possessed ; and it was wholly southern and shut off from the north. To the prime necessities of great strength and a tolerable water-supply, to the further advantages of a position on the trunk-road and not far from the head of an easily defended pass into the western plain, Jerusalem added the supreme excellence of a neutral site which had belonged neither to Judah nor to the northern tribes, and was therefore without bias in the delicate balance of interests, which it strained David to preserve throughout the rest of his reign. Nor within the basin in which Jerusalem lies could there be any question between the exact site of the Jebusite stronghold and the other fortifiable hills around. The capture of many an eastern city has meant the abandonment of its site and the rise of a new town at some little distance. But, as we have seen,[1] in that large basin the position most favourable for sustaining the population of a town is where the waters of the basin gather and partly come to the surface before issuing by their one outlet—to the south-east. Here flowed the only spring or springs. There was thus no other way for it. *David dwelt in the stronghold*,[2] in the ancient Jebusite fortress which lay on the East Hill of the present Jerusalem, and immediately above Giḥon.[3]

---

[1] Vol. i. 79.

[2] 2 Sam. v. 6.

[3] Vol. i. 142 ff. ; vol. ii. 22 f.

David, then, being, or about to be, monarch of all Israel, supplied his monarchy with its correlative, a capital; strong by natural position, and politically The Capital suitable by neutrality towards the rival in- of all Israel. terests of his kingdom, north and south. The European analogy, which one remembers, is that of Madrid. Like Jerusalem, with fewer natural advantages than other cities of its land, Madrid was nevertheless largely for the same reasons created the capital by the will of the sovereign.[1] David's conquest gave him complete power over Jerusalem. No tribe or family, except his own, had henceforth predominant rights in the City.[2] It seems indeed as if at first she was attached to neither of the neighbouring tribal territories, for later on her tribal connection was still ambiguous: some writers reckoning her to Judah, David's own tribe, and some to Benjamin.[3] There were no Israelite institutions to supplant, nor authorities to conciliate. As the citadel became David's-Burgh, so the town belonged to the king or his house. In no other town in Israel was the government so directly royal.[4] All this meant an immediate addition to the population. In the East, when a monarchy replaces the ancient tribal constitution, a royal bodyguard is always formed: mercenary and mostly foreign. David set the example in Israel, and it was followed by every king up to the time of Herod. He brought his *Gibbôrîm* or

---

[1] Philip II. in 1561 ; but the fortunes of the city previous to this were not the same as those of Jerusalem had been. Madrid had always been the seat of the Spanish court.

[2] Vol. i. 377 ff.

[3] The Jahwist, Josh. xv. 63, to Judah ; the Priestly Writer, Josh. xv. 7, xviii. 15 f. 28, to Benjamin ; Deut. xxxiii. 12 may not refer to Jerusalem.

[4] Vol. i. 377 ff.

*Bravos* to Jerusalem, and built them barracks beside his residence. They were partly foreigners and partly Israelites, who in the disturbed days of Saul had become detached from their tribal or family interests.[1]   Among them—witness the devotion of the sons of Zeruiah, and the passionate loyalty of Ittai the Gittite[2]—David found his most steady support against the rival jealousies of his still incohesive people. They added sensibly to the numbers of the capital, and must have introduced mixed and wild strains into her blood.   Besides the Gibbôrîm there were David's numerous family, his counsellors, numbers of his fellow-tribesmen, and the other Israelites whom he attracted to his court, with all their clients and servants, and with the traders who were certain to follow them.

*Mixed Character of the Population.*

Historians who have recounted the advantages of Jerusalem as a capital have sometimes included among these a central position for the trade of the land.[3]   But, as we have seen, this judgment is lacking in discrimination.   Jerusalem does not lie, as is sometimes asserted, upon two of the trade-routes of Palestine, that running north and south along the main ridge of the land and that climbing the ridge from east to west. She lies only on the former, and it is not a main route. The other traverses the ridge not at the gates of Jerusalem but twelve miles away, near Bethel ; hence a market as well as a sanctuary.   Jerusalem has no natural command of traffic, as either Bethel, or Hebron, with her more open roads to the coast and her market for the nomads, enjoyed. If, then, Jerusalem did compel the trade of the land to

*Organisation of Trade.*

---

1 Vol. i. 346 f.                                            2 2 Sam. xv. 21.
3 So Kittel, *Gesch. Hebr.* ii. 134.

concentrate upon her bazaars, this was by virtue of her
political supremacy and the commercial organisation of
her kings. Such an organisation always attends the
rise of a new monarchy,—we find a modern Oriental
instance in Telal Ibn Rashîd's policy at Ḥa'îl in the
middle of last century,[1]—and there is evidence that
David began it for Israel. His alliance with Ḥiram ;
his introduction of foreigners, some of whom must have
been traders like those tempted to Ḥa'îl by Ibn Rashîd ;
his stamping of shekels,[2] a sure sign of other regulations
of commerce ; his maintenance of a mercenary army and
his numerous buildings—invariable results of commercial
success—are proofs that he inaugurated the policy which
Solomon developed. But from all this Jerusalem would
chiefly benefit in the increase of her population and
resources.

David reprieved the Jebusite inhabitants from the
massacre or deportation which usually followed the
capture of an Eastern city.[3] He put them out
of their citadel, and probably also from its
immediate environs, but he spared their lives,
to the necessary extension of the City, and he left them
their property. We are not told that he destroyed their
sanctuary or forbade the continuance of their worship.
But, whatever may have happened to these, it is clear
that a considerable heathen population, with the attractions which a god in ancient possession of a definite
territory has always had for the invaders of the latter,
persisted in Jerusalem. If we are to understand the

*The Survival
of the Jebusite
Population.*

---

[1] Palgrave, *Central and E. Arabia*, 93, 112, 133.    [2] 2 Sam. xiv. 26.
[3] 2 Sam. v. 8, according to the reading given above on p. 32 : cf. xxiv.
18 ff.

subsequent history of her religion, we must, with Ezekiel, keep in mind this heathen strain. *Thine origin*, he tells her, when exposing her affection for debased rites, *thine origin and nativity is of the land of the Canaanites ; an Amorite was thy father and thy mother was a Hittite.*[1]

To such a capital David brought the symbol of his people's God.  This was a movable chest, the sanctuary

The Bringing in of the Ark.

and palladium of a nomad people ; which, except for intervals, had never settled anywhere ; which had been carried into their battles ; which had even fallen into the hands of their foes.  With the prestige of victory over the latter, and as if its work of war were over, David brought it for the first time within walls.  He still covered it with the nomad tent ; yet, as the Psalm says,[2] he gave it a *resting-place, a resting-place for ever.*  We can have little doubt that what moved David to recover an object which had so long fallen out of his people's history, and to place it in the new capital, was not merely that the Ark was the only relic of the past with which Israel's memories of their national unity were associated.  David was moved by a religious inspiration. The national unity had never been maintained, or when lost had never been recovered, except by loyalty to the nation's One God and Lord.  His Ark implied Himself. It was His Presence which sealed the new-formed union, and consecrated the capital.

The nation, then, appeared to be made ; and in every

David thus only began Jerusalem.

respect, military, political and religious, Jerusalem stood for its centre.  Yet such achievements could not be the work of one day nor of one man.  Least of all could this happen in the case of

---

[1] Ezek. xvi. 3.  See above, pp. 16 f.          [2] cxxxii. 8, 14.

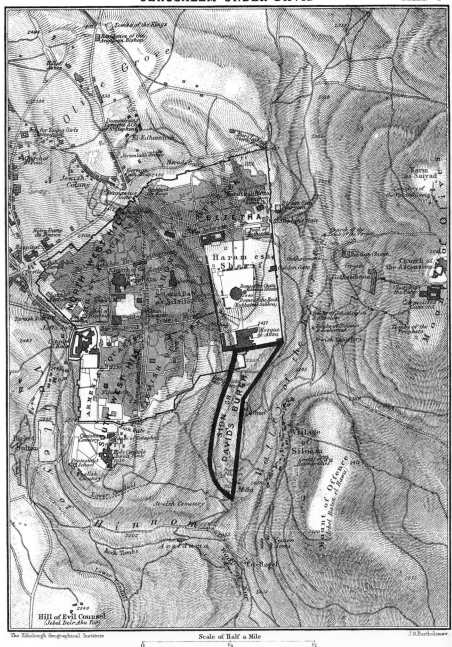

The certain lines of Wall are shown by red lines. There were also suburbs on
the S.W. Hill, probably not walled; they were of uncertain extent.
The Modern City is shown in black.

This map has not been printed in the original color. The red line
has been replaced by a heavy black line.

a town so lately adopted, and with so many natural disadvantages, among a people so recently welded together. Historians are premature who at this point celebrate all the meaning of Jerusalem in the history of Israel, as if due to David alone. The work was Divine and required the ages for its fulfilment. The most we can say of David, beyond the splendid insight with which he met the exigencies of his own day, and his religious devotion, is that in giving Israel Jerusalem he gave them the possibility of that which was yet to be. But for centuries the position of the City remained precarious. She was violated by Shishak; harassed by the Northern Kingdom, so far as she was a capital, and ignored so far as she was a sanctuary. Elijah passed her by when he went to seek Jahweh at Horeb; and according to Amos[1] the Israelite devotees of Jahweh in the eighth century preferred Beersheba' to Sion. It required the disappearance of the Northern Kingdom; the desecration of the rural sanctuaries by the Assyrians, the proof of her own inviolableness by Isaiah, and the centralisation of worship in the Temple by the Deuteronomists of the seventh century, before Jerusalem became the heart and soul of the nation, from which all their life beat forth and with whose fall they died.

It was on the East Hill that David fixed his residence and built or commenced his buildings. We have seen that the town occupied at least as much of David's this Hill as lies to the south of the present Buildings. Ḥaram area. It was grouped round *the stronghold Sion*. This lay above Gihon upon an elevation (now

[1] viii. 14.

cleared away) which in some books of the Old Testament is called *The 'Ophel* or *The Swelling*.[1] But we shall use the name Ophel (without the article) in the conventional sense, in which it is employed by modern writers, for *all* the East Hill south of the Ḥaram area.

Immediately upon the fact of his taking up his abode in Ṣion we read, *and David built* or *fortified round about from the Millo and inward*,[2] or as the Greek version gives it, *and he fortified it, the city, round about from the Millo, and his house*.[3] Whichever of these readings we select, it is evidently the same site on which he dwelt that David fortified. A new feature appears in the Millo.

It has been argued [4] that the Millo was the Jebusite sanctuary, which David destroyed and rebuilt for his own God; but the evidence for this is strained, and is opposed by the data of the text.[5] The Millo, literally *The Filling*, is usually taken as a dam, rampart or solid tower. Such a meaning is confirmed by the use of the root in other North Semitic dialects.[6] The Septuagint render it by 'the Citadel.'[7] The account implies that it was not a line of fortification,

*The Millo.*

---

[1] For all these points see vol. i. Bk. I. ch. vi.      [2] 2 Sam. v. 9.

[3] Καὶ ᾠκοδόμησεν αὐτὴν πόλιν (as if עָר or עִיר הַבָנֵה) κύκλῳ ἀπὸ τῆς Ἄκρας καὶ τὸν οἶκον αὐτοῦ. Cf. 1 Chron. xi. 8: *and he built the city round about from the Millo, even round about.* The Chronicler's text is awkward and appears to betray his difficulties with the data at his disposal. Note that Absalom came to Jerusalem=City of David, 2 Sam. xv. 37.

[4] Winckler, *Gesch.* ii. 198, 249 ff. ; *K.A.T.*[(3)] 239.

[5] David built not *round the Millo* (Wi.), but *from the Millo round about*.

[6] The Assyrian verb in one form = 'heap up an earthen rampart'; mulû and tamlû=artificial terrace. The Targumic מְלִיתָא = a rampart of earth filled up between walls. Compare the LXX. τὸ ἀνάλημμα in 2 Chron. xxxii. 5.

[7] Ἡ Ἄκρα: LXX. B. x. 23, etc. This, if the Greek Ἄκρα is intended, shows that the LXX. translators believed it to be on the East Hill. LXX. A. in 1 Kings ix. 15, 24, Μελω ; 2 Ki. xii. 20 Μααλω, Luc. Μαλλων.

but occupied a definite spot; it is stated that David started his building from it. Either, then, it was an isolated rampart, covering some narrow approach from the north on the level, towards the stronghold, which was otherwise surrounded by steep rocks; or it was one of those solid towers[1] which were often planted on city walls. The Millo is variously placed by modern topographers at the north-east corner of Ophel, because of the words which follow it, *and inward*; or at the north-west corner;[2] or as a rampart across the Tyropœon to bar the approach from the north.[3] But it may have lain off the south end of Ophel, to retain and protect the old Pool. To the Chronicler the Millo was in the city of David.[4]

David's fortifications, then, were on the East Hill, and compassed Ophel[5]; they included an ancient tower or rampart somewhere on the circumference. Within this fortification, all of which perhaps bore the name of David's - Burgh, he built, with the aid of Phœnician workmen, a house for

The King's House and other Buildings.

---

[1] Cf. Josephus, v. *B.J.* iv. 3 : square solid towers on the wall of Agrippa : τετράγωνοί τε καὶ πλήρεις.    [2] Stade, *Gesch.* i. 343.

[3] G. St. Clair, *P.E.F.Q.*, 1889, 90, 96 ; Schick, *id.* 1893, plan, p. 191 ; cf. *id.* 1892, 22, where the Khatuniyeh is suggested as the Millo, separated from the Temple by a passage 15 ft. 4 in. wide, and connected by a bridge. St. Clair, *id.* 1891, 187 f., suggests S. end of Tyropœon.    On Benzinger's plan, p. 217 of his *Kings* (*Kurzer Hand-Commentar* series) Millo ? is marked on the east slope of the West Hill above the Tyropœon.    But this position is *excluded* by the datum of 2 Chron. xxxii. 5.    I do not see how Benzinger (on 1 Kings ix. 16) concludes from 2 Sam. v. 9 and the parallel passage in 1 Chron. xi. 8 that the Millo served for the protection of the western town.    On the contrary, these connect it too closely for such an assumption with David's occupation of the Eastern Hill.

[4] 2 Chron. xxxii. 5.

[5] No trace of an ancient wall has yet been discovered up the west bank or slope of Ophel ; some scarps occurring there cannot be certainly identified as part of a city wall.    But see vol. i. 230.

himself of stone and cedar,[1] which subsequent notices
imply was small,[2] and a house for the Gibbôrîm, or bodyguard ; and here also he pitched a tent for the Ark of the
Lord, which he brought up, and in, to David's-Burgh.[3]
The rest of Ophel below the stronghold, and perhaps the
gorge to the west, were occupied by houses.  At least
there is mention of houses below David's own.[4]

The next question is : did David's Jerusalem extend
beyond Ophel?   On the east the town was certainly
East Limit of  bounded by the bed of the Ḳidron, for we
the City.    read that when the King fled from Jerusalem
before Absalom he tarried till his soldiers passed him at
Beth-ham-merḥaḳ, *house of the distance* or *farthest house*,
that is the utmost building on that side of the town, and
then crossed the brook Ḳidron.[5]  Jerusalem never spread
beyond this natural limit to the East, though the present
suburb of Silwân probably existed from very ancient times.[6]

The opinion that David's Jerusalem extended to the
West Hill is supported even by some who place Ṣion on
Possible West  the East.[7]  For this we have no direct evi-
Extension.   dence.   Only it is difficult to see how the
undoubted increase of the City under David could have
been accommodated upon Ophel.  New ground must

---

[1] 2 Sam. v. 11.

[2] 1 Kings iii. 1 ; ix. 15.  The Chronicler indeed (2 Chron. viii. 11) says
that the daughter of Pharaoh could not live in the house of David because
it was rendered holy by the proximity of the Ark.  But as the new palace of
Solomon was next the Temple this can hardly have been the reason (Stade,
*Gesch.* i. 311 ff.).

[3] 2 Sam. vi. 15, 17.        [4] *Id.* xi. 2, 8, 13.        [5] *Id.* xv. 17, 18, 23.

[6] If, as I have suggested (vol. i. p. 111), 'En-Rogel was the name of a
village as well as of a fountain, it may have occupied the site of Silwân.

[7] Sir Charles Wilson, art. 'Jerusalem,' Smith's *D.B.*[(2)]; Benzinger,
*Comm. on Kings*, 1 Kings iii. 1, and Plan, p. 217 ; Guthe, Hauck's *R.E.*
viii. 676, 678.

have been occupied by the Jebusite population evicted
from the citadel and its environs, and by the settlements
of native and foreign merchants. Besides these, the
large garrison,[1] the great number of royal officials,[2]
their families,[3] the priests and singers,[4] the different
provincials whom David drew to his court,[5] and the
households of the members of his large family separate
from his own,[6] must have greatly expanded the size of
the town. Some of those various houses seem to have
been close to the king's;[7] others were at a distance,
for Absalom dwelt two years in Jerusalem without seeing
the king's face.[8] But all the extension doubtless consisted of suburbs. The town within the walls was still
small; it appears to have had but one principal gate;
the phrase *the way of the gate*[9] contrasts with the
numerous gates of later centuries.

One bit of the orientation of David's Jerusalem has
been preserved by the Greek version of 2 Sam. xiii., the
tale of how Absalom invited the king's sons The North
to a feast at *the shearing of his sheep in Baal-* Road.
*Ḥaṣôr which is beside Ephraim,* that is the modern 'Aṣûr,
near eṭ-Ṭaiyibeh, fourteen miles from Jerusalem, on the
great north road. At this feast Amnon was murdered in
revenge for his humbling of Tamar, Absalom's sister, and
the rest of the king's sons fled. The rumour preceded
them that all were murdered. But, as the king and
his courtiers rent their clothes, Jonadab declared that

---

[1] 2 Sam. x. 14; xii. 31; xv. 18; xx. 7.
[2] 2 Sam. viii. 15-18; xx. 23-26; xxiii. 8 ff.    [3] *Id.* xi. 3, etc.
[4] *Id.* viii. 17 f. ; xix. 35.    [5] *Id.* ix. ; xix. 33 ff. ; 1 Kings ii. 36.
[6] 2 Sam. v. 13-15 ; xiii. ; xiv. 24, 28; 1 Kings i. 5, 53, etc.
[7] 2 Sam. xi. 2, 10.
[8] *Id.* xiv. 24, 28 : cf. Adonijah banished from the court to his own house
(1 Kings i. 53).    [9] 2 Sam. xv. 2.

Amnon alone was slain, and the watchman reported the coming of much people on the Horonaim road : the road from the two Beth-horons, which coincides with the road from Baal-Hasôr, a few miles north of Jerusalem. *And the young man, the watchman, lifted up his eyes and looked, and, behold, much people coming on the road behind him, from the side of the mountain on the descent, and the watchman came and reported to the king, and said, I have seen men out of the Horonaim road from the part of the mountain.*[1] Doubtless the watchman stood on some high tower on the royal residence ; that he saw the Horonaim road *behind him* does not mean that he looked out of the back of his head, but that this road was to the west or north-west of his station, descending as the present road does from the hills on the north, and probably passing down the central wâdy, west of the present Haram area, to the royal residence at the head of Ophel. The phrase *behind him*, or *to the west of him*, is an interesting confirmation that David's house lay on the East Hill. Had it been on the West Hill, the watchman could not have had the north road to the west of him. And it further shows that Jerusalem was not as yet so extended to the north, that in this direction the view was not open.

The only other road made visible by the records is that pursued by David when he fled before Absalom.[2] It is called the *Way of the Wilderness*. There seems to have been an exit from the David's-Burgh on the north into the Kidron valley, for later, when Joab had taken Adonijah to feast by 'En-Rogel, the modern Job's Well, their company were not aware of the descent of another company from the king's

The Way of the Wilderness.

---

[1] 2 Sam. xiii. 34 ; LXX.　　　　　[2] Chap. xv.

house to crown Solomon at Giḥon till the acclamation
which followed this came down the valley towards them.[1]
Compare the later mention of a water-gate near Giḥon,
which must always have been there.   Once across Ḳidron
the Way of the Wilderness led up *the ascent of Olives*,[2]
to the top where there was a sanctuary—*there he was
wont to worship God*.[3]   A little beyond the summit Ziba
met him with provisions for the wilderness, and David
proceeded to Bahurim,[4] which the Targum identifies with
Almon, perhaps the present 'Almît near 'Anathoth.   If
this be correct, the Wilderness was that of Benjamin, and
the way led not round nor over the south shoulder of the
Mount of Olives, but north-east up the hill.[5]   In that case
Beth-ham-merḥaḳ lay not under the north end of Ophel,
but some way up the Ḳidron, and there were probably
a few houses along the valley on the west of the stream.

Standing, then, on the Mount of Olives, we may discern
the following to have been the aspect of Jerusalem under
David.   Where the great Temple platform is   Aspect of
now spread upon large substructions there   the City.
was a rocky summit with a small plateau, the threshing-
floor of 'Araunah.   The southern flank of this fell steeply to
the northern fortifications of David's-Burgh with (according to some) the Millo,[6] a solid bulwark or tower.   A
narrow gateway opened on the north, on a steep descent
to Giḥon, and the road from this turned northwards for a
little with a few houses straggling up it till the Far-house
was reached and then crossed the Ḳidron.   Within the

---

[1] I Kings i. 9, 41 ff.          [2] 2 Sam. xv. 30.
[3] *Ibid.* 32.   Probably the spot to which Ezekiel saw the God of Israel
remove from the Temple (xi. 23; xliii. 1 ff.).          [4] *Id.* xvi. 1-5.
[5] For alternatives for the further course of the road, see *Z.D.P.V.* iii. 8 ff.,
xiii. 93 ff.          [6] More probably S. of Ophel; see p. 43.

walls stood the Stronghold, the small house of David, the house of the Gibbôrîm, with some other buildings, and close to the king's house the Tent of the Ark. Some further open space there must have been for the later graves of the kings. The wall compassed Ophel, with one principal gate, at probably the lower end of Ophel, from which the houses thickly climbed towards the Citadel. On the West Hill our records leave a mist. Probably its slopes into the central wâdy, opposite the north end of Ophel, were also covered with dwellings. Dr. Benzinger, indeed,[1] thinks that 'under David the southern part and eastern slopes of the West Hill were already built upon.' This may have been so. But the more natural growth outwards from the 'City of David' would rather have been from its northern end into the central wâdy and up the opposite slopes of the West Hill. In any case we have no proof, nor even probability, that the whole of the South-West Hill was built upon in David's time. Whatever its size may have been, the new town does not seem to have had a wall around it during David's reign. The first record of such a wall is given under Solomon.[2]

But in all this scene nothing is so vivid as the King himself. I have said that it is easy to exaggerate, as The Figure of some historians have done, David's share the King. in the making of Jerusalem. Her full influence and sacredness were a Divine achievement, which required the ages for its consummation. The Prophets and the Deuteronomic legislation were perhaps the greatest factors in the development of the City; much of her glory, which the later literature throws back upon David, is only the reflection of their work. Neverthe-

---

[1] On 1 Kings iii. 1.        [2] 1 Kings iii. 1, etc.

less it was his choice of her which started everything; which brought history to her walls and planted within them that which made her holy. The Man, whose individual will and policy seem essential to the career of every great city, Jerusalem found in David. He made her the capital of a kingdom; he brought to her the shrine of Israel's God; he gave her a new population: and, if we remember the personal rôle which the sovereigns of antiquity filled in the development and regulation of trade, we shall see his hand in the first drawing to her— little as she was fitted by nature for so central a position —of those industrial and commercial influences which in our modern world are less dependent on the control of kings, however powerful. But besides thus standing behind the City and providing the first impetus to her career, the figure of David stands out among the early features of her life more conspicuous than any of them. Of all the actors on that stage, from David himself to Titus, there is none who moves more clearly, whether under the stress of the great passions or through the details of conduct and conversation. We see him in temptation, in penitence, in grief or dancing with that oriental ecstasy of worship which had not yet died out of the Hebrew religion; now bent beneath the scandals of his family; now rending his garments at the death of Adonijah; now weeping on the way to the wilderness when he flees from Absalom; or listening to the arguments of his subjects against himself; or besought by his soldiers to remain within the walls while they go out to war, *that the lamp of Israel be not quenched*; or tenderly nourished through the feebleness of old age. The drama of Jerusalem is never more vivid than while David is its hero.

CHAPTER III

SOLOMON AND THE TEMPLE

*c.* 970-933 B.C.

WHEN we pass from David to Solomon, from
Second Samuel to First Kings, we are conscious

The Change<br>in the Royal<br>Spectacle. of a change in both the quality of the drama
and the character of its hero. Instead of the
palpable figure, the vivid features of a man,
there rises an apparition more majestic indeed, but, just
by reason of its grandeur, nebulous and vague. *Solomon
in all his glory*—we see the glory, but are dazzled as to
the man behind it. In part, at least, this haze may be
attributed to the style of the narrators. Of the history
of David, the bulk is the precious bequest of a contemporary,[1] who has not lost sight of the man in the
monarch. But of Solomon's history much more is due
to writers at a distance from their subject, and even
where the text is taken from contemporary annals it
seems to be the work of courtiers to whom the King, the
Royal Personage, is everything.[2] Even so, however, the

---

[1] Cf. Budde, *Gesch. der althebr. Litteratur,* 43 : ' Die Geschichte Davids
und seines Zeitalters, von zeitgenössischer Hand verfasst oder doch von eines
Zeitgenossen Mund erzählt wird immer der feste und älteste Kern israeli-
tischer Geschichtsschreibung bleiben.'

[2] For the critical analysis of 1 Kings i.-xi., see the commentaries, I. Benzinger, *Die Bücher der Könige,* 1899 ; C. F. Burney, *Notes on the Heb. Text
of the Books of Kings,* 1903 ; B. Stade and F. Schwally, *The Books of Kings :
crit. ed. of the Heb. Text* (Haupt's *S.B.O.T.*), 1904 ; J. Skinner, ' Kings ' (in

questions arise, whether some of the haze may not be due to the want in Solomon himself of the character and passion that give distinctness to all the movements of David ; or whether the features of the great Sultan are hidden from us only by the largeness and splendour of his policy, and through lack of that atmosphere of adversity which alone reveals a man to his contemporaries and posterity.

Solomon had not to fight his way to the throne ; his succession was managed for him by others.[1] Nor do we find originality in the three swift blows by which he followed it up. These are the in-evitable consequences of the movement which bore him so high, sheer flashes from the thundercloud that had been gathering in Jerusalem since his birth. Prince by the blood-stained marriage of his father, and king through his mother's intrigues, Solomon was obliged to secure this double usurpation by removing all possible stays of the legitimate succession. So when Adonijah imprudently gave him occasion by seeking for wife their father's companion, he slew Adonijah ; he slew Joab, the general of his father's forces, appointing to the post Benaiah, the captain of the bodyguard ; and had he dared he would have slain the chief priest Abiathar, but he banished him and gave the office to Sadok, with whose family it remained for centuries.[2] None of these actions

*Personal Powers of Solomon.*

*The Century Bible*) n.d. Winckler's theories, that the histories of David and Solomon reflect, or were written upon the scheme of, a Babylonian mythology under Canaanite influence, is unfolded in several works, but fully stated in his edition of Schrader, *K.A.T.*[(3)] 222 ff., 233 ff. For Cheyne's treatment of Solomon's history in accordance with his Jerahmeel theories, see *Enc. Bibl.*, art. 'Solomon,' and *Critica Biblica*.

[1] 1 Kings i.
[2] 1 Kings ii. 12 ff.

evince either character or inventiveness; they were compelled from him by the forces which had made him king.
Nor had Solomon the opportunity of distinguishing himself in battle; he did not extend, but on the contrary lost
some of, the conquests of his father. Nor through the rest
of his reign are there any of those personal adventures
which bring David out of his state and present his figure
throbbing before us. Solomon's appearances are all official
—on the judgment-seat, on the throne, consecrating the
Temple. Even such as are religious are after a more
sober style of religion. They have lost the primitive
ecstasy which distinguished the worship of both of his
predecessors. He sleeps, it is true, in a sanctuary in
order to induce a dream; but we cannot conceive of
Solomon either tearing his clothes and lying prostrate
like Saul, or dancing before the Ark as David his father
did. Even the wisdom which exalts his personality sub-
limates it at the same time. Even the one personal
temper imputed to him,—*now King Solomon loved women
. . . he took foreign wives*,[1] may have been only the result
of policy and a love of splendour. His establishment of
many strange shrines in Jerusalem was certainly due to
such motives as well as to the exigencies of the foreign
trade upon which he adventured.[2] In short, behind his
wealth, his wisdom, his wives and his idols, it is difficult
to discern the real man. Yet through that long and
prosperous reign the throne must have been filled by a
personality of unusual power. Of the early concentration of his mind upon the highest duties, we are assured

---

[1] 1 Kings xi. 1, after the LXX.
[2] See the author's 'Trade and Commerce,' *Enc. Bibl.*, §§ 21-24,
50.

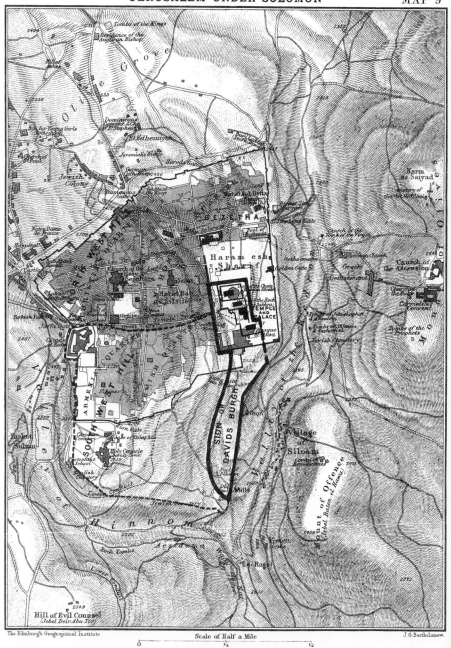

The certain lines of Wall are shown by red lines, and the uncertain by red
dotted lines. There may have been a suburb on the N.W. Hill.
The Modern City is shown in black.

This map has not been printed in the original color. The red line
has been replaced by a heavy black line.

by a narrative from probably an ancient source.[1] Having been asked by the Lord what gift he desired, Solomon chose neither wealth, honour nor the life of his enemies, but the mind to govern wisely; *an understanding heart to judge Thy people.* The Lord gave this, and there follows an instance of its use ; of a kind to win the admiration of any Eastern people, for whom justice depends so exclusively upon the discrimination and cleverness of their prince.[2] Even if we consent to the criticism which consigns so much of the splendour of the reign to legend, this will but prove the memory of his high capacity for ruling. The tradition of so wide a kingdom, and such influence abroad, the facts of so great an activity in building, so elaborate an organisation of the state, so large an enterprise of trade—these imply that if Solomon was the fortunate heir of his father's conquests, his mind rose to the splendid heritage, and easily, as would appear, maintained its authority to the end. We read of no intrigues or revolts within the palace ; and the spirit of opposition in Northern Israel was ineffective so long as Solomon lived.

Such was the new lord of Jerusalem : fateful to her in more ways than one. He found her little but a fortress, and he left her a city. For the tent which covered her wandering Ark[3] he built a temple Their Effect on Jerusalem. of stone on a site which kept its holiness through his people's history and is still sacred to religion. He devoted

---

[1] 1 Kings iii. 4-28. Besides the passages usually marked as Deuteronomic, verses 6*b*, 14, there are other traces of the editorial hand ; *e.g.* the language in which Solomon is made to ask his desire is Deuteronomic.

[2] The story of Solomon and the two mothers is very like some still current in the Lebanon concerning the wise judgments of the Emir Beshir at the beginning of the nineteenth century.

[3] It had left the City even in David's time.

to his capital the labours of the whole nation and the wealth of a very distant trade; embellishing her with buildings which raised her once for all above every other town in Israel, and gave her rank with at least the minor capitals of Asia. But, though all this concentration of the national resources worked towards her future fame, and enabled her to endure through the next two centuries of misfortune, it must also be estimated as one of the causes of the latter. The discontent excited among the Northern Tribes by the drain upon their men and their wealth was the strongest of the influences which led to the disruption of the kingdom and the deposition of Jerusalem from the rank of capital of all Israel to that of the chief town in the petty principality of Judah, precariously situated near the frontier of her most jealous neighbour. Nor, as we shall see, did even the erection of the Temple ensure the immediate religious fame of the City.

We may now trace the centralising policy of Solomon, the directions in which it bore in upon Jerusalem, and what necessary exceptions there were to it.

In the first place, we notice some increase of the Court and the Household. David's ministers were a General of the troops, a Captain of the guard, two Priests, a Recorder, a Scribe or Secretary of State, a Master of the Levies, and one who is described as the King's Friend.[1] Solomon had all these, along with a second Scribe, a Steward or Officer of the Household, a Finance-minister or chief of the provincial governors; and seems to have given the King's Friend a more definite position in the official list of

*Solomon's Centralising Policy.*
*1. The Ministers of State.*

[1] 2 Sam. viii. 17 ff.; xx. 23 ff.; xv. 37; xvi. 16; 1 Chron. xxvii. 33.

ministers than he occupied under David.[1] These, and a
large number of lesser officers of court and household,
formed the centre from which the following organisations
were worked.

In the next place, there was the division of the kingdom into twelve provinces, each of which furnished the
king's court, and perhaps the wider circle of
his workmen, with food for one month a year.
The list of the provinces may have been drawn
up late in the king's reign, and is therefore out of place
where it stands in the history,[2] but we may conveniently
take it now. The fragmentary state of the text forbids
dogmatic inferences as to the size of the various provinces, or whether, as some assert, the impost was arranged
to lie more heavily on those with a non-Israelite population. But one feature is striking. It has been pointed
out that neither Jerusalem, Bethlehem nor Hebron is
included ; as if Solomon relieved from the duty the seats
of his own family. In any case, those national contributions poured into Jerusalem, not only for the nourishment
of the court, but directly or indirectly for the enrichment
of the whole population. Their reception and consumption must have increased the number and business of the
latter. Many provincials must thus have formed the
habit of visiting the capital, and this would lead to

2. The
Twelve
Provinces.

[1] 1 Kings iv. 2-6 ; LXX. has two lists, here and at ii. 46*h* (Swete's ed.),
which Benzinger suggests belong to different periods of the king's reign. The
King's Friend is an old Egyptian title (Maspero, *R.P.* sec. ser. ii. 18), and is
also found in the Tell el-Amarna letters, Winckler, i. 19 (?).

[2] 1 Kings iv. 7 ff. There is no reason to doubt the reliableness of the list.
The late date in the king's reign assigned to it is inferred, not so much from
the mention of two of the king's sons-in-law among the officers, as from the
fact that the court could hardly have reached the size implied till after he
had reigned some years.

the settlement of some of them within and about its walls.

Another influence of the same kind was the employment for thirteen years at least[1] of a number of Phœnician workmen,[2] and of a mass of Israelites,
**3. The National Levies.** stated at 30,000[3] (with 3300 overseers), who quarried stones in the mountains of Judah, and helped the Phœnicians in their building. That Solomon drew his levies of labour only from his non-Israelite subjects[4] is a statement which does not agree either with the data in Chronicles v., nor with the intimation that Jeroboam was *over the levy of the house of Joseph*,[5] and must therefore be the insertion of a later hand.[6] It is probable that some of these labourers were added to the permanent population of Jerusalem. But in any case their sight of her, and their sense of her new importance, were carried across the land, and made Jerusalem far better known. The cedars cut in Lebanon and conveyed through the Phœnician ports, the mines in Lebanon,[7] and the foundries in the Jordan Valley[8]—all for a city which a few years before was a mere Jebusite *enclave*—must of themselves have created for her a foreign reputation, and brought an influx of trade to her gates.

---

[1] 1 Kings vii. 1. If the building of the Temple, which is stated to have taken seven years (vi. 1, 38), was not contemporaneous with the thirteen years of the building of the palace, then the operations took twenty years in all (ix. 10). But this is doubtful.

[2] 1 Kings v. 18.    [3] *Id.* v. 13 ff.    [4] ix. 22.    [5] xi. 28.

[6] Cf. too the words 'unto this day' in ix. 21.

[7] In the LXX. version, chapter ii. 46c, we read : καὶ Σαλώμων ἤρξατο ἀνοίγειν τὰ δυναστεύματα τοῦ Λιβάνου : this is explained by Winckler (*A. T. Untersuchungen*, p. 175) as referring to mines in Lebanon, where ancient workings have been found. Cf. Benzinger on 1 Kings ix. 19. Cf. Jeremiah xv. 12.    [8] vii. 46.

On the frontiers of his territory Solomon fortified certain cities: Ḥaṣôr, Megiddo, Gezer, Bêth-Ḥorôn the nether, Ba'alath, and Tamar in the wilderness.[1] With the exception of Ba'alath the sites of all these are known, and one of them, Gezer, has been laid bare by excavation in a more thorough fashion than the ruins of any other town in Palestine. Mr. Macalister is 'strongly inclined to seek, in the square towers inserted at irregular intervals along the [outer] wall, for the tangible traces' of Solomon's fortification of Gezer after the probable breaching of the wall by the king of Egypt.[2] Ḥaṣôr, probably the present Tell-Khurêbe above the Lake of Huleh, commanded the main entrance into Palestine from the North; Megiddo, the passage from Esdraelon to Sharon; Bêth-Ḥorôn, the most open ascent from Sharon, Jafa and the group of towns about the latter to Jerusalem; Gezer (as in the time of the Maccabean kingdom) the approach up the Vale of Ayyalôn from the coast, and a road which probably entered the hills by the town of Ayyalôn, and thence travelled by the present Ḳuriet el-'Eynab[3] to Jerusalem more directly than the Bêth-Ḥorôn road. Ba'alath lay either on this last road nearer to Jerusalem than Gezer, or on a more southerly approach to the capital. *Tamar in the wilderness* is the Roman Thamara,[4] on the road up the Negeb to Hebron from the Gulf of 'Aḳaba. If we may draw a deduction from the absence of towns in Moab, Gilead and Bashan, Solomon had nothing to fear upon those frontiers of his kingdom; and in fact Ḥaṣôr

*4. The Screen of Frontier Fortresses*

---

[1] ix. 15*b*, 17, 18.
[2] *P.E.F. Quart. Statement*, January 1905, pp. 30 f.
[3] I followed this natural and ancient track in 1904.
[4] Probably the present El-Kurnub.

and Tamar confronted the only two foreign peoples from whom he is reported to have had trouble—the Arameans and the Edomites; while the absence of Jericho and Ephraimite cities proves how quietly he held Northern Israel.   Megiddo and Gezer controlled the main trade route between Damascus and Egypt; but besides protecting the international traffic, and thus enabling Solomon to fulfil his engagements with other potentates,[1] these two fortresses may have been further intended as a signal to the Phœnicians of the power of Israel.

Each of these cities, then, on the borders of the proper territory of Israel, covered an important trade route and secured the tolls upon it;[2] while three of them,

and their<br>Protection of<br>the Capital.

Bêth-Ḥorôn, Gezer and Baʿalath, protected the more immediate approaches to the capital. Tamar was in hardly less close connection with Jerusalem, as one feels to-day at the occasional sight of a caravan from Sinai or the Gulf of ʿAḳaba at the Hebron gate of the City.   Imagine these secure roads drawing in on Jerusalem!  We can believe that with the completion of the fortresses upon them, a new sense of being at the centre of things, and an assurance of security, inspired her inhabitants, and contributed to her increase.

Besides those six fortified towns Solomon had a number of *store cities, and cities for his chariots, and cities for his horsemen.*[3]   These were the necessary excep-

5. The Store<br>and Garrison<br>Towns.

tions to his centralising policy.   That he did not assemble his cavalry or chariots at the capital was due to the character of its surroundings,

---

[1] Cf. the Tell el-Amarna letters, in which a king of Mesopotamia complains to the King of Egypt of the lawlessness from which his caravans had suffered in Palestine, then Egyptian territory.   See above, p. 9.

[2] See vol. i. 343.                                   [3] 1 Kings ix. 19.

destitute of rich pasture, and too steep and broken for wheels. In contrast with the more open Samaria and Esdraelon, we seldom read of the use of chariots about Jerusalem.[1] Solomon kept his where they could manœuvre. Some horses, no doubt, appeared at the City. Solomon was the first to introduce horses into Israel, importing them, not from Egypt as the Hebrew text declares, but from the northern Muṣri and Ḳuë or Cilicia, as the more correct Greek version enables us to discover.[2] They would replace at his court the mules on which royal personages had hitherto ridden.[3]

We may infer, then, a considerable increase of the population of Jerusalem under Solomon, not only during the thirteen or twenty years in which his buildings were in progress, but permanently. The sites on which the new inhabitants settled *Consequent Increase of Jerusalem.* can only have been the South-West Hill and the Central Valley. The extent of the enlarged City we shall consider when we treat of the wall which he built.

Besides a few scattered notes of the buildings erected by Solomon, the history of his reign contains a detailed account, 1 Kings v.-vii., of his preparations for, and his construction of, the Temple, the *The Account of the Temple, etc.* Palace, and their adjacent Halls. Unfortunately the text has suffered from the wear of tradition, from attempts at repair, and from insertions by a later age, to which the Temple was of more importance—the object at once of greater superstition and of more careful definition between the degrees of holiness ascribed to its

---

[1] There are three instances: in one case the chariot carried a dead, in another a dying, man (2 Kings ix. 28; 2 Chron. xxxv. 24). See *H.G.H.L.* 330, with Appendix v. See vol. i. 325.

[2] 1 Kings x. 28; vol. i. 324.  [3] Vol. i. 326.

various parts—than it was under Solomon himself. For details the reader must be referred to the commentaries and various special treatises.[1] There is no doubt that the basis of the description of the Temple and adjacent buildings is a contemporary document, whether from the royal annals or the Temple archives.[2]

That at first Solomon dwelt in the David's-Burgh, the former Ṣion, is clear from the statement that he brought

Sites of the Temple, Palace and Royal Halls.

there the daughter of Pharaoh, till he should finish his new buildings.[3] These it was most natural for him to raise in proximity to the David's-Burgh and the barracks of the Gibbôrîm ; that is on the East Hill, on which there appears to have been open ground to the north. Here, it is generally agreed, lay the site which he chose for the Temple, the threshing-floor of 'Araunah on which David had erected an altar. For here in the time of the Maccabees we find the Second Temple, and there can be no doubt that this occupied the site of Solomon's, nor that the Mosque of Omar with its immediate platform occupies much the same site to-day :[4] the Mount Ṣion of several Old Testament writers, the 'Mount Moriah' of the Chronicler.[5] Round es-Ṣakhra, which is the summit of this part of the East Hill, the rock has been frequently levelled and scarped, but the present contours ascertained by the Ordnance

---

[1] See the commentaries mentioned on p. 48 *n.* 2, and especially Burney's with its valuable suggestions on the text of 1 Kings v.-vii. Of special treatises there are Stade, *Z. A. T. W.*, 1883, 129 ff., 'Der Text des Berichts über Salomo's Bauten' (cf. *Gesch. Isr.* i. 311 ff.); I. Benzinger, *Hebr. Archäologie*, 1894, §§ 35, 53, and arts. 'Palace' and 'Temple' in the *Enc. Bibl. ;* Nowack, *Lehrbuch der Hebr. Arch.*, 1894 ; T. Witton Davies, art. 'Temple' in Hastings' *D.B.*, 1902.

[2] See below, pp. 109 f.     [3] 1 Kings iii. 1 ; ix. 24.

[4] Vol. i. 230 ff.     [5] Vol. i. 267.

# PLAN OF SOLOMON'S BUILDINGS

### (after Stade)

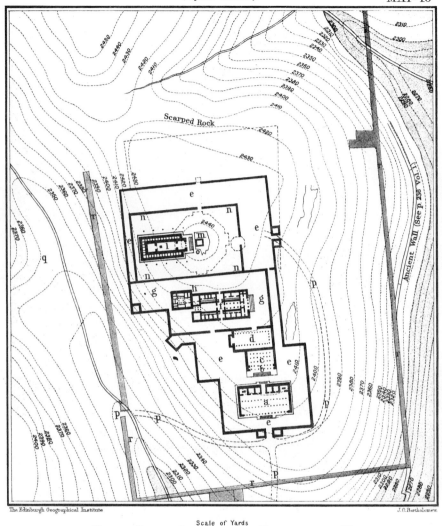

The Edinburgh Geographical Institute

J.G.Bartholomew

Scarped Rock

Ancient Wall (See p. 236 Vol. I)

Scale of Yards

100  50  0  100  200

a  The House of the Forest of Lebanon
b  Threshold
c  Hall of Pillars
d  The Throne Hall
e  The "Great" or Outer Court
f  The King's House
g  The "Other" or "Middle" Court

h  House of Pharaoh's Daughter
l  The Temple
m  Altar of Burnt Offering
n  The Upper Court or C. of the House of Yahweh
pp  Ascents to Palace and Temple
q  Ḥammam esh-Shefa
r  Wall of present Ḥaram-esh-Sherif

London; Hodder and Stoughton.

Survey are sufficient evidence that there was upon it ample room for 'Araunah's threshing-floor.[1] Here, then, Solomon's Temple was built, surrounded by a Court of its own. But both Temple and Court were only the highest part of a complex of buildings and courts within one greater court, surrounded by a strong wall. To the south of the Temple Court, below it and separated by a wall[2] with an entry, lay a second inner court containing the *King's House* and the *House of the Daughter of Pharaoh*. And this being so, the rest of the buildings, *the Throne Hall, the Pillared Hall*, and *the House of the Forest of Lebanon*, must have lain on the other side of the Palace from the Temple. Such, too, is the order in which they are described in the account of their construction. In any case it is clear that the Palace lay above the David's-Burgh, for Pharaoh's daughter *came up* from the latter into the house which Solomon built for her,[3] and that the Temple lay above the Palace.[4] On all these data most moderns accept the general plan of the buildings drawn upon the ascertained contours of the hill by Professor Stade.[5] This is here reproduced but with the contour lines corrected after the data of the Ordnance Survey.[6]

The exact position of the Temple may be reasonably

[1] *Rec. of Jer.* 298, with plan.
[2] Separated only by a wall from the Temple-court, Ezek. xliii. 8 ; below the Temple-court, 2 Kings xi. 19 : *they brought down the king from the house of Jahweh to the king's house*. Jer. xxvi. 10 : the princes of Judah *came up* from the king's house to the house of Jahweh : cf. xxxvi. 11 ff.
[3] 1 Kings ix. 24.
[4] See last note but one.
[5] *Gesch. des Volkes Israel*; between pp. 314 and 315, with the contours supplied by Schick.
[6] *P.E.F. Excav. at Jerusalem*, Portfolio Plan VI. ; *Rec. of Jerus.*, 298.

estimated from the data of Josephus and the Mishna and
from the character of the Rock eṣ-Ṣakhra and

The Exact Site of the Temple and Altar of Burnt-Offering. its surrounding contours. Josephus says that 'at first the highest level ground on the Hill

was hardly sufficient for the Temple and the Altar,'[1] that is the Altar of burnt-offering in front of the Temple; and that Solomon and the people of subsequent periods built walls and banks till the Hill was made broad. But the summit of the Hill is eṣ-Ṣakhra, and the rock-levels about it suit the levels of the Temple-Courts as given in the Mishna.[2] Moreover, the Rock eṣ-Ṣakhra, now under the dome of the Mosque of Omar, is venerated by Mohammedans as second only to the shrine of Mecca. From the tenacity with which such sites in the East preserve their character, we may infer that in ancient times also the Rock was holy; and Professor Stade points out that as angels are represented in the Old Testament appearing on rocks, it is probable that the appearance of the angel to David by the threshing-floor, *between earth and heaven*, was believed to have taken place on this very summit.[3] Moreover, the Rock itself bears proofs of having been used as an altar. A channel penetrates from the surface to a little cave below, whence a conduit descends through the body of the Hill; obviously designed to carry off either the blood or the refuse of sacrifices.[4] Similar arrangements are seen on other Semitic altars. From all these data the conclusion is reasonable that the Rock, eṣ-Ṣakhra, represents the Altar of Burnt-offering. But as

[1] I *B.J.* v. I.        [2] Conder, *Tent-Work* (6), 288.
[3] *Gesch. des Volkes Israel*, i. 314; cf. Judges vi. 11 ff., 20; xiii. 19; I Chron. xxi. 16.
[4] *Rec. of Jerus.* 221.

this lay to the east of the Temple, we must place the site of the latter to the west of eṣ-Ṣakhra. In that case the western end of the Temple stood upon some of those substructures which, as Josephus emphasises, were frequently laid down from the time of Solomon onwards.[1]

From the description in First Kings, even when its omissions and obscurities are supplemented by Ezekiel's plans,[2] it is not possible to achieve such an Description of exact reconstruction of Solomon's Temple as the Temple. several moderns have attempted. The ground-plan may be drawn with some certainty, and we can realise the bulk of the whole as seen from the outside, along with the general aspect of the interior. But we are ignorant both of some of the exact proportions and of the general style of the architecture. The following facts must be

[1] On the improbability of the theory which places the Temple in the south-west corner of the Ḥaram area, see vol. i. 231. The Temple is placed on the eṣ-Ṣakhra summit of the East Hill by the great majority of modern authorities: *e.g.* Robinson, Warren (*Rec. of Jerus.* 313); Thomson (*L. and B.* 688); Stade and Conder as cited above; Schick, Henderson (*Palestine*, 146); Socin and Benzinger (in *Baedeker* and elsewhere) ; Nowack (*Hebr. Archä.* 27 f.); Sanday (*Sacred Sites*, etc., 58); Rix (*Tent and Testament*, 304). Of these Thomson, Stade, Socin, Benzinger, Nowack and Rix take eṣ-Ṣakhra as the site of the altar of burnt-offering. Conder, Henderson and Schick take it to have been the ʻstone of foundation' (אבן שתייה, *Mishna* ʻYôma,' v. 2) on which the Ark rested within the Holy of Holies. But the dimensions of eṣ-Ṣakhra, 17·7 m. by 15·5 and 1·25 to 2 m. above-ground (according to *Baedeker*: about 58 feet by 50¾, and from over 4 feet to 6½ high), are too great for it to have stood in the Holy of Holies, a cube of little over 30 feet; and the ʻstone of foundation' was not a rock but a stone. Besides, to place the Holy of Holies at eṣ-Ṣakhra would leave too little space to the east for the Temple court. Warren places the altar of burnt-offering to the south of eṣ-Ṣakhra, which, arguing from the *Mishna* tract ʻMiddoth,' he takes to have been the site of the Gate Nitzotz (*P.E.F. Mem.* ʻJerus.' 98 f.).

[2] Ezek. xl. ff. Ezekiel's plans are of course ideal, but must be based on his knowledge as a priest of the First Temple.

kept in mind. A Temple was indeed no novelty in
Israel. There had been one in Shiloh.[1] But Solomon's
Temple appears to have been constructed after foreign
patterns. It was built by Phœnician workmen, yet the
description shows more likeness to the Egyptian than to
the Phœnician type of sanctuary.[2] Again, we must not,
in accordance with modern ideas, conceive of the Temple
as a house for worshippers (whose place of assembly was
rather in the court in front of it), but as the dwelling
of the Deity; for by this we shall be prepared for
its comparative smallness. Solomon's Temple lay east
and west, a thick-walled, rectangular building of large
squared stones and cedar beams, about 124 feet long by
55 broad and over 52 high;[3] with a porch of uncertain
height on the east side, and round the others three

---

[1] Cf. 1 Sam. ii. 22; the second half, which speaks of *the tent of meeting*,
is wanting in the Greek, and is no doubt an addition from a Priestly Writer,
who supposed that the great tabernacle of P. had been set up in Shiloh. It
contradicts the rest of the narrative, in which the Shiloh sanctuary is called
a *hekal* or *temple*, with doorposts and a *lishkah* (i. 9 after the LXX. and
Klostermann, iii. 3); cf. Jer. vii. 12 ff.; xxvi. 6, 9. (The other passages
quoted in support of this which speak of the *house of Jahweh* (1 Sam. i. 7,
24; cf. Judg. xviii. 31) are not conclusive, for *house* might be a tent.)
Opposed to this is another tradition (2 Sam. vii. 6 ff.), the author of which
cannot have been acquainted with 1 Sam. i.-iii. (cf. Kennedy in *The Century
Bible*). Fergusson's theory that Solomon's Temple was built on the model
but twice the scale of the Tabernacle breaks down on the figures available,
even if we were to allow that the Tabernacle of the Priestly Writer ever
existed.

[2] Benzinger, *Hebr. Archä.* 385; cf. Pietschmann, *Gesch. der Phönizier*,
200 f. There is a very striking resemblance between the description of
Solomon's Temple and that of the Temple of Hierapolis by Lucian (*De Dea
Syra*).

[3] These figures are reckoned from what are evidently the internal dimensions, but without the breadth of the wall between the two chambers (viz.
60 by 20 by 30 cubits, which at 20·7 inches to the cubit equal 103½ by
34½ by 52 feet), *plus* the thickness of two walls each 6 cubits, and an allowance
for the roof.

stories of *side chambers*—literally *ribs*—to a height of about 17 feet *plus* their roof. The interior was divided by a wall into two apartments. The outer, the *Hekal* or *Palace* of the Deity, called in later times *The Holy Place*, was nearly 70 feet long by 34½ broad and 52 high. The inner, the *Debîr* or *Back*, later the *Holy of Holies*, was a cube of 34½ feet, with apparently a chamber above it. Both were panelled with cedar and floored with cypress wood;[1] *there was no stone seen*; the cedar appears to have been richly carved. The *debîr*, the actual dwelling of the Deity, contained the Ark, overhung by the Cherubim; it was absolutely dark, save perhaps for a single lamp. The high lattice windows in the main wall above the side chambers can have given but scanty light to the *hekal*, which contained the cedarn *Table of Shew-Bread*, or *Bread of the Presence*,[2] and perhaps *candlesticks* or *lampstands*.[3] At the entrance, either within or before the Porch, stood two bronze columns, of which that on the right was called *Yakîn* and that on the left *Boaz*;[4] probably representations of the *maṣṣebôth* or sacred pillars usual in Semitic sanctuaries, and once

---

[1] The overlaying of the walls with gold is a later addition to the description, as Stade has shown from the fact that the various statements of it are out of order and partly wanting in the LXX.

[2] 1 Kings vi. 20, LXX.: *and he made an altar of cedar*; vii. 48 : *the table on which the Bread of the Face* or *Presence was, of gold.* The last word is doubtful. Ezekiel's was of cedar, xli. 22. In P. (Nu. iv. 7) the bread is called *the continual bread*; in Chron. (1 Chron. ix. 32; 2 Chron. xiii. 11) *the b. of arrangement* or *ordering.* 1 Kings vii. 48 is altogether doubtful; it mentions *a golden* altar which is not mentioned in vi., and is obviously the insertion of a later hand in order to introduce the altar of incense of the Second Temple. There was no incense in the first; see below.

[3] 1 Kings vii. 49, another late passage; the lampstands are not mentioned in vi., but in themselves are probable.

[4] 1 Kings vii. 21 : יָכִין *he establishes* (?); בֹּעַז *in him is strength* (?).

legal, but afterwards condemned, in the worship of
Israel.[1]

Round all the Temple, yet so that the greater part of
its space extended upon the eastern front, lay the *Court*
The Temple<br>Forecourt, *of the House of Jahweh,* called also the *Inner
Court,* to distinguish it from *The Other Court*
round the Palace, and from *The Great Court* which
compassed all the buildings.[2]   In later times the first
two were named *The Upper* and *Middle Courts* respectively.[3]  With the sanctuary proper, *The Inner* or *Upper
Court* was included under the name of *The House of
Jahweh.*[4]  That is, it was part of the Holy Place, and there
the great bulk of the sacrifices were accomplished ; for
there, as we have seen, stood the Altar of the Burnt-
with the Altar<br>of Burnt-<br>Offering. Offering.  In the description of Solomon's
Temple there is no word of his having con-
structed an altar.  Though in other parts of
his history *a bronze altar before Jahweh* is mentioned,
the probability is that this was a subsequent invention,
and that Solomon, at least at first, simply used the bare
Rock es-Ṣakhra for his sacrifices.[5]  In a later reign we

---

[1] Gen. xxviii. 18 ; xxxv. 14, etc. ; Ex. xxiv. 4 ; Hos. iii. 4 (cf. Is. xix.
19) contrasted with Deut. xvi. 22 ; Lev. xxvi. 1.   Robertson Smith (*Rel. of
the Sem.* 191, 468) takes Yakîn and Boaz to have been altar-pillars, with
hearths on their tops.

[2] *C. of the House of Jahweh,* חֲצַר בֵּית־יהוה, 1 Kings vii. 12.  *Inner Court,*
הֶחָצֵר הַפְּנִימִית vi. 36, vii. 12.  *Other Court,* חָצֵר הָאַחֶרֶת vii. 8.  *Great Court,*
הֶחָצֵר הַגְּדוֹלָה vii. 9, 12.  Burney emends 1 Kings vii. 12 after the LXX. so
as to bring out all three courts.

[3] See below, pp. 256 ff.          [4] Jer. xxxv. 4, etc.

[5] See above, p. 60.  The theory that 1 Kings v. originally contained a
description of the *bronze altar,* and that this was deleted by a later editor, is
answered by Burney, p. 103.  Robertson Smith explains the omission by
his theory that Yakîn and Boaz were altar hearths (above *n.* 1), but
this is improbable.  The solution adopted above (cf. Skinner on viii. 64),
that Solomon required to construct no altar, because the Rock now

shall find *a bronze altar* in the forecourt of the Temple,
but this also may have been constructed on the same
Rock, the surface of which is sufficient for its stated
dimensions.[1] Between the Altar of Burnt-Offering and
the Temple, but to the south-east of the latter, stood the
*Bronze Sea*,[2] a huge cast-bronze tank, some  The Bronze
seventeen feet in diameter, supported on the  Sea.
backs of twelve Bronze Bulls, facing by threes to the
four quarters of heaven.[3] It is difficult to think that
such a construction was meant for use only as a laver;
and the plausible suggestion has been made that it
embodied certain ideas which prevailed in the Babylonian and Canaanite religions, and, as various parts
of the Old Testament prove, influenced at some time or
other the religion of Israel. According to this theory
*The Sea* was the symbol of the Great Deep, the primeval
chaos subjugated (according to the Babylonians) by
Marduk, whose symbol was the Bull, at this time
a frequent image of deity also throughout Canaan and
even within Israel. How much of this symbolism the

called eṣ-Ṣakhra was already used as such, has this in its favour, that a rock-
altar, but not a bronze one, would conform to the practice in early Israel and
the directions in Ex. xx. 24 f. But this does not amount to much, for
Solomon introduced many innovations. The reference to a *bronze altar* in
I Kings viii. 64 may be late; for the passage has other late elements, and
the material of Solomon's altar in ix. 25 is not stated (yet note, it was *built*).
2 Chron. iv. 1, Ḥuram-abi's construction of a bronze altar, is late; and the
earliest reliable mention of such an altar is therefore that in the story of
Aḥaz, 2 Kings xvi. 14.

[1] 2 Chron. iv. 1; cf. Ezek. xliii. 13 ff.   [2] I Kings vii. 39.
[3] הַיָּם מוּצָק vii. 23; יָם הַנְּחֹשֶׁת 2 Kings xxv. 13, or simply הַיָּם
I Kings vii. 39, 44; 2 Kings xvi. 17. I Kings vii. 23 ff. states 10 cubits as
the diameter, 30 (approximately) as the circumference, and 5 as the depth.
The capacity, either as given here (verse 26, 2000 baths) or as in 2 Chron.
iv. 5 (3000 baths), is too great for these dimensions. The casting may not
have been in one piece; some have thought of a wooden basin plated with
bronze castings.

VOL. II.

Israelites of Solomon's day recognised in the Bronze Sea with its twelve Bulls facing the four quarters of heaven is, of course, quite uncertain; but that the whole was associated with Babylonian notions is rendered probable by the fact that under the later and more exclusive monotheism, the Bronze Sea is either ignored, or studiously explained as a mere laver, or replaced by a laver.[1] If the theory be sound, we must add the Bronze Sea and its twelve Bulls to the other proofs afforded by the furniture of the Temple that under Solomon the religion of Israel still included a number of pagan elements, the elimination of which we shall have to watch in the course of Jerusalem's religious history. Besides the Sea there were ten travelling lavers on wheels, *mekonôth*,[2] five on the south and five on the north of the Temple. They too were decorated with mythological figures, lions, bulls and cherubim, and like the Sea are absent from the Temple arrangements of Ezekiel and the Priestly Writer. Upon the forecourt, thus furnished, were performed the daily and the greater sacrifices of king and nation; and here till the time of the Exile the mass of the people gathered without restriction for the

---

[1] The theory is due to Kosters (*Theol. Tijdschrift*, 1879, 445 ff.). Aḥaz took away the Bulls and put the Sea on a pavement, rather, it would appear, because he wanted the bronze than from a reforming motive, 2 Kings xvi. 17. Ezekiel has no place for the Sea; his Temple-spring seems its substitute. 2 Chron. iv. 6 explains it as a laver. In the Priestly writing a laver כִּיּוֹר stands in the place of the Sea, Exod. xxx. 18 ff.; xl. 7, 30. For Babylonian analogies see Gunkel, *Schöpfung und Chaos*, 153; Sayce, *Hibbert Lectures*, 63; *Rec. of the Past*, new series, i. 65; inscription of Ur-nina at Telloh, col. iii.: 'The temple of the goddess Gatumdug he has erected, the great *apzu* he has constructed,' . . . 'the apzu or deep was the basin for purification attached to a Babylonian temple, corresponding to the "sea" of Solomon.'

[2] 1 Kings vii. 27 ff. On the whole passage see especially Stade, *Z. A. T. W.*, 1883. *Mekonôth* may mean *bases*, but by some is compared with the Greek *mechanē*.

worship of God. The Rock eṣ-Ṣakhra became the
national altar, the court around it the national auditorium. That high platform which Solomon spread
about his Temple was to be identified with both the
rival institutions of Israel's religion; the ritual and the
ethic, sacrifice and prophecy. The king surrounded it, we
are told, by a wall of three courses of hewn stone, and
a course of cedar beams.[1] Through this an entry led to
the palace-court. There was one gate on the north,[2] and
certainly another, though it is not mentioned, on the east.
At what date the lodges or chambers were added, which
Baruch notices over these gates and in other parts of the
court, we do not know.

South of the Temple-Court, separated only by a wall,
but on a lower terrace, lay *The Other* or *Middle Court*,[3]
enclosing *the House of the King*. This was The Palace
built of hewn stone and cedar like the other and its Court.
royal buildings; which are described in 1 Kings vii. in the
opposite order from that in which we now take them.
Here, too, and most probably behind the Palace, was *the
House of the Daughter of Pharaoh*;[4] and from the first
there were doubtless many of those other buildings for
the king's household, officials and stores which are mentioned in the time of Jeremiah.[5]

South of the Palace, and immediately adjacent to its
Court, stood the *Hall of Justice* or *The Throne Hall*[6]
panelled in cedar from floor to rafters, and distinguished
by a great ivory throne supported by lions.[7] South

---

[1] 1 Kings vi. 36.    [2] Below, p. 257.    [3] Above, p. 64 *n.* 2.

[4] 1 Kings vii. 8, slightly emended: *and his house in which he was to dwell,
in the other court, inwards from the Hall* of Justice, *was like the construction
of this; also the House for the daughter of Pharaoh was like this Hall.*

[5] Below, pp. 258 f.    [6] vii 7, אוּלָם הַמִּשְׁפָּט or אֻלָם הַכִּסֵּא.
[7] x. 18-20.

of this and probably constructed as its vestibule, was

The Throne, and Pillars, Halls. the *Hall of Pillars*,[1] some 86 feet by 52, which had a pillared porch and a flight of steps or heavy eaves—the Hebrew term is uncertain.[2]

And finally, to the south of these, stood the *House of the Forest of Lebanon*,[3] deriving its name from its com-
House of the Forest of Lebanon. plicated structure in that northern timber which was so strange to the people of Judah. It was the largest of all the buildings, 172 feet by 86 by 52. There seem to have been two stories: in the lower forty-five pillars in three rows supported the floor of the upper. An early document says that Solomon deposited in this House the three hundred shields of beaten gold, probably among the forest of pillars in the lower story.[4] The upper story, so firmly supported on the pillars, may have been designed for popular gatherings. Josephus says that Solomon 'prepared this House to receive a multitude for judgments and for the decision of public business, and to provide room for an assembly of men convened for cases of justice:'[5] that is, not to wait for the decisions of judges, but in order themselves to decide, as a popular assembly, upon the affairs of the state and of justice. If Josephus be not merely reflecting upon the reign of Solomon the conditions of his own times, we have here a curious illustration of the existence of that popular power which we have seen prevailing throughout the history of Israel, even under the most despotic of her kings.[6]

[1] vii. 6, אוּלָם הָעַמּוּדִים.        [2] עֵב; cf. Ezek. xi. 25 f.

[3] viii. 2 ff., בֵּית יַעַר הַלְּבָנוֹן.

[4] x. 17; cf. Is. xxii. 8, *the armour in the House of the Forest.*
[5] Jos. viii. *Ant.* v. 2.        [6] Vol. i. Bk. ii. ch. x.

All these buildings, rising upon their successive terraces from the Forest House to the Temple—as attested
no less by the ancient description of them Spectacular
than by the modern discovery of the and Historical Effects of the
contours of their sloping site — must have whole.
presented to the eyes of a people, still mainly in the
agricultural stage of development, a very imposing
spectacle; the effect of which we must not measure
by the fact that the whole complex lay in all probability within the southern section of the present
Ḥaram area, or at the most extended but a little way
beyond it.[1] *All these,* says the historian, *were of costly
stones, according to the* usual *dimensions of ashlar, sawn
with saws, inside and outside, from foundation to coping,
from the Court of the House of Jahweh even to the Great
Court.*[2] The latter encompassed the whole, and was itself
surrounded by a great wall *of three courses of ashlar and
one of cedar beams; round about the court of the House of
Jahweh and the court of the porch of the palace.*[3] Not a
fragment of these edifices or lines of wall has remained
recognisable to the present day; but the relative positions of the edifices, and the directions of the walls, are
tolerably clear from the data of their description and the
natural contours of their rocky site. Above all, we must
grasp in our minds two results of our investigation. The
Temple was built by Solomon, and till the Exile remained,
only as a part of the royal house and the government
offices. And thus, both by the strength of the site
which he chose, and by the wall with which he embraced
it, Solomon created a separate citadel in Jerusalem, whose

[1] Vol. i. 230 ff.　　　[2] 1 Kings vii. 9 ; see Burney.
[3] vii. 12 ; Burney after the LXX.

distinctness from the rest of the City remained a factor of importance in the history, especially of her sieges, to the very end.

Besides the detailed account of Solomon's buildings on the East Hill, there are inserted at different points of

Solomon's further Fortifications. 1 Kings ii.-xi. fragmentary statements about his fortifications of the City:—(a) Solomon *brought Pharaoh's daughter into the David's-Burgh until he had finished building his own house, the house of Jahweh and the wall of Jerusalem round about ;*[1] (b) . . . *to build the house of Jahweh, his own house, and the Millo and the wall of Jerusalem . . . but the daughter of Pharaoh came up from the David's-Burgh to her house which he had built for her ; at that time he built the Millo*[2] ; (c) *And Solomon built the Millo and stopped the breach of the David's-Burgh.*[3] These fragments, so variously placed and rendered in the Hebrew and the Greek texts, apparently belong to one original statement[4] from an ancient source, probably the annals of Solomon's

---

[1] Heb. text iii. 1, parallel to the Greek (Swete's ed.), ii. 35*c* : *until he had finished the house of Jahweh at first and the wall of Jer. round about* ; and iv. 31 : *the house of Jahweh, his own h. and the w. of Jer.*

[2] Heb. text ix. 15*b*, 24, parallel to the Greek, x. 23 : *house of Jahweh, h. of the king, w. of Jer., and the citadel* (τὴν ἄκραν), *to complete the fortification of the city of David* ; cf. ii. 35*e* : *and he built the citadel a defence upon it, he cut through, or off, the city of David* ; 35*f* : *thus the daughter of Ph. came up from the city of D. to her house which he built for her ; then he built the citadel* ; 35*k* adds that he built Gezer and other cities *after* he built the palace, the Temple, and the wall of Jerusalem.

[3] Heb. text, xi. 27, exactly translated at the same point by the Greek ; which in xii. 24*b* adds that it was Jeroboam who (under Solomon) enclosed the city of David.

[4] Wilson (Smith's *D.B.*[(2)], 1598*a*), following Josephus (viii. *Ant.* ii. 1, vi. 1), takes 1 Kings iii. 1 and ix. 15 as referring to two different buildings of the wall of Jerusalem by Solomon before and after he built the Temple. But in all its repetitions the statement is apparently the same.

reign; there is no reason to doubt it. It tells us first that Solomon *built* or *fortified* the Millo. Had there not been a credible account of the Millo The Millo. under David,[1] we might have inferred that this was an earthwork or dam to connect David's-Burgh, across the intervening hollow, with the new citadel to the north. But the account under David leads, as we have seen, to the conclusion that the Millo was an earth-bastion or solid tower on either the north-east, north-west, or at the south end of the David's-Burgh, or perhaps a dam across the Central Valley. It is significant that the Greek translators call it 'the Akra,' the name of the citadel which in Greek times occupied the site of the David's-Burgh.[2] Further, Solomon *stopped the breach of the David's-Burgh*, which we are unable to define except as a gap left by David in the fortifications of his citadel. And, lastly, *he built the wall of Jerusalem round about.* Did this run round the East Hill only, or include in whole or part the South-west Hill? Josephus regards it as identical with his First Wall, The Wall round about Jerusalem. which from the Temple-cloisters crossed the Tyropœon, ran up the northern edge of the South-west Hill to 'the Tower of David,' and thence round that Hill to Siloam;[3] and many moderns accept the identification Dr. Guthe doubts if it was Solomon who carried the northern stretch of this wall across the Central Valley, and thinks that the circumvallation ran round the slopes of the South-west Hill, to which (he believes) the name Jerusalem, as distinct from David's-Burgh, was confined.[4] Dr. Bliss suggests that the south-west angle of Solomon's

---

[1] Above, p. 40 f.; but some think it unhistorical.     [2] Vol. i. 156 ff.
[3] v. *B.J.* iv. 2.                    [4] Hauck's *R.-E.* viii. 678.

fortifications was 'Maudslay's Scarp,' traces their line thence south-east on another scarp he uncovered to a rectangular wall above the Central Valley, and infers a continuation to the present Burj-el-Kibrit, and so across the valley to the East Hill.[1] On these theories Solomon's wall enclosed either the whole or the northern part of the South-west Hill, a conclusion in itself by no means improbable ; for in that direction, as we have seen, must have spread the undoubted increase of the population. Still, it is possible that this was accommodated in suburbs. None of the remains recovered on the South-west Hill are recognisable as Solomon's.  It has not been proved that the name Jerusalem was confined in early times to that Hill.  And we ought to observe that none of the statements quoted above afford the slightest evidence for the inclusion of the Hill, or of any part of it, within Solomon's wall.  On the contrary, this wall is associated by them only with buildings on the East Hill ; and all they appear to prove is that the wall ran round both the David's-Burgh with the houses which covered the rest of the ridge falling to Siloam, and the new buildings which Solomon had erected to the north upon the same East Hill.  In that uncertainty we must leave the question.

An exact appreciation of Israel's religion under Solomon is one of the hardest tasks that await their historian ; requiring as it does the difficult justice which is due alike to the high spiritual rank the religion had already attained, and to those facts, which conflict or seem to conflict with this, in the text of Solomon's annals : the little ethical

*Religious Problems of Solomon's Reign.*

---

[1] Vol. i. 213 ff., 218.  See especially 1 Kings iii. 1.

emphasis found in the oldest parts of that text, the
evidence of elements in the national worship alien to
its higher spirit; and the tradition of some doubt or
even controversy among the prophets as to the Divine
will regarding the Temple itself. We want to know
what features of high and permanent value the religion
already displayed; what Solomon and his Temple contributed to its subsequent development; and what ruder
elements, either surviving in the ritual from its racial
origins or perhaps introduced by Solomon from neighbouring nations, had to be thrown out of it, as in later
centuries the prophets became more conscious of the real
character of the religion. But for reasons already stated
—the mixed style of the narrative and the obscurity
which rests on Solomon's own character—all these are
difficult to estimate.

Some points indeed are sufficiently clear. The Temple
was built in the Name and at the Word of Jahweh
alone. No other god was worshipped there. Israel's
Nor was He represented by any image. The Creed,
Ark, which from the days of Sinai He was believed to
inhabit, was reverently laid in the darkness of the
inner chamber, and towards this empty shrine wrapt
in gloom the people, gathering on the sunlit court outside, worshipped as towards His Presence and the seat
of His Power. On the day of Dedication (we are told),
when the priests had deposited the Ark, and while a
cloud immediately filled the empty House, Solomon pronounced certain words expressive of the nature of the
God who had chosen it for His dwelling. Of this solemn
utterance the Hebrew text has preserved only a part,
but the Greek version yields us the whole—two couplets

marked by the elliptic diction, the rhythm and the parallelism which are characteristic of Hebrew poetry:—

> *The Sun hath Jahweh set in the Heavens*
> *But* Himself *hath decreed to dwell in the Darkness.*
> *Build Me a House, a Homestead for Me,*
> *To inhabit for ever.*

The second of these couplets is rendered by the Hebrew as if it were Solomon's answer to the first:—

> *I have built thee a House, an Abode,*
> *Seat of Thy Habitation for ever.* [1]

The great antiquity of this verse is assured by a note in the Greek version which says that it is taken from the Book of Jashar,[2] the same to which we owe David's incomparable elegy on Saul and Jonathan. The four lines are therefore very precious: Israel's Creed, when they had built their Temple and assembling before it under the open heaven, lifted their hearts not thither but towards the dark and empty cell in front of them. The sources of this Creed are simple and significant, Nature and the Word: man's constant resorts for the knowledge of God, reacting upon, explaining and supplementing each other. Upon the one is manifest His creative power, *the Sun hath Jahweh set in the Heavens.* The other affirms His distinctness from all that is seen, His invisibleness and His inscrutable nature. *He hath*

---

[1] The Hebrew, which omits the first of the four lines, is found in 1 Kings viii. 12, 13. The Greek, giving all four lines, is inserted after verse 53. See Wellhausen, *Comp. des Hexateuchs*, etc., 271; Cheyne, *Origin of the Psalter*, 193, 212; Benzinger, Burney and Skinner *in loco*.

[2] Greek: ἐν βιβλίῳ τῆς ᾠδῆς=בְּסֵפֶר הַשִּׁיר; but as Wellhausen suggests, transposing two letters, we ought probably to read בְּסֵפֶר הַיָּשָׁר. This, of course, does not prove that Solomon himself uttered the words, but it ensures at least that they cannot be later than the age immediately after him.

*said*—this term is the simplest in the language—*He hath
said He will dwell in the Darkness.* Without form He
has formed all things. Maker of the light, His home
is the cloud. His Power is high as heaven, but His
Presence and local habitation are with men. These are
the abiding antitheses of religion for which we still seek
an adequate expression. Obedient to the Word, Israel,
in contrast with all the peoples about them, have made
no image of their God, but within and around His
imageless shrine they have planted certain and
symbols or mythical types, of which we Symbols.
cannot say whether they had all descended from an
earlier stage of the national religion or whether some
of them were now borrowed by Solomon from his
Canaanite neighbours. These are the two Cherûbîm
towering above the empty Ark, the other Cherûbîm
carved on the walls of the sanctuary, the Bronze Serpent,
the position of which is unknown, the two Pillars in the
Temple-Porch, and the Bronze Sea upon its twelve Bulls.
As with the origin of these so with their meaning, we
cannot tell what exactly they typified. Nor, perhaps,
could the worshippers themselves, beyond some vivid
suggestion of the various forms and forces of life which
were at the command of the unseen Deity. The Cherubs
are evidently intended as guardians or supporters of His
Presence.[1] The Bronze Serpent is said to have been a

---

[1] No satisfactory etymology has been found for the name *Kěrûb* (cherub)
either in Hebrew or any other language. The Hebrew idea of them greatly
altered in the course of the history. As here, so in the Paradise story they
are conceived as guards, and further associated with fire (Gen. iii. 24). So
in Ezek. xxviii. 13 f. 16. In Ezek. i., x. the conception seems influenced
by the Babylonian winged, human-headed bulls, which also stand as guards
or sentinels. In Ps. xviii. 9, 10 the Kerûbîm are parallel to the storm-
clouds or winds; the Deity rides on them. In the Apocalyptic literature

relic of the days and acts of Moses; but in accordance
with Canaanite ideas Israel came to 'impute to it a
special divinity and to offer it the smoke of their
sacrifices.'[1]  Pillars, like the two in the Temple-Porch,
had been a part of Israel's ritual, as of that of every
Semitic people, from the earliest times; and we have
already seen the probability that the Bronze Sea on the
twelve Bulls represented the subjection of the forces of
nature to the Deity.[2]  All these symbols, along with the
Ark itself, disappeared gradually from the worship of
Israel.  The Bronze Serpent was removed by Ḥezeḳiah's
reformation, the Bulls by the sordid necessity of another
king for their bronze; the Sea was replaced by a
Laver; the Pillars were forbidden by the Deuteronomic
Law.[3]  All were evidently found incompatible with the
spiritual growth of the religion.  In Solomon's time they
represented those 'beggarly rudiments' from which the
progressive faith of Israel had not yet shaken itself free.

We cannot fail to notice that the Creed attributed to
Solomon gives expression to neither of the two elements
Ethical Ques-  which, from other sources, we know to have
tions.        been already powerful in the religion of the
people—the historical and the ethical.  Nothing is said
of the great events by which Jahweh had made Himself known to Israel as their God; and nothing of the
conduct which He required of them.  This silence is
curiously abetted by the rest of the older texts.  Though
the prophet Nathan, who had rebuked the sin of David,

they are, with the Seraphim and the Ophannim, *the angels of power* (Enoch
lxi. 10 ff. ; cf. xx. 7), guardians of the Divine Throne (lxxi. 7).  Some have
associated the early Hebrew form with that of the Hittite griffin (Cheyne,
art. 'Cherub,' *Enc. Bibl.*).

[1] 2 Kings xviii. 4.     [2] Above, pp. 65 f.     [3] Above, pp. 64, 66.

was among the forces which made Solomon king, there
is no mention of prophetic influence throughout the rest
of the latter's reign ; and the only historical or ethical
references which occur are those found in the great
addresses attributed to Solomon at the Dedication of
the Temple. That these, as they stand, are the work
of some centuries later cannot be doubted ; they are
written throughout from the Deuteronomist's standpoint
and in his own characteristic style. But it would be
wrong to suppose that he had no authentic material from
which to elaborate them. As remarked above, both the
historical and ethical elements were already developed
in the religion of Israel, and we cannot believe that the
consciousness of either was absent from the men who
built the Temple or that it failed to find some expression on so great a festival as that of the Dedication.
But it would be precisely such an expression on which
the Deuteronomist would sympathetically fasten, and
on which he would naturally bestow a more elaborate
form.

Even while imputing to the aged king a serious de-
linquency from the virtue of his youth, the Deuteronomist
nowhere asserts that Solomon himself sacrificed to another god than Jahweh. Nor are
there ascribed to Solomon any of the horrors
The Presence
of other Cults
in Jerusalem.
which more than one of his successors imported from
Canaanite faiths into the national worship: neither the
sacrifice of children nor the orgies of the *ḳedeshim.* ' But
we have no reason to doubt the substance of the tradition[1] that Solomon provided shrines in Jerusalem for
many foreign deities. This was the inevitable conse-

---

[1] Elaborated by the Deuteronomist in I Kings xi. 1-13.

quence, according to the ideas of the time, of the king's treaties with monarchs of other faiths, his marriages with their daughters, and his trade with their merchants. It implies, of course, not only a conception of religion still below a perfect monotheism, but an evil effect upon the man whom his policy forced to it. The king, however exclusively he had dedicated the Temple to the God of Israel, could not live with so many wives nor provide for so many alien forms of worship without himself deteriorating in character and without tempting his people to that confusion of their own higher worship with the other cults of Canaan, which was of constant peril to Israel, but especially dangerous at a time when the ancient Canaanite communities were being absorbed into the nation.

As to the Temple itself, we are left in some doubt by the conflicting reports of the motives which led to its erection. One narrative recounts how prophecy had at first conveyed to David the Divine permission to build it ; and had then, in the same Lord's name, withdrawn this permission on the ground that He had never inhabited a House but had gone about in a Tent and a Tabernacle.[1] Another asserts that Solomon explained to Hiram how David could not build a House for the name of his God, because wars were about him on every side ;[2] and similar is the reason given by the Chronicler, that David's hands were stained with blood.[3] These three statements occur in texts which criticism has good grounds for judging to be late. But in the second

*Probable Motives for the Erection of the Temple.*

[1] 2 Sam. vii. : see Kennedy in the *Century Bible.*
[2] 1 Kings v. 2 f.          [3] 1 Chron. xxii. 8 ff. ; xxviii. 2 f.

the description of so sudden a change in the Divine
purpose can hardly be a pure invention.  It probably
preserves the memory that David's proposal had raised
a controversy among the prophets.  There were two
opinions as to whether a Temple was right.  Those who
objected to it may have done so with the instinct, which
afterwards developed into articulate expression, that to
conceive of the dwelling of so great a God as confined
to a house made with hands, was to contradict His true
nature.  But their opposition more probably arose from
the feelings expressed by the narrator, that all the proposed splendour was an innovation upon that plainer
investment of the Divine Presence with which the nation
had been content from the days of their nomadic sim-
plicity.  And, indeed, it is clear that the converse was
at least one of the motives of Solomon in designing this
new departure.  The erection of a Temple was part of
the imperial policy in which he imitated the greater
monarchs of his time.  The Temple (as we have seen)
was upon a foreign model.  It arose as one of a complex
of royal buildings, and within the same walls by
which the king fortified his palace, his court and his
halls of justice.  He himself sacrificed upon its altar,
assuming the dignity which afterwards belonged to the
priests alone.  Not only did his foreign guards act as
its police, but there are reasons for supposing that they
also discharged the duty of slaughtering the animals for
its sacrifices.[1]  All this is so contrary to the later Jewish
systems, which carefully exclude foreigners from the

[1] See Robertson Smith, *O. T. J. C.* p. 262 *n.* 1.  The phrase *captain of the guard* literally means *chief of the slaughterers*, as altar is literally *slaughter-place*.

Temple and reserve to one priestly tribe both the sacrificial offices and the duty of watching the sacred courts, as to confirm us in the belief that in instituting the Temple Solomon was also in no way moved by the later policy of centralising the national worship. In fact, the Deuteronomic editor admits that this centralisation did not take place for a very long time afterwards. For at least a couple of centuries no king proposed or attempted the removal of the rural high-places at which Jahweh was worshipped. It will be our duty to observe the first faint beginnings of the idea, with their evident motives in the circumstances of Judah's history. For long Solomon's Temple did not even become the most important sanctuary of Israel's God. About 750 the pilgrims of Northern Israel not only preferred the more ancient shrines of Bethel and Gilgal, but still passed by Jerusalem for Beersheba',[1] as Elijah had done for Sinai.

But these facts must not be permitted to weaken our sense of the influence of Solomon and his Temple upon The Religious the subsequent religious development of Influence of Israel. The Temple, not only because it was Solomon and the Temple. more imposing than any other in the land, and was identified with the one enduring dynasty of the nation, but because it preserved the shrine of ancient Israel and a purer form of the worship of God than elsewhere prevailed, could wait for that future which lay beyond the calamities that were immediately to assail it. So far Solomon was the pioneer of the prophets and the Deuteronomists in the creation of the unique sacredness of Ṣion and of the religious service which Jerusalem

[1] Amos viii. 14.

has achieved for humanity. Nor was his share in this history merely of a formal or material character. By his peaceful reign and his organisation of the national life Solomon provided opportunity[1] for the beginning of those habits of reflection, the growth of that wisdom, which tradition so generously imputes to him. To a reign which has left such memories, the most sceptical historian cannot grudge the rudiments at least of the reflective literature of Israel. And what food for reflection was furnished by Solomon's Temple and his Creed! Both were pregnant with those religious antitheses through controversy on which the truth appears to be providentially developed towards its fullest expression. On the one side the fact that a local habitation was built for God the Creator, and that this was believed to be His *habitation for ever*; on the other side the fact that He chose to dwell in the cloud, and that the inmost shrine of His Temple was dark and imageless—these represent the two poles between which religious controversy in Israel oscillated through Isaiah, Jeremiah, Ezekiel, the Evangelists of the Exile, the Priestly legislators and the Psalmists of Judaism down to the conversation of Jesus with the woman of Samaria and the speech of Stephen before the Sanhedrin of Jerusalem. In his Temple Solomon, like every other founder of a religious institution, bequeathed to future generations the material for dogmas that were superstitious and enslaving. But the history will show us that at the same time he gave to their purer worship and more spiritual conceptions the only home and fortress in which these could come to maturity. After all, *salvation was of the Jews*; and the sum of

---

[1] On this see Ewald, *History of Israel*, Eng. Trans. iii.

our judgment must be that if the religion of Israel under Solomon had not yet escaped bondage to the things which are seen, nor for many centuries to come could do so, it had already the instinct at its heart that the things which are unseen are the things which are eternal.

## CHAPTER IV

## FROM REHOBOAM TO AHAZ

### *c.* 933–720

THE period of Jerusalem's history upon which we now enter is bounded by two dominant events which across it confront each other with opposite effects upon the fortunes of the City: the Disruption of the Kingdom about 933 B.C., and the Fall of Northern Israel in 721-720. The Disruption of the Kingdom deposed Jerusalem from her brief glory as the capital of all Israel, and left to her only the small province of Judah and a Temple whose reputation, in spite of its greater splendour and purer worship, was still below those of more ancient sanctuaries in the land. The Fall of Samaria restored Jerusalem to the rank of the single metropolis of her people, commanding indeed a smaller territory, but one that was more compact and secluded, and about to be endowed with the greater fame of the one inviolable shrine of the true God. Between these distant and opposite crises there came a long ebb and a gradual flow of the City's fortunes. At first Jerusalem suffered additional despoiling and disgrace, but under the later of the twelve monarchs of the period she more than recovered her former strength. It would be wrong, however, to assume

*The General Importance of the Period.*

83

that the time of her sufferings was one only of loss.
Jerusalem preserved the Ark with its more spiritual cult
of the national God, and remained true to the dynasty
of David, the guardian of its bright and pregnant traditions.　Thus both her misfortunes and her recoveries
during the period made for the glory of her future : the
misfortunes by the memories and the hopes in which
they disciplined her people ; the recoveries by preparing
the material basis on which her unique holiness was to
be vindicated by the hand of God Himself.　Some recent
historians have minimised the importance of Jerusalem
during the period of the Double Kingdom.　They have
been moved to do so by a natural reaction from the
tradition that the incomparable sacredness of the City
was already realised under Solomon and by a just desire
to emphasise the influence of the prophets in the creation
of her greatness.　But the duty of showing how slowly
this greatness came, and how essential to it were the
contributions of prophecy, cannot be properly discharged
without some appreciation of the political and religious
importance which Jerusalem achieved before the time of
the prophets, and of which their tributes to the City are
the strongest certificates.　Whatever Solomon may have
done for Jerusalem, it is during the long and broken
period on which we now enter that we shall find the
first slow developments of that material and spiritual
grandeur with which the Prophets and the Law finally
endowed her.

## 1. REHOBOAM : *c.* 933–917

The Biblical history of the Disruption of the Kingdom

consists of two narratives. According to one which is generally, but too hastily, assigned to a writer of Northern Israel, Rehoboam upon the death of his father went to Shechem, where all Israel gathered to make him king.[1] Did this narrative stand alone, it would be evidence that in spite of David's choice and Solomon's embellishment of Jerusalem the City was not yet regarded as the focus of the national life, but that the latter still found a more natural centre at Shechem.[2] Such an impression, however, is dispelled by another account preserved in the Septuagint.[3] According to this Rehoboam had begun to reign in Jerusalem before Jeroboam returned from Egypt on hearing of Solomon's death, and went to Shechem only after Jeroboam's appearance there at the head of the revolt.[4] Whether the negotiations between Rehoboam and the northern Israelites took place before or after the

The Revolt of Northern Israel, *c.* 933.

---

[1] 1 Kings xii. 1 ff. The addition, that at this time Jeroboam also came to Shechem, which the Hebrew text contains, is not original, as we see both from its omission by the LXX. and from the statement, in verse 20, that Jeroboam was sent for and came to Shechem only after the revolt had begun. This narrative has been assigned to a northern writer, both because the blame of the Disruption is imputed by it to Rehoboam (hardly a sufficient reason, considering that Judæan historians did not hesitate otherwise to condemn the early kings of Judah) and because a Judæan writer would hardly have allowed that the succession to the throne was decided upon Solomon's death by the popular election implied in this account (nor is this conclusive, for a Judæan scribe might be glad to record the popular confirmation of a son of Solomon).

[2] See *Hist. Geog. of the Holy Land*, 119 ff., 332.

[3] Swete's ed. 1 Kings xii. 24 *a-z*. This account is generally assigned to a Judæan writer, as it opens with the usual formula for the beginning of a reign of a king of Judah, assumes Rehoboam's succession as a matter of course, and imputes the blame of the Disruption to Jeroboam. On the whole question of the relation of the two accounts and their comparative value see Skinner's Appendix, note ii., to *Kings* in the *Century Bible*.

[4] Verse 24*n* (Swete). The arguments against this account by Kuenen and Kittel are not conclusive. It appears the more natural.

arrival of the former at Shechem is uncertain. The result was that Reḥoboam, discarding the advice of his father's counsellors for that of his younger contemporaries, refused to lighten the burdens laid on the people by Solomon. He answered the suppliants with an insult, and wantonly aggravated this by sending them Adoniram, *who was over the levy.* They killed Adoniram, and Reḥoboam saved himself only by flight to Jerusalem. The Disruption was complete.

The effect upon Jerusalem is clear. The City remained loyal to the dynasty to which she owed her rank, and re-

Effects on Jerusalem. tained her supremacy over Judah;[1] but she was deprived of the resources, both religious and commercial, which she had enjoyed under Solomon. She still held the ancient shrine of Jahweh; but Jeroboam, whom a prophet of Jahweh had acclaimed as king of Northern Israel, established His worship in two sanctuaries at either end of the kingdom, a striking contrast to the centralising policy of Solomon. The Temple[2] was cut off from the vast majority of Israel, for the trans-Jordanic tribes joined the Northern Kingdom. The loss to Jerusalem was not only religious. The sanctuaries of the time were its principal markets as well,[3] and the trade, which a monarch so vigilant for the commercial interests of his realm must have included among his designs in building the Temple, would be largely diverted from its courts. At Bethel, which, besides possessing more

---

[1] 1 Kings xii. 20: *the tribe of Judah only.* This is confirmed by the list of cities fortified by Jeroboam; they are all in Judah (2 Chron. xi. 5 ff.). Thus the words *and the tribe of Benjamin* in 1 Kings xii. 21 must be a later addition.

[2] It is uncertain how much adhesion the Temple had secured among Northern Israelites in Solomon's time.      [3] Vol. i. 354.

ancient religious associations than Jerusalem, stood near the junction of two trade routes, Jeroboam instituted at harvest-time a great festival which would also be a great fair.[1] This was only twelve miles from Jerusalem, and in times of peace would attract, by its double temptation, numbers of traders from Judah.[2] Jerusalem, too, had lost the sumptuousness of her court.[3] The low morale of the City under these losses may be judged from the spirit of the counsellors whom Rehoboam had chosen, as well as from the abandonment of the campaign against the Northern Kingdom which they proposed. Prophecy had too emphatically blessed the secession for any immediate hope of victory against it. The impression of this fact upon the people of Judah may even have led to the formation of a party favourable to the North, unless the sympathies of those likely to join it were alienated by the establishment of the images at Dan and Bethel. In any case it was a shaken and dispirited people in Judah who now faced inevitable war with the larger and richer tribes that had broken away from them.

The state of war lasted sixty years.[4] Soon after it began Judah suffered in addition from an Egyptian invasion. This was the first of many warnings to Israel of the necessity of her union, for Egypt, though in possession of the Philistine coast, had not dared to attack the united kingdom under David and Solomon. But *in the fifth year of Rehoboam*

*Invasion of Judah by Shoshenk of Egypt.*

---

[1] 1 Kings xii. 32.

[2] Cf. the appearance of Amos at Bethel; he may have gained his experience of life in North Israel and of the ritual at Bethel by his journeys as a woolseller. Cf. *The Book of the Twelve Prophets*, i. pp. 79 ff.; and Driver, 'Joel and Amos' in the *Cambridge Bible for Schools*, p. 105.

[3] See above, pp. 52 f.

[4] 1 Kings xiv. 30; xv. 6, 16; xxii. 44.

*Shishak* (or *Shoshak̇*), *king of Egypt*, that is Shoshenḳ I.,
of the twenty-second dynasty, *came up against Jerusalem,
and took away the treasures of the house of Jahweh, and
the treasures of the king's house, and all the golden shields
which Solomon had made*, and which the king's guards
used when escorting him to the Temple.[1]   It is not said
that Jerusalem was forcibly taken by Shoshenḳ, nor is
this necessarily implied by the Chronicler's account,
which adds that Shoshenḳ *took the fenced cities of Judah*.[2]
Shoshenḳ's own list of the cities affected by his campaign
covers Israel as well as Judah, but his enumeration may
include cities which sent him tribute besides those which
he took by force of arms.[3]   Among them the name of
Jerusalem has not been deciphered.[4]   Reḥoboam replaced
the golden shields by shields of bronze, and is said by
the Chronicler to have fortified a number of cities in
Judah.[5]   These were Bethlehem, 'Eiṭam (Arṭās, just south
of Bethlehem), Teḳoa' and Beth-ṣūr (Bêt-ṣūr), all between Jerusalem and Hebron ;  Hebron itself ;  Zīph (Tell
Zīf, south-east of Hebron), Mareshah, Adoraim (Dora)

---

[1] 1 Kings xiv. 25 ff.   For Shishak LXX. B reads Σουσακειμ, and says that
the shields were those which David took from the Arameans: 2 Sam. viii. 7.
The consonants of the Hebrew text of verse 25 read Shoshak̇.

[2] 2 Chron. xii. 4.

[3] See W. Max Müller, *Enc. Bibl.*, arts. ' Egypt,' § 63 (with a reproduction of part of Shoshenḳ's list), and ' Shishak,' according to which the
enumeration of the northern cities ' merely means that the northern kingdom
was tributary ; it is only the second half of the list which contains details
pointing to the actual conquest, and these seem to belong to Judah.' This
seems a more natural explanation than that given by C. Niebuhr and
Winckler (*Gesch. Israels*, i. 160 *n.* 1) that the northern cities in the list
were conquered by Shoshenḳ for Rehoboam.   Had the Miṣraim to which
Jeroboam fled been the Arabian Muṣri, as Cheyne argues (cf. the art.
' Shiskak '; cf. Winckler, *Gesch.* ii. 273), it is difficult to see why Shoshenḳ
should have interfered so partially with the two kingdoms.

[4] But see vol. i. 268.                           [5] 2 Chron. xi. 5 ff.

and Lakīsh, all guarding the approaches to Hebron from
the south ; Soko, 'Adullam, Gath and 'Azeḳah, all on or
near the border between the Shephelah and the hill-
country of Judah ;[1] Ṣor'a and Ayyalôn commanding two
passes to Jerusalem from the coast.[2] This list, in contrast with that of the cities fortified by Solomon,[3] exhibits
how shrunken was the territory of which Jerusalem was
now the capital. On the east her connection with Jericho
was severed ; and Jericho, if we may judge from the
care which so many invaders of Judæa took to possess it
before advancing on Jerusalem, was always a convenient
source of supplies for the latter. No cities to the north
of Jerusalem are mentioned on the list. In Reḥoboam's
time that border must have been drawn immediately
above Jerusalem. Her own walls confronted it without
any intervening fortress.

## 2. ABIYAH : *c.* 916-914

After a reign of seventeen years, Rehoboam was succeeded by Abiyah, his son by Maakah, the daughter of
Absalom. Abiyah reigned three years.[4] The
Deuteronomic editor passes on this king an
adverse judgment, which is explained by the first acts of
his successor. War continued between him and Jeroboam. The Chronicler gives a detailed account (which,
to say the least, is much coloured by the circumstances of
a later age)[5] of a battle between Abiyah and Jeroboam

War with
N. Israel.

---

[1] *Hist. Geog. of the Holy Land*, 205 ff.

[2] The position of Hebron on the list—last, both in the Hebrew and in the
LXX.—is curious. [3] Above, pp. 55 f.

[4] 1 Kings xv. 1-8. The Hebrew text spells the name Abiyam ; but Abiyah
is confirmed by the LXX., 'Aβιου, and by 2 Chron. xiii. 1. On Maakah see
the commentaries. [5] 2 Chron. xiii. 2 ff.

at Ṣemaraim, near Bethel, in consequence of which Abiyah was able to push his frontier north to Bethel, to Jeshana, probably the present 'Ain Sīnīyeh,[1] and to Ephron or Ephraim, the present eṭ-Ṭaiyibeh. Abiyah was not able to keep these cities, for under his successor the frontier appears south of Ramah.

### 3. ASA: *c.* 913-873

Abiyah was succeeded by his son[2] Asa, who is said to have reigned over forty years, the round number for a generation. The first record of his reign is one of religious reform.[3] He removed the idols which *his fathers had made*, along with an image erected by the Queen-mother, Maakah. He did not remove the *high places*, or local sanctuaries of Jahweh, but he gathered into the Temple the *holy things which he and his father* had dedicated. The text calls the image erected by Maakah *a horrible* or *grisly*[4] *thing belonging to an Asherah*; but *grisly thing* may be a substitute for a word which either moral or religious delicacy forbade the later scribes to write. Asa *cut down* the thing and burned it at the Ḳidron. This record is from the Deuteronomic editor, but as the reforms described in it fall short of the Deuteronomic standard, it must be founded on an earlier source, and we have no reason to doubt the details. They illustrate the congenital and obdurate heathenism

*First Religious Reforms.*

---

[1] Cf. Josephus, xiv. *Ant.* xv. 12.

[2] As Asa's mother is given the same name as Abiyah's, *Maakah the daughter of Absalom* (1 Kings xv. 2, 10), some would read *brother* for *son* in verse 8. Alternatively Maakah, the mother of Abiyah, continued to enjoy the rank of Queen-mother in the beginning of Asa's reign. Or there is a confusion of the two names. [3] 1 Kings xv. 9-15.

[4] LXX. σύνοδος; Jerome, a phallic object.

with which Ezekiel charges Jerusalem. The original Jebusite population remained among their Hebrew conquerors ; and their ritual, as of gods of ancient association with the place, must have been a constant temptation to the latter. That it was native gods whose idols Asa removed is confirmed by the survival to a later age of the foreign cults established by Solomon in connection with his trade and treaties with the Phœnicians and other nations. The most interesting detail, however, is Asa's gathering of *holy things* to the Temple. These must have been brought from other sanctuaries. Was this done for their greater security? Or may we see in the fact the first step towards that gradual centralisation of the worship which the Deuteronomic reform was to consummate? In this connection we notice that, according to the Chronicler, Asa attracted to the purer worship of the Temple a number of the Northern Israelites.[1] This is very probable.

The political events of Asa's reign are mainly taken from the early annals both of Judah and Israel.[2] In Northern Israel Jeroboam was succeeded for Successful two years by his son Nadab, who while laying Campaigns. siege to Gibbethon,[3] a Philistine town, was slain by Ba'sha, of the house of Issachar, and Ba'sha carried on the war both against Judah and the Philistines.[4] Against the former he fortified Ramah of Benjamin, five miles north of Jerusalem, *that he might not suffer any to go out or*

---

[1] 2 Chron. xv. 9 ff.

[2] Judah, I Kings xv. 16-22; Israel, *id.* 27-29a; xvi. 9-11, 15b-18, 21-24 (except 23). The other verses are from the Deuteronomic editor.

[3] I Kings xv. 27 : a frontier town of Dan, Josh. xix. 44 ; xxi. 23.

[4] According to I Kings xvi. 15, Gibbethon was still besieged by Israel when 'Omri rose to take the crown.

*come in to Asa king of Judah.*[1]  To relieve the pressure,
Asa stripped the Temple and his own house of their
silver and gold, and sent this to Ben-hadad of Damascus
to bribe him to break his league with Israel.  Ben-hadad
invaded the northern provinces of Israel; and when
Ba'sha in consequence suspended the fortification of
Ramah, Asa carried off the material and fortified there-
with Geba' of Benjamin—either Geba' on the natural
frontier formed by the valley of Michmash,[2] or Gibe'ah,
three miles from Jerusalem[3]—and Mizpah, either the
present Neby Samwil[4] or Scopus on the north road.
Jerusalem had now these screens between her and the
frontier of Israel, yet Asa did not dare to carry his arms
across the latter, not even during the civil war which
followed the overthrow of Ba'sha's dynasty.[5]  According
to the Chronicler, Asa won a decisive victory over Zerah
the Kushite, near Mareshah, and pursuing him to Gerar
took much spoil.[6]  These invaders, who are usually understood to have been the Ethiopian Kushites, were more
probably from Arabia, where there were tribes of the
name.  The booty taken from them points to their being
Arabs.  If this was so, then we see the first of many
Arab failures to invade Judah from the south.  Fortified
towns which yielded to more civilised invaders proved a
sufficient screen to Jerusalem against the Nomads; and,
near as she lay to the Desert, no Arab invasion reached

---

[1] xv. 16 f.  [2] The present Geba' on the Wâdy Suweinit.
[3] Tell el-Ful.
[4] In whose neighbourhood we find a fortification, Bethome (Beitunî?), in
the days of Alexander Jannæus.  [5] xvi. 9-22.
[6] 2 Chron. xiv. 8-14.  The Hebrew text says that the battle took place in
the glen of Sephathah, *i.e.* צְפָתָה, for which the LXX. read צָפֹנָה, κατὰ βορρᾶν,
*to the North of.*

her walls[1] till the time of the Hasmoneans, when the Nabateans, aided by a force of Jews, besieged the Holy City.

Asa lived through the reign of 'Omri and saw the genius of the latter create from its foundations the one city which was to prove, in history as in prophecy, The Rise of the counterpart and rival of Jerusalem. It is Samaria. remarkable how from the beginning Shechem disappeared out of the politics of Northern Israel. The geographical centre of the whole land, on the main trade route across the Western Range, and endowed with abundant fertility, Shechem appears to have lost her supremacy through the military weakness of her site.[2] When Jeroboam formed his kingdom, he removed his residence from Shechem to Tirzah, commanding one of the eastern avenues to his land; and Tirzah was retained as their capital by the following dynasty. But 'Omri, partly because of his alliance with Phœnicia, crossed to the western face of Mount Ephraim, and selected a new site on an isolated hill at the head of the chief pass to the coast. He called this, according to the Hebrew text of the Old Testament, Shōmerōn, which might be taken to mean the same as the German Wartburg; but the Greek and Aramaic forms preserve what is probably an older vocalisation, Shamrain, from which the form Samaria is derived.[3]

The new capital rapidly gathered the Northern Kingdom under her lead—*the head of Ephraim is Samaria*[4]

---

[1] Unless we take as historical, and as referring not to the Philistines, but to the Arabs alone, 2 Chron. xxi. 16.

[2] *Hist. Geog. of the Holy Land*, 346 ff.

[3] LXX. B of 1 Kings xvi. 24, Σεμερων, Σαημερων; Aramaic, Ezra iv. 10, 17, Shamrain; cf. the Samarina of the Assyrian inscriptions.

[4] Isaiah vii. 9.

—and gave her name to the whole of it. To the earlier prophets of Judah Samaria was already the double of their own Jerusalem, both in character and in the consequent doom which their God sent upon His people. That later prophecy should remember her as Jerusalem's elder sister[1] is explained by her position. Young and upstart as she was, Samaria derived from the greater fertility and openness of her surroundings a precocity of growth which lifted her above Jerusalem in wealth and energy.

*Comparison with Jerusalem,*

Grey, shrunken and withdrawn, Jerusalem must sometimes have envied the brilliance of her younger rival. Yet envy cannot have been the only nor the prevailing temper of her people in this period. Jerusalem held the Ark, was constant to her one dynasty, and lay more aloof from the probability of invasion. Samaria did not contain the principal sanctuary of her kingdom,[2] was the creature of a usurping dynasty that at any time might pass away like its brief predecessors, and besides had to endure, on her open and forward position, one siege after another from powerful invaders. On these facts wise minds in Jerusalem knew that their City could wait, and nursed for her the promises of David. They were inspired by the possession of a poetry, popular and national, which not only, as in the *Oracles of Balaam*, sang the glories of Israel undivided; but signalised, as in the *Blessing of Jacob*, the political pre-eminence of Judah.[3] It is certain that Judæan writers of the period

*to the latter's advantage.*

[1] Ezekiel xxiii. 4.

[2] Which was in Bethel, Deut. xxxiii. 12 (see below, p. 96), Amos vii. 13.

[3] It is hard to believe that the longer oracles of Balaam are later than the days of Saul and David. 'The Blessing of Jacob,' Gen. xlix. 1-27, is assigned by Driver (*Genesis*, p. 380) to 'the age of the Judges or a little later,' by

were busy with new works. Among these we may place
the strong and spirited narratives of the reigns of David
and Solomon (obviously based on earlier documents), which
emphasise Jerusalem as the centre of the national life they
celebrate. Many also assign to this period the Judæan
constituent of the Pentateuch, the Jahwist Document,
and this breathes a more confident spirit, a firmer sense
of possessing the future, than the parallel northern
narrative of the Elohist. There is not, however, either in
the poetry or in the histories just cited, any expression or
even foreboding of that unique sacredness which future
events and legislation were to confer upon Jerusalem.
Whether or not the Book of the Covenant[1] was known
and obeyed in Judah at this time, the practice which it
sanctions of worshipping Jahweh at many altars was
recognised as freely there as in Northern Israel. His
*high places* were not yet removed. But though none of
the literature of Judæa predicts the Single Sanctuary,
it reveals the moral and political elements which were
unconsciously working towards the ultimate centralisation of the worship of Jahweh.

By the Northern Kingdom, Jerusalem at this time
seems to have been wholly disregarded. To begin with,
that Kingdom called itself Israel, flying high
its title to be regarded as the actual people     Jerusalem
ignored in
of Jahweh. Permeated by a strong, self-     the North.
reliant temper, its annals and narratives do not even

Duhm (*Enc. Bibl.* col. 3797) to the early reign of David, and by Kautzsch
(*Abriss d. Gesch. d. A.-T. Schrifttums*, p. 142) to at least as early as
Solomon's reign, though he admits the possibility of a later date. See also
G. B. Gray, *Numbers*, pp. 313 f. Wellhausen and others, because of verse
23, date the blessing after the Aramean invasions. The collections of poems
known as *The Book of Jashar* and *The Book of the Wars of Jahweh*, used by
the Jahwist, were also in existence.     [1] Exod. xx. 22 to xxiii. 19.

mention Jerusalem. The drought of Elijah's time must
have afflicted Judah as well as Israel and Phœnicia, yet
in his splendid story the name of Judah occurs but once,
and then casually as defining the position of Beersheba.[1]
When Elijah himself sought Jahweh, it was not the
Temple which was the goal of his pilgrimage but Horeb.
This is not to be explained by the probability that Judah
was already the vassal of Israel, and that the fugitive
prophet sought a shrine of his God beyond the influence
of Ahab. The truth is that for the prophecy of the
Northern Kingdom, Jerusalem at this time had no religious significance. If the Blessing of the Tribes (in
Deuteronomy xxxiii.), as its contents and spirit seem
to prove, is an Ephraimitic work from the beginning of
the double kingdom, its eulogy of Benjamin, as containing the dwelling of Jahweh, must refer to Bethel, for,
as we have seen, the documents of the period do not
include the tribe of Benjamin in the Southern Kingdom.[2]

## 4. JEHOSHAPHAT : *c.* 873–850

It is not easy to estimate the effects upon Jerusalem
of the reign of Jehoshaphat. Owing to the character of the traditions we must deal largely
with inferences. Yet the general facts from
which these have to be drawn are well
attested. The war between Israel and Judah had at

*The High
Character of
Jehoshaphat,*

---

[1] 1 Kings xix. 3 ; but 2 Chron. xxi. 12 ff. records a writing from Elijah to
Jehoram (below, pp. 99 f.).

[2] On the date of Deut. xxxiii. see the commentaries. Driver and others
incline to the reign of Jeroboam I.; Moore (*Enc. Bibl.* col. 1090) and others
to that of Jeroboam II. The northern origin of the poem is universally
admitted, and indeed is very obvious.

last come to an end. Asa's efforts must have so far
strengthened the latter as to render the house of 'Omri
willing to enter an alliance. Had it been otherwise, so
ambitious a dynasty, increasing in wealth and political
influence, would hardly have consented to a relation in
which there was probably more equality between the
contracting parties than modern historians have perceived. 'Athaliah, the daughter of Ahab, was married
to Jehoram, the son of Jehoshaphat ;[1] and Jehoshaphat
assisted both Ahab at Ramoth-Gilead and Ahab's son,
Jehoram, against Moab.[2] It is true that on each of
these occasions the king of Israel made the proposal,
and that Jehoshaphat unreservedly complied. The terms
in which he did so are, however, no stronger than the
forms of Oriental politeness demand from an ally. As
leader of the smaller force Jehoshaphat took, of course,
the second place in the expeditions. But when Ahab's
second successor, Ahaziah, offered to share in the voyage
down the Red Sea, Jehoshaphat was able to refuse him ;
and even on the campaigns against Aram and Moab he
is said—by, be it observed, records which are not Judæan,
but Israelite—to have shown a firm and independent
temper. Before the battle of Ramoth-Gilead it was he
who proposed to consult a prophet of Jahweh, and it was
by his repeated urgency that the true prophet was at last
found. On the Moabite campaign he showed a similar
insistence, and this time the prophet, who was Elisha,
consented to give an answer only for his sake. These
things testify to religious insight and force of character.
A Judæan record adds that Jehoshaphat completed the
removal of the immoral elements in Judah's worship

[1] 2 Kings viii. 18.      [2] 1 Kings xxii.; 2 Kings iii. 4 ff.

which Asa had begun.[1]  He also maintained the supremacy of Judah over Edom, and used it not only for the land-trade which Edom commanded, but in order to launch a ship on the Red Sea.[2]

We may take the high qualities of Jehoshaphat as indicative of the morale of Judah and Jerusalem at this time. Whatever lower elements remained, the City possessed an amount of piety and energy which were preparing for her future.  The Chronicler[3] indeed supplies an account of Jehoshaphat's reign according to which Jerusalem must already have become a place of great magnificence.  His story has sometimes been regarded as an entire fabrication, both because of the number of soldiers described as waiting on the king[4] in Jerusalem—one million one hundred and sixty thousand in all—and because the organisation attributed to Jehoshaphat has some features characteristic of the Jewish constitution after the Exile.[5]  Yet there is evidence that the Chronicler has employed older sources;[6] it is hardly possible that the personal names he cites are inventions; and there is no sufficient motive to adduce for his assigning to Jehoshaphat so thorough an organisation of religion and justice if that monarch had not achieved some results of the kind.  Written law was certainly in existence, and those who attribute to this or

*and of his Government.*

---

[1] 1 Kings xxii. 46.

[2] *Ibid.* 47 ff.  The text reconstructed after the LXX. and the Hebrew consonants reads thus : *And there was no king in Edom; the deputy of king Jehoshaphat made a ship of Tarshish to go to Ophir for gold, but it went not, for the ship was broken in Ezion-Geber.*  So Stade and others.

[3] 2 Chron. xvii.-xx.

[4] *Besides those whom the king put in the fenced cities* (*Id.* xvii. 13-19).

[5] Wellhausen, *Proleg.* 2nd ed. 198 f.  See above, vol. i. 379 *n.* 6 ; 387 f.

[6] xvii. 7-9 and xix. 4-11 are parallel and independent accounts of the establishment of the Law.

a previous period the Book of the Covenant[1] naturally see in it the code which Jehoshaphat is said to have promulgated and organised. Whether this was so or not, we cannot be wrong in believing that under Jehoshaphat life and religion in Judah were inspired and regulated as they had not been since the days of Solomon. But every such achievement, however small, and even if followed as this was by a time of reaction, must have heightened the position of the City in the eyes of all Israel, and trained the more serious classes of her population in those ideals and habits which fitted her for her future career.

### 5 and 6. JEHORAM AND AHAZIAH: *c.* 850–842

But the course of the purer faith was not yet clear. Jehoram, the son of Jehoshaphat, was married to 'Athaliah, a daughter of Aḥab, and introduced to Judah the idolatry favoured by his
*A Reaction.*
wife's family.[2] The strange gods did not help him. First Edom revolted, then Judah was invaded by Philistines and Arabs.[3] Libnah fell away,[4] the king lost to the invaders his treasure, his wives and his sons save one,[5] and finally himself succumbed to an incurable disease.[6] These fatalities must have strengthened the party of the purer religion, and the impression would be confirmed when, after reigning a year, Aḥaziah, the next king,

---

[1] See above, p. 95.

[2] It may have been in consequence of opposition to this that he found it necessary to slay all his brothers and other princes of Judah. 2 Chron. xxi. 1-7. In verse 4 for Israel read Judah.

[3] 2 Kings viii. 20 ff.; 2 Chron. xxi. 8 ff., 16 f.      [4] 2 Kings viii. 22.

[5] 2 Chron. xxi. 17. 2 Kings x. 13 ff. describes the brethren of Aḥaziah as slain by Jehu.      [6] 2 Chron. xxi. 18 f.

was slain along with Jehoram of Israel by Jehu, the fanatic destroyer of the worship of Baal.[1]

### 7. 'ATHALIAH: *c.* 842-836

In the Book of Kings we now encounter a series of more detailed narratives of the history of Judah, and as
The fuller Records. their stage is Jerusalem we recover that close and vivid view of the City which we have lost since the days of Solomon, but which henceforth is visible at intervals for some centuries. These records, which are fragmentary,[2] may be supplemented from the narrative of the Chronicler, who drew from the same sources. The Chronicler has greatly altered the story in harmony with the conditions of his own time, but he has preserved some original data omitted by the compiler of Kings.[3]

Our increased materials commence by presenting us with the most perplexing event in the history of the
Perplexing Character of 'Athaliah's Usurpation, dynasty of David. We encounter an apparent paradox. At the very time that the revolution in favour of the religion of Jahweh succeeds in Northern Israel, and the house of Ahab is extinguished by it, in Judah, on the contrary, we see a daughter of Ahab seize the throne, slaughter (as she supposes) all the seed of David, and reign securely for a period of six years. How was this possible? How could Judah tolerate so long the one interregnum from

[1] 2 Kings ix. 27.

[2] Observe, for instance, in the narrative of the revolt against 'Athaliah, 2 Kings xi., how abruptly Jehoiada' is introduced, as if he had been already mentioned. Plainly the compiler is here employing only part of the documents at his disposal ; see next note.

[3] *E.g.* the Chronicler in 2 Chron. xxiii. has substituted for the foreign guard, by whom, according to Kings, Jehoiada' effected the revolution against 'Athaliah, the priests and Levites ; but he adds in its proper place what the editor of Kings has omitted of the original data, viz. who Jehoiada' was: *Id.* xxii. 11.

which her dynasty suffered? Recent historians have called the fact a mystery, but we find at least partial explanations of it in three features of the revolt which overthrew 'Athaliah, and which is described in detail by the sources.

In that revolt a decisive part was played by a body of foreign troops, called the Carians,[1] whose presence was natural at the court of virtually a Phœnician princess, and by whose aid doubtless she had achieved her usurpation. Secondly, it is clear that during her reign 'Athaliah, whose name, *and its Explanation— the Foreign Elements in the City,* be it remembered, implies a certain recognition of Jahweh,[2] had left untouched His worship in the Temple. This may explain the temporary acquiescence of His adherents in the new régime. But, thirdly, the queen had probably on her side a strong native party. The policy of her house made for increased culture among their peoples. It not only favoured commerce, but in opposition to the conservative elements of Hebrew society, as represented by the Rechabites, emphasised (in accordance with the characteristic Phœnician polity) the City as the chief factor in the national life. There were sufficient temptations to form a strong Athalian party in Jerusalem. One of the most remarkable features of the subsequent history is the ease with which Jerusalem produced factions in favour of foreign influences. These not only meant a wider and a freer life,

---

[1] Kari, 2 Kings xi. 4. In the consonantal text of 2 Samuel xx. 23 the same name is used for David's bodyguard, but is corrected by the Massoretes to Kerethi. It has been proposed by some modern scholars to make the same correction in 2 Kings xi. 4, but it is more probable that here it is really Carians who are meant: 'a famous mercenary people in antiquity' whom 'it would not surprise us to find at Jerusalem in the days of 'Athaliah (G. F. Moore, *Enc. Bibl.*). [2] 'Athalyahu, 2 Kings viii. 26, etc.

but were especially favourable to the enhancement of the City at the expense of the country. Just as a strong Greek faction existed in Jerusalem in Maccabæan times, and was enthusiastic for Greek fashions which led to the embellishment of the City and the exhilaration of her life; so it is natural that among the Jews of 'Athaliah's time there should be a Canaanite or Phœnician faction inspired by similar motives. The story of the revolution indicates that Jehoiada' feared opposition from the City, and relied upon *the people of the land.*

But above all there was the personality of the queen herself. 'Athaliah was the only woman who ever reigned in Jerusalem till the accession of the widow of Alexander Jannæus in the first century before Christ. It is noteworthy that the Phœnician race produced about this time several strong women: Jezebel, 'Athaliah, Dido. The attractions of the culture and the worship, which she represented, the support she derived from foreign troops, and the security which she temporarily enjoyed from rebellion through her tolerance of the native religion, could not have existed in so effective a combination without her own strong capacity for organising. In themselves, therefore, her usurpation and reign are perfectly explicable. The one mystery is why Jehu, in alliance as he was with movements like that of the Rechabites, which had a strong hold on Judah, did not interfere with her. Probably he was too much engrossed by the attacks of the Arameans.

In the revolution against 'Athaliah, we have the first of those many outbreaks, mixed of priests, soldiers and people, which have the Temple courts for their stage,

and so often recur in the history of Jerusalem. The revolt
was carefully arranged, but the disorder of the text
which describes it[1] disables us from following
the exact details. The main features, however, are clear. The author of the movement
was Jehoiada' the priest, who held hid in the Temple
the six-year-old Joash, saved by the wife of Jehoiada'
from the massacre of the rest of Ahaziah's children.
The priest's plan was to bring forward in the Temple this
sole survivor of David's house, to have him crowned
King, and then to put 'Athaliah to death. The time
he chose for this was the Sabbath, and the instruments
the soldiery: the Carians and other guards, who kept
both the Palace and the Temple. He secured their
Centurions, and arranged with these the details of action.
Here it is that obscurity falls on the story, the text
hovering between a statement of the usual routine of
the guard and directions for their procedure at the crisis.
Dr. Wellhausen elides verse 6 as a gloss, and explains
the rest as follows. He infers that on week-days two
divisions of the guard were at the Palace and one in
the Temple; but that on the Sabbath two were in the
Temple and one at the Palace. Jehoiada' planned to
bring out Joash on the Sabbath at that hour, at which
the two divisions who had *come out* from their quarters
in the Palace were relieving at the Temple the one about
to *go in*, and indeed verse 9 says that the Centurions
brought to Jehoiada' for the crisis *each his men, those
coming in on the Sabbath with those going out on the
Sabbath.* This implies that the Palace, where 'Athaliah
lived, was for the time divested of the whole guard. The

*The Revolt against her: its Plan.*

[1] 2 Kings xi. 4 ff.

explanation is at first sight plausible and has been accepted by recent writers. But it is hardly credible that in the ordinary routine of the guard all the force should thus be periodically withdrawn from the Palace, which, it must be remembered, was in those days still the principal object of their duty. And although the text is difficult, it seems to imply, in verse 7, that Jehoiada‘ directed only two of the bands—defined *as all who come out on Sabbath and keep the watch of the house of Jahweh for the king*—to surround the young king (verse 8). The remaining third has already been assigned by verse 5 to guard the Palace.[1] It is true that verse 9 states that the Centurions brought to Jehoiada‘ both the men who turned into quarters on the Sabbath and the men who turned out. But, as we see from the Septuagint, the text of this verse is uncertain. In our ignorance of the custom of the guard as well as of the stations assigned to them [2] we must leave the matter undecided.

In the story of how the conspirators achieved their end Dr. Stade has seen the fusion of two differing accounts,[3] and Achievement. one of which, 4-12, 18*b*-20, reads the event as wholly political, achieved by Jehoiada‘ and the royal guards; while the second, 13-18*a*, gives it a religious character, brings into it *the people of the land*, and adds ‘Athaliah’s dramatic appearance in the Temple, which the first ignores. This analysis has been accepted by most recent writers,[4] but it seems to me very doubtful. To us it is easy to separate the political from the religious, but what writer of those times would think of doing so? Surely not one who, on Dr. Stade’s own showing, has

[1] So the LXX.    [2] See below.    [3] *Z.A.T.W.* v. 279 ff.
[4] *E.g.* Kittel, Benzinger and Skinner.

described the chief priest as the prime conspirator. Why, again, was the Sabbath chosen for the revolt, if not with regard to religion and the people?[1] Besides, the supposed second narrative testifies in verse 15 to the soldiers' share in the transaction, and the first, in verse 19, to the association of the people of the land with the priests and the military.[2] There remain the two statements of 'Athaliah's death, in 16 and 20; but these agree as to where and how this took place; and it would be very arbitrary to suppose that the annalist, not distinguished for his style, could not have thus repeated himself. The story may therefore be regarded as a unity, and the conspiracy as one which was—what such a conspiracy in favour of the house of David against 'Athaliah could not but be—at once political and religious. The movement started with the priest, and naturally he took care to arrange for the support of the soldiers; but he was evidently sure of the people of the land, and probably he chose the Sabbath for his action in order to secure their presence in large numbers. In verse 20 it is said that *the people of the land rejoiced, and the City*— observe how it is distinguished from them—*was quiet.* We see, therefore, that it was against the mixed population of Jerusalem, favourable (for reasons given above) to 'Athaliah and her worship, that Jehoiada' took his precautions. These were successful; the City did not rise. The opposition between the City and the Country at so early a stage of the history is exceedingly interesting.

As to the topographical details of the narrative, we

---

[1] Except on what we have shown above to be the unlikely assumption that *all* the guard was on that day assembled at one time in the Temple.

[2] The hypothesis of a double account takes these clauses to be harmonising insertions.

only learn that the passage of the king between the
Topo-graphical. Temple and the Palace was made by a gate
called the *Gate of the Foot-Guards.*[1] There
was probably also a horse-gate, whose name may be
disguised in the *Gate of Sûr*;[2] but it was not necessarily the same as *the entry of the horses* through which
'Athaliah sought to escape. This is the earliest proof we
have found of horses being established in Jerusalem.[3]

## 8. JOASH: *c.* 836-798

The story of the Temple revolt is succeeded by one of
its administration and repair. The succession of records,
which have the Temple for their scene or subject, raises
a question which will be more conveniently answered after
we have examined this new addition to them.

Joash was brought up by Jehoiada' the priest, and, at
least so long as the latter survived, the king remained
Repair and Administra-tion of the Temple. loyal to the purer religion.[4] The sanctuary of
Baal was destroyed,[5] and the only qualifica-
tion which the Deuteronomic editor makes
in his praise of the new régime is the one usual with
him at this date: *the high places were not removed,* or, in
other words, the worship of Jahweh was not yet confined to the Temple.[6] But the growing importance of
the latter, its increasing command of the popular regard

[1] שַׁעַר הָרָצִם : verse 19.

[2] Verse 6: שַׁעַר סוּר, for which the LXX. gives πύλη τῶν ὁδῶν, and 2
Chron. xxiii. 5 שַׁעַר הַיְסוֹד, *gate of the foundation.* For סוּר, סוּם has been
suggested. But verse 6 appears to be an intrusion.

[3] See vol. i. 324 ff. and vol. ii. 56 f.

[4] 2 Kings xii. 2 ; the Hebrew text is ambiguous ; the LXX., *all the days
in which Jehoiada' the priest instructed him,* is more explicit in its limitation.

[5] 2 Kings xi. 18.            [6] 2 Kings xii. 1-4.

and consequently of the people's contributions, is well illustrated by the story just alluded to. By this time Solomon's buildings were at least a century old, and dilapidated.[1] Orders were given by the young king to the priests to make the necessary repairs from their revenues. Besides offerings in kind, these revenues included three classes of payment in the money of the period, which was, of course, not coined money but weights of metal attested by the king's stamp.[2] There were, first, assessments of individuals for religious purposes; second, freewill offerings; and third, *sin* and *guilt moneys*—quit-moneys, which probably covered omissions in ritual as well as moral faults.[3] Joash ordered that the first two of these classes of revenue should be devoted to the repairs;[4] and directed the priests to see to this individually — *each from his own transactions, takings* or *possessions* (? the word occurs only here and is uncertain[5]). Such a direction implies at least the

---

[1] 2 Chron. xxiv. 7 imputes the dilapidations to '*Athaliah the malefactor and her sons* (LXX. ? *priests*).

[2] 2 Sam. xiv. 26. On the whole subject see above, Bk. II. ch. vii.

[3] The atonement for these in the Levitical legislation was by sacrifices. In the above list nothing is said of payments to the priests for their delivery of the Torôth; cf. Micah iii. 11.

[4] 2 Kings xii. 5 (Engl. 4) must be amended to read thus: *And Joash said to the priests, All the money of the hallowed things that is brought into the house of Jahweh: the money that every man is rated at* (read with LXX. כֶּסֶף אֶרֶךְ אִישׁ, and omit the next clause, כֶּסֶף נַפְשׁוֹת עֶרְכּוֹ as a gloss referring to Lev. xxvii. 2 ff.) *and all the money which comes into any man's heart to bring into the house of Jahweh.*

[5] מֵאֵת מַכָּרוֹ (verse 6 = Eng. 5). Following the Targum, the Eng. versions render this *from his acquaintance*, taking the word מַכָּר from the root נכר. But the word may be as naturally derived from מכר, *to exchange, give over* or *sell*, and is so taken by the LXX., ἀπὸ τῆς πράσεως αὐτοῦ. Cf. the Assyrian makkeru (the same form as the Hebrew, with the

beginnings of those individual and hereditary rights in the Temple revenues which we know to have existed in other sanctuaries of the time.[1]

But the arrangement failed. By the twenty-third year of the king the priests had not repaired the dilapidations.

*Re-arrange-ment by Joash.* Joash therefore arranged, with their consent, that they should resign their income from the two sources above-mentioned and give it to others to do the work. Jehoiada' set a box with a hole in the lid on the right of the entrance to the Temple,[2] and in it the priests of the threshold put *all the money* that came into the Temple. At intervals, when the box was full, the king's scribe came up from the Palace, weighed the money, and gave it to those in charge of the Temple business, who paid it out to the workmen in wages and for the purchase of materials. The money was confined to repairing the dilapidations; none of it was used to provide vessels or ornaments for the House.[3] The priests were allowed to retain the sin and guilt moneys.

doubled middle radical) rendered by Delitzsch (*Assyr. Handwörterbuch*) 'property,' 'possessions.' It is not improbable that the Hebrew had the same general sense; yet it may rather mean *transactions*. *Enc. Bibl.* col. 3843 suggests 'customers.'

[1] For Babylonia compare Johns, *Babyl. and Assyr. Laws, Contracts and Letters* (1904), p. 215; and see above, Bk. II. chap. vii.

[2] The Hebrew of 2 Kings xii. 10 (Eng. 9) states that the box was set *beside the altar on the right as a man comes into the house of Jahweh*. But the altar lay in the middle of the court; and 2 Chron. xxiv. 8, omitting mention of it, says only that they set the box *outside the Temple gate.* . . . Stade, following LXX. A, reads for הַמִּזְבֵּחַ, הַמַּצֵּבָה, *the maṣṣebah*; Klostermann אֵצֶל הַמְּזוּזָה חַיְמִינִית, *beside the right doorpost.* If Robertson Smith's argument be admitted, that the pillars, Yakîn and Boaz, were originally altars (*Rel. of the Semites*, Add. Note L), this might be the solution. See above, p. 64 *n.* 1.

[3] Verses 13 f. The Chronicler reports differently.

The story is instructive. The Temple is still a royal sanctuary, and the king has the disposal of its revenues, with the consent of the priests, whose interests are forming but not yet fully vested. The annalist does not conceal the negligence of the priests, as the Chronicler does, who confines to the Levites the blame of not carrying out the repairs. The superior honesty of the lay administrators is emphasised. With the king's hold upon the revenues we may take the fact mentioned further on, that when Ḥazael of Aram threatened Jerusalem with the forces which had swept across Northern Israel and taken Gath, Joash bought him off with the gifts which he and his predecessors had consecrated to the Temple, as well as with the treasures of the Temple and the Palace.[1] These last included, of course, the king's own accumulations of precious metals, partly deposited in the sanctuary for security. But if we may judge from the analogy of other ancient temples, they also comprised the Temple funds, and deposits by private persons. The sanctuaries of those days were banks, and as other monarchs, when they drew upon such stores, either afterwards replaced them or gave an equivalent in land, Joash would doubtless do the same. This is the third instance of the spoliation of the Temple to buy off an invader or to bribe an ally.[2]

We can now discuss the question raised by these detailed narratives which have the Temple for their subject or for their scene. Are we to consider them as borrowed from a work which was exclusively a history of the Temple? Or do they belong to the general annals of Judah? The former

*Royal Powers over the Temple.*

*The Source of these Records.*

[1] 2 Kings xii. 17, 18.      [2] 1 Kings xiv. 26 ; xv. 18.

hypothesis, first advanced by Dr. Wellhausen, is much favoured at present. Struck by the features which the story of Joash's repair of the Temple and that of Josiah's (chs. xxii., xxiii.) possess in common, Dr. Wellhausen [1] proposed to assign them to a pre-Deuteronomic history of the Temple, and to trace to the same source the narratives of the Temple revolt against 'Athaliah and of the rearrangement of the altars by Aḥaz; [2] as well as the account of the building of the Temple and the various records of its spoliation. [3] Yet in a work written in the interests of the Temple we should hardly have expected to find the subordination of the priests to the king and their gross negligence so explicitly set forth, as we have seen them to be, in a section of the supposed book which deals with the Temple only; while in others of the alleged extracts the events treated—the Temple building, the crowning of Joash, and the murder of 'Athaliah, the finding of the law-book, and the successive borrowings from the Temple treasures—have not to do with the Temple alone, but are of general political interest. [4] We may therefore consider as insufficient the argument for the existence of a special history of the Temple, and as more probable the hypothesis that these detailed narratives were drawn by the editor of the Book of Kings from the national annals of Judah.

But if that be so, we have to infer the rapid growth of the importance of Solomon's Temple. Of this growth the records provide us with the most natural explanations.

---

[1] 4th ed. of Bleek's *Einleitung*.      [2] 2 Kings xi., xvi.

[3] So also Kittel, Cornill, Benzinger.

[4] Since the above was first written in the *Expositor*, April 1905, I find that Professor Skinner also raises the second of these objections to Wellhausen's theory, *Century Bible, Kings*, p. 343.

We see from them that the prominence of the Temple
is not the exaggeration of a priestly narrator, but the
solid result of causes which may be illus- Growing
trated from the history of other sanctuaries Influence of
Temple and
in the Semitic world. For, first, the Temple Priests.
in Jerusalem was the king's; strongly situated in the
closest proximity to the palace and the garrison, which
rendered it a natural centre for political movements. The
stability of the Davidic dynasty ensured for the priesthood
a sense of security and an opportunity to form traditions
and rights which cannot have been enjoyed to the same
degree by the priests of the sanctuaries in Northern
Israel. But, secondly, the Temple, besides being the
royal sanctuary, had won considerable command of the
national life outside Jerusalem. *The people of the land*
came up to it, and the priests could count on their
adherence.[1] Thirdly, the Temple was growing in material
wealth. Its treasures were accumulating, and when these
were taken from it to meet some national emergency,
they seem to have been quickly restored. To other
Temples, kings repaid their forced loans by gifts of
lands or new treasure, and that this happened also in
the case of the Judæan Temple appears from the fact
that there were always funds in it when they were required.
But, above even these royal and popular opportunities,
with all the training and influence in affairs which they
provided, the Temple priesthood enjoyed the inspiration
and the credit of the purer religion of which they were
the guardians. Everything points to the fact that in
politics, as in religion, they played a part similar to that
of the prophets of Northern Israel. It is certainly to

[1] See above on the revolt against 'Athaliah, pp. 104 f.

them that we owe the legal code and most of the other literature of the period.[1]

We see then that the Deuteronomic exaltation of Jerusalem was no sudden or artificial achievement, but the

Preparations for the Deuteronomic Centralisation.

result of a slow growth which took centuries for its consummation, and was due to a multitude of processes, political and religious, of which indeed we have only seen the beginnings.

The Chronicler states that after Jehoiada‘ died Joash, enticed by the princes of Judah, forsook the house of

The rest of the Reign of Joash.

Jahweh and worshipped Asherim and idols.[2] Prophets were raised up to testify against him, and one of these he ordered to be stoned in the Temple. With this crime the Chronicler connects the invasion of Ḥazael, emphasising the divine justice of the penalty by recording that Ḥazael's army was a small one compared with the great host of Judah,[3] and that it destroyed the princes of the people.[4] The Chronicler adds that the same crime caused a conspiracy against Joash, who, overcome by disease, was slain on his bed. The Hebrew text of Kings says that the conspirators *smote* Joash *in the house of Millo that goes down to Silla.* As it stands this gives little sense, and the versions testify to so early a corruption of the text that it is perhaps vain to attempt to restore it.[5]

[1] See above, pp. 95, 98 f.  [2] 2 Chron. xxiv. 15 ff.
[3] Cf. Deuteronomy xxxii. 30.
[4] The Chronicler cannot have invented the story (so also Benzinger).
[5] The readiest emendation is suggested by Lucian's version: *at the house of Millo which is on the descent* (of Silla). Silla may be taken as *a street* or *way* (Thenius = מְסִלָּה); Assyr. sul(l)u. This would suit the southern location for Millo (above, pp. 41, 71). Other Greek versions found no word for *the descent,* and read Silla with an initial 'Ayin for Samekh, or even as Galaad; cf. Winckler, *Gesch.* i. 178, who places the assassination in Gilead; this is improbable.

## 9. AMAZIAH : *c.* 797-789 or 779

The murdered king was succeeded by his son, Amaziah: proof that the assassins had been provoked not by hatred to the dynasty, but by what they regarded as their victim's personal fault, whether in the surrender to Ḥazael or in the murder of Zechariah. Amaziah, indeed, appears to have

Stability of the Davidic Dynasty.

owed his elevation to the assassins, for we read that *as soon as* (which means *not until*) *the kingdom was firmly in his grasp he slew his servants which had slain the king his father.*[2] It is noteworthy not only that a usurping faction should thus find the house of David indispensable to the kingdom, but that the dynasty should so bravely show its independence of every faction and its ability to punish even more or less justifiable assaults upon its representatives.

This endurance of the dynasty is not the only relief to the depressing tales of intrigue, tumult and bloodshed, of which the history of Jerusalem at this period so largely consists. The execution of the murderers of Joash was signalised

An instance of Ethical Progress.

by an innovation, which betrays the existence of impulses—to whatever source they may be assigned—surely making for a higher morality. The editor records that Amaziah did not also slay the children of the murderers, and recognises in this his obedience to the Deuteronomic law : *the fathers shall not be put to death for the children nor the children for the fathers, every man shall be put to death for his own sin.*[3] The institution

---

[1] 2 Kings xiv. 1 ff.    [2] *Id.* 5.    [3] 2 Kings xiv. 6 f. ; Deut. xxiv. 16.

VOL. II.

of such a law is of itself proof that once Israel had
shared the opposite feeling of the time, that in the
guilt of an individual all the members of his family
were involved.[1]  Early society regarded the family as a
moral unit.  In the absence of a law and of a public
opinion to the contrary, the passion of private revenge,
to which ancient jurisprudence largely left the punishment for murder, did not hesitate to work itself out
upon the family of the criminal, as it still does among
the Bedouin.  And it is easy to see how even public
justice could go to that extreme under the prevailing
idea of the moral solidarity of the family.  In Israel
there were current during our period traditions of
how the children of criminals had, at certain crises,
been put to death for their fathers' crimes by the
supreme authority;[2] and in the Book of the Covenant,
the only code of the period, there was no law to the
contrary.  Deuteronomy is the earliest code which contains such a law.  We may be sure, too, that the editor
of the Book of Kings did not invent the story of
Amaziah's sparing of the murderers' children.  He must
have found it in the sources from which he drew his
materials; and he hails it, as he does every other
approximation to the Deuteronomic standards.  But if
the annals of Judah mentioned the fact, this can only
have been because it was recognised as something unusual; and that it was unusual is proved by Joshua's
execution of the family of Achan, by David's con-

---

[1] It is not certain whether this feeling was universal in antiquity.  In the
Code of Ḥammurabi there is no trace of the extension of the capital penalty
from a criminal to his children ; but these could be sold into slavery for their
father's debts : § 117.

[2] Josh. vii. 24 ff. ; 2 Sam. xxi. 1 ff. ; 2 Kings ix. 26.

viction that he must surrender Saul's sons to the vengeance of the Gibeonites, and by the slaughter of Naboth's sons along with their father.[1]  We may, therefore, add this leniency on the part of Amaziah to the symptoms which the troubled period reveals of the presence of influences gradually elevating the social ethics of Judah.  The particular innovation was not, as we have seen, inspired by the Book of the Covenant. Whence, then, did it spring?  From the king's own resolution, or from his religious advisers, or from such public discontent with the cruelty of the ancient custom as would probably arise in the generally improved ethics of the community?  We cannot tell.  But we may be reasonably sure that thus gradually, and even sporadically, many ameliorations of ancient custom began in Israel, which were finally articulated and enforced in such definite codes as form our Book of Deuteronomy.  The Spirit of the God of Israel, working on individuals or on the general conscience of the community, modified or annulled, one by one, the harsher and baser elements of that consuetudinary law, which Israel had inherited as a member of the Semitic race. A code like the Book of Deuteronomy was not brought forth at a stroke, but was the expression of the gradual results of the age-long working of the Spirit of the Living God in the hearts of His people.

The vigour and the originality which this episode evinces were next illustrated by Amaziah in defeating the Edomites.  The scene was the *Ravine of Salt*, probably the present Wâdy el-Milḥ, in the south of Judah.[2]

---

[1] See previous note.

[2] 2 Kings xiv. 7 : נֵי or נַיְא does not suit the valley of the 'Arabah, which Benzinger takes as the battlefield.  He takes *the Sela'* as Petra.

*The Sela'*, or *Rock*, which Amaziah took and called *Yoktheel*, can hardly have been the later Nabatean capital, Petra;

Opening of<br>the Road to<br>the Red Sea.

which is probably not mentioned in the Old Testament.[1] It was surely no chief town of Edom that fell to Amaziah, or else the subjection of the Edomites to Judah would have been mentioned, but rather some citadel guarding the road from Judah to the Red Sea. Amaziah had sought to open this road, and his success is proved by the fact that its goal, Elath, was held and fortified by his successor.[2]

Elated by this victory, Amaziah sent a wanton challenge to Joash of Israel. Their armies met at Beth-Shemesh. If this was the Beth-Shemesh at

Israel's vic-<br>tory at Beth-<br>Shemesh and<br>capture of<br>Jerusalem.

the mouth of one of the passes from the Philistine country towards Jerusalem, Israel's choice of such a point of attack on Judah may be explained either by an alliance between them and the Philistines or by the same tactics which led many of the Seleucid generals to approach Jerusalem from the Shephelah rather than upon a more direct road from the north. But there may have been another place of the same name on the northern frontier of Judah. In any case, after defeating Amaziah, Joash did deliver his attack on Jerusalem from the north—the first of many recorded assaults on that side of the City where alone the fortifications are not surrounded by deep ravines—*and brake down four hundred cubits of the wall from the gate of Ephraim to the corner-gate*, probably at the north-western corner of the City, and despoiled the Temple and the Palace.[3]

[1] As Buhl has shown, *Gesch. der Edomiter*, 35 ff.  [2] 2 Kings xiv. 22.
[3] 2 Kings xiv. 8-14, perhaps from an Israelite document.

It was perhaps in consequence of this defeat that the people of Jerusalem conspired against Amaziah.[1]  He fled to Lakîsh, but they sent after him and <sup>Conspiracy</sup> slew him.  Once again the dynasty of David <sup>against Amaziah.</sup> survived the fall of its chief.  Whatever the <sup>His death.</sup> plans of the Jerusalem conspirators had been, *all the people of Judah took 'Azariah and made him king in room of his father Amaziah.*  In these events it is, perhaps, unnecessary to see another instance of the opposition we perceived in 'Athaliah's time between the citizens of the capital and the country population.  But we may take the opportunity to recall the different in-<sup>Different</sup> terests and parties which we have found <sup>Parties in</sup> moving in the history of Judah at this time. <sup>Judah.</sup> These are the dynasty, the priesthood, the princes or nobles of Judah, the populace of Jerusalem, the people of the land, and, for a time, the foreign, heathen elements.

## 10. 'UZZIAH OR 'AZARIAH : 789 or 779-740

With the moral and political factors in her life which have been noted in this chapter, Jerusalem entered the long and prosperous reign of 'Uzziah.

The editor of the Books of Kings records from his sources but two events in this reign, the restoration of the Red Sea port of Elath to Judah, to which <sup>The King's</sup> we have already referred, and the king's <sup>Leprosy and</sup> <sup>Retirement.</sup> leprosy.  When this stroke befell 'Uzziah *he lived in his own house relieved* of the duties of governing, *and Jotham the king's son judged the people of the*

---

[1] 2 Kings xiv. 19 ff., probably from the Judæan annals ; but another writer (*id.* 17) says Amaziah lived fifteen years after the death of Joash of Israel.

*land.*[1] At what date this happened we are not told. It has been supposed that the variant numbers assigned to Jotham's reign in 2 Kings xv. 30 and 33 refer—the *sixteen* years to Jotham's regency during his father's life, and the *twenty* to that *plus* the years of his reign after his father's death. In this case 'Uzziah resigned the government about 755, for Jotham died in 735. But it is equally probable that 'Uzziah did not resign till 750.

On the other hand, the Chronicler's account of the reign is very full.[2] Apart from his explanation of 'Uzziah's leprosy, which is obviously due to the influence of the Levitical system in his own time, and such details as the size of the Judæan army (and perhaps the engines ascribed to 'Uzziah), the account is evidently drawn from earlier sources, and is confirmed by what the prophets tell us of the state of Judah at the end of 'Uzziah's reign. According to the Chronicler, then, 'Uzziah made expeditions against the Philistines,[3] the Arabs in Gûr or Gerar,[4]

*The Chronicler's Account of his Reign.*

---

[1] 2 Kings xv. 5. The Hebrew text has בֵּית הַחָפְשִׁית, which some of the Versions (ancient and modern) render *a separate house*, others *a house of freedom* (*i.e.* instead of being shut up with other lepers). Klostermann emends בְּבֵיתֹה חָפְשִׁית, *in his own house, free* or *unmolested*. But if we accept this reading, it is most natural, both because of the clause which follows (*and Jotham the king's son was over the palace, judging the people of the land*) and because of other uses of חָפְשִׁי, to take it as meaning *free from the duties of government*; cf. the use of חָפְשִׁי in Mishnic Hebrew, *free* as a corpse is from the obligations of the law, or as Saul was by his death from the kingly office.

[2] 2 Chron. xxvi.

[3] Verse 6. As the building of cities by 'Uzziah in Philistine territory is questionable, it has been proposed to read וַיִּבְנֶה עִיר בְּאַשְׁדֹּד, *now Jabneh is a city in Ashdod*; and to take וּבַפְּלִשְׁתִּים as a superfluous gloss.

[4] Verse 7. For והמעונים בעל read וְעַל־הַמְּעוּנִים בעל, Winckler (*Gesch.* i. 46)

and the Meʿûnîm—all of them tribes upon the avenues of Judah's commerce with the south. In the southern desert the king built towers, the best means (as also the Romans and the Turks have known) of keeping the nomads in subjection and the desert roads open.[1] *And he hewed many cisterns, for he had much cattle in the Shephelah and the Mishōr or Plain,* most probably the level land at the foot of the Shephelah hills, *and vinedressers in the mountains and the garden-land, for he was a lover of husbandry.*[2]

In Jerusalem, according to the Chronicler, ʿUzziah made some simple additions to the walls. *He built towers in Jerusalem over the Gate of the Corner,* that is on the extreme north-east, *and over the Gate of the Gai,*[3] on the south of the City,

ʿUzziah's Fortification of Jerusalem.

then proposes to read גּוּר as the same name as Gari in the Tell el-Amarna Letters (Lond. 64, l. 23), which he takes as equivalent to Edom. גּוּר, however, may be a corruption of גְּרָר, Gerar, which is read by the Targum: cf. 2 Chronicles xiv. 13. For בגור־בעל Kittel proposes בְּטוּר־בַּעַל, which is found in Cod. Amiatinus of the Vulgate: *in Turbaal.*

[1] Cf. Doughty, *Arabia Deserta,* I. *passim.*

[2] 2 Chron. xxvi. 10. This sentence seems compounded from more than one source, or at least to have had additions made to it, and is therefore as it stands ambiguous. If the Hebrew text be retained, its accents must be discarded, and אכרים, without a conjunction, taken with the preceding *and in the Shephelah and on the Plain.* But if with the LXX. we omit אכרים as well as the conjunction before בשפלה, then the verse will run as given above. The verse is interesting as giving the different kinds of land of which Judah was composed. The Mīshōr cannot be, as Ewald and Buhl assert (*Geog. des Alten Palästinas,* p. 104), the Moabite Mīshōr or Plateau, for that lay outside Uzziah's domains, but either part of the ʿArabah south of the Dead Sea or the level land at the foot of the Shephelah hills. The latter is most probable because of the conjunction of the Mīshōr with the Shephelah. But if this be so, we have another reason (besides those given in my *H. G. H. L.* p. 202) for confining the name Shephelah to the range of low hills west of the Judæan range, and holding it to have been distinct from the maritime Plain; this against Buhl, *loc. cit.*

[3] Vol. i. 176 ff., 215.

*and upon the angles* or *turnings* of the walls, *and made
them strong.*[1]    This is a notice credible both in itself and
from the great increase in building which distinguished
the king's reign.[2]    It represents a development of the
fortifications of Jerusalem which is well within the ascertained achievements of the˙age in military engineering,
and which was probably forced upon the defenders of
Jerusalem by their experience of the ease with which the
Israelite army had made a long breach in the northern
wall.    From as early as the fourth millennium[3] Babylonian engineers built the walls of fortresses with a
regular sequence of right angles, out and in, with heavy
towers over the gates and at the corners, so that the
besieged could command with their bows the foot of the
walls and prevent these from being breached by the
besiegers.[4]    The Syrian and other fortresses attacked
by the Assyrians in the ninth and eighth centuries are
represented, almost without exception, as polygonal.[5]
Very frequently the walls are double or even treble, and
in general they are furnished with battlements, casemates and loopholes.    But the main feature is the tower
projecting from the wall and manned by archers, who
shoot over its breast-work at the advancing foe.[6]    Of the
results of this long-developed science 'Uzziah's engineers
are said to have employed the gate towers and the flanking towers at angles where the walls turned round the

---

[1] 2 Chron. xxvi. 9.    The Hebrew has the singular, but the LXX. gives
the more probable plural, angles.

[2] See below, pp. 122 f.

[3] See the plan of a fortress engraved on the lap of the statue of Gudea.

[4] *Die Festungsbau im Alten Orient*, by A. Billerbeck in *Der Alte Orient*
series, 1900, Heft 4, pp. 11, etc., with plans.

[5] *Idem*, p. 14.

[6] So in nearly all Assyrian and Egyptian pictures of sieges.

City or bent with the natural line of rock. Probably this
was all that was required on the walls of Jerusalem,
which for the most part were planted on the edge of
deep ravines high above the reach of breaching engines.
But it is well to keep in mind also the series of buttresses, or forward towers, which Dr. Bliss uncovered
upon the most ancient of the lines of wall traced by
him across the mouth of the Tyropœon.[1] 'Uzziah's
flanking towers fully served their purpose. Where before his reign the comparatively small forces of Northern
Israel had made a long breach on the northern wall, the
only breachable part of the defences, after his reign the
engines of Assyria herself failed to effect an entrance. On
all these grounds we may accept the Chronicler's report
of 'Uzziah's fortification of his capital. We shall find
this developed by the king's immediate successors.

It is different, however, with the armament which the
Chronicler declares 'Uzziah to have placed upon the walls.
*And he made in Jerusalem engines, the inven-* Engines of
*tion of an engineer,* or *ingenious man, to be on* War (?).
*the towers and the angles to shoot arrows and great stones.*[2]
Benzinger thinks that the redundant expressions 'speak
for the age of this notice; at the time of the Chronicler
there were no more such marvels. It is true that nowhere
else in the Old Testament are such engines mentioned.
But since the Assyrians had them, they cannot have
remained unknown to the Israelites.' This reasoning is
doubtful both in its premises and conclusion. Billerbeck
states that 'the ancient artillery,' with its engines for

---

[1] See above, vol. i. 220 ff., and the frontispiece to Bliss, *Excav. at Jerus.*,
showing the restoration of the wall.
[2] 2 Chron. xxvi. 15.

shooting arrows and throwing stones, first appears in
the fifth century before Christ.[1]  Nor can I find any such
engines pictured on the Assyrian or Egyptian pictures
of battles or sieges in the eighth or previous centuries,
and it is strange that if 'Uzziah had used engines the
prophets who describe other novel constructions of the
time should fail to speak of them.  The next earliest
notice of shooting instruments in Jewish writings is
1 Maccabees vi. 51.[2]

The Chronicler also ascribes to 'Uzziah the organisation and equipment of a huge army.[3]  We may question
*Size of the Army.* the total number given, 307,500; but the
number of heads of families who had to
furnish the fighting men, 2600, is not improbable, and
the Chronicler cannot have invented the names of the
officials charged with the levy.  'Uzziah re-armed his
host.

Those records of 'Uzziah's activity, in which we have
seen no inherent improbability, are confirmed by the
*Great Increase of Building under 'Uzziah,* evidence of the Prophets at the close of
that monarch's reign.  As we should expect,
there is a background of agriculture and pasture to the pictures of the national life presented by
Amos and Isaiah.[4]  But against that background rises,
in a way novel in Israel's history, an extraordinary
enterprise in building [5]—the instruments and material

---

[1] *Op. cit.* p. 5.
[2] The דָּיֵק of 2 Kings xxv. 1 and Ezek. iv. 2, etc., are towers manned by
archers and pushed forward on wheels or rollers.
[3] 2 Chron. xxvi. 11-14.
[4] Amos ii. 13, iii. 12, iv. 9, v. 11, 16 f., vi. 12, vii. 1 ff., viii. 6.  Cf.
Isaiah i. 3, 8, iii. 14, v. 1-10, 17, vii. 23, ix. 3, etc.
[5] Amos iii. 15, v. 11, etc.; Hos. viii. 14; Isaiah ii. 15, ix. 10 (9).

of which are used familiarly as religious figures,[1] while
one of the names, *'armōn*, hitherto limited to royal
castles, is applied to private dwellings—with an increase
of all manner of wealth and luxury.[2]   But   and of
these imply a great development of trade;   Trade.
and of this and of the tempers it breeds the Prophets
give us direct evidence.   Amos describes an excessive
zeal in buying and selling.   Hosea calls Northern Israel
a very *Canaan*, or trader.[3]   Isaiah says *Judah is filled
from the East, she strikes hands with the sons of strangers*,[4]
and mentions ships of Tarshish and caravans.[5]   The sins
of trade : the covetousness which oppresses the poor
and threatens the old religious festivals, false weights
and lying are exposed and condemned.[6]   Whether
'Uzziah throughout his long reign remained under that
subjection to Northern Israel which was confirmed by
Amaziah's defeat at Beth-shemesh, or gradually advanced
to more equal relations with Jeroboam II., it is difficult
to say.   In either case the two kingdoms were at peace,
and between them commanded the trade from Elath to
the borders of Phœnicia and Damascus.   So great a
commerce was in the hands mainly of foreigners—Arabs
according to Isaiah,[7] and doubtless also Arameans.[8]
They must have brought into Judah many foreign
products and inventions; also a familiarity with life and
institutions in Assyria and Egypt.   The armies of
Asshur had been as far south as Damascus and were

---

[1] Amos vii. 7 ff. ; cf. Isaiah xxviii. 16, xxx. 13.
[2] Amos iii. 15, iv. 4 f., v. 11, vi. 4-8 ; Hos. xii. 8 ; Isaiah ii. 7, etc.
[3] xii. 7 ; cf. vii. 8, viii. 10.   See vol. i. 369 f.
[4] ii. 6.                                    [5] ii. 16, xxx. 6.
[6] Amos ii. 6, iv. 1, viii. 4 ff. ; Hos. xii. 7 ; Isaiah iii. 15, v. 8, 23, etc.
[7] ii. 6.                 [8] *Enc. Bibl.*, 'Trade and Commerce,' § 51.

still moving in Northern Syria. Isaiah describes the aspect of their ranks; and through the other prophets there beats the sense of their irresistibleness.

The effects of all this on Jerusalem may be easily conceived. The City must have regained much of the

The Effects on Jerusalem. prosperity which she enjoyed under Solomon, and despite her political separation from Northern Israel may even have risen beyond that. As through the rest of her history before the Exile, we are without any data for estimating the number of her population, and with very few for determining the space covered by her buildings. But we have seen grounds for the assurance that by this time, or at the latest by Ḥezeḳiah's, the South-west Hill was within the City walls.[1] The passages quoted above from Isaiah imply a large increase of the foreign elements in her population. Many at least of these alien traders would be accommodated outside the walls: most probably in a suburb along the outer or second northern wall, which there is no reason to doubt ran from the Corner Gate near the present Jaffa Gate eastwards to the north end of the Temple enclosure. Within the walls the inhabitants would be more crowded than before, the buildings more numerous, compact and lofty. Isaiah, as we shall see in the next chapter, prophesies in presence of the characteristic tempers of a large city life. In the national wealth the Temple must have shared; its revenues would be rapidly increasing. Thus, in every direction, the material, political and moral forces, with which Jerusalem entered the long reign of 'Uzziah, were greatly developed before its close.

[1] Vol. i. 38, 177, 207, 218.

## 11. Jotham, Regent from 755 or 750; King 740-735

The only addition to the buildings of Jerusalem ascribed to Jotham by the Books of Kings is *the upper gate of the Temple*,[1] probably the same as Jeremiah's *upper gate of Benjamin*, and Eze- kiel's *gate of the inner court towards the north*.[2] The Chronicler adds that Jotham *built much on the wall of The 'Ophel*.[3] The position of The 'Ophel is clearly determined by the data of Nehemiah and Josephus. It lay on the East Hill south of the Temple and above Giḥon; and, as we have seen, was to the Chronicler and other writers the name which they prefer for Ṣion.[4] From an early time a wall ran up the eastern edge of the hill, and this wall Jotham now strengthened, probably in the same style as that of his father's additional fortifications.

*Further Building.*

## 12. Aḥaz: 735-720 (?)

The fortifications of Jerusalem strengthened by 'Uzziah and Jotham were speedily to be tested. The political calm in which Israel and Judah had lived for a number of years began to be disturbed soon after 745 by forces both from without and from within. In that year the Assyrian throne was ascended by a strong soldier who, under the title of Tiglath-Pileser III., revived a vigorous policy of conquest, which, however, owing to the numerous directions on which it had to be prosecuted, could not be steadily

*The uncertain advance of Assyria.*

---

[1] 2 Kings xv. 35.　　[2] Jer. xx. 2; Ezek. viii. 3, ix. 2.
[3] 2 Chron. xxvii. 3.　　[4] See above, vol. i. 152 ff.

maintained along any one of them. For the next fifteen years politics in Palestine swung upon the ebb and flow of Assyrian invasion. In Northern Israel this oscillation was aggravated after the close of Jeroboam's long reign by the overthrow of his dynasty and the succession of various short-lived usurpers. In 738 the second of these, Menahem, became, along with some of his neighbours, tributary to Tiglath-Pileser, then moving south on one of his Syrian campaigns. But for the next three years Tiglath-Pileser was occupied to the north of Assyria, and taking advantage of his absence, short-sighted factions in all the Syrian states dared to form a new league against him.

When Menahem died in 735, those in Israel who sympathised with this movement slew his son, and, rais-

League of Aram and Israel against Judah,

ing their leader, Pekah, a Gileadite, to the throne, made alliance against Assyria with Rĕṣîn, or Raṣon, of Damascus. It seems to have been Jotham's refusal to join them which stirred the allies against him.[1] But Jotham died in 735, and left his son Ahaz, or Jehoahaz, to face their invasion of Judah,[2] with its aim of displacing the king by a creature of their own.[3] Isaiah has himself described the panic which ensued in Jerusalem under this danger to the City and the dynasty of David. *Now it was told to the house of David that Aram was pitched in Ephraim, and his heart and the heart of his people quivered as the trees of the jungle quiver before the wind.*[4] Probably it was under this alarm that the superstitious king *made his son to pass through the fire;*[5] which can only mean a sacrifice by burning in

---

[1] 2 Kings xv. 37.　　　　[2] *Id.* xvi. 5.
[3] Isaiah vii. 6.　　　　[4] Isaiah vii. 2.
[5] 2 Kings xvi. 3; LXX. reads *sons,* so 2 Chron. xxviii. 3.

order to propitiate the divine powers in some extreme danger. Isaiah nowhere alludes by word to this horror. But we may perhaps find the prophet's rebuke of so awful a sacrifice to despair in his taking with him to meet the king his own son, whom he also had dedicated, but to hope, by the symbolic name She'ar-yashûb, *a remnant shall return.* They met *at the end of the conduit of the Upper Pool on the highway by the Fuller's field.* It is the same spot from which in 701 the Assyrian Rab-shaḳeh addressed his challenge to the defenders of Jerusalem. It lay, therefore, outside the walls; note also the command to Isaiah *to go forth* to it. Beyond this we cannot tell certainly where it lay, but more probably off the mouth of the Tyropœon than to the north of the City.[1]

Aḥaz, when Isaiah found him, was probably inspecting

---

[1] For the opposing arguments see vol. i. 105, 114 ff. On the one hand, it is reasonable to seek for the Fuller's field in the Ḳidron valley, where the only springs are found. Here the Upper Pool might be identified with the inner of the two pools of Siloam, and the conduit with the rock-cut channel leading directly to the Ḳidron gardens. We should then have the explanation of the existence of *the end* of a conduit outside the City walls, for in this case the conduit was for the purpose of irrigating the gardens. Or we may take the Upper Pool to have been the basin into which Giḥon (the Virgin Fountain) issues, and the conduit that which Dr. Masterman discovered along the foot of Ophel. But, on the other hand, if the Upper Pool and its conduit were any part of the system of Shiloaḥ, it is singular that this name is not given to them. Sir Charles Wilson thinks that 'the conduit of the Upper Pool must have been on the north of the City, because no general commanding an army would go down to the mouth of the Tyropœon valley to parley with the men on the wall, but would speak to them from some plateau on the north': this is not conclusive. He suggests that the Upper Pool was one which in the eleventh century existed under the name of 'the Lake of Legerius,' at the head of the Tyropœon valley, and that the conduit was one on the east hill by which water was led from the same locality to the Temple enclosure. In any case the Upper Pool can hardly have been, as many have thought, the Birket Mamilla.

the water supplies in order to prevent their use by the
and its approaching invaders. Against these the forti-
Results. fications of 'Uzziah and Jotham were found
sufficient. Syria and Israel came up against Jerusalem,
but were not able to breach or to storm it.[1] The invasion, however, meant losses to Judah in other directions. The Edomites recovered Elath from the Jews,[2]
and the Philistines took several towns in the Shephelah.[3]

The waters of the Shiloah are mentioned by Isaiah in
another address during the reign of Ahaz: *forasmuch as*
*this people despises the waters of the Shiloah*
The Shiloah
and the *which flow gently and . . . therefore the Lord*
Euphrates. *will bring against them the waters of the*
*River.*[4] As we saw in the study of the Waters of
Jerusalem, the Shiloah, which means *sent* or *conducted*,
must refer to some part of the system of aqueducts by
which the waters of Gihon were led to the mouth of the
Tyropœon. If the famous tunnel which still carries them
under Ophel to the Pool of Siloam was the work of the
engineers of Hezekiah,[5] Isaiah must intend some other
part of the system: perhaps the ancient channel traced by
Dr. Masterman along the eastern foot of Ophel. In any
case Isaiah takes the gentle and fertilising streams of the
Shiloah as symbolic of the spiritual influences of Judah's
God, from which the people were turning impatiently to
seek their salvation through submission and tribute to

[1] Isaiah vii. 1.
[2] 2 Kings xvi. 6, where with the LXX. read Edom for Aram.
[3] 2 Chron. xxviii. 18. The greater part of this chapter on Ahaz is
obviously a very late Midrash on the history of Judah; but the section,
vs. 17-19, which is in a different style from, and disturbs the connection of,
the rest, is, as Benzinger says, 'at least not improbable.'
[4] Isa. viii. 6; vol. i. 103 f.    [5] Vol. i. 93 ff., 102.

Assyria. For such was the fateful step on which Ahaz
was resolved, and it brings us into that new period of the
City's history which is identified with Isaiah's name.

To raise his first tribute to Assyria, Ahaz imitated
certain of his predecessors and despoiled the Palace
and Temple treasuries.[1] Tiglath-Pileser im- Evil fruits of
mediately rewarded him by invading the the Assyrian
policy of
territories of his principal foes: the Philistines Ahaz.
of Gaza, Northern Israel and Aram (734-732), who
alone of the Palestine states formed a league against
Assyria, all the others joining Ahaz in his submission.
They doubtless relied upon help from Egypt, but in
vain. Tiglath-Pileser swept south as far as Gaza, which
he captured and sacked. Either on his way there, or
more probably on his return, he overran the northern
frontier of Israel, Galilee and Gilead, and carried the
inhabitants into captivity.[2] Only Samaria remained to
Israel, and even there the discredited Pekah was slain by
a conspiracy of his own people, whose leader, Hoshea',
ascended the throne as a vassal of Assyria. In 732
Tiglath-Pileser took Damascus,[3] and thither Ahaz re-

---

[1] 2 Kings xvi. 8.    [2] Isa. ix. 1.

[3] The evidence of the Assyrian inscriptions is as follows :—(1) The Eponym
Canon (see *C.O.T.* ii. 194 f.) records campaigns of Tiglath-Pileser III. to
'Pilista' in 734, and to Damascus in 733 and 732. 'Pilista' is either
Philistia, or (to judge from the following) Philistia and the neighbouring
countries (in this case a remarkable anticipation of the name Palestine).
(2) According to his Nimrud Inscr. (British Museum, K. 3751 ; published by
Rawlinson, *W.A.I.* ii. 67 ; transl. in *R.P.* sec. series, v. 120 ff. ; see also
*C.O.T.* 249) Tiglath-Pileser received tribute from (among others) the kings
of 'Ammon, Moab, Edom, 'Jehoahaz of Judah,' Ashkelon and Gaza. (3) His
Annals (227 f., see *K.A.T.*[(3)] 264 f.) record that Tiglath-Pileser overran a
land, supposed to be Bit Khumria (*i.e.* Kingdom of 'Omri, by which name
N. Israel was known to the Assyrians), and left to its ruler only Samaria.
(4) A mutilated fragment (Rawlinson, iii. 10, No. 2 ; *C.O.T.* i. 246 f.) records
that Tiglath-Pileser took two towns, 'Ga-al . . . and . . bel . .' (Gilead

paired to do him homage. Anxious as a vassal to imitate his lord, and impressed by an altar which he saw in Damascus, he sent the pattern to Uriyah, the priest at Jerusalem, had one like it constructed for the Temple, and himself sacrificed upon this when he returned. Some further changes which he ordered in the Temple and the ritual are not intelligible to us, but the account of them brings out clearly the undiminished supremacy of the crown over the Temple and its methods of worship.[1] Previous tributes to foreign monarchs, taken from the Temple treasures, had been occasional, and once paid were done with. But in the Assyrian Aḥaz met a more persistent master to whom tribute had to be sent annually. There was no time to replenish the emptied treasuries, and Aḥaz had to strip the metal from some of the most ancient of the Temple furnishings. Among these were the machines on which the Lavers ran, and the twelve Bronze Bulls that bore the Bronze Sea.[2]

The chronology of the Books of Kings offers alternative dates for the death of Aḥaz, 727 or 720. The latter alone leaves room for the sixteen years over which his reign is said to have extended,[3] suits other symptoms of the text, and is conformable to data in the following reign of Ḥezekiah.[4] If it

*The Fall of Samaria, 721 B.C.*

and Beth Maacah ?) 'above Bit Khumria,' which, 'in its entire extent,' was made Assyrian; that he took Gaza, whose king, Hanno, fled; that all the inhabitants of Bit Khumria were deported to Assyria; that Peḳaḥ, their king, was slain and Hosheaʻ appointed in his stead. In what order these events happened is uncertain: see Schrader, *C.O.T.* i. 246 ff.; Winckler, *K.A.T.*(³ 56 f., 264 f.; Whitehouse, *Isaiah* (*Century Bible*) 13 f.

[1] On the whole passage, 2 Kings xv. 10-16, see the commentaries.

[2] 2 Kings xvi. 17 f. (text uncertain); see above, pp. 65 f.     [3] 2 Kings xvi. 2.

[4] See the commentaries, especially Benzinger's and Skinner's; also Winckler's argument that Samaria fell in the end of the reign of Aḥaz. The date 720 for Aḥaz's death is accepted by a growing number of scholars.

be correct, Aḥaz lived to see the end of the Northern Kingdom. After resisting for three years a siege by Shalmaneser IV., Samaria fell, in 721, to his successor, Sargon, who carried away 27,000 of the inhabitants and destroyed the state. Judah alone was left to represent the people of Jahweh, and Jerusalem had no longer any rival either as the capital of Israel or as the chief sanctuary of the national God.

We have now finished our survey of the history of Jerusalem from Rehoboam to Aḥaz. We have seen her lose the high rank and great prosperity which she had enjoyed under Solomon ; but gradu- Summary of the Period, ally regain much of both, while preserving the 933-720 B.C. dynasty of David and the Ark of the God of Israel. We have seen her grow stronger than she ever was before both in material and spiritual resources. But a novel danger and one more pregnant than she has yet encountered begins to loom upon her in that subjection to Assyria into which Aḥaz has just drawn her. With all this Jerusalem is now to pass into the hands of the greatest statesman who ever swayed her life. What he inherited from her and what in return he gave her ; how he interpreted her history, developed her spiritual forces, rallied her dynasty and her military strength, and by his almost solitary faith arrested the destruction which threatened her, will form the subject of the next two chapters.

# CHAPTER V

## ISAIAH'S JERUSALEM

### FROM 740 ONWARDS

ACCORDING to his own reading of her history, Isaiah inherited so much through Jerusalem, that (at the risk of repetition) we must attempt to register the endowments, spiritual and material, which he owed to her before we can estimate the supreme service which in return he rendered to his City. The Disruption had deposed Jerusalem from her brief reign as the capital of all Israel. Of her territory only the small province of Judah was left, while the reputation of her Temple was still below that of many other sanctuaries in the land. Yet in the dynasty of David and the Ark of Jahweh with its comparatively pure worship, Jerusalem held stronger pledges for the future than Israel at the time anywhere else possessed. It is true that neither of these securities had escaped challenge and serious danger. From the congenital heathenism of a part of her population,[1] and the foreign alliances of some of her kings, the City was liable to outbreaks of idolatry ; while the House of David suffered at least one overthrow and was almost extirpated.[2] But from such disasters both the dynasty and the religion emerged with a brighter lustre and a more articulate

*Isaiah's Inheritance in Jerusalem.*

---

[1] Ezek. xvi. 3.    [2] By 'Athaliah.

confidence in their destiny. Behind them a considerable
force of piety and virtue is visible in all classes of the
population. With few exceptions the kings were loyal to
Jahweh, and many evinced both character and wisdom.
They were aided and corrected by the priesthood. The
bulk of the country people were on the same side. In
some royal measures we can trace the growth and refine-
ment of the moral sense. Rude customs were abolished
and reforms effected. Religion was organised and the
Law codified. We perceive the increase, if not the first
appearance, of a literature of patriotism and religious
faith, breathing a strong confidence of the future. The
Temple, though avoided by the great majority of the
Tribes and ignored by the main currents of prophecy
which ran in the Northern Kingdom, steadily grew in
its command of the Judæan people and in the influence
of its priesthood. It is true that down to Ahaz the
supremacy of the King was maintained over both the
administration and the ritual of the Temple; but the
inference is unjust, that therefore the Temple was little
more than the Chapel Royal. Its very proximity to the
Palace meant the training of its priests in public affairs;
and in politics and religion they undoubtedly played a
part analogous to that of the more famous prophets of the
North. Several episodes in the history prove the increasing popularity of the Temple and the consequent growth
both of its revenues and of its spiritual influence. The
people of the land gathered to it; its treasures, though
often exhausted, were always again sufficient for national
emergencies. The Temple was regarded, if not as the
only, yet as the chief, sanctuary of Jahweh in Judah: it
was not merely a royal but a national and a popular

shrine. To all this we have to add, at least from 'Uzziah onwards, the development of the trade of the City and the increase of her military strength. The walls which fell before Joash of Israel were so fortified by 'Uzziah and Jotham that they resisted not only the confederate troops of Israel and Aram, but, after Hezekiah's additions to them, the arms of Assyria.

Such was the Jerusalem in which Isaiah grew up : the City of David and of the Temple; soon to be the sole His Double Vision of her. capital and unrivalled sanctuary of Israel; strongly walled and fairly wealthy; with a trained priesthood, a comparatively pure worship and a large body of religious law and literature; but with a very mixed and fickle population under rulers who were entangling her fortunes with the perilous policy of Assyria. The vision which Isaiah gives of Jerusalem is twofold, actual and ideal. On both sides it confirms that story of her growth from Rehoboam to Aḥaz, which we have read from the annals of Judah.

First, then, we find portrayed, as by one who, for forty 1. The Actual City: years at least, walked the pavements of Jerusalem and watched her from his housetop, line after line of her material features, and phase after phase of her crowded life.

We get not a few glimpses of her position and shape— *Mount Ṣion* and *the hill of Jerusalem,*[1] so described for the Material Features, the first time ; of fragments of her architecture and engineering—*the conduit of the Upper Pool on the highway of the Fuller's Field,*[2] *the Shiloaḥ,* and

---

[1] x. 12 (?) 32 ; xxxi. 4.　　　　[2] vii. 3 ; vol. i. 103 ff., vol. ii. 128.

its *softly flowing waters,*[1] *the armour in the Forest-house,*[2]
*the waters of the Lower Pool, and the tank between the
two walls for the water of the Old Pool* ;[3] of the lines of
wall,[4] the Temple with its Courts,[5] and the house-tops,[6]
at all times in this City of covered lanes the only stages
on which crowds are visible; of the *lifted* look of the
new buildings;[7] and of the *carven sepulchres on high,*[8] the
like of which are still so conspicuous from Jerusalem.
The environing hills stand clear; Nob is named upon
them, and behind Nob the train of villages up the great
North Road.[9] There are also the *wâdies between preci-
pices* and *the clefts of the rocks,*[10] characteristic of the
immediate surroundings of the City; *the standing wheat
in the Vale of Rephaim* ;[11] and the whole background of
pasture and agriculture, vineyards and olive groves, with
large single trees scattered across it, terebinths and oaks.[12]

We see, too, by Isaiah's eyes, the habits and fashions
of the citizens. The various religions are visible : on the
one side the Temple-courts, thronged with
worshippers, and above them the smoke of
the lavish sacrifices, the new moons and the
Sabbaths ;[13] on the other heathen rites and magic, the
many idols and soothsayers,[14] the necromancy and spirit-
raising,[15] the Adonis gardens and the worship of trees.[16]

*and the
Fashions of
her life.*

---

[1] viii. 6.     [2] xxii. 8 ; see above, p. 68.
[3] xxii. 9, 11 ; but it is uncertain whether these verses are of Isaiah's date.
[4] ii. 15 ; xxxvi. 11, etc.     [5] vi. 1 ; i. 11 ff.     [6] xxii. 1.
[7] ii. 12, 15.     [8] xxii. 16.     [9] x. 28 ff.
[10] vii. 19.     [11] xvii. 5.
[12] v. 1-6, 8-10 ; vi. 13 ; vii. 21 ff. ; xvii. 6 ; i. 29-30 ; xxviii. 23 ff. (though
Cheyne and others deny this passage to Isaiah) ; xviii. 4 ff. ; i. 8.
[13] i. 11-15.     [14] ii. 6, 8, 18, etc.
[15] viii. 19 : the objections to the authenticity of these verses are not cogent.
[16] xvii. 10 f. ; i. 29 f.

We see a great deal of luxury and vice; the parade and foppery of the women,[1] and, in verses which Juvenal might have written of the Romans of his day, the drunkenness in the streets and at the banquets: *priest and prophet reel with new wine, and totter while giving judgment; all tables are covered with vomit, filth everywhere.*[2] The rulers are childish and effeminate; the judges are corrupt; the poor are oppressed; tyranny in high places and insolence among the young and the mean.[3] Through all this moves the prophet himself, austere, clamant, persistent: confronting the king at the end of the conduit;[4] displaying a large tablet with plain characters;[5] leading about his children with the ominous names;[6] walking for three years through the streets stripped of his upper robe and barefoot.[7] In short, we have seen nothing of Jerusalem so near or so vivid since the days of David.

Most significant for the history of the City are the movement and noise everywhere audible round the prophet. The land has become full of silver and gold, full of horses and chariots.[8] There are strong foreign elements;[9] and other prophets of the time emphasise the increase of trade and building. All this must have found its focus in Jerusalem, *her pomp, her throng, her tumult, and the boisterous in her*;[10] while the rural districts, under the new economic conditions, were being stripped of their people and their wealth.[11] Isaiah prophesies in presence of the characteristic

*The Crowds and Tumult.*

---

[1] iii. 16 ff.    [2] xxviii. 7 f. ; cf. v. 11 f.    [3] Chs. i., iii. and v.
[4] vii. 3 ff.    [5] viii. 1 ff.
[6] vii. 3 ; viii. 3 ff. ; 18.    [7] xx. 1 ff.    [8] ii. 7 ff.
[9] ii. 6 ; cf. Shebna, the secretary with the Aramaic name.    [10] v. 14.
[11] v. 8 ff. ; cf. Micah ii. 2 ; and see vol. i. 281, 295 f.

tempers of a large city-life: the religion of crowds,[1] their fickleness and desperate levity—

*What has come to thee, then, that the whole of thee*
*Is up on the house-tops?*
*O full of uproar, city tumultuous,*
*Boisterous town!*
*The Lord Jahweh Ṣebaôth, was calling on that day*
*To tears, lamentation, baldness, girding with sackcloth;*
*And lo, there was joyaunce, merriment, slaying of oxen, killing of sheep,*
*Eating of flesh and drinking of wine; eating and drinking for—*
  *'To-morrow we die.'* [2]

In this connection we must notice how Isaiah mentions Jerusalem as parallel to the rest of Judah—*the Lord removes from Jerusalem and from Judah every stay and support; Jerusalem comes to ruin and Judah falls;*[3] *ye dwellers in Jerusalem and men of Judah,*[4] and as parallel even to both houses of Israel.[5]   The capital is already approaching that preponderance of influence which in coming centuries is to render the rest of the country but the fringe upon her walls.   Nothing could more confirm the fact of her growth during the previous period: the change which the development of trade, the new economic conditions alluded to above, and the increasing importance of her Temple had made in her relation to the rest of the land.

*Preponder-*
*ance of the*
*Capital.*

But all these visions of the material size, strength and *noise* of the City, vivid and near as they be, are dim beside the burning words in which Isaiah reveals her moral and her religious significance. From such words we receive ample confirmation of the evidence we have gathered of Jerusalem's

2. The Ideal
City: her
Divine Origin
and Purpose.

---

[1] i. 11 ff.
[2] xxii. 1, 12 f. (probably in 701); עֲלִיזָה, *boisterous* (cf. v. 14), is also used of Jerusalem by Zephaniah, ii. 15.
[3] iii. 1, 8.          [4] v. 3.                    [5] viii. 14.

ethical development in the age of the Double Kingdom. Her present vice and corruption of justice do
not prevent Isaiah from affirming that she had been *the
faithful city, full of justice, where righteousness abode*.[1]
The Lord had made *a vineyard on a fruitful and sunny
hill. He had dug it and cleared it of stones, planted choice
vines, built a tower in the midst, hewed a wine-vat and
looked to find grapes*—such is the prophet's account of the
City's discipline in the centuries leading up to his own.[2]
The outcome ought to have been justice and righteousness, but behold it was *bloodshed and screaming*.[3] Nevertheless God has still His purposes for her: He has not
Himself forsaken her. *The Lord hath founded Ṣion*.[4]
She is Ariel, *God's altar-hearth*,[5] *who has a fire in Ṣion
and a furnace in Jerusalem*.[6] *He dwells in Ṣion*.[7] Therefore, even before Samaria fell, and Jerusalem was left
without a rival, and even before her vindication in 701
as Jahweh's inviolate shrine, the City was identified by
Isaiah with the One True God and with His religion.[8]

It is not wonderful, therefore, that from the beginning
of his career the prophet should have beheld Jerusalem
The Break of in a supernatural glory. This breaks even
Apocalypse. upon his inaugural vision. The actual Temple
is indeed the stage: the walls raised by Solomon and
repaired by Joash. But before the eyes of the young

---

[1] i. 21.  [2] v. 1 ff.  [3] v. 7.
[4] xiv. 32 (721 ?).  [5] xxix. 1 (probably about 704).
[6] xxxi. 9: unless, as some think, this is a later addition to Isaiah's
prophecies.
[7] viii. 18. Cheyne dates this oracle as late as 701, but with a mark of
interrogation. It is probably earlier.
[8] Not to speak of the opening words of the Book of Amos (i. 2): *Jahweh
roareth from Ṣion and uttereth His voice from Jerusalem*—words which
some, but I think on insufficient grounds, deny to be original.

seer these give way, and open upon the Divine Court itself and the immediate Presence of the Lord. The foundations of the thresholds rock at the thunderous song of the seraphim, and through the smoke a seraph flies with a glowing stone to the prophet's lips. Nor does Isaiah fail to see the whole City and Land in the same or a similar apocalypse. In one of the very earliest of his discourses he describes *the terror of Jahweh, and the glory of His majesty, when He rises to strike through the land. In that day shall Jahweh*—He whom he had seen *on a throne high and lifted up*—*be alone exalted.*[1] *The Lord shall cleanse the filth of the daughters of Ṣion, and sweep from her midst the blood of Jerusalem by a blast of judgment and a blast of burning.*[2] There is a vision of Sheol *enlarging her appetite and opening her mouth without measure,* and of *Ṣion's pomp and throng and tumult and boisterousness plunging into it.*[3] The day of Jahweh *is the overthrow of all that is high.*[4] *Behold there will be distress and darkness, the gloom of anguish and pitch darkness.*[5] *Suddenly shall she be visited by Jahweh of Hosts with thunder and with earthquake and a great noise, with whirlwind and storm and flame of devouring fire.*[6] Now these visions are not apocalypse technically so-called, the beginnings of which in prophecy we are wont to trace to Zephaniah. But they travel in that direction, with a desire for the manifestation of God, and a conviction of the fulness of His judgment, which the material

---

[1] ii. 10, 11, 17, 19 (under Aḥaz).

[2] iv. 4 (under Aḥaz: but denied by some to Isaiah and his time).

[3] v. 14 (under Aḥaz).

[4] ii. 11 f.      [5] viii. 22 under Aḥaz).

[6] xxix. 6 (*circa* 703 B.C.): for the material of such visions see above, Book I. ch. iv. on the Earthquakes.

of this dispensation cannot satisfy, and which look to the
hidden world for their fulfilment. Occurring as some of
the visions do in discourses, unanimously attributed to
Isaiah's earlier years, they arrest us from following the
recent tendency of criticism to deny to the prophet a
number of other passages[1] on the ground that these
must be the product of a later age more at home in
apocalyptic vision. The verses just quoted prove that
the young Isaiah knew how to paint pictures of the
Divine presence and judgment with colours from another
world and atmosphere than the present. But however
we may settle this point of literary criticism, what is
now of interest to us is, that to Isaiah on the threshold
of his career Jerusalem had already that supreme ethical
and religious significance, out of his conviction of which
alone he could see her singularly bare and unromantic
site enveloped in the glories and terrors of the Divine
presence.

To this, her religious significance, is due the cardinal
place, which Isaiah claimed for a city so aloof and so
unendowed by nature, in the politics and history of the world. Isaiah was the first to set
Jerusalem on high among the nations; nor
had the conditions for such an exaltation been present
before his day. What gave the mind of Israel the
earliest opportunity of realising the world as a whole was
the advance of the Assyrian Empire and its reduction of
the peoples under its sway.[2] The religion of Israel rose
to the opportunity. The God whom its prophets saw

The Cardinal
Position of
Jerusalem.

---

[1] *E.g.* iv. 5 f. ; v. 30; xxx. 27 f. etc.: see Whitehouse, *Isaiah* (*Century Bible*).
[2] Cf. the present writer's *Book of the Twelve Prophets*, I. ch. iv., 'The
Influence of Assyria upon Prophecy.'

*exalted in righteousness* could not but be supreme over
the novel, world-wide forces which had risen upon history.
His old national name, *Jahweh Ṣebaōth*, meant no more
Jahweh of the armies of Israel, but Lord of the great
powers. Assyria was but the tempest in His hand,[1]
*the rod of His anger and the staff of His indignation.*[2]
When He had done with it, He should *break it on His
own land, and tread it under foot upon His mountains.*[3]
Of these movements of history what could be the centre
but the city where God had set His hearth and His
dwelling, and where He had provided *a refuge for the
afflicted of His people*?[4] Jerusalem was inviolable whether
against the confederacy of Aram and Israel,[5] or against
the Assyrian invasion itself.[6] God was with her,[7] and
would save her by His own arm and in His own way.
This was the conviction which sustained Isaiah in his
predictions that Jerusalem could not be taken. It was
independent of her material strength. But the latter,
along with the City's withdrawn and exalted site, afforded
that earthly basis which every such spiritual conviction
needs for its realisation in history. Without her hills
and her walls Jerusalem could not have existed at all,
nor Isaiah himself have had ground whereon to stand
and answer her enemies. So that even 'Uzziah's and
Ḥezeḳiah's fortifications were part of the preparation
for the prophet and for his vindication of his City as
inviolable.

[1] Isa. xxviii. 2.      [2] x. 5. See Cheyne's reading in *S.B.O.T.*
[3] xiv. 25.      [4] xiv. 32.      [5] vii. 4 ff.
[6] x. 28 ff. (there is no valid objection against the authenticity of verses
33, 34); xiv. 29-32.
[7] vii. 14; viii. 8, 10. The occurrence of the phrase in these last two
verses is denied to Isaiah by Cheyne and others.

In modern criticism there has been a tendency to deny that Isaiah insisted upon the inviolableness of Jerusalem, or predicted her deliverance. He was 'pro-

Did Isaiah predict the Deliverance of Jerusalem? bably content,' it has been maintained, 'to express the general idea of the purgation and renewal of the people.'[1] The reasons for this denial are two: on the one hand, a general theory that Hebrew prophecy before the Exile was wholly judicial and minatory; on the other, that Isaiah himself was purely an ethical teacher, the prophet of faith in the moral might of Jahweh, and not a practical statesman who concerned himself with military issues or the precise political forms in which Israel's future was to be realised; it is later legend which has transformed him into the predictor of exact events, such as the siege and deliverance of Jerusalem. The first of these presuppositions is in itself improbable, and can be sustained only by an arbitrary elimination from the text of the prophets of all passages which contradict it. The second, the attempt to sublimate a great intellect like Isaiah's till it is confined to one consistent line of thought and activity, can be achieved only by grave injustice at once to the genius of the prophet, to the text of his undoubted oracles, and to such evidence as we have of the religious exigencies of his time. That practical statesmanship is not incompatible with a purely spiritual faith, that political sagacity aiming at apparently material ends may exist in the same mind with a lofty idealism which seems to soar above all earthly expediencies, are possibilities which have been frequently realised in history. It is not difficult, there-

---

[1] Guthe, *Jesaia* in the *Religionsgeschichtliche Volksbücher*, 1907; a different opinion from that expressed in his *Das Zukunftsbild des Jesaias*, 1885.

fore, to reconcile Isaiah's doctrine of sheer faith in God
with his insistence on the material security of the City,
or even with a prediction, when at last the Assyrians
closely threatened her, of her deliverance by God Himself. Sion was the dwelling-place of God. He had
designed Jerusalem as a City of Righteousness, and
although she had morally forfeited her destiny, she
remained the only possible site for that reconstruction of
her people which, it is admitted, Isaiah foresaw. He
emphatically predicted the survival of a Remnant, but
the Remnant required a home, and there was no home
left for it outside the walls of Jerusalem. Hence his
insistence that *in Sion* the Lord would lay a foundation-
stone; and hence the probability that the predictions of
her deliverance imputed to him are genuine. Such an
emphasis does not detract from the spiritual character of
the faith which the prophet proclaimed. Common-sense
in face of the practical necessities of the time is not
incompatible with the loftiest idealism. Indeed, there is,
next to faith, no quality on which Isaiah more insists
than on practical wisdom, sagacity in the conduct of
affairs. He reminds the politicians that God also is
*wise; wonderful in counsel and excellent in the quality
which carries things through.*[1] But the things dearest to
the prophet's heart could not be carried through if Jerusalem were taken. It is true that Isaiah appears sometimes to have abandoned his hope for the City, but this
was on ethical grounds. There seem to have been outbursts of folly among the people, even in the hour of
their greatest danger, and at such moments Jerusalem

[1] xxxi. 1-3; xxviii. 29.

must have appeared to Isaiah as not worth saving. These are not impossible inconsistencies. The tendency of the criticism, to which we have alluded, to confine each prophet to one line of temper or ideal, is also on this point astray and misleading. The prophets were *men of like passions with ourselves*—as the story of Elijah might save us from forgetting—capable, that is, of real as well as apparent inconsistencies. If we keep in mind that they were also confronted with swift changes in the temper of their people, and had therefore to apply their principles to emergencies of very opposite kinds, we must judge the criticism, which denies to them more than a single rôle of thought, as both psychologically and historically inaccurate. That freedom which Jeremiah attributed to his God of changing His purpose for a nation when He found the latter change its disposition for good or evil, may also be attributed to the God in whom Isaiah believed through those great variations of political experience and popular temper that characterised the history of Judah in his day.[1]

Of the characteristics of Jerusalem, developed from David's time onward and used or enhanced by Isaiah, we

---

[1] The above paragraph is condensed from a review by the author of Professor Guthe's *Jesaia* and other works, in Dr. Menzies's *Review of Theology and Philosophy* for July 1907. Cf. Budde, *Gesch. der alt-Hebr. Litteratur*, 85. 'Frequently as our prophet's view of the future vacillated during his long career, this [the survival of a Remnant] remained constantly certain to him, and condensed itself particularly towards the end of his activity, into the firm promise of the deliverance of Jerusalem from the Assyrian blockade. It is not only attributed to him in the popular legend about the prophet, chaps. xxxvi. f., but occurs also in the original constituents of xxviii. ff., is clearly expressed in x. 5-15, 24-34 (cf. also xiv. 24-27), and is presupposed in xxii. 14 ; i. 9, 21-26 ; iv. 1-4, as self-evident. It is, therefore, impossible to stamp Isaiah as the prophet of unconditional destruction, strongly as a powerful school of to-day inclines to do so.'

have now only to deal with her relation to David's dynasty. How did Isaiah treat this? Or did he touch upon it at all? The latter question is ren- Isaiah and the Dynasty of David. dered necessary by the criticism of Drs. Hackmann, Cheyne, Volz and Marti. Partly on grounds of language, but largely on the theory that all prophecies of the Messiah are late, they deny to Isaiah those passages [1] in which the advent is promised of a victorious Leader and Ruler of Israel, a scion of the house of David. I have already argued against both their premises and their conclusions,[2] and here need only add that the objections to the authenticity of the passages offered by Dr. Marti in his recent Commentary[3] do not seem to me more cogent than those of the others. It is not conclusive to say that Isaiah laboured for the preservation of only a spiritual community, while the functions ascribed to the promised Prince are purely political; or that Isaiah's expectation of the appearance of God Himself leaves no room for the rise of so imposing a figure. Isaiah laboured for the continuance of the Jewish state as strenuously as for the security of Jerusalem. He lamented the corruption of justice and the imbecility into which the government had fallen under Aḥaz. At the time no need was more urgent than that of a wise and righteous prince; if, as Isaiah predicted, invasion and devastation were imminent, it would not be unnatural to paint him a victorious captain as well. But how was such an one to be found outside the House of David, which in Judah knew no rival, and had already, when almost

---

[1] Ch. ix. 2-7, and xi. 1-8.
[2] Hastings' *Dictionary of the Bible, Isaiah,* ii. 487-89.
[3] In the *Kurzer Hand-Commentar.*

extirpated, proved its powers of recuperation? Thus all the moral and political conditions were present for such prophecies as we are now discussing. He who, following Amos, took the popular idea of a coming day of the Lord and transformed it into a purely ethical conception, was equally capable of choosing some common hope of the advent of a powerful prince, and of giving it those moral elements with which the popular religion was incapable of endowing it. To say that Isaiah 'set his hope on Jahweh and upon a religious community, but not upon the Davidic dynasty and a political dominion,'[1] is to detach the prophet—who was a statesman as well—from those political conditions of his age along which we elsewhere find him working for the future. That Isaiah should invest his hope in the recovery and continuance of the Dynasty need give us therefore no more difficulty than the fact of his insisting upon the survival of the City. We may feel even less objection to the military features in the description of the Prince of the Four Names. The title *Father of Spoil* —if that be indeed the correct rendering—is overborne by the others; whilst the defeat of Israel's enemies, associated with the Prince's advent,[2] is as directly imputed to God as it is in the unquestioned oracles of Isaiah.[3] We need not doubt, therefore, Isaiah's authorship of the Messianic passages.[4]

---

[1] Marti, p. 94 f.     [2] ix. 4.     [3] *E.g.* xiv. 24 f.

[4] To those who argue for the late origin of these passages it may be pointed out that neither of them attributes to the Ideal Prince any of the measures for achieving the establishment of Israel which were required either by the immediately pre-exilic or the post-exilic generations of Israel, *e.g.* the recovery of the people from Exile or the (post-exilic) dream of a world-empire. Guthe (*Jesaia*) admits the compatibility of the programmes of the two passages with Isaiah's other prospects for Judah; Isaiah's ability as a

Thus, then, the fires which David and Solomon kindled in Jerusalem, and which have been smouldering—sometimes, one might say, without betraying any-
thing but smoke—leap into high, bright flame at the powerful breath of Isaiah. The City has found her Prophet: the mind to read her history and proclaim her destiny. Her long labours and obscure growth from Rehoboam to Hezekiah have received their vision and interpretation. Without that history behind him, Isaiah could not have spoken as he did of the character and destiny of Jerusalem. But he was the first to read and proclaim their full meaning; and therefore Jerusalem may be said to be Isaiah's Jerusalem even more than she was David's or Solomon's.

Isaiah the real Maker of Jerusalem.

poet to paint so ideal a figure; and that an ancient parallel for his teaching about the Spirit's endowment of the Prince and the consequent peace of nature exists in Genesis ii., 'which probably goes back upon very ancient models.' But he denies that we have any proof that the passages are from Isaiah himself, and points to their want of connection with the context. On the other hand, Cornill (*Introduction* [5] Eng. Trans.) considers the prophecies conceivable 'as marking the zenith of Isaianic ideas,' but 'an unmixed marvel if they are the production of a post-exilic teacher of the law,' while the origin and development of the Messianic hope is 'an inexplicable enigma if in Isaiah it is confined to chap. i. 26.' See also Whitehouse's *Isaiah* in the *Century Bible*, 151 ff., a full and convincing argument.

# CHAPTER VI

## HEZEKIAH AND SENNACHERIB

### c. 720-685 B.C.

W E have now to follow Isaiah, as with these convictions about the City he carried her—it would
appear almost unaided—through the great crises which
fell upon her during the reign of Ḥezeḳiah.

When Ḥezeḳiah came to the throne remains uncertain,
729, 720 (most probably), or 715; as also when he died,
soon after 701 or about 692, or even as late as
685. But the discussion of the exact year is
not necessary to our present purpose. What is clear is
that Ḥezeḳiah had already reigned some years before
the campaign of Sennacherib in 701; and if a second
attempt of Sennacherib on Jerusalem be found described
in Isaiah xxxvii., and dated as late as 690 or thereabouts,
Ḥezeḳiah was then still on the throne.

In 721 Samaria fell, the Northern Kingdom came to
its end, and its people were carried into exile. Judah
remained the sole trustee of the hope of
Israel, and the Temple was left without a
possible rival. What emphasis this gave to
Isaiah's earlier words about the City and Mount Ṣion
need not be detailed. But it may be noted that in
addition (as some have rightly conjectured) the fall of

148

the Northern State would lead to the immigration of a number of fugitives to Jerusalem, as well as to the occasional pilgrimages of any of the Israelite population who were left in the land of Samaria.

In the same year, 721, Merodak Baladan, chief of a small Chaldean state at the head of the Persian Gulf, became King of Babylon, in revolt from Assyria, Merodak and maintained his position till 710. Some- Baladan. where between these years, therefore, we must place his embassy to Ḥezekiah:[1] many date it immediately after Merodak Baladan's accession,[2] and suppose it to have been connected with revolts against Assyria by the North-Syrian states, Gaza and the Arabian Muṣri. These were subdued by Sargon in 720. Ḥezekiah does not appear to have taken part with them. For nearly a decade no further rising was attempted in Palestine. But the power, or at least the pretensions, of Egypt were growing, and like other Syrian states Judah developed a party sympathetic to her. With the Philistine cities Edom and Moab Ḥezekiah seems to have formed a Isaiah's warning against coalition. It was at least as a warning against reliance on Egypt. such a policy that Isaiah received the Divine command to walk disrobed and barefoot for three years: for Jahweh said, *As my servant Isaiah hath walked disrobed and barefoot three years for a sign and a portent against Egypt and Ethiopia,[3] so shall the kingdom of Assyria lead away the captives of Egypt and the exiles of Ethiopia stripped, barefoot and with buttocks uncovered, to the*

---

[1] Isaiah xxxix. 1-8.

[2] *E.g.* Winckler, *A. T. Untersuchungen,* 146 ff.

[3] Winckler and others take these to have been the Arabian Muṣri and Kush. On this see below, pp. 155 f.

*shame of Egypt. . . . And the inhabitants of this coastland shall say in that day : Lo, such is our expectation, whither we had fled for help to deliver ourselves from the king of Assyria, and we, how shall we escape ?*[1]  The warning was effectual.  Ashdod alone revolted, in 711, and was easily subdued by the Assyrian Tartan.

No further attempt against Assyria was made till the death of Sargon and the accession of Sennacherib in 705.

Revolt from Sennacherib's Reliance on Egypt.

Then, or soon after, a wider coalition of the Palestine states was formed, not wholly on their own strength, but with hope of support from Egypt.  It is significant of the growing reputation of Jerusalem that in this coalition Ḥezeḳiah seems to have played a leading rôle.  The Egyptian party in his Court ruled its politics, and Isaiah's oracles at the time describe their temper.  He has now no word of idols, he implies that the people worship Jahweh ; yet their religion is purely formal, *a precept of men learned by rote.*[2]  They have rejected the spiritual teaching of the prophet ; and are trusting in embassies to Egypt, in her promises, in her gifts of horses and chariots, expected or actually received.[3]  They appear also to have sought assistance in other quarters.  In the narrative of his advance on Jerusalem Sennacherib says that Ḥezeḳiah had reinforced his garrison with Arab mercenaries; and it is the account of an embassy to Arabia which some critics find under the present form of the *Oracle on the Beasts of the South.*[4]

---

[1] Isaiah xx. 1-6: *in the year that Tartan*—the title of the Assyrian commander in chief—*came to Ashdod when Sargon the King of Assyria sent him and he fought against Ashdod and took it.*

[2] xxix. 13 (about 703 B.C.).

[3] xxx. 1 ff., 12, 16 ; xxxi. 1.　　　　　　　　　[4] xxx. 6 ff.

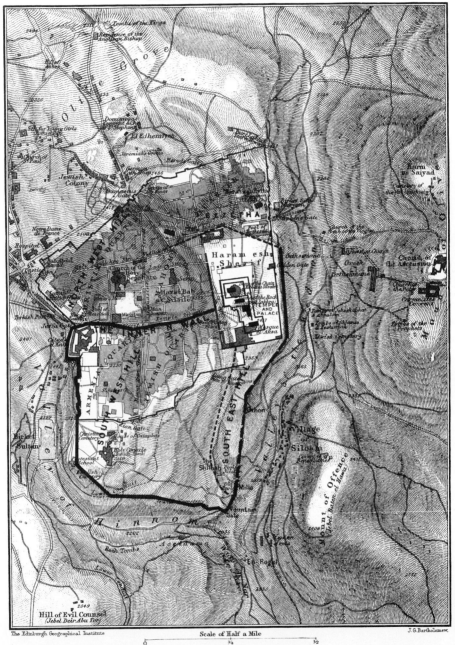

The certain lines of Wall are shown by red lines, and the probable lines of Wall by red dotted lines; but the course of the outer Wall is left blank between the Central Valley and the present citadel as it is quite unknown.

This map has not been printed in the original color. The red line has been replaced by a heavy black line.

To the same crisis we may assign Ḥezeḳiah's work on the fortifications of Jerusalem, though some of this was so extensive that it may have been carried out in the earlier and less strained years of his reign. According to the Deuteronomic editor of the Books of Kings, the annals of the Kings of Judah held an account of a new *pool* and a *conduit* by which Ḥezeḳiah *brought the waters within the City*.[1] The Chronicler says that *Hezeḳiah sealed the issue of the waters of Gîhon, the upper, and directed them down, westwards, to the City of David*.[2] In another passage he explains the King's purpose: *much people were gathered, and they sealed all the springs and the Naḥal*, or *Brook, flowing through the midst of the land, saying, why should the Kings of Assyria come and find much water?*[3] The Chronicler evidently describes the same work as that referred to by the editor of Kings; and there can be no doubt that he understood by it the tunnel which runs under Ophel from the Virgin's Well, or Gihon,[4] and carries the waters of the latter to the Pool of Siloam. Whether he only inferred this to have been the conduit which Ḥezeḳiah made, or found a statement of the fact in the official annals of Judah, does not matter much. The characters of the inscription in the Tunnel cannot be later than the time of Ḥezeḳiah;[5] and the inscription speaks of the *issue*, called by the Chronicler *Gihon the upper*, and of *the pool* mentioned in 2 Kings xx. 20. We may therefore reasonably assume that the Tunnel is *the conduit* by which Ḥezeḳiah *brought*

*Ḥezeḳiah's preparations for Siege: 1. the Tunnel from Gihon.*

---

[1] 2 Kings xx. 20.
[2] 2 Chron. xxxii. 30 (see vol. i. 102).
[3] *Ibid.* 4 (vol. i. 102).
[4] Vol. i. 93 ff.
[5] Vol. i. 95 f.

*the waters into the City of David.*[1]   His purpose was very
practical.   The main difficulty with which besiegers of
Jerusalem have had to contend—and it has sometimes
proved insuperable—is, as we have seen,[2] the waterlessness of the City's surroundings.   Gihon, if not the only
fountain of the neighbourhood, was the principal one, and
sprang just beneath the City walls.   By covering the
aperture of the cave in which it issued, and by leading
the water under the 'City of David' to a reservoir in the
mouth of the central valley between Ophel and the
South-west Hill, Hezekiah deprived the invader of its
use and secured this for himself.   But the formation of
a pool where the Tunnel issues in the central valley
furnishes us with unambiguous evidence of the extension
of Jerusalem over the South-west Hill.   We have seen
that part of this was probably covered with buildings
under David and Solomon, and possibly enclosed with
walls.[3]   But what is only possible under these monarchs
is now seen to be certain under Hezekiah.   His purpose
of securing the waters of Gihon for the besieged by
bringing them to a pool in the central valley could not
have been effected unless he held at the same time the
South-west Hill.[4]   This rises immediately from the Pool
at the end of the Tunnel, and if it had been outside the
City and unfortified, a blockading force could easily with
their darts and stones have prevented the besieged from
using the Pool.   We may confidently assert, then, that
Hezekiah's Jerusalem included the South-west Hill, that

---

[1] In that case the Shiloah mentioned by Isaiah in the reign of Ahaz was
another conduit by which they were still led outside the walls of Ophel ;
perhaps, as we have seen (i. 104), the channel partly cut in the rock and
partly built, which Messrs. Hornstein and Masterman have traced from
Gihon southwards.                           [2] Vol. i. 15, 79 ff., 102 f.
[3] Above, pp. 42 f., 57, 72.               [4] Vol. i. 38, 103, etc.

this was surrounded by walls, and contained some of the lofty buildings which Isaiah describes.

The Chronicler adds that *Hezekiah built* again *all the wall which had been breached, and raised upon it towers, and outside another wall.*[1] If *the wall which had been breached* refers to some definite part of the walls of the City, it can only be the northern wall breached by Joash and repaired by 'Uzziah.[2] In that case Hezekiah further strengthened this most vulnerable part of the fortifications, and *the other wall without* was also on the north, enclosing some new suburb sprung up in the prosperous times of 'Uzziah and Jotham. But the phrase *the wall which had been breached* may bear a more general signification, as of all the fortifications wherever they were in disrepair. Of *the two walls* with *a ditch between them*, mentioned in Isaiah xxii. 11, we have already sufficiently treated.[3]

> 2. The new Walls.

The Chronicler also tells us that Hezekiah *strengthened the Millo*,—perhaps, as we have seen, the dam across the mouth of the Tyropœon, below the Birket el-Hamra, where Dr. Bliss uncovered not merely a wall, but a very broad and well-buttressed stone rampart. A later hand has added the words, *City of David.*[4]

> 3. The Millo.

When in 705 the transfer of the Assyrian throne became the occasion for a general revolt among its vassals, the most formidable of these, Merodak Baladan of Bīt Jakīn on the northern coast of the Persian Gulf, who in 709 had been driven from Babylon, now regained that great capital with all

> Progress of Sennacherib.

---

[1] 2 Chronicles xxxii. 5, reading וַיַּעַל עָלֶיהָ מִגְדָּלוֹת for וַיַּעַל עַל־הַמִּגְדָּלוֹת; the LXX. omits the letters יעל על־ל־ה.

[2] 2 Kings xiv. 13 ; 2 Chronicles xxvi. 9.     [3] Vol. i. 225 f.

[4] 2 Chron. xxxii. 5 ; the LXX. renders *The Millo* by τὸ ἀνάλημμα.

the commercial and religious influence which its possession conferred. He enjoyed besides the support of
Elam. In 703 Sennacherib, on his first campaign, drove
Merodak Baladan out of Babylon, and set' up there, as
'king of Sumer and Akkad,' a vassal of his own, named
Bel-Ibni. Sennacherib's second campaign in 702 was
northwards, towards Media. In 701 he began his third—
against Phœnicia and Palestine.[1]

His swift overthrow of the Phœnicians terrified a
number of the southern states into submission but Judah,

His Palestine
Campaign,
701.

Ashḳelon, 'Eḳron—where the Assyrian vassal,
Padi, had been deposed—and others continued
to resist. The head of this coalition was
Ḥezeḳiah, by virtue alike of the size of his territory, the
strength of his capital, and the repute of his arms, which
had recently overrun Philistia as far as Gaza.[2]   Padi,

---

[1] There are six Assyrian accounts of, or references to, this campaign :—
(1) 'The Rassam Cylinder' of 700 B.C., recording Sennacherib's first three
campaigns. (2) 'The Taylor Cylinder' of 691 (in the British Museum,
reproduced at p. 188 of *Light from the East*, by Rev. C. S. Ball, London,
1899), recording eight campaigns, the account of the first three based on
'The Rassam Cylinder.' (3) 'The Bull Inscription' (on slab I. of the
Kuyunjik Bulls in the British Museum, translated in *Records of the Past*, vii.
57 ff., by Rodwell). (4) Cylinder C. (5) The Neby Yunus Inscription of
Sennacherib (now at Constantinople ; translated in *Records of the Past*, xi.
45 ff., by Budge), with a very brief notice of the campaign of 701, lines 13-15.
(6) The Bas-Relief from Sennacherib's Palace at Nineveh (now in the British
Museum ; reproduced in *Light from the East*, 190 ff.), with the inscription,
'Sennacherib, king of the world, king of Assyria, sate on a throne and
caused the spoil of Lakîsh to pass before him.' Of all these the most useful
to the historian of Ḥezeḳiah's reign is 'The Taylor Cylinder,' along with the
additional information of the Bas-Relief of the Siege of Lakîsh. For the
following pages I have used the various translations, or summaries, of 'The
Taylor Cylinder,' by Talbot, Schrader, Sayce, Ball, Winckler, Weber, Price,
and Rogers.

[2] 2 Kings xviii. 8. Cheyne (*Enc. Bib.* column 2059) seems to me rightly
to date this campaign of Ḥezeḳiah *before* Sennacherib's arrival, as against
Stade and Kittel, who date it later.

upon his deposition—which, perhaps, occurred on this campaign—was delivered into the keeping of Hezekiah. As we have seen,[1] the league against Assyria did not rely solely upon its own forces. Sennacherib tells us that the garrison of Jerusalem had been increased by a number of Arab mercenaries,[2] and among the forces he encountered at Eltekeh, near 'Ekron, were 'bowmen, chariots and horses of the king of Melukhkha,' which used to be considered as Ethiopia, but is now by Assyriologists held to be a state or territory of Northern Arabia.[3] It may be to negotiations before 701 between the South Palestine States and such Arab princes that Isaiah's *Oracle of the Beasts of the South* refers with its description of the passage of an embassy bearing treasure through the terrible desert.[4]

Till recently Old Testament scholars and Assyriologists alike held that Hezekiah and his allies relied also upon help from Egypt, and that in response What was an Egyptian force appeared at the Battle of Musri? Eltekeh. Sennacherib includes among his foes there, along with the king of Melukhkha, 'the king' or 'kings of Musuri';[5] and Musuri was understood to be the

---

[1] Above, p. 150.

[2] Taylor Cylinder, col. iii. line 31. The Assyrian word is *urbi*. Schrader, Sayce, Ball (with a query), Price, Nagel, etc., render it 'Arabians.' Others leave it untranslated.

[3] Taylor Cylinder, col. ii. line 74. Schrader in the second edition of the *K.A.T.*, English translation, 289 f., still took Melukhkha as Ethiopia. In his map to the third edition, Winckler places it south of the Gulf of 'Akaba on the Red Sea coast. Budge (preface to vol. vi., *History of Egypt*, p. xv.) thinks that Winckler's previous hypothesis of Melukhkha = Sinai and Midian has much probability. If Melukhkha be an Arabian state, it is surprising to find chariots mentioned among its forces.

[4] Isaiah xxx. 6 f. See above, p. 150.

[5] Taylor Cyl. ii. 23, 'Kings'; but other readings give ' King'; cf. the Bull Inscr. l. 23.

Hebrew Miṣraim or Egypt, divided at this time under several rulers. But since Dr. Winckler elaborated his arguments for the existence of an Arabian Muṣri, Sennacherib's foes of that name at Elteḳeh are considered by a number of authorities to have been as certainly Arabs as their allies of Melukhkha were. This opinion has been further supported by an appeal to the political condition of Egypt. In the second half of the eighth century, and indeed till the appearance of Taharḳō in 691,[1] Egypt, it is argued, owing to her division, was not capable of interfering in the politics of Palestine. Dr. Winckler indeed holds that wherever the Assyrian inscriptions of that period mention Muṣri they mean an Arabian Muṣri—that, for example, it was not Egypt, as we have always supposed, but an independent Arab state of the same (or a very similar) name which Sargon had met at Raphia in 720, and which conspired with Ashdod and other South Palestine states in the rising against him of 713-711. The present is not the connection in which to discuss exhaustively the question between Dr. Winckler and those who deny that he has proved the existence of an Arabian Muṣri,[2] but the problem and its most probable solution may at least be stated. Dr. Winckler has produced evidence for an Arabian Muṣri which has convinced a number of leading scholars both in Germany and this country,[3]

---

[1] According to W. Max Müller, *Enc. Bib.* col. 1245, this is the proper date for Taharḳo's achievement of the sovereignty of all Egypt. The formerly accepted date, 704, is 'certainly improbable' (*n.* 2). See also the detailed argument for 691 in Prášek, *Sanheribs Feldzüge gegen Juda*, i. 34 ff., 1903.

[2] *E.g.* Dr. Budge, in the preface to vol. vi. of his *History of Egypt*.

[3] The English reader will of course consult Cheyne's 'Mizraim,' § 2*b* and other articles in the *Enc. Bib.*; cf. Hommel, 'Assyria,' in Hastings' *D.B.* i. 187 f.; in German, Guthe, *Gesch.* 219 f.

including some who do not think him justified in all the assertions which he makes of the appearance of this state in the Assyrian and Jewish records.[1] At the same time there are great difficulties, one of which is the existence of two independent states, bordering on each other and bearing names which are practically the same : MSR. We must keep in mind that (as in modern times) Egypt, that is Muṣr or Miṣr (Miṣraim), was not confined to Africa, but included the fringe of Asia as far as the Gulf of 'Aḳaba on the east, and Raphia near Gaza on the north—or just the territory which Dr. Winckler claims for his Arabian Muṣri. It may have been thus that the name Muṣr came to cover the latter and the Arab tribes which inhabited it ;[2] and, if the real Egypt between 745 and 691 was too weak to interfere with Assyrian operations in Palestine, it is quite possible that it is Arab tribes *only* whom the Assyrian inscriptions mean by Muṣur or Muṣuri. But though this is possible, to say that it is certain would be somewhat rash in our present fragmentary knowledge of Egypt at the time. Bokenrenf, the Bocchoris of the Greeks, who reigned at Sais in the last quarter of the century, evinced some power and left a great reputation. Either he or the vigorous Shabako who overcame him about 706[3] may have been strong enough to attract the hopes of the South

---

[1] *E.g.* Nagel, *Der Zug des Sanheribs gegen Jerusalem*, 1902, p. 98, who admits the existence of an Arabian Muṣri and its appearance at Elteḳeh in 701, but argues that the Muṣri of Sargon's inscriptions is Egypt.

[2] Since I made this suggestion, which still seems to me the most probable solution of the Muṣr problem, in *The Expositor* for September 1905, Professor Flinders Petrie has independently made it also.

[3] '706 (?),' W. Max Müller, *Enc. Bib.* col. 1245. Shabako certainly corresponded with Assyria ; two of his seals have been discovered in the royal library at Nineveh.

Palestine cities in their fear before Sennacherib's advance.

In such uncertainty we must leave the question. But it does not much affect our present purpose. What is clear is that on the approach of Sennacherib, Hezekiah and his allies sought and found support from Arab tribes and kingdoms; this is proved from the presence of Arab mercenaries in Jerusalem, and of the forces of the king of Melukhkha at the Battle of Eltekeh. What is not certain is whether Egyptian soldiers were also present at Eltekeh. The name Muṣuri applied by Sennacherib to some of his foes there may mean Egyptians (as all scholars used to think) or Arab tribes from Asiatic Egypt (as the present writer thinks most probable), or, on Dr. Winckler's argument, the forces of an Arabian land, Muṣur, which at the time was independent of Egypt.[1]

*(margin: Hezekiah's Arabian and Egyptian (?) allies.)*

Sennacherib, having settled affairs in Phœnicia, advanced upon Hezekiah and his allies. We need not suppose that his inscriptions give the exact chronological order of his operations. For instance, they report the restoration of Padi immediately after the capture of 'Eḳron, while it is more probable that Hezekiah did not deliver up Padi till after his own submission and payment of tribute. But in the main the inscriptions follow the natural course of such a campaign.[2] Coming down the sea-coast Sennacherib

*(margin: Sennacherib's account of his Advance on Jerusalem.)*

---

[1] If Dr. Winckler be right, that Egypt was too weak to interfere in South Palestine before Taharḳō's accession in 691, or to attract the hopes of Hezekiah and his allies, whose only reliance, when Sennacherib approached to attack them, was on an Arabian Muṣri, then we may have to remove the oracles of Isaiah on Egypt in chaps. xxx. ff. from 705-701 (to which they are generally assigned) to the next decade.

[2] See *Hist. Geog. of the Holy Land*, pp. 235 f.

took first Ashḳelon and its subject cities: Beth-dagon, Joppa, Bene-beraḳ and Azur. Next he turned to meet the southern forces, whom the allies had summoned to their help: the kings of Muṣur and the warriors of the king of Melukhkha; and defeated them at Elteḳeh (unknown but probably on the Philistine plain). Then he took 'Eḳron and was free to turn against the most secure and formidable of the allies, Ḥezeḳiah. Sennacherib appears not to have immediately advanced on Jerusalem. Whether because his victory at Elteḳeh had not finally dispersed the danger of an attack by an army from the south, and he could not therefore afford to lead his main force against Jerusalem; or because, like the Seleucid generals and Vespasian, he appreciated the strength of Jerusalem and the waterlessness of her surroundings, so dangerous to all her besiegers, and knew that he must not hope to take her before making sure of the rest of the land, he began with the latter. ' But Ḥezeḳiah of Jerusalem, who had not submitted to me, forty-six of his walled towns, numberless forts and small places in their neighbourhood I invested and took by means of battering-rams and the assault of scaling-ladders (? siege towers), the attack of foot-soldiers, mines, breaches and . . .[1] Two hundred thousand one hundred and fifty, great and small, men and women, horses, mules, asses, camels, oxen and sheep without number I carried off from them and counted as spoil.'[2] While these operations proceeded,[3] part of the Assyrian army blockaded

---

[1] So after Ball and Nagel, the former of whom renders the last three terms, 'mines, bills and axes': Taylor Cyl. iii. 11-17.        [2] *Id.* 17-20.

[3] Because later, when Ḥezeḳiah submitted, we find Sennacherib still investing Lakîsh, doubtless one of the Judæan towns, since Ḥezeḳiah had already overrun Philistia up to Gaza.

Jerusalem. ' Himself I shut up like a bird in a cage in Jerusalem his royal city. I raised forts about him and the exits of (*or* whatever came forth from) the chief gate of his city I barred. His towns which I spoiled I severed from his territory and gave them to Mitinti, king of Ashdod, Padi, king of 'Ekron, and Silbil, king of Gaza ; so I diminished his territory.'[1] The blockade of Jerusalem brought Hezekiah to terms. ' Himself the fear of my august Lordship overpowered. The Arabians and his faithful ones, whom he had brought in for the defence of Jerusalem his royal city, fell away.[2] Along with 30 talents of gold and 800 of silver, precious stones, carbuncles, *kassû* stones, great pieces of lapis lazuli, ivory thrones, elephant hides [and] tusks, *ushu* wood, boxwood, all sorts of things, a huge treasure, and his own daughters, the women-folk of his palace, men and women singers he brought after me to Nineveh the city of my Lordship ; and for the payment of the tribute and to do homage, he despatched his envoy.'[3]

This account asserts or implies the following: the conquest of Judah, with the overthrow of all the prin-

Judah overrun, Jerusalem blockaded, but not taken.

cipal cities except Jerusalem, and the captivity of a large portion of the country population ; the blockade of Jerusalem, but neither its siege[4] nor its capture ; the payment by Hezekiah of a costly tribute ; and the departure of Senna-

---

[1] Taylor Cyl. 20-26, after Schrader and Ball.

[2] So Ball and Nagel ; cf. Delitzsch, *Assyr. Handwörterbuch*, 171*a*. Others translate differently.

[3] Taylor Cyl. iii. 29-41 : after Ball and Schrader.

[4] The inscription does not use the usual word for siege, but a word that probably means 'blockade': cf. Prášek, *Sanheribs Feldzüge gegen Juda*, 21 ; in the *Mitteilungen der Vorderasiatischen Gesellschaft*, 1903, 4. Cf. Winckler, *A. T. Untersuchungen*, 31 (1892).

cherib to Nineveh, before even the tribute could be paid. The Bas-Relief in the British Museum proves in addition that among the cities taken and spoiled by Sennacherib was Lakîsh. For the reason of Sennacherib's swift return to Nineveh we cannot be at a loss. It must have been news of the revolt of his vassal Bel-Ibni in Babylon, for Sennacherib's next campaign in 700 was directed against this rebel.

There is no doubt that the Biblical parallel to Sennacherib's record of his suddenly ended campaign in Southern Palestine is found in 2 Kings xviii. 13-16: *In the fourteenth year of king Ḥizḳiyah Sanherîb, king of Ashshûr, came up against all the fortified cities of Judah and took them; and Ḥizḳiyah, king of Judah, sent to the king of Ashshûr to Lakîsh saying: I have sinned; turn from against me, what thou layest upon me I will bear; and the king of Ashshûr laid upon Ḥizḳiyah, king of Judah, 300 talents of silver and 30 talents of gold. And Ḥizḳiyah gave up all the silver, found in the House of Jahweh and in the treasuries of the Palace. At that time Ḥizḳiyah stripped the doors of the Temple of Jahweh and the pillars which Ḥizḳiyah (?), king of Judah had overlaid and gave it to the king of Ashshûr.* The first verse of this passage is found in Isaiah xxxvi. 1, the rest are omitted. The independence of the passage from what follows it will be shown below.

*The Biblical Parallels: 1. Narrative.*

To the same campaign of Sennacherib in 701 we may reasonably refer the long discourse by Isaiah, now placed as a preface to his prophecies, ch. i. 2-26; but it is right to mention that some refer this to the previous invasion of Judah by Aram and Israel in 734. Verses 7-9 run as follows:—

*2. Prophecy.*

> *Your land is a waste, your cities are burned with fire,*
> *Your soil before you strangers devour it*
> (*It is waste as the overthrow of Sodom*).[1]
> *The daughter of Ṣion is left like a hut in a vineyard,*
> *Like a lodge in a garden of cucumbers,*
> *Like a city beleaguered.*[2]
> *Had Jahweh of hosts not left us a remnant,*
> *Almost as Sodom had we been,*
> *To Gomorrah had been levelled.*

To the same year of 701 is usually assigned chap. xxii.
1-14. It seems hardly possible to take this passage as a
unity.[3] Owing to the corruption of the text it is difficult,
if not impossible, to detect the seam between the two
pieces: hence the diverse modern divisions of the passage. But not only are the opening verses (1-5 at least)
in one rhythm, and the closing (11*b*-14) in another; they
do not appear to describe the same phase of the fickle
temper of the City. Verses 1-2*a* exhibit the people on

---

[1] So Ewald, Lagarde, Cheyne, and others, reading סדם for the unmeaning
זרים. The clause, however, is taken by some as a later insertion, on the
ground that it breaks into the couplets of the verse-form.

[2] This clause is strange after the previous comparisons, unless Isaiah spoke
it before the actual blockade of Jerusalem.

[3] Formerly the universal opinion (shared by the present writer, *Expositor's
Bible*, Isaiah i.-xxxix.), and still held by Prof. Skinner (*Camb. Bible*, 162 ff.);
cf. Robertson Smith, *Prophets*, 1st ed., 346 f. Duhm divides the passages into
two oracles of Isaiah: (*a*) 1-7, on an unknown occasion which moved the
City to mirth, which the prophet answers by a vision of destruction; (*b*) 8-14,
the prophet's rebuke of the City's trust in its preparations against a siege and
its subsequent desperate levity. Marti distinguishes three pieces: (*a*) 1-5, in
the Ḳinah measure: to the City, in an exultant mood, Isaiah announces his
vision of the overthrow of its leaders without resistance; (*b*) 6-11, the work
of a later writer, because of the mention of Elam, which cannot have been
among the Assyrian forces in 701; (*c*) 12-14, Isaiah's, from the same occasion
as 1-5, the thoughtless joy of the citizens at the withdrawal of the Assyrians
in 701. Cheyne (*S.B.O.T.* p. 163: see further *Crit. Bibl.*) distinguishes 1-5
and 6-14, both on the Assyrian withdrawal, the latter describing the rebound
of the citizens from despair to hope. He thinks something has fallen out
from the beginning of the second piece. All three take vs. 9*b*-11*a* as a
gloss.

the housetops in a joyous celebration, to which the prophet opposes, in 2*b*-5, his vision of an imminent flight of the garrison merging into a picture of *a day of the Lord*.   On the other hand, verses 8-14[1] rebuke the people for trusting in their preparations for a siege instead of in God ; and then, as if even that material confidence had given way, depicts them, while God calls them to repentance, plunging into a desperate self-indulgence— *for to-morrow we die*.   This is a very different mood from that pictured in the opening verses.   Let us take verses 11-14 first.   Professors Cheyne, Skinner and Marti refer this oracle to the people's relief upon the sudden withdrawal of the Assyrians : ' in the rebound from despair to hope the citizens of Jerusalem give expression to the wildest joy.'[2]   But this does not suit the cry, *for to-morrow we die*.   These words compel us to refer the passage to a panic, when the people imagined that their end was near, and instead of penitence gave way to wild excesses.   Now the occasion of this panic may have been that alluded to in Sennacherib's statement : during the blockade of the City, Hezekiah's ' Arab mercenaries and his faithful ones ' deserted.   At an earlier moment, when no fear of their end possessed the citizens, but they had gone up to the housetops in great joy, Isaiah appears to have anticipated some such desertion of their cause, even by the rulers themselves : verses 1-3 :—

> *What aileth thee now, thou art up*
> *All to the housetops ?*
> *O full of uproar, city of tumult,*
> *Boisterous town.*

---

[1] Perhaps this passage begins earlier ; for verses 12 f. see p. 137.
[2] Cheyne, *S.B.O.T.*, ' Isaiah,' p. 163.

> *Thy slain are not slain with the sword,*
> *Nor fallen in battle.*
> *Thy rulers are fled altogether.*
>
> .     .     .     .     .[1]
>
> *Thy strong ones have yielded[2] together,*
> *Afar have they hurried.*

An alternative is to take the exultation of the people
on the housetops as happening on the departure of the
Assyrians, while the prophet predicts the certain return
of the latter.   But this is less likely, for verses 8-9*a*
go on to describe hasty preparations *before* a siege,
*when He had removed the screen of Judah*: that is, when
the frontier fortresses strengthened by Ḥezeḳiah and
previous kings as screens to the capital had already
been captured by Sennacherib.   It is therefore more
reasonable to take the exultation upon the housetops as
happening upon the arrival of some addition to the
strength of Jerusalem—possibly the entry of the Arabian
mercenaries ; while, as we have seen, the different mood
of the people, described in verses 11-14, emerged before
rather than after the blockade was lifted, and possibly
on the desertion of these same hirelings along with a
number of the native Jews.

So much, then, at least happened in 701, and is covered
by Sennacherib's inscription and the passages of narrative
and prophecy we have quoted.   Ḥezeḳiah
strengthened his garrison with a number of
Arab mercenaries.   Sennacherib, having devastated Judah, blockaded Jerusalem.   The blockade
was lifted, and Ḥezeḳiah sent tribute to Sennacherib

*Summary of
Events in
these pas-
sages.*

---

[1] The text of this line is uncertain : as it stands it reads, *Without the bow
they are bound.*   Perhaps for מקשת we should read מקשר.

[2] For אסרו, wrongly repeated from the previous line, read סְרוּ.

either at Lakîsh or at Nineveh, whither the Assyrian king implies that he suddenly returned.

The short Biblical summary of these proceedings[1] is, by the style of it, evidently drawn from the annals of Judah. But there immediately follow two further accounts of Assyrian expeditions against Jerusalem,[2] which, besides differently spelling the name Hezekiah, are couched not in the annalist's but in a narrative style, and are usually taken to be from that class of prophets' biographies upon which the compiler of the Books of Kings has so largely drawn.[3] These two narratives contain obvious editorial additions.[4] The compiler certainly did not finish his work before the Exile, or more exactly before the middle of the sixth century, and to him may be assigned the possibly late features which the language of the two accounts exhibits.[5] The foreshortening of the period

*Two further Narratives: their historical value.*

---

[1] 2 Kings xviii. 13-16 (verse 13 is parallel to Isaiah xxxvi. 1).

[2] (a) 2 Kings xviii. 17-xix. 8 parallel with Isa. xxxvi. 2-xxxvii. 8; (b) 2 Kings xix. 9-37 parallel with Isa. xxxvii. 9-38.

[3] As *e.g.* in the cases of Elijah and Elisha.

[4] *E.g.* xviii. 17: *the Tartan and the Rabsaris*, in addition to the Rabshakeh; for verses 17-19 imply the presence only of the Rabshakeh, cf. xix. 8; xix. 2, 20, *son of Amos*, cf. Kautzsch *in loco*; xix. 10: *Thus shall ye speak to H. King of Judah, saying* (Kautzsch).

[5] For example, the name *Jewish* (instead of Hebrew) for the language of the people of Jerusalem (2 Kings xviii. 26, 28), not elsewhere used in the O.T. except in the post-exilic Neh. xiii. 24, and objected to on the ground that it could not have come into use so soon after the fall of Samaria and the sole survival of Judah as the end of the eighth or beginning of the seventh century. Nagel argues that its use was possible after 681, subsequent to which year he places the two accounts because of Sennacherib's death. Other expressions alleged to be late are the Deuteronomic phrases in Hezekiah's prayer, xix. 15 ff.; the words שארית and פלטה, xix. 31, which Cheyne calls post-Isaian, but this is doubtful (see Nagel's answer); and the expressions *for My sake*, and *for the sake of My servant David* (so Kuenen and others).

between Sennacherib's return from Palestine and his murder in 681 may also be due to the distance of the compiler from these events.[1]   More precarious evidence of the compiler's alteration of his materials is found by some in the religious temper of the two accounts.   The monotheism especially of Ḥezeḳiah's prayer is said to be too pure for a date before Deuteronomy and the 'Second Isaiah';[2] while the representation of Isaiah as a mediator between God and man is held to be a conception of the prophetic office not formed till later.   This line of argument is very uncertain.   Isaiah, during his long career and by the vindication of several of his predictions, may well have achieved an authority sufficient to create among his contemporaries the conception of him prevailing in these narratives.   Again, Ḥezeḳiah's expectation of help from Egypt, and the Assyrian assertion that he will be disappointed, are not impossible (as some have alleged) before Tirhaḳah's conquest of Egypt in 691 ; but are consistent with Isaiah's own oracles so generally assigned to 705-701.   On the other hand, many of the details in the two accounts can hardly be the invention of a late compiler.   The case for the credibility of the narratives may have been overstated,[3] but their graphic description is most adequately explained as the work of a contemporary, if not of an eye-witness.   The two accounts, then, owe their present form, including some overlapping and probably some errors not always possible to distinguish, to their late

[1]  2 Kings xix. 36, 37 : so Kuenen.
[2]  So Meinhold and others.
[3]  As by Nagel in his sections on ' The Credibility of the Hebrew Accounts ' in *Der Zug des Sanheribs gegen Jerusalem.*

compilation; but the attempt to prove them substantially unsound cannot be maintained.[1]

The contents of these two accounts are as follows. The First (2 Kings xviii. 17-xix. 8)[2] relates that the Assyrian Rabshakeh, or Chief Minister, was sent by Sennacherib from Lakîsh with an army to Jerusalem, to demand her surrender; The Contents of the two Narratives. but Isaiah emboldened Hezekiah to defiance by predicting that the king of Assyria would hear a rumour, return to his own land, and there perish by the sword. So the Rabshakeh rejoined his master at Libnah. The Second (2 Kings xix. 9-37)[3] relates that Sennacherib, hearing that Tirhakah[4] of Egypt was advancing, sent a letter to Hezekiah once more demanding the surrender of Jerusalem; Hezekiah spread the letter with prayer before God; Isaiah told him that the Assyrian was overruled by God and would return without coming near Jerusalem; an angel smote of the Assyrians 185,000 in a single night; Sennacherib returned to Nineveh and was murdered by his sons in the temple of Nisroch.[5]

Two serious questions are raised by these similar yet

[1] Prašek (*op. cit.* 25 ff.) divides the first into a short summary from the annals of Judah, 2 Kings xviii. 17, 18, xix. 8, of historical value, and a prophetic narrative of the time of the Exile; but so definite a division cannot be pronounced successful. The oracles attributed to Isaiah in xix. 21-34 have been doubted. They vary in rhythm, and some of the verses contain the later features noted above. But even if parts, or all, of them be omitted, a substantial narrative remains.

[2] Parallel with Isaiah xxxvi. 2-xxxvii. 8.

[3] Parallel with Isaiah xxxvii. 9-38.     [4] The Hebrew form of Taharḳō.

[5] The line between the two accounts is very sharp. 2 Kings xix. 8 tells of the return of the Rabshakeh from Jerusalem to Sennacherib at Libnah. But the subject of the verb, *and he heard*, in verse 9, is not the Rabshakeh but the king. With this verse, then, a new narrative obviously begins. The verses xix. 35-37 describing the visitation on the Assyrian army, the return of Sennacherib and his murder, are assigned by some to the first account.

differing narratives of expeditions to Jerusalem from
The Questions Sennacherib.   Are they parallel versions of
they raise. one and the same expedition, or the accounts
of two separate expeditions?   And do they refer to the
events of 701, as given by Sennacherib's inscription and
the extract from the annals of Judah, or to some later
campaign of Sennacherib in Palestine?   To both these
questions diametrically opposite answers have been given
with equal confidence.   The evidence is incomplete, and
as it stands somewhat conflicting.   We can reach only
probable answers—and even when most probable not
entirely harmonious.

The recent tendency of criticism[1] has been to take
the narratives as parallel versions of the same course of
Are they          events in 701.   Stress is laid upon their
parallel
Versions of      common elements: the despatch of a mission
the same
Expedition in    by Sennacherib to demand the surrender of
701?             Jerusalem; the similarity of the speech of
the Rabshakeh in the First to the letter given in the
Second; Hezekiah's submission of both speech and letter
to God; the intervention in both cases of Isaiah and his
encouragement of Hezekiah to defy Sennacherib; while
the discrepancies between the two narratives are held to
be 'perhaps not greater than between parallel accounts
in the four gospels.'[2]   This is by no means conclusive.
Other explanations of the similarities are, to say the least,
equally probable.   For in part these may be due to the
borrowing by one account of the exact terms of the other;[3]

---

[1] Since Stade's analysis of the narratives in *Z.A.T.W.* vi. 1886.   See
Skinner, *Kings*, 388, where the argument is maintained against the new
hypothesis of Winckler; Whitehouse, *Isaiah*, 353.

[2] Skinner, *Isaiah, i.-xxxix.* 262.

[3] For example, the list of towns conquered by Assyria.

and still more they may have arisen from the analogies between two similar situations in which the principal actors were the same. If Sennacherib sent two different missions to demand the surrender of Jerusalem, it is probable that he would repeat himself, nor is it less likely that Ḥezekiah and Isaiah would return him similar replies. On the other hand, the discrepancies between the two narratives are greater than the advo- *or the Accounts of two successive Expeditions?* cates of their parallelism allow; and more consistent with the explanation which refers the narratives to two successive missions. In the Second there is no allusion to the fall of Samaria, which is explicable if this narrative deals with events later than the First. In the Second, Sennacherib no longer taunts Ḥezekiah with the futility of reliance on Egypt; again a natural omission if, as the Second narrative states, Taharḳō was at last able to march into Palestine. There is also a difference in the positions assigned to Sennacherib by the two narratives. In the First he is in Judah, not far from Jerusalem, to which he is able to send a corps detached from his great host; in the Second he is not near, and Isaiah asserts he will not come near.[1] There is also a great difference between the panic ascribed to Ḥezekiah in the First narrative, and his calm demeanour in the Second; the change is naturally explained, both if we assume that Ḥezekiah had already passed through the discipline described in the first narrative, and if we suppose (as we have just seen reason to do) that on the second occasion the Assyrians were at a much greater distance from the capital. In the First

---

[1] Prašek's contention (*op. cit.* 32, 37) that the letter of Sennacherib in the Second narrative implies that Jerusalem was besieged by the Assyrians and hard pressed, is unfounded ; on the contrary, Winckler, *A. T. Unters.*, 42.

narrative Ḥezeḳiah sends a formal embassy to Isaiah; in the Second Isaiah sends of his own accord to Ḥezeḳiah. And finally, while, in the First, Isaiah announces that Sennacherib's departure from Palestine will be due to a rumour, in the Second this is not implied, but the cause of his departure is a pestilence.[1]

While, then, the similarities in the two narratives are explicable on other grounds than that they are parallel

They are the accounts of two Assyrian Expeditions.

versions of the same expedition, their differences are less consistent with such a theory than they are with the interpretation of the two narratives as the accounts of successive missions from Sennacherib to Jerusalem. We take it, that Sennacherib sent twice to Jerusalem to demand her surrender, and twice was defied by Ḥezeḳiah under the influence of her great prophet.[2]

This leads to our other question: Did both of these separate missions sent by Sennacherib to Jerusalem take

Were there two Campaigns of Sennacherib in Palestine?

place in 701; or is the first alone to be assigned to that year, and the second to another campaign of Sennacherib some years later? The hypothesis that Isaiah xxxvi.-xxxvii. records the results of two Assyrian invasions of Palestine was advanced by British scholars from a comparatively early date,[3] but met with opposition,[4] and was generally

---

[1] There is no sufficient reason for assigning the story of the pestilence to the first narrative.

[2] Even some of the adherents of the theory of parallelism between the two narratives admit that the latter 'allow themselves' to be read as a continuous whole.

[3] Hincks, followed for a time by Cheyne and Schrader, dated the first in Sargon's campaign of 711, the second in Sennacherib's of 701. Sir Henry Rawlinson distinguished between a first successful campaign of Sennacherib, and a later unsuccessful one by the same monarch (G. Rawlinson's *Herodotus*, 1862).   [4] From Schrader.

supposed to be disproved on the grounds that there is no room in the Biblical records for a second campaign, and no word about it in the Assyrian annals.[1]

Recently, however, additional evidence has appeared which, though not conclusive, points towards the fact of a second Palestine campaign by Sennacherib some years later than that of 701. First of all we have an allusion in the annals of Asarḥaddon to a campaign by Sennacherib in Northern Arabia.[2] As Asarḥaddon repeated this expedition of his predecessor and continued its probable purpose in the invasion of Egypt, it was argued that Sennacherib himself had advanced from his Arabian conquests at least as far as the frontier of Egypt; and appeal was made to the Egyptian tradition of an Assyrian overthrow and retreat, reported by Herodotus,[3] which calls Sennacherib 'King of the Arabians and Assyrians,' a title that implies his Arabian conquests. On this ground alone Dr. Winckler has argued for a second appearance of Sennacherib in Palestine, after 690, of which the Biblical account is found in the Second of the narratives which we have been discussing;[4] and his argument has received considerable support.[5] But,

*Assyrian evidence for a second Palestine Campaign by Sennacherib.*

---

[1] Cheyne, *Intro. to the Book of Isaiah*, 234 f. ; Rogers, *Hist. of Babyl. and Assyria*, ii. 203 *n.* 4. Cf. Meinhold, *Jesaia u. seine Zeit*, ii. ff.

[2] In which he took the fortress of Adumu, variously identified with Petra of Edom, and with Dumât in the Jôf (the Dumata of Pliny): cf. Duma, Isaiah xxi. 11. [3] ii. 141.

[4] 2 Kings xix. 8-37 ; Winckler, *Alt. Or. Untersuchungen*, 1889, especially p. 259; *A. T. Untersuchungen* (1895), 41 ff. ; *K.A.T.*(3), 1902, 272 f.

[5] Hommel, Hastings' *D.B.* i. 188 ; Benzinger, *Die Bücher der Könige* ; Guthe, *Gesch.*, 221 ; Budge (*Hist. of Egypt*, vi. 141 f.). Budge (*Hist. of Egypt*, vi. 149) says that the compiler of the Books of Kings ' seems to have confused ' two sieges of Jerusalem, one when Shabataka was king of Egypt, and one when Taharḳô was king.

secondly, Father Scheil has discovered a fragment of Sennacherib's own annals,[1] which implies that between 691 and 689, in consequence of a revolt of his western vassals encouraged by the activity of Taharḳō, Sennacherib undertook a campaign westwards; unfortunately the fragment does not carry his progress farther than Northern Arabia.

In this inconclusive state of the Assyrian evidence it may be pointed out how far the hypothesis of a second Its Harmony with the Biblical Narratives. campaign by Sennacherib to the South suits the Biblical record. Before Father Scheil's discovery this was supposed to have taken place in the eighties of the seventh century.[2] But we now know that the campaign, whether or not it extended to Palestine, took place between 691 and 689, which would bring it within the possible extent of Ḥezeḳiah's reign and Isaiah's career. By that time, too, Taharḳō had certainly become lord of all Egypt, the most probable date being 691.[3] With all this are consistent the introduction of his name at the beginning of our Second narrative,[4] and the omission from Sennacherib's letter of the emphasis which the Rabshaḳeh's speech had laid upon the futility of Judah's reliance on Egypt. Such reliance was not futile now that Taharḳō was advancing. And finally, if the Second narrative refers to a campaign of Sennacherib in 690 or 689, we can more easily understand why there was included in it a notice of Sennacherib's murder in 681, than if it refers to the campaign of 701, which was distant twenty years from that murder.

---

[1] Announced in the *Orient. Litteraturzeitung* for 1904, p. 2. Cf. Weber, *Sanherib*, Heft 3 of *Der Alte Orient*, 1905.  [2] Winckler, *A. T. Unters.*, 36 f.  [3] See above, p. 156 *n.* 1.  [4] 2 Kings xix. 9.

On the present evidence, then, imperfect though it is, the theory seems most probable that the First narrative describes what happened in 701, either after, Summary of or (alternatively) along with, Hezekiah's sub- the Probable<br>Course of mission and the raising of the Assyrian Events. blockade. Having received Hezekiah's tribute, Sennacherib sent by his Rabshakeh a fresh and insolent summons for the surrender of Jerusalem ; the despairing king was inspired by Isaiah to defy it, and, in accordance with the prophet's foresight, Sennacherib was hastily summoned from Palestine by news of Bel-Ibni's revolt in Babylon. Alternatively, and some will feel more probabiy, the mission of the Rabshakeh was simultaneous with the blockade of the City, which was raised in consequence of the news from Babylon. The Second narrative, on the other hand, describes what happened some years later, in 690 or 689, when Taharkō had gained command of all Egypt, and Sennacherib was marching to meet him, after some conquests in Northern Arabia. In this campaign the Assyrian did not come near Jerusalem, but sent a letter demanding her surrender. Hezekiah received it with calmness, and Isaiah defied its pretensions in the name of his God. The Assyrian army, before it met the Egyptians, was visited by a pestilence, and Sennacherib again hastily retreated to his own land. Eight or nine years later, in 681, he was murdered in Nineveh. The compiler of Kings, working more than a century afterwards, has compressed the two narratives into one of the first campaign in 701. It is his preservation of the name of Tirhakah, who did not come to power over Egypt till 691, that enables us to separate the Second narrative and assign its different story to that second southern campaign of Sennacherib, which the Assyrian evidence gives us some ground to suppose took place between 691 and 689.

Therefore, certainly once, and probably twice, Jerusalem was delivered from capture by the Assyrians, and her

Vindication of the Unique Holiness of Șion,

people were saved from the deportation and destruction which had overtaken the northern tribes of Israel in 721. A remnant remained in their own uncaptured City, and the altar and dwelling-place of Jahweh were inviolate. As the Assyrians had overrun the rest of Judah, more or less discrediting the influence, if not actually destroying the fabric, of every other shrine at which Jahweh was worshipped, we can appreciate the increased sacredness which the deliverance conferred upon Jerusalem. Mount Șion and the Temple stood at last alone: the one inviolable sanctuary of the One True God. Isaiah's predictions were vindicated by a glorious Fact in which not the

and of Isaiah's Interpretation of her History.

arms nor the powers of men were manifest, but only the Hand of God for the salvation of His people. We must not, however, forget the previous history of the City and its religious and moral meaning, upon which Isaiah had ventured his predictions of her security. To all that history and its prophetic interpretation the Deliverance of Jerusalem came as God's own signature. We are prone to consider the great event by itself, and to trace to it alone the subsequent prestige of the City. But apart from the previous history and prophecy, the Deliverance would have been as a seal without any document accompanying it.

In estimating the effect of all this upon the destiny

of Jerusalem, we must distinguish the various powers of imagination and conscience which it roused among her mixed and fickle people. Of such powers there were at least three: the conscience of the executive statesmen, the popular imagination, and the more spiritual convictions of the prophets themselves.

*The Threefold Effects of all this:*

As to the first, we find explicit statements in the Second Book of Kings. The Deuteronomic editor of that book attributes to King Ḥezeḳiah a number of religious reforms, some of which are sympathetic with, while others were actually required by, the earlier teaching of the great prophet.[1] Ḥezeḳiah (we are told) *brake in pieces the bronze serpent, which Moses had made, for unto those days were Israel offering to it the smoke of sacrifice,*[2] *and it was called Neḥushtan.* There can be no doubt about the fact of this particular reform, and we may safely assume that it implies the removal, or at least the attempt to remove, all the idolatries against which Isaiah had inveighed. Isaiah's indictment of the idols and the sacred trees had been so absolute, that it is hard to believe that Ḥezeḳiah postponed their abolition to so late a date in his reign as after 701. But the acceptance which has been granted to the record of this reform has been denied to the clause which precedes it—*he removed the high places and brake the pillars and cut down the Ashērôth*[3]—on the grounds that the grammatical form of the clause is late, that there is no evidence of Isaiah's hostility to the three objects which it mentions, and that

*1. Upon the Statesmen; Religious Reforms.*

---

[1] 1 Kings xviii. 4.   [2] E. V. *incense.*
[3] Plural, after the LXX.

these were still in use at the beginning of Josiah's reign. The question is difficult, and an answer perhaps not now attainable. But, because the Book of Deuteronomy, which contains explicit laws against the high places, the pillars and the Asherôth, is certainly compiled from earlier sources, and because such written laws were (as we have seen in other cases) connected with specific acts of reform, it is quite possible that Hezekiah took measures for the abolition of all those three institutions of the earlier religion of Israel. That his reforms were of a drastic character [1] is proved by the violence of the reaction against them under Manasseh. Nor is it a conclusive objection to the introduction of those particulars in the list of Hezekiah's reforms, that Isaiah does not enforce them by name. In such a movement there are always some details achieved, which its spiritual leaders have not actually defined in their statement of its principles. We have seen the faint beginnings of a tendency towards the centralisation of the worship of Judah nearly a century before Isaiah.[2] And, indeed, so pure a faith as he urged upon his people involved such

Possible attempts to centralise the Worship.

a centralisation as one of its most practical consequences. To us it may seem paradoxical that the doctrine of the One God should carry as its corollary the doctrine of the One Sanctuary : *neither in this mountain nor in Jerusalem shall ye worship the Father : the hour now is, when the true worshippers shall worship the Father in spirit and in truth.* But in

---

[1] ' Die erste Durchführung der Forderungen des Jahvismus ' ; ' eine völlige Durchführung des Jahvismus in seiner streng monotheistischen Bedeutung mit teilweiser Beseitigung anderer Kulte.' Winckler, *K.A.T.*[(3)] 271 ; cf. Guthe, *Gesch.* 223.

[2] Above, pp. 90 f., 111 f., 130, 133 f., 137 f., 140 f., 174.

the religious circumstances of that time there was indeed
no greater safeguard of monotheism than the concentration of the national worship on the Temple.   Most of the
rural shrines of Jahweh had been shrines of local gods,
and in their ritual, as in their worshippers' conceptions
of the godhead, must have perpetuated the influences of
the ancient polytheism.   In name belonging to Jahweh,
in reality they were devoted to the Baalim—*according to
the number of thy cities are thy gods, O Judah !*[1]   The
worship of *one Jahweh*, spiritual and not idolatrous,
was practicable only in the Temple.   Again, the rural
sanctuaries had all been violated by the Assyrian invasion of 701 ; and further, the smallness of the Israelite
territory since the collapse of the Northern Kingdom in
721 and the exile of its people, rendered possible the
periodical assembly at Jerusalem of all the worshippers
of Jahweh.   Even, therefore, if Hezekiah did not actually
succeed in centralising the national cult in the capital,
there is no reason to doubt that he attempted such a
policy.   The political and religious motives for it were
all present before the end of his reign.   It need not have
been started at the same time as the measures for removing the idols.   Centralisation may have first suggested
itself when the suppression of idolatry was found to be
impossible so long as the rural sanctuaries remained; and
it was, no doubt, greatly facilitated by the violation of
these sanctuaries in 701, and by the vindication of the
unique inviolableness of Jerusalem.   The *removal of the
high places* by Hezekiah is therefore more probable after
than before that date.[2]

[1] Jer. xi. 13.

[2] Nevertheless we find it asserted in the speech of the Rabshakeh in the first
narrative which, as we have seen, refers to 701: Isa. xxxvi. 7; 2 Kings xviii. 22.

Of the effect of the Deliverance of Jerusalem on the popular imagination we can have no doubt.   For a century Assyria had been the terror of the peoples of Palestine.   The citizens of Jerusalem heard Isaiah himself describe, in periods which marched like their subject, the progress of the monstrous hosts of the North: their unbroken ranks, their pitiless and irresistible advance.   Further and further south had this pressed, overwhelming Northern Israel, spreading around Judah, and rising upon the land to the very walls of Jerusalem.   From these the citizens at last saw with their own eyes the predicted and long-imagined forms of their terror, knowing that behind lay exile and destruction for the people of God.   Then suddenly the Assyrian army vanished and Jerusalem was left the one unviolated fortress on the long, ruin-strewn path of the conqueror.   We need not wait for answers to the difficult questions of the date and value of the Scriptures which celebrate the Deliverance.   The bare facts, about which there is no doubt, convince us of their effects in the temper of the Jewish people.   Upon minds too coarse to appreciate Isaiah's reading of the moral vocation and destiny of their City, her signal relief (or reliefs) from so invincible a foe, must have made a profound impression.   The Jews had seen the rest of the sacred territory violated, and a great proportion of its population carried into exile.   Here alone the foe had been kept back.   Alone the Temple remained secure. From this time, therefore, rose the belief, which seventy years later we find hardened into a dogma, that Jerusalem was inviolable. No article of religion could have been more popular.

2. Upon the Popular Imagination.

Dogma of the Inviolable-ness of Jerusalem.

Among the mass of the citizens, undoubtedly increased by the devastation of the rest of the country, it must have spread with rapidity; and the measures for centralising the national worship in the Temple, in so far as they were successful, can only have assisted its propagation.

But we must not suppose that such a belief was accepted by the more spiritual of the prophets. Micah had predicted that *Sion should be ploughed as a field, Jerusalem become heaps, and the mountain of the House as the high places of a jungle.*[1] 

3. The Ethical Attitude of the Prophets.

And although Isaiah had foretold the Deliverance, and almost alone had sustained the courage of Jerusalem till it came, he did not, we may be sure, believe in any survival of the City apart from those moral conditions which the popular faith in her inviolableness was certain to ignore, but upon which it had been the constant energy of his long career to insist. We may not even assert that Isaiah was devoted to the centralisation of the national worship. No share in this is imputed to him by the records. His practical genius may have felt that centralisation was necessary for the purity of the religion, but in his old age he may also have foreseen its tendency towards formality and superstition, which seventy years later became obvious to Jeremiah.

Whatever may have been the extent of the reforms under Ḥezeḳiah and Isaiah, their stability became endangered by the disappearance of the two personalities, on whom they had depended, soon after the (probable) second Deliverance of the City about 690. Ḥezeḳiah died not

Deaths of Ḥezeḳiah and Isaiah: Manasseh's accession.

[1] iii. 12.

later than 685, perhaps even a few years earlier,[1] and with him or soon after him Isaiah, whose ministry had lasted more than fifty years. The new king Manasseh was a boy. Aḥaz, who had favoured the religious fashions of the Canaanites and Assyrians, was his grandfather. All the conditions, therefore, made a reaction against the reforms an easy possibility. But to understand the extent as well as the character of the reaction, we must look at the political history of the period.

[1] 2 Kings xxi. 1 assigns 55 years to the reign of Manasseh. If we take 641 as the year of his death, this would fix the death of Ḥezeḳiah in 696 or 695; if we take 638, then Ḥezeḳiah on the Biblical datum lived till 692 (Rost) or 691 (cf. Guthe, *Gesch.* 253). The accession of Taharḳō was in 691, and the probable second Deliverance of Jerusalem, as we have seen, between 691 and 689. Winckler (*K.A.T.*[3] 274) suggests that Manasseh and not Ḥezeḳiah was king of Judah at this time, but there are not sufficient grounds for such a hypothesis. Accepting the Biblical statement that the king of Judah was still Ḥezeḳiah after Taharḳō's accession in 691, two hypotheses become possible : that the second Deliverance took place in 690, that Ḥezeḳiah died immediately after it, and that Manasseh reigned till at least 637, which is not probable; or that there is a mistake of ten years in the datum of 2 Kings xxi. 1, and that we should read 45 instead of 55 as the years of Manasseh's reign. This would give us 683 as the year of Ḥezeḳiah's death, reckoning back from 638 or 639, or 685 reckoning back from 641. According to the Biblical data Ḥezeḳiah reigned 29 years (2 Kings xviii. 2), his sixth year was 722-1, that of the fall of Samaria (*Ibid.* 10), and his fourteenth 701, that of Sennacherib's invasion of Judah (*Ibid.* 13) ! To which of these latter contradictory statements are we to adhere? Each has its supporters. Or are we to say both are wrong, and with Winckler and others place Ḥezeḳiah's accession in 720 as we have done above (pp. 130, 148), and his death in 692? The latter, of course, is only possible on the hypothesis that not Ḥezeḳiah but Manasseh was king when Taharḳō advanced on Sennacherib's army in Palestine—a hypothesis for which, as we have said, there are no grounds.

# CHAPTER VII

# JERUSALEM UNDER MANASSEH

*c.* 685-640

THERE is no period of Jewish history more full of darkness and vague sound. The record of Manasseh's long reign in the Books of Kings Ominous Character of Manasseh's Reign. is brief and late; but it is resonant with the echoes both of great movements external to the Jewish state, for the exact course of which the Assyrian annals supply considerable evidence; and of convulsions within Jerusalem, the precipitates from which lie heavy on the memory of the Jewish nation and deeply imbue the substance of their religion.

The record of Manasseh's reign [1] is not even in part an extract from the annals of the kings of Judah, but merely a summary of the king's evil deeds, The Biblical Record. judged from the Deuteronomic standpoint. Though thus subordinate to a distinct ethical intention, the passage is not a unity. It contains repetitions, and apparently gradual accretions from more than one hand.[2] It presupposes the Exile.[3] On the other hand, many of

---

[1] 2 Kings xxi. 1-18.

[2] The passage has been variously divided between the two Deuteronomic redactions of the Books of Kings. To the earlier of these Skinner assigns verses 1-6, 16-18, to the other 7-15. To the former Benzinger assigns only 1, 2a and 16. For another analysis see *Bks. of Kings* in *S.B.O.T.*, by Stade and Schwally.

[3] Verse 8. Verse 5, because it speaks of *two* courts to the Temple, is also generally taken as post-exilic; but in addition to the forecourt proper

the deeds which it attributes to Manasseh are accredited from other sources: from Deuteronomy and the prophets the revival of Canaanite forms of worship, Baal-altars and Asherôth, with the introduction of the worship of the host of heaven;[1] from Jeremiah, the drenching of Jerusalem with innocent blood.[2]

The lateness of this record is in nothing more manifest than in its silence with regard to the Palestine campaigns of Asarḥaddon and Ashurbanipal, and the close traffic of Judah with Assyria which took place during Manasseh's reign. Of all this the record transmits only one clear echo, the introduction of *the worship of the host of heaven.* That cult was Babylonian, and its adoption at this time by Jerusalem was due to the political and social subjection of Judah to Assyria. In spite of the great Deliverance from Sennacherib the Jewish state remained, or early in Manasseh's reign again became, Assyria's vassal. 'Manasseh of Judah' appears twice as an Assyrian tributary: once in 677-6, when among twenty-two kings he paid homage to Asarḥaddon as 'king of the *city* of Judah,'[3] and again as one of the same group who furnished 'men and ships in addition to the customary

Manasseh the Vassal of Assyria.

of Solomon's Temple there was an outer court within the boundary wall of the whole complex of his buildings; cf. 1 Kings vi. 36 with vii. 12. This against Benzinger on 2 Kings xxi. 5.

[1] Deut. iv. 19, xvi. 21 f., xvii. 3; Zeph. i. 5; Jer. viii. 2, xix. 5, 13, xliv. 17 ff.    [2] Jer. xix. 4.

[3] C. H. W. Johns in *Enc. Bibl.* col. 1332; cf. H. F. Talbot, *Records of the Past,* 1st series, iii. 107 (Kouyunjik Inscr. of Asarḥaddon, now in British Museum); and Winckler, *K.A.T.*[(3)] 87. Col. v. of the 2nd, Nebi Yunus, Inscription of Asarḥaddon (lines 11 to 26) records a review of the twenty-two kings apparently at Nineveh, to which they brought materials for the adornment of the palace (Talbot, *op. cit.* 120). On 'city of Judah,' cf. vol. i. 268.

tribute' on Ashurbanipal's first campaign against Egypt in 668.[1]

In 678 the king of Ṣidon, in alliance with a Cilician prince, revolted from Assyria. Asarḥaddon's vengeance was immediate and complete. He destroyed the ancient city and apparently on another site built a new town, named after himself, in which he established an Assyrian adminis- tration and the worship of the Assyrian pantheon.[2]  In 676 the arms of Assyria for the first time crossed the border of Egypt, only, however, to suffer defeat.[3]  But in 671-670 a second Egyptian campaign was success- ful, and Egypt became an Assyrian province.  When Taharḳō, from the south, recovered it in the following year, Asarḥaddon prepared a third expedition, continued, upon his death (668 or 667) by Ashurbanipal, who within two years had twice to drive back the restless Taharḳō into Ethiopia, suppress an Egyptian revolt, and then capture Thebes from Taharḳō's successor.  The fall of Thebes resounded through Western Asia,[4] but failed to place a permanent stamp on the Assyrian power in Egypt, for about 660 or perhaps a few years later[5] Psameṭik I. asserted his independence.  Tyre had sub- mitted to Ashurbanipal in 668, and in spite of the Egyptian revolt all Palestine remained quiet for the next decade.  Then the revolt of Babylon (652-648) roused the tribes

*Campaigns in Palestine and Egypt of Asarḥaddon and Ashur- banipal.*

---

[1] L. W. King, *Enc. Bibl.* coll. 372 f. ; cf. Winckler, *K.A.T.*[(3)] 87. G. Smith, *Rec. of the Past,* 1st series, i. 62, does not give Manasseh's name.

[2] *Hexagonal Prism,* Nebi Yunus Inscr. col. I.

[3] *Babyl. Chron.* iv. 10, 16 ; see Winckler, *K.A.T.*[(3)] 88.

[4] Cf. Nahum iii. 8.

[5] 'About 660 (but this is uncertain),' W. Max Müller in the *Enc. Bibl.* col. 1245.  Guthe, *Gesch.* 233, puts the date as late as 'about 645.

of Northern Arabia, Edom, Moab and Hauran, and even the Phœnicians in Usu and 'Akko; and must have excited Judah and her immediate neighbours, who, however, did not actively rebel. It has been supposed that the historical fact underlying the Jewish Chronicler's account
Manasseh at Babylon. of Manasseh's captivity in Babylon is that, in order to clear himself of the suspicion of complicity in the revolt of 652 onwards, Manasseh paid homage in person to Ashurbanipal, when the latter had at last conquered, and was residing in, Babylon.[1] But it is equally possible to suppose that, as the Chronicler says, Manasseh's temporary residence in Babylon was an enforced one, and this may have taken place earlier. Asarhaddon's annals seem to imply that the twenty-two kings of Syria and the Levant, of whom Manasseh was one, appeared before him at Nineveh.[2]

Such, so far as Palestine is concerned, is the history of the Assyrian Empire during the long reign of Manasseh.
Spread of Babylonian Influence. Under Asarhaddon and Ashurbanipal that Empire reached its widest bounds, and— though the final collapse was near—the summit of its culture and of its ability to impress this upon its subject peoples. Intellectually and religiously the Assyrian culture was Babylonian. Never, since the time of the Tell el-Amarna correspondence, had the civilisation of Mesopotamia so permeated the life of Palestine. We have seen how Asarhaddon established his officials and

---

[1] So Winckler in *A. T. Untersuchungen*, 122, followed by Benzinger on 2 Chron. xxxiii. 10-13, and Guthe, *Gesch.* 227. Winckler has altered his opinion and placed Manasseh's visit to Babylon under Asarhaddon: *K.A.T.*[(3)] 274 f.

[2] See p. 182 *n.* 3.

his gods at Ṣidon,[1] how he and Ashurbanipal organised an Assyrian administration in Egypt, and how Jewish soldiers were brought in to the Assyrian armies. Both monarchs appear to have added to the number of Mesopotamian colonists in Samaria,[2] who introduced the worship of their own gods, and whose influence upon the native customs of the province may be easily imagined by those who have seen the changes effected in social life East of the Jordan through the Circassian colonies introduced by the Turkish Government. Nor are we without contemporary records of Assyrian administration and influence in Palestine during the period. Mr. Macalister has recently discovered at Gezer two cuneiform tablets, deeds of the sale of lands, which there is no reason to suppose are not 'genuine products of the ancient dwellers at Gezer.'[3] The dates of these documents are 651 and 649, and they prove that under Ashurbanipal fields at Gezer, one of which belonged to a man with a Jewish name, Nathaniah, were sold, and the sales were registered, according to Assyrian formulas, in the Assyrian language, and in the one case by a notary with so unmistakable an Assyrian name as Nêrgal-sharuṣur.[4]

It will be observed that while most of these instances

[1] As early as 711 Sargon had introduced some measure of Assyrian administration into Ashdod.

[2] 2 Kings xvii. 24 ff.—which appears to assign this settlement wholly to Sargon after 721, but evidently contains later elements—compared with the Book of Ezra in which the Samaritans assert their descent from colonists settled by Asarhaddon (iv. 2), and this is also traced to those settled by Osnappar, or Ashurbanipal (iv. 10).

[3] Rev. C. H. W. Johns, *P.E.F.Q.*, 1905, 206.

[4] Cf. Nergal-sareṣer, one of the princes of the king of Babylon mentioned by Baruch, Jer. xxxix. 3, 13.

of the enforcement of the Assyrian discipline are from
Its appear- ance in Judah. the neighbourhood of Judah—Gezer and the Samarian territory were not twenty miles from Jerusalem—two of them are from Judah itself: the visit of Manasseh to Babylon and the employment of Jewish auxiliaries in the Assyrian army. Moreover, the inclusion of all Western Asia and Egypt in one great Empire, which, besides, contained the still active centre of ancient civilisation, must have effected an extraordinary increase of commerce and mental intercourse all the way between the Tigris and the upper Nile, from the influences of which it was impossible that Judah, a tributary of the Empire, could stand aloof. Hence the establishment at Jerusalem of the Babylonish worship *of the host of heaven*—a worship so elaborate and offered to so many deities that its altars may well have spread, as the Biblical historian affirms, over both of the open courts before the Temple.[1]

The host of heaven were the sun, moon and stars,[2] and at this time probably added to the significance of
Worship of the Host of Heaven. one of the most sacred names of the God of Israel: *Jahweh of Hosts*.[3] But because belief in them as real deities had not died out of Israel—compare the language of even those genuine monotheists the authors of Deuteronomy[4]—it was the more easy to introduce their worship into Jerusalem. The first reasons for this were doubtless political. Their altars and rites were the official acknowledgment of the subjection of the Jewish state to the Empire, among whose most popular deities was Ishtar, the planet Venus,

---

[1] See above, p. 181 f. *n*. 3.    [2] Deut. iv. 19; xvii. 3.
[3] Originally this had meant God of the armies of Israel.    [4] iv. 19.

'queen of heaven.' That the mass of the population of Jerusalem readily yielded to the attractions of a worship which was performed on arenas they were accustomed to throng, and with which so many of their native instincts and conceptions of the universe were in sympathy, is proved by the evidence alike of the prophets, the legislators and the annalists of Judah. The Book of Deuteronomy twice specially distinguishes the host of heaven as objects which Israel must not let themselves be drawn away to adore.[1] The site of the City, high and open to heaven—within view, too, of the long edge of the Moabite plateau over which the moon and the planets rise with impressive majesty—was particularly suitable for a worship conducted without idols, by direct adoration of its heavenly objects, and by offerings so simple as to be within reach of the poorest worshippers. Accordingly Jeremiah and Zephaniah both record that the cult of the host of heaven spread from the courts of the Temple to the house-tops in Jerusalem;[2] while the former describes the domestic preparation, in which children, fathers and mothers alike engaged, of *cakes* to the Queen of Heaven;[3] and the cakes are called by a name borrowed

---

[1] iv. 19; xvii. 3.   [2] Jer. xix. 13; Zeph. i. 5.

[3] Jer. vii. 18; cf. xliv. 15 ff.   Stade's contentions (*Z.A.T.W.*, 1886, 123 ff., 289 ff.), following the hint of the Massoretic vocalisation of מְלֶכֶת הַשָּׁמַיִם, that מלכת is an abstract noun signifying *dominion* or *governing powers* of heaven; or an abbreviation for מְלֶאכֶת *work*, and in either case an equivalent of the name *host of heaven*, have been generally rejected by Assyrian and Hebrew scholars (*e.g.* Schrader, *Zeitschr. f. Assyriologie*, iii. 353 ff.; iv. 74 ff.; Kuenen, *Gesammelte Abhandlungen*, Budde's tr. 186 ff.; G. F. Moore, *Enc. Bibl.* 3992 f.; Zimmern, *K.A.T.*(3) 441). Read therefore with LXX. of xliv. 17, מַלְכַּת, *queen of*. Ishtar is 'queen of heaven,' sharrat shamê; the Hebrew name for the cakes offered to her in Jerusalem, כַּוָּן, is the same as for those offered to Ishtar in Babylonia, kamânu (Zimmern, *loc. cit.*).

from the Assyrian. In recounting Josiah's reforms the annalist says,[1] *he put down . . . them that offered unto the sun, the moon, the mazzālōth and all the host of heaven . . . and he took away the horses that the kings of Judah had set up for the sun at the entrance of the House of Jahweh, by the chamber of Nathan-melek the chamberlain, which was in the precincts, and he burned the chariots of the sun with fire, and the altars which were on the roofs,*[2] *and the altars which Manasseh had made in the two courts of the House of Jahweh.* Mazzālōth is the same word as the Babylonian *manzaltu.* They were either the twelve signs of the zodiac or the divine 'stations' in the heavens.[3] - The horses and chariot of the sun were also borrowed from Babylonia.[4] In this case, too, there had been an ancient worship near Jerusalem, the instincts of which had probably not died out of her mixed population and would now spring to welcome its Babylonian analogy. In the fourteenth century Abd-Khiba's letters from Jerusalem mention, within the territory of the City, a place called Bit-Ninib, or house of Ninib, a Babylonian deity regarded as solar.[5]

---

[1] 2 Kings xxiii. 5, 11, 12.

[2] The following phrase, *the upper chamber of Ahaz,* is from its ungrammatical connection with what precedes obviously a gloss. *The roof* is usually taken to be that of the Temple, but it may well be a collective for the *roofs* from which the domestic worship of the host of heaven took place. In that case the next clause *which the Kings of Judah had made* would be part of the gloss. In itself the plural *kings* raises doubts.

[3] Zimmern, *K.A.T.*[(3)] 628.     [4] *Id.* 368 ff.

[5] *Id.* 411. Cf. Budde on Judg. i. 34 f., Mount Ḥeres (הַר־חֶרֶם or עִיר־חֶרֶם, Cheyne, *Enc. Bibl.* 2019), where he proposes to identify Bit-Ninib with Beth-Shemesh; while Cheyne suggests that Ḥeres is a 'Hebraised form of Uraš, a synonym of the Ass. god Ninib, who is primarily the fierce morning sun (see Jensen, *Kosmol.* 458)'; and connects Ḥeres with 'the gate Ḥarsith,' Jer. xix. 2. On Bit-Ninib see above, pp. 21, 25 *n.* 6; on Beth-Shemesh, 116.

Jerusalem, then, was permeated during Manasseh's reign by the astral worship of Babylonia, which did not merely obtain, for political reasons, a station in the royal sanctuary, but found an eager welcome from many ancient and popular instincts, still unsubdued by the progress of monotheism. Its rites were domesticated in shapes which long outlived the drastic reforms of Josiah.

To the same Assyrian influences we may assign the change which appears soon after this in the Jewish system of dating the year. In earlier times the Israelite year had been the agricultural; it began, as appears from the oldest stratum of the legislation, with the end of autumn and the fall of the early rains.[1]  But in the latest legislation and other post-exilic literature we find a system of reckoning the year, as in the Babylonian calendar, from the spring month. The date of this change is usually assigned to the Exile: ‘in the Exile,’ says Professor Marti, ‘comes in the custom of placing the first month in spring.’[2] Yet the custom was already followed by the scribe Baruch. In the narrative of Jeremiah's dictation of the roll of his prophecies, Baruch says he read this in the Temple in the ninth month of the fourth year of Jehoiakim, which was a winter month.[3] There is no reason for supposing that these data of the narrative are due to an exilic editor.[4] Taking them as Baruch's own, we see that the influence of the Assyrian

*Adoption of the Babylonian Calendar.*

---

[1] The autumn feast, the last of the annual series of festivals, is dated at *the outgoing of the year* (Ex, xxiii. 16) or at *the year's circuit* or *revolution* (Ex. xxxiv. 22).

[2] *Enc. Bibl.* col. 5366.      [3] Jer. xxxvi. 9 and 22 ; cf. xli. 1.

[4] So Marti would dispose of them : *loc. cit.*

administration during Manasseh's reign extended so far as to impose upon Jewish scribes the Babylonian system of dating the year.[1]

But Manasseh also encouraged the revival of the Canaanite idolatries, which Hezekiah had removed: the

Revival of Canaanite Idolatries.

worship of the Baalim and the graven image of the Asherah, with the use of the pillars and the Asherôth, soothsaying, necromancy, and the practice of sacrificing children by fire.[2] When we wonder that such a recrudescence of baser cults could happen so speedily after Hezekiah's reforms, we must recall the congenital heathenism of Jerusalem on which Ezekiel insists; the prevalence of such forms of worship all round Judah, but especially in Samaria; and also the probable additions to the population from the Judæan towns devastated by Sennacherib in which Canaanite cults still survived, from the Philistine and Phœnician cities that had suffered by the campaigns of Asarhaddon and Ashurbanipal, and from the great increase of trade under the Assyrian lordship of Western Asia.

From all sides, then, the monotheism proclaimed by Isaiah and established by Hezekiah was, within a few

Extreme peril to the Mono- theism of Israel.

years from their deaths, assailed by forms of polytheism which enjoyed the support both of the supreme political power and of the most ancient popular instincts. We see clearly that the historians and prophets[3] have not exaggerated the extreme peril of Manasseh's reign to the higher religion of Israel, upon the only stage where it was

---

[1] Another effect of the Assyrian administration may perhaps be found in the registry of the sale of land recorded in Jer. xxxii.

[2] 2 Kings xxi. 6 ff., xxiii. 5 ff. ; cf. Jer. xv. 4.     [3] Cf. Jer. xv. 4, etc.

now possible for that religion to persist. Both the Assyrian devastation of Judah and the reforms of Hezekiah had tended to confine the worship of Jahweh to Sion. And now, when it has no longer behind it that rural population, which we have seen rally to its support in previous crises of its betrayal by its royal patrons, we find the higher faith of Israel exposed within the courts of its own sanctuary to the invasion of rival forms of worship, enforced by the policy of a great Empire and welcomed by the memories of many of the population about it.

Its adherents did not yield without a struggle; but Manasseh met them with the sword. *He shed,* says the historian, *innocent blood very much, till he had filled Jerusalem from mouth to mouth*[1] of her savage appetite, and Jeremiah testifies that her population was with him; *because they have forsaken me . . . and filled this place with the blood of innocents.*[2] It is strange that there is no echo of this in the Book of Deuteronomy, the authors of which are nowhere troubled by the problem of the sufferings of the righteous. But the problem had come to stay. By its statement in lines of blood upon her streets Jerusalem matriculated in a profounder school of religion than that through which Isaiah had brought her; and by her sufferings at the hands of her own sons was learning a lesson more useful for her mission to humanity than even the truth which her great deliverance from the foreign oppressor had stamped upon her mind. For through

*Persecution of its Adherents.*

[1] 2 Kings xxi. 16: part of the Deuteronomic text, but the Deuteronomists are not unreliable witnesses of a reign so near their own time as that of Manasseh. [2] Jer. xix. 4.

all these savage cruelties the nucleus of the true people of God remained loyal, and was purified. Isaiah's The Suffering *Remnant* became *a Suffering Remnant.* The Remnant. times forbade the appearance of public prophets. Persecution drove their faith to anonymous methods of expression,[1] to the secret treasuring of earlier prophecies, perhaps also to the codifying of the social and religious teaching of these (which codes were hidden away in the Temple against the recurrence of happier times[2]), and certainly to more spiritual and personal communion with their God. While the majority of her people gave way to the heathen customs and rites which Manasseh had introduced, and delivered to the next generation a number of men and women with totem names,[3] there were still in Jerusalem families who feared the Lord, and, as we see from the genealogies of the prophets in Josiah's reign, dedicated their children to His Name.

Nor did they fail to learn from their oppressors and from the systems of belief which threatened to destroy Intellectual their own. The Babylonian religion had Gain from nothing ethical to teach to the disciples of Babylon. Amos, Hosea and Isaiah. But, if we may judge from the subsequent use of Babylonian literature in the cosmogonies and psalms of Israel, there entered her religion at this time from that foreign source new impressions of the order and processes of the universe with fresh explanations of the beginnings of history and culture, all of which the Spirit of her God enabled her to use for His glory and to interpret in the light

---

[1] *E.g.* 'Micah,' vi. 6-8.    [2] 2 Kings xxii. 8 ff.
[3] *E.g.* Ḥuldah, *Weasel*; Shaphan, *Badger*; 'Achbor, *Mouse.*

of those purposes of grace and righteousness which He had long revealed to her. The Assyrian dominance of Jerusalem during Manasseh's reign was thus not altogether for loss to the higher religion, against which it provoked so cruel a reaction. While the faith of the righteous was purified by the sufferings it imposed, the intellect of the people was fertilised by the ideas it introduced. Their observation of the universe was stimulated, and their habits of writing and recording were developed.

We have already touched a number of reasons for a considerable increase in the population of the City since 701 : the devastation of the rest of the land in that year,[1] Ḥezeḳiah's attempt to centralise the national worship, the peace of Judah during the long reign of Manasseh, while neighbouring lands were harried by Assyrian armies, the introduction of the Babylonian cults, and the increase of trade across Western Asia. *Probable Increase of the Population of Jerusalem.*

For the large share which Jerusalem took in the trade of Palestine during the seventh century, we have three independent testimonies. First, there is the presence of commercial regulations in the Book of Deuteronomy, as contrasted with their absence from the earlier legislation.[2] Second, there is the epithet, *gate of the peoples*, applied to Jerusalem by Ezekiel[3] in his description of Tyrian commerce. And third, there is the reason, which the king of Persia gave *Evidence for the Growth of the City's Trade.*

---

[1] Compare the parallel case during Nebuchadrezzar's invasion, Jer. xxxv. 11.

[2] For details see § 54 of 'Trade and Commerce' by the present writer in the *Enc. Bibl.*, column 5175.

[3] xxxvi. 2 ; LXX.

for his veto upon the rebuilding of the City's walls in the time of Zerubbabel: *there have been mighty kings over Jerusalem . . . and tribute, custom and toll was paid unto them.*[1]  Whether the terms imposed by Assyria reserved to Manasseh those rights of levying customs at his frontiers which the kings of Judah, both before and after him, thus appear to have enjoyed, we do not know ; but at least he and his subjects would benefit in other ways from the immense increase of traffic caused by the inclusion of Egypt and Western Asia under one Empire.  The political rank of Jerusalem secured to her the chief markets of the internal commerce of Judah, as well as the gifts which it was customary for foreign traders to leave with the lords of the territories they visited ;[2] and thus in spite of the commercial disadvantages of its site the City must have become a considerable emporium.

From all these causes the increase of the population is certain, the incomers being largely accommodated in New Quarters and Walls of the City. the new quarters of which we first hear from Zephaniah.  But the circuit of the walls was not widened.  No achievement of this kind is attributed to Manasseh.  The Chronicler, drawing upon a source which there is no reason to doubt, tells us that Manasseh built an outer wall to the 'City of David' on the steep slope *to the west of Gihon in the valley* of the Ḳidron, and that it extended *to the entrance of the Fish-Gate* which lay on the north.  *He compassed about the 'Ophel and raised it up a very great height.*[3]  The only other topographical notice is that of the king's burial.

---

[1] Ezra iv. 20.          [2] See vol. i. 343 *n.* 3.
[3] 2 Chron. xxxiii. 14 ; see vol. i. 208.

Hezekiah is the last king said to have been buried in the royal sepulchres.   They laid Manasseh *in the garden of his own house, the garden of 'Uzza* or 'Uzziah.   Here also his son Amon was buried after a reign of little over one year.   These, and perhaps Josiah's, are the graves of the kings which Ezekiel condemns as too near the sacred precincts of the Temple.[1]   Was the new site for the royal burials due to some of the novel religious ideas introduced under Manasseh?

From 701 Jerusalem began to assume that excessive predominance which gradually rendered the rest of the country but the fringe of her walls.   We shall see this in several of Jeremiah's allusions.   Meantime it is perhaps worth repeating that Manasseh is described by Asarhaddon as king not of the land, but 'of the City, of Judah.'[2]

---

[1] Ezekiel xliii. 7-9.          [2] Above, vol. i. 268; vol. ii. 182.

## CHAPTER VIII

## JOSIAH: JERUSALEM AND DEUTERONOMY

### c. 638-608 B.C.

DURING the long reign of Manasseh, c. 685-640, the land of Judah had time to recover from the devastation of 701. What became of the 200,000 captives whom Sennacherib claims to have taken,[1] how many he carried to Assyria and how many his sudden departure forced him to release, we do not know. But the numbers of the slain must have been large, and it is certain that of his captives and of those who fled before him to Jerusalem, not all were able to return to their lands. In any case the rural economy was radically disturbed. An invasion such as Sennacherib wrought upon Judah—and its drastic character is emphasised both by himself and by Isaiah[2]—had effects far more terrible than the modern conditions of warfare allow us to conceive. In those times wars were waged not between armies alone, but between peoples and between their gods. The inexhaustible jealousy of the latter infected their worshippers and sanctioned the uttermost ruthlessness. Women and children were savagely treated. Whole families, sometimes whole communities, were destroyed or carried into exile. The fields

*Recovery of Judah under Manasseh.*

---

[1] See above, p. 160.　　　　　[2] Ch. i.

196

were wasted, the very seed was burned. The local cults were broken up, and with them the pieties, the rights, the entire framework of society, which they controlled and defended. On the disappearance of the invader, these disasters to a nation became the opportunity of the more energetic and unscrupulous survivors. It happened almost always that lands formerly possessed by many individuals passed into the hands of a few, and only seldom that the domains of a slain or an exiled landholder were divided among his serfs or adherents. Additional consequences may be attributed to Sennacherib's war. Some of the Jewish domains which he wasted must, as so often in the history of Palestine, have been seized by the nomad tribes which have always hovered on the borders of the cultivated territory ; and some fell to the Philistines. Even in those which remained to the Jews, the fact that it was the God of Israel whom Sennacherib had seemed to defeat may have shaken His authority with many of the Jewish rustics, and led to a recrudescence of Canaanite forms of worship.[1] The religion of the rural districts thus tended to become more confused and impure than before. Upon this state of affairs descended the long peace and prosperity of Manasseh's reign,[2] repairing the material ravages of Sennacherib's invasion but not the religious confusion. By 625 the rural population of Judah was again large. From 'Anathôth Jeremiah heard across the land the noise of much people [3] and saw idolatrous shrines everywhere—*as many as thy cities so be thy gods, O Judah, where hast thou not*

---

[1] Witness the similar feelings among Jews after the devastations by Nebuchadrezzar.

[2] See above, pp. 193 f.    [3] iii. 21 (?), 23 ff., etc.

*been defiled?*[1] Yet this part of the nation was not without considerable moral force. Of the second group of Judæan prophets, Jeremiah himself, and perhaps Nahum, came from the villages, and, as we shall see, the Deuteronomic legislation is strongly influenced by provincial interests. The capital, of course, retained its lead, but when a party of officials slew Amon, son of Manasseh, it was *the people of the land*[2] who executed the murderers, and, as in the case of 'Uzziah, raised the murdered man's son to the throne.

The motives of the intrigue against Amon are not clear. Manasseh's persecutions, apparently confined to Jerusalem, must have created a bitterness against his house, which would naturally become effective under his weaker successor. But the conspiracy is said to have been formed among *the servants of Amon,* and was therefore more probably due to political opinions,[3] restrained so long as Manasseh lived and no alternative was possible to the Assyrian supremacy. By the time Manasseh died Psameṭik of Egypt had thrown off the Assyrian yoke,[4] and according to a credible tradition was already interfering in southeastern Palestine.[5] The Egyptian party at the court of Jerusalem, which had controlled affairs towards the close of the previous century and was again active about 625,[6]

*Political Motives for the Murder of Amon.*

[1] ii. 28, iii. 2 ; cf. iii. 9, xi. 13, etc.

[2] 2 Kings xxi. 24 : it does not seem to be exclusive of the population of Jerusalem ; though Kittel renders it by 'the party of the country people.'

[3] This seems to me more probable than Kittel's explanation that it was adherents of the purer religion who killed Amon.

[4] 'Before 660,' Rogers' *Hist. of Bab. and Assyria,* ii. 254. 'It may have been about 660, but this is uncertain,' W. Max Müller, *Enc. Bibl.* art. 'Egypt.' 'Certainly by 645,' M'Curdy, *Hist. Proph. and the Monuments,* ii. 355.     [5] Herodotus, ii. 151.     [6] Jer. ii. 18, 36.

but lay powerless during the reign of Manasseh, may
have sought by the death of Amon to remove the chief
obstacle to their policy. Or his courtiers may have had
some private grudge against him. In any case the
motives of the conspirators were not economic; their
punishment by *the people of the land* proves how contented
the latter had been under the government of Manasseh.

There is no evidence that the elevation of Amon's
eight-year old son, Josiah,[1] was due to the party of the
purer religion, formed by Isaiah. But from
the first that party had included many of the
leading men in Jerusalem,[2] and, in spite of
Accession<br>of Josiah,<br>*c.* 637.
its decimation by Manasseh, probably retained some
adherents of high rank. After the murder of Amon,
the slaughter of the king's *servants*, nominees of
Manasseh, may have opened to such influential followers of the prophets several offices at court. It
was certainly to the advantage of their principles that
the new king was too young to have been trained in
the policy of Manasseh. At the age of eight he was
chiefly under the care of the women of the household;[3]
and through them, or some of his ministers or some of
the priests, his character, on which so much depended,
was moulded by the principles of his great-grandfather,
Ḥezeḳiah. There must also have been sober and con-

---

[1] 2 Kings xxi. 24, xxii. 1.

[2] Smend, *A. T. Religionsgeschichte.*

[3] His mother was Yedidah, daughter of 'Adayah of Bozḳath (mentioned
with Lakîsh and Eglon, Josh. xv. 39). His own name, like that of the
latter (?), was compounded with the name of Jahwe' Yoshiyahu = *Jahweh
supports*: in contrast, be it noted, with those of his father Amon and his
grandfather Manasseh, both of which may be derived from other gods.
That Manasseh and Amon alone break a long list of Judæan kings named
after Jahweh is significant.

servative Jews who, though their minds did not appreciate the spiritual doctrine of the prophets, revolted against the foreign cults and cruelties of Manasseh, and who were ready to welcome the restored supremacy of the national God. And there was always the party favourable to Egypt. But so long as the Assyrian domination remained effective—Ashurbanipal had apparently accepted Josiah as his vassal—no one of these parties nor all of them together could carry their desires into action. The Assyrian sovereignty both awed and divided them. While it remained there would be many who feared it, and some, among the prophetic party, who, following Isaiah, would judge rebellion or the appeal to Egypt, which others proposed, as an impious course for the Lord's people to pursue. The various parties could, therefore, only wait and prepare, each in its own way and perhaps by some compromise with the others, for a change in the political situation. Of this there were many omens. The Assyrian Empire, apparently as strong as ever at its centre, was suffering in its extremities. Egypt was independent, and her forces, increased by Greek and Carian mercenaries, threatened the southern provinces ; while swift and terrible hordes, races new to history, stirred upon the northern frontier. During the youth of Josiah all Jews must have gathered hope and courage, but the eyes of their various factions rested upon different rifts in the horizon. At last in 625, by the death of Ashurbanipal, a gap was suddenly opened wide enough for all to move forward together, and a religious influence descended under which they became for the first time since Hezekiah's death a united nation.

The editor of the Books of Kings dates the beginning of Josiah's reforms in the eighteenth year of his reign, 621 or 620 B.C.[1]  The previous repair of the Temple which he records was a periodical function instituted by Joash.[2]  The Chronicler Reforms under Josiah: their Record. asserts that the reforms began earlier.  He dates the king's adhesion to the purer religion in the eighth year of his reign, and the *commencement*[3] of the destruction of the high-places and the idols in the twelfth year, and says that the work was complete by the eighteenth when the Temple was repaired and the Book of the Law discovered.  But if the king had already achieved such drastic reforms, there was no cause for the consternation ascribed to him when the Book was read.  We must therefore prefer the statement in Kings, that the high places and idols began to be removed *after* the discovery of the Book.  Still the definite dates of the Chronicler, read in the light of the history of the time, suggest that he worked upon reliable material.  The eighth year of Josiah's reign was the sixteenth of his life, when we may suppose that his character was formed and he began to assert himself.  And the twelfth year of his reign was 626

---

[1] 2 Kings xxii. 3.  The narrative of the reforms lasts till xxiii. 25.  It contains some editorial and other intrusions.  Stade and Schwally (*S.B.O.T.*) excise the following : xxii. 6 f. (from xii. 9 ff.), 15-20, Ḥuldah's prophecy (but see below, p. 203 *n.* 1), part of 3 from the Deuteronomic editor; 10*b*, last clause, 5, 8*b*, 10, 12, last clause, 13-20, 24 f.

[2] Erbt, *Die Sicherstellung des Monotheismus durch die Gesetzgebung im Vorexil. Juda* (1903), assumes that Josiah ordered a reconstruction (Umbau) of the Temple, and illustrates, what he believes must have followed from this on the discovery of its foundation-stone and the documents of its constitution (Urkunde), from Babylonian parallels.  But there is no evidence of so thorough a rebuilding.  On Joash, see above, pp. 107 ff.

[3] Josiah *began to purge Judah and Jerusalem from the high places, the Asherim, the graven images*, etc., 2 Chron. xxxiv. 2 ff.

or 625, the year of Ashurbanipal's death, which, as we have seen, left Judah more free to govern herself.

We may therefore infer that with the gradual growth of opportunity, as depicted above, the stages of the move-

Their three<br>Stages and<br>Motives.

ment under Josiah were three. *First*, there was the king's adolescence and his adhesion to the purer religion. Whatever influences brought this about, the personal fact is too well credited to remain doubtful. Between the kings who preceded and

1. The<br>Character of<br>Josiah.

those who followed him, Josiah stands by himself, and we need not hesitate to ascribe to him, as both his historians do, that power of personality which it is so easy but so fallacious to ignore in religious movements.[1] *Second*, there were some tentative efforts at reform after 625, when Ashurbanipal's

2. The Death<br>of Ashur-<br>banipal.

death gave Josiah and his counsellors political freedom ; but the king and all the parties may have been too dazzled by the sudden opportunity and too much at variance among themselves to effect at once a decisive change. *Third*, in 621 or 620,

3. The Dis-<br>covery of the<br>Law-Book.

a sacred Law-Book was discovered in the Temple which not only did justice in its details to the various national interests, but by its general spirit impressed all their representatives with the awe of a supreme religious obligation.[2] It is

---

[1] Since the above was published in the *Expositor* for November 1905, Cornill in *Das Buch Jeremia* has done full justice to the character and influence of Josiah: the best study of the king, see pp. xiii, etc.

[2] Erbt (*op. cit.*) and Dr. John Cullen (*The Book of the Covenant in Moab : a Critical Enquiry into the Original Form of Deuteronomy*, Glasgow, Maclehose, 1903) both do justice, upon the Chronicler's data, to the gradual character of the movement. Cullen (p. 17): 'The author of Kings has telescoped into one account a series of reforms.' Erbt (p. 8) places the first stage at the accession of Josiah, yet, as we have seen, there is no

this religious influence, gathered from the prophets of the eighth century, fostered by loyal hearts under Manasseh, and giving itself forth as divine, to which the great Reform, the establishment of Monotheism in Israel, was essentially due. It acted on the priests of the Temple, on a king whose character was predisposed to receive it, and through them on the whole people of Judah, at a time when the political situation was favourable to its national enforcement. Without the Divine call and the faith of the men who received it, the political situation, the compromises of parties, and the wonderful adaptation of the Law itself to the rival ecclesiastical and social interests, would have availed little. The effect upon the nation was immediate and complete. The king was overcome by the denunciations against the neglect of its laws which the Book contained. Further moved by a message from the prophetess Ḥuldah,[1] he gathered *the men of Judah and all the inhabitants of Jerusalem* to the Temple and had the Book read in their hearing. Then with due sacrificial forms, and as the representative of the people, he *made a covenant* before God to keep the words of the Book, *and all the people stood to the covenant.*[3]

There can be little doubt that the discovered Book which formed the basis of this national covenant was

evidence that this was due to the spiritual party in Judah; and does not accept as reliable the Chronicler's first datum in Josiah's conversion, but takes it as a mere easy assumption that the king's adolescence was marked by his adhesion to the prophetic principles: yet here, as elsewhere, Erbt seems to me to ignore too much the personality of Josiah.

[1] 2 Kings xxii. 15-20. Ḥuldah's oracle as here given is probably not in its original form, but the fact that it predicts a peaceful death for Josiah, who fell in battle at Megiddo, is proof that some at least of the original contents have been preserved.   [3] 2 Kings xxiii. 1-3.

part at least of our Book of Deuteronomy. Such a conclusion is independent of the question of its origin and inevitable upon the evidence of the Biblical narra-

The dis-
covered
Law-book
part at least
of Deuter-
onomy.
tive. For the discovered Book is called by the names which Deuteronomy uses for itself: the *Book of the Law*, the *Book of the Covenant*. The consternation of Josiah when he heard it read and the urgency of his measures to fulfil its commands are adequately explained by the stern temper of Deuteronomy and its denunciations not only of foreign cults but of practices hitherto followed by the worship of Israel, whether in the Temple or throughout the land. The reforms which Josiah introduced correspond to the requirements of Deuteronomy as they do not to those of the other codes of Israel; in particular, the removal of the high-places of Jahweh and the concentration of His worship in the Temple, which Josiah was the first to carry out, are the central and most distinctive principles of the Deuteronomic system. We have seen, too, how so radical a measure as this centralising of the worship was facilitated and prepared for by the events of the history between the building of the Temple and the time of Josiah;[1] and how by the latter date they had also become necessary for the purity of Israel's religion and the assurance of monotheism.[2] And, finally, it is precisely from this time onward that the style and phraseology

---

[1] The building of the Temple; the possession of the Ark and the purest form of Israel's worship; their identification with the house of David, the one permanent dynasty in Israel; the growth of the Temple in resources and influence; the fall of the Northern Kingdom; Isaiah's views on the Temple; the Assyrian devastation of all the other sanctuaries of Judah; the vindication of the Temple in 701 as the one inviolable sanctuary of Jahweh.

[2] See above, pp. 176 f., and below, pp. 212 f., 219 f.

which are characteristic of Deuteronomy begin to affect the literature of Israel.[1]

But how much of our Book of Deuteronomy the discovered Law-Book contained it is difficult and perhaps impossible to determine. The whole of Deuteronomy in the form in which we now have it can hardly have been extant by 621. Parts The Structure of Deuteronomy. of the canonical text are held by some to presuppose the Exile and echo exilic writers, while parts have been taken from sources of the Pentateuch other than the Deuteronomist.[2] But not even is the rest of the Book an obvious unity. It consists of a Code of Laws with denunciations of those who transgress them (chapters xii.-xxvi., xxviii.) and two separate introductions of a hortatory and historical character (chapters i.-iii., iv. 1-40, and chapters iv. 45-xi.). The existence of these divisions,

---

[1] For the fuller exhibition of these proofs the English reader is referred to the translation of Wellhausen's *Prolegomena to the Hist. of Isr.* ; Robertson Smith's *O.T.J.C.*[(2)] (with his *Additional Answer to the Libel*, 1878, and *Answers to the Amended Libel*, 1879) ; Driver's ' Deuteronomy ' and the articles by Ryle in Hastings' *D.B.*, and Moore in the *Enc. Bibl.* Recent attempts to question these proofs cannot be pronounced successful : *Are the Critics Right?* by Möller (tr. by Irwin, 1903) ; ' The Date of Deuteronomy,' by Kennett, *Jour. of Theol. Studies*, 1904. The latter would date the Book in the sixth cent. by seeking to show the dependence of the Deuteronomic language on Jeremiah ; by pointing out features in our Book of Deuteronomy suitable to the Exile (this has never been doubted) ; and (p. 492) explaining Josiah's consternation by some denunciation of sacrifice by one of the prophets, and his preservation of sacrifice at the Temple alone by the fact that it was his own royal chapel !

[2] iv. 1-40 is held by many to be not connected with i.-iii., varying from these chapters both in its substance and in its diction, which recalls that of Jeremiah, Ezekiel and the Priestly Document; but this is questionable ; xxix. 2-xxx. Eng. = xxix. 1.-xxx. Heb. is separated from what precedes it by the formal close of the latter, xxix. 1 Eng. = xxviii. 69 Heb., and its diction recalls that of Jeremiah. The long poem in xxxii. has also traces of the Exile. In xxvii., xxxi., xxxiv. are pieces from E. and J., earlier than the Deuteronomist and from P. later.

each with its own title and with some distinctions of substance and diction,[1] has made possible several theories of their relation to each other and to the primitive Deuteronomy. On the one hand emphasis has been laid on the fact that the Book discovered in the Temple was a Law-Book, and the conclusion has been drawn that this consisted of the Code alone, which furnished the programme for Josiah's reforms, the hortatory and historical introductions being added by a later writer or writers of the same school.[2] On the other hand, it has been argued that the hortatory sections by themselves were the more likely to have inspired the reforms, and that the Code is the precipitate or codification of these.[3] Between such extremes there is a more reasonable mean. *The Book of the Law* found in the Temple and inspiring the Reforms of Josiah, must have contained some laws—the abolition of images, the abolition of the high-places of Jahweh, and the centralisation of His worship—such as we find in the Code; but a Code so obviously due to prophetic influence may well have had a prophetic introduction and explanation attached to it. These are supplied by the section iv. 45-xi., which besides in standpoint and style very closely agrees with the Code. On such grounds many take the primitive Deuteronomy to have been chapters iv. 45-xxvi. of our Book along with the substance at least of xxviii., the denunciations in which would account for Josiah's terror when the Book was read to him.[4] Some

---

[1] The unity of the Book is arguable, but that the evidence for it is 'overwhelming' (Orr, *Problem of the Old Testament*, p. 253) cannot be maintained upon a full consideration of the above facts.

[2] Wellhausen, Stade and others.

[3] Cullen, *The Book of the Covenant in Moab.* He takes v. 29-xi. 28 and some other passages to have been the original discovered in the Temple.

[4] Kuenen, Dillmann, Driver, Moore, Budde (virtually), and others.

would add the other introduction i.-iii., with its separate
title but somewhat varying diction and standpoint;
others would take i.-iii. as originally the introduction to a
variant edition of the Code. That there was more than
one such edition of the Deuteronomic laws is rendered
probable by an analysis of the Code, which discovers
doublets or different forms of the same laws.[1] The
double fashion in which the people are addressed, now
as *thou* and now as *you*, which runs through both the
hortatory and legal sections, would not of course by itself
prove different styles; but these two forms of address
so often coincide with different phraseologies for the
same events, and with different conceptions of the
previous history of Israel, that the coincidence can
hardly be accidental, and the probability is that they
are frequently the work of different authors. These
materials, however, have been so interwoven with each
other, and the text has undergone so much revision, that
an exact analysis of its constituents is no longer possible.
But enough is clear to let us see that the original Deuteronomy was composed from more than one source, or
alternatively that there were several variant editions of
it;[2] and this complicates the already difficult question of
the origin and date of the Book.

The full discussion of the question is beyond the scope
of our present task. It is only necessary to recall the

---

[1] *E.g.* xii., the law of the central sanctuary (here there are traces of four
laws); the laws of the cities of refuge and others.

[2] The analysis of Deuteronomy according to the *Thou* and *You* forms of
address was first made by Steuernagel and by Staerk about 1894. Another
was given by Mitchell in the *Journal of Biblical Literature*, 1899, 61 ff.; and
another by the present writer in a paper before the Oxford Society of
Historical Theology in 1902.

main proofs upon which the late date of Deuteronomy is
now so widely accepted, and to express the

Proofs of the
Late Date of conviction that to fix that date exactly is a
Deuteronomy. task for which we have no sufficient material.
The evidence for the late date of Deuteronomy consists
of the perspective in which it views the time of Moses;[1]
its implication that the monarchy has long been in
existence; its reflection of a more elaborate economy
than is shown in the earlier legislation; its polemic
against forms of idolatry prevalent in Israel during the
Assyrian period; and (most of all) the testimony of
the historical books that up to the end of the eighth
century the religious practice of Israel neither conformed,
nor sought to conform, to the Deuteronomic prohibition
of pillars in the worship of Jahweh and insistence on a
single sanctuary;[2] while the appearance of such provisions just about this date is naturally explained by the
events and processes in the previous history of Jerusalem
which we have seen leading up to them and by the
practical necessities of the monotheism. Besides, Deuteronomy is clearly inspired by the eighth-century prophets.

[1] In the title to the second introduction, iv. 46, Israel's defeat of Sîhon
is described as happening *after their coming forth out of Egypt*, and in the
Code, xxiii. 4, it is said that Israel was not given bread and water by 'Ammon
and Moab *in their coming out of Egypt.* These expressions could not have
been used by one speaking to Israel a few weeks or months after 'Ammon's
and Moab's refusal and the war with Sîhon ; but they are natural to a writer to
whom the whole forty years of wandering were foreshortened by the distance
at which he lived from them.

[2] The earlier legislation permits sacrifice to Jahweh at many places
(Ex. xx. 24), and does not forbid the masseboth or *pillars.* In harmony with
this is the testimony of the historical books. Elijah and other religious
leaders either build or permit altars to Jahweh in a way that renders the
existence of the Deuteronomic Code in their days inconceivable. Hezekiah
is the first king who is said to have attempted the removal of the high-places,
Jeremiah the first prophet to declaim against *the pillars.*

On these grounds the conclusion is reasonable that the code or codes from which Deuteronomy is compiled were constructed towards the end of the eighth or during the seventh century. A more exact date is not within our reach. Some regard as the most probable time the reign of Manasseh, when the adherents of the purer religion, prevented from carrying out their principles in the worship of the Temple, betook themselves to the codification of these against the arrival of happier times. For this there is much to be said ; yet the fact that Deuteronomy nowhere reflects the division of the people into a persecuting majority and a suffering remnant, but consistently treats Israel as a moral whole, seems to the present writer a strong argument against a date in Manasseh's reign. The alternatives to this are the years after and the years before Manasseh. In the early reign of Josiah the *rapprochement* of the rival parties in Jerusalem may explain Deuteronomy's silence upon national divisions. But if, as we have seen, Hezekiah's reforms were in the direction of the Deuteronomic requirements, we may trace the beginnings at least of the Deuteronomic legislation to the end of his reign, by which time both its political and its religious premises were already in existence.[1] Possibly different essays were made at different points between the middle of Hezekiah's and the middle of Josiah's reign.

We must emphasise, however, that what these reformers did was not to create a body of fresh and novel laws. The dependence of Deuteronomy upon the earlier legisla-

---

[1] As the present writer suggested in reviewing Driver's *Deuteronomy* in the *Critical Review* for 1895, vol. v. 339 ff. Erbt, following Steuernagel, distinguishes two Deuteronomic codes, one under Hezekiah and one under Josiah.

tion of Israel is very apparent.[1]  But both codes reveal
their development from far older sources.  The similarity

*Deutero-nomy's Service to Religion.*
of their provisions to the customs and rites of
the surrounding peoples indicates that early
Israel in common with these, and by virtue of
her Semitic descent, had inherited a body of consuetudinary law.  Upon this had become operative the higher
ethical influences of the revelation which through Moses
God had made of Himself as the national God of
Israel.  How real and how great the service of Moses
had been is proved not only by all the lines of the
people's historical tradition, but by the later fame which
has attributed to him the sole authorship of the legislation.  But Moses did not complete the elevating and
purifying process.  By Israel's living faith in a living
God this continued through the subsequent centuries.
We have seen it at work under the kings and priests
of Judah;[2] it was no less active through the early
prophets of the north.  Then came the further revelation
of God by the prophets of the eighth century, and the
light which this reflected alike on the religious practices
of the nation and the new temptations which came to
them from abroad.  Simultaneously the possibilities
of conserving and developing these religious gains from
so long a divine guidance were being manifestly limited
by the events of history to Jerusalem and the Temple.
For so great a crisis, for so divine a call, a gifted school
of writers in Judah were found sufficient.  Equally alive
to the real origins of their religion under Moses and to
the workings of God's Spirit in their own day, they recast

[1] For details see the introduction to Driver's *Deuteronomy*, § ii., especially pp. viii. ff.    [2] Above, pp. 74, 90, 94 ff., 113 ff., etc.

the ancient laws of Israel in the temper of the prophets and with regard to the changed historical conditions of the nation.   In particular they were concerned with some religious practices which their fathers had pursued without questioning, but which recent experience had shown to be dangerous to a spiritual faith; as well as with certain foreign forms of idolatry, Canaanite and Babylonian, which were beginning to fascinate the people or to be imposed upon them by their subjection to Assyria. Hence the sincerity, the vitality, the power of the work they produced.   Deuteronomy is a living and a divine Book, because, like every other religious reformation in which God's spirit may be felt, it is at once loyal to the essential truth revealed in the past, while daring to cast off all tradition however ancient and sacred that in practice has become dangerous and corruptive; vigilant to the new perils and exigencies of faith and receptive of the fresh directions of the living God for their removal or conquest.

The Book of Deuteronomy, then, applies the revelation of the eighth-century prophets to the life and consuetudinary law of Israel: interpreting the people's history, modifying their institutions, regulating their daily habits, inspiring their individual hearts and minds, and dealing in addition with the latest features of their political and economic development.  The governing principle of the Book is Monotheism, slightly qualified, it is true, by current popular conceptions, and limited in its applications by the practical necessities of the time; yet so earnestly moral and warmly spiritual in its exposition of the relation between God and the people, that our Lord has

*The Principle of Deuteronomy: the One God.*

accepted one of its central expressions as the supreme law of religion: *Hear, O Israel, Jahweh thy God is one Jahweh, and thou shalt love Jahweh thy God with all thine heart, and with all thy soul, and with all thy might.*   He is to be loved because He is Love.   His grace in the choice of Israel, His tenderness in their guidance and training, with the high moral destiny He has conceived for them, are urged upon the people in language of extraordinary power and beauty.   Therefore He alone is God: the one and only Deity by His character and deeds of love and power.   The worship of every other god is absolutely forbidden, and, in the spirit of the times, on the penalty of death.   Equally excluded is the representation of the Deity in any material form; and His ritual is purged of all immoral elements, *abominations* as they are called: images, *maṣṣeboth*, Asherim, all tainted and foolish rites, all mutilations of the body and unclean practices, all witchcraft and necromancy.   The whole of the practice of religion is winnowed and ordered by a spirit as certain of its own reasonableness as it is passionately pure and, in most directions, humane.

The distinctive feature of Deuteronomy, however, is the centralisation of the national worship.   We have already seen how inevitable a corollary this was to the ethical monotheism of the prophets.   The ritual of Israel's religion had always been a menace to its intellectual and moral elements, partly because men are ever disposed to assign to the performance of rites a higher place in the Divine will than they do to morality, and partly because the rites used by Israel were akin to those of the religions around them, and thus constantly tempted the worshippers to confuse the character

The Central Law : the One Altar.

of their God with the characters of others. That is why the prophets of the eighth century did not refrain from demanding the abolition of all sacrifice and ritual. Instead of this the practical reformers of the seventh century proposed their limitation to one place, not only in order to secure the purity of the ritual but to avert that dissolution of the Divine Unity which was almost inseparable in the popular mind from the identification of God with many sanctuaries. Therefore, besides enforcing the extirpation of the cult of every other god from the land, Deuteronomy decrees the destruction of all the *bamoth* or *high-places* at which Jahweh Himself was worshipped, and confines His sacrifices and the celebration of His feasts to a single sanctuary. Such a measure was not, as some recent writers labour to prove, the invention of any interested locality or corporation of priests, and it could never have been carried out by mere party motives, however powerful or skilfully organised. The removal of the high-places was nothing less than a religious and ethical necessity, demanded in the name of the One God, and proved by the bitter experience of centuries. Unless we appreciate this we shall not understand how so great a revolution in the national worship was so successfully effected in Judah, without serious opposition from the interests which it disturbed.

The ideal of the Book is political as well as religious. The establishment of many idolatries in Jerusalem had been the sacramental token of the nation's servitude to a foreign power. But the Deuteronomic Israel is a free people, owning no overlord save their God, and governing themselves in obedience to His revealed will. This will is applied, we shall

Its Political Outlook: the One People.

immediately see, to every department of the national life in as comprehensive a system of national religion as the world has ever known. Yet the system is limited to Israel. Beyond directions for the admission to the covenant of individual Edomites and Egyptians,[1] there is no attempt to deal with the world outside. There is no missionary programme, no provision for mankind. This may not have been practical in the conditions of the time but in any case its omission is one of the limitations of the monotheism of the Book that have been already referred to. Next to devotion to the national Deity comes pride in the nation itself: a pride, of course, subject to the austere moral conditions imposed on its life. As there is one Jahweh so there is one Israel, the only righteous people and wise above all others. For no other possesses a religion or laws so high and so pure. The intellectual tempers of monotheism—the sense of a loftier mental position, the scorn of idolatry—appear if not in the original Deuteronomy, yet in its immediate additions. *Keep therefore and do them, for this is your wisdom and your understanding in the sight of the peoples, which shall hear all these statutes and say, Surely this great nation is a wise and understanding people. For what great nation is there that hath God so nigh to them as Jahweh our God is whensoever we call upon Him? And what great nation is there that hath statutes and judgments so righteous as all this law which I set before you this day? Jahweh hath avouched thee to be a peculiar people to Himself . . . and to make thee high above all nations, which He hath made, in praise, renown and honour.*[2]

---

[1] xxiii. 3-8 : against which note the frequent command to extirpate other peoples, *e.g.* xxv. 17 ff.        [2] iv. 6 ff. ; xxvi. 18.

Further, there is the frequent insistence by Deuteronomy upon its absolute sufficiency for Israel. The Word of God is no more *hidden*, nor has its meaning or interpretation to be brought *from afar*. The Word has come *very nigh* to the people, *in their mouth and heart*. All that remains is to practise it : *that thou mayest do it*.[1] Some maintain that its authors even conceive of Deuteronomy as the exhaustive and final revelation of God to His people, and quote the verses : *ye shall not add to the word which I command you, neither shall ye diminish it ; whatsoever thing I am commanding you, observe to do it : thou shalt not add thereto nor diminish it*.[2] Now it would indeed be a paradox if Deuteronomy, the fruit of a long development of religion, the manifest proof in all its parts of the progressive character of revelation, had thus foreclosed the question of further progress and shut the mouth of prophecy for ever. But this is not so, as its own words explicitly prove : *I will raise them up a prophet from among their brethren like unto thee, and will put my words in his mouth and he shall speak unto them all that I command him*.[3] Yet while we must acquit the Book itself of regarding revelation as finally complete, this was exactly what its words almost immediately led their readers to do. The legal mind forgot the promise of a new prophet, and interpreted the other sayings we have quoted as if the Book were the final and exhaustive Word of God. Men fastened upon and worshipped the very letter of it, opposing and preferring the written revelation to the new and living word which Jeremiah brought to them. As Dr. Davidson remarks : 'Pharisaism and

*Its Sufficiency and Ethical Absolutism : the One Book (?)*

---

[1] xxx. 11-14.     [2] iv. 2 ; xii. 32.     [3] xviii. 15-19.

Deuteronomy came into the world the same day.'[1]
The rise of this narrow temper was also assisted by
the Deuteronomists' constant and vigorous conjunction
of righteousness with good fortune. They were not
without the perception that God sometimes afflicted His
people for the purpose of testing and humbling them. So
far as it refers to the nation's past, they have expressed
this truth in language of exquisite beauty.[2] But for
the future they insist unwearyingly and without qualification on the certainty that righteousness will bring
prosperity, but wickedness ill-fortune; and that it is the
*doing* of the Law, the observance of its manifold laws
both ethical and ceremonial, which comprises the duty,
and will ensure the political and economic stability, of
the people. Such sayings the predecessors of Pharisaism hardened into a dogma, the contradiction of which
by the facts of experience led to the rise of scepticism
in Israel—a scepticism that we find first expressed by
Jeremiah[3] and Habakkuk.

But while confined to Israel, and exhibiting the
other limitations we have defined, Deuteronomy covers
The Great every department of the national life—not the
Width of the
Book's Interest worship alone, nor merely the duties and rights
and Care. of the Priesthood, but the monarchy, the discharge of justice, the character and judgment of prophecy,
the conduct of war, agriculture and commerce, the interests of the family and education, the relief of the poor
and the treatment of the lower animals, in as complete
a system of public religion as the world has ever seen.
The obligation, which the authors feel, of limiting the
national worship to one locality, has neither shortened

[1] Art. 'Jeremiah,' Hastings' *D.B.*    [2] viii. 2-5.    [3] xii. 1 f.

their vision of the land nor restrained their hearts from
the whole compass of the people's life. There is no
stage of Israel's legislation from which we enjoy so wide
and sympathetic a prospect of land and people. One of
the most frequently enforced obligations to love and
serve God is His gift of *this land,* whose singular pre-
ciousness and beauty is as lavishly described[1] as its
sacredness is solemnly proclaimed : *Thou shalt not cause
the land to sin which Jahweh thy God giveth thee for an
heritage. Thy cities* and *thy gates* are among the most
often recurring formulas by which the laws (except
those relating to the central sanctuary) are   Its regard for
affirmed to be applicable throughout the   the Provinces.
whole country ; and the laws are designed for a widely
scattered people still mainly employed in agriculture.[2] To this stage of life the blessings and the
curses are, with one exception,[3] confined, and the
happiness of the people is described as in rural
wealth and pleasures. It is remarkable how the very
fringes of country life are considered—dropped sheaves,
strayed animals, and the like ; and also how much care
is taken for remote persons and places—for fugitives
from blood at a distance from the central sanctuary,[4] for
escaped slaves,[5] and for the victims of murder and outrage
in lonely fields far from houses.[6] If the writers belonged
to Jerusalem, they did not write from behind her walls.
The whole country was upon their conscience and their
heart ; its townships and villages, farms and homesteads,
vineyards, fields and mines, long roads and desert places.
One would think that not the law of the central sanc-

---

[1] xi. 10 ff.   [2] This even in xiv. 22-29.   [3] xxviii. 12*b*, 43 f.
[4] iv. 41 ff.   [5] xxiii. 15.   [6] xxi. 1 ; xxii. 25 ff.

tuary, but the interests of the rest of the land, were the main anxiety of the Book; so careful, for instance, are its provisions for the priests of the disestablished shrines, and for the domestic convenience of the people in whose gates sacrifice, hitherto the invariable form of the slaughter of animals for food, is no longer to be allowed. Down to small details and to the remotest distances, interests, whether vested or not, are safeguarded, and compensation is made for the disturbance caused to the rural economy by the centralisation of the cultus. But such provisions form only part of the wide and mindful humanity of the Book. Its ethics are the social justice and pure charity of the great prophets. Its care is vigilant for the poor, the widow, the fatherless, the slave, the debtor, and *the stranger that is within thy gates.* Nor are the animals forgotten.

It is only when we thus realise all the tempers which inspire Deuteronomy—some of them, it may be, not yet articulate by the date of the Reform, of which

The Secrets of the Book's Influence.

parts of the Book were the cause and parts the precipitate—that we can explain the rapid and unanimous adoption of the system by the nation : in spite of the fact that it involved the alteration of so many sacred customs and the disturbance of so many interests throughout the land. The religious instincts and natural conscience of the people, headed by their pious king, were stirred. Truly God Himself came near to the heart of the people in such a story of grace, such repeated and urgent calls to righteousness: we cannot but believe that the chief influence of the Book lay in its religion proper—the revelation of Him which it

conveyed. Then Israel's patriotism was inflamed, their
intelligence aroused, and their affections drawn forth by
the humane ideals presented to them. Every home,
every heart was appealed to. Every interest found
itself respected. Upon the poor and the oppressed a
great hope dawned. But to all this volume of movement, the edge and point was the conviction of the
zealous leaders of reform—sharpened as it had been by
the cruel experiences of Manasseh's reign—that only
such radical and rigorous measures as Deuteronomy
enjoins could save their religion from submergence by
heathenism, and their nation from destruction. And
now for the full operation of all these motives the
political situation gave the opportunity which had been
denied to the efforts of Ḥezekiah. Israel was free for the
moment from foreign servitude—free to obey its God
and to govern itself in His fear.

The Book of Deuteronomy is singularly reticent as to
the name of the place which Jahweh would choose for
His one altar and sanctuary. Jerusalem is *It does not*
not mentioned ; neither in the laws nor in the *name Jeru-*
introductions and supplements.[1] We can *salem.*
hardly doubt the reason of this. The authors of the
policy were more concerned to state the religious principle involved in it than to advocate the claims of a
particular locality. Nor did the latter need to be
asserted. Jerusalem was the only possible candidate for
the unique position designated by Deuteronomy. We
have seen the gradual growth of Temple and City at a
time when they had still many ancient and more powerful

---

[1] And that although the cities of refuge are given by name, and sacred
functions are appointed at Ebal and Gerizim, the natural centre of the land.

rivals in the land. We have seen how Isaiah interpreted the Divine purpose in their history and unveiled their glory as the habitation and the hearth of God, and how this sacredness had been vindicated in 701 when every other sanctuary in the land was despoiled. Nowhere else could the centralised ritual be kept so pure as on a site which, never having been used by another deity before Jahweh chose it for Himself, had passed through such a history of divine deed and word. David's, Solomon's, Isaiah's, Ḥezeḳiah's work was completed by Josiah, and the Temple became the single sanctuary of the One God.

The record of how Josiah carried out the Deuteronomic reforms[1] is composite, and beset with later intrusions. But it is certain that the Temple, the City and their surroundings were largely purged of heathen altars, rites and ministries; and that from Geba' to Beersheba'—the limits of Judah— the high-places of Jahweh were abolished, His rural priests brought to Jerusalem, and His sacrifices and festivals established there alone. The former side of the Reform does not appear to have been so successful as the latter. The heathen cults may have ceased for the rest of Josiah's reign, but upon his death they immediately revived. But the centralisation of the national worship of Jahweh, the establishment of the one sanctuary for the One God, was settled once for all. And this was the main thing. Whether cleansed or not from heathen cults, Jerusalem became, not merely the principal school and shrine of the one great system of ethical and intellectual monotheism in the ancient world; but its

The Reforms which it effected.

---

[1] 2 Kings xxiii. : see above, p. 201 *n.* 1.

material sign and sacrament, its only altar, and for centuries almost an equal object with its God of confidence
and longing.

While it was thus possible to execute the formal
decrees of Deuteronomy with regard to the worship, it
was by no means so easy to realise the ethical
ideals, and one after another these faded even
in Josiah's time. Removed from close contact
with the agricultural and pastoral habits of
the people, which moulded the uses of the rural shrines,
the ritual was relieved from the debasing infections of
nature-worship. But at the same time there was danger
that the healthy influence of association with the simple
life of the common people and their domestic interests
would be lost. As a matter of fact the sensuous but
naïve credulities of the country were replaced by another
materialism. Jeremiah reports that a more sophisticated
and tyrannous superstition grew up about the one altar
and the letter of the Law on which its ritual was
founded.[1] The vivid sympathy which we have seen in
Deuteronomy for the whole land and its life was replaced
by a fanaticism for the Temple and the City. Even so
definite an ordinance as that for the admission of the
rural priests to equal office and privilege with those of
Jerusalem was ignored. And in general the social
legislation of Deuteronomy was neglected. As the
prophets complain, the people of Jerusalem learned
neither justice nor mercy toward the poor and the
slave.

The great influx of rural priests undoubtedly introduced to the capital a measure of moral vigour and

*Observance of its formal, neglect of its ethical, Demands.*

---

[1] See above, pp. 215 ff.

independence of thought: witness Jeremiah himself. But it also meant the increase of the number of religious

**Double Character of the Increase of the Temple Priesthood.**

idlers, especially when those priests were refused admission to the full work and honour of the altar. Divorced more or less from local and domestic interests, deprived of the highest ambitions of their profession, and reduced in many cases to a degrading beggary and subsistence on chance, the Levites were left to develop a narrow and a hollow patriotism without responsibility or healthy discipline. Thus there was constituted a body of zealots and fanatics, who are already apparent in the days of Jeremiah, and who never ceased in the sacred courts till the days of Titus: men who turned the Temple into a fortress and neglected the rest of their land and its interests.

Thrice every year the manhood of the people gathered to Jerusalem, and what that meant for the national unity,

**The Temple the National Auditorium.**

discipline and instruction in great causes cannot be exaggerated. We see it already in Jeremiah's choice of such seasons for the delivery of his prophecies. He could then address the whole of Judah in the courts of the Temple. But at the same time these mobs were prone to be as fuel to the false fire of the zealots. Instead of bringing to the capital the health and sanity of the country, they too often took back to the provinces the fever of the City.

In short, from the very morrow of the Deuteronomic centralisation of the cultus in Jerusalem, we see at work all the forces, good and bad, which form the mingled glory and horror of her future history.

# CHAPTER IX

## JEREMIAH'S JERUSALEM
### c. 625-586 B.C.

THE ministry of Jeremiah to Jerusalem covered as long and as critical a period of the City's history as did that of Isaiah, and was exercised upon the same wide complex of affairs: the ethics, the worship and the politics of her people. Isaiah and Jeremiah scourged the same vices, and enforced the same principles of righteousness. Both inveighed against prevalent idolatries; both wrought with reforming kings, who not only sought to extirpate the idols, but, for the further security of a pure faith, took measures to concentrate the national worship upon the Temple. As for politics, Jeremiah, as well as Isaiah, had to fight a party which intrigued for alliance with Egypt, to confront the armies of a northern empire, and to live with his city through the terrors of a siege.

*Isaiah and Jeremiah: the Resemblances of their Ministries.*

In spite, however, of so much outward resemblance, the respective attitudes of the two prophets towards Jerusalem were distinguished by inherent differences, which are perceptible even in the ethical tempers of their ministries, while in the political issues they become so wide as almost to appear irreconcilable. Ethically, Jeremiah was more

*The Differences: 1. Ethical*

rigorous and hopeless than Isaiah. The evil reign of
Manasseh had come between and revealed the incorrigible
bias of the people to idolatry and immorality. The
efforts of Ḥezekiah to purify and concentrate the national
worship did not succeed, and Isaiah was therefore spared
the duty of criticising the popular effects of such measures.
But Jeremiah lived through a reform and a centralisation
of the worship only to be confronted by their moral
failure and their many abuses. In other words, while
the one prophet led up to Deuteronomy, the ministry of
the other was compelled to lead away from Deuteronomy.
Isaiah had interpreted to Jerusalem God's purpose in her
selection by David and throughout her history since. It
had been God's will to make Jerusalem *the City of
Righteousness*; and even though she had failed of that
ideal, she was still His dwelling, whose eternal throne
the prophet saw behind the altar of her Temple. She was
still, in a shaken and distracted world, the only refuge of
His Remnant. Upon the faith roused by such visions,
Isaiah, almost alone, carried the City inviolate through
the Assyrian invasion; and her deliverance in 701 set
God's signature to the interpretation which he had given
of her history. But Jeremiah saw no visions of the
unique sacredness of Jerusalem. His inaugural sacraments were provided not in the Temple, but in the open
air of the country, to which he belonged: in a blossom-
ing almond twig, and a boiling caldron with its face to
the fateful north, out of whose smoke came actual, vivid
heathen to set their thrones in the gates of Jerusalem.
Ḥezekiah's efforts to translate Isaiah's ideals for the City
into fact had failed, in spite of the miraculous attestation of
her inviolableness, and had been succeeded by the relapse

into the idolatries of Manasseh. Josiah's measures, though thorough and apparently successful, effected only a formal and unethical fulfilment of the prophetic ideals. Therefore where Isaiah had travailed with the hearts of his generation in order to prove that the City was sacred and impregnable to the forces of the world, Jeremiah was compelled to contend with that superstition of her security, to which the faith of his great predecessor had been perverted by her people, and to doom to destruction what Isaiah had triumphantly saved. Isaiah inspired her timid king to defy the northern foes and tell them that God would turn them back before they touched her walls. Jeremiah had to scorn the immoral confidence of the citizens in her invincibility, and to call the prophets false who predicted that she would not be taken.

It was not, however, only ethical reasons or disappointment with the effects of reform which thus drove Jeremiah into an attitude towards Jerusalem anti-
thetic to that of Isaiah. The political situa- 2. In the Political Situation.
tion had also changed. By Jeremiah's time Jerusalem was no longer the indispensable fortress of God's Remnant which the statesmanship of Isaiah had seen her to be in the Assyrian world of his day. The empire, which now threatened Judah, bore a different policy to the victims of its sword. Conquest by Assyria had meant national annihilation. Northern Israel did not survive it, and we may be sure that if Jerusalem had fallen to Sennacherib in 701 Judah must have perished with her sister. But, with political insight equal to Isaiah's, Jeremiah perceived the wide difference of the Babylonian policy. This also meant exile for the peoples whom its armies had conquered, but it did not involve

their utter destruction. A people uprooted from their own land might live and even flourish when replanted in the soil of Babylonia and surrounded by a political climate which—we do not exactly know why—was more favourable to their survival than the Assyrian had been. So Jeremiah not only refrained from predicting the inviolableness of Jerusalem, but actively counselled her surrender to the Chaldeans, advised her banished people to adapt themselves to their servitude, and foresaw with hopefulness their long residence in a foreign land.

These, then, are the two reasons why the watchword of Isaiah's ministry was the Remnant, secure upon their immovable City, while that of Jeremiah's may be said to have been the Return, after the City had been *wiped as a dish* and her people scattered among the nations.

I have hinted that one difference between the two prophets was that of their local origins; and the emphasis of this also must be put into our contrast. Isaiah was Isaiah of Jerusalem. The City was his platform and the scenery of all his visions. He moved about her a free and commanding figure, sure of his influence upon her rulers, and with an imagination never more burning than when exercised upon her Temple and her walls. But Jeremiah was a countryman, whose earliest landscapes were the desert hills and stony fields of Benjamin, with their agricultural shrines; who found his first sacraments, as has been said, in the simple phenomena of rural life; and whose youthful ears were filled, not like Isaiah's with the merrymaking of the crowds of *the boisterous City*, but with the cry of the defenceless villages. When at last

3. Isaiah of Jerusalem; Jeremiah of the Country.

Jeremiah came to the capital it was to see the Temple of
Isaiah's vision turned into a fetish by the people; it was
to be treated as a traitor by her rulers; it was to find in
her his repeated prison.   And even when the siege was
close about the City, and the prophet himself was shut up
in the court of the guard, his hope still anchored in the
country.   His pledge for the future of the nation he gave
neither in the Temple nor in anything else of which
Jerusalem boasted, but in the purchase from his uncle of
one of the family fields in 'Anāthôth: for his heart was
set not upon the survival of civic or priestly glory, but
on the restoration of agriculture throughout the land
which was now desolate and in the hands of the foe.[1]
We must count it one not only of the most pathetic but
of the most significant episodes in this rural prophet's
career that he should stake his hope upon those derelict
acres.   It was there, forty winters before, he had seen
the almond-tree blossom, and knew that God was awake.[2]

Jeremiah was born of a family of priests at 'Anāthôth[3]
between the years 650 and 645, or about the same time
as Josiah himself.   It was to *his own fields*
at this same 'Anāthôth that the chief priest
Abiathar had been banished when Solomon
gave his office to Ṣadok.[4]   The chief priesthood had
since remained in Ṣadok's family; and if, as is probable,
Jeremiah belonged to the stock of Abiathar, he was born
in opposition and with no hereditary interest in the religious authorities of his time.   But 'Anāthôth lies only four
miles from Jerusalem, and its inhabitants have constantly
been in the closest economic relations with their capital.

*Jeremiah
and
'Anāthôth.*

---

[1] Ch. xxxii., especially verses 15, 41, 43 ff. (probably a later commentary
on the episode), contrasted with 29 and 31.

[2] Ch. i. 11, 12.          [3] Jer. i. 1.          [4] See above, p. 49.

We may therefore infer Jeremiah's familiarity from his earliest years with the Temple and other buildings in Jerusalem, with her commercial and religious life, and later with the store of literature that she possessed. Jerusalem is hidden from 'Anāthôth by that branch of the watershed which runs south-east from the main line to the Mount of Olives.[1]   The outlook of the village is upon those rural landscapes which Jeremiah has chiefly reflected in his oracles: the rocks, stony fields, villages and high places of Benjamin, Ramah being especially conspicuous,[2] the hills of Ephraim out of which the great north road comes down upon the capital, the bare heights of the wilderness, the valley of the Jordan, and the hills of Gilead.[3]   But though hidden from the City, 'Anāthôth is within earshot of her life and of all the foreign rumour of which in those times she was full.   Nor should we omit the effect of a boy's accession to the throne and of the growth of his character upon the imagination of this other boy scarcely four miles away.   When both the king and the young provincial priest were about twenty-one, there came the crisis in the history of Western Asia which we have noted on the death of Ashurbanipal.[4]   It was just then, about 625 B.C., *in the thirteenth year of Josiah's reign*, that Jeremiah received God's call to prophesy.   The nation was unreformed and impenitent; full of idolatry and immoral ways of life.   The ominous North was once more boiling like a caldron.[5]   *Kingdoms and Nations—*

Jeremiah's Call.

---

[1] See vol. i. 31.                          [2] xxxi. 15.

[3] Few visitors to Jerusalem go out to 'Anāthôth, now 'Anâtâ, and yet in all the surroundings of the City there is no more instructive site.   Its equal neighbourhood to Jerusalem and the Desert, and its wild outlook, illustrate many passages in the Book of Jeremiah.                     [4] See above, p. 200.

[5] i. 13, 14.

the troubled masses to which Jeremiah constantly refers[1]
—were astir; among them races new to Israel: the
Medes, the Chaldeans, the Scythians. But above this
confusion, so Jeremiah was assured by the sacrament of
the almond-blossom, God was watching, *watching over
His Word to perform it*,[2] His Word of Judgment on
Israel and His promise of their sanctification. The
judgment was certain even if the politics of Western
Asia were still too confused for the discrimination of its
direction and its exact instruments. For a time indeed
one long and terrible movement appeared to embody it.
About 625 a force of Scythians[3] swept through the
Assyrian Empire as far as the frontier of Egypt;[4]
and a number of oracles by Jeremiah[5] are The
generally interpreted as reflecting the char- Scythians.
acteristic warfare of these hordes of horsemen, incapable
of setting a regular siege but rushing the open country
and unfenced towns. The Scythians, however, appear
to have retired from Palestine without invading Judah.
Among such events Jeremiah had been four or five years
a prophet before the discovery of Deuteronomy and the
beginning of Josiah's reforms, 621.[6] The history assigns
to him no part in the transactions connected with the
former. These were all carried through in Jerusalem;

---

[1] Duhm's denial to Jeremiah of such references as well as of all consciousness of a mission to peoples beyond Israel, is contradicted by the circumstances of the prophet's time, his geographical position, and the traditions of
Hebrew prophecy, on which he at first so strongly leant. See also ch. xxvii.

[2] i. 11, 12.

[3] This is the Greek form of their name, Σκύθαι, supposed to be derived
from an original Sku or Saka which (with the prosthetic aleph) appears in the
Assyrian Ashkuza and the Hebrew Ashkenaz, Gen. x. 3; 1 Chron. i. 6;
Jer. li. 27. See Winckler, *K.A.T.*[(3)] 76 *n.* 1, 101 ff. ; Ramsay, *Galatians*, 28 f.

[4] Herodotus, i. 103 ff.

[5] As well as Zephaniah ii.                    [6] See above, pp. 202 f.

he was still at 'Anāthôth.[1] But that he was in sympathy with the religion of the Book we cannot doubt. Its

*Jeremiah and Deuteronomy.* creed, its conceptions of the early relations of Jahweh and Israel, its tenderness and rigour, its dependence on the eighth-century prophets and especially on Hosea, were all also his own. There is even evidence that he accepted the centralisation of the worship, for he includes this in one of his pictures of the ideal future of Israel;[2] and his assistance in effecting it would explain his ill-treatment by the people of 'Anāthôth jealous for their local shrine.[3] On these grounds we may accept the substance at least of the narrative which describes his share in the promulgation of Deuteronomy among the townships of Judah, and his use, on that mission and at other times, of the Deuteronomic phraseology. If in his verse this young prophet echoed Hosea, it is not hard to believe that in his appeals on behalf of the Reforms he adopted the prose style, so infectious and so adapted for hortatory purposes, of the Law-Book which inspired them. But his mind was just of the kind to perceive very soon the inevitable failure of the movement: the superstitious acceptance by the people of the formal side of Deuteronomy, with their neglect of its ethics and spiritual religion.[4] We have no evidence of his further activity

---

[1] His father Hilḳiah being of the stock of Abiathar, cannot have been the same as the chief priest Hilḳiah who discovered the Law-Book, for the latter was of the family of Ṣadoḳ.

[2] xxxi. 6 ff; see below, pp. 253 f.

[3] xi. 18 ff.

[4] Between the extremes of Winckler on the one hand, who reckons Jeremiah as a 'legalist,' and therefore far below Isaiah, and of Duhm on the other hand, who denies to him any sympathy with law or legal reforms, there is the more reasonable mean of allowing to the prophet the

during the rest of the reign of Josiah. He may have
been in doubt for a time, as he was on other subjects during his long career, and have chosen to be
silent; but it is not unlikely that those thoughts were
already at work in his mind which led him to abandon
the national conception of religion that his early
ministry had shared with Deuteronomy, and to develop
the individual aspects of faith and duty of which he
was the first great prophet in Israel. With the defeat
and death of the righteous king at Megiddo   The Battles
in 608, the Deuteronomic movement re-   of Megiddo
ceived a serious if not a fatal check. The centralisation of the worship remained, and the people of Judah
continued to gather to the Temple; but idolatries of
various kinds appear to have revived, and the spirit of
the new king Jehoiakim was very different from that of
his father Josiah. To quote an expression of Ḥabakkuk,
*the Torah was paralysed, and the Mishpat did not march
on.* Judah had passed under a new foreign lordship.
By right of her victory at Megiddo Egypt appointed the
new king and exacted a heavy tribute.[1] The teaching of
Deuteronomy, that the due fulfilment of the Law would
be certainly followed by Israel's victory over other
nations and her great prosperity, was contradicted by
these facts; and the result was the growth of scepticism.

liberty of changing his mind with regard to the Deuteronomic movement as
experience showed him its true character. This interpretation of Jeremiah
is at once the more natural and the more true to the evidence of the Biblical
text. On recent tendencies of modern criticism to confine the interest and
activity of each of the great prophets to one consistent temper and line of
action, see a review by the present writer in the *Review of Theology and
Philosophy* (edited by Menzies) for July and August 1907.

[1] 2 Kings xxiii. 33-35. On the possibility that the tyranny of which
Ḥabakkuk complains was that of Egypt, see the present writer's *Book of
the Twelve Prophets*, ii. 123 f.

In the fourth year of Jehoiakim, 604, Egypt was defeated
<sub>and</sub>        by the Babylonians at Carchemish, and a
Carchemish.   Babylonian supremacy of Western Asia
became certain.   It was then that Jeremiah received the
command to write out all the oracles he had uttered
*from the day I spake unto thee, from the days of Josiah*
Jeremiah     *even unto this day,* and sent Baruch to read
dictates his  them to the people in the Court of the
earlier Oracles
to Baruch.    Temple, that Judah might have one more
opportunity to repent.   Jeremiah dictated the oracles to
Baruch, and we can understand how with this immediate
ethical purpose in view he altered them in the light of
the new political conditions.  When the roll was destroyed
by Jehoiakim, Jeremiah and Baruch made another, and
*added many like oracles.*[1]   This roll is generally understood to have been the source from which our Book of
Jeremiah has derived all its oracles of the prophet up to
Difficulty of   the year 604.   The absence of dates from so
dating them.   many, the circumstances of their dictation,
their probable revision in the light of the now certain
Babylonian supremacy, and the intrusion of so many
titles, glosses and passages of prophecy by later writers,
render the task of arranging them in chronological
order extremely difficult, and in many cases impossible.
Still we can often mark whether an oracle was uttered
before or after the prophet left 'Anâthôth for Jerusalem ;
whether an oracle implies the existence of the rural
high-places or the effects of the Deuteronomic legislation ; whether the battle of Megiddo was past ; and
whether that of Carchemish had been fought.   As
already said, some of the oracles referring to invasion

[1] xxxvi. 32.

reflect the distinctive warfare of the Scythians, but in one or two cases the prophet seems to have altered his description to suit the methods of the new enemies from the north, who, as he was now certain, were to be the instruments of God's judgment upon His impenitent people. After 604, thanks to Baruch, the dates of different events and oracles are either definitely stated, not, however, always correctly, or are clearly betrayed.

We have now before us, first, the distinctive features of Jeremiah's attitude to Jerusalem, explained in the light of his people's conduct and the politics of the *The Details of Jeremiah's Treatment of Jerusalem.* time; second, the main facts of his life and experience up to 604; and third, the character of his oracles before that date. In the light of these we may proceed to trace the details of his treatment of Jerusalem, his judgment of her people, and his predictions of their future, along with the materials which he and Baruch incidentally provide for the topography of the City.

In what are apparently some of the earliest oracles of Jeremiah, now found in chapters ii.-iv. of the Book,[1] the prophet is engaged with the nation as a *The Earliest Oracles, ii.-iv.* whole; her first loyalty to God, her subsequent apostasy increasing from her entrance to the Promised Land, and her present incredible misunderstanding of His ways with her. In these chapters the name of Jerusalem, when used either by itself or in precedence to the land, appears almost exclusively in passages which for other reasons may be assigned to a later date.[2] It is all-Israel

---

[1] Erbt's arguments for a later date for ii. (*Jeremia und seine Zeit*, 129, 235 ff.) are hardly sufficient.

[2] *E.g.* in the title ii. 2*a*, which is not found in the LXX., while the original oracle begins with 2*b* (*I remember the true love of thy youth*, etc.) ; and it is clearly not Jerusalem (which the inserted title names) but the nation as a whole

or Judah with which these early oracles deal.[1] If Jerusalem is mentioned it is as second to Judah,[2] or as the strongest of the fenced cities of the land,[3] or as the public centre at which it was most natural to proclaim the coming disaster.[4] Throughout these oracles the young Jeremiah has on his heart the unprotected villages and the interests of all the *townships of Judah.*[5] The first outbreak of his anxiety for Jerusalem alone occurs at the end of this collection of oracles in a taunt-song,[6] which is one of the pieces that have been reasonably assigned to the Scythian invasion. Two of these so-called 'Scythian Songs' may be given as specimens of his style. The first sounds the alarm of the invasion, and summons the country people to the walled cities :—

> *In Judah make known and Jerusalem,*
> *Proclaim and announce ;*
> *Blow ye the trump through the land,*
> *Call with full voice,*
> *And say, 'Sweep together, come in*
> *To the towns that are fenced.*
> *Lift up the signal towards Sion,*
> *Rouse ye and stay not !'*
> *For evil I bring from the North,*
> *Ruin immense.*

that is addressed (this against Erbt, *Jer. u. seine Zeit*, 128 f.) ; iii. 14-18, which implies the Exile ; iv. 14, which Duhm is right in regarding as an interpolation, for it breaks the connection and weakens the emphasis of the context.

[1] Addressed by name ii. 14, 28, 31 ; iii. 6-13 (this passage may not all be from Jeremiah), 20, 23 ; iv. 1 ; and implied elsewhere.

[2] *Men of Judah and Jerusalem,* iv. 3 ; *men of Judah and inhabitants of Jerusalem,* iv. 4 ; *declare in Judah and publish in Jerusalem,* iv. 5 ; *this people and Jerusalem,* iv. 11*a* (the genuineness of this clause is doubtful).

[3] iv. 5, 6.

[4] iv. 16 : even here Duhm elides the words, *publish against Jerusalem.*

[5] *E.g.* iv. 16.      [6] iv. 29-31.

*The Lion is up from his thicket,*
*Mauler of nations.*
*He hath broke, he hath marched from his place*
*—Thy cities are burning—*
*To turn to a desert thy land,*
*Swept of its people.*
*Gird ye with sackloth for this,*
*Lament and bewail,*
*For His anger turneth not from us,*
*The wrath of the Lord.*[1]

The other piece is held by many to be from the same period, and in that case the prophet predicts, as in the last, the effects of the feared Scythian raids. But if we read the opening verses as the description of an actual invasion, we must refer the verses to another period, either when the Egyptians or when the Babylonians came on the land. The prophet taunts Jerusalem with the same levity which we have seen Isaiah impute to her people. The City hopes to flatter off her enemies; but these are no wooers. It is her life that they seek.

*From the noise of the horse and the bowmen*
*All the land*[2] *is in flight.*
*They are into the caves, they hide in the thickets,*[3]
*Are up on the crags.*
*Every town of its folk is forsaken,*
*No habitant in it!*
*All is up! Thou destined to ruin,*
*What doest thou now?*[4]

---

[1] iv. 5-8. In the Ḳinah measure, alternately three and two accents. In verse 7 two of the clauses have been transposed so as to make this regular.

[2] The correct Greek reading: Heb. *every city*.

[3] So the fuller text of the LXX.

[4] The text of these three lines is uncertain. The reading I conjecture is

וְאֵין יוֹשֵׁב בָּהּ
נוֹאָשׁ וְאַתְּ שְׁדוּדָה
מַה־תַּעֲשִׂי לָךְ

*That thou deck'st thee with deckings of gold—*
*That thou clothest in scarlet,*[1]
*That thou widenest thine eyes with the stibium,*[2]
*In vain dost thou prink!*
*Though lechers they be,-they do loathe thee,*
*Thy life are they seeking!*
*I hear cries of woman in travail,*
*Shrieks of her that beareth.*[3]
*The voice of the daughter of Ṣion, she gaspeth,*
*She spreadeth her hands,*
*' Woe unto me now! For it faileth,*
*My life to the slayers!'*

There are oracles farther on in the Book which apparently are as early as those in chapters ii.-iv.; in Other Early Oracles. them also the interest of the prophet is for all the townships of Judah,[4] and the whole country,[5] on which Jerusalem is conspicuous as the capital, but by no means has a unique sacredness, for he continues to name her second to the country, equally involved in the horrors of the impending invasion, and certain of siege and destruction if her inhabitants do not repent.[6]

To sum up—what Jeremiah has before him in these earlier oracles is the whole land of Judah, with its many In all these Jerusalem secondary to the Land. shrines rank with idolatry, its rural landscapes and figures, its villages defenceless to the foe, and Jerusalem merely as the strongest and most wicked of its cities, to which the country folk

---

[1] These two lines have been transposed, with Duhm and others, to suit the rhythm.

[2]
    ' Ceruse nor stibium can prevail,
       Nor art repair when age makes fail.'
           Collop: *Poesie Reviv'd,* 1656.

[3] Heb. *as of one that beareth for the first time.*

[4] *E.g.* v. 15-17; x. 19-22: apparently from the Scythian period.

[5] xiv. 17, 18; xvii. 1-4 (date uncertain).

[6] vi. 1-8 (but this may be later: see below, p. 246), 23.

flee before the invader, and which, as the climax of all, must fall before him. Many of the passages of which Jerusalem forms the sole or the predominant subject are of later date.

In Chapter v. Jeremiah brings a searching indictment against all classes of the City's population. Professor Duhm has argued that the oracle marks Jeremiah's removal from 'Anāthôth to Jeru- salem, and that this therefore took place before the centralisation of the national worship in the Temple in 620. But he forgets how close 'Anāthôth lay to the capital, and how familiar Jeremiah must have been with the citizens even before he became one of them. More probably the prophet's final migration to Jerusalem took place when the rural shrines, of which 'Anāthôth was one, were abolished, and he and other of their priests were brought by Josiah to the Temple. However that may be, the effects of the centralisation of the worship become very evident in the records of Jeremiah's activity as a prophet. After 620 he is able to address the manhood of the nation in the Temple Courts, where, obedient to Deuteronomy, they gather to the national festivals or fasts. For such addresses we have no dates during the reign of Josiah. Hitzig, Keil and others have assigned to the reign of Josiah chapter vii. 1-15, a passage which contains a speech by Jeremiah to *all Judah*[1] assembled in the Temple; distinguishing it from an address to *all the cities of Judah which are come to worship in Jahweh's house*, chapter xxvi. 1 ff., dated *in the beginning of the reign of Jehoiakim*. These two accounts, however, seem to refer to the same event. In any case

*Oracles after the Deuteronomic Reforms.*

---

[1] vii. 2. The shorter LXX. text is here to be preferred : see next note.

the periodical gatherings in the Temple of all the men of Judah, which are enjoined by Deuteronomy, had become by the end of Josiah's reign so firmly established that they survived through the reign of his very differently minded successor ; and Jeremiah used these gatherings in order to reach the national conscience. *Stand in the court of the House of Jahweh and speak to all the cities of Judah which are come to worship in the house of Jahweh.*[1] And again, in the fourth year of Jehoiakim, when the prophet dictated his oracles to Baruch, he ordered him to read the roll of them *in the ears of the people in the house of Jahweh on a Fast-day, and also in the ears of all Judah who are come in from their cities.*[2] The City in fact has become the auditorium of the nation. Yet even so, it is only because the nation is massed upon the courts of her Temple that the prophet's activity is confined to her. In other words, he concentrates his teaching upon Jerusalem for practical and not for doctrinal reasons ; and neither he himself nor his biographer, Baruch, gives her any precedence (with perhaps one exception [3]) before the rest of the land. In the passages just quoted from xxv. and xxxvi., in chapter xiii.,

*The Temple the National Auditorium.*

*But Jerusalem still secondary to the Land.*

---

[1] xxvi. 2.   The parallel passage in vii. 2 runs thus in the Hebrew text : *Stand in the gate of the house of Jahweh and proclaim there this word, and say, Hearken to the word of Jahweh, all Judah—ye that are entering by these gates to worship Jahweh ;* for which the LXX. has only *Hear the word of Jahweh, all Judah.*

[2] xxxvi. 6.   Compare xxv. 1 f., where it is said that in the fourth year of Jehoiakim Jeremiah *spake with all the people of Judah and to all the inhabitants of Jerusalem.*

[3] ix. 11 [Heb. 10].   *I will make Jerusalem heaps . . . and the cities of Judah a desolation.*   The date of this verse and even its origin from Jeremiah himself are uncertain.

if this be genuine,[1] in chapter xiv., the Great Drought,
and in the Parable of the Potter (chapter xviii.) and the
Symbol of the Potter's Vessel (chapter xix.) the precedence of the Land to the City is constant, in spite of
the fact that the national worship has already been concentrated in the City.[2]

Jeremiah's sermon, recorded in chapter vii. 1-15,[3] reflects another result of the centralisation of the worship:
the popular perversion of the Deuteronomic
insistence on the unique sacredness of Jerusalem. By the beginning of the reign of
Jehoiakim,[4] and in all probability before this
and during the reign of Josiah, the people had come
to regard the Temple as a fetish. *Put not*, he says to
the crowds assembled from all Judah in the Temple
courts, *put not your faith in false words: ' The Temple
of Jahweh, the Temple of Jahweh, the Temple of Jahweh,
there they are.'* [5] He turns his fellow-countrymen to the
amendment of their ways. If they do justice between
man and man, cease to oppress the orphan and widow
and to shed innocent blood *in this place* and to go after

*Jeremiah
rebukes super-
stitious con-
fidence in the
Temple,*

---

[1] A difficult question, but on the whole Erbt's defence of it against Duhm
seems to me strong. Cornill takes xiii. as a unity and the bulk of it from
Jeremiah.

[2] xiii. 9, 13; xiv. 2, 19; xviii. 11; xix. 7, 11; cf. xxv. 1, 18.

[3] Duhm regards this passage as the work of a later expander of some
genuine ideas of Jeremiah, obtained through Baruch's biography: 'great
thoughts, weakly elaborated.' Duhm's view is governed by his quite unsub-
stantial theory that we have no genuine prose discourses from Jeremiah.
Disallow this theory and there remains no objection to the substantial
autnenticity of ch. vii. The ideas are certainly Jeremiah's, and there is
no improbability in his having expressed them in the then current and very
infectious style of Deuteronomy.

[4] Cf. with vii. 1-15 the date in xxvi. 1.

[5] Literally *those*. Cf. our Lord's words, Matt. xxiv. 1 and 2.

other gods; then God will dwell with them in the place
which He gave to their fathers. *Lo, ye are trusting to
false words that profit nothing! Is it* possible? *Ye steal,
murder, commit adultery, perjure yourselves, sacrifice to
Baal and go after other gods whom ye have not known,
and then ye come in and stand before Me in this House,
which is called by My Name, and say, ' We have saved
ourselves! '—In order to do all these abominations! Has
this House become a den of thieves?*[1]

The ecclesiastical ideals of Deuteronomy have been
fulfilled, only to become a superstitious substitute for
its ethical demands. The people have made

and threatens
its destruc-
tion.

obedience to its programme of ritual an
atonement for their evil lives; and impiously
congratulate their blood-stained and lustful hearts that
they are as safe behind the sacred walls as the pure
faith of Isaiah had known itself to be. To all that
kind of sham there is but one end—the destruction
of the abused sanctuary. For this there is a precedent.
*Go now to my sacred place*[2] *which was in Shilo, where at
the first I caused My Name to dwell, and see what I
have done to it for the wickedness of My people Israel.
So now, because ye have done all these deeds (although I
spoke to you in time, but ye hearkened not, and although
I called you, but ye did not answer), I will do to the
House which is called by My Name, in which ye put your
trust, and to the sacred place which I gave to you and
to your fathers, just as I have done to Shilo, and I will
cast you out from My Presence just as I cast out all your
brethren, the whole of the seed of Ephraim.*

[1] Cf. Mark xi. 15 ff.
[2] מָקוֹם here in the same sense as the Arabic Makâm.

We must observe that on this occasion Jeremiah addressed himself not to the nation as a unit (as he had done in his earlier discourses and as the Book of Deuteronomy generally does) but to the separate individuals who compose the nation. This is clear from the parallel account in chapter xxvi. 3: *peradventure they will hear and turn, every man from his evil way*; and is in accordance with the increasing individualism of Jeremiah's ethics, when the failure of the national system of Deuteronomy became apparent and the collapse of the state grew more certain.

*Increasing Individualism of the Prophet's Ethics.*

Jeremiah's prediction of the ruin of the Temple in which the people trusted was addressed to practically the whole nation gathered to a Temple festival.[1] At its close the Temple prophets and priests[2] laid hold on him with the words, *Thou shalt verily die.* To them it was the sheerest sacrilege to say a word against either Temple or City. But the matter, being public, *for all the people were gathered to Jeremiah in the Temple,*[3] the news of it speedily reached the nobles of Judah, and they came up at once from the palace to the Temple and took their seats *in the opening of the new gate of Jahweh.* The prophets and priests then formally accused Jeremiah *to the nobles and all the people*[4] of a capital crime in threatening *this City.* Jeremiah made a calm and dignified reply: the Lord had sent him to prophesy

*Prophets and Priests therefore seek his Death.*

[1] xxvi. 2, 7.

[2] Verse 8. Omit the words *and all the people,* which have been wrongly repeated from verse 7.

[3] Verse 9. But this clause really belongs to the following verse, and explains how the report quickly reached the nobles in the palace.

[4] Verse 11. *The people* were therefore not among his accusers: see the note before the last.

against the Temple and the City; but there was still time by amending their ways to move God to relent. As for himself, he was in their hands, let them do what seemed good to them, only they must know that if they killed him they would bring the guilt of innocent blood upon themselves and the City, for in truth it was Jahweh who had sent him. The nobles and all the people then said he was not guilty of a capital crime, for he had spoken to them in the name of Jahweh; and some of the oldest of the men present testified to the assemblage that when Micah the Morasthite proclaimed a destruction of the City and Temple, Ḥezeḳiah and the men of Judah instead of putting him to death feared God and He averted the disaster. This precedent prevailed and Jeremiah escaped. The king, who was absent on the occasion—it is remarkable that neither now nor in the events related in chapter xxxvi. is Jehoiaḳim present in the Temple—pursued even to Egypt another prophet who spoke as Jeremiah had done, and put him to death.

*Acquitted by the Princes and the People.*

The people's relapse into idolatry after the collapse of the Deuteronomic ideals in the disaster at Megiddo (608 or 607 B.C.) confirmed Jeremiah in his belief of the inevitableness of the destruction of Jerusalem. In the fact of the Potter at his wheel, changing his first plans for a lump of clay, as he finds it under his hand unsuitable to them, chapter xviii. 1 ff.,[1] Jeremiah sees an illustration of how God may change His purpose for Israel. Chapter xix.,

*Other Oracles under Jehoiaḳim, 608-597.*

---

[1] Undated, but most probably from Jehoiaḳim's reign. Cornill dates xviii. 1-4 between 620 and 610, denies the genuineness of 5-12, and puts 13-17 and 18-20 under Jehoiaḳim.

the story of how Jeremiah broke a potter's jar at the Gate Harṣith, concentrates this lesson upon Jerusalem and the Temple.[1] The prophets of Jerusalem, now the religious centre of the land, are themselves immoral and the source of all the national sin. We must note that Jeremiah considers their immorality as more horrible than the Baal-worship of the prophets of Samaria.[2] Therefore Jeremiah is certain of her fall. For this foe is not one who will be turned as the Scythians were. The prophet varies a line he had used in the Scythian songs about fleeing into the fenced cities, and adds to it a note of despair. For walls are no refuge from the Babylonians. The measure of the piece is broken and uncertain.[3]

> *Why sit we still !   Sweep together,*
> *Let us enter the fortified cities,*
> *    That there we may perish !*
> *For our God, He hath doomed us to perish,*
> *He hath given us the poisonous water :*
> *    Against Him we have sinned.*
> *Hope of peace there was once,*
> *    Now there is panic.*[4]

---

[1] Also undated ; some place it in Jehoiaḳim's (so Cornill), some in Ṣedeḳiah's reign. Duhm's objections to the authenticity of the narrative are arbitrary.

[2] xxiii. 3-15 : certainly to be dated after the centralisation of the worship and probably in the reign of Jehoiaḳim, though some assign it to Ṣedeḳiah's. Even Duhm admits this oracle as genuine.

[3] viii. 14-ix. i. [Eng. =viii. 14-23, Heb.]. The various opinions as to the date of this oracle are proof of the impossibility of assigning it with certainty to any definite point in the prophet's career. Cornill (pp. 112, 123) takes the whole section viii. 4-23 as an original unity connected by Jeremiah himself with the Temple discourse which precedes it, and therefore one with the latter in subject if not in date. But it may be one of those pieces which the prophet added in 604 to his earlier oracles, when he came to dictate the second roll (xxxvi. 32).

[4] Verse 15 has been expanded from xiv. 19. For בעתה read with LXX. בהלה. See Giesebrecht, Duhm, and Cornill.

*From Dan a sound has been heard,*
*The hinnying of his horses,*
*With the noise of the neigh of his stallions*
*The earth is aquake.*
' *Lo, I am sending upon you*
*Serpents and basilisks,*
*Against whom availeth no charm,*
*But they will bite you.*'
*For that this grief hath no comfort,*[1]
*Sick is my heart.*
*Hark to the cry of my people*
*Wide o'er the land!*
' *Is Jahweh no longer in Ṣion?*
*Is there no King in her?*'
' *Why have they vexed Me with idols,*
*Vanities alien?*'
*Harvest is over, the summer is ended;*
*We are not saved!*
*For the breaking of the daughter of my people*
*I break, I darken.*
*Horror hath seizèd upon me,*
*Pangs of a woman.*[1]
*Is there no balm still in Gilead?*
*Is there no healer?*
*Why will the wounds not be staunched*[2]
*Of the daughter of my people?*
*Oh that my head were but waters,*
*Mine eyes springs of tears,*
*Night and day would I weep*
*For the slain of my people!*

*Is there no Jahweh in Ṣ̀ion, is there no king there?*—
it is an echo on the lips of the people of that same

Once more
against the
Temple super-
stition.

superstitious belief in the inviolableness of the
Temple which we have heard before : the
perversion of Isaiah's faith in her sacredness.
Immediately the voice of God replies that He is wearied
with their idolatry. This quotation from the lips of
the people of what might have been the very words of

---

[1] After the LXX.　　　　[2] Heb., *Why mounts not the healing skin.*

Isaiah is an instructive proof of how the pure ethical faith of one generation may become the desperate fetish of the next.

Another piece definitely anticipates the fall and destruction of the City. The order of some of the lines has been altered in translation.[1]

> *Jerusalem, who shall console thee,*
> *Who shall bemoan thee?*
> *Who shall but turn him to ask*
> *After thy welfare?*
> *'Tis Me whom thou hast rejected,*
> *Turned thy back to,*
> *And I stretch My hand to destroy,*
> *Sick of relenting.*
> *I will winnow you out with the fan*
> *In the gates of the land,*
> *Bereave and extirpate My people*
> *Because of their ways.*
> *More are their widows become*
> *Than sand of the sea.*
> *I will bring upon mother and son*
> *Destroyers at noon,*
> *In a moment let fall on them*
> *Terror and panic.*
> *The mother of seven hath fainted,*
> *Breathed out her life;*
> *Set is her sun in the daytime,*
> *Baffled and shamèd.*
> *Their remnant I give to the sword*
> *In face of their foes.*

And again the beautiful lines—

> *Call ye the keening women to come,*
> *Send for the wise ones,*
> *That they hasten and sing us a dirge*
> *Till with tears our eyes run down,*
> *Our eyelids with water.*

> .    .    .    .    .    .

---

[1] xv. 5-9.

> *For death is come up to our windows*
> *And into our palaces;*
> *The children are cut from the streets,*
> *The youths from the places;*
> *And the corpses of men are fallen*
> *Like dung on the field,*
> *Like wisps that the reaper has dropped,*
> *And nobody gathers.*[1]

From this time, then, about 604 or 603 B.C., Jeremiah was certain of the fall of the City, which less than a century before Isaiah had so triumphantly saved. Nor had he any doubt of the quarter from which her executioner was to come. The battle of Carchemish left Nebuchadrezzar, the Chaldean, master of Western Asia.

*Jerusalem Delenda.*

For want of a date it is impossible to say whether an oracle with so early a position in the Book as chapter vi. 1 ff. arose from this time: it describes enemies besieging the City, who are certainly not the Scythians, for these appear not to have cast mounts or ramps against fortified places, but when they attacked them did so by 'rushing' the walls. But the kind of siege described suits the Egyptians as well as the Babylonians; and the oracle is as dateable from the years immediately after Megiddo when Necho had Palestine in his power, as from those after Carchemish when he had yielded this sovereignty to Nebuchadrezzar. But if, as is reasonable, we allow any genuine elements in chapter xxv. 1-14,[2] we have among them a distinct statement that Jerusalem shall fall to the king of Babylon. Jehoiakim seemed to have turned the edge of this sentence upon his capital by

*Arrival of the Babylonians.*

---

[1] ix. 16 (partly), 17, 20, 21.  [2] See Giesebrecht and Cornill on this passage.

submission to Nebuchadrezzar, and remained his vassal for three years, 604-601. Then he rebelled, and Judah was invaded by a Babylonian army aided by bands of Aram, 'Ammon and Moab. The country people and even such nomads from the desert as the Rechabites, flocked for refuge to Jerusalem : an illustration of how the population of the City was always increased upon the threats of invasion.[1] What happened to Jehoiakim is uncertain. From the Book of Kings[2] we may infer that he died a natural death, while the statement in Chronicles[3] that he was taken by the Babylonians and carried into exile, is difficult to reconcile with the fact that three months later Jerusalem, under Jehoiakin, was besieged by Nebuchadrezzar himself, and almost immediately surrendered. The king, the royal family, and the court, *Siege of Jerusalem and First Captivity, 601 B.C.* with the flower of the population,[4] were carried into Babylonia; but a further respite was granted to Jerusalem under Mattaniah or Ṣedeḳiah, whom Nebuchadrezzar placed on the throne as his vassal.

To these events we have no reference by Jeremiah himself beyond a short elegy upon the exiled Jehoahaz.[5] Perhaps, till they were over, the prophet re- *Silence of Jeremiah.* mained hidden outside Jerusalem[6] in the refuge to which he had fled from Jehoiakim. This suggestion is strengthened by the fact that he escaped the deportation of the notables of the City to Babylonia.

---

[1] xxxv. : this chapter is dated in Jehoiakim's reign (verse 1). Many transfer it to Ṣedeḳiah's reign, 588-87. It is possible that the text gives a wrong date, like ch. xxvii. 1. But 2 Kings xxiv. 1 ff. describes a Chaldean invasion of Judah in Jehoiakim's days. [2] 2 Kings xxiv. 6.
[3] 2 Chron. xxxvi. 6 ; cf. Daniel i. 2 ; Josephus x. *Ant.* vi. 3.
[4] Jeremiah xxiv. 1. [5] xxii. 10 ff. [6] As Erbt suggests, p. 19.

Ṣedeḳiah, whom Nebuchadrezzar installed in place of Jehoiakin, was master neither of his throne nor of him-
*Ṣedeḳiah : his Character.* self. A vassal, in the hand of his powerful lord, yet constantly goaded to revolt by his neighbours and a restless faction of his own subjects; deprived of the strongest of his people and dependent upon a council of inexperienced upstarts, yet tempted to rebel by the strength of his walls and the popular belief in their inviolableness; sensitive, if only from superstition, to the one high influence left him, yet urged in a contrary direction by prophets who appealed to the same God as Jeremiah did—the last king of Judah is one of the most pathetic figures even in her history and forms a dramatic centre for its closing tragedy.

During the first years of his reign there was nothing for Ṣedeḳiah and his people but to remain submissive to
*His first years : establishment of Idolatry.* their Babylonian lord. This was in agreement with the convictions of Jeremiah, and therefore these years bring us no record of action by him, unless we are to assign to them any of those denunciations of idolatry which he is usually supposed to have published under Jehoiaḳim. As in the time of Manasseh, the servitude to a heathen empire involved the admission to the national sanctuary of the gods of that empire. Ezekiel[1] gives us a picture of the Babylonian idolatry which invaded the Temple under Ṣedeḳiah, and to which it is possible that some of Jeremiah's descriptions of the worship of *the host of heaven* may refer. Ezekiel also describes Jerusalem as full of moral wrong and the stupid pride of the baser people left to her. They, forsooth, were Jahweh's true

---

[1] Ch. viii.

remnant, because they alone were spared to the City![1]
They had usurped the offices and estates of their
exiled countrymen. They were full of the Foolishness of
arrogance of the upstart and of those who, the Rulers.
having been saved only because of their inferiority, impute their salvation with equal folly either to their own
merits or to the special favour of Heaven. Their self-
confidence grew, till it inevitably turned upon its patron,
and, fortified by proposals from others of his vassals, they
began to intrigue against Nebuchadrezzar.

It is at this point that the record of Jeremiah's public
ministry is resumed. Ambassadors having arrived from
Moab and 'Amnon, Tyre and Ṣidon—perhaps Resumption
in the fourth year of Ṣedeḳiah, that is 593,[2]— of Jeremiah's
Public
Jeremiah was directed to meet their proposals Ministry.
for common revolt against Babylon by making yokes
for himself and for them, as symbols that the Babylonian
yoke would not be broken. But the party of revolt had
also its prophets who spake in the name of Jahweh, and
we can easily understand how sincerely these men felt
the truth of their message. Jahweh was Judah's God,
who had already delivered her from an invader as

---

[1] Ch. xi. 15 ; cf. Jeremiah xxiv.

[2] Jeremiah xxvii., xxviii. xxvii. 1, which fixes these events *in the beginning of the reign of Jehoiaḳim*, is both a late addition (which the LXX. Version
is still without) and a false one: as even our English Revisers allow themselves to affirm, substituting on the margin the name of Ṣedeḳiah for that
of Jehoiaḳim, and appealing to verses 3, 12, 20, and xxviii. 1. Chaps.
xxvii.-xxix. form a group by themselves, being distinguished by certain
literary characteristics from the rest of the Book of Jeremiah. But xxvii.
also differs much from xxviii. ; it is more diffuse, and its Hebrew text contains many additions, whose style no less than their absence from the Greek
version proves them to be late. In xxvii., too, Jeremiah is introduced in the
first person, while in xxviii. he appears in the third. In the text above use
is mainly made of xxviii. The date suggested for the events of which both
chapters treat, the fourth year of Ṣedeḳiah, is by no means certain.

powerful as the Babylonian. In affirming that He would do so once more those prophets were not solely inflamed by a fanatic patriotism and a mere military confidence in the nation's Divine leader. No doubt they desired as much as Jeremiah himself did to banish from Jahweh's Temple the foreign gods and their impure rites. It was a plausible opposition with which Jeremiah was confronted, and the way in which he dealt with it, uncertain at first whether it might not be genuinely inspired of Jahweh, forms one of the most interesting episodes in the history of prophecy. Only observe how, unlike his contemporary Ezekiel, Jeremiah is indifferent to the part which the question of the Temple plays in the controversy. This is to be solved, he feels, by no dogmas connected with the Temple or the Law, but upon principles which are purely ethical and political.

*His Doubt*

When Jeremiah was going about with the bar upon his neck he was met by *a prophet*, Hananiah ben-'Azzur, who in the name of Jahweh told him that the Babylonian yoke would be broken, Jehoiakin be restored, and the sacred vessels brought back which Nebuchadrezzar had carried away. Jeremiah did not contradict this, but prayed that it might be as Hananiah said, and solemnly left the question to the issue of events ; evidently in doubt for the moment as to whether the word of Jahweh was with himself or with the other. The confident Hananiah broke the bar on Jeremiah's neck, the symbol of the Babylonian yoke, *and the prophet Jeremiah went his way.* Later, Jeremiah's confidence was restored. He denounced Hananiah as false, and—in the spirit of Deuteronomy itself—predicted his

*and Debate with Hananiah.*

death.[1]  Thenceforth he remained constant in his conviction that the only hope for Judah was in submission
to the Babylonians.  If Ṣedeḳiah revolted, Jerusalem
must fall.

If the date we have assumed for this episode be correct,
Ṣedeḳiah did not venture to break his homage to Nebuchadrezzar for four or five years.  But in 588
a new monarch ascended the throne of Egypt,
Ḥophra [2] by name, and began to interfere in
the politics of Palestine.  The Egyptian party

*Activity of Egypt: Nebuchadrezzar besieges Jerusalem.*

in Jerusalem found its opportunity, and Ṣedeḳiah appears
to have come to an understanding with the Pharaoh.[3]
Against this coalition Nebuchadrezzar moved south in
person, and established his headquarters at Riblah on the
Orontes.  On the tenth day of the tenth month of the
ninth year of Ṣedeḳiah, January 588-587 B.C., a Babylonian army began the siege of Jerusalem.

In this swift act of arms Ṣedeḳiah and his people
might have seen the contradiction of Ḥananiah's prophecy; and at first sight it is surprising that
they did not surrender the City.  Their resolution to defend it proves the sincerity of

*Spirited Defence of the City.*

the party whom Jeremiah himself at first treated with
respect.  And in truth, besides their religious beliefs,
this party of resistance had much that was substantial
on which to rely.  The walls of Jerusalem were strong
and well garrisoned.  The Babylonian general did not
attempt to storm them, but, like Titus centuries after, he

---

[1] The verses stating this, xxviii. 16 f., are doubted by some critics.

[2] 'The Hebrew transcription is rather exact.'—W. M. Müller, *Enc. Bibl.*
col. 2107.  Herodotus: 'Ἀπρίης.  He is the Pharaoh of Jer. xxxvii. 5, 7, 11.

[3] Ezek. xvii. 15.

built a rampart round the City. Egypt, too, was really ready to move to her relief; and in order to show the sincerity of their faith in the help of Jahweh, the king and his council took the first real step towards fulfilling the spirit of the Deuteronomic laws by engaging in the Temple to enfranchise all their Jewish slaves.[1] The atonement appeared to be successful. An Egyptian army advanced towards Jerusalem, and the Babylonians raised the siege. The confidence of Jeremiah's opponents revived. To the sincerely religious among them it may have appeared as if Jahweh was repeating the wonderful relief of 701. But king and people forgot their oath to release the slaves; and on this ethical ground, if also from his saner estimate of the political situation, Jeremiah proclaimed that the Egyptians would withdraw and the Babylonians come back to besiege and to take the City. Either then, or previously, he replied to a deputation from the king, who inquired whether Jahweh had not been propitiated, that Jahweh's purpose was clear. They must not flatter themselves that the Chaldeans would depart. Even if the expedition of Pharaoh were not futile, even if he had smitten the whole Chaldean army and only the wounded were left to it, *these would rise up every man in his tent and burn the City*.[2] That is to say, Jeremiah, now indifferent as to the military issue of the imminent conflict between Egypt and Babylon, was ethically convinced of the doom of Jerusalem. But the opposition to him remained. When, taking advantage of the withdrawal of the Chaldeans, he tried to go out to 'Anāthôth to secure his patrimony, a captain of the guard arrested him on the charge of deserting to

*Temporary Raising of the Siege.*

*Predictions and Imprisonment of Jeremiah.*

[1] Jer. xxxiv. 8 ff.    [2] xxxvii. 1-10.

the enemy. In spite of his denial, *the princes*—how changed from those of Jehoiakim's reign!—*smote him and put him in a pit in the house of Jonathan the scribe.* Here he received a secret message from the distracted king inquiring if there was any word from the Lord. He replied firmly that Ṣedeḳiah would be delivered into the hands of the king of Babylon, and then claimed that he ought to be set free. He was innocent, and if left in this dungeon, would die. Ṣedeḳiah answered with a sordid compromise. He took Jeremiah out of the pit, but confined him in *the court of the guard, and gave him daily a loaf from the bakers' bazaar, till all the bread in the City was done.*[1]

The Babylonians returned, and the siege was held closer than before. Jeremiah appears to have got his release, but was a second time imprisoned,[2] without doubt on the charge of *weakening the men of war* by persisting in his call to surrender.[3] They cast him into a cistern in the house of Malkiah, from the mire of which he was drawn by Ebed-Melek, the Ethiopian, and placed in the court of the guard, where the king again consulted him. It is uncertain whether it was during his first or this second imprisonment that, confident as ever of the fall of the City, he pledged his hope for the future of the nation by purchasing from his uncle the fields in 'Anāthôth.[4] But though Jerusalem should be burnt, he predicted its rebuilding[5] and its restoration as a centre of worship.[6] The form in which the latter prediction is put is very significant.

*Resumption of Siege: Jeremiah's second Imprisonment.*

*His Confidence in the Future.*

---

[1] xxxvii. 11-21.  [2] xxxiii. 1-13.  [3] xxxviii. 4.
[4] xxxii. Stade assigns this to the first incarceration. See above, p. 227.
[5] xxxiii. 1-13.
[6] xxxi. 2-6, which even Duhm admits to be an authentic oracle.

*For a day shall be when the watchers call*
*Upon Mount Ephraim—*
*'Rise, let us go up to Ṣion,*
*To Jahweh our God.'*

That is to say, Jeremiah not only was confident of the resumption of worship in the Temple, but he conceived of the national worship as centralised there, in obedience to the Deuteronomic Law.  This means, that in common with all his countrymen, he had accepted the great change in the ritual prescribed by that law and carried out by Josiah.  But that is evidence that Dr. Duhm's theory of Jeremiah's indifference, or even hostility, to the Deuteronomic reforms is impossible.

The end was not far off.  The timid, those who in their despair felt that Jahweh had forsaken the City, and those who had before deserted Him for the Babylonian gods, went over to the enemy.[1] Famine ensued, and pestilence.[2]  The enemy pressed, as every besieger before and after them did, upon the northern wall, where the ground was level, and their engines were not confronted as on other sides by high rocks.  At last, on the ninth day of the fourth month of the eleventh year of Ṣedeḳiah, July 586, a breach was made.  As the Chaldeans were thus about to enter on the north, the king and his guards fled by the gate in the south-east corner of the City, through the royal gardens, towards the Jordan.  They had better have sought the deserts of Judah.  They were pursued, captured, and taken to Riblah, where, after his sons were slain before him, the last king of Judah had his eyes put out and was carried to Babylon.  The Chaldeans burned the Temple, the Palace, and many of the other houses.

*Fall of the City, 586 B.C.*

---

[1] xxxviii. 19.  [2] *Id.* 2.

The walls were ruined. And the most of the population were carried away to Babylonia.

To complete this account of Jeremiah's Jerusalem, we have now to gather the topographical details, a few of which occur in the prophet's own oracles; but by far the most are given incidentally and in the plainest prose by Baruch, his biographer. The result is a picture of the City of a different character from that which we received from Isaiah. In his case the details come to us through a prophet's imagination of her ideal, or through the warmth of a heart that, while indignant with her careless crowds, still loved and pitied them. The like of this we cannot expect either from Jeremiah, who had no such love nor vision of Jerusalem, nor from Baruch, who was not a prophet but a scribe. But Baruch had the invaluable pedestrian sense of the ups and downs of his City's site, and the plain man's memory of the exact scenes of his hero's adventures. The result is a picture, grey indeed, but more accurate than any we have yet had, of the outlines and disposition of Jerusalem, as well as of her common buildings and more obscure receptacles. We may begin with the Temple, the centre and crown of the whole, cross its courts and come down through their gates to the Palace and its outhouses; thence pass through the City to the walls and City-gates, and so out upon the immediate surroundings.

*Topography of the City given by Jeremiah and Baruch.*

Nothing is said of the architecture of the Temple; but it is referred to in the plural, *the Temple of Jahweh, the Temple of Jahweh are those*,[1] probably as including its

---

[1] vii. 4; cf. Matthew xxiv. 1, 2.

courts and the separate buildings on them, for elsewhere these are implied as part of the Beth-Jahweh.[1] The

The Temple and its Courts.

usual term for visiting the Temple was to *go in* to it.[2] The contents of the sanctuary are not mentioned, beyond a notice that Nebuchadrezzar carried away its furniture and vessels.[3] Whether the Ark was still there or had disappeared we do not know.[4] Round the Temple lay its court: *the court of the house of Jahweh*, where the prophet spoke because *all the people* gathered there;[5] *the upper court*, as Baruch calls it in distinction from the lower, *other* or *middle* court of the Palace, and *the great-court* which surrounded both.[6] There were thus from Solomon's time to Jeremiah's *three* courts, of which only *one*, the *upper* or *inner*, was the Temple-court proper ; and to it, as we see from the Books of Kings and from Baruch's narratives, the people were freely admitted both before and after the Deuteronomic reforms. (The courts about the Second Temple were different. That next the sanctuary, corresponding to Solomon's *inner* court but apparently smaller, was called *the court of the priests*,[7] and either

---

[1] xxxv. 4, etc.      [2] xxxvi. 5 ; cf. xxvi. 2.

[3] xxviii. 3 ; lii. 18 (from the Book of Kings), etc.

[4] The words in iii. 16, which imply that it had disappeared, occur in an obviously exilic passage : verses 14-18. Whether verse 16 be a quotation from Jeremiah himself (so Erbt) it is impossible to say. There was a tradition after the Exile that Jeremiah hid the Ark : 2 Esdras x. 22 ; 2 Macc. ii. 5. This was the most unlikely thing for him to do.

[5] xix. 14 ; xxvi. 2 : *the inner court* of 1 Kings vi. 36.

[6] *Upper court*, xxxvi. 10 ; *other court*, 1 Kings vii. 8 ; *middle court*, 2 Kings xx. 4 ; *great court*, 1 Kings vii. 9, 12 : Burney's emendation of this verse after the LXX. brings out all *three* courts. See above, pp. 59, 64, 67 ff.

[7] The Chronicler (2 Chron. iv. 9) antedates this court, existing in his own time, to the time of Solomon, and calls an outer Temple-court the *New court* (xx. 5). Schlatter (*Zur Topogr. u. Gesch. Paläst.* 173) assigns this to Asa, and quotes 2 Kings xxi. 5 for the existence of two courts of the Temple

at the beginning in accordance with Ezekiel's directions or at some later stage in its history the laity were
excluded from it.) Within the upper court were *chambers*,
or lodges, for priests and Temple-officers. Some of these
are named: *the sons*, or *guild, of Ḥanan ben-Gedaliah, the
man of God*, whose chamber was *beside the chamber of the
officers*, and this *above* that of *Maʿaseyahu ben-Shallum, a
keeper of the threshold*;[1] and *Gemariahu ben-Shaphan, the
scribe*, from the door or window of whose chamber Baruch
read Jeremiah's roll *in the ears of all the people*.[2] That
Jeremiah himself sometimes held one of those chambers
seems probable from two occasions on which the command came to him to *go down—to the king's house, to
the house of the potter*.[3] The upper court had several
gates known as *the gates of the House of Jahweh*.[4] One
or two are named. First there was *the new gate of
Jahweh* or *of the House of Jahweh*,[5] probably that which
Jotham built or rebuilt.[6] Where this stood is uncertain.
The princes took their seats at it[7] on coming up from
the Palace, and so some place it on the south. But so
public a gate could hardly have been next the Palace.
It may have stood on the east. More probably it was the
same as the next one, on the north of the upper court—
the gate of Benjamin, called also *the upper*,[8] perhaps to

in Manasseh's time. But if pre-exilic (which is doubtful), this verse regards
the great court as a Temple-court proper. And Schlatter's whole argument
(from p. 167 onwards) for the pre-exilic Temple-courts is founded on the
evidence of the Chronicler and the Rabbis, who speak only of post-exilic
conditions.

[1] Jer. xxxv. 4.  [2] xxxvi. 10.
[3] xxii. 1; xviii. 1.  [4] vii. 2.
[5] xxvi. 10; xxxvi. 10.  [6] 2 Kings xv. 35; see above, p. 125.
[7] Heb. פֶּתַח, LXX. ἐν προθύροις.

[8] Jer. xx. 2. ἐν πύλῃ οἴκου ἀποτεταγμένου τοῦ ὑπερῴου, the *north gate* of
Ezek. viii. 3, ix. 2, and *gate of altar*, viii. 5.

distinguish it from the corresponding gate of Benjamin on the City Wall. There stood *the stocks*—or rather the low vault in which a prisoner had to sit bent—where Pashḥur, the royal overseer of the Temple, confined Jeremiah. Another entry into this court is called *the third entry that is in the House of Jahweh*, but perhaps we should read *the entry of the Shalishim*, either a certain grade of officers, or the three divisions of the Temple and Palace guards.[1] The Septuagint, however, takes it as one of the houses in the court.

That the Palace, which was to the south of the Temple, lay upon a lower level than the latter, is proved by the verbs which Baruch uses for passing between them. The princes of Judah, when they heard in the Palace the noise in the Temple court, *came up* from the king's house to the house of Jahweh.[2] Micaiah ben-Gemariah *went down* from the upper court to tell the princes of Baruch's reading of the roll.[3] Like the upper court, the court of the Palace had its chambers or lodges for officials, of which one at least is mentioned, *the chamber of the king's scribe* or chancellor.[4] Part of the Palace court was railed off as *the court of the ward*,[5] in which prisoners were kept. As still in Oriental prisons, they were allowed to transact business with their friends through the rail, and receive food

*The Palace, and its Courts.*

---

[1] Jer. xxxviii. 14. Shalish is the title of a certain officer in N. Israel (2 Kings vii. 2). On the divisions of the guard, see 2 Kings xi. 5-7. The LXX. of Jeremiah xxxviii. 14 gives, instead of this entry, the house of 'Aseleisel or Shealtiel: εἰς οἰκίαν ἀσελεισηλ (B), ασαλιηλ (א), σαλαθιηλ (A).

[2] xxvi. 10.

[3] xxxvi. 12 ; cf. xxii. 1 : *go down to the house of the king of Judah*.

[4] xxxvi. 12.

[5] xxxii. 2 : חֲצַר הַמַּטָּרָה, *which was in the king's house* (thus, as in the case of the Temple, the name *the king's house* covered the court round it).

from the outside.[1]   When it was felt that Jeremiah was
not securely confined by such conditions, he was cast into
a cistern in the court, described as that *of Malkiyahu, son
of the king*, or *of Hammelek* ;[2] and when more room was
needed for political prisoners it was found in *the house of
the cistern*, a vault with a cistern, under *the house of the
scribe* or chancellor.[3]   From this house the princes *went
in to the king, to the* presence-*chamber*.[4]   This was in *the
winter-house*, where the king sat before a brasier ;[5] the
summer-house would be on an upper story, to which
lattices admitted the breeze.[6]   Within the Palace was
also the house of the royal women ;[7] and a *treasury* or
*storehouse* is mentioned, with vaults or pits beneath for
cast clothes.[8]

The other buildings of Solomon on the East or Temple
Hill are not mentioned in the Book of Jeremiah.

Outside the Temple and Palace lay *the streets* or
*bazaars of Jerusalem and her broad places*[9]—the narrow
lanes for which the compact City[10] has always ⎫ The Streets
been notorious, and the comparatively small ⎭ and Bazaars.
open spaces within the gates.   The various crafts
gathered in their own bazaars.   Of these only *the bakers'
street*[11] and the *house of the potter* are named ;[12] but the
gold- and silversmiths, the weavers,[13] the image-makers,[14]

---

[1] Jer. xxxii. 8, 12 ; xxxvii. 21 ; xxxviii. 28 ; cf. xxxiii. 1 ; xxxix. 14 f.
[2] xxxviii. 6.                                        [3] xxxvii. 15 f.
[4] xxxvi. 20 ; for חָצֵרָה (εἰς τὴν αὐλήν) *into the court*, where the king
could hardly have sat in the winter, read הַחַדְרָה (after 1 Kings i. 15),
generally the interior of a house (Deut. xxxii. 25), but especially the private
room of the master (Jud. iii. 24, etc.).                [5] *Id*. 22.
[6] עֲלִיַּת הַמְּקֵרָה, *upper chamber of cooling*, Judges iii. 20, 24.   The upper
story is called *'aliyah* in Arabic.        [7] xxxviii. 22, etc.
[8] *Id*. 11.          [9] v. 1, etc. etc.      [10] Ps. cxxii. 3.
[11] Jer. xxxvii. 21.      [12] xviii. 2.      [13] x. 9 ; vi. 29.      [14] x. 14.

the workers in wood, stone and metal,[1] the locksmiths (?),[2] and the wine-sellers[3] had each their own bazaar. The fish-sellers were by the Fish-gate.[4] No other public buildings are mentioned. Beyond the Palace and the Temple and the lodges in their courts, we hear only of *the houses of the people*;[5] but among these were, as in the time of Amos, some *palaces*,[6] and *wide houses cieled with cedar and painted with vermilion*.[7] The roofs were flat, and the bazaars probably covered as in later days. Before the reforms of Josiah there was an altar in every street, and on the housetops family services were performed to Baal and the host of heaven.[8] Neither the size of the town nor its divisions are given; the name *City of David* does not occur. But from Zephaniah[9] we learn that Jerusalem comprised the *Mishneh* or *Second-town* and the *Maktesh* or *Mortar*, perhaps the hollow between the West and the East Hills where the Phœnician merchants and money-dealers had their quarters.[10]

We hear, of course, of the City's walls and gates.[11] Of the latter four at least are named: the gate Ḥarsith

The Gates of the City. (Potsherds?) on the valley of Hinnom;[12] *the gate between the two walls* to *the king's garden*,[13] in the extreme south-east by Siloam; *the middle gate*,[14]

---

[1] All included under the common name חָרָשׁ, Jer. xxiv. 1.

[2] *Ibid.* מַסְגֵּר; alternatively *yoke-makers*, or *gold-refiners* (vol. i. 328 *n.* 2).

[3] xiii. 12.　　　　　　　[4] Zephaniah i. 10: see below.

[5] Jer. xxxix. 8; lii. 13 (=2 Kings xxv. 9).　　[6] ix. 20 (Heb.).

[7] xxii. 14.　　　　[8] xxxii. 29, etc.　　　[9] Zeph. i. 10, 11.

[10] Mishneh: 2 Kings xxii. 14; 2 Chron. xxxiv. 22, which state that the prophetess Ḥuldah lived there; cf. Nehemiah iii. 9, 12; xi. 9. Maktesh: Zeph. i. 11.

[11] Jer. i. 15; xvii. 19 ff.　　　[12] xix. 2: see vol. i. 173; vol. ii. 188 *n.* 5.

[13] xxxix. 4; vol. i. 226.　　　[14] xxxix. 3.

probably on the north wall, and *the city gate of Benjamin*,[1] on the north-east; and, from Zephaniah, the *Fish-gate.* In exilic additions to the Book we find also the *Corner-gate* and *Horse-gate*,[2] and the *Gate of the Children of the People* (?).[3] The two former occur in a passage which defines the boundaries of the City, beginning with the north-east corner: *from the tower Hananeel to the Gate of the Corner*, on the north-west, *the measuring line shall go out to the hill Gareb* (which is a place-name or designation of a field in other Semitic languages),[4] presumably at the south-west corner, *and it shall turn round towards Goah* (or, as the Syriac gives it, Gabatha or Gibeah),[5] *and . . .* [6] *and all the fields to the torrent of Ḳidron to the angle of the Horse-gate eastward.*

In the topography of the Book of Jeremiah nothing is more distinctive than its treatment of the surroundings of Jerusalem. We hear, by name or feature, The of places further afield: of 'Anāthôth, Ramah, Environs. Bethhak-Kerem, Teḳoa', Mizpah, the trench which King Asa made against Baasha of Israel, the great waters that are in Gibeon, and Geruth (or Gidroth) Chimham, near Bethlehem. But of the immediate suburbs of the City, their names or features, almost none are given. We

---

[1] Jer. xxxvii. 13.    [2] xxxi. 38, 40: see vol. i. 199, 201 ff., 206, 325.

[3] xvii. 19: *by which the kings of Judah go in and out.*

[4] Sabean נרבם, a place-name. In Arabic different forms of the root mean rough, scaly, rusty, a measure of corn or size of field on which it can be sown, and cold north wind. Aram., an earthen vessel, measure of corn and size of field which can be sown with it, leprosy, and northward. Assyr., leprous. On Gareb in the Talmud, three miles from Shiloh, see *Talmud Bab.*, 'Sanhedrin,' 103*a*; Neubauer, *Géog. du Talmud*, 150 ff., where a Wâdy Gourab west of Jerusalem is mentioned.

[5] LXX.: ἐξ ἐκλεκτῶν λίθων.

[6] *All the valley of the corpses and the ashes of the fat* omitted by LXX., and perhaps a gloss.

hear nothing of Nob, the Mount of Olives, or the Plain of Rephaim ; nothing of Giḥon, 'En-Rogel, the conduits or the highways ; nothing of the near sky-lines nor the woods, nor (till the very end) of the King's Garden. Jeremiah and his biographers behold his Jerusalem only as the City of Doom—doomed by the sins which burst into their wildest orgies beneath her walls, doomed to the assaults which must presently fill her environs. And, therefore, these environs, so striking in their features and so brilliant in their memories, are described only as the haunts of idolatry, the scenes of siege, the site of graves. It is as if to the prophet's eye Jerusalem had no longer any suburbs save guilt and war and death.

Thus the oracles upon the Scythian and Babylonian invasions predict in their vivid way the defenceless Overrun by country-folk streaming for refuge to Ṣion,[1] besiegers. the approach of the foe always from the north, the setting of his first posts,[2] his felling of the trees and casting of ramps against the walls,[3] the corpses scattered over the fields,[4] and the final acres of graves.[5] But for all we are told of the shape or disposition of the stage on which such scenes are to be enacted, it might be a level plain, without feature, name or memory. And the only waft of its natural atmosphere which we feel is the sirocco blowing in from the bare heights of the desert, *a hot wind neither to fan nor to cleanse, towards the daughter of my people.*[6]

The single variation to these prospects of suburban war is introduced in connection with the national sin. The prophet's eye, to which the whole land was defiled,

---

[1] Jer. iv. 6.      [2] iv. 16 ; vi. 3.      [3] vi. 6 ff.
[4] ix. 22 ; vii. 33.      [5] vii. 32.      [6] iv. 11.

saw the pollution concentrated upon the valleys and slopes about the Holy City. The curse of Manasseh was upon them. The worst rites of the idolatries The idolatries which that king had introduced or revived of Hinnom. could not be performed within the walls of the capital. The adoration of the host of heaven might be offered from every housetop and upon the Temple-courts themselves. But the sacrifice of children, prompted by a more malignant superstition, had to be performed, in accordance with the conscience of the ancient world, outside the walls, and in one of the ravines which entrench them. Except the Kidron this is the only suburb which the oracles or narratives of Jeremiah mention : the Hollow of the Son of Hinnom.[1]

In this lay the Topheth. If one may judge from Phœnician analogies—and the rites were borrowed from Phœnicia—a great fire pit, a development of The the primitive hearth, was dug on the floor of Topheth. the gorge; and upon a pile of fuel or more elaborate structure, called the Topheth, or more correctly Tephath,[2] the victim after being slain was laid, a whole burnt offering. The deity who was supposed to demand so cruel an oblation is named by the Hebrew text Molek,[3] but there are grounds for believing that this was a divine title, Melek[4] or King, rather than a name ; and that the awful Despot who demanded such a propitiation was

---

[1] See vol. i. Bk. I. ch. vii.

[2] The Hebrew vocalisation Topheth is apparently modelled upon Bosheth = shame, and the vowels also give it the same sound as the word for a thing *spat at* or *abhorred*. The Greek gives Ταφεθ. The word is probably borrowed from the Aramaic, in which תפיא means *fireplace*. See Robertson Smith, *Rel. of the Sem.* (2nd ed.) 377.

[3] Jer. vii. 31, xxxii. 35 ; 2 Kings xxiii. 10.

[4] Changed to Molek by the vowels of Bosheth as in the case of Topheth.

regarded by the Jews as none other than their own God. The terms in which the prophets of the seventh century remonstrate against the practice show that the people imagined they had Jahweh's command for it.[1] They could quote the letter of an ancient law to that effect,[2] and they had strong motives to so extreme a propitiation in that sense of Jahweh's wrath which one national disaster after another stirred up within them.[3] The practice of sacrificing children is said to have been begun by Ahaz in the despair to which he was reduced by Aram and Israel,[4] and it was revived by Manasseh and spread among his subjects. The horror which it excited is vividly expressed in the remonstrances of Jeremiah. The place was accursed. God would slay His people upon it till it *should no more be called the Hollow of the Son of Hinnom, but the Hollow of Slaughter,*[5] and be covered with graves: a Polyandrion, as the Greek Version calls it, a place populous with the dead. This prediction has been fulfilled not there alone, but in all the encircling valleys of Jerusalem, which are choked with her *débris* and the dust of her slain. The name itself, obliterated from the spot,[6] was translated to a still more

---

[1] 'Micah' vi. 6 f. ; Jer. vii. 31 ; Ezekiel xx. 18-26.

[2] Exod. xiii. 12, quoted by Ezekiel, *loc. cit.*

[3] The best discussion of this subject is the rich and careful argument by G. F. Moore, *Enc. Bibl.*, art. 'Molech.'

[4] Moore indeed argues that the reference to Ahaz (2 Kings xvi. 4) cannot be correct, for the prophets of the eighth century do not condemn the sacrifice of children as those of the seventh century do. But it is difficult to perceive why the historian's attribution of the practice to Ahaz should have been invented any more than that to Manasseh, which Moore accepts. And, as we have seen (vol. i. 127), the fact that Isaiah, when confronting Ahaz, took with him his own son dedicated by the symbolic name to hope, appears to have been the prophet's rebuke to the king for dedicating *his* son to despair.

[5] Jer. vii. 32.           [6] See vol. i. 172 ff.

awful use, and became, as Gehinnom, Geenna, Gehenna and Jahannum, the Hell alike of the Jewish, the Christian and the Moslem theologies. In the case of the Jews this Hell, as we have seen, was located in the Ķidron valley below the Temple.[1]

So Jeremiah saw Jerusalem awaiting her doom—an apostate City, beleaguered by her sins, her relentless foes, and the graves of her perpetually slaughtered people.

[1] Vol. i. 174.

# CHAPTER X

## THE DESOLATE CITY

### 586-537 B.C.

THAT the destruction of Jerusalem by Nebuchadrezzar was thorough, and that he drained her
population to the dregs, cannot be doubted.

Difficulty of estimating the Numbers: But when we attempt to estimate how much
of the City remained habitable, or how
many Jews were left in the land after the successive
removals to Babylonia and the migration to Egypt, we
encounter difficulties which prevent any near view of a
result.

To begin with the people. There are no reliable data
for the population of Judah or of Jerusalem before the

1. Of the Population of Judah; Babylonian invasion. In 701 Sennacherib
claims to have 'carried off and counted as
spoil' 200,150 Jewish men, women and children. If this means that he deported them, it must be
an exaggeration. The number, which Sargon took into
exile when he captured Samaria, is stated as only 27,290;
who, if we count them as the fighting-men, even then
represent little more than a third of Sennacherib's vast
figure. The alternative is to interpret the 200,150 as the
whole population of the 'forty-six walled cities and forts
without number' which Sennacherib took captive: that
is, practically all Judah outside the walls of Jerusalem.

266

If we add to them a few tens of thousands for the capital, the result is a very reasonable figure for the population of a land of the size and fertility of Judah. An estimate has been made, from official lists of the inhabitants of practically the same extent of territory,[1] in the year 1892. Without Jerusalem or Hebron and its many villages, this amounts to over 170,000 souls.[2] Adding 40,000 for Jerusalem and the very moderate conjecture of 15,000 for the Hebron district, we get 225,000, which is very near Sennacherib's figure, increased by an allowance for the population of Jerusalem. As we have seen,[3] Judah must have fully recovered from the disasters of 701 during the long and prosperous reign of Manasseh. We cannot therefore be far from the truth in estimating the Jewish nation in the end of the seventh century as comprising *at least* 250,000 souls. That would make it somewhat greater than the present population on the same territory. But such is not unlikely to have been the case.

The Biblical statements of the numbers deported by Nebuchadrezzar are conflicting. The Book of Kings says that in 598-7 Nebuchadrezzar carried to Babylon 8000 *men*.[4] Another passage, wanting in the Septuagint and therefore probably a later insertion in the Hebrew text of Jeremiah,[5] gives the number for 598-7 B.C. as 3023 *Jews* ; and adds for

2. of the Jews deported by Nebuchadrezzar.

---

[1] By Baurath Schick in the *Z.D.P.V.* xix.

[2] Not 120,000, as Guthe states in his *Geschichte*, p. 256.

[3] Above, pp. 196 ff.

[4] 2 Kings xxiv. 15, 16. The preceding verses, which give 10,000 (or *all Jerusalem*), are apparently a later insertion, borrowed (Stade thinks, but without much reason) from an account of the later deportation in 586.

[5] Jer. lii. 28-30.

that of 586 B.C. 832 *souls from Jerusalem*, and for a third deportation in 581 B.C. 745 *souls, Jews*: in all, 4600. Although thus described as *souls* and *Jews* it is probable that according to the Oriental fashion fighting men only are intended. But from the Assyrian bas-reliefs it appears that upon those deportations families were not separated but marched away together; and the accounts of the Babylonian captivity imply that this included the women and children. The 4600 fighting men will, therefore, on the usual calculation, have to be increased by half that number in order to represent all the males carried captive; and this sum must be at least doubled so as to include the women and girls. On that basis the Jews deported to Babylonia amounted to at least 14,000, but may have been as many as 19,000 or 20,000. But if we prefer to take the datum of the Book of Kings for 598-7, 8000 fighting men, and add to it another 8000 for 586 (a generous estimate, for we may reasonably infer that a second gleaning of the manhood and the prosperous classes of Judah was less than the first) we raise (on the method of reckoning adopted above) the total number deported by Nebuchadrezzar to 48,000 or 50,000. While if we put these two estimates together, on the ground that the three deportations, given in the Hebrew text of Jeremiah as 4600, refer to other occasions than 597 and 586,[1] we get as the very highest figures possible on our data 62,000 or 70,000. There fall to be added the unknown but probably large number of the organised migration into Egypt,[2] as well as the scattered groups which would drift in the same direction.

---

[1] Ewald would read in Jer. lii. 28-30, *17th* for *7th*, year of Nebuchadrezzar.

[2] Numerous enough to form several settlements, Jer. xliv.

Even then it is clear, on our estimate of the total population, that a large majority of the Jewish people remained on their land. This conclusion may startle us, with our generally received notions of the whole nation as exiled. But there are facts which support it. Before the migration to Egypt, the people were themselves confident of a prosperous agriculture; and even after Joḥanan and his bands had left the country the Babylonians did not find it necessary to introduce colonists from other parts of the empire. It is true that the necessity may have been obviated, without Nebuchadrezzar's interference, by the encroachment of neighbouring tribes upon the territories of the depleted and disorganised people. The Samaritans pushed south into Ayyalôn and the neighbourhood. The Edomites drew in upon the Negeb. 'Ammonites and Moabites doubtless took their shares; and the desert nomads, always hovering upon the borders of cultivation and even in times of peace encamped across its pastures, would take advantage of this crisis as they have done of every similar one to settle down in deserted fields and buildings. Yet the fact persists, that upon a much diminished territory some scores of thousands of Jews remained in Judah through all the period of the Exile. They were, as the Biblical narratives testify, *the poorest of the land*, from whom every man of substance and of energy had been sifted; mere groups of peasants, without a leader and without a centre; disorganised and depressed; bitten by hunger and compassed by enemies; uneducated and an easy prey to the heathenism by which they were surrounded. We can appreciate the silence which reigns in the Bible

*Large number of Jews left in Judah.*

*The Poorest of the Land.*

regarding them, and which has misled us as to their numbers. They were a negligible quantity in the religious future of Israel: without initiative or any influence except that of a dead weight upon the efforts of the rebuilders of the nation when these at last returned from Babylonia.

We may now consider the position of Jerusalem in this desperate condition of the land. Penetrating the City by a breach in her northern walls, the Babylonians had sacked, burned and ruined her. Any treasure that remained and the whole of the costly furniture of the Temple were carried to Babylon.[1] The Temple itself, the Palace, and probably every other conspicuous building, with many of the common houses, were burned.[2] What could not be burned was dismantled: *the walls of Jerusalem he brake down round about.*[3]

Ruin of Jerusalem.

The whole fighting force of the City, the men of substance, and the skilled workmen, with their families, were deported to Babylon. Some of the baser sort of the people doubtless continued to herd in the ruins; and among them may have been priests, for an interesting story (preserved probably by Baruch[4]) tells of a band of pilgrims from Shechem, Shilo and Samaria, intent upon still obeying the Deuteronomic behests and passing with every sign of mourning to sacrifice in the ruined house of the Lord. With this exception Jerusalem seems to have been

Only the Dregs of the Population left to her.

---

[1] 2 Kings xxv. 13-17, and the fuller text in Jer. lii. 17-23.

[2] 2 Kings xxv. 9. The last clause of this verse, *and every great house burned he with fire*, is probably from the awkward repetition a later addition. Still that is no reason why we should doubt so probable an assertion.

[3] *Ibid.* verse 10.         [4] Jer. xli. 4 ff.

avoided by the remnants of the conquered people. They set their political centre at Mizpah, and in all their proceedings which follow up to the migration to Egypt their ancient capital and its temple are ignored. This silence is significant. It is as if the shock of the fall of the City had been felt as a curse from heaven. Therefore there is practically no exaggeration in the statement which is so much doubted in that narrative of very mixed value, Jeremiah xliv. : *Ye have seen all the evil I have brought on Jerusalem and all the cities of Judah : they are a desolation, and no man dwelleth therein.*[1] Even the last clause may be accepted for Jerusalem at least, with only the slight qualification mentioned above. God's curse had fallen upon His ancient abode, and even the hopes of the people were hunted away from it.

But if the Jews who remained in the land thus avoided Jerusalem, the hearts of her exiles continued to haunt her, and in the languor of their banishment still brooded over the scenes of her carnage and ruin. One of these visitants to that awful past has described it with a wealth and a vividness of detail which justify the conclusions we have reached from the meagre data of the records. The second and fourth chapters of the Book of Lamentations or Dirges are generally, and on the whole rightly, attributed to an eyewitness of the siege, the famine and the fall of Jerusalem. He composes, it is true, with deliberate art, ranging his verses by their initial letters so as to form two acrostic poems under the twenty-two letters of the alphabet. But this is the only symptom of his work which tempts us to

*How the hearts of the Exiles haunted her.*

*Lamentations ii., iv.*

[1] Verse 2 : note, however, the precedence given to Jerusalem.

think of him at a distance from the events he bewails;
and it is overborne not merely by the vivid glimpses
which we may reasonably suppose only a contemporary
or eyewitness would have selected, but by the fervid
passion of one who himself has suffered the horrors he
paints, by the indignation he feels towards those who,
still alive, were responsible for them, and by the unrelieved darkness and grief of both poems.
Their Date
All this implies a date before 561. The
tradition that Jeremiah himself was the poet is due to
the Greek version alone, and finds no support in the
Hebrew, where the work is anonymous. The poetry,
grand as it is, is inferior to Jeremiah's own; the 'rhetoric'
with which it has not unjustly been charged could never
be imputed to him. Nor had he the passion for the
City or the Temple which these poems reveal. The fall
of Jerusalem could not have come upon Jeremiah (as we
have seen) with such a shock, unrelieved by hope.[1] The
poet writes as if he had been among the dupes
and Author.
of the prophets, whom he bitterly blames. He
stands outside both their circle and that of the priests.
He is a layman, probably a member of one of the
upper and ruling classes of the city, of whom the Book
of Jeremiah gives us so much evidence. He is in sympathy with the delicately nurtured. The fall of the
monarch and the princes, to whom he imputes no blame,
he feels as a desecration. He is pious, but not after
the temper of Jeremiah. The fact that, as he puts it,
Jahweh could *take post as the foe* of His own people,
that the Lord could become *the Enemy*, had startled and
shocked him. He comes back to it with amazement

---

[1] Above, pp. 224 ff., 235 f., 240 ff., 245 f., 251 ff.

even now, when he appreciates the ethical reasons. To
a citizen of Jerusalem, then, we owe these poems, a
member or client of one of the governing families; and
he sings of what he has seen, and has been stunned by,
but now he is roused to the blame and the bitterness
of it all. Some who acknowledge the original experience
of the writer have thought of him as the victim with his
City of one of her subsequent disasters. But it is plainly
of Nebuchadrezzar's overthrow that he writes; of a
destruction of City and Temple which was never repeated except by Titus; and of the flight and capture
of Ṣedekiah.[1]

A few words are necessary on the rhythm. This is
the elegiac measure, of which Professor Budde first made
us aware. It has gradually become probable *Their
Rhythm:
the Ḳinah
Measure.* that the dominant factor in Hebrew metre
was accent or stress, and not the quality or
the number of the syllables. The basis of the Ḳinah is a
couplet, of which the first line with a rising cadence has
generally three accented syllables; the second, with a
falling cadence, generally two. These numbers may
sometimes have varied; but the proportion seems to
have been constant. In chapter ii. three couplets
go to one acrostic verse: in chapter iv., two. The
Hebrew text has passed through a succession of scribes
who were aware of the verses but not of the structure
of the lines. Therefore the text of the lines invites
amendment; some as they stand are too short, some
too long. But we must beware of applying the principle of the metre too rigorously to the text. Oriental
artists have always avoided an absolute symmetry: and

[1] Jer. iv. 20.

it may be that some of the irregularities, which we are inclined to get rid of as editorial additions, belong to the original forms of the poems. The following translation aims at reproducing the cardinal features of the rhythm — alternate lines usually of three and two accents or stresses. I have had to admit three accents to some of the shorter lines, in which the epithet *daughter of Sion* occurs. For while the Hebrew for that has only one accent, the English has two. But, as I am convinced, for the reasons given above, that Hebrew poets were not averse to admitting irregularities to their rhythms, I have no bad conscience about such inevitable exceptions in the translation. In order to avoid similar ones in other lines, I have sometimes rendered *daughter of my people* simply by *my people.* And occasionally I have reversed the position of two lines for the sake of the English rhythm or for the sake of a better climax. Otherwise the translation follows the original line by line. Where it is not literal, this has been indicated in the notes. Words that have been supplied are in italics.

## LAMENTATIONS II.

*Circa* 570 B.C.

### 1. א

How the Lord beclouds with his wrath
　　The daughter of Sion.[1]
From heaven to earth hath he hurled
　　The pomp of Isräel.
He did not remember his Footstool
　　In the day of his wrath.

### 2. ב

The Lord hath engulfed without pity
　　The homesteads of Jacob.

---

[1] *Or,* How the cloud of the wrath of the Lord
　　Enshrouds the daughter of Sion.

He ruined [*and trod*][1] in his wrath
   The strongholds of Judah.
He smote to the earth, he profaned
   The realm and its princes.

### 3. ‫ג‬

In the glow of his wrath he hath hewn
   Each horn of Isräel.
He drew back his right hand
   In face of the foe.
On Jacob he burned like a fire,
   Devouring all round.

### 4. ‫ד‬

He hath bent his bow like a foe,
   Taken post to besiege.[2]
He hath slain each delight of the eye,
   In the tent of the daughter of Ṣion,
He hath poured out his fury like fire.
   *      *      *      *      *[3]

### 5. ‫ה‬

The Lord hath Himself turned foe
   To envelope Isräel,
Engulfing her palaces all,
   Razing her strongholds.
On the daughter of Judah he lavished
   Lamentation and woe.

### 6. ‫ו‬

He hath torn from *his* Garden his Booth,[4]
   Demolished his Temple,[5]
Jah hath forgotten in Ṣion
   Tryst-day and Sabbath,
And spurned with the curse of his wrath
   Monarch and priest.

---

[1] Word wanting in the original.

[2] Delete *his right hand* as too long for the rhythm and unnecessary.

[3] Line wanting in the original.

[4] Read ‫מִגַּן‬.   The Garden, of course, is the Land, the Booth the Temple.

[5] The parallel line and the verb used in this line show that ‫מוֹעֵד‬ *tryst*

means here the *place of tryst*.   In the fourth line (as in verse 7) it means *the day* or *time of tryst*.

7. ז

The Lord hath discarded his Altar,
  Scornèd his Sanctuary,
Hath locked in the grasp of the foe
  Its fortifications.[1]
How they shout through the house of the Lord
  Like one of the tryst-days !

8. ח

Of purpose did Jahweh destroy
  The wall of the daughter of Sion.
He stretched out the line nor withdrew
  His hand from the ruin.
Fortress and rampart he wrung,
  Together they tottered.[2]

9. ט

Sunk to the earth are her gates,
  Her bars he hath shattered.
Her king and her princes are exiles.[3]
  The Torah is spent !
Even her prophets obtain not
  Vision from Jahweh !

10.

They sit on the ground and are dumb,
  The elders of Sion ;
They lift up the dust on their heads,
  They gird them with sackcloth.
And brought to the ground are the heads
  Of Jerusalem's maidens.

11. כ

Mine eyes are wasted with tears,
  My bowels are troubled,
My heart[4] is poured out on the ground
  For the wreck of my people,
For the infants and sucklings that perish
  On the streets of the city.

---

[1] The sense is plain, the text uncertain.   [2] Heb. : *shrivelled, withered.*
[3] Literally : *are among the Gentiles.*   [4] Literally : *my liver.*

## 12. ל

They are saying to their mothers, Ah, where
    Are the corn and the wine?
As like one that is wounded they swoon
    On the streets of the City,
As they pour out their lives [*to the death* ?][1]
    On the laps of their mothers.

## 13. מ

How shall I rank,[2] how compare thee,
    Daughter of Jerusalem?
How shall I liken, how comfort thee,
    Virgin of Ṣion?
Vast as the sea is thy ruin ;
    Who will restore thee?

## 14. נ

Thy prophets? They dreamt[3] for thee
    Falsehood and flattery.
They did not uncover thy guilt
    To turn thy captivity,
But they dreamt[3] for thee runes
    That lied and misled.[4]

## 15. ס

They were clapping their hands at thee
    All who passed by.
They were hissing and wagging their heads
    At the daughter of Jerusalem :—
' Is this what they called the Perfection of Beauty,
    Joy of the earth ! '

## 16. פ

Against thee they opened their mouths,
    Thine enemies all,

---

[1] Another accented word is needed for this line.

[2] Read with Meinhold (quoted by Budde) אֶעֱרָךְ (Isa. xl. 18) : or at least with the Qerî אֲעִידֵךְ : *I take thee as a parable* or *warning*.

[3] Literally : *saw in vision*; used of prophetic vision, but here in a bad sense.     [4] Budde : *expulsion*.

Hissing and gnashing their teeth :[1]
　' We have swallowed her up !
Just this is the day we have looked for,
　We meet it, we see it !'

### 17. ע

Jahweh hath done what he planned,
　Discharging his word.
As in days long ago he decreed,
　Ruthless he ruins.
He hath given thee up to their joy,
　Exalted[2] thy foes.

### 18. צ

Let thy heart cry aloud to the Lord,[3]
　Clamour,[4] O Ṣion,
Let tears run down like a stream
　By day and by night.
Give to thyself no respite,
　No rest to thine eye.

### 19. ק

Get thee up, sing out in the night
　At the start of the watches !
Pour out like water thy heart
　In the face of the Lord !
Lift up before him thy hands
　For the life of thy children.[5]

---

[1] Omit אָמְרוּ, *they said,* which is unnecessary to the meaning (having probably been inserted to mark what follows as a quotation), and makes an accent too many for the rhythm. With LXX. read בִּלַּעֲנוּהָ.

[2] Omit קֶרֶן, *horn,* for the reasons given in the previous note.

[3] This line as it stands in the Hebrew gives no sense. Ṣion is addressed, and an imperative is necessary for the verb. Read צַעֲקִי לִבֵּךְ with Ewald and others ; Löhr, צַעֲקִי קוֹלֵךְ. The Heb. has *daughter of Ṣion.*

[4] Read with Budde הֱמִי for the meaningless הוֹמַת ; Löhr, בְּתוּלַת, *virgin.*

[5] To this verse a fourth couplet is added in the Hebrew ::
　　They that have fainted for hunger
　　At the top of all the streets.

### 20. ר

' Behold, O our God, and consider
    Whom thou maltreatest.
Shall women devour their offspring,
    The infants they fondle ?
Or men in thy sanctuary slay
    The priest with the prophet ?

### 21. ש

' They are strewn on the face of the streets,
    Young men and old,
My youths and my virgins are fallen
    At the edge of the sword.
In the day of thy wrath thou hast slaughtered,
    Ruthlessly butchered.

### 22. ת

' Thou summonest as to a tryst
    Terrors around.
Not one did escape or was left
    In the day of his wrath.
Those whom I nursed and brought up
    My foes have destroyed.'

## LAMENTATIONS IV.

### 1. א

How bedimmed is the gold, how changed
    The best of the gold !
The hallowèd jewels are poured
    Down every street.[1]

### 2. ב

The children of Ṣion, the priceless,
    Weighed against gold,[2]
Are reckoned as earthenware pitchers,
    The work of the potter.

---

[1] The reference is not, as in the English versions, to the stones of the Temple, but to the *living stones* of the holy people.
[2] As we say : ' worth their weight in gold.'

### 3. ג

Even the jackals[1] give breast
  And suckle their whelps,
*But* the daughters[2] of my people are cruel
  As ostriches wild.

### 4. ד

Cleaves to the palate for thirst
  Tongue of the nursling.
The children are asking for bread,
  None to dispense it.

### 5. ה

They that were fed upon dainties
  Rot on the streets;
They who were nourished in scarlet
  Huddle on ashheaps.

### 6. ו

The guilt of my people[3] exceeded
  The sins of Sĕdŏm,[4]
Whose overthrow came in a flash
  Ere a hand could be wrung.[5]

### 7. ז

Her princes were whiter than milk,
  More radiant than snow.[6]
Ruddier in body than coral,
  Veined with the sapphire.[7]

### 8. ח

*Now* darker than blackness their visage,
  Unknown as they pass,[8]
Their skin drawn tight on their bones,
  Dry as a stick.

---

[1] Others : *monsters.*       [2] So Bickell, reading בְּנֹת for בַּת.
[3] *Of the daughter of my people.*
[4] The Hebrew for Sodom.      [5] Omit בָּהּ.
[6] In the original these two comparisons are reversed.
[7] Literally : *sapphire their threading* or *filaments.*
[8] Literally : *they are not recognised in the streets.*

### 9. ס

For the wounds of the sword are more kind
　　Than the wounds of starvation,[1]
They, *too*, drain their blood who are stabbed
　　By the dearth of the harvest.

### 10. י

The hands of the delicate women
　　Have sodden their children,
*These* are become their food,
　　In the wreck of my people.

### 11. כ

God hath accomplished his fury,
　　Exhausted his wrath,[2]
He kindled in Ṣion a fire,
　　*It* sapped her foundations.

### 12. ל

No kings of the earth had believed,
　　No man in the world,
That foe or besieger could enter
　　Jerusalem's gates.

### 13. מ

For the sins of her prophets *it was*,[3]
　　For the crimes of her priests,
They who had shed in her midst
　　Blood of the just.

### 14. נ

They straggle like the blind in the streets,
　　Polluted with blood.
What they could not endure, they must *now*
　　Sweep with their robes.

---

[1] Literally: *happier they who are stabbed with the sword than they who are stabbed by famine!*

[2] Budde omits חָרוֹן as too much for the line, but in the construct before אַפּוֹ it may have no stress, and therefore suit the Hebrew cadence. In the English rhythm, however, we must omit it.

[3] To be regular, the Hebrew needs a third accented word.

## 15. ס

'Bear off, O unclean,' men adjure them,
  'Bear off[1] and avoid!'
So they stagger and straggle about
  Homeless for ever![2]

## 16. פ

Jahweh himself hath dispersed them
  Out of his heeding;
None to pay homage to the priests
  Nor court to the elders!

## 17. ע

We were straining, were straining[3] our eyes,
  Our help was a dream.
While we looked for, we looked for a people
  That never brought help.[4]

## 18. צ

They hunted our steps till we could not[5]
  Walk our own streets.
Our days were cut short and completed,[6]
  Our end was come.

## 19. ק

Swifter were they that pursued us
  Than eagles of heaven.
They hunted us over the mountains,
  They ambushed the desert.

---

[1] Delete the second סוּרוּ and אָמְרוּ בַגּוֹיִם, which are too many for the lines. The latter, as Budde remarks, is senseless.

[2] Literally: *They will no more become guests.*

[3] There is a repetition here of the musical syllable ênu. 'Odhênu tikhlenah 'enênu.'

[4] The allusion is plainly to the failure of Egypt to bring relief.

[5] Perhaps we should supply צַר or צָרִים in the Hebrew of this line.

[6] Omit קרב as both obscure and superfluous for the rhythm.

### 20. ר

The breath of our life,[1] God's anointed
  Was trapped in their toils,
Of whom we had said, we shall live
  On in his shadow.[2]

### 21. שׁ

Be glad and rejoice, O daughter of Edom,
  With a land to inhabit.[3]
To thee, too, the cup must pass round *till*
  Thou 'rt drunk and dishevelled.

### 22. ת

Thy guilt is exhausted, Daughter of Ṣion.
  No more shall he banish !
Daughter of Edom, He hath summed up thy guilt,
  Thy sins are laid bare.

In these poems a note is struck which echoes throughout the literature of the Exile: *God hath accomplished
His fury, exhausted His wrath . . . Daughter
of Ṣion, thy guilt is exhausted.* As the Evangelist of the Exile said of the City: *her iniquity
is pardoned: she hath received of the Lord's
hand double for all her sins.*[4] Even the resources of the
Divine wrath could do no more to Israel. The sufferings
of the people had expiated their guilt. This is the
stripped bed-rock, the dead foundation, from which
Israel's hope was to revive. But there is another consequence. The actual Jerusalem has perished—and has had
to perish—in order that the ideal Jerusalem, liberated
from all the evil associations of the past, may be con-

The Fall of the Real, the Rise of the Ideal Jerusalem.

---

[1] Literally : *the breath of our nostrils.*

[2] The Hebrew adds, *among the Gentiles.* The allusion in this verse is of
course to the capture of Ṣedeḳiah.

[3] Omit ישׁבתי.         [4] ' Isaiah ' xl. 1.

structed in the faith of her people. In this chapter we have seen what the overthrow of Jerusalem meant, how thorough, how terrible it was. In the next we are to trace the resurrection of the Ideal City in the hearts of her exiles. For the work of David, of Solomon, of Isaiah and of the Deuteronomists upon Jerusalem, required the Exile to make it perfect.

## CHAPTER XI

## THE IDEAL CITY AND THE REAL

I N previous chapters we have seen how very gradual
was the rise of Jerusalem to pre-eminence among
the shrines of Israel. Of her long and dis- The Gradual
turbed promotion, the two most rapid factors Exaltation of
Jerusalem:
had been Isaiah's argument of the Divine 1. Religious;
purpose in her history and her vindication in 701 as the
only inviolable city of the One God. But it was Josiah
who rendered this rank indefeasible by realising the ideal
of Deuteronomy and concentrating the national worship
in the Temple. Jeremiah, it is true, scorned the popular
superstitions which assumed the unique holiness of the
Temple, and never set the City of his own day in any
precedence to the rest of the land, save a precedence of
sin. Yet the Deuteronomic conceptions prevailed; and
in looking to the future, even Jeremiah saw the worship
of the northern tribes returning to the Temple.

For such centralisation of the worship, the religious
motives, as we have seen, were high and strong.[1] But
they would hardly have achieved so full a
2. Political
victory without the aid of others, which were and Economic.
partly political, having begun with David, and
partly economic, having been at work since at least the

[1] Above, pp. 176 f.

eighth century. The Monarchy implied the Capital, which replaced the tribal centres and attracted to itself the forces of the national life. To the same focus gathered the trade which 'Uzziah had fostered, and which must have largely increased through the reign of Manasseh, and by virtue of his position as a vassal in the wide empire of Assyria. Thus the urban forms of society replaced the agricultural, and the capital absorbed the political talent, the military strength and the industrial efficiency of the people. But the classes which represented these were the classes whom Nebuchadrezzar carried into captivity. It was the wisdom of this conqueror to leave to his new province her peasantry, with a few of their leaders; but he brought away with him the royal family, the statesmen, the soldiers, the priesthood, the men of substance and the artisans, all of whom he found concentrated in the capital. Thus it came about that the bulk of the Jewish exiles in Babylonia were the men of Jerusalem, to whom their City was everything, and the rest of the land but a fringe about her walls; while such of their fellow-captives as came from the country had lived for a generation under the spell of the religious rank conferred on her by the Deuteronomic reforms. Thus at the moment of the Exile, Jerusalem represented not only the actual and efficient nation, but the Divine idea for which the nation lived.

*The Bulk of the Exiles were from Jerusalem.*

These facts explain what would otherwise appear as a paradox. Jerusalem has hardly fallen, and been drained of her population, when we find her regarded in Jewish literature, not only as still alive, but as if she comprised in herself all the significance of Israel. This is the case even with Ezekiel, who

*Jerusalem represents the Nation.*

was so careful to keep in sight the rest of the land up to its ideal boundaries. Not only does he call Jerusalem the *gate of the peoples*,[1] thus emphasising the commercial power which the Jewish capital had gained through the long reign of Manasseh; not only does he see her restored, as the head and heart of the people, marvellously elevated and fenced from all profane influences by his disposition of the country about her; but to him Jerusalem is Israel. The nation's guilt in the past has been her guilt.[2] Their king is *the King of Jerusalem*.[3] It is Jerusalem that from beginning to end of the long history has conducted those foreign intrigues in which the national apostasy consists, and has been unfaithful with Egypt, Assyria and Babylonia.[4] Not Judah but Jerusalem is *Aholibah*, the adulterous wife of Jahweh.[5] To Ezekiel, then, the City not only is, but always has been, the People.

*In Ezekiel.*

As with Ezekiel, so with his contemporary, the author of the two great dirges, Lamentations ii. and iv.[6] These pour their grief chiefly on the City, and similarly use her name for the whole Nation. *Daughter of Sion* is as national a designation as *daughter of Edom*.[7] The body of Jerusalem is broken, but her spirit still lives, and is called by the poet to bewail her ruin and the death of her children; to pray for her restoration and revenge upon her enemies. We find the same in the somewhat later dirge, Lamentations i. This

*In Lamentations.*

[1] Ezek. xxvi. 2, after the LXX.
[2] Especially xvi., xxii., xxiii.      [3] xvii. 12.
[4] xvi., xxiii.      [5] xxiii.
[6] See previous chapter.
[7] Lam. iv. 22; cf. ii. 13. *Israel, Judah, daughter of Judah* are also used, but not so often.

breaks full upon Jerusalem, and contrasts her not with
other towns, but with provinces and nations.

> *How alone sits the City*
> *That swarmed with people!*
> *Become as a widow is she,*
> *Chief among nations.*
> *Once princess of provinces,*
> *Thrall is she now.* [1]

*Judah* is mentioned but twice, the City much oftener.
*Jacob* comes in but as a third between Ṣion and
*Jerusalem.*

> *Ṣion spreadeth her hands,*
> *None to relieve her.*
> *Of Jacob hath Jahweh commanded:*
> *'Round him his foes!'*
> *Jerusalem hath come to be*
> *Noisome among them.*[2]

In all these dirges Jerusalem or Ṣion stands for the
whole people of God; not merely mother or mistress
of the nation, but the ideal figure in whom Israel is
concentrated.

Such, too, is the sense in which she is regarded by the
great prophet of the Exile, the author of ' Isaiah ' xl.-lv.
In one passage he describes the exiles as
*naming themselves by the Holy City.*[3] He
accepts the identification. He opens by
addressing *Jerusalem* and *my people* as one.[4] He is
commanded to *say unto Ṣion, My people art thou.*[5] God,
he says, *hath comforted His people, hath redeemed Jeru-*
*salem.*[6] *Behold, I have graven thee on the palms of my*

*In 'Isaiah' xl.-lv., and later Prophets;*

---

[1] Verse 1.　　　　[2] Verse 17.　　　　[3] 'Isaiah' xlviii. 2.
[4] 'Isaiah' xl. 1, 2.　　[5] li. 16.　　　　[6] lii. 9; cf. xlvi. 13.

*hands, thy walls are continually before me.*[1] When he addresses a promise to *Jacob-Israel,* it is *Sion-Jerusalem* who answers.[2] This identification, we must note, does not occur in the passages on the Servant of the Lord, who is always Israel or Jacob;[3] but everywhere else *Sion the daughter of Sion,* or *Jerusalem,* is the name of the banished Israel,[4] the spiritual figure of God's people. This use is continued by later prophets.[5]

The same note is struck in the Psalms of the Exile and of the Return. The Babylonian captivity is *the captivity of Sion; the songs of Jahweh* are *the songs of Sion.*[6] It is Jerusalem which the exiles cannot forget, and upon which they pour out their hearts. Psalm cxxxvii. is the work of a poet who had lived through the fall of the City and was carried to Babylon. The metre, as it now stands, is an irregular form of the Ḳinah.

*and in the Psalms of Exile.*

> *By the rivers of Babel we sat down and wept*
> > *Remembering Sion,*
> *On the willows in the midst of her*
> > *We hung up our harps.*
> *For there had our banishers asked us for songs,*
> *Our torturers mirth, ' Sion's-songs sing us ! '*[7]
> *' How can we sing the songs of Jahweh*
> > *On the land of the stranger !*[8]

---

[1] 'Isaiah' xlix. 16.

[2] xlix. 14, compared with 5, 7, 13 ; see, too, xli. 27 compared with 8 ; li. 3 compared with 1, 2.

[3] xli. 8 ; xliv. 1, 21 ; xlv. 4 ; xlix. 3 (if, indeed, *Israel* be genuine in this passage).

[4] In addition to passages quoted above, lii. 2.

[5] 'Zeph.' iii. 14 ; cf. 'Isaiah' lix. 20, lxvi. 8.

[6] Ps. cxxvi. 1, cxxxvii. 3 f.

[7] By elision some reduce these lines to regularity.

[8] Michaelis aptly quotes Quintus Curtius, vi. 2 : 'Captivæ feminarum jubebantur suo ritu canere in ludis, inconditum et abhorrens peregrinis auribus carmen.'

*Jerusalem, if I forget thee,*
  *My right hand be withered!* [1]
*My tongue to my mouth cleave*
*If thou do not haunt me,*
*If I set not Jerusalem*
  *Above my chief joy.*

If the Fifty-first Psalm be wholly from the time of the Exile, then we see how the most spiritual of all the exilic writers was able to set the hope of the rebuilding of Ṣion and of the resumption of the legal sacrifices side by side with his expression of the faith that the *sacrifices of God are a broken spirit and a contrite heart.*

Such, then, are the stages which we have been able to trace in the gradual exaltation of Jerusalem: her

Summary:
the Stages of
Jerusalem's
Rise.

choice by David as the Capital; the building of her Temple by Solomon; the revelation by Isaiah of God's purpose in her history, with the seal put upon this by her deliverance in 701; the concentration of the national worship upon the Temple by Josiah; and now her captivity, effecting the release of her life from the guilt and the habits of a history which, however divinely guided, had been full of apostasy, and affording to her children the vision of her, seen through the distance and the tears of exile, as the image and the name of the spiritual people of God. Hereafter, whatever may happen to her earthly frame, there will still be, free of its fluctuating fortunes, a Ṣion

Her
Apotheosis.

and Jerusalem—ideal and immortal. It is from such premises that future generations will construct their doctrines of *the new Jerusalem* and *the heavenly Jerusalem*, the first sketches of which are indeed already traced by Ezekiel.

---

[1] So Grätz, transposing the letters תשכח *forget*, to תכחש *be withered.*

Our present duty, however, is to follow the hopes of the restoration of the earthly Sion, till after many disappointments and delays these resulted in the return of some of her people, the re- building of the Temple, and then many years later the rebuilding of the City's walls and the organisation of the community under their full Law.

*Restoration of the earthly City.*

When the Babylonian exiles began to form such hopes with any distinctness is uncertain. A number of predictions, probably from the period of the Exile, are found in the Book of Jeremiah, but it is impossible to give them an exact date. We must confine ourselves to those whose years we can fix with some approximation. The writers of Lamentations ii. and iv., about 570, and of Lamentations i. and Psalm cxxxvii., probably somewhat later, are stunned by the completeness of the City's ruin and the utterness of her fall. None of them speculate upon any recovery which may come to her either through the clemency of her destroyers,[1] or by their overthrow; for though this is described with sufficient vividness, it is felt that the matter is one between God and His people. *He* has been *the Foe, He has ruthlessly ruined and slaughtered.* Hence the finality of the disaster: divinely planned and foretold and divinely performed. Yet just because the worst possible has happened, the air is at last clear. Even God can have nothing left to wreak upon His people. Their *guilt is exhausted*, and His wrath must now turn on their enemies.[2] To so full an end did the

*First Hopes of it and their Foundation.*

---

[1] It was about 560 that Jehoiakin or Jekoniah was kindly treated by the Babylonian king: 2 Kings xxv. 27 ff.

[2] Lam. i. 21, 22; iv. 22; Ps. cxxxvii. 7-9.

Jews believe their sacred history to have run; from so
low and bare a level must it start again.[1]

It is to this mood of the exiles that their great
Evangelist addresses his gospel, weaving his verse to the
same measure as that of their dirges.[2]

> *'Comfort ye, comfort my people,'*
>   *Sayeth your God.*
> *'Speak home to the heart of Jerusalem*
>   *And call to her,*
> *That fulfilled is her servitude,*
>   *Her guilt is discharged;*
> *From the hand of the Lord she hath gotten*
>   *Double her sins.'*[3]

But not immediately does the prophet pass to the
return and the restoration.  It is his greatness (we see
from the arguments which follow) to conceive
of his task as first and mainly religious; the
creation of faith in God, the rousing of the
nation's conscience to their calling, the purging of their mind from all prejudice as to the ways the
Divine action shall take.   Therefore, to begin with, he
speaks to his people of God; in aspects of His majesty
so sovereign and omnipotent that not only must the
night of despair vanish before them, but Israel's trust
in Him shall include a willingness to believe in two
new and very wonderful things : their world-wide destiny,
and the selection, not of one of their own princes, but
of a Gentile conqueror, to be their deliverer.   Thus out
of all that glory of God in nature, and in history, which
the opening chapters so greatly unfold—His sway of the

*Their Re-
ligious
Strength,
'Isaiah' xl.
ff.*

---

[1] Compare above, p. 283.
[2] The *Ḳinah* or Elegiac : alternate lines of usually three and two beats or
accents.          [3] 'Isaiah' xl. I, 2.

stars and of the nations, His tenderness to His people and His passion to redeem them—there issue gradually the two figures of the Servant and the Anointed ; the blind and plundered captive of Babylon, whom God yet destines to be the herald of His religion to the ends of the earth ; and the visible and accredited conqueror, whom God has raised *from the north, from the east,* anywhere out of the far and the unknown, and now— somewhere between 545 and 538—is leading against Babylon to effect His judgment on the tyrant and to set His people free.   Only when this great prologue has been achieved do there break the particular promises of the return and the rebuilding :—

> *Who saith to the City, Be peopled,*
> *To the Temple, Be founded!*
> *To the towns of Judah, Be built,*
> *Her ruins I raise.*
> *Who saith to the flood, Be dry,*
> *The streams will I parch.*
> *Who saith to Cyrus, My friend,*
> *My purpose he perfects.*
> *Thus saith Jahweh, the God,*
> *Of Cyrus, his christ;*
> *Whose right hand I grasped*
> *To bring down the nations,*
> *To open before him the doors,*
> *No gate shall be closed.*[1]
> *I, I have raised him in troth;*[2]
> *His ways will I level.*
> *'Tis he who shall build up My City,*
> *My captives send forth.*

---

[1] 'Isaiah' xliv. 26-xlv. 1: reconstructed by bringing the last clause of xliv. 28 to 26, and adding from the LXX. *the God* to xlv. 1 ; so Duhm, Cheyne, Marti.   It is, of course, conjectural, but the result renders the measure regular. On this ground I have omitted a clause in xlv. 1.

[2] xlv. 13.   The English phrase, *in troth,* but imperfectly renders בצדק, *in righteousness,* which does not refer to the character of Cyrus, but to that of the action of God, who means to see Cyrus through.

The same exalted comforter, or (as some think) another, puts no limit to the numbers who shall return, or to the glory of the restoration. *Then thou wilt be too narrow for thine inhabitants . . . thou wilt say in thine heart, Who hath borne me these? . . . Lo, I was left solitary ; these, where were they?* [1]

> *Arouse thee, arouse thee, put on*
> *    Thy power, O Ṣion!*
> *Thy glorious apparel put on,*
> *    City of Holiness!*
> *Rise, shake the dust from thee,*
> *    Captive Jerusalem!*
> *Loosen thy shackles, O captive*
> *    Daughter of Ṣion!* [2]
> *How beautiful on the mountains*
> *    The feet of the herald!*
> *Who publisheth peace and good news,*
> *    Proclaiming salvation,*
> *Who saith to* [*the daughter of*] *Ṣion :*
> *    Reigneth thy God!*
> *Hark, 'tis thy sentinels calling!*
> *    Together they shout,*
> *As the Lord, eye to eye, they behold*
> *    Returning to Ṣion.*
> *'Break ye out, sing together,*
> *    Jerusalem's ruins,*
> *For Jahweh hath pitied His people,*
> *    Delivered Jerusalem.'* [3]

Cyrus the Great became master of Babylon and the Babylonian Empire in 538.  He entered the city without fighting; welcomed and escorted (he claims) by her deity Marduk, who recognised him as his vicegerent.[4]  He speaks of restoring to their own shrines the other Assyrian and Babylonian gods whom Nabonidus had removed to Babylon,

Cyrus, Master of Babylon.

[1] 'Isaiah' xlix. 21.  LXX. reads : *These of mine, where were they?*
[2] lii. 1, 2.          [3] lii. 7-9.          [4] The Cyrus Cylinder.

and of giving them back their lands. But he says nothing of the Jews or of any other of the tribes captive on Babylonian soil.

At this point the compiler of the Book of 'Ezra takes up the story. According to him, Cyrus, soon after his capture of Babylon, gave permission to the Jews to return; and immediately, it would seem,[1] over forty thousand left Babylonia for Jerusalem, under *Sheshbaṣṣar, prince of Judah*, who is described in an Aramaic document incorporated by the compiler, as Peḥah, or *governor of a province*, and as laying the foundation of the Temple.[2] There is also mentioned in command of the people a Tirshatha (Persian Tarsāta), similarly *governor of a province*.[3] On their arrival at Jerusalem, *in the seventh month*,[4] the people are said to be under Jeshua' ben-Joṣadak and Zerubbabel ben-She'alti'el,[5] who is called by his contemporary Ḥaggai, *Peḥah*, or *governor, of Judah*.[6] The returned exiles at once rebuild the altar of the burnt-offering, resume the morning and evening sacrifices, keep the feast of Tabernacles and thereafter *all the feasts of Jahweh*; and engage masons and carpenters to erect the Temple, and Phœnicians to bring cedar from Lebanon.[7] Another section from the compiler's hand[8] states that they set to work in *the second month of the second year*; but certain *adversaries*,[9] by whom the compiler means Samaritans, demanded a

*Permits the Jews to return.*

*Resumption of the Worship in Jerusalem.*

---

[1] Ezra i. compared with ii. 1.
[2] Ezra v. 14, 16.      [3] *Ibid.* ii. 63.
[4] We are not told the year: 538 or 537.
[5] Ezra iii. 2, like Ezra i. 1-8, from the compiler.
[6] Ḥaggai i. 14; ii. 2, 21.
[7] Ezra iii. 3-7.      [8] *Ibid.* 8-13.      [9] iv. 1 ff.

share in the work, and when Jeshua' and Zerubbabel refused this, *the people of the land* frustrated the building, and it was postponed till the reign of Darius ; to the second year of which, 520, Haggai and Zechariah assign the beginning of new measures to build the Temple.

The present form of the Book of 'Ezra is so late, and the different sections so confused, we cannot be surprised that all its data have been questioned. Following Kosters,[1] a number of scholars have recently

Doubts of the Narrative.

asserted (1) that there was no attempt to build the Temple before 520; (2) that there was no return of exiles under Cyrus ; and (3) that when the Temple was built the work was that of Jews who had never left the country. I have elsewhere discussed these negative theories,[2] and here need give only a summary of my argument against them.

It is true that Haggai and Zechariah do not speak of a Return, nor call the builders of the Temple Golah or B'ne hag-Golah, *Captivity* or *Sons of the Captivity*,

Argument for the Reality of the Return under Cyrus.

but simply *this people*, or *remnant of the people*, or *Judah*. But we must remember that prophets bent, as these two were, upon encouraging the people to use their own resources and trust in God, had little reason for appealing either to the Return, or to the royal power which had decreed the rebuilding of the Temple. All the less reason had they that the first effects of the Return were, in contrast with the promises of the 'Second Isaiah,' so bitterly disappointing. Besides, if Haggai ignores any Return in the past, he equally ignores a Return to come, and in

---

[1] *Het Herstel van Israel*, 1894 ; German translation by Basedow, 1896.
[2] *Book of the Twelve Prophets*, vol. ii. chap. xvi.

fact says nothing at all about the Exile itself. The
argument from his silence, therefore, proves nothing.
On the other hand, the testimony that a Return did
take place under Cyrus cannot be wholly denied. Even
if we set aside the list of the returned families as belonging to a later date, we still have the Aramaic document,
which agrees with Ḥaggai and Zechariah in assigning the
real beginnings of the new Temple to the second year of
Darius, under the leadership of Jeshua' and Zerubbabel; [1]
and therefore need not be disbelieved in its statement of
the facts under Cyrus. 'Ezra, too, talks of the Golah in a
way [2] which shows that he means by it not the Jews who
came up from Babylon with himself, but an older community whom he found in Judah. That such had returned
under Cyrus, and at once attempted the rebuilding of the
Temple, is in itself extremely probable. The real effective
Jerusalem, as we have seen, was the Jerusalem in Exile.
It was among the Exiles that upon the advance of Cyrus
the hopes of restoration had so confidently appeared, that
they expressed them as if already realised. We cannot
believe that none of these enthusiasts took advantage of
the opportunity which there can be no doubt it was consonant to the whole policy of Cyrus to give them, but
waited for nearly a century before seeking to return, and
meantime left the rebuilding of the Temple to *the people
of the land*, who were not only unlikely to have energy
for the work, but would have done it in a very different
spirit to that which inspires the prophecies of Ḥaggai
and Zechariah. 'Without the leaven of the Golah, the
Judaism of Palestine is in its origin incomprehensible.' [3]
And finally, if *the people of the land* had effected by

[1] Ezra iv. 24, etc.     [2] ix. 4; x. 6, 7.     [3] Wellhausen, *Geschichte*, p. 160.

themselves the restoration of the Temple, it would not have been possible to treat them with the contempt which was shown by those exiles who returned under 'Ezra and Nehemiah. These considerations appear to render a Return under Cyrus and an immediate attempt to rebuild the Temple very probable. Indeed, some of the scholars who have called Kosters' conclusions inevitable, recognise that the history of Jerusalem before the arrival of 'Ezra cannot be explained except by the presence of those higher elements of the national life which had been fostered in Babylonia. They admit a return of some of the exiles before the days of Haggai.

Accordingly the probable course of events was as follows. Cyrus gave orders for the reconstruction of the Temple, and despatched to Jerusalem Sheshbaṣṣar, an imperial officer, with an escort of soldiers. Some Jews must have accompanied him, both priests and laymen, of a rank suitable to the high purpose before them. The Book of 'Ezra includes Jeshua' and Zerubbabel.[1] That a more general permission was given to the Exiles to return seems certain from the urgency of the appeals to take advantage of it, which their prophet addressed to them.[2] But, as we shall see, few appear to have responded. Those who did return first rebuilt the altar of the burnt-offering. There is no record, and but little probability,[3] of this having been regularly used since the fall of the City. We saw how Jerusalem was avoided by the Jews left in the land,

*Its probable Course.*

---

[1] Professor Sellin, on the ground of Zech. iii. 8*b*, vi. 12, 13, 15, argues that Zerubbabel did not reach Jerusalem till after Zechariah had begun to prophesy, but the verses quoted are inconclusive.

[2] Isa. xlviii. 20 ; lii. 11 ; lv.

[3] See above, p. 270, for proof of an occasional worship.

and Ezekiel charges them with idolatry.[1] Had sacrifice been continued, the fact must have been memorable enough to be handed down. But now the morning and evening oblations were resumed, the Feast of Tabernacles observed and afterwards the other feasts. Next Sheshbaṣṣar laid the foundation-stone of the Temple and began the building.[2] Obstruction arose from two directions. The people left in the land had from the very beginning claimed a right to it;[3] and now, we are told, *they weakened the hands of the people of Judah*—these the Exiles claimed to be, in harmony with the passages quoted above—*intimidated them from building, and hired counsellors against them all the days of Cyrus, even until the reign of Darius.*[4] Thus from the very foundation of the new Temple began those intrigues with their foreign lords which faction wages against faction down to the end of the City's history.

Foundation of Second Temple, *c.* 536.

Obstruction to the Building

The other source of hostility was also to prove perennial. The Samaritans, claiming to have worshipped Jahweh since the days of Asarhaddon,[5] asserted now or later their right to a share in the building of the Temple. If all the host of exiles, registered in 'Ezra ii., had been present at this time in Jerusalem, they could, with the aid of the Imperial authority, easily have overcome the opposition. That this prevailed shows how small a number had really returned. They now found themselves far from their patron and with no hold as yet upon the land they had come to. The very material they required was in the hands of their adversaries. Stone lay about them in

---

[1] Ezek. xxxiii. 24 f.　　[2] Ezra v. 16.　　[3] Ezek. xxxiii. 24.
[4] Ezra iv. 4, 5.　　[5] ? Sargon, iv. 2 ; cf. 2 Kings xvii. 27.

plenty, but even common timber grew at a distance, and if the story be correct that they made a contract for cedar with the Phœnicians, this had to be carried from Joppa by roads which were either in the possession of, or open to, the Samaritans.[1]   Apparently the authors of the imperial mandate had not foreseen such obstacles, and its officers felt that their powers were exhausted.   Sheshbassar seems to have gone back to Babylon.   Cyrus died in 529 and was succeeded by Cambyses (529-522), who can have had little sympathy with Jewish ambitions.   Bad seasons ensued.   The new colonists had to provide for their own shelter and sustenance, and their hearts, like those of many other emigrants to a promised land, grew callous to higher interests.   We cannot be surprised that the Temple was neglected, or that the builders began to explain the disillusions of the Return by arguing that God's time for the restoration of His house had not yet come.[2]

*till 522 B.C.*

To such a state of mind the prophet Ḥaggai addressed himself upon one of those political occasions, which prophecy had always been ready to use.   In 521 a new king had ascended the Persian throne, Darius, son of Hystaspes, and political agitations were impending.   Like their Syrian neighbours, the Jews remained loyal to the throne, and appear as a reward to have had a scion of their own royal house, Zerubbabel, confirmed, or now for the first time appointed, as their Peḥah or governor.   To him and to Jeshua' the high priest, on the first day of the sixth month of the second year of Darius—that is on the festival of a new moon,

*The work of Haggai, 520.*

---

[1] See the *Book of the Twelve Prophets,* ii. 219 f., for a modern analogy.
[2] Haggai i. 2.

520 B.C.—Ḥaggai brought the word of the Lord: a command to build the Temple. It is significant that to men whose experience had fallen so far short of the former promises, the message did not repeat the glories of these. Like every living word of God, it struck the immediate situation, and summoned the people to the duty lying within reach of them. *Go up into the mountain*—the hill country of Judah—*and bring in timber and build the House, that I may take plea-* His First *sure in it and show My glory, saith Jahweh.*[1] Oracle. There is no talk here of Phœnician cedar, nor as yet of the desirable things of the nations miraculously poured into the City's lap. Let the people do what they could for themselves; this was the indispensable condition of the Lord showing His glory. The appeal to their conscience reached it. *God stirred the spirit of Zerubbabel, and the spirit of Jehoshua,*[2] *and the spirit of all the rest of the people; and they went and did work in the House of their God on the twenty-fourth day of the sixth month.* The unflattering words of the prophet had effected a purely spiritual result. Not in vain had the people suffered disillusion under Cyrus, if now their history was to start again from sources so pure.

On the twenty-first day of the next month, when the people had worked long enough to realise the scarcity of their materials and began to murmur that His other the new Temple would never be like the old, Oracles. Ḥaggai came with another word, this time of encouragement and of hope. *Courage, all ye people. Get to work, for I am with you—oracle of Jahweh of Hosts—and My Spirit stands in your midst! It is but a little while*

---

[1] Hag. i. 8.  [2] Jehoshua' is the full form of Jeshua'.

*and I will shake heaven and earth, . . . and the costly
things of all nations shall come in, and I will fill this
house with glory. Mine is the silver and mine the gold.
Greater shall the later glory of this house be than the
former, saith Jahweh of Hosts, and in this place will I
give peace.*[1] In two other oracles Ḥaggai explained to
the impatient people the tardiness of the moral and
material results of their vigour, and promised to Zerubbabel, in an impending overturn of the nations, the manifest recognition of his God.[2]

There is need only to summarise the oracles of
Zechariah. (1) Between the second and third oracles
of Ḥaggai, he published a word that affirmed
their place in the succession of the prophets
of Israel;[3] (2) two months later, in January
or February 519, came his Eight Visions,[4] of which the
third showed Jerusalem rebuilt no longer as a narrow
fortress but spread abroad for the multitude of her population, and the fourth Jeshua' vindicated from Satan his
Accuser, cleansed from his foul garments and invested
with the apparel of his office; (3) the Visions are followed
by an undated oracle, on the use of gifts which have
arrived from Babylonia; from the silver and the gold
a crown is to be made, and, according to the present
form of the text, to be placed on the head of Jeshua'.
But there is evidence that it was originally meant for
Zerubbabel, at whose right hand the priest is to stand,
and there shall be peace between them.[5] (4) In the
ninth month of the fourth year of Darius, when the
Temple was approaching completion, Zechariah gave a

*Zechariah's Oracles, 520-516.*

---

[1] Hag. ii. 6-9.  [2] ii. 10-19, 20-23.  [3] Zech. i. 1-6.
[4] Zech. i. 7-vi. 8.  [5] vi. 9-15. See vol. i. 381 f.

historical explanation of how the Fasts of the Exile arose.[1] (5) And finally there are ten undated oracles [2] summarising all Zechariah's teaching up to the question of the cessation of the Fasts upon the completion of the Temple in 516, with promises for the future. Jerusalem shall be restored with fulness of old folk and children in her streets. Her people shall return from east and west. God's wrath towards her has changed to grace; but her people themselves must do truth and justice, ceasing from perjury and thoughts of evil against each other. The Fasts instituted to commemorate her siege and overthrow shall be replaced by festivals; and the Gentiles shall come to worship in her the God of Israel.

These prophecies of Zechariah reveal, during the years that the Temple was building, certain processes which were characteristic of, and results which were decisive for, the whole of the subsequent history of Jerusalem. There was apparently a contest between the civil and religious heads of the community for the control of the Temple and its environs. Here before the Exile the king was paramount, and it was natural for Zerubbabel to claim to continue his authority. But the vision of the prophet decided in favour of the high priest,[3] and to him the crown was ultimately given that at first had been designed for the Prince.[4] Zerubbabel, indeed, from what cause we know not, disappears. In the last stages of the building of the Temple we do not hear of a Persian governor, but of *the elders of the Jews*.[5] In fact, the exiles, with or without struggles

Supremacy of the Priest.

---

[1] Zech. vii.     [2] viii.     [3] iii.     [4] vi. 9-15.
[5] Ezra v. 3-vi. 15; cf. Guthe, *Geschichte*, p. 268.

for their national independence, settled down to that state of life which lasted in Jerusalem till the times of the Maccabees.[1] 'The exiles returned from Babylon to found not a kingdom but a church.'[2] 'Israel is no longer a kingdom but a colony':[3] a colony in their own land indeed, but the heart and efficiency of the nation are still in Babylonia, where the system is being constructed under which their life for centuries shall be subject to priestly government and ideals.

Yet the civic hopes which the older prophecy had revealed for Jerusalem are not abandoned.  Starting from the glowing love of Jahweh for His people, the last prophecies of Zechariah not only promise a full glory to her restoration and a world about her converted to faith in her God, but the conversion of her citizens from the jealousy and fierce rivalry which beset them to justice, kindness and hearty labour bringing forth a great prosperity. *Judge true judgment and practise loyalty and love every man with his brother.  Oppress not the widow nor the orphan, the stranger nor the poor, and plan not evil in your hearts every man against his brother. . . . For Jerusalem shall be called the City of Troth. . . . There shall yet be old men and old women sitting in the streets of Jerusalem, and the streets of the City shall be full of boys and of girls, at play in her streets.*

Civic hopes.

---

[1] See vol. i. 380 ff.          [2] Kirkpatrick.
[3] *Book of the Twelve Prophets*, ii. 189.

# CHAPTER XII

# THE SECOND TEMPLE, FROM ZECHARIAH
# TO 'MALACHI'

## 516-460 B.C.

THE builders of the Second Temple completed their work in March 516 B.C., the last month of the sixth year of Darius.[1] The data of its size, appearance and furniture are meagre and ambiguous. No inference can be drawn from the words of Ḥaggai,[2] that in the eyes of them who had seen Solomon's Temple, the new House was as nothing; for when the prophet spoke the builders had been but a few weeks at work. Their disappointment was not with the scale of their building, which was probably that of the old one, but with the lack of materials to enrich it, for the prophet answers them that God will provide these later.[3] Nor does Ḥaggai's expression, *Who among you is left that saw this House in its former glory*, imply, as has been supposed,[4] that the fabric of the old House, though dilapidated, was still standing. This is contradicted by the thoroughness with which annalists and poets alike describe the destruction by Nebuchad-

*Completion of the Second Temple : 516.*

---

[1] Adar, the last of the Babylonian year; on the 3rd day, according to the Aramaic document in the Book of Ezra, vi. 15; on the 23rd, according to 1 Esdras.

[2] Hag. ii. 3.      [3] ii. 7, 8.      [4] Guthe, *Gesch.* 264 ; cf. 270.

rezzar, and by the accounts of the rebuilding under Darius. The latter was started from the foundation, *before a stone was laid on a stone*,[1] and it took four and a half years to accomplish—ample time for an entire reconstruction, for which little or no quarrying would be required. It is most probable that the outlines of the First Temple could still be traced, and that these were followed in the reconstruction, particularly of the Sanctuary itself.[2] This consisted, as before, of two parts: the Holy Place, and the Holy of Holies, the *hêkal* and the *děbîr*.[3] In front of the *hêkal* was the *'ulam*, the Porch or Vestibule. There were also, as formerly, *chambers* or *cells*, built against the Sanctuary and round its court.[4]

On the lines of the First.

It is impossible to determine exactly what the furniture of the Sanctuary was before the institution by 'Ezra and Nehemiah of the Priestly Code. The historical references to the subject are all later than this. Only this is certain: that the Holy of Holies, which in Solomon's Temple had held the Ark, was in

Its furnishings.

---

[1] Hag. ii. 15.

[2] Ezra vi. 3 states that Cyrus had decreed that the new Temple should be 60 cubits high and 60 broad (Solomon's having been 60 long, 20 broad, and 30 high). But the text of this verse is not reliable. Ewald (*Hist.*, Eng. tr., v. 113) accepts the height of 60 cubits, but confines the enlargement to the external three-storied building. Josephus (*C. Apion.* i. 22) quotes from the Περὶ Ἰουδαίων—a work ascribed to Hecatæus of Abdera, *c.* 300 B.C., perhaps wrongly, but quoted as early as the Letter of Aristeas, *c.* 200 B.C. (?)—a statement that the whole area of the Second Temple, within the *enceinte* of its court, was 5 plethra long by 100 (Greek) cubits broad, either 505 ft. by 172½ or 485½ ft. by 145 ; see below, Ch. XVI.

[3] See above, pp. 62 f.

[4] Ezra viii. 29 ; Neh. x. 37 f. ; xiii. 4, 7-9. Cf. *the storehouse* for tithes, Mal. iii. 10. On these *chambers* in the First Temple see above, pp. 62 f. 1 Macc. iv. 38, 57 describes παστοφορεῖα, or priests' cells, as by the gates in the walls of the court.

Zerubbabel's empty;[1] and that in the Holy Place, which was probably already separated from the inner sanctuary by a curtain,[2] stood the Table of Shewbread, and, instead of the former ten several candlesticks, one seven-branched Lamp.[3]

What provision was made for the offering of incense? It is uncertain whether incense had been used in the worship of Israel before the reign of Manasseh. Provision for There is no clear mention of it, in either Incense. the earlier historical books, or the first two codes, or the descriptions of ritual by the eighth-century prophets.[4] Jeremiah is the earliest to speak of frankincense, and as though it were an innovation in the worship of Jahweh.[5] Ezekiel is the first to use the term *ḳeṭoreth*, which in the earlier literature means *the*

---

[1] Cf. *Talm. Bab.* 'Yoma,' 22*b*. Josephus, in a well-known passage, v. *B.J.* v. 5, says of the Holy of Holies, ἔκειτο δὲ οὐδὲν ὅλως ἐν αὐτῷ : cf. the 'inania arcana' of Tac. *Hist.* v. 9. According to the *Mishna*, 'Yoma,' v. 2, the foundation stone אֶבֶן שְׁתִיָּה, three finger-breadths high, lay in the *debir*, and on it the high priest laid his censer; and (later) on the day of Atonement set the blood. On the disappearance of the Ark see above, p. 256.

[2] Later on *veils or curtains* hung in the doorways both of the sanctuary and the Holy of Holies (1 Macc. i. 22; iv. 51), as in the description of the Tabernacle (Exod. xxvi. 31, 36).

[3] On the Table of Shewbread see above, p. 63. On the seven-branched Lamp, Zech. iv. Cf. 1 Macc. i. 21; iv. 49, 50; Jos. xiv., *Ant.* iv. 4. Ezekiel xli. 22 and xliv. 16 f. prescribes an altar-like table of wood, *the table before Jahweh*, and he speaks of the priests as serving the table.

[4] In Deut. xxxiii. 10 and Isa. i. 13, קְטֹרֶת or קְטֹרָה, rendered *incense* in the English versions, is the *smoke of the burnt-offering*, and so with the use of the verb קִטֵּר (1 Sam. ii. 16; Amos iv. 5). All these refer to Israel's ritual. In the same sense the verb is used of heathen ritual: Hos. iv. 13, xi. 2; Jer. xix. 13 (?). Before the 7th century there is no proof that incense was employed in Israel, though in use in Babylonian and Egyptian temples from a very early date, and at Taanach by the 8th century (next page, *n.* 4). See vol. i. 333; vol. ii. 63 *n.* 2.

[5] לְבֹנָה. Jer. vi. 20.

*smoke* or *savour of the burnt offering*, for a cloud of incense smoke, and he does so in connection with idolatrous worship.[1] The earliest prophet to imply that incense may have a place in the legal worship of Israel is the great Evangelist of the Exile;[2] and after the Return, some time (as we shall see) before 450 B.C., another prophet predicts that in the approaching glory of Jerusalem frankincense shall be brought to her from Sheba.[3] We may therefore assume that even before the worship was arranged in conformity with the Priestly Code, which makes ample provision for incense, the latter was used in the Second Temple. But we cannot tell whether as yet it was burned only in censers in the hands of the priests, or whether the altar of incense which afterwards stood in the Holy Place of the Second Temple was there from the beginning.[4]

The only altar mentioned during this period[5] is that of the burnt-offering raised by the returned exiles in 536 on the site of Solomon's in the court before the Sanctuary. Josephus quotes Hecatæus, who describes it as a square of twenty cubits and ten in height, built of undressed stones.[6] Probably this was the same which stood there from the days of the Return;

Altar of Burnt-Offering.

---

[1] In Ezek. xvi. 18 and xxiii. 41, where Jahweh charges His people with offering קְטָרְתִּי (Eng. versions, *mine incense*) to idols, it is doubtful whether *incense* or *the smoke of the burnt offering* is intended.

[2] 'Isa.' xliii. 23.

[3] 'Isa.' lx. 6. In the contemporary 'Malachi,' i. 11, מֻקְטָר (if genuine?) means only *is burnt* or *sacrificed*; cf. the Deuteronomic passage, 1 Sam. ii. 28.

[4] Hecatæus (above, 306 *n.* 2) describes in the Sanctuary an altar as well as a lamp, both of gold. Ezekiel (see note 3 on previous page) prescribes no altar in the Sanctuary, but *an altar-like table*, i.e. of the shewbread. Two incense altars have been unearthed at Taanach, *M.u.N.D.P.V.* 1902, 35; 1903, 2.

[5] 'Mal.' i. 10 f.　　　　　[6] *C. Apion.* i. 22; cf. 1 Macc. iv. 44, 47.

it occupied, of course, the site of Solomon's altar.[1] The Pillars Yakîn and Boaz would not be repeated in consequence of the Deuteronomic Law against the Masseboth; nor was the Bronze Sea with its twelve bronze bulls.[2]

The Court before the Sanctuary had walls with doors.[3] But there were more courts than one: *they that have gathered the wine*, says a prophet already cited,[4] *shall drink it in the courts of my Sanctuary.* Probably the Courts were two,[5] as in the programme of Ezekiel. But, contrary to his reservation of the Inner Court to the priests, the laity (as we see from the verse just quoted) were admitted to both; and this right seems to have lasted till the time of Alexander Jannæus, who as he stood by the Altar was pelted with citrons by a crowd of worshippers, and retaliated by building a wooden fence round the Altar, within which only priests were admitted.[6] To the gates of these Courts we will return with Nehemiah.

*The Temple Courts.*

Thus, then, stood the Second Temple on the lines of, and as large as, the First, but doubtless barer and more rough: the work of a smaller and poorer people, without commerce, threatened by many adversaries, and with the walls of their City still in ruin. One great difference between the new and the old House must have impressed itself upon the people, and was certainly significant of their future history. The First Temple had risen as but a part of a

*No Palace or Judgment Halls.*

---

[1] See above, p. 60.

[2] See above, pp. 65 f., 76; the first reference to a laver in the Second Temple is in the *Mishna*, 'Middoth,' iii. 6.

[3] 'Mal.' i. 10.  [4] 'Isa.' lxii. 9.  [5] See above, pp. 256 f.

[6] Josephus, xiii. *Ant.* xiii. 5.

great complex of royal buildings—a palace, a judgment hall, barracks and an arsenal—round the whole of which there ran one enclosure. Of these none was now rebuilt. The Second Temple rose alone, without civic or political rival, a religious Capitol within its own courts and surrounding wall. This wall is probably referred to in the ambiguous statement of the Book of 'Ezra : *three courses of great stones and a course of new timber.*[1]

For Israel as a whole the completion of the Temple meant the full return of their God to Jerusalem. We have already seen in what various and even conflicting forms this faith might be held. At Solomon's time the Presence of God had been conceived as entering with the Ark into the inner shrine of the Temple and finding there *a habitation for ever*;[2] yet this conception was not held in so exclusive a fashion as to forbid His worship at other sanctuaries throughout the land. But when these were abolished by Josiah, and the national worship, in conformity with the Deuteronomic principles, was confined to the Temple, new problems were set to Israel's thoughts about the Divine Presence. Of the practical necessity for this centralisation there can be no doubt. It was required in the interests not only of a pure ritual, but of those spiritual conceptions of the Godhead which to our mind are difficult to harmonise with it ;[3] and that was why even so spiritual a prophet as Jeremiah acquiesced in the centralisation of

*Various Views of the Relation of God to the Temple :—*

*1. under Solomon.*

---

[1] Ezra vi. 4 ; LXX., *one course of timber.* Cf. 1 Kings vi. 36, where the wall of the single court of the First Temple is said to have *three courses of hewn stones and a course of cedar beams.*

[2] See above, pp. 73 f., 80 f.  [3] See above, pp. 176 f., 212 f.

the worship.  But these very conceptions of God, in the interests of which the practice of His Presence was confined to the Temple, were themselves the contradiction of the idea that He dwelt only there.  No part of heaven or earth could contain the omnipresent Deity who had made all.  If it was irrational to embody Him in an image carven by men's hands, it was equally so to suppose Him confined to a house built by the same.  And as the Deuteronomists condemned the former of these errors, so from their phraseology they appear to have guarded against the latter.  The prayer of Solomon at the Dedication of the Temple which they have given us, contains the question, *Will God indeed dwell on the earth?  Lo, heaven and the heaven of heavens cannot contain Thee, how much less this House that I have builded?*[1]  And they repeatedly assert that it is *His Name* which God has *set* or *caused to dwell there*, which means that in the Temple men may call upon Him, and may know what He is as they cannot do anywhere else on earth;[2] or, as one passage explains, the Temple is the place where *His Eyes and Heart may be constantly*,[3] where Israel may be sure of His regard and of His answer to their prayers.  So practical was the Deuteronomists' conception of God's particular connection with the Temple!  But we have seen how it was abused by the unspiritual among the priests, the prophets and the common people.  From this particular sacredness of the Temple

2. Practical Truth of the Deuteronomists.

3. Superstitions of the People.

---

[1] I Kings viii. 27.

[2] *Ibid.* 43.  This, rather than the explanation of the phrase given by Stade, *Gesch.* ii. 247, seems to be the most natural.  Stade's further assertion that these phrases occur *only* in the secondary strata of Deuteronomy is very doubtful.

[3] I Kings ix. 3.

they developed the dogma of its inviolableness, and, absorbed by a superstitious confidence in God's habitation of it, neglected the ethical conditions of His covenant with them. The true prophets condemned this abuse of a real

4. Ethical Views of the Prophets.

truth, insisting that God would not dwell in Jerusalem if the people cherished their idols and their immorality, but at the same time they recognised that only in Sion was the real knowledge of Him to be found, and that after her purgation Jerusalem would be the religious centre and resort of the whole earth. Meantime her wickedness nullified the Divine purpose. Jeremiah doomed the City to destruction, Ezekiel had a vision of the removal of the Divine Presence from the Temple.[1] The destruction of both in 586 made manifest to the whole nation that Jahweh

5. Effects of 586 B.C.

had abandoned His Building, His Altar, His Footstool. His Name was removed from Jerusalem, and His oracles were silenced ; no more was His ear open there to the prayers of His people. To us it might seem as if, the Deuteronomic principles having been tested and found wanting, the hour had already come for the birth of that new dispensation when *neither in this mountain nor at Jerusalem* men should worship the

6. Promise of a more spiritual Dispensation.

Father. There are, indeed, traces of the dawn of such a faith in the minds of many in Israel: Jeremiah's increasing insistence upon the individual aspects of religion, and his advice to the exiles to settle to life in Babylonia, and to pray to the Lord for the peace of their new home ; as well as the more explicit utterances, which we find in some prophets of the Return, that God needs no Temple to dwell in, and rests

[1] Ezek. xi. 23 ; cf. xliii. 2 ff.

in no one locality, but *the High and Lofty One who inhabiteth eternity and dwells in the high and holy place, dwells also with him that is of a contrite and a humble spirit*.[1] But in the Providence of God the time had not yet come for the realisation of these principles. Jeremiah himself looked for a Return of the people to Jerusalem, and the restoration of the Temple;[2] he announced a new covenant, but again it was with Israel alone.[3] The Evangelist of the Exile proclaims a wider gospel of God's sovereignty than his predecessors, and unfolds to Israel their mission to the whole world; yet even to him the indispensable start of this great future is the Return of the People to Jerusalem, and the rebuilding of God's House. Under God these things happened, and the earliest prophets of the Return accepted their leading. Ḥaggai and Zechariah looked forward to the completion of the Temple as to the full return of God to His City and His people.

7. Prevalence of the National and Local Ideals.

God returns to the completed Temple.

These convictions inspired the two prophets with the immediate expectation of a period of material and spiritual glory. The droughts and barren years had been due to the people's negligence in building the House of the Lord;[4] but now He would bless their labours. There had been no hire for man or beast, and with so many adversaries trade was impossible; but God *was already sowing the seed of peace; the vine should yield her fruit, the land her*

The Hopes roused by this.

---

[1] 'Isa.' lxvi. 1 f.; lvii. 15.   [2] See above, p. 254.
[3] For the genuineness of the prophecy of the New Covenant, xxxi. 31 ff., see the unanswerable argument of Cornill.
[4] Hag. i. 10 f.; ii. 16-19.

*increase, the heavens their dew, and all was to be a heritage to the remnant of this people.*[1] The Fasts instituted in the Exile to commemorate the destruction of the City must be changed to Feasts.[2] The sorry populations of Jerusalem and the other towns should grow and overflow the land: *Jerusalem shall be inhabited as villages without walls,* spreading by suburbs far into the country, *by reason of the multitude of men and cattle therein*:[3] her streets full of men and women living to a comfortable old age, and of boys and girls at play;[4] her festivals crowded with pilgrims, yea even with *many peoples and strong nations coming to seek Jahweh of Hosts in Jerusalem and to entreat His favour.*[5] For *the Lord has returned to Ṣion,* and *Jerusalem shall be called The City of Troth, and the mountain of Jahweh of Hosts the Holy Mountain.*[6] The iniquity of the land shall be removed in one day.[7]

This prediction from the standpoint of the new community repeats the three essential notes of the older

*Repeat three notes of the Older Prophecy.*

prophecy. First, the conditions of its fulfilment are ethical. Zechariah summons the people to put away their civic wickedness and rise to a purer and more unselfish life.[8] Again, the promised restoration is connected with the prophet's expectancy of an immediate *shaking* of the whole world.[9] As with the older prophets so with Ḥaggai and Zechariah, the reasons of such an assurance are the political signs of their own times. Darius has not yet made his throne secure. In some of the provinces there are revolts, in

---

[1] Hag. i. 6; Zech. viii. 9-12.
[2] Zech. viii. 18 f.
[3] Zech. ii. 4.
[4] viii. 4 ff.
[5] viii. 20 ff.; cf. ii. 11.
[6] viii. 3; cf. ii. 10 ff.
[7] v. 5 ff.
[8] i. 4, vi. 15, viii. 16 f.
[9] Hag. ii. 6 ff., 21 ff.; Zech. i. 15, ii. 8 ff.

others restlessness. And finally, Ḥaggai and Zechariah concentrate their political hopes for Israel on the person of a descendant of David: yet he is no future and unnamed prince, as with their predecessors, but their own contemporary and governor, Zerubbabel, who, in the day that the world is shaken, shall be as a *signet ring*,[1] so manifest an authority is to descend upon him. *The mountain* of obstacles, says Zechariah, *shall become as a plain before him.*[2] *He shall bear the glory and rule from his throne with the priest at his right hand.*[3]

These great hopes for the immediate future were not fulfilled. Darius crushed his adversaries and organised his Empire in peace. The world was not shaken. Zerubbabel vanished. What became *Disappointed by Events.* of him we are not told. It has been variously conjectured that he succumbed to the intrigues of the party among his own countrymen who favoured the supremacy of the high priest; that his governorship was abolished when Darius divided the Empire into twenty Satrapies; that he fell in an unsuccessful revolt against his Persian lord. The hypothesis has even been ventured that his fall involved the destruction of the new Temple by the enraged Persians.[4] For none of these suppositions have

---

[1] Hag. ii. 21, 23.    [2] Zech. iv. 7.

[3] Zech. vi. 13, LXX.; see vol. i. 382 *n.* 1.

[4] So Sellin, dating it between 515 and 500, on the grounds (1) of the present text of Isa. lxiii. 18 (*thy holy people were in possession but a little while; our adversaries have trodden down thy sanctuary*), and lxiv. 10 ff. (*thy holy cities . . . and Jerusalem a desolation; our holy house . . . is burned with fire*); and (2) because only so great a catastrophe could explain the sudden collapse of the Messianic hopes centred on Zerubbabel. But the text of the above passages is uncertain; their reference to the destruction by Nebuchadrezzar very possible (see below, p. 317); and equally great Messianic hopes had been abandoned in earlier times without requiring so great a catastrophe as the cause. Sellin (*Serubbabel*, 31 f. 197) holds that Zerubbabel

we any evidence ; the last of them is not only extremely improbable, but if the new Temple had fallen
some allusion must have been preserved in the Book
of 'Ezra.  All we are sure of is the disappearance of the
last prince of the House of David, who ruled or bore a
semblance of rule in Jerusalem.  Not in vain had the
returned exiles refrained from restoring the Palace beside
the Temple.  Zerubbabel's end meant the end of the
dynasty with whose founder the City had risen, and to
whose kings alone she had given her allegiance.  No
other scion of the family was henceforth to be acknowledged by her ; they sank into obscurity.  Even prophecy,
which had flourished round their throne, and pledged its
faith in their permanence, gave up its hope of them
before it too expired, as if unable to exist apart from the
independent national life with which they had been
identified.  The Temple, the Temple alone, remained ;
and the Priest, as we have seen from the significant
alterations in the text of Zechariah's oracles, bare rule
over a kingless and a prophetless people.

For the next fifty or sixty years, till the arrival of
'Ezra and Nehemiah, we owe our information to some
of the last efforts of prophecy, in forms no
longer original but resting either upon the
Law or upon the prophetic literature of earlier
times.  One anonymous prophet, to whom our

The next
Sixty Years :
'Malachi,'
'Isaiah,' lvi.-
lxvi.

Canon gives the name of ' Malachi,'[1] uttered his oracles
either just before or just after the arrival of 'Ezra ; and
another series of prophecies, ' Isaiah ' lvi.-lxvi., are most

restored the walls under Darius i., but later (*Studien zur Entstehungsgesch.*
121 f. 182) places the rebuilding under Cambyses or Cyrus, and ascribes its
frustration and their ruin to the Samaritans.

[1] See the *Book of the Twelve Prophets* (*Expositor's Bible*), ii. ch. xxiv.

probably assigned to the same period, because, though containing apparently earlier elements from the period of the Exile, they not only reflect what we know were the main features of life in Jerusalem between Zechariah and 'Ezra, but exhibit some parallels to ' Malachi,' and contain echoes of Ezekiel, of the great Evangelist of the Exile and of Zechariah.[1]

[1] In *Isaiah xl.-lxvi.* (*Expositor's Bible*, 1890), I suggested that ' Isaiah ' lvi.-lxvi. was from a number of hands (cf. Cheyne, *Enc. Brit.*[9] ; of late their unity has been asserted by Duhm, and their origin in the time of 'Malachi.' See also Cramer, *Der geschichtliche Hintergrund d. Kap.* lv.-lxvi. *Buch. Jesaia,* 1905, and Budde, *Gesch. d. alt. Hebr. Litt.,* 1906, 176 ff. The existence of the Temple is implied throughout the greater part of Isa. lvi.-lxvi., especially lvi. 7, 8, lxii. 9 (the courts of the Temple), lxvi. 6. Some exiles have returned ; others have still to be gathered (lvi. 8, lvii. 14, 19, lx. 4 ff.). The walls of Jerusalem are still unbuilt, and there are many *old* waste places (lviii. 12, lx. 10). There are very many idolaters practising, amidst scenery that is Palestinian (lvi. 9-lvii.), cults that are recognisable as those of the Western Semites (lvii. 9, lxv. 11 ; cf. lxv. 1-5). Some of these are undoubtedly Jews, *apostates* (lxvi. 24) ; others may be (not certainly are, as some commentators assert about lvii. 3 ff.) Samaritans. There is a great deal of trouble and strife with adversaries : this is implied in the many promises of peace. The faithful community is also abused by its governors, and its poor by the rich (lviii.-lix.). Altogether Jerusalem is like a pregnant mother who cannot bring her children to the birth (lxvi. 7-9).

Among other parallels with ' Malachi' are lvi. 1-8 with ' Mal.' iii. 5 (*turn aside the stranger*), lvi. 10 ff. with ' Mal.' i. 10, ii. 1 ff. ; the temper of lxiii. 7-lxiv. (on this see ' Isaiah' in Hastings' *B.D.*) ; and the prediction of the separation of the good from the apostates and the judgment of the latter ('Mal.' iii. 13-21, Heb.—Eng. iii. 13-iv. 2—with 'Isa.' lxv.-lxvi.) The treatment of the Fasts (lviii.) may be compared with Zech. viii. 14-19, and the phrase *my holy mountain* (lvi. 7, lvii. 13, lxv. 11, 25, lxvi. 20) recalls the prediction of Zechariah (viii. 3) ; lxv. 20 recalls Zech. viii. 4 ; and lxv. 16, *God of troth,* recalls Zech. viii. 3, *City of troth,* 8, *their God in troth.* There is not space to enumerate other parallels with Zechariah, or the one or two echoes of Ezekiel, or the adoption of many texts from ' Isaiah ' xl.-lv.

The only difficulties in the way of assigning these chapters to this period are the references to the destruction of the Temple, but these belong to a distinct section of the prophecies, lxiii. 7-lxiv. 11, which is probably from the period of the Exile ; and the assertion in lxvi. that God does not dwell in temples made with hands, which, however, does not preclude the existence of the Temple (on this see Skinner, *Cambr. Bible for Schools*).

The picture which these writings present to us is one
of anarchy and depression, both in religion and in civic
Condition of affairs. The tone of the prophets is, therefore,
the Jews. for the most part, sombre, critical and minatory; but it is relieved by passages of truth so spiritual,
of charity so broad, and of hope so strong and dazzling,
that they have ever been esteemed by the Church of
God as among the most precious of her Scriptures. It is
not the City alone which is under review, but the land;
yet not, as with some older prophets, extended to its
ideal boundaries, but shrunken almost to the limits of
the people's actual possession: *Judah ana Jerusalem* as
'Malachi' calls it;[1] while the other prophet dares not,
even in promise, to define it as wider than from Sharon
to 'Akôr, mere *pasture and a place for herds to lie down
in*.[2] The religious symbols and promises of these prophets are largely pastoral and agricultural,[3] as if the
returned exiles had already spread beyond Jerusalem to
such forms of life, and particularly, we may note, to the
cultivation of the vine. Three classes of the population
are discernible: the faithful Jews returned from Babylon;
the apostate Jews, consisting both of those who had never
left the land and those of the Return who had fallen away
to them; and the Samaritans, who had spread into the
Vale of Ayyalôn and held many of the approaches to the
City. In addition the Edomites had come up the Negeb
as far as Hebron; there were some 'Ammonite settlements occupying fields from which Nebuchadrezzar took
away their Jewish owners and introducing the cult of

[1] iii. 4.　　　　　　　　　　　　[2] 'Isa.' lxv. 10.
[3] 'Mal.' iii. 11, iv. 2 (Eng.); 'Isa.' lxi., lxii., lxiii. 2 f., 13 f., lxv. 8,
22 ff., etc.

Molok or Melek ;[1] while the Phœnician coast towns, as of yore, sent their traders through the land and with them their own forms of worship.[2]

To all these temptations the Jewish community was exposed, and the worship of the Temple had to compete with them. A Persian had succeeded Zerub- Moral and babel.[3] We cannot suppose that he was Religious sympathetic with the ideals or careful of the Abuses, religious discipline of the City.[4] Priests and laity were left to themselves and grew lax in their worship. The former neglected the more spiritual of their duties ;[5] the latter cheapened their sacrifices and withheld their tithes.[6] The Sabbath was abused ;[7] the pilgrimages to Ṣion fell off.[8] Jews divorced their wives in order to marry the heathen.[9] And the minds of the people reaped the natural fruit of such laxity, in the persuasion that right conduct mattered nothing. There was a prevalent scepticism.[10] Sorcery, perjury, oppression of the poor, shedding of innocent blood, with a general covetousness and envy of the rich, are the sins charged against the community.[11]

From all this we can see how the work of 'Ezra and Nehemiah upon their arrival in Jerusalem was at once difficult and easy—difficult because the com- awaiting munity was corrupted by nearly two genera- 'Ezra and Nehemiah. tions of so much temptation and so much carelessness ; but easy because in the resultant anarchy

---

[1] 'Isa.' lvii. 9.  [2] lxv. 11.  [3] 'Mal. i. 8.
[4] Ryle, *Ezra-Nehemiah* (*Camb. Bible for Schools*), p. xxxvii.
[5] 'Mal.' ii. 1-9 ; cf. 'Isa.' lvi. 10 ff.
[6] 'Mal.' i. 6 ff., iii. 7 ff.  [7] 'Isa.' lvi. 1-8, lviii. 13 f.
[8] lxv. 11.  [9] 'Mal.' ii. 10-16.  [10] ii. 17, iii. 13 ff.
[11] iii. 5, 15 ; 'Isa.' lvii. 17, lviii., lix. 3-8, 13-15.

there was no force, either moral or physical, sufficient to compete with the movement for reform. In estimating the work of 'Ezra and Neḥemiah, the rapidity with which they imposed a new and elaborate constitution upon the life of their people, we must appreciate the fact that these reformers had to reckon, not with an established political system nor long traditions nor a disciplined hierarchy, but with a popular life broken into fragments and dispirited —corrupt, indeed, but flexible and at the disposal of any definite and straightforward purpose of repair.

This is not the place to follow or appraise the loftier flights upon which 'Malachi' and his fellow prophets rose above their sombre tasks of tracking and dragging to light the vices and superstitions of their people. But we must not fail to notice how, at a time when prophecy indulged in no great hopes for the political future of the community and was engrossed with practical proposals for the improvement of the details of their life, it also possessed the power to rise to far visions of the world and to the widest charity and hope for other peoples. There are no passages of Scripture which breathe a more tender or a more liberal spirit than some of these utterances from so narrow and dispirited an age. 'Malachi' turns from his disgust with the blemished sacrifices of the Temple to the thought of how God is honoured everywhere among the heathen: *for from the rising of the sun to his setting My Name is great among the nations, and in every sacred place smoke of sacrifice ascends to My Name and a pure offering, for great is My Name among the nations, saith Jahweh of Hosts.*[1] A wonderful thought to rise

*Loftier Visions in this Period.*

---

[1] 'Mal.' i. 11.

from that starved and corrupt City, a wonderful claim to make for her God at such a time! How it anticipates the words of Christ in the same place centuries later, that God has rejected Israel and called the Gentiles to Himself! The other prophet or prophets are in their own way equally catholic, equally spiritual. They make provision within Israel for the eunuch and the stranger;[1] declare that God *who inhabits the high and holy place dwells also with him that is of a contrite and humble spirit*;[2] proclaim that the service which He seeks is *to loosen the bonds of wickedness, to undo the knots of the yoke, to let the crushed go free, to rend every yoke*;[3] and publish that programme of service which Christ took as His own: *to tell good tidings to the suffering, to bind up the broken-hearted, to proclaim liberty unto the captives, and open ways to the prisoners, to proclaim an acceptable year for the Lord and a day of vengeance for our God; to comfort all that mourn; to provide for the mourners of Sion, to give them a garland for ashes, the oil of joy for mourning, the mantle of praise for the spirit of dulness.*[4]

With regard to the City herself, the pictures are double and contradictory. Not in 'Malachi,' for he says as little of Jerusalem and as much implies her, as does the Deuteronomic law, upon which he prophesies. But in 'Isaiah' lvi.-lxvi. the City is represented now as the glorified centre of the whole world, embellished by its tribute and attracting its nations, and now as the floor of judgment on which her own people have to be separated and

*Double Aspect of Jerusalem.*

---

[1] 'Isa.' lvi. 1-8.  [2] lvii. 15.
[3] lviii. 6 ff.  [4] lxi. 1 ff.

punished. Let this chapter conclude with an instance of each of these : either from the same author in different moods or from different authors but of the same period.

In the Sixtieth Chapter we see Jerusalem bidden to rise to her glory, which is described as the spiritual

The glorious Hope of the City—East and West. counterpart of a typical Eastern day in the sudden splendour of its dawn, the fulness and apparent permanence of its noon, the spaciousness it reveals on land and sea, and the barbaric profusion of life, which its strong light is sufficient to flood with glory.[1] The prophet has caught that high central position of the City on the ridge which runs between sea and desert, east and west, the ends of her world. We have seen that her exposure is eastward,[2] and with this he begins.[3] Arabia, whose border is Jerusalem's horizon, is pouring into her : *Profusion of camels shall cover thee, young camels of Midian and 'Ephah, all of them from Sheba shall come : gold and frankincense shall they bring and publish the praises of Jahweh. All the flocks of Kedar shall be gathered unto thee ; the rams of Nebaioth shall minister to thee· they shall come up with acceptance on Mine altar and the house of My glory will I glorify.* Then turning from this, the natural prospect of every housetop in the City, the prophet overlooks the ridge which hides Jerusalem from the sea, and starts her hope in what till the days of her exile was a direction unknown. Nay, as if she had left her secluded mountain and taken her stand by the sea, he describes her with all its light thrown up in her face and all its wealth

[1] From *Isaiah* xl.-lxvi. (*Expositor's Bible*), p. 429.
[2] Vol. i. 10 ff.  [3] Verses 6-9.

drifting to her feet. *Then shalt thou see and be radiant, thy heart shall throb and grow large ; for there shall be turned upon thee the tide of the sea, and the wealth of the nations shall come to thee. . . . Who are these like a cloud that fly, like doves to their windows ? Surely the Isles* [1] *are stretching towards me, ships of Tarshish in the van to bring thy sons from afar, with their silver and their gold to the name of Jahweh thy God and to the Holy of Israel, for He hath glorified thee.* It is a picture, wonderful at this time when the life of the City was at its lowest, of the far future, when all the Western world should draw to Jerusalem with their gifts and their spiritual homage. But *the least was to become a thousand and the smallest a strong nation.*

The counterpart of this is seen in Chapter lxvi.,[2] which tells how the glory of Jerusalem must be preceded by a great and searching judgment: between her citizens who are faithful and those who are apostate. The high notes of the future to which we have been listening are repeated. Yet the *Her Division between Worship and Judgment.* prophet's last vision of the City is not that of a holy mountain, the abode of a holy people and the centre of a redeemed humanity, but with her narrow surface and her little people divided between worship and a horrible woe—Gehenna underneath the walls of the Temple. What was to have been the Lord's garner is still only His threshing-floor, and heaven and hell as of old shall from new moon to new moon lie side by side in her. For from the day that Araunah the Jebusite threshed out his sheaves upon that high, wind-swept rock to the

---

[1] Or coastlands.

[2] And equally in ' Malachi ' iii. 18 ff.

day when the Son of Man standing over against her divided the sheep from the goats, the wise from the fools, and the loving from the selfish, Jerusalem has been appointed of God for trial, separation and judgment.[1]

[1] *Isaiah* xl.-lxvi. (*Expositor's Bible*), p. 466.

# CHAPTER XIII

EZRA AND NEHEMIAH

458 (?)-431 B.C.

I N the history of Jerusalem, when we come to the
Books of 'Ezra and Neḥemiah, it is as if a mist
lifted, for we regain that near view of the
City which has been more or less obscured
since Baruch's stories of Jeremiah and the
A close sight
of the City
regained.
Dirges of the desolate Ṣion.   Not only are precise
narratives resumed and dated to the month and day—a
custom with Jewish writers since Baruch—documents of
state are also offered ; and, most valuable of all, we have
the memoirs of the principal actors, written in the first
person singular.  This is a form of literature to which the
only precedents, so far as Jerusalem is concerned, have
been Isaiah's account of his vision in the Temple, some
passages of his earlier life dictated by Jeremiah to
Baruch, and the visions of Ezekiel.  The new memoirs,
however, not being those of prophets, with whom the
spiritual vision always tends to overwhelm the material
circumstance and personal detail, provide of the latter
a wealth unprecedented in the literature of Jerusalem.
The authors, in explaining their policy and describing
their conduct—their conversations, their passions and
even their gestures—reveal the characters behind these,

and enrich the long drama of Jerusalem with two of its eight or ten most vivid personalities. To our view of the stage itself the gain is considerable. What Baruch did for the hills of Jerusalem and for the courts of the Palace and Temple, Neḥemiah now does, and more, for the full circuit of the City walls. There is, too, an atmosphere through which the voices and the tempers of men rise with a distinctness we hardly ever again feel about the grey town till Josephus comes upon her with his Romans. We see a wet day in December, with a crowd on the broad place before the Temple, *shivering for their business, and because of the winter rains*;[1] and a September day when the people fill the same space *and feast and send portions to one another and make great mirth, bringing in from the mountain branches of olive, wild olive, myrtle, palm and thick trees* to build booths, every citizen on the roof of his house and the pilgrims on the broad places by the Water-gate and the Gate of Ephraim.[2] Most vivid of all is the building of the Walls, half the force at work with their swords girt to their sides—as a few years ago I saw Circassian immigrants building their houses from the ruins of 'Ammân under fear of an Arab attack — and half behind them under the Wall with spears, bows and habergeons; Neḥemiah in the centre and a bugler by his side all the long hours from *the rise of the dawn till the stars come out.*[3] Between these crises and festivals the daily life of the people unfolds before us; country-folk and Tyrian fish-dealers waiting till the gates open of a morning, and bringing in to the markets the City's food and the offerings for the Temple; the daily

---

[1] Ezra x. 9.    [2] Neh. viii. 12 ff.    [3] Neh. iv. 15 ff.

table of the hospitable governor, *one ox a day and six choice sheep, also fowls, and once in ten days store of all wines* ; [1] and the discontent of an over-taxed people with their fields mortgaged to the usurer—in fact very much that we wanted to know about Jerusalem and now see, not only for that year or two of Nehemiah's reports but for all the centuries of the common unchanging life on either side of him.

Yet the whole story is beset with difficulties arising from the composition of its text—difficulties about the sources, the chronology and the relations of the two principal actors—all of which are hard and some perhaps insoluble, but with which we must come to terms before the Jerusalem of 'Ezra and Nehemiah grows certain to us. To avoid undue disturbance of the narrative, I propose to discuss a number of details in the Appendix, and to state here only the principal questions and conclusions.

Difficulties of the Text.

In our Bible the Books of 'Ezra and Nehemiah are separated ; but in the Hebrew Canon they were originally one Book : manifestly the compilation of a writer who worked after the fall of the Persian Empire, and whose style, in the summary and connective passages which he contributes, very closely resembles that of the compiler of the Book of Chronicles. On this ground, and because 'Ezra-Nehemiah continues the Books of Chronicles, he is to be identified with the Chronicler himself, whose date was about 300 B.C., or more than a century after 'Ezra and

'Ezra-Nehemiah a Compilation by the Chronicler from several sources.

---

[1] Neh. v. 17 ff.

Nehemiah visited Jerusalem.[1]  Among the constituents
of the Book are a historical summary written not in
Hebrew but in Aramaic;[2] several 'State-documents' in
the direct form;[3] and two long fragments of Memoirs
in which 'Ezra and Nehemiah respectively speak in the
first person singular.[4]  As suddenly as these memoirs
are introduced, so are they again broken off, but other
parts of them appear to form the basis of narratives
which continue their story with 'Ezra or Nehemiah in
the third person.[5]  Nor (as we shall see) does the compiler observe the regular sequence of events.  All these
features, visible on the surface of this double Book, and
complicated by others of a more subtle kind, have provoked what is perhaps the most considerable controversy
in the past ten years of Old Testament scholarship.
Some of it is not very relevant to the story of Jerusalem; but we have to determine at least the most
probable answers to the questions raised by the Memoirs
and the Chronology.

No serious objections have been taken to the Memoirs
Memoirs of of Nehemiah.[6]  Written in classical Hebrew
Nehemiah.  —in the vocabulary there are, of course,
some late elements—and with the spirit and directness

---

[1] For the proofs of this, which are obvious and accepted by critics of all
schools (cf. even Sayce, *The Higher Criticism and the Ancient Monuments*,
537), see Driver, *Introd.*, 6th ed. 544 f., with list of phrases characteristic
of the Chronicler, 535 ff. ; and § 5 of Ryle's *Ezra and Neh.*, *Camb. Bible
for Schools.*                         [2] Ezra iv. 8-vi. 18, ? after 450 B.C.

[3] Ezra i. 2-4 ; iv. 11-16, 18-22 ; v. 7-17 ; vi. 3-12 ; vii. 12-26, all but the
first in Aramaic : for convincing proof of their genuineness see Meyer,
*D. Entstehung des Judenthums.*

[4] Ezra vii. 27-ix. ;  Neh. i.-vii. 5 (6-73*a*?); xii. 31 (32-36?), 37-40 ;
xiii. 4-31.               [5] Ezra x. ;  Neh. vii. 73*b*, viii., xii. 30.

[6] Neh. i.-vii. 5 (6-73*a*?); xii. 31 (32-36?), 37-40; xiii. 4-31.  Renan
characteristically guards himself from a final opinion on their authenticity.
*Histoire*, iv. 67, 68.

of an actor in the scenes they describe, these Memoirs
form one of the most valuable documents in the history
and topography of Jerusalem. To be used with more
discrimination are the passages that continue the story
of Nehemiah, but present him in the third person.[1]

The question of the Memoirs of 'Ezra [2] is more difficult. They also are written in the first person singular,
but objection has been taken to their authen-  Memoirs of
ticity [3] on the ground that their vocabulary  'Ezra.
and syntax are those of the compiler himself; that they
contain unhistorical elements; that the whole story of
'Ezra's activity is improbable; that Nehemiah does not
mention 'Ezra; and that 'Ezra is unknown both to the
Son of Sira and the author of Second Maccabees, to
whom Nehemiah is the sole champion of Judaism at
this period.[4] For these reasons the ' Memoirs of 'Ezra '
are held to be the merest fiction, invented by the priests
of a later age in order to place beside the layman
Nehemiah a priestly colleague in the restoration of the
Law and the Congregation of Israel. It is even denied
that 'Ezra himself existed, except as an ordinary priest

[1] Neh. vii. 73*b*-x. and xi. ; xi. is the immediate continuation of vii.;
viii.-x., in which Nehemiah appears in the third person, appear to be founded
not on his ' Memoirs ' but on 'Ezra's, as I stated in the *Expositor* for July
1906, p. 10. This is also the view of Budde, *Gesch. d. alt. Hebr. Litt.* 236,
and indeed is most probable ; cf. Cornill, *Introd.* (Eng. trans.) 247 f.

[2] Ezra vii. 27-ix. ; only viii. 35 f. seem to be from another hand.

[3] Principally by Renan (1893), *Hist.* iv. 96 ff. ; C. C. Torrey (1896),
*The Compos. and Histor. Value of Ezra and Neh.* (*Beihefte z.Z.A.T.W.* ii.),
in which the 'Ezra memoirs are subjected to a searching analysis with the
conclusion that they are the work of the Chronicler himself; H. P. Smith
(1903), *O. T. Hist.* 390 ff., and Foster Kent (1905), *Israel's Hist. and Biogr.
Narratives* (in *The Students' O. T.*), 29-34—these last two following Torrey,
Foster Kent more moderately. Cf. also Winckler, *Alt-Orient. Forschungen*
and *K.A.T.*[(3)], 294.

[4] Ecclus. xlix. 12 ff. ; 2 Macc. i. 10 ff.

whose name descended to the generation which made
so much of him. As we know from the Apocrypha and
from Talmudic literature, 'Ezra became an attractive
centre for legend ; according to this argument, the legend
was already begun by the forger of these Memoirs.
To the theory as a whole two answers at once suggest
themselves. So lavish and detailed a story can hardly
be conceived as developing except from the actual
labours of a real and impressive personality. And
against the hypothesis that a later generation of priests,
jealous for the history of their order, invented a man
learned in the Law as colleague to the layman Nehemiah,
may be urged the necessity of the actual appearance of
such a man in the conditions in which Nehemiah found
himself at Jerusalem. A layman like Nehemiah could
hardly have ventured to enforce the religious reforms
to which he was obliged after his work upon the Walls
was completed, without some more authoritative exposition of the Divine Law of his people than he could
himself give. The presence of 'Ezra, then, by the side
of Nehemiah, is perfectly natural, if not necessary, to the
crisis which the latter encountered and overcame. Nor
is the great expedition, which 'Ezra is said to have led
to Jerusalem, historically improbable. On the contrary,
the achievements of Nehemiah—his triumph over habits
of worship which, as ' Malachi ' tells us, were nearly
universal among the priesthood and laity of Jerusalem,
and his foundation of a compact community which
remained loyal to the stricter law brought from Babylon,
and resisted, as Judaism before Nehemiah had not
been able to resist, the surrounding heathenism—are
best explained through his reinforcement by a large

number of Babylonian Jews under just such a leader as 'Ezra. When we turn with these considerations to the text of the Memoirs, we find this to be consonant with the authorship of 'Ezra himself. A large number of the words and phrases which are alleged to be characteristic of the Chronicler are employed as well by other post-exilic writers. 'Ezra may easily have used most of them; if there are any besides which only the Chronicler could have employed, they are due to his redaction of the Memoirs.[1]

Besides the Memoirs of 'Ezra and Nehemiah, which refer to their own times—from 457 or alternatively 445 onwards—the Chronicler has embodied in his compilation a document written in the Aramaic language,[2] which relates a number of transactions *The Aramaic Document.* between the Jews of Jerusalem and their Persian lords before the arrival of 'Ezra and Nehemiah. He has prefixed to this[3] an account of the Return of the Jews under Cyrus, in which there is much to question. But we have no reason to doubt the reliableness of his Aramaic source, which is generally assigned to the fifth century. Many of its data, concerning the building of the Temple under Darius (521-485), are exactly confirmed by the Books of Ḥaggai and Zechariah; the rest, obstructions which the *peoples of the land* put in the way of the rebuilding of the walls of the City under Xerxes and Artaxerxes, agree with the testimony of constant and harassing opposition from that quarter, which is given by these prophets and by Nehemiah.

From such reliable sources the following facts may

---

[1] See further, Appendix II.
[2] Ezra iv. 8-vi. 18; vii. 12-26 is also in Aramaic.          [3] Ezra i.-iii.

be accepted. *First*, after the Temple was built there were several efforts to restore the walls of the City under Xerxes I. (485-464), and especially under Artaxerxes I. (464-424), but these were frustrated on the appeal of the other peoples in Palestine to the Persian throne. *Second*, sometime in the reign of Artaxerxes, 'Ezra, a priest and scribe, sought and obtained permission from the king to lead from Babylonia to Jerusalem a great company of priests and levites; and upon his arrival attempted with no success to reform the worship and the customs of the Jewish community, which, as we have seen from ' Malachi,' suffered from lax discipline and many abuses. *Third*, in 445 Nehemiah, the cupbearer of Artaxerxes in the palace at Shushan, being grieved by a report of the defenceless state of Jerusalem, asked and obtained leave from his master to go and rebuild the walls; by September 444, in spite of opposition from *the peoples of the land*, he accomplished his task, and the walls were dedicated. *Fourth*, in 432 Nehemiah, again as Tirshatha, or governor of the Jewish province, paid a second visit to Jerusalem and achieved many reforms. *Fifth*, about one or other of these dates, or between them, 'Ezra brought forth the Law to the Jews of Jerusalem and Judah, gathered in a national assembly, and by a covenant on the basis of the Law the sacred community was anew established and organised.

*Certain Events of the Period.*

But though the compiler has thus preserved for us a great amount of contemporary and authentic information as to events in Jerusalem both before and after the arrival of 'Ezra and Nehemiah in the City, it is clear from his arrangement

*Confusion of their Chronological Order.*

of his materials that he was either ignorant of or indifferent to the proper chronological order of these
events.[1]   In the first place, either he or the author of
the Aramaic document before him has mixed into each
other the building of the Temple under Darius and the
attempts to build the City walls under Xerxes I. and
Artaxerxes I.   Again, in arranging the Memoirs of 'Ezra
and Neḥemiah he has broken up and re-sorted his
materials; some of his dates are capable of different
interpretations; and in two cases at least he has separated passages which belong to each other.

Such confusion has naturally given rise to
different theories of the exact course of the
ascertained events.   Some accept the definite statements that 'Ezra, with his bands, reached Jerusalem in
*the seventh year of Artaxerxes*, 458, and attempted his
reforms up to April 457.[2]   To the following years they
refer the account, in the Aramaic document, of the
frustrated efforts to rebuild the walls,[3] manifestly
out of place where the compiler has put it.   To the
wreck of these efforts they attribute Neḥemiah's grief in
445, and his request to Artaxerxes to be allowed to
visit Jerusalem and rebuild the Walls.   The other
theory is that 'Ezra's expedition to Jerusalem did not
take place till some years after the Walls were rebuilt
by Neḥemiah; that there had been no attempt at rebuilding before Neḥemiah, but that what caused his
grief at Shushan was the report of the ruin in which the
Walls had lain ever since the overthrow of the City
by Nebuchadrezzar in 586.   'Ezra is not mentioned in

*Opposite Theories as to this.*

---

[1] For the exhibition of this in detail see Appendix II.
[2] Ezra vii. 8, x. 16.   [3] Ezra iv. 8-vi.

Neḥemiah's story of the rebuilding: Neḥemiah's reforms
are not intelligible if 'Ezra's institution of the Law preceded them. On these grounds 'Ezra's expedition and
institution of the Law must be postponed either to the
interval between Neḥemiah's two visits in 444 and 432
—in which case we must read *the twenty-seventh* instead
of *the seventh year of Artaxerxes* as its date, that is 437—
or to the second of these visits.

I have explained in the Appendix the impossibility
of deciding between these rival chronologies, upon the
Impossibility　evidence at our disposal. It is strange how
of deciding　'Ezra and Neḥemiah avoid mentioning each
between
these.　　　other, but this may be due to the fact that
we have only part of the Memoirs of each of them.
We must be content to leave the order of the great
events to which they contributed, uncertain. Only one
thing seems probable in this order, that (for reasons I
shall give) before Neḥemiah came there had been
attempts to rebuild the Walls, and that it was the report
of the wreck of these which moved his passion to go
and do the work himself.

Having examined the documents upon the period,
and seen that recent objections to the authenticity of
'Ezra's Memoirs are insufficient, but that we cannot form
exact conclusions as to his relations with Neḥemiah and
the dates of his appearances in Jerusalem, we proceed
now to an account of the events which happened during
the governorship of Neḥemiah.

The policy of Neḥemiah and 'Ezra may be regarded as
twofold, but the end it pursued was virtually one. *First,*
there was the Rebuilding of the Walls of the City which
had lain breached since their overthrow by Nebuchad-

rezzar in 586 ; and *second*, during the rebuilding there became evident to the leaders the necessity of raising a Wall or Fence of Law about the community itself : bulwarks to keep pure the blood, the language, the worship and the morals of Israel.

Twofold Policy of 'Ezra and Nehemiah.

Nehemiah himself tells us that it was an account of the ruin of the Walls and of *the affliction and reproach* to which in consequence his returned countrymen were exposed which moved him to crave leave from Artaxerxes to go to Judah and *rebuild the place of my fathers' sepulchres : it lieth waste, and the gates thereof are consumed with fire.*[1] The petition was granted, and in 445 Nehemiah arrived in Jerusalem under military escort and with letters-royal to *the Keeper of the King's Forest, that he might give me timber to make beams for the gates of the castle which appertaineth to the House, and for the wall of the City, and for the house that I shall enter into.*[2] The Aramaic document in the Book of 'Ezra reports earlier attempts to rebuild the walls and their frustration by Samaritan intrigue ;[3] these attempts (the account of which the compiler has obviously misplaced in his arrangement of the Book of 'Ezra) have been attributed by several moderns to 'Ezra himself.[4] Whether they actually took place under 'Ezra or not, Nehemiah alludes neither to them nor to him. After a survey of the ruins he induced a large number of his fellow-Jews to begin the restoration, which he carefully describes not as an entire rebuilding, but as a *strengthening*,

1. The Restoration of the Walls.

---

[1] Neh. i.-ii. 5.        [2] ii. 8, 9.

[3] Aramaic document = Ezra iv. 8-vi. 18. The account of the attempts to build *the walls* is given in iv. 6-23 (verses 6, 7 are in Hebrew).

[4] See above, p. 333.

a '*pointing*' or *cementing*, a *healing*, and a *sealing* or *stopping of the breaches*.[1]    The restoration, which took fifty-two days, was finished by September 444, and the gates set up.[2]    After an interval of one hundred and forty-two years, Jerusalem was again *a fenced city*.   Gate-keepers and police were appointed with Ḥanani, Nehe-miah's brother, and Ḥananiah, the governor of the castle, in charge of the whole town.[3]

During the process of rebuilding, Nehemiah encoun-tered opposition from the same quarters from which the

*Opposition from the peoples of the land.*

earlier attempts are said to have been frus-trated.    *Sanballaṭ the Ḥoronite and Ṭobiyah the servant* or *slave, the 'Ammonite*, had been alarmed at his coming *to seek the welfare of the children of Israel*, and unable to stop his operations, along with *Gashmu the Arab, began to laugh us to scorn*, and to spread the old story that by rebuilding the walls the Jews intended rebellion against the king.[4]   The names of these persons, if they have been accurately transmitted, reflect the curious mixture of *the peoples of the land* which had taken place during the Jewish exile.   Sanballaṭ is a

*Samaritans.*

Ḥoronite, that is, from Beth-ḥoron, then a Samaritan town ; for according to a probable emendation of the text he is described as *saying before his brethren, Is this the power of Samaria, that these Jews*

---

[1] *Strengthening* (Hiphil of the verb חזק *to be strong*, and once, iii. 19, Piel) throughout ch. iii., E.V. *repairing*. '*Pointing*' or *cementing* (Kal of עזב, probably a technical term, for which see the lexicons), iii. 8, E.V. *fortified*. *Healing* and *sealing of the breaches*, A.V. *that the walls of Jerusa-lem were made up, and that the breaches began to be stopped ;* R.V. *that the repairing of the walls of Jerusalem went forward*, etc., iv. 7 (Eng.)=iv. I (Heb.).

[2] Neh. iii. I, 3, 6, 13 ff. ; vi. 15, vii. I ; cf. Ecclus. xlix. 13.

[3] vii. I, 2.                              [4] ii. 10, 19 ; iv. I ff.

*are fortifying their city ?* [1] and with a Samaritan nationality his Assyrian name, ' The Moon-god-gives-life,'
would agree. Tobiyah, on the other hand, like   Recreant
his son Jehôhanan, has a name compounded   Jews
of that of the God of Israel ; he is called *the 'Ammonite*,
but this may mean from Kephar Ha'ammoni, or ' Village
of the 'Ammonite,' which lay in the territory
                              and Arabs.
of Benjamin. Gashmu is an Arabian name ;
these nomads have always been scattered across Judah.
It is true that other meanings, as well as different readings,
of those names have been suggested ; but the latter are
mere conjectures, and as the meanings just given suit
the conditions of the time, it is reasonable to accept them.[2]
Samaritans, Jews, probably of that poorer class who had
never left Judah,[3] and Arabs, whose assistance rival
political powers in Palestine have always been eager to
enlist—the trio represent an alliance, frequent in the
history of Syria, between persons of different tribes
and cults, all of them Semitic, and therefore more or less
merging into each other, but bound only by a temporary
community of material interests.

An effort has been made to impute to these allies some
nobility of aim by representing them as a racial league,

---

[1] So the LXX. version, cod. B in 'Εσδρας B xiv. 4 : the Greek equivalent
of the Hebr. Neh. iii. 34=Eng. iv. 2.

[2] For other meanings that *Ḥoronite* is from Ḥoronaim in Moab, and that
*'Ammonite* means one of the neighbouring children of 'Ammon, see Schlatter,
*Zur Topogr. u. Gesch. Paläst.* 4, and Winckler, *Alt-Orient. Forschungen*, ii.
228 ff. ; for other readings Cheyne, artt. ' Sanballaṭ ' and ' Ṭobiah ' in *Encl.
Bibl.*, and the present writer's ' Beth-ḥoron ' in the same.

[3] Winckler, *K.A.T.*[(3)] 296, takes Sanballaṭ and Ṭobiyah as father and son,
' representatives,' whether genuine or not, ' of that branch of the royal family
which had remained in the land,' and now claimants for the leadership. There
are no grounds for either of these hypotheses—not even in the fact that later
' Tobiades ' appear in opposition to the high priests (below, ch. xv.).

eclectic in faith, and ambitious to create a common

Their character. national cause among the factions of the land. But their eclecticism was obviously of that petty sort which, without either strong intellectual force or sense of the supremacy of ethics in religion, or conscience of the moral unity of mankind, maintains its alliances and mixtures upon merely local or family considerations, or motives of gain, or sometimes only by the hostility of all its ingredients to the advocates of a higher moral standard. The attempt to argue that Neḥemiah has misrepresented his opponents is futile, and its conclusions are disproved, first by the fact that Neḥemiah and the allies faced each other from the beginning with a mutual and instinctive feeling of their essential hostility,

Incompatibility between their aims and Neḥemiah's. and secondly, by our knowledge of the subsequent fortunes of the tribes and cults of Palestine outside of Israel. In the alarm of the allies at Neḥemiah's arrival *to seek the welfare of the children of Israel,* and in his retort to them, *You have no portion nor right nor memorial in Jerusalem,*[1] we touch those ultimate elements of human consciousness, in which Neḥemiah was not rash in feeling the inspiration of God Himself. The low character of the popular cults of Syria, which recent excavations have revealed to us, and the ease with which those cults allowed themselves to be absorbed by Hellenism, prove that for Neḥemiah and 'Ezra to have yielded to the attempts to mingle the Jews with *the peoples of the land* would have been fatal both to the nation and the religion of Israel.

During his operations upon the Walls, Neḥemiah learned, from Jews living outside, of a plan of his enemies

---

[1] Neh. ii. 10, 19, 20.

to attack the builders; whom, therefore, in one of the most gallant scenes in all the drama of Jeru-salem's history, he armed as they built, and supported by a force of bowmen and lancers drawn up behind the Walls.[1] When the work was finished, Sanballaṭ, Ṭobiyah, and Gashmu sought four times to entice Neḥemiah to a conference on the plain of Ono, intending to do him a mischief; and then accused him of aiming at kingship.[2] But he discovered that such assaults from the outside were not all he had to fear. The alliance against him, with its right wing merging into Judaism, had friends within the Walls, such as we shall find every heathen power hereafter able to reckon upon in Jerusalem. They hired prophets, Neḥemiah says, to work upon his fears, and to seduce him to discredit himself with his people by taking refuge in the Temple from plans for his assassination.[3]

Ṭobiyah, of the Jewish name, was in close correspondence with the *nobles of Judah*,[4] that is with some of the returned Jews, for no nobles had been left in the land after the Babylonian deportations and the flight into Egypt. He and his son Jehoḥanan were married to the daughters of such families, and were thus related to the high priest Eliashib,[5] who allowed Ṭobiyah, even after the Walls were built but during Neḥemiah's absence from the City, to store his household stuff in one of the consecrated chambers of the Temple courts.[6] The Jews themselves had not recovered command of the trade of the country, and held

*Conspiracies against the Building*

*and against Neḥemiah.*

*These perils and the many abuses*

---

[1] Neh. iv. 7-23.    [2] vi. 1-9.    [3] vi. 10-14.
[4] vi. 17.    [5] vi. 18; xiii. 4.    [6] xiii. 4-9.

close commerce with Tyrians for fish, and with travelling dealers in other kinds of wares, who found quarters
within the walls.[1]  Consequently, as in later days from
the same cause, the Sabbath was profaned equally with
the Temple.  Commerce nearly always implies *connubium* ;
the blood of the Jews was mixed with that of other
tribes, and the children grew up ignorant even of the
Hebrew tongue.  *In those days also I saw Jews who had
married wives of Ashdod, 'Ammon and Moab, and their
children spake half in the dialect of Ashdod, and could not
speak the Jewish language, but according to the language of
each people.*[2]  These evils are the same as 'Ezra reports
having encountered upon his arrival at Jerusalem, either
before or after Nehemiah ; and as having infected likewise the immigrant Jews, fresh from the more bracing
atmosphere of Babylonian Jewry.[3]  But in addition,
Nehemiah the governor discovered among the noble and
ruling Jews a cruel oppression of their poorer brethren,
whose lands they mortgaged and whose persons they
enslaved for debt.[4]  From all these things
require (2) the
Fence of the   experienced after their arrival in Jerusalem,
Law.
'Ezra, whose mission had been to enrich the
Temple with gifts, and Nehemiah, who had set out to
build the Walls, developed that wider policy, the success
of which constituted them the founders of Judaism.  To
men of such a conscience towards God and their race
such a policy was inevitable in the conditions we have
sketched.  The mere Walls of the City and the Temple
were not enough ; the circumstances revealed during their
construction demanded the more effectual ' Fence of the
Law.'

[1] Neh. xiii. 15-22.     [2] xiii. 24.     [3] Ezra ix. f.     [4] Neh. v.

Nor is it less natural to believe that, as his singularly candid Memoirs testify, Neḥemiah achieved the beginnings of this wider policy largely on the strength of his own personality. By his immediate recognition of the wrongs of the poor, by his unselfish example and resignation of his rights as governor, by casting the household stuff of Ṭobiyah out of the Temple Courts, by regulating the Temple organisation and the distribution of tithes to the Levites, by shutting the City gates on the Sabbath, by contending with the men who had married foreign wives, and even by using (as he confesses) personal violence to them, Neḥemiah, upon his own strength of spirit and body, started the necessary reforms.[1] His Memoirs reveal a strong personality, full of piety towards God and his people, with a power both of sincere prayer and the persuading of men ; cut to the quick by the thought of *the place of the graves of his fathers* lying waste, but more concerned for the affliction and reproach of his living brethren, and with a conscience, too, of their sins, especially towards the poor and the easily defrauded Levites. Without Isaiah's vision or Jeremiah's later patience, Neḥemiah fulfils the prophetic ideal of the ruler, whose chief signs shall be that he draws breath in the fear of the Lord, that he defends the cause of the poor, that he has gifts of persuasion and inspiration, that he is quick to distinguish between the worthy and the evil, and that he does not spare the evil in their way. Neḥemiah is everywhere dependent upon God, and conscious *of the good hand of his God upon him.* He has the strong man's power of

*How much was done by Neḥemiah himself.*

*His character and sympathies.*

[1] Neh. i.-vii. ; xii. 31, 37-40 ; xiii. 4-31.

keeping things to himself, but when the right moment
comes he can (unlike 'Ezra) persuade and lift the people
to their work.  He has a keen discernment of character
and motive.  He is intolerant of the indulgent, the com-
promising and the lazy, even when they are nobles—who,
as he expresses it, *put not their necks to the work of the
Lord.*[1]  In the preparations for his mission and its first
stages at Jerusalem he is thoroughly practical.  In his
account of his building he proves himself careful and
true to detail.  As he becomes familiar with the conditions on which he has been called to act, and gradually
realises how much he must do beyond the mere building
of walls, the growth of his sense of the grandeur of his
His                work is very beautiful ; the sense of his loneli-
loneliness.        ness not less pathetic.  *I am doing a great
work, so that I cannot come down : why should the work
cease, whilst I leave it and come down to you ?*[2]  There
were few whom he could trust in charge of the City and
its gates : he had to draw his police from the bands of
Levites and musicians whose rights he had defended.[3]

   If sometimes his loneliness made Neḥemiah too suspicious of his opponents or of his own people, this was but
Criticisms         the defect of his qualities or inevitable in the
of him             atmosphere of intrigue that he had to breathe.
answered.
         To be able to criticise the personal violence
which he confesses, *his smiting of some* of those who had
married foreign wives, and *his plucking of their hair*, we
would need to have stood by him through all his troubles.
The surmise is reasonable that such extreme measures
may have been best for the lax and self-indulgent
among his contemporaries ; with Orientals, treatment of

---

[1] Neh. iii. 5.          [2] vi. 3.          [3] vii. 1 ; cf. xiii. 10 ff.

this kind from a man whom they trust or fear oftener enhances respect than induces resentment.[1] By the followers of Him who in that same desecrated City over-turned the tables of the money-changers, and scourged with a scourge of cords, much may be forgiven to an anger which is not roused by selfish disappointments or the sense of weakness, but by sins against national ideals, and which means expense to him who displays it. Anger is often selfish, but may also be one of the purest and most costly forms of self-sacrifice. The disciples, who saw the exhaustion to which it put our Lord, said of Him, *the zeal of Thine House hath eaten me up.* Had we been present with this lonely governor, aware of the poorness of the best of the material he had to work with, and conscious, as we are to-day, of the age-long issues of his action, we might be ready to accord to his passion the same character of devotion and self-sacrifice. Such an ' Apologia pro Nehemiâ' is necessary in face of recent criticisms on his conduct, all the materials for which have been supplied by his own candour. One of not the least faults of a merely academic criticism is that it never appeals to Christian standards except when it would dis-parage the men of the Old Covenant; who at least under-stood as we cannot the practical conditions and ethical issues of the situations on which God set them to act.

In the great work which was then achieved at Jeru-salem the presence of 'Ezra by Nehemiah's side is, as we have seen,[2] natural and authentic; but it is impossible to date 'Ezra's appearances and difficult to relate the two men, who almost never allude to each other. 'Ezra's contributions to the

'Ezra's con-tributions to the work.

---

[1] Witness John Nicholson and the Punjaubees.    [2] Above, p. 330.

work were the large reinforcement which he brought out
of Babylonia to the loyal Jewish population of the land,
his own zeal for reform, and above all his learning in the
Law, without which the layman Nehemiah could hardly
have succeeded in organising the community. 'Ezra
His character. the man is scarcely so clear to our eyes as
Nehemiah; his Memoirs are more overlaid
with the work of the Chronicler. Yet we can see in him
certain differences, some of which at least are natural to
the priest as distinguished from the governor. Nehemiah
came to Jerusalem with a military escort, and, as he had
prayed to God to move the king's heart to his request,
so he saw nothing in these Persian guards inconsistent
with the Divine protection. 'Ezra, on the contrary, tells
us: *I was ashamed to ask of the king a band of soldiers
and horsemen to help us against the enemy in the way
because we had spoken unto the king, saying, The hand of
our God is upon all them that seek Him for good, but His
power and His wrath are against all who forsake Him*;
and instead 'Ezra proclaimed a fast at the river Ahava,
from which his company started, *that we might humble
ourselves before God and seek of Him a straight way*.[1] As
some one has said, while Nehemiah smote and plucked
the hair of those who had married foreign women,
'Ezra in face of the same sinners rent his clothes and
plucked the hair of his own head and beard and sat
down stunned.[2] His dialect of Hebrew is legal and
priestly; Nehemiah's is his own. 'Ezra has not, at first
at least, the governor's powers of persuasion and inspiration; the people put him off from month to month.[3]
When Nehemiah speaks they act at once. Still, if, as

---

[1] Ezra viii. 21-23.  [2] ix. 3.  [3] ix., x.

the compiler says, 'Ezra came to Jerusalem before Nehemiah, his frustrated labours no doubt prepared the way for the latter's success. What is hard to understand is that the two scarcely if at all mention one another. Would this mutual silence have been explained if we had had the rest of their Memoirs? Was it due to the differences of their temperaments? Or was Nehemiah, who found his only reliable officers, beyond his kinsfolk, among the Levites and musicians, suspicious of all priests; and did the priest 'Ezra take the other side from him in his efforts to get the Levites their tithes? These are questions, naturally arising from the materials at our disposal, but impossible to answer.

His contrast and relations to Nehemiah.

Yet this is certain, that it was 'Ezra who brought and expounded the Law to Jerusalem. It is not necessary here to discuss the origins of that Law: all we need to keep in mind is that (as we have seen) the life and worship of the community had hitherto been regulated by the Deuteronomic Code, and that most of the reforms effected by 'Ezra and Nehemiah were on the lines of the Priestly Code. The Book which 'Ezra brought to the people was, besides, new to them.[1] We can have little doubt, therefore, that the Priestly Code was what 'Ezra introduced, and what he and Nehemiah moved the people to adopt. Except for a few later additions the Pentateuch was complete, and Jerusalem in possession of the Law-book which was to govern her life, till she ceased to be Jewish. In our survey of the constitutional history we have sufficiently discussed the forms of government, foreign and native, to

Institution of the Law.

[1] Ezra vii. 14, 25; Neh. viii. 9 ff.

which the Jews were subject when Nehemiah arrived, as well as the reorganisation of the people under their new Law.[1]

Most of the details of the topography of Nehemiah's Jerusalem have also been already discussed:[2] the course Topographi- of the Walls and positions of the Gates with cal: the Walls. the character of his reconstruction. Nehemiah rebuilt the Walls of Jerusalem on the lines on which they had run before the Exile.[3] That is, the Walls again enclosed both the East and the South-west Hills. From somewhere about the present Citadel they ran on the brow of the South-west Hill above Hinnom, south and then east to the Fountain Gate near the mouth of the Central Valley, crossed this below Siloam, on one of the five lines discovered by Dr. Bliss,[4] continued north up the brow of the East Hill above Kidron towards the Temple enclosure, ran under this and then round the Temple mount, west and south-west on the unknown line of the Second Wall of Josephus back to the point from which we have started. On this circuit there were eight, perhaps nine, Gates: the Gate of the Gai at the south-west

---

[1] Vol. i. Bk. ii. ch. ix., 'Government and Police,' sections iii. and iv., pp. 382 ff.

[2] Vol. i. Bk. i. ch. iv. p. 74, and ch. v. p. 111 on the Dragon's Well; ch. vii. pp. 177 ff. on the Gate of the Gai and the Dung-Gate; ch. viii. 'The Walls of Jerusalem,' pp. 195-204, on the course of the walls in Nehemiah's time and his rebuilding of them. Since those chapters were passed for press I have received a new essay on Nehemiah's walls and gates in Mommert's *Topographie des Alten Jerusalem*: ivter Theil (1907), the first four sections of which deal with Nehemiah's ride of inspection, his North, West and South Walls with their gates, his 'inner wall' which Mommert supposes to have crossed the South-west Hill, and the East Wall, and the routes of the two choirs (pp. 1-76).

[3] Vol. i. 195 ff.                    [4] Vol. i. 220 ff.

corner, the Dung-Gate on the south stretch, the Fountain
Gate at the south-east corner, a Water-Gate on Ophel,
apparently a Horse-Gate, probably an East-Gate under
the Temple, and—on the north stretch—the Sheep-Gate,
the Fish-Gate, and the *Gate of the Old* . . . (?), which
may have been the same as the Corner-Gate. The same
amount of labour was not required on every part of this
circuit : Wall and Gates seem to have been much less
ruined on the west and south stretches than on the east
and north. The stones for repair lay to hand in the
ruins themselves, hence the short time the work occupied.
Whether the timber that Nehemiah required from the
King's Forest[1] was used for a course in the walls,
as in the case of Solomon's Wall round the Temple,[2]
or only for the posts and doors of the Gates,[3] is
uncertain.

Nehemiah tells that he also required wood *to timber
the gates of the Birah of the Temple. Birah*[4] is a new
word in Hebrew, meaning *Castle.* Does it The Birah of
apply here—as it does in late Hebrew—to the Temple.
the whole Temple-mount with its enclosure, which
formed a separate citadel within the City ; or is it some
particular fortress attached to the Temple? Nehemiah
says no more about it except to mention a governor of
the Birah.[5] This might indicate a separate castle, either
the old David's-Burgh, or a fortified building on the site

---

[1] Neh. ii. 8.                        [2] See above, p. 67.

[3] So Mommert, *Topog. des alt. Jerus.*, iv[ter] Theil 4. In his somewhat
harsh criticism of Rückert, Mommert has forgotten the course of timber in
Solomon's walls.

[4] בִּירָה, perhaps fr$_o$m the Assyrian *birtu* through Aramaic, found in the
O.T. only in Nehemiah, Chronicles, Esther and Daniel.

[5] Neh. vii. 2.

of the palace of Solomon, or less probably one to the
north of the Temple on the site afterwards occupied by
the Baris of the Hasmoneans and the Antonia of Herod.[1]
But it is possible that by the Birah Neḥemiah meant the
separately fortified Temple-Mount, which we know had
its own gates. Where Neḥemiah's own house stood we
do not know.

Of other buildings Neḥemiah mentions only the Turret
of the Corner at the north-east angle of the City ; Towers
Hammeah and Ḥananeel to the north of the
Temple ; the Tower of the Ovens on the
West wall ; and—south of the Temple—the
House of the Gibbôrim (the old Barracks of David) ;
the Armoury ; the House of the High Priest, evidently a
large building, from the length of the wall in front of it ;
the upper House of the King with the Court of the
Guard ; the Projecting Tower (or Towers), the houses of
the Priests and of the Nethinim.[2] It is significant that
except the Tower of the Ovens all these
buildings lie on the East Hill : a striking
confirmation of the conclusion we have come
to that till the time of Herod not only the Temple
but the military and civil centre of Jerusalem was here,
and not on the South-west Hill.[3] But indeed Neḥemiah's location of the stairs of the David's-Burgh would
by itself be sufficient to prove the correctness of the
East-Hill theory.

When the City walls were rebuilt on the old lines, it

*Other public
or prominent
buildings.*

*All but one
on the East
Hill.*

---

[1] This, the site usually accepted (cf. Josephus xv. *Ant.* xi. 4 ; xviii. *Ant.*
iv. 3), can hardly have been the Birah of Neḥemiah, for on it or close to it
stood the towers Hammeah and Ḥananeel.

[2] All these are given in ch. iii.      [3] Vol. i. Bk. i. ch. vi.

was found that the space was too great for the shrunken population.   This   has   been   estimated   at   Size of the 10,000.[1]   Nehemiah took measures to increase   Population. it by drafts from the other Jewish settlements.   But probably it was long before Jerusalem was again as full as she had been before the Exile.

[1] By Guthe (Hauck's *R.E.* viii. 683, on the basis of Neh. xi. 4-19).

# CHAPTER XIV

## THE REST OF THE PERSIAN PERIOD

### 431-332 B.C.

F ROM the close of Nehemiah's Memoirs to the opening of the Maccabean histories—or more

*The Obscurity which rests on this Period.* exactly from 431 B.C. to the fall of the Persian Empire before Alexander in 331, and from this onwards under the Ptolemies to the Seleucid conquest of Palestine in 197—the history of Jerusalem lies under an almost unbroken obscurity; from which many have too hastily turned as though it were a winter-fog and below lay a frosted City and a benumbed People. Far rather is it that mellow haze beneath which life in field and town runs perhaps the more busily that the horizons are narrow; and in the diffused light men's minds, though unable to read the past correctly or take clear views of the future, are the more disposed to reflect upon things which have little to do with time. We who stand so far from that haze fail to discern through it either the definite figures of men, the presence of powerful personalities, or even the exact character of such events as we otherwise know to have happened within it. And we observe, too, that one who, like Josephus, lived so much nearer to the period, confused its chronology and believed that he saw moving through its mists apparitions of a legendary character.

Yet there is much in the period of which we may be sure besides the constant labour of the olive, the vine and the corn, the increasing smoke of sacrifice from the Temple, the great annual festivals, and—this is equally undoubted—the increase of population both in the City and over the narrow territory which she commanded. The flash of war breaks the haze more than once. We learn that Jerusalem was taken and perhaps sacked under Artaxerxes Ochus about 350, and 'was destroyed' by Ptolemy Soter in 312.[1] We have already seen[2] how the Law which the nation had adopted under Nehemiah became, with additions, gradually operative, and the supreme national authority was absorbed by the High Priest, the only chief whom the Law recognised; while around but beneath him there developed out of the loosely organised body of nobles and priests, whom we found under Nehemiah, an aristocratic council or senate, room for which had also been provided by the Law. The Samaritan schism was completed, a Samaritan Temple was built on Mount Gerizim, and round it a community was organised under a scarcely differing edition of the Law, yet so definitely in disruption from the Jews that these were no more haunted by fears of the intrusion into their life of elements so menacing to their higher ideals. The Jews passed from the Persian beneath a Greek dominion. Even earlier than this change of masters, they came into contact with the Greeks, and we have the first notices of them by Greek writers. After Alexander's Asian conquests (333-331)

*Things certain in it.*

*Assaults on the City.*

*The Law, High Priest and Council.*

*The Samaritan Temple and Community.*

*Palestine passes under Greek influence.*

---

[1] See below, p. 359 f.    [2] Vol. i. Bk. II. ch. ix. pp. 384-98.

their life began to be influenced by Greek culture and polity. Still rooted on their own soil and tenacious of their ancestral institutions and beliefs, as none of the neighbouring nations except the Samaritans continued to be, they felt the influences of a new climate which could not but affect their polity, and, compact as the nation was, test it with new solvents and split it into fresh factions which last through the New Testament period. All these general movements and changes are un-doubted; and, though the haze does not (as we have said) permit even the nearest historians to discern a succession of dominant personalities through the period (beyond the roll of the governing High Priests); and though the literature which has come down to us from it is nearly all anonymous; we cannot, with the testimony of the latter before us, hesitate to believe that Israel was still the mother of great sons. When out of the mists rivers flow to our feet, we know that there are mountains behind.

As our authorities for this period we have five or six chapters of the *Antiquities* of Josephus,[1] but for reasons given above they are among the least reliable in that book of very various values; the notices of Greek historians and other writers which are either confined to the general history and geography of the time or merely mention such events as happened to Jerusalem, or (perhaps with one exception)[2] describe the City and the Jews from a very distant point of view; and some of the later literature of the Old Testament. This, however, is difficult to

Our Authori-
ties for the
Period.

---

[1] xi. *Ant.* vi.-viii. ; xii. *Ant.* i., ii., and part of iii.

[2] The exception is the Pseudo-Aristeas. On that and the other Greek notices see next chapter.

assign to definite dates. We must beware of the temptation, offered us by an age of whose history we know so little, to use it as a last resort for literature which we have had difficulty in assigning to other periods just because of our better knowledge of these.[1] At the same time, we know with what amount of Law, History and Prophecy Israel entered the period after Nehemiah ; that in particular the Priestly Law had been accepted as canonical, and that the Pentateuch in its present form was complete before the establishment of the Samaritan community. By 250 B.C. it was translated into Greek. Recent criticism has given fair reasons for assigning to the period between Nehemiah and 300 B.C. some additions to the Priestly Law, the Books of Chronicles, certain Psalms, the Book of Joel, ' Zechariah ' ix.-xiv., the Book of Jonah, and probably the Book of Ruth and ' Isaiah ' xxiv.-xxvii.[2] We may be sure, too, that certain processes, which were consummated during the Greek period, such as the collection, with additions, of the Prophets, the construction of the Book of Proverbs, and the collection of Psalms for the Temple - service, had already begun ; and some of them were perhaps even finished, under the Persians. For the rest, which include Job and a number of Psalms, we can only say that they more probably belong to the Persian Period than to any other. Ecclesiastes falls to be discussed in the next chapter.

[1] We must also remember that in the case of some writings which certainly belong to this age, it is impossible always to say definitely whether they come from the Persian or from the Greek half of it.

[2] To those some would add ' Isaiah ' lvi.-lxvi., but we have seen reason for assigning these prophecies to the exilic and immediately post-exilic age : above, pp. 316 ff.

In this chapter we shall deal with Jerusalem through the remainder of the Persian Period : the century between the date of Nehemiah's second visit to the City in 431, and the fall of the Persian Empire in 331. The Jewish territory formed part of the great Persian Satrapy called '*Abar-Naharah, Beyond-the-River*, both in the documents given in the Book of 'Ezra,[1] and on the coins of the rebellious Satrap Mazaeus:[2] the fifth of the 'Nomoi' or Satrapies described by Herodotus as 'all Phœnicia and Syria called the Palestinian, Cyprus . . .' with part of Arabia.[3] The boundaries were : on the north a line from the mouth of the Orontes to the great bend of the Euphrates near Tiphsah; on the south the Egyptian border at Mount Casius, and on the east an unknown line through the desert.[4] The seat of government appears to have been Samaria, the natural centre for Western Palestine, and in easy communication with the lands east of Jordan.[5]

*Geographical and Political Condition.*

Within this Satrapy lay the Jewish *Mĕdinah* or *Province* : Jerusalem, its suburban territory and such other towns with their fields as loyal Jews had held during the Exile or those returned from Babylon had reoccupied. After Nehemiah Judah appears to have had still a separate governor, but the Satrap sometimes held his court at Mispah,[6]

*The Extent of the Jewish Territory.*

---

[1] עֲבַר־נַהֲרָה, Ezra v. 6 ; vi. 6, Aramaic ; cf. the Hebrew עֵבֶר הַנָּהָר Neh. iii. 7.

[2] Head, *Hist. Num.* 615. Compare 1 Macc. iii. 32, vii. 8, but not, as Wellhausen (*Isr. u. Jüd. Gesch.* 150) and Hölscher (*Palästina in der Pers. u. Hellenist. Zeit*, 5) do, xi. 60 ; for in the latter verse *the River* cannot be the Euphrates.　　　　　　　[3] Herodotus iii. 89-94.

[4] Cf. Hölscher, *op. cit.* 4-6.　　　　　[5] *H.G.H.L.* 332 f.

[6] This is a natural interpretation of the phrase in Neh. iii. 7, *the Mispah to* or *of the throne of the Pehah of 'Ēber-han-Nahar*. Mispah cannot

where the Babylonians had formerly posted Gedaliah as governor.[1] The extent of the Jewish territory is uncertain. The following districts, mentioned as those from which the Levites were summoned to Jerusalem, are all in the neighbourhood of the City ; *the Kikkar* or *Circuit round Jerusalem,* the suburban territory ;[2] *the villages of the Netôphâthites,* Netôphah being either the modern Liftā or the modern Bet-Nettîf;[3] *Beth-hag-Gilgal,* probably *the Gilgal which is over against the ascent of Adummim,* or about as far east of Jerusalem as Geba' is to the north ;[4] and *the fields of Geba' and 'Azmaveth.*[5] From the following places came the Jews who helped to rebuild the walls: *Jerusalem and its Kikkar*; to the north *Gibe'on* and *Mispah*; to the west or south *Beth-hak-Kerem,* according as this is Jebel Fureidis or the modern 'Ain Kārim ; to the east *Jericho* ; and to the south *Tekoa', Keilah, Beth-Sur* and *Zanoah.*[6] It is significant that no town is mentioned farther south than these: neither Hebron nor its neighbours Mareshah, Tappuah and

have been the usual seat of the Satrap, as Hölscher (29) infers, for there is evidence that this was Samaria (Ezra iv. 10 ff.). The recently discovered Papyri (Sachau, *Drei Aramäische Papyrusurkunden aus Elephantine*) mention a Pehah of Judah in 411 B.C.

[1] Jer. xl. 6 ; 2 Kings xxv. 23.    [2] Vol. i. Bk. II. ch. iii.

[3] Henderson, *P.E.F.Q.*, 1878, 198, proposes its identification with Nephtoah (Josh. xv. 9; xviii. 15), near Bethlehem.

[4] Josh. xv. 7. This identification was suggested independently by Professor Cheyne and myself, artt. Gallim and Gilgal (§ 6) in the *Enc. Bibl.* The ascent of Adummim is the modern Tal'at ed-Dum on the road from Jerusalem to Jericho. Hölscher (28) suggests Tell Jeljul, near Jericho, but this is too far from the City.

[5] Neh. xii. 28 f., probably from the Chronicler.

[6] Neh. iii. There is hardly sufficient reason to suppose with Smend (*Die Listen der Bücher Ezr. u. Neh.*) that only fragments have been preserved of the full list of the builders of the wall. Probably the wall was not equally ruined throughout its circuit, and some stretches of it required less restoration than others.

Ma'on, nor any place in the Negeb. In all probability
these former seats of the Calebites were
Hebron and
southward already occupied by the children of Edom who
was Edomite.
had come upon them during the Exile, and
who certainly held them through the Maccabean period.
With Hebron there would also fall the valuable oasis of
Engedi, always a dependence of the Hebronites.[1] According to the Chronicler, the dispossessed Calebites occupied
*Bethlehem, Ḳiriath-ye'arim* and *Beth-Gader* (perhaps the
modern Khurbet Jedireh), *Sorea'* and *Eshtaol.*[2] For the
same reason—that the Chronicler knew them as Jewish—
*Ono, Lod* or Lydda, *Ayyalôn,*[3] the *Beth-Ḥorons, Bethel,
Yeshanah* and *'Ephron,*[4] have been added to the Jewish
territory by some scholars. But Lydda and
Lydda, Beth-
horon and 'Ephron or Ephraim[5] were still Samaritan
'Ephron
probably in the beginning of the Maccabean period,
Samaritan.
and Beth-Ḥoron (as we have seen)[6] was
probably the town of Sanballat, Nehemiah's Samaritan
foe. These places must, therefore, be left doubtful. Herr
Hölscher argues that Jericho lay outside the
Jericho
probably Jewish territory and in possession of the
Jewish.
Arabs.[7] His reasons are that a prophet whom
he takes to be of the Persian Period[8] gives the eastern
boundary of Judah as *the Vale of 'Akôr,* the Wâdy Kelt,
and that Hieronymus of Kardia describes the whole
circuit of the Dead Sea along with the balsam fields of
the Ghôr as in possession of the Nabateans.[9] To these

---

[1] *H.G.H.L.* 271 f.   [2] 1 Chron. ii. 50-55.
[3] *Id.* viii. 12 f.   [4] vii. 24; 2 Chron. xiii. 19 (Eng.).
[5] Hölscher, *op. cit.* 30 ff.   [6] Above, p. 336.
[7] *Op. cit.* 46-50.   [8] 'Isa.' lxv. 10. See above, p. 316 ff.
[9] Diod. Sic. xix. 98, the data of which are reasonably attributed to
Hieronymus.

reasons might be added the fact that even when the kingdom of Judah was strong it did not hold Jericho, which belonged to Israel. The separableness of Jericho from Judah is therefore assured. But at the same time neither of those testimonies is exactly relevant to the geographical conditions in the time of Nehemiah, the third quarter of the fifth century.[1] Since Nehemiah himself states that men from Jericho took part in the rebuilding of the walls, we may assume that Jericho was then Jewish. It was a town which often and easily passed from one lord to another.[2] But even if we include Jericho, the Jewish territory was very small—some 20 miles north and south by 32 east and west (about 33 kilometres by 52), a large part desert, and the rest containing, at least in Nehemiah's time, several settlements of a non-Jewish population.

Beyond Judæa, in Gilead and Galilee, there may already have been a few Jewish *enclaves* as there certainly were by the Maccabean period,[3] but the grounds on which the attempt is sometimes made to prove this are precarious. The Jewish communities which Simon and Judas Maccabeus brought away from Galilee and Gilead were very small, and the inference is reasonable that if they had been already planted in these provinces by an active Jewish propaganda during the Persian Period, they would have grown to something more powerful under the favourable reigns of the earlier Ptolemies.

*Jewish Settlements beyond Judah.*

---

[1] ' Isaiah' lxv. is, as we have seen, more probably contemporary with Haggai and Zechariah, or a little later with ' Malachi'; and Hieronymus of Kardia wrote towards the end of the fourth century.

[2] *H.G.H.L.* 266 f. See also below, p. 359.

[3] Stade, *Gesch.* ii. 198; Wellhausen, *Isr. u. Jüd. Gesch.* 160 ff. ; Guthe, *Gesch.* 292 ; Hölscher, *op. cit.* 31-37.

Such was the small territory of which Jerusalem was
the capital.  The prophet Joel, about 400 B.C., repre-

Joel's Picture
of the
Jewish com-
munity.

sents its people as existing solely by agriculture and for the worship of their God.  His
vivid pictures, so far as they relate to the
present, are divided between fields devastated by the
locusts and a people gathered in Ṣion to implore the pity
of Jahweh and to expect, one and all, the spirit of prophecy.  Even when he discloses the future Joel betrays
no ambition for a wide land and a great empire.  It is
remarkable how content he is to promise the fertility of
Judah and the inviolableness of Jerusalem.  From his
emphasis on the latter we learn that the Holy City
was full of foreigners;[1] probably her trade was still in
their hands.[2]   There had also been a selling by the
heathen of a number of young Jews into the hands of
the Greeks: a distant and, without Divine aid, an irre-
coverable captivity.[3]

From 400 B.C. onwards Syria was the scene of many
military expeditions and conflicts.  For more than fifty

Probable
Disasters to
Jerusalem,
*circa* 350 B.C.

years (408-343) Egypt endeavoured to assert
her independence of Persia ; and Artaxerxes II. Mnemon (404-358) and Artaxerxes III.
Ochus (358-337) fought her, across the natural obstacles
which defend her from Asian invasion, with many failures
and the loss of large forces.  The Persians were compelled to war during part of the same time with
Evagoras of Cyprus, and those Phœnician cities which
had put themselves under his protection.  The gravity
of the double crisis, and its uncertainties, must have
tempted into revolt the other peoples of Palestine, and

---

[1] iii. 17 (Heb. iv. 17).            [2] See above, pp. 319, 326, 339 f.
[3] iii. 6 (Eng. = iv. 6 Heb.).

have embittered towards them the temper of the Persian kings; a dynasty which, so long as their power was secure, treated their subjects with considerable kindness. The tides of war rolled up and down the coast of the Levant; many of its towns were given to fire and sword. We have two traditions that under one or other Artaxerxes, Jerusalem became involved in these disasters. On the one hand, it is stated by Syncellus, and in the *Chronicon* of Eusebius, that 'Ochus, son of Artaxerxes, when on a campaign against Egypt, made a partial captivity of the Jews, of whom he settled some in Hyrkania on the Caspian Sea, and some in Babylonia, who are even now there, as many of the Greeks relate.'[1] Solinus contributes a very mixed reminiscence of what seems to be the same event. 'The capital of Judæa was Jerusalem, but it was destroyed; Jericho succeeded, but it also has disappeared, having been conquered in the war of Artaxerxes.'[2] On the other hand, Josephus records[3] that when the high-priest John, the grandson of Nehemiah's contemporary Eliashib, slew Jesus his brother and rival in the Temple, Bagōses, 'the general of another Artaxerxes' (that is, another than Artaxerxes I., Longimanus), came in anger to Jerusalem, for he had promised the high-priesthood to Jesus, forcibly entered the Temple, and imposed on the Jews a tax of fifty drachms for every lamb offered in the daily sacrifices. These are the two traditions: both late, but independent of each other. There is no reason against the substance of either of them: that under the second or third

[1] Eusebius, *Chron.*, ed. Schoene, ii. 112 f. ; Syncellus, ed. Dindorf, i. 486. Cf. Orosius, III. vii. 6 f.

[2] Reinach, *Textes d'Auteurs Grecs et Romains relatifs au Judaïsme*, 339, from the *Collectanea* of Solinus, Mommsen's ed. 1864.

[3] xi. *Ant.* vii. I.

Artaxerxes Jerusalem was punished by the Persians, a number of Jews carried into exile (it must have been for an actual or a threatened revolt), and the Temple defiled by the entrance of the Persian general. The time to which these events have been assigned is that of the campaigns of Artaxerxes Ochus from 353 onwards, especially after the defeat of the Persians in 352 by Egypt, and the consequent revolt of the Phœnician states. A certain Bagōas was the Persian general in Phœnicia in 348-346.[1] A religious revolt by the Jews, during those disturbances in Syria when the Persian power was shaken to its foundations, was likely; not less probably Artaxerxes Ochus, or his general Bagōas, punished it, as they punished the risings in Egypt and Phœnicia, by profaning, if not destroying, the Temple, and putting the Jews under heavier tribute. But the Papyri discovered at Assouan state that in 411 B.C. Bagohi was Peḥah of Judah, and Iehoḥanan High-Priest at Jerusalem.[2] Professor Robertson Smith suggested that the story in Josephus of the forcible entrance to the Temple by Bagōses is really a pragmatical invention in order to soften the catastrophe to the Jews, and partly to explain it by the sin of the High-Priest. This was accepted by Professor Cheyne, and both scholars transferred to the campaign of Bagōas Psalms xliv., lxxiv., and lxxvii., which had been generally regarded as Maccabean.[3] The latter two Psalms,

---

[1] The stratum of fact which may underlie the Book of Judith has been referred to the same events on account of the likeness of the name Holophernes to that of Orophernes, the leader at the time of a Persian army (Diod. Siculus, xxxi. 19). [2] Above, pp. 354 f., *n.* 6.

[3] W. R. Smith, *O. T.J. C.*(2), 207, 438 ff. ; Cheyne, *Introd. to Isaiah*, 358 ff. On the other side see A. B. Davidson, *Critical Review*, 1893, 19; A. R. S. Kennedy, *Expository Times* (1892), 247. Cf. Cheyne, *Ib.* 320.

however, as well as 'Isaiah' lxiv. 10, which has also been referred to the same period, reflect a much more disastrous attack upon both City and Temple than we have a right to infer (in spite of Professor Robertson Smith's theory) from the meagre data of the traditions; and while the passage in Isaiah is referable to the destruction by Nebuchadrezzar,[1] those in the Psalms are possibly Maccabean, or if so late a date for them be deemed improbable, may refer to the destruction of Jerusalem by Ptolemy Soter.[2]

Whatever may have been the facts we have just discussed, and apart from the question of Jewish settlements at this time in Gilead, Galilee and elsewhere, there can be no doubt that during the last century of the Persian dominion the Jewish nation developed considerably in numbers, in resources and in institutions. As to the numbers, we have seen that the population of Jerusalem in Nehemiah's time proved too small for the restored City, and that a levy was made upon the Jews of other townships to supply what was lacking. But by the beginning of the Greek Period we have evidence, both from the Chronicler and other sources, that the population was comparatively large and fairly prosperous, and that there prevailed among them the spirit of a people which not only felt itself worthy of its great past, but was quietly confident of the future. Still, we must not suppose that the vast numbers, in which the Chronicler indulges, are correct. A quarter of a million would be a generous estimate for the population of Judah at this period.

Of the development of the institutions we find evidence

Development of the Nation

---

[1] See also above, p. 315 *n.* 4.      [2] See below, p. 376.

by a comparison between the Priestly Law, with which
the people started upon the century from Nehemiah
and of its to Alexander the Great, and the Chronicler's
Institutions. description, which may be taken as reflecting
the conditions prevalent at its close. Nehemiah had
secured for his nation the full practice of their Law, and
there is no reason to suppose that their Persian lords
seriously interfered with this. We are to conceive the
Jews, through the rest of the Persian Period, as settling
into those habits of life which ever afterwards distinguished them. There is a significant contrast between
the complaints of Nehemiah and some prophets immediately before him about the popular neglect of the
Sabbath, and the unanimous refusal of the nation to fight
on that day, which enabled Ptolemy I., in 321, to take
Jerusalem. The observance of the Sabbath, and the
three great annual festivals, the system of sacrifices, the
application of the ritual to the routine and emergencies
of life, whether individual or national, the appointment,
duties and rights of the priests, the influence of the
High-Priest without a rival to dispute his gradual advancement to the political headship of the nation, and
the institution around him of a college of priests and
nobles,[1]—all these, organised or suggested in the Priestly
Code, must have been developed and confirmed. Of
High-Priests during the time we read of only three,[2]
an indication that in religious matters the Jews

---

[1] Vol. i. 386 ff.

[2] Eliashib, Nehemiah's contemporary, was succeeded by his son Ioiada;
he by his son Iohanan, according to Josephus, a contemporary of Bagōas,
the servant of Artaxerxes II. (according to the Assouan Papyrus both I. and
B. were in office in 411 B.C.); and he by his son Iaddua, a contemporary,
according to Josephus, of Alexander (xi. *Ant.* viii. ; cf. Neh. xii. 11, 22).

were left to themselves. But while the Law was thus
carried out, and even developed, it is plain from the
Books of Chronicles that the development included a
number of features for which the Law finds no place.
Priests and Levites were divided each into twenty-four
courses;[1] the Temple singers, musicians and doorkeepers had become large and equally organised bodies,
which were recognised as of Levitical rank.[2] The elabora-
tion of the Temple music is especially interesting. We
must not suppose that its origins were recent, or that the
Chronicler had no grounds for carrying these back to the
beginnings of the Temple itself; but when we compare
the Priestly Code with the Chronicler's descriptions
of the Temple organisation and worship, we cannot
doubt that during the century after Nehemiah the
Levitical choirs and the whole personnel of the Temple
service had been extraordinarily increased. There are
no parts of the Old Testament so impossible to date with
exactness as the vast majority of the Psalms. Yet it is
a reasonable inference, from the development of the
Jewish ritual during this age, that to the latter belong a
number of the liturgical Psalms, as well as some of those
collections of earlier hymns and their adaptation to the
Temple-service, of which so much evidence is found in
the Psalter. The Pilgrim Psalms have also been assigned
by some to the Persian age. Like everything else
ordained by the Law, the three festivals of the sacred

---

[1] 1 Chron. xxiii. f. ; cf. 2 Chron. xxiii. 4, 8.

[2] 1 Chron. xxiii. 3-5 (cf. vi. 16-48), xxvi. 1-19; 2 Chron. xx. 19. The
singers are not mentioned in the Law, and in Nehemiah they are a class
lower than the Levites, while the doorkeepers are lower still, and only 138 in
number : Neh. vii. 44 f. Cf. Wellhausen, *Prolegomena*, 150 ff. ; *Isr. u. Jüd.
Gesch.* 151 ff. ; Guthe, *Gesch. des Volkes Israel*, 296 f.

year became more than ever fundamental institutions; and Jerusalem herself—not merely the one large town which the nation possessed, but their only valid shrine and altar—absorbed nearly all their patriotism and religious zeal. We cannot say *all*, if the Song of Songs and the Books of Jonah and of Job belong to this period.

Similarly stimulated and organised were other functions of the national energy, which were also of the Development utmost importance for the future of Jerusalem of the Scribes. and her religion. We have seen how the figure of 'Ezra the Scribe dominates equally with that of Neḥemiah the historical writings of the Persian Period,[1] and to what eminence among the people his whole profession had attained by the beginning of the second century.[2] Before 300 B.C. the Scribes, both priests and laymen, were organised in companies or guilds.[3] The Scribes were the guardians and interpreters of the sacred writings, the scholars and canonists of their age. First and foremost they were doctors of the Law, declaring its meaning, developing its details, and applying them to particular cases. They rewrote—in the Books of Chronicles—the nation's history in light of the doctrines and institutions of the Law. They taught the Law and the History to the people and their rulers. The religious instruction of the nation was in their hands. They used the Temple-Courts and the Synagogues for this purpose. There they read and expounded the sacred books in the hearing of the people; but besides reasoning on the details of the Law, they composed in

---

[1] Above, p. 330.
[2] See the eulogy of the Scribes by the Son of Sira, Ecclesiasticus xxxviii. 24-xxxix. 12 ; cf. vol. i. 392, and below, pp. 386 f.     [3] 1 Chron. ii. 55.

its praise hymns for popular use, and framed of its
ethical substance discourses of warning and consolation.

But the life of Israel had always been wider and more
rich than even the spirit of the Law expressed. The
Scribes could not be in contact with that *Their wider*
life, whether as calling to them from the *Sympathies and Enterprises.*
ancient literature of which they were masters,
or as throbbing less articulately in the ethical experience
and intellectual problems of the common people of their
own day, from whom most of them were sprung, without the stronger minds among them being drawn away
from the legal centre of their profession upon enterprises
more free and humane. Both their literary acumen
and their conscience as educators were greater than
was the case among the Scribes of our Lord's time.
Besides *meditating on the Law of the Most High*, it was
the duty of the Scribe, according to the Son of Sira, *to
be occupied in prophecies, to seek out the wisdom of all
the ancients and the hidden meaning of proverbs, and to be
conversant in the dark sayings of parables.*[1]

We cannot deny some of the development of these
interests to the Scribes of the Persian Period. The
study of the Prophets, and the feeling, be- *The Scribes*
trayed by many alterations and additions *and the Wise Men.*
to their text, of its lasting religious worth,
of its message to each new generation, which led to
the completion of the Canon of the Prophets by 250
B.C.,[2] were already operative. The Scribes of the
Persian Period worked with the great horizons of the
Prophets before them, and in touch with the passion
and originality of the Prophets' ethics. But besides

[1] Ecclesiasticus xxxix. 1-3.   [2] Or, at the latest, 200 B.C.

the Priests and the Prophets there had been in the
nation, at least since Jeremiah's time, another definite class of active minds, *the Wise Men*.[1] Not at all
concerned with the ritual and little with the national
interests of Israel's faith, they occupied themselves with
the general elements of religion, and were more free to
develop that Scepticism which we found originating
among the Prophets themselves.[2] From these Wise Men
it is not possible, with Ben Sira's words before us, to distinguish part at least of the Scribal profession.   But
whether it was Scribes during the Persian Period, or the
Wise Men of an earlier age, who produced such works
as the Book of Job and certain Psalms on the problems
of life and immortality; or whether the powers of synthesis and imagination evinced in the Prologue to the
Book of Proverbs are to be assigned to the Persian or
to the Greek period—are questions which we are without
the material to answer.   The collections of *Proverbs* and
*dark sayings of parables* which that Prologue introduces
must have had a very early origin, but probably were
not complete till the Greek period.   We can hardly doubt
that the Scribes of the Persian age had a share in the
formation of them.

[1] Jer. xviii. 18.
[2] For example, in Jeremiah and Habakkuk.

# CHAPTER XV

## THE JEW AND THE GREEK

### 332-168 B.C.

O F all the movements of history, none are more fitted
to attract our curiosity than those by which Jew
and Greek first came into contact: when When Jew
the minds were confronted and the spiritual met Greek.
heritages began to be exchanged, whose concurrence and
interaction were destined to exercise so enormous an
influence upon civilisation. The first attitudes of the
two races to each other: their recognition of a common
temper, their earliest criticisms, and their gradual discovery of an antagonism between their principles, all
took place in Egypt and Syria under Alexander the
Great and his successors—the period of the history of
Jerusalem which we have now reached. But the early
promises of this intimacy, and the gradual approaches to
it, are also of interest. I may summarise them in a
paragraph, but I must leave the details, so far as they
have been discovered, to another occasion.[1]

### 1. BEFORE ALEXANDER THE GREAT.

Representatives of the ancient civilisations of Mycenæ

[1] I regret that I have not space for an Appendix I had prepared giving
these details in full.

and Crete, men of Greek race from the isles and coasts of the Ægean, found their way to Egypt in very early times, and formed settlements on the Delta and in south-western Palestine. The Israel of Saul and David encountered them in the Philistines, and some of their adventurers constituted the royal bodyguard in Jerusalem. It is probable that a few of their military and political terms passed into Hebrew and appear in the Old Testament. But for such earlier movements we await the clearer light which is promised from the excavations in Crete and at Gezer. More discernible are fresh settlements of Greek traders on the Delta from 700 onwards, and the enlistment of Greek mercenaries by Psametik about 660. During the following century both of these classes increased, and the Jewish refugees to Egypt in 586 must have come into contact with them. We know of Greeks in the court or army of Nebuchadrezzar (604-561), acquaintance with whom can hardly have been missed by some of his captives from Jerusalem. The Phœnicians had for centuries been in communication with Greek lands and peoples. And finally, there was the long war between the Greeks and the Persian masters of the Jews, 499-449.

*Earliest Contacts of Greeks with Egypt and W. Asia.*

It is in writings of the Babylonian and Persian periods that we find the first Hebrew references to Greeks under the name Iawan : that is Ionian, spelt with the original digamma. Ezekiel mentions them among the traffickers with Tyre in slaves and bronze.[1] The Priestly Document names

*Earliest References in Hebrew to the Greeks.*

[1] Ezek. xxvii. 13. The reference to Iawan in 19 is doubtful; the text is not certain.

Iawan as a son of Japhet and *father* of the western peoples, or settlements, of Elisha (Sicily or Carthage), Tarshish (most probably in Spain), Kittim or Cyprus, and the Rodanim or Rhodians.[1] To a post-exilic prophet Iawan is a *coastland afar off*, which has not heard of the fame of the God of Israel;[2] and about 400 Joel (as we have seen) speaks of sons of Judah and Jerusalem who were sold by the Phœnicians to the sons of the Iĕwanîm.[3]

But remote as the Greeks still appear in Jewish literature, the Jews are even less distinguishable in Greek writings of the same period. It is doubtful whether the fragment quoted by Josephus from the fifth-century poet Choerilos actually refers to them;[4] if it does, it shows knowledge neither of their name nor of their characteristics. Herodotus, who was acquainted with some of the peoples of Syria,[5] does not mention Jerusalem or Judah, and, more strangely, takes no notice of the Jewish settlements in Egypt. In the works of Aristotle there is no mention of the Jews, not even when he touches with reserve upon a report which he heard of the Dead Sea.[6] But a pupil of his, Clearchus of Soli,[7] quotes him as describing a Jew whom he had met in Asia Minor, and who had evidently contributed some authentic information about the people, for Clearchus is the only Greek writer who gives an exact transliteration of the name of Jerusalem.[8] Adopting a fashion in which his countrymen rapidly became expert, the Jew had emphasised or exaggerated the resemblance

*Earliest Greek References to the Jews.*

---

[1] Gen. x. 2, 4. Cf. 1 Chron. i. 5, 7.
[2] 'Isa.' lxvi. 19.
[3] Joel iii. 6 (Eng. = iv. 6 Heb.).
[4] See vol. i. 262.
[5] *Hist.* ii. 104.
[6] *Meteor.* ii. iii. 39.
[7] In Josephus, *C. Apion.* i. 22.
[8] Vol. i. 260.

between the principles of his religion and those of the illuminated Greeks to whom he was talking. Clearchus calls the Jews 'the philosophers of the Syrians,' and with the perspective of a distant observer of the East, derives them from the 'Kalanoi' or 'philosophers of India.' This Jew, then, talked Greek, and understood the sympathies of his Greek interrogants. But it is implied that he was the first of his kind in their experience, which (we must remember) already included the beginnings of trade with the Further East; and his information apparently left them unconscious of the separate polity of the Jews among the peoples of Syria.[1] In Egypt the Greek ignorance of the Jews, the mutual sense of remoteness between the two races, cannot have been so great. They had been in contact on the Delta since 600, and must have discovered to each other something of their respective qualities and institutions.

## 2. ALEXANDER AND THE JEWS: 332-323 B.C.

In any case a very great difference in the relations of the two races was effected by the Asian conquests of
Alexander's Asian Policy. Alexander, and by the policy which his successors believed he had bequeathed to them. These not only brought Jews and Greeks together in the comradeships and rivalries of endless campaigns, but surrounded Judah with a host of Greek communities, and drew her people abroad into residence and citizenship all over the Greek world. Whatever may have been

[1] It is possible, from the date of Clearchus, that the incident he reports fell not before but after Alexander's invasion; yet this would only make the incident still more significant of the Greek world's ignorance of the Jews.

the motives from which his father designed and he embarked upon the war against Persia,[1] there is no doubt that Alexander developed, and that his successors, but especially the Seleucids, accepted, the ambition of Hellenising the East, or, more exactly, of founding an empire which should enlist all the virtues and energies of Asian life, but organise them in a system and with a spirit that were Greek.[2] There is one essential resemblance between Alexander's invasion of the East and Napoleon's. Besides the military ambitions which inspired them, both expeditions felt the impulses of intellectual revolutions which had liberated the minds of their leaders from at least the forms of their national religions, and had sent them forward ready to sympathise with many elements in the civilisations they came to conquer. In Alexander's army, and still more among the Greeks who thronged into Asia behind it, there were numbers of philosophic Greeks who, as appears from the story of Clearchus, were eager to discover among the barbarians resemblances to their own intellectual tempers. But of all the peoples of Western Asia none, as we shall see, were more fitted to satisfy this desire than the Jews.[3]

---

[1] Polybius, iii. 6, defines the *cause* as the discovery, in the expeditions of Xenophon and Agesilaus, of the cowardice and inefficiency of the Persians ; and the *pretext* the desire to avenge the injuries inflicted by Persia on Greece. There was also the avowed intention of freeing the Greek cities in Asia. But the pupil of Aristotle doubtless already cherished the aims which he afterwards developed, of Hellenising the Asiatics. It is even reported that he rejected Aristotle's advice to treat the Greeks as masters and the peoples he subdued as slaves, and expressed the hope of uniting victors and vanquished, without distinctions, in one commonwealth (Plutarch, *Mor.*, ' On the Fortune of Alexander ').

[2] On the Seleucid policy, Ramsay, *Cities of St. Paul*, 181 ff.

[3] The ancient authorities for this period are the historians of Alexander's expedition; the Greek writers from about 300 onwards who have left notices

By 331 Alexander had overthrown the Persian Empire and established his own in Western Asia. He had

His Arrival in Syria, 333 B.C.,

besieged and taken Tyre (333-332), had marched down the coast of Palestine and taken Gaza, had been welcomed in Egypt and founded Alexandria, had returned through Palestine and finally defeated Darius at Arbela.[1] Josephus relates that the High-Priest Jaddua, because of his oath of fealty to the Persians, refused to obey the conqueror's summons from Tyre; that to punish him Alexander marched on Jerusalem from Gaza, and Jaddua, being instructed of God in a dream, went to meet him at Sapha, arrayed in the robes of his office and the mitre with the sacred Name; and that, to the astonishment of his generals, Alexander immediately saluted the solemn

and alleged Visit to Jerusalem, 332.

figure and adored the Name, for in the former he recognised one who had appeared to him in a dream in Macedonia and inspired him to march against the Persians. The conclusion of the

of the Jews (collected by Th. Reinach, *Textes d'Auteurs Grecs et Romains relatifs au Judaïsme*, 1895), fragments of Diodorus Siculus, Polybius and Appian; and of Jewish writers Daniel vii. ff., Ecclesiasticus, 1 Maccabees i., 2 Macc. i.-vii., Josephus, *Contra Apionem* and *Antiquities* XI. viii.-XII. v. Of moderns these will be found useful:—O. Holtzmann in Stade's *Gesch. des Volkes Israel*, vol. ii. pt. ii. pp. 273 ff. (1888); J. Wellhausen, *Isr. u. Jüd. Gesch.* ch. xvi. (1888, 4th ed. 1901); Schürer, *Gesch. des Jüd. Volkes* (3rd ed. 1901); Mahaffy, *Greek Life from Alexander to the Roman Conquest* (1887), *Greek World under Roman Sway* (1890), and *Empire of the Ptolemies* (1895); H. Willrich, *Juden u. Griechen vor der Makkabäischen Erhebung* (1895); A. Büchler, *Die Tobiaden u. die Oniaden* (1899); G. Hölscher, *Pal. in der Pers. u. Hellenistichen Zeit* (1903); A. Schlatter, *Gesch. Israels von Alex. dem Grossen bis Hadrian* (2nd ed. 1906); E. R. Bevan, *The House of Seleucus.* Consult also W. R. Ramsay, *Cities of St. Paul* (1907), Schürer's art. 'Diaspora' in Hastings' *D.B.*, extra vol., and H. Guthe's art. 'Dispersion' in the *Enc. Bibl.*

[1] 'The passage of the Granicus rendered Alexander master of the Greek colonies; the battle of Issus gave him Tyre and Egypt; the battle of Arbela gave him the whole earth.'—Montesquieu, *Esprit des Lois*, x. 14.

story is that Alexander went with the High-Priest into the Temple, offered sacrifices, was shown the prophecies of Daniel concerning himself, and gave permission to the Jews, not only of Judah but of Media and Babylonia, to live under their own laws.[1] The whole of this narrative has a legendary appearance, its geographical data are difficult, its chronology is mixed up with that of San-ballaṭ, the contemporary of Neḥemiah; and no other writer even hints that Jerusalem was visited by Alexander.[2] Some recollection of such a visit would surely have been preserved by other Jews. As it is, Alexander appears by name in only one Jewish book,[3] and neither there nor in the prophecies of Daniel is there a suggestion of any contact between him and Jerusalem, or of special treatment of the Jews in his policy. Had he and his officers enjoyed a close acquaintance with the Temple, its ceremonies and its books, some effects of This im-this would have been visible in the histories of probable. his expedition,[4] or in the writings of those Greeks who soon began to take an interest in Jerusalem. Their silence rather implies that Alexander and his army left

---

[1] Jos. xi. *Ant.* viii. 3-5.

[2] If Alexander went from Gaza to Jerusalem, it is curious that Jaddua should have met him at Sapha, for this, 'from which there is a prospect both of Jerusalem and the Temple,' can only be Scopus on the *northern* approach to the City; yet compare below the tradition of his capture of Samaria. Arrian, *Anab. of Alex.* iii. 1, states that Alexander went 'in seven days' from Gaza to Pelusium, as if his march into Egypt followed immediately upon his capture of Gaza. Justin, in his epitome of Trogus Pompeius, xi. 10, says 'many kings wearing fillets met him'; but Curtius, iv. 5, adds that 'he visited some cities who as yet refused the yoke of his government.' The prophecies of Daniel, as we have them, were not yet written.

[3] 1 Macc. i. 1-8; vi. 2.

[4] Which describe his visit to Gordium after the battle of Issus, his relations with the oracle of Ammon, and his care for the worship of Bel at Babylon.

Palestine unaware of the distinctive customs of the inhabitants of Jerusalem. All that is probable is that, with the other 'chiefs wearing fillets,' whom Justin mentions,[1] the High-Priest made his submission to the conqueror; and that Alexander confirmed the people in the practice of their own laws. At least no grudge against him is expressed in Jewish literature,[2] which only records that after his overthrow of the Persian empire and his *slaughter of the kings of the earth, the earth was quiet before him.*[3] A credible tradition says that he settled Macedonians in Samaria,[4] the only capital of ancient Israel on the western watershed. 'Omri had chosen the site in pursuance of his Phœnician policy, and Herod, with his further western outlook, was to rebuild it before constructing his new port of Cæsarea. Near the natural centre of the land, but in sight of the sea, there was no fitter capital for the Greek authorities in Palestine.[5] Jerusalem would have been of far less use to them. But it is probable that Jews entered the army of Alexander,[6] and certain that a number settled

---

[1] See previous page, *n.* 2.    [2] Cf. Schlatter, p. 8.

[3] 1 Macc. i. 3. The prophecies of Daniel emphasise the destructive force of his conquests, but similarly do not attribute to him any oppression of the Jews. Wellhausen, pp. 182 f. *n.* 1, assigns to the time of his conquests Psalm xlvi., which reflects a disturbance of the whole earth, the overthrow of the heathen not at, but away from, Jerusalem, and the inauguration of a great peace. 'An Alexander konnten in der Tat eben so grosse Hoffnungen geknüpft werden wie an Cyrus und die Begrüssung wäre seiner und nur seiner wert.'

[4] Eusebius, *Chron.*, ed. Schoene, ii. 114. See also below, p. 376.

[5] We must clearly distinguish between the *town* Samaria, the Greek capital, and the surrounding *country* of Samaria, from which the Samaritans derived their Greek name. The latter had nothing to do with the *town* Samaria; their centre, however, was an hour and a half distant in Shechem and on Mount Gerizim. The two are easily confounded, as by Mahaffy, *Greek World under Roman Sway*, 43 f.

[6] Hecatæus, quoted by Josephus, *C. Apion.* i. 22.

in his new foundation of Alexandria. We may believe
that with the versatility of their race, who knew how
to make themselves useful to each fresh conqueror,
individual Jews assisted his officers with the collection
of the tribute and furnished him with supplies and information.[1]   Like the Ptolemies after him, Alexander would
find among the Jews of Egypt men at once acquainted
with his own tongue and familiar with the social conditions of Palestine.   These are the probable    The Truth
facts, but the story of his visit to Jerusalem   behind the
embodies also this truth, that the illuminated   Legend.
Greeks who thronged to Syria with him or in his wake,
soon discovered a sympathy between themselves and the
equally versatile Jews.   Looking back from a later period,
Hellenised Jews remembered what Alexander had done
for them, and invented the story that it was their own
High-Priest who had appeared to the King in Macedonia
with the appeal : ' Come over to Asia and help us.'

### 3. Wars of the Ptolemies and Seleucids for Palestine: 323-198 b.c.

On Alexander's death in 323 peace was again disturbed. *His servants bare rule each in his place ; they did
all put on diadems after he was dead, and*   The immedi-
*so did their sons after them many years ; and*   ate Successors
of Alexander,
*they multiplied evils upon the earth.*[2]   Perdiccas   323-320.
took charge of affairs at Babylon, Antigonus obtained
' Asia,' Ptolemy, son of Lagus, seized Egypt.   Among

---

[1] Mahaffy, *Greek Life*, ch. xx., says that Alexander got valuable information from Jews about the interior of Asia.          [2] 1 Macc. i. 8, 9.

these rival heirs of Alexander and their successors
Palestine lay, as from the beginning it had lain between
the empires of Mesopotamia and the Nile, the highway of
their wars, the prey of their rival ambitions. Perdiccas
appears to have been its first master. He is said to have
rebuilt or fortified Samaria,[1] and he invaded Egypt; but,
being repulsed, he was slain by his officers, and Seleucus
succeeded him in 321. In this year Ptolemy invaded
Palestine, and is said to have seized Jerusalem, for what
reason is not apparent. Disturbances may have arisen
between the Jews and Samaritans;[2] or either or both may
have chosen to keep their allegiance to the northern Greeks.
In any case there is nothing in the circumstances of the
time to move us to doubt the story. Josephus says
that Ptolemy came to the City on a Sabbath, as if to
sacrifice, and took the Jews by surprise; but
he quotes Agatharchides to the effect that
the Jews desisted from fighting because it
was the Sabbath.[3] Ptolemy led a large number of the
nation captive to Egypt; and of his treatment of Jerusalem herself Appian uses a term which may denote either
that he 'destroyed' or 'reduced' her.[4] In the former case
it would be possible to refer to the disaster some of
the Psalms usually assigned either to evils inflicted by
Artaxerxes Ochus about 350, or to those by Antiochus
Epiphanes in 168.[5]

Seleucus was obliged to flee from Babylon before

*Assault on Jerusalem by Ptolemy I.*

---

[1] Eusebius, as above.

[2] Who (as explained on p. 374 *n.* 5) had nothing to do with the now Greek
Samaria, but had their centre four or five miles from it on Mount Gerizim.

[3] Jos. xii. *Ant.* i.; *C. Apion.* i. 22.

[4] Καθῃρήκει: *Syr.* 50.

[5] See above, p. 359, and below, p. 434 f.

Antigonus, and found refuge with Ptolemy. In 314 Antigonus occupied Palestine, but in 312 his army was defeated by Ptolemy, whose fleet Seleucus commanded. Seleucus re-entered Babylon, and therefore from 312 the Seleucid era was started, upon which by the peoples of Palestine the years were dated down to, and in part after, the arrival of the Romans. Ptolemy held Palestine for only a year, when it again passed to Antigonus. In 306 the latter's son Demetrius defeated the Egyptian fleet and took Cyprus. But in 301 Antigonus fell at Ipsus before a fresh coalition of his Greek rivals, and (though till about 285 Demetrius held sway over Tyre, Sidon and the sea) Seleucus took northern Syria and Ptolemy regained Palestine. All these struggles for the possession of Palestine appear to have been limited to the sea-board and to Samaria,[1] which was twice captured and once destroyed. Jerusalem lay aloof from the path and the main interest of the campaigners, experiencing only rapid changes in the direction in which her High-Priest had to despatch the national tribute. It is possible that the two fine prophecies 'Zechariah' ix.-xi. and xii.-xiv. date from these disturbances; but, while both are post-exilic and apparently of the Greek period, we cannot give them an exact date.

*Jerusalem aloof from the subsequent struggles, 320-301.*

The story of Alexander's conquests and of the fortunes of his immediate successors will have made clear to us the change that has come over the political world of Jerusalem. This had been wonderfully anticipated by the Prophets of the Exile

*The new Disposition of Jerusalem's World.*

---

[1] For the course of them see Diod. Sic. xix.; the fragments assigned to Hecatæus in Jos., *C. Apion.* i. 22; Appian, *Syr.* 53 ff.; and Eusebius, *Chron.*

and of the following century, in their outlook upon the isles and coasts of the Mediterranean and in their vision of Jerusalem on the sea, radiant with its light and with the new hopes that were dawning across it.[1]  The old political centres have passed away—Nineveh, Babylon, Shushan.  The centre of gravity, if we may speak of such a thing in a condition of affairs still so unstable, has moved to the west; and the sovereignty of Palestine is decided on the sea as well as on the land.  Alexandria has been founded and Babylon replaced as a centre both of trade and of culture.  Palestine still lies, as of old, between an Egyptian power and one sufficiently in possession of the ancient Asiatic centres to be called by the name of Assyria.  But both powers are Greek; with Eastern ambitions indeed, yet of an inspiration and resources that are largely of the West.  Even the internal arrangements of Palestine have felt the fact in the fixing of the local centre of authority in the seaward Samaria.[2]

By seizing Egypt Ptolemy obtained what for the time was the best share of his master's empire, because not only did it include Alexandria, with the *The Ptolemies the most stable of the Greek Dynasties,* trade from the Red Sea and the issues to Europe, but because the whole land lay apart, entrenched by sea and desert from all his rivals, whose domains were not secluded from each other by any such barriers.  Hence Ptolemy's kingdom and *and at first the most constant Masters of Palestine.* dynasty remained the most stable of the powers into which Alexander's empire was divided; and hence, too, they were at first the most constant masters of Palestine.  During the

[1] See above, pp. 322 f.          [2] See above, p. 374.

next century, 301 to 198, they held it with but few interruptions. Jerusalem lay under Egyptian rule, and Alexandria was the centre of her world.

But when, about 300, Seleucus mastered his other rivals, and under the same attraction to the Mediterranean established a capital at Antioch *Their inevit-* on the Orontes, with a port at Seleucia, he *able replace-* *ment by the* ensured for Palestine, at however distant a *Seleucids.* date, a change to the north in her unchanging servitude to foreign lords. For the country which, instead of Mesopotamia, Seleucus made the centre of his kingdom— the country which lies between the Euphrates and the Lebanons, and which received the distinctive name of Seleucis—is not separated [1] from Palestine, as Egypt is, by a great stretch of desert. Palestine belongs with it to the same physical system, and neither Seleucus nor his successors ever resigned their claims to the whole of this.[2] From 264 to 248 they fought for Palestine with the second Ptolemy, Philadelphus (285-246), and, after a short peace, with Ptolemy III., Euergetes (246-221). He not only held his own but overran Seleucis to its limit, the Euphrates; and in particular Seleucia, the port

---

[1] The southern boundary of Seleucis was held to be the river Eleutherus, north of Beyrout: so Strabo, xvi. ch. 11 § 12 (quoting Posidonius?); cf. Hölscher, *op. cit.* 51-55.

[2] This is made clear in Polybius v. 67, on the debate at Seleucia between Antiochus III. and Ptolemy IV. (218 B.C.) as to which was the legitimate heir to Coelesyria. The elastic name of Coelesyria was given at this time to all Palestine from the Lebanons southward; Hölscher (*op. cit.* 51-55) argues that it consisted of four satrapies, Idumæa, Samaria, Phœnicia, and probably Coelesyria in the narrower sense of the name. Idumæa is placed among the satrapies of Seleucus in Diod. Sic. xix. 95, 98, which, as based on the nearly contemporary evidence of Hieronymus of Kardia, is proof that Seleucus regarded all Coelesyria in the broader sense (even its most southern province of Idumæa) as constituting part of his kingdom.

of Antioch, remained Egyptian till 220. Meantime Antiochus III., the Great (223-187), had come to the Seleucid throne and imagined that he saw a weaker Ptolemy, Ptolemy IV. (221-204), succeed to that of Egypt. Antiochus overran Palestine in 218, but next year was beaten back at Raphia, a historic battlefield between Asia and Africa, on the desert road south of Gaza. The fifth Ptolemy, Epiphanes (204-181), was a child at the date of his accession, and Antiochus had become a great conqueror. In 202 he ventured once more into Palestine, but in 200 Scopas recovered it for Egypt. This was for the last time. In 198 Antiochus defeated Scopas at Paneas and took Ṣidon, Samaria, and other cities of Coelesyria. The Jews welcomed him with his elephants to Jerusalem, and helped him to besiege the Egyptian garrison in the Akra. Josephus produces certain alleged letters and a decree of Antiochus recounting the services of the Jews to himself, honouring their Temple and remitting much of their tribute.[1] Thus the Jews exchanged the sovereignty of the Greek Ptolemies for that of the Greek Seleucids. If it be true that they welcomed the latter, they were speedily disappointed. The Syrian taxes became heavier than those of Egypt had been, and the Syrian persecutions led to the destruction of the Temple in 168, and the subsequent wars for religious and political liberty.

#### 4. JERUSALEM AND JUDAH UNDER THE GREEKS.

During this period the territory which Jerusalem commanded was little larger than that which we traced

---

[1] Jos. xii. *Ant.* iii. 3 f. ; see vol. i. 392 f. On the preceding events see, besides Josephus, Polybius v. 68 ff. ; xvi. 18 ; xxviii. 1 ; Daniel xi. 10-19.

as Jewish under the Persians.[1] The northern frontier against the Samaritans was uncertain, but it crossed the watershed beyond Bethel.[2]  Under Jonathan, The Territory Emmaus, Beth-horon, Bethel and Timnath of Jerusalem. were in Judah;[3] but Aphairema, Lydda and Ramathaim were Samaritan *nomoi* or toparchies.[4]  Probably all of these places had long been in debate between the Jews and the Samaritans.[5]  On the west the border was probably the line between the Shephelah and the range of Judah.[6]  The territory of the Philistine cities, now largely Phœnician and Hellenised, came inland as far as 'Ekron and that outpost of the Shephelah, Gezer, some nineteen miles from Jerusalem.[7]  Emmaus, the present 'Amwâs, nearly fifteen miles from Jerusalem, was in Judah.  The southern border crossed the Judæan range between Beth-ṣûr and Hebron.  The former, probably the modern Burj- or Beit-ṣûr, some fifteen miles south of Jerusalem and four north of Hebron, was Jewish;[8] Hebron and Mareshah, or Marissa, had been taken by the Idumeans, but the latter, on the highroad from the coast, became Hellenised.[9]  On the east, Tekoa' and its pastures were Jewish; but Engedi probably still went with Hebron, though Jonathan and Simon found a refuge close to

---

[1] See above, pp. 354 ff.          [2] *H.G.H.L.* 252 ff.

[3] 1 Macc. ix. 50.          [4] *Id.* xi. 28, 34; xiii. *Ant.* iv. 9.

[5] In 'Amwâs (Emmaus) was found a bilingual inscription in Samaritan and Greek; Cl.-Ganneau, *Arch. Res.* i. 484; 'Zechariah' xiv. 10 gives the northmost Jewish town as Geba'.

[6] *H.G.H.L.* 205 f.

[7] With Tyre and Ṣidon, Ashḳelon, Gaza, 'Ekron and Ashdod are mentioned in 'Zech.' ix. 2-5; their people are called Philistine; but *mamzer, mongrel* or *hybrid race* is the name given to the people of Ashdod. 'Ekron became Jewish under Jonathan, 1 Macc. x. 88 f., Gezer under Simon, *id.* xiii. 43 ff.

[8] Neh. iii. 16; 1 Macc. iv. 28 ff. (Lysias invades Judah at Bethsura), 61.

[9] See below, p. 388; also *H.G.H.L.* 233.

it at the Pool of Asphar.[1]  Jericho, and even the flanks
of Ephraim to the north-west of Jericho, may also have
become Idumean.[2]  The territory of Jerusalem was
thus confined to the hills, and within these covered only
part of the ancient Judah, or not thirty miles north
and south by little over twenty east and west.[3]  To the
Greek writers of the period it is Jerusalem and little else.
They call Solomon 'king of Jerusalem';[4] the Jews 'those
who dwell about the sanctuary called Hierosolyma';[5]
Judæa 'the places round Hierosolyma.'[6]  What a speck
it must have seemed to the Greeks who had pushed
their conquests as far as the Indus—what a speck, and
how aloof!

[1] I Macc. ix. 33 ; probably Bir Selhub (Robinson, *B.R.* ii. 202), a little
S.W. of Engedi, the hills round which still bear the name Sufra (I have
suggested this identification in the *Enc. Bib.*, art. 'Asphar') rather than the
cistern ez-Za'ferâneh (suggested by Buhl, *G.A.P.* 158), the letters of which
name do not correspond to Asphar, while the site is too near the W. edge of
the desert.

[2] In I Macc. v. 3 Judas is said to have *fought the children of Esau in
Judah for Akrabattene, for they surrounded Israel.*  If the reading in the
Codices ℵ and V, of *Idumæa* for *Judæa*, be correct, then Akrabattene is the
district about the ascent of 'Akrabbim (Num. xxxiv. 4, etc.), the steep approach
from the 'Arabah, south of the Dead Sea, towards Hebron.  But a separate
campaign by Judas against the Idumeans *of the south* is recorded later,
verses 65-68 ; and this first Idumean campaign of Judas is associated with
another against the sons of Baean, from whom Judas *passed over* (? the Jordan)
to 'Ammon and his campaigns in Gilead and Bashan (verses 4 ff.).  There is
therefore some reason for taking Akrabattene as the Judæan toparchy mentioned by Josephus (ii. *B.J.* xx. 4, xxii. 2 ; iii. *B.J.* iii. 4 f. ; iv. *B.J.* ix. 3 f.
9), which lay next to, and probably S. and E. of, Gophna.  This would explain the expression that the Idumeans *surrounded Israel.*  So Ewald, and
lately also Hölscher, *op. cit.* pp. 69 ff.

[3] A fragment attributed to Hecatæus (see p. 384 *n.* 1) states its extent
at three millions of *arourae* (Egyptian acres), about two millions forty
thousand English acres.

[4] Dios and Menander (of Ephesus) about 275, quoted in *C. Apion.* i. 17 f. ;
Manetho (in the same century) hardly speaks of Jewish territory beyond
Jerusalem, *C. Apion.* i. 26 ff.

[5] Polybius xvi. 39, in Jos. xii. *Ant.* iii. 3.      [6] Diod. Sic. xxxiv. 1, 2.

Under the mild rule of the Ptolemies, and until Antiochus III. began his invasions of Palestine,[1] Jerusalem enjoyed an unbroken peace. The country was properly cultivated, commerce was secure, and in the management of the national tribute the ruling families had opportunities of finance which augmented the wealth of the City.[2] Ptolemy II. is said to have restored the 120,000 Jews whom his father deported to Egypt.[3] There must have been a considerable increase of the vigorous and fertile population and of their various energies; for we shall see that large emigrations became possible. The dominant features of the national life continued to be the Temple and its worship. The Ptolemies did not interfere with these, but, on the contrary, if later stories be true, they encouraged and fostered them.[4] For all this prosperity we have evidence both from the beginning and the end of the period. The earliest Greek writer who has accurate information about the Jews, Hecatæus of Abdera, about 300 B.C., affirms their fertility, and details their wise and vigorous organisation.[5] Another writing of the period, also ascribed to Hecatæus and at least using his materials, enlarges upon the agriculture of Judah and the strength of Jerusalem. It gives a description of the City with a population, it says, of 120,000, a possible but hardly a probable

*Prosperity of the Jews under the Ptolemies.*

*Evidence from Hecatæus, c. 300,*

---

[1] See above, p. 380; cf. Jos. xii. *Ant.* iii. 3.

[2] Vol. i. 368; Jos. xii. *Ant.* iv.

[3] Jos. xii. *Ant.* ii. 1; *C. Apion.* i. 22.

[4] For a list of such stories see below, p. 392 *n.* 3.

[5] 'Αεὶ τὸ γένος τῶν 'Ιουδαίων ὑπῆρχε πολυάνθρωπον. On what he says of the number, the revenues and the political influence of the priests, and the absolute supremacy of the High-Priest, see vol. i. 389 f.

figure; of the Temple *enceinte* with double cloisters; of the Altar of Burnt-offering; and of the Sanctuary with the Golden Altar and Lamp, but ' no image nor anything planted, neither groves nor anything of that kind.' [1]

By the end of the period the evidence is more lavish and emphatic; [2] but that furnished by Jesus Ben Sira is of itself sufficient for our purpose. Throughout, Ben Sira's book reflects a quiet and a prosperous community with a developed civilisation. The land is secure and settled. A hedge is enough for the defence of property. If a man is homeless he is suspect — *who will trust a man that hath no nest and lodgeth wherever he findeth himself at nightfall?* [3] Agriculture is unharassed : *he that tilleth his land shall raise high his heap.* [4] *Great travail is created for every man and a heavy yoke is on the sons of Adam.* Fears, strifes and disappointments await them ; but *all bribery and injustice shall be*

*and from Ben Sira.*

*Security and Comfort of Life in Judah.*

---

[1] It is by no means certain that this evidence is not from Hecatæus of Abdera himself. The latter wrote a history of Egypt, from which the first fragment quoted above has been preserved in Diodorus Siculus, xl. 3. Two other works circulated under his name concerning the Jews, and concerning Abraham. The latter, cited by Jos. i. *Ant.* vii. 2 and Clem. Alex. *Strom.* v. 14, is not genuine. But that on the Jews, used by Josephus in *C. Apion.* i. 22, from which this second piece of evidence given above is taken, may quite well be genuine. All fragments ascribed to Hecatæus are given by Müller, *Frag. Histor. Graec.* ii. 384-96. Reinach gives the fragment through Diodorus alone to Hecatæus (*Textes . . . relatifs au Judaisme,* 14 ff.), the rest under Pseudo-Hecatæus (227 ff.). On the whole question see Schürer, *Gesch.*[(3)] ii. § 33, and Schlatter's note, *Gesch.* 31, 318.

[2] Particularly so if we take the date of the Letter of Aristeas as about 200 : see next chapter.

[3] xxxvi. 25 f.

[4] xx. 28 : there are several references to agriculture, *e.g.* xxxiii. 16 ; xxxviii. 25.

*blotted out and good faith shall stand for ever. The life of one that laboureth and is content shall be made sweet.*

> *Children and the building of a city establish a name,*
> *And a blameless wife is reckoned above both.*
> *Wine and music rejoice the heart,*
> *And the love of wisdom is above both.*
> *The pipe and the psaltery make pleasant melody,*
> *And a pleasant tongue is above both.*
> *Thine eye shall desire grace and beauty,*
> *But above both the green blade of corn.*
> *Gold and silver will make the foot stand sure,*
> *And counsel is esteemed above them both.*
> *Riches and inheritance will lift up the heart,*
> *And the fear of the Lord is above both.*[1]

Zechariah's promise of a full population and a secure old age[2] has at last come to pass. Ben Sira dwells on the beauty of the aged and their wisdom : *as the lamp that shineth on the holy candlestick, so is the beauty of the face in ripe age.*[3] Jerusalem is a large and a carefully organised City. The Book reflects crowds ; professions and industries ; a wide commerce ; assemblies and courts ; rumour, intrigue, slander, mob-law and dema- gogues ; the sins of harlotry and drunken- ness. There are temptations on the one hand to depression in the crowd—*say not I am hidden from the Lord . . . I am not known among so many people*—and on the other to the dissipation of one's energies among manifold interests—*winnow not with every wind, nor walk in every path.*[4] No detail of the topography of the City is given ; but those who have built and fortified are remem- bered with their works.[5] We hear of one great builder

*Size and Business of Jerusalem.*

---

[1] xl. 1-26.  [2] See above, pp. 304, 314.

[3] xviii. 9 ; xxv. 3 ff. ; xxvi. 17 ; cf. xlii. 8, etc.

[4] xvi. 17 ; v. 9 ; for the rest of the above see especially iii.-v., vii., ix., xxiii., xxv. ff., xxxviii.

[5] xlvii. 13 ; xlviii. 17 ; xlix. 12 f. ; l. 1 ff.

within the period itself: Simon, son of Joḥanan (Onias)
—either Simon I., son of Joḥanan I., about
*Fortification of the City and Temple.* 310-290, or Simon II., son of Joḥanan II., about
218-198 [1]—*who repaired the House and forti-fied the Temple*, building reservoirs and *lofty substructures*
for the sacred platform; *who took thought for his people
against the spoiler, and strengthened the City against
siege.*[2] As significant are the references to its *pavements*
and *battlements*; *the timber girt and bound into a building
which cannot be shaken* and the *ornaments of plaster on a
polished wall*, which are used as illustrations by the writer.[3]
There is no talk of breaches, of dilapidation or of the need
of rebuilding; the City is compact, embellished, secure.
All the developments of ritual, all the sacred studies
and literary habits which we have traced through
the Persian period, continued in Jerusalem under the
Ptolemies. Ben Sira describes the glory of the national
worship, when Simon came forth before the priests and
the congregation, and *the sons of Aaron sounded the
*Glory of the Worship.* trumpets of beaten work and made a great
noise, to be heard for a remembrance before the
Most High, while the people together hasted and fell down
on their faces to worship their Lord, the Almighty God
Most High; the singers also praised Him with their
voices, in the whole House was there made sweet melody.*[4]
But, as we have seen, it is the growing influence of the
Scribes to which Ben Sira chiefly bears witness. By
250[5]—when also the Law was translated into Greek—

[1] On the evidence which leaves us in doubt see Toy, *Enc. Bibl.* 1170 f.
He inclines to Simon II., but there is much to be said for the other.

[2] l. 4 (see vol. i. 391 *n.* 3); the text is uncertain, but the above data are clear.

[3] xx. 18; ix. 13; xxii 16; cf. xxi. 8; xxvii. 2; xxxiv. 23, etc.

[4] l. 5-21; cf. vii. 29 ff. on duties to the priests.    [5] Or 200.

they had completed and closed the canon of the Prophets,[1] but were busy too with *the wisdom of all the ancients, the hidden meanings of proverbs, the dark sayings of parables.*[2] No profession stood higher in repute, was more open to able youths of all ranks in the community, or was fitted to exert greater influence in both of the directions between which the life of the Jews was about to divide. For by their primary studies and their judicial work, the Scribes preserved the national law and tradition, upholding the Fence within which Israel lived distinct and secure from other peoples. But by their pursuit of a wider wisdom, and by the questions which this encountered, they prepared the habits of inquiry and more liberal sympathies of the mind, for which Hellenism provided so much opportunity and material.

The Scribes— their double influence on the National Mind.

For we must next note that on nearly all sides this tiny territory and this active life of the Jews were surrounded by rapidly increasing centres of Greek culture. Even before Alexander's time the influence of Greece had begun to work upon the coast; under the Persians the coins of Gaza were already of the Athenian type and standard.[3] All the maritime towns save Tyre and Gaza appear

Establishment of numerous Greek Communities round Judah.

---

[1] That is both the former prophets, Joshua—2 Kings; and the latter—Isaiah, Jeremiah, Ezekiel and the Book of the Twelve.

[2] See above, p. 365.

[3] Head, *Hist. Num.* 680 (after Six, *Num. Chron.*, 1877, 221), states that its coinage in the fifth and fourth centuries was of Attic weight and various types, and describes a type of silver drachm with Janiform diademed heads, or head of Pallas, 'sometimes closely imitated from Athenian coins even with letters ΑΘΕ,' and on reverse עזה in Phœnician letters; Macdonald, *Greek Coins in the Hunterian Collection*, iii. 282, a silver drachm 'of Euboic-Attic standard . . . borrowed directly from Athenian models,' Pl. LXXVII. 30.

to have welcomed Alexander and accepted his policy.[1]
Their younger nobles, taking Greek names, enlisted
among his officers. In the following century their
polity, customs and religion were largely Hellenised.
Their gods assumed the names and borrowed the attributes of those of Greece; Greek legends received new
scenery from their neighbourhoods.[2] As Tyre obtained
a fresh population from Alexander, so did Gaza either on
its old or on a new site.[3] Ashdod had a mixed population.[4] The foreign influence came inland as far as 'Ekron
and Gezer. Further south, in Idumean territory at Mareshah or Marissa, a Sidonian colony with considerable
Greek culture was settled before 190.[5] On the north
'Akko had become Ptolemais as early as the second
Ptolemy.[6] From this, the nearest good harbour on the
Syrian coast, it was more than three hundred miles oversea to Alexandria, about one hundred and fifty to Cyprus,
and two long days' march inland to Samaria, which, as
we have seen, was occupied by Macedonians and by the
central Greek authority of the land. Beth-shan, less than
two days from Ptolemais across Esdraelon, was also
settled by the Greeks under the name of Nysa. Besides
these ancient towns, Alexander, the Ptolemies, Seleucus
and his successors built upon sites hitherto unoccupied,
save by villages, a considerable number of new towns

---

[1] The replacement of the Persic standard by the Euboic-Attic appears to
have taken place in the coinage of all the Phœnician and other coast towns
immediately after Alexander's conquests. See Head, 665 ff. ; Macdonald,
iii. 225 ff. ; 249 f. 263.

[2] See Stark's *Gaza u. die Philist. Küste.*     [3] *H. G. H. L.* 184 ff.

[4] Zech. ix. 6. See above, p. 381 *n.* 7.

[5] So recent discoveries have made clear; see Peters and Thiersch, *Painted
Tombs in the Necropolis of Marissa*, P.E.F., 1905.

[6] See the present writer's art. ' Ptolemais' in the *Enc. Bibl.*

mostly Greek in their population, and wholly so in their constitution and culture.[1] Among those nearest to Judah were Anthedon, a harbour near Gaza;[2] Apollonia, north of Joppa, the present Arsûf; inland, Patras and Arethusa;[3] a number of small 'cities' on the coast by Carmel,[4] including 'Sykaminōn Polis,' which is Haifa; and Philoteria on the Lake of Galilee. On the latter also was the Greek settlement of Taricheae,[5] but industrial, not political. East of the Jordan were Pella, Dion, Gerasa, and Philadelphia, the ancient Rabbath-'Ammon—all of them almost within sight of the Mount of Olives, and not three days off—besides the smaller Greek settlements in Moab. With some or all of these places the people of Jerusalem had to trade; to sell them oil, and to buy wheat, metals and pottery through their markets.[6] Their coins were the only ones Jews could use. Their language was becoming in Palestine as common as Aramaic; yet we must not suppose that it was mastered by many of the Jews of Judah. Josephus asserts the contrary.[7]

---

[1] On the question which of the above-named monarchs was the greatest builder see Hölscher, *op. cit.* 58 ff. He decides for Seleucus, but not on grounds that are certain. Besides his section on the subject and the authorities quoted above, see Schürer, *Gesch.*[(3)] ii. (Eng. trans. div. ii. vol. i.).

[2] The name still survives as Tedûn over some ruins on the coast, a little N.W. from Gaza. See below, p. 482.

[3] Sites uncertain; Schlatter, pp. 10 f. *n.* 1, suggests Kh. Badras, near Lydda, and Artâs at Solomon's Pools.

[4] For the full list see Hölscher, *op. cit.* 66.

[5] The date of the settlement is unknown; Taricheae first appears in the time of Josephus, but there must have been large fish-curing establishments (the name means this) on the lake in the time of our Lord. See vol. i. p. 318.

[6] See vol. i. Bk. II. ch. v.  [7] xx. *Ant.* xi. 2.

## 5. The New Jewish Diaspora.

But the rumour of these Greek and Græcised towns around them spoke loudly to the Jews of the greater Greek world beyond, and tempted them forth to it by manifold voices of promise and sympathy. Hitherto exile had been a horrible thing to Israel,[1] the compulsory migration of their families to remote lands, the ways to which they trod blinded by tears and with no hope in their hearts; for it is singular how in all their copious literature of exile none of them has traced the stages by which they were carried away. The desperate feeling with which Jews had universally regarded their banishment has been expressed by Jeremiah in some lines on the removal of Jehoahaz into Egypt:—[2]

*The New and Voluntary Dispersion of the Jews.*

> *Weep ye not for the dead*
> *Nor bemoan him,*
> *But weeping weep for him that goeth away;*
> *He turneth not again*
> *Nor seeth the land of his birth.*

But now to Jewish eyes the paths out into the world ran shining. Jews went into exile of their own will; there was a new and an eager Diaspora. From Gaza by the desert road to Pelusium; from Joppa and Ptolemais oversea to Alexandria; or northward by earlier Jewish settlements and a train of Greek stations to Antioch, they swarmed into the new world intent and expectant.

---

[1] The last certain captivity of the Jews till the fall of Jerusalem before the Romans was that by Ptolemy I. (above, p. 376). The statement of Josephus that Antiochus III. deported two thousand Jewish families to Lydia and Phrygia is possible but doubtful (xii. *Ant.* iii. 4). Cf. Willrich, 39 f.

[2] Jer. xxii. 10 ff.

The old fears were lifted. Ţobias the traveller had an angel for his guide.[1] With the lines of Jeremiah just quoted we may contrast those of Ben Sira :—

> *He that hath no experience knoweth few things,*
> *But he that hath wandered shall increase skill.*
> *In my wandering I have seen many things,*
> *And more than my words is my understanding.*
> *Ofttimes was I in danger even unto death;*
> *And I was preserved because of these things.*[2]

When we seek for the attractions to this new Dispersion of the Jews, we find them to be numerous and of a mixed character. First, there were the opportunities we have noted of military service and of political and financial usefulness to the new lords of the world. Though it may bè impossible to credit all the stories of this which Josephus has provided,[3] it is clear that even more brilliant fortunes awaited some Jews under the Greeks than had fallen to the Jewish favourites of the Persian court. Greek rulers, and especially the earlier Ptolemies, appreciated the abilities of Jews and their practical knowledge of Eastern life, advanced some of them to high rank in their service, and employed many others in humbler positions. Second, there was the hunger for lands more fertile than their own, of which the inhabitants of Judah were constantly hearing from their brethren in Egypt [4] and elsewhere. To this we may attribute some of the Jewish settlements in Samaria, Galilee, Gilead and Bashan, their ancient claims to which Israel

*Attractions to it:—1. Military and Political Employment.*

*2. Hunger for more fertile Lands.*

---

[1] Book of Tobit.      [2] Ecclesiasticus xxxiv. 10 ff.

[3] See below, p. 392 *n*. 3.

[4] Jos. xii. *Ant.* i. : ‘Jews, who of their own accord went into Egypt, invited by the goodness of the land.’

had never relinquished,[1] which were very fruitful, and in which the Ptolemaic sovereignty of Palestine could provide for them openings that had not existed for cen-

3. Opportunities of Commerce.

turies. Third, and principally, there were the opportunities of commerce which were few in Judah, but in Egypt and elsewhere exceedingly abundant. Alexandria rapidly grew as a centre of trade under Ptolemy II., and by his measures for the development of commerce on the Red Sea;[2] the land of Goshen, where numbers of Jews were settled, occupied a favourable intermediary position; Cyrene began to flourish on the coast west of Alexandria. Fourth, there were

4. Facilities for Residence and Rights of Citizenship.

the facilities granted to the Jews for settling in the larger Greek cities. Josephus states that Alexander himself, as a reward for their assistance against the Egyptians, gave to the Jews equal rights with the Greeks in Alexandria, while his successors assigned to them a special quarter in the city and the further privilege 'that they should be called Macedonians.' In this the truth seems to be that the Jews became clients of the Macedonian 'Phyle' in Alexandria, and that their special quarter of the city formed part of it.[3] In Cyrene,

---

[1] 'Micah' vii. 14, a prophecy of uncertain date ; Psalm lx. 6 ff. (Eng. =Heb. 8 ff.).    [2] See art. 'Trade and Commerce,' *Enc. Bibl.* § 63.

[3] Guthe, *Enc. Bibl.* 1109, where it is argued (against Willrich) that the Jews must have received these privileges under the earlier Ptolemies and before the second century.   The favour of Alexander and the earlier Ptolemies to the Jews is emphasised and detailed by Josephus as follows :—ii. *B.J.* xviii. 7, Alexander gave the Jews equal privileges with the Greeks in Alexandria (cf. *C. Apion.* ii. 4), and his successors granted the special quarter of the city and the right to be called Macedonians ; xii. *Ant.* i., Ptolemy I., after his deportation of Jews to Egypt, attracted others by his liberality, gave them equal rights with the Macedonians, and according to *C. Apion.* ii. 4 (after Hecatæus) entrusted them with Egyptian fortresses and settled some at Cyrene ; xii. *Ant.* ii., Ptolemy II. released the captives of his father, sent an embassy with presents to the High-priest, and brought to Alexandria the

says Strabo,[1] the Jews formed a fourth class of the population beside the citizens, the peasants and the *metoikoi* ;
while in their quarter in Alexandria they lived under an
ethnarch of their own who had powers as absolute as the
ruler of an independent state. The Seleucids, it is said,
were equally forward to favour the Jews. Josephus
states that Seleucus I. himself granted them the rights of
citizenship in all the cities of his foundation in Asia and
the Lower Syria, including Antioch.[2] The statement has
been denied, but we can understand how even Seleucus,
with his claims upon Palestine, would be eager to outbid
his Egyptian rivals, who possessed it, by the promise, at
least, of civic rights to its natives who had settled in his
domains ; and we know that by the following century
his successors had granted all the above privileges.[3] The
enjoyment of these must have led to a great increase
among the Jews of political experience and capacity.
But, fifthly, we have to appreciate the general
freedom and exhilaration of life in the Greek
cities of the East as a powerful temptation
to the Jew to leave his somewhat sombre fatherland.

5. Freedom and Exhilaration of Greek Life.

scribes who translated the Scriptures into Greek (cf. Letter of Aristeas and
*C. Apion.* ii. 4) ; xii. *Ant.* iv. 2 ff., the story of Joseph, son of Tobias, and
his management of the Syrian finances of Ptolemy, and *C. Apion.* ii. 5,
Ptolemy III. offered sacrifices to God in Jerusalem; xiii. *Ant.* iii., Ptolemy VI.,
a friend of the Jews, let Onias build a temple at Leontopolis, decided against
the Samaritans in favour of the Temple at Jerusalem, and according to
*C. Apion.* ii. 5, 'entrusted his whole kingdom to Jews' by making two of
them his chief generals. Ptolemy VII. (Euergetes II.) was hostile to the Jews
who had supported his brother Philometor, but even he in later years is
known from papyri to have favoured them (Willrich, 142 ff.).

[1] In a fragment of his Ὑπομνήματα Ἱστορικά preserved by Josephus, xiv.
*Ant.* vii. 2 (Müller, *Frag. Histor. Graec.* iii. 492). It is doubtful if he is
giving the state of affairs in his own day or drawing on more ancient sources.

[2] xii. *Ant.* iii. 1 ; *C. Apion.* ii. 4.

[3] Cf. Ramsay, *Cities of St. Paul*, 180 ff., 255 ff., 321.

Life in Judah was starved of the political excitement, the artistic feeling, the sheer physical enjoyment of which the Greek communities were full. The heathen world broke upon the shores of Judah no longer, as Isaiah heard it, with the wrathful crash of the stormy sea upon the harbourless coast of Palestine, but with the music of freedom, adventure, wealth and a liberal and boundless happiness.

Such, then, were the more obvious attractions which created the increase of the Jewish Diaspora, of its occupa-
Proofs of the tion in the commerce and politics of the world,
Results. and of its engagement in other foreign in-
terests. We have many proofs of the results. Before the end of the period Jewish communities were established in the Greek cities of Egypt and Syria, by then or the beginning of the next period in some of Cilicia and the rest of Asia Minor. Strabo says: 'These Jews have penetrated to every city, and it would not be easy to find a single place in the inhabited world which has not received this race, and where it has not become master.' [1] We have no exact evidence as to the numbers of the
Dispersion, but by 200 B.C. they must have
The large
Numbers of risen to hundreds of thousands, for in the
the Diaspora. time of Philo the Jews in Egypt alone amounted to a million,[2] and on a temperate reckoning from this datum there were from three to four millions throughout the Roman world.[3] Egyptians and Greeks rapidly became jealous of the Jews. The later Greek charge against them, that they had produced no useful invention, is an unmistakable sign of bitterness at

[1] In Jos. xiv. *Ant.* vii. 2 ; see above, p. 393 *n.* 1.     [2] *In Flacc.* 6.
[3] Guthe, *Enc. Bibl.* 1112.

their commercial successes.[1]   The Book of Tobit
(about 150) illustrates easy habits of travel, a wide
acquaintance with foreign lands, and a liberal adoption of
their legends and folklore.   The assumption of Greek
names instead of or along with their own was a common
practice with the Jews of the time; and it was accompanied by a lavish borrowing of characteristic Greek
customs in social life and military and athletic exercises.
But above all, the Jewish Diaspora added another language
to their own.   As their fathers of the Baby-   Their Adop-
lonian captivity had accepted Aramean, the   tion of the
*lingua franca* of the time, so these new exiles   Language.
accepted and employed Greek.   Not only did they use
it in commerce and society, but for the purposes of
religion.   The translation of the Law, the first five books
of the Old Testament, into Greek, can hardly be later
than 250.   It is in the colloquial dialect of Alexandria
and Lower Egypt; the rest of the Septuagint which was
later shows other and wider influences.[2]   The dispersed
Jews learned to pray, to preach, and to argue in Greek.
Of all this Hellenism there was a considerable reflection
on Jerusalem herself.   There, too, Greek names for Jews
were common before the Maccabean period ; and we have
seen the inestimable advantages which Ben Sira imputes
to travel, the openings to commerce, the distractions and
dissipations which he describes in the life of the City.
Some of the new social fashions of which he approves
were borrowed from the Greeks;[3] and for the fact that

---

[1] See vol. i. 372 f. on Apollonius of Rhodes.

[2] On the Greek of the Septuagint see the chapter under that title (pp. 289-
314) in Swete's *Introd. to the O.T. in Greek*, with the literature there cited.

[3] *E.g.* xxxii. 1-4.

these had invaded Jerusalem we have other proofs. The
institution of a Gymnasium, with all that it meant
of mental intercourse as well as physical exercise,[1] was
one of the causes of the final revolt against foreign
influence. When we consider these things, and the
associations of the fiscal and political officials in Jerusalem with the Greek courts, we see that the statement
of Josephus that but one or two Jews spoke Greek must
be received with a great qualification.[2]

But the Jews of this Dispersion, so widely scattered and
for the most part so thoroughly Hellenised, were not therefore cut off from Jerusalem, nor did they forget
her. With all their absorption in commerce,
with all their religious privileges in their
local synagogues and the Greek translation of the
Scriptures, with all their duties to the self-government
granted to their communities, their devotion to the Holy
City and their loyalty to the Temple remained undiminished. Exile only enhanced the fervour with which
Jerusalem was regarded; the pressure of the heathen
world but confirmed the discipline of which she was
the mistress. Just as we saw that the Babylonian
Captivity led to the exaltation of the City above the
sordid realities of her history to an idealism richer than
any prophet had dared for her before; so, through the
Greek dispersion, Jerusalem was raised to an even rarer
sacredness and endowed with a far wider empire of the
spirit. Things now came true which were then only seen
in vision. The Isles were strewn with them *that waited
for her ; the ships of Tarshish brought her sons from afar
their silver and their gold with them, for the Name of the*

*The new
world-wide
Influence of
Jerusalem.*

----

[1] See below, pp. 405 f.　　　　　　[2] xx. *Ant.* xi. 2.

*Lord her God and for the Holy One of Israel, because He had glorified her.* Sacrifice for the whole nation was accomplished only in her courts, and the nation was world-wide. The most distant Jew knew that prayer was being offered for him there and atonement made for his sins.[1] When he himself prayed he turned to Jerusalem.[2] Every year he sent his half-shekel for the support of the national worship; and the sums were collected and forwarded from every province by a careful administration.[3] When it was possible he went on pilgrimage to her festivals. We cannot suppose that as yet the pilgrims came up to Ṣion in the vast numbers which Josephus records for the Roman period.[4] But the streams which ran annually to the Temple along every great road of the world must already have been considerable. Of their own will they had gone forth, and instinctively they flew home again—*like doves to their windows.* They brought to their Mother their questions of law and life, and took back her answers as binding; they also took back upon their hearts her fresh sorrows and needs. There was nothing else like this in the ancient world, and all modern instances of so wide a spiritual empire are only its imitations.

---

[1] 2 Macc. I, 6, etc.

[2] Daniel vi. 10.

[3] Philo, *de Mon.* ii. 3 ; Josephus, xviii. *Ant.* ix. 1. In xiv. *Ant.* vii. 2 Josephus quotes from Strabo's *Hypomnemata* that the Jews (of Asia Minor) had deposited 800 talents, about £292,000, in Cos, and explains this large sum as the Temple tribute. Reinach, however, argues that it was the private money of the Jews of Alexandria and Leontopolis, who had sent it to Cos to escape confiscation by Ptolemy Lathyrus (*Textes*, etc., 91 *n.* 2).

[4] Under Cestius Gallus (63-66 A.D.) he says a census was taken of those at a Passover, and the number was 2,700,200 ; vi. *B.J.* ix. 3.

## 6. Spiritual Intercourse of Jews and Greeks.

If the intercourse and exchanges of the two races were so intimate upon all the outer and lower levels of life which we have surveyed in the last section, they could not possibly have been confined to these. On both sides were eager and earnest minds working not merely in the strength of their individual curiosity or interests, but with the pressure behind of ancient and vast heritages of thought. How far did they enter and convince each other's souls? In this sphere the facts are naturally less capable of exact appreciation than in those we have surveyed. But we may at least assume the following.

Possibilities of such an Intercourse.

On the one side there was Israel's heritage of a mission to the whole world. The Jews of the new Dispersion could not have trodden those roads or sailed those seas, upon which the prophets of three centuries back had foreseen Israel carrying the knowledge of God to the heathen, without some sense of their obligation to this duty, and some endeavours to fulfil it. Of the missionary conscience there is something in Ben Sira. With his knowledge of the world beyond and of its advantages to the mind of the Jew, his ethical ideals and interests are not as limited to Israel as we have seen those of Deuteronomy to be.[1] He has a wider conception of Providence than the Deuteronomists,[2] and speaks as they do not of mankind in general.[3] The Divine Wisdom which he adores *covers the earth as a mist, she has got a possession in every people and nation;*[4] but not even does this sense of a

Israel's Heritage of a Mission to the Gentiles.

---

[1] Above, p. 214.   [2] i. 10; xvii. 17; xxiv. 6.   [3] xvii. 1.   xxiv. 3, 6.

favourable atmosphere for her in the world outside rouse within him a very great hope of carrying to the latter[1] her full and articulate authority which he affirms to have been established in Ṣion.[2] So little feeling of missionary hopes and duties on the part of a writer who was both familiar with the world and convinced of the unique and priceless wisdom of his own religion is very striking. But that was not the only temper with which the prophetic ideals of Israel had to contend in Jerusalem. Among untravelled Jews, nursed in the religious pride and natural hopes of vengeance, which centuries of instruction in their Law and of oppression by foreign peoples had produced, there grew a bitter and relentless hostility to the idea of the conversion of the heathen and their participation in the covenant mercies of Israel. The Book of Jonah, which may be earlier than the Greek period,[3] was written in order to expose the folly of this jealousy and to declare that God had permitted repentance even to the Gentiles. If the Book of Tobit belongs to the end of this period, we may point in addition to these lines of Tobit's *Prayer for Rejoicing* :—

> *I, in the land of my captivity, give Him thanks,*
> *And shew His strength and majesty to a nation of sinners.*
> *Turn, ye sinners, and do righteousness before Him :*
> *Who can tell if He will accept you and have mercy upon you ? . . .*
> *Let all men speak, and let them give Him thanks in Jerusalem . . .*
> *Many nations shall come from afar to the Name of the Lord God*
> *With gifts in their hands, even gifts to the King of Heaven.*[4]

---

[1] But see xxxvi. 1-17.   [2] xxiv. 1-12.

[3] For the question arises whether in the Greek period a Jewish writer would have sent his fugitive prophet a voyage on the western sea in order to escape from the God of Israel.

[4] Tobit, xiii. 6, 8, 11.

We cannot tell whether such expressions were exceptional in our period. That many prayed for the conversion of the heathen is certain. We may also assume that some took advantage of their close intercourse with the Greeks in politics and in commerce not only to explain the resemblances between their principles and those of Greek philosophers, which we saw to be a habit with some Jews, but to urge upon Greek individuals and families the benefits of a full conversion to the Jewish faith and practice. All that we know is that there was a great zeal for making proselytes among the Pharisees of our Lord's time,[1] and a large number of Gentile believers by that date throughout the Greek world. We can hardly refuse to our period the beginnings of such missionary zeal.

On the other side, we have seen a readiness in some Greeks to inquire into the principles of the Jewish religion, and a recognition at least of their distinction and their value. The first Greeks who wrote about the Jews were impressed by the absorption of the nation in its religious exercises. They emphasised the absence of images and other sensuous objects of worship from the Temple.[2] Just as the Jews of the time had discovered that the Divine Wisdom was also found among other nations, brooding upon them like a mist, to use Ben Sira's figure; so the Greeks recognised a philosophy among the Jews, so characteristic of their life, that they appeared to be little or nothing but philosophers. As to this there is a remarkable unanimity among the first Greek writers about

*Attitude of the Greeks to the Jewish Religion.*

---

[1] Matt. xxiii. 15.
[2] See on Hecatæus, vol. i. 389 f., and vol. ii. 383 f.

the Jews ; they call them a 'race of philosophers.'[1]  Their
testimony is the more striking by its contrast to that
of the Egyptian priest Manetho of the third century
before Christ, whose bitter account of the Jews—as originally a race of vile shepherds, lepers and other outcasts,
who defiled the images of gods and turned their sanctuaries into kitchens where they roasted the animals,
deemed by Egyptians to be sacred[2]—reads like an intentional answer to the favourable Greek opinions.[3]
The singular difference of Judaism from the other cults
of Western Asia must have been as obvious to the
intelligent Greek as to the European of to-day is
the difference of the Mohammedan or the Sikh from
the Hindoos who still worship a multitude of gods ;
while in the religion of the Greek there was far less
to restrain him from sympathising with this Asiatic sect
than the Christian European is conscious of in those
other monotheists.  And as we have seen, the Jews of
the Dispersion, from various motives high and low,
were eager to explain the spiritual affinities between
their religion and the philosophy of the Greeks.  Nor,
of course, had the Greeks those prejudices against animal
sacrifice which provoked the Egyptian Manetho to write

---

[1] Besides Hecatæus of Abdera (who, at least, emphasises the wise prin-
ciples of Jewish government) and Clearchus of Soli, quoted above, the term
philosophers is applied to the Jews by Theophrastus (quoted by Porphyry *de
Abstinentia*, ii. 26; Reinach, *Textes . . . relatifs au Judaïsme*, 7 f.);
Megasthenes (quoted by Clem. Alex., *Strom.* i. 15; Müller, *Frag. Hist.
Graec.* ii. 437), who (cf. Clearchus) compares them with the Brahmans of
India; Hermippus of Smyrna (quoted by Josephus, *C. Apion.* i. 22, and
Origen, *C. Celsum*, i. 15; Müller, iii. 36, 41).  Theophrastus and Megas-
thenes wrote about 300 B.C., Hermippus sixty or seventy years later.

[2] Quoted by Josephus, *C. Apion.* i. 14 f., 26 f. ; Müller, ii. 580; Reinach, 33.

[3] According to Josephus, *C. Apion.* i. 14, Manetho accused Herodotus of
having been led into falsehood by his ignorance of the history of Egypt.

with such disgust of the Jewish ritual. Yet when they were confronted with the question of their adoption into the Jewish system, the Greeks, and especially the men among them, had some reason to draw back. For there were, as we shall see, other rites and institutions of the Jewish system which, to the Greek mind, were repulsive or ridiculous: the Sabbath, circumcision, and the narrow nationalism with which faith in one only God was so paradoxically identified. In spite of these difficulties, however, the Jewish propaganda made some way among the Greeks. There were, of course, the same unworthy motives at work, as the Book of Esther exposes among the Persians.[1] In certain cities fear of the political influence of the Jews, and, among Hellenised Orientals at least, an ambition to share in their civil status would be strong. But doubtless higher motives also operated upon Greek individuals and families of all ranks. The decay of their own popular faiths, the example of the many pure and constant lives among the Jews, the reading of the Torah in Greek, and still more, as time went on, of the Prophets and the Psalmists, cannot have failed to tell upon religious minds; and numerous conversions are more probable than the literature of the time allows us to see. Those who write books do not always notice such movements.

Even more difficult to appreciate, not because it was less real, but because it worked in ways less definite, was the influence of the Greek mind upon the mind

---

[1] Esther viii. 17 : the Talmud speaks of 'Esther' proselytes as well as of 'lion' and other self-interested proselytes, 'Yeb.' 24*b*, Ḥull. 36 ; cf. Levy, *Neuhebr. u. Chald. Wörterbuch*, i. 353.

of Israel. Yet not only may we assume great results
from this for reasons already described,   Intellectual
but there are many detailed symptoms and   Influence of
the Greeks on
in the general tempers of Jewish literature   the Jews.
more than one change, in which we may confidently trace
its operation.

To begin with, the Greek arts were conspicuous and
attractive. The Jew loved and practised Music both in
his worship and for secular purposes ;[1] he
   The Greek
must have learned much from its develop-   Arts:
   1. Music.
ments in Egypt and Mesopotamia. But the
Greeks also had something to teach him. It is significant
that some of the earliest Greek words in Jewish literature are musical ;[2] and in Ben Sira there is an unusual
emphasis on music for its own sake, which has reasonably been traced to Greek influence.

> *Speak, thou that art the elder, for it becometh thee, with sound*
>    *knowledge,*
> *And hinder not music.*
> *Pour not out talk where there is a performance of music,*
> *And display not thy wisdom out of season.*
> *A signet of carbuncle in a setting of gold*
> *Is a concert of music in a banquet of wine.*
> *A signet of emerald in a work of gold*
> *Is a strain of music with pleasant wine.*[3]

The practical benefits of Architecture and Medicine were
too obvious to be resisted ; in the former the Greek was
expert far beyond the Jew. It is the next period which

---

[1] On the development of music in worship see above, p. 353 ; on secular
music, cf. Isa. xxiii. 15 ff. ; Canticles, etc.

   Dan. iii. 5, 7, 10, 15 (Aramaic), the instruments קִיתָרֹס or קַתְרֹס,
κίθαρις ; פְּסַנְתֵּרִין, ψαλτήριον ; סוּמְפֹּנְיָה, συμφωνία or (as in 10) סִיפֹּנְיָא,
σιφώνια (?) ; סַבְּכָא or שַׂבְּכָא, σαμβύκη, seems rather of Syrian or Egyptian
origin.

[3] Ecclesiasticus xxxii. 3-6.

yields the first undoubted examples of Greek style and ornament in the construction of buildings in Jerusalem,[1]

2. Architecture. and in his metaphors derived from building Ben Sira does not go beyond the styles usual among the Semites.[2] But from the remains of the palace of Hyrkanus at 'Arâḳ el-Emîr,[3] it is probable that Simon and other builders of this period were already borrowing from Greek architects. As to Medicine we have more certain evidence. Ben Sira's advice to the people of

3. Medicine. Jerusalem to honour the Physician and to use his skill in their need of it, and his emphasis on the Divine origin of the art and the high place of the profession among great men, read like an argument against objections to the introduction of a foreign practice. In that age religious men had no objections to medicine in itself; many remedies were already practised among the people, and there was apparently a body of healers or physicians.[4] But on the part of the orthodox a strong feeling existed against physicians who did not associate their healing with the ceremonies enjoined by the Law; and it is clear that the priests were regarded as experts in medicine.[5] Greek physicians were probably the first in Jewish experience who used no religious formulæ in their art; [6] and it is such rational

---

[1] See vol. i. 217.

[2] The mingled courses of wood and stone, see above, pp. 67, 69, 386.

[3] See below, pp. 425 ff.

[4] Jer. viii. 22; 2 Chron. xvi. 12; Isai. i. 6, xxxviii. 21; cf. the frequent use of the term *to heal* in metaphor. See, too, Ex. xxi. 19; 2 Kings iv. 19 ff., v. 1 ff.; Isai. iii. 7.

[5] See the various Levitical laws on leprosy, with the implication that the priests could distinguish the various kinds of it; cf. 2 Chron. xvi. 12.

[6] Oriental healers almost invariably do so; cf. for Babylonia Johns, *Assyr. Deeds and Documents*, 63; Jastrow, *Relig. of Bab. and Assyr.*, 269 ff.; Benzinger, *Heb. Arch.*(2) § 38. Among the other sons of the East against whom the prophets warn Israel there were doubtless many exorcisers.

healers whom Ben Sira commends to his fellow citizens, when they fall ill, along with the use of their own religious forms.

> *Honour a physician according to thy need,*[1] *with the*
>    *honours due to him,*
> *For verily the Lord hath created him,*
> *For from the Most High cometh healing,*
> *And from the King shall he receive a gift.*
> *The skill of the physician shall lift up his head,*
> *And in the sight of great men shall he be admired.*
> *The Lord created medicines out of the earth,*
> *And a prudent man will have no disgust at them.*

This is apparently an answer to objections against remedies not sanctioned by religion, and therefore 'unclean.' Ben Sira goes on to counsel his fellow Jews not to be negligent in sickness of the appointed religious means : prayer, repentance and offerings. But when these are performed,

> *Then give place to the physician, for verily the Lord hath created*
>    *him ;*
> *And let him not go from thee, for thou hast need of him.*
> *There is a time when in their very hands is the issue for good.*
> *For they also shall beseech the Lord that He prosper them*
> *In relief and in healing for the maintenance of life.*
> *He that sinneth before His Maker,*
> *Let him fall into the hands of the physician.*[2]

Apart from the question with which we are now dealing, these words are of interest as giving a glimpse into the life of the Jerusalem of this period. We may also trace the intellectual influence of the Greek upon the Jew in the adoption of another Greek institution. The Gymnasium was used by the Greeks not only for bodily exercises. Throughout

4. The Gymnasium and its Opportunities for Debate ;

---

[1] That is, without respect to other considerations of religion or of race.
[2] Ecclesiasticus xxxviii. 1-15.

the Greek world it was a place for conversation and discussion both political and philosophic. This opportunity for the ventilation of liberal opinions was no doubt a principal reason for the hostility to the establishment of the Gymnasium in Jerusalem. But the influence of the latter prevailed: and in later times the Xystos became a centre for popular gatherings. Finally,[1] command of the Greek language opened to the Jewish mind the treasures of Greek literature and philosophy. Ptolemy II. had collected a very large library in Alexandria; and just as we have seen that some Jewish

5. Greek Literature and Philosophy.

writers freely borrowed from the folklore of the Eastern peoples around them, so there is abundant proof that others with equal freedom and more method used the materials and absorbed the spirit of Greek literature. This proof is found largely in a number of quotations preserved by Alexander Polyhistor (*c.* 80-40 B.C.) from authors who, while using the Greek language, exhibit obvious signs of their Jewish nationality.[2] Among them are both historians and poets. Before this, Jewish historians had not so absolutely confined their interest in history to its religious and ethical lessons as some moderns seem to imply; there had been annals of Israel which the compilers of our Old Testament histories employed, and even in the original

---

[1] Schlatter, pp. 24 ff., indeed suggests that if the Jews did not owe their new interest in Astronomy and Astrology to Greek teaching, the openness of the Jewish mind to Hellenism facilitated its opening also to that Eastern culture which had especially elaborated these sciences. But more probably the Jewish interest in Astronomy was developed before the Greek period.

[2] The list of them with their fragments, as quoted by Alexander and handed down by Eusebius and Clement of Alexandria, is given by Müller, *Frag. Histor. Graec.* iii. 206-244 ; see what he says on the obviously Jewish origin of the writings in question, p. 207*b* ; cf. Schürer, *Gesch.*[3] ii. § 33.

work of the latter there are notes upon the origins of
the races of mankind and other antiquarian matters
which reveal an interest in history for its own sake.[1]
But in the Hellenistic Jews quoted by Alexander,
especially Demetrius, Eupolemus and Artapanus, this
interest is much developed; while in the Letter of
Aristeas we find signal evidence of the way in which
a Jew of the period sought to put himself into the
Greek attitude and write about his people from a Greek
standpoint. Of Jewish poets in the Greek language
Alexander mentions two: Philo, who wrote an epic on
Jerusalem,[2] and Ezekiel, who wrote 'Jewish tragedies,'
among them one on the Exodus.[3] Of the absorption
of Greek philosophy by the Jews of the Diaspora, we have
some illustration in passages which have survived from
the works of Aristobulus of Alexandria under Ptolemy
Philometor (181-146). They betray not only the direct
and dominant influence of Aristotle, but a knowledge of
Plato and other leaders of Greek thought. Aristobulus,
who is said to have been of the High-priestly family
and in correspondence with Judas Maccabeus, was certainly not the first of his countrymen who, while striving
to prove that Greek philosophy derived its principles
from the Hebrew Scriptures, succeeded only in showing
how much their own minds were governed by the Greek
language and the Greek methods.[4] We must also keep

---

[1] This small addition is necessary to Schürer's contrasts between the historians of Pharisaic, and those of Hellenistic, Judaism, *Gesch.*[3] ii. § 33, p. 345.

[2] Eusebius, *Praep. Evang.* (ed. Gaisford, ii. 378, 392, 434) ix. 20, 24, 37,
from Alex. Pol. ; Müller, iii. 213, 219, 229 (extracts 6, 11, 23). See below,
p. 462.

[3] Eusebius, *Praep. Evang.* ix. 28, 29 (ed. Gais. 404 ff.) ; Müller, iii. 224 f.

[4] In 2 Macc. i. 10 it is said he belonged not merely to the priestly but to
the *high*-priestly stock (ἀπὸ τοῦ τῶν χριστῶν ἱερέων γένους = הַמָּשִׁיחַ הַכֹּהֵן).

in mind another work of the Diaspora, the Book of Wisdom, which, while showing more dependence on orthodox Palestinian Judaism than the works just cited, clearly reveals the direct influence both of Plato and the Stoics.

By all these and other avenues the Greek mind poured its rich influences upon the mind of the Jew. In The Welcome the latter there was already much to give of the Hebrew them welcome. For till the arrival of the Mind to the Greek. Greeks in Western Asia, the Jew felt himself a solitary among the nations. These were all, except the Samaritans, worshippers of images. As many of his Scriptures reminded him, he alone was *wise*. Next to his faith in a righteous God, what most sustained him through his persecutions by the heathen was his strong sense of intellectual superiority. He knew his height above these grovellers before animals and the stocks and stones which their own hands had shaped. The scorn which he poured on them was a sweet relief to the misery he endured from their oppression. But in the philosophic Greek he thought he had at last found a fellow. The rational element in this Gentile mind appealed to him ; the Greek, too, was *wise*. In the powers of synthesis and construction which he discovered in Greek literature he could not but recognise abilities in which his own mind was deficient, forces which promised to complete the efforts he had already begun in these

and a letter is given from Judas Maccabeus to him, in which he is addressed as 'the teacher of Ptolemy.' We owe our knowledge of his writings to fragments preserved in Clement of Alexandria, *Strom.* i. v. vi. ; Eusebius, *Praep. Evang.* vii. 14, viii. 10, xiii. 12 (ed. Gaisford, ii. 185, 291, iii.) For accounts and discussions of Aristobulus, see Ewald's *Hist.* (Eng. trans.) v. 259, 357, 488 ; Schürer, *Gesch.*[3] ii. 384 f. (Eng. trans.) div. ii., vol. iii. 237 ff.) ; and Schlatter, *Gesch.* 39 ff.

directions. On the other side he must have welcomed
the rationalising of religions and mythologies by Greek
philosophy,[1] for had he not already by himself employed
the stuff of Oriental myths in his monotheistic interpretations of the Universe and history?[2] Nor could
he escape the further influences of Greek scepticism.
Confident theories have therefore been formed of the
Greek origin of both the constructive and the sceptical
elements in the later literature of the Jewish Wisdom.
The conception of the Cosmos and of the Divine
Wisdom which pervades it, the identification of knowledge and virtue, the division of mankind into wise and
fools, with its emphasis upon the intellectual basis of
character—these features of the Prologue to the Book
of Proverbs, of Ecclesiastes and of Ben Sira, have been
traced directly to the same Greek example and influence
which we have seen so operative among Jewish writers
of the Diaspora. But in the case of the former, all of
them written in Palestine and probably in Jerusalem,
much more discrimination is necessary than in that of
the latter. Even if on other grounds we grant that

[1] Cf. Schlatter, p. 31, on Euhemerus.

[2] There is a charming tale attributed by Josephus to Hecatæus (*C. Apion.*
i. 22) which might be used to illustrate the innate sympathy between the
mind of the Jew and that of the enlightened Greek, if we were sure that it
was from Hecatæus himself and not the work of a Jewish writer who used
his name; for the author of the story evidently regards with approval the
Jewish rebuke of superstition which it recounts. A troop of Greeks marching towards the Red Sea was suddenly ordered to halt by their Mantis. A
Jewish archer (Mosollamos or Meshullam) among them asked why, and the
augur pointed to a bird by whose movements he said their own must be
determined. Whereupon Meshullam shot the bird. The augur and others
were indignant. 'Why, are you mad?' said M.; 'how could this bird,
which did not provide for its own safety, tell us anything sound about our
march? If it was able to foretell the future it would never have come to this
place, fearing that Meshullam the Jew would shoot it dead.'

Proverbs, like Ben Sira, belongs to the Greek Period, we must remember that some conception of the Universe and of the one Divine Wisdom which runs through nature and history had been reached by Hebrew prophets centuries before; and that prophets as well as Deuteronomists had emphasised the connection between knowledge and virtue—which indeed is implied in the elastic meaning and practical bearings of the Hebrew verb *to know*. In this case, as in that of the doctrine of immortality,[1] the germs and first shoots of her wisdom were Israel's own. But the new climate, which Hellenism had brought upon Western Asia, was peculiarly favourable to their growth, and at least some of them were ripened by its influences. Even for the sceptical forms of Hebrew wisdom we have found precedents in prophecy as far back as before the Exile, while the Book of Job, that epic of scepticism, is entirely due to the experience of the East and is untouched by Greek speculation. The Book of Ecclesiastes, however, introduces us to a wider subject than scepticism, and requires separate treatment.

To Ecclesiastes, the lateness of whose language is obvious, various dates have been assigned from the end of the Persian Period to the reign of Herod the Great.[2]

---

[1] See the author's *Modern Criticism and the Preaching of the O.T.*, 207 f.

[2] Later Persian Period, Ewald, Ginsburg, Delitzsch; that or Greek Period during wars of Ptolemies and Seleucids, but earlier than the rise of the national spirit under the Maccabees, A. B. Davidson, *Enc. Bibl.* 1161; similarly Driver, *Introd.*[(6)] 476; Wildeboer, *Kurzer Hand-Comm.* 113 f.; Budde, *Gesch. d. alt-Hebr. Litt.* 304, and others; the original book before Ben Sira with additions till 100 B.C., Siegfried in Nowack's *Hand-Komm.* Winckler, *Alt-Orient. Forsch.*[(2)], assigns the kernel to Alkimos; reign of Alex. Jannæus, König, *Einl.* 432 ff.; Herod, Grätz, *Monatsschrift für Gesch. u. Wissensch. des Judenthums*, 1885 (not seen); cf. Cheyne, *Jewish Relig. Life after the Exile*, 183 ff., and *Enc. Bibl.* 1163 f.

He calls himself *Koheleth*,[1] *Preacher*, literally *one who calls together*, or *takes part in*, a *Kahal* or *ecclesia*, a public *assembly* or *congregation*, and as we shall see he was a Jew of Jerusalem, with disciples and exercising authority. His indebtedness to the Greek mind has been widely asserted, but is very doubtful. To begin with, there are only a few traces of Greek in his language,[2] and these uncertain; otherwise his speech, his style, and his way of thinking, are all Semitic. They are as different as possible from those of his Hellenised contemporaries of the Diaspora. This far more original Jew of Jerusalem betrays no such influence as is obvious in the case of Aristobulus or the Book of Wisdom. The various parallels which moderns have drawn between the thoughts and phrases of Ecclesiastes and those of Greek philosophers [3] are only exhibitions of the rationalism and the humanity common to them both.

Ecclesiastes—
Hebraic Character of his Style, Methods,

---

[1] הַקֹּהֶלֶת, a femin. participle, but always with the masc. form of the verb (vii. 27 read אמר הקהלת). Elsewhere in Heb. a fem. is used for a masc. as if for the office or rank which the verb expresses, and hence for the holder of the office, Ezra ii. 55, 57. A similar use of the fem. is found in Arabic, *e.g.* Khalifah; as expressing the full realisation of the duty or ideal of the office (for instances see W. Wright, *Arab. Gram.* i. § 233 rem. *c*). The Greek Ἐκκλησιαστής, *one who sits*, or *speaks, in the* ἐκκλησία, is therefore an exact translation.

[2] These have been marked (Wildeboer, 114). יָפֶה, *beautiful*, is like καλός used for seemly or excellent, and is joined with טוֹב *good* (v. 17), like καλὸς κἀγαθός; תּוּר, *to look round about*, is compared with σκέπτεσθαι (i. 13, ii. 3); and the constant תחת השמש, *under the sun* = ὑφ᾽ ἡλίῳ. But none is certainly from the Greek; the first seems the most probable; see also next note.

[3] ʻThe idea of Tyler, who is followed by Plumptre, that the Book is a blend of the Stoic and Epicurean philosophies, seems extraordinarily superficial, and is supported mainly by what appears misinterpretation of its language. . . . Determinism is, of course, a prevailing idea in the Book. That, however, is just the fundamental idea of the Wisdom, or indeed of the Hebrew mind— that God is the causality in all things—with the inevitable development which time gave it. At first sight the phrase " to do good " in the sense of "to

The principles, upon which the Preacher falls back from the exhaustion of his research and his experience of the

and Prin- resultlessness of life, are all native to Israel.
ciples. We need not look elsewhere for his convictions that God has made the world and made it beautiful, that He has a purpose in it though this be not discoverable by us, that He has appointed to men their labours and their pleasures alike, that there is an order in life, a set time for everything, that even by the worst disorders God is proving or testing men, and that, all experience to the contrary, the wise man *is* better than the fool;[1] nor for the Preacher's practical precepts to fear God, to be sincere and restrained in His worship, to remember His care of the righteous and His bringing into judgment all that is done.[2] One remarkable passage enjoins men,

see good" to enjoy life (iii. 12) has a startling resemblance to the Gk. εὖ πράτ- τειν; but after all, the senses of the two phrases are somewhat different, and there is no reason to suppose the Hebrew expression to be an imitation; though not occurring elsewhere, its opposite "to do badly" (i.e. *to be sad*) is used in early literature (2 Sam. xii. 18, and perhaps Eccles. v. 1), and possibly the phrase itself may be ancient.'—A. B. Davidson, *Enc. Bibl.* 1162. Similar also is the summary verdict of Budde (*Gesch. d. alt-Hebr. Litt.* 305):—'Seine eigen- tümliche Grösse gewinnt noch dadurch, dass man seine Gedanken vergeblich aus dem Einfluss griechischer Philosophie herzuleiten sucht; *in ihrer eigen- tümlichen Unfolgerichtigkeit sind sie vielmehr*, so viel oder so wenig er von jenem mag gewusst haben, durchaus sein persönliches Eigentum.' Cf. Wildeboer (*Kurzer Hand-Commentar*, 113): 'deutlich erkennbarer Einfluss der gr. Philosophie lässt sich nicht nachweisen.' A good monograph on the subject is that of Kleinert, *Stud. u. Krit.*, 1883, 761 ff., whose conclusion is that all that the Book betrays is the influence of the general atmosphere of the later Greek mind. See too Genung, *Words of Koheleth*, 1904.

[1] iii. 10-15, 17; v. 18 ff.; vii. 13 f.; viii. 15; ix. 1, 13-16, 17 ff.; xi. 5. To these we might add ii. 24 ff. and vii. 26; though the more positive clauses in them are taken by some to be interpolations, they go little further than the sayings cited above, which are allowed to be original.

[2] iii. 14; v. 1-7; vii. 18; viii. 12 f.; xi. 9. The authenticity of viii. 12*b*, 13, is denied by some, and certainly 12*a* is not harmonious with 13. On the other hand, there is no reason to take xi. 9 as an addition; the *judgment* mentioned in it is not the one last judgment in a life to come, but the con- tinual process apparent in this life.

though God's processes be unknowable, to strike into the opportunities these afford, with unceasing vigilance and labour.[1] *Send forth thy bread on the face of the waters, for thou shalt find it after many days. Divide a portion into seven, yea even into eight, for thou knowest not what evil shall be on the earth. . . . As thou knowest not what is the way of the Wind, or the Spirit, nor how the bones grow in the womb of her that is with child; even so thou knowest not the work of God who doeth all. In the morning sow thy seed, and in the evening withhold not thy hand; for thou knowest not which shall prosper, whether this or that, or whether they both alike shall be good. Truly the light is sweet, and a pleasant thing it is for the eyes to behold the sun. Yea, if a man live many years, let him rejoice in them all, but remember the days of darkness for they shall be many.* Another said in Jerusalem: *The Wind, or the Spirit, bloweth where it listeth, and thou hearest the noise thereof, but knowest not whence it cometh nor whither it goeth; so is every one that is born of the Spirit*; and again, *We must work the works of Him that sent me while it is day, for the night cometh when no man can work.*[2] Ecclesiastes, it is commonly said, is nowhere quoted in the New Testament, yet these words of our Lord sound like an echo of the words of the Preacher—an echo in that higher sphere into which Jesus carried the sayings of those who were before Him.[3] But no teacher in Israel required to go to the Greek for such things, even if the Greek knew and had already expressed them in his own inimitable way.

---

[1] xi. 1-8.    [2] John iii. 8; ix. 4; cf. xii. 35 f.
[3] The whole subject of the influence of the Books of Wisdom upon our Lord's teaching requires fresh and thorough study; see Foster Kent, *The Wise Men of Israel*, and *Modern Criticism and the Preaching of the O.T.*, Lecture viii.

Nor did the Preacher even require to borrow from 'the Greek Spirit' his sense of the indifferent flux of nature or of all the resultlessness of life.[1] These may be confidently ascribed to his own mind and to the influence of his times, but far more to the former than to the latter. The times were in part unsettled and evil. The rapid changes of rank and fortune which the Preacher notices.[2] were very possible in Israel of the Greek age. Injustice and oppression, such as he laments,[3] were bound to be rife, when the supreme authority was foreign and far off and the factions at home were so eager for its patronage, so jealous of each other and so unscrupulous. But there was another side to these times, which modern writers on the Book tend to overlook. *Great works* were undertaken and carried through: *houses, vineyards, gardens, parks, pools of water.* Herds and flocks, troops of servants and singers, wealth and treasures, could be accumulated.[4] With all his griefs, the man who toiled could have joy in his work, men would envy him for it, and he had peace to heap up its gains.[5] There was freedom for study, for the growth of wisdom, and for the joys of life.[6] Such reflections upon the Book allow us to assign it—in spite of its shadows, and if we keep in view the real source of these in the mind of its author—to the same age as produced the kindred but sunnier spirit of Ben Sira. The temper of the Preacher is his own : *I communed with mine own heart*,[7] he says, and by variations of this phrase,

*His reflection of his Times.*

*His originality.*

---

[1] i. 2 ff. ; 14 ff. ; ii. 11, 17, etc. etc.

[2] ii. 21 ; iv. 14 ; v. 13 ff. ; vi. 2 ; ix. 13 ff. ; x. 5 ff.

[3] iii. 16 ; iv. 1 ; v. 8.   [4] ii. 1-11 ; cf. v. 10-12, etc.

[5] ii. 24 ; iii. 13, 22 ; iv. 4 ; v. 10-12, 18-20, etc.   [6] ix. 7-10, etc.

[7] i. 13, 16, 17 ; viii. 16 ; ix. 1, and so the frequent *I have seen, I turned, I proved, I said in my heart, I applied my heart.*

which always emphasise the first personal pronoun, he insists that it is his individual experience and musings which he unfolds. The things which affected him had touched many in Israel before him : that the righteous man got the wicked's deserts, and that the wicked reaped the reward of the righteous ; that men might labour anxiously and with wisdom, but must leave their gains to the idler; that men won wealth but in the winning lost the power to enjoy it; that death always came so fast and so certain, the wise had no advantage above the fool, nor man above the beasts—and all this in spite of the truth, to which he returns again and again, that wisdom *is* better than folly.[1] Only the Preacher broods more upon these facts than any of his predecessors in Jerusalem have done. He has none of the national enthusiasm and very little of the personal passion for God which enabled them to triumph over life and death itself. For the moment Israel seemed to have lost not only its hope, but also in minds like the Preacher's its sense of distinction. In his fascination by the chances and the last fate which befall all men alike, it was impossible to feel that Israel was different from other peoples. Deuteronomy [2] was no longer true. *All things come alike to all ; there is one event to the righteous and to the wicked, to the good and to the evil,[3] to the clean and to the unclean, to him that sacrificeth and to him that sacrificeth not ; as is the good so is the sinner, he that sweareth as he that feareth an oath ; [4] this is an evil in all that is done under the sun, that there is one event unto all : yea also the heart of the sons of men is full*

---

[1] ii. 13, 14 ff., 18-22 ; iii. 18-21 ; v. 13-17 ; vi. 1-9 ; viii. 14 ; ix. 1 ff., 11 f., 13-16.

[2] See above, p. 216.  [3] So the LXX.

[4] Or *he that forsweareth himself as he that reverenceth an oath* (?).

*of evil, madness is in their heart while they live and after that—to the dead!* [1] We may reasonably ascribe such generalising, as extreme in one direction as the teaching of Deuteronomy was in another, to that experience of life upon the same levels with foreign peoples to which the Greek empire in Asia so lavishly introduced the Jew. Whether the intellectual atmosphere of Hellenism had also told upon the Preacher —whether he was aware of the questions started by Greek philosophers,[2] and was directly disturbed by them—is very doubtful. The most reasonable conclusion appears to be that if the interest of Israel was no longer confined to the nation and its fortunes, but had spread with the Preacher upon all *the sons of men* and *all that is done under the Sun,*[3] this was due more to the opportunity, than to the example, provided by Greece; while the novel width of his survey and of his consequent sympathies and his peculiar temperament are, in themselves and without any resort to Greek philosophy, sufficient to account for the weariness of his spirit and the scepticism which prevails in so much of his thinking.

*His sense of Humanity as a Whole.*

But however we may decide this question of Greek influence, the great fact is certain that from the spirit of the Preacher, and through the assemblies he addressed, Israel were learning what the Book of Jonah, in its simpler way, represents them as learning in the person of that prophet when he fled across the sea, their commonness with all the sons of men; and were winning the power to realise humanity as a whole. For this essential moment in their discipline

*His unique Service to Israel.*

---

[1] ix. 2 f. : cf. ii. 14, etc.  [2] Kuenen, *Onderzoek*, § 105, 9.
[3] Constant phrases of his, *e.g.* i. 3, 13 f. ; ii. 18, etc. etc.

the nation not only required to undertake those stormy voyages with the heathen, and to come face to face with those populous cities to which the Greek dispensation called them, and the effects of both of which the Book of Jonah so graphically describes;[1] but they must embark, too, upon the more perilous seas of research and of doubt over which the Preacher steered his solitary craft. Cut loose from their sense of distinction and religious privilege, Israel had to reflect upon the labour, the baffled thought, the sorrow and the death which made them one with all the sons of men, before their experience and sympathy became adequate for their mission to the world. It is thus that the Book vindicates its rank in the religious history of Israel. Whatever may have been the motives which led to its official embodiment in the Canon, Ecclesiastes by its very scepticism, its sympathy with the groping and disappointed mind of man, deserved a place among the sacred writings. The school of Hillel which accepted it were right, and the school of Shammai which sought its rejection were wrong.[2] In the Providential discipline of Israel the Book of Ecclesiastes was as indispensable as was its opposite pole the Book of Deuteronomy.

And equally with the Deuteronomists, Ecclesiastes was a son of Jerusalem. The Preacher was not a Jew

---

[1] If the Book be of the Persian Period this would only date earlier the beginnings of the lesson which Israel principally owed to the Greeks. See above, p. 399 *n. 2.*

[2] The Epilogue to Ecclesiastes, xii. 9-14, is of course later and by another hand than the rest of the Book; the Preacher is described in it in the third person. Probably it was this defence of him, and the very orthodox utterance with which it closes, that assisted the official reception of the Book into the Canon.

of the Dispersion, nor does he even appear to have been
a traveller like Ben Sira. For one of his
troubles is that he has seen the wicked
peacefully gathered to the graves of their
fathers, while *they that did right went away from the Holy
Place and were forgotten in the City.*[1] Those whom he
addresses live close to the Temple, can sacrifice and
fulfil their vows.[2] The royal mask which he assumes
in the beginning of his Book[3] is soon dropped, and even
for the short time he wears it is so detachable that we
cannot argue from it as to his location. But that he
belonged to the City remains clear, both from the
passages just cited and from another expression, in which
Solomon is made to speak of Jerusalem only : *I had
great possessions of herds and flocks above all who were
before me in Jerusalem.* Under the shadow of the
Temple, then, did *Ḳoheleth, Ḳahal-minister* and *Master of
Assemblies,* gather his audiences, *teach the people,* and,
according to the Epilogue, found his school.[4] That
baptism of Israel in the common sorrows and doubts
of humanity, of which he was the minister, took place
in Jerusalem, just like every other crisis in the history of

*Jerusalem the Mother of Ecclesiastes.*

---

[1] viii. 10 : a difficult verse, but such, following the Greek reading, seems to be the true sense.   [2] v. 1 ff.

[3] For the conclusion that the Preacher himself assumed the personality of Solomon, and that it was not forced on him by a later hand, and for the greater probability of this both on textual and psychological grounds, I have not space to give the detailed argument.

[4] On Ḳoheleth see above, p. 411 *n* 1. The phrase xii. 11, בַּעֲלֵי אֲסֻפּוֹת,
is probably correctly rendered by our version, *masters of assemblies,* for such is the meaning of אספה in Phoen. (Block, *Phön. Glossar.* 14) and Mishnic Hebrew (Levy, *Neuhebr. Wörterbuch,* i. 127); but others take it to mean collections of sentences ; see Nowack *in loco.* In any case the tradition about the Preacher given in the Epilogue is clear : he was one of the wise, a teacher of the people, whose influence remained.

the nation's mind ; for, as we have seen, even the pregnant sufferings of the Babylonian Exile were no less really endured within Sion [1] than were those which happened behind her actual walls. Jerusalem was always the Mother of Sorrows to Israel—even now also when the sorrows were not national, but the universal grief and darkness of mankind.

### 8. THE REACTION AGAINST HELLENISM.

But all these effects on the Jew, both of the opportunities which Greek empire afforded and of the direct influence of Greek example and doctrine, represent only one side of Israel's attitude to Hellenism. Within the same small population which produced the humane and liberal spirit of Ben Sira, proud of the advantages of travel and favourable to foreign fashions, and the universal sorrow of the Preacher, too vast to nestle on the breast of any mother, but moaning like the sea round every coast of the sons of men, there were being fostered, during these same years, the hopes of national freedom, the passionate loyalty to Law and Temple and the fierce intolerance of other faiths, which were immediately to break out in the Maccabean Revolt. We have, therefore, now to inquire what it was which in spite of his long experience of a mild Greek rule and the welcome which he gave to Greek fashions, discovered to the Jew the essential hostility between himself and the Greek, and drove him to fight to the death for his national institutions and the faith of his fathers.

Jewish reaction against Hellenism.

[1] See above, pp. 287 ff.

Forebodings of this discovery we have seen in both Greek and Jew from the very beginnings of their intimacy with each other. Hecatæus emphasised the absence of images in the Temple and of every sensuous object of worship.[1] Behind the similarities of temper and the common political interests which drew the two races together, especially in Egypt, other Greeks soon[2] detected that same national tenacity, that pride of distinction and destiny, and those peculiar rites and institutions, by all of which Israel had already provoked the hostility of their Semitic and Egyptian neighbours. Alike to the philosophers and the statesmen of Greece, the spirit and the customs of the Jew were perplexing and offensive. For the sake of his absurd Sabbath he would not defend his city or temple, and was therefore to Greek eyes no patriot; yet his nationalism was

*Causes and Progress of this Reaction (1) among the Greeks.*

---

[1] See above, p. 384. He adds that Moses conceived the Heaven which surrounds the earth to be God alone and the Lord of the universe (μόνον εἶναι θεὸν καὶ τῶν ὅλων κύριον, quoted by Diodorus Sic. xl. 3; Müller, *Frag. Histor. Graec.* ii. 391 f.). This statement, so often repeated by Greek and Latin writers, was probably due to the divine title common in later Hebrew literature, אֱלֹהֵי הַשָּׁמַיִם, *God of Heaven*; in Aramaic, אֱלָהּ שְׁמַיָּא, or even שְׁמַיָּא alone (Dan. ii. 18, iv. 23, the Books of the Maccabees and the Mishna).

[2] It is striking that the worst outbursts extant of Greek hatred and contempt for the Jews, emphasising their exclusiveness and misanthropy, do not occur till after the Maccabean revolt and reorganisation of Israel (cf. Posidonius of Apamaea, *c.* 135-51 B.C.: *apud* Diodorus, xxxiv. 1, Jos. *C. Apion.* ii. 7, Müller, iii. 256; and Apollonius of Rhodes, *c.* 100-75 B.C., *apud* Jos. *C. Apion.* ii. 7, 14, 33, 36); but we find the same feelings already expressed by Agatharchides of Cnidos under Ptolemy Philometor (181-146 B.C., quoted by Jos. *C. Apion.* i. 22; Müller, iii. 196). The common fable that the Jews worshipped the head of an ass is found as early as Mnaseas of Patras (beginning of second century B.C.; Jos. *C. Apion.* ii. 9; Reinach, *Textes,* 49 f.). On Manetho, who wrote in Greek, though expressing Egyptian feeling, see above, p. 401.

so fanatic that of all the peoples of Syria he alone refused to be absorbed by Hellenism. There was, too, the awkwardness of his geographical position. Had Israel lived on the Levant, it might have been possible to Hellenise them. But so far from the sea, with the desert behind and all that the desert meant to Israel, mentally as well as physically, the nation was an extremely dangerous one for its Greek sovereigns to provoke. That these felt the danger is apparent from all the policy of the Ptolemies and Seleucids towards Jerusalem. They sought her subjection to Hellenism less by the invasion of their arms than by the gradual infection of her life through the Greek cities with which they surrounded her, and by the creation among her citizens of parties favourable to themselves. But whether they treated her with force or with intrigue, their sense is constant of the uniqueness of Jerusalem among the states subject to them, of the essential hostility of her spirit and her system to the spirit and the aims of Hellenism.

On the other side Israel became equally conscious of the antagonism. Even the illuminated Jew, of the most liberal views, could not forget the unique- (2) Among ness of his history or the superiority of his the Jews. ethics. Even in Alexandria, Aristobulus employed his Greek scholarship in the endeavour to prove that the Hebrew scriptures were the source of all the wisdom of Greece. Ben Sira, for all his foreign culture, is proud of the story of his little people, and carried away by the glory of their worship. It surprises one to see his prudence change to passion when he turns to these subjects; to find a man so travelled, so aware of the

world and liberal in his views as in his tastes, celebrate
like any Deuteronomist the divine story of Israel and
the splendours of the national ritual. Wisdom might
brood over all the peoples of the world, but *in Şion was
she established, and in Jerusalem was her authority.*[1]
Salvation was of the Jews! Ben Sira's concluding prayer
is not only for the joy and peace of his people, but for
their deliverance : *let Him deliver us in His time.*[2] He
curiously adds, *with two nations is my soul vexed, and the
third is no nation : they that sit on the Mount of Samaria,
and the Philistines, and that foolish people which dwelleth
in Sichem.* These last, of course, are the Samaritans. If
the reading of the first be correct,[3] Ben Sira means the
Greeks, whose centre of authority in Palestine was established in Samaria,[4] while by *the Philistines* he covers the
Hellenised inhabitants of the formerly Philistine cities.[5]
If such reactions are apparent in the green trees, upon
which Hellenism had been so liberally grafted, what
must it have been in the old, main stocks of Judaism?
Even Ecclesiastes is driven back from his wide doubts
upon the simple principles of his fathers—nothing else
for him abides sure—and even he does not dissuade his
people from the *House of God*, nor says more against
sacrifice than the Prophets had said before him.[6] The
devotees of the Law can have viewed the results of a
century of Greek progress only with hatred and alarm.
They were as hostile to and scornful of idols as their
fathers, as jealous of circumcision and the Sabbath, as

---

[1] xxiv. 10 f. ; on his Jewish ethics see ix. 3 ff.
[2] l. 24 : cf. xxxvi. 1-11.    [3] Some versions read *Seir* for *Samaria*.
[4] Above, pp. 374, 376 ff.
[5] The LXX. translates *Philistines* in Isa. ix. 12 by Ἕλληνες.
[6] v. 1 ff. : cf. Ecclesiasticus xxxv. 1 ff.

sure of the sufficient wisdom of the Law, as proud of the uniqueness of their race. But they discovered that Hellenism, instead of destroying the idols of their neighbours, left these alone or gave them the names of the gods of Greece. Centuries of contact had taught them, what recent excavations have revealed to ourselves, the uncleanness and the cruelty of the cults of Canaan. They were finding that for such sores Hellenism had no remedies. *The fear of Jahweh*, says one of their Psalmists, thinking of those other impure and changeable religions, *the fear of Jahweh is clean and enduring for ever*. They heard the Sabbath ridiculed by Greeks, and in the new stir of life which Hellenism excited they found it ever more difficult to keep. They saw some Jews becoming ashamed of circumcision and otherwise neglecting the Law, and a number lapsing through such stages into open revolt. Amid the influx of Greek thought and fashion they keenly felt their own and their children's danger : *keep back thy servant*, says the same Psalmist, *from overweening men*; *let them not have dominion over me, then shall I be perfect and guiltless of the great apostasy*.[1] This inevitable reaction against Hellenism appears to have been organised. By the time of the Maccabees a party had been formed, whose Its organisa-name, Asidaeoi or *Ḥasîdîm*, testifies at once tion. to their loyalty to Israel's God and their sense of His distinctive mercies to themselves.[2] From so influential a group the feeling must have spread left and right throughout Israel—to the simpler country folk ignorant of Greek and tenacious of the customs of their fathers, to the fanatics for national liberty, and, upon the questions

[1] Psalm xix. 13 f.  [2] Vol. i. 401 f.

of the idols and the ethics, to the more liberal *wise men*. But while all these experiences supplied material for the crisis, the occasion of this would hardly have arrived but for two other causes—the old curse of political factions in Jerusalem herself, and the persecutions of Antiochus IV., in strange contrast to the policy of the Ptolemies.

## 9. THE JEWISH FACTIONS AND ANTIOCHUS EPIPHANES.

We have already seen[1] how a certain Joseph, son of Ṭobiah, had secured towards 200 B.C. the management

Factions in Jerusalem: Oniads and Tobiads. of the Egyptian tribute from Palestine, and was thereby risen to great wealth and influence in Jerusalem. His family and adherents, known as the Tobiadæ, formed a powerful party over against the Oniadæ, the family with whom the High-priest's office still remained,[2] and divided with them the allegiance of 'the multitude.'[3] Joseph lived through the Seleucid conquest of Palestine and into the reign of Seleucus IV. (187-175). Under the Seleucids he or his family retained the farm of the taxes, and Josephus gratefully records

Joseph Ben-Ṭobiah. that he brought his people 'out of a state of poverty into one which was more splendid.' Probably it was by his services that the transference of the Jews to Antiochus the Great was facilitated and the favourable terms secured which that monarch granted to them.[4] Joseph had several legitimate sons and one illegitimate, whose Greek name was Hyrkanus.[5] Hyr-

---

[1] Vol. i. 368, 399.

[2] Vol. i. 393, 398 f., they were descended from Ṣadok, whom Solomon had instituted as chief priest in place of Abiathar ; vol. ii. p. 49.

[3] Josephus, xii. *Ant.* v. 1.          [4] Above, p. 380.

[5] For what follows see xii. *Ant.* iv. 11.

KAṢR EL-'ABD—PALACE OF THE SLAVE.

Remains of the Ancient Tyrus or Ṣûr built by Hyrkanus (Ṭobiyah) Son of Joseph, C. 180 B.C.

*Plate XII.*

*Plate XIII.*

KASR EL-'ABD—PALACE OF THE SLAVE.

Gateway outside the Moat of the Palace of Tyrus or Ṣûr.

kanus resided at the Egyptian court, but the other sons with their father at Jerusalem. From what happened afterwards it appears that while they accepted the Seleucid régime he endeavoured to restore that of the Ptolemies ; and thus the old and familiar situation was repeated in Jerusalem. There was a party for Egypt and a party for the North. Hyrkanus marched upon Judah with an armed force, was opposed by his brethren, and slew two of them; but although 'the multitude was divided in this war,' 'when he came to the City nobody would receive him.' The High-priest being related to the elder Tobiadæ took sides with them, and hopeless of his Egyptian schemes Hyrkanus retired beyond Jordan, where for seven years, warring with the Arabs, he sustained a principality of his own. The ruins of Ḳaṣr el-'Abd and the adjacent caves of 'Arâḳ el-Emîr, the Cliffs-of-the-Prince, still testify to the accuracy of Josephus's description of the fortress which Hyrkanus built, and furnish us with proofs of the wealth of his generation and the styles of its architecture. In the neighbouring Khurbet eṣ-Ṣâr there is perhaps an echo of the name which he gave to his place, Ṣûr, in Greek Tyros or Tyre.[1] The remains of a rude and lavish grandeur are everywhere visible. A high and dry plateau was converted, by a strong dam and by an aqueduct from the distant sources of the stream above which it lies, into a lake or broad moat. In the middle

*Hyrkanus and his Fortress, Ṣûr.*

[1] According to the *P.E.F. Mem.*, 'Eastern Palestine,' Kh. [eṣ] Ṣâr, W. of 'Arâḳ el-Emîr, was itself a place of importance on a site 500 yards square by an ancient road from 'Ammân. The identifiable masonry is Roman ; but the ruined tower may have been an outpost of Hyrkanus's fortress. Close by there is a Kh. es-Ṣûr, whether spelt with a Sin or a Ṣad is doubtful. The Wâdy es-Sir, above which Ḳaṣr el-'Abd and 'Araḳ el-Emîr lie, has its name from another root, and means W. of the Sheepfold (so 'E. Palestine,' 277).

of this, upon an artificial mound connected with the
shore by a causeway, a considerable palace was erected.
The stones, all large, some vast, were carefully dressed, and
on the walls were the figures of great animals.[1]  In the
cliff which rises to the west two tiers of caves open, one
from the ground, the other from a terrace which is
approached by a sloping ramp and has at one end a
great detached block curiously carved with pigeon-holes.[2]
Some of the upper caves, with their side chambers, have
many mangers; they were the stables of the cavalry used
by Hyrkanus against the Arabs.  Others with corniced
roofs and deep carvings were, as Josephus describes, for
sleeping, feeding and living in.  On the sides of the
entrances to two on the lower tier are inscribed the
consonants of the name Ṭobiah, either the Hebrew name

---

[1] Josephus's description is in xii. *Ant.* iv. II.  The part of the plateau converted into a lake is some 320 yards broad ; walled to the N.W. by the long
cliff and protected on the N. by a knoll ; the dam runs round the S. and E. ;
the aqueduct is from the N. ; the causeway runs N.E. from the island.
The palace is 126 ft. by 62, and was probably 21 or 22 ft. high.  The
stones, boss and margin, are pick-dressed ; two of the largest are 20 ft. by
10, and 17, 4 by 8 by 2, 8.  The capitals of some pillars are peculiar, most
nearly resembling Egyptian, but other details seem a rough reproduction of
the Greek.  I take the figures from the *P.E.F. Mem.*, ' E. Palestine,' where
the account is clear and thorough, but the description I give from my own
examination of the site.  The nomads have already begun to settle upon it,
and we must expect the ruins to diminish.  I found a man building a
house whose fathers had been tent-dwellers (see above, vol. i. 286).  See
further both for the ruins and the caves Duc de Luynes, *Voyage*, 138 ff. ;
De Vogüé, *Temple de Jérusalem*, Pl. 35, and *Revue Archéol.*, 1864, 208 ff.,
1865, 31 ff. ; De Saulcy, *Ibid.* 137 ff. ; Merrill, *E. of the Jordan*, 106 ff. ;
Conder, *Heth and Moab*, 170; Gautier, *Au delà du Jourdain*, 118 ff. ;
Driver, *Text of the Bks. of Samuel*, xxi. ; and especially Clermont-Ganneau,
*Arch. Researches in Palestine*, ii. 261 ff.

[2] The purpose of this (16½ feet high by 12½ broad and 7 thick) and its
twenty-six niches or pigeon-holes is uncertain.  Was it to light up the
terrace ?  Our Arab guide said there is a similar one at Merj el Ḥammâm,
N.W. of Madaba, on the road from 'Ammân.

'ARÁḲ EL-EMÎR—CLIFF OF THE PRINCE
with the Two Tiers of Caves, part of the fortress of Tyrus or Sûr C. 180 B.C.

Plate XIV.

of Hyrkanus himself, or the proof of his continued pride in his family.[1] To have seen these remains is to understand the character and ambitions of this Jewish clan from whom their nation had gained so much, but was destined to suffer unspeakable evils. If one of their bastards, whom they had themselves disowned, could build a fortress and a state like this and hold it seven years in defiance of the Seleucid authority and against the fierce tribes of Arabia, we can appreciate the influence of the family in Jerusalem and at the court of Antioch : the wealth of their resources, the undaunted front they showed to foreign powers, the ambition they cherished of being kings themselves. With their command of the fiscal arrangements of the country, with their unscrupulous energy and skill, they easily outmatched the priestly aristocracy of Jerusalem, and made themselves indispensable to the Greek monarchy. The impecuniousness of this dynasty and its eagerness to Hellenise its subjects were equal temptations to the Jewish factions to outbid each other for its patronage, by promises of increased tribute and of the adoption of Greek fashions.

*Proofs of the Power of the Tobiads.*

So at least the author of Second Maccabees makes

---

[1] See Cl.-Ganneau *op. cit.*, who cites the custom among Jews of the time of having two names, Greek and Hebrew, and reminds us that Hyrkanus may have had his Hebrew name from his grandfather Tobiah, according to another Jewish fashion, and appeals to 2 Macc. iii. 11, where some of the treasure in the Temple is said to be that of Ὑρκανοῦ τοῦ Τοβίου, which may be translated Hyrkanus Tobias and not Hyrkanus son of Tobias. Most accounts of the inscription treat it as if it were single ; but I saw and photographed *two* copies, one on the *left* of the entrance to a large cave on the lower tier which the peasants call ej-Jâyah, the other on the *right* of the entrance to another cave to which our guide gave the same name. This second is the inscription described in the *P.E.F. Mem.* ; it is the better preserved of the two. See Plate XIII.

clear, and as he ascribes the original cause of his people's
misfortunes to her factions rather than to the
tyranny of her foreign lords, we may receive
the substance of his narrative as true. According to him everything was going well at Jerusalem when
Onias III. was High-priest in the early years of Seleucus IV.
(187-175). The High-priesthood remained secure with
its hereditary possessors. The Temple was respected
by the Greeks, and 'of his own revenues the King bore all
the costs belonging to the service of the sacrifices.'[1] It
is no wonder that the whole population rejected the
Egyptian offers of Hyrkanus about 182. They had
reason to be content with their present lords and looked
forward to years of peace. But then a Tobiad named
Simon, the elder brother of Hyrkanus according to some,[2]
and at least an adherent of the family, who was the civil
guardian of the Temple, having quarrelled with the High-
priest about the management of the city-market, went off
to Apollonius the governor of Coelesyria, with a story
that the Temple treasury was full of moneys not devoted
to sacred purposes but exigible by the King. Apollonius
reported the news to Seleucus, who sent his chancellor
Seleucus IV.
sends Helio-
dorus to ex-
amine the
Temple
Treasures.
Heliodorus to make inquiry. Onias received
the chancellor courteously, and explained that
the Treasury held only 400 talents of silver
and 200 of gold, and that these were the
deposits of widows and orphans with other private
moneys, including some belonging to Hyrkanus; to con-
fiscate them would be to violate the trust which men put
in the sanctity of a Temple honoured over the world.[3]

---

[1] 2 Macc. iii. 3.  [2] See above, vol. i. 399 *n*. 1.
[3] On the Temple as a Bank see above, vol. i. 354, 365.

Plate XV.

'ARÂḲ EL-EMÎR—CLIFF OF THE PRINCE.

Entrance to one of the Caves on the lower Tier with the Inscription: ṬOBIYAH.

But Heliodorus claimed everything for the King, and asserted his right of search. It was at once a sacrilege and an assault upon public security. Consternation fell upon the priesthood and people, and they cried unto God. 'When Heliodorus and his guards appeared over against the treasury, the Sovereign of Spirits and of all authority caused a great apparition so that all who had presumed to enter fainted and were sore afraid.' A horse with a terrible rider in golden armour rushed fiercely at Heliodorus and smote him with its forefeet, while two young men who stood by scourged him with many sore stripes, and he was carried off dying. But Onias magnanimously prayed for his life, and the same figures that beat him having assured him in a dream that he was revived for Onias's sake, he sacrificed and returned with his strange story to the King. When the King asked him what manner of man he should send to Jerusalem to complete the business, Heliodorus with grim humour advised him 'to despatch any enemy or conspirator against the state, and thou shalt have him back again well scourged, for of a truth there is about the place a power of God.'[1]

Simon, however, declared to Apollonius that the 'apparition' had been arranged by Onias, and further slandered the latter as a conspirator against the state.[2] Onias therefore travelled straight to the King, careful not so much for his own defence as for the interest of the commonwealth, 'for he saw that without the King's providence it was impossible for the state to have peace any more, and that Simon would not cease from his madness.' He was detained at the court, and his brother Jeshua' or Jason, in intrigue with the

*Onias ousted by Jason his brother.*

---

[1] 2 Macc. iii.  [2] 'Επίβουλον τῶν πραγμάτων : 2 Macc. iv. 2.

Tobiadæ, took advantage of his absence to supplant him.

Antiochus IV.
Epiphanes,
175-164.

In 175 Seleucus was murdered and succeeded by his brother Antiochus IV., who called himself Epiphanes, The God-Manifest, but was nicknamed Epimanes, The Maniac.[1] Both epithets are required to characterise the monarch, on whose powerful but unbalanced mind the fortunes of Israel now depended. Sensible people, says Polybius, knew not what to make of him; some thought him a plain, blunt fellow,[2] others a madman. For nearly fourteen years he had lived as a hostage at Rome, in the corrupt idleness of such a life; and then for some time at Athens, where he acted as a magistrate.[3] He knew the world, and as king could conceive great things: in religion, in art, in liberality, and even in war. In sacrifices in various cities and in honours to the gods he exceeded all who had reigned before him.[4] When he heard of the games celebrated in Macedonia by Æmilius Paulus, resolving to surpass their magnificence, he provided and personally marshalled at

---

[1] Epiphanes is not the ordinary epithet 'illustrious' (though Athenæus, v. 25, seems to take it in this sense), but an abbreviation of the title Θεὸς Ἐπιφανής, which Antiochus himself assumes on some of his coins (Head, *Hist. Num.* 641 ; Macdonald, *Catalogue of Greek Coins in the Hunterian Museum*, iii. pp. 44 ff., Nos. 21 ff.), and which means 'the God who manifests himself.' It seems Egyptian in origin (cf. above on Amenhotep IV., pp. 19 f., 24), and the first Greek monarch who assumed it was Ptolemy V. Of Antiochus IV., Macdonald *op. cit.* p. 41 says: 'Evidence of the divine honours accorded him in his lifetime is borne by his coins, not merely through the inscription (Nos. 21 ff.), but also through the appearance of stars on the diadem (Nos. 4, etc.), and through the idealisation of the head (Nos. 5, etc.).' It is Polybius who reports that he was nicknamed Epimanes (Pol. xxvi. 10, preserved in Athenæus x.). For further literature on the subject see Schürer, *Gesch.*[(3)] i. 192 f. *n.* 21, and add Ramsay, *Cities of St. Paul*, 252.

[2] Ἀφελῆ : Shuckburgh translates 'a good-natured, easy-going man.'

[3] His name stands the first of three magistrates on a coin of Athens described by Macdonald, *op. cit.* ii. 61, No. 96.

[4] Polybius, xxvi. 10 ; Athenæus, x. 63.

Daphne an extraordinary parade and festival.[1] Polybius
also calls him an able general and worthy of the royal
name.[2] He remembered his magistracy at Athens, and
putting on a citizen's cloak he canvassed the Agora of
Antioch for the offices of Agoranomos and of Demarch.[3]
When elected he would give his decisions upon the
market-cases with great zest. He mixed with the common
people of his capital, and chattered on art with all the
craftsmen. But he was also a heavy drinker,[4] and indulged in the oddest pranks. He joined in the horseplay
of the public baths, and when he heard of parties of young
people feasting together he would break in upon them,
with horn and bagpipe, to their terror and instant flight.
His freaks of favour and liberality were extraordinary:
on some he would lavish gold, on others dice, dates,
drenches of ointment.[5] In short, Antiochus IV. was a
monster of impulses, with these additional dangers: that
he never forgot he had a mission in life and was never out
of need of money. The Roman world remembered him
as the monarch who undertook to replace the superstitions of his Asian subjects by the gift of Greek manners,[6]
and Polybius says that he sacrilegiously plundered most
of the Temples within his reach.[7] His boisterousness
and his piety, his equal zest for games and for civic

---

[1] Polybius, xxxi. 3 f. (Oxf. ed., 1823, iv. 118 ff.), preserved in Athenæus,
v. 22-24, x. 53.

[2] xxvii. 17, Oxf. ed., Tom. iv. p. 40; xxviii. 18, in Shuckburgh's translation. Polybius excepts the bad tactics of Antiochus at Pelusium.

[3] Ædile and Tribune.

[4] Athenæus, x. 52, quoting the *Hypomnemata* of Ptolemy Euergetes II.;
Müller, *Frag. Hist. Graec.* iii. 186.

[5] The above description is abridged from Polybius, xxvi. 10, preserved by
Athenæus, v. 21; cf. x. 52: Oxford ed. of Polybius, 1823, Tom. iv.
pp. 15 ff.

[6] Tacitus, *Hist.* v. 8.          [7] xxxi. 4, in Athenæus, v. 24.

duties, testify to a nature saturated with the spirit with which he believed it to be his divine duty to infect his peoples. Alike in its lowest and its highest forms Antiochus Epiphanes was Hellenism incarnate, but Hellenism with its head turned and gnawed by a hunger for gold. He is reported to have died mad.[1]

If ever a nemesis were apparent in the history of men, it was so now, in the conjunction of this Greek monster

*Jason intro-*
*duces Greek*
*Fashions to*
*Jerusalem.*

with the Hellenising factions in Jerusalem. Having received an audience from Antiochus, Jason promised in return for the gift of the High-priesthood a large addition to the Jewish tribute, 440 talents of silver; and undertook to furnish 150 more if authority were given him to erect a Gymnasium in Jerusalem and to register the inhabitants as Antiochenes. Confirmed as High-priest, Jason ' forthwith brought over them of his own race to the Greek fashion.' He built the Gymnasium under the Akra, where it enjoyed the protection of the Greek garrison, but was near enough to the Temple to attract the younger priests by its summons to the game of the Discus.[2] He also caused the youths of priestly families and other young nobles to wear the Greek cap. 'And thus,' says the pious chronicler, to whom we owe these details,[3] 'there was an extreme of Greek fashions and the advance of an alien religion by reason of the exceeding profaneness of Jason, that ungodly man and no High-priest.' But in such measures Jason would not have succeeded without the influence of

---

[1] Polybius, xxxi. 11 (Oxf. ed., iv. 131). The more favourable view by Ramsay, *Cities of St. Paul*, 181 ff., does not refer to the above data.

[2] It lay either in the Tyropœon or the Ḳidron Valley, probably on the same site on which Herod built his Hippodrome (see below, ch. xvii.).

[3] For all this paragraph see 2 Macc. iv. 7-22 ; cf. 1 Macc. i. 11-15.

a strong Hellenic party among the citizens, some welcoming the exhilaration of Greek life and some the intellectual power of Greek institutions.[1] Further, he sent to Tyre three hundred silver drachmæ, as the contribution of the now Antiochene citizens of Jerusalem to the sacrifices of Heracles or Baal-Melkart.[2] Antiochus visited Jerusalem and Jason received him magnificently. The wily King saw for himself the political situation. But, although doubtless after his manner he roistered with all the Hellenisers, he would be ignorant of the strong and still silent force of the opposite party.

In 171 another Tobiad, Menelaus, the brother of Simon,[3] was sent by Jason to Antioch with the annual tribute. He used his opportunity to secure the High-priesthood for himself, outbidding Jason by three hundred talents of silver! On his return to Jerusalem, bringing, says the historian, nothing worthy of the High-priesthood but having the passion of a tyrant and the rage of a beast, he drove out Jason, who fled across Jordan. Failing to furnish the increased moneys he had promised, Menelaus was summoned to Antioch along with Sostratus the Greek governor of the Akra, who was responsible for the tribute. On their arrival Antiochus was absent in Cilicia, and Menelaus bribed the deputy to kill Onias, while Lysimachus his brother, whom he had left in charge of his office in Jerusalem in order to supply him with money, laid unholy hands upon the golden vessels of the Temple. This sacrilege was too much for the common people, who

*Menelaus supplants Jason.*

---

[1] See above, pp. 393 f., 402 ff.  [2] Vol. i. Plate IX., Nos. 5 and 6.
[3] Vol. i. p. 399 *n.*

rose against the armed bands of Lysimachus, while the Senate sent three legates to Tyre to accuse Menelaus before the King.[1]  By bribing certain officials Menelaus won the King to his side, and the legates were executed. ' Menelaus, through the covetousness of them that were in power, remained in office.' [2]

The factions at Jerusalem were still influenced by the rivalry between Egypt and Syria for the possession of Palestine.[3]  In 170 Antiochus marched into Egypt, and upon a rumour of his death there, Jason with a thousand men took Jerusalem by surprise, and Menelaus threw himself into the Akra, which still had its Greek garrison.  Antiochus, stung by this revolt, abandoned his unsuccessful campaign against Egypt, and in a frenzy marched on Jerusalem.  He took the City, drove out Jason, and for three days delivered the population to massacre.  Eighty thousand are said to have perished, but the number is doubtless exaggerated.  Under the guidance of Menelaus the King presumed to enter the Temple, polluted the sacred vessels with his own hands, dragged down the offerings dedicated by other kings, and took his departure with one thousand eight hundred talents from the treasury.[4]  He left Philip, a barbarous Phrygian, in command of the

*Occupation of Jerusalem by Antiochus, 170 B.C.*

---

[1] See vol. i. 392 f.

[2] 2 Macc. iv. 23-50.

[3] Josephus, i. *B.J.* i. 1:—Antiochus Epiphanes, quarrelling with Ptolemy VI. about his right to the whole country of Syria, a great sedition arose among the δυνατοί in Judæa.  Onias (this is an error for Jason) having got the upper hand, cast the sons of Tobias out of the City, who fled to Antiochus. He took Jerusalem and slew many of the adherents of Ptolemy.

[4] So 2 Macc. v. 21 ; 1 Macc. i. 20 ff. says that he carried off the golden altar and candlestick, the table of shewbread, the plated gold and silver and the hidden treasures.

Akra and Menelaus as High-priest, 'who worse than all the rest exalted himself against his fellow-citizens.'[1]

In 168 Antiochus resumed operations against Egypt, but was presented by a Roman ambassador, Popilius Laenas, with a decree of the Senate forbidding him to make further attempts on that country. This was the first effective interference by Rome in the affairs of Egypt and Palestine; it secured the safety of the former, but it drove the energy of Antiochus to a more thorough Hellenising of the latter.[2] He sent Apollonius, one of his principal fiscal officers, into Judæa. Pretending peace, Apollonius took Jerusalem on a Sabbath, put a great number of the citizens to the sword, and strengthened the Akra with better walls and a larger garrison. The City walls were torn down, Jerusalem organised as a Greek city, and the worship of Greek deities enforced throughout the land at the point of the sword. The surrounding Greek populations were enlisted in the work. Circumcision and the observance of the Sabbath were forbidden. Jews were compelled to eat swine's flesh and to sacrifice to idols. But worst of all, in December 168, on the 15th Kislev of the 145th Seleucid year, a heathen altar was built on the site of the Altar of Burnt Offering, and on the

*Capture and Devastation by Apollonius, 168 B.C.*

[1] 2 Macc. v. 1-23; Jos. i. *B.J.* i. 1. As Schürer points out (*Gesch.*[(3)] i. 196 *n.* 30), the former account from Jewish sources displays more knowledge of the internal affairs of the Jews, the latter from Greek sources more of the wider political situation—the rivalry of the Ptolemies and Seleucids, the adherence of Menelaus and the Tobiads to Antiochus, the adherence of the rest to Ptolemy VI. The accounts are thus independent of each other, and the errors of Josephus (see p. 434 *n.* 2) explicable. Cf. the summary, 1 Macc. i. 16-28.

[2] Polybius, xxix. ii.; Diod. Siculus, xxxi. 2; Livy, xlv. 12; Appian, *Syr.* 66.

25th Kislev — how the exact dates were branded on the memory of the Jews!—sacrifices were offered upon it to Zeus Olympios. This was *the abomination of desolation spoken of by Daniel the prophet.* The finest buildings in the town were burned, and the walls, as of the town, so of the Sanctuary, were breached. The Temple itself was not destroyed, but stripped and 'filled with riotings and revels.' 'The Sanctuary was laid waste like a wilderness.'[1]

---

[1] 2 Macc. v. 24-vi. ; 1 Macc. i. 29-64, iv. 38, 60 ; Josephus, i. *B.J.* i. 1 f., xii. *Ant.* v. 4 f.

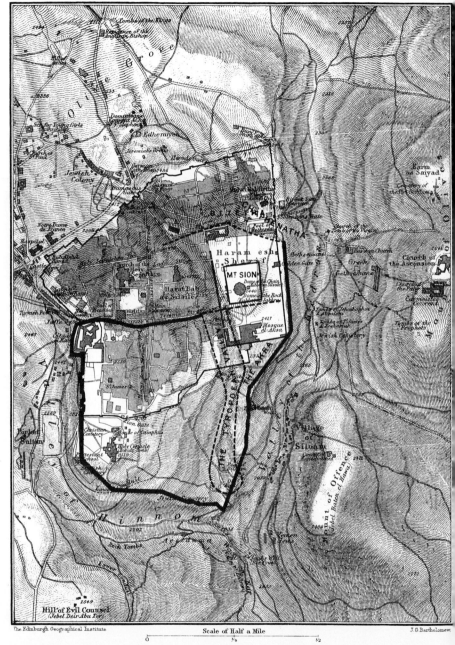

The continuous red lines are the Ancient City Walls, destroyed and restored during this Period. The dotted red lines on either side of the Tyropoeon are alternative suggestions for the rampart built to shut off the Akra from Jerusalem. The dotted red line round the North of the Haram area, is the supposed line of the Second North Wall of the Period. Its course is unknown from the N.W. corner of the area to the present Citadel.

This map has not been printed in the original color. The red line has been replaced by a heavy black line.

# CHAPTER XVI

## JERUSALEM UNDER THE MACCABEES AND HASMONEANS

### 168-38 B.C.

FROM this point onwards it will not be necessary to treat the History with so much detail as we have hitherto devoted to it, for in our survey of the government and institutions of Israel we have had occasion to record[1] most of the Plan of the Rest of this Work. events which determined the fortunes of Jerusalem under the Maccabees, the Hasmoneans, Herod and the Romans. We may confine ourselves to descriptions of the City and of the character of her population during those periods, with brief historical summaries where such are still needed. In the present chapter we begin with Jerusalem under the Maccabees (using this conventional term for Judas and his brothers)[2] and under the Hasmonean Kings and High Priests, from John Hyrkanus to Antigonus, whom Sosius slew in 37 B.C.

[1] Vol. i. Bk. II. chs. ix. and x. ; cf. for the buildings of the walls, etc., Bk. I. ch. viii.

[2] The name Maccabee (Gr. μακκαβαιος or μακαβαιος, Syr. Maḳabî) is properly either the personal name or the title of Judas, and is confined to him till as late as Josephus. But the collector of the Apocrypha gave the plural form as the title of Four Books, dealing not only with Judas and his brethren and John Hyrkanus, but with all who acted or suffered with them (as well as, in 3rd Macc., with events before them), and from this the term Maccabees has come to be applied to all Jewish heroes and martyrs of the

437

Maccabean Jerusalem occupied virtually the same site within the same lines of fortification which we have traced for the time of Nehemiah :[1] that is to say, most of the East Hill and all the South-West Hill, with part of the North-West Hill and the Tyropœon valley. The West, South and East Walls still followed the natural lines of fortification above the encompassing valleys and across the mouth of the Tyropœon ;[2] but the North Wall, the Second of Josephus, ran along an uncertain line from the present citadel to the rock at the north-west corner of the Ḥaram area, and thence on the southern slope of the tributary ravine to the Ḳidron, somewhere near the present 'Solomon's Throne.'[3] These limits represent approximately a circumference of 12,000 feet, or over twenty stadia.[4] If we include the northern suburb up

*Maccabean Jerusalem: Its Size,*

time. The meaning of the name is uncertain. It is usually taken from the Hebrew מַקֶּבֶת, *hammer*, and treated as a title bestowed on Judas after his numerous beatings of the Greeks. But neither its form (adjectival) nor the use of it in 1st or 2nd Macc. supports this idea. The latter rather suggests that it was given at birth to the son of Mattathias, in which case the possible derivations of it are many (whether from מקב or נקב). It is also doubtful whether it was originally spelt with a single or double *ḳ* (ק) for the Greek κκ sometimes stands for the Semitic ḳ ; and in Niese's ed. of Josephus the Greek is four times out of five spelt with a single k. See S. I. Curtiss, *The Name Machabee* (he derives it from כבה, *to quench*); Schürer, *Gesch.*[(3)] § 4 note 47 ; Niese, *Kritik der beiden Makkabäerbücher*, 1 ; Fairweather, 'Maccabees' in Hastings' *D.B.* ; C. C. Torrey, 'Maccabees (Family)' in *Enc. Bibl.* § 1 ; Winckler, *K.A.T.*[(3)] 304 (a mythol. origin of the name).—On the name Hasmonean, which properly covers the Maccabean brethren as well as the dynasty that Simon founded, see vol. i. 407 *n.* 3.

[1] Vol. i. 196 ff.

[2] Vol. i. Bk. I. chs. i. f., vi.-viii. Timochares (see below, p. 439 *n.* 2), the biographer of an Antiochus, either IV. or VII., describes steep ravines on *every* side, which, of course, is wrong.

[3] Vol. i. 33 f., 200 ff., 243, 247 ff.    [4] If the stadium = 582 ft.

to the present wall we get nearly 16,000 feet, which is about the twenty-seven stadia stated for the perimeter of the City by Xenophon the topographer in the first century B.C.[1] But we should require to go out some distance upon the northern plateau in order to compass the forty and fifty stadia which are reckoned by other writers of the Greek period.[2] They have probably exaggerated. Even Josephus, after the Third Wall was built, does not venture on more than thirty-three.[3]

Apart from her suburbs the City thus covered an area of about three-fourths of a mile north and south by three-fifths east and west;[4] and consisted of three divisions, for the clear distinction of which in the records of the time we are prepared by her previous history: (1) the Town, or bulk of the City, generally called Jerusalem; (2) the Temple Mount, separately fortified; and (3) the Akra, or Citadel, which threatened and embarrassed, if it did not actually dominate, the Temple.

*and its Three Divisions.*

One of the later Pilgrim-Psalms has praised Jerusalem

---

[1] Identified with the author of the *Triangulation of Syria.* Quoted by Alexander Polyhistor and Eusebius, *Praep. Evang.* ix. 36; Müller, *Frag. Hist. Graec.* iii. 228-9; Reinach, *Textes*, etc., 54.

[2] Hecatæus of Abdera, or the Pseudo-Hecatæus (quoted by Josephus, *C. Apion.* i. 22; Müller, ii. 392; Fr., 14; Reinach, 227 ff.), gives 50 stadia; the Letter of Aristeas (p. 538 of Thackeray's ed. in Swete's *Introd. to O.T. in Gk.*), 40, 'so far as one can guess.' The 40 stadia of Timochares (quoted by Alex. Polyh. and Eus. *Praep. Evang.* ix. 35; Müller, iii. 228; Reinach, 53) are apparently reckoned round the edges of the encompassing ravines. Even if the circuit be reckoned along the beds of the ravines, this does not give more than 30 stadia.

[3] v. *B.J.* iv. 2. See last sentence of previous note.

[4] More exactly, from the south-east angle of the City to the rock at the north-west corner of the Ḥaram area, 4000 feet (nearly 1220 metres), and from the south-east corner of the Ḥaram area to the outside of the present citadel 3200 feet (about 975 metres).

as *built like a city that is compact together*.[1]  Such was
also the impression which the town made on
1. The Town.
another visitor within our period.  He says
that ' the mould or form of the City is well-proportioned.' [2]
Standing upon the Akra, which, as we shall see, lay on
the East Hill, this observer had the bulk of the town
before him on the South-West and North-West Hills,
and with remarkable fidelity to their configuration he
describes it thus : ' In the disposition of its towers and
of the thoroughfares which appear, some below, some
above, with the cross-streets through them, it has the
familiar [3] aspect of a theatre.[4]  For the ground is broken

---

[1] Psalm cxxii. 3.   The expression (a late Aramaic one) is taken by some in
an ethical sense (*e.g.* Coverdale : *that is at unity with itself*, cf. the LXX. ;
and Duhm : *built like the city where they gather in one mind*), but the term
*built* seems to shut us up to a material meaning for the phrase which is
parallel to it.   And so this is usually taken, though it seems true that the
writer has in view rather the sense of physical compactness and proportion,
as if *well-gathered together*, than that of recent and solid fortification.   In
Aramaic the root חבר is sometimes used in a physical sense : cf. Levy,
*Neuhebr. u. Chald. Wörterbuch*, ii. 7 f.

[2] Τῆς δὲ πόλεώς ἐστι τὸ χύμα [cod. B. σχῆμα] συμμέτρως ἔχον : Letter of
Aristeas, Thackeray's ed. in Swete's *Intro. to O.T. in Gr.* 538.   In his
translation (London : Macmillan, 1904) Thackeray renders 'the extent of
the city is moderate,' but from what follows the above seems the more
probable meaning of the original, though Thackeray's translation suits better
a later use by the author of the same expression.

[3] Reading with Redpath (*apud* Thackeray) εἰθισμένως for εἰθισμένων.

[4] 'Thoroughfares,' διόδοι : 'cross-streets,' διεξόδοι.   Thackeray (*Trans.*
24 *n.*) reverses these meanings, taking the latter to be the 'thoroughfares'
(cf. xxii. 9) and the former to be the 'cross-streets' (cf. the LXX. addition
to Jer. ii. 28).   But the thoroughfares or main streets of Jerusalem which
have persisted to the present day are those which alone could be described
as appearing some above and some below, for they run from north to south
of the City, whereas the cross-streets are those which descend at right
angles to them.   Besides, in Matt. xxii. 9, which refers to country roads,
the main roads are ὅδοι, and the διεξόδοι, those which lead through and out of
them.   But the proof seems to me clenched by the stairs which are said
to lead to the διόδοι : the stairs would mostly (though not altogether) be as
to-day, towards the thoroughfares running north and south.

up, as the City is built on a mountain. And there are stairs towards the thoroughfares.' Another sentence seems to refer to that use of the housetops and roofs of lanes which was characteristic of Jerusalem. 'Some persons take their way above, others underneath; this distinction of travelling being chiefly on account of those who are undergoing purification, so that they may touch nothing improper.'[1] Thus the aspect of the City must have been what it has so constantly remained: the houses thickly packed, the main lines of street perhaps a little more visible than they are to-day; but with no conspicuous buildings, save the towers at the gateways and elsewhere round the walls. No palace nor citadel is noted by this observer looking west on the town from his point of vantage on the East Hill. But as to that we shall find a change under the Hasmonean kings, and especially under Herod.[2] As to the fortifications of the City—in distinction from those of the Temple and the Akra—we are left in doubt. We have seen that they were repaired to some effect by a High-priest Simon in the course of the third century.[3] That Jason required only one thousand men to take the town as distinct from the Akra, or that Apollonius easily captured it,[4] is no proof that

---

[1] The original indeed connects this sentence with what has gone before by γὰρ; but this seems to be due to some confusion, because a person desirous of avoiding unholy contacts could as little effect his purpose on the higher as on the lower thoroughfares, and the higher were the further from the Temple. The other meaning given above seems the only possible one.

[2] This seems to me one proof of the early date of the Letter of Aristeas, or at least of the material embodied in this part of his work. Schürer assigns it on other grounds to about 200 B.C. If the author had written, as some maintain, in the first century B.C. or later, he could not have failed to notice the palace of the Hasmoneans and Herod's palace and citadel, as he looked west from the East Hill.

[3] Vol. i. 391 ; vol. ii. 386.          [4] Above, pp. 434 f.

the walls were poor or badly breached. There were other reasons for the ease with which these conquests were effected. None of the observers in our period, however, seems to have been so much impressed with the town's fortifications as he was with those of the Temple. Ben Sira, Hecatæus (or the Pseudo-Hecatæus) and the Letter of Aristeas say little, or nothing, of the City Walls, while they emphasise the strength of the Sanctuary.[1]

The fortification of the Temple, for which it was so well adapted by its site, was inaugurated (as we have seen) by Solomon,[2] who, however, included also his palace and other government build-ings. After the Exile the Second Temple was separately fortified long before the walls of the City were restored;[3] and, in the third century, one or other of the two High-priests called Simon not only increased its substructures and cisterns, but built a wall and bulwark round it: *in his days the Temple was fortified.*[4] Hecatæus, or his imitator, in describing Jerusalem, says:[5] 'About the middle of the City is a circumvallation of stone 5 plethra long by 100 cubits broad [about 485 feet by 145, or 172][6] with double gates.' The Letter of Aristeas, after stating that Jerusalem lies on a mountain in the middle

2. The Temple-Fortress.

---

[1] Ecclesiasticus li. 4; Hec. or the Ps.-Hec. in *C. Apion.* i. 22; Letter of Arist. in Thackeray's ed., cf. p. 534 on the Temple with 538 on the City.

[2] Above, p. 69 f.     [3] Above, pp. 310, 332, 335 f.

[4] Ecclesiasticus l. 1-4 (the Hebr. text in Schechter and Taylor; *Wisdom of Ben Sira*, pp. xlvi. and (19).

[5] In Josephus *C. Apion.* i. 22 (see above, p. 383) it must always be remembered that even if we have to do here with the work not of the real but of a Pseudo-Hecatæus, many of the details given were probably borrowed from the former.

[6] Taking the plethron at 97 Eng. feet and the Gk. cubit at 17½ inches. *Enc. Bibl.* col. 4942 takes the 5 pl. as 485½ Eng. ft. If the longer Egyptian cubit be meant the breadth is 172¼ Eng. ft.

of Judæa, proceeds : ' Upon the crest was built the Temple, of magnificent appearance ; and the three encompassing walls, more than 70 cubits [120 feet] high, and of a breadth and length suitable to the House, the whole built off with unrivalled profusion and munificence.' It also describes the huge doorway of the House with the great curtain ; the Altar of Burnt Offering of a size in keeping with the place, and with the number of sacrifices upon it ; the House itself facing east ; the sloping floors of the Court flushed with water from the marvellous and indescribable reservoirs below the surface, so that the blood of the sacrifices is swept away in the twinkling of an eye ; and it adds the well-known report (which it gives us no means of verifying) of a copious natural spring within the precincts.[1] From all these testimonies—as also from the natural contours of the site—the separate standing and the fortification of the Temple are clear to us. The Second Temple was a fortress by itself, and its surrounding walls—said by the Letter to be three in number, though probably it includes the wall of the inner court— were apparently much more formidable than the walls of the City. The only calculation of the dimensions which is given [2] is at once striking and puzzling: the length, 485 feet, is approximately that, east and west, of the present platform round the Dome of the Rock, and is probably correct; nor does the breadth, 145 or 172 feet, seem inadequate when we remember that Solomon's Sanctuary was only 55 feet broad,[3] and that the Second Temple

---

[1] Thackeray's ed. in Swete's *Intr. to O. T. in Greek*, 534 f. On the question of the Temple Spring see vol. i. 85 f. ; on the Temple reservoirs (which it declares extend for five stadia round the Temple foundations !), vol. i. 119 ff.

[2] Above, p. 442.      [3] Above, p. 62.

was doubtless built to the same scale. It is interesting to notice that if the 100 cubits which Hecatæus gives as the breadth of the Temple enclosure were Egyptian cubits (and therefore about 172 English feet), this is exactly the dimension which Ezekiel prescribes in both directions for his inner court.[1] In any case we must conceive of the Maccabean Temple and its courts as occupying at the most little more than the space of the present platform round the Dome of the Rock. All the rest of the Temple Mount, now masked by the level surface of the Ḥaram area, at that time steeply descended on its natural contours from the base of the Temple Walls, and was perhaps covered as in Neḥemiah's day by the houses of priests and traders. Solomon's Palace and other government buildings had long ago disappeared. For what we have now to discuss about the Akra let us keep in mind that the Temple-fortress of this time did not in all probability extend more than 100 feet south of the Rock eṣ-Ṣakhra.

The earliest notice of the Akra or citadel is the one preserved by Josephus: that it was occupied by an Egyptian garrison when in 198 B.C. the Jews welcomed Antiochus the Great to Jerusalem, and that they helped him to besiege it.[2] In the subsequent contests of the factions the Akra was garrisoned by Seleucid soldiers, and when Jason took the town by surprise his rival Menelaus, the creature of the Seleucids, fled to it for refuge.[3] Through all the Maccabean wars the Akra remained in Seleucid hands till Simon took it in 142. In the First Book of Maccabees the Akra is

3. The Akra.

---

[1] Ezek. xl. 47.
[2] Josephus xii. *Ant.* iii. 3; see above, p. 380.
[3] See above, p. 434; 2 Macc. v. 5-7.

described as fortified by *a great and strong wall with strong towers*, so that *it became a great trap, an ambush against the Sanctuary*;[1] its garrison were able to *shut up Israel in the holy places*;[2] and in order to blockade it Jonathan built *a great mound between the Akra and the City*.[3]  Such passages assure us of the distinctness of the Akra both from the City and the Temple.

Its Distinctness.

But when we try to fix the exact site of this citadel, difficulties arise and opinion is divided.  By the author of First Maccabees the Akra is identified with 'the City of David,'[4] that is the earlier Jebusite stronghold of Ṣion.  If we accept this identification the question is at once solved, for, as we have seen, the stronghold Ṣion lay on the East Hill, south of and below the Temple, or immediately above Giḥon.[5]  But both because some refuse to accept this position for Ṣion, and because even if all were convinced of the fact it would still be possible that by 100 B.C., the date of First Maccabees, the name 'City of David' had migrated from its original position to some other prominent point in Jerusalem, it will be best to investigate anew the evidence for the site of the Akra.

Question of its Site.

Theories of the position of the Akra are almost as numerous as the writers who have devoted attention to the subject; and the mere statement of them will show the difficulty, if not the impossibility, of reaching a certain decision.  We may select six of

Various Theories.

[1] I Macc. i. 33, 35 f. ; cf. Josephus xiii. *Ant.* vi. 7: 'a base from which the foe might assault Jerusalem'; and see on the whole subject above, vol. i. 157 ff.

[2] I Macc. vi. 18.

[3] *Ibid.* xii. 36.

[4] I Macc. i. 33; vii. 32; xiv. 36.

[5] Vol. i. Bk. I. ch. vi.

the principal: three which place the Akra west of the
Tyropœon and three which place it east of that valley.
(1) Some, holding still that Ṣion lay on the South-West
Hill, and accepting the identification of it with the Akra,
find the site on that of the present citadel by the Jaffa
Gate.[1] (2) Others place it on the lowest terrace of the
South-West Hill just above the Tyropœon, opposite the
south of the Ḥaram area.[2] (3) Many, not less convinced
that Ṣion lay on the South-West Hill, but refusing the
identification of it with the Akra, place the latter on the
North-West Hill, between the two branches of the Tyropœon, on an assumed rocky knoll east of the Holy
Sepulchre.[3] Those who hold that the Akra lay on the
East Hill are divided as to whether it was north or south
of the Temple. Thus (4) some place it on the prominent
rock at the north-west of the Temple area, where the
Hasmonean Baris was erected, and afterwards Herod's
Antonia, the site of the present Turkish barracks.[4] Of
those who hold that it must have stood south of the

---

[1] Rückert, *Die Lage des Berges Ṣion*, 87 ff. ; he further defends this position by arguing that the Akra lay on the periphery of Jerusalem.

[2] Tobler, *Topographie von Jerusalem*, etc., I. 29 ff. ; Mommert, *Topogr.
des alten Jerus.* i[er] Theil, 8[es] Kapitel ; iv[er] Theil, 6[es] Kap.

[3] Robinson, *B.R.* 410 ff., 567 ; *L.B.R.* 204 ff. ; Warren, *Temple and
Tomb*, 37 ; Conder, *Handbook to the Bible*, 346, and in Hastings' *D.B.* ii.
594 ; Henderson, *Palestine* (plan of ancient Jerusalem) ; Gatt, *Die Hügel von
Jerusalem*, 45 f.; Tenz, *P.E.F.Q.*, 1906, 158 (*two* Akras, the second being
south of the Temple), 1907, 290 ff.; Pierotti, *Jerus. Expl.*, appears to place
it in the Tyropœon, west of the Ḥaram wall.

[4] Thrupp, *Antient Jer.* 19 f., 178 f. ; W. R. Smith, 'Jerus.' in *Enc. Brit.*,[(9)]
*Enc. Bibl.* § 27 i. ('presumably') ; Wilson, Smith's *D.B.*[(2)] 'Jerus.' 1644 ;
in *P.E.F.Q.*, 1893, 164 ff., he argues against Birch for the north site ; cf.
Nevin, quoted by Watson, *P.E.F.Q.*, 1907, 206.  Rix, *Tent and Testament*,
226, suggests that the Akra rock was south of the present barracks, and was
cut down to the present flat surface there, the rock on which the barracks
stand being 'in fact a mere remnant of the Akra rock.'

Temple,[1] the most (5) equate it with the site which we have preferred for Ṣion, or 'the City of David,' immediately above Giḥon, the present Virgin's Spring;[2] but recently (6) a site closer to the Temple has been suggested, on the natural surface between the Rock eṣ-Ṣakhra and the south Ḥaram wall.[3]

The ancient evidence is conclusive that the Akra lay near enough to the Temple to threaten, but not to dominate, the circumvallations of the latter (which we must remember ran on a lower level than the Temple and its inner court), and to harass both its defenders and those who came up to sacrifice. We have seen the testimony to this in First Maccabees.[4] We refrain from adding that of the Letter of Aristeas, for its date is uncertain, and what it describes may be not the Akra but the later Baris. We can, however, quote the evidence of Josephus. He says that the Akra was adjacent to the Temple, so that the garrison, by sudden sorties, could destroy those who came up to sacrifice;[5] and elsewhere he calls it the Syrians' 'base of attack' from which they could harass Jerusalem.[6] Such evidence excludes the position proposed for the Akra on or by the site of the present citadel, which is certainly too far away from the Temple.

*The Akra most probably on East Hill, south of Temple.*

---

[1] So first Olshausen, *Zur Topogr. des alten Jerus.* (1833), pp. 4 f.; see Robinson, *B.R.* i. 567.

[2] Birch, *P.E.F.Q.*, 1886, 25 ff.; 1888, 44 f.; 1893, 324; 1906, 157; Benzinger, *Hebr. Arch.*(1) 47; Buhl, *G.A.P.* 142; G. A. Smith, *Enc. Bibl.* 'Jerus.' § 27 iii.; Schürer, *Gesch.*(3) i. 198 f. *n.* 37; Masterman, art. 'Jerus.' in Hastings' *Dict. of Christ and the Gospels*.

[3] Ch. Watson, *P.E.F.Q.*, 1906, 50 ff.; 1907, 204 ff.; Kuemmel, *Materialien zur Topogr. des alten Jerus.* 138 (he suggests it occupied the site of the Palace of Solomon, but reserves his argument).

[4] Above, p. 445.      [5] xii. *Ant.* ix. 3.

[6] xiii. *Ant.* vi. 7: ὁρμητήριον.

The sites proposed on the lower terrace of the South-West Hill, and on the North-West Hill below Calvary, are nearer. Though they are separated from the Temple Hill by the Tyropœon, a citadel upon either of them would overlook part, at least, of the wall surrounding the Temple Hill; and its garrison would be able by sorties to interfere with the approach of worshippers. But neither site agrees with the repeated statement of First Maccabees that the Akra was 'The City of David,' nor with the data of Josephus. His well-known description of Jerusalem, though of tantalising ambiguity, is most reasonably interpreted, in the light of other passages of his works, as associating the name Akra with the East Hill, south of the Temple area.[1] Here lay his Lower City in contrast to the Upper City on the South-West Hill, and separated from it by the Tyropœon 'which extended to Siloam.' Besides telling us that the Akra was built in the Lower City,[2] Josephus twice says that in

[1] v. *B.J.* iv. 1 describes Jerusalem as built on two hills divided by the Tyropœon, which 'extended as far as Siloam'; the higher and straighter hill sustaining the Upper City called the 'Upper Agora,' the lower and 'gibbous' (ἀμφίκυρτος) sustaining the Lower City called 'Akra.' These details suit the South-West, and the southern end of the East, Hills respectively. No one would have doubted this identification but for the addition that there was a third hill 'naturally lower than Akra,' and 'formerly parted from it by a broad valley.' Was this the Temple Summit, as distinct from the rest of the East Hill to the south of it? I agree with those who think it was, for as we have seen, there is a good deal of evidence that in O.T. times the East Hill after falling southward from the Temple summit rose into another separate elevation : Şion or The 'Ophel (*hump* or *swelling*; vol. i. Bk. i. ch. vi.). But in that case Josephus, writing of what had disappeared long before his time, was wrong in describing the Temple-summit as 'naturally lower' than it and dominated (xii. *Ant.* v. 4) by it. Those who maintain that the Upper Agora and Akra were the South-West and North-West Hills respectively, while the third hill was the East Hill, have to account for this fact, that in Josephus's own time the N.W. Hill was still separated by a valley, the Upper Tyropœon, from the East Hill.

[2] xii. *Ant.* v. 4.

his time the Lower City was called Akra;[1] while in another passage he connects the Akra with Siloam.[2] But such evidence is not only against the proposed sites on the South-West and North-West Hills; it is equally adverse to the site proposed on the East Hill north of the Temple, the rock on which the present Barracks stand, the site successively of the ancient Baris and Antonia. For this position is not in harmony with the statement that the Akra was 'the city of David,' and it lies too far from Siloam. Nor is it overlooked by the site of the Temple courts, as Josephus says the Akra rock was overlooked after this was cut down; nor can we conceive the Hasmoneans to have first reduced this rock and then raised a new Baris upon its site. On the whole, then, the evidence that the Akra stood on the East Hill and south of the Temple is stronger than the argument for any of the other sites which have been proposed for it.

We have still to inquire whether the Akra was so close to the Temple as both Sir Charles Watson and Herr Kuemmel have independently suggested, or whether it lay further south upon the site which we have selected for Sion or 'the City of David.'[3] Herr Kuemmel thinks that it occupied the site of Solomon's Palace, but reserves his argument for a future work. Sir Charles Watson's attractive theory implies that some five hundred feet south-east of es-Sakhra, the East Hill originally swelled up into another summit, forty feet higher than the Temple site, and that

*Rival Sites south of the Temple.*

---

[1] i. *B.J.* i. 4; v. *B.J.* iv. 1.
[2] v. *B.J.* vi. 1.
[3] See above, p. 445; cf. vol. i. Bk. I. ch. vi.

this summit was the position first of Ṣion, the Jebusite stronghold, and then of the Akra ; when the Hasmoneans destroyed the latter and reduced the rock on which it stood, the material was cast into the Tyropœon valley and the south-west corner of Herod's Temple was built down through it, as the excavations of Sir Charles Warren have shown. Sir Charles Watson says that his conclusions appear to him 'compatible with every statement in the authorities';[1] but this is a claim which students of the ancient documents upon Jerusalem will hardly regard as a recommendation to any theory. In fact, however, his premises and conclusions do not agree with the data of the Old Testament and First Maccabees. For while Sir Charles Watson identifies the site of Ṣion, the Jebusite stronghold, with that of the Akra, he sepa-rates from, and puts to the south of, it, 'the City of David'; whereas (as we have seen) 'the city of David' is identified with Ṣion by the Old Testament and with the Akra by First Maccabees.[2] Nor is it clear how Sir Charles Watson would find room for the Palace and other government buildings of Solomon, which lay below and to the south of the Temple,[3] if the fortress Ṣion lay so close, as he suggests, to the site of the latter. Again, can we receive without question the statement of Josephus that 'the third hill,' which Sir Charles Watson accepts as the Temple-hill,[4] was 'naturally lower' than the Akra, when elsewhere Josephus himself informs us that the Temple was built on 'the highest level part' of the East Hill,[5] that is the highest part level enough to carry a

---

[1] *P.E.F.Q.*, 1906, 52.

[2] Vol. i. Bk. I. ch. vi. ; vol. ii. 445.

[3] Above, p. 59.

[4] *P.E.F.Q.*, 1907, 209.

[5] v. *B.J.* v. I ; see above, p. 60.

building?[1] The whole theory requires for its establishment a wider as well as a more critical use of the ancient data. In our present ignorance of so much of the original surface of the East Hill no one will venture to say that there are no possibilities in the proposal; but at present it seems unworkable if we are to accept the evidence of the First Book of Kings and the Book of Jeremiah upon the Palace and other royal buildings.

While granting that there is still much uncertainty, I am inclined on the whole to adhere to the conclusions reached in the first volume of this work that the Akra occupied the same site as the ancient citadel, Ṣion, above Giḥon, or the Virgin's Spring. *Most probable Conclusion: Akra= Ṣion.* This suits the repeated statement of First Maccabees that the Akra was 'the City of David'; though it is possible that, like that of Ṣion, the name 'City of David' had shifted between Neḥemiah and the Maccabees. It suits the evidence of Josephus, for it places the Akra in closer connection with Siloam than does any of the other proposals. And it also agrees with the descriptions, in both those authorities, of the menace and danger which the Akra constituted towards the Temple and those who came up to worship. For while the position above Giḥon lies further from the site of the Temple than the other proposed positions for the Akra on the East Hill — indeed it is nearly five hundred yards distant — yet it is clear that even at that distance a strong and well-garrisoned citadel,

---

[1] Cf. also the testimony of the Letter of Aristeas that the Temple stood upon the crest of the hill on which Jerusalem was built; see above, p. 443. I do not quote in support the statement of I Macc. vii. 32 f., that Nikanor *went up* from the Akra to the Temple; for the Greek ἀνέβη may be used here in its technical sense of advancing with a hostile purpose.

upon an independent summit of the ridge such as rose here, before the Hasmoneans cut it down, was capable of doing all the mischief that the Akra is said to have done to the City and the Temple and the crowds which came up to the latter to sacrifice. We cannot fail to notice that Josephus emphasises this mischief as inflicted mainly by sorties from the Akra, which he calls 'a base of attack' against the Temple and the Town.[1] First Maccabees says that the garrison of the Akra were able to *shut up Israel in the holy places*;[2] but they would have as much difficulty in doing this if the Akra stood on any of the other proposed sites as if it stood on the site of Sion above Gihon. And it must be remembered that the garrison of the Akra held out against the Jews both of the Temple and the Town for many years. A position at some little distance from the Temple, and on the edge of the Kidron valley, better suits this fact than the position proposed by Sir Charles Watson. With the reservations, then, that we have still a great deal to learn from excavation, and that the historical data are far from conclusive, we may accept the opinion that the Akra most probably stood on the ridge of 'Ophel, somewhere above Gihon, upon a former summit which the Hasmoneans reduced to the level of the rest of the slope.

Throughout the Maccabean struggles these three parts of Jerusalem remain distinct: the Town, the Temple, and the Akra or Citadel. The condition in which each was left by the invasion and outrage of 168 B.C. is also clear. The Town was sacked and set on fire ; *its houses and walls were pulled down on*

Effects of the Outrages, 168 B.C.

---

[1] See above, p. 447.  [2] vi. 18,

*every side*; the inhabitants who escaped massacre and captivity fled to the wilderness; their places were filled by Greeks and apostate Jews, so that Jerusalem became *a habitation of strangers*, and *at the doors of the houses and in the streets they burnt incense.*[1] The Temple was *laid waste like a desert*; that is, while the sanctuary itself still stood, the priests were driven forth, the ritual ceased, *the priests' chambers were pulled down*, the courts and shrine were *profaned* by pagan feet, a Greek altar was built on the altar of burnt-offering, and sacrifices performed to the Olympian Zeus — *the appalling abomination*, as it is called in the Book of Daniel.[2] The Akra was re-fortified and more strongly garrisoned.[3]

For a time, therefore, the history shifts from Jerusalem

---

[1] I Macc. i. 31 f., 37 f., 54 f. When iii. 45 says that *Jerusalem was without inhabitant as a wilderness*, this is immediately explained as a reference to her own faithful people, *none of her offspring went in or out.* 2 Macc. v. 24 ff. describes the massacre.

[2] I Macc. i. 37, 39, 46, 54, 59; ii. 8 f., 12; iii. 45, 51; iv. 38; 2 Macc. vi. 2 ff. *The abomination of desolation.* (τὸ) βδέλυγμα τῆς ἐρημώσεως is the LXX. translation of Daniel's הַשִׁקּוּץ מְשֹׁמֵם (xi. 31) and שִׁקּוּץ שֹׁמֵם (xii. 11), either *the abomination that appals* or *the abomination that maketh desolate* (cf. viii. 13; ix. 27). The phrase *they builded it upon the altar* (I Macc. i. 54) implies that it was the altar to Zeus, the βωμός, which the Greeks constructed upon the altar of burnt-offering, θυσιαστήριον (*id.* 59). Some, however, take it as an image of Zeus set on or by the altar. Nestle (*Z.A.T.W.*, 1884, 248) reads the name as a travesty of בַּעַל שָׁמַיִם, in Phœn. בעל שמם, the Semitic analogue of Zeus. (Bevan, *Daniel*, 193, quotes from *Bereshith Rabba* 4 a derivation of שֹׁמֵם from שמים, because men are *astounded* by it.) Bevan (*Journal of Hell. Studies*, xx., 1900, 26 ff.) conjectures that the worship was that of Antiochus himself as Zeus Olympius (2 Macc. vi. 7 ff.). Cf. above, p. 430 *n.* 1. Winckler (*K.A.T.*[(3)] 303 *n.* 2) takes שקוּץ משמם for 'a distortion of אל משמם as a transcript of ἐπιφανής (as a "translation" of ἐπιφανής, "wonderful" or as re-echoing שֵׁ "Name," *i.e.* Incarnation; presumably with the design of indicating both).'

[3] I Macc. i. 33 ff.

to the country : the villages, from which the faithful
were largely recruited,[1] the mountains,[2] and
the surrounding wastes, always hospitable to
the forces of revolt and religious reform.
Israel fled to their ancient home and unfailing ally,
the wilderness.[3]  We have already followed, in that
sympathetic air, the rallies of the faithful and their em-
battlement under Judas.[4]  In addition, we need only
emphasise the large spoil which fell to them from their
four or five victories over the Seleucid forces.[5]  Inspired,
organised and enriched, they marched on Jerusalem
and occupied the Temple Hill.  No resistance was
offered to them.  The Greeks seem to have tired of
abusing the sanctuary, for Judas and his men found the
courts overgrown with shrubs.  The whole was rapidly
cleansed.  The altar of Zeus was torn down and the
materials stowed away till a prophet should arise to give
directions regarding them.  A new altar was built of
unhewn stones, according to the Law.  The courts were
hallowed, and the sanctuary furnished with vessels, golden
lamp, altar, and table of shewbread.[6]  Incense arose once
more to the God of Israel; and on the 25th day of Kislev,
exactly three years from the date of its pollution, the

*Restoration of the Temple, 165 B.C.*

---

[1] 1 Macc. ii. 1, 15 ff. 70 ; iii. 8, 46, 56 ; 2 Macc. viii 1.

[2] 1 Macc. ii. 28.           [3] See vol. i. 451, 454.

[4] Vol. i. 400 ff.

[5] 1st, 166 B.C., between the Jewish frontier and the town of Samaria ;
2nd, on the ascent of Bethhoron (1 Macc. iii. 10-26); 3rd, 165 B.C., at
Emmaus with a pursuit to Gezer, Ashdod and Jamnia (iii. 38-iv. 27 ;
2 Macc. viii. 8 ff., which account Niese prefers) ; 4th, 165 B.C. (autumn), at
Beth-ṣur (1 Macc. iv. 28-35).  According to 2 Macc. viii. 30 there was still
another previous to that over Lysias at Beth-ṣur, which is placed subsequently
to the possession and purification of the Temple (2 Macc. xi. 1 ff.).

[6] See above, pp. 63, 307 f.

high altar of burnt-offering was rekindled and the legal sacrifices resumed. Mount Ṣion, which throughout First Maccabees is the name for the Temple Hill, was surrounded by high walls with towers. Judas, who had serious work awaiting him elsewhere, left in it some priests and a garrison, besides detaching a number of men to engage the Greeks in the Akra.[1] For the next twenty-two years Greeks and Jews faced each other from the walls of these fortresses hardly a quarter of a mile apart, the citadel of David and the Temple of Solomon. Nothing is said of the Town, which appears to have remained in possession of the Greeks and the apostates, protected by the garrison of the Akra.

Thus Mount Ṣion was not yet again the centre of Judaism, but only one of its two fortified posts, the other being Beth-ṣur. For a time the centre was Judas, and if he had a base this was still the wilderness. Up to his death and for some years after, the narrative significantly mentions no place, not even Mizpah, as the headquarters of the Jewish forces. There was indeed a land of Judæa, for which Judas and his brothers fought, over which they put deputies when they went on distant campaigns, and to which they brought back the Jews from Galilee and Gilead.[2] Within its uncertain frontiers[3] Jews built houses, cultivated fields, reaped harvests, and supplied the armies of Judas with the resources of war.[4] But

*Its continued Isolation.*

[1] 1 Macc. iv. 36-61. From this arose the Jewish feast of the Ḥanukah or Dedication. Wellhausen suggests (*Isr. u. Jüd. Gesch.* 210 *n.* 2) that the 25th Kislev or December was originally the feast of the winter solstice ; 2 Macc. i. 9, x. 5-8 ; xii. *Ant.* vii. 7, φῶτα, 'Lights'; but φῶς was also used for 'joy' or 'deliverance.' John x. 22, τὰ ἐγκαίνια.

[2] 1 Macc. v. 8, 18, 23, 45, 53, 55 ff., 68 ; vi. 5.

See above, pp. 380 ff. [4] iii. 56; vi. 49, 53.

even this narrow surface was crossed by lines of Greek posts, and contained communities sympathetic with Hellenism. When Judas returned from Gilead he celebrated Pentecost in the Temple.[1] In B.C. 163-2, when apparently the only fortifications he had were Mount Ṣion and Beth-ṣur, he laid siege to the Akra, raising *mounds to shoot from and engines of war.*[2] This, and not the occupation of the Temple, provoked the return of the Syrians. Lysias, the general in power, with the young king Antiochus V., invaded Judæa from the south, defeated the Jews at Beth-ṣur, and beleaguered the Temple. It was a Sabbatic year, and both Greeks and Jews suffered from the scantiness of supplies. The former were further embarrassed by their rivals in Antioch, the latter by the number of Jews from Gilead who had taken refuge with them. Peace was therefore concluded, with an engagement that the Jews should live under their own laws. But when they opened the gates of Mount Ṣion and the king saw the strength of the place, he broke his oath and ordered the walls to be pulled down.[3]

The general lines, which the history of Israel thenceforth pursued, have already been indicated;[4] we give here a summary only of such events as concerned the City. Nikanor's visit to the Temple is of interest, for it shows that the priests who held this were no longer in open confederation with Judas. Alkimus, the creature of the Greeks, was High-Priest and had gotten the mastery in Judæa; with him were the Ḥasidîm, content to have secured liberty of worship according to their own laws; Judas, in com-

Summary of events in Jerusalem, 162-142 B.C.

[1] 1 Macc. v. 54; 2 Macc. xii. 31 f.    [2] 1 Macc. vi. 18 ff.
[3] vi. 21-62.    [4] Vol. i. 402 ff.

mand of a remnant, still fought for national independence.[1]
When Nikanor was slain, Judas could hang up his head
and right hand beside Jerusalem.[2] But when Judas fell his
brothers were driven back into the desert;[3] and Alkimus
for the few months which elapsed before his death exercised his powers unthreatened. He attempted a daring
innovation in pursuance of his Hellenising policy. The
Temple had still but two courts: the inner, which Israelites,
both priests and laity, alone could enter, and the outer,
which was apparently open to Gentiles. Alkimus gave
orders *to pull down the wall of the inner court*, so that there
would have remained no barrier to the entrance of the
Gentiles. The work was begun, but his death put a stop
to it.[4] At last the Syrians retired, and Jonathan established a government at Mikmash.[5] In 153 he moved his
residence to Jerusalem, and for the first time we hear of
the Town as in possession of the Maccabees. Jonathan
began to rebuild it, the separate fortifications of Mount
Sion were restored, and only the Akra and Beth-ṣur
continued to hold Greek garrisons.[6] About 146 Jonathan
besieged the Akra, but failed to take it. Soon after he
built a great rampart, which was designed to shut it off
from the Town, and must therefore have run either on
the east or on the west of the Lower Tyropœon with a

---

[1] 1 Macc. vii. 21-38.    [2] vii. 47.    [3] ix. 33 f.; above, p. 382 *n.* 1.
[4] 1 Macc. ix. 54-56; cf. Jos. xii. *Ant.* x. 6. The expression αὐλὴ
ἐσώτερα implies *two* courts. In the Herodian Temple there were more, as we
shall see. Some, holding this to have been also the case through the Greek
Period, have supposed the τεῖχος, or wall, of the inner court to have been
the Soreg of Herod's Temple, which a tradition in the Mishna (Middôth ii. 3)
avers had been breached 'by the Greek kings' in thirteen places. But it
is doubtful whether the Soreg existed at so early a time; besides, it was a
mere barrier and not a τεῖχος.
[5] Vol. i. 403.    [6] 1 Macc. x. 1-14.

continuation across the East Hill south of the Temple.[1] In 142 the blockade succeeded, and the starved garrison surrendered to Simon. We have seen how the rock on which the Akra stood, and which 'the City of David' and the Jebusite Ṣion had occupied before it, was cut down to the level of the rest of the ridge.[2]

The double office of High Priest and Ethnarch, with rights of coinage, in which Simon was confirmed by the

The Hasmo-<br>nean Princes<br>—their Char-<br>acter and<br>Circumstance.

dwindling authority of the Seleucids, received from his grateful people powers that were practically absolute, and under his successors developed into the formal and explicit rank of kingship.[3] 'A royal kind of men, but, at their best, not royal enough'[4]—this description of another brilliant but unhappy dynasty, also sprung from the liberators of their nation, sufficiently characterises the descendants of Simon. Embarrassed by their own discordant, perhaps incompatible, duties, and distracted between the two ideals which divided their people into the rapidly organising parties of the Pharisees and Sadducees, the Hasmonean princes took the line most natural to men of inferior character through such circumstance, and employed their hereditary vigour in large enterprises of conquest and aggrandisement, for which the weakness of Syria and the distance of Rome afforded them opportunity.[5] It was another of the many occasions we have

---

[1] Vol. i. 225.     [2] Vol. i. 159 f.     [3] As we have seen, vol. i. 404 ff.

[4] Carlyle, *Historical Sketches*, p. 3, on the Stuarts.

[5] Cf. Tacitus, *Hist.* v. 8: 'Tum Iudaei, Macedonibus invalidis, Parthis nondum adultis (et Romani procul erant) sibi ipsi reges imposuere. Qui mobilitate vulgi expulsi, resumpta per arma dominatione, fugas civium, urbium eversiones, fratrum, conjugum, parentum neces, aliaque solita regibus ausi, superstitionem fovebant: quia honor sacerdotii firmamentum potentiae assumebatur.'

had to note in the history of Israel, in which an outburst of national glory was due less to the vigour of her kings than to the temporary disablement of the empires about her. By their permanent conquests of Idumea, Galilee, and part of Samaria, by their campaigns in Gilead and Philistia, the Hasmoneans immensely increased the resources and the honour of their state; but it was their unscrupulousness, the barbarity of their warfare, their political crimes and savage family quarrels, which broke up the state and brought upon Jerusalem the arms and irresistible authority of Rome. The Hasmonean wealth was illustrated by the usual signs, large mercenary armies and a great revival of building.[1] Upon their capital the effects were immediate and permanent. Not only was Jerusalem generally strengthened and embellished; we see, in particular, two departures in her construction, which were destined to revolutionise the topography. A palace was built on the West Hill, and a citadel was raised on the north of the Temple to replace that which from the time of the Jebusites had stood to the south. The erection of these two buildings sharply divides the topography of the Old Testament and Maccabean Jerusalem from that of the Herodian, the Christian, and the Moslem City.

*The Effects on Jerusalem and the Topography.*

When Antiochus Sidetes received the surrender of Jerusalem from John Hyrkanus in 134 B.C.,[2] he overthrew part at least of the City's walls.[3] But so pro-

---

[1] Strabo (*apud* Jos. xiv. *Ant.* iii. 1) records that he saw in Rome the present which Aristobulus gave to Pompey a Damascus, an artificial 'vine or garden,' which was called Terpōlē or 'delight'; it bore the inscription, ' Of Alexander, King of the Jews,' and was valued at 500 talents.

[2] Vol. i. 408.

[3] Jos. xiii. *Ant.* viii. 3 : the στεφάνη of the City which this passage says that he destroyed is not merely, as some take it, the crown of the wall, but is

sperous a prince as Hyrkanus, so vigorous a warrior and engineer, must speedily have restored them, and,

The Reign of John Hyrkanus, 135-104 B.C.

indeed, we have an ancient testimony to this effect in the First Book of Maccabees.[1] Probably those portions of the southern City wall in which Dr. Bliss discovered fragments of Graeco-Jewish moulding are the work of John Hyrkanus.[2] His long years of peace, his use of the treasure found in the tomb of David, his rich spoils and many captives, endowed him with opportunities for building which none of his successors so fully enjoyed. We may therefore assign to him not only the particular buildings which Josephus describes as the work of the Hasmoneans, but that general embellishment of the City to which witness is borne by writers almost contemporary with his reign.

About the Baris or Castle there can be no doubt. Josephus expressly assigns it to Hyrkanus, and his

The Baris or Birah.

earliest record of its use is under the next king,[3] Aristobulus, who caused his brother to be slain in a dark passage in one of its towers.[4] We cannot tell the size of the Baris; Josephus was familiar with it only after its enlargement by Herod. But we know that it lay on the rock, north-west of the Temple, now occupied by the Turkish barracks.[5] This had been the site of the towers Hammeah and Ḥananeel;[6] some maintain that the Syrian Akra also stood here, but that,

the technical term for the whole circumvallations. Other authorities are equally emphatic: Diod. Sic. xxxiv. 1; Porphyrius (quoted by Eusebius). See Müller, *Frag. Hist. Graec.* iii. 256, 712.

[1] xvi. 23.      [2] Vol. i. 216 f.
[3] xviii. *Ant.* iv. 3; cf. xv. *Ant.* xi. 4.
[4] xiii. *Ant.* xi. 2. The tower is called Straton's.
[5] xv. *Ant.* xi. 4: κατὰ δὲ τὴν βόρειον πλευράν.
[6] Vol. i. 201.

as we have seen, is very improbable.[1]   The Birah of
Neḥemiah had been either the palace of Solomon or the
whole fortified Temple Hill.   The latter is the more
reasonable hypothesis, and explains the limitation of the
name Birah or Baris to the Hasmonean castle, which lay
on the Temple Hill, and from the time of Hyrkanus became
the real Temple citadel.

Besides the Baris there was a Hasmonean Basileion or
Palace, the position of which is also clearly indicated by
Josephus.[2]   This occupied an elevation to the
west of the Temple, close to the Xystus.   It   The Palace
of the
has been correctly located upon the middle   Hasmoneans.
terrace of the South-West Hill above the scarp,[3] whence
it afforded a view across the Tyropœon to the Temple.
Who built it we are not told.   The earliest certain notice
of it is that just cited, which refers to its enlargement by
Agrippa II.   But it may have been the house from which
Alexander Jannæus, feasting with his women, watched
the massacre of captives of war;[4] the palace occupied
by Queen Alexandra,[5] and the residence of Hyrkanus II.,
from which he took refuge in the Baris and which he
gave up to Aristobulus II.[6]   It was connected with the
Temple by a bridge, the earliest evidence for which is
the account of Pompey's siege in 63 B.C.[7]   This bridge
cannot have existed in the Maccabean period when the

---

[1] Above, pp. 446, 449.

[2] xx. *Ant.* viii. 11 ; ii. *B.J.* xvi. 3.

[3] Vol. i. 35 ; Robinson, *B.R.* i. 392 f. *n.* ; Mommert, *Topog. d. alt.
Jerus.* iv. 160 ff.   None of the remains found here appear to be older than
Crusading times ; *P.E.F Mem.*, 'Jerus.,' 272 f.

[4] xiii. *Ant.* xiv. 2 ; 1 *B.J.* iv. 6.                    [5] xiii. *Ant.* xvi. 2.

[6] 1 *B.J.* vi. 1.   But see Mommert, p. 169 : it may be that it was the
Baris which Hyrkanus II. resigned to his brother, and the palace which he
received in exchange.                    [7] 1 *B.J.* vii. 2 ; xiv. *Ant.* iv. 2.

Temple was entirely isolated from the Town, but may, with the Palace, have been the work of Hyrkanus I. In any case the South-West Hill at last contained a public building directly connected with the Temple Courts. Which of the remains of approaches to the latter across the Tyropœon now represents the bridge we cannot say; probably something lower than those which, when complete, were on a level with the Temple Courts.[1]

It has already been suggested that John Hyrkanus may have built the High Level Aqueduct.[2] In support of this there is some remarkable evidence from the period itself.[3] Besides a statement from a *Survey of Syria*,[4] that Jerusalem contained a spring with a copious jet of water, doubtless Gihon, there are two records of other streams and conduits. Timochares, the biographer of Antiochus VII., says that 'the whole city runs down with waters, so that even the gardens are irrigated by the water which flows off from it.' And the Jewish Philo, who wrote a poem on Jerusalem, describes, besides the spring, 'another most marvellous thing,' 'a powerful current filling a deep stream'; 'a high-shining stream winding among towers'; irrigating the thirsty dust; apparently high up and conspicuous from afar; 'headlong the conduits gush forth by underground pipes.' The construction of the lines is very obscure, but the epithets used suit the issue of the

*John Hyr-kanus and the High Level Aqueduct.*

---

[1] It is interesting that on undoubtedly ancient remains just outside the W. Ḥaram wall (*P.E.F. Mem.*, 'Jerus.,' 200), the pilasters should have Ionic capitals of peculiar shape, the volute being something similar to that on one of the capitals found at Ṭobiah-Hyrkanus's palace at 'Arâḳ el-Emir. See above, p. 426.     [2] Vol. i. 129, 131.

[3] Handed down by Alex. Polyhistor of the first century B.C. through Eusebius, *Praep. Evang.* ix. 35 ff.; Müller, *Frag. Hist. Graec.* iii. 228 f.

[4] Τῆς Συρίας Σχοινομέτρησις. Above, p. 439 *n.* 1.

High Level Aqueduct, which entered the City from above on the west, as they do not suit either Gihon or Siloam. The fountain, too, is called that of the High Priest. The evidence, therefore, for assigning the High Level Aqueduct to Hyrkanus is considerable; and there appears to have been an ancient channel from the place, near which it probably entered the City walls, in the direction at least of the Hasmonean Palace.[1]

The only other structure mentioned in this period is the wooden barrier erected by Alexander Jannæus round the Temple and the Altar, after he was pelted by the people with citrons when serving at the latter. His purpose was to exclude the laity; and this is the earliest notice we have of an inner court open only to the priests.[2]  The remarkable tombs in the Ḳidron valley, now called Absalom's and the Pyramid of Zecharias, belong either to the Hasmonean or to the Roman period.

*Alexander Jannæus and a Temple Barrier.*

Such were the changes which the Hasmoneans had effected on Jerusalem, when the quarrels of Hyrkanus II. and Aristobulus II., upon the death of their mother Alexandra (66 B.C.), broke up the dynasty, provoked the interference of Rome, and introduced to the centre of Jewish affairs a new and fateful influence in the person of Antipater, the father of Herod. The Roman sovereignty and this Idumean family remain the dominant factors in the history of the City till her fall in 70 A.D.[3]

*The Break-up of the Hasmonean Dynasty.*

---

[1] *P.E.F. Mem.*, 'Jerus.,' 270 f.     [2] xiii. *Ant.* xiii. 5.

[3] For the rest of this chapter the authorities besides Josephus, xiv. *Ant.*, 1 *B.J.* vi.-xviii., with his various excerpts from writers of the first century B.C. (for which see Reinach, *Textes*, 77 ff.), are the *Psalms of Solomon* (Ps. of

After a reign of three months Hyrkanus resigned the kingship to Aristobulus. But Antipater, perceiving his opportunity with so facile a character, convinced Hyrkanus that he was still in danger of his life, and persuaded him to appeal to Aretas (Ḥarîth III.), King of the Nabateans. In the end of 66, or the beginning of 65, a Nabatean army marched into Judæa, and after defeating Aristobulus was reinforced by a large number of Jews who, under the influence of the Pharisees, sympathised with Hyrkanus. As the Nation was divided, so also the City. Aristobulus shut himself up in the Temple Mount with the priests and probably the chiefs of the Sadducean party. Whether he also held the Baris is not stated, but is probable. The rest of Jerusalem was occupied by the supporters of Hyrkanus and the Nabateans. The siege lasted some months. When the Passover came round, the besieged begged from their countrymen animals with which to celebrate the feast. After putting an enormous price on each of these, and receiving the money, the besiegers treacherously refused to fulfil their engagement.[1] It is a welcome relief to so sordid a story when Josephus tells us that the holy Onias, brought by the besiegers to bless their arms, uttered instead this noble prayer: 'O God,

the Pharisees), text and translation, by Ryle and James, Cambridge, 1891 ; Diodorus Siculus, xl., second fragment ; fragments in Cicero, Livy, Plutarch's *Lives*, and Appian alluded to below ; Tacitus (*Hist.* v. 9) ; Dion Cassius, xxxvii. 15 ff. ; xxxix. 55 ff. ; xli. 18 ; xlvii. 28 ; xlviii. 26, 39 ff. ; xlix. 19 ff. (ed. Sturzius, vols. i. f.). Modern works : besides the histories already cited for the Greek period, the student will find a valuable and accurate guide in *The Jews under Roman Rule*, by W. D. Morrison ('The Story of the Nations' Series): London, Unwin ; New York, Putnam, 1890.

[1] Cf. the account of the generous behaviour of Antiochus VII. in the siege of 135 B.C., xiii. *Ant.* viii. 2.

Ruler of all men, since these standing with me are Thy people and the besieged are Thy priests, I pray that Thou wilt hearken neither to those against these, nor bring into effect what these beseech against those.' The enraged Hyrkanians immediately stoned him to death.[1] This Onias, of whom we know nothing else than his power of prayer, is thus worthy to stand in the ranks of the City beside Isaiah and Jeremiah. The prayer was answered through one of those sudden and incalculable events which so often, in the history of Jerusalem, have overruled the rage of her factions or her foes and vindicated the faith of her purer minds—sometimes, as apparently in this case, beyond all their anticipations. Soon after the Passover the siege was raised not by force of arms, but by the sudden menace of Rome. Pompey, then with his legions in Armenia, had despatched southwards a force which took Damascus. Thither he now sent Marcus Scaurus, who, hearing of the troubles in Judæa, came on to judge the situation for himself. Aristobulus and Hyrkanus both offered him money; but, adds Josephus, Aristobulus was the more able to pay; and besides, 'to take by force a city specially fortified and powerful, was a different thing from expelling fugitives and a multitude of Nabateans who were not much disposed to war.'[2] Scaurus commanded Aretas to withdraw, on pain of Rome's hostility, and Aretas yielded. It was a repetition of what happened in the case of Antiochus IV.[3] The word of a Roman legate altered the history of Syria.

When Pompey, after his conference at Damascus with the rival princes,[4] marched on the Nabateans, he learned that Aristobulus, anticipating a decision adverse to

[1] xiv. *Ant.* ii. 1.    [2] *Id.* 3.    [3] Above, p. 435.    [4] Vol. i. 410 f.

himself, was preparing to resist it. He therefore turned into Judæa, and having secured Jericho, advanced on Jerusalem. On the way he was met by Aristobulus with his submission, and sent forward Gabinius to receive the surrender of the City. This was refused, and Pompey appeared in force before the walls. The supporters of Hyrkanus admitted him to the Town and the Palace;[1] but those of Aristobulus who occupied the Temple[2] cut down the bridge over the Tyropœon and prepared for a siege. Pompey pitched his camp to the north of the Temple,[3] where the assault was most practicable. Even here 'were great towers and a ditch had been dug,' which Strabo defines as 250 feet broad by 60 deep.[4] Pompey filled the ditch with a bank, that might never have been completed but for the inactivity of the defenders on the Sabbath. Across this bank he rolled his engines and battering-rams from Tyre, and so breached the Temple wall that at last, after a blockade of three months, it was taken on a Sabbath,[5] and the Romans poured into the courts. The priests, who had never remitted their ministrations, were cut down in the

*Pompey's Siege and Conquest, 63 B.C.*

---

[1] Dion Cassius, xxxvii. 16; Josephus, xiv. *Ant.* iv. 2; cf. *Ps. of Solom.* viii. 18 ff.

[2] Josephus does not mention the Baris, but, as the adherents of Aristobulus already occupied it, it was included in the Temple (Ewald otherwise, *Hist.* v. 400, but he confounds the Baris with the Basileion or Palace on the South-West Hill). Dion Cassius also mentions only the Temple as occupied by Aristobulus: 'for it lay on a lofty place and was fortified by walls of its own.'

[3] Josephus, xiv. *Ant.* iv. 2, adds ἔωθεν ('at dawn'); so Niese's text. The Latin reads *mane*. Some MSS. read ἔσωθεν, which Whiston translates 'within [the wall],' meaning the wall which Pompey is said to have built round the Temple Mount. The present east wall north of the Temple Mount was not built till the time of Agrippa; vol. i. 238 f., 244 ff.

[4] *Geog.* xvi. 40.

[5] Ἐν τῇ τοῦ Κρόνου ἡμέρᾳ, Dion Cassius, xxxvii. 16. Strabo and Josephus call it a fast-day. *Ps. of Solom.* ii. 1: 'cast down strong walls with a ram.'

act of sacrificing.   Pompey penetrated to the Holy of
Holies, and saw that which was unlawful for any but the
High-priests to see; yet he touched nothing of all the
valuable furnishings and treasure of the sanctuary, 'on
account of his respect for religion, and in a manner
worthy of his virtue.'[1]   The empty shrine impressed the
Romans as it had impressed the earlier Greeks.  'Inde
vulgatum,' says Tacitus, 'nulla intus deum effigie, vacuam
sedem, inania arcana.'[2]   Having destroyed the walls of
Jerusalem, restored the High-priesthood to Hyrkanus,
and arranged for the administration under Scaurus,
Pompey went away to his triumph, carrying captive
Aristobulus and his sons.   'Noster Hierosolymarius,'
Cicero calls him[3]—in the year of whose consulship the
City thus suffered its first Roman occupation.

The other critical events in Jerusalem before the last
of the Hasmoneans was deposed and Herod became king
in fact as well as by the authority of Rome,
are these: a momentary seizure of all the
City save the citadel by Alexander, the son of
Aristobulus; the spoliation of the Temple by Crassus in
54 B.C.; Cæsar's confirmation of Hyrkanus as High-
priest, and appointment of Antipater as procurator, with
licence to restore the walls of Jerusalem; the conquest of
the City, in 40, by the Parthians, who drove out Herod
and established as king Antigonus, the other son of
Aristobulus;[4] the siege and storming of the City, in 37, by
the combined forces of Herod and of Sosius, the representative of Mark Antony.   Josephus says that on this
occasion no fewer than eleven legions, with six thousand

*Events in the City, 63-37 B.C.*

---

[1] Jos. xiv. *Ant.* iv. 4; Cicero, *Pro Flacco*, 67; but cf. *Ps. of Solom.* ii. 2.
[2] *Hist.* v. 9.          [3] *Ad Atticum*, ii. 9.          [4] Vol. i. 412.

horsemen and a number of auxiliaries, encamped against
Jerusalem, which appears to have been wholly one in
resisting Herod. As in all other cases, so in this, the
assault was delivered on the north. The outer wall took
forty days to carry, the inner fifteen more. The defenders
concentrated in the Temple, but had to yield its outer
court, parts of the cloisters of which were reduced to ashes.
In the 'Upper City'[1] and the inner court of the Temple,
the besieged held out for some time longer. At their
request, Herod gave them beasts to sacrifice, thinking
the request indicated their speedy surrender. But they
persisted, and their obduracy embittered the besiegers to
great cruelty. In the end the refuges were stormed, and
a terrible slaughter ensued. Herod, who did his best to
restrain the excesses of the Romans, was master of the
City. The last of the Hasmonean kings was carried away
by Sosius and put to death.[2] Herod became King of the
Jews in fact as well as by title of the Roman authority.[3]

[1] One wonders if Josephus employs this term in the meaning he usually
gives to it. If so, the defenders held two separated parts of the City. But
it seems as though by the 'Upper City' he here meant the Baris.

[2] Vol. i. 412. For the exact date of the siege, summer 37 B.C., see
Schürer, *Gesch.*(3) i. § 14 *n.* 11. It was a Sabbatic year, says Josephus.

[3] For the siege described above, see xiv. *Ant.* xvi.

# CHAPTER XVII

# HEROD, THE ROMANS AND JERUSALEM
## 37-4 B.C.

I F the title Great be ever deserved by the cruel and the unjust, history has not erred in granting it to Herod the son of Antipater. His father had Herod the Great. dared for him a name, the full spelling of which is 'hero-id,' and not all his crimes, which have turned it into a proverb of ferocity, can obscure the power that was in him to rise to the challenge it rang out.[1] That Herod was great in all but goodness, and had a nature capable at least of explosions in that direction, is manifest upon the mere summary of his fortunes and achievements. Josephus writes of the 'high-mindedness'

---

[1] Ἡρώδης : so Niese throughout his ed. of Josephus; 'idem est quod Ἡρώδης, siue Ἡρώνδας, quare iota non patitur' (Pref. to vol. iii. p. vii.). But the Cod. Ambrosianus of Josephus's works reads Ἡρώιδης, and Westcott and Hort in their N.T. give Ἡρῴδης, with the iota subscript: it 'is well supported by inscriptions and manifestly right' (ii. 314). For example, Le Bas and Waddington, *Inscriptions Grecques et Latines recueillies en Grèce et Asie Mineure*, iii. No. 3 (2364; cf. *H.G.H.L.* 618). So also Schürer, *Gesch.*[(3)] i. 375 *n.* 20. The coins of H. naturally omit the iota. The name occurs as early as the fifth century B.C., and contemporary with H. the Idumean was an Archon H. in Athens; Cicero (*ad Att.* II. ii. 2, etc.) mentions an Athenian H. as the teacher of his son. Other Greek instances occur. There is no possibility of a Semitic derivation for the name. The Talmudic הוֹרְדוֹם is clearly a transcription of the Greek. An adjective from the name was applied to tamed pigeons ! Levy, *Chald. u. N. Hebr. Wörterbuch*, i. 491.

of his youth, and the worst his enemies could then say of him was that 'he was forcible, daring, and ambitious of absolute power.' At twenty-five, by his own energy he swept the robber-ridden Galilee free of its pests, so that 'the villages and townships sang songs in his praise.' For this he had to answer to the Sanhedrin; and the character of these authorities at Jerusalem may be seen from their intention to try him on the capital charge, because the brigands whom he exterminated were Jews! Instead of appearing before them, like other accused persons, with hair dishevelled and in black, Herod came 'in purple, with his hair finely trimmed,' and with his guards about him; so that his judges were all silenced except Sameas, who predicted the day when the young soldier would have them in his power. His contempt for the sophistries and false patriotism of these pedants is one of his most characteristic tempers. Indeed all his valour, though it often seemed reckless, was inspired by an accurate knowledge of men, a strong grasp of circumstances, and an unfailing assurance of his abilities and of other men's need of them. His skill in the art of war was not less conspicuous. He sustained the severest proofs of generalship, winning battles against heavy odds, and rallying a beaten army to victory. The worst defeats left him unbroken and elastic; men stood amazed at his courage under disaster and his resources of recovery. When his ambitions of conquest were frustrated, he fell back on reducing to order the territory already in his possession, and won new moral influence which rendered possible the conquest he had only postponed. When the powers he had espoused were defeated, he knew how to make himself necessary to the victors.

His personality—or his eloquence—prevailed alike with
his soldiers, though on the verge of mutiny; with his
turbulent people, though his policy outraged their most
sacred convictions; and with the successive lords of his
world, though he had previously intrigued or openly
fought against them. Josephus, who never writes with
greater effect—because never with more insight and discrimination—than when Herod is his subject, convinces
us that it was the sheer ability of the man, working in
very various directions, which stunned his foes and kept
about him through all the uncertainties of his time a
group of devoted and capable servants—besides that wider
Herodian party among the people which even after his
death and the removal of his sons from Judah continued
to believe that his dynasty was indispensable to the
nation. There has seldom been a more thorough master
of the forces of disorder; or, considering his means, a
more ready financier and energetic builder; or, when he
liked, a better administrator. The methods by which he
overcame the emergencies of the famine and pestilence
of 25 B.C. were altogether admirable, and succeeded in
restoring for a time that popular trust in him which his
exactions and his crimes had shattered. Had Herod
lived when his world was open, he would have been
among the greater kings of the East, and might have
proved a famous, if a transient, conqueror; for he had the
imperial vision, and while conscious of the value of his
people's patriotism and able to sway it, he was not
embarrassed by merely national ideals. As it was, he
understood and used for his own ends every limit which
the Roman dispensation imposed on his career. But,
whether he derived it from his father, who was a good

man and a strong governor, or whether he learned it from
the example of Rome, Herod had at heart the fundamental
sense of order, and it was his ability to create order in
very difficult circumstances which, in spite of his breaches
of the Jewish law and the care of Rome to ensure its
enforcement, commended him to one after another of her
representatives. For nothing else than because he was
the strong man of the East, Sextus Cæsar supported him
in his youth against the Sanhedrin, and Augustus committed to him in his prime the wild provinces beyond
Jordan. Yet he did more than persuade each of the
masters of Palestine that he was necessary to their policy.
His capacity for winning the friendship of the greatest
Romans of his day is as striking as his power to withstand the temptress to whom more than one of them
succumbed. Cæsar, Sextus Cæsar, Cassius, Antony,
Augustus and Marcus Agrippa, Herod knew how to
charm them all ; and he baffled the intrigues as well as
resisted the fascinations of Cleopatra herself. His secret
is clear. He read men through and through. Thus he
bribed Mark Antony, but showed himself a frank and
magnanimous soldier before Augustus. Never had prince
more tragic dissensions in his family or more dangerous
conspiracies among his people ; yet it is remarkable how
often his troubles at home culminated along with some
fresh success of his influence upon the Roman authorities ;
and if he had done nothing more than keep the balance
between the demands of his lords that he should introduce
a western civilisation to Judæa, and the demands of his
people that he should keep it out,—because every constructive act to which he was obliged provoked the
suspicions of the one or of the other—his ability would

still have claims upon our admiration. He has been likened to several eastern princes who have played the same arduous part between a fanatic people and an aggressive foreign civilisation, for which they had more or less sympathy. Perhaps the nearest analogy is that of Ismail, Khedive of Egypt : on the one side with the intellectual centre of Islam in his capital, with so many violent deaths among his family and courtiers and with so cruel an oppression of his peasantry ; and on the other side a lavish finance, enormous public works after the western fashion, a western theatre, fêtes for European magnates, numerous palaces, and even the introduction of statues in defiance of the precepts of his people's religion. On all these points the parallel is complete.[1] Only, Herod's reign did not prematurely close in bankruptcy. Nothing stopped his flow. The careers of great men have been likened to rivers. Herod was more : he was a tide, whose inevitable ebb came only after his death. The volume and the spaciousness of his success were extraordinary. He quelled every sedition among his people ; swayed every institution ; in turn provoked and mastered every interest. Though not by race a Jew, he impressed himself on the fabric of the Jewish religion, as hardly any native ruler had done since Solomon ; and he founded a dynasty which endured, more or less, till the state itself disappeared. He covered his land with buildings, and gave to its inhospitable coast the one harbour which this ever possessed. But his generalship and his munificence spread also abroad. Besides his

---

[1] I do not know if the parallel has been drawn before. It occurred to me as I stood in the Khedivial Mausoleum at Cairo, where to so many of the tombs a tragic story is attached.

successful conduct of Roman armies over the sands between Judæa and Egypt, he tamed the Arabs of the Lejá, rendered possible a large population in Ḥauran, and assisted in the erection of many public buildings, the remains of one of which, near the borders of the desert, still testify to his work as the pioneer of civilisation in that region.[1] He poured gifts upon the Phœnician towns, Damascus and the Syrian Antioch, many cities of Asia Minor, Athens, Sparta and Nicopolis; and by his liberal endowments revived the splendour of the Olympian games. The influence which he thus earned he exerted loyally on behalf of the Jews of the Dispersion, and succeeded in securing their rights as well as additional privileges to many of those communities. But with all that he did for Judaism Herod had no religious convictions. He sprang from a race notorious for their irreligion, and though he patronised the faith of Israel, the people were never really deceived by him. The hands that gave the gifts might appear to be those of Jacob, the heart behind was Esau's from first to last. And, therefore, just because he was without either faith or a national enthusiasm, he was obliged to maintain his position by a series of unparalleled crimes. His passions were never controlled except, as in his dealings with Cleopatra, by barriers of policy; and being indulged they soon broke through even these in a series of blunders which forced him to fresh outrage. They turned his own house into a cage of beasts, into a slaughterhouse. He had married Mariamme out of mere ambition, and she tortured him with her contempt for his family; his wild nature came to conceive for her a brutal affection, and she repulsed it

[1] See *H.G.H.L.* 617 f.

with reproaches. Her murder was the inevitable resource
of such a nature so baffled; and his remorse, one of the
most terrible in history, derives its horror from being less
a sense of guilt than the hunger of a balked passion, with
perhaps the exasperating recollection that he had slain
the queen who alone lent an appearance of legitimacy to
his usurped position. Of his next marriage with another
Mariamme, a woman of great beauty, Josephus says that
'he suffered not his reason to hinder him from living as
he pleased'; and this new passion also had its woes to
work. The crowded crimes of his last years were all
either the direct consequences of these passions, or due
to the sense of his own danger. Herod never started a
religious persecution; but he filled his prisons as full,
he indulged in as wide a carnage for his own interests,
as ever any fanatic in the remorselessness of a holy
war. In all this the similitude we have suggested for
him is still deserved. His storms were like the storms of
the sea; their wreckage strewed every coast he rose upon.
One cannot estimate the individuals, the families, the
circles and hosts of men who disappeared in his cruel
and relentless depths.[1]

[1] For the career of Herod the sources are Josephus xiv.-xvii. *Ant.*,
and 1 *B.J.* vi.-xxxiii. Josephus largely uses, but with criticism (especially when Herod is in question), the *Histories* of Nicolaus of Damascus,
Herod's younger contemporary and confidant (for these and other fragments of
Nicolaus see Müller, *Frag. Hist. Graec.* iii. 348 ff.). There is no reason to
doubt the accuracy and justice of Josephus's accounts of Herod. The passages
I have found most enlightening, as to the latter's character and the extraordinary difficulties which it mastered, are xiv. *Ant.* ix., xiii f.; xv. *Ant.* iii.,
iv., v. 2 f. 5, vi., vii., viii., ix. 2 f., xi. 1; xvi. *Ant.* v., vii. f., x. f.; xvii. *Ant.* i. v.-
viii.; xix. *Ant.* vii. 3. The title Great is given by Josephus to Herod only in
xviii. *Ant.* v. 4, and may be interpreted as simply used to distinguish him
from others of the same name. So Schürer (*Gesch.*[3] i. 418), who holds that
it can only be justified in that relative sense, and quotes with approval
Hitzig's remark that Herod 'was only a common man.' But as I have tried

The methods by which Herod governed Jerusalem have already been sketched;[1] and the principal events of his reign may now be briefly summarised. Upon his capture of the City in 37 B.C., there followed that execution of the adherents of Antigonus which cost the Sanhedrin more than half its members. Herod had connected himself with the Hasmonean house by marrying Mariamme,[2] a granddaughter of Hyrkanus II. At the instigation of her mother, Alexandra, he appointed his wife's brother, Aristobulus III., High-priest (35 B.C.); but finding the young prince dangerously popular, he is said to have arranged for his death, which took place treacherously in the bath at Jericho. Henceforth Herod's nominees to the

*Summary of Events in his Reign.*

to show, his record as a soldier, his instincts and powers of order, the maintenance of his position against his own people, his management of the great Romans of his time, or (if this be too strong a phrase) his convincing them of his indispensableness to their policy, his numerous enterprises, his grasp of emergencies and occasional feats of sound statesmanship, raise him far above ' the common man.' Cf. the higher estimates of Ewald, *Hist.* v. 418 f. ; and Headlam, *Enc. Bibl.* The references to him in Greek and Latin writers are not very numerous, but sufficient to show that he had impressed himself on the mind not only of his own, but of the succeeding, age. Horace alludes to his palm-groves at Jericho (*Ep.* ii. 2, 185). Josephus quotes one reference from Strabo's Ὑπομνήματα (xv. *Ant.* i. 2 ; Müller, iii. 494) ; and in the latter's *Geogr.* there are two references, xvi. 34, 46. The second runs : ' Herod, a man of the country, having usurped the high-priesthood (!) so excelled his predecessors through his friendly relations with Rome and his government, that he even became king, first Antony and then Augustus granting him the power.' Persius calls the Sabbath by his name : ' Herodis dies ' (*Sat.* v. 180). By Appian (*Bell. Civ.* v. 75) he is entitled King ' of the Idumeans and Samarians.' To Dion Cassius he is only ' a certain Herod,' to whom Antony conveyed the government of the Jews (xlix. 22, ed. Sturzii, ii. 120), and Augustus the tetrarchy of Zenodorus (liv. 9, ed. St. iii. 262). Cf. Plutarch, *Anton.* 61, 71 f. ; Pliny, *H.N.* v. 13 ; Tacitus, *Hist.* v. 9. A saying about Herod is attributed to Augustus (Macrobius, *Saturnalia*, II. iv. 11) : ' Mallem Herodis porcus esse quam filius,' but the original was probably Greek with a pun upon ὗς and υἱός.

[1] Vol. i. 412.  [2] So, and *not* Mariamne.

sacred office were from families as far removed as possible from the legitimate succession ; none of them was even a Palestinian Jew.[1] In 34 he visited Antony at Laodicea, and succeeded in persuading his patron that he was innocent of the murder of Aristobulus. The same year Cleopatra came to Jerusalem and tried her charms upon the still handsome king. He wanted to kill her, in the hope of freeing Antony from her toils and himself from her spite ; but his counsellors dissuaded him, and the only result was that he undertook the campaign against the Arabs, by which she hoped to get rid both of him and their king. Herod was saved by this engagement from the necessity of taking arms against Octavian, and at the same time won fresh fame through his defeat of the Arab forces. In 31 a great earthquake shook Judæa ;[2] and later in the same year the battle of Actium transferred the Roman power in the East, and Herod's allegiance, from Antony to Octavian. In 30 Herod made his peace in person with the latter at Rhodes, and was confirmed in his kingdom. In 30 the aged Hyrkanus, in 29 Mariamme, and a little later Alexandra, were executed. Herod received accessions of territory, and rebuilt Samaria as a Greek town under the name of Sebastē.[3] There followed the most prosperous years of his reign : his buildings in Jerusalem, his construction of Cæsarea,[4] and the extension of his territory by Augustus over Trachonitis, Auranitis, Batanæa, and in 20 over the domains of Zenodorus. In 25 a famine fell on Judæa, and Herod organised vigorous measures of relief. About

---

[1] Cf. Edersheim, *Life and Times of Jesus the Messiah*, i. 24.
[2] See vol. i. 64.
[3] *H.G.H.L.* 139 f.            [4] *Ibid.*, also 348.

22 he visited Marcus Agrippa at Mytilene, and about 18 he went to Rome. In 15 Agrippa came as his guest to Jerusalem and sacrificed in the Temple. The next year Herod returned the visit in Asia Minor. Then began his troubles with his two sons by Mariamme, and they dragged on (with visits to Rome in 12 and 10) till he had the princes strangled in 7 B.C.[1] A couple of years later he imprisoned his eldest son Antipater, and in 4 B.C. came the revolt of the rabbis in Jerusalem;[2] Antipater's execution; the final testament appointing Archelaus as successor to the kingdom of Judæa and Antipas and Philip to tetrarchies over the rest of the territories; and Herod's death.[3]

Before we consider the details of Herod's work in Jerusalem, it is necessary to form an idea of the changed world in which the City lay since the advent of the Roman power, and to which her life, largely by Herod's instrumentality, rapidly adapted itself. The last great change we have had to note in Israel's world came with the conquests of Alexander and the division of his Asiatic empire among the dynasties founded by his generals. The centre of politics and culture moved from its ancient Oriental seats into the West. The fortunes of Palestine were decided by Greek minds, and not only upon the soil of Asia but out on the Mediterranean. Trade and mental intercourse increased rapidly with the West, and in a limited degree with the far East as well. The horizons of Israel were immensely widened. The intellectual sympathies of the nation were

The Roman World of Israel.

[1] Vol. i. 443 ff.　　　　　　　　[2] Vol. i. 445.
    A most useful chronology of the reign, with footnotes, is given by Schürer, *Gesch.*[3] i. 360 ff.

engaged by a culture utterly different from that which had previously influenced them. There was a new and enormous Jewish dispersion. Jerusalem became the seat of a far-spread spiritual empire.[1] Now Rome did not materially widen those horizons. Unlike the Phœnicians and the Greeks, the Romans were not explorers. But they gave peace to the world, whose extent the enterprise of their predecessors had made known, and by their thorough administration they multiplied its commerce and its wealth. The world was not a new one, but, to use the famous figure of Pliny, the Romans were a new day, a new sun, to it. His words are not too proud: '. . . immensa Romanae pacis majestate, non homines modo diversis inter se terris gentibusque, verum etiam montes et excedentia in nubes juga, partusque eorum et herbas quoque invicem ostentante. Aeternum quaeso Deorum sit munus istud. Adeo Romanos, velut alteram lucem, dedisse rebus humanis videntur.'[2] In this new day Jerusalem also flourished.

The effects of the Roman conquest on Western Asia may be stated as five.[3] First, the centre of trade as well as of politics was transferred to the other end Its Five of the Mediterranean, from Alexandria to Features. Rome. Secondly : the Roman Empire excelled all before it in the construction of roads—long lines of firm highways, fit for wheels as well as animals. Palestine, it is true, did not (except in the neighbourhood of colonial and other centres of Roman life) benefit by the characteristic Roman 'streets' till the time of the Antonines. But

---

[1] See above, Bk. III. ch. xv.    [2] *H.N.* xxvii. I.

[3] This paragraph is abridged from the author's article 'Trade and Commerce' in the *Enc. Bibl.* §§ 68-73, to which the reader is referred for the authorities cited.

the security of the ancient lines of traffic was a matter of care to the provincial governors; and even the *reges socii*, like Herod, in whose domains brigandage was apt to be rife, knew that the favour of Rome depended upon the success with which they kept order and the roads open. By the beginning of the Empire the security of land travel was immensely increased. Thirdly: at sea the greatest change was the reduction of the Mediterranean under one power, and the consequent clearance of piracy, first by Pompey and then by Augustus. Herod's own life offers remarkable illustrations of this. None of his predecessors voluntarily set foot on shipboard; he visited Rhodes, Lesbos, the Ionian coast, Sinope on the Black Sea, and four times went to Rome. Fourthly: trade down the Red Sea and across the Indian Ocean was multiplied. Ceylon, with its markets for the further East, became familiar. The Tiber and the Indus were not more than four months apart. All this secured the continued importance of Alexandria, which therefore did not succumb before Rome as Babylon had succumbed before herself. Fifthly: the civilised world found itself for the first time under a common system of law. We have seen the effect on Judæa after this became a Roman province;[1] but even in Herod's time, and through all the arbitrariness of his government, that effect was manifest. He was constantly referring cases of justice to Augustus.[2] The common languages of Syria continued to be Greek and Aramaic, the intellectual atmosphere that of Hellenism. But the Roman discipline and many Roman customs penetrated even the semi-independent states. And as all princes and their peoples were equally sub-

---

[1] Vol. i. 413.                    [2] See vol. i. 442 ff.

jects of Rome, there was more intercourse among them and more intermarriage.

To the imperial example and opportunity the genius of Herod responded—to the good that was in both as well as to the evil with which the latter tempted his ambitious and versatile mind. Our admiration has already been claimed for

Herod's Response to these.

the strong foundation of order from which Herod raised his services to the Empire. When he came to the full resources of his position, part of his method was the construction of fortresses. He rebuilt the Hasmonean castles of Alexandrium in the Jordan valley, Masada in the desert of Judæa, Machaerus in Moab, and Hyrkania the site of which is unknown.[1] He erected two new fortresses, each of which he called Herodium,[2] and a citadel by Jericho named after his mother, Kypros. That he could explain all these as necessary to the maintenance of order is proved by his exhibition of three of them to Marcus Agrippa. Those who have inspected the remains of the Herodian castles can testify to the skill with which they were designed and the power with which they were constructed—the strength of their sites, the ingenuity of their approaches, the number and thickness of their walls, the thoroughness of their masonry. In all these respects Herod might confidently show them to an able Roman. He also fortified Heshbon in Peræa, and,

---

[1] For the first three see *H.G.H.L.* 353, 512 ff., 569 (with my article on Machaerus in *P.E.F.Q.*, 1905, 224 ff.). Hyrkania must have lain west of the Jordan, for Herod took Marcus Agrippa to see it as well as Alexandrium and Herodium : xvi. *Ant.* ii. 1.

[2] Ἡρώδειον : one about three miles S.E. of Jerusalem on the Frank Mountain : Jebel el-Fureidis (Hill of Paradise), in which modern name it is possible to conjecture a corruption of his own. The site of the other has not been recovered ; it lay 'in the mountains towards Arabia.'

as a centre for his cavalry, Gaba on Esdraelon—one is reminded of Solomon's cities for chariots [1]—besides planting guard-houses all over the land. The next work which the Roman dispensation demanded from him was an open and secure gateway to the west. This he gave in Cæsarea—city, fortress and harbour. Its rank as the capital of the Roman province of Judæa, with all its commercial and religious importance in New Testament times, proved his foresight and the solidity of his building.[2] In the hills behind Cæsarea stood the already fortified Sebastē, upon the site of Samaria, which Herod selected, like Omri, Alexander and Perdiccas before him, for its western outlook.[3] On the maritime plain somewhere by the road between Cæsarea and Jerusalem he founded Antipatris in memory of his father,[4] and further south, near Gaza, he rebuilt the town and port of Anthedon,[5] under the name Agrippeion, thereby securing control of the Nabatean trade, which spread from Arabia as far as Italy.[6] He also founded a town Phasaelis, called after his brother, in the Jordan valley, which he brought under a wide and profitable cultivation.

The effects upon Jerusalem herself were of a double and opposite character. On the one hand, Herod was never at home in his capital. Besides their political purpose, a number of his constructions provided him with relief from the legalism of the City, which he detested, and with refuges from her fanatic turbulence, which he had increasing reason to fear. Sebastē was wholly Greek, and Josephus says that

Effects on Jerusalem.

---

[1] Above, pp. 56 f.    [2] *H.G.H.L.* 138 ff.    [3] Above, pp. 374, 376.
[4] *H.G.H.L.* 165, and the present writer's 'Antipatris' in the *Enc. Bibl.*
[5] *H.G.H.L.* 189.                [6] Vol. i. 341.

Herod built it ' for his own security.' His later years he seems to have spent almost constantly at Jericho, protected by his new citadel. It was the local Assembly of Jericho before which he brought the case of his sons, and other legal questions. In this he strictly conformed to the Law ;[1] but he was also more sure of the verdicts he wanted than if the trials had taken place in Jerusalem. Herodium, with its aqueduct, gardens[2] and luxurious apartments, not only gave him a residence near to Jerusalem yet fortified against her multitude, but lay on the way to Masada, where he had built himself a retreat from Jewish revolt and Roman caprice. That he also made the military road between the two is unlikely ;[3] it is probably Roman. But while this prudent distribution of his resources must have diminished in some degree the importance of the capital, it also increased her security, her population and her wealth. Except from Rome, Jerusalem had now nothing to fear. Fortresses controlled most of the ways to her gates. She had a coast of her own from Anthedon to Carmel and a spacious port towards Europe. The summer voyage from Cæsarea to Cyprus might be accomplished within two days, to Alexandria in four, to Athens in ten, to Rome within three weeks.[4] In other words, Jerusalem was sometimes, though not regularly, almost as near to Rome as Calcutta is to London. Roman emissaries and officials, Italian, German and Gaulish mercenaries, with traders from all the coasts of the Mediterranean, became familiar figures in her streets. The pickled fish

[1] Vol. i. 443 f.          [2] Vol. i. 130.

[3] Traces of which I followed in the desert : *H.G.H.L.* 273.

[4] See the writer's ' Trade and Commerce,' *Enc. Bibl.*, where the uncertainties of the voyage over the Mediterranean are also illustrated.

of the Lake of Galilee, the wheat of Hauran and Moab, the olives of Judæa, the gold and incense of Arabia, paid tolls from which Herod's capital directly benefited. From this time onward the majority of foreign terms in the Hebrew language are still Greek, but Latin words appear in increasing number. It is difficult to determine when each of these entered the language; many are certainly later than Herod's day, and imply the creation of the Roman province of Judæa in 6 A.D.; but a summary of them all may be given here as on the whole illustrative of Roman influence on Jewish life during New Testament times.[1] Greek terms of civil or military administration were already fairly numerous, for the Jews had been under Greek kings and familiar with their garrisons since Alexander; while the fact that nearly all the names for popular forms of government are Greek is significant of that influence of Hellenic cities upon Jewish politics which has been already described.[2] The political or military terms which Hebrew borrowed from Latin signify various military officers, several kinds of private soldiers, and parts of the characteristic Roman uniform or armour; courtiers, guards, police-officers, spies and informers; some taxes, weights and coins. In architecture the foreign terms are mostly Greek; we have seen traces of Greek influence in

---

[1] I have not been able to see the monographs on Greek and Latin words in the Mishna and Talmuds cited by Strack in his *Einleitung*, pp. 119, 121. Schürer, *Gesch.*[(3)] § 22, gives an interesting list. I have used it for checking and extending the summary which is given above, and which is mainly derived from my own reading. An exact study would discriminate between those in the Mishna and those in the Talmuds : the former are not nearly so many as the latter. Another difficulty would be to decide whether certain terms common to both languages were directly derived from the one or the other.     [2] Vol. i. Bk. I. ch. x.

the remains both of Hasmonean and Herodian buildings.[1]
But there are Latin words, as also Greek, for streets,
roads and footpaths. The terms for inn and harbour
and for many things connected with the sea are Greek.
In astrology, geometry, literature, medicine, philosophy
and religion the foreign terms are, of course, almost
exclusively Greek; yet Latin words sometimes occur,
and it is interesting to meet the Roman *disciplina* side
by side with the Greek *nomos*. Foreign expressions for
the industrial arts and their materials, especially spinning, weaving, fish-curing and writing, for the processes
and objects of trade, especially the names of various
traders and of jars for the conveyance of goods, are
nearly all Greek. Greek and Latin garments are
frequent: boots, trousers, robes and caps; names of
games, baths, feasts and articles of luxury are borrowed
from both languages. But the names of European
countries and peoples are given mostly in their Latin
form.

Through Herod's reign Jerusalem probably increased
in size and in the number of her inhabitants. But for
neither have we any exact data. The First Size and
and Second Walls ran as before, and the Population of<br>the Herodian
divisions of the City were the same. On the City.
crest of the East Hill lay the Temple with Baris to the
north, and to the south the Lower City falling to Siloam.
On the South-West Hill lay the Upper City, protected to
the north by the First Wall; beyond which lay the
northern quarter or slope enclosed by the Second Wall.[2]
That to the north of this there were already suburbs we

---

[1] Vol. i. 192, 217; vol. ii. 404, 426.
[2] Τὸ προσάρκτιον κλίμα: Jos. v. *B.J.* iv. 2.

know from the account of Herod's siege in 37,[1] but how far they reached at that time or were increased under Herod, how much of Bezetha was covered, or whether outlying houses with gardens had yet appeared on the northern plateau, are questions we have no means of answering. The population, too, is unknown. At the end of the reign and through the New Testament period it has been estimated as from 200,000 to 250,000, but the figure seems far too high.

From such uncertainties we turn to the increased fortifications and the new buildings which we definitely know to have been due to the lavish energy

The Revolution in the Topography.

of Herod. We must examine these with care, for they not only brought into bolder relief the outlines of the City and of her divisions, they not only enriched and dignified her whole appearance; but they altered her centre of gravity, in a political sense, they determined the topography of the New Testament, and they perverted the tradition of that of the Old Testament.[2]

When Herod captured Jerusalem in 37 B.C. the two northern lines of wall were breached, some of the Temple-cloisters burned, and other parts of the

The Walls and Great Towers.

town probably dilapidated, for the sack that followed the capture was ruthless.[3] Herod's first care as king must have been the repair of the fortifications. Although there is no record of his work upon the walls, we may infer from the towers he built, as well as from his thorough construction of other strongholds, that his engineers were busy with them all round

[1] Τὰ προάστεια : i. *B.J.* xvii. 8.   [2] Vol. i. 161 ff.
[3] xiv. *Ant.* xvi. 2 f. ; i. *B.J.* xviii.

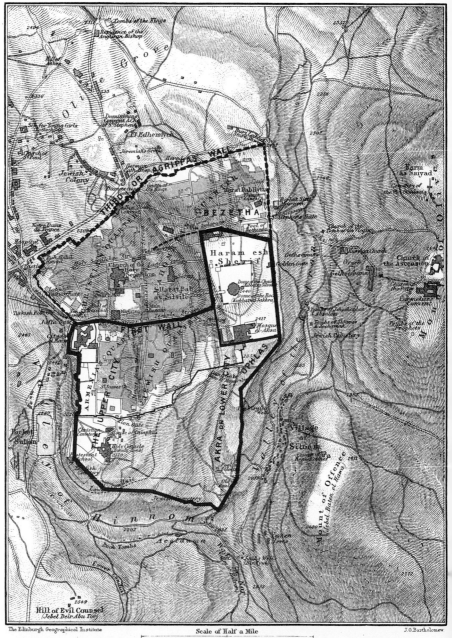

The Edinburgh Geographical Institute      Scale of Half a Mile      J.G.Bartholomew

The Walls in Herod's time are shown by red lines, except the course of the Second
Wall on the North which is unknown. The Third Wall added by Agrippa is
shown by red dotted lines on the line of the present North Wall of the City.

This map has not been printed in the original color. The red line
has been replaced by a heavy black line.

the City, and that the First and Second Walls which
so stubbornly resisted Titus in 70 A.D. had all been
strengthened or elevated by Herod.[1]  From the west wall
of the Temple to the present citadel and round the
South-West Hill to the Tyropœon the First Wall ran as
before.  It still enclosed Siloam,[2] and when it reached
the eastern boundary of the Temple area as extended by
Herod it coincided with this above Ḳidron, and then
turning round the northern slopes of the Temple-mount
reached the Baris, now called Antonia,[3] from which the
Second Wall struck across the Tyropœon on an unknown line to the Gate Genath on the stretch of the
First Wall along the north of the South-West Hill.
Here, on this same stretch of the First Wall, Herod
raised three lofty towers, which with a fourth to the
north of them greatly changed the western outline of the
City.  The three were Hippicus, perhaps where the north-
west tower of the present citadel stands ; Phasael, the
base of which still bears the tower known as ' David's ' ;
and a little to the east of this Mariamme [4]—the last two
certainly, and Hippicus perhaps also, on the Old or First
north wall.[5]  The fourth tower, Psephinus, an octagon,
stood to the north, probably on the site of the present
Ḳaṣr Jâlûd, at first isolated but afterwards connected
with the others by the Third, or Agrippa's Wall.[6]  Phasael
was ninety cubits high, Hippicus eighty, Psephinus
seventy, Mariamme fifty ; Phasael was forty cubits

---

[1] Vol. i. 193.          [2] Vol. i. 223.          [3] Vol. i. 234 f.

[4] On these three see vol. i. 242, and further on Phasael, 191 f.

[5] Josephus, v. *B.J.* iv. 3, seems to imply that only Phasael and Mariamme
were on the Old or First north wall, Hippicus being close by ; but in the
next section (4) he places them all on the old wall.

[6] Vol. i. 11 (*n.* 1), 240, 244.

square, Hippicus twenty-five, Mariamme twenty. Each of the four was built on a high, solid base of huge stones without mortar, with a revetment such as we see on the still extant base of Phasael.[1] Above this the structures differed, but all the towers were provided with battlements and turrets.[2]

The three towers, Hippicus, Phasael and Mariamme, lay then at the north-west angle of the Old or First Wall, where Herod's Court or Palace. this already formed a crest of thirty cubits high[3] on the South-West Hill, within and near the site of the present citadel. In touch with them, to the south and within the wall, Herod constructed a new Royal Court or Palace, 'the Palace in the Upper City.'[4] The wall of this was on the north and west the Old or First City wall; on the south and east a wall of the same height, thirty cubits, was erected, and there were towers at intervals. It was, in fact, a citadel as well as a palace. Within were two halls, each the size of the sanctuary with couches for a hundred guests, and many other chambers richly furnished. There were colonnades all round, courts open to the air in which everything was green, and groves or shrubberies with long walks among them. The whole was rendered possible by the High-

---

[1] Vol. i. 192, with Plate VI. This cubit was probably about 17·5 inches.

[2] See further the description of Phasael in *P.E.F. Mem.* 'Jerus.' 267 ff., especially the interesting comparison of the Josephan datum of a cloister which went round the tower ten cubits above the base with a similar outwork still extant.        [3] v. *B.J.* iv. 4: about 43¾ feet.

[4] Ἡ τοῦ βασιλέως αὐλή, v. *B.J.* iv. 4; τὸ ἑαυτοῦ βασίλειον κατὰ τὴν ἄνω πόλιν, i. *B.J.* xxi. 1; cf. xv. *Ant.* ix. 3; xvii. *Ant.* x. 2. After describing its various parts, in the first of these three passages, Josephus calls it by the plural, τὰ βασίλεια, in ii. *B.J.* iii. 1, xvii. 6; cf. ἡ ἀνωτέρω αὐλή. xv. *Ant.* vii. 8 calls it the Phrourion of the City as contrasted with that of the Temple; and in other passages the Akrai of Jerusalem are mentioned, xvii. *Ant.* x. 1; ii. *B.J.* ii. 2, iii. 1. See below, pp. 574 ff.

Level Aqueduct, which distributed water through deep conduits and metal fountains.[1] It was here that Herod kept those flocks of tamed pigeons to which, oddly enough, his name has been attached in later Hebrew.[2] The Palace was destroyed by fire in 70 A.D., and only the base of Phasael, parts of its other towers and of its western wall, remain to witness to its strength. But of the site there can be no doubt. Herod built his Palace on the highest of the three terraces of the South-West Hill.[3] The north and west walls were, as we have seen, the north-west angle of the First City Wall, and it therefore occupied the site of the present citadel and barracks, with an unknown extension southwards over the gardens of the Armenian monastery. Its breadth would most naturally be the breadth of the terrace, and its eastern wall therefore probably followed the line of the present street leading to the Sion Gate.[4] The Palace and Towers of Herod overlooked the whole City, as well as her approaches from the south and the west.[5]

Thus at last one, and this perhaps the most formidable, of the centres of authority in the City had been planted on the crest of the South-West Hill; and it was never to be shifted from here. Here Herod resided when he was in Jerusalem, and here he kept a large garrison of his mercenaries. Here also would reside Archelaus and Agrippa I.[6] The Palace

*Permanent Removal of the Seat of Authority to the S.W. Hill.*

---

[1] Vol. i. 129; vol. ii. 462 f.     [2] Above, p. 469 *n.* 1.     [3] Vol. i. 35.

[4] Schick (*Z.D.P.V.* xvii. 85) conjectures the breadth as extending from the west City wall nearly to the English church, and that the W. wall of the Armenian monastery stands on the E. wall of the Palace. 'The market-place east of the fosse which surrounds the Citadel appears to be supported on vaults' (*P.E.F. Mem.* 'Jerus.' 270). Could these be excavated some remains of Herod's Palace might be found.

[5] Vol. i. 26.     [6] xvii. *Ant.* ix. 3; ii. *B.J.* ii. 1 f.; xix. *Ant.* vii. 3.

of Herod was the Prætorium or residence of the Roman procurators,[1] the tower Phasael was the stronghold of Simon through the siege.[2] The Legionary Camp had its strongest angle here ;[3] here lay the castle of the Byzantines and the Moslems,[4] the Crusaders' Tower of David and Castle of the Pisans,[5] and here still stands the Turkish Castle, el-Ḳala'a. Herod's choice and parts of Herod's construction have endured, through all these dispensations, to the present day. And, as we have seen, it was his removal of the centre of the City's authority from the East to the South-West Hill which carried with it the names of the ancient stronghold on the former Ṣion, the 'City of David,' and perverted the whole tradition of the Old Testament topography.[6]

On the lowest terrace of this same South-West Hill, and, in fact, due east from the site of Herod's Palace, lay (as we saw) the Palace of the Hasmoneans ;[7] the first short step which the government of Jerusalem had taken from the East Hill and across the Tyropœon. After Herod extirpated the Hasmoneans this palace would pass into the use of his family, if indeed Mariamme had not already brought it with her as a dowry. Below this, in the Tyropœon, had long lain an open place of exercise, perhaps the Gymnasium which Jason had built.[8] Hereafter it is called the Xystos, the Greek name for a covered colonnade in a gymnasium.[9]

*The Hasmonean Palace and the Xystos.*

---

[1] xvii. *Ant.* ix. 3 ; ii. *B.J.* ii. 2, xiv. 8 ; see below, pp. 574 ff.
[2] v. *B.J.* iv. 3.      [3] Wilson, *Golgotha*, 142 ff.
[4] Muḳaddasi, 167, Istakhri, 56, quoted by Le Strange, *Pal. under the Moslems*, 213.
[5] That is Phasael ; cf. Will. of Tyre, viii. 3 ; ix. 3.
[6] Vol. i. 161 ff.      [7] Above, p. 461.      [8] Above, p. 432.
[9] So called from its polished floor ; it is first mentioned in xx. *Ant.* viii. 11 under Festus ; ii. *B.J.* xvi. 3, just before the siege by Titus.

Herod may have remade it under this name. The Hippodrome also, which it is probable (though not certain) that Herod built, is placed by some on the South-West Hill,[1] and they conjecture that a memory of it survives in the Ḥaret el-Meidān, or street of the racecourse. But the single notice of the Hippodrome seems to imply that it did not lie in the western part of the City.[2]

While by these edifices Herod not only altered the appearance of the South-West Hill, but the relative significance of all parts of the City, he effected also, by constructions still more massive, a transformation of the East Hill and of the Central Valley.[3] For on the third summit of the East Hill he rebuilt and amplified its citadel, the Baris.[4] On the fourth he rebuilt the Temple, greatly heightening the House itself, widely extending the courts, so as to cover all this part of the hill and project over the Central Valley, and surrounding the whole with a huge wall. And he appears to have made the east stretch of this wall coincident, for the first time in its history, with the East Wall of the City above the Ḳidron.[5] The extent and character of many of these changes has been disclosed by the work of the Palestine Exploration Fund, but some of them remain obscure, and have provoked much controversy. For such reasons, but also because of the place which the two buildings occupy in New Testament

*Transformation of the East Hill and CentralValley.*

---

[1] Guthe, Hauck's *R.-E.* viii. 686.

[2] xvii. *Ant.* x. 2 ; it was held by a band of the Jews who revolted against Sabinus, a second band held the temple, and a third band 'the western part of the city.'

[3] For these constituents of the site of Jerusalem, see vol. i. Bk. I. ch. i.

[4] On these summits see vol. i. p. 34.        [5] Vol. i. 234 f.

history and through the last siege, Herod's Castle and Temple are treated by themselves in the next chapter.

In this chapter we have still to notice his Theatre and Amphitheatre, with the gorgeous shows exhibited in them. Somewhere about 25 B.C. Herod founded an Athletic Gathering, to be celebrated every five years, in honour of Augustus.[1]

Herod's Athletic Gatherings.

He spared no expense, for, like Antiochus Epiphanes, this patron of the Olympian Games was determined to rival on his own soil the finest of the Greek and Roman spectacles. Athletes from all lands were invited to Jerusalem, to contend for costly prizes amid magnificent surroundings that flashed with ascriptions to the Emperor and trophies of the nations he had subdued, all wrought in silver and gold. There came also musicians and choral actors, whose name, Thymelikoi, would remind a cultured Jew of their original association with Greek worship. In a region unsuitable to wheels,[2] chariot-races were run, with two, three and four pairs of horses. Wild beasts were collected to fight with each other, or with men. To these shows Gentiles flocked with admiration. But it was a sore sight to Jerusalem, as though the most Hellenising of her Seleucid tyrants the very monster against whom the Maccabeans had risen, were come again, and in the person of her own king. We cannot wonder that the first festival marked the beginning of a period of trouble for Herod.

The sites of these spectacles are, therefore, of more

---

[1] Josephus, xv. *Ant.* viii. i.: ἀγῶνα πενταετηρικὸν ἀθλημάτων κατεστήσατο Καίσαρι. The name 'gathering,' used in the Highlands of Scotland for athletic and musical contests, is the exact equivalent of the Greek Agōn.

[2] See above, vol. i. 325. Herod must have improved the roads of his kingdom.

than ordinary interest.   Josephus says that ' Herod built
a theatre in Jerusalem, and a very great   His Theatre
amphitheatre on the plain.'[1]   If we conclude,
from its contrast with the other position, that the phrase
' in Jerusalem ' is to be taken literally, we must seek for
Herod's Theatre inside the walls, where two sites have
been suggested.[2]   But it is improbable that he would so
violently affront the religious authorities, and possible
to understand the words of Josephus in a more general
sense.   To the south of the City, on the hill beyond
the Jebel Deir Abu Ṭor,[3] the remains of a great theatre
were recently discovered, and we know of no other name
to call it by than Herod's.   It is of the usual form : a
semicircle on the hillside, with traces of stepped seats
and chambers below, and in front a level space for the
stage.   The diameter is rather large for a Palestine
theatre, 132 or 136 feet.   Facing north, the theatre is
visible from several parts of Jerusalem : the spectators
looked across the Jebel Deir Abu Ṭor onwards to the
City.[4]

The site of Herod's Amphitheatre ' on the plain ' is not
certainly known.   It may have been out on the Buḳêi'a,
or on the plateau to the north of Jerusalem.   and Amphi-
But an equally suitable position, and one   theatre.
with which tradition connects great games, may be seen
as we look from the north-east corner of the City north-
east into the great basin on the Olivet range.   I often

---

[1] As above, xv. *Ant.* viii. 1.

[2] On the S.W. Hill, south of the Burj el-Kibrit, and on the East Hill
south of the Ḥaram.                    [3] Vol. i. 31 and Plate v.

[4] The discovery was made by Schick, who, however, wrongly calls it
an *amphitheatre*, while his description and plans are, as above, of a *theatre* ;
*P.E.F.Q.*, 1887, 161 ff.

wondered whether this level space was ever utilised in ancient times, till I heard that the people have a story of its having been 'a Meidan, or place of exercise, where strong men wrestled and made games.' This may embody a genuine recollection of Herod's athletic gatherings in honour of Augustus, and indicate the site of his Amphitheatre.[1]

---

[1] I was walking in the neighbourhood one afternoon with Dr. Percy D'Erfe Wheeler and his servant, when the latter told us this story as current among the people. He called a clump of ruins on the site er-Raṣâṣ. Cf. Bîr er-Raṣâṣ or Raṣâṣîyeh, a little further north (*P.E.F. Large Map*, sheet xvii., and Schick's map of the nearer environs). Raṣâṣ does not necessarily mean 'lead'; the root is applied to any joining, ranging, or piling, especially of stones.

# CHAPTER XVIII

## HEROD'S CASTLE AND TEMPLE

IN this chapter we shall treat of Herod's two most conspicuous and significant reconstructions, which, standing together on the East Hill, were destined to be the principal scenes of the remaining Jewish history of Jerusalem—his Castle, the Antonia, and his Temple. The Castle was built first, and we begin with it.

The Baris, or Akropolis of the Hasmoneans, stood (as we have seen) on the north of the Temple.[1] According to Josephus, Herod refortified this castle and enlarged it at a vast expense, calling it 1. The the Antonia, in honour of Mark Antony.[2] Antonia—its character: He says that the Antonia 'lay at' or 'near to the angle of the two cloisters of the first Temple, that to the west and that to the north.'[3] Its basis was 'a rock 50 cubits high, and precipitous all round.' Herod deprived the sides of foothold by covering them with slabs of stone. Round the edge ran a rampart, three cubits high, within which 'the whole erection of the Antonia was carried to

---

[1] Above, p. 460.

[2] xv. *Ant.* viii. 5, xi. 4 ; xviii. *Ant.* iv. 3 ; xx. *Ant.* v. 3 ; i. *B.J.* xxi. 1. The description of it given above is abridged from v. *B.J.* v. 8.

[3] v. *B.J.* v. 8 : Ἡ δ' Ἀντωνία κατὰ γωνίαν μὲν δύο στοῶν ἔκειτο τοῦ πρώτου ἱεροῦ, τῆς τε πρὸς ἑσπέραν καὶ τῆς πρὸς ἄρκτον. The *First Temple* here is to be taken in the sense of the outer Temple ; cf. v. *B.J.* v. 2, where the inner Temple is called *the second.* See below, pp. 513 *n.* 2, 518 *n.* 1.

a height of 40 cubits.[1]   The interior contained every
kind of dwelling and other convenience, colonnades,
baths and broad courts for encampments, so that in
possessing all manner of utilities it seemed a city, but in
sumptuousness a palace.'  'The whole plan was tower-
like,'[2] but at the corners it carried four other towers,
three 50 cubits high, and a fourth, at the south-east
corner, 70, so as to overlook the Temple.  Stairs or
sloping gangways led down to the two adjoining cloisters.
They appear to have crossed a rocky incline between the
Antonia and the Temple; for, though some of the
language used by Josephus may be interpreted as though
the Antonia immediately adjoined, or even abutted upon,
the Temple cloisters, this is not the only possible
meaning;[3] and in his description of the struggles between the Romans and the Jews, after Titus had taken
the Castle, Josephus implies that some little space inter-
vened between the latter and the *peribolos* of the
sanctuary.[4]   On the north, again, the Antonia was

[1] As to the figures given by Josephus, it must be remembered that he
wrote some years after the destruction of the Temple, and at a distance
from Jerusalem, that his figures for the Temple dimensions frequently
exceed those given in the Mishna (which are preferred below); but also
that in one or two cases in which we can test others of his figures by
extant remains, these have been found to be very near the truth.   The
heights which he gives for the Antonia towers seem needlessly great.

[2] Cf. Tacitus, *Hist.* v. 11 : 'Conspicuoque fastigio turris Antonia in
honorem M. Antonii ab Herode appellata.'

[3] ii. *B.J.* xv. 5 f: when Gessius Florus sought to reach the Temple
'through the Antonia,' the Jews 'cut through the Temple cloisters adjoining': ἀναβάντες εὐθέως τὰς συνεχεῖς στοὰς τοῦ ἱεροῦ πρὸς τὴν 'Αντωνίαν
διέκοψαν ; xvi. 5, however, calls them the στοαῖ of the Antonia itself, and
this suggests that they were the (covered) passages connecting the two ;
xvii. 1: the people going up to the Temple began the rebuilding of these
στοαῖ.

[4] vi. *B.J.* i. 7 ff ; ii. 6 ; 'neither side had any length of space whether for
flight or pursuit.'

isolated from the higher summit of Bezetha by a deep ditch 'designedly cut through' the ridge which joined them.[1] So far Josephus. With his data agrees Luke's description of Paul's adventures between the Temple and the Castle. When Paul was dragged *out* of the Temple, and the gates were shut, the Chiliarch came down with soldiers and brought him up *the ascents* to the Castle. From these gangways Paul addressed a crowd standing below them, but outside the great sanctuary wall. There was, therefore, a space of open ground on the saddle of the hill between the Temple and the Castle.[2]

For those who hold that the Temple stood to the west of the rock eṣ-Ṣakhra, there can be no doubt about part at least of the site of the Antonia.[3] This was the rock at the north-west corner of the *and its Site.* Ḥaram, upon which the Turkish barracks now stand. The southern face of the rock is a scarp from 20 to 32 feet high. The east face is hidden by buildings. On the west the conditions are not so clear. But it has been amply verified that on the north a broad, deep ditch is cut across the hill, so as to separate the rock from

---

[1] v. *B.J.* iv. 2: διεταφρεύθη γὰρ ἐπίτηδες, ὡς μὴ τῷ λόφῳ συνάπτοντες οἱ θεμέλιοι τῆς 'Αντωνίας εὐπρόσιτοί τε εἶεν καὶ ἧττον ὑψηλοί (see vol. i. 244); cf. v. 8.

[2] Acts xxi. 30 ff. (cf. above, vol. i. 246): castle=παρεμβολή. The reference to the gates cannot mean the gates of the inner sanctuary, and that the crowd stood in the court of the Gentiles. Paul could not have addressed them through the massive outer wall and its cloisters.

[3] Those who place the Temple in the S.W. corner of the Ḥaram (vol. i. 231; vol. ii. 61) are forced to place the Antonia much further south than the rock described above, and, in fact, where there is no outstanding rock at all, in the Tyropœon valley! Fergusson (*Temples of the Jews*, 172 ff.) assumes that Wilson's arch and the underground chambers to the W. of this are parts of the substructions of the Antonia. But this is also to remove the Antonia too far from Bezetha, its nearness to which is placed by Josephus beyond all doubt.

Bezetha, just as Josephus describes.[1] Above these scarps, then, stood part at least of the Antonia. But the rock is not a simple oblong; it has an offshoot to the south. At right angles from the west end of its southern face, another scarp, facing east across the Ḥaram, runs to the Bab es-Serai. The space between the two scarps is natural rock, falling south-east to the Ḥaram level. It is probable, therefore, that the high site of the Antonia was an irregular gnomon with its prolongation southwards to the Bab es-Serai. This hypothesis provides more of the room needed for the interior of the Castle as described by Josephus; it provides a longer western face for the Antonia which seems required by the account of the fighting under Titus; it brings the end of the Castle nearer to the north-west angle of the Temple, which cannot have been situated much further north than the Bab en-Nâzir;[2] and at the same time it leaves space, partly sloping, partly level, for the interval which Josephus describes between the cloisters and Antonia, and which was apparently crossed by the sloping gangways.[3] In this space traces of a ditch across the saddle are said to have been discovered.[4] If such a ditch ever existed, it was before Herod's day, in order to separate between the Baris and the Second Temple, and it must have been filled up by Herod, for there is no description or hint of a ditch between the Antonia and Herod's Temple.

---

[1] For these particulars see *P.E.F. Mem.* 'Jerus.' 212 ff., with Plans II. and XXXVII. of the Portfolio. The northern ditch and its scarps are described by Clermont-Ganneau, *Arch. Res.* i. 49 ff. The street to the Bab Sitti Mariam (St. Stephen's Gate) runs along the ditch, which extended far to the west, part of its N. scarp having been discovered in the grounds of the Austrian hospice. Here it was probably the fosse outside the Second Wall.

[2] See vol. i. 231.        [3] Above, p. 496.

[4] *Recovery of Jerus.* 13, 312.

Therefore the supposition that a bridge, or pair of bridges, connected the two is unfounded.[1]

As the name implies, Herod built his Antonia before the fall of Mark Antony in 31 B.C.   His Palace on the South-West Hill was finished by 23,[2] and even earlier his Hippodrome, Theatre and Amphitheatre.[3]  Sebaste was built in 27, and Cæsarea begun about 22.   In these and other cities he had erected shrines to Greek and Roman deities; while in sight of Jerusalem he had established heathen games and spectacles.[4]  It became necessary to his policy to do something for Judaism.   His fresh and costly structures in Jerusalem, built in Hellenic style with limestone that showed like marble, rendered the Temple of Zerubbabel, in spite of its embellishment during the Greek period, meagre and shabby.   Herod had difficulty, however, in gaining the consent of 'the multitude' to his plans;[5] and Josephus says that he began by explaining to them that his previous works were undertaken in order to advance the fame of the Jews among other nations!   But now piety urged them all to do something great for their own God. The Second Temple, he averred, was not so lofty as the First, and his predecessors had never been able to heighten

2. The Temple—Herod's Reasons for Rebuilding.

---

[1] Sanday and Waterhouse (*Sacred Sites of the Gospels*, 108, with Plan 116; see also frontispiece) suppose a 'valley' crossed by 'a double bridge' between the Temple and Antonia, for which there is 'some reason' (108).   But there is no 'valley' across this part of the East Hill, only a saddle between two summits, the Antonia rock and the rock eṣ-Ṣakhra.   If there had been a ditch before Herod's time, Herod must have filled it up, for there is not the faintest allusion to either a ditch or 'a bridge' in all the subsequent relations of the Temple and Antonia.   Nothing is described between them from Herod to Titus, except 'no long space of ground' (on which the fighting took place between Romans and Jews) and the stairs or gangways.

[2] Above, pp. 488 f.          [3] Above, p. 491 ff.          [4] Above, p. 492.

[5] xv. *Ant.* xi. 2 ; see above, vol. i. 443.

it. But his friendship with the Romans, the peace with which God had blessed His people, made it possible to repair this defect and prove their gratitude to God. Still the Jews hesitated, and Herod won them over only by promising that he would not pull down the old House till he was ready to build the new. That no profane hand might touch the inner sanctuary, he put a thousand priests into training as masons and carpenters. Then, in the eighteenth year of his reign, the winter of 20-19 B.C., he began to build. The Naos or House itself was finished in

Dates and Period of Con- struction.

eighteen months, and was dedicated on the anniversary of his accession; but the construc- tion of the cloisters and the massive outer en- closures occupied eight years.[1] Even then much remained to be done, and the work dragged on long after Herod's death. During one of our Lord's visits to Jerusalem it was said *forty-and-six years has this Temple been building*,[2] which fixes the date of that visit as 27 or 28 A.D. Not

[1] For all the above particulars see xv. *Ant.* xi. 5 f. In i. *B.J.* xxi. 1 the Temple is said to have been begun in Herod's fifteenth year. If this be correct it refers to the preliminary operations. See Schürer's full note *Gesch.*(3) § 15 *n.* 12.

[2] John ii. 20: Ναός; *the Naos*, in its proper sense of the House itself, was finished in 1½ years, and objection has therefore been taken to the Evangelist's accuracy, which Drummond meets by saying that the phrase 'takes up the word used by Jesus and might be loosely applied to the Temple with all its connected ornaments and buildings' (*Character and Authorship of the Fourth Gospel*, 370). But that *Naos* was used by Jewish writers of Greek to describe not only the House itself, but the inner enclosure and even the outer, may be seen both in the N.T. and Josephus. In Matt. xxvii. 5 Judas is said to have *thrown the silver pieces into the Naos*, which cannot have been the House but one of the courts about it. (For ναός in its proper sense see Matt. xxiii. 35; Luke i. 21 f.; in ii. 27, 37, 46, and in Acts xxi., Luke correctly uses ἱερόν.) Similarly Josephus, v. *B.J.*, v. 3 § 201, speaks of 'one gate, that outside the Naos, of Corinthian bronze'; it stood outside the Court of Israel, if not even outside the Court of Women. And in xv. *Ant.* xi. 3, while employing Naos of the House itself (§ 391, etc.) he

till the Procuratorship of Albinus (63-64), says Josephus,
'was the Temple finished.'[1]  Six years later the House
with all its cloisters sank in fire, never to be replaced.

Solomon's Temple had consisted of a House, with an
inner chamber known as the Debîr or Back, and an outer
called the Hêkal, Palace, or Temple.  In front   Its Various
it had a Porch, a Fore-Court, with the Altar    Divisions.
of Burnt-Offering, to which all Israel were admitted, and
a great Outer or Lower Court which surrounded also the
Palace-Court and other royal buildings.[2]   The Second
Temple was a House of the same scale and disposition as
the First.  It had more than one court, probably two, as
Ezekiel prescribes ; but his reservation of the inner one to
the priests does not appear to have been enforced for a
considerable period.[3]   The first recorded exclusion of the
laity from the neighbourhood of the Great Altar is under
Alexander Jannæus (103-78 B.C.), who put up a barrier
'round House and Altar,' after the crowd pelted him with
citrons.[4]   But it is precarious to conclude that so personal
a trouble was the whole origin of the reservation of the
inner court to the priests.  Along with other developments,
like the Court of Women and the exclusion of foreigners
from the inner Temple, the reservation of the Altar-court
to the priests may have been realised during earlier
centuries, when the Temple area was enlarged by new
substructures ;[5] and when the rigorous distinctions of the

also applies it both to the inner (401) and to the whole Temple, inner and
outer, τὸν ναὸν ἅπαντα (396).   In the conversation described in John ii., our
Lord and the Jews used either *Baith* or *Hêkal*, both of which were applicable
either in the stricter or looser sense ; and whichever was used it was natural
for the Evangelist to employ the same Greek word to translate it in both cases.

[1] xx. *Ant.* ix. 7 ; in xv. *Ant.* xi. 3 Josephus states that part of the Naos
fell and was rebuilt under Nero.          [2] Above, pp. 61 f.

[3] Above, p. 309.        [4] Vol. i. 410.        [5] Above, p. 386.

Law were gradually enforced, if not in the Persian period then under the Maccabees. In any case the following delimitations appear in the area of Herod's Temple, and he cannot be supposed to have invented any of them. Herod's Temple consisted of a House divided like its predecessor into the Holy of Holies, and the Holy Place; a Porch; an immediate Fore-court with the Altar of Burnt-offering; a Court of Israel; in front of this a Court of Women; and, round the whole of the preceding, a Court of the Gentiles.[1]

'The House' itself, the Naos proper, occupied the site of its predecessors, to the west of the rock eṣ-Ṣakhra.

The House proper: Divisions and Contents.

The ground-plan was the same, the interior being 60 cubits by 20, divided into the Holy of Holies and the Holy Place. Before the former, still a dark and empty cube of 35 feet, known by its ancient name Dĕbîr, but also as the House of Atonement, hung a Veil, *the Veil of the Naos* according to the Gospels, the *second veil* of Hebrews;[2] the Rabbinic tradition was of two curtains with a cubit between them.[3] The Holy Place or Hêkal proper

---

[1] The data for Herod's Temple are found in Josephus, xv. *Ant.* xi. 3, 5; v. *B.J.* v., with other passages describing the revolt under Gessius Florus and the siege by Titus. The Mishna tractate 'Middoth' (ed. Surenhusius, vol. v., with R. Obadiah of Bartenora's and other commentaries; an Eng. trans. is given in the *P.E.F.Q.*, 1886, f.). See also the *Beth hab-Bechereh* of Maimonides (which I do not have in the original; Eng. trans. in *P.E.F.Q.*, 1885). Modern descriptions and reconstructions are many, of which there may be mentioned Lightfoot, *Descriptio Templi Hierosolymitani*; *Opera Omnia*, 2nd ed. vol. i. 333 f. (1699); Fergusson, *The Temples of the Jews*, pt. ii. (1878); Perrot and Chipiez, *History of Art in Sardinia, Judæa*, etc., i. 142 ff. (1890); Waterhouse in *Sacred Sites of the Gospels*, 106 ff. (1903); see also the various Bible dictionaries and manuals of archæology.

[2] Mark xv. 38; Matt. xxvii. 51; Luke xxiii. 45; Heb. ix. 3.

[3] *Mishna*, 'Middoth' iv. 7, with R. Obadiah's note: 'Yoma' v. 1; Moses Maimonides, *Beth hab-Bechereh*, iv. 2.

was still 40 cubits by 20, but 40 instead of 30 high.
Over it lay a second chamber of 40 more, which with
the solid foundations, 6 cubits high, the ceilings and
roof, made 100 cubits in all.   The Holy Place held
the same furniture as the Second Temple: the Altar
of Incense, the Table of Shewbread and the Lamp,
now with seven branches.[1]   After what we have seen of
the symbolism of Solomon's Temple, it is interesting
that Josephus should ascribe to these objects a cosmic
meaning.[2]   The doorway was 20 cubits by 10, and had
double doors with a magnificent Babylonian curtain
on the outside, of various colours symbolising the
elements, ' as it were an image of the universe.'   Upon
beams in front of this trailed the Golden Vine, of the
size of a man, to which liberal worshippers contributed
leaves and clusters.   The Porch was rebuilt as a great
propylæum, 11 cubits deep and of the same height,
100 cubits, as the House behind it.   But it was also 100
cubits broad, or 15 more on either side than the exterior
breadth of the House behind, which was 70 cubits.[3]   The
vast entrance, 70 cubits high by 15 broad, lay open
without doors, manifesting, says Josephus, 'the unobstructed openness of heaven.'[4]

Herod outraged Jewish feelings by hanging above this
symbol of heaven a golden eagle with the name of his
friend Marcus Agrippa.   When the eagle was pulled

[1] As shown on the arch of Titus in Rome.

[2] v. *B.J.* v. 5 ; see below, p. 527.

[3] Josephus makes it 20 cubits broader on each side, but agrees with the
Mishna ('Middoth' iv. 6 f.) on 100 cubits as the breadth and height. .

[4] v. *B.J.* v. 4 : τοῦ γὰρ οὐρανοῦ τὸ ἀφανὲς καὶ ἀδιάκλειστον ἐνέφαινε. Τὸ
ἀφανές might be taken as Jew-Greek for a prospect on which 'nothing appears '
to obstruct the vision ; but Bekker emends to τὸ ἀχανές, which Aristotle
uses for ' the void of space ' (Liddell and Scott).   In either case the meaning
is the same.   ' Middoth ' iii. 7 gives the opening as 40 by 20 cubits.

down in the riots of 4 B.C., he seems to have felt the act
more as an affront to himself than as sacrilege against
God. He was naïvely right. The imperial eagle and some
distinguished Roman or other were always fixed in
Herod's heaven.[1]

We are thus asked to conceive of a building 172 feet
long from east to west, and (if all its base was visible)

Its General      172 feet high, whose propylæum was also
Appearance.      172 broad, while the House behind was only
120. 'As a lion is narrow behind but broad in front, so
the Temple was narrow behind but broad in front.'[2] The
height may seem excessive, but besides being attested
by Josephus and the Mishna independently,[3] it is very
credible in the light of Herod's ambitions and the limits
within which these had to work. He did not dare to
alter the ground-plan or interior arrangements, but he

---

[1] The names given in 'Middoth' (cf. 'Kelîm' i. 9) are כָּל־הַבַּיִת, the whole
House, applied to the building with the porch (iv. 1); the Naόs proper (see
above, p. 500 *n.* 2); הַהֵיכָל, ha-hêkal, palace or temple properly (as before)
the Holy Place (iv. 7, Maimonides, *Beth hab-Bechereh*, vii. 22); perhaps also
applied to the House as distinct from its porch (iii. 8, iv. 1 : so certainly in
the Talmud); and to the House inclusive of the porch (iv. 6 f.). The Holy
of Holies was בֵּית קֹדֶשׁ הַקֳּדָשִׁים, also הַקֹּדֶשׁ and בֵּית הַכַּפֹּרֶת, or House
of Atonement (O.T. כַּפֹּרֶת). It is also called דְּבִיר, but an interesting
instance of how the original meanings of names are forgotten is the
Talmudic derivation of this, from דבר, word or oracle (*Talm. Jerush.*,
'Ber.' iv. 8 *c.*). The Holy Place was הֵיכָל, as we have seen. The Porch
was אוּלָם. The chambers were תָּאִים. The whole was sometimes called
בֵּית הַמִּקְדָּשׁ (used also in a wider sense); and בֵּית אַחֲרוֹן and בֵּית שֵׁנִי, the
latter and second House.

[2] 'Middoth' iv. 7, ha-hêkal; cf. Jos. v. *B.J.* v. 4, 'in front it had what
may be called shoulders on each side.'

[3] The above reckoning (more exactly 172·25 ft.) is on the basis of 20·67
inches to the (sacred) cubit. If we take the later Greek cubit of 17·47 inches,
the Temple was 145·58 feet in all three dimensions, the 'House' 101·9 broad.

could amplify the less sacred porch and increase the
height of the whole. If he was forbidden to extend the
House, he would at least make it soar! The whole was
built of huge blocks of white stone,[1] with plates of gold
upon the front, so that at a distance it appeared like
a mountain covered with snow. The roof was protected
from birds by a multitude of sharp spikes. It is interesting to note that above the great entrance the courses were
five oak beams with a course of stone between each two.
Such a detail warns us against attributing to the architecture of the House that Greek style, which many are
tempted to give it, because of the Corinthian pillars of
the outer cloisters and the Grecian qualities of Herod's
military architecture. It was one thing to plan cloisters
for the court of the Gentiles, or revetments at the base of
fortresses, but quite another to replace an ancient Jewish
Temple. While the Temple of Herod was much more
lofty than that of Zerubbabel, jealous care would be
exercised to model it on the same lines, and priests
alone effected its construction. We may conceive of
its style either as Babylonian, the builders of the Second
Temple having come from long residence in Babylon, or
as perpetuating the Phœnician and Egyptian traits which
distinguished the Temple of Solomon.[2] Neither Herod
nor his generation were likely to feel incongruous the
conjunction of several styles of building on the same area.
And that is why all modern reconstructions of the work,
except the outer cloisters, must be more or less fanciful.

Twelve broad steps descended from the House to
the Court of the Priests,[3] covering nearly all the 22

---

[1] Twenty-five by 8 by 12 cubits; xv. *Ant.* xi. 3.
[2] Above, p. 62.     [3] עזרת הכהנים.

cubits which separated the Porch from the Altar.[1]  This
The Court of the Priests.  was the space *between the Temple and the Altar*.[2]  No one might stand here while the priest was within offering incense.[3]  A little to the south of the steps stood the great Laver which had replaced the Bronze Sea of Solomon's Temple.[4]  We have seen reason to believe that the Altar rose upon the rock eṣ-Ṣakhra. In Herod's Temple the Altar, of unhewn stones, was a massive structure whose base must have been adapted to the irregular surface of the rock ; and, conformably to this, tradition says it was laid in concrete.[5]  The base was 32 cubits square and one high.  Above it the structure, 30 cubits square, rose five high to a ledge one cubit broad, on which were the horns of the altar ; a little higher another ledge, also a cubit broad, ' the place for the feet of the priests ' who officiated ; and above this the hearth itself, 24 cubits square.[6]  Two apertures drained the blood into a channel, which carried it off to the Ḳidron.[7] On the south a slope of masonry led to the ledge on which the ministering priests stood.  To the north were the shambles : rings in the pavement, to which the victims were bound and so slain ; marble tables on which they were flayed and washed ; pillars with cross

---

[1] *Mishna*, ' Middoth ' iii. 6.

[2] Matt. xxiii. 35 : *between the Naos and the Altar*, for which the Mishnic phrase is ' between the Porch and the Altar,' ' Kelîm ' i. 9.

[3] ' Kelîm ' i. 9.    Lightfoot (cap. xxxvi. p. 641) suggests a spiritual application of this.   ' Kelîm ' i. 9 adds none might come here who was blemished or had his head uncovered.

[4] Above, p. 65.  Some tables stood beside it for the victims.

[5] R. Obadiah of Bartenora's note to ' Middoth ' iii. 1.

[6] Ezekiel xliii. 16 had fixed the altar as 12 cubits long and broad, but the Rabbis interpreted this as 12 each way *from the centre*, which harmonised with the 24 of each side given above ; ' Middoth' iii. 1.

[7] ' Yoma' v. 6 ; ' Middoth ' iii. 2 ; cf. on the Ṣakhra above, p. 60.

beams and hooks from which they were hung and (when necessary) quartered.[1] It is said that the plentiful supply of water rapidly flushed off the blood and refuse; but both on the greater festivals and on ordinary days, when the number of private sacrifices was frequently very large, the court must have reeked with blood and flesh. The exact size of the Priests' Court is unknown, for the data conflict. Josephus says that the barrier of stone, which marked it off from the Court of Israel, encompassed the House and the Altar,[2] that is, ran round at least three sides, if not also the back, of the former. But according to the Mishna the barrier ran only on the east of the Court of the Priests.[3]

Therefore, except that it was railed off from the Court of the Priests, and that part, if not the whole of it, lay to the east of this, we do not know the disposition of the Court of Israel.[4] Josephus implies that it spread round at least three sides of the House and the Priests' Court; the Mishna, that it lay only on the east of the latter.[5] The Mishna, followed by its commentaries and several modern reconstructions, defines the Court of Israel as an oblong, 135 cubits north and south by 11 east and west. But this appears far too small a space for what was the gathering-ground of all the men

The Court of Israel.

---

[1] *Mishna*, 'Middoth' iii. 5; v. 2; cf. 'Pesaḥim' v., 'Zebaḥim' v., and 'Tamîd' iii. For the slaughter of victims on the north of the altar, see Leviticus i. 10 f.

[2] v. *B.J.* v. 6; cf. the barrier of Alex. Jannæus, xiii. *Ant.* xiii. 5.

[3] 'Middoth' ii. 6, where the extension north and south of the Priests' Court and of the Ct. of Israel is the same (see p. 509 *n.* 1), so that the barrier did not run round the House. If we prefer the evidence of Josephus, we have still to decide whether his 'encompassed' means round all four sides of the House. If it does, the Court of Israel included the space of 11 cubits between the Holy of Holies and the inner west wall.

[4] עזרת ישראל : 'Middoth' ii. 6.     [5] Above, *n.* 3.

of the Congregation; and there is thus a semblance of
reason for Mr. Waterhouse's reconstruction, which,
ignoring the Mishna, assigns to the Court of Israel a
greater breadth than 11 cubits to the east of the Court
of Priests; carries it besides with Josephus round at
least the north and south sides of the latter; and
interprets 'the place for the tread of Israel,' which the
Mishna identifies with the Court of Israel, as merely a strip
of 11 cubits (to the east of 'the place for the tread of
the priests'), on which the laymen stood whose presence
was required with their victims near the altar.    There
are, however, objections to this, and the data of the
Mishna though confused appear capable of another
explanation.    It seems to me probable that the ambiguity of the Mishna reflects these facts : *first*, that there
was once no distinction, but the Court for Israel and the
Priests was one;[1] and *second*, that when the distinction
was made and the laity were driven back from the altar,[2]
controversies arose about the new delimitation, and that
its lines remained for a time (perhaps always) uncertain.
The names 'place for the tread of priests' and 'place
for the tread of Israel' probably represent the first stage
in the delimitation when there was still (as before the
Exile and for some time afterwards) only one inner court
to the Temple.    The name 'Courts' was applied to these
separate spaces only later, while the name 'the whole
Court' continued to cover both divisions.    Hence the
Mishna's undoubted equation of the places for the tread

[1] See above, p. 501.
[2] Except in cases in which the offerer had to come forward into the Priests'
Court for the purpose of slaying his victim himself, or putting his hands on it,
or waving it : 'Kelîm' i. 8.

of the priests and of Israel respectively with the Courts
of the Priests and of Israel may not be wrong, but may
merely represent the gradual evolution of the single
inner court of the Temple, with 'places marked off for
priests and laity,' into the two or three inner courts of
Herod's Temple.[1]

On the east the Court of Israel was separated by
a wall (running north and south) from the Court of
Women, which lay fifteen steps lower,[2] but The Court
had a gallery high enough to allow the of Women.
women to view the services in the Court of the Priests.[3]

---

[1] *Mishna*, 'Middoth' ii. 6, first states the dimensions of both courts;
each was 135 cubits long (north to south) by 11 broad (east to west); then
the dimensions of 'the whole court,' 187 long (east to west) by 135 broad
(north to south); v. i. gives the same dimensions for 'the whole court': in
the length (east to west) it includes 'the place for the tread of Israel' and
that 'for the tread of the priests,' which are also 11 cubits each, and therefore obviously the same as the Court of Israel and the Court of the Priests in
ii. 6. Lightfoot (cap. xvi. p. 590), who treats this part of the subject with
an unusual disregard of detail, calls the Court of Israel and the Court of the
Priests one court, evidently feeling that the delimitation of them is impossible. Nearly all modern descriptions fight shy of the conflicting data;
most of them follow the Mishna in giving the breadth of the Court of Israel
at 11 cubits, but with Josephus (and against the Mishna) they carry the
court round the north and south of the House, some of them even round the
back of it. Waterhouse (*Sacred Sites of the Gospels*, 111 f.) treats the
difficult question more carefully and with originality. In opposition to the
Mishna he takes 'the whole court' as meaning only the Court of the Priests,
and the 'place for the tread of Israel' a strip within this to which laymen
were permitted for purposes of sacrifice (see above), and assigns to the
Court of Israel a considerable extension to the east. One cannot but
sympathise with so reasonable an arrangement. At the same time, it is
only possible if we assume that 'Middoth' is altogether wrong in identifying the Court of Israel with 'the place for the tread of Israel': a precarious assumption. On the whole, I think the explanation which I have
suggested above is the most probable.

[2] The Court of Israel (or at least its eastern end) lay on substructions
which were necessary from the slope of the hill, and which formed vaults
opening into the Court of Women : עֶזְרַת נָשִׁים ; 'Mid.' ii. 5 f.

[3] 'Middoth' ii. 5.

Except this gallery, all the Women's Court was open to men. It was a large court, 135 cubits square, and probably the finance with much other business of the Temple was transacted within it. There is no direct statement of this.[1] But we may infer so from the comparative size of the court, from the large chambers at its corners and the vaults under the Court of Israel which opened on to it, and from the fact that the treasures and private deposits[2] which the Temple held were certainly kept within the inner Temple, while the business they involved would more naturally be transacted in the Court of Women than in either the Court of Israel or the Court of the Priests, which were devoted to the worship and to processes immediately pertaining to this. In the Women's Court, then, we are to place the Temple strong-rooms and the thirteen trumpet-shaped money-boxes into which the faithful put their legal and voluntary offerings.[3] The Gospels certainly imply that women had access to these, and describe them by one word—the Treasury: *the crowd cast money into the Treasury, and a poor widow coming up cast in two lepta.*[4] In another passage the name seems to be given to the Women's Court as a whole.[5]

---

[1] Compare the statement that it was 'the camp of Levi.'

[2] See vol. i. 365; vol. ii. 428.

[3] For the size of the court and the chambers, 'Middoth' ii. 5. Of the שופרות or 'trumpets,' 'Shekalim' vi. 1, 5, says merely that they stood in the Miḳdash or Miḳdash shel-baith, the sanctuary of the House; that six were for freewill offerings and seven for specific dues which are named. Josephus, xix. *Ant.* vi. 1, says that the γαζοφυλάκιον was in the inner enclosure of the Temple; the γαζοφυλάκια, which he mentions in v. *B.J.* v. 2 and vi. *B.J.* v. 2, are all the chambers or לשכות which lay round the walls of the whole inner court, and not merely the treasuries in the Women's Court. Yet in the former passage he associates them with this Court. [4] Mark xii. 41 ff.; Luke xxi. 1 f.

[5] John viii. 20; cf. 2 Macc. iii. 24, 28.

The Court of Israel was surrounded by a high wall (25 cubits=43 feet), with a cloister and chambers on the inside, while round the outside ran a narrow terrace known as the Ḥêl, or fortification,[1] and outside this the Soreg, a latticed barrier, with copies of the inscription warning foreigners not to pass within on pain of death.[2] The question is whether the Court of the Women did not also lie within this double boundary of Ḥêl and Soreg, fortification and ritual fence. Josephus appears to imply that it did.[3] In one passage the Mishna implies that it lay outside, but in others that it was included.[4] The inclusion has thus a large balance of evidence in its favour, and is in itself the more probable supposition. The notices on the Soreg warned off only foreigners, and not Israelite women. The Jews would hardly have left their women outside the protective enclosure, and nearer to the Gentiles in the great outer court than to themselves. The same consideration applies to the treasuries, which were always placed within the Sanctuary,[5] and to the money-boxes, to which indeed the Gospels clearly state that women had access. On the whole, therefore, the inclusion of the Women's Court within the Inner Sanctuary is extremely probable, if not certain ; and we must again read the ambiguities of the Mishna as reflect-

Did it lie in the Inner Temple?

[1] The Ḥêl (חיל) was properly both the wall and the terrace of 11 cubits round the outside of it : ' Kelîm ' i. 8.

[2] Vol. i. 425.                [3] xix. *Ant.* vi. 1.

[4] ' Middoth ' i. 4, which gives only three gates on each of the north and south sides of ' the Court.' ' Middoth ' ii. 6, which gives four gates on each of the north and south sides—and calls one of the former ' the gate of women.' ' Kelîm ' i. 8 distinctly states that the Ct. of Women lay within, and was holier than, the Ḥêl.

[5] See the LXX. of Neh. xiii. 7 ; also 2 Macc. iii. 24 ff.

ing a dim recollection of different stages in the history of the Temple : one when 'the Court' had but three gates on the north and on the south respectively ; and one when a separate Women's Court was constructed to the east of it, or (at least) included within it, and 'the Court' had four gates on each side : the latest and most easterly of each row opening into the Women's Court.[1]  The Women's Court, then, was one of the latest developments of the growth of the Temple, and the memory of this was preserved in the wall which ran between it and the court of Israel ; as in the tradition that it was less holy than the latter.[2]  In the last years of the Temple, when the Evangelists and Josephus knew it, the Women's Court had become an integral part of the Inner Sanctuary, within the Ḥêl and the Soreg ; and of this the Mishna, too, has preserved a tradition.  The surrounding wall, then, had nine gates, four on the south, four on the north, and one on the east, out of the Women's Court into the Court of the Gentiles.  In addition there was a gate between the Courts of Israel and the Women, the gate of Corinthian bronze.  Which of these two gates opening to the east is to be identified with the Gate of Nikanor and *the Gate Beautiful* is uncertain.[3]  The Mishna implies that the Gate of Nikanor was the inner of the two.[4]

Everything that has been described up to this point—

[1] For an argument that the Ct. of the Women lay outside the wall, the Ḥêl and the Soreg, see Büchler, *Jew. Quart. Rev.*, 1898, July and October.

[2] 'Kelîm' i. 8.          [3] Acts iii. 2.

[4] 'Middoth' i. 4 ; in ii. 3 it seems to set this gate on the boundary wall of the Inner Temple, which it now (ii. 6) implies enclosed the Women's Court. These passages, as we have seen, may reflect different stages in the growth of the Temple.

the House proper, the Court of Priests with the great
Altar, the Court of Israel, the Court of Women The Inner
with the Treasury — possessed a special Temple or<br>Sanctuary of
sanctity and lay within their own double en- the House.
closure: a high, towered and gated wall, surrounded by a
narrow terrace, the Ḥêl, and a ritual fence, the Soreg.
They formed the Inner Temple, the Second Temple, the
Sanctuary, as Josephus variously defines it;[1] the Temple
(proper) according to the Soreg inscription;[2] in the
Mishna the Sanctuary, or the Sanctuary of the House,[3]
or even the House and House of the Sanctuary,[4] in that
wider sense to which both these terms might be stretched
according to an ancient practice of the language.[5] *Minus*
the Women's Court, it is also called by the Mishna 'The
Court' or 'The Whole Court.'[6] Only Israelites, and
these only when ceremonially clean, could enter the
Inner Temple. From the Soreg inwards all was holy
ground, though, of course, with varying degrees of
sanctity.[7] But the Ḥêl or 'fortification' constituted the
Inner Sanctuary into a fortress as well — a separate
citadel which in 70 A.D. the Jews were able to hold for
some time after Titus had taken the outer cloisters on
the north and penetrated the Court of the Gentiles.[8]

Fourteen steps lower than the Ḥêl lay the wide outer

---

[1] Tὸ ἔνδον ἱερόν, vi. *B.J.* iv. 4, τοῦ ἐνδοτέρω ναοῦ, v. 3; τὸ δεύτερον ἱερὸν ἅγιον ἐκαλεῖτο, v. *B.J.* v. 2. For the 'First Temple' see above, p. 495 *n.* 3.

[2] Vol. i. 425, within its double enclosure of τρύφαξ, that is the Soreg, and περιβολός, that is the Ḥêl and the wall together.

[3] מקדש or בית של מקדש, 'Shekalim' vi. 1, 5.

[4] הבית; בית המקדש, 'Mid.' i. 1.    [5] Above, p. 256.

[6] 'Middoth' i. 4, 'the Court' with seven gates (*i.e. minus* the Women's Court, which added two more; see above, p. 512); *Id.* ii. 6, v. 1, 'the whole Court.'

[7] For these degrees see *Mishna*, 'Kelim' i. 8 f.    [8] vi. *B.J.* iv. 4 ff.

VOL. II.

Court, the Court of the Gentiles, surrounding the Inner

The Outer
Court or
Court of the
Gentiles.
Temple on all sides, but with much the greatest space on the south, and with the next greatest on the east.[1] The Inner Temple, therefore, did not lie in the middle of the Court of the Gentiles, but towards its north-western corner, round the summit of the Temple-Mount, now the rock es-Ṣakhra, on which the Altar was placed. We have seen that Herod built vast substructions on the lower slopes of the mount and over the Tyropœon Valley, in order to form this spacious outer Court and lift its surface near to the level of the Inner Sanctuary, about the summit: thus creating the immense platform, still extant as the outer Ḥaram area. The passages in which Josephus compares the Temple areas of Solomon and Herod respectively[2] are somewhat obscure. Their construction is involved, and not without traces (in one passage at least) of confusion between the very different operations of the two kings upon the Outer Court and its surrounding walls. To begin with, although Josephus states in one place that fresh banks, enlarging the Temple area, were added at some periods between Solomon and Herod[3]— and we have seen this to be the case, during the Greek period, with Zerubbabel's or the intermediate Temple— yet in general he speaks of only two Temples, and in one passage as if that of Solomon had been succeeded immediately by that of Herod.[4] We must understand that by Solomon's Temple area Josephus means in this passage the Temple area of Zerubbabel enlarged by the

---

[1] *Mishna*, 'Middoth' ii. 1.
[2] xv. *Ant.* xi. 3; 1 *B.J.* xxi. 1; v. *B.J.* v. 2.
[3] v. *B.J.* v. 1.     [4] xv. *Ant.* xi. 3.

High-Priest Simon in the third century B.C., and by others also, as it stood just before Herod began his reconstructions. Again, although Josephus distinctly states that Herod's Temple area was double that which preceded it,[1] yet in another passage he describes Solomon's outer and lower Temple wall as 'starting from the root' or 'bottom,' that is of the Temple-Mount.[2] But if Solomon's Temple area had covered the whole Temple-Mount from the bottom (as the Ḥaram area now does), no room would have been left, at least on the eastern slope, for Herod's extension of the sacred precincts ; and besides, we have seen that in Nehemiah's time there were houses on this eastern slope between the Temple enclosure and the City wall above the Kidron.[3] Solomon's outer and lower Temple wall must therefore have risen on the east, not from the bottom of the Mount but some way up it. In fact, in this last passage the description of the outer enclosure—'carried to a [great] height[4] so that the extent and altitude of the structure, which was rectangular, was immense, . . . and he filled up the hollows round [the inside of] the wall till he made them of the same level as, and flush with, the surface of the upper parts of the Mount'—reads as if it had been originally intended for a description rather of Herod's Temple area than of Solomon's.[5] In any case the description agrees

[1] 1 *B.J.* xxi. 1 : 'he rebuilt the Naos, and round it he walled in a space double that which was' already enclosed.

[2] xv. *Ant.* xi. 3 (398 in Niese's edition).

[3] Vol. i. 199 f.

[4] Or 'carried forward to the depth [outside],' xv. *Ant.* xi. 3 (398).

[5] As it stands the passage, xv. *Ant.* xi. 3 (398-400), is undoubtedly arranged so as to read as a description of Solomon's Temple, for (1) Solomon's is the name mentioned immediately before it, 398 ; and (2) immediately after, it is still the older Temple area which is described, as being a

with the present disposition of the Ḥaram, whose enclosing walls spring from 'the root' of the Temple-Mount,
whose outer area rests upon 'hollows filled up' by vast
substructions, and whose higher central platform, representing, in part at least, the Inner Temple of Josephus,
lies 'round the summit' of the Mount, the rock eṣ-Ṣakhra.
And we have already seen evidence that at least the
south-west corner of the Ḥaram, the south wall and the
east wall as far north as the so-called ' Golden Gate,' is
Herod's masonry.[1]   It is true that the colonnade along the
inside of this wall was called Solomon's, and that Phœnician letters have been discovered on some of its lowest
courses.   But neither of these facts can be taken as proof
either that the wall dates from Solomon's time or that
Solomon's outer and lower Temple wall stood so far east
as this.   For the name Solomon's Porch, like many other
structures called after that monarch, does not imply that he
built it, and the Phœnician letters may have been mason-
marks as late as the time of Herod.[2]   We have also seen
that the north wall of the Ḥaram is probably not Herod's.
The north wall of his Court of the Gentiles lay further
south, crossing the present Ḥaram from a point a little
north of the Golden Gate to near the Bab en-Nâzir.   The
Mishna defines the Temple area as a square of 500 cubits,
that is 860 feet.[3]

Inside these outer walls Herod erected magnificent
colonnades.   The finest was the southern, the Stoa

stadium in each direction, and as having been adorned by many kings in
former times, and by Herod himself with the spoils he had taken from the
Arabians.   But either Josephus has written the whole section hurriedly, and
in the description quoted above Herod must be taken as the nominative to
the verbs ; or else the sentences have become disarranged.

[1] Vol. i. 232 f.        [2] Vol. i. 233, 238 *n.* 3.        [3] 'Mid.' ii. 1.

Basilica or Royal Cloister, with 162 Corinthian columns
in four rows. Each of the others had two rows. The
eastern was known as Solomon's.[1] At least
eight gates pierced the walls. On the north
was the Gate Tadi.[2] On the east was the Gate
Shushan, probably that now called 'the Golden,' the
masonry of which appears to belong to a later period
than the Herodian. On the south, low down in the wall,
were at least the two Gates of Ḥuldah, the present Double
and Triple Gates, with passages leading up under the
Royal Cloister to the Inner Temple. These gave way to
the Temple from the Lower City. On the west the
Mishna records only one gate, Kiponus ; but, with the
bulk of the City on the West Hill, there must have been
more. Josephus mentions four. The fragment known
as Robinson's Arch, the lintel of an old gateway which
appears a little to the north, and, still further north,
Wilson's Arch, probably indicate the positions of three of
these gates.

*The Outer Cloisters and Gates.*

The Outer Court within its massive, strongly gated
walls, was known to the Jews as the Mountain of the
House.[3] The name, so far as Herod's Temple
is concerned, is an anachronism ; reminiscent
of days when this part of the East Hill was
an actual mount, with the Temple disposed round its
summit, and, below the Temple wall, houses down the
slopes to Ophel on the south, and to the edges of the
valleys which encompassed it west, east and north-east.

*Other Names for the Outer Temple.*

---

[1] John x. 23 ; Acts iii. 11 f., v. 12.  [2] 'Mid.' i. 3.

[3] הר הבית distinguished in 'Middoth' i. 1 from 'the Court' or Inner Sanctuary (cf. i. 3, five gates to the Mt. of the H. with i. 4, seven to the Court),
and still more clearly in ii. 1, where it is described as east, west, north and
south of the latter ; cf. ii. 3 where the Soreg is said to be inside of it.

But now the mount was masked beneath an artificial plateau within walls that rose from 'its root' nearly to the level of its summit. The Jews seem, too, to have applied to the Outer Court the name Birah or Castle, yet this may also have been used as in former times for the whole Temple.[1] The Court of the Gentiles is variously designated by Josephus as the First, Outer and Lower Temple.[2] Taken along with the Inner Temple, he calls it 'the whole Temple.'[3]

Such, then, was the Third Temple of Jerusalem : sanctuary within sanctuary, fortress within fortress—with an Appearanceof adjunct and dominating castle off its north-the Whole. west corner. We are standing on the road from Bethany as it breaks round the Mount of Olives, and are looking north-west; this is what we see. Instead of the round and steep Temple-Mount, which has hitherto been visible, the fourth eminence of the East Hill, with a Temple disposed about its summit, but on its lower slopes houses girdled by the eastern wall of the City; there spreads a vast stone stage, almost rectangular, some 400 yards north and south by 300 east and west, held up above Ophel and the Ḳidron valley by a high and massive wall, from 50 to 150 feet and more in height, according to the levels of the rock from which it rises.[4] Deep cloisters surround this platform on the inside of the walls. Upon the east one large gate gives way from it

---

[1] בירה ' Middoth ' i. 9 ; from the house Moḳed on the Ḥêl a winding passage led under the Birah, by which priests who became unclean could pass outside the Temple without treading on consecrated ground. This implies that the Birah here means all outside the Ḥêl. Yet R. Obadiah in his note says that the whole sanctuary was called the Birah. Cf. ' Tamîd ' i.

[2] v. *B.J.* v. 8 ; vi. *B.J.* iv. 4.      [3] xv. *Ant.* xi. 3, § 402.

[4] The best idea of the height of the Ḥaram walls is got from Warren's elevations in the *Recovery of Jerus.* facing p. 118. The lowest height was above Ophel, 52 feet ; the highest over Ḳidron, 170.

into the Ḳidron. On the south, two and perhaps three gates pierce the wall below the level of the cloisters and lead up under these to the middle of the platform. Through the west wall four gates give entrance from the Upper City, which rises theatre-wise in the background and is topped by Herod's Towers and Palace. On the north wall one gate leads in from the overlooking suburb of Bezetha. Every gate has its watch, and other guards patrol the courts.[1] The crowds, which pour through the south gates upon the great platform, for the most part keep to the right; the exceptions, turning westwards, are excommunicated or in mourning.[2] But the crowd are not all Israelites. Numbers of Gentiles mingle with them; there are costumes and colours from all lands. In the cloisters sit teachers with groups of disciples about them. On the open pavement stand the booths of hucksters and money-changers; and from the north sheep and bullocks are being driven towards the Inner Sanctuary. This lies not in the centre of the great platform, but towards its north-west corner. It is a separately fortified, oblong enclosure; its high walls with their nine gates rising from a narrow terrace at a slight elevation above the platform, and the terrace encompassed by a fence, within which none but Israelites may pass. This Inner Sanctuary and fortress is nearly 185 yards from east to west and some 77 from north to south.[3] Upon its

---

[1] Philo, *De Praemiis Sacerdotum*, vi. The *Mishna*, 'Mid.' i. 1 f., describes the watches at the corners, and at only some of the gates, besides the patrols; but the whole passage seems to refer to the discipline during the night.

[2] 'Middoth' ii. 2.

[3] 'The whole court,' 187 cubits, *plus* 'the Court of Women,' 135 cubits ('Mid.' ii. 5 f. v. i.)=322 cubits. At 20·67 inches to the sacred cubit, most probably the one used, we get 554·64 feet, or nearly 185 yards. If we add to this twice the breadth of the Hêl, 20 cubits=34·45 ft., we get 589 ft. The breadth (N. to S.) without the Hêl was 135 cubits, which on the same reckoning is 232·53 ft.

higher western end rises a House, 'like a lion, broad in front and narrow behind'—57 yards broad in front and of that length and height throughout. From the open porch of this House stone steps descend to a great block of an Altar, perpetually smoking with sacrifices; and to the north of the Altar are its shambles with living animals and rows of carcases. Priests in white garments move to and fro among these objects, or ascend the slope to the Altar, or stand round its hearth serving the sacrifices, or pass up and down the steps to the House. East of all this runs a barrier, and the space outside is packed with men. Then a wall and the lower eastern end of the Inner Sanctuary: the Temple-Treasury and exchange, filled with a crowd of Levites in charge of the people's offerings, hucksters, money-changers and worshippers on their way to the inner court, and above them a gallery of women. Off the north-west of the Outer Sanctuary a castle dominates the whole from its four lofty towers. Beyond, as has been said, the Upper City rises in curved tiers like a theatre. Against that crowded background, the Sanctuary with its high House gleams white and fresh. But the front of the House glittering with gold plates is obscured by a column of smoke rising from the Altar; and the Priests' Court about the latter is coloured by the slaughters and sacrifices—a splash of red as our imagination takes it in the centre of the prevailing white. At intervals there are bursts of music; the singing of psalms, the clash of cymbals and a great blare of trumpets, at which the people in their court in the Inner Sanctuary fall down and worship.[1]

[1] 2 Chron. xxix. 26 ff.; *Mishna*, 'Tamîd' vii. 3, etc.

# CHAPTER XIX

## THE TEMPLE AND THE LORD

SUCH were the Shrine, Altar and Courts which constituted the last Temple of Jerusalem. We have now to examine the worship they embodied, and this not merely in order to complete our survey of the Jewish religion The Temple : Israel and Christianity. through the history of the First and Second Temples,[1] but because from the short-lived Third Temple, Israel's final and most elaborate sanctuary, tradition has dated the origins of Christianity [2]—in the promise of an immediate Messiah, revealed during the routine of its worship and to the prayers of its regular congregation. The Third Temple was that to which Christ came, which He used, and which He judged ; that to which for a time His disciples adhered, and their relinquishment of which formed the most potential crisis in the history of the Church. Part of the historical connection between the two religions thus ran through the Third Temple. And whatever of essential difference distinguished the new from the old is best illustrated by the principles of its worship. In the main the difference was one between an Institution and a Person. The Messiah promised to the Temple supplanted the Temple.

---

[1] Above, pp. 72 ff., 310 ff.  [2] Luke i., ii.

It is this religious revolution which forms the subject of
the present chapter, and leads our long work—begun
among the physical rudiments of the life of Jerusalem,
and pursued through the closely interwoven developments of her economy, politics and religion—to its end
in Jesus Christ.  Put what meaning we may into the
facts, History has nowhere else such facts to offer.  Nor
is our assurance of them dependent on still unfinished
processes of criticism.  About the broad results there is
no question ; the rise of a new religion from the heart
and the home of the old one, the hesitating steps upon
which at first it ventured, and its final break from the
Jewish system in the faith that all which this had
mediated was become more directly and surely possible
through the Person and Work of Jesus.  Even before
the great Sanctuary perished at the hands of Rome, and
Israel's Altar was for ever quenched, Jesus in the experience of His followers had taken the place of the Temple
and of everything for which it stood.

The Temple was the approach of a Nation to their
God.  Israelites alone could enter its Inner Sanctuary,
and its standard rites were performed in the
name and for the sake of the whole People.
At the crisis of the Sacred Year, the Day of
Atonement, when the High Priest entered the Holy of
Holies alone, he did so as the representative of Israel ;
conversely his sins were theirs, and the additional offering
which he made for himself covered them also.[1]  The
Tamîd or 'Standing Sacrifice,' offered twice a day on the

The Temple
Worship—
1. The Nation.

---

[1] Lev. iv. 3 : Patrick Fairbairn's *Typology*, ii. 263 f.

high altar, was the offering of the Nation.[1]  Every Jew
contributed to its maintenance.[2]  So closely was it identified with the public welfare, that in times of stress all
other sacrifices were abandoned before it was, and its
stoppage meant the utmost calamity to the state.[3]  Each
of its celebrations was attended by a formal committee
of the nation,[4] and its national character was further
expressed by the seven Psalms appointed for its weekly
rotation.[5]  The Gospel of Luke opens with the service of
incense accompanying the Tamîd.  *And the whole multitude of the people were without praying at the hour of
incense :*[6] this, though it seems an exaggerated expression, is a formally correct description of the lay congregation which attended every service of the Tamîd.
Compare the communal phrases which follow: *to make
ready for the Lord a people prepared ; the throne of his
father David, and he shall reign over the house of Jacob ;
He hath holpen Israel His servant that He might remember
covenant mercy towards Abraham and his seed for ever ;*
the similar phrases, of which the Song of Zacharias is
full; and finally, *looking for the consolation of Israel.*[7]
That Luke, the Gentile evangelist, should have depicted

---

[1] התמיד or עלת התמיד : Num. xxviii. 3 ff. ; Dan. viii. 11 ff., xi. 31 ;
*Mishna,* 'Tamîd'; a whole burnt-offering and meal-offering accompanied
with a service of incense.  [2] Vol. i. 357, 359.

[3] Daniel viii. 11 ff. ; xi. 31; xii. 11; Josephus vi. *B.J.* ii. 1 ; *Mishna,*
'Ta'anith' iv. 6: בטל התמיד.

[4] Israel was divided for the purpose into twenty-four 'watches,' representatives of each of which in succession formed with the corresponding
'watch' of Priests and Levites a 'station' for the service.  *Mishna,*
'Ta'anith' iv. 2 ff.; to be corrected by the corresponding passage in the
*Tosephta*; cf. *Mishna,* 'Tamîd' v. 6.  For details see Lightfoot, *Minis-
terium Templi,* vii. 3 (*Opera* i. 700); Schürer, *Gesch.*[(3)] ii. § 24 *n.*

[5] Psalms xxiv., xlviii., lxxxii., xciv., lxxxi., xciii., xcii. ; 'Tamîd' vii. 4.

[6] Luke i. 10.

[7] Luke i. 17, 32 f., 54, 68 ff.; ii. 25.

this communal character of the Temple worship is proof of his fidelity to historical situations of which he had not been an eye-witness, nor with which he had any congenital sympathy; and the proof is the more emphatic if, as Professor Harnack has argued, the early chapters of the Gospel are not a translation from an Aramaic document, but Luke's own reproduction of oral tradition.[1] Thus the worship of the Temple was corporate, communal, national. Although, as we shall see, there was room for the individual piety which Jeremiah asserted contemporaneously with the Deuteronomic proclamation of the Covenant as one with all-Israel, yet the latter was the dominant and organic principle of the worship; and the individual took his part in this only as a member of the Chosen Nation.

But secondly, the Prophets had predicted the coming of the Gentiles *to the mount of the House of the Lord—My House shall be called a House of Prayer for all peoples*;[2] and the Law had provided for the 2. The Gentiles and their Sacrifices. admission of proselytes and implied that sacrifices might be rendered by those who were alien to Israel.[3] The kinds of offerings acceptable from them were even defined.[4] Such hopes and tolerances were signalised by the Court of the Gentiles. The most spacious of all the divisions of the Temple, it typified a

---

[1] *Luke the Physician*, Eng. trans., especially 12 f., 24, 96-105, 199. If, as Harnack argues, Luke composed the Magnificat and the Song of Zacharias, their fidelity to the essential form of the Jewish religion is evidence that he must have been an enthusiastic proselyte to Judaism for some time before he became a Christian. But to an Old Testament student, the other alternative, of translation from Aramaic originals, seems the more probable.

[2] Isa. ii. 2 f.; lvi. 7.      [3] Lev. xxii. 25.

[4] *Mishna*, 'Shekalim' i. 5, vii. 6; 'Zebahim' iv. 5; 'Menahoth' v. 3, 5 f., vi. 1, ix. 8. Gentiles could not place their hands on their offerings.

world gathered about Mount Sion, and suggested the short and single step which still separated the Gentiles from full communion with Israel.    More obscure is the meaning of the Gentile sacrifices.    Offerings had been accepted from the Greek sovereigns of Judæa and other notable foreigners, but the national party were hostile to their admission.[1]    Even if they could be technically regarded as gifts to Israel, to enable the nation to fulfil its own dues to God, the thought can never have been far away that the persons of their donors were also acceptable before Him.    We must guard, however, against the opinion that the crowds of Hellenist Jews, and their familiarity with the Greek world, favoured liberal views on the subject.    From various motives the Hellenists were even less disposed to relaxation than the Hebrews of Jerusalem.[2]    To all alike, the Nation, Israel, was still the human partner in the Covenant with God.

But the nation did not make its approach to God, at least through the most intimate stages of this, in the persons of all its members.    Whereas in the First Temple the laity had been admitted to the inmost Court, and Solomon had ministered 3. The Mediating Priesthood at the Altar, in the Third Temple the laity were excluded by a barrier, and Herod, though king, could not present his own offerings.[3]    Every most sacred rite was performed by priests, and the Holy of Holies was entered by the High Priest alone.    This reservation of the immediate Presence of God to one hereditary order, the sons of Aaron, was connected with a change of emphasis among

---

[1] And protested in 6 A.D.  See Schürer, *Geschichte d. jüd. Volkes, etc.*[(3)] ii. § 24, Appendix.

[2] Cf. Acts vi. 9 ; ix. 29.          [3] Josephus, xv. *Ant.* xi. 5.

the various values attributed to Sacrifice. In primitive
times every slaughter of a domestic animal was
*and Sacrifices.*　a sacrament, and every house-father might
perform it. In the first sanctuaries of the people the
feast shared with the Deity by the worshippers determined if not the sole, yet the predominant, character of
the ritual. Even in Deuteronomy, worship is *eating and
rejoicing before God.* The priest burnt the fat, the
Deity's share of the Covenant feast, and had his own legal
due from the flesh ; but his office seems to have been
connected more with the oracle than with the victim.
The earlier priest was a teacher and a judge,[1] rather
than a mediator or minister of expiation. This festival
character of sacrifice was not destroyed by the centralisation of the cultus, but it was greatly diminished. The
proportion of sacrifices, which were not feasts but services
wholly of atonement, gradually increased, as we may see
by comparing the Deuteronomic code with the Levitical,
and both with the practice of the earlier kingdom. In
the third century B.C., Theophrastus the Greek observed
that 'the Jews do not eat their offerings, but burn them
entire.' [2] So absolute a negative is, of course, wrong ;
yet it is certain that in the Third Temple the piacular
aspects of sacrifice prevailed over every other. And in
consequence, the position of the priests as the necessary
mediators between God and man was deeply confirmed.
The consummation of every sacrifice, the offering of
blood and incense, the entrance to the Presence of God,
were lawful for priests alone. This requirement of a
mediating priesthood and of sacrifice, Christianity

---

[1] Hosea iv. 6 ; Micah iii. 11 ; cf. Deut. xxxiii. 10, for both offices.
[2] The passage is given in Reinach, *Textes*, etc., 7 f.

took over from Judaism, as an assumed principle of religion.

Israel's approach to God through priests and sacrifices was made in order to fulfil the Covenant into which He of His mercy had called them, that they might become a holy Nation to Himself. He was 4. The God of the Temple. very jealous of sins, whether against the moral conditions of the Covenant or against the ceremonial law, which at once expressed and guarded the awfulness of His Presence. He demanded restitution for sins, but in the Temple service He had provided the means for this, and upon the use of the means was ready to forgive and to restore His erring people. Thus the God of Israel, He was also Creator of all things, God alone, Omnipotent in Nature and History alike. In the Third Temple we miss some cosmic symbols which were present in Solomon's.[1] But the seven Psalms of the Tamîd celebrate both God's deeds in History and His cosmic power: the latter especially in the verse which opens the series, and in the Psalms of the fifth and sixth days of the week.[2] And, if Josephus be right, the vast entrance of the Porch symbolised Heaven, the colours of the First Veil the elements, the Seven Lamps the Seven Planets, the twelve loaves of the Presence the signs of the Zodiac and the circuit of the year: while 'the Altar of Incense with its thirteen odorous spices signified that God is the possessor of all things, in both the uninhabitable and the habitable world.'[3] Yet amid all this symbolism God Himself was not adored in any material form. One could

---

[1] Above, p. 75 f.    [2] Ps. xxiv. 1; lxxxi., xciii.
[3] v. *B.J.* v. 4 f. There are similar ideas in Philo. Against them see Patrick Fairbairn, *Typology*, ii. 253 f.

represent only His Presence or Dwelling, and this was double. God was both the Far and the Near; above all things, filling the Heavens and yet abiding with His people. The antithesis is similar to that in the creed and worship of the First Temple.[1] During the later centuries and in the silence of the living word of Prophecy, the impression of God's Transcendence prevailed over the experience of His Intimacy, and 'God of Heaven,' or even 'Heaven' alone, came to be one of His commonest designations. Yet this conception was linked to the other and nearer by the closest name men have ever found for Him: 'your Father in Heaven.'[2] He had chosen Israel for His own, and He dwelt with Israel. The Temple was His earthly seat; and the Rabbis accepted the Deuteronomic explanation of this by saying that 'His Name dwelt there':[3] the practical and experimental meaning of which we have already learned.[4]

Conformably to this double conception of God's Presence — transcendent and indwelling — the Temple The Double contained a great Altar beneath the open Worship— heavens and a Mercy-Seat within a dark *a.* Towards Heaven. and windowless House. From the Altar sacrifices ascended in smoke to the Divine Throne. Smoke symbolised many things to the religious feelings of Israel: God's Presence, the confusion of mortals when they encountered it, His wrath, the torments of the wicked, the evanescence of everything material before the blast of His Spirit. The smoke of sacrifices of which the worshippers consumed part had been conceived as the Deity's share in the feast. But the smoke of the whole

---

[1] Above, p. 74.
[2] *Mishna,* 'Yoma' viii. 9.
[3] *Id.* i. 5.
[4] Above, p. 311.

burnt-offering was the people's confession of their sin, their surrender through death and fire of the lives He was pleased to take in place of their guilty and forfeit selves. The sin, the contrition, the repentance of a nation—this was what the dark column meant which rose from the Altar and melted away in the infinite purity of the skies. *I have blotted out as a thick cloud thy transgressions, and as a cloud thy sins.* If ethical processes must be expressed in material forms, no sacrament could be more adequate than this, which proved at once the death deserved by sin, its purification by fire, and the disappearance of its blackness and bitterness in the unfathomable mercy of Heaven.

Behind the Altar rose the House, the dwelling of God with men. The vast and doorless Porch was the symbol of an approach as free and clear as opened above the Altar: 'the unobstructed openness of Heaven.'[1] *b.* Towards the House. But behind were a veil and a door, and after the Holy Place another veil and then a dark and empty room. For as God was invisible and inscrutable yonder, so was He even here. His Presence was darkness itself, and no mind nor hand might image Him. As from the Altar the smoke ascended to the heavens, so into 'the House of the Atonement' they brought the Blood, that also was expiation by death, the Bread of the Presence, and the Incense, which, whatever may have suggested its first use, was regarded as well-pleasing to God, a propitiation (therefore offered first in the outer chamber), and perhaps, too, a symbol of the people's prayers.[2]

---

[1] Above, p. 503.

[2] Perfumes shed in the presence of kings, cf. Ephes. v. 2; for the placating of wrath, atonement, Num. xvi. 46 ff. (Eng. =xvii. 11 ff. Heb.); prayers, Ps. cxli. 2; Rev. v. 8, viii. 3 f.

The ethical effect of all this must have been double
and contradictory. On the one hand, the faith of the
Ethical Effects. worshippers was drawn into the unseen:
*it was anchored within the veil.* From
the visible, the material, the finite, their hearts went
out to an empty darkness which was the most fruitful
suggestion possible of the invisibleness and imma-
teriality of the things which are eternal. From their
own works, from rites performed by themselves, their
faith was lifted to a work done *for* them and accepted
solely of the grace of God. Such, we may take it, was
in the main the beneficial influence exercised by the
Jewish system on the minds of the worshippers. The
Temple carried faith at least in the right direction. *My
soul longeth, yea even fainteth, for the courts of the Lord :
my heart and my flesh cry out for the living God.* Nor
did the rites, though predominantly national, fail to meet
the individual as well. Save in a pedantic logic, these
two ideas of religion, the corporate and the personal, are
not incompatible. As none know better than we Christians, they may sincerely, and indeed inevitably do,
exist together in the consciousness of the worshipper.
Moreover, the multitude of private sacrifices for which
the Temple provided were wholly personal, while the
Psalms of its most national service, the Tamîd, emphasise
the moral purity required from every individual worshipper.[1] Men *went up into the Temple to pray*, each
for himself and after his own temper.[2] For the day of
Atonement the Mishna details not only the duties of
the High Priest, but the proper conduct of the private
Israelite, and inculcates the sincere repentance of every

---

[1] Especially Psalm xxiv. 3 ff.    [2] Luke xviii. 10.

man.[1]  It is true that the sacrifices atoned only for sins
of ignorance, whether against the ethical or the ritual
laws—*the ignorances of the people*, says the Epistle to the
Hebrews[2]—and that, as in the same epistle, conscious
crime or apostasy was not remediable by them.[3]  But
while this was the technical meaning of the Law, spiritual
minds must have found in the worship the seals of a
more ethical pardon, the means of a deeper sanctification.
Behind all was the infinite mercy of God, and the keenest
eyes which ever looked into the heart of man saw one
who, if not formally excommunicated, was yet an outcast,
appeal to that mercy not in vain and go down to his
house justified.[4]

On the other hand, the imperfect character of the
system must have been felt by those who cherished the
loftier ideals and promises of the prophets. Other Ideals
That a man could not by himself come —Prophecy.
through the Inner Sanctuary to God, that a professional
priesthood could alone enter the most secret communion with the Deity, that things not ethical inter-
vened between the worshipper and God — such facts
were bound to raise questions in the more earnest minds
and to leave them unsatisfied.[5]  The Temple itself had
not always been monopolised by priestly ideals : it had

---

[1]  *Mishna,* ' Yoma ' viii., especially section 9.  For a noble exposition of
the relation of the modern Jew to the Day of Atonement, see C. G. Monte-
fiore, *The Bible for Home Reading,* Part i. 146 ff.

[2]  ix. 7 (not *errors*): cf. Lev. iv. 2, 13, 22, 27 ; v. 15; Num. xv. 24 ff.  '

[3]  Heb. x. 26 ; Num. xv. 30.

[4]  Luke x. 13 f.  On the exclusion, if not the excommunication, of the
publican, see vol. i. 368 *n.* 2.

[5]  In this connection the reported disuse of animal sacrifices by the
Essenes is instructive : Josephus xviii. *Ant.* i. 5 ; cf. Schürer, *Gesch.*[(3)] § 30,
' The Essenes.'

also been the platform of a purely ethical prophecy.[1]
To devout Jews familiar with their Scriptures, their
Sanctuary must have seemed as loud with voices hostile
to sacrifice as with the bleating of animals, the murmur
of the priests at their ministry, and the cries and music
which accompanied the public services. In these very
courts Isaiah had announced that God's only requirements
from Israel were pure hearts and ethical service. He
proclaimed a pardon, free of all rites, to that conviction
which comes when God Himself has reasoned with the
soul. Jeremiah, too, had here protested that God gave
no commandments concerning burnt-offerings and sacrifices, but called upon His people only for obedience.[2]
Others outside the Temple had said the same: *I will
not smell a savour in your solemn gatherings, . . . but let
justice roll down as waters, and righteousness like a
perennial stream. I desire mercy and not sacrifice, the
knowledge of God more than burnt-offerings.*[3] We must
also remember that both the ideals of prophecy and
the actual experience of the nation had accustomed the
mind of Israel to the assurance of pardon apart from
ritual. Jeremiah's promise in the New Covenant, *I will
forgive their iniquity and their sin I will remember no
more*, rested upon the immediate and spiritual knowledge
of God possessed by all the individuals of the nation.[4]
And the greatest *consolation of Israel* which their history
knew had been achieved while the Temple was in ruins
and sacrifice impossible, upon the sole basis of the people's
sufferings and the free grace of God: *Comfort ye, com-*

---

[1] Above, p. 67.          [2] Isa. i. 10-20; Jer. vii. 22.
[3] Amos v. 21 ff. ; Hosea vi. 6 ; cf. the sublime passage, xi. 8 f.
[4] Jer. xxxi. 31 ff.

*fort ye my people, saith your God. Speak ye comfortably to Jerusalem, and proclaim to her that her service is accomplished, her iniquity pardoned, that she hath received of the Lord's hand double for all her sins.*[1]

But Prophecy had also associated the redemption of Israel with the virtue and even with the self-sacrifice of a single Personality. He is described in various forms and under different names, yet with this idea common to them all, that the mediation by which the recovery and the righteousness of the nation are effected is neither material nor mechanical, but lies in the character and service of a voluntary agent.  To the earlier prophets this Person is a King.  Israel are to be saved from their enemies by his prowess, and to fulfil their life with God under his just government and the influence of his strong and pure individuality.[2]  Another prophecy emphasises that in the ideal age everything will depend on personal influence:[3] *A man shall be as an hiding-place from the wind and a covert from the tempest; as rivers of water in a dry place, as the shadow of a great rock in a weary land. And the eyes of them that see shall not be dim, and the ears of them that hear shall hearken.*  So with the Messiah, or promised King.[4]  It is remarkable that there is no mention of Temple or sacrificial rites in connection with his office; his personal power counts for everything.  Sometimes, however, and in reflection of the political conditions prevailing, the Priest is associated with the Prince. Theirs is 'the equal and co-ordinate duty of sustaining the

*Hope of a Personal Mediation.*

---

[1] 'Isa.' xl. 1 f.  See above, p. 283.
[2] Isa. ix. 1 ff. ; xi. 1 ff. (on the genuineness of which see above, pp. 145 f.).
[3] Isa. xxxii. 1 ff.
[4] The name Messiah, or Anointed, is given to him in Psalm ii. 1

Temple and ensuring the brightness of its revelation. The Temple is nothing without the monarch and priest behind it, and these stand in the presence of God,' the essential mediators of the whole system.[1] In Psalm cx. Priest and King are identified as one, again in consonance with the conditions of the |time, for the High Priest is now become also the civil ruler of the people. Thus, however the form may change with the changing politics, the idea is constant. The virtue of the mediation is personal. In the Servant of the Lord this truth reaches its fullest expression. A righteous Israelite or the righteous nucleus of Israel, atone by their sufferings for the sins of the people, and through death rise to glory. In the fifty - third of Isaiah it does not matter whether the Servant be still, as in the preceding chapters, the people personified, or whether at last he be conceived as a single personality.[2] The point is, that the atonement of the nation proceeds through an ethical agent who consciously and intelligently undertakes his mission, and the virtue of whose service lies in the voluntary offering of himself.[3]

[1] The present writer's *Twelve Prophets*, ii. 298 on Zechariah iv.

[2] The *Targum of Jonathan* interprets 'Isa.' lii., liii. of the Messiah, and later Jewish theology dwells on the sufferings of the Messiah, with explicit reference to 'Isa.' lii., liii. : Wünsche, *Die Leiden des Messias*; Driver and Neubauer, *The Fifty-Third Chapter of Isaiah According to the Jewish Interpreters*; Dalman, *Der leidende u. sterbende Messias*. The *Targum* excepts the verses on the atoning virtue of the Servant's sufferings as inapplicable to the Messiah, and although certain rabbis appear to have admitted that he bore the sins of the wicked, the idea was foreign and even repulsive to Judaism in our Lord's time. See Schürer, *Gesch.*[(3)], Appendix to § 29.

[3] Edghill, *Evidential Value of Prophecy*, 306 (the whole of this work is valuable for a presentation of the essence of the O.T. religion and its connection with the N.T.), appositely quotes the 'magnificent mistranslation of the Vulgate—oblatus est quia ipse voluit. But the other point ought also to be emphasised : *My servant shall deal wisely* ; that is, knows what he is doing, is conscious from the first of the practical value of his humiliation and sacrifice which to others seems useless and repulsive.

In the presence of such a substitute there is no need of the Temple and its victims. All the virtue associated with the priesthood and the sacrifices is transferred to him, and transferred in the very language of the ritual : *God hath laid on Him the iniquity of us all. For the transgression of My people was He stricken. His life is an offering for guilt. By His knowledge shall My righteous Servant justify many, and He shall bear their iniquities. He bears the sin of many, He makes intercession for the transgressors.*[1]

But Prophecy had also spoken, as though God Himself shared all this travail and suffering. He makes His people's salvation His own concern and effort, and accomplishes this not in power only but in pain and self-sacrifice. His love is not complacent but sympathetic, passionate. *In all their affliction He is afflicted.* He *pleads* for their loyalty, *reasons* with them in their sin, and *travails* for their new birth. Their guilt costs Him pain as well as anger. Their sins and sorrows are set not only in the light of His countenance, but upon His heart. The Evangelist of the Exile uses of God the same heavy word, *to bear with pain and difficulty*, as he has used of the Servant.[2]

The Travail and Passion of God.

Finally, these truths of Prophecy, or the most of them, had passed before the end of the Temple history, through the forms of vision and of literature, which we know as Apocalypse. Despairing of the redemption of Israel in the present dispensation, and yet believing in the Divine justice, certain ardent souls and schools in Israel predicted the sudden intervention of

The Jewish Apocalypses.

---

[1] 'Isa.' liii. 6, 8, 10 ff.

[2] For a fuller expression of the above truth see the present writer's *Modern Criticism and the Preaching of the Old Testament*, 174 ff.

God Himself with supernatural forces, resulting in the purgation of this world or even in its overthrow and replacement by new heavens and a new earth. Such ideas had indeed started long before Prophecy closed, and are uttered in several parts of the Old Testament.[1] But they reached their most ardent and systematic expression in a series of Jewish works of the last two centuries before Christ and the first of the Christian era. The various writings from which *The Book of Enoch* has been compiled, *The Book of the Secrets of Enoch, The Testaments of the Twelve Patriarchs, The Book of Jubilees, The Psalms of Solomon, The Apocalypse of Baruch,* and the older *Sibylline Oracles,* are the most important survivals of what must have been a much larger mass of apocalyptic literature produced in this period by Jews of Palestine and Egypt.[2] The general standpoint described above was occupied by all these writers; and we may easily conceive how the institutions and ideals of Israel's religion would become modified through the apocalyptic expectations visible from it. But, naturally, the different minds which shared this standpoint assumed different attitudes towards, and laid different emphases upon, the forms which the Law had instituted and the promises which Prophecy had bequeathed to the nation.

---

[1] See above, pp. 138 ff., on Isaiah. Zephaniah is usually regarded as the first prophet with an apocalypse (*Book of the Twelve Prophets*, ii. 55 f.) The most notable apocalyptic passages of the O.T. are in 'Isaiah' xxiv.-xxvii., Joel, 'Zechariah' xii.-xiv., and Daniel.

[2] English readers will consult 'Apocalyptic Literature' in *Enc. Bibl.* by R. H. Charles, and the other works of this leading authority on the subject (especially his *Book of Enoch*); the *Psalms of Solomon*, by Ryle and James; Schürer, *Hist.* (Eng. trans.), div. ii. vols. ii., iii., §§ 29, 32 f.; J. E. H. Thomson, *Books which influenced our Lord and His Apostles*; W. J. Deane, *Pseudepigrapha.*

As for their theology, the Apocalypses emphasise the Transcendence of God. Heaven is His dwelling and He is the Holy One in the Heavens, the God of glory; who when He would work for men comes down to them in awful manifestations of power and majesty. Amid these super- Their treat-<br>ment of the<br>Beliefs and<br>Institutions<br>of Israel. natural phenomena, the Prophets' sense of God's intimacy with His People, of His ethical travail and passion, is overwhelmed. Yet Israel is still the human unit for which He works. The Nation is His interest: He will overthrow the heathen oppressors and recreate Israel into a kingdom for Himself. Within the Nation He will discriminate between the righteous and the wicked; and He will have respect to the individual: even in death, for the righteous dead shall be raised to a share in the kingdom. In fact, the vindication of the individual and the development of belief in his resurrection are among the most signal services of the Jewish Apocalypse to the cause of religion; it contains no nobler passages than those which enforce the hope of the righteous. With regard to the exact form of so awful a future, we can understand that, as among Christians, so with these Jewish seers, considerable diversity prevailed. Many of them have a strong sense of the steadfastness of the present order of nature; all the more impressive is the obligation, which their ethical convictions lay upon them, to expect its convulsion and catastrophe. Sometimes they are content to say that God's kingdom will be realised upon this same earth, cleansed and restored to the order which the sin of men has disturbed. The whole of the earth shall be the heritage of the pious: its centre a renewed Jerusalem, from whose security the righteous shall behold the torments of the wicked in Gehenna,[1] and themselves enjoy incredible length of days and a serene old age. But sometimes this is not enough, and beyond the present world there breaks the vision of another.[2]　A new heaven and earth are revealed, with the righteous translated to everlasting bliss in the presence of God.　Some writers almost entirely ignore the Temple, saying nothing about it except that it shall be rebuilt, and absolutely nothing about the Law or Sacrifices.　Others carry the origins of the cultus back to primæval times, from which we may infer their belief in its eternal validity ; and they insist upon animal sacrifices and the punctilious observance of the Law.　Some see God alone in the supernatural intervention, which they expect, and in the foundation of the kingdom.　Others continue the prophetic hope of a Messiah proceeding from the community ; and in one, the seventeenth of the Psalms of Solomon, He is figured in the prophetic style as a son of David, purging Jerusalem, overcoming the heathen, yet not trusting in military force, but governing by the word of His mouth. Sinless Himself, He shall rule a holy people and tend the flock of God in faith and righteousness.　In 'The Similitudes' of the *Book of Enoch* [3] the doctrine of the Messiah assumes an original form destined to have great influence on the New Testament　In Daniel, the name *the Son of Man* had been applied to Israel ; but in 'The Similitudes' it is the title of a Person who takes the attributes and name of the Messiah, yet is regarded as

[1] As we have seen even under Prophecy, above, pp. 323 f.

[2] Cf. Mark x. 30 ; Matt. xii. 32 ; Luke xviii. 30.

[3] Chs. xxxvii.-lxx., assigned by Charles either to 94-79 or 70-64 B.C., and 'reasonably' to the former.

supernatural. He has existed with God, in name at least, from before the Creation, the deliverer and preserver of the elect Israel. He is the Lord's Anointed, who rules over all and judges all, on whose mercy all men at the last shall set their hope.[1] There is also a difference as to the fate of the Gentiles. For the most part their destruction is predicted, but some of them shall be converted and serve Israel.

To understand what Jesus taught of the Kingdom of God and of Himself, and what through the faith of His followers He effected, it is necessary to ap- Summary— preciate in due proportion all the beliefs and Three Main Streams in institutions which we have just surveyed. Judaism. And if an Old Testament student may venture to criticise recent New Testament criticism, it appears to him that this suffers, and in certain quarters'suffers radically, from failure to allow to one of these religious elements its proper and direct influence on the origins of Christianity. As we have seen, the principal factors in the later religion of Israel were these three. *First*, the Law with its central emphasis upon Institutions, the Temple, the 1. The Law Priesthood, the Ritual; founded, as much of —Institutions. the Law was, on Prophecy, this emphasis did not ex- haust its influence, yet in the practice of the Law by the generation contemporary with Jesus, the Institutions were the main things. *Second*, Prophecy with its de- preciation of the Ritual and the Priestly Institutions, and with its three great protestations of the sole, eternal value of Personality: that God requires from 2. Prophecy— men only ethical obedience; that their Personalities. redemption and atonement shall be effected through a

[1] See especially *Book of Enoch*, chs. xlvii. f., lxii., lxix.

heroic character and his self-sacrifice, the personality of the Servant of the Lord ; and that God Himself is not mere Law nor Love at a distance, but that even His Personality is engaged in the ethical warfare and passion to which ours are subject. And *third*, Apocalypse, starting within Prophecy as this became conscious of want of room and power in the historical conditions of Israel for the fulfilment of its hopes ; and predicted the fulfilment of these in another dispensation, which is beyond and above the present world, and in which, while the personalities described by prophecy gain in transcendence and supernatural majesty, this is achieved only at the cost of much of their ethical character.

3. Apocalypse —the Super- natural.

These, then, are the three. There never has been any doubt about the discipline of the Law. But if an older generation of critics did less than justice to the influence of Apocalypse upon the conditions out of which Christianity arose, it seems to the present writer, coming up to the study of recent New Testament criticism from long following of the history of Israel, that much of this criticism fails to allow enough to the immediate action of Prophecy. Carried away by the influences on our Lord's time of the Apocalypses, the full appreciation of which has but recently become possible, some critics almost entirely ignore the direct influence, untinged by Apocalypse, of the Hebrew Prophets. By others the main tendencies of religion during the period are defined as only two, the Legal and the Apocalyptic, while the Prophetic is regarded and treated as subordinate. This may be true of some, but not of all, of the popular religion. It is not true of the circles in which Christianity arose, nor of our Lord's

Their Treat- ment by recent Criticism.

mind whether about the Jewish system or about Himself.
While it is impossible to ignore in these certain contributions from Apocalypse, they prove the immediate and
the dominant influence of Prophecy.

No one may understand the origins of Christianity who
does not realise in them a revival—after a silence of many
centuries—of Prophecy,[1] which, whatever relation it might assume to the ritual and
institutions of Israel, felt itself independent
of these and delivered its own direct message
from God. So in the early chapters of Luke's Gospel.

*Dominant Influence of Prophecy in the Prepara- tion for Jesus*

Be their source what it may, they testify to the Church's
consciousness of her birth in Prophecy—Prophecy which,
though it started in the Temple, was not concentrated on
that or any other institution, but struck again its high
and earliest notes of the advent of a great Personality,
the Messiah of God. This Prophecy (so far as the
records go) shows no tinge of Apocalypse. So too with
John the Baptist, whose ministry had nothing to do
with either Jerusalem or the Temple, but was accomplished outside these, with another sacrament, upon
methods purely prophetic, and concentrated on the
coming of the Messiah. The colours upon John's
preaching may be cast from the Apocalypse; the ideas
are all to be found within Prophecy.[2]

And so, too, with Jesus Himself. It is everywhere the
essential ideas and tempers of Prophecy which pervade
His ministry—especially the three emphases
upon the sole, eternal value of personality in
religion: that what God requires of men is

*and in the ministry of Jesus.*

ethical obedience, that their redemption is to be effected

---

[1] Cf. *Ecce Homo*, ch. i.    [2] Luke iii. 2 ff.

through the virtue and self-sacrifice of a single Personality; and that the Love of God Himself has come to share the ethical warfare and passion of men. But all these are concentrated by Jesus in a new and wonderful way upon His own Person and His unique significance for men. They are complicated, too, by His attitude to the Law, and they reveal the influence of conceptions characteristic of the Apocalypse.

The child of a Jewish family loyal to the Law and the Temple,[1] Jesus was *born under the Law.*[2] He was circumcised, and at the usual age He became 'a son of the Law.' It has been said that 'the New Testament gives us no means whatever of judging how the passive, unconscious relation to the Law was changed into the conscious and responsible one which we see when our Lord entered His public work.'[3] But we must remember that Prophecy, with its free and sometimes hostile attitude to the Law, was also powerful in the circles in which His boyhood was spent; and that throughout His ministry He not only appealed to the Prophets as well as the Law, and constantly quoted their very words, but used these just on the great points on which they differed from the Law: that God *will have mercy and not sacrifice,* and that the atonement for the sins of men is to be effected by an ethical agent. This, however, is to anticipate, and we now proceed with the details which led to it. The loyalty of Jesus to the ritual was on some sides unexceptionable. The only

His Practice relative to the Law and the Temple.

---

[1] Luke i., and especially ii. 41 (see Plummer's note).

[2] Gal. iv. 4.

[3] Denney, art. 'Law (in N.T),' Hastings' *D.B.* See the whole very illuminating article; also Mackintosh, *Christ and the Jewish Law.*

faults of ceremonial with which His vigilant enemies charged Him were His use of the Sabbath, His neglect of fasts, and his neglect of the washing of hands.[1] He sent the leper, whom He healed, to the priest to fulfil the rites required by the Law.[2] He bade His disciples offer their gifts at the Altar after they were reconciled to their brethren.[3] In defence of His conduct He appealed to the authority of the Temple and the example of the Priests.[4] The sanctity of the Temple, He said, was greater than that of its gold, the sanctity of the Altar than that of the gifts laid upon it.[5] He paid the half-shekel which was the Temple-tax.[6] He attended the statutory Temple feasts. And if all these are only instances of accommodation to the customs of His people, we have besides His anger at the desecration of the Temple which moved Him to the one violent action imputed to Him.[7] But in general the whole system had for Him a Divine authority. God spake through Moses. The way of life was in keeping the commandments. He Himself had come to fulfil the Law.[8] Yet, on the other hand, the inaugural sacrament of His ministry was, as in the case of Jeremiah,[9] altogether outside the Temple service; and it is striking that there is no record of His participation in any of the central rites of the Sanctuary. We do not read of Him as going

---

[1] In the fragment of an Apocryphal Gospel discovered by Messrs. Grenfell and Hunt, a chief priest blames Jesus for neglect of the Temple lustrations. *Oxyrhynchus Papyri*, Part v. 1 ff.

[2] Mark i. 44 ; Matt. viii. 4 : which incident recalls the orthodox feeling against physicians, who did not observe religious forms prescribed by the Law. Above, p. 404.

[3] Matt. v. 23 f.    [4] Matt. xii. 1 ff.    [5] Matt. xxiii. 16 ff.
[6] Matt. xvii. 14 ; see above, vol. i.    [7] Mark xi. 15, etc.
[8] Matt. v. 17 (18) ; xix. 17 ; Mark vii. 19.    [9] Above, p. 224.

further into the Temple than the Treasury, in the Court of Women.[1] All the Gospels agree on this. *Over against the Treasury, in Solomon's Porch,*[2] or generally *walking in the Temple, teaching in the Temple,*[3] are phrases that imply no more than the same outer Court in which He overturned the tables of the money-changers. These comprise all His recorded visits to the Temple. It is also remarkable that while His parables reflect every other aspect of the national life, they do not reflect the worship of the Inner Sanctuary nor the ministration of the Priests. His story of the Pharisee and the Publican is the only one that has the Temple for its scene. Jesus visited the Temple as a Prophet. He *sat in the Temple teaching.*[4] As to Jeremiah, so to Him it was the auditorium of the nation, an opportunity of getting at the hearts of men.[5] And, therefore, it will not be surprising nor seem the after-thought of a later generation, that the great freedom, which the Prophets had shown towards the ritual and even towards the sacred fabric itself, is also imputed to this new Prophet: for instance, in His saying about the Temple-tax, *the children are free, notwithstanding lest we should offend them, go thou . . . and give unto them for thee and me*; or *I desire mercy and not sacrifice*;[6] or His condemnations of the additional laws and ceremonies imposed by the Scribes. To be able to doubt that such sayings were His, is to forget the precedents for them in Prophecy before the Exile: the hostility of some prophets to the whole ritual, and the charge which one at least made

---

[1] Above, p. 510.

[2] Mark xii. 41; cf. Luke xxi. 1 f.; John viii. 20; x. 23.

[3] Mark xi. 27 (Matt. xxi. 12); xii. 35: ἱερόν is the word used; see above, p. 500. Cf. Swete, *The Gospel according to St. Mark*, 246.

[4] Matt. xxvi. 55.     [5] Above, p. 237 f.     [6] Matt. xvii. 26 f.

against the Scribes of his time of falsifying the Torah.[1]
Doubts have been expressed of His prediction that the
Temple would be destroyed.[2]  In spite of its occurrence
in all the Synoptics and the echo of it in John, in spite of
the fact that it formed the charge against Him before the
Sanhedrin, it has been declared conceivable only as 'a
prophecy after the event,' a prediction invented for Him
when the Temple had perished and His followers had
transferred its virtue to Himself.  No one can say so
who remembers Jeremiah's attitude to the Temple and
his predictions of its ruin.[3]  To take the lowest ground,
Jesus was prophesying only what others in Jerusalem had
already declared.  And in connection with this we must
keep in mind His words about the necessity of new
bottles for new wine.[4]  In the association in which these
appear they can only mean the insufficiency of the forms
of the Old Covenant for the new truths and tempers
which were on the point of being realised, or which in a
sense were already realised, in Himself and in those who
believed on Him.  His statement: *Think not that I am
come to destroy the Law and the Prophets, I come not to
destroy but to fulfil,*[5] must be interpreted upon the
antithesis which we have seen between Law and Prophecy and in the light of His other saying that *the
whole of the Law and the Prophets* is to love God and
one's neighbour.

All this, then, is the spiritual liberty of the greater

---

[1] Jer. viii. 8 f. ; but cf. Isa. xxix. 13.

[2] Mark xiii. 1 ff. ; Matt. xxiv. 1 f. ; Luke xxi. 5 f. ; cf. John ii. 19.
There is also the reference in Matt. xxiii. 38 f. (Luke xiii. 35), *your House is
left unto you desolate* ; cf. Jer. xxii. 5, *this House shall become a desolation.*

[3] Jer. vii., xxvi.       [4] Matt. ix. 14 ff. ; Mark ii. 18 ff. ; Luke v. 33 ff.

[5] Matt. v. 17.

prophets.  Only by the new Prophet the liberty is

His Sovereign use of Law and Liberty.

exercised (to speak moderately), with a larger patience and the sense of a loftier authority than by any of His predecessors or than by any of His apostles after Him.  Jesus shows Himself Lord of both aspects of the religion, rather than as the mere reformer of the one, the mere champion of the other.  There is a sovereign quality about His attitude to both the legal and the spiritual sides of the worship which is wanting in theirs.  He vindicates His use of the liberty as His own right ; nor does he feel fettered or burdened by the Law when He submits Himself to its discipline, whether He does so out of regard for others or because it is the Law of God.  The Law is no 'painful problem' to Jesus as to His apostles.[1]  Law or Liberty, He uses both as master of both.  We can see how very hard it must have been for His disciples to understand this dominant, characteristic quality of His conduct ; yet they lived to understand it.[2]

With this attitude of Jesus to the Law, we must take His sense of His difference from the Prophets before Him:[3]

His Sense of the Virtue and Significance of His Person.

they were servants, He was the Son.  We must take His proclamation of the close of the dispensation, which the Law and the Prophets *until John* had mediated, and the opening with Himself of a new age in which they were replaced by something else.[4]  We must take the facts that His disciples came to believe in Him as the Messiah—not merely the greatest

[1] Wellhausen calls this 'das Eigentümliche' in Christ's relation to the Law ; *Einleitung*, 137.

[2] Especially Galatians ii., iii. 19, v. 6.        [3] Mark xii. 1 ff., etc.

[4] Luke xvi. 16 ; Matt. xi. 12 f.  Cf. Denney as above, Hastings' *D.B.* ii. 74*b*.

of Prophets, but the Person to whom Prophecy pointed as
the agent of Israel's redemption—and that in some sense
He accepted their homage and confessed Himself King
of the Jews, for otherwise the Roman procurator would
never have decided against Him. He was not Elijah,
but John was Elijah. Himself He identified with the
Son of Man in the Messianic and transcendental sense of
that title given to it in 'the Similitudes' of the Book of
Enoch. Towards Prophetic and Apocalyptic ideals of
the Messiah He maintained the same sovereign attitude
as we have seen Him hold towards the Law and its
institutions. He exercised a liberty of selection. He
discarded the political rôles assigned to the Christ, but
He assumed the ethical authority and the transcendental
powers. He set His own word against the Law, and
He declared Himself the future and ultimate Judge of
men. Finally, there was His announcement that by His
submission to death, He became to the New Covenant
what sacrifice had been to the Old, or, in other words
attributed to Him, He *gave His life a ransom for many.*
The exact meaning of these sayings has been variously
interpreted. But to understand Him it is sufficient to
remember that the redemptive value of the sufferings of
the righteous, an atonement made for sin not through
material sacrifice but in the obedience and spiritual
agony of an ethical agent, was an idea familiar to Prophecy. It is enough to be sure, as we can be sure, that
He whose grasp of the truths of the Old Testament
excelled that of every one of His predecessors, did not
apply this particular truth to Himself in a vaguer way,
nor understand by it less, than they did. His people's
pardon, His people's purity—foretold as the work of a

righteous life, a perfect service of God, a willing self-sacrifice—He now accepted as His own work, and for it He offered His life and submitted unto death. The ideas, as we have seen, were not new ; the new thing was that He felt they were to be fulfilled in *His* Person and through *His* passion. But all this implies two equally extraordinary and amazing facts : that He who had a more profound sense than any other of the spiritual issues in the history of Israel, was conscious that all these issues were culminating to their crisis in Himself; and that He who had the keenest moral judgment ever known on earth, was sure of His own virtue for such a crisis— was sure of that perfection of His previous service without which His self-sacrifice would be in vain. Nor was the agony of the sacrifice abated by His trust in the promise of a glory that should follow. No man questions the story of His mental sufferings or of their crisis in Gethsemane. Yet these were not due to any doubt of His own purity. The records which so faithfully describe His temptations may be equally trusted when throughout they imply His innocence. It is a very singular confidence. Men there have been who felt themselves able to say, ' *I know*,' and who died like Him for their convictions. But He was able to say ' *I am*. I am that to which Prophecy has pointed,' and was able to feel Himself worthy to be that. Thus Jesus fulfilled the second of the great ethical emphases of Prophecy : He was the Messiah, the Servant of the Lord, through whose self-sacrifice the redemption of men was assured.

But in Jesus there was also fulfilled the third of the Prophetic demands for personal action and sacrifice as the fulfilment of religion. That the love of God was not merely transcendent and complacent, but travailing and passionate, sharing the moral struggle, the weakness, the pain, even the shame and curse of the souls of men, is illustrated in Jesus as it is nowhere else. And this not merely in such a parable as that of the Prodigal and all He has told us of the love of the Father, but in Himself and His wonderful expressions of His sufficiency for the needs of the people: such as His *Come unto Me all ye that labour and are heavy laden, and I will give you rest.* None of these is more wonderful than His appeal to Jerusalem, with its *How often would I have gathered you,* and its conclusion that since she has rejected Him she has rejected all.

The travail of the Love of God in Jesus.

In all this, however, He went beyond every precedent in the history and prophecy which we have followed ; and we must seek another scale than that either of the prophet or even of the personality to whom prophecy pointed, by which to measure Him. Just because of this His disciples failed as yet to understand Him, and we must look to the last years of our City's history for the development of, and the full reasons for, their recognition of what He was and what He did.

Conclusion of foregoing Data.

Two things are certain about the earliest community of His disciples, the Church in Jerusalem : first, their belief in the Messiahship of Jesus, confirmed to them by the evidence of His Resurrection ; and second, their continued adhesion to their Jewish nationality and to the services of the Temple. A third is equally clear—it was the power of His personality upon them which alone enabled them to break

The Church in Jerusalem and the Temple.

from Judaism and its ritual. In the earlier chapters of Acts we find the same communal conception of religion prevailing as in the first chapters of Luke's Gospel.[1] The apostles address themselves to Israel, the Nation, in forms similar to those which the Prophets used. The whole Christian community is observant of the Law and shares in the national worship of the Temple. 'Perhaps it is no exaggeration to say that the early Christians were Jews first and Christians afterwards in more than the sequence of their own experience. They did not indeed value their Christianity less than their Jewish nationality, but they had not yet learned even in thought to separate them.'[2] Even while acknowledging that God had *visited the Gentiles to take out of them a people for His Name*, James, the head of the Church in Jerusalem, quoted the prophecy, *I will build again the tabernacle of David which is fallen, I will build again the ruins thereof and set it up*.[3] The student of the Old Testament will readily understand this attitude of the Christians of Jerusalem to the Temple and their Jewish nationality. There is a precedent for it in the prophecies of the Evangelist of the Exile.[4] In these, too, a great Redemption is in process, but not yet completed. Israel has to be restored and the Gentiles converted. The Servant by whom the results are to be achieved is an Israel within Israel, the spiritual nucleus of the nation, the rest of which is still blind and unredeemed. Precisely such a Remnant might the early Christians in Jerusalem feel themselves to be: distinct from other Jews by their redemption and

---

[1] See above, pp. 523 f.
[2] W. R. Sorley, *Jewish Christians and Judaism*, 33.
[3] Acts xv. 14 ff.      [4] 'Isaiah' xl.-lv.

enlightenment through Christ, yet in Israel and of Israel still, with a duty to the national institutions ; while, at the same time, they sought to lift the whole people to their own spiritual level and were not forgetful of their mission to the Gentiles.

We need not dwell on the troubles which ultimately rose out of this loyalty to the National Covenant : the controversies about Law, Temple and cir- Stephen, cumcision, that threatened to rend the Church Paul and Hebrews. in twain. But it is necessary to remark the following. The movement which finally divorced Christianity from Israel may have begun in Jerusalem in disputes between Hebrews and Hellenists,[1] and he who started the controversy was in all probability a Hellenist. Yet it is fallacious to suppose that the Grecian Jews as a body were less loyal than the Jews of Jerusalem to the national institutions. Stephen's most bitter opponents were of the Hellenist synagogues.[2] His own line of argument, as recorded by Luke, has nothing to do with racial questions, but lies within the method of the Hebrew prophets when dealing with their own people. We are accustomed to call the Baptist the last of the Hebrew prophets, but Stephen was the last ; speaking as Jeremiah himself would have spoken,[3] with the same appeal to precedents in the history of Israel, the same emphasis on the incurable sinfulness of the nation, the same indifference to the sanctity of the Temple, the same fearlessness of death. But the power upon Stephen is throughout the power of Jesus. Stephen is the prophet of the new Messiah, who to him is everything that the Temple and what it stands for is to his opponents. We

[1] Acts vi.　　[2] Acts vi. 9 ; and so with Paul, ix. 29.　　[3] Jer. xxvi.

see the same, but more articulately, in Paul and the author of the Epistle to the Hebrews. In neither of these Jews has the change been wrought by a gradual solution of the national idea and system in the influences of the larger Greek world, nor by the prospect, nor by the fact, of the fall of the Temple. What alone tells with both is the significance of the Personality of Christ. To both He has taken the place of the Temple, the Sacrifices, the Priesthood, just because of what He has proved Himself to be in His people's experience—an atonement for sin, a living way to God, the seeking and suffering Love of God, the Risen Saviour and Intercessor. It is also striking to find how His Person has become the substitute of the national idea, which had been organic in the religion of Israel. The communal conception of religion still prevails, but Christ is the new secret of the unity and the common life. Though the Epistle to the Hebrews is based on the assumption that the old Dispensation has passed, it presents the New Covenant as one not with individuals, but with *a people*,[1] through their great High Priest, Jesus Christ. Though Paul accounts for the rejection of Israel by the words, *I will provoke you to jealousy with that which is no nation*,[2] and affirms that all racial distinctions are abolished in Christ, in whom is neither Greek nor Jew, barbarian nor Scythian; yet he tells the Galatians that they are *Abraham's seed, the Israel of God*.[3] Here, again, the bond is clear. The new community gathered out of many nations are one people, because they are one in Christ. His rank as the Messiah, Lord and King, con-

---

[1] A. B. Davidson, *Hebrews*, 166.  [2] Romans x. 19.
[3] Galatians iii. 28 f. ; vi. 16.

stitutes them a nation—*a holy nation, a peculiar people,*
as Peter expresses it. Therefore in the reconstruction of
religion, which was effected in place of the Jewish system,
even before the fabric of this had fallen, the creative force
was everywhere the significance of Christ's Person and
Christ's work. Everything reaches back to Him and to
His ' infinite longing to open the soul of man to the life
in God, unhindered by the mediation of priest and ritual.
Thus the fountain of catholicity is in no confluence of
philosophies, no combination of external conditions, but
in the unique personality of Jesus of Nazareth.' [1]

To the Old Testament student who, like ourselves, has
come upon this last stage of the history of Jerusalem
through the long centuries of Israel's life and *Parallel be-*
religion, which lead up to it, there is only one *tween the Influence of*
parallel to the influence of Jesus upon the *the Divine Character in*
nation, their institutions and their ideals. As *Israel's Religion*
we followed the gradual elevation of Israel's
faith and ethics from obscure beginnings to the clear
monotheism of the prophets with its sublime ideals for
daily life, the elevating factor of which we were aware
was throughout the character of the Deity: God's revelation of His Nature and His Will. We found this at work
within the ritual, the customs and the intellectual conceptions of God which Israel had inherited as part of
the great Semitic family of mankind; purifying, expand-
ing and articulating these into the most perfect system
of national religion the world has ever seen.[2] We have
seen it break the bounds of this nationalism, at once

---

[1] Martineau, *The Seat of Authority*, 632.
[2] Above, pp. 115, 210.

displaying its sovereignty over the world, and drawing the individual man directly to the breast of God. Had the scope of our task been wider, we should have perceived this same influence of the character of God acting upon an ancient folklore and mythology, purging it of its grosser elements, and rendering it expressive of the One Creator and Preserver of the world and men; we should have followed its effects upon popular religious imaginations—such, for instance, as that of the Day of the Lord, a day of the national deity's vengeance on the heathen, or that of the physical marriage of the deity with his people or with his land—and we should have watched it transform these into the most ethical of hopes and experiences. We should have seen all this done gradually, and, as it were, naturally; with the age-long patience of the Divine methods in Nature, and yet with the urgent travail and the passion which become the Love of God in the education and redemption of men.

Very similar, in these last years of the history of Jerusalem, is the working of the influence of the Person of Jesus: gradual and slow to be understood, like all the works of God; patient and yet full of travail and agony; in the end transforming and creative. He also started from the names, the forms, the symbols, the intellectual conceptions of the religion of His time. He also selected those which He would use, and put new meanings into them: meanings which are not yet exhausted, but remain as infinite to us as to the hearts that first heard them. And just as in the former development it was the Person, the Character and the Work of God which was everywhere the active Power, so here it is the Person, the Character and the Work of Jesus. Not

His interpretation of God was the new thing which appeared with Jesus, but the new thing was Himself. Not the ideas of the mission which He assumed, for these had all been defined by Prophecy, but the Fact that He felt Himself able for the mission and the Fact that He fulfilled it. The authority which He claimed, the sufficiency for men of which He was conscious—these are His own testimonies to what He was. And the experience of His followers from the time of the Resurrection onward is that He was no less than Lord and God, the fulness of the Divine Grace and Truth.

As a Fact in history all this is not less credible than its anticipation by the prophets ages before. The Love of God could not be satisfied nor perfected in sending to men the knowledge of itself through Prophets and Priests or by the discipline of their own sufferings; but must itself share, by their side, their weakness, their sorrow, their ethical warfare and passion.

# CHAPTER XX

## JERUSALEM OF THE GOSPELS

THE Jerusalem of the Gospels was the Jerusalem of
Herod, a great engineer and builder of strongholds.[1]  Seated on her two hills and girt by massive
walls, ingeniously constructed with curves and re-entrant
angles, the City to which Christ came presented the appearance of a gigantic fortress;
impregnable on three sides, for here the walls
rose from the precipitous flanks of her hills, but on the
north they struck across the backs of these and were
further fortified by a deep-cut fosse, beyond which lay a
suburb of uncertain extent.  Round this the Third or
outmost wall, probably on the line of the present north
wall, had not yet been built.  At intervals upon the
others towers rose from solid bases, so closely constructed
as to seem single masses of stone; while in front of the
gates and other assailable points the rock bristled with
counterscarps and similar outworks.[2]  Nor did all these
exhaust the embattled aspect of the City.  Her outer
walls embraced a number of separate and independent
strongholds.  On the East Hill the ramparts of the
Temple towered over the Lower City, falling from their
feet to Siloam; and, as the Temple was to the City, so
was Antonia to the Temple, a still more eminent citadel.[3]

*Warlike aspect of the City.*

---

[1] Above, pp. 481 ff.  [2] Vol. i. 181 f., 187 ff., 191 f., 244 ff.
[3] Vol. i. 426; vol. ii. 495 ff.

Beyond the Tyropœon rose the longer and loftier West Hill, its streets and terraces disposed theatre-wise,[1] but with the old First Wall running down the middle of it and so over the Tyropœon to the Temple ramparts.[2] The Hasmonean House, with the Xystus below, stood upon this wall towards its lower end;[3] in its topmost north-west angle Herod's castellated Palace and three Towers crowned, or rather helmeted, the war-girt figure of Israel's metropolis. But for the broad Sanctuary in her lap, with its snow-white shrine and smoking altar, Jerusalem must have seemed more devoted to war than to religion, more suggestive of siege than of pilgrimage. It is singular to think of the cradle of Christianity in so formidable a fortress.

We have also realised the politics of the City and the tempers of her population. There was, first, the Roman garrison, quartered in the two highest citadels: the Antonia, which communicated by a double passage with the outer Court of the Temple, and Herod's Palace, now the Prætorium or seat of the Roman Procurator when he came up from Cæsarea to the Jewish feasts.[4] There was the Sanhedrin, seated in the Temple, with religious and civil jurisdiction over Judæa (but in capital cases subject to the Procurator) and with considerable influence in Galilee and elsewhere.[5] There were the Sadducees and Chief Priests, an ecclesiastical but unspiritual aristocracy, arrogant and unscrupulous, without popular ideals or influence, but ready to employ popular passions, 'able to persuade none save

*Politics and Tempers of the Population.*

---

[1] Vol. ii. 440 ff.  [2] Vol. i. 242 f.  [3] Vol. ii. 459, 461 f.
[4] Vol. i. 413 ff. (cf. 28) ; vol. ii. 488 ff.  See below, pp. 573 ff.
[5] Vol. i. 415 ff. ; vol. ii. 470.

the rich,' but with gangs of bravos in their pay.[1]   There
were the Pharisees and Scribes, influential with the multitude and zealous in education ; patriotic and religious
in their ideals, but in their methods professional and
pedantic, who with one hand kindled the soul of the
nation and with the other smothered the soul they
kindled by their cumbrous and often desperate legalism.[2]
There was the army of Priests, Levites and Temple
servants with a warlike as well as a spiritual discipline,
a financial as well as a religious training, under captains
as well as chief priests, like one of the great military
orders of Christianity ; accustomed to sentinel the walls
of their sanctuary, but ready when these were taken to
die round its altar rather than remit their sacred rites.[3]
There were a considerable number of wealthy families,[4]
a considerable volume of commerce and industry ;[5] but,
on the other hand, swarms of idlers and mendicants,
much poverty, and because of the comparative sterility
of the surroundings, a general precariousness of subsistence, which under drought or invasion, especially if the
latter coincided with a Sabbatic year, rapidly became
famine.[6]   Of clean and ardent souls we descry not a few ;
there must have been many more, keeping themselves
from the world and nursing the most spiritual of the
national promises ; and a still larger number of simple
men, ignorant, brave, devoted, the innocent prey of leaders
with less lofty ambitions for Israel.   We have seen the
character of the City's ' multitude ' : intensely jealous for

[1] Vol. i. 423.   See below, p. 572.
[2] Vol. i. 416, 447, 452.                    [3] Vol. i. 351 ff., 423 ff.
[4] Vol. i. 368.                               [5] Vol. i. 374 ff.
[6] Vol. i. 298 ff. ; vol. ii. 456 ; cf. below, p. 563.

the Law and the purity of public worship, but even more bent on their political freedom ; accustomed to be consulted by their rulers, expert in discussion, conscious of their power, and easily stirred to revolt.[1]  To them were added at the feasts 'an innumerable throng from the country,' so that at such seasons Jerusalem was less a City than a nation concentrated like a city to one man's voice and influence.[2]  And finally, we have appreciated the double exposure of all this life : on the one side, its recent openness, through the Hellenised cities of Palestine and the new port of Cæsarea, to the Greek and Roman world ;[3] on the other, its ancient neighbourhood to the Desert, so hospitable to its forces of fanaticism and revolt.[4]

In the Gospels, the story of a Galilean Prophet and His disciples, Jerusalem appears mainly as a Place of Pilgrimage, and, with but few exceptions,[5] only on the occasion of the great Festivals.[6] She is *the Holy City*.[7]  So long as Jesus is the master of His movements, we hear of little but the Sanctuary, and only of its outer courts.[8]  He does not go elsewhere within the walls except to Bethesda and to the house selected for His last Passover ;[9] He does not

Jerusalem of the Gospels. 1. A place of Pilgrimage.

---

[1] Vol. i. 442 f., 445, 449 ff., 454.   [2] Vol. i. 455.

[3] Vol. i. 453 f. ; vol. ii. 478 ff.

[4] Vol. i. 11 ff., 400, 451, 454 ; vol. ii. 454, 457, 483.

[5] Luke i.-ii. 40 ; Matt. ii. 1 ff. (the dates of which are uncertain) ; cf. iv. 5, the Second Temptation.

[6] Luke ii. 41 ; John ii. 13, 23 (the Passover) ; v. 1 (the Feast) ; vii. 2, 10 (Tabernacles); x. 22 (F. of the Dedication, see above, 454 f.); and the accounts of our Lord's last Passover in all the Gospels ; cf. Acts ii. (Pentecost).

[7] Matt. iv. 5 ; xxvii. 53 ; see vol. i. 270.   [8] Cf. above, pp. 543 f.

[9] John v. 2 ff. ; Mark xiv. 12 ff., etc.  We are not told where Nicodemus came to Him.

speak of any other place except Siloam.[1]  The Temple
bulks before everything else, the wonder of all visitors
to the City; its dizzy pinnacles the scene of His own
Temptation[2] — a remarkable proof of the impression
which the lofty House had left on His boyhood.  Beside
the Temple neither the walls nor Herod's Castle nor his
Towers are noticed, but they are implied in that utterance
of our Lord, on His approach round Olivet, when the
whole military appearance of the place burst upon Him
and He foretold its siege and overthrow.[3]  Perhaps
there are also allusions to the characteristic housetops of
the town,[4] and to its market-places and numerous synagogues,[5] but these features were equally conspicuous in
other towns.

The rest of the time in which He was master of His
movements, Jesus spent with His disciples outside the
walls, and (it is interesting to observe) only
in that part of the environs which lay opposite
the Temple.    From Jericho they came up
past Bethany and Bethphage.  The full strength, the full
pity, of the City burst upon Him as He crossed either the
shoulder or the summit of the Mount of Olives.[6]  The
last nights they passed in Bethany and out on the Mount
itself.  This bivouac was His custom : *they went every man
to his own house, but Jesus went to the Mount of Olives;
He came out and went, as His custom was, to the Mount*

2. Our Lord's
Resorts in the
Environs.

---

[1] John ix. 7, 11.          [2] Mark xi. 11 ; xiii. 1 ff ; cf. Luke xxi. 5 ff.
[3] Luke xix. 43 ff.          [4] Mark xiii. 15, etc.
[5] Matt. xx. 3 ; xxiii. 7 ; John xviii. 20 ; cf. Acts vi. 9.
[6] Luke xix. 41 ff.  What line the road from Jericho took in those days is
uncertain.  There is trace of an ancient road over the top of Olivet (above,
pp. 44 f.) ; but the mention of Bethany and Bethphage suggests that, as now,
the road came round the Mount.  See the fine description in Stanley, *Sinai
and Palestine,* 190 ff.

*of Olives.*[1] There He taught as He taught in the Temple.[2] His parables and illustrations in Jerusalem include marriage feasts and trading with pounds or talents, also the Temple figures of the Pharisee and the Publican, and of the Widow putting her mite into the Treasury; but otherwise they are of vines and figs, vineyards and sheepfolds, the fountain of living water, and the white tombs conspicuous round the City —all of them visible from His haunts on the Mount. There *He sat over against the Temple.*[3] And thither He crossed the Ḳidron to His agony in Gethsemane.

In the religious expectation of the time, Jerusalem bore further aspect than as the place of pilgrimage or of a prophet's teaching. The Apocalypses pre- 3. How the dicted that the City should be the glorious West Hill comes into centre of the new dispensation.[4] There the the Story. Kingdom was to come and the Messiah appear to reign : most probably at one of the great feasts when the Nation would be gathered to meet Him. The popular revolts, at the call of some ' prophet ' or other,[5] doubtless happened during such seasons, when the excitable populace was reinforced by the simple and credulous peasantry. That such ideas held the imagination of some of the disciples of Jesus is plain from the petition of James and John, while *they were in the way going up to Jerusalem: Grant that we may sit one on Thy right hand and one on Thy left hand in Thy glory.*[6] He knew that Jerusalem held not His throne, but the cup whereof

---

[1] John vii. 53, viii. 1, the section on the Woman taken in Adultery ; Luke xxii. 39 ; cf. xxi. 37.

[2] Matt. xxiv. 3.  [3] Mark xiii. 3.

[4] Above, pp. 537 f.  [5] Vol. i. 451.

[6] Mark x. 32, 35 ff. ; Matt. xx. 17 ff: see Bengel on verse 22.

He must drink. The chief priests were waiting for Him there. There sat the Sanhedrin and the Gentile governor into whose hands they would deliver Him to death.[1] When His anticipations were fulfilled, and He was arrested, He was brought beyond the Temple, and so for the first time the West Hill comes into the story. He was taken to the house of the High Priest, to the Prætorium, to the residence of Herod Antipas, back to the Prætorium, and thence through a northern gate to His crucifixion beyond the walls, where also He was buried.

Of the neighbourhood of the Desert to Jerusalem, and the conspiracy of its wild freedom with the turbulence and fanaticism of her people,[2] there is not so much reflection in the Gospels as in Josephus, with his stories of prophets who called the multitude to ' see the signals of liberty in the wilderness,' or led them back to behold the walls fall. But Jesus alludes to the same popular hope in the Desert when in His last discourse He says : *If they should say unto you, Behold, He is in the wilderness, go not forth* ;[3] and it is significant that two of His temptations are laid in the Desert and in the Temple. In a similar connection with the City the Jordan appears, and for the first time in its history. To its banks the populace of the City follow John, and afterwards Theudas.[3]

4. The Neighbourhood of the Desert.

Of the opposite, and recent, exposure of Jerusalem to the western world, there is ample illustration in the drift of the story through the Book of Acts : down the hills on which the City stood, by the Gaza road, to the maritime plain, and to Ashdod,

5. The Openness to the West.

---

[1] Vol. i. 451, 454.      [2] Matt. xxiv. 26.      [3] Vol. i. 449.

or more directly to Lydda, Joppa, and out through
Cæsarea to Cyprus,[1] Asia Minor, Greece and Rome.
The Gospels are already ominous of this decentralisa-
tion of the religion. They contain no such promises of
the glory of Jerusalem as we find in the Apocalypses
with their narrow Jewish outlook. The destruction of the
City is foretold, and no restoration. The disciples are
bidden to tarry at Jerusalem, only till they are endued
with power from on high. We have seen how, for a time,
they clung to the Temple and the Law, and that before
the destruction of 70 they had finally broken from these
and other national institutions.

One other feature has to be considered. In the course
of the history it has become clear how unable the City
was to support herself from her own resources, 6. The Poverty
and how many non-productive members her of the City.
population contained.[2] Jerusalem was naturally a poor
City. This condition is reflected in all that the Book of
Acts affirms about the poverty of her Christians and
their need of support from abroad. The first practical
measures of the Church were the voluntary surrender by
the wealthy members of their estates, that no brother
might be in need.[3] The earliest development of her
system had to do with the *daily ministrations*.[4] When a
famine threatened *the world*, it was at once felt that the
brethren in Judæa would suffer most, and accordingly
the council in Antioch determined that relief should
be sent to them, of which Barnabas and Saul were the
ministers.[5]

[1] Acts viii. 26 ; ix. 30, 32 ff., x., etc.
[2] Vol. i. 3, 14 f., 297 f., 327, 372 ; vol. ii. 222.
[3] Acts ii. 44 ; iv. 32, 34 ff. ; cf. iii. 6.     [4] Acts vi. 1 ff.
[5] Acts xi. 27 ff.; xii. 25; cf. Galatians ii. 10.

To the student of the Gospels and the Acts it is more important to feel these general aspects of the Christian story of Jerusalem, than that he should know, or think he knows, its exact topography. And indeed no part of the topographical tradition of the City is more difficult than that which deals with the data of the Gospels. The textual uncertainties are many. The most sacred sites of all, Calvary and the Sepulchre, lie in that part of the City where the destruction by Titus was complete and continuous excavation has been least possible.

*These Aspects more important than the exact Topography.*

Perhaps the most difficult datum is the verse which speaks of the Pool of Bethesda.[1] The name has been handed down in three different forms: Bethesda, as in our Authorised Version, but derived from sources of inferior value; Bethzatha or Bezatha, with good manuscript evidence and accepted by leading authorities of our own time; and Bethsaida, with early and apparently independent traditions in its favour.[2] Nor is the meaning of any of these quite clear. Bethesda is usually taken as *house of mercy*, but this is not certain.[3] Bethzatha was the name of the quarter of

*The Topography— 1. The Pool of Bethesda.*

---

[1] John v. 2.

[2] Βηθεσδα, textus receptus, Peshiṭto; cod. leid., *O.S.* Eus. and Jerome, ed. Larsow-Parthey, 112 f. Βηθζαθα, א, L., Tischendorf, W. H., and Moffatt; or Βηζαθα, Eusebius in Lag. *O.S.* 251; or Βελζεθα, D. Βηθσαιδα, B., several versions, Tertullian, Bordeaux Pilgrim (333 A.D.) and Jerome in Lag. *O.S.* 142; 'the combination of two authorities so wide apart as Tertullian and B., carrying it back to a remote antiquity' (Sanday, *S.S.* 57); so too the Vulgate. J. B. Lightfoot, *Biblical Essays*, 29 *n.*, prefers Βηθσαιδα with Βηθζαθα as an alternative.

[3] Aram. Beth-ḥisda, Syr. Beth-ḥesda; it is doubtful whether an original *ḥi* or *ḥe* would be represented in Greek by ε. Mediæval tradition took it as בית אשדא, 'locus' or 'domus effusionis,' from the belief that there poured into it the washings of the altar and inner court and the blood of the victims (Eus., Jer., as above; Quaresmius, *Elucid.* vol. ii. 80*b*, where the name,

the City to the north of the Temple.[1]  Bethsaida, 'house of hunting,' or 'of fishing,' though well supported, is hardly appropriate to Jerusalem,[2] and may easily have arisen, through an error of the ear, for Bethzaitha, 'place of olives,' or by confusion with the Galilean place-name. The rest of the verse is also ambiguous.  As it stands, it reads: *there was in Jerusalem by the Probatikē a Pool called in Hebrew B., having five porches.  Probatikē* is the adjective used by the Septuagint to translate *sheep* in the name *the Sheep-Gate*;[3] and the clause is therefore translated *by the Sheep-Gate a Pool, called B.*  Another reading with considerable support runs: *there was in Jerusalem a Sheep-Pool called in Hebrew B.*[4]  The suggestion also has been made: *there was by the Sheep-Pool that which was called in Hebrew B.*[5]  But it is possible that *Probatikē* is the reproduction of an Aramaic noun *Pĕrobatayah, Bath* or *Baths.*[6]  In any

however, is Bethsaida; Reland, *Pal.* 856; Bochart, *Phaleg* 680). So Ewald (*Hist.* vi. 282 *n.*), Conder (Hastings' *D.B.* i. 279*b*, אשדה=stream), but thinking rather of a natural emission of water which would suit the Virgin's Spring=Gihon 'the gusher.' Lewin (*Sketch of Jerus.* 268), בית אסדא, 'house of washing.' Brose (*St. u. Kr.*, Jan. 1902) goes back to the mediæval idea.  Westcott (*St. John*) quotes Delitzsch, בית אסטין, οἶκος στοᾶς, 'house of the Portico.'

[1] Vol. i. 247.　　　　[2] See, however, on fish-ponds, vol. i. 317 *n.* 4.

[3] Neh. iii. 1, 32; xii. 39: ἡ πύλη ἡ προβατική, vol. i. 200.

[4] Cod. א. Eusebius and Jerome apply the adjective to the Pool. So Chrysostom. Vulgate, *probatica piscina.*

[5] Smith, *D.B.*[(2)] art. 'Bethesda' by Grove and Wilson.

[6] Cf. Buxtorf (*Lex. Chald.*, etc.), פְּרוֹבְטִיָא, *balneae*, with references to the Targum and Midrash on Eccles. ii. 8, which explain *the delights of men* in that verse as *baths.*  Baths among the Jews were introduced by Greeks or Romans.  The Aramaic word is variously derived: from the Greek προβατικός, or περίπατος, or the Latin *privata*, at first applied to private baths as distinguished from public ones (Levy, *Neu. Hebr. u. Chald. Wörterbuch*, פרובטייה).  Note that Eccles. ii. 8 was referred to Solomon, and that one of the proposed sites for Bethesda may be Solomon's Pool (below, p. 567). This explanation of Probatikē suggested itself to me on coming across

case we are not tied down by the text to a site in
the neighbourhood of the Sheep-Gate.  At least six sites
have been proposed: the Ḥammam esh-Shefâ,[1] the Twin-
Pools adjoining the north-west corner of Antonia, the
Birket Israin, the Twin-Pools at St. Anne's,[2] the Virgin's
Well or Giḥon, and Siloam.   Tradition supports in succession the second, third and fourth of these.   The Twin-
Pools by Antonia are probably those identified with
Bethesda by the Bordeaux Pilgrim, Eucherius, Eusebius
and Jerome; the Birket Israin has been connected with
our passage since the thirteenth century; and the Pools
of St. Anne's at least since the Crusades.   If the *troubling
of the waters* was due to the emptying of the lavers and
conduits of the Temple, that would be possible in the
Twin-Pools near Antonia and in the Birket Israin, assuming that these existed before 70 A.D., which is uncertain.
If *the troubling* was due to a natural syphonic spring,
this, if it ever existed north of the Temple, has been
destroyed or masked by the earthquakes.   All three
sites suit the well-supported reading Bethzatha, and lie
in the neighbourhood of the old Sheep-Gate.   But, as we
have seen, neither of these reasons is decisive.   If *Probatikē*

Perobatayah in Buxtorf and Levy; but I have since found that it was
suggested by Sepp, *Jerusalem* (1863), i. 331, and by Bishop Lightfoot in his
Lecture-notes, published posthumously in *Biblical Essays* (1893), p. 170.
There must, therefore, be something in it.

[1] By Sepp, *Jerusalem*, i. 329, 331, and by Furrer; see vol. i. 84 *n.* 4.

[2] On these three see vol. i. 116 f. : and add to the references there
Clermont-Ganneau, *Arch. Res.* i. 118 f. : ' The Sanctuary of the *House of
St. Anne*, built on the actual site of Bethesda, has for its origin a play
upon the words *Bethesda* and *Béit Hanna*, both of which mean " House
of Grace."   We have a decisive material proof of this, the marble foot
discovered at St. Anne's itself, and bearing . . . an *ex voto* in Greek, of
Pompeia Lucilia in gratitude for his cure at the Sheep-Pool.'   But this
proves only that in Greek times the pool was identified with Bethesda.
See also Mommert, *Topogr. d. alt. Jerus.* iii. 97 ; Sanday, *S.S.* 55 ff. ; Rix,
*Tent and Testament*, 205-208.

may be taken absolutely as a proper name, whether meaning *Bath* or something else, and the reading Bethesda, or even Bethsaida, be possible, then one of the two sites south of the Temple is open to us; and on each of these we have a pool periodically disturbed by a natural spring which would suit the reading Bethesda and its equation, 'house of emission.' The ancient name of the Virgin's Spring was Gihon, 'the Gusher'; there lies a Pool— in ancient times there may have been a larger one— which still has the reputation of healing diseases.[1] The water of the Pool of Siloam was also disturbed at intervals by the intermittent rush from Gihon; the Pool was possibly rebuilt in Herod's time.[2] But, on the other hand, Siloam is separately mentioned in the Fourth Gospel: to the writer it can hardly have been the same as Bethesda.[3] The balance of evidence, therefore, is in favour of the Virgin's Spring, but the whole is uncertain.

Three questions arise concerning the Upper Room in which our Lord kept the Passover with His disciples. *First:* Is it the same as that in which the disciples gathered after His ascension? *Second:* Did it remain the usual meeting-place of the Church till the destruction of Jerusalem? *Third:* Did either the Supper Room or the Church, or both, occupy the site with which a very old tradition has identified them —the present Cœnaculum in the complex of buildings

2. The Upper Room—the Cœnaculum.

---

[1] Vol. i. 87 ff.; on the supposed pool here, 91, 198 *n.* 2. It may have been 'Solomon's Pool' of Josephus (v. *B.J.* iv., *the King's Pool*, Neh. iii. 15). The late Yusuf Pasha informed me that in his boyhood he was sent to bathe in this pool when he was ill. On this identification see Lightfoot, *Opera* ii. 588; Robinson, *B.R.* i. 508; Conder, 'Bethesda' in Hastings' *D.B.*          [2] Bliss, *Excav. at Jerus. 1894-1897*, 330.

[3] Rix, *Tent and Test.* 255, argues for Siloam, but does not give enough weight to the above reason against it.

known as Neby Daûd, on the South-West Hill (the 'traditional Sion') and connected with, among other 'places,' that of the death or *Dormitio* of the Virgin? These questions have recently been answered in the affirmative by writers of different schools.[1] Dr. Sanday, for example, does 'not think there is any reason to doubt that where the "upper room" is mentioned in the Gospels and Acts, it is the same upper room that is meant.' Nor does he think it 'a very precarious step to identify this upper room as in the house of Mary the mother of Mark. . . . It seems to me' (he continues) 'that the combinations are quite legitimate, and only give unity and compactness to the history, if we suppose that the house of Mary and her son was the one central meeting-place of the Church of Jerusalem throughout the Apostolic age. Our latest evidence for it is on the occasion of the release of St. Peter in 44 A.D. But there is no reason to think that there would be any change between that date and the flight of the threatened community to Pella in the year 66.' The present writer would willingly agree with these opinions, both for their own attractiveness and from his respect for the authority of those who hold them. But while the facts alleged are within the bounds of possibility, they are not very probable. One need not, indeed, be hindered by the objection that Luke uses one word for *upper chamber* in the Gospel and another in Acts.[2] But Luke

---

[1] C. Mommert, *Die Dormitio u. das Deutsche Grundstück auf dem traditionellen Zion*, 1899; Th. Zahn, 'Die Dormitio Sanctae Virginis u. das Haus des Johannes Markus,' in the *Neue Kirchliche Zeitschrift*, x. (1899), 377 ff. (not seen); also *Einl.*[(2)] ii. 212 f.; W. Sanday, *S.S.* 77 ff.; J. Weiss, *D. älteste Evang.* 409. Mommert distinguishes between the Dormitio and the Cœnaculum.

[2] Luke xxii. 11 f., ἀνάγαιον μέγα, *a great upper chamber* (cf. Mark xiv. 14 f., which has also τὸ κατάλυμά μου, *my guest-chamber*); Acts ii. 13, τὸ ὑπερῷον, *the upper chamber where they were abiding*.

would surely have noticed the identity ; in the Gospel he implies that the first upper chamber was only for the purpose of the Passover. It is still more precarious to argue both that this was in the house of Mark's mother, and that it remained the meeting-place of the Church till 66 A.D. Considering the rapid growth of the community and other circumstances of their life, it is more probable that their meeting-place changed from time to time. Then Dr. Sanday finds that the New Testament data are met by evidence 'from the time of Hadrian.' But this is the testimony of Epiphanius, who lived in the fourth century (312-403).[1] He reports that forty-seven years after the ruin by Titus, Hadrian, on his arrival at Jerusalem, found 'the whole city levelled . . . save a few dwellings and the little Church of God, whither the disciples returned when the Saviour was taken up from Olivet, and they went up to the upper room ; for it had been built there, that is in the quarter of Sion. [The church] had been left over from the destruction, and parts of the dwellings about Sion, and the seven synagogues which alone remained standing in Sion, like huts, one of which survived till the time of the bishop Maximonas and the Emperor Constantine, like *a booth in the vineyard*, according to the Scripture.' Similar testimonies exist from the same period.[2] Dr. Sanday remarks that the historical character of the tradition need not be questioned. Surely all that can be said is that it is not impossible. The tradition has the same antiquity as that of the Holy Sepulchre. From the fourth century till now it has been constant. As in the case of the Holy Sepulchre, other scenes of the sacred history have been grouped in and round the Upper Room or Cœnaculum :

---

[1] *De Mensuris et Ponderibus*, xiv.　　[2] See Zahn, *Einl.*[(2)] 213.

the place of Pentecost, the house of St. John with the scene of the Dormitio, or death, of the Blessed Virgin, the house of Caiaphas, the pillar at which our Lord was scourged, the place where He appeared 'in Galilee.' There has been much rebuilding on the site : including the restoration of a basilica after the Persian destruction in 614 A.D. ; a church of two stories in the time of the Crusades ; and a reconstruction by the Franciscans in 1333, from which the present form of the Cœnaculum dates. In 1547 it passed into the hands of the Moslems, who still hold it.

The Synoptic Gospels agree that after the Supper our Lord and His disciples *went out to the Mount of Olives*, Luke adds, *as was His custom*; *to an enclosed piece of ground named Gethsemane*, or *Oil-Press*, Luke simply says *at the place*, but John that it was *a garden across the winter-brook, Ḳidron*.[1] The traditional site, in possession of the Franciscans, received its present form so recently as 1848.[2] But a 'Grotto of the Agony' is shown some paces to the north, and is reached by a passage from the forecourt of the Church of the Virgin's Tomb: it may have been a cistern or oil-vat. The Church represents 'St. Mary in the Valley of Jehoshaphat,' one of the principal sanctuaries of Jerusalem during the Latin kingdom ;[3] doubtless that which the Moslem geographers of the tenth and twelfth centuries call 'El Jismâniyah,' 'The Place of the Incarnation,' a corruption of Gethsemane.[4] From this the

*3. Gethsemane.*

---

[1] Mark xiv. 26, 32 ; Matt. xxvi. 30, 36 ; Luke xxii. 39 f. ; John xviii. 1. Γεθσημανεῖ or-νη, *i.e.* שְׁמָנָא גַּת; another reading, γεσσ-, implies the same, and hardly גֵּיא, Oil-glen. On the Ḳidron see vol. i. 80 f.

[2] Robinson, cf. *B.R.* i. 346 and *L.B.R.* 188.

[3] Frequent references in Röhricht's *Regesta*.

[4] So Mas'ûdi and Idrisi. Le Strange, *Pal. under Moslems*, 203, 210.

tradition is pretty constant back to the fourth century, where the data of the Bordeaux Pilgrim, 333 A.D., and Eusebius, are not against the present site, and the position is defined by Jerome as at the roots of Olivet with a church built over it.[1] Whether all this rests on earlier tradition we cannot tell. The Gospels assure us of a site on Olivet opposite the Temple, for this was our Lord's usual resort. It is not necessary to suppose that the garden lay much higher up the hill. But wherever it was —and the slopes have suffered much these nineteen centuries—any of the olive-groves on the Mount which have not been dressed as the Franciscan garden has, will give the pilgrim a more natural impression of the scene of our Lord's agony than the latter can.

After the arrest on Olivet, Jesus was led to the *house of the High Priest*,[2] which might also be described as his *Aulē* or *Court*.[3] It was evidently a large building with a court in front, and before this a Proaulion or Pulon.[4] In all probability it

4. The House of the High Priest.

lay with the Hasmonean and Herodian Palaces, and other notable buildings, on the South-West Hill. That is where Josephus places the residence of a later High

---

[1] Eusebius (in Lag. *O.S.* 257), Γεθσιμανῆ, χωρίον, ἔνθα πρὸ τοῦ πάθους ὁ Χριστὸς προσηύξατο. κεῖται δὲ καὶ πρὸς τῷ ὄρει τῶν ἐλαιῶν, ἐν ᾧ καὶ νῦν τὰς εὐχὰς οἱ πιστοὶ ποιεῖσθαι σπουδάζουσιν. The church upon it was therefore built between the time of Eusebius and that of Jerome.

[2] Εἰς τὴν οἰκίαν τοῦ ἀρχιερέως: Luke xxii. 54; locality is implied also in Mark xiv. 53 ff., Matt. xxvi. 57.

[3] John xviii. 15 ff. : εἰς τὴν αὐλὴν τοῦ ἀ. Here Aulē seems to be the whole residence of the High Priest (cf. in Josephus above, p. 488), and so too, possibly, even in Mark xiv. 54, Matt. xxvi. 58. Elsewhere Aulē is the court in front of the house, in which Peter remained *outside* (Matt. xxvi. 69), or *below* (Mark xiv. 66). The questions raised by John's story (xviii. 12-24), that Jesus was led first to Annas, then to Caiaphas, do not concern us here. But notice, in illustration of John's two chief priests, Josephus iv. *B.J.* iii. 7.

[4] Mark xiv. 66, 68 ; Matt. xxvi. 69, 71.

Priest, Ananias.[1] To this house were gathered *the chief priests, elders and scribes*,[2] the members of the Sanhedrin. It seems also implied, though not necessarily, that a formal meeting of the Council was held : now *the chief priests and the whole Sanhedrin sought witness against Jesus that they might put Him to death*.[3] We have seen that the Sanhedrin usually sat in their chamber in the Temple, but that under stress of circumstances they might meet elsewhere.[4] If this midnight meeting in the house of Caiaphas was a formal one, the uncanonical hour may be explained by the desire to complete the punishment in the case before the Sabbath,[5] the unusual place by the fact that at that hour the Temple gates were shut.[6] We have seen how ready both Herod and the Zealots were, on the one hand, to seem to observe the forms, and on the other to violate the spirit, of the Law.[7] The Sadducees were also reputed, on other occasions than this, to have been unscrupulous and irregular in their management of the Sanhedrin.[8] No one familiar with the constitutional history of the period can doubt

---

[1] ii. *B. J.* xvii. 6.      [2] Mark xiv. 53 ; Matt. xxvi. 59.

[3] Mark xiv. 55 ; Matt. xxvi. 59 (false witness). It is possible to refer this either to a previous procedure of the whole Sanhedrin, or to an informal meeting at this time.      [4] Vol. i. 420.

[5] The procedure both in money-cases, דיני ממונות, and capital cases, דיני נפשות, is explained in the *Mishna*, 'Sanhedrin' iv. 1. The former could be finished in one day, in the latter the sentence could be pronounced only on the day after the trial ; 'accordingly there were no courts or judgments on the evening before the Sabbath or a feast day.'

[6] Vol. i. 424.      [7] Vol. i. 433, 444 ff.

[8] Keim, *Jesus of Nazara*, 41 f., with references to Josephus, xx. *Ant.* ix. 1, the trial and stoning of James, in which the illegality of the procedure under the leadership of the younger Ananias and the Sadducees is indicated (the Pharisees contrasted with them in this respect, xiii. *Ant.* x. 6 ; ii. *B.J.* viii. 14.) For a detailed criticism, with the conclusion that no formal sentence was passed, see J. Weiss, *D. älteste Evang.* 306 ff.

the possibility of such procedure as the Evangelists describe. Another meeting of the Sanhedrin—to pass the sentence arrived at during the night, or to have further consultation—was held at sunrise, within the canonical hours, and probably in the regular chamber.[1]

From the Sanhedrin Jesus was led to Pilate, the Procurator.[2] John says that He was led straight from Caiaphas to the Prætorium,[3] into which He was taken to Pilate, while the Jews remained outside; during the rest of John's account Pilate comes and goes between Jesus in the Prætorium and the multitude in front of it; finally, he brings Jesus out to them and takes his seat on *the Bema, or judgment-seat, at a place called the Pavement, but in Hebrew Gabbatha.*[4] Matthew also speaks of Pilate sitting on the Bema in face of the multitude,[5] and Mark and Luke recount that Pilate's decision was given before the multitude.[6] Matthew and Mark then describe how the soldiers of the governor took Jesus into the Prætorium.[7] The name Prætorium, originally the Prætor's (or general's) quarters in a Roman camp, was also applied to the official residence of the governor of a Province.[8] In this sense it is used in Acts: the Prætorium of Herod in Cæsarea

5. The Prætorium = Herod's Palace.

---

[1] Mark xv. 1; Matt. xxvii. 1; Luke xxii. 66. See J. Weiss, *op. cit.* 308 ff.
[2] Mark xv. 1; Matt. xxvii. 2 (who alone gives the title); Luke xxiii. 1. On *Governor*, see vol. i. 413. [3] John xviii. 28 ff. [4] John xix. 13.
[5] Matt. xxvii. 19; cf. 17. [6] Mark xv. 8 ff. ; Luke xxiii. 4 ff., 18 ff.
[7] Matt. xxvii. 27; Mark xv. 16, *into the Court which is the Prætorium.* Brandt (*Die Evang. Gesch.* 107), quoted with approval by Canney, *Enc. Bibl.* 3823, says that *which is the Prætorium* 'is a strange addition, a gloss occasioned by the text of Matthew.' But such a criticism is strange to any one who knows the history of Herod's Palace. Josephus called it an Aulē; this was evidently the common Greek name for it, and it was now the Prætorium. Mark's expression therefore is both natural and exactly correct. [8] Cicero, *In Verrem*, II. iv. 28; v. 35.

was the palace which Herod built there and which was used by the Procurator as his residence.[1] But the name was also given to those residences which either the governor or other officials occupied when on tour through their province.[2] The Prætorium in Jerusalem was therefore the Government House; in front of it stood the Procurator's tribunal, and it contained a detachment of soldiers.[3] The sites advocated are naturally two: the Castle Antonia, because tradition places the House of Pilate [4] near it, and in it was the larger part of the garrison,[5] while the Pavement is identified with the space between the Castle and the Temple; and Herod's Palace on the West Hill.[6] I think we can have little hesitation in deciding for the latter. It was in the Palace of Herod, says Philo,[7] that Pilate hung up the golden shields which brought him into trouble with the Jews. It was, says Josephus, 'in the Palace that Florus the Procurator took up his quarters, and having placed his tribunal in front of it, held his sessions, and the chief priests, influential persons, and notables of the city appeared before the tribunal.' Provoked by their arguments, 'he shouted to the soldiers

---

[1] Acts xxiii. 35. See Schürer, *Gesch.*[(3)] 457 f.

[2] Cf. Domaszewski in Brünnow and D. *Die Provincia Arabia*, ii. 58, on the inscription at Ḳuṣr Bsher, 'castra praetorii Mobeni,' with reference to Mommsen, *Hermes*, 1900, p. 436 *n.* 3. Vincent, *Rev. Bibl.*, 1898, p. 436, quotes from Cagnat, *L'Armée Romaine d'Afrique* (578 *n.* 7), to the effect that in a certain case Prætorium signifies 'non pas un établissement militaire, mais un gîte d'étape comme on en contruisait le long des grandes routes pour servir d'abri aux officiers et aux fonctionnaires en voyage.'

[3] ὅλην τὴν σπεῖραν (Mark xv. 16; Matt. xxvii. 27), not necessarily *the whole cohort*, vol. i. 426.

[4] Mommert, *Das Prätor. des Pilatus* (1903), argues for a site in the central valley, on the ground of the Un. Armenians; see especially pp. 23 ff. 69-81.

[5] Weiss, Westcott, Swete (*Mark* on xv. 16) and others.

[6] Sepp, Ewald, Keim, Meyer, Schürer, Edersheim, Kreyenbühl (*Z.N.T.W.*, 1902, 15 ff.), Sanday (*S.S.* 52 ff.), Purves in Hastings' *D.B.*, an excellent article.          [7] *Leg. ad Caium*, 31.

to plunder the Upper Market and to slay those they fell in with,' and many of the moderate citizens they brought up before Florus, whom with stripes he first scourged and then crucified.[1]  Later he tried to force his way to the Antonia with such soldiers 'as were with him out of the Royal Aulē,' but they had to fall back on the camp, which was at the Palace.[2]  We have seen other proofs that part of the Roman garrison of Jerusalem were stationed here.[3]  There is no need, therefore, for calling in the Antonia and its guardroom ; everything indicates that the Roman trial of our Lord happened in or before the Palace of Herod on the South-West Hill. But above all this is distinctly stated by Mark : *He was taken into the Aule, which is the Prætorium.*[4]  That Pilate's tribunal was set on *Pavement* or *Mosaic*[5] was in accordance with Roman custom.  Gabbatha may not be given as its translation, but as the Hebrew name of the place.  It means either an elevated place or a bare and open one, or even possibly mosaic.[6]  In front, then, of Herod's

---

[1] Josephus, ii. *B.J.* xiv. 8.

[2] *Id.* xv. 5 ; with βασιλικὴ αὐλὴ cf. αὐλὴ βασιλέως, v. *B.J.* iv. 4 ; and above, pp. 488, 571.　　　　　[3] Vol. i. 426.

[4] See above, p. 573 *n.* 7.　　　[5] Λιθόστρωτον : Ἑβραϊστὶ δὲ Γαββαθά.

[6] Cf. גַּב, גַּבָּא, emphatic state, גַּבְתָא, *elevation, raised back, ridge* ; גַּבַּחַת, *elevation,* also *bald* place on the forehead ; Levy, *Neu. Hebr. u. Chald. Wörterbuch,* s. vv.  Dalman (*Worte Jesu,* i. 6) prefers the latter in its definite form, גַּבַּחְתָּא.  But it is not to be overlooked that there is a root גבב in the Hebrew of the time, to bring or pack together a lot of little things (applied to an argument made out of trifles), and that גבבה means anything composed of fragments, loppings, chips (Levy).  This comes very near a *mosaic.*  Only there are other Aramaic terms for that.  The suggestion that the name is 'a purely artificial formation, the writer himself attaching no meaning to it' (*Enc. Bibl.* 3640), is incredible.  That a writer, otherwise regarded by the author of this theory as writing continually in symbols, should be supposed to have invented a meaningless name, is surely an inconsistent piece of criticism.

Palace, the site now occupied by the Turkish citadel, stood the Procurator's tribunal, where Jesus was tried by Pilate, presented to the people along with Barabbas, rejected by the multitude and scourged. In the Palace itself, or in 'the camp' which Josephus says was attached to it, He endured the mockery of the soldiers.

Luke alone tells us that Pilate, hearing that Jesus was a Galilean and of the jurisdiction of Herod Antipas, sent

6. Residence of Herod Antipas= Hasmonean Palace.

Him to the latter, *who himself also was at Jerusalem in these days.* After questioning our Lord, who gave him no answer, *Herod with his soldiers set Him at nought and mocked Him, and arraying Him in gorgeous apparel sent Him back to Pilate.*[1] Ewald has suggested that upon their visits to Jerusalem the children of Herod the Great found quarters in a wing of the Prætorium, their father's Palace. It is more probable that Antipas occupied the Palace of the Hasmoneans, where indeed we find Agrippa and Bernice living.[2]

Then *they led Him away, they led Him out, to crucify Him, and as they came out they found a man of Cyrene*

The Cruci-fixion.

*coming from the country, and laid on him the cross to bear it after Jesus.*[3] In the neighbour-hood of the Palace was a City-gate, Gennath.[4] Probably by this the procession left the town, and came to the place Golgotha, at which they crucified Him. Where Golgotha stood, and where the neighbouring garden lay in which He was buried, we do not know, because, for reasons already explained, we cannot tell how the Second Wall, at this time the outer wall on the north, exactly ran.[5]

---

[1] Luke xxiii. 4 ff.        [2] ii. *B.J.* xvi. 3 ; see above, pp. 461 f.
[3] Matt. xxvii. 31 f. ; Mark xv. 20 f. ; Luke xxiii. 26.
[4] Vol. i. 243.        [5] Vol. i. 247 ff. ; vol. ii. 564.

While for such topographical details we seek, and perhaps in the case of some of them seek in vain, let us not fail to lift our eyes to those general aspects of the crisis with which we began this chapter. They are certain. We see our Lord's relations to the several parts of the City and her environs: how while He was master of His movements He kept—save for His ministries at Bethesda and in the Upper Room— to the outer Courts of the Temple and to the Mount of Olives; but after His arrest He was taken to the West Hill with its Palaces, and thence by a City-Gate to His Crucifixion in the northern suburb. We feel the bare, fierce days of argument and menace within the walls, the hospitable darkness among the olives beyond. We can hear the wild call of the Desert stirring the City's blood, while she sits deaf to the pleadings of the Love of God. Our study of the authorities, the parties, and the popular forces in Jerusalem has enabled us to appreciate how various and confused were the motives of their unnatural conspiracy against this solitary Prophet; but our criticism of them is controlled by that utterance which some ancient authorities attribute to Jesus and which certainly bears the proof of His spirit: *Father forgive them, for they know not what they do!* Ignorance, whatever may have been its causes, is indeed the appalling fact that covers every other aspect of this terrible crime. It was (as we have seen) a believing, an eager and enthusiastic people, with a tumult of hopes in their breast: ready to die by their thousands for leaders whose aims were low enough to flash upon their imagination or to stir their fanatic patriotism; but equally ready to call for the death of the Prophet, whose ideals were beyond

*Review of the General Aspects.*

their conceiving, and who, they therefore thought, had
betrayed their interests.   It was a Priesthood with some
noble and many brave and zealous spirits ; but blinded—
by professional prejudices, by panic for their influence
with the people, by homage to tradition, and by the
curiously close and rigorous logic of their scribes—to the
spiritual realities, to the fulfilment of the highest promises
of their religion, which no prophet had ever brought so
near as this one now did.   The Supreme Authority, with
whom the final sentence lay, was foreign, perplexed, and
therefore vacillating.   How often in history has the fate
of the earnest and the unselfish been decided by judges,
at once racially and religiously as incapable as Pilate of
understanding the issues before them !   *Sursum corda !*
After the Passion and Crucifixion of Jesus no cause of
justice, no ministry of truth, no service of one's fellow-
men, need despair.   Though the People, Religion and
the State together triumph over them, beyond the brief
day of such a triumph *the days*—to use a prophetic
promise which had often rung through Jerusalem—*the
days are coming.*   The centuries, patient ministers of
God, are waiting as surely for them as they waited for
Christ beyond His Cross.

Thus, then, did the City and the Man confront each
other: that great Fortress, with her rival and separately
entrenched forces, for the moment confederate
The End.          against Him ; that Single Figure, sure of His
sufficiency for all their needs, and, though His flesh might
shrink from it, conscious that the death which they conspired for Him was His Father's will in the redemption
of mankind.   As for the embattled City herself, lifted
above her ravines and apparently impregnable, she sat

prepared only for the awful siege and destruction which He foresaw; while all her spiritual promises, thronging from centuries of hope and prophecy, ran out from her shining into the West: a sunset to herself, but the dawn of a new day to the world beyond.

# APPENDIX

## A LIST OF BLOCKADES, SIEGES, CAPTURES, AND DESTRUCTIONS SUFFERED BY JERUSALEM

Besides the capture by David, about 1000 B.C., the following are known to history :—Plunder of Temple and City by Shoshenk I. of Egypt, about 930 (1 Kings xiv. 25 f. ; 2 Chron. xii. 2 ff.) ; partial overthrow by Jehoash of Israel about 790 (2 Kings xiv. 13 ff.) ; attack by Aram and N. Israel about 734 ; siege by Sennacherib, 701 ; surrender to Nebuchadrezzar, 597 ; his siege and destruction, 587-6 ; probable sack by the Persians about 350 ; destruction by Ptolemy Soter, 320 (καθῃρήκει : Appian, *Syr.* 350) ; siege of Akra by Antiochus III., 198 ; capture by Jason, 170 ; destruction by Antiochus Epiphanes, 168 ; sieges of Akra and Temple, 163-2 ; siege of Akra, 146 ; siege and levelling of walls by Antiochus VII., 134 ; brief and unsuccessful siege by the Nabateans, 65 ; siege, capture and much destruction by Pompey, 63 ; sack of Temple by Crassus, 54 ; capture by the Parthians, 40 ; siege and partial destruction by Herod and Sosius, 37 ; insurrection and some ruin on the visit of Florus, 65 A.D. ; brief and unsuccessful siege by Cestus Gallus, 66 ; the great siege and destruction by Titus, 70 ; seizure by the Jews under Bar Cocheba, 131 ; capture and devastation by Hadrian, 132 ; capture and plunder by Chosroes the Persian, 614 ; re-capture by Heraclius, 628 ; occupation by Omar, 637 ; capture by Moslem rebels, 842 ; ruin of Christian buildings, 937 ; occupation by the Fatimite Dynasty, 969 ; some destruction by the Khalîf Hakîm, 1010 ; occupation by the Seljuk Turks, 1075 (?) ; siege and capture by Afdhal, 1096 ; siege, capture and massacre by Godfrey, 1099 ; occupation by Saladin, 1187 ; destruction of walls, 1219 ; capture by the Emir of Kerak, 1229 ; surrender to Frederick II., 1239 ; capture and sack by the Kharesmians, 1244 ; plunder by Arabs, 1480 ; occupation by Turks, 1547 ; bombardment by Turks, 1825 ; Egyptian occupation, 1831 ; re-occupation by Turks, 1841.

## BUILDING AND REBUILDING OF CITY

Before the Exile by David, Solomon, Uzziah, Jotham, Hezekiah and Manasseh ; after the Exile, at first by the few Jews who returned from Babylon to rebuild the Temple, and then in the reconstruction of the walls and other buildings under Nehemiah ; after the Persian sack in 350 (?) ; and that by Ptolemy in 320 ; by Simon the High Priest in the third century ; by the Maccabees after 168, and then more thoroughly by Simon ; by John Hyrkanus ; by Antipater after Pompey (Jos. i. *B.J.* x. 4) ; by Herod the Great and by Agrippa ; imposition of the Legionary Camp by Titus after 70 A.D. ; building of walls, etc., by Hadrian from 136 onward ; by Constantine (churches), the Empress Eudocia (walls, churches, etc.), and Justinian (churches and convents) ; by the Moslems, especially the Khalîfs Omar and Maimûn (mosques and walls) ; by Christians (churches) under the earliest Moslem supremacy, and especially during the time of the Crusades ; after destruction of walls in 1219 ; some churches built in the fourteenth century ; building of the present walls under Suleiman the Magnificent ; much ruin of the remains of ancient walls, and building of churches, synagogues and other edifices during the nineteenth and present centuries.

# GENERAL INDEX TO VOLUME II.

# SPECIAL INDEX I.

## PASSAGES OF THE BIBLE AND THE APOCRYPHA

# SPECIAL INDEX II.

## JOSEPHUS

### I. THE ANTIQUITIES OF THE JEWS

(Cited as *Ant.*)

## II. WARS OF THE JEWS

### (Cited as *B.J.*)

## III. AGAINST APION

### (Cited as *C. Ap.* or *C. Apion.*)

# SPECIAL INDEX III.

## TALMUDIC LITERATURE

### I. THE MISHNA (ed. Surenhusius)

*\*\** The Tractates are given below in the order in which they occur in the Mishna.

On the Mishna generally see 31 *n.*, 60, 420, 484, 496 *n.* ('Middôth'), 507 *f.*, 517, 530.

## II. THE TOSEPHTA

## III. THE TALMUD